Oxford
Colour Spanish
Dictionary Plus

Revised second edition

SPANISH–ENGLISH
ENGLISH–SPANISH

ESPAÑOL-INGLÉS
INGLÉS-ESPAÑOL

OXFORD

UNIVERSITY PRESS

Great Clarendon Street, Oxford OX2 6DP

Oxford University Press is a department of the University of Oxford.
It furthers the University's objective of excellence in research, scholarship,
and education by publishing worldwide in

Oxford New York
Auckland Cape Town Dar es Salaam Hong Kong Karachi Kuala Lumpur
Madrid Melbourne Mexico City Nairobi New Delhi Shanghai Taipei Toronto

With offices in
Argentina Austria Brazil Chile Czech Republic France Greece
Guatemala Hungary Italy Japan South Korea Poland Portugal
Singapore Switzerland Thailand Turkey Ukraine Vietnam

Oxford is a registered trade mark of Oxford University Press
in the UK and in certain other countries

Published in the United States
by Oxford University Press Inc., New York

First published as the Oxford Colour Spanish Dictionary 1995
Revised edition published 1998
This edition published 2001
Revised second published 2004

British Library Cataloguing in Publication Data

Data available

Library of Congress Cataloging in Publication Data

Data available

ISBN 0-19-860903-5   978-0-19-860903-2
ISBN 0-19-860902-7   978-0-19-860902-5 (US edition)

10 9 8 7 6 5 4 3

Typeset by Tradespools
Printed in Italy by
Lito Terrazzi S.r.l.

Contents

Preface

The *Oxford Colour Spanish Dictionary Plus* is a dictionary
designed primarily for students of Spanish. The clear
presentation and colour headwords make it easily accessible.
It contains completely new sections, not found in the *Oxford
Colour Spanish Dictionary*, on Spanish life and culture, letter-
writing, and Spanish grammar, making it even more useful
for students at intermediate level.

List of contributors

Revised Second Edition

Editor:

Nicholas Rollin

Second Edition

Editors:

Carol Styles Carvajal
Michael Britton
Jane Horwood

Supplementary Material:

Ana Cristina Llompart
John Butt
Michael Britton
Valerie Grundy
Josephine Grundy

Data Capture:

Susan Wilkin
Anne McConnell
Anna Cotgreave

Proof-reading:

Andrew Hodgson

First Edition

Editor:

Christine Lea

Introduction

The word list for this dictionary has been comprehensively revised to reflect recent additions to both languages.

A new feature of the dictionary is the special status given to more complex grammatical words which provide the basic structure of both languages. Boxed entries in the text for these *function words* provide extended treatment, including notes to warn of possible pitfalls.

The dictionary has an easy-to-use, streamlined layout. Bullets separate each new part of speech within an entry. Nuances of sense or usage are pinpointed by indicators or by typical collocates with which the word frequently occurs. Extra help is given in the form of symbols to mark the register of words and phrases. An exclamation mark ① indicates colloquial language, and a cross ✖ indicates slang.

The swung dash (∼) is used to replace a headword or that part of a headword preceding the vertical bar (|).

In both English and Spanish only irregular plurals are given. Normally Spanish nouns and adjectives ending in an unstressed vowel form the plural by adding *s* (e.g. *libro*, *libros*). Nouns and adjectives ending in a stressed vowel or a consonant add *es* (e.g. *rubí*, *rubíes*, *pared*, *paredes*). An accent on the final syllable is not required when *es* is added (e.g. *nación*, *naciones*). Final *z* becomes *ces* (e.g. *vez*, *veces*).

Spanish nouns and adjectives ending in *o* form the feminine by changing the final *o* to *a* (e.g. *hermano*, *hermana*). Most Spanish nouns and adjectives ending in anything other than final *o* do not have a separate feminine form, with the exception of those denoting nationality etc.; these add *a* to the masculine singular form (e.g. *español*, *española*). An accent on the final syllable is then not required (e.g. *inglés*, *inglesa*). Adjectives ending in *án*, *ón*, or *or* behave like those denoting nationality, with the following exceptions: *inferior, mayor, mejor, menor, peor, superior*, where the feminine has the same form as the masculine. Spanish verb tables will be found at the back of the book.

The Spanish alphabet

In Spanish ñ is considered a separate letter and in the
Spanish–English section, therefore, is alphabetized after *ny*.

Proprietary terms

This dictionary includes some words which have, or are
asserted to have, proprietary status as trademarks. Their
inclusion does not imply that they have acquired for legal
purposes a non-proprietary or general significance, nor any
other judgement concerning their legal status. In cases where
the editorial staff have some evidence that a word has
proprietary status this is indicated in the entry for that word
by the symbol (P), but no judgement concerning the legal
status of such words is made or implied thereby.

Pronunciation of Spanish

Vowels

a   between pronunciation of *a* in English *cat* and *arm*

e   like *e* in English *bed*

i   like *ee* in English *see* but a little shorter

o   like *o* in English *hot* but a little longer

u   like *oo* in English *too*

y   when a vowel is as Spanish **i**

Consonants

b   (1) in initial position or after a nasal consonant is like English *b*

    (2) in other positions is between English *b* and English *v*

c   (1) before **e** or **i** is like *th* in English *thin*. In Latin American Spanish is like English *s*.

    (2) in other positions is like *c* in English *cat*

ch like *ch* in English *chip*

d   (1) in initial position, after nasal consonants, and after **l** is like English *d*

    (2) in other positions is like *th* in English *this*

f   like English *f*

g   (1) before **e** or **i** is like *ch* in Scottish *loch*

    (2) in initial position is like *g* in English *get*

    (3) in other positions is like (2) but a little softer

h   silent in Spanish but see also **ch**

j   like *ch* in Scottish *loch*

k   like English *k*

l	like English *l* but see also **ll**
ll	like *lli* in English *million*
m	like English *m*
n	like English *n*
ñ	like *ni* in English *opinion*
p	like English *p*
q	like English *k*
r	rolled or trilled
s	like *s* in English *sit*
t	like English *t*
v	(1) in initial position or after a nasal consonant is like English *b*
	(2) in other positions is between English b and English *v*
w	like Spanish **b** or **v**
x	like English *x*
y	like English *y*
z	like *th* in English *thin*

Glossary of grammatical terms

Abbreviation A shortened form of a word or phrase: **Mr = Sr.**

Active In the active form the subject of the verb performs the action: **Pedro** *kisses* **Ana = Pedro** *besa* **a Ana**

Adjective A word describing a noun: **a** *red* **pencil = un lápiz** *rojo*; *my* **house = mi casa**

Adverb A word that describes or changes the meaning of a verb, an adjective, or another adverb: **he ran** *quickly* **= corrió** *rápidamente*; *very* **pretty = muy bonito; she sings** *very* **badly = canta** *muy* **mal**

Apocope The omission of the final sound of a word, as in Spanish **algún** (alguno), **tan** (tanto)

Article The definite article, **the = el/la/los/las,** and indefinite article, **a/an = un/una**

Attributive An adjective or noun is attributive when it is used directly before a noun: **a** *good* **wine = un b***uen* **vino;** *business* **hours = horas** *de* **oficina**

Auxiliary verb A verb used with another verb to form compound tenses, as English **be, do,** and **have: I** *have* **eaten = *he* comido; he** *was* **sleeping = *estaba* durmiendo**

Cardinal number A whole number representing a quantity: **one/two/three = uno/dos/tres**

Clause A self-contained section of a sentence that contains a subject and a verb

Collective noun A noun that is singular in form but refers to a group of individual persons or things, e.g. **royalty, government**

Collocate A word that regularly occurs with another; in Spanish, **libro** is a typical collocate of the verb **leer**

Comparative The form of an adjective or adverb that makes it "more": **smaller = más pequeño; better = mejor**

Compound An adjective, noun, or verb formed from two or more separate words: **self-confident (self + confident) = seguro de sí mismo; airmail (air + mail) = correo aéreo; outdo (out + do) = superar**

Conditional tense A tense of a verb that expresses what would happen if something else occurred: **he would go = iría**

Conjugation Variation of the form of a verb to show tense, person, mood, etc

Conjunction A word used to join clauses together: **and = y; because = porque**

Countable noun A noun that can form a plural and, in

the singular, can be used with the indefinite article, e.g. **a book, two books**

Definite article: the = el/la/los/las

Demonstrative adjective An adjective indicating the person or thing referred to: *this* table = *esta* mesa

Demonstrative pronoun A pronoun indicating the person or thing referred to: *this* is my sister = *ésta* es mi hermana

Direct object The noun or pronoun directly affected by the verb: I bought *a book* = compré *un libro*

Direct speech A speaker's actual words or the use of these in writing: he said: *be quiet!* = dijo: *¡cállense!*

Ending Letters added to the stem of verbs to show tense, and to nouns to show plurality

Feminine One of the genders in Spanish, applied to nouns, pronouns, adjectives, and articles: **la casa blanca = the white house; ella = she**

Future tense The tense of a verb that refers to something that will happen in the future: he *will arrive* late = llegará tarde

Gender Spanish nouns, pronouns, adjectives, and articles almost all fall into two genders, masculine and feminine; in addition, Spanish uses the neuter pronouns **esto, eso,** and **aquello,** and the neuter article **lo**

Gerund The part of a verb

used in Spanish to form continuous tenses: **muriendo = dying; cantando = singing**

Imperative A form of a verb that expresses a command: **come here! = ¡ven aquí!**

Imperfect tense The tense of a verb that refers to an uncompleted or a habitual action in the past: **the children** *were playing* = los niños *jugaban*; I *went/used to go* there every Monday = *iba* allí todos los lunes

Impersonal verb A verb in English used only with it: **it is raining = está lloviendo**

Indefinite article a/an = un/una

Indefinite pronoun A pronoun that does not identify a specific person or object: **one, something**

Indicative form The form of a verb used when making a statement of fact or asking questions of fact: **I'm not hungry = no tengo hambre**

Indirect object The noun or pronoun indirectly affected by the verb, at which the direct object is aimed: I wrote a letter *to my mother* = le escribí una carta *a mi madre*

Indirect speech A report of what someone has said which does not reproduce the exact words: **she said that they had gone out = dijo que habían salido; he told me to be quiet = me dijo que me callara**

Infinitive The basic part of a verb: **to sing = cantar**

Inflect To change the ending or form of a word to show its tense or its grammatical relation to other words: **gone** and **went** are inflected forms of **to go**

Interjection A sound, word, or remark expressing a strong feeling such as anger, fear, or joy, or attracting attention: **ouch!** = **¡ay!**; **good heavens!** = **¡Dios mío!**

Interrogative An adjective, adverb, or pronoun that asks a question: **what?** = **¿qué?**; **how much?** = **¿cuánto?**; **who?** = **¿quién?**

Intransitive verb A verb that does not have a direct object: **he died suddenly** = **murió repentinamente**

Invariable noun A noun that has the same form in the plural as the singular: **sheep, species**

Irregular verb A verb that does not follow one of the set patterns and has its own individual forms, e.g. English **to be**, Spanish **ser**

Masculine One of the genders in Spanish applied to nouns, pronouns, adjectives, and articles: **el perro negro** = **the black dog**; **él** = **he**

Modal verb A verb that is used with another verb to express necessity or possibility, e.g. **might, should, will**

Mood A category of verb use, expressing fact (indicative), command (imperative), or wish or conditionality (subjunctive)

Negative expressing refusal or denial

Neuter One of the genders in Spanish, used only in the pronouns **esto, eso**, and **aquello**, and the article **lo**

Noun A word that names a person or a thing

Number The state of being either singular or plural

Object The word or words naming the person or thing acted upon by a verb or preposition: **John studies** *geography* = **John estudia** *geografía*

Ordinal number A number that shows a person's or thing's position in a series: **first** = **primero**

Part of speech A grammatical term for the function of a word; noun, verb, adjective, etc, are parts of speech

Passive In the passive form the subject of the verb experiences the action rather than performs it – common in English, but not in Spanish: **Ana** *is kissed by* **Pedro** = **Ana es besada por Pedro**

Past participle The part of a verb used to form past tenses: **she had** *gone* = **había** *ido*

Perfect tense The tense of the verb that refers to an event that has taken place in a period of time that includes the present: **I have eaten** = **he comido**

Person Any of the three groups of personal pronouns

and forms taken by verbs; the **first person** (e.g. **I/yo**) refers to the person(s) speaking, the **second person** (e.g. **you/tú**) refers to the person(s) spoken to; the **third person** (e.g. **he/él**) refers to the persons spoken about

Personal pronoun A pronoun that refers to a person or thing: **I/he/she** = yo/él/ella

Phrasal verb A verb in English combined with a preposition or an adverb to have a particular meaning: **run away** = huir; **go past** = pasar

Phrase A self-contained section of a sentence that does not contain a full verb

Pluperfect tense The tense of a verb that refers to something that happened before a particular point in the past: **he had left** = había salido

Plural Of nouns etc, referring to more than one: **the houses** = las casas

Possessive adjective An adjective that shows possession, belonging to someone or something: **my/your** = mi/tu

Possessive pronoun A pronoun that shows possession, belonging to someone or something: **mine/yours** = mío/tuyo

Predicative An adjective is predicative when it comes after a verb such as **be** or **become**: **she is beautiful** = es hermosa

Prefix A letter or group of letters added to the beginning of a word to change its meaning:

*im*possible = *im*posible, *un*lucky = *des*afortunado

Preposition A word that stands in front of a noun or pronoun, relating it to the rest of the sentence: **with** = con; **without** = sin

Present participle The part of a verb that in English ends in –**ing**, and is used in forming continuous tenses: **doing** = haciendo

Present tense The tense of a verb that refers to something happening now: **I *open* the door** = *abro* la puerta

Preterite tense A simple tense referring to a completed action in the past: **I *did* it yesterday** = lo *hice* ayer

Pronominal verb A Spanish verb conjugated using the pronouns **me**, **te**, **se**, **nos**, and **os**, in which the pronoun refers to the subject of the verb: **(yo) me equivoqué** = I was wrong. A subgroup of these verbs are REFLEXIVE VERBS

Pronoun A word that stands instead of a noun: **he/she** = él/ella; **someone** = alguien; **mine** = el mío/la mía

Proper noun A name of a person, place, institution, etc, in English written with a capital letter at the start: **Spain, the Atlantic, London, Juan, Madrid** are all proper nouns

Reflexive pronoun A pronoun that refers back to the subject of the clause in which it is used: **myself** = me; **themselves** = se

Reflexive verb A verb whose object is the same as its subject; in Spanish, it is used with a reflexive pronoun: **he washed himself = se lavó**

Regular verb A verb that follows a set pattern in its different forms

Relative pronoun A pronoun that introduces a subordinate clause, relating to a person or thing mentioned in the main clause: **the man *who* visited us = el hombre *que* nos visitó**

Reported speech Another name for INDIRECT SPEECH

Sentence A sequence of words, with a subject and a verb, that can stand on their own to make a statement, ask a question, or give a command

Singular Of nouns etc, referring to just one: **the house = la casa**

Stem The part of a word to which endings are added: **care** is the stem of **careful** and **careless**; in Spanish **cuidado** is the stem of **cuidadoso**

Subject In a clause or sentence, the noun or pronoun that causes the action of the verb: ***John* studies geography = *John* estudia geografía**

Subjunctive A verb form that is used to express wishes or

conditionality: **long *live* the King! = ¡*viva* el Rey!; if it *was* or *were* possible = si *fuera* posible**

Subordinate clause A clause which adds information to the main clause of a sentence but cannot be used as a sentence by itself, e.g. **she answered the phone *when it rang***

Suffix A letter or group of letters joined to the end of a word to make another word, e.g. **quick*ly* = rápida*mente***

Superlative The form of an adjective or adverb that makes it "most": **the smallest = la más pequeña; the best = el mejor**

Tense The form of a verb that tells when the action takes place: present, future, imperfect, perfect, pluperfect are all tenses

Transitive verb A verb that is used with a direct object: **she *read* the book = *leyó* el libro**

Uncountable noun A noun that cannot form a plural in ordinary usage and is not used with the indefinite article: **china, luggage**

Verb A word or group of words that describes an action: **the children *are playing* = los niños *están jugando***

Abbreviations/Abreviaturas

adjective	*a*	adjetivo
abbreviation	*abbr/abrev*	abreviatura
administration	*admin*	administración
adverb	*adv*	adverbio
American	*Amer*	americano
anatomy	*Anat*	anatomía
architecture	*Archit/Arquit*	arquitectura
definite article	*art def*	artículo definido
indefinite article	*art indef*	artículo indefinido
astrology	*Astr*	astrología
motoring	*Auto*	automóvil
auxiliary	*aux*	auxiliar
aviation	*Aviat/Aviac*	aviación
biology	*Biol*	biología
botany	*Bot*	botánica
British	*Brit*	británico
commerce	*Com*	comercio
conjunction	*conj*	conjunción
cookery	*Culin*	cocina
electricity	*Elec*	electricidad
school	*Escol*	enseñanza
Spain	*Esp*	España
feminine	*f*	femenino
familiar	*fam*	familiar
figurative	*fig*	figurado
philosophy	*Fil*	filosofía
photography	*Foto*	fotografía
geography	*Geog*	geografía
geology	*Geol*	geología
grammar	*Gram*	gramática
humorous	*hum*	humorístico
interjection	*int*	interjección
interrogative	*inter*	interrogativo
invariable	*invar*	invariable
legal, law	*Jurid*	jurídico
Latin American	*LAm*	latinoamericano
language	*Lang*	lengua(je)
masculine	*m*	masculino
mathematics	*Mat(h)*	matemáticas
mechanics	*Mec*	mecánica
medicine	*Med*	medicina

Spanish–English Dictionary

Mexico	*Mex*	México
military	*Mil*	militar
music	*Mus*	música
mythology	*Myth*	mitología
noun	*n*	nombre
nautical	*Naut*	náutica
oneself	*o. s.*	uno mismo, se
proprietary term	*P*	marca registrada
pejorative	*pej*	peyorativo
philosophy	*Phil*	filosofía
photography	*Photo*	fotografía
plural	*pl*	plural
politics	*Pol*	política
possessive	*poss*	posesivo
past participle	*pp*	participio pasado
prefix	*pref*	prefijo
preposition	*prep*	preposición
present participle	*pres p*	participio de presente
pronoun	*pron*	pronombre
psychology	*Psych*	psicología
past tense	*pt*	tiempo pasado
railroad	*Rail*	ferrocarril
relative	*rel*	relativo
religion	*Relig*	religión
school	*Schol*	enseñanza
singular	*sing*	singular
slang	*sl*	argot
someone	*s. o.*	alguien
something	*sth*	algo
subjunctive	*subj*	subjuntivo
technical	*Tec*	técnico
television	*TV*	televisión
university	*Univ*	universidad
auxiliary verb	*v aux*	verbo auxiliar
verb	*vb*	verbo
intransitive verb	*vi*	verbo intransitivo
pronominal verb	*vpr*	verbo pronominal
transitive verb	*vt*	verbo transitivo
transitive & intransitive verb	*vti*	verbo transitivo e intransitivo
vulgar	*vulg*	vulgar
colloquial	**!**	coloquial
slang	**✖**	argot

a

● *preposición*

Note that **a** followed by **el** becomes **al**, e.g. **vamos al cine**

····➤ (dirección) to. **fui a México** I went to Mexico. **muévete a la derecha** move to the right

····➤ (posición) **se sentaron a la mesa** they sat at the table. **al lado del banco** next to the bank. **a orillas del río** on the banks of the river

····➤ (distancia) **queda a 5 km** it's 5 km away. **a pocos metros de aquí** a few metres from here

····➤ (fecha) **hoy estamos a 5** today is the 5th. **¿a cuánto estamos?**, (LAm) **¿a cómo estamos?** what's the date?

····➤ (hora, momento) at. **a las 2** at 2 o'clock. **a fin de mes** at the end of the month. **a los 21 años** at the age of 21; (después de) after 21 years

····➤ (precio) **¿a cómo están las peras?** how much are the pears? **están a 500 pesetas el kilo** they're 500 pesetas a kilo. **salen a 30 pesetas cada uno** they work out at 30 pesetas each.

····➤ (medio, modo) **fuimos a pie** we went on foot. **hecho a mano** handmade. **pollo al horno** (LAm) roast chicken

····➤ (cuando precede al objeto directo de persona) *no se traduce.* **conocí a Juan** I met Juan. **quieren mucho a sus hijos** they love their children very much

····➤ (con objeto indirecto) to. **se lo di a Juan** I gave it to Juan. **le vendí el coche a mi amigo** I sold my friend the car, I sold the car to my friend. **se lo compré a mi madre** I bought it from my mother; (para) I bought it for my mother

⟹ Cuando la preposición **a** se emplea precedida de ciertos verbos como **empezar, faltar, ir, llegar** etc., ver bajo el respectivo verbo

ábaco *m* abacus

abadejo *m* pollack

abadía *f* abbey

abajo *adv* (down) below; (dirección) down(wards); (en casa) downstairs. ● *int* down with. ∼ **de** (LAm) under(neath). **calle** ∼ down the street. **el** ∼ **firmante** the undersigned. **escaleras** ∼ down the stairs. **la parte de** ∼ the bottom (part). **más** ∼ further down

abalanzarse [10] *vpr* rush (**hacia** towards)

abanderado *m* standard-bearer; (Mex, en fútbol) linesman

abandon|ado *adj* abandoned; (descuidado) neglected; <*persona*> untidy. ∼**ar** *vt* leave <*un lugar*>; abandon <*persona, cosa*>. ● *vi* give up. ◻ ∼**arse** *vpr* give in; (descuidarse) let o.s. go. ∼**o** *m* abandonment; (estado) neglect

abani|car [7] *vt* fan. ∼**co** *m* fan

abaratar *vt* reduce

abarcar [7] *vt* put one's arms around, embrace; (comprender) embrace

abarrotar *vt* overfill, pack full

abarrotes *mpl* (LAm) groceries; (tienda) grocer's shop

abast|ecer [11] *vt* supply. ~**ecimiento** *m* supply; (acción) supplying. ~**o** *m* supply. no dar ~**o** be unable to cope (con with)

abati|do *a* depressed. ~**miento** *m* depression

abdicar [7] *vt* give up. ● *vi* abdicate

abdom|en *m* abdomen. ~**inal** *a* abdominal

abec|é *m* 🔢 alphabet, ABC. ~**edario** *m* alphabet

abedul *m* birch (tree)

abej|a *f* bee. ~**orro** *m* bumble-bee

aberración *f* aberration

abertura *f* opening

abeto *m* fir (tree)

abierto *pp* ⇒ABRIR. ● *a* open

abism|al *a* abysmal; (profundo) deep. ~**ar** *vt* throw into an abyss; (fig, abatir) humble. □ ~**arse** *vpr* be absorbed (en in), be lost (en in). ~**o** *m* abyss; (fig, diferencia) world of difference

ablandar *vt* soften.□ ~**se** *vpr* soften

abnega|ción *f* self-sacrifice. ~**do** *a* self-sacrificing

abochornar *vt* embarrass. □ ~**se** *vpr* feel embarrassed

abofetear *vt* slap

aboga|cía *f* law. ~**do** *m* lawyer, solicitor; (ante tribunal superior) barrister (Brit), attorney (Amer). ~**r** [12] *vi* plead

abolengo *m* ancestry

aboli|ción *f* abolition. ~**cionismo** *m* abolitionism.

~**cionista** *m & f* abolitionist. ~**r** [24] *vt* abolish

abolla|dura *f* dent. ~**r** *vt* dent

abolsado *a* baggy

abomba|do *a* convex; (LAm, atontado) dopey. ~**r** *vt* make convex. □ ~**rse** *vpr* (LAm, descomponerse) go bad

abominable *a* abominable

abona|ble *a* payable. ~**do** *a* paid. ● *m* subscriber. ~**r** *vt* pay; (en agricultura) fertilize. □ ~**rse** *vpr* subscribe. ~**o** *m* payment; (estiércol) fertilizer; (a un periódico) subscription

aborda|ble *a* reasonable; <persona> approachable. ~**je** *m* boarding. ~**r** *vt* tackle <un asunto>; approach <una persona>; (Naut) come alongside; (Mex, Aviac) board

aborigen *a & m* native

aborrec|er [11] *vt* loathe. ~**ible** *a* loathsome. ~**ido** *a* loathed. ~**imiento** *m* loathing

abort|ar *vi* have a miscarriage. ~**ivo** *a* abortive. ~**o** *m* miscarriage; (voluntario) abortion. hacerse un ~**o** have an abortion

abotonar *vt* button (up). □ ~**se** *vpr* button (up)

abovedado *a* vaulted

abrasa|dor *a* burning. ~**r** *vt* burn. □ ~**rse** *vpr* burn

abraz|ar *vt* [10] embrace. ~**arse** *vpr* embrace. ~**o** *m* hug. un fuerte ~**o de** (en una carta) with best wishes from

abre|botellas *m invar* bottle-opener. ~**cartas** *m invar* paper-knife. ~**latas** *m invar* tin opener (Brit), can opener

abrevia|ción *f* abbreviation; (texto abreviado) abridged text. ~**do** *a* brief; <texto> abridged. ~**r** *vt* abbreviate; abridge <texto>; cut

short <*viaje etc*>. ● *vi* be brief.
~**tura** *f* abbreviation.

abrig|ado *a* <*lugar*> sheltered;
<*persona*> well wrapped up.
~**ador** *a* (Mex, ropa) warm. ~**ar**
[12] *vt* shelter; cherish
<*esperanza*>; harbour <*duda,
sospecha*>. □ ~**arse** *vpr* (take)
shelter; (con ropa) wrap up. ~**o** *m*
(over)coat; (lugar) shelter

abril *m* April. ~**eño** *a* April

abrillantar *vt* polish

abrir (*pp* **abierto**) *vt/i* open.
□ ~**se** open; (extenderse) open
out; <*el tiempo*> clear

abrochar *vt* do up; (con botones)
button up

abruma|dor *a* overwhelming. ~**r**
vt overwhelm

abrupto *a* steep; (áspero) harsh

abrutado *a* brutish

absentismo *m* absenteeism

absolución *f* (Relig) absolution;
(Jurid) acquittal

absolut|amente *adv* absolutely,
completely. ~**o** *a* absolute. **en** ~**o**
(not) at all

absolver [2] (*pp* **absuelto**) *vt*
(Relig) absolve; (Jurid) acquit

absor|bente *a* absorbent; (fig,
interesante) absorbing. ~**ber** *vt*
absorb. ~**ción** *f* absorption. ~**to**
a absorbed

abstemio *a* teetotal. ● *m*
teetotaller

absten|ción *f* abstention.
□ ~**erse** [40] *vpr* abstain, refrain
(de from)

abstinencia *f* abstinence

abstra|cción *f* abstraction. ~**cto**
a abstract. ~**er** [41] *vt* abstract.
□ ~**erse** *vpr* be lost in thought.
~**ído** *a* absent-minded

absuelto *a* (Relig) absolved; (Jurid)
acquitted

absurdo *a* absurd. ● *m* absurd
thing

abuche|ar *vt* boo. ~**o** *m* booing

abuel|a *f* grandmother. ~**o** *m*
grandfather. ~**os** *mpl*
grandparents

ab|ulia *f* apathy. ~**úlico** *a*
apathetic

abulta|do *a* bulky. ~**r** *vt* (fig,
exagerar) exaggerate. ● *vi* be
bulky

abunda|ncia *f* abundance. **nadar
en la** ~**ncia** be rolling in money.
~**nte** *a* abundant, plentiful. ~**r**
vi be plentiful

aburguesarse *vpr* become
middle-class

aburri|do *a* (con estar) bored;
(con ser) boring. ~**dor** *a* (LAm)
boring. ~**miento** *m* boredom;
(cosa pesada) bore. ~**r** *vt* bore.
□ ~**rse** *vpr* get bored

abus|ar *vi* take advantage. ~**ar de
la bebida** drink too much. ~**ivo** *a*
excessive. ~**o** *m* abuse

acá *adv* here. ~ **y allá** here and
there. **de** ~ **para allá** to and fro.
de ayer ~ since yesterday. **más** ~
nearer

acaba|do *a* finished; (perfecto)
perfect. ● *m* finish. ~**r** *vt/i*
finish. □ ~**rse** *vpr* finish;
(agotarse) run out; (morirse) die. ~**r
con** put an end to. ~**r de** (+
infinitivo) have just (+ *pp*). ~ **de
llegar** he has just arrived. ~**r por**
(+ *infinitivo*) end up (+ *gerundio*).
¡se acabó! that's it!

acabóse *m*. **ser el** ~ be the end,
be the limit

acad|emia *f* academy. ~**émico** *a*
academic

acallar *vt* silence

acalora|do *a* heated; <*persona*>
hot. □ ~**rse** *vpr* get hot; (fig,
excitarse) get excited

acampar *vi* camp

acantilado *m* cliff

acapara|r *vt* hoard; (monopolizar) monopolize. **~miento** *m* hoarding; (monopolio) monopolizing

acariciar *vt* caress; <*animal*> stroke; <*idea etc*> nurture

ácaro *m* mite

acarre|ar *vt* transport; <*desgracias etc*> cause. **~o** *m* transport

acartona|do *a* <*piel*> wizened. □ **~rse** *vpr* (ponerse rígido) go stiff; <*piel*> become wizened

acaso *adv* maybe, perhaps. ● *m* chance. **~ llueva mañana** perhaps it will rain tomorrow. **por si ~** (just) in case

acata|miento *m* compliance (**de** with). **~r** *vt* comply with

acatarrarse *vpr* catch a cold, get a cold

acaudalado *a* well off

acceder *vi* agree; (tener acceso) have access

acces|ible *a* accessible; <*persona*> approachable. **~o** *m* access, entry; (Med, ataque) attack

accesorio *a & m* accessory

accident|ado *a* <*terreno*> uneven; (agitado) troubled; <*persona*> injured. **~al** *a* accidental. □ **~arse** *vpr* have an accident. **~e** *m* accident

acci|ón *f* (incl Jurid) action; (hecho) deed; (título) share. **~onar** *vt* work. ● *vi* gesticulate. **~onista** *m & f* shareholder

acebo *m* holly (tree)

acech|ar *vt* lie in wait for. **~o** *m* spying. **al ~o** on the look-out

aceit|ar *vt* oil; (Culin) add oil to. **~e** *m* oil. **~e de oliva** olive oil. **~te de ricino** castor oil. **~era** *f* cruet; (para engrasar) oilcan. **~ero** *a* oil. **~oso** *a* oily

aceitun|a *f* olive. **~ado** *a* olive. **~o** *m* olive tree

acelera|dor *m* accelerator. **~r** *vt* accelerate; (fig) speed up, quicken

acelga *f* chard

acent|o *m* accent; (énfasis) stress. **~uación** *f* accentuation. **~uar** [21] *vt* stress; (fig) emphasize. □ **~uarse** *vpr* become noticeable

acepción *f* meaning, sense

acepta|ble *a* acceptable. **~ción** *f* acceptance; (éxito) success. **~r** *vt* accept

acequia *f* irrigation channel

acera *f* pavement (Brit), sidewalk (Amer)

acerca de *prep* about

acerca|miento *m* approach; (fig) reconciliation. **~r** [7] *vt* bring near. □ **~rse** *vpr* approach

acero *m* steel. **~ inoxidable** stainless steel

acérrimo *a* (fig) staunch

acert|ado *a* right, correct; (apropiado) appropriate. **~ar** [1] *vt* (adivinar) get right, guess. ● *vi* get right; (en el blanco) hit. **~ar a** happen to. **~ar con** hit on. **~ijo** *m* riddle

achacar [7] *vt* attribute

achacoso *a* sickly

achaque *m* ailment

achatar *vt* flatten

achicar [7] *vt* make smaller; (fig, 🄻, empequeñecer) belittle; (Naut) bale out. □ **~rse** *vpr* become smaller; (humillarse) be intimidated

achicharra|r *vt* burn; (fig) pester. □ **~rse** *vpr* burn

achichincle *m & f* (Mex) hanger-on

achicopalado *a* (Mex) depressed

achicoria *f* chicory

achiote *m* (LAm) annatto

achispa|do *a* tipsy. □ **~rse** *vpr* get tipsy

achulado *a* cocky

acicala|do *a* dressed up. ~**r** *vt*
dress up. □ ~**rse** *vpr* get dressed
up

acicate *m* spur

acidez *f* acidity; (Med) heartburn

ácido *a* sour. ● *m* acid

acierto *m* success; (idea) good
idea; (habilidad) skill

aclama|ción *f* acclaim; (aplausos)
applause. ~**r** *vt* acclaim; (aplaudir)
applaud

aclara|ción *f* explanation. ~**r** *vt*
lighten <*colores*>; (explicar) clarify;
(enjuagar) rinse. ● *vi* <*el tiempo*>
brighten up. □ ~**rse** *vpr* become
clear. ~**torio** *a* explanatory

aclimata|ción *f* acclimatization,
acclimation (Amer). ~**r** *vt*
acclimatize, acclimate (Amer).
□ ~**rse** *vpr* become acclimatized,
become acclimated (Amer)

acné *m* acne

acobardar *vt* intimidate. □ ~**se**
vpr lose one's nerve

acocil *m* (Mex) freshwater shrimp

acog|edor *a* welcoming;
<*ambiente*> friendly. ~**er** [14] *vt*
welcome; (proteger) shelter; (recibir)
receive. □ ~**erse** *vpr* take refuge.
~**ida** *f* welcome; (refugio) refuge

acolcha|do *a* quilted. ~**r** *vt* quilt,
pad

acomedido *a* (Mex) obliging

acomet|er *vt* attack; (emprender)
undertake. ~**ida** *f* attack

acomod|ado *a* well off. ~**ador** *m*
usher. ~**adora** *f* usherette. ~**ar**
vt arrange; (adaptar) adjust. ● *vi*
be suitable. □ ~**arse** *vpr* settle
down; (adaptarse) conform

acompaña|miento *m*
accompaniment. ~**nte** *m & f*
companion; (Mus) accompanist.
~**r** *vt* go with; (hacer compañía)
keep company; (adjuntar) enclose

acondicionar *vt* fit out; (preparar)
prepare

aconseja|ble *a* advisable. ~**do** *a*
advised. ~**r** *vt* advise. □ ~**rse** *vpr*
~**rse con** consult

acontec|er [11] *vi* happen.
~**imiento** *m* event

acopla|miento *m* coupling; (Elec)
connection. ~**r** *vt* fit; (Elec)
connect; (Rail) couple

acorazado *a* armour-plated. ● *m*
battleship

acord|ar [2] *vt* agree (upon);
(decidir) decide; (recordar) remind.
□ ~**arse** *vpr* remember. ~**e** *a* in
agreement; (Mus) harmonious. ●
m chord

acorde|ón *m* accordion. ~**onista**
m & f accordionist

acordona|do *a* <*lugar*> cordoned
off; <*zapatos*> lace-up. ~**r** *vt* lace
(up); (rodear) cordon off

acorralar *vt* round up
<*animales*>; corner <*personas*>

acortar *vt* shorten; cut short
<*permanencia*>. □ ~**se** *vpr* get
shorter

acos|ar *vt* hound; (fig) pester. ~**o**
m pursuit; (fig) pestering

acostar [2] *vt* put to bed; (Naut)
bring alongside. ● *vi* (Naut) reach
land. □ ~**se** *vpr* go to bed;
(echarse) lie down. ~**se con** (fig)
sleep with

acostumbra|do *a* (habitual) usual.
~**do a** used to. ~**r** *vt* get used. **me
ha** ~**do a levantarme por la noche**
he's got me used to getting up at
night. ● *vi*. ~**r a** be accustomed
to. **acostumbro a comer a la una** I
usually have lunch at one
o'clock. □ ~**rse** *vpr* become
accustomed, get used (**a** to)

acota|ción *f* (nota) margin note;
(en el teatro) stage direction; (cota)
elevation mark. ~**miento** *m* (Mex)
hard shoulder

acrecentar [1] *vt* increase.
□ ∼**se** *vpr* increase

acredita|do *a* reputable; (Pol)
accredited. ∼**r** *vt* prove; accredit
<*diplomático*>; (garantizar)
guarantee; (autorizar) authorize.
□ ∼**rse** *vpr* make one's name

acreedor *a* worthy (de of). ● *m*
creditor

acribillar *vt* (a balazos) riddle (a
with); (a picotazos) cover (a with);
(fig, a preguntas etc) bombard (a
with)

acr|obacia *f* acrobatics. ∼**obacias
aéreas** aerobatics. ∼**óbata** *m & f*
acrobat. ∼**obático** *a* acrobatic

acta *f* minutes; (certificado)
certificate

actitud *f* posture, position; (fig)
attitude, position

activ|ar *vt* activate; (acelerar)
speed up. ∼**idad** *f* activity. ∼**o** *a*
active. ● *m* assets

acto *m* act; (ceremonia) ceremony.
en el ∼ immediately

act|or *m* actor. ∼**riz** *f* actress

actuación *f* action; (conducta)
behaviour; (Theat) performance

actual *a* present; <*asunto*>
topical. ∼**idad** *f* present; (de
asunto) topicality. **en la** ∼**idad** (en
este momento) currently; (hoy en día)
nowadays. ∼**idades** *fpl* current
affairs. ∼**ización** *f*
modernization. ∼**izar** [10] *vt*
modernize. ∼**mente** *adv* now, at
the present time

actuar [21] *vi* act. ∼ **de** act as

acuarel|a *f* watercolour. ∼**ista** *m
& f* watercolourist

acuario *m* aquarium. **A**∼
Aquarius

acuartelar *vt* quarter, billet;
(mantener en cuartel) confine to
barracks

acuático *a* aquatic

acuchillar *vt* slash; stab
<*persona*>

acuci|ante *a* urgent. ∼**ar** *vt* urge
on; (dar prisa a) hasten. ∼**oso** *a*
keen

acudir *vi*. ∼ **a** go to; (asistir)
attend; turn up for <*a una cita*>.
∼ **en auxilio** go to help

acueducto *m* aqueduct

acuerdo *m* agreement. ● *vb*
⇒ACORDAR. **¡de** ∼**!** OK! **de** ∼ **con**
in accordance with. **estar de** ∼
agree. **ponerse de** ∼ agree

acuesto *vb* ⇒ACOSTAR

acumula|dor *m* accumulator. ∼**r**
vt accumulate. □ ∼**rse** *vpr*
accumulate

acunar *vt* rock

acuñar *vt* mint, coin

acupuntura *f* acupuncture

acurrucarse [7] *vpr* curl up

acusa|do *a* accused; (destacado)
marked. ● *m* accused. ∼**r** *vt*
accuse; (mostrar) show; (denunciar)
denounce; acknowledge <*recibo*>

acuse *m*. ∼ **de recibo**
acknowledgement of receipt

acus|ica *m & f* Ⓕ telltale. ∼**ón** *m*
Ⓕ telltale

acústic|a *f* acoustics. ∼**o** *a*
acoustic

adapta|ble *a* adaptable. ∼**ción** *f*
adaptation. ∼**dor** *m* adapter. ∼**r**
vt adapt; (ajustar) fit. □ ∼**rse** *vpr*
adapt o.s.

adecua|do *a* suitable. ∼**r** *vt*
adapt, make suitable

adelant|ado *a* advanced; <*niño*>
precocious; <*reloj*> fast. **por** ∼**ado**
in advance. ∼**amiento** *m*
advance(ment); (Auto) overtaking.
∼**ar** *vt* advance, move forward;
(acelerar) speed up; put forward
<*reloj*>; (Auto) overtake. ● *vi*
advance, go forward; <*reloj*> gain,
be fast. □ ∼**arse** *vpr* advance,

move forward; <*reloj*> gain; (Auto) overtake. ● *int* come in!; (¡siga!) carry on! **más ~e** (lugar) further on; (tiempo) later on. **~o** *m* advance; (progreso) progress

adelgaza|miento *m* slimming. **~r** [10] *vt* make thin; lose <*kilos*>. ● *vi* lose weight; (adrede) slim. □ **~rse** *vpr* lose weight; (adrede) slim

ademán *m* gesture. **en ~ de** as if to. **ademanes** *mpl* (modales) manners.

además *adv* besides; (también) also; (lo que es más) what's more. **~ de** besides

adentr|arse *vpr*. **~arse en** penetrate into; study thoroughly <*tema etc*>. **~o** *adv* in(side). **~ de** (LAm) in(side). **mar ~o** out at sea. **tierra ~o** inland

adepto *m* supporter

aderez|ar [10] *vt* flavour <*bebidas*>; (condimentar) season; dress <*ensalada*>. **~o** *m* flavouring; (con condimentos) seasoning; (para ensalada) dressing

adeud|ar *vt* owe. **~o** *m* debit

adhe|rir [4] *vt/i* stick. □ **~rirse** *vpr* stick; (fig) follow. **~sión** *f* adhesion; (fig) support. **~sivo** *a* & *m* adhesive

adici|ón *f* addition. **~onal** *a* additional. **~onar** *vt* add

adicto *a* addicted. ● *m* addict; (seguidor) follower

adiestra|do *a* trained. **~miento** *m* training. **~r** *vt* train. □ **~rse** *vpr* practise

adinerado *a* wealthy

adiós *int* goodbye!; (al cruzarse con alguien) hello!

adit|amento *m* addition; (accesorio) accessory. **~ivo** *m* additive

adivin|anza *f* riddle. **~ar** *vt* foretell; (acertar) guess. **~o** *m* fortune-teller

adjetivo *a* adjectival. ● *m* adjective

adjudica|ción *f* award. **~r** [7] *vt* award. □ **~rse** *vpr* appropriate. **~tario** *m* winner of an award

adjunt|ar *vt* enclose. **~o** *a* enclosed; (auxiliar) assistant. ● *m* assistant

administra|ción *f* administration; (gestión) management. **~dor** *m* administrator; (gerente) manager. **~dora** *f* administrator; manageress. **~r** *vt* administer. **~tivo** *a* administrative

admira|ble *a* admirable. **~ción** *f* admiration. **~dor** *m* admirer. **~r** *vt* admire; (sorprender) amaze. □ **~rse** *vpr* be amazed

admi|sibilidad *f* admissibility. **~sible** *a* acceptable. **~sión** *f* admission; (aceptación) acceptance. **~tir** *vt* admit; (aceptar) accept

adobar *vt* (Culin) pickle; (condimentar) marinade

adobe *m* sun-dried brick

adobo *m* pickle; (condimento) marinade

adoctrinar *vt* indoctrinate

adolecer [11] *vi*. **~ de** suffer from

adolescen|cia *f* adolescence. **~te** *a* adolescent. ● *m & f* teenager, adolescent

adonde *adv* where

adónde *adv* where?

adop|ción *f* adoption. **~tar** *vt* adopt. **~tivo** *a* adoptive; <*hijo*> adopted; <*patria*> of adoption

adoqu|ín *m* paving stone; (imbécil) idiot. **~inado** *m* paving. **~inar** *vt* pave

adora|ción f adoration. **~r** vt adore

adormec|er [11] vt send to sleep; (fig, calmar) calm, soothe. □ **~erse** vpr fall asleep; <un miembro> go to sleep. **~ido** a sleepy; <un miembro> numb

adormilarse vpr doze

adorn|ar vt adorn (**con**, **de** with). **~o** m decoration

adosar vt lean (**a** against); (Mex, adjuntar) to enclose

adquiri|r [4] vt acquire; (comprar) purchase. **~sición** f acquisition; (compra) purchase. **~sitivo** a purchasing

adrede adv on purpose

adrenalina f adrenalin

aduan|a f customs. **~ero** a customs. ● m customs officer

aducir [47] vt allege

adueñarse vpr take possession

adul|ación f flattery. **~ador** a flattering. ● m flatterer. **~ar** vt flatter

ad|ulterar vt adulterate. **~ulterio** m adultery

adulto a & m adult, grown-up

advenedizo a & m upstart

advenimiento m advent, arrival; (subida al trono) accession

adverbio m adverb

advers|ario m adversary. **~idad** f adversity. **~o** a adverse, unfavourable

advert|encia f warning. **~ir** [4] vt warn; (notar) notice

adviento m Advent

adyacente a adjacent

aéreo a air; <foto> aerial; <ferrocarril> overhead

aeróbico a aerobic

aerodeslizador m hovercraft

aero|ligero m microlight. **~lito** m meteorite. **~moza** f (LAm)

flight attendant. **~puerto** m airport. **~sol** m aerosol

afab|ilidad f affability. **~le** a affable

afamado a famous

af|án m hard work; (deseo) desire. **~nador** m (Mex) cleaner. **~anar** vt ⊠ pinch ①. □ **~anarse** vpr strive (**en**, **por** to)

afear vt disfigure, make ugly; (censurar) censure

afecta|ción f affectation. **~do** a affected. **~r** vt affect

afect|ivo a sensitive. **~o** m (cariño) affection. ● a. **~o a** attached to. **~uoso** a affectionate. **con un ~uoso saludo** (en cartas) with kind regards. **suyo ~ísimo** (en cartas) yours sincerely

afeita|do m shave. **~dora** f electric razor. **~r** vt shave. □ **~rse** vpr shave, have a shave

afeminado a effeminate. ● m effeminate person

aferrar vt grasp. □ **~se** vpr to cling (**a** to)

afianza|miento m (refuerzo) strengthening; (garantía) guarantee. □ **~rse** [10] vpr become established

afiche m (LAm) poster

afici|ón f liking; (conjunto de aficionados) fans. **por ~ón** as a hobby. **~onado** a keen (**a** on), fond (**a** of). ● m fan. **~onar** vt make fond. □ **~onarse** vpr take a liking to

afila|do a sharp. **~dor** m knifegrinder. **~r** vt sharpen

afilia|ción f affiliation. **~do** a affiliated. □ **~rse** vpr become a member (**a** of)

afín a similar; (contiguo) adjacent; <personas> related

afina|ción f (Auto, Mus) tuning. **~do** a (Mus) in tune. **~dor** m

afinar tuner. **~r** vt (afilar) sharpen; (Auto, Mus) tune. □ **~rse** vpr become thinner

afincarse [7] vpr settle

afinidad f affinity; (parentesco) relationship by marriage

afirma|ción f affirmation. **~r** vt make firm; (asentir) affirm. □ **~rse** vpr steady o.s. **~tivo** a affirmative

aflicción f affliction

afligi|do a distressed. **~r** [14] vt distress. □ **~rse** vpr distress o.s.

aflojar vt loosen; (relajar) ease. ● vi let up. □ **~se** vpr loosen

aflu|encia f flow. **~ente** a flowing. ● m tributary. **~ir** [17] vi flow (a into)

afónico a hoarse

aforismo m aphorism

aforo m capacity

afortunado a fortunate, lucky

afrancesado a Frenchified

afrenta f insult; (vergüenza) disgrace

África f Africa. **~ del Sur** South Africa

africano a & m African

afrodisíaco, afrodisiaco a & m aphrodisiac

afrontar vt bring face to face; (enfrentar) face, confront

afuera adv out(side) ¡**~**! out of the way! **~ de** (LAm) outside. **~s** fpl outskirts

agachar vt lower. □ **~se** vpr bend over

agalla f (de los peces) gill. **~s** fpl (fig) guts

agarradera f (LAm) handle

agarr|ado a (fig, 🄵) mean. **~ar** vt grasp; (esp LAm) take; (LAm, pillar) catch. □ **~arse** vpr hold on; (🄵, reñirse) have a fight. **~ón** m tug; (LAm 🄵, riña) row

agarrotar vt tie tightly; <el frío> stiffen; garotte <un reo>. □ **~se** vpr go stiff; (Auto) seize up

agasaj|ado m guest of honour. **~ar** vt look after well. **~o** m good treatment

agazaparse vpr crouch

agencia f agency. **~ de viajes** travel agency. **~ inmobiliaria** estate agency (Brit), real estate agency (Amer). □ **~rse** vpr find (out) for o.s.

agenda f diary (Brit), appointment book (Amer); (programa) agenda

agente m agent; (de policía) policeman. ● f agent; (de policía) policewoman. **~ de aduanas** customs officer. **~ de bolsa** stockbroker

ágil a agile

agili|dad f agility. **~zación** f speeding up. **~zar** vt speed up

agita|ción f waving; (de un líquido) stirring; (intranquilidad) agitation. **~do** a <el mar> rough; (fig) agitated. **~dor** m (Pol) agitator

agitar vt wave; shake <botellas etc>; stir <líquidos>; (fig) stir up. □ **~se** vpr wave; <el mar> get rough; (fig) get excited

aglomera|ción f agglomeration; (de tráfico) traffic jam. **~r** vt amass. □ **~rse** vpr form a crowd

agnóstico a & m agnostic

agobi|ante a <trabajo> exhausting; <calor> oppressive. **~ar** vt weigh down; (fig, abrumar) overwhelm. **~o** m weight; (cansancio) exhaustion; (opresión) oppression

agolparse vpr crowd together

agon|ía f death throes; (fig) agony. **~izante** a dying; <luz> failing. **~izar** [10] vi be dying

agosto m August. **hacer su ~** feather one's nest

agota|do *a* exhausted; (todo vendido) sold out; <*libro*> out of print. **~dor** *a* exhausting. **~miento** *m* exhaustion. **~r** *vt* exhaust. □ **~rse** *vpr* be exhausted; <*existencias*> sell out; <*libro*> go out of print

agracia|do *a* attractive; (que tiene suerte) lucky. **~r** *vt* make attractive

agrada|ble *a* pleasant, nice. **~r** *vt/i* please. **esto me ~** I like this

agradec|er [11] *vt* thank <*persona*>; be grateful for <*cosa*>. **~ido** *a* grateful. ¡muy **~ido!** thanks a lot! **~imiento** *m* gratitude

agrado *m* pleasure; (amabilidad) friendliness

agrandar *vt* enlarge; (fig) exaggerate. □ **~se** *vpr* get bigger

agrario *a* agrarian, land; <*política*> agricultural

agrava|nte *a* aggravating. ● *f* additional problem. **~r** *vt* aggravate; (aumentar el peso) make heavier. □ **~rse** *vpr* get worse

agravi|ar *vt* offend; (perjudicar) wrong. **~o** *m* offence

agredir [24] *vt* attack. **~ de palabra** insult

agrega|do *m* aggregate; (diplomático) attaché. **~r** [12] *vt* add; appoint <*persona*>. □ **~se** *vpr* to join

agres|ión *f* aggression; (ataque) attack. **~ividad** *f* aggressiveness. **~ivo** *a* aggressive. **~or** *m* aggressor

agreste *a* country; <*terreno*> rough

agriar *regular, o raramente* [20] *vt* sour. □ **~se** *vpr* turn sour; (fig) become embittered

agr|ícola *a* agricultural. **~icultor** *m* farmer. **~icultura** *f* agriculture, farming

agridulce *a* bitter-sweet; (Culin) sweet-and-sour

agrietar *vt* crack. □ **~se** *vpr* crack; <*piel*> chap

agrio *a* sour. **~s** *mpl* citrus fruits

agro|nomía *f* agronomy. **~pecuario** *a* farming

agrupa|ción *f* group; (acción) grouping. **~r** *vt* group. □ **~rse** *vpr* form a group

agruras *fpl* (Mex) heartburn

agua *f* water; (lluvia) rain; (marea) tide; (vertiente del tejado) slope. **~ abajo** downstream. **~ arriba** upstream. **~ bendita** holy water. **~ corriente** running water. **~ de colonia** eau-de-cologne. **~ dulce** fresh water. **~ mineral con gas** fizzy mineral water. **~ mineral sin gas** still mineral water. **~ potable** drinking water. **~ salada** salt water. **hacer ~** (Naut) leak. **se me hizo ~ la boca** (LAm) it made my mouth water

aguacate *m* avocado pear; (árbol) avocado pear tree

aguacero *m* downpour, heavy shower

aguado *a* watery; (Mex, aburrido) boring

agua|fiestas *m & f invar* spoilsport, wet blanket. **~mala** *f* (Mex), **~mar** *m* jellyfish. **~marina** *f* aquamarine

aguant|ar *vt* put up with, bear; (sostener) support. ● *vi* hold out. □ **~arse** *vpr* restrain o.s. **~e** *m* patience; (resistencia) endurance

aguar [15] *vt* water down

aguardar *vt* wait for. ● *vi* wait

agua|rdiente *m* (cheap) brandy. **~rrás** *m* turpentine, turps Ⅱ

agud|eza *f* sharpness; (fig, perspicacia) insight; (fig, ingenio) wit. **~izar** [10] *vt* sharpen. □ **~izarse** *vpr* <*enfermedad*> get worse. **~o**

a sharp; *<ángulo, enfermedad>* acute; *<voz>* high-pitched

agüero *m* omen. **ser de mal ~** be a bad omen

aguijón *m* sting; (vara) goad

águila *f* eagle; (persona perspicaz) astute person; (Mex, de moneda) heads. ¿**~ o sol?** heads or tails?

aguileño *a* aquiline

aguinaldo *m* Christmas box; (LAm, paga) Christmas bonus

aguja *f* needle; (del reloj) hand; (Arquit) steeple. **~s** *fpl* (Rail) points

agujer|ear *vt* make holes in. **~o** *m* hole

agujetas *fpl* stiffness; (Mex, de zapatos) shoe laces. **tener ~** be stiff

aguzado *a* sharp

ah *int* ah!, oh!

ahí *adv* there. **~ nomás** (LAm) just there. **de ~ que** that is why. **por ~** that way; (aproximadamente) thereabouts

ahija|da *f* god-daughter, godchild. **~do** *m* godson, godchild. **~dos** *mpl* godchildren

ahínco *m* enthusiasm; (empeño) insistence

ahog|ado *a* (en el agua) drowned; (asfixiado) suffocated. **~ar** [12] *vt* (en el agua) drown; (asfixiar) suffocate; put out *<fuego>*. □ **~arse** *vpr* (en el agua) drown; (asfixiarse) suffocate. **~o** *m* breathlessness; (fig, angustia) distress

ahondar *vt* deepen. ● *vi* go deep. **~ en** (fig) examine in depth. □ **~se** *vpr* get deeper

ahora *adv* now; (hace muy poco) just now; (dentro de poco) very soon. **~ bien** however. **~ mismo** right now. **de ~ en adelante** from now on, in future. **por ~** for the time being

ahorcar [7] *vt* hang. □ **~se** *vpr* hang o.s.

ahorita *adv* (esp LAm 🄸) now. **~ mismo** right now

ahorr|ador *a* thrifty. **~ar** *vt* save. □ **~arse** *vpr* save o.s. **~o** *m* saving. **~os** *mpl* savings

ahuecar [7] *vt* hollow; fluff up *<colchón>*; deepen *<la voz>*

ahuizote *m* (Mex) scourge

ahuma|do *a* (Culin) smoked; (de colores) smoky. **~r** *vt* (Culin) smoke; (llenar de humo) fill with smoke. ● *vi* smoke. □ **~rse** *vpr* become smoky; *<comida>* acquire a smoky taste

ahuyentar *vt* drive away; banish *<pensamientos etc>*

aimará *a & m* Aymara. ● *m & f* Aymara Indian

airado *a* annoyed

aire *m* air; (viento) breeze; (corriente) draught; (aspecto) appearance; (Mus) tune, air. **~ acondicionado** air-conditioning. **al ~ libre** outdoors. **darse ~s** give o.s. airs. **~ar** *vt* air; (ventilar) ventilate; (fig, publicar) make public. □ **~arse** *vpr*. **salir para ~arse** go out for some fresh air

airoso *a* graceful; (exitoso) successful

aisla|do *a* isolated; (Elec) insulated. **~dor** *a* (Elec) insulating. **~nte** *a* insulating. **~r** [23] *vt* isolate; (Elec) insulate

ajar *vt* crumple; (estropear) spoil

ajedre|cista *m & f* chess-player. **~z** *m* chess

ajeno *a* (de otro) someone else's; (de otros) other people's; (extraño) alien

ajetre|ado *a* hectic, busy. **~o** *m* bustle

ají *m* (LAm) chilli; (salsa) chilli sauce

ajillo *m* garlic. al ~illo cooked with garlic. ~o *m* garlic. ~onjolí *m* sesame

ajuar *m* furnishings; (de novia) trousseau; (de bebé) layette

ajust|ado *a* right; <vestido> tight. ~ar *vt* fit; (adaptar) adapt; (acordar) agree; settle <una cuenta>; (apretar) tighten. ● *vi* fit. □ ~arse *vpr* fit; (adaptarse) adapt o.s.; (acordarse) come to an agreement. ~e *m* fitting; (adaptación) adjustment; (acuerdo) agreement; (de una cuenta) settlement

al = a + el

ala *f* wing; (de sombrero) brim.● *m* & *f* (deportes) winger

alaba|nza *f* praise. ~r *vt* praise

alacena *f* cupboard (Brit), closet (Amer)

alacrán *m* scorpion

alambr|ada *f* wire fence. ~ado *m* (LAm) wire fence. ~e *m* wire. ~e de púas barbed wire

alameda *f* avenue; (plantío de álamos) poplar grove

álamo *m* poplar. ~ temblón aspen

alarde *m* show. hacer ~ de boast of

alarga|do *a* long. ~dor *m* extension. ~r [12] *vt* lengthen; stretch out <mano etc>; (dar) give, pass. □ ~rse *vpr* get longer

alarido *m* shriek

alarm|a *f* alarm. ~ante *a* alarming. ~ar *vt* alarm, frighten. □ ~arse *vpr* be alarmed. ~ista *m* & *f* alarmist

alba *f* dawn

albacea *m* & *f* executor

albahaca *f* basil

albanés *a* & *m* Albanian

Albania *f* Albania

albañil *m* builder; (que coloca ladrillos) bricklayer

albarán *m* delivery note

albaricoque *m* apricot. ~ro *m* apricot tree

albedrío *m* will. libre ~ free will

alberca *f* tank, reservoir; (Mex, piscina) swimming pool

alberg|ar [12] *vt* (alojar) put up; <vivienda> house; (dar refugio) shelter. □ ~arse *vpr* stay; (refugiarse) shelter. ~ue *m* accommodation; (refugio) shelter. ~ue de juventud youth hostel

albino *a* & *m* albino

albóndiga *f* meatball, rissole

albornoz *m* bathrobe

alborot|ado *a* excited; (aturdido) hasty. ~ador *a* rowdy. ● *m* trouble-maker. ~ar *vt* disturb, upset. ● *vi* make a racket. □ ~arse *vpr* get excited; <el mar> get rough. ~o *m* row, uproar

álbum *m* (*pl* ~es *o* ~s) album

alcachofa *f* artichoke

alcald|e *m* mayor. ~esa *f* mayoress. ~ía *f* mayoralty; (oficina) mayor's office

alcance *m* reach; (de arma, telescopio etc) range; (déficit) deficit

alcancía *f* money-box; (LAm, de niño) piggy bank

alcantarilla *f* sewer; (boca) drain

alcanzar [10] *vt* (llegar a) catch up; (coger) reach; catch <un autobús>; <bala etc> strike, hit. ● *vi* reach; (ser suficiente) be enough. ~ a manage

alcaparra *f* caper

alcázar *m* fortress

alcoba *f* bedroom

alcoh|ol *m* alcohol. ~ol desnaturalizado methylated spirits, meths ~ólico *a* & *m* alcoholic. ~olímetro *m* Breathalyser. ~olismo *m* alcoholism

alcornoque *m* cork-oak; (persona torpe) idiot

aldaba *f* door-knocker

aldea *f* village. **~ano** *a* village.
● *m* villager

alea|ción *f* alloy. **~r** *vt* alloy

aleatorio *a* uncertain

aleccionar *vt* instruct

aledaños *mpl* outskirts

alega|ción *f* allegation; (LAm,
disputa) argument. **~r** [12] *vt*
claim; (Jurid) plead. ● *vi* (LAm)
argue. **~ta** *f* (Mex) argument. **~to**
m plea

alegoría *f* allegory

alegr|ar *vt* make happy; (avivar)
brighten up. □ **~arse** *vpr* be
happy; (emborracharse) get merry.
~e *a* happy; (achispado) merry,
tight. **~ía** *f* happiness

aleja|do *a* distant. **~amiento** *m*
removal; (entre personas)
estrangement; (distancia) distance.
~r *vt* remove; (ahuyentar) get rid
of; (fig, apartar) separate. □ **~rse**
vpr move away

alemán *a* & *m* German

Alemania *f* Germany. **~**
Occidental (historia) West Germany.
~ Oriental (historia) East Germany

alenta|dor *a* encouraging. **~r** [1]
vt encourage. ● *vi* breathe

alerce *m* larch

al|ergia *f* allergy. **~érgico** *a*
allergic

alero *m* (del tejado) eaves

alerta *a* alert. ¡**~**! look out! **estar**
~ be alert; (en guardia) be on the
alert. **~r** *vt* alert

aleta *f* wing; (de pez) fin

aletarga|do *a* lethargic. **~r** [12]
vt make lethargic. □ **~rse** *vpr*
become lethargic

alet|azo *m* (de un ave) flap of the
wings; (de un pez) flick of the fin.
~ear *vi* flap its wings, flutter

alevosía *f* treachery

alfab|ético *a* alphabetical.
~etizar [10] *vt* alphabetize;

teach to read and write. **~eto** *m*
alphabet. **~eto Morse** Morse code

alfalfa *f* alfalfa

alfarería *m* pottery. **~ero** *m*
potter

alféizar *m* (window)sill

alférez *m* second lieutenant

alfil *m* (en ajedrez) bishop

alfile|r *m* pin. **~tero** *m*
pincushion; (estuche) pin-case

alfombr|a *f* (grande) carpet;
(pequeña) rug, mat. **~ado** *a* (LAm)
carpeted. **~ar** *vt* carpet. **~illa** *f*
rug, mat; (Med) type of measles

alforja *f* saddle-bag

algarabía *f* hubbub

algas *fpl* seaweed

álgebra *f* algebra

álgido *a* (fig) decisive

algo *pron* something; (en frases
interrogativas, condicionales) anything.
● *adv* rather. ¿**~ más?** anything
else? ¿**quieres tomar ~?** would
you like a drink?; (de comer)
would you like something to eat?

algod|ón *m* cotton. **~ón de azúcar**
candy floss (Brit), cotton candy
(Amer). **~ón hidrófilo** cotton wool.
~onero *a* cotton. ● *m* cotton
plant

alguacil *m* bailiff

alguien *pron* someone,
somebody; (en frases interrogativas,
condicionales) anyone, anybody

alguno *a* (delante de nombres
masculinos en singular **algún**) some;
(en frases interrogativas, condicionales)
any; (pospuesto al nombre en frases
negativas) at all. **no tiene idea alguna**
he hasn't any idea at all. **alguna**
que otra vez from time to time.
algunas veces, alguna vez
sometimes. ● *pron* one; (en plural)
some; (alguien) someone

alhaja *f* piece of jewellery; (fig)
treasure. **~s** *fpl* jewellery

alharaca *f* fuss

alhelí *m* wallflower

alia|do *a* allied. ● *m* ally. **~nza** *f* alliance; (anillo) wedding ring. **~r** [20] *vt* combine. □ **~rse** *vpr* be combined; (formar una alianza) form an alliance

alias *adv & m* alias

alicaído *a* (fig, débil) weak; (fig, abatido) depressed

alicates *mpl* pliers

aliciente *m* incentive; (de un lugar) attraction

alienado *a* mentally ill

aliento *m* breath; (ánimo) courage

aligerar *vt* make lighter; (aliviar) alleviate, ease; (apresurar) quicken

alijo *m* (de contrabando) consignment

alimaña *f* pest. **~s** *fpl* vermin

aliment|ación *f* diet; (acción) feeding. **~ar** *vt* feed; (nutrir) nourish. ● *vi* be nourishing. □ **~arse** *vpr* feed (**con, de** on). **~icio** *a* nourishing. **productos** *mpl* **~icios** foodstuffs. **~o** *m* food. **~os** *mpl* (Jurid) alimony

alinea|ción *f* alignment; (en deportes) line-up. **~r** *vt* align, line up

aliñ|ar *vt* (Culin) season; dress <*ensalada*>. **~o** *m* seasoning; (para ensalada) dressing

alioli *m* garlic mayonnaise

alisar *vt* smooth

alistar *vt* put on a list; (Mil) enlist. □ **~se** *vpr* enrol; (Mil) enlist; (LAm, prepararse) get ready

alivi|ar *vt* lighten; relieve <*dolor, etc*>; (✗, hurtar) steal, pinch 🅘. □ **~arse** *vpr* <*dolor*> diminish; <*persona*> get better. **~o** *m* relief

aljibe *m* tank

allá *adv* (over) there. ¡**~ él!** that's his business. **~ fuera** out there.

~ por 1970 back in 1970. **el más ~** the beyond. **más ~** further on. **más ~ de** beyond. **por ~** that way

allana|miento *m*. **~miento (de morada)** breaking and entering; (LAm, por la autoridad) raid. **~r** *vt* level; remove <*obstáculos*>; (fig) iron out <*dificultades etc*>; break into <*una casa*>; (LAm, por la autoridad) raid

allega|do *a* close. ● *m* close friend; (pariente) close relative. **~r** [12] *vt* collect

allí *adv* there; (tiempo) then. **~ fuera** out there. **por ~** that way

alma *f* soul; (habitante) inhabitant

almac|én *m* warehouse; (LAm, tienda) grocer's shop; (de un arma) magazine. **~enes** *mpl* department store. **~enaje** *m* storage; (derechos) storage charges. **~enar** *vt* store; stock up with <*provisiones*>

almanaque *m* almanac

almeja *f* clam

almendr|a *f* almond. **~ado** *a* almond-shaped. **~o** *m* almond tree

alm|íbar *m* syrup. **~ibarar** *vt* cover in syrup

almid|ón *m* starch. **~onado** *a* starched; (fig, estirado) starchy

almirante *m* admiral

almizcle *m* musk. **~ra** *f* muskrat

almohad|a *f* pillow. **consultar con la ~a** sleep on it. **~illa** *f* small cushion. **~ón** *m* large pillow, bolster

almorranas *fpl* haemorrhoids, piles

alm|orzar [2 & 10] *vt* (a mediodía) have for lunch; (desayunar) have for breakfast. ● *vi* (a mediodía) have lunch; (desayunar) have breakfast. **~uerzo** *m* (a mediodía) lunch; (desayuno) breakfast

alocado *a* scatter-brained

jirafa *f* giraffe

jirón *m* shred, tatter

jitomate *m* (Mex) tomato

jorna|da *f* working day; (viaje) journey; (etapa) stage. **~l** *m* day's wage. **~lero** *m* day labourer

joroba *f* hump. **~do** *a* hunchbacked. ● *m* hunchback. **~r** *vt* 🗋 annoy

jota *f* letter J; (danza) jota, popular dance. **ni ~** nothing

joven (*pl* **jóvenes**) *a* young. ● *m* young man. ● *f* young woman

jovial *a* jovial

joy|a *f* jewel. **~as** *fpl* jewellery. **~ería** *f* jeweller's (shop). **~ero** *m* jeweller; (estuche) jewellery box

juanete *m* bunion

jubil|ación *f* retirement. **~ado** *a* retired. **~ar** *vt* pension off. ▫ **~arse** *vpr* retire. **~eo** *m* jubilee

júbilo *m* joy

judaísmo *m* Judaism

judía *f* Jewish woman; (alubia) bean. **~ blanca** haricot bean. **~ escarlata** runner bean. **~ verde** French bean

judicial *a* judicial

judío *a* Jewish. ● *m* Jewish man

judo *m* judo

juego *m* play; (de mesa, niños) game; (de azar) gambling; (conjunto) set. **estar en ~** be at stake. **estar fuera de ~** be offside. **hacer ~** match. **~s** *mpl* **malabares** juggling. **J~s** *mpl* **Olímpicos** Olympic Games. ● *vb* ⇒JUGAR

juerga *f* spree

jueves *m invar* Thursday

juez *m* judge. **~ de instrucción** examining magistrate. **~ de línea** linesman

juga|dor *m* player; (habitual, por dinero) gambler. **~r** [3] *vt* play.

● *vi* play; (apostar fuerte) gamble. ▫ **~rse** *vpr* risk. **~r al fútbol**, (LAm) **~r fútbol** play football

juglar *m* minstrel

jugo *m* juice; (de carne) gravy; (fig) substance. **~so** *a* juicy; (fig) substantial

juguet|e *m* toy. **~ear** *vi* play. **~ón** *a* playful

juicio *m* judgement; (opinión) opinion; (razón) reason. **a mi ~** in my opinion. **~so** *a* wise

juliana *f* vegetable soup

julio *m* July

junco *m* rush, reed

jungla *f* jungle

junio *m* June

junt|a *f* meeting; (consejo) board, committee; (Pol) junta; (Tec) joint. **~ar** *vt* join; (reunir) collect. ▫ **~arse** *vpr* join; <gente> meet. **~o** *a* joined; (en plural) together. **~o a** next to. **~ura** *f* joint

jura|do *a* sworn. ● *m* jury; (miembro de jurado) juror. **~mento** *m* oath. **prestar ~mento** take an oath. **~r** *vt/i* swear. **~r en falso** commit perjury. **jurárselas a uno** have it in for s.o.

jurel *m* (type of) mackerel

jurídico *a* legal

juris|dicción *f* jurisdiction. **~prudencia** *f* jurisprudence

justamente *a* exactly; (con justicia) fairly

justicia *f* justice

justifica|ción *f* justification. **~r** [7] *vt* justify

justo *a* fair, just; (exacto) exact; <ropa> tight. ● *adv* just. **~ a tiempo** just in time

juven|il *a* youthful. **~tud** *f* youth; (gente joven) young people

juzga|do *m* (tribunal) court. **~r** [12] *vt* judge. **a ~r por** judging by

kilo *m*, **kilogramo** *m* kilo, kilogram

kil|ometraje *m* distance in kilometres, mileage. **~ométrico** *a* 🆒 endless. **~ómetro** *m* kilometre. **~ómetro cuadrado** square kilometre

kilovatio *m* kilowatt

kiosco *m* kiosk

....
la

●*artículo definido femenino* (*pl* **las**)

····▸ the. **la flor azul** the blue flower. **la casa de al lado** the house next door. **cerca de la iglesia** near the church
No se traduce en los siguientes casos:

····▸ (con nombre abstracto, genérico) **la paciencia es una virtud** patience is a virtue. **odio la leche** I hate milk. **la madera es muy versátil** wood is very versatile

····▸ (con algunas instituciones) **termino la universidad mañana** I finish university tomorrow. **no va**

nunca a la iglesia he never goes to church. **está en la cárcel** he's in jail

····▸ (con nombres propios) **la Sra. Díaz** Mrs Díaz. **la doctora Lara** doctor Lara

····▸ (con partes del cuerpo, artículos personales) *se traduce por un posesivo*. **apretó la mano** he clenched his fist. **tienes la camisa desabrochada** your shirt is undone

····▸ **la + de. es la de Ana** it's Ana's. **la del sombrero** the one with the hat

····▸ **la + que** (persona) **la que me atendió** the one who served me. (cosa) **la que se rompió** the one that broke

····▸ **la + que** + *subjuntivo* (quienquiera) whoever. **la que gane pasará a la final** whoever wins will go to the final. (cualquiera) whichever. **compra la que sea más barata** buy whichever is cheaper
....

laberinto *m* labyrinth, maze

labia *f* gift of the gab

labio *m* lip

labor *f* work. **~es de aguja** needlework. **~es de ganchillo** crochet. **~es de punto** knitting. **~es domésticas** housework. **~able** *a* working. **~ar** *vi* work

laboratorio *m* laboratory

laborioso *a* laborious

laborista *a* Labour. ● *m & f* member of the Labour Party

labra|do *a* worked; <*madera*> carved; <*metal*> wrought; <*tierra*> ploughed. **~dor** *m* farmer; (obrero) farm labourer. **~nza** *f* farming.

~r *vt* work; carve *<madera>*; cut *<piedra>*; till *<la tierra>*. □ **~rse** *vpr*. **~rse un porvenir** carve out a future for o.s.

labriego *m* peasant

laca *f* lacquer

lacayo *m* lackey

lacio *a* straight; (flojo) limp

lacón *m* shoulder of pork

lacónico *a* laconic

lacr|ar *vt* seal. **~e** *m* sealing wax

lactante *a* *<niño>* still on milk

lácteo *a* milky. **productos** *mpl* **~s** dairy products

ladear *vt* tilt. □ **~se** *vpr* lean

ladera *f* slope

ladino *a* astute

lado *m* side. **al ~** near. **al ~ de** next to, beside. **de ~** sideways. **en todos ~s** everywhere. **los de al ~** the next-door neighbours. **por otro ~** on the other hand. **por todos ~s** everywhere. **por un ~** on the one hand

ladr|ar *vi* bark. **~ido** *m* bark

ladrillo *m* brick

ladrón *m* thief, robber; (de casas) burglar

lagart|ija *f* (small) lizard. **~o** *m* lizard

lago *m* lake

lágrima *f* tear

lagrimoso *a* tearful

laguna *f* small lake; (fig, omisión) gap

laico *a* lay

lament|able *a* deplorable; (que da pena) pitiful; *<pérdida>* sad. **~ar** *vt* be sorry about. □ **~arse** *vpr* lament; (quejarse) complain. **~o** *m* moan

lamer *vt* lick

lámina *f* sheet; (ilustración) plate; (estampa) picture card

lamina|do *a* laminated. **~r** *vt* laminate

lámpara *f* lamp. **~ de pie** standard lamp

lamparón *m* stain

lampiño *a* beardless; *<cuerpo>* hairless

lana *f* wool. **de ~** wool(len)

lanceta *f* lancet

lancha *f* boat. **~ motora** motor boat. **~ salvavidas** lifeboat

langost|a *f* (de mar) lobster; (insecto) locust. **~ino** *m* king prawn

languide|cer [11] *vi* languish. **~z** *f* languor

lánguido *a* languid; (decaído) listless

lanilla *f* nap; (tela fina) flannel

lanudo *a* woolly; *<perro>* shaggy

lanza *f* lance, spear

lanza|llamas *m invar* flamethrower. **~miento** *m* throw; (acción de lanzar) throwing; (de proyectil, de producto) launch. **~miento de peso**, (LAm) **~miento de bala** shot put. **~r** [10] *vt* throw; (de un avión) drop; launch *<proyectil, producto>*. □ **~rse** *vpr* throw o.s.

lapicero *m* (propelling) pencil

lápida *f* tombstone; (placa conmemorativa) memorial tablet

lapidar *vt* stone

lápiz *m* pencil. **~ de labios** lipstick. **a ~** in pencil

lapso *m* lapse

larg|a *f*. **a la ~a** in the long run. **dar ~as** put off. **~ar** [12] *vt* (Naut) let out; (🔢, dar) give; 🔢 deal *<bofetada etc>*. □ **~arse** *vpr* 🔢 beat it 🔢. **~o** *a* long. ● *m* length. **¡~o!** go away! **a lo ~o** lengthwise. **a lo ~o de** along. **tener 100 metros de ~o** be 100 metres long

laring|e *f* larynx. **~itis** *f* laryngitis

L

larva *f* larva

las *art def fpl* the. *véase tb* LA. ● *pron* them. ~ **de** those, the ones. ~ **de Vd** your ones, yours. ~ **que** whoever, the ones

láser *m* laser

lástima *f* pity; (queja) complaint. **da ~ verlo así** it's sad to see him like that. **ella me da ~** I feel sorry for her. **¡qué ~!** what a pity!

lastim|ado *a* hurt. ~**ar** *vt* hurt. □ ~**arse** *vpr* hurt o.s. ~**ero** *a* doleful. ~**oso** *a* pitiful

lastre *m* ballast; (fig) burden

lata *f* tinplate; (envase) tin (esp Brit), can; (🔲, molestia) nuisance. **dar la ~** be a nuisance. **¡qué ~!** what a nuisance!

latente *a* latent

lateral *a* side, lateral

latido *m* beating; (cada golpe) beat

latifundio *m* large estate

latigazo *m* (golpe) lash; (chasquido) crack

látigo *m* whip

latín *m* Latin. **saber ~** 🔲 know what's what 🔲

latino *a* Latin. **L~américa** *f* Latin America. ~**americano** *a & m* Latin American

latir *vi* beat; <herida> throb

latitud *f* latitude

latón *m* brass

latoso *a* annoying; (pesado) boring

laúd *m* lute

laureado *a* honoured; (premiado) prize-winning

laurel *m* laurel; (Culin) bay

lava *f* lava

lava|ble *a* washable. ~**bo** *m* wash-basin; (retrete) toilet. ~**dero** *m* sink. ~**do** *m* washing. ~**do de cerebro** brainwashing. ~**do en seco** dry-cleaning. ~**dora** *f* washing machine. ~**ndería** *f* laundry. ~**ndería automática** launderette, laundromat (esp Amer). ~**platos** *m & f invar* dishwasher. ● *m* (Mex, fregadero) sink. ~**r** *vt* wash. ~**r en seco** dry-clean. □ ~**rse** *vpr* have a wash. ~**rse las manos** (incl fig) wash one's hands. ~**tiva** *f* enema. ~**vajillas** *m invar* dishwasher; (detergente) washing-up liquid (Brit), dishwashing liquid (Amer)

laxante *a & m* laxative

lazada *f* bow

lazarillo *m* guide for a blind person

lazo *m* knot; (lazada) bow; (fig, vínculo) tie; (con nudo corredizo) lasso; (Mex, cuerda) rope

le *pron* (acusativo, él) him; (acusativo, Vd) you; (dativo, él) (to) him; (dativo, ella) (to) her; (dativo, cosa) (to) it; (dativo, Vd) (to) you

leal *a* loyal; (fiel) faithful. ~**tad** *f* loyalty; (fidelidad) faithfulness

lección *f* lesson

leche *f* milk; (golpe) bash. ~ **condensada** condensed milk. ~ **desnatada** skimmed milk. ~ **en polvo** powdered milk. ~ **sin desnatar** whole milk. **tener mala ~** be spiteful. ~**ra** *f* (vasija) milk jug. ~**ría** *f* dairy. ~**ro** *a* milk, dairy. ● *m* milkman

lecho *m* (en literatura) bed. ~ **de río** river bed

lechoso *a* milky

lechuga *f* lettuce

lechuza *f* owl

lect|or *m* reader; (Univ) language assistant. ~**ura** *f* reading

leer [18] *vt/i* read

legación *f* legation

legado *m* legacy; (enviado) legate

legajo *m* bundle, file

legal *a* legal. **~idad** *f* legality.
~izar [10] *vt* legalize; (certificar)
authenticate. **~mente** *adv* legally

legar [12] *vt* bequeath

legible *a* legible

legi|ón *f* legion. **~onario** *m*
legionary

legisla|ción *f* legislation. **~dor**
m legislator. **~r** *vi* legislate.
~tura *f* term (of office); (año
parlamentario) session; (LAm, cuerpo)
legislature

leg|itimidad *f* legitimacy. **~ítimo**
a legitimate; (verdadero) real

lego *a* lay; (ignorante) ignorant. ●
m layman

legua *f* league

legumbre *f* vegetable

lejan|ía *f* distance. **~o** *a* distant

lejía *f* bleach

lejos *adv* far. **~ de** far from. **a lo
~** in the distance. **desde ~** from
a distance, from afar

lema *m* motto

lencería *f* linen; (de mujer) lingerie

lengua *f* tongue; (idioma)
language. **irse de la ~** talk too
much. **morderse la ~** hold one's
tongue

lenguado *m* sole

lenguaje *m* language

lengüeta *f* (de zapato) tongue.
~da *f*, **~zo** *m* lick

lente *f* lens. **~s** *mpl* glasses. **~s
de contacto** contact lenses

lentej|a *f* lentil. **~uela** *f* sequin

lentilla *f* contact lens

lent|itud *f* slowness. **~o** *a* slow

leñ|a *f* firewood. **~ador** *m*
woodcutter. **~o** *m* log

Leo *m* Leo

le|ón *m* lion. **~ona** *f* lioness

leopardo *m* leopard

leotardo *m* thick tights

lepr|a *f* leprosy. **~oso** *m* leper

lerdo *a* dim; (torpe) clumsy

les *pron* (acusativo) them; (acusativo,
Vds) you; (dativo) (to) them; (dativo,
Vds) (to) you

lesbiana *f* lesbian

lesi|ón *f* wound. **~onado** *a*
injured. **~onar** *vt* injure; (dañar)
damage

letal *a* lethal

let|árgico *a* lethargic. **~argo** *m*
lethargy

letr|a *f* letter; (escritura)
handwriting; (de una canción)
words, lyrics. **~a de cambio** bill of
exchange. **~a de imprenta** print.
~ado *a* learned. **~ero** *m* notice;
(cartel) poster

letrina *f* latrine

leucemia *f* leukaemia

levadura *f* yeast. **~ en polvo**
baking powder

levanta|miento *m* lifting;
(sublevación) uprising. **~r** *vt* raise,
lift; (construir) build; (recoger) pick
up. □ **~rse** *vpr* get up; (ponerse de
pie) stand up; (erguirse, sublevarse)
rise up

levante *m* east; (viento) east wind

levar *vt*. **~ anclas** weigh anchor

leve *a* light; <*sospecha etc*> slight;
<*enfermedad*> mild; (de poca
importancia) trivial. **~dad** *f*
lightness; (fig) slightness

léxico *m* vocabulary

lexicografía *f* lexicography

ley *f* law; (parlamentaria) act

leyenda *f* legend

liar [20] *vt* tie; (envolver) wrap up;
roll <*cigarrillo*>; (fig, confundir)
confuse; (fig, enredar) involve.
□ **~se** *vpr* get involved

libanés *a & m* Lebanese

libelo *m* (escrito) libellous article;
(Jurid) petition

libélula *f* dragonfly

libera|ción *f* liberation. **~dor** *a*
liberating. ● *m* liberator

liberal *a & m & f* liberal. **~idad** *f* liberality

liber|ar *vt* free. **~tad** *f* freedom. **~tad de cultos** freedom of worship. **~tad de imprenta** freedom of the press. **~tad provisional** bail. **en ~tad** free. **~tador** *m* liberator. **~tar** *vt* free

libertino *m* libertine

libido *f* libido

libio *a & m* Libyan

libra *f* pound. **~ esterlina** pound sterling

Libra *m* Libra

libra|dor *m* (Com) drawer. **~r** *vt* free; (de un peligro) save. □ **~rse** *vpr* free o.s. **~rse de** get rid of

libre *a* free. **estilo ~** (en natación) freestyle. **~ de impuestos** tax-free

librea *f* livery

libr|ería *f* bookshop (Brit), bookstore (Amer); (mueble) bookcase. **~ero** *m* bookseller; (Mex, mueble) bookcase. **~eta** *f* notebook. **~o** *m* book. **~o de bolsillo** paperback. **~o de ejercicios** exercise book. **~o de reclamaciones** complaints book

licencia *f* permission; (documento) licence. **~do** *m* graduate; (Mex, abogado) lawyer. **~ para manejar** (Mex) driving licence. **~r** *vt* (Mil) discharge; (echar) dismiss. **~tura** *f* degree

licencioso *a* licentious

licitar *vt* bid for

lícito *a* legal; (permisible) permissible

licor *m* liquor; (dulce) liqueur

licua|dora *f* blender. **~r** [21] liquefy; (Culin) blend

lid *f* fight. **en buena ~** by fair means. **~es** *fpl* matters

líder *m* leader

liderato *m*, **liderazgo** *m* leadership

lidia *f* bullfighting; (lucha) fight. **~r** *vt/i* fight

liebre *f* hare

lienzo *m* linen; (del pintor) canvas; (muro, pared) wall

liga *f* garter; (alianza) league; (LAm, gomita) rubber band. **~dura** *f* bond; (Mus) slur; (Med) ligature. **~mento** *m* ligament. **~r** [12] *vt* bind; (atar) tie; (Mus) slur. ● *vi* mix. **~r con** (fig) pick up. □ **~rse** *vpr* (fig) commit o.s.

liger|eza *f* lightness; (agilidad) agility; (rapidez) swiftness; (de carácter) fickleness. **~o** *a* light; (rápido) quick; (ágil) agile; (superficial) superficial; (de poca importancia) slight. ● *adv* quickly. **a la ~a** lightly, superficially

liguero *m* suspender belt

lija *f* dogfish; (papel de lija) sandpaper. **~r** *vt* sand

lila *f* lilac. ● *m* (color) lilac

lima *f* file; (fruta) lime. **~duras** *fpl* filings. **~r** *vt* file (down)

limita|ción *f* limitation. **~do** *a* limited. **~r** *vt* limit. **~r con** border on. **~tivo** *a* limiting

límite *m* limit. **~ de velocidad** speed limit

limítrofe *a* bordering

lim|ón *m* lemon; (Mex) lime. **~onada** *f* lemonade

limosn|a *f* alms. **pedir ~a** beg. **~ear** *vi* beg

limpia|botas *m invar* bootblack. **~parabrisas** *m invar* windscreen wiper (Brit), windshield wiper (Amer). **~pipas** *m invar* pipe-cleaner. **~r** *vt* clean; (enjugar) wipe. **~vidrios** *m invar* (LAm) window cleaner

limpi|eza *f* cleanliness; (acción de limpiar) cleaning. **~eza en seco** dry-cleaning. **~o** *a* clean; <cielo> clear; (fig, honrado) honest; (neto) net. **pasar a ~o**, (LAm) **pasar en ~o**

make a fair copy. ● *adv* fairly.
jugar ~o play fair

linaje *m* lineage; (fig, clase) kind

lince *m* lynx

linchar *vt* lynch

lind|ar *vi* border (**con** on). **~e** *f* boundary. **~ero** *m* border

lindo *a* pretty, lovely. **de lo ~** 🆒 a lot

línea *f* line. **en ~s generales** broadly speaking. **guardar la ~** watch one's figure

lingote *m* ingot

lingü|ista *m & f* linguist. **~ística** *f* linguistics. **~ístico** *a* linguistic

lino *m* flax; (tela) linen

linterna *f* lantern; (de bolsillo) torch, flashlight (Amer)

lío *m* bundle; (jaleo) fuss; (embrollo) muddle; (amorío) affair

liquida|ción *f* liquidation; (venta especial) sale. **~r** *vt* liquify; (Com) liquidate; settle <*cuenta*>

líquido *a* liquid; (Com) net. ● *m* liquid; (Com) cash

lira *f* lyre; (moneda italiana) lira

líric|a *f* lyric poetry. **~o** *a* lyric(al)

lirio *m* iris

lirón *m* dormouse; (fig) sleepyhead. **dormir como un ~** sleep like a log

lisiado *a* crippled

liso *a* smooth; <*pelo*> straight; <*tierra*> flat; (sencillo) plain

lisonj|a *f* flattery. **~eador** *a* flattering. ● *m* flatterer. **~ear** *vt* flatter. **~ero** *a* flattering

lista *f* stripe; (enumeración) list. **~ de correos** poste restante. **a ~s** striped. **pasar ~** take the register. **~do** *a* striped

listo *a* clever; (preparado) ready

listón *m* strip; (en saltos) bar; (Mex, cinta) ribbon

litera *f* (en barco, tren) berth; (en habitación) bunk bed

literal *a* literal

litera|rio *a* literary. **~tura** *f* literature

litig|ar [12] *vi* dispute; (Jurid) litigate. **~io** *m* dispute; (Jurid) litigation

litografía *f* (arte) lithography; (cuadro) lithograph

litoral *a* coastal. ● *m* coast

litro *m* litre

lituano *a & m* Lithuanian

liturgia *f* liturgy

liviano *a* fickle; (LAm, de poco peso) light

lívido *a* livid

llaga *f* wound; (úlcera) ulcer

llama *f* flame; (animal) llama

llamada *f* call

llama|do *a* called. ● *m* (LAm) call. **~miento** *m* call. **~r** *vt* call; (por teléfono) phone. ● *vi* call; (golpear en la puerta) knock; (tocar el timbre) ring. **~r por teléfono** phone, telephone. ◻ **~rse** *vpr* be called. **¿cómo te ~s?** what's your name?

llamarada *f* sudden blaze; (fig, de pasión etc) outburst

llamativo *a* flashy; <*color*> loud; <*persona*> striking

llamear *vi* blaze

llano *a* flat, level; <*persona*> natural; (sencillo) plain. ● *m* plain

llanta *f* (Auto) (wheel) rim; (LAm, neumático) tyre

llanto *m* crying

llanura *f* plain

llave *f* key; (para tuercas) spanner; (LAm, del baño etc) tap (Brit), faucet (Amer); (Elec) switch. **~ inglesa** monkey wrench. **cerrar con ~** lock. **echar la ~** lock up. **~ro** *m* key-ring

llega|da *f* arrival. **~r** [12] *vi* arrive, come; (alcanzar) reach;

(bastar) be enough. **~r a** (conseguir) manage to. **~r a saber** find out. **~r a ser** become. **~r hasta** go as far as

llen|ar *vt* fill (up); (rellenar) fill in; (cubrir) cover (**de** with). **~o** *a* full. ● *m* (en el teatro etc) full house. **de ~** entirely

lleva|dero *a* tolerable. **~r** *vt* carry; (inducir, conducir) lead; (acompañar) take; wear <*ropa*>. **¿cuánto tiempo ~s aquí?** how long have you been here? **llevo 3 años estudiando inglés** I've been studying English for 3 years. □ **~rse** *vpr* take away; win <*premio etc*>; (comprar) take. **~rse bien** get on well together

llor|ar *vi* cry; <*ojos*> water. **~iquear** *vi* whine. **~iqueo** *m* whining. **~o** *m* crying. **~ón** *a* whining. ● *m* cry-baby. **~oso** *a* tearful

llov|er [2] *vi* rain. **~izna** *f* drizzle. **~iznar** *vi* drizzle

llueve *vb* ⇨LLOVER

lluvi|a *f* rain; (fig) shower. **~oso** *a* rainy; <*clima*> wet

lo *art def neutro*. **~ importante** what is important, the important thing. ● *pron* (él) him; (cosa) it. **~ que** what, that which

loa *f* praise. **~ble** *a* praiseworthy. **~r** *vt* praise

lobo *m* wolf

lóbrego *a* gloomy

lóbulo *m* lobe

local *a* local. ● *m* premises. **~idad** *f* locality; (de un espectáculo) seat; (entrada) ticket. **~izar** [10] *vt* find, locate

loción *f* lotion

loco *a* mad, crazy. ● *m* lunatic. **~ de alegría** mad with joy. **estar ~ por** be crazy about. **volverse ~** go mad

locomo|ción *f* locomotion. **~tora** *f* locomotive

locuaz *a* talkative

locución *f* expression

locura *f* madness; (acto) crazy thing. **con ~** madly

locutor *m* broadcaster

lod|azal *m* quagmire. **~o** *m* mud

lógic|a *f* logic. **~o** *a* logical

logr|ar *vt* get; win <*premio*>. **~ hacer** manage to do. **~o** *m* achievement; (de premio) winning; (éxito) success

loma *f* small hill

lombriz *f* worm

lomo *m* back; (de libro) spine. **~ de cerdo** loin of pork

lona *f* canvas

loncha *f* slice; (de tocino) rasher

londinense *a* from London. ● *m* Londoner

Londres *m* London

loneta *f* thin canvas

longaniza *f* sausage

longev|idad *f* longevity. **~o** *a* long-lived

longitud *f* length; (Geog) longitude

lonja *f* slice; (de tocino) rasher; (Com) market

lord *m* (*pl* **lores**) lord

loro *m* parrot

los *art def mpl* the. *véase tb* EL. ● *pron* them. **~ de Antonio** Antonio's. **~ que** whoever, the ones

losa *f* (baldosa) flagstone. **~ sepulcral** tombstone

lote *m* share; (de productos) batch; (terreno) plot (Brit), lot (Amer)

lotería *f* lottery

loto *m* lotus

loza *f* crockery; (fina) china

lozano *a* fresh; *<vegetación>* lush; *<persona>* healthy-looking

lubina *f* sea bass

lubrica|nte *a* lubricating. ● *m* lubricant. **~r** [7] *vt* lubricate

lucero *m* bright star. **~ del alba** morning star

lucha *f* fight; (fig) struggle. **~dor** *m* fighter. **~r** *vi* fight; (fig) struggle

lucid|ez *f* lucidity. **~o** *a* splendid

lúcido *a* lucid

luciérnaga *f* glow-worm

lucimiento *m* brilliance

lucio *m* pike

lucir [11] *vt* (fig) show off. ● *vi* shine; *<joya>* sparkle; (LAm, mostrarse) look. □ **~se** *vpr* (fig) shine, excel; (presumir) show off

lucr|ativo *a* lucrative. **~o** *m* gain

luego *adv* then; (más tarde) later (on); (Mex, pronto) soon. ● *conj* therefore. **~ que** as soon as. **desde ~** of course

lugar *m* place; (espacio libre) room. **~ común** cliché. **dar ~ a** give rise to. **en ~ de** instead of. **en primer ~** first. **hacer ~** make room. **tener ~** take place. **~eño** *a* local

lugarteniente *m* deputy

lúgubre *a* gloomy

lujo *m* luxury. **de ~** luxury. **~so** *a* luxurious

lujuria *f* lust

lumbago *m* lumbago

luminoso *a* luminous; (fig) bright; *<letrero>* illuminated

luna *f* moon; (espejo) mirror. **~ de miel** honeymoon. **claro de ~** moonlight. **estar en la ~** be miles away. **~r** *a* lunar. ● *m* mole; (en tela) spot

lunes *m invar* Monday

lupa *f* magnifying glass

lustr|abotas *m invar* (LAm) bootblack. **~ar** *vt* shine, polish.

~e *m* shine; (fig, esplendor) splendour. **dar ~e a**, **sacar ~e a** polish. **~oso** *a* shining

luto *m* mourning. **estar de ~** be in mourning

luz *f* light; (electricidad) electricity. **luces altas** (LAm) headlights on full beam. **luces bajas** (LAm), **luces cortas** dipped headlights. **luces antiniebla** fog light. **luces largas** headlights on full beam. **a la ~ de** in the light of. **a todas luces** obviously. **dar a ~** give birth. **hacer la ~ sobre** shed light on. **sacar a la ~** bring to light

macabro *a* macabre

macaco *m* macaque (monkey)

macanudo *a* 🄳 great🄳

macarrones *mpl* macaroni

macerar *vt* macerate *<fruta>*; marinade *<carne etc>*

maceta *f* mallet; (tiesto) flowerpot

machacar [7] *vt* crush. ● *vi* go on (**sobre** about)

machamartillo. a ~ *adj* ardent; (como adv) firmly

machet|azo *m* blow with a machete; (herida) wound from a machete. **~e** *m* machete

mach|ista *m* male chauvinist. **~o** *a* male; (varonil) macho

machu|car [7] *vt* bruise; (aplastar) crush. **~cón** *m* (LAm) bruise

macizo *a* solid. ● *m* mass; (de plantas) bed

madeja *f* skein

madera m (vino) Madeira. ● f wood; (naturaleza) nature. ~**ble** a yielding timber. ~**men** m woodwork

madero m log; (de construcción) timber

madona f Madonna

madr|astra f stepmother. ~**e** f mother. ~**eperla** f mother-of-pearl. ~**eselva** f honeysuckle

madrigal m madrigal

madriguera f den; (de conejo) burrow

madrileño a of Madrid. ● m person from Madrid

madrina f godmother; (en una boda) matron of honour

madrug|ada f dawn. de ~**ada** at dawn. ~**ador** a who gets up early. ● m early riser. ~**ar** [12] vi get up early

madur|ación f maturing; (de fruta) ripening. ~**ar** vt/i mature; <fruta> ripen. ~**ez** f maturity; (de fruta) ripeness. ~**o** a mature; <fruta> ripe

maestr|ía f skill; (Univ) master's degree. ~**o** m master; (de escuela) schoolteacher

mafia f mafia

magdalena f fairy cake (Brit), cup cake (Amer)

magia f magic

mágico a magic; (maravilloso) magical

magist|erio m teaching (profession); (conjunto de maestros) teachers. ~**rado** m magistrate; (juez) judge. ~**ral** a teaching; (bienhecho) masterly. ~**ratura** f magistracy

magn|animidad f magnanimity. ~**ánimo** a magnanimous. ~**ate** m magnate, tycoon

magnavoz m (Mex) megaphone

magnético a magnetic

magneti|smo m magnetism. ~**zar** [10] vt magnetize

magn|ificar vt extol; (LAm) magnify <objeto>. ~**ificencia** f magnificence. ~**ífico** a magnificent. ~**itud** f magnitude

magnolia f magnolia

mago m magician; (en cuentos) wizard

magro a lean; <tierra> poor

magulla|dura f bruise. ~**r** vt bruise. □ ~**rse** vpr bruise

mahometano a Islamic

maíz m maize, corn (Amer)

majada f sheepfold; (estiércol) manure; (LAm) flock of sheep

majader|ía f silly thing. ~**o** m idiot. ● a stupid

majest|ad f majesty. ~**uoso** a majestic

majo a nice

mal adv badly; (poco) poorly; (difícilmente) hardly; (equivocadamente) wrongly; (desagradablemente) bad. ● a. **estar** ~ be ill; (anímicamente) be in a bad way; (incorrecto) be wrong. **estar** ~ **de** (escaso de) be short of. véase tb MALO. ● m evil; (daño) harm; (enfermedad) illness. ~ **que bien** somehow (or other). **de** ~ **en peor** from bad to worse. **hacer** ~ **en** be wrong to. ¡**menos** ~! thank goodness!

malabaris|mo m juggling. ~**ta** m & f juggler

mala|consejado a ill-advised. ~**costumbrado** a spoilt. ~ **crianza** f (LAm) rudeness. ~**gradecido** a ungrateful

malagueño a of Málaga. ● m person from Málaga

malaria f malaria

Malasia f Malaysia

malavenido a incompatible

malaventura a unfortunate

malayo a Malay(an)

malbaratar vt sell off cheap; (malgastar) squander

malcarado a nasty looking

malcriado a <niño> spoilt

maldad f evil; (acción) wicked thing

maldecir [46] (pero imperativo **maldice**, futuro y condicional regulares, pp **maldecido** o **maldito**) vt curse. ● vi curse; speak ill (**de** of)

maldi|ciente a backbiting; (que blasfema) foul-mouthed. ~**ción** f curse. ~**to** a damned. ¡~**to sea**! damn (it)!

maleab|ilidad f malleability. ~**le** a malleable

malea|nte m criminal. ~**r** vt damage; (pervertir) corrupt. □~**rse** vpr be spoilt; (pervertirse) be corrupted

malecón m breakwater; (embarcadero) jetty; (Rail) embankment; (LAm, paseo marítimo) seafront

maledicencia f slander

mal|eficio m curse. ~**éfico** a evil

malestar m discomfort; (fig) uneasiness

malet|a f (suit)case. **hacer la** ~**a** pack (one's case). ~**ero** m porter; (Auto) boot, trunk (Amer). ~**ín** m small case; (para documentos) briefcase

mal|evolencia f malevolence. ~**évolo** a malevolent

maleza f weeds; (matorral) undergrowth

mal|gastar vt waste. ~**hablado** a foul-mouthed. ~**hechor** m criminal. ~**humorado** a bad-tempered

malici|a f malice; (picardía) mischief. □~**arse** vpr suspect. ~**oso** a malicious; (pícaro) mischievous

maligno a malignant; <persona> evil

malintencionado a malicious

malla f mesh; (de armadura) mail; (de gimnasia) leotard

Mallorca f Majorca.

mallorquín a & m Majorcan

malmirado a (con estar) frowned upon

malo a (delante de nombre masculino en singular **mal**) bad; (enfermo) ill. ~ **de** difficult to. **estar de malas** (malhumorado) be in a bad mood; (LAm, con mala suerte) be out of luck. **lo** ~ **es que** the trouble is that. **por las malas** by force

malogr|ar vt waste; (estropear) spoil. □~**arse** vpr fall through

maloliente a smelly

malpensado a nasty, malicious

malsano a unhealthy

malsonante a ill-sounding; (grosero) offensive

malt|a f malt. ~**eada** f (LAm) milk shake. ~**ear** vt malt

maltr|atar vt ill-treat; (pegar) batter; mistreat <juguete etc>. ~**echo** a battered

malucho a 🔢 under the weather

malva f mallow. (**color de**) ~ a invar mauve

malvado a wicked

malvavisco m marshmallow

malversa|ción f embezzlement. ~**dor** a embezzling. ● m embezzler. ~**r** vt embezzle

Malvinas fpl. **las (islas)** ~ the Falklands, the Falkland Islands

mama f mammary gland; (de mujer) breast

mamá f mum; (usado por niños) mummy

mama|da f sucking. ~**r** vt suck; (fig) grow up with. ● vi <bebé> feed; <animal> suckle. **dar de** ~ breastfeed

M

mamario *a* mammary

mamarracho *m* clown; (cosa ridícula) (ridiculous) sight; (cosa mal hecha) botch; (cosa fea) mess. **ir hecho un ~** look a sight

mameluco *m* (LAm) overalls; (de niño) rompers

mamífero *a* mammalian. ● *m* mammal

mamila *f* (Mex) feeding bottle

mamotreto *m* (libro) hefty volume; (armatoste) huge thing

mampara *f* screen

mampostería *f* masonry

mamut *m* mammoth

manada *f* herd; (de lobos) pack; (de leones) pride. **en ~** in crowds

mana|ntial *m* spring; (fig) source. **~r** *vi* flow; (fig) abound. ● *vt* drip with

manaza *f* big hand

mancha *f* stain; (en la piel) blotch. **~do** *a* stained; (sucio) dirty; <*animal*> spotted. **~r** *vt* stain; (ensuciar) dirty. □ **~rse** *vpr* get stained; (ensuciarse) get dirty

manchego *a* of la Mancha. ● *m* person from la Mancha

manchón *m* large stain

mancilla *f* blemish. **~r** *vt* stain

manco *a* (de una mano) one-handed; (de las dos manos) handless; (de un brazo) one-armed; (de los dos brazos) armless

mancomun|adamente *adv* jointly. **~ar** *vt* unite; (Jurid) make jointly liable. □ **~arse** *vpr* unite. **~idad** *f* union

manda *f* (Mex) religious offering

manda|dero *m* messenger. **~do** *m* (LAm) shopping; (diligencia) errand. **hacer los ~dos** (LAm) do the shopping. **~miento** *m* order; (Relig) commandment. **~r** *vt* order; (enviar) send; (gobernar) rule.

● *vi* be in command. **¿mande?** (Mex) pardon?

mandarin|a *f* (naranja) mandarin (orange). **~o** *m* mandarin tree

mandat|ario *m* attorney; (Pol) head of state. **~o** *m* mandate; (Pol) term of office

mandíbula *f* jaw

mando *m* command. **~ a distancia** remote control. **al ~ de** in charge of. **altos ~s** *mpl* high-ranking officers

mandolina *f* mandolin

mandón *a* bossy

manducar [7] *vt* 🔲 stuff oneself with

manecilla *f* hand

manej|able *a* manageable. **~ar** *vt* use; handle <*asunto etc*>; (fig) manage; (LAm, conducir) drive. □ **~arse** *vpr* get by. **~o** *m* handling. **~os** *mpl* scheming

manera *f* way. **~s** *fpl* manners. **de alguna ~** somehow. **de ~ que** so (that). **de ninguna ~** by no means. **de otra ~** otherwise. **de todas ~s** anyway

manga *f* sleeve; (tubo de goma) hose; (red) net; (para colar) filter; (LAm, de langostas) swarm

mango *m* handle; (fruta) mango. **~near** *vt* boss about. ● *vi* (entrometerse) interfere

manguera *f* hose(pipe)

manguito *m* muff

maní *m* (*pl* **~es**) (LAm) peanut

manía *f* mania; (antipatía) dislike. **tener la ~ de** have an obsession with

maniaco *a*, **maníaco** *a* maniac (al). ● *m* maniac

maniatar *vt* tie s.o.'s hands

maniático *a* maniac(al); (obsesivo) obsessive; (loco) crazy; (delicado) finicky

manicomio *m* lunatic asylum

manicura f manicure; (mujer) manicurist

manido a stale

manifesta|ción f manifestation, sign; (Pol) demonstration. **~nte** m demonstrator. **~r** [1] vt show; (Pol) state. □ **~rse** vpr show; (Pol) demonstrate

manifiesto a clear; <error> obvious; <verdad> manifest. ● m manifesto

manilargo a light-fingered

manilla f (de cajón etc) handle; (de reloj) hand. **~r** m handlebar(s)

maniobra f manoeuvre. **~r** vt operate; (Rail) shunt. ● vt/i manoeuvre. **~s** fpl (Mil) manoeuvres

manipula|ción f manipulation. **~r** vt manipulate

maniquí m dummy. ● m & f model

mani|rroto a & m spendthrift. **~ta** f, (LAm) **~to** m little hand

manivela f crank

manjar m delicacy

mano f hand; (de animales) front foot; (de perros, gatos) front paw. **~ de obra** work force. **~s arriba!** hands up! **a ~** by hand; (próximo) handy. **a ~ derecha** on the right. **de segunda ~** second hand. **echar una ~** lend a hand. **tener buena ~ para** be good at. ● m (LAm, 🄸) mate (Brit), buddy (Amer)

manojo m bunch

manose|ar vt handle. **~o** m handling

manotada f, **manotazo** m slap

manote|ar vi gesticulate. **~o** m gesticulation

mansalva: **a ~** adv without risk

mansarda f attic

mansión f mansion. **~ señorial** stately home

manso a gentle; <animal> tame

manta f blanket

mantec|a f fat. **~oso** a greasy

mantel m tablecloth; (del altar) altar cloth. **~ería** f table linen

manten|er [40] vt support; (conservar) keep; (sostener) maintain. □ **~erse** vpr support o.s.; (permanecer) remain. **~se de/con** live off. **~imiento** m maintenance

mantequ|era f butter churn. **~illa** f butter

mant|illa f mantilla. **~o** m cloak. **~ón** m shawl

manual a & m manual

manubrio m crank; (LAm, de bicicleta) handlebars

manufactura f manufacture. **~r** vt manufacture, make

manuscrito a handwritten. ● m manuscript

manutención f maintenance

manzana f apple; (de edificios) block. **~ de Adán** (LAm) Adam's apple. **~r** m (apple) orchard

manzan|illa f camomile tea. ● m manzanilla, pale dry sherry. **~o** m apple tree

maña f skill. **~s** fpl cunning

mañan|a f morning. **~a por la ~a** tomorrow morning. **pasado ~a** the day after tomorrow. **en la ~a** (LAm), **por la ~a** in the morning. ● m future. ● adv tomorrow. **~ero** a who gets up early. ● m early riser

mañoso a clever; (astuto) crafty; (LAm, caprichoso) difficult

mapa m map

mapache m racoon

maqueta f scale model

maquiladora f (Mex) cross-border assembly plant

maquilla|je m make-up. **~r** vt make up. □ **~rse** vpr make up

máquina *f* machine; (Rail) engine.
~ **de afeitar** shaver. ~ **de escribir**
typewriter. ~ **fotográfica** camera

maquin|ación *f* machination.
~**al** *a* mechanical. ~**aria** *f*
machinery. ~**ista** *m & f* operator;
(Rail) engine driver

mar *m & f* sea. **alta** ~ high seas. **la**
~ **de** 🅵 lots of

maraña *f* thicket; (enredo) tangle;
(embrollo) muddle

maratón *m & f* marathon

maravill|a *f* wonder. **a las mil**
~**as, de** ~**as** marvellously. **contar/**
decir ~**as de** speak wonderfully
of. **hacer** ~**as** work wonders. ~**ar**
vt astonish. □ ~**arse** *vpr* be
astonished (**de** at). ~**oso** *a*
marvellous, wonderful

marca *f* mark; (de coches etc)
make; (de alimentos, cosméticos)
brand; (Deportes) record. ~ **de**
fábrica trade mark. **de** ~ brand
name; (fig) excellent. **de** ~ **mayor**
🅵 absolute. ~**do** *a* marked.
~**dor** *m* marker; (Deportes)
scoreboard. ~**r** [7] *vt* mark;
(señalar) show; score <*un gol*>; dial
<*número de teléfono*>. ● *vi* score

marcha *f* (incl Mus) march; (Auto)
gear; (desarrollo) course; (partida)
departure. **a toda** ~ at full speed.
dar/hacer ~ **atrás** put into
reverse. **poner en** ~ start; (fig) set
in motion

marchante *m* (*f* **marchanta**) art
dealer; (Mex, en mercado) stall
holder

marchar *vi* go; (funcionar) work,
go; (Mil) march. □ ~**se** *vpr* leave

marchit|ar *vt* wither. □ ~**arse**
vpr wither. ~**o** *a* withered

marcial *a* martial

marciano *a & m* Martian

marco *m* frame; (moneda alemana)
mark; (deportes) goal-posts

marea *f* tide. ~**do** *a* sick; (en el
mar) seasick; (aturdido) dizzy;
(borracho) drunk. ~**r** *vt* make feel
sick; (aturdir) make feel dizzy;
(confundir) confuse. □ ~**rse** *vpr* feel
sick; (en un barco) get seasick; (estar
aturdido) feel dizzy; (irse la cabeza)
feel faint; (emborracharse) get
slightly drunk; (confundirse) get
confused

marejada *f* swell; (fig) wave

mareo *m* sickness; (en el mar)
seasickness; (aturdimiento)
dizziness; (confusión) muddle

marfil *m* ivory

margarina *f* margarine

margarita *f* daisy; (cóctel)
margarita

marg|en *m* margin; (de un camino)
side. ● *f* (de un río) bank. ~**inado**
a excluded. ● *m* outcast. **al** ~**en**
(fig) outside. ~**inal** *a* marginal.
~**inar** *vt* (excluir) exclude; (fijar
márgenes) set margins

mariachi *m* (Mex) (música popular de
Jalisco) Mariachi music; (conjunto)
Mariachi band; (músico) Mariachi
musician

maric|a *m* 🅵 sissy 🅵. ~**ón** *m*
🅵 homosexual, queer 🅵; (LAm,
cobarde) wimp

marido *m* husband

mariguana *f*, **marihuana** *f*
marijuana

marimacho *f* mannish woman

marimba *f* (type of) drum (LAm,
especie de xilofón) marimba

marin|a *f* navy; (barcos) fleet;
(cuadro) seascape. ~**a de guerra**
navy. ~**a mercante** merchant
navy. ~**ería** *f* seamanship;
(marineros) sailors. ~**ero** *a* marine;
<*barco*> seaworthy. ● *m* sailor. **a**
la ~**era** in tomato and garlic
sauce. ~**o** *a* marine

marioneta *f* puppet. ~**s** *fpl*
puppet show

maripos|a *f* butterfly. **~a nocturna** moth. **~ear** *vi* be fickle; (galantear) flirt. **~ón** *m* flirt

mariquita *f* ladybird (Brit), ladybug (Amer). ● *m* 🛈 sissy 🛈

mariscador *m* shell-fisher

mariscal *m* marshal

maris|car *vt* fish for shellfish. **~co** *m* seafood, shellfish. **~quero** *m* (pescador de mariscos) seafood fisherman; (vendedor de mariscos) seafood seller

marital *a* marital; <vida> married

marítimo *a* maritime; <ciudad etc> coastal, seaside

marmita *f* cooking pot

mármol *m* marble

marmota *f* marmot

maroma *f* rope; (Mex, voltereta) somersault

marqu|és *m* marquess. **~esa** *f* marchioness. **~esina** *f* glass canopy; (en estadio) roof

marran|a *f* sow. **~ada** *f* filthy thing; (cochinada) dirty trick. **~o** *a* filthy. ● *m* hog

marrón *a* & *m* brown

marroqu|í *a* & *m* & *f* Moroccan. ● *m* (leather) morocco. **~inería** *f* leather goods

Marruecos *m* Morocco

marsopa *f* porpoise

marsupial *a* & *m* marsupial

marta *f* marten

martajar *vt* (Mex) crush <maíz>

Marte *m* Mars

martes *m invar* Tuesday. **~ de carnaval** Shrove Tuesday

martill|ar *vt* hammer. **~azo** *m* blow with a hammer. **~ear** *vt* hammer. **~eo** *m* hammering. **~o** *m* hammer

martín pescador *m* kingfisher

martinete *m* (del piano) hammer; (ave) heron

martingala *f* (ardid) trick

mártir *m* & *f* martyr

martir|io *m* martyrdom; (fig) torment. **~izar** [10] *vt* martyr; (fig) torment, torture

marxis|mo *m* Marxism. **~ta** *a* & *m* & *f* Marxist

marzo *m* March

más *adv* & *a* (comparativo) more; (superlativo) most. **~ caro** dearer. **~ doloroso** more painful. **el ~ caro** the dearest; (de dos) the dearer. **el ~ curioso** the most curious; (de dos) the more curious. ● *prep* plus. ● *m* plus (sign). **~ bien** rather. **~ de** (cantidad indeterminada) more than. **~ o menos** more or less. **~ que** more than. **~ y ~** more and more. **a lo ~** at (the) most. **dos ~ dos** two plus two. **de ~** too many. **es ~** moreover. **nadie ~** nobody else. **no ~** no more

masa *f* mass; (Culin) dough. **en ~** en masse

masacre *f* massacre

masaj|e *m* massage. **~ear** *vt* massage. **~ista** *m* masseur. ● *f* masseuse

mascada *f* (Mex) scarf

mascar [7] *vt* chew

máscara *f* mask

mascar|ada *f* masquerade. **~illa** *f* mask. **~ón** *m* (Naut) figurehead

mascota *f* mascot

masculin|idad *f* masculinity. **~o** *a* masculine; <sexo> male. ● *m* masculine

mascullar [3] *vt* mumble

masilla *f* putty

masivo *a* massive, large-scale

mas|ón *m* Freemason. **~onería** *f* Freemasonry. **~ónico** *a* Masonic

masoquis|mo *m* masochism. **~ta** *a* masochistic. ● *m* & *f* masochist

mastica|ción f chewing. **~r** [7] vt chew

mástil m (Naut) mast; (de bandera) flagpole; (de guitarra, violín) neck

mastín m mastiff

mastodonte m mastodon; (fig) giant

masturba|ción f masturbation. □ **~rse** vpr masturbate

mata f (arbusto) bush; (LAm, planta) plant

matad|ero m slaughterhouse. **~or** a killing. ● m (torero) matador

matamoscas m invar fly swatter

mata|nza f killing. **~r** vt kill <personas>; slaughter <reses>. **~rife** m butcher. □ **~rse** vpr kill o.s.; (en un accidente) be killed; (Mex, para un examen) cram. **~rse trabajando** work like mad

mata|polillas m invar moth killer. **~rratas** m invar rat poison

matasanos m invar quack

matasellos m invar postmark

mate a matt. ● m (ajedrez) (check) mate (LAm, bebida) maté

matemátic|as fpl mathematics, maths (Brit), math (Amer). **~o** a mathematical. ● m mathematician

materia f matter; (material) material; (LAm, asignatura) subject. **~ prima** raw material. **en ~ de** on the question of

material a & m material. **~idad** f material nature. **~ismo** m materialism. **~ista** a materialistic. ● m & f materialist; (Mex, constructor) building contractor. **~izar** [10] vt materialize. □ **~izarse** vpr materialize. **~mente** adv materially; (absolutamente) absolutely

matern|al a maternal; <amor> motherly. **~idad** f motherhood;

(hospital) maternity hospital; (sala) maternity ward. **~o** a motherly; <lengua> mother

matin|al a morning. **~ée** m matinée

matiz m shade; (fig) nuance. **~ación** f combination of colours. **~ar** [10] vt blend <colores>; (introducir variedad) vary; (teñir) tinge (de with)

mat|ón m bully; (de barrio) thug. **~onismo** m bullying; (de barrio) thuggery

matorral m scrub; (conjunto de matas) thicket

matraca f rattle. **dar ~** pester

matraz m flask

matriarca f matriarch. **~do** m matriarchy. **~l** a matriarchal

matr|ícula f (lista) register, list; (inscripción) registration; (Auto) registration number; (placa) licence plate. **~icular** vt register. □ **~icularse** vpr enrol, register

matrimoni|al a matrimonial. **~o** m marriage; (pareja) married couple

matriz f matrix; (molde) mould; (Anat) womb, uterus

matrona f matron; (partera) midwife

matutino a morning

maull|ar vi miaow. **~ido** m miaow

mausoleo m mausoleum

maxilar a maxillary. ● m jaw(bone)

máxim|a f maxim. **~e** adv especially. **~o** a maximum; <punto> highest. ● m maximum

maya f daisy. ● a Mayan. ● m & f (persona) Maya

mayo m May

mayonesa f mayonnaise

mayor a (más grande, comparativo) bigger; (más grande, superlativo) biggest; (de edad, comparativo) older; (de edad, superlativo) oldest; (adulto) grown-up; (principal) main, major; (Mus) major. ● *m & f* (adulto) adult. **al por ~** wholesale. **~al** *m* foreman. **~azgo** *m* entailed estate

mayordomo *m* butler

mayor|ía *f* majority. **~ista** *m & f* wholesaler. **~itario** *a* majority; *<socio>* principal. **~mente** *adv* especially

mayúscul|a *f* capital (letter). **~o** *a* capital; (fig, grande) big

mazacote *m* hard mass

mazapán *m* marzipan

mazmorra *f* dungeon

mazo *m* mallet; (manojo) bunch; (LAm, de naipes) pack (Brit), deck (Amer)

mazorca *f* cob. **~ de maíz** corncob

me *pron* (acusativo) me; (dativo) (to) me; (reflexivo) (to) myself

mecánic|a *f* mechanics. **~o** *a* mechanical. ● *m* mechanic

mecani|smo *m* mechanism. **~zación** *f* mechanization. **~zar** [10] *vt* mechanize

mecanograf|ía *f* typing. **~iado** *a* typed, typewritten. **~iar** [20] *vt* type

mecanógrafo *m* typist

mecate *m* (Mex) string; (más grueso) rope

mecedora *f* rocking chair

mecenas *m & f invar* patron

mecer [9] *vt* rock; swing *<columpio>*. □ **~se** *vpr* rock; (en un columpio) swing

mecha *f* (de vela) wick; (de explosivo) fuse. **~s** *fpl* highlights

mechar *vt* stuff, lard

mechero *m* (cigarette) lighter

mechón *m* (de pelo) lock

medall|a *f* medal. **~ón** *m* medallion; (relicario) locket

media *f* stocking; (promedio) average. **a ~s** half each

mediación *f* mediation

mediado *a* half full; (a mitad de) halfway through. **~s** *mpl*. **a ~s de marzo** in mid-March

mediador *m* mediator

medialuna *f* (*pl* **mediaslunas**) croissant

median|a *f* (Auto) central reservation (Brit), median strip (Amer). **~amente** *adv* fairly. **~era** *f* party wall. **~ero** *a* *<muro>* party. **~o** *a* medium; (mediocre) average, mediocre

medianoche *f* (*pl* **mediasnoches**) midnight; (Culin) *type of roll*

mediante *prep* through, by means of

mediar *vi* mediate; (llegar a la mitad) be halfway through; (interceder) intercede (**por** for)

medic|ación *f* medication. **~amento** *m* medicine. **~ina** *f* medicine. **~inal** *a* medicinal

medición *f* measurement

médico *a* medical. ● *m* doctor. **~ de cabecera** GP, general practitioner

medid|a *f* measurement; (unidad) measure; (disposición) measure, step; (prudencia) moderation. **a la ~a** made to measure. **a ~a que** as. **en cierta ~a** to a certain extent. **~or** *m* (LAm) meter

medieval *a* medieval. **~ista** *m & f* medievalist

medio *a* half (a); (mediano) average. **dos horas y media** two and a half hours. **~ litro** half a litre. **las dos y media** half past two. ● *m* middle; (Math) half; (manera) means; (en deportes) half(-back). **en ~** in the middle (**de** of).

M

por ~ de through. ~ **ambiente** *m* environment

medioambiental *a* environmental

mediocr|e *a* mediocre. ~**idad** *f* mediocrity

mediodía *m* midday, noon; (sur) south

medioevo *m* Middle Ages

Medio Oriente *m* Middle East

medir [5] *vt* measure; weigh up <*palabras etc*>. ● *vi* measure, be. **¿cuánto mide de alto?** how tall is it? □ ~**se** *vpr* (moderarse) measure o.s.; (Mex, probarse) try on

medita|bundo *a* thoughtful. ~**ción** *f* meditation. ~**r** *vt* think about. ● *vi* meditate

mediterráneo *a* Mediterranean

Mediterráneo *m* Mediterranean

médium *m* & *f* medium

médula *f* marrow

medusa *f* jellyfish

megáfono *m* megaphone

megalómano *m* megalomaniac

mejicano *a* & *m* Mexican

Méjico *m* Mexico

mejilla *f* cheek

mejillón *m* mussel

mejor *a* & *adv* (comparativo) better; (superlativo) best. ~ **dicho** rather. **a lo** ~ perhaps. **tanto** ~ so much the better. ~**a** *f* improvement. ~**able** *a* improvable. ~**amiento** *m* improvement

mejorana *f* marjoram

mejorar *vt* improve, better. ● *vi* get better. □ ~**se** *vpr* get better

mejunje *m* mixture

melanc|olía *f* melancholy. ~**ólico** *a* melancholic

melaza *f* molasses

melen|a *f* long hair; (de león) mane. ~**udo** *a* long-haired

melindr|es *mpl* affectation. **hacer** ~**es con la comida** be picky about food. ~**oso** *a* affected

mellizo *a* & *m* twin

melocot|ón *m* peach. ~**onero** *m* peach tree

mel|odía *f* melody. ~**ódico** *a* melodic. ~**odioso** *a* melodious

melodram|a *m* melodrama. ~**ático** *a* melodramatic

melómano *m* music lover

melón *m* melon

meloso *a* sickly-sweet; <*canción*> slushy

membran|a *f* membrane. ~**oso** *a* membranous

membrete *m* letterhead

membrill|ero *m* quince tree. ~**o** *m* quince

memo *a* stupid. ● *m* idiot

memorable *a* memorable

memorando *m*, **memorándum** *m* notebook; (nota) memorandum, memo

memori|a *f* memory; (informe) report; (tesis) thesis. ~**as** *fpl* (autobiografía) memoirs. **de** ~**a** by heart; <*citar*> from memory. ~**al** *m* memorial. ~**ón** *m* good memory. ~**zación** *f* memorizing. ~**zar** [10] *vt* memorize

menaje *m* household goods. ~ **de cocina** kitchenware

menci|ón *f* mention. ~**onado** *a* aforementioned. ~**onar** *vt* mention

mendi|cidad *f* begging. ~**gar** [12] *vt* beg for. ● *vi* beg. ~**go** *m* beggar

mendrugo *m* piece of stale bread

mene|ar *vt* wag <*rabo*>; shake <*cabeza*>; wiggle <*caderas*>. □ ~**arse** *vpr* move; (con inquietud) fidget; (balancearse) swing). ~**o** *m* movement; <*sacudida*> shake

menester *m* occupation. **ser ~** be necessary. **~oso** *a* needy

menestra *f* vegetable stew

mengano *m* so-and-so

mengua *f* decrease; (falta) lack. **~do** *a* diminished. **~nte** *a* <luna> waning; <marea> ebb. **~r** [15] *vt/i* decrease, diminish

meningitis *f* meningitis

menjurje *m* mixture

menopausia *f* menopause

menor *a* (más pequeño, comparativo) smaller; (más pequeño, superlativo) smallest; (más joven, comparativo) younger; (más joven, superlativo) youngest; (Mus) minor. ● *m & f* (menor de edad) minor. **al por ~** retail

menos *a* (comparativo) less; (comparativo, con plural) fewer; (superlativo) least; (superlativo, con plural) fewest. ● *adv* (comparativo) less; (superlativo) least. ● *prep* except. **al ~** at least. **a ~ que** unless. **las dos ~ diez** ten to two. **ni mucho ~** far from it. **por lo ~** at least. **~cabar** *vt* lessen; (fig, estropear) damage. **~cabo** *m* lessening. **~preciable** *a* contemptible. **~preciar** *vt* despise. **~precio** *m* contempt

mensaje *m* message. **~ro** *m* messenger

menso *a* (LAm, ⊺) stupid

menstru|ación *f* menstruation. **~al** *a* menstrual. **~ar** [21] *vi* menstruate

mensual *a* monthly. **~idad** *f* monthly pay; (cuota) monthly payment

mensurable *a* measurable

menta *f* mint

mental *a* mental. **~idad** *f* mentality. **~mente** *adv* mentally

mentar [1] *vt* mention, name

mente *f* mind

mentecato *a* stupid. ● *m* idiot

mentir [4] *vi* lie. **~a** *f* lie. **~ijillas** *fpl.* **de ~ijillas** for a joke. **~oso** *a* lying. ● *m* liar

mentís *m invar* denial

mentor *m* mentor

menú *m* menu

menud|ear *vi* happen frequently; (Mex, Com) sell retail. **~encia** *f* trifle. **~encias** *fpl* (LAm) giblets. **~eo** *m* (Mex) retail trade. **~illos** *mpl* giblets. **~o** *a* small; <lluvia> fine. **a ~o** often. **~os** *mpl* giblets

meñique *a* <dedo> little. ● *m* little finger

meollo *m* (médula) marrow; (de tema etc) heart

merca|chifle *m* hawker; (fig) profiteer. **~der** *m* merchant. **~dería** *f* (LAm) merchandise. **~do** *m* market. **M~do Común** Common Market. **~do negro** black market

mercan|cía(s) *f(pl)* goods, merchandise. **~te** *a* merchant. ● *m* merchant ship. **~til** *a* mercantile, commercial. **~tilismo** *m* mercantilism

merced *f* favour. **su/vuestra ~** your honour

mercenario *a & m* mercenary

mercer|ía *f* haberdashery (Brit), notions (Amer). **~io** *m* mercury

mercurial *a* mercurial

Mercurio *m* Mercury

merec|edor *a* worthy (de of). **~er** [11] *vt* deserve. □ **~erse** *vpr* deserve. **~idamente** *adv* deservedly. **~ido** *a* well deserved. **~imiento** *m* (mérito) merit

merend|ar [1] *vt* have as an afternoon snack. ● *vi* have an afternoon snack. **~ero** *m* snack bar; (lugar) picnic area

merengue *m* meringue

M

meridi|ano *a* midday; (fig) dazzling. ● *m* meridian. **~onal** *a* southern. ● *m* southerner

merienda *f* afternoon snack

merino *a* merino

mérito *m* merit; (valor) worth

meritorio *a* praiseworthy. ● *m* unpaid trainee

merluza *f* hake

merma *f* decrease. **~r** *vt/i* decrease, reduce

mermelada *f* jam

mero *a* mere; (Mex, verdadero) real. ● *adv* (Mex, precisamente) exactly; (Mex, casi) nearly. ● *m* grouper

merode|ador *m* prowler. **~ar** *vi* prowl

mes *m* month

mesa *f* table; (para escribir o estudiar) desk. **poner la ~** lay the table

mesarse *vpr* tear at one's hair

meser|a *f* (LAm) waitress. **~o** *m* (LAm) waiter

meseta *f* plateau; (descansillo) landing

Mesías *m* Messiah

mesilla *f*, **mesita** *f* small table. **~ de noche** bedside table

mesón *m* inn

mesoner|a *f* landlady. **~o** *m* landlord

mestiz|aje *m* crossbreeding. **~o** *a* <persona> half-caste; <animal> cross-bred. ● *m* (persona) half-caste; (animal) cross-breed

mesura *f* moderation. **~do** *a* moderate

meta *f* goal; (de una carrera) finish

metabolismo *m* metabolism

metafísic|a *f* metaphysics. **~o** *a* metaphysical

met|áfora *f* metaphor. **~afórico** *a* metaphorical

met|al *m* metal; (de la voz) timbre. **~ales** *mpl* (instrumentos de latón)

brass. **~álico** *a* <objeto> metal; <sonido> metallic

metal|urgia *f* metallurgy. **~úrgico** *a* metallurgical

metamorfosis *f invar* metamorphosis

metedura de pata *f* blunder

mete|órico *a* meteoric. **~orito** *m* meteorite. **~oro** *m* meteor. **~orología** *f* meteorology. **~orológico** *a* meteorological. **~orólogo** *m* meteorologist

meter *vt* put; score <un gol>; (enredar) involve; (causar) make. □ **~se** *vpr* get involved (**en** in); (entrometerse) meddle. **~se con uno** pick a quarrel with s.o.

meticulos|idad *f* meticulousness. **~o** *a* meticulous

metida de pata *f* (LAm) blunder

metido *m* reprimand. ● *a*. **~ en años** getting on. **estar ~ en algo** be involved in sth. **estar muy ~ con uno** be well in with s.o.

metódico *a* methodical

metodis|mo *m* Methodism. **~ta** *a & m & f* Methodist

método *m* method

metodología *f* methodology

metraje *m* length. **de largo ~** <película> feature

metrall|a *f* shrapnel. **~eta** *f* submachine gun

métric|a *f* metrics. **~o** *a* metric; <verso> metrical

metro *m* metre; (tren) underground (Brit), subway (Amer). **~ cuadrado** square metre

metrónomo *m* metronome

metr|ópoli *f* metropolis. **~opolitano** *a* metropolitan. ● *m* metropolitan; (tren) underground (Brit), subway (Amer)

mexicano *a & m* Mexican

México *m* Mexico. **~ D. F.** Mexico City

mezcal *m* (Mex) mescal

mezc|la *f* (acción) mixing; (substancia) mixture; (argamasa) mortar. ∼**lador** *m* mixer. ∼**lar** *vt* mix; shuffle *<los naipes>*. □ ∼**larse** *vpr* mix; (intervenir) interfere. ∼**olanza** *f* mixture

mezquin|dad *f* meanness. ∼**o** *a* mean; (escaso) meagre. ● *m* mean person

mezquita *f* mosque

mi *a* my. ● *m* (Mus) E; (solfa) mi

mí *pron* me

miau *m* miaow

mica *f* (silicato) mica

mico *m* (long-tailed) monkey

microbio *m* microbe

micro|biología *f* microbiology. ∼**cosmos** *m invar* microcosm. ∼**film(e)** *m* microfilm

micrófono *m* microphone

microonda *f* microwave. ∼**s** *m invar* microwave oven

microordenador *m* microcomputer

micros|cópico *a* microscopic. ∼**copio** *m* microscope. ∼**urco** *m* long-playing record

miedo *m* fear (a for). **dar** ∼ frighten. **morirse de** ∼ be scared to death. **tener** ∼ be frightened. ∼**so** *a* fearful

miel *f* honey

miembro *m* limb; (persona) member

mientras *conj* while. ● *adv* meanwhile. ∼ **que** whereas. ∼ **tanto** in the meantime

miércoles *m invar* Wednesday. ∼ **de ceniza** Ash Wednesday

mierda *f* (vulgar) shit

mies *f* ripe, grain

miga *f* crumb; (fig, meollo) essence. ∼**jas** *fpl* crumbs; (sobras) scraps. ∼**r** [12] *vt* crumble

migra|ción *f* migration. ∼**torio** *a* migratory

mijo *m* millet

mil *a & m* a/one thousand. ∼**es de** thousands of. ∼ **novecientos noventa y nueve** nineteen ninety-nine. ∼ **pesetas** a thousand pesetas

milagro *m* miracle. ∼**so** *a* miraculous

milen|ario *a* millenial. ∼**io** *m* millennium

milésimo *a & m* thousandth

mili *f* [1] military service. ∼**cia** *f* soldiering; (gente armada) militia

mili|gramo *m* milligram. ∼**litro** *m* millilitre

milímetro *m* millimetre

militante *a & m & f* activist

militar *a* military. ● *m* soldier. ∼**ismo** *m* militarism. ∼**ista** *a* militaristic. ● *m & f* militarist. ∼**izar** [10] *vt* militarize

milla *f* mile

millar *m* thousand. **a** ∼**es** by the thousand

mill|ón *m* million. **un** ∼**ón de libros** a million books. ∼**onada** *f* fortune. ∼**onario** *m* millionaire. ∼**onésimo** *a & m* millionth

milonga *f* popular dance and music from the River Plate region

milpa *f* (Mex) maize field, cornfield (Amer)

milpies *m invar* woodlouse

mimar *vt* spoil

mimbre *m & f* wicker. □ ∼**arse** *vpr* sway. ∼**ra** *f* osier. ∼**ral** *m* osier-bed

mimetismo *m* mimicry

mímic|a *f* mime. ∼**o** *a* mimic

mimo *m* mime; (a un niño) spoiling; (caricia) cuddle

mimosa *f* mimosa

mina *f* mine. ∼**r** *vt* mine; (fig) undermine

M

minarete *m* minaret

mineral *m* mineral; (mena) ore. **∼ogía** *f* mineralogy. **∼ogista** *m* & *f* mineralogist

miner|ía *f* mining. **∼o** *a* mining. ● *m* miner

miniatura *f* miniature

minifundio *m* smallholding

minimizar [10] *vt* minimize

mínim|o *a* & *m* minimum. **como ∼** at least. **∼um** *m* minimum

minino *m* 🅸 cat, puss 🅸

minist|erial *a* ministerial; <reunión> cabinet. **∼erio** *m* ministry. **∼ro** *m* minister

minor|ía *f* minority. **∼idad** *f* minority. **∼ista** *m* & *f* retailer

minuci|a *f* trifle. **∼osidad** *f* thoroughness. **∼oso** *a* thorough; (detallado) detailed

minúscul|a *f* lower case letter. **∼o** *a* tiny

minuta *f* draft copy; (de abogado) bill

minut|ero *m* minute hand. **∼o** *m* minute

mío *a* & *pron* mine. **un amigo ∼** a friend of mine

miop|e *a* short-sighted. ● *m* & *f* short-sighted person. **∼ía** *f* short-sightedness

mira *f* sight; (fig, intención) aim. **a la ∼** on the lookout. **con ∼s a** with a view to. **∼da** *f* look. **echar una ∼da a** a glance at. **∼do** *a* careful with money; (comedido) considerate. **bien ∼do** highly regarded. **no estar bien ∼do** be frowned upon. **∼dor** *m* viewpoint. **∼miento** *m* consideration. **∼r** *vt* look at; (observar) watch; (considerar) consider. **∼r fijamente a** stare at. ● *vi* look <edificio etc>. **∼ hacia** face. □ **∼rse** *vpr* <personas> look at each other

mirilla *f* peephole

miriñaque *m* crinoline

mirlo *m* blackbird

mirón *a* nosey. ● *m* nosy parker; (espectador) onlooker

mirto *m* myrtle

misa *f* mass. **∼l** *m* missal

misántropo *m* misanthropist

miscelánea *f* miscellany; (Mex, tienda) corner shop (Brit), small general store (Amer)

miser|able *a* very poor; (lastimoso) miserable; (tacaño) mean. **∼ia** *f* extreme poverty; (suciedad) squalor

misericordi|a *f* pity; (piedad) mercy. **∼oso** *a* merciful

mísero *a* miserable; (tacaño) mean; (malvado) wicked

misil *m* missile

misi|ón *f* mission. **∼onero** *m* missionary

misiva *f* missive

mism|ísimo *a* very same. **∼o** *a* same; (después de pronombre personal) myself, yourself, himself, herself, itself, ourselves, yourselves, themselves; (enfático) very. ● *adv*. **ahora ∼** right now. **aquí ∼** right here. **lo ∼** the same

misterio *m* mystery. **∼so** *a* mysterious

místic|a *f* mysticism. **∼o** *a* mystical. ● *m* mystic

mistifica|ción *f* mystification. **∼r** [7] *vt* mystify

mitad *f* half; (centro) middle. **cortar algo por la ∼** cut sth in half

mitigar [12] *vt* mitigate; quench <sed>; relieve <dolor etc>

mitin *m*, **mitín** *m* meeting

mito *m* myth. **∼logía** *f* mythology. **∼lógico** *a* mythological

mitón *m* mitten

mitote *m* (Mex) Aztec dance

mixt|o *a* mixed. **educación mixta** coeducation

mobiliario *m* furniture

moce|dad *f* youth. **~río** *m* young people. **~tón** *m* strapping lad. **~tona** *f* strapping girl

mochales *a invar.* **estar ~** be round the bend

mochila *f* rucksack

mocho *a* blunt. ● *m* butt end

mochuelo *m* little owl

moción *f* motion

moco *m* mucus. **limpiarse los ~s** blow one's nose

moda *f* fashion. **estar de ~** be in fashion. **~l** *a* modal. **~les** *mpl* manners. **~lidad** *f* kind

model|ado *m* modelling. **~ador** *m* modeller. **~ar** *vt* model; (fig, configurar) form. **~o** *m & f* model

módem *m* modem

modera|ción *f* moderation. **~do** *a* moderate. **~r** *vt* moderate; reduce <*velocidad*>. □ **~rse** *vpr* control oneself

modern|idad *f* modernity. **~ismo** *m* modernism. **~ista** *m & f* modernist. **~izar** [10] *vt* modernize. **~o** *a* modern; (a la moda) fashionable

modest|ia *f* modesty. **~o** *a* modest

módico *a* moderate

modifica|ción *f* modification. **~r** [7] *vt* modify

modismo *m* idiom

modist|a *f* dressmaker. **~o** *m* designer

modo *m* manner, way; (Gram) mood; (Mus) mode. **~ de ser** character. **de ~ que** so that. **de ningún ~** certainly not. **de todos ~s** anyhow. **ni ~** (LAm) no way

modorra *f* drowsiness

modula|ción *f* modulation. **~dor** *m* modulator. **~r** *vt* modulate

módulo *m* module

mofa *f* mockery. □ **~rse** *vpr*. **~rse de** make fun of

mofeta *f* skunk

moflet|e *m* chubby cheek. **~udo** *a* with chubby cheeks

mohín *m* grimace. **hacer un ~** pull a face

moho *m* mould; (óxido) rust. **~so** *a* mouldy; <*metales*> rusty

moisés *m* Moses basket

mojado *a* wet

mojar *vt* wet; (empapar) soak; (humedecer) moisten, dampen

mojigat|ería *f* prudishness. **~o** *m* prude. ● *a* prudish

mojón *m* boundary post; (señal) signpost

molar *m* molar

mold|e *m* mould; (aguja) knitting needle. **~ear** *vt* mould, shape; (fig) form. **~ura** *f* moulding

mole *f* mass, bulk. ● *m* (Mex, salsa) chilli sauce with chocolate and sesame

mol|écula *f* molecule. **~ecular** *a* molecular

mole|dor *a* grinding. ● *m* grinder. **~r** [2] grind

molest|ar *vt* annoy; (incomodar) bother. **¿le ~a que fume?** do you mind if I smoke? ● *vi* be a nuisance. **no ~ar** do not disturb. □ **~arse** *vpr* (ofenderse) take offence. **~ia** *f* bother, nuisance; (inconveniente) inconvenience; (incomodidad) discomfort. **~o** *a* annoying; (inconveniente) inconvenient; (ofendido) offended

molicie *f* softness; (excesiva comodidad) easy life

molido *a* ground; (fig, muy cansado) worn out

molienda *f* grinding

molin|ero *m* miller. **~ete** *m* toy windmill. **~illo** *m* mill; (juguete) toy windmill. **~o** *m* mill. **~ de agua** watermill. **~o de viento** windmill

molleja *f* gizzard

mollera *f* (de la cabeza) crown; (fig, sesera) brains

molusco *m* mollusc

moment|áneamente *adv* momentarily. **~áneo** *a* (breve) momentary; (pasajero) temporary. **~o** *m* moment; (ocasión) time. **al ~o** at once. **de ~o** for the moment

momi|a *f* mummy. **~ficar** [7] *vt* mummify. □ **~ficarse** *vpr* become mummified

monacal *a* monastic

monada *f* beautiful thing; (niño bonito) cute kid; (acción tonta) silliness

monaguillo *m* altar boy

mon|arca *m & f* monarch. **~arquía** *f* monarchy. **~árquico** *a* monarchical

monasterio *m* monastery

monda *f* peeling; (piel) peel. **~dientes** *m invar* toothpick. **~adura** *f* peeling; (piel) peel. **~ar** *vt* peel <fruta etc>. **~o** *a* (sin pelo) bald

mondongo *m* innards

moned|a *f* coin; (de un país) currency. **~ero** *m* purse (Brit), change purse (Amer)

monetario *a* monetary

mongolismo *m* Down's syndrome

monigote *m* weak character; (muñeco) rag doll; (dibujo) doodle

monitor *m* monitor

monj|a *f* nun. **~e** *m* monk. **~il** *a* nun's; (como de monja) like a nun

mono *m* monkey; (sobretodo) overalls. ● *a* pretty

monocromo *a & m* monochrome

monóculo *m* monocle

mon|ogamia *f* monogamy. **~ógamo** *a* monogamous

monogra|fía *f* monograph. **~ma** *m* monogram

mon|ologar [12] *vi* soliloquize. **~ólogo** *m* monologue

monoplano *m* monoplane

monopoli|o *m* monopoly. **~zar** [10] *vt* monopolize

monos|ilábico *a* monosyllabic. **~ílabo** *m* monosyllable

monoteís|mo *m* monotheism. **~ta** *a* monotheistic. ● *m & f* monotheist

mon|otonía *f* monotony. **~ótono** *a* monotonous

monseñor *m* monsignor

monstruo *m* monster. **~sidad** *f* monstrosity; (atrocidad) atrocity. **~so** *a* monstrous

monta *f* mounting; (valor) total value

montacargas *m invar* service lift (Brit), service elevator (Amer)

monta|dor *m* fitter. **~je** *m* assembly; (Cine) montage; (teatro) staging, production

montañ|a *f* mountain. **~a rusa** roller coaster. **~ero** *a* mountaineer. **~és** *a* mountain. ● *m* highlander. **~ismo** *m* mountaineering. **~oso** *a* mountainous

montaplatos *m invar* dumb waiter

montar *vt* ride; (subirse a) get on; (ensamblar) assemble; cock <arma>; set up <una casa, un negocio>. ● *vi* ride; (subirse) mount. **~ a caballo** ride a horse

monte *m* (montaña) mountain; (terreno inculto) scrub; (bosque) woodland. **~ de piedad** pawnshop

montepío *m* charitable fund for dependents

montés *a* wild

montevideano *a & m* Montevidean

montículo *m* hillock

montón *m* heap, pile. **a montones** in abundance. **un ~ de** loads of

montura *f* mount; (silla) saddle

monument|al *a* monumental; (fig, muy grande) enormous. **~o** *m* monument

monzón *m & f* monsoon

moñ|a *f* ribbon. **~o** *m* bun; (LAm, lazo) bow

moque|o *m* runny nose. **~ro** *m* 🅸 handkerchief

moqueta *f* fitted carpet

moquillo *m* distemper

mora *f* mulberry; (de zarzamora) blackberry; (Jurid) default

morada *f* dwelling

morado *a* purple

morador *m* inhabitant

moral *m* mulberry tree. ● *f* morals. ● *a* moral. **~eja** *f* moral. **~idad** *f* morality. **~ista** *m & f* moralist. **~izador** *a* moralizing. ● *m* moralist. **~izar** [10] *vt* moralize

morar *vi* live

moratoria *f* moratorium

mórbido *a* soft; (malsano) morbid

morbo *m* illness. **~sidad** *f* morbidity. **~so** *a* unhealthy

morcilla *f* black pudding

morda|cidad *f* sharpness. **~z** *a* scathing

mordaza *f* gag

morde|dura *f* bite. **~r** [2] *vt* bite; (Mex, exigir soborno a) extract a bribe from. ● *vi* bite. □ **~rse** *vpr* bite o.s. **~rse las uñas** bite one's nails

mordi|da *f* (Mex) bribe. **~sco** *m* bite. **~squear** *vt* nibble (at)

moreno *a* (con ser) dark; (de pelo obscuro) dark-haired; (de raza negra) dark-skinned; (con estar) brown, tanned

morera *f* white mulberry tree

moretón *m* bruise

morfema *m* morpheme

morfin|a *f* morphine. **~ómano** *m* morphine addict

morfol|ogía *f* morphology. **~ógico** *a* morphological

moribundo *a* dying

morir [6] (*pp* muerto) *vi* die; (fig, extinguirse) die away; (fig, terminar) end. **~ ahogado** drown. □ **~se** *vpr* die. **~se de hambre** starve to death; (fig) be starving. **se muere por una flauta** she's dying to have a flute

morisco *a* Moorish. ● *m* Moor

morm|ón *m* Mormon. **~ónico** *a* Mormon. **~onismo** *m* Mormonism

moro *a* Moorish. ● *m* Moor

morral *m* (mochila) rucksack; (de cazador) gamebag; (para caballos) nosebag

morrillo *m* nape of the neck

morriña *f* homesickness

morro *m* snout

morrocotudo *a* 🅸 (tremendo) terrible; (estupendo) terrific 🅸

morsa *f* walrus

mortaja *f* shroud

mortal *a & m & f* mortal. **~idad** *f* mortality. **~mente** *adv* mortally

mortandad *f* loss of life; (Mil) carnage

mortecino *a* failing; <color> pale

mortero *m* mortar

mortífero *a* deadly

mortifica|ción *f* mortification. **~r** [7] *vt* (atormentar) torment. □ **~rse** *vpr* distress o.s.

mortuorio *a* death

M

mosaico *m* mosaic; (Mex, baldosa) floor tile

mosca *f* fly. ~**rda** *f* blowfly. ~**rdón** *m* botfly; (de cuerpo azul) bluebottle

moscatel *a* muscatel

moscón *m* botfly; (mosca de cuerpo azul) bluebottle

moscovita *a & m & f* Muscovite

mosque|arse *vpr* get cross. ~**o** *m* resentment

mosquete *m* musket. ~**ro** *m* musketeer

mosquit|ero *m* mosquito net. ~**o** *m* mosquito

mostacho *m* moustache

mostaza *f* mustard

mosto *m* must, grape juice

mostrador *m* counter

mostrar [2] *vt* show. □ ~**se** *vpr* (show oneself to) be. **se mostró muy amable** he was very kind

mota *f* spot, speck

mote *m* nickname

motea|do *a* speckled. ~**r** *vt* speckle

motejar *vt* call

motel *m* motel

motete *m* motet

motín *m* riot; (de tropas, tripulación) mutiny

motiv|ación *f* motivation. ~**ar** *vt* motivate. ~**o** *m* reason. **con** ~**o de** because of

motocicl|eta *f* motor cycle, motor bike 🔟. ~**ista** *m & f* motorcyclist

motoneta *f* (LAm) (motor) scooter

motor *a* motor. ● *m* motor, engine. ~ **de arranque** starter motor. ~**a** *f* motor boat. ~**ismo** *m* motorcycling. ~**ista** *m & f* motorist; (de una moto) motorcyclist. ~**izar** [10] *vt* motorize

motriz *a* motor

move|dizo *a* movable; (poco firme) unstable; *<persona>* fickle. ~**r** [2] *vt* move; shake *<la cabeza>*; (provocar) cause. □ ~**se** *vpr* move; (darse prisa) hurry up

movi|ble *a* movable. ~**do** *a* moved; (Foto) blurred

móvil *a* mobile. ● *m* motive

movili|dad *f* mobility. ~**zación** *f* mobilization. ~**zar** [10] *vt* mobilize

movimiento *m* movement, motion; (agitación) bustle

moza *f* young girl. ~**lbete** *m* lad

mozárabe *a* Mozarabic. ● *m & f* Mozarab

moz|o *m* young boy. ~**uela** *f* young girl. ~**uelo** *m* young boy/ lad

mucam|a *f* (LAm) servant. ~**o** *m* (LAm) servant

muchach|a *f* girl; (sirvienta) servant, maid. ~**o** *m* boy, lad

muchedumbre *f* crowd

mucho *a* a lot of; (en negativas, preguntas) much, a lot of. ~**s** a lot of; (en negativas, preguntas) many, a lot of. ● *pron* a lot; (personas) many (people). **como** ~ at the most. **ni** ~ **menos** by no means. **por** ~ **que** however much. ● *adv* a lot, very much; (tiempo) long, a long time

mucos|idad *f* mucus. ~**o** *a* mucous

muda *f* change of clothing; (de animales) shedding. ~**ble** *a* changeable; *<personas>* fickle. ~**nza** *f* move, removal (Brit). ~**r** *vt* change; shed *<piel>*. ~**rse** *vpr* (de ropa) change one's clothes; (de casa) move (house)

mudéjar *a & m & f* Mudejar

mud|ez *f* dumbness. ~**o** *a* dumb; (callado) silent

mueble *a* movable. ● *m* piece of furniture. ~**s** *mpl* furniture

mueca *f* grimace, face. **hacer una ~** pull a face

muela *f* back tooth, molar; (piedra de afilar) grindstone; (piedra de molino) millstone. **~ del juicio** wisdom tooth

muelle *a* soft. ● *m* spring; (Naut) wharf; (malecón) jetty

muérdago *m* mistletoe

muero *vb* ⇒MORIR

muert|e *f* death; (homicidio) murder. **~o** *a* dead. ● *m* dead person

muesca *f* nick; (ranura) slot

muestra *f* sample; (prueba) proof; (modelo) model; (señal) sign. **~rio** *m* collection of samples

muestro *vb* ⇒MOSTRAR

muevo *vb* ⇒MOVER

mugi|do *m* moo. **~r** [14] *vi* moo

mugr|e *m* dirt. **~iento** *a* dirty, filthy

mugrón *m* sucker

mujer *f* woman; (esposa) wife. ● *int* my dear! **~iego** *a* fond of the women. **~iego** womanizer. **~zuela** *f* prostitute

mula *f* mule. **~da** *f* drove of mules

mulato *a* of mixed race (black and white). ● *m* person of mixed race

mulero *m* muleteer

muleta *f* crutch; (toreo) stick with a red flag

mulli|do *a* soft. **~r** [22] *vt* soften

mulo *m* mule

multa *f* fine. **~r** *vt* fine

multi|color *a* multicoloured. **~copista** *m* duplicator. **~forme** *a* multiform. **~lateral** *a* multilateral. **~lingüe** *a* multilingual. **~millonario** *m* multimillionaire

múltiple *a* multiple

multiplic|ación *f* multiplication. **~ar** [7] *vt* multiply. □ **~arse** *vpr* multiply. **~idad** *f* multiplicity

múltiplo *m* multiple

multitud *f* multitude, crowd. **~inario** *a* mass; <concierto> with mass audience

mund|ano *a* wordly; (de la sociedad elegante) society. **~ial** *a* worldwide. **la segunda guerra ~ial** the Second World War. **~illo** *m* world, circles. **~o** *m* world. **todo el ~o** everybody

munición *f* ammunition; (provisiones) supplies

municip|al *a* municipal. **~alidad** *f* municipality. **~io** *m* municipality; (ayuntamiento) town council

muñe|ca *f* (Anat) wrist; (juguete) doll; (maniquí) dummy. **~co** *m* doll. **~quera** *f* wristband

muñón *m* stump

mura|l *a* mural, wall. ● *m* mural. **~lla** *f* (city) wall. **~r** *vt* wall

murciélago *m* bat

murga *f* street band

murmullo *m* (incl fig) murmur

murmura|ción *f* gossip. **~dor** *a* gossiping. ● *m* gossip. **~r** *vi* murmur; (criticar) gossip

muro *m* wall

murria *f* depression

mus *m* card game

musa *f* muse

musaraña *f* shrew

muscula|r *a* muscular. **~tura** *f* muscles

músculo *m* muscle

musculoso *a* muscular

muselina *f* muslin

museo *m* museum. **~ de arte** art gallery

musgo *m* moss. **~so** *a* mossy

música *f* music

musical *a & m* musical

M

músico *a* musical. ● *m* musician

music|ología *f* musicology.
~**ólogo** *m* musicologist

muslo *m* thigh

mustio *a* <*plantas*> withered;
<*cosas*> faded; <*personas*>
gloomy; (Mex, hipócrita) two-faced

musulmán *a & m* Muslim

muta|bilidad *f* mutability. ~**ción**
f mutation

mutila|ción *f* mutilation. ~**do** *a*
crippled. ● *m* cripple. ~**r** *vt*
mutilate; maim <*persona*>

mutis *m* (en el teatro) exit. ~**mo** *m*
silence

mutu|alidad *f* mutuality;
(asociación) friendly society.
~**amente** *adv* mutually. ~**o** *a*
mutual

muy *adv* very; (demasiado) too

nabo *m* turnip

nácar *m* mother-of-pearl

nac|er [11] *vi* be born; <*pollito*>
hatch out; <*planta*> sprout. ~**ido**
a born. **recien** ~**ido** newborn.
~**iente** *a* <*sol*> rising. ~**imiento**
m birth; (de río) source; (belén)
crib. **lugar** *m* **de** ~**imiento** place of
birth

naci|ón *f* nation. ~**onal** *a*
national. ~**onalidad** *f*
nationality. ~**onalismo** *m*
nationalism. ~**onalista** *m & f*
nationalist. ~**onalizar** [10] *vt*
nationalize. □ ~**onalizarse** *vpr*
become naturalized

nada *pron* nothing, not anything.
● *adv* not at all. **¡~ de eso!**
nothing of the sort! **antes que** ~
first of all. **¡de** ~**!** (después de
'gracias') don't mention it! **para** ~
(not) at all. **por** ~ **del mundo** not
for anything in the world

nada|dor *m* swimmer. ~**r** *vi*
swim. ~**r de espalda(s)** do (the)
backstroke

nadería *f* trifle

nadie *pron* no one, nobody

nado *m* (Mex) swimming. ● *adv* **a**
~ swimming

naipe *m* (playing) card. **juegos**
mpl **de** ~**s** card games

nalga *f* buttock. ~**s** *fpl* bottom.
~**da** *f* (Mex) smack on the bottom

nana *f* lullaby

naranj|a *f* orange. ~**ada** *f*
orangeade. ~**al** *m* orange grove.
~**ero** *m* orange tree

narcótico *a & m* narcotic

nariz *f* nose. **¡narices!** rubbish!

narra|ción *f* narration. ~**dor** *m*
narrator. ~**r** *vt* tell. ~**tivo** *a*
narrative

nasal *a* nasal

nata *f* cream

natación *f* swimming

natal *a* native; <*pueblo etc*>
home. ~**idad** *f* birth rate

natillas *fpl* custard

nativo *a & m* native

nato *a* born

natural *a* natural. ● *m* native.
~**eza** *f* nature. ~**eza muerta** still
life. ~**idad** *f* naturalness. ~**ista**
m & f naturalist. ~**izar** [10] *vt*
naturalize. □ ~**izarse** *vpr*
become naturalized. ~**mente** *adv*
naturally. ● *int* of course!

naufrag|ar [12] *vi* <*barco*> sink;
<*persona*> be shipwrecked; (fig)
fail. ~**io** *m* shipwreck

náufrago *a* shipwrecked. ● *m* shipwrecked person

náuseas *fpl* nausea. **dar ~s a uno** make s.o. feel sick. **sentir ~s** feel sick

náutico *a* nautical

navaja *f* penknife; (de afeitar) razor. **~zo** *m* slash

naval *a* naval

nave *f* ship; (de iglesia) nave. **~ espacial** spaceship. **quemar las ~s** burn one's boats

navega|ble *a* navigable; <barco> seaworthy. **~ción** *f* navigation; (tráfico) shipping. **~dor** *m* (Informática) browser. **~nte** *m & f* navigator. **~r** [12] *vi* sail; (Informática) browse

Navid|ad *f* Christmas. **~eño** *a* Christmas. **en ~ades** at Christmas. **¡feliz ~ad!** Happy Christmas! **por ~ad** at Christmas

nazi *a & m & f* Nazi. **~smo** *m* Nazism

neblina *f* mist

nebuloso *a* misty; (fig) vague

necedad *f* foolishness. **decir ~es** talk nonsense. **hacer una ~** do sth stupid

necesari|amente *adv* necessarily. **~o** *a* necessary

necesi|dad *f* need; (cosa esencial) necessity; (pobreza) poverty. **~dades** *fpl* hardships. **no hay ~dad** there's no need. **por ~dad** (out) of necessity. **~tado** *a* in need (de of). **~tar** *vt* need. ● *vi*. **~tar de** need

necio *a* silly. ● *m* idiot

néctar *m* nectar

nectarina *f* nectarine

nefasto *a* unfortunate; <consecuencia> disastrous; <influencia> harmful

nega|ción *f* denial; (Gram) negative. **~do** *a* useless. **~r** [1 &

12] *vt* deny; (rehusar) refuse. □ **~rse** *vpr* refuse (a to). **~tiva** *f* (acción) denial; (acción de rehusar) refusal. **~tivo** *a & m* negative

negligen|cia *f* negligence. **~te** *a* negligent

negoci|able *a* negotiable. **~ación** *f* negotiation. **~ante** *m & f* dealer. **~ar** *vt/i* negotiate. **~ar en** trade in. **~o** *m* business; (Com, trato) deal. **~os** *mpl* business. **hombre** *m* **de ~os** businessman

negr|a *f* black woman; (Mus) crotchet. **~o** *a* black; <ojos> dark. ● *m* (color) black; (persona) black man. **~ura** *f* blackness. **~uzco** *a* blackish

nen|a *f* little girl. **~o** *m* little boy

nenúfar *m* water lily

neocelandés *a* from New Zealand. ● *m* New Zealander

neón *m* neon

nepotismo *m* nepotism

nervio *m* nerve; (tendón) sinew; (Bot) vein. **~sidad** *f*, **~sismo** *m* nervousness; (impaciencia) impatience. **~so** *a* nervous; (de temperamento) highly-strung. **ponerse ~so** get nervous

neto *a* clear; <verdad> simple; (Com) net

neumático *a* pneumatic. ● *m* tyre

neumonía *f* pneumonia

neur|algia *f* neuralgia. **~ología** *f* neurology. **~ólogo** *m* neurologist. **~osis** *f* neurosis. **~ótico** *a* neurotic

neutr|al *a* neutral. **~alidad** *f* neutrality. **~alizar** [10] *vt* neutralize. **~o** *a* neutral; (Gram) neuter

neva|da *f* snowfall. **~r** [1] *vi* snow. **~sca** *f* blizzard

nevera *f* refrigerator, fridge (Brit)

N

nevisca *f* light snowfall

nexo *m* link

ni *conj.* ~... ~ neither... nor. ~ **aunque** not even if. ~ **siquiera** not even. **sin...** ~ ... without ... or...

Nicaragua *f* Nicaragua

nicaragüense *a & m & f* Nicaraguan

nicho *m* niche

nicotina *f* nicotine

nido *m* nest; (de ladrones) den

niebla *f* fog. **hay** ~ it's foggy. **un día de** ~ a foggy day

niet|a *f* granddaughter. ~**o** *m* grandson. ~**os** *mpl* grandchildren

nieve *f* snow; (Mex, helado) sorbet

niki *m* polo shirt

nimi|edad *f* triviality. ~**o** *a* insignificant

ninfa *f* nymph

ningún ⇒ NINGUNO

ninguno *a (delante de nombre masculino en singular* **ningún***)* no; (con otro negativo) any. **de ninguna manera, de ningún modo** by no means. **en ninguna parte** nowhere. **sin ningún amigo** without any friends. ● *pron* (de dos) neither; (de más de dos) none; (nadie) no-one, nobody

niñ|a *f* (little) girl. ~**era** *f* nanny. ~**ería** *f* childish thing. ~**ez** *f* childhood. ~**o** *a* childish. ● *m* (little) boy **de** ~**o** as a child. **desde** ~**o** from childhood

níquel *m* nickel

níspero *m* medlar

nitidez *f* clarity; (de foto, imagen) sharpness

nítido *a* clear; (foto, imagen) sharp

nitrógeno *m* nitrogen

nivel *m* level; (fig) standard. ~ **de vida** standard of living. ~**ar** *vt* level. □ ~**arse** *vpr* become level

no *adv* not; (como respuesta) no. ¿~? isn't it? **¡a que** ~! I bet you don't! **¡cómo** ~! of course! **Felipe** ~ **tiene hijos** Felipe has no children. **¡que** ~! certainly not!

nob|iliario *a* noble. ~**le** *a & m & f* noble. ~**leza** *f* nobility

noche *f* night. ~ **vieja** New Year's Eve. **de** ~ at night. **hacerse de** ~ get dark. **hacer** ~ spend the night. **media** ~ midnight. **en la** ~ (LAm), **por la** ~ at night

Nochebuena *f* Christmas Eve

noción *f* notion. **nociones** *fpl* rudiments

nocivo *a* harmful

nocturno *a* nocturnal; <clase> evening; <tren etc> night. ● *m* nocturne

nodriza *f* wet nurse

nogal *m* walnut tree; (madera) walnut

nómada *a* nomadic. ● *m & f* nomad

nombr|ado *a* famous; (susodicho) aforementioned. ~**amiento** *m* appointment. ~**ar** *vt* appoint; (citar) mention. ~**e** *m* name; (Gram) noun; (fama) renown. ~**e de pila** Christian name. **en** ~**e de** in the name of. **no tener** ~**e** be unspeakable. **poner de** ~**e** call

nomeolvides *m invar* forget-me-not

nómina *f* payroll

nomina|l *a* nominal. ~**tivo** *a & m* nominative. ~**tivo a** <cheque etc> made out to

non *a* odd. ● *m* odd number. **pares y** ~**es** odds and evens

nono *a* ninth

nordeste *a* <región> north-eastern; <viento> north-easterly. ● *m* northeast

nórdico *a* Nordic. ● *m* Northern European

noria f water-wheel; (en una feria) big wheel (Brit), Ferris wheel (Amer)

norma f rule

normal a normal. ● f teachers' training college. ~**idad** f normality (Brit), normalcy (Amer). ~**izar** [10] vt normalize. ~**mente** adv normally, usually

noroeste a <región> north-western; <viento> north-westerly. ● m northwest

norte a <región> northern; <viento, lado> north. ● m north; (fig, meta) aim

Norteamérica f (North) America

norteamericano a & m (North) American

norteño a northern. ● m northerner

Noruega f Norway

noruego a & m Norwegian

nos pron (acusativo) us; (dativo) (to) us; (reflexivo) (to) ourselves; (recíproco) (to) each other

nosotros pron we; (con prep) us

nostalgia f nostalgia; (de casa, de patria) homesickness. ~**álgico** a nostalgic

nota f note; (de examen etc) mark. **de** ~ famous. **de mala** ~ notorious. **digno de** ~ notable. ~**ble** a notable. ~**ción** f notation. ~**r** vt notice. **es de** ~**r** it should be noted. **hacerse** ~**r** stand out

notario m notary

noticia f (piece of) news. ~**as** fpl news. **atrasado de** ~**as** behind with the news. **tener** ~**as de** hear from. ~**ario**, (LAm) ~**ero** m news

notifica|ción f notification. ~**r** [7] vt notify

notori|edad f notoriety. ~**o** a well-known; (evidente) obvious; (notable) marked

novato a inexperienced. ● m novice

novecientos a & m nine hundred

noved|ad f newness; (cosa nueva) innovation; (cambio) change; (moda) latest fashion. **llegar sin** ~**ad** arrive safely. ~**oso** a novel

novel|a f novel. ~**ista** m & f novelist

noveno a ninth

noventa a & m ninety; (nonagésimo) ninetieth

novia f girlfriend; (prometida) fiancée; (en boda) bride. ~**r** vi (LAm) go out together. ~**zgo** m engagement

novicio m novice

noviembre m November

novill|a f heifer. ~**o** m bullock. **hacer** ~**os** play truant

novio m boyfriend; (prometido) fiancé; (en boda) bridegroom. **los** ~**s** the bride and groom

nub|arrón m large dark cloud. ~**e** f cloud; (de insectos etc) swarm. ~**lado** a cloudy, overcast. ● m cloud. ~**lar** vt cloud. □ ~**larse** vpr become cloudy; <vista> cloud over. ~**oso** a cloudy

nuca f back of the neck

nuclear a nuclear

núcleo m nucleus

nudillo m knuckle

nudis|mo m nudism. ~**ta** m & f nudist

nudo m knot; (de asunto etc) crux. **tener un** ~ **en la garganta** have a lump in one's throat. ~**so** a knotty

nuera f daughter-in-law

nuestro a our. ● pron ours. ~ **amigo** our friend. **un coche** ~ a car of ours

nueva f (piece of) news. ~**s** fpl news. ~**mente** adv again

N

Nueva Zelanda, (LAm) **Nueva Zelandia** *f* New Zealand

nueve *a & m* nine

nuevo *a* new. **de ~** again. **estar ~** be as good as new

nuez *f* walnut. **~ de Adán** Adam's apple. **~ moscada** nutmeg

nul|idad *f* nullity; (🔲, persona) dead loss 🔲. **~o** *a* useless; (Jurid) null and void

num|eración *f* numbering. **~eral** *a & m* numeral. **~erar** *vt* number. **~érico** *a* numerical

número *m* number; (arábigo, romano) numeral; (de zapatos etc) size; (billete de lotería) lottery ticket; (de publicación) issue. **sin ~** countless

numeroso *a* numerous

nunca *adv* never. **~ (ja)más** never again. **casi ~** hardly ever. **como ~** like never before. **más que ~** more than ever

nupcial *a* nuptial. **banquete ~** wedding breakfast

nutria *f* otter

nutri|ción *f* nutrition. **~do** *a* nourished, fed; (fig) large; <aplausos> loud; <fuego> heavy. **~r** *vt* nourish, feed; (fig) feed. **~tivo** *a* nutritious. **valor** *m* **~tivo** nutritional value

nylon *m* nylon

ñapa *f* (LAm) *extra goods given free*

ñato *adj* (LAm) snub-nosed

ñoñ|ería *f*, **~ez** *f* insipidity. **~o** *a* insipid; (tímido) bashful; (quisquilloso) prudish

o *conj* or. **~ bien** rather. **~... ~** either ... or

oasis *m invar* oasis

obed|ecer [11] *vt/i* obey. **~iencia** *f* obedience. **~iente** *a* obedient

obes|idad *f* obesity. **~o** *a* obese

obispo *m* bishop

obje|ción *f* objection. **~tar** *vt/i* object

objetivo *a* objective. ● *m* objective; (foto etc) lens

objeto *m* object. **~r** *m* objector. **~r de conciencia** conscientious objector

oblicuo *a* oblique

obliga|ción *f* obligation; (Com) bond. **~do** *a* obliged; (forzoso) obligatory; **~r** [12] *vt* force, oblige. □ **~rse** *vpr*. **~rse a** undertake to. **~torio** *a* obligatory

oboe *m* oboe. ● *m & f* (músico) oboist

obra f work; (acción) deed; (de teatro) play; (construcción) building work. ~ **maestra** masterpiece. **en ~s** under construction. **por ~ de** thanks to. ~**r** vt do

obrero a labour; <clase> working. ● m workman; (de fábrica, construcción) worker

obscen|idad f obscenity. ~**o** a obscene

obscu... ⇨ OSCU...

obsequi|ar vt lavish attention on. ~**ar con** give, present with. ~**o** m gift, present; (agasajo) attention. ~**oso** a obliging

observa|ción f observation. **hacer una ~ción** make a remark. ~**dor** m observer. ~**ncia** f observance. ~**r** vt observe; (notar) notice. ~**torio** m observatory

obses|ión f obsession. ~**ionar** vt obsess. ~**ivo** a obsessive. ~**o** a obsessed

obst|aculizar [10] vt hinder; hold up <tráfico>. ~**áculo** m obstacle

obstante: **no ~** adv however, nevertheless; (como prep) in spite of

obstar vi. **eso no obsta para que vaya** that should not prevent him from going

obstina|do a obstinate. □ ~**rse** vpr. ~**rse en** (+ infinitivo) insist on (+ gerundio)

obstru|cción f obstruction. ~**ir** [17] vt obstruct

obtener [40] vt get, obtain

obtura|dor m (Foto) shutter. ~**r** vt plug; fill <muela etc>

obvio a obvious

oca f goose

ocasi|ón f occasion; (oportunidad) opportunity. **aprovechar la ~ón** take the opportunity. **con ~ón de** on the occasion of. **de ~ón** bargain; (usado) second-hand. **en ~ones** sometimes. **perder una ~ón** miss a chance. ~**onal** a chance. ~**onar** vt cause

ocaso m sunset; (fig) decline

occident|al a western. ● m & f westerner. ~**e** m west

océano m ocean

ochenta a & m eighty

ocho a & m eight. ~**cientos** a & m eight hundred

ocio m idleness; (tiempo libre) leisure time. ~**sidad** f idleness. ~**so** a idle; (inútil) pointless

oct|agonal a octagonal. ~**ágono** m octagon

octano m octane

octav|a f octave. ~**o** a & m eighth

octogenario a & m octogenarian

octubre m October

ocular a eye

oculista m & f ophthalmologist, ophthalmic optician

ocult|ar vt hide. □ ~**arse** vpr hide. ~**o** a hidden; (secreto) secret

ocupa|ción f occupation. ~**do** a occupied; <persona> busy. **estar ~do** <asiento> be taken; <línea telefónica> be engaged (Brit), be busy (Amer). ~**nte** m & f occupant. ~**r** vt occupy, take up <espacio>. □ ~**rse** vpr look after

ocurr|encia f occurrence, event; (idea) idea; (que tiene gracia) witty remark. ~**ir** vi happen. **¿qué ~e?** what's the matter? □ ~**irse** vpr occur. **se me ~e que** it occurs to me that

oda f ode

odi|ar vt hate. ~**o** m hatred. ~**oso** a hateful; <persona> horrible

oeste a <región> western; <viento, lado> west. ● m west

ofen|der vt offend; (insultar) insult. □ ~**derse** vpr take offence. ~**sa**

O

f offence. ~**siva** *f* offensive.
~**sivo** *a* offensive.

oferta *f* offer; (en subasta) bid. ~**s de empleo** situations vacant. **en ~** on (special) offer

oficial *a* official. ● *m* skilled worker; (Mil) officer

oficin|a *f* office. ~**a de colocación** employment office. ~**a de turismo** tourist office. **horas** *fpl* **de ~a** business hours. ~**ista** *m & f* office worker

oficio *m* trade. ~**so** *a* (no oficial) unofficial

ofrec|er [11] *vt* offer; give <*fiesta, banquete etc*>; (prometer) promise. □ ~**erse** *vpr* <*persona*> volunteer. ~**imiento** *m* offer

ofrenda *f* offering. ~**r** *vt* offer

ofuscar [7] *vt* blind; (confundir) confuse. □ ~**se** *vpr* get worked up

oí|ble *a* audible. ~**do** *m* hearing; (Anat) ear. **al** ~**do** in one's ear. **de** ~**das** by hearsay. **conocer de** ~**das** have heard of. **de** ~**do** by ear. **duro de** ~**do** hard of hearing

oigo *vb* ⇒**oír**

oír [50] *vt* hear. **¡oiga!** listen!; (al teléfono) hello!

ojal *m* buttonhole

ojalá *int* I hope so! ● *conj* if only

ojea|da *f* glance. **dar una ~da a, echar una ~da a** have a quick glance at. ~**r** *vt* have a look at

ojeras *fpl* rings under one's eyes

ojeriza *f* ill will. **tener ~ a** have a grudge against

ojo *m* eye; (de cerradura) keyhole; (de un puente) span. **¡~!** careful!

ola *f* wave

olé *int* bravo!

olea|da *f* wave. ~**je** *m* swell

óleo *m* oil; (cuadro) oil painting

oleoducto *m* oil pipeline

oler [2] (*las formas que empezarían por* **ue** *se escriben* **hue**) *vt* smell. ● *vi* smell (**a** of). **me huele mal** (fig) it sounds fishy to me

olfat|ear *vt* sniff; scent <*rastro*>. ~**o** *m* (sense of) smell (fig) intuition

olimpiada *f*, **olimpíada** *f* Olympic games, Olympics

olímpico *a* Olympic; (fig, 🛈) total

oliv|a *f* olive. ~**ar** *m* olive grove. ~**o** *m* olive tree

olla *f* pot, casserole. ~ **a/de presión, ~ exprés** pressure cooker

olmo *m* elm (tree)

olor *m* smell. ~**oso** *a* sweet-smelling

olvid|adizo *a* forgetful. ~**ar** *vt* forget. □ ~**arse** *vpr* forget. ~**arse de** forget. **se me ~ó** I forgot. ~**o** *m* oblivion; (acto) omission

ombligo *m* navel

omi|sión *f* omission. ~**tir** *vt* omit

ómnibus *a* omnibus

omnipotente *a* omnipotent

omóplato *m*, **omoplato** *m* shoulder blade

once *a & m* eleven

ond|a *f* wave. ~**a corta** short wave. ~**a larga** long wave. **longitud** *f* **de ~a** wavelength. ~**ear** *vi* wave; <*agua*> ripple. ~**ulación** *f* undulation; (del pelo) wave. ~**ular** *vi* wave

onomásti|co *a* <*índice*> of names. ● *f* saint's day

ONU *abrev* (**Organización de las Naciones Unidas**) UN

OPA *f* take-over bid

opac|ar [7] (LAm) make opaque; (deslucir) mar; (anular) overshadow. ~**o** *a* opaque; (fig) dull

opci|ón *f* option. ~**onal** *a* optional

ópera *f* opera

opera|ción f operation; (Com) transaction. **~dor** m operator; (TV) cameraman; (Mex, obrero) machinist. **~r** vt operate on; work <milagro etc>; (Mex) operate <máquina>. ● vi operate; (Com) deal. **~rio** m machinist. □ **~rse** vpr take place; (Med) have an operation. **~torio** a operative

opereta f operetta

opin|ar vi express one's opinion. ● vt think. **~ que** think that. **¿qué opinas?** what do you think? **~ión** f opinion. **la ~ión pública** public opinion

opio m opium

opone|nte a opposing. ● m & f opponent. **~r** vt oppose; offer <resistencia>; raise <objeción>. □ **~rse** vpr be opposed; <dos personas> oppose each other

oporto m port (wine)

oportun|idad f opportunity; (cualidad de oportuno) timeliness; (LAm, ocasión) occasion. **~ista** m & f opportunist. **~o** a opportune; (apropiado) suitable

oposi|ción f opposition. **~ciones** fpl public examination. **~tor** m candidate; (Pol) opponent

opres|ión f oppression; (ahogo) difficulty in breathing. **~ivo** a oppressive. **~or** m oppressor

oprimir vt squeeze; press <botón etc>; <ropa> be too tight for; (fig) oppress

optar vi choose. **~ por** opt for

óptic|a f optics; (tienda) optician's (shop). **~o** a optic(al). ● m optician

optimis|mo m optimism. **~ta** a optimistic. ● m & f optimist

óptimo a ideal; <condiciones> perfect

opuesto a opposite; <opiniones> conflicting

opulen|cia f opulence. **~to** a opulent

oración f prayer; (Gram) sentence

ora|dor m speaker. **~l** a oral

órale int (Mex) come on!; (de acuerdo) OK!

orar vi pray (por for)

órbita f orbit

orden f order. **~ del día** agenda. **órdenes** fpl **sagradas** Holy Orders. **a sus órdenes** (esp Mex) can I help you? **~ de arresto** arrest warrant. **en ~** in order. **por ~** in turn. **~ado** a tidy

ordenador m computer

ordena|nza f ordinance. ● m (Mil) orderly. **~r** vt put in order; (mandar) order; (Relig) ordain; (LAm, en restaurante) order

ordeñar vt milk

ordinario a ordinary; (grosero) common; (de mala calidad) poor-quality

orear vt air

orégano m oregano

oreja f ear

orfanato m orphanage

orfebre m goldsmith, silversmith

orfeón m choral society

orgánico a organic

organillo m barrel-organ

organismo m organism

organista m & f organist

organiza|ción f organization. **~dor** m organizer. **~r** [10] vt organize. □ **~rse** vpr get organized

órgano m organ

orgasmo m orgasm

orgía f orgy

orgullo m pride. **~so** a proud

orientación f orientation; (guía) guidance; (Archit) aspect

oriental a & m & f oriental

O

orientar vt position; advise
<persona>. □ ~se vpr point;
<persona> find one's bearings

oriente m east

orificio m hole

orig|en m origin. **dar ~en a** give
rise to. **~inal** a original;
(excéntrico) odd. **~inalidad** f
originality. **~inar** vt give rise to.
~inario a original; (nativo) native.
ser ~inario de come from.
□ **~inarse** vpr originate;
<incendio> start

orilla f (del mar) shore; (de río)
bank; (borde) edge. **a ~s del mar**
by the sea

orina f urine. **~l** m chamber-pot.
~r vi urinate

oriundo a native. **ser ~ de**
<persona> come from; <especie
etc> native to

ornamental a ornamental

ornitología f ornithology

oro m gold. **~s** mpl Spanish card
suit. **~ de ley** 9 carat gold.
hacerse de ~ make a fortune.
prometer el ~ y el moro promise
the moon

orquesta f orchestra. **~l** a
orchestral. **~r** vt orchestrate

orquídea f orchid

ortiga f nettle

ortodoxo a orthodox

ortografía f spelling

ortopédico a orthopaedic

oruga f caterpillar

orzuelo m sty

os pron (acusativo) you; (dativo) (to)
you; (reflexivo) (to) yourselves;
(recíproco) (to) each other

osad|ía f boldness. **~o** a bold

oscila|ción f swinging; (de precios)
fluctuation; (Tec) oscillation. **~r** vi
swing; <precio> fluctuate; (Tec)
oscillate

oscur|ecer [11] vi get dark. ● vt
darken; (fig) obscure. □ **~ecerse**
vpr grow dark; (nublarse) cloud
over. **~idad** f darkness; (fig)
obscurity. **~o** a dark; (fig)
obscure. **a ~as** in the dark

óseo a bone

oso m bear. **~ de felpa, ~ de
peluche** teddy bear

ostensible a obvious

ostent|ación f ostentation. **~ar**
vt show off; (mostrar) show. **~oso**
a ostentatious

osteópata m & f osteopath

ostión m (esp Mex) oyster

ostra f oyster

ostracismo m ostracism

Otan abrev (**Organización del
Tratado del Atlántico Norte**)
NATO, North Atlantic Treaty
Organization

otitis f inflammation of the ear

otoño m autumn, fall (Amer)

otorga|miento m granting. **~r**
[12] vt give; grant <préstamo>;
(Jurid) draw up <testamento>

otorrinolaringólogo m ear, nose
and throat specialist

otro, otra

● adjetivo

····▸ another; (con artículo, posesivo)
other. **come ~ pedazo** have
another piece. **el ~ día** the other
day. **mi ~ coche** my other car.
otra cosa something else. **otra
persona** somebody else. **otra vez**
again

····▸ (en plural) other; (con numeral)
another. **en otras ocasiones** on
other occasions. **~s 3 vasos**
another 3 glasses

····▸ (siguiente) next. **al ~ día** the
next day. **me bajo en la otra**

estación I get off at the next station

● *pronombre*

····▸ (cosa) another one. **lo cambié por ~** I changed it for another one

····▸ (persona) someone else. **invitó a ~** she invited someone else

····▸ (en plural) (some) others. **tengo ~s en casa** I have (some) others at home. **~s piensan lo contrario** others think the opposite

····▸ (con artículo) **el ~** the other one. **los ~s** the others. **uno detrás del ~** one after the other. **los ~s no vinieron** the others didn't come. **esta semana no, la otra** not this week, next week. **de un día para el ~** from one day to the next

➡Para usos complementarios ver **uno, tanto**

ovación *f* ovation

oval *a*, **ovalado** *a* oval

óvalo *m* oval

ovario *m* ovary

oveja *f* sheep; (hembra) ewe

overol *m* (LAm) overalls

ovillo *m* ball. **hacerse un ~** curl up

OVNI *abrev* (**objeto volante no identificado**) UFO

ovulación *f* ovulation

oxida|ción *f* rusting. **~r** *vi* rust. □ **~rse** *vpr* go rusty

óxido *m* rust; (en química) oxide

oxígeno *m* oxygen

oye *vb* ⇒ oír

oyente *a* listening. ● *m & f* listener; (Univ) occasional student

ozono *m* ozone

pabellón *m* pavilion; (en jardín) summerhouse; (en hospital) block; (de instrumento) bell; (bandera) flag

pacer [11] *vi* graze

pachucho *a* <fruta> overripe; <persona> poorly

pacien|cia *f* patience. **perder la ~cia** lose patience. **~te** *a & m & f* patient

pacificar [7] *vt* pacify. □ **~se** *vpr* calm down

pacífico *a* peaceful. **el (Océano) P~** the Pacific (Ocean)

pacifis|mo *m* pacifism. **~ta** *a & m & f* pacifist

pact|ar *vi* agree, make a pact. **~o** *m* pact, agreement

padec|er [11] *vt/i* suffer (**de** from); (soportar) bear. **~er del corazón** have heart trouble. **~imiento** *m* suffering

padrastro *m* stepfather

padre *a* 🗍 terrible; (Mex, estupendo) great. ● *m* father. **~s** *mpl* parents

padrino *m* godfather; (en boda) *man who gives away the bride*

padrón *m* register. **~ electoral** (LAm) electoral roll

paella *f* paella

paga *f* payment; (sueldo) pay. **~dero** *a* payable

pagano *a & m* pagan

pagar [12] *vt* pay; pay for <compras>. ● *vi* pay. **~é** *m* IOU

página *f* page

pago *m* payment

país *m* country; (ciudadanos) nation. ∼ **natal** native land. **el P∼ Vasco** the Basque Country. **los P∼es Bajos** the Low Countries

paisaje *m* landscape, scenery

paisano *m* compatriot

paja *f* straw; (en texto) padding

pájaro *m* bird. ∼ **carpintero** woodpecker

paje *m* page

pala *f* shovel; (para cavar) spade; (para basura) dustpan; (de pimpón) bat

palabr|a *f* word; (habla) speech. **pedir la** ∼**a** ask to speak. **tomar la** ∼**a** take the floor. ∼**ota** *f* swearword. **decir** ∼**otas** swear

palacio *m* palace

paladar *m* palate

palanca *f* lever; (fig) influence. ∼ **de cambio (de velocidades)** gear lever (Brit), gear shift (Amer)

palangana *f* washbasin (Brit), washbowl (Amer)

palco *m* (en el teatro) box

palestino *a* & *m* Palestinian

paleta *f* (de pintor) palette; (de albañil) trowel

paleto *m* yokel

paliativo *a* & *m* palliative

palide|cer [11] *vi* turn pale. ∼**z** *f* paleness

pálido *a* pale. **ponerse** ∼ turn pale

palillo *m* (de dientes) toothpick; (para comer) chopstick

paliza *f* beating

palma *f* (de la mano) palm; (árbol) palm (tree); (de dátiles) date palm. **dar** ∼**s** clap. ∼**da** *f* pat; (LAm) slap. ∼**das** *fpl* applause

palmera *f* palm tree

palmo *m* span; (fig) few inches. ∼ **a** ∼ inch by inch

palmote|ar *vi* clap. ∼**o** *m* clapping, applause

palo *m* stick; (de valla) post; (de golf) club; (golpe) blow; (de naipes) suit; (mástil) mast

paloma *f* pigeon; (blanca, símbolo) dove

palomitas *fpl* popcorn

palpar *vt* feel

palpita|ción *f* palpitation. ∼**nte** *a* throbbing. ∼**r** *vi* beat; (latir con fuerza) pound; <*vena, sien*> throb

palta *f* (LAm) avocado (pear)

paludismo *m* malaria

pamp|a *f* pampas. ∼**ero** *a* of the pampas

pan *m* bread; (barra) loaf. ∼ **integral** wholewheat bread, wholemeal bread (Brit). ∼ **tostado** toast. ∼ **rallado** breadcrumbs. **ganarse el** ∼ earn one's living

pana *f* corduroy

panader|ía *f* bakery; (tienda) baker's (shop). ∼**o** *m* baker

panal *m* honeycomb

panameño *a* & *m* Panamanian

pancarta *f* banner, placard

panda *m* panda

pander|eta *f* (small) tambourine. ∼**o** *m* tambourine

pandilla *f* gang

panecillo *m* (bread) roll

panel *m* panel

panfleto *m* pamphlet

pánico *m* panic

panificadora *f* bakery

panor|ama *m* panorama. ∼**ámico** *a* panoramic

panque *m* (Mex) sponge cake

pantaletas *fpl* (Mex) panties, knickers (Brit)

pantalla *f* screen; (de lámpara) (lamp)shade

pantalón *m*, **pantalones** *mpl* trousers

pantano *m* marsh; (embalse) reservoir. ∼**so** *a* marshy

pantera *f* panther

panti m, (Mex) **pantimedias** fpl tights (Brit), pantyhose (Amer)

pantomima f pantomime

pantorrilla f calf

pantufla f slipper

panz|a f belly. ~**udo** a pot-bellied

pañal m nappy (Brit), diaper (Amer)

paño m material; (de lana) woollen cloth; (trapo) cloth. ~**o de cocina** dishcloth; (para secar) tea towel. ~**o higiénico** sanitary towel. **en** ~**os menores** in one's underclothes

pañuelo m handkerchief; (de cabeza) scarf

papa m pope. ● f (LAm) potato. ~**s fritas** (LAm) chips (Brit), French fries (Amer); (de paquete) crisps (Brit), chips (Amer)

papá m dad(dy). ~**s** mpl parents. **P~ Noel** Father Christmas

papada f (de persona) double chin

papagayo m parrot

papalote m (Mex) kite

papanatas m invar simpleton

paparrucha f (tontería) silly thing

papaya f papaya, pawpaw

papel m paper; (en el teatro etc) role. ~ **carbón** carbon paper. ~ **de calcar** tracing paper. ~ **de envolver** wrapping paper. ~ **de plata** silver paper. ~ **higiénico** toilet paper. ~ **pintado** wallpaper. ~ **secante** blotting paper. ~**eo** m paperwork. ~**era** f waste-paper basket. ~**ería** f stationer's (shop). ~**eta** f (para votar) (ballot) paper

paperas fpl mumps

paquete m packet; (bulto) parcel; (LAm, de papas fritas) bag; (Mex, problema) headache. ~ **postal** parcel

Paquistán m Pakistan

paquistaní a & m Pakistani

par a <número> even. ● m couple; (dos cosas iguales) pair. **a** ~**es** two by two. **de** ~ **en** ~ wide open. ~**es y nones** odds and evens. **sin** ~ without equal. ● f par. **a la** ~ (Com) at par. **a la** ~ **que** at the same time

. . . .

para

● *preposición*

····▸ for. **es** ~ **ti** it's for you. ~ **siempre** for ever. **¿~ qué?** what for? ~ **mi cumpleaños** for my birthday

····▸ (con infinitivo) to. **es muy tarde** ~ **llamar** it's too late to call. **salió** ~ **divertirse** he went out to have fun. **lo hago** ~ **ahorrar** I do it (in order) to save money

····▸ (dirección) **iba** ~ **la oficina** he was going to the office. **empújalo** ~ **atrás** push it back. **¿vas** ~ **casa?** are you going home?

····▸ (tiempo) by. **debe estar listo** ~ **el 5** it must be ready by the 5th. ~ **entonces** by then

····▸ (LAm, hora) to. **son 5** ~ **la una** it's 5 to one

····▸ ~ **que** so (that). **grité** ~ **que me oyera** I shouted so (that) he could hear me.

Note that **para que** is always followed by a verb in the subjunctive

. . . .

parabienes mpl congratulations

parábola f (narración) parable

parabólica f satellite dish

para|brisas m invar windscreen (Brit), windshield (Amer). ~**caídas** m invar parachute. ~**caidista** m & f parachutist; (Mil) paratrooper. ~**choques** m invar bumper (Brit), fender (Amer); (Rail) buffer

P

parad|a *f* (acción) stop; (lugar) bus
stop; (de taxis) rank; (Mil) parade.
~**ero** *m* whereabouts; (LAm, lugar)
bus stop. ~**o** *a* stationary;
<*desempleado*> unemployed. **estar
~** (LAm, de pie) be standing

paradoja *f* paradox

parador *m* state-owned hotel

parafina *f* paraffin

paraguas *m invar* umbrella

Paraguay *m* Paraguay

paraguayo *a & m* Paraguayan

paraíso *m* paradise; (en el teatro)
gallery

paralel|a *f* parallel (line). ~**as**
fpl parallel bars. ~**o** *a & m*
parallel

par|álisis *f invar* paralysis.
~**alítico** *a* paralytic. ~**alizar** [10]
vt paralyse

paramilitar *a* paramilitary

páramo *m* bleak upland

parangón *m* comparison.

paraninfo *m* main hall

paranoi|a *f* paranoia. ~**co** *a*
paranoiac

parar *vt/i* stop. **sin ~**
continuously. □ ~**se** *vpr* stop;
(LAm, ponerse de pie) stand

pararrayos *m invar* lightning
conductor

parásito *m* parasite

parcela *f* plot. ~**r** *vt* divide into
plots

parche *m* patch

parcial *a* partial. **a tiempo ~** part-
time. ~**idad** *f* prejudice

parco *a* laconic; (sobrio) sparing,
frugal

parear *vt* put into pairs

parec|er *m* opinion. **al ~er**
apparently. **a mi ~er** in my
opinion. ● *vi* [11] seem;
(asemejarse) look like; (tener aspecto
de) look. **me ~e** I think. ~**e fácil** it

looks easy. **¿qué te ~e?** what do
you think? **según ~e** apparently.
□ ~**erse** *vpr* resemble, look like.
~**ido** *a* similar. **bien ~ido** good-
looking. ● *m* similarity

pared *f* wall. **~ por medio** next
door. ~**ón** *m* (de fusilamiento) wall.
llevar al ~ón shoot

parej|a *f* pair; (hombre y mujer)
couple; (compañero) partner. ~**o** *a*
the same; (LAm, sin desniveles) even;
(LAm, liso) smooth; (Mex, equitativo)
equal. ● *adv* (LAm) evenly

parente|la *f* relations. ~**sco** *m*
relationship

paréntesis *m invar* parenthesis,
bracket (Brit); (intervalo) break. **entre
~** in brackets (Brit), in
parenthesis; (fig) by the way

paria *m & f* outcast

paridad *f* equality; (Com) parity

pariente *m & f* relation, relative

parir *vt* give birth to. ● *vi* give
birth

parisiense *a & m & f*, **parisino** *a
& m* Parisian

parking /'parkin/ *m* car park
(Brit), parking lot (Amer)

parlament|ar *vi* talk. ~**ario** *a*
parliamentary. ● *m* member of
parliament (Brit), congressman
(Amer). ~**o** *m* parliament

parlanchín *a* talkative. ● *m*
chatterbox

parlante *m* (LAm) loudspeaker

paro *m* stoppage; (desempleo)
unemployment; (subsidio)
unemployment benefit; (LAm,
huelga) strike. **~ cardíaco** cardiac
arrest

parodia *f* parody

parpadear *vi* blink; <*luz*> flicker

párpado *m* eyelid

parque *m* park. **~ de atracciones**
funfair. **~ eólico** wind farm. **~
infantil** playground. **~ zoológico**
zoo, zoological gardens

parquímetro *m* parking meter

parra *f* grapevine

párrafo *m* paragraph

parrilla *f* grill; (LAm, Auto) luggage rack. **a la ~** grilled. **~da** *f* grill

párroco *m* parish priest

parroquia *f* parish; (iglesia) parish church. **~no** *m* parishioner; (cliente) customer

parte *m* (informe) report. **dar ~** report. **de mi ~** for me ● *f* part; (porción) share; (Jurid) party; (Mex, repuesto) spare (part). **de ~ de** from. **¿de ~ de quién?** (al teléfono) who's speaking? **en cualquier ~** anywhere. **en gran ~** largely. **en ~** partly. **en todas ~s** everywhere. **la mayor ~** the majority. **la ~ superior** the top. **ninguna ~** nowhere. **por otra ~** on the other hand. **por todas ~s** everywhere

partera *f* midwife

partición *f* division; (Pol) partition

participa|ción *f* participation; (noticia) announcement; (de lotería) share. **~nte** *a* participating. ● *m & f* participant. **~r** *vt* announce. ● *vi* take part

participio *m* participle

particular *a* particular; <*clase*> private. **nada de ~** nothing special. ● *m* private individual. **~mente** *adv* particularly

partida *f* departure; (en registro) entry; (documento) certificate; (de mercancías) consignment; (juego) game; (de gente) group

partidario *a & m* partisan. **~ de** in favour of

parti|do *m* (Pol) party; (encuentro) match, game; (LAm, de ajedrez) game. **~r** *vt* cut; (romper) break; crack <*nueces*>. ● *vi* leave. **a ~r de** from. **~ de** start from. □ **~rse** *vpr* (romperse) break; (dividirse) split

partitura *f* (Mus) score

parto *m* labour. **estar de ~** be in labour

parvulario *m* kindergarten, nursery school (Brit)

pasa *f* raisin. **~ de Corinto** currant

pasa|da *f* passing; (de puntos) row. **de ~da** in passing. **~dero** *a* passable. **~dizo** *m* passage. **~do** *a* past; <*día, mes etc*> last; (anticuado) old-fashioned; <*comida*> bad, off. **~do mañana** the day after tomorrow. **~dos tres días** after three days. **~dor** *m* bolt; (de pelo) hair-slide

pasaje *m* passage; (pasajeros) passengers; (LAm, de avión etc) ticket. **~ro** *a* passing. ● *m* passenger

pasamano(s) *m* handrail; (barandilla de escalera) banister(s)

pasamontañas *m invar* balaclava

pasaporte *m* passport

pasar *vt* pass; (atravesar) go through; (filtrar) strain; spend <*tiempo*>; show <*película*>; (tolerar) tolerate; give <*mensaje, enfermedad*>. ● *vi* pass; (suceder) happen; (ir) go; (venir) come; <*tiempo*> go by. **~ de** have no interest in. **~lo bien** have a good time. **~ frío** be cold. **~ la aspiradora** vacuum. **~ por alto** leave out. **lo que pasa es que** the fact is that. **pase lo que pase** whatever happens. **¡pase Vd!** come in!, go in! **¡que lo pases bien!** have a good time! **¿qué pasa?** what's the matter?, what's happening? □ **~se** *vpr* pass; <*dolor*> go away; <*flores*> wither; <*comida*> go bad; spend <*tiempo*>; (excederse) go too far

pasarela *f* footbridge; (Naut) gangway

pasatiempo *m* hobby, pastime

P

Pascua *f* (fiesta de los hebreos) Passover; (de Resurrección) Easter; (Navidad) Christmas. ∼**s** *fpl* Christmas

pase *m* pass

pase|ante *m & f* passer-by. ∼**ar** *vt* walk <*perro*>; (exhibir) show off. ● *vi* walk. ir a ∼**ar**, salir a ∼**ar** walk. □ ∼**arse** *vpr* walk. ∼**o** *m* walk; (en coche etc) ride; (calle) avenue. ∼**o marítimo** promenade. **dar un** ∼**o, ir de** ∼ go for a walk. ¡**vete a** ∼**o!** 🔲 get lost! 🔲

pasillo *m* corridor; (de cine, avión) aisle

pasión *f* passion

pasivo *a* passive

pasm|ar *vt* astonish. □ ∼**arse** *vpr* be astonished

paso *m* step; (acción de pasar) passing; (camino) way; (entre montañas) pass; (estrecho) strait(s). ∼ **a nivel** level crossing (Brit), grade crossing (Amer). ∼ **de cebra** zebra crossing. ∼ **de peatones** pedestrian crossing. ∼ **elevado** flyover (Brit), overpass (Amer). **a cada** ∼ at every turn. **a dos** ∼**s** very near. **de** ∼ in passing. **de** ∼ **por** just passing through. **prohibido el** ∼ no entry

pasota *m & f* drop-out

pasta *f* paste; (masa) dough; (🔲, dinero) dough 🔲. ∼**s** *fpl* pasta; (pasteles) pastries. ∼ **de dientes**, ∼ **dentífrica** toothpaste

pastel *m* cake; (empanada) pie; (lápiz) pastel. ∼**ería** *f* cake shop

pasteurizado *a* pasteurized

pastilla *f* pastille; (de jabón) bar; (de chocolate) piece

pasto *m* pasture; (hierba) grass; (LAm, césped) lawn. ∼**r** *m* shepherd; (Relig) minister. ∼**ra** *f* shepherdess

pata *f* leg; (pie de perro, gato) paw; (de ave) foot. ∼**s arriba** upside down. **a cuatro** ∼**s** on all fours. **meter la** ∼ put one's foot in it. **tener mala** ∼ have bad luck. ∼**da** *f* kick. ∼**lear** *vi* stamp one's feet; <*niño pequeño*> kick

patata *f* potato. ∼**s fritas** chips (Brit), French fries (Amer); (de bolsa) (potato) crisps (Brit), (potato) chips (Amer)

patente *a* obvious. ● *f* licence

patern|al *a* paternal; <*cariño etc*> fatherly. ∼**idad** *f* paternity. ∼**o** *a* paternal; <*cariño etc*> fatherly

patético *a* moving

patillas *fpl* sideburns

patín *m* skate; (con ruedas) roller skate. **patines en línea** Rollerblades (P)

patina|dor *m* skater. ∼**je** *m* skating. ∼**r** *vi* skate; (resbalar) slide; <*coche*> skid

patio *m* patio. ∼ **de butacas** stalls (Brit), orchestra (Amer)

pato *m* duck

patológico *a* pathological

patoso *a* clumsy

patraña *f* hoax

patria *f* homeland

patriarca *m* patriarch

patrimonio *m* patrimony; (fig) heritage

patri|ota *a* patriotic. ● *m & f* patriot. ∼**otismo** *m* patriotism

patrocin|ar *vt* sponsor. ∼**io** *m* sponsorship

patrón *m* (jefe) boss; (de pensión etc) landlord; (en costura) pattern

patrulla *f* patrol; (fig, cuadrilla) group. ∼**r** *vt/i* patrol

pausa *f* pause. ∼**do** *a* slow

pauta *f* guideline

paviment|ar *vt* pave. ∼**o** *m* pavement

pavo *m* turkey. ∼ **real** peacock

pavor *m* terror

payaso m clown

paz f peace

peaje m toll

peatón m pedestrian

peca f freckle

peca|do m sin; (defecto) fault. **∼dor** m sinner. **∼minoso** a sinful. **∼r** [7] vi sin

pech|o m chest; (de mujer) breast; (fig, corazón) heart. **dar el ∼o a un niño** breast-feed a child. **tomar a ∼o** take to heart. **∼uga** f breast

pecoso a freckled

peculiar a peculiar, particular. **∼idad** f peculiarity

pedal m pedal. **∼ear** vi pedal

pedante a pedantic

pedazo m piece, bit. **a ∼s** in pieces. **hacer(se) ∼s** smash

pediatra m & f paediatrician

pedicuro m chiropodist

pedi|do m order; (LAm, solicitud) request. **∼r** [5] vt ask for; (Com, en restaurante) order. ● vi ask. **∼r prestado** borrow

pega|dizo a catchy. **∼joso** a sticky

pega|mento m glue. **∼r** [12] vt stick (on); (coser) sew on; give <enfermedad etc>; (juntar) join; (golpear) hit; (dar) give. **∼r fuego a** set fire to. ● vi stick. □ **∼rse** vpr stick; (pelearse) hit each other. **∼tina** f sticker

pein|ado m hairstyle. **∼ar** vt comb. □ **∼arse** vpr comb one's hair. **∼e** m comb. **∼eta** f ornamental comb

p.ej. abrev (por ejemplo) e.g.

pejerrey m (americano) silverside; (europeo) sand smelt

pelado a <fruta> peeled; <cabeza> bald; <terreno> bare

pela|je m (de animal) fur; (fig, aspecto) appearance. **∼mbre** m (de animal) fur; (de persona) thick hair

pelar vt peel; shell <habas>; skin <tomates>; pluck <ave>

peldaño m step; (de escalera de mano) rung

pelea f fight; (discusión) quarrel. **∼r** vi fight; (discutir) quarrel. □ **∼rse** vpr fight; (discutir) quarrel

peletería f fur shop

peliagudo a difficult, tricky

pelícano m pelican

película f film (esp Brit), movie (esp Amer). **∼ de dibujos animados** cartoon (film)

peligro m danger. **poner en ∼** endanger. **∼so** a dangerous

pelirrojo a red-haired

pellejo m skin

pellizc|ar [7] vt pinch. **∼o** m pinch

pelma m & f, **pelmazo** m bore, nuisance

pelo m hair. **no tener ∼os en la lengua** be outspoken. **tomar el ∼o a uno** pull s.o.'s leg

pelota f ball. **∼ vasca** pelota. **hacer la ∼ a uno** suck up to s.o.

pelotera f squabble

peluca f wig

peludo a hairy

peluquer|ía f hairdresser's. **∼o** m hairdresser

pelusa f down

pena f sadness; <lástima> pity; (LAm, vergüenza) embarrassment; (Jurid) sentence. **∼ de muerte** death penalty. **a duras ∼s** with difficulty. **da ∼ que** it's a pity that. **me da ∼** it makes me sad. **merecer la ∼** be worthwhile. **pasar ∼s** suffer hardship. **¡qué ∼!** what a pity! **valer la ∼** be worthwhile

penal a penal; <derecho> criminal. ● m prison; (LAm,

P

penalty) penalty. **~idad** *f*
suffering; (Jurid) penalty. **~ty** *m*
penalty

pendiente *a* hanging; *<cuenta>*
outstanding; *<asunto etc>*
pending. ● *m* earring. ● *f* slope

péndulo *m* pendulum

pene *m* penis

penetra|nte *a* penetrating;
<sonido> piercing; *<viento>* bitter.
~r *vt* penetrate; (fig) pierce. ● *vi*.
~r en penetrate; (entrar) go into

penicilina *f* penicillin

pen|ínsula *f* peninsula. **~insular**
a peninsular

penique *m* penny

penitencia *f* penitence; (castigo)
penance

penoso *a* painful; (difícil) difficult;
(LAm, tímido) shy; (LAm, embarazoso)
embarrassing

pensa|do *a*. **bien ~do** all things
considered. **menos ~do** least
expected. **~dor** *m* thinker.
~miento *m* thought. **~r** [1] *vt*
think; (considerar) consider. **cuando
menos se piensa** when least
expected. **¡ni ~rlo!** no way! **pienso
que sí** I think so. ● *vi* think. **~r
en** think about. **~tivo** *a*
thoughtful

pensi|ón *f* pension; (casa de
huéspedes) guest-house. **~ón
completa** full board. **~onista** *m* &
f pensioner; (huésped) lodger

penúltimo *a* & *m* penultimate,
last but one

penumbra *f* half-light

penuria *f* shortage. **pasar ~s**
suffer hardship

peñ|a *f* rock; (de amigos) group;
(LAm, club) folk club. **~ón** *m* rock.
el P~ón de Gibraltar The Rock (of
Gibraltar)

peón *m* labourer; (en ajedrez)
pawn; (en damas) piece

peonza *f* (spinning) top

peor *a* (comparativo) worse;
(superlativo) worst. ● *adv* worse. **de
mal en ~** from bad to worse. **lo ~**
the worst thing. **tanto ~** so much
the worse

pepin|illo *m* gherkin. **~o** *m*
cucumber. **(no) me importa un ~o**
I couldn't care less

pepita *f* pip; (de oro) nugget

pequeñ|ez *f* smallness; (minucia)
trifle. **~o** *a* small, little; (de edad)
young; (menor) younger. ● *m* little
one. **es el ~o** he's the youngest

pera *f* (fruta) pear. **~l** *m* pear
(tree)

percance *m* mishap

percatarse *vpr*. **~ de** notice

perc|epción *f* perception. **~ibir**
vt perceive; earn *<dinero>*

percha *f* hanger; (de aves) perch

percusión *f* percussion

perde|dor *a* losing. ● *m* loser.
~r [1] *vt* lose; (malgastar) waste;
miss *<tren etc>*. ● *vi* lose. □ **~rse**
vpr get lost; (desaparecer)
disappear; (desperdiciarse) be
wasted; (estropearse) be spoilt.
echar(se) a ~r spoil

pérdida *f* loss; (de líquido) leak; (de
tiempo) waste

perdido *a* lost

perdiz *f* partridge

perd|ón *m* pardon, forgiveness.
pedir ~ón apologize. ● *int* sorry!
~onar *vt* excuse, forgive; (Jurid)
pardon. **¡~one (Vd)!** sorry!

perdura|ble *a* lasting. **~r** *vi* last

perece|dero *a* perishable. **~r**
[11] *vi* perish

peregrin|ación *f* pilgrimage. **~o**
a strange. ● *m* pilgrim

perejil *m* parsley

perengano *m* so-and-so

perenne *a* everlasting; (Bot)
perennial

perez|a *f* laziness. **∼oso** *a* lazy
perfec|ción *f* perfection. **a la ∼ción** perfectly, to perfection. **∼cionar** *vt* perfect; (mejorar) improve. **∼cionista** *m & f* perfectionist. **∼to** *a* perfect; (completo) complete
perfil *m* profile; (contorno) outline. **∼ado** *a* well-shaped
perfora|ción *f* perforation. **∼dora** *f* punch. **∼r** *vt* pierce, perforate; punch <papel, tarjeta etc>
perfum|ar *vt* perfume. □ **∼arse** *vpr* put perfume on. **∼e** *m* perfume, scent. **∼ería** *f* perfumery
pericia *f* skill
perif|eria *f* (de ciudad) outskirts. **∼érico** *a* <barrio> outlying. ● *m* (Mex) ring road
perilla *f* (barba) goatee
perímetro *m* perimeter
periódico *a* periodic(al). ● *m* newspaper
periodis|mo *m* journalism. **∼ta** *m & f* journalist
período *m*, **periodo** *m* period
periquito *m* budgerigar
periscopio *m* periscope
perito *a & m* expert
perju|dicar [7] *vt* damage; (desfavorecer) not suit. **∼dicial** *a* damaging. **∼icio** *m* damage. **en ∼icio de** to the detriment of
perla *f* pearl. **de ∼s** *adv* very well
permane|cer [11] *vi* remain. **∼ncia** *f* permanence; (estancia) stay. **∼nte** *a* permanent. ● *f* perm. ● *m* (Mex) perm
permi|sivo *a* permissive. **∼so** *m* permission; (documento) licence; (Mil etc) leave. **∼so de conducir** driving licence (Brit), driver's license (Amer). **con ∼so** excuse me. **∼tir** *vt* allow, permit. **¿me**

∼te? may I? □ **∼tirse** *vpr* allow s.o.
pernicioso *a* pernicious; <persona> wicked
perno *m* bolt
pero *conj* but. ● *m* fault; (objeción) objection
perogrullada *f* platitude
perpendicular *a & f* perpendicular
perpetrar *vt* perpetrate
perpetu|ar [21] *vt* perpetuate. **∼o** *a* perpetual
perplejo *a* perplexed
perr|a *f* (animal) bitch; (moneda) coin, penny (Brit), cent (Amer); (rabieta) tantrum. **estar sin una ∼a** be broke. **∼era** *f* dog pound; (vehículo) dog catcher's van. **∼o** *a* awful. ● *m* dog. **∼o galgo** greyhound. **de ∼os** awful
persa *a & m & f* Persian
perse|cución *f* pursuit; (política etc) persecution. **∼guir** [5 & 13] *vt* pursue; (por ideología etc) persecute
persevera|nte *a* persevering. **∼r** *vi* persevere
persiana *f* blind; (LAm, contraventana) shutter
persignarse *vpr* cross o.s.
persist|ente *a* persistent. **∼ir** *vi* persist
person|a *f* person. **∼as** *fpl* people. **∼aje** *m* (persona importante) important figure; (de obra literaria) character. **∼al** *a* personal. ● *m* staff. **∼alidad** *f* personality. □ **∼arse** *vpr* appear in person. **∼ificar** [7] *vt* personify
perspectiva *f* perspective
perspica|cia *f* shrewdness; (de vista) keen eyesight. **∼z** *a* shrewd; <vista> keen
persua|dir *vt* persuade. **∼sión** *f* persuasion. **∼sivo** *a* persuasive

P

pertenecer [11] *vi* belong

pértiga *f* pole. **salto** *m* **con** ~ pole vault

pertinente *a* relevant

perturba|ción *f* disturbance. ~**ción del orden público** breach of the peace. ~**r** *vt* disturb; disrupt *<orden>*

Perú *m*. **el** ~ Peru

peruano *a* & *m* Peruvian

perver|so *a* evil. ● *m* evil person. ~**tir** [4] *vt* pervert

pesa *f* weight. ~**dez** *f* weight; (de cabeza etc) heaviness; (lentitud) sluggishness; (cualidad de fastidioso) tediousness; (cosa fastidiosa) bore, nuisance

pesadilla *f* nightmare

pesado *a* heavy; *<sueño>* deep; *<viaje>* tiring; (duro) hard; (aburrido) boring, tedious

pésame *m* sympathy, condolences

pesar *vt* weigh. ● *vi* be heavy. ● *m* sorrow; (remordimiento) regret. **a** ~ **de (que)** in spite of. **pese a (que)** in spite of

pesca *f* fishing; (peces) fish; (pescado) catch. **ir de** ~ go fishing. ~**da** *f* hake. ~**dería** *f* fish shop. ~**dilla** *f* whiting. ~**do** *m* fish. ~**dor** *a* fishing. ● *m* fisherman. ~**r** [7] *vt* catch. ● *vi* fish

pescuezo *m* neck

pesebre *m* manger

pesero *m* (Mex) minibus

peseta *f* peseta

pesimista *a* pessimistic. ● *m* & *f* pessimist

pésimo *a* very bad, awful

peso *m* weight; (moneda) peso. ~ **bruto** gross weight. ~ **neto** net weight. **al** ~ by weight. **de** ~ influential

pesquero *a* fishing

pestañ|a *f* eyelash. ~**ear** *vi* blink

pest|e *f* plague; (hedor) stench. ~**icida** *m* pesticide

pestillo *m* bolt; (de cerradura) latch

petaca *f* cigarette case; (Mex, maleta) suitcase

pétalo *m* petal

petardo *m* firecracker

petición *f* request; (escrito) petition

petirrojo *m* robin

petrificar [7] *vt* petrify

petr|óleo *m* oil. ~**olero** *a* oil. ● *m* oil tanker

petulante *a* smug

peyorativo *a* pejorative

pez *f* fish; (substancia negruzca) pitch. ~ **espada** swordfish

pezón *m* nipple

pezuña *f* hoof

piadoso *a* compassionate; (devoto) devout

pian|ista *m* & *f* pianist. ~**o** *m* piano. ~**o de cola** grand piano

piar [20] *vi* chirp

picad|a *f*. **caer en** ~**a** (LAm) nosedive. ~**o** *a* perforated; *<carne>* minced (Brit), ground (Amer); (ofendido) offended; *<mar>* choppy; *<diente>* bad. ● *m*. **caer en** ~**o** nosedive. ~**ura** *f* bite, sting; (de polilla) moth hole

picaflor *m* (LAm) hummingbird

picante *a* hot; *<chiste etc>* risqué

picaporte *m* door-handle; (aldaba) knocker

picar [7] *vt* *<ave>* peck; *<insecto, pez>* bite; *<abeja, avispa>* sting; (comer poco) pick at; mince (Brit), grind (Amer) *<carne>*; chop (up) *<cebolla etc>*; (Mex, pinchar) prick. ● *vi* itch; *<ave>* peck; *<insecto, pez>* bite; *<sol>* scorch; *<comida>* be hot

picardía *f* craftiness; (travesura) naughty thing

pícaro a crafty; <*niño*> mischievous. ● m rogue

picazón f itch

pichón m pigeon; (Mex, novato) beginner

pico m beak; (punta) corner; (herramienta) pickaxe; (cima) peak. **y ~** (con tiempo) a little after; (con cantidad) a little more than. **~tear** vt peck; (🍴, comer) pick at

picudo a pointed

pido vb ⇒PEDIR

pie m foot; (Bot, de vaso) stem. **~ cuadrado** square foot. **a cuatro ~s** on all fours. **al ~ de la letra** literally. **a ~** on foot. **a ~(s) juntillas** (fig) firmly. **buscarle tres ~s al gato** split hairs. **de ~** standing (up). **de ~s a cabeza** from head to toe. **en ~** standing (up). **ponerse de ~** stand up

piedad f pity; (Relig) piety

piedra f stone; (de mechero) flint

piel f skin; (cuero) leather

pienso vb ⇒PENSAR

pierdo vb ⇒PERDER

pierna f leg

pieza f piece; (parte) part; (obra teatral) play; (moneda) coin; (habitación) room. **~ de recambio** spare part

pijama m pyjamas

pila f (montón) pile; (recipiente) basin; (eléctrica) battery. **~ bautismal** font. **~r** m pillar

píldora f pill

pilla|je m pillage. **~r** vt catch

pillo a wicked. ● m rogue

pilot|ar vt pilot. **~o** m pilot

pim|entero m (vasija) pepperpot. **~entón** m paprika; (LAm, fruto) pepper. **~ienta** f pepper. **grano m de ~ienta** peppercorn. **~iento** m pepper

pináculo m pinnacle

pinar m pine forest

pincel m paintbrush. **~ada** f brush-stroke. **la última ~ada** (fig) the finishing touch

pinch|ar vt pierce, prick; puncture <*neumático*>; (fig, incitar) push; (Med, 💉) give an injection to. **~azo** m prick; (en neumático) puncture. **~itos** mpl kebab(s); (tapas) savoury snacks. **~o** m point

ping-pong m table tennis, pingpong

pingüino m penguin

pino m pine (tree)

pint|a f spot; (fig, aspecto) appearance. **tener ~a de** look like. **~ada** f graffiti. **~ar** vt paint. **no ~a nada** (fig) it doesn't count. □ **~arse** vpr put on make-up. **~or** m painter. **~oresco** a picturesque. **~ura** f painting; (material) paint

pinza f (clothes-)peg (Brit), clothespin (Amer); (de cangrejo etc) claw. **~s** fpl tweezers

piñ|a f pine cone; (fruta) pineapple. **~ón** m (semilla) pine nut

pío a pious. ● m chirp. **no decir ni ~** not say a word

piojo m louse

pionero m pioneer

pipa f pipe; (semilla) seed; (de girasol) sunflower seed

pique m resentment; (rivalidad) rivalry. **irse a ~** sink

piquete m picket; (Mex, herida) prick; (Mex, de insecto) sting

piragua f canoe

pirámide f pyramid

pirata a invar pirate. ● m & f pirate

Pirineos mpl. **los ~** the Pyrenees

piropo m flattering comment

pirueta f pirouette

pirulí m lollipop

P

pisa|da f footstep; (huella) footprint. **~papeles** m invar paperweight. **~r** vt tread on. • vi tread

piscina f swimming pool

Piscis m Pisces

piso m floor; (vivienda) flat (Brit), apartment (Amer); (de autobús) deck

pisotear vt trample (on)

pista f track; (fig, indicio) clue. **~ de aterrizaje** runway. **~ de baile** dance floor. **~ de carreras** racing track. **~ de hielo** ice-rink. **~ de tenis** tennis court

pistol|a f pistol. **~era** f holster. **~ero** m gunman

pistón m piston

pit|ar, (LAm) **~ear** vt whistle at; <conductor> hoot at; award <falta>. • vi blow a whistle; (Auto) sound one's horn. **~ido** m whistle

pitill|era f cigarette case. **~o** m cigarette

pito m whistle; (Auto) horn

pitón m python

pitorre|arse vpr. **~arse de** make fun of. **~o** m teasing

pitorro m spout

piyama m (LAm) pyjamas

pizarr|a f slate; (en aula) blackboard. **~ón** m (LAm) blackboard

pizca f 🔢 tiny piece; (de sal) pinch. **ni ~** not at all

placa f plate; (con inscripción) plaque; (distintivo) badge. **~ de matrícula** number plate

place|ntero a pleasant. **~r** [32] vi. **haz lo que te plazca** do as you please. **me ~ hacerlo** I'm pleased to do it. • m pleasure

plácido a placid

plaga f (also fig) plague. **~do** a. **~do de** filled with

plagio m plagiarism

plan m plan. **en ~ de** as

plana f page. **en primera ~** on the front page

plancha f iron; (lámina) sheet. **a la ~** grilled. **tirarse una ~** put one's foot in it. **~do** m ironing. **~r** vt iron. • vi do the ironing

planeador m glider

planear vt plan. • vi glide

planeta m planet

planicie f plain

planifica|ción f planning. **~r** [7] vt plan

planilla f (LAm) payroll; (personal) staff

plano a flat. • m plane; (de edificio) plan; (de ciudad) street plan. **primer ~** foreground; (Foto) close-up

planta f (Anat) sole; (Bot, fábrica) plant; (plano) ground plan; (piso) floor. **~ baja** ground floor (Brit), first floor (Amer)

planta|ción f plantation. **~r** vt plant; deal <golpe>. **~r en la calle** throw out. □ **~rse** vpr stand; (fig) stand firm

plantear vt (exponer) expound; (causar) create; raise <cuestión>

plantilla f insole; (nómina) payroll; (personal) personnel

plaqué m plating. **de ~** plated

plástico a & m plastic

plata f silver; (fig, 🔢, dinero) money. **~ de ley** hallmarked silver

plataforma f platform

plátano m plane (tree); (fruta) banana. **platanero** m banana tree

platea f stalls (Brit), orchestra (Amer)

plateado a silver-plated; (color de plata) silver

pl|ática f talk. **~aticar** [7] vi (Mex) talk. • vt (Mex) tell

platija *f* plaice

platillo *m* saucer; (Mus) cymbal. **~ volador** (LAm), **~ volante** flying saucer

platino *m* platinum. **~s** *mpl* (Auto) points

plato *m* plate; (comida) dish; (parte de una comida) course

platónico *a* platonic

playa *f* beach; (fig) seaside

plaza *f* square; (mercado) market (place); (sitio) place; (empleo) job. **~ de toros** bullring

plazco *vb* ⇒PLACER

plazo *m* period; (pago) instalment; (fecha) date. **comprar a ~s** buy on hire purchase (Brit), buy on the installment plan (Amer)

plazuela *f* little square

pleamar *f* high tide

pleb|e *f* common people. **~eyo** *a* & *m* plebeian. **~iscito** *m* plebiscite

plega|ble *a* pliable; <silla> folding. **~r** [1 & 12] *vt* fold. □ **~rse** *vpr* bend; (fig) yield

pleito *m* (court) case; (fig) dispute

plenilunio *m* full moon

plen|itud *f* fullness; (fig) height. **~o** *a* full. **en ~o día** in broad daylight. **en ~o verano** at the height of the summer

plieg|o *m* sheet. **~ue** *m* fold; (en ropa) pleat

plisar *vt* pleat

plom|ero *m* (LAm) plumber. **~o** *m* lead; (Elec) fuse. **con ~o** leaded. **sin ~o** unleaded

pluma *f* feather; (para escribir) pen. **~ atómica** (Mex) ballpoint pen. **~ estilográfica** fountain pen. **~je** *m* plumage

plum|ero *m* feather duster; (para plumas, lápices etc) pencil-case. **~ón** *m* down; (edredón) down-filled quilt

plural *a* & *m* plural. **en ~** in the plural

pluriempleo *m* having more than one job

plus *m* bonus

pluscuamperfecto *m* pluperfect

plusvalía *f* capital gain

pluvial *a* rain

pobla|ción *f* population; (ciudad) city, town; (pueblo) village. **~do** *a* populated. ● *m* village. **~r** [2] *vt* populate; (habitar) inhabit. □ **~rse** *vpr* get crowded

pobre *a* poor. ● *m* & *f* poor person; (fig) poor thing. **¡~cito!** poor (little) thing! **¡~ de mí!** poor (old) me! **~za** *f* poverty

pocilga *f* pigsty

poción *f* potion

....

poco

● *adjetivo/pronombre*

····▸ **poco, poca** little, not much. **tiene poca paciencia** he has little patience. **¿cuánta leche queda? - poca** how much milk is there left? - not much

····▸ **pocos, pocas** few. **muy ~s días** very few days. **unos ~s dólares** a few dollars. **compré unos ~s** I bought a few. **aceptaron a muy ~s** very few (people) were accepted

····▸ **a ~ de llegar** soon after he arrived. **¡a ~ !** (Mex) really? **dentro de ~** soon. **~ a ~,** (LAm) **de a ~** gradually, little by little. **hace ~** recently, not long ago. **por ~** nearly. **un ~ (cantidad)** a little; (tiempo) a while. **un ~ de a** (little) bit of, a little, some

● *adverbio*

····▸ (con verbo) not much. **lee muy ~** he doesn't read very much

P

····▶ (con adjetivo) **un lugar** ∼
conocido a little known place. **es**
∼ **inteligente** he's not very
intelligent

! Cuando **poco** modifica a un
adjetivo, muchas veces el
inglés prefiere el uso del
prefijo *un-*, p. ej. **poco**
amistoso *unfriendly*. **poco**
agradecido *ungrateful*

··

podar *vt* prune
poder [33] *v aux* be able to. **no**
voy a ∼ **terminar** I won't be able
to finish. **no pudo venir** he
couldn't come. **¿puedo hacer algo?**
can I do anything? **¿puedo pasar?**
may I come in? **no** ∼ **con** not be
able to cope with; (no aguantar) not
be able to stand. **no** ∼ **más** be
exhausted; (estar harto de algo) not
be able to manage any more. **no**
∼ **menos que** have no alternative
but. **puede que** it is possible that.
puede ser it is possible. **¿se puede**
...? may I...? ● *m* power. **en el** ∼
in power. ∼**es** *mpl* **públicos**
authorities. ∼**oso** *a* powerful
podrido *a* rotten
po|ema *m* poem. ∼**esía** *f* poetry;
(poema) poem. ∼**eta** *m & f* poet.
∼**ético** *a* poetic
polaco *a* Polish. ● *m* Pole;
(lengua) Polish
polar *a* polar. **estrella** ∼ polestar
polea *f* pulley
pol|émica *f* controversy.
∼**emizar** [10] *vi* argue
polen *m* pollen
policía *f* police (force); (persona)
policewoman. ● *m* policeman.
∼**co** *a* police; <novela etc>
detective
policromo *a*, **polícromo** *a*
polychrome

polideportivo *m* sports centre
polietileno *m* polythene
poligamia *f* polygamy
polígono *m* polygon
polilla *f* moth
polio(mielitis) *f* polio(myelitis)
polític|a *f* politics; (postura) policy;
(mujer) politician. ∼ **interior**
domestic policy. ∼**o** *a* political.
familia ∼**a** in-laws. ● *m* politician
póliza *f* (de seguros) policy
poll|o *m* chicken; (gallo joven)
chick. ∼**uelo** *m* chick
polo *m* pole; (helado) ice lolly (Brit),
Popsicle (P) (Amer); (juego) polo.
P∼ **norte** North Pole
Polonia *f* Poland
poltrona *f* armchair
polución *f* pollution
polv|areda *f* dust cloud; (fig,
escándalo) uproar. ∼**era** *f* compact.
∼**o** *m* powder; (suciedad) dust.
∼**os** *mpl* powder. **en** ∼**o**
powdered. **estar hecho** ∼**o** be
exhausted. **quitar el** ∼**o** dust
pólvora *f* gunpowder; (fuegos
artificiales) fireworks
polvoriento *a* dusty
pomada *f* ointment
pomelo *m* grapefruit
pómez *a*. **piedra** *f* ∼ pumice stone
pomp|a *f* bubble; (esplendor) pomp.
∼**as fúnebres** funeral. ∼**oso** *a*
pompous; (espléndido) splendid
pómulo *m* cheekbone
ponchar *vt* (Mex) puncture
ponche *m* punch
poncho *m* poncho
ponderar *vt* (alabar) speak highly
of
poner [34] *vt* put; put on <ropa,
obra de teatro, TV etc>; lay <la
mesa, un huevo>; set <examen,
deberes>; (contribuir) contribute;
give <nombre>; make <nervioso>;
pay <atención>; show <película,

interés>; open *<una tienda>*; equip *<una casa>*. **∼ con** (al teléfono) put through to. **∼ por escrito** put into writing. **∼ una multa** fine. **pongamos** let's suppose. ● *vi* lay. □ **∼se** *vpr* put o.s.; (volverse) get; put on *<ropa>*; *<sol>* set. **∼se a** start to. **∼se a mal con uno** fall out with s.o.

pongo *vb* ⇒**PONER**

poniente *m* west; (viento) west wind

pont|ificar [7] *vi* pontificate. **∼ifice** *m* pontiff

popa *f* stern

popote *m* (Mex) (drinking) straw

popul|acho *m* masses. **∼ar** *a* popular; *<costumbre>* traditional; *<lenguaje>* colloquial. **∼aridad** *f* popularity. **∼arizar** [10] *vt* popularize.

póquer *m* poker

poquito *m*. **un ∼** a little bit. ● *adv* a little

....

por

● *preposición*

····▶ for. **es ∼ tu bien** it's for your own good. **lo compró ∼ 5 dólares** he bought it for 5 dollars. **si no fuera ∼ ti** if it weren't for you. **vino ∼ una semana** he came for a week

⇨ Para expresiones como **por la mañana**, **por la noche** etc., ver bajo el respectivo nombre

····▶ (causa) because of. **se retrasó ∼ la lluvia** he was late because of the rain. **no hay trenes ∼ la huelga** there aren't any trains because of the strike

····▶ (medio, agente) by. **lo envié ∼ correo** I sent it by post. **fue**

destruida ∼ las bombas it was destroyed by the bombs

····▶ (a través de) through. **entró ∼ la ventana** he got in through the window. **me enteré ∼ un amigo** I found out through a friend. **∼ todo el país** throughout the country

····▶ (a lo largo de) along. **caminar ∼ la playa** to walk along the beach. **cortar ∼ la línea de puntos** cut along the dotted line

····▶ (proporción) per. **cobra 30 dólares ∼ hora** he charges 30 dollars per hour. **uno ∼ persona** one per person. **10 ∼ ciento** 10 per cent

····▶ (Mat) times. **dos ∼ dos (son) cuatro** two times two is four

····▶ (modo) in. **∼ escrito** in writing. **pagar ∼ adelantado** to pay in advance

⇨ Para expresiones como **por dentro**, **por fuera** etc., ver bajo el respectivo adverbio

····▶ (en locuciones) **∼ más que** no matter how much. **¿∼ qué?** why? **∼ si** in case. **∼ supuesto** of course

....

porcelana *f* china

porcentaje *m* percentage

porcino *a* pig

porción *f* portion; (de chocolate) piece

pordiosero *m* beggar

pormenor *m* detail

pornogr|afía *f* pornography. **∼áfico** *a* pornographic

poro *m* pore; (Mex, puerro) leek. **∼so** *a* porous

porque *conj* because; (para que) so that

porqué *m* reason

porquería f filth; (basura) rubbish; (grosería) dirty trick

porra f club

porrón m wine jug (with a long spout)

portaaviones m invar aircraft carrier

portada f (de libro) title page; (de revista) cover

portadocumentos m invar (LAm) briefcase

portador m bearer

portaequipaje(s) m invar boot (Brit), trunk (Amer); (encima del coche) roof-rack

portal m hall; (puerta principal) main entrance. ~**es** mpl arcade

porta|**ligas** m invar suspender belt. ~**monedas** m invar purse

portarse vpr behave

portátil a portable

portavoz m spokesman. ● f spokeswoman

portazo m bang. **dar un ~** slam the door

porte m transport; (precio) carriage; (LAm, tamaño) size. ~**ador** m carrier

portento m marvel

porteño a from Buenos Aires

porter|**ía** f porter's lodge; (en deportes) goal. ~**o** m caretaker, porter; (en deportes) goalkeeper. ~**o automático** entryphone

pórtico m portico

portorriqueño a & m Puerto Rican

Portugal m Portugal

portugués a & m Portuguese

porvenir m future

posada f inn. **dar ~** give shelter

posar vt put. ● vi pose. □ ~**se** vpr <pájaro> perch; <avión> land

posdata f postscript

pose|**edor** m owner; (de récord, billete, etc) holder. ~**er** [18] vt own; hold <récord>; have <conocimientos>. ~**sión** f possession. □ ~**sionarse** vpr. ~**sionarse de** take possession of. ~**sivo** a possessive

posgraduado a & m postgraduate

posguerra f post-war years

posib|**ilidad** f possibility. ~**le** a possible. **de ser ~le** if possible. **en lo ~le** as far as possible. **si es ~le** if possible

posición f position; (en sociedad) social standing

positivo a positive

poso m sediment

posponer [34] vt put after; (diferir) postpone

posta f. **a ~** on purpose

postal a postal. ● f postcard

poste m pole; (de valla) post

póster m (pl ~**s**) poster

postergar [12] vt pass over; (diferir) postpone

posteri|**dad** f posterity. ~**or** a back; <años> later; <capítulos> subsequent. ~**ormente** adv later

postigo m door; (contraventana) shutter

postizo a false, artificial. ● m hairpiece

postrarse vpr prostrate o.s.

postre m dessert, pudding (Brit)

postular vt postulate; (LAm) nominate <candidato>

póstumo a posthumous

postura f position, stance

potable a drinkable; <agua> drinking

potaje m vegetable stew

potasio m potassium

pote m pot

poten|**cia** f power. ~**cial** a & m potential. ~**te** a powerful

potro *m* colt; (en gimnasia) horse

pozo *m* well; (hoyo seco) pit; (de mina) shaft; (fondo común) pool

práctica *f* practice. **en la ~** in practice

practica|nte *m & f* nurse. **~r** [7] *vt* practise; play <*deportes*>; (ejecutar) carry out

práctico *a* practical; (conveniente, útil) handy. ● *m* practitioner

prad|era *f* meadow; (terreno grande) prairie. **~o** *m* meadow

pragmático *a* pragmatic

preámbulo *m* preamble

precario *a* precarious; <*medios*> scarce

precaución *f* precaution; (cautela) caution. **con ~** cautiously

precaverse *vpr* take precautions

precede|ncia *f* precedence; (prioridad) priority. **~nte** *a* preceding. ● *m* precedent. **~r** *vt/i* precede

precepto *m* precept. **~r** *m* tutor

precia|do *a* valued; <*don*> valuable. □ **~rse** *vpr*. **~rse de** pride o.s. on

precio *m* price. **~ de venta al público** retail price. **al ~ de** at the cost of. **no tener ~** be priceless. **¿qué ~ tiene?** how much is it?

precios|idad *f* (cosa preciosa) beautiful thing. **¡es una ~idad!** it's beautiful! **~o** *a* precious; (bonito) beautiful

precipicio *m* precipice

precipita|ción *f* precipitation; (prisa) rush. **~damente** *adv* hastily. **~do** *a* hasty. **~r** *vt* (apresurar) hasten; (arrojar) hurl. □ **~rse** *vpr* throw o.s.; (correr) rush; (actuar sin reflexionar) act rashly

precis|amente *a* exactly. **~ar** *vt* require; (determinar) determine.

~ión *f* precision. **~o** *a* precise; (necesario) necessary. **si es ~o** if necessary

preconcebido *a* preconceived

precoz *a* early; <*niño*> precocious

precursor *m* forerunner

predecesor *m* predecessor

predecir [46], (*pero imperativo* **predice**, *futuro y condicional regulares*) *vt* foretell

predestinado *a* predestined

prédica *f* sermon

predicar [7] *vt/i* preach

predicción *f* prediction; (del tiempo) forecast

predilec|ción *f* predilection. **~to** *a* favourite

predisponer [34] *vt* predispose

predomin|ante *a* predominant. **~ar** *vi* predominate. **~io** *m* predominance

preeminente *a* pre-eminent

prefabricado *a* prefabricated

prefacio *m* preface

prefer|encia *f* preference; (Auto) right of way. **de ~encia** preferably. **~ente** *a* preferential. **~ible** *a* preferable. **~ido** *a* favourite. **~ir** [4] *vt* prefer

prefijo *m* prefix; (telefónico) dialling code

pregonar *vt* announce

pregunta *f* question. **hacer una ~** ask a question. **~r** *vt/i* ask (**por** about). □ **~rse** *vpr* wonder

prehistórico *a* prehistoric

preju|icio *m* prejudice. **~zgar** [12] *vt* prejudge

preliminar *a & m* preliminary

preludio *m* prelude

premarital *a*, **prematrimonial** *a* premarital

prematuro *a* premature

premedita|ción *f* premeditation. **~r** *vt* premeditate

P

premi|ar vt give a prize to; (recompensar) reward. **~o** m prize; (recompensa) reward. **~o gordo** jackpot

premonición f premonition

prenatal a antenatal

prenda f garment; (garantía) surety; (en juegos) forfeit. **en ~ de** as a token of. **~r** vt captivate. □ **~rse** vpr fall in love (**de** with)

prende|dor m brooch. **~r** vt capture; (sujetar) fasten; light <cigarrillo>; (LAm) turn on <gas, radio, etc>. • vi catch; (arraigar) take root. □ **~se** vpr (encenderse) catch fire

prensa f press. **~r** vt press

preñado a pregnant; (fig) full

preocupa|ción f worry. **~do** a worried. **~r** vt worry. □ **~rse** vpr worry. **~rse de** look after

prepara|ción f preparation. **~do** a prepared. • m preparation. **~r** vt prepare. □ **~rse** vpr get ready. **~tivos** mpl preparations. **~torio** a preparatory

preposición f preposition

prepotente a arrogant; <actitud> high-handed

prerrogativa f prerogative

presa f (cosa) prey; (embalse) dam

presagi|ar vt presage. **~o** m omen

presb|iteriano a & m Presbyterian. **~ítero** m priest

prescindir vi. **~ de** do without; (deshacerse de) dispense with

prescri|bir (pp prescrito) vt prescribe. **~pción** f prescription

presencia f presence; (aspecto) appearance. **en ~ de** in the presence of. **~r** vt be present at; (ver) witness

presenta|ble a presentable. **~ción** f presentation; (de una persona a otra) introduction. **~dor** m presenter. **~r** vt present; (ofrecer) offer; (entregar) hand in; (hacer conocer) introduce; show <película>. □ **~rse** vpr present o.s.; (hacerse conocer) introduce o.s.; (aparecer) turn up

presente a present; (actual) this. • m present. **los ~s** those present. **tener ~** remember

presenti|miento m premonition. **~r** [4] vt have a feeling (**que** that)

preserva|r vt preserve. **~tivo** m condom

presiden|cia f presidency; (de asamblea) chairmanship. **~cial** a presidential. **~ta** f (woman) president. **~te** m president; (de asamblea) chairman. **~te del gobierno** prime minister

presidi|ario m convict. **~o** m prison

presidir vt be president of; preside over <tribunal>; chair <reunión, comité>

presi|ón f pressure. **a ~ón** under pressure. **hacer ~ón** press. **~onar** vt press; (fig) put pressure on

preso a. **estar ~** be in prison. **llevarse ~ a uno** take s.o. away under arrest. • m prisoner

presta|do a (de uno) lent; (a uno) borrowed. **pedir ~do** borrow. **~mista** m & f moneylender

préstamo m loan; (acción de pedir prestado) borrowing; (acción de prestar) lending

prestar vt lend; give <ayuda etc>; pay <atención>. □ **~se** vpr. **~se a** be open to; (ser apto) be suitable (**para** for)

prestidigita|ción f conjuring. **~dor** m conjurer

prestigio m prestige. **~so** a prestigious

presu|mido a conceited. **~mir** vi show off; boast (**de** about). **~der** vt try to; (afirmar) claim; (solicitar) apply for; (cortejar) court. **~ción** f conceit; (suposición) presumption. **~nto** a alleged. **~ntuoso** a conceited

presup|oner [34] vt presuppose. **~uesto** m budget; (precio estimado) estimate

preten|cioso a pretentious. **~der** vt try to; (afirmar) claim; (solicitar) apply for; (cortejar) court. **~diente** m pretender; (a una mujer) suitor. **~sión** f pretension; (aspiración) aspiration

pretérito m preterite, past

pretexto m pretext. **con el ~ de** on the pretext of

prevalecer [11] vi prevail (**sobre** over)

preven|ción f prevention; (prejuicio) prejudice. **~ido** a ready; (precavido) cautious. **~ir** [53] vt prevent; (advertir) warn. **~tiva** f (Mex) amber light. **~tivo** a preventive

prever [43] vt foresee; (planear) plan

previo a previous

previs|ible a predictable. **~ión** f forecast; (prudencia) precaution

prima f (pariente) cousin; (cantidad) bonus

primario a primary

primavera f spring. **~l** a spring

primer a ⇒PRIMERO. **~a** f (Auto) first (gear); (en tren etc) first class. **~o** a (delante de nombre masculino en singular **primer**) first; (mejor) best; (principal) leading. **la ~a fila** the front row. **lo ~o es** the most important thing is. **~a enseñanza** primary education. **a ~os de** at the beginning of. **de ~a** first-class. ● n (the) first. ● adv first

primitivo a primitive

primo m cousin; Ⓘ fool. **hacer el ~** be taken for a ride

primogénito a & m first-born, eldest

primor m delicacy; (cosa) beautiful thing

primordial a fundamental; <interés> paramount

princesa f princess

principal a main. **lo ~ es que** the main thing is that

príncipe m prince

principi|ante m & f beginner. **~o** m beginning; (moral, idea) principle; (origen) origin. **al ~o** at first. **a ~o(s)** de at the beginning of. **desde el ~o** from the start. **en ~o** in principle. **~os** mpl (nociones) rudiments

prión m prion

prioridad f priority

prisa f hurry, haste. **a ~** quickly. **darse ~** hurry (up). **de ~** quickly. **tener ~** be in a hurry

prisi|ón f prison; (encarcelamiento) imprisonment. **~onero** m prisoner

prismáticos mpl binoculars

priva|ción f deprivation. **~da** f (Mex) private road. **~do** a (particular) private. **~r** vt deprive (**de** of). **~tivo** a exclusive (**de** to)

privilegi|ado a privileged; (muy bueno) exceptional. **~o** m privilege

pro prep. **en ~ de** for, in favour of. ● m advantage. **los ~s y los contras** the pros and cons

proa f bow

probab|ilidad f probability. **~le** a probable, likely. **~lemente** adv probably

proba|dor m fitting-room. **~r** [2] vt try; try on <ropa>; (demostrar) prove. ● vi try. □ **~rse** vpr try on

P

probeta f test-tube

problema m problem. **hacerse ~as** (LAm) worry

procaz a indecent

proced|encia f origin. **~ente** a (razonable) reasonable. **~ente de** (coming) from. **~er** m conduct. ● vi proceed. **~er contra** start legal proceedings against. **~er de** come from. **~imiento** m procedure; (sistema) process; (Jurid) proceedings

proces|ador m. **~ de textos** word processor. **~al** a procedural. **costas ~ales** legal costs. **~amiento** m processing; (Jurid) prosecution. **~amiento de textos** word-processing. **~ar** vt process; (Jurid) prosecute

procesión f procession

proceso m process; (Jurid) trial; (transcurso) course

proclamar vt proclaim

procrea|ción f procreation. **~r** vt procreate

procura|dor m attorney, solicitor; (asistente) clerk (Brit), paralegal (Amer). **~r** vt try; (obtener) obtain

prodigar [12] vt lavish

prodigio m prodigy; (maravilla) wonder; (milagro) miracle. **~ioso** a prodigious

pródigo a prodigal

produc|ción f production. **~ir** [47] vt produce; (causar) cause. □ **~irse** vpr (suceder) happen. **~tivo** a productive. **~to** m product. **~tos agrícolas** farm produce. **~tos alimenticios** foodstuffs. **~tos de belleza** cosmetics. **~tos de consumo** consumer goods. **~tor** m producer

proeza f exploit

profan|ación f desecration. **~ar** vt desecrate. **~o** a profane

profecía f prophecy

proferir [4] vt utter; hurl <insultos etc>

profes|ión f profession. **~ional** a professional. **~or** m teacher; (en universidad) lecturer. **~orado** m teaching profession; (conjunto de profesores) staff

prof|eta m prophet. **~etizar** [10] vt/i prophesize

prófugo a & m fugitive

profund|idad f depth. **~o** a deep; (fig) profound. **poco ~o** shallow

progenitor m ancestor

programa m programme; (de estudios) syllabus. **~ concurso** quiz show. **~ de entrevistas** chat show. **~ción** f programming; (TV etc) programmes; (en periódico) TV guide. **~r** vt programme. **~dor** m computer programmer

progres|ar vi (make) progress. **~ión** f progression. **~ista** a progressive. **~ivo** a progressive. **~o** m progress. **hacer ~os** make progress

prohibi|ción f prohibition. **~do** a forbidden. **prohibido fumar** no smoking. **~r** vt forbid. **~tivo** a prohibitive

prójimo m fellow man

prole f offspring

proletari|ado m proletariat. **~o** a & m proletarian

prol|iferación f proliferation. **~iferar** vi proliferate. **~ífico** a prolific

prolijo a long-winded

prólogo m prologue

prolongar [12] vt prolong; (alargar) lengthen. □ **~se** vpr go on

promedio m average. **como ~** on average

prome|sa f promise. **~ter** vt promise. ● vi show promise.

□ ~**terse** vpr <novios> get engaged. ~**tida** f fiancée. ~**tido** a promised; <novios> engaged. ● m fiancé

prominente f prominence

promiscu|idad f promiscuity. ~**o** a promiscuous

promo|ción f promotion. ~**tor** m promoter. ~**ver** [2] vt promote; (causar) cause

promulgar [12] vt promulgate

pronombre m pronoun

pron|osticar [7] vt predict; forecast <tiempo>. ~**óstico** m prediction; (del tiempo) forecast; (Med) prognosis

pront|itud f promptness. ~**o** a quick. ● adv quickly; (dentro de poco) soon; (temprano) early. **de ~o** suddenly. **por lo ~o** for the time being. **tan ~o como** as soon as

pronuncia|ción f pronunciation. ~**miento** m revolt. ~**r** vt pronounce; deliver <discurso>. □ ~**rse** vpr (declararse) declare o.s.; (sublevarse) rise up

propagación f propagation

propaganda f propaganda; (anuncios) advertising

propagar [12] vt/i propagate. □ ~**se** vpr spread

propasarse vpr go too far

propens|ión f inclination. ~**o** a inclined

propici|ar vt favour; (provocar) bring about. ~**o** a favourable

propie|dad f property. ~**tario** m owner

propina f tip

propio a own; (característico) typical; (natural) natural; (apropiado) proper. **el ~ médico** the doctor himself

proponer [34] vt propose; put forward <persona>. □ ~**se** vpr. ~**se hacer** intend to do

proporci|ón f proportion. ~**onado** a proportioned. ~**onal** a proportional. ~**onar** vt provide

proposición f proposition

propósito m intention. **a ~** (adrede) on purpose; (de paso) by the way. **a ~ de** with regard to

propuesta f proposal

propuls|ar vt propel; (fig) promote. ~**ión** f propulsion. ~**ión a chorro** jet propulsion

prórroga f extension

prorrogar [12] vt extend

prosa f prose. ~**ico** a prosaic

proscri|bir (pp proscrito) vt exile; (prohibir) ban. ~**to** a banned. ● m exile; (bandido) outlaw

proseguir [5 & 13] vt/i continue

prospecto m prospectus; (de fármaco) directions for use

prosper|ar vi prosper; <persona> do well. ~**idad** f prosperity

próspero a prosperous. **¡P~ Año Nuevo!** Happy New Year!

prostit|ución f prostitution. ~**uta** f prostitute

protagonista m & f protagonist

prote|cción f protection. ~**ctor** a protective. ● m protector; (benefactor) patron. ~**ger** [14] vt protect. ~**gida** f protégée. ~**gido** a protected. ● m protegé

proteína f protein

protesta f protest; (manifestación) demonstration; (Mex, promesa) promise; (Mex, juramento) oath

protestante a & m & f Protestant

protestar vt/i protest

protocolo m protocol

provecho m benefit. **¡buen ~!** enjoy your meal! **de ~** useful. **en ~ de** to the benefit of. **sacar ~ de** benefit from

proveer [18] (pp proveído y provisto) vt supply, provide

P

provenir [53] *vi* come (**de** from)

proverbi|al *a* proverbial. ~**o** *m* proverb

provincia *f* province. ~**l** *a*, ~**no** *a* provincial

provisional *a* provisional

provisto *a* provided (**de** with)

provoca|ción *f* provocation. ~**r** [7] *vt* provoke; (causar) cause. ~**tivo** *a* provocative

proximidad *f* proximity

próximo *a* next; (cerca) near

proyec|ción *f* projection. ~**tar** *vt* hurl; cast <*luz*>; show <*película*>. ~**til** *m* missile. ~**to** *m* plan. ~**to de ley** bill. **en** ~**to** planned. ~**tor** *m* projector

pruden|cia *f* prudence; (cuidado) caution. ~**te** *a* prudent, sensible

prueba *f* proof; (examen) test; (de ropa) fitting. **a** ~ on trial. **a** ~ **de** proof against. **a** ~ **de agua** waterproof. **poner a** ~ test

pruebo *vb* ⇒PROBAR

psicoan|álisis *f* psychoanalysis. ~**alista** *m & f* psychoanalyst. ~**alizar** [10] *vt* psychoanalyse

psic|ología *f* psychology. ~**ológico** *a* psychological. ~**ólogo** *m* psychologist. ~**ópata** *m & f* psychopath. ~**osis** *f invar* psychosis

psiqu|e *f* psyche. ~**iatra** *m & f* psychiatrist. ~**iátrico** *a* psychiatric

psíquico *a* psychic

ptas, **pts** *abrev* (**pesetas**) pesetas

púa *f* sharp point; (Bot) thorn; (de erizo) quill; (de peine) tooth; (Mus) plectrum

pubertad *f* puberty

publica|ción *f* publication. ~**r** [7] *vt* publish

publici|dad *f* publicity; (Com) advertising. ~**tario** *a* advertising

público *a* public. ● *m* public; (de espectáculo etc) audience

puchero *m* cooking pot; (guisado) stew. **hacer** ~**s** (fig, 🔲) pout

pude *vb* ⇒PODER

pudor *m* modesty. ~**oso** *a* modest

pudrir (*pp* **podrido**) *vt* rot; (fig, molestar) annoy. □ ~**se** *vpr* rot

puebl|ecito *m* small village. ~**erino** *m* country bumpkin. ~**o** *m* town; (aldea) village; (nación) nation, people

puedo *vb* ⇒PODER

puente *m* bridge; (fig, 🔲) long weekend. ~ **colgante** suspension bridge. ~ **levadizo** drawbridge. **hacer** ~ 🔲 have a long weekend

puerco *a* filthy; (grosero) coarse. ● *m* pig. ~ **espín** porcupine

puerro *m* leek

puerta *f* door; (en deportes) goal; (de ciudad, en jardín) gate. ~ **principal** main entrance. **a** ~ **cerrada** behind closed doors

puerto *m* port; (fig, refugio) refuge; (entre montañas) pass. ~ **franco** free port

puertorriqueño *a & m* Puerto Rican

pues *adv* (entonces) then; (bueno) well. ● *conj* since

puest|a *f* setting; (en juegos) bet. ~**a de sol** sunset. ~**a en escena** staging. ~**a en marcha** starting. ~**o** *a* put; (vestido) dressed. ● *m* place; (empleo) position, job; (en mercado etc) stall. ● *conj*. ~**o que** since

pugna *f* struggle. ~**r** *vi*. ~**r por** strive to

puja *f* struggle (**por** to); (en subasta) bid. ~**r** *vt* struggle; (en subasta) bid

pulcro *a* neat

pulga *f* flea. **tener malas** ~**s** be bad-tempered

pulga|da f inch. ~**r** m thumb; (del pie) big toe

puli|do a polished; <modales> refined. ~**r** vt polish; (suavizar) smooth

pulla f gibe

pulm|ón m lung. ~**onar** a pulmonary. ~**onía** f pneumonia

pulpa f pulp

pulpería f (LAm) grocer's shop (Brit), grocery store (Amer)

púlpito m pulpit

pulpo m octopus

pulque m (Mex) pulque, alcoholic Mexican drink. ~**ría** f bar

pulsa|ción f pulsation. ~**dor** m button. ~**r** vt press; (Mus) pluck

pulsera f bracelet

pulso m pulse; (firmeza) steady hand. **echar un** ~ arm wrestle. **tomar el** ~ **a uno** take s.o.'s pulse

pulular vi teem with

puma m puma

puna f puna, high plateau

punitivo a punitive

punta f point; (extremo) tip. **estar de** ~ be in a bad mood. **ponerse de** ~ **con uno** fall out with s.o. **sacar** ~ **a** sharpen

puntada f stitch

puntaje m (LAm) score

puntal m prop, support

puntapié m kick

puntear vt mark; (Mus) pluck; (LAm, en deportes) lead

puntería f aim; (destreza) markmanship

puntiagudo a pointed; (afilado) sharp

puntilla f (encaje) lace. **en** ~**s** (LAm), **de** ~**s** on tiptoe

punto m point; (señal, trazo) dot; (de examen) mark; (lugar) spot, place; (de taxis) stand; (momento) moment; (punto final) full stop (Brit), period (Amer); (puntada) stitch. ~ **de vista** point of view. ~ **com** dot-com. ~ **final** full stop (Brit), period (Amer). ~ **muerto** (Auto) neutral (gear). ~ **y aparte** full stop, new paragraph (Brit), period, new paragraph (Amer). ~ **y coma** semicolon. **a** ~ on time; (listo) ready. **a** ~ **de** on the point of. **de** ~ knitted. **dos** ~**s** colon. **en** ~ exactly. **hacer** ~ knit. **hasta cierto** ~ to a certain extent

puntuación f punctuation; (en deportes, acción) scoring; (en deportes, número de puntos) score

puntual a punctual; (exacto) accurate. ~**idad** f punctuality; (exactitud) accuracy

puntuar [21] vt punctuate; mark (Brit), grade (Amer) <examen>. ● vi score (points)

punza|da f sharp pain; (fig) pang. ~**nte** a sharp. ~**r** [10] vt prick

puñado m handful. **a** ~**s** by the handful

puñal m dagger. ~**ada** f stab

puñ|etazo m punch. ~**o** m fist; (de ropa) cuff; (mango) handle. **de su** ~**o** (**y letra**) in his own handwriting

pupa f (🄸, en los labios) cold sore

pupila f pupil

pupitre m desk

puré m purée; (sopa) thick soup. ~ **de papas** (LAm), ~ **de patatas** mashed potatoes

pureza f purity

purga f purge. ~**torio** m purgatory

puri|ficación f purification. ~**ificar** [7] vt purify. ~**sta** m & f purist. ~**tano** a puritanical. ● m puritan

puro a pure; <cielo> clear. **de pura casualidad** by sheer chance. **de** ~ **tonto** out of sheer stupidity. ● m cigar

púrpura f purple

pus *m* pus
puse *vb* ⇒PONER
pusilánime *a* fainthearted
puta *f* (vulg) whore

que *pron rel* (personas, sujeto) who;
(personas, complemento) whom;
(cosas) which, that. ● *conj* that.
¡∼ **tengan Vds buen viaje!** have a
good journey! ¡∼ **venga!** let him
come! ∼ **venga o no venga**
whether he comes or not. **creo ∼
tiene razón** I think (that) he is
right. **más** ∼ more than. **lo** ∼
what. **yo** ∼ **tú** if I were you
qué *a* (con sustantivo) what; (con a o
adv) how. ● *pron* what. ¡∼ **bonito!**
how nice! ¿**en** ∼ **piensas?** what
are you thinking about?
quebra|da *f* (riña) gorge; (paso) pass.
∼**dizo** *a* fragile. ∼**do** *a* broken;
(Com) bankrupt. ● *m* (Math)
fraction. ∼**ntar** *vt* break; disturb
<*paz*>. ∼**nto** *m* (pérdida) loss;
(daño) damage. ∼**r** [1] *vt* break. ●
vi break; (Com) go bankrupt.
□ ∼**rse** *vpr* break
quechua *a* Quechua. ● *m & f*
Quechan. ● *m* (lengua) Quechua
quedar *vi* stay, remain; (estar) be;
(haber todavía) be left. ∼ **bien** come
off well. □ ∼**se** *vpr* stay. ∼ **con**
arrange to meet. ∼ **en** agree to.
∼ **en nada** come to nothing. ∼ **por**
(+ *infinitivo*) remain to be (+ *pp*)
quehacer *m* work. ∼**es
domésticos** household chores
quej|a *f* complaint; (de dolor)
moan. □ ∼**arse** *vpr* complain (**de**

about); (gemir) moan. ∼**ido** *m*
moan
quema|do *a* burnt; (LAm,
bronceado) tanned; (fig) annoyed.
∼**dor** *m* burner. ∼**dura** *f* burn.
∼**r** *vt/i* burn. □ ∼**rse** *vpr* burn
o.s.; (consumirse) burn up; (con el
sol) get sunburnt. ∼**rropa** *adv*. **a
∼rropa** point-blank
quena *f* Indian flute
quepo *vb* ⇒CABER
querella *f* (riña) quarrel, dispute;
(Jurid) criminal action
quer|er [35] *vt* want; (amar) love;
(necesitar) need. ∼**er decir** mean. ●
m love; (amante) lover. **como quiera
que** however. **cuando quiera que**
whenever. **donde quiera** wherever.
¿**quieres darme ese libro?** would
you pass me that book? ¿**quieres
un helado?** would you like an
ice-cream? **quisiera ir a la playa** I'd
like to go to the beach. **sin** ∼**er**
without meaning to. ∼**ido** *a* dear;
(amado) loved
querosén *m*, **queroseno** *m*
kerosene
querubín *m* cherub
ques|adilla *f* (Mex) tortilla filled
with cheese. ∼**o** *m* cheese
quetzal *m* (unidad monetaria
ecuatoriana) quetzal
quicio *m* frame. **sacar de** ∼ **a uno**
infuriate s.o.
quiebra *f* (Com) bankruptcy
quien *pron rel* (sujeto) who;
(complemento) whom
quién *pron interrogativo* (sujeto)
who; (tras preposición) ¿**con** ∼? who
with ?, to whom? ¿**de** ∼ **son estos
libros?** whose are these books?
quienquiera *pron* whoever
quiero *vb* ⇒QUERER
quiet|o *a* still; (inmóvil) motionless;
<*carácter etc*> calm. ∼**ud** *f*
stillness

quijada *f* jaw

quilate *m* carat

quilla *f* keel

quimera *f* (fig) illusion

químic|a *f* chemistry. ~**o** *a* chemical. ● *m* chemist

quince *a & m* fifteen. ~ **días** *a* fortnight. ~**na** *f* fortnight. ~**nal** *a* fortnightly

quincuagésimo *a* fiftieth

quiniela *f* pools coupon. ~**s** *fpl* (football) pools

quinientos *a & m* five hundred

quinquenio *m* (period of) five years

quinta *f* (casa) villa

quintal *m* a hundred kilograms

quinteto *m* quintet

quinto *a & m* fifth

quiosco *m* kiosk; (en jardín) summerhouse; (en parque etc) bandstand

quirúrgico *a* surgical

quise *vb* ⇒QUERER

quisquill|a *f* trifle; (camarón) shrimp. ~**oso** *a* irritable; (exigente) fussy

quita|esmalte *m* nail polish remover. ~**manchas** *m invar* stain remover. ~**nieves** *m invar* snow plough. ~**r** *vt* remove, take away; take off <*ropa*>; (robar) steal. ~**ndo** (ⅠⅠ, a excepción de) apart from. □ ~**rse** *vpr* get rid of <*dolor*>; take off <*ropa*>. ~**rse de** (no hacerlo más) stop. ~**rse de en medio** get out of the way. ~**sol** *m* sunshade

quizá(s) *adv* perhaps

quórum *m* quorum

rábano *m* radish. ~ **picante** horseradish. **me importa un** ~ I couldn't care less

rabi|a *f* rabies; (fig) rage. ~**ar** *vi* (de dolor) be in great pain; (estar enfadado) be furious. **dar** ~**a** infuriate. ~**eta** *f* tantrum

rabino *m* rabbi

rabioso *a* rabid; (furioso) furious

rabo *m* tail

racha *f* gust of wind; (fig) spate. **pasar por una mala** ~ go through a bad patch

racial *a* racial

racimo *m* bunch

ración *f* share, ration; (de comida) portion

raciona|l *a* rational. ~**lizar** [10] *vt* rationalize. ~**r** *vt* (limitar) ration; (repartir) ration out

racis|mo *m* racism. ~**ta** *a* racist

radar *m* radar

radiación *f* radiation

radiactiv|idad *f* radioactivity. ~**o** *a* radioactive

radiador *m* radiator

radiante *a* radiant; (brillante) brilliant

radical *a & m & f* radical

radicar [7] *vi* lie (**en** in). □ ~**se** *vpr* settle

radio *m* radius; (de rueda) spoke; (LAm) radio. ● *f* radio. ~**actividad** *f* radioactivity. ~**activo** *a* radioactive. ~**difusión** *f* broadcasting. ~**emisora** *f* radio station.

~**escucha** *m & f* listener.
~**grafía** *f* radiography
radi|ólogo *m* radiologist.
~**oterapia** *f* radiotherapy
radioyente *m & f* listener
raer [36] *vt* scrape; (quitar) scrape off
ráfaga *f* (de viento) gust; (de ametralladora) burst
rafia *f* raffia
raído *a* threadbare
raíz *f* root. **a ~ de** as a result of. **echar raíces** (fig) settle
raja *f* split; (Culin) slice. ~**r** *vt* split. □ ~**rse** *vpr* split; (fig) back out
rajatabla. a ~ rigorously
ralea *f* sort
ralla|dor *m* grater. ~**r** *vt* grate
ralo *a* <pelo> thin
rama *f* branch. ~**je** *m* branches. ~**l** *m* branch
rambla *f* watercourse; (avenida) avenue
ramera *f* prostitute
ramifica|ción *f* ramification. □ ~**rse** [7] *vpr* branch out
ram|illete *m* bunch. ~**o** *m* branch; (de flores) bunch, bouquet
rampa *f* ramp, slope
rana *f* frog
ranch|era *f* (Mex) folk song. ~**ero** *m* cook; (Mex, hacendado) rancher. ~**o** *m* (LAm, choza) hut; (LAm, casucha) shanty; (Mex, hacienda) ranch
rancio *a* rancid; <vino> old; (fig) ancient
rango *m* rank
ranúnculo *m* buttercup
ranura *f* groove; (para moneda) slot
rapar *vt* shave; crop <pelo>
rapaz *a* rapacious; <ave> of prey
rape *m* monkfish

rapidez *f* speed
rápido *a* fast, quick. ● *adv* quickly. ● *m* (tren) express
rapiña *f* robbery. **ave** *f* **de ~** bird of prey
rapsodia *f* rhapsody
rapt|ar *vt* kidnap. ~**o** *m* kidnapping; (de ira etc) fit
raqueta *f* racquet
rar|eza *f* rarity; (cosa rara) oddity. ~**o** *a* rare; (extraño) odd. **es ~o que** it is strange that. **¡qué ~o!** how strange!
ras *m*. **a ~ de** level with
rasca|cielos *m invar* skyscraper. ~**r** [7] *vt* scratch; (raspar) scrape
rasgar [12] *vt* tear
rasgo *m* characteristic; (gesto) gesture; (de pincel) stroke. ~**s** *mpl* (facciones) features
rasguear *vt* strum
rasguñ|ar *vt* scratch. ~**o** *m* scratch
raso *a* <cucharada etc> level; <vuelo etc> low. **al ~** in the open air. ● *m* satin
raspa|dura *f* scratch; (acción) scratching. ~**r** *vt* scratch; (rozar) scrape
rastr|a. **a ~as** dragging. ~**ear** *vt* track. ~**ero** *a* creeping. ~**illar** *vt* rake. ~**illo** *m* rake. ~**o** *m* track; (señal) sign. **ni ~o** not a trace
rata *f* rat
ratero *m* petty thief
ratifica|ción *f* ratification. ~**r** [7] *vt* ratify
rato *m* moment, short time. ~**s libres** spare time. **a ~s** at times. **a cada ~** (LAm) always. **hace un ~** a moment ago. **pasar un mal ~** have a rough time
rat|ón *m* mouse. ~**onera** *f* mousetrap; (madriguera) mouse hole

raudal *m* torrent. **a ~les** in abundance

raya *f* line; (lista) stripe; (de pelo) parting. **a ~s** striped. **pasarse de la ~** go too far. **~r** *vt* scratch. **~r en** border on

rayo *m* ray; (descarga eléctrica) lightning. **~ de luna** moonbeam. **~ láser** laser beam. **~s X** X-rays

raza *f* race; (de animal) breed. **de ~** *<caballo>* thoroughbred; *<perro>* pedigree

raz|ón *f* reason. **a ~ón de** at the rate of. **tener ~ón** be right. **~onable** *a* reasonable. **~onar** *vt* reason out. ● *vi* reason

RDSI *abrev* (= Red Digital de Servicios Integrados) ISDN

re *m* D; (solfa) re

reac|ción *f* reaction; (LAm, Pol) right wing. **~ción en cadena** chain reaction. **~cionario** *a & m* reactionary. **~tor** *m* reactor; (avión) jet

real *a* real; (de rey etc) royal; *<hecho>* true. ● *m* real, old Spanish coin

realidad *f* reality; (verdad) truth. **en ~** in fact. **hacerse ~** come true

realis|mo *m* realism. **~ta** *a* realistic. ● *m & f* realist

realiza|ción *f* fulfilment. **~r** [10] *vt* carry out; make *<viaje>*; fulfil *<ilusión>*; (vender) sell. □ **~rse** *vpr* *<sueño, predicción etc>* come true; *<persona>* fulfil o.s.

realzar [10] *vt* (fig) enhance

reanimar *vt* revive. □ **~se** *vpr* revive

reanudar *vt* resume; renew *<amistad>*

reavivar *vt* revive

rebaja *f* reduction. **en ~s** in the sale. **~do** *a <precio>* reduced. **~r** *vt* lower; lose *<peso>*

rebanada *f* slice

rebaño *m* herd; (de ovejas) flock

rebasar *vt* exceed; (dejar atrás) leave behind; (Mex, Auto) overtake

rebatir *vt* refute

rebel|arse *vpr* rebel. **~de** *a* rebellious; *<grupo>* rebel. ● *m* rebel. **~día** *f* rebelliousness. **~ión** *f* rebellion

rebosa|nte *a* brimming (**de** with). **~r** *vi* overflow; (abundar) abound

rebot|ar *vt* bounce; (rechazar) repel. ● *vi* bounce; *<bala>* ricochet. **~e** *m* bounce, rebound. **de ~e** on the rebound

reboz|ar [10] *vt* wrap up; (Culin) coat in batter. **~o** *m* (LAm) shawl

rebusca|do *a* affected; (complicado) over-elaborate. **~r** [7] *vt* search through

rebuznar *vi* bray

recado *m* errand; (mensaje) message

reca|er [29] *vi* fall back; (Med) relapse; (fig) fall. **~ída** *f* relapse

recalcar [7] *vt* stress

recalcitrante *a* recalcitrant

recalentar [1] *vt* reheat; (demasiado) overheat

recámara *f* small room; (de arma de fuego) chamber; (Mex, dormitorio) bedroom

recambio *m* (Mec) spare (part); (de pluma etc) refill. **de ~** spare

recapitular *vt* sum up

recarg|ar [12] *vt* overload; (aumentar) increase; recharge *<batería>*. **~o** *m* increase

recat|ado *a* modest. **~o** *m* prudence; (modestia) modesty. **sin ~o** openly

recauda|ción *f* (cantidad) takings. **~dor** *m* tax collector. **~r** *vt* collect

recel|ar *vt* suspect. ● *vi* be suspicious (**de** of). **~o** *m* distrust; (temor) fear. **~oso** *a* suspicious

R

recepci|ón f reception. **~onista** m & f receptionist

receptáculo m receptacle

receptor m receiver

recesión f recession

receta f recipe; (Med) prescription

rechaz|ar [10] vt reject; defeat <moción>; repel <ataque>; (no aceptar) turn down. **~o** m rejection

rechifla f booing

rechinar vi squeak. **le rechinan los dientes** he grinds his teeth

rechoncho a stout

recib|imiento m (acogida) welcome. **~ir** vt receive; (acoger) welcome. ● vi entertain. □ **~irse** vpr graduate. **~o** m receipt. **acusar ~o** acknowledge receipt

reci|én adv recently; (LAm, hace poco) just. **~ casado** newly married. **~ nacido** newborn. **~ente** a recent; (Culin) fresh

recinto m enclosure; (local) premises

recio a strong; <voz> loud. ● adv hard; (en voz alta) loudly

recipiente m receptacle. ● m & f recipient

recíproco a reciprocal; <sentimiento> mutual

recita|l m recital; (de poesías) reading. **~r** vt recite

reclama|ción f claim; (queja) complaint. **~r** vt claim. ● vi appeal

réclame m (LAm) advertisement

reclamo m (LAm) complaint

reclinar vi lean. □ **~se** vpr lean

reclus|ión f imprisonment. **~o** m prisoner

recluta m & f recruit. **~miento** m recruitment. **~r** vt recruit

recobrar vt recover. □ **~se** vpr recover

recodo m bend

recog|er [14] vt collect; pick up <cosa caída>; (cosechar) harvest. □ **~erse** vpr withdraw; (ir a casa) go home; (acostarse) go to bed. **~ida** f collection; (cosecha) harvest

recomenda|ción f recommendation. **~r** [1] vt recommend; (encomendar) entrust

recomenzar [1 & 10] vt/i start again

recompensa f reward. **~r** vt reward

reconcilia|ción f reconciliation. **~r** vt reconcile. □ **~rse** vpr be reconciled

reconoc|er [11] vt recognize; (admitir) acknowledge; (examinar) examine. **~imiento** m recognition; (admisión) acknowledgement; (agradecimiento) gratitude; (examen) examination

reconozco vb ⇒RECONOCER

reconquista f reconquest. **~r** vt reconquer; (fig) win back

reconsiderar vt reconsider

reconstruir [17] vt reconstruct

récord /'rekor/ m (pl ~s) record

recordar [2] vt remember; (hacer acordar) remind. ● vi remember. **que yo recuerde** as far as I remember. **si mal no recuerdo** if I remember rightly

recorr|er vt tour <país>; go round <zona, museo>; cover <distancia>. **~ mundo** travel all around the world. **~ido** m journey; (trayecto) route

recort|ar vt cut (out). **~e** m cutting (out); (de periódico etc) cutting

recostar [2] vt lean. □ **~se** vpr lie down

recoveco m bend; (rincón) nook

recre|ación f recreation. ~**ar** vt recreate; (divertir) entertain. □ ~**arse** vpr amuse o.s. ~**ativo** a recreational. ~**o** m recreation; (Escol) break

recrudecer [11] vi intensify

recta f straight line. ~ **final** home stretch

rect|angular a rectangular. ~**ángulo** a rectangular; <triángulo> right-angled. ● m rectangle

rectifica|ción f rectification. ~**r** [7] vt rectify

rect|itud f straightness; (fig) honesty. ~**o** a straight; (fig, justo) fair; (fig, honrado) honest. **todo** ~**o** straight on. ● m rectum

rector a governing. ● m rector

recubrir (pp recubierto) vt cover (con, de with)

recuerdo m memory; (regalo) souvenir. ~**s** mpl (saludos) regards. ● vb ⇒RECORDAR

recupera|ción f recovery. ~**r** vt recover. ~ **el tiempo perdido** make up for lost time. □ ~**rse** vpr recover

recur|rir vi. ~**rir a** resort to <cosa>; turn to <persona>. ~**so** m resort; (medio) resource; (Jurid) appeal. ~**sos** mpl resources

red f network; (malla) net; (para equipaje) luggage rack; (Com) chain; (Elec, gas) mains. **la R**~ the Net

redac|ción f writing; (lenguaje) wording; (conjunto de redactores) editorial staff; (oficina) editorial office; (Escol, Univ) essay. ~**tar** vt write. ~**tor** m writer; (de periódico) editor

redada f catch; (de policía) raid

redecilla f small net; (para el pelo) hairnet

redentor a redeeming

redimir vt redeem

redoblar vt redouble; step up <vigilancia>

redomado a utter

redond|a f (de imprenta) roman (type); (Mus) semibreve (Brit), whole note (Amer). **a la** ~**a** around. ~**ear** vt round off. ~**el** m circle; (de plaza de toros) arena. ~**o** a round; (completo) complete; (Mex, boleto) return, round-trip (Amer). **en** ~**o** round; (categóricamente) flatly

reduc|ción f reduction. ~**ido** a reduced; (limitado) limited; (pequeño) small; <precio> low. ~**ir** [47] vt reduce. □ ~**irse** vpr be reduced; (fig) amount

reduje vb ⇒REDUCIR

redundan|cia f redundancy. ~**te** a redundant

reduzco vb ⇒REDUCIR

reembols|ar vt reimburse. ~**o** m repayment. **contra** ~**o** cash on delivery

reemplaz|ar [10] vt replace. ~**o** m replacement

refacci|ón f (LAm) refurbishment; (Mex, Mec) spare part. ~**onar** vt (LAm) refurbish. ~**onaria** f (Mex) repair shop

referencia f reference; (información) report. **con** ~ **a** with reference to. **hacer** ~ **a** refer to

referéndum m (pl ~**s**) referendum

referir [4] vt tell; (remitir) refer. □ ~**se** vpr refer. **por lo que se refiere a** as regards

refiero vb ⇒REFERIR

refilón. de ~ obliquely

refin|amiento m refinement. ~**ar** vt refine. ~**ería** f refinery

reflector m reflector; (proyector) searchlight

R

reflej|ar vt reflect. ~a reflex.
● m reflection; (Med) reflex; (en el pelo) highlights

reflexi|ón f reflection. **sin ~ón** without thinking. ~**onar** vi reflect. ~**vo** a <persona> thoughtful; (Gram) reflexive

reforma f reform. ~**s** fpl (reparaciones) repairs. ~**r** vt reform. □ ~**rse** vpr reform

reforzar [2 & 10] vt reinforce

refrac|ción f refraction. ~**tario** a heat-resistant

refrán m saying

refregar [1 & 12] vt scrub

refresc|ar [7] vt refresh; (enfriar) cool. ● vi get cooler. □ ~**arse** vpr refresh o.s. ~**o** m cold drink. ~**os** mpl refreshments

refrigera|ción f refrigeration; (aire acondicionado) air-conditioning; (de motor) cooling. ~**r** vt refrigerate; air-condition <lugar>; cool <motor>. ~**dor** m refrigerator

refuerzo m reinforcement

refugi|ado m refugee. □ ~**arse** vpr take refuge. ~**o** m refuge, shelter

refunfuñar vi grumble

refutar vt refute

regadera f watering-can; (Mex, ducha) shower

regala|do a as a present, free; (cómodo) comfortable. ~**r** vt give

regalo m present, gift

regañ|adientes. a ~adientes reluctantly. ~**ar** vt scold. ● vi moan; (dos personas) quarrel. ~**o** m (represión) scolding

regar [1 & 12] vt water

regata f boat race; (serie) regatta

regate|ar vt haggle over; (economizar) economize on. ● vi haggle; (en deportes) dribble. ~**o** m haggling; (en deportes) dribbling

regazo m lap

regenerar vt regenerate

régimen m (pl **regímenes**) regime; (Med) diet; (de lluvias) pattern

regimiento m regiment

regi|ón f region. ~**onal** a regional

regir [5 & 14] vt govern. ● vi apply, be in force

registr|ado a registered. ~**ar** vt register; (Mex) check in <equipaje>; (grabar) record; (examinar) search. □ ~**arse** vpr register; (darse) be reported. ~**o** m (acción de registrar) registration; (libro) register; (cosa anotada) entry; (inspección) search. ~**o civil** (oficina) registry office

regla f ruler; (norma) rule; (menstruación) period. **en ~** in order. **por ~ general** as a rule. ~**mentación** f regulation. ~**mentar** vt regulate. ~**mentario** a regulation; <horario> set. ~**mento** m regulations

regocij|arse vpr be delighted. ~**o** m delight

regode|arse vpr (+ gerundio) delight in (+ gerund). ~**o** m delight

regordete a chubby

regres|ar vi return; (LAm) send back <persona>. □ ~**arse** vpr (LAm) return. ~**ivo** a backward. ~**o** m return

regula|ble a adjustable. ~**dor** m control. ~**r** a regular; (mediano) average; (no bueno) so-so. ● vt regulate; adjust <volumen etc>. ~**ridad** f regularity. **con ~ridad** regularly

rehabilita|ción f rehabilitation; (en empleo etc) reinstatement. ~**r** vt rehabilitate; (en cargo) reinstate

rehacer [31] *vt* redo; (repetir) repeat; rebuild <*vida*>. □ ~**se** *vpr* recover

rehén *m* hostage

rehogar [12] *vt* sauté

rehuir [17] *vt* avoid

rehusar *vt/i* refuse

reimpr|esión *f* reprinting. ~**imir** (*pp* **reimpreso**) *vt* reprint

reina *f* queen. ~**do** *m* reign. ~**nte** *a* ruling; (fig) prevailing. ~**r** *vi* reign; (fig) prevail

reincidir *vi* (Jurid) reoffend

reino *m* kingdom. **R~ Unido** United Kingdom

reintegr|ar *vt* reinstate <*persona*>; refund <*cantidad*>. □ ~**arse** *vpr* return. ~**o** *m* refund

reír [51] *vi* laugh. □ ~**se** *vpr* laugh. ~**se** laugh at. **echarse a** ~ burst out laughing

reivindica|ción *f* claim. ~**r** [7] *vt* claim; (rehabilitar) restore

rej|a *f* grille; (verja) railing. **entre** ~**as** behind bars. ~**illa** *f* grille, grating; (red) luggage rack

rejuvenecer [11] *vt/i* rejuvenate. □ ~**se** *vpr* be rejuvenated

relaci|ón *f* connection; (trato) relation(ship); (relato) account; (lista) list. **con** ~**ón a, en** ~**ón a** in relation to. ~**onado** *a* related. **bien** ~**onado** well-connected. ~**onar** *vt* relate (**con** to). □ ~**onarse** *vpr* be connected; (tratar) mix (**con** with)

relaja|ción *f* relaxation; (aflojamiento) slackening. ~**do** *a* relaxed. ~**r** *vt* relax; (aflojar) slacken. □ ~**rse** *vpr* relax

relamerse *vpr* lick one's lips

relámpago *m* (flash of) lightning

relatar *vt* tell, relate

relativ|idad *f* relativity. ~**o** *a* relative

relato *m* tale; (relación) account

relegar [12] *vt* relegate. ~ **al olvido** consign to oblivion

relev|ante *a* outstanding. ~**ar** *vt* relieve; (substituir) replace. ~**o** *m* relief. **carrera** *f* **de** ~**os** relay race

relieve *m* relief; (fig) importance. **de** ~ important. **poner de** ~ emphasize

religi|ón *f* religion. ~**osa** *f* nun. ~**oso** *a* religious. ● *m* monk

relinch|ar *vi* neigh. ~**o** *m* neigh

reliquia *f* relic

rellano *m* landing

rellen|ar *vt* refill; (Culin) stuff; fill in <*formulario*>. ~**o** *a* full up; (Culin) stuffed. ● *m* filling; (Culin) stuffing

reloj *m* clock; (de bolsillo o pulsera) watch. ~ **de caja** grandfather clock. ~ **de pulsera** wrist-watch. ~ **de sol** sundial. ~ **despertador** alarm clock. ~**ería** *f* watchmaker's (shop). ~**ero** *m* watchmaker

reluci|ente *a* shining. ~**r** [11] *vi* shine; (destellar) sparkle

relumbrar *vi* shine

remach|ar *vt* rivet. ~**e** *m* rivet

remangar [12] *vt* roll up

remar *vi* row

remat|ado *a* (total) complete. ~**ar** *vt* finish off; (agotar) use up; (Com) sell off cheap; (LAm, subasta) auction; (en tenis) smash. ~**e** *m* end; (fig) finishing touch; (LAm, subastar) auction; (en tenis) smash. **de** ~**e** completely

remedar *vt* imitate

remedi|ar *vt* remedy; repair <*daño*>; (fig, resolver) solve. **no lo pude** ~**ar** I couldn't help it. ~**o** *m* remedy; (fig) solution; (LAm, medicamento) medicine. **como último** ~**o** as a last resort. **no hay más**

R

~o there's no other way. **no tener
más ~o** have no choice

remedo *m* poor imitation

rem|endar [1] *vt* repair. ~**iendo**
m patch

remilg|ado *a* fussy; (afectado)
affected. ~**o** *m* fussiness;
(afectación) affectation. ~**oso** *a*
(Mex) fussy

reminiscencia *f* reminiscence

remisión *f* remission; (envío)
sending; (referencia) reference

remit|e *m* sender's name and
address. ~**ente** *m* sender. ~**ir** *vt*
send; (referir) refer ● *vi* diminish

remo *m* oar

remoj|ar *vt* soak; (fig, 🔟)
celebrate. ~**o** *m* soaking. **poner a
~o** soak

remolacha *f* beetroot. ~
azucarera sugar beet

remolcar [7] *vt* tow

remolino *m* swirl; (de aire etc)
whirl

remolque *m* towing; (cabo) tow-
rope; (vehículo) trailer. **a ~** on tow.
dar ~ a tow

remontar *vt* overcome. ~ **el vuelo**
soar up; <avión> gain height.
□ ~**se** *vpr* soar up; (en el tiempo)
go back to

remord|er [2] *vi*. **eso le remuerde**
he feels guilty for it. **me remuerde
la conciencia** I have a guilty
conscience. ~**imiento** *m*
remorse. **tener ~imientos** feel
remorse

remoto *a* remote; <época> distant

remover [2] *vt* stir <líquido>; turn
over <tierra>; (quitar) remove; (fig,
activar) revive

remunera|ción *f* remuneration.
~**r** *vt* remunerate

renac|er [11] *vi* be reborn; (fig)
revive. ~**imiento** *m* rebirth.
R~imiento Renaissance

renacuajo *m* tadpole; (fig) tiddler

rencilla *f* quarrel

rencor *m* bitterness. **guardar ~ a**
have a grudge against

rendi|ción *f* surrender. ~**do** *a*
submissive; (agotado) exhausted

rendija *f* crack

rendi|miento *m* performance;
(Com) yield. ~**r** [5] *vt* yield;
(agotar) exhaust; pay <homenaje>;
present <informe>. ● *vi* pay;
(producir) produce. □ ~**rse** *vpr*
surrender

renegar [1 & 12] *vt* deny. ● *vi*
grumble. ~**r de** renounce <fe
etc>; disown <personas>

renglón *m* line; (Com) item. **a ~
seguido** straight away

reno *m* reindeer

renombr|ado *a* renowned. ~**e** *m*
renown

renova|ción *f* renewal; (de edificio)
renovation; (de mobiliario) complete
change. ~**r** *vt* renew; renovate
<edificio>; change <mobiliario>

rent|a *f* income; (Mex, alquiler) rent.
~**a vitalicia** (life) annuity. ~**able**
a profitable. ~**ar** *vt* yield; (Mex,
alquilar) rent, hire. ~**ista** *m & f*
person of independent means

renuncia *f* renunciation; (dimisión)
resignation. ~**r** *vi*. ~**r a**
renounce, give up; (dimitir) resign

reñi|do *a* hard-fought. **estar ~do
con** be incompatible with <cosa>;
be on bad terms with <persona>.
~**r** [5 & 22] *vt* scold. ● *vi* quarrel

reo *m & f* (Jurid) accused;
(condenado) convicted offender;
(pez) sea trout

reojo. mirar de ~ look out of the
corner of one's eye at

reorganizar [10] *vt* reorganize

repar|ación *f* repair; (acción)
repairing (fig, compensación)

reparation. **~ar** *vt* repair; (fig)
make amends for; (notar) notice.
● *vi*. **~ar en** notice; (hacer caso de)
pay attention to. **~o** *m* fault;
(objeción) objection. **poner ~os**
raise objections

repart|ición *f* distribution. **~idor**
m delivery man. **~imiento** *m*
distribution. **~ir** *vt* distribute,
share out; deliver <*cartas, leche
etc*>; hand out <*folleto, premio*>.
~o *m* distribution; (de cartas, leche
etc) delivery; (actores) cast

repas|ar *vt* go over; check
<*cuenta*>; revise <*texto*>; (leer a la
ligera) glance through; (coser)
mend. ● *vi* revise. **~o** *m*
revision; (de ropa) mending. **dar un
~o** look through

repatria|ción *f* repatriation. **~r**
vt repatriate

repele|nte *a* repulsive. ● *m*
insect repellent. **~r** *vt* repel

repent|e. de ~ suddenly. **~ino** *a*
sudden

repercu|sión *f* repercussion.
~tir *vi* reverberate; (fig) have
repercussions (**en** on)

repertorio *m* repertoire

repeti|ción *f* repetition; (de
programa) repeat. **~damente** *adv*
repeatedly. **~r** [5] *vt* repeat; have
a second helping of <*plato*>;
(imitar) copy. ● *vi* have a second
helping of

repi|car [7] *vt* ring <*campanas*>.
~que *m* peal

repisa *f* shelf. **~ de chimenea**
mantlepiece

repito *vb* ⇒REPETIR

replegarse [1 & 12] *vpr*
withdraw

repleto *a* full up. **~ de gente**
packed with people

réplica *a* reply; (copia) replica

replicar [7] *vi* reply

repollo *m* cabbage

reponer [34] *vt* replace; revive
<*obra de teatro*>; (contestar) reply.
□ **~se** *vpr* recover

report|aje *m* report; (LAm,
entrevista) interview. **~ar** *vt* yield;
(LAm, denunciar) report. **~e** *m* (Mex,
informe) report; (Mex, queja)
complaint. **~ero** *m* reporter

repos|ado *a* quiet; (sin prisa)
unhurried. **~ar** *vi* rest; <*líquido*>
settle. **~o** *m* rest

repost|ar *vt* replenish. ● *vi*
(Aviac) refuel; (Auto) fill up. **~ería**
f pastrymaking

reprender *vt* reprimand

represalia *f* reprisal. **tomar ~s**
retaliate

representa|ción *f*
representation; (en el teatro)
performance. **en ~ción de**
representing. **~nte** *m*
representative. **~r** *vt* represent;
perform <*obra de teatro*>; play
<*papel*>; (aparentar) look. □ **~rse**
vpr imagine. **~tivo** *a*
representative

represi|ón *f* repression. **~vo** *a*
repressive

reprimenda *f* reprimand

reprimir *vt* supress. □ **~se** *vpr*
control o.s.

reprobar [2] *vt* condemn; (LAm,
Univ, etc) fail

reproch|ar *vt* reproach. **~e** *m*
reproach

reproduc|ción *f* reproduction.
~ir [47] *vt* reproduce. **~tor** *a*
reproductive; <*animal*> breeding

reptil *m* reptile

rep|ública *f* republic. **~ublicano**
a & *m* republican

repudiar *vt* condemn; (Jurid)
repudiate

repuesto *m* (Mec) spare (part). **de
~** spare

R

repugna|ncia f disgust. ~**nte** a repugnant; <*olor*> disgusting. ~**r** vt disgust

repuls|a f rebuff. ~**ión** f repulsion. ~**ivo** a repulsive

reputa|ción f reputation. ~**do** a reputable. ~**r** vt consider

requeri|miento m request; (necesidad) requirement. ~**r** [4] vt require; summons <*persona*>

requesón m curd cheese

requete... pref extremely

requis|a f requisition; (confiscación) seizure; (inspección) inspection; (Mil) requisition. ~**ar** vt requisition; (confiscar) seize; (inspeccionar) inspect. ~**ito** m requirement

res f animal. ~ **lanar** sheep. ~ **vacuna** (vaca) cow; (toro) bull; (buey) ox. **carne de** ~ (Mex) beef

resabido a well-known; <*persona*> pedantic

resaca f undercurrent; (después de beber) hangover

resaltar vi stand out. **hacer** ~ emphasize

resarcir [9] vt repay; (compensar) compensate. □ ~**se** vpr make up for

resbal|adilla f (Mex) slide. ~**adizo** a slippery. ~**ar** vi slip; (Auto) skid; <*líquido*> trickle. □ ~**arse** vpr slip; (Auto) skid; <*líquido*> trickle. ~**ón** m slip; (de vehículo) skid. ~**oso** a (LAm) slippery

rescat|ar vt rescue; (fig) recover. ~**e** m ransom; (recuperación) recovery; (salvamento) rescue

rescoldo m embers

resecar [7] vt dry up. □ ~**se** vpr dry up

resenti|do a resentful. ~**miento** m resentment. □ ~**rse** vpr feel

the effects; (debilitarse) be weakened; (ofenderse) take offence (**de** at)

reseña f summary; (de persona) description; (en periódico) report, review. ~**r** vt describe; (en periódico) report on, review

reserva f reservation; (provisión) reserve(s). **de** ~ in reserve. ~**ción** f (LAm) reservation. ~**do** a reserved. ~**r** vt reserve; (guardar) keep, save. □ ~**rse** vpr save o.s.

resfria|do m cold. □ ~**rse** vpr catch a cold

resguard|ar vt protect. □ ~**arse** vpr protect o.s.; (fig) take care. ~**o** m protection; (garantía) guarantee; (recibo) receipt

resid|encia f residence; (Univ) hall of residence (Brit), dormitory (Amer); (de ancianos etc) home. ~**encial** a residential. ~**ente** a & m & f resident. ~**ir** vi reside; (fig) lie (**en** in)

residu|al a residual. ~**o** m residue. ~**os** mpl waste

resigna|ción f resignation. □ ~**rse** vpr resign o.s. (**a** to)

resist|encia f resistence. ~**ente** a resistent. ~**ir** vt resist; (soportar) bear. ● vi resist. **ya no resisto más** I can't take it any more

resol|ución f resolution; (solución) solution; (decisión) decision. ~**ver** [2] (pp **resuelto**) resolve; solve <*problema etc*>. □ ~**verse** vpr resolve itself; (resultar bien) work out; (decidir) decide

resona|ncia f resonance. **tener** ~**ncia** cause a stir. ~**nte** a resonant; (fig) resounding. ~**r** [2] vi resound

resorte m spring; (Mex, elástico) elastic. **tocar (todos los)** ~**s** (fig) pull strings

respald|ar *vt* back; (escribir) endorse. □ **~arse** *vpr* lean back. **~o** *m* backing; (de asiento) back

respect|ar *vi*. **en lo que ~a a** with regard to. **en lo que a mí ~a** as far as I'm concerned. **~ivo** *a* respective. **~o** *m* respect. **al ~o** on this matter. **(con) ~o a** with regard to

respet|able *a* respectable. ● *m* audience. **~ar** *vt* respect. **~o** *m* respect. **faltar al ~o a** be disrespectful to. **~uoso** *a* respectful

respir|ación *f* breathing; (ventilación) ventilation. **~ar** *vi* breathe; (fig) breathe a sigh of relief. **~o** *m* breathing; (fig) rest

respland|ecer [11] *vi* shine. **~eciente** *a* shining. **~or** *m* brilliance; (de llamas) glow

responder *vi* answer; (replicar) answer back; (reaccionar) respond. **~ de** be responsible for. **~ por uno** vouch for s.o.

responsab|ilidad *f* responsibility. **~le** *a* responsible

respuesta *f* reply, answer

resquebrajar *vt* crack. □ **~se** *vpr* crack

resquemor *m* (fig) uneasiness

resquicio *m* crack; (fig) possibility

resta *f* subtraction

restablecer [11] *vt* restore. □ **~se** *vpr* recover

rest|ante *a* remaining. **lo ~nte** the rest. **~ar** *vt* take away; (substraer) subtract. ● *vi* be left

restaura|ción *f* restoration. **~nte** *m* restaurant. **~r** *vt* restore

restitu|ción *f* restitution. **~ir** [17] *vt* return; (restaurar) restore

resto *m* rest, remainder; (en matemática) remainder. **~s** *mpl* remains; (de comida) leftovers

restorán *m* restaurant

restregar [1 & 12] *vt* rub

restri|cción *f* restriction. **~ngir** [14] *vt* restrict, limit

resucitar *vt* resuscitate; (fig) revive. ● *vi* return to life

resuello *m* breath; (respiración) heavy breathing

resuelto *a* resolute

resulta|do *m* result (en in). **~r** *vi* result; (salir) turn out; (dar resultado) work; (ser) be; (costar) come to

resum|en *m* summary. **en ~en** in short. **~ir** *vt* summarize; (recapitular) sum up

resur|gir [14] *vi* re-emerge; (fig) revive. **~gimiento** *m* resurgence. **~rección** *f* resurrection

retaguardia *f* (Mil) rearguard

retahíla *f* string

retar *vt* challenge

retardar *vt* slow down; (demorar) delay

retazo *m* remnant; (fig) piece, bit

reten|ción *f* retention. **~er** [40] *vt* keep; (en la memoria) retain; (no dar) withhold

reticencia *f* insinuation; (reserva) reluctance

retina *f* retina

retir|ada *f* withdrawal. **~ado** *a* remote; *<vida>* secluded; (jubilado) retired. **~ar** *vt* move away; (quitar) remove; withdraw *<dinero>*; (jubilar) pension off. □ **~arse** *vpr* draw back; (Mil) withdraw; (jubilarse) retire; (acostarse) go to bed. **~o** *m* retirement; (pensión) pension; (lugar apartado) retreat; (LAm, de apoyo, fondos) withdrawal

reto *m* challenge

retocar [7] *vt* retouch

retoño *m* shoot; (fig) kid

retoque *m* (acción) retouching; (efecto) finishing touch

R

retorc|er [2 & 9] vt twist; wring <ropa>. □ ~erse vpr get twisted up; (de dolor) writhe. ~ijón m (LAm) stomach cramp

retóric|a f rhetoric; (grandilocuencia) grandiloquence. ~o m rhetorical

retorn|ar vt/i return. ~o m return

retortijón m twist; (de tripas) stomach cramp

retractarse vpr retract. ~se de lo dicho withdraw what one said

retransmitir vt repeat; (radio, TV) broadcast. ~ en directo broadcast live

retras|ado a (con ser) mentally handicapped; (con estar) behind; <reloj> slow; (poco desarrollado) backward; (anticuado) old-fashioned. ~ar vt delay; put back <reloj>; (retardar) slow down; (posponer) postpone. ● vi <reloj> be slow. □ ~arse vpr be late; <reloj> be slow. ~o m delay; (poco desarrollo) backwardness; (de reloj) slowness. traer ~o be late. ~os mpl arrears

retrato m portrait; (fig, descripción) description. ser el vivo ~o de be the living image of

retrete m toilet

retribu|ción f payment; (recompensa) reward. ~ir [17] vt pay; (recompensar) reward; (LAm) return <favor>

retroce|der vi move back; (fig) back down. ~so m backward movement; (de arma de fuego) recoil; (Med) relapse

retrógrado a & m (Pol) reactionary

retrospectivo a retrospective

retrovisor m rear-view mirror

retumbar vt echo; <trueno etc> boom

reum|a m, **reúma** m rheumatism. ~ático a rheumatic. ~atismo m rheumatism

reuni|ón f meeting; (entre amigos) reunion. ~r [23] vt join together; (recoger) gather (together); raise <fondos>. □ ~rse vpr meet; <amigos etc> get together

revalidar vt confirm; (Mex, estudios) validate

revalorizar [10] vt, (LAm) **revaluar** [21] vt revalue; increase <pensiones>. □ ~se vpr appreciate

revancha f revenge; (en deportes) return match. tomar la ~ get one's own back

revela|ción f revelation. ~do m developing. ~dor a revealing. ~r vt reveal; (Foto) develop

revent|ar [1] vi burst; (tener ganas) be dying to. □ ~arse vpr burst. ~ón m burst; (Auto) blow out; (Mex, fiesta) party

reveren|cia f reverence; (de hombre, niño) bow; (de mujer) curtsy. ~ciar vt revere. ~do a (Relig) reverend. ~te a reverent

revers|ible a reversible. ~o m reverse; (de papel) back

revertir [4] vi revert (a to)

revés m wrong side; (de prenda) inside; (contratiempo) setback; (en deportes) backhand. al ~ the other way round; (con lo de arriba abajo) upside down; (con lo de dentro fuera) inside out

revesti|miento m coating. ~r [5] vt cover

revis|ar vt check; overhaul <mecanismo>; service <coche etc>; (LAm, equipaje) search. ~ión f check(ing); (Med) checkup; (de coche etc) service; (LAm, de equipaje) inspection. ~or m inspector

revista f magazine; (inspección) inspection; (artículo) review;

(espectáculo) revue. **pasar** $\sim$ **a** inspect

revivir *vi* revive

revolcar [2 & 7] *vt* knock over. □ $\sim$**se** *vpr* roll around

revolotear *vi* flutter

revoltijo *m*, **revoltillo** *m* mess

revoltoso *a* rebellious; *<niño>* naughty

revoluci|ón *f* revolution. $\sim$**onar** *vt* revolutionize. $\sim$**onario** *a & m* revolutionary

revolver [2] (*pp* **revuelto**) *vt* mix; stir *<líquido>*; (desordenar) mess up

revólver *m* revolver

revuelo *m* fluttering; (fig) stir

revuelt|a *f* revolt; (conmoción) disturbance. $\sim$**o** *a* mixed up; *<líquido>* cloudy; *<mar>* rough; *<tiempo>* unsettled; *<huevos>* scrambled

rey *m* king. **los** $\sim$**es** the king and queen. **los R**$\sim$**es Magos** the Three Wise Men

reyerta *f* brawl

rezagarse [12] *vpr* fall behind

rez|ar [10] *vt* say. ● *vi* pray; (decir) say. $\sim$**o** *m* praying; (oración) prayer

rezongar [12] *vi* grumble

ría *f* estuary

riachuelo *m* stream

riada *f* flood

ribera *f* bank

ribete *m* border; (fig) embellishment

rico *a* rich; (Culin, ▯) good, nice. ● *m* rich person

rid|ículo *a* ridiculous. $\sim$**iculizar** [10] *vt* ridicule

riego *m* watering; (irrigación) irrigation

riel *m* rail

rienda *f* rein

riesgo *m* risk. **correr (el)** $\sim$ **de** run the risk of

rifa *f* raffle. $\sim$**r** *vt* raffle

rifle *m* rifle

rigidez *f* rigidity; (fig) inflexibility

rígido *a* rigid; (fig) inflexible

rig|or *m* strictness; (exactitud) exactness; (de clima) severity. **de** $\sim$**or** compulsory. **en** $\sim$**or** strictly speaking. $\sim$**uroso** *a* rigorous

rima *f* rhyme. $\sim$**r** *vt/i* rhyme

rimbombante *a* resounding; *<lenguaje>* pompous; (fig, ostentoso) showy

rímel *m* mascara

rin *m* (Mex) rim

rincón *m* corner

rinoceronte *m* rhinoceros

riña *f* quarrel; (pelea) fight

riñón *m* kidney

río *m* river; (fig) stream. $\sim$ **abajo** downstream. $\sim$ **arriba** upstream. ● *vb* ⇒REÍR

riqueza *f* wealth; (fig) richness. $\sim$**s** *fpl* riches

ris|a *f* laugh. **desternillarse de** $\sim$**a** split one's sides laughing. **la** $\sim$**a** laughter. $\sim$**otada** *f* guffaw. $\sim$**ueño** *a* smiling; (fig) cheerful

rítmico *a* rhythmic(al)

ritmo *m* rhythm; (fig) rate

rit|o *m* rite; (fig) ritual. $\sim$**ual** *a & m* ritual

rival *a & m & f* rival. $\sim$**idad** *f* rivalry. $\sim$**izar** [10] *vi* rival

riz|ado *a* curly. $\sim$**ar** [10] *vt* curl; ripple *<agua>*. $\sim$**o** *m* curl; (en agua) ripple

róbalo *m* bass

robar *vt* steal *<cosa>*; rob *<banco>*; (raptar) kidnap

roble *m* oak (tree)

robo *m* theft; (de banco, museo) robbery; (en vivienda) burglary

robusto *a* robust

roca *f* rock

R

roce *m* rubbing; (señal) mark; (fig, entre personas) regular contact; (Pol) friction. **tener un ~ con uno** have a brush with s.o.

rociar [20] *vt* spray

rocín *m* nag

rocío *m* dew

rodaballo *m* turbot

rodaja *f* slice. **en ~s** sliced

rodaje *m* (de película) shooting; (de coche) running in. **~r** [2] *vt* shoot <*película*>; run in <*coche*>. ● *vi* roll; <*coche*> run; (hacer una película) shoot

rodear *vt* surround; (LAm) round up <*ganado*>. □ **~arse** *vpr* surround o.s. (**de** with). **~o** *m* detour; (de ganado) round-up. **andar con ~os** beat about the bush. **sin ~os** plainly

rodilla *f* knee. **ponerse de ~as** kneel down. **~era** *f* knee-pad

rodillo *m* roller; (Culin) rolling-pin

roedor *m* rodent. **~r** [37] *vt* gnaw

rogar [2 & 12] *vt/i* beg; (Relig) pray; **se ruega a los Sres. pasajeros...** passengers are requested.... **se ruega no fumar** please do not smoke

rojizo *a* reddish. **~o** *a & m* red. **ponerse ~o** blush

rollizo *a* plump; <*bebé*> chubby. **~o** *m* roll; (de cuerda) coil; (Culin, rodillo) rolling-pin; (fig, 🔲, pesadez) bore

romance *a* Romance. ● *m* (idilio) romance; (poema) ballad

romano *a & m* Roman. **a la ~a** (Culin) (deep-)fried in batter

romanticismo *m* romanticism. **~ántico** *a* romantic

romería *f* pilgrimage; (LAm, multitud) mass

romero *m* rosemary

romo *a* blunt; <*nariz*> snub

rompecabezas *m invar* puzzle; (de piezas) jigsaw (puzzle). **~olas** *m invar* breakwater

romper (*pp* **roto**) *vt* break; tear <*hoja, camisa etc*>; break off <*relaciones etc*>. ● *vi* break; <*novios*> break up. **~er a** burst out. □ **~erse** *vpr* break

ron *m* rum

roncar [7] *vi* snore. **~o a** hoarse

roncha *f* lump; (por alergia) rash

ronda *f* round; (patrulla) patrol; (serenata) serenade. **~r** *vt* patrol. ● *vi* be on patrol; (merodear) hang around

ronquera *f* hoarseness. **~ido** *m* snore

ronronear *vi* purr

roña *f* (suciedad) grime. **~oso** *a* dirty; (oxidado) rusty; (tacaño) mean

ropa *f* clothes, clothing. **~a blanca** linen, underwear. **~a de cama** bedclothes. **~a interior** underwear. **~aje** *m* robes; (excesivo) heavy clothing. **~ero** *m* wardrobe

rosa *a invar* pink. ● *f* rose. ● *m* pink. **~áceo** *a* pinkish. **~ado** *a* pink; <*mejillas*> rosy. ● *m* (vino) rosé. **~al** *m* rose-bush

rosario *m* rosary; (fig) series

rosca *f* (de tornillo) thread; (de pan) roll; (bollo) type of doughnut. **~co** *m* roll. **~quilla** *f* type of doughnut

rostro *m* face

rotación *f* rotation. **~r** *vt/i* rotate. □ **~rse** *vpr* take turns. **~tivo** *a* rotary

roto *a* broken

rótula *f* kneecap

rotulador *m* felt-tip pen

rótulo *m* sign; (etiqueta) label; (logotipo) logo

rotundo *a* categorical

rotura *f* tear; (grieta) crack

rozadura *f* scratch

rozagante *a* (LAm) healthy

rozar [10] *vt* rub against; (ligeramente) brush against; (raspar) graze. □ ~**se** *vpr* rub; (con otras personas) mix

Rte. *abrev* (**Remite**(**nte**)) sender

rubéola *f* German measles

rubí *m* ruby

rubicundo *a* ruddy

rubio *a* <*pelo*> fair; <*persona*> fair-haired; <*tabaco*> Virginia

rubor *m* blush; (Mex, cosmético) blusher. □ ~**izarse** [10] *vpr* blush

rúbrica *f* (de firma) flourish; (firma) signature; (título) heading

rudeza *f* roughness

rudiment|ario *a* rudimentary. ~**os** *mpl* rudiments

rudo *a* rough; (sencillo) simple

rueca *f* distaff

rueda *f* wheel; (de mueble) castor; (de personas) ring; (Culin) slice. ~ **de prensa** press conference

ruedo *m* edge; (redondel) bullring

ruego *m* request; (súplica) entreaty. ● *vb* ⇒ROGAR

rufián *m* pimp; (granuja) rogue

rugby *m* rugby

rugi|do *m* roar. ~**r** [14] *vi* roar

ruibarbo *m* rhubarb

ruido *m* noise. ~**so** *a* noisy; (fig) sensational

ruin *a* despicable; (tacaño) mean

ruin|a *f* ruin; (colapso) collapse. ~**oso** *a* ruinous

ruiseñor *m* nightingale

ruleta *f* roulette

rulo *m* curler

rumano *a & m* Romanian

rumbo *m* direction; (fig) course; (fig, esplendidez) lavishness. **con** ~ **a** in the direction of. ~**so** *a* lavish

rumia|nte *a & m* ruminant. ~**r** *vt* chew; (fig) brood over. ● *vi* ruminate

rumor *m* rumour; (ruido) murmur. ~**ear** *vt.* **se** ~**ea que** rumour has it that. ~**oso** *a* murmuring

runrún *m* (de voces) murmur; (de motor) whirr

ruptura *f* breakup; (de relaciones etc) breaking off; (de contrato) breach

rural *a* rural

ruso *a & m* Russian

rústico *a* rural; (de carácter) coarse. **en rústica** paperback

ruta *f* route; (fig) course

rutina *f* routine. ~**rio** *a* routine; <*trabajo*> monotonous

S.A. *abrev* (**Sociedad Anónima**) Ltd, plc, Inc (Amer)

sábado *m* Saturday

sábana *f* sheet

sabañón *m* chilblain

sabático *a* sabbatical

sab|elotodo *m & f invar* know-all ▣. ~**er** [38] *vt* know; (ser capaz de) be able to, know how to; (enterarse de) find out. ● *vi* know. ~**er a** taste of. **hacer** ~**er** let know. **¡qué sé yo!** how should I know? **que yo sepa** as far as I know. **¿~es nadar?** can you swim? **un no sé qué** a certain sth. **¡yo qué sé!** how should I know? **¡vete a ~er!** who knows? ● *m* knowledge. ~**ido** *a* well-known.

~**iduría** f wisdom; (conocimientos) knowledge

sabi|endas. a ~ knowingly; (a propósito) on purpose. ~**hondo** m know-all **I**. ~**o** a learned; (prudente) wise

sabor m taste, flavour; (fig) flavour. ~**ear** vt taste; (fig) savour

sabot|aje m sabotage. ~**eador** m saboteur. ~**ear** vt sabotage

sabroso a tasty; <chisme> juicy; (LAm, agradable) pleasant

sabueso m (perro) bloodhound; (fig, detective) detective

saca|corchos m invar corkscrew. ~**puntas** m invar pencil-sharpener

sacar [7] vt take out; put out <parte del cuerpo>; (quitar) remove; take <foto>; win <premio>; get <billete, entrada>; withdraw <dinero>; reach <solución>; draw <conclusión>; make <copia>. ~ **adelante** bring up <niño>; carry on <negocio>

sacarina f saccharin

sacerdo|cio m priesthood. ~**te** m priest

saciar vt satisfy; quench <sed>

saco m sack; (LAm, chaqueta) jacket. ~ **de dormir** sleeping-bag

sacramento m sacrament

sacrific|ar [7] vt sacrifice; slaughter <res>; put to sleep <perro, gato>. □ ~**arse** vpr sacrifice o.s. ~**io** m sacrifice; (de res) slaughter

sacr|ilegio m sacrilege. ~**ílego** a sacrilegious

sacudi|da f shake; (movimiento brusco) jolt, jerk; (fig) shock. ~**da eléctrica** electric shock. ~**r** vt shake; (golpear) beat. □ ~**rse** vpr shake off; (fig) get rid of

sádico a sadistic. ● m sadist

sadismo m sadism

safari m safari

sagaz a shrewd

Sagitario m Sagittarius

sagrado a <lugar> holy, sacred; <altar, escrituras>) holy; (fig) sacred

sal f salt. ● vb ⇒SALIR

sala f room; (en casa) living room; (en hospital) ward; (para reuniones etc) hall; (en teatro) house; (Jurid) courtroom. ~ **de embarque** departure lounge. ~ **de espera** waiting room. ~ **de estar** living room. ~ **de fiestas** nightclub

salado a salty; <agua del mar> salt; (no dulce) savoury; (fig) witty

salario m wage

salchich|a f (pork) sausage. ~**ón** m salami

sald|ar vt settle <cuenta>; (vender) sell off. ~**o** m balance. ~**os** mpl sales. **venta de** ~**os** clearance sale

salero m salt-cellar

salgo vb ⇒SALIR

sali|da f departure; (puerta) exit, way out; (de gas, de líquido) leak; (de astro) rising; (Com, venta) sale; (chiste) witty remark; (fig) way out; exit. ~**da de emergencia** emergency exit. ~**ente** a (Archit) projecting; <pómulo etc> prominent. ~**r** [52] vi leave; (ir afuera) go out; (Informática) exit; <revista etc> be published; (resultar) turn out; <astro> rise; (aparecer) appear. ~**r adelante** get by. □ ~**rse** vpr leave; <recipiente, líquido etc> leak. ~**rse con la suya** get one's own way

saliva f saliva

salmo m psalm

salm|ón m salmon. ~**onete** m red mullet

salón m living-room, lounge. ~ **de actos** assembly hall. ~ **de clases** classroom. ~ **de fiestas** dancehall

salpica|dera *f* (Mex) mudguard.
~dero *m* (Auto) dashboard.
~dura *f* splash; (acción)
splashing. **~r** [7] *vt* splash; (fig)
sprinkle

sals|a *f* sauce; (para carne asada)
gravy; (Mus) salsa. **~a verde**
parsley sauce. **~era** *f* sauce-boat

salt|amontes *m invar*
grasshopper. **~ar** *vt* jump (over);
(fig) miss out. ● *vi* jump;
(romperse) break; <*líquido*> spurt
out; (desprenderse) come off;
<*pelota*> bounce; (estallar) explode.
~eador *m* highwayman. **~ear** *vt*
(Culin) sauté

salt|o *m* jump; (al agua) dive. **~o**
de agua waterfall. **~ mortal**
somersault. **de un ~o** with one
jump. **~ón** *a* <*ojos*> bulging

salud *f* health. ● *int* cheers!;
(LAm, al estornudar) bless you!
~able *a* healthy

salud|ar *vt* greet, say hello to;
(Mil) salute. **lo ~a atentamente** (en
cartas) yours faithfully. **~ con la**
mano wave. **~o** *m* greeting; (Mil)
salute. **~os** *mpl* best wishes

salva *f* salvo. **una ~ de aplausos** a
burst of applause

salvación *f* salvation

salvado *m* bran

salvaguardia *f* safeguard

salvaje *a* (planta, animal) wild;
(primitivo) savage. ● *m & f* savage

salva|mento *m* rescue. **~r** *vt*
save, rescue; (atravesar) cross
(recorrer); travel (fig) overcome.
□ **~rse** *vpr* save o.s. **~vidas** *m &*
f invar lifeguard. ● *m* lifebelt.
chaleco *m* **~vidas** life-jacket.

salvo *a* safe. ● *adv & prep*
except (for). **a ~** out of danger.
poner a ~ put in a safe place. **~**
que unless. **~conducto** *m* safe-
conduct

San *a* Saint, St. **~ Miguel** St
Michael

sana|r *vt* cure. ● *vi* recover; heal
<*herida*>. **~torio** *m* sanatorium

sanci|ón *f* sanction. **~onar** *vt*
sanction

sandalia *f* sandal

sandía *f* watermelon

sándwich /'saŋgwitʃ/ *m* (*pl* **~s**,
~es) sandwich

sangr|ante *a* bleeding; (fig)
flagrant. **~ar** *vt/i* bleed. **~e** *f*
blood. **a ~e fría** in cold blood

sangría *f* (bebida) sangria

sangriento *a* bloody

sangu|ijuela *f* leech. **~íneo** *a*
blood

san|idad *f* health. **~itario** *a*
sanitary. ● *m* (Mex) toilet. **~o** *a*
healthy; <*mente*> sound. **~o y**
salvo safe and sound. **cortar por lo**
~o settle things once and for all

santiamén *m*. **en un ~** in an
instant

sant|idad *f* sanctity. **~ificar** [7]
vt sanctify. □ **~iguarse** [15] *vpr*
cross o.s. **~o** *a* holy; (delante de
nombre) Saint, St. ● *m* saint; (día)
saint's day, name day. **~uario** *m*
sanctuary. **~urrón** *a*
sanctimonious

saña *f* viciousness. **con ~**
viciously

sapo *m* toad

saque *m* (en tenis) service; (inicial en
fútbol) kick-off. **~ de banda**
throw-in; (en rugby) line-out. **~ de**
esquina corner (kick)

saque|ar *vt* loot. **~o** *m* looting

sarampión *m* measles

sarape *m* (Mex) colourful blanket

sarc|asmo *m* sarcasm. **~ástico**
a sarcastic

sardina *f* sardine

sargento *m* sergeant

sarpullido *m* rash

S

sartén *f or m* frying-pan (Brit), fry-pan (Amer)

sastre *m* tailor. **~ría** *f* tailoring; (tienda) tailor's (shop)

Sat|anás *m* Satan. **~ánico** *a* satanic

satélite *m* satellite

satinado *a* shiny

sátira *f* satire

satírico *a* satirical. ● *m* satirist

satisf|acción *f* satisfaction. **~acer** [31] *vt* satisfy; (pagar) pay; (gustar) please; meet <*gastos, requisitos*>. □ **~acerse** *vpr* satisfy o.s.; (vengarse) take revenge. **~actorio** *a* satisfactory. **~echo** *a* satisfied. **~echo de sí mismo** smug

satura|ción *f* saturation. **~r** *vt* saturate

Saturno *m* Saturn

sauce *m* willow. **~ llorón** weeping willow

sauna *f*, (LAm) **sauna** *m* sauna

saxofón *m*, **saxófono** *m* saxophone

sazona|do *a* ripe; (Culin) seasoned. **~r** *vt* ripen; (Culin) season

....

se

● *pronombre*

····▶ (en lugar de le, les) **se lo di** (a él) I gave it to him; (a ella) I gave it to her; (a usted, ustedes) I gave it to you; (a ellos, ellas) I gave it to them. **se lo compré** I bought it for him (*or* her *etc*). **se lo quité** I took it away from him (*or* her *etc*). **se lo dije** I told him (*or* her *etc*)

····▶ (reflexivo) **se secó** (él) he dried himself; (ella) she dried herself; (usted) you dried yourself; (sujeto no humano) it dried itself. **se**

secaron (ellos, ellas) they dried themselves; (ustedes) you dried yourselves. (con partes del cuerpo) **se lavó la cara** (él) he washed his face. (con efectos personales) **se limpian los zapatos** they clean their shoes

····▶ (recíproco) each other, one another. **se ayudan mucho** they help each other a lot. **no se hablan** they don't speak to each other

····▶ (cuando otro hace la acción) **va a operarse** she's going to have an operation. **se cortó el pelo** he had his hair cut

····▶ (enfático) **se bebió el café** he drank his coffee. **se subió al tren** he got on the train

⟹ **se** also forms part of certain pronominal verbs such as **equivocarse, arrepentirse, caerse** etc., which are treated under the respective entries

····▶ (voz pasiva) **se construyeron muchas casas** many houses were built. **se vendió rápidamente** it was sold very quickly

····▶ (impersonal) **antes se escuchaba más radio** people used to listen to the radio more in the past. **no se puede entrar** you can't get in. **se está bien aquí** it's very nice here

····▶ (en instrucciones) **sírvase frío** serve cold

....

sé *vb* ⇒SABER *y* SER

sea *vb* ⇒SER

seca|dor *m* drier; (de pelo) hair-drier. **~nte** *a* drying. ● *m* blotting-paper. **~r** [7] *vt* dry. □ **~rse** *vpr* dry; <*río etc*> dry up; <*persona*> dry o.s.

sección *f* section

seco *a* dry; *<frutos, flores>* dried; (flaco) thin; *<respuesta>* curt. **a secas** just. **en ~** (bruscamente) suddenly. **lavar en ~** dry-clean

secretar|ía *f* secretariat; (Mex, ministerio) ministry. **~io** *m* secretary; (Mex, Pol) minister

secreto *a & m* secret

secta *f* sect. **~rio** *a* sectarian

sector *m* sector

secuela *f* consequence

secuencia *f* sequence

secuestr|ar *vt* confiscate; kidnap *<persona>*; hijack *<avión>*. **~o** *m* seizure; (de persona) kidnapping; (de avión) hijack(ing)

secundar *vt* second, help. **~io** *a* secondary

sed *f* thirst. ● *vb* ⇒SER. **tener ~** be thirsty. **tener ~ de** (fig) be hungry for

seda *f* silk. **~ dental** dental floss

sedante *a & m* sedative

sede *f* seat; (Relig) see; (de organismo) headquarters; (de congreso, juegos etc) venue

sedentario *a* sedentary

sedici|ón *f* sedition. **~oso** *a* seditious

sediento *a* thirsty

seduc|ción *f* seduction. **~ir** [47] *vt* seduce; (atraer) attract. **~tor** *a* seductive. ● *m* seducer

seglar *a* secular. ● *m* layman

segrega|ción *f* segregation. **~r** [12] *vt* segregate

segui|da *f*. **en ~da** immediately. **~do** *a* continuous; (en plural) consecutive. **~de** followed by. ● *adv* straight; (LAm, a menudo) often. **todo ~do** straight ahead. **~dor** *m* follower; (en deportes) supporter. **~r** [5 & 13] *vt* follow. ● *vi* (continuar) continue; (por un camino) go on. **~ adelante** carry on

según *prep* according to. ● *adv* it depends; (a medida que) as

segunda *f* (Auto) second gear; (en tren, avión etc) second class. **~o** *a & m* second

segur|amente *adv* certainly; (muy probablemente) surely. **~idad** *f* security; (ausencia de peligro) safety; (certeza) certainty; (aplomo) confidence. **~idad en sí mismo** self-confidence. **~idad social** social security. **~o** *a* safe; (cierto) certain, sure; (estable) secure; (de fiar) reliable. ● *adv* for certain. ● *m* insurance; (dispositivo de seguridad) safety device. **~o de sí mismo** self-confident. **~o contra terceros** third-party insurance

seis *a & m* six. **~cientos** *a & m* six hundred

seísmo *m* earthquake

selec|ción *f* selection. **~cionar** *vt* select, choose. **~tivo** *a* selective. **~to** *a* selected; (fig) choice

sell|ar *vt* stamp; (cerrar) seal. **~o** *m* stamp; (precinto) seal; (fig, distintivo) hallmark; (LAm, en moneda) reverse

selva *f* forest; (jungla) jungle

semáforo *m* (Auto) traffic lights; (Rail) signal; (Naut) semaphore

semana *f* week. **S~ Santa** Holy Week. **~l** *a* weekly. **~rio** *a & m* weekly

semántic|a *f* semantics. **~o** *a* semantic

semblante *m* face; (fig) look

sembrar [1] *vt* sow; (fig) scatter

semeja|nte *a* similar; (tal) such. ● *m* fellow man. **~nza** *f* similarity. **a ~nza de** like. **~r** *vi*. **~ a** resemble

semen *m* semen. **~tal** *a* stud. ● *m* stud animal

semestr|al *a* half-yearly. **~e** *m* six months

S

semi|circular *a* semicircular. ~**círculo** *m* semicircle. ~**final** *f* semifinal

semill|a *f* seed. ~**ero** *m* seedbed; (fig) hotbed

seminario *m* (Univ) seminar; (Relig) seminary

sémola *f* semolina

senado *m* senate. ~**r** *m* senator

sencill|ez *f* simplicity. ~**o** *a* simple; (para viajar) single ticket; (disco) single; (LAm, dinero suelto) change

senda *f*, **sendero** *m* path

sendos *a pl* each

seno *m* bosom. ~ **materno** womb

sensaci|ón *f* sensation; (percepción, impresión) feeling. ~**onal** *a* sensational

sensat|ez *f* good sense. ~**o** *a* sensible

sensi|bilidad *f* sensibility. ~**ble** *a* sensitive; (notable) notable; (lamentable) lamentable. ~**tivo** *a* <órgano> sense

sensual *a* sensual. ~**idad** *f* sensuality

senta|do *a* sitting (down); **dar algo por ~do** take something for granted. ~**dor** *a* (LAm) flattering. ~**r** [1] *vt* sit; (establecer) establish. ● *vi* suit; (de medidas) fit; <comida> agree with. □ ~**rse** *vpr* sit (down)

sentencia *f* (Jurid) sentence. ~**r** *vt* sentence (**a** to)

sentido *a* heartfelt; (sensible) sensitive. ● *m* sense; (dirección) direction; (conocimiento) consciousness. ~ **común** common sense. ~ **del humor** sense of humour. ~ **único** one-way. **doble** ~ double meaning. **no tener** ~ not make sense. **perder el** ~ faint. **sin** ~ senseless

sentim|ental *a* sentimental. ~**iento** *m* feeling; (sentido) sense; (pesar) regret

sentir [4] *vt* feel; (oír) hear; (lamentar) be sorry for. **lo siento mucho** I'm really sorry. ● *m* (opinión) opinion. □ ~**se** *vpr* feel; (Mex, ofenderse) be offended

seña *f* sign. ~**s** *fpl* (dirección) address; (descripción) description. **dar ~s de** show signs of

señal *f* signal; (letrero, aviso) sign; (telefónica) tone; (Com) deposit. **dar ~es de** show signs of. **en ~ de** as a token of. ~**ado** *a* <hora, día> appointed. ~**ar** *vt* signal; (poner señales en) mark; (apuntar) point out; <manecilla, aguja> point to; (determinar) fix. □ ~**arse** *vpr* stand out

señor *m* man, gentleman; (delante de nombre propio) Mr; (tratamiento directo) sir. ~**a** *f* lady, woman; (delante de nombre propio) Mrs; (esposa) wife; (tratamiento directo) madam. **el ~** Mr. **muy ~ mío** Dear Sir. **¡no ~!** certainly not!. ~**ial** *a* <casa> stately. ~**ita** *f* young lady; (delante de nombre propio) Miss; (tratamiento directo) miss. ~**ito** *m* young gentleman

señuelo *m* lure

sepa *vb* ⇒SABER

separa|ción *f* separation. ~**do** *a* separate. **por ~do** separately. ~**r** *vt* separate; (de empleo) dismiss. □ ~**rse** *vpr* <amigos> part. ~**tista** *a & m & f* separatist

septentrional *a* north(ern)

septiembre *m* September

séptimo *a* seventh

sepulcro *m* sepulchre

sepult|ar *vt* bury. ~**ura** *f* burial; (tumba) grave. ~**urero** *m* gravedigger

sequ|edad *f* dryness. ~**ía** *f* drought

séquito *m* entourage; (fig) train

ser [39]

●*verbo intransitivo*

····▸ to be. **es bajo** he's short. **es abogado** he's a lawyer. **ábreme, soy yo** open up, it's me. **¿cómo es?** (como persona) what's he like?; (físicamente) what does he look like? **era invierno** it was winter

····▸ **ser de** (indicando composición) to be made of. **es de hierro** it's made of iron. (provenir de) to be from. **es de México** he's from Mexico. (pertenecer a) to belong to. **el coche es de Juan** the car belongs to Juan, it's Juan's car

····▸ (sumar) **¿cuánto es todo?** how much is that altogether? **son 40 dólares** that's 40 dollars. **somos 10** there are 10 of us

····▸ (con la hora) **son las 3** it's 3 o'clock. **~ía la una** it must have been one o'clock

····▸ (tener lugar) to be held. **~á en la iglesia** it will be held in the church

····▸ (ocurrir) to happen **¿dónde fue el accidente?** where did the accident happen? **me contó cómo fue** he told me how it happened

····▸ (en locuciones) **a no ~ que** unless. **como sea** no matter what. **cuando sea** whenever. **donde sea** wherever. **¡eso es!** that's it! **es que** the thing is. **lo que sea** anything. **no sea que, no vaya a ~ que** in case. **o sea** in other words. **sea ... sea ...** either ... or ... **sea como sea** at all costs

●*nombre masculino*

····▸ being; (persona) person. **el ~ humano** the human being. **un ~**

amargado a bitter person. **los ~es queridos** the loved ones

seren|ar *vt* calm down. □ **~arse** *vpr* calm down. **~ata** *f* serenade. **~idad** *f* serenity. **~o** *a* serene; <cielo> clear; <mar> calm

seri|al *m* serial. **~e** *f* series. **fuera de ~e** (fig) out of this world. **producción** *f* **en ~e** mass production

seri|edad *f* seriousness. **~o** *a* serious; (confiable) reliable; **en ~o** seriously. **poco ~o** frivolous

sermón *m* sermon; (fig) lecture

serp|enteante *a* winding. **~entear** *vi* wind. **~iente** *f* snake. **~iente de cascabel** rattlesnake

serr|ar [1] *vt* saw. **~ín** *m* sawdust. **~uchar** *vt* (LAm) saw. **~ucho** *m* (hand)saw

servi|cial *a* helpful. **~cio** *m* service; (conjunto) set; (aseo) toilet; **~cio a domicilio** delivery service. **~dor** *m* servant. **su (seguro) ~dor** (en cartas) yours faithfully. **~dumbre** *f* servitude; (criados) servants, staff. **~l** *a* servile

servidor *m* server; (criado) servant

servilleta *f* napkin, serviette

servir [5] *vt* serve; (en restaurante) wait on. ●*vi* serve; (ser útil) to be of use. □ **~se** *vpr* help o.s. **~se de** use. **no ~ de nada** be useless. **para ~le** at your service. **sírvase sentarse** please sit down

sesent|a *a & m* sixty. **~ón** *a & m* sixty-year-old

seseo *m* pronunciation of the Spanish *c* as an *s*

sesión *f* session; (en el cine, teatro) performance

seso *m* brain

seta *f* mushroom

S

sete|cientos *a & m* seven hundred. **∼nta** *a & m* seventy. **∼ntón** *a & m* seventy-year-old

setiembre *m* September

seto *m* fence; (de plantas) hedge. **∼ vivo** hedge

seudónimo *m* pseudonym

sever|idad *f* severity; (de profesor etc) strictness. **∼o** *a* severe; <*profesor etc*> strict

sevillan|as *fpl* popular dance from Seville. **∼o** *m* person from Seville

sexo *m* sex

sext|eto *m* sextet. **∼o** *a* sixth

sexual *a* sexual. **∼idad** *f* sexuality

si *m* (Mus) B; (solfa) te. ● *conj* if; (dubitativo) whether; **∼ no** otherwise. **por ∼ (acaso)** in case

sí[1] *pron reflexivo* (él) himself; (ella) herself; (de cosa) itself; (uno) oneself; (Vd) yourself; (ellos, ellas) themselves; (Vds) yourselves; (recíproco) each other

sí[2] *adv* yes. ● *m* consent

sida *m* Aids

sidra *f* cider

siembra *f* sowing; (época) sowing time

siempre *adv* always; (LAm, todavía) still; (Mex, por fin) after all. **∼ que** if; (cada vez) whenever. **como ∼** as usual. **de ∼** (acostumbrado) usual. **lo de ∼** the usual thing. **para ∼** for ever

sien *f* temple

siento *vb* ⇒SENTAR *y* SENTIR

sierra *f* saw; (cordillera) mountain range

siesta *f* nap, siesta

siete *a & m* seven

sífilis *f* syphilis

sifón *m* U-bend; (de soda) syphon

sigilo *m* stealth; (fig) secrecy

sigla *f* abbreviation

siglo *m* century; (época) age. **hace ∼s que no escribe** he hasn't written for ages

significa|ción *f* significance. **∼do** *a* (conocido) well-known. ● *m* meaning; (importancia) significance. **∼r** [7] *vt* mean; (expresar) express. **∼tivo** *a* meaningful; (importante) significant

signo *m* sign. **∼ de admiración** exclamation mark. **∼ de interrogación** question mark

sigo *vb* ⇒SEGUIR

siguiente *a* following, next. **lo ∼** the following

sílaba *f* syllable

silb|ar *vt/i* whistle. **∼ato** *m*, **∼ido** *m* whistle

silenci|ador *m* silencer. **∼ar** *vt* hush up. **∼o** *m* silence. **∼oso** *a* silent

sill|a *f* chair; (de montar) saddle; (Relig) see. **∼a de ruedas** wheelchair. **∼ín** *m* saddle. **∼ón** *m* armchair

silueta *f* silhouette; (dibujo) outline

silvestre *a* wild

simb|ólico *a* symbolic(al). **∼olismo** *m* symbolism. **∼olizar** [10] *vt* symbolize

símbolo *m* symbol

sim|etría *f* symmetry. **∼étrico** *a* symmetric(al)

similar *a* similar (**a** to)

simp|atía *f* friendliness; (cariño) affection. **∼ático** *a* nice, likeable; <*ambiente*> pleasant. **∼atizante** *m & f* sympathizer. **∼atizar** [10] *vi* get on (well together)

simpl|e *a* simple; (mero) mere. **∼eza** *f* simplicity; (tontería) stupid thing; (insignificancia) trifle. **∼icidad** *f* simplicity. **∼ificar** [7] *vt* simplify. **∼ista** *a* simplistic. **∼ón** *m* simpleton

simula|ción f simulation. ~**r** vt simulate; (fingir) feign

simultáneo a simultaneous

sin prep without. ~ **saber** without knowing. ~ **querer** accidentally

sinagoga f synagogue

sincer|idad f sincerity. ~**o** a sincere

sincronizar [10] vt synchronize

sindica|l a (trade-)union. ~**lista** m & f trade-unionist. ~**to** m trade union

síndrome m syndrome

sinfín m endless number (**de** of)

sinfonía f symphony

singular a singular; (excepcional) exceptional. □ ~**izarse** vpr stand out

siniestro a sinister. ● m disaster; (accidente) accident

sinnúmero m endless number (**de** of)

sino m fate. ● conj but

sinónimo a synonymous. ● m synonym (**de** for)

sintaxis f syntax

síntesis f invar synthesis; (resumen) summary

sint|ético a synthetic. ~**etizar** [10] vt synthesize; (resumir) summarize

síntoma f symptom

sintomático a symptomatic

sinton|ía f tuning; (Mus) signature tune. ~**izar** [10] vt (con la radio) tune (in) to

sinvergüenza m & f crook

siquiera conj even if. ● adv at least. **ni** ~ not even

sirena f siren; (en cuentos) mermaid

sirio a & m Syrian

sirvient|a f maid. ~**e** m servant

sirvo vb ⇒SERVIR

sísmico a seismic

sismo m earthquake

sistem|a m system. **por** ~**a** as a rule. ~**ático** a systematic

sitiar vt besiege; (fig) surround

sitio m place; (espacio) space; (Mil) siege; (Mex, parada de taxi) taxi rank. **en cualquier** ~ anywhere. ~ **web** website

situa|ción f situation; (estado, condición) position. ~**r** [21] vt place, put; locate <edificio>. □ ~**rse** vpr be successful, establish o.s.

slip /es'lip/ m (pl ~**s**) underpants, briefs

smoking /es'mokin/ m (pl ~**s**) dinner jacket (Brit), tuxedo (Amer)

sobaco m armpit

sobar vt handle; knead <masa>

soberan|ía f sovereignty. ~**o** a sovereign; (fig) supreme. ● m sovereign

soberbi|a f pride; (altanería) arrogance. ~**o** a proud; (altivo) arrogant

soborn|ar vt bribe. ~**o** m bribe

sobra f surplus. **de** ~ more than enough. ~**s** fpl leftovers. ~**do** a more than enough. ~**nte** a surplus. ~**r** vi be left over; (estorbar) be in the way

sobre prep on; (encima de) on top of; (más o menos) about; (por encima de) above; (sin tocar) over. ~ **todo** above all, especially. ● m envelope. ~**cargar** [12] vt overload. ~**coger** [14] vt startle; (conmover) move. ~**cubierta** f dustcover. ~**dosis** f invar overdose. ~**entender** [1] vt understand, infer. ~**girar** vt (LAm) overdraw. ~**giro** m (LAm) overdraft. ~**humano** a superhuman. ~**llevar** vt bear. ~**mesa** f. **de** ~**mesa** after-dinner. ~**natural** a supernatural. ~**nombre** m nickname. ~**pasar** vt exceed. ~**peso** m (LAm) excess

S

baggage. **~poner** [34] *vt* superimpose. □ **~ponerse** *vpr* overcome. **~saliente** *a* (fig) outstanding. ● *m* excellent mark. **~salir** [52] *vi* stick out; (fig) stand out. **~saltar** *vt* startle. **~salto** *m* fright. **~sueldo** *m* bonus. **~todo** *m* overcoat. **~venir** [53] *vi* happen. **~viviente** *a* surviving. ● *m & f* survivor. **~vivir** *vi* survive. **~volar** *vt* fly over

sobriedad *f* moderation; (de estilo) simplicity

sobrin|a *f* niece. **~o** *m* nephew. **~os** (varones) nephews; (varones y mujeres) nieces and nephews

sobrio *a* moderate, sober

socavar *vt* undermine

soci|able *a* sociable. **~al** *a* social. **~aldemócrata** *m & f* social democrat. **~alismo** *m* socialism. **~alista** *a & m & f* socialist. **~edad** *f* society; (Com) company. **~edad anónima** limited company. **~o** *m* member; (Com) partner. **~ología** *f* sociology. **~ólogo** *m* sociologist

socorr|er *vt* help. **~o** *m* help

soda *f* (bebida) soda (water)

sodio *m* sodium

sofá *m* sofa, settee

sofistica|ción *f* sophistication. **~do** *a* sophisticated

sofo|cante *a* suffocating; (fig) stifling. **~r** [7] *vt* smother *<fuego>*; (fig) stifle. □ **~rse** *vpr* get upset

soga *f* rope

soja *f* soya (bean)

sojuzgar [12] *vt* subdue

sol *m* sun; (luz) sunlight; (Mus) G; (solfa) soh. **al ~** in the sun. **día** *m* **de ~** sunny day. **hace ~, hay ~** it is sunny. **tomar el ~** sunbathe

solamente *adv* only

solapa *f* lapel; (de bolsillo etc) flap. **~do** *a* sly

solar *a* solar. ● *m* plot

solariego *a* <casa> ancestral

soldado *m* soldier. **~ raso** private

solda|dor *m* welder; (utensilio) soldering iron. **~r** [2] *vt* weld, solder

soleado *a* sunny

soledad *f* solitude; (aislamiento) loneliness

solemn|e *a* solemn. **~idad** *f* solemnity

soler [2] *vi* be in the habit of. **suele despertarse a las 6** he usually wakes up at 6 o'clock

sol|icitar *vt* request, ask for; apply for *<empleo>*. **~ícito** *a* solicitous. **~icitud** *f* request; (para un puesto) application; (formulario) application form; (preocupación) concern

solidaridad *f* solidarity

solid|ez *f* solidity; (de argumento etc) soundness. □ **~ificarse** [7] *vpr* solidify

sólido *a* solid; *<argumento etc>* sound. ● *m* solid

soliloquio *m* soliloquy

solista *m & f* soloist

solitario *a* solitary; (aislado) lonely. ● *m* loner; (juego, diamante) solitaire

solloz|ar [10] *vi* sob. **~o** *m* sob

solo *a* (sin compañía) alone; (aislado) lonely; (sin ayuda) by oneself; (único) only; (Mus) solo; *<café>* black. ● *m* solo; (juego) solitaire. **a solas** alone

sólo *adv* only. **~ que** except that. **no ~... sino también** not only... but also.... **tan ~** only

solomillo *m* sirloin

soltar [2] *vt* let go of; (dejar ir) release; (dejar caer) drop; (dejar salir,

decir) let out; give <*golpe etc*>.
□ ~**se** *vpr* come undone; (librarse)
break loose

solter|a *f* single woman. ~**o** *a*
single. ● *m* bachelor

soltura *f* looseness; (fig) ease,
fluency

solu|ble *a* soluble. ~**ción** *f*
solution. ~**cionar** *vt* solve; settle
<*huelga, asunto*>

solvente *a* & *m* solvent

sombr|a *f* shadow; (lugar sin sol)
shade. **a la** ~**a** in the shade.
~**eado** *a* shady

sombrero *m* hat. ~ **hongo** bowler
hat

sombrío *a* sombre

somero *a* superficial

someter *vt* subdue; subject
<*persona*>; (presentar) submit.
□ ~**se** *vpr* give in

somn|oliento *a* sleepy. ~**ífero** *m*
sleeping-pill

somos *vb* ⇒SER

son *m* sound. ● *vb* ⇒SER

sonámbulo *m* sleepwalker. **ser** ~
walk in one's sleep

sonar [2] *vt* blow; ring <*timbre*>.
● *vi* sound; ring <*timbre, teléfono etc*>
ring; <*despertador*> go off; (Mus)
play; (fig, ser conocido) be familiar.
~ **a** sound like. □ ~**se** *vpr* blow
one's nose

sonde|ar *vt* sound out; explore
<*espacio*>; (Naut) sound. ~**o** *m*
poll; (Naut) sounding

soneto *m* sonnet

sonido *m* sound

sonoro *a* sonorous; (ruidoso) loud

sonr|eír [51] *vi* smile. □ ~**eírse**
vpr smile. ~**isa** *f* smile

sonroj|arse *vpr* blush. ~**o** *m*
blush

sonrosado *a* rosy, pink

sonsacar [7] *vt* wheedle out

soñ|ado *a* dream. ~**ador** *m*
dreamer. ~**ar** [2] *vi* dream (**con**
of). **¡ni** ~**arlo!** not likely!

sopa *f* soup

sopesar *vt* (fig) weigh up

sopl|ar *vt* blow; blow out <*vela*>;
blow off <*polvo*>; (inflar) blow up.
● *vi* blow. ~**ete** *m* blowlamp.
~**o** *m* puff

soport|al *m* porch. ~**ales** *mpl*
arcade. ~**ar** *vt* support; (fig) bear,
put up with. ~**e** *m* support

soprano *f* soprano

sor *f* (Relig) sister

sorb|er *vt* sip; (con ruido) slurp;
(absorber) absorb. ~ **por la nariz**
sniff. ~**ete** *m* sorbet, water-ice.
~**o** *m* (pequeña cantidad) sip; (trago
grande) gulp

sordera *f* deafness

sórdido *a* squalid; <*asunto*>
sordid

sordo *a* deaf; <*ruido etc*> dull. ●
m deaf person. **hacerse el** ~ turn
a deaf ear. ~**mudo** *a* deaf and
dumb

soroche *m* (LAm) mountain
sickness

sorpre|ndente *a* surprising.
~**nder** *vt* surprise. □ ~**nderse**
vpr be surprised. ~**sa** *f* surprise

sorte|ar *vt* draw lots for; (fig)
avoid. ~**o** *m* draw. **por** ~**o** by
drawing lots

sortija *f* ring; (de pelo) ringlet

sortilegio *m* sorcery; (embrujo)
spell

sos|egar [1 & 12] *vt* calm. ~**iego**
m calmness

soslayo. de ~ sideways

soso *a* tasteless; (fig) dull

sospech|a *f* suspicion. ~**ar** *vt*
suspect. ● *vi*. ~ **de** suspect.
~**oso** *a* suspicious. ● *m* suspect

sost|én *m* support; (prenda
femenina) bra 🇮, brassière. ~**ener**

S

[40] vt support; bear <*peso*>; (sujetar) hold; (sustentar) maintain; (alimentar) sustain. □ **~enerse** vpr support o.s.; (continuar) remain. **~enido** a sustained; (Mus) sharp. ● m (Mus) sharp

sota f (de naipes) jack

sótano m basement

soviético a (Historia) Soviet

soy vb ⇨SER

Sr. abrev (**Señor**) Mr. **~a.** abrev (**Señora**) Mrs. **~ta.** abrev (**Señorita**) Miss

su a (de él) his; (de ella) her; (de animal, objeto) its; (de uno) one's; (de Vd) your; (de ellos, de ellas) their; (de Vds) your

suav|e a smooth; (fig) gentle; <*color, sonido*> soft; <*tabaco, sedante*> mild. **~idad** f smoothness, softness. **~izante** m conditioner; (para ropa) softener. **~izar** [10] vt smooth, soften

subalimentado a underfed

subarrendar [1] vt sublet

subasta f auction. **~r** vt auction

sub|campeón m runner-up. **~consciencia** f subconscious. **~consciente** a & m subconscious. **~continente** m subcontinent. **~desarrollado** a under-developed. **~director** m assistant manager

súbdito m subject

sub|dividir vt subdivide. **~estimar** vt underestimate

subi|da f rise; (a montaña) ascent; (pendiente) slope. **~do** a <*color*> intense. **~r** vt go up; climb <*mountain*>; (llevar) take up; (aumentar) raise; turn up <*radio, calefacción*>. ● vi go up. **~r a** get into <*coche*>; get on <*autobús, avión, barco, tren*>; (aumentar) rise. **~ a pie** walk up. □ **~rse** vpr climb up. **~rse a** get on <*tren etc*>

súbito a sudden. **de ~** suddenly

subjetivo a subjective

subjuntivo a & m subjunctive

subleva|ción f uprising. □ **~rse** vpr rebel

sublim|ar vt sublimate. **~e** a sublime

submarino a underwater. ● m submarine

subordinado a & m subordinate

subrayar vt underline

subsanar vt rectify; overcome <*dificultad*>; make up for <*carencia*>

subscri|bir vt (pp **subscrito**) sign. □ **~birse** vpr subscribe (**a** to). **~pción** f subscription

subsidi|ario a subsidiary. **~o** m subsidy. **~o de desempleo, ~ de paro** unemployment benefit

subsiguiente a subsequent

subsist|encia f subsistence. **~ir** vi subsist; (perdurar) survive

substraer [41] vt take away

subterráneo a underground

subtítulo m subtitle

suburb|ano a suburban. **~io** m suburb; (barrio pobre) depressed area

subvenci|ón f subsidy. **~onar** vt subsidize

subver|sión f subversion. **~sivo** a subversive. **~tir** [4] vt subvert

succi|ón f suction. **~onar** vt suck

suce|der vi happen; (seguir) **~ a** follow. ● vt (substituir) succeed. **lo que ~de es que** the trouble is that. **¿qué ~de?** what's the matter? **~sión** f succession. **~sivo** a successive; (consecutivo) consecutive. **en lo ~sivo** in future. **~so** m event; (incidente) incident. **~sor** m successor

suciedad f dirt; (estado) dirtiness

sucinto a concise; <*prenda*> scanty

sucio *a* dirty; <*conciencia*> guilty.
en ~ in rough

sucre *m* (unidad monetaria del Ecuador)
sucre

suculento *a* succulent

sucumbir *vi* succumb (**a** to)

sucursal *f* branch (office)

Sudáfrica *f* South Africa

sudafricano *a & m* South
African

Sudamérica *f* South America

sudamericano *a & m* South
American

sudar *vi* sweat

sud|este *m* south-east. **~oeste**
m south-west

sudor *m* sweat

Suecia *f* Sweden

sueco *a* Swedish. ● *m* (persona)
Swede; (lengua) Swedish. **hacerse
el ~** pretend not to hear

suegr|a *f* mother-in-law. **~o** *m*
father-in-law. **mis ~os** my
in-laws

suela *f* sole

sueldo *m* salary

suelo *m* ground; (dentro de edificio)
floor; (territorio) soil; (en la calle etc)
road surface. ● *vb* ⇒SOLER

suelto *a* loose; <*cordones*>
undone; (sin pareja) odd;
<*lenguaje*> fluent. **con el pelo ~**
with one's hair down. ● *m*
change

sueño *m* sleep; (lo soñado, ilusión)
dream. **tener ~** be sleepy

suerte *f* luck; (destino) fate; (azar)
chance. **de otra ~** otherwise. **de
~ que** so. **echar ~s** draw lots. **por
~** fortunately. **tener ~** be lucky

suéter *m* sweater, jersey

suficien|cia *f* (aptitud) aptitude;
(presunción) smugness. **~te** *a*
enough, sufficient; (presumido)
smug. **~temente** *adv* sufficiently

sufijo *m* suffix

sufragio *m* (voto) vote

sufrimiento *m* suffering. **~r** *vt*
suffer; undergo <*cambio*>; have
<*accident*>. ● *vi* suffer

suge|rencia *f* suggestion. **~rir**
[4] *vt* suggest. **~stión** *f* (Psych)
suggestion. **es pura ~stión** it's all
in one's mind. **~stionable** *a*
impressionable. **~stionar** *vt*
influence. **~stivo** *a* (estimulante)
stimulating; (atractivo) sexy

suicid|a *a* suicidal. ● *m & f*
suicide victim; (fig) maniac.
□ **~arse** *vpr* commit suicide. **~io**
m suicide

Suiza *f* Switzerland

suizo *a & m* Swiss

suje|ción *f* subjection. **con ~** a in
accordance with. **~tador** *m* bra
🔳, brassière. **~tapapeles** *m
invar* paper-clip. **~tar** *vt* fasten;
(agarrar) hold. □ **~tarse** *vpr*. **~se
a** hold on to; (someterse) abide by.
~to *a* fastened; (susceptible)
subject (**a** to). ● *m* individual;
(Gram) subject.

suma *f* sum; (Math) addition;
(combinación) combination. **en ~** in
short. **~mente** *adv* extremely.
~r *vt* add (up); (totalizar) add up
to. ● *vi* add up. □ **~rse** *vpr*. **~rse
a** join in

sumario *a* brief; (Jurid) summary.
● *m* table of contents; (Jurid) pre-
trial proceedings

sumergi|ble *a* submersible. **~r**
[14] *vt* submerge

suministr|ar *vt* supply. **~o** *m*
supply; (acción) supplying

sumir *vt* sink; (fig) plunge

sumis|ión *f* submission. **~o** *a*
submissive

sumo *a* great; (supremo) supreme.
a lo ~ at the most

suntuoso *a* sumptuous

supe *vb* ⇒SABER

S

superar *vt* surpass; (vencer) overcome; beat <*marca*>; (dejar atrás) get over. □ ~**se** *vpr* better o.s.

superchería *f* swindle

superfici|al *a* superficial. ~**e** *f* surface; (extensión) area. **de** ~**e** surface

superfluo *a* superfluous

superior *a* superior; (más alto) higher; (mejor) better; <*piso*> upper. ● *m* superior. ~**idad** *f* superiority

superlativo *a* & *m* superlative

supermercado *m* supermarket

supersticl|ón *f* superstition. ~**oso** *a* superstitious

supervis|ar *vt* supervise. ~**ión** *f* supervision. ~**or** *m* supervisor

superviv|encia *f* survival. ~**iente** *a* surviving. ● *m* & *f* survivor

suplantar *vt* supplant

suplement|ario *a* supplementary. ~**o** *m* supplement

suplente *a* & *m* & *f* substitute

súplica *f* entreaty; (Jurid) request

suplicar [7] *vt* beg

suplicio *m* torture

suplir *vt* make up for; (reemplazar) replace

supo|ner [34] *vt* suppose; (significar) mean; involve <*gasto, trabajo*>. ~**sición** *f* supposition

suprem|acía *f* supremacy. ~**o** *a* supreme

supr|esión *f* suppression; (de impuesto) abolition; (de restricción) lifting. ~**imir** *vt* suppress; abolish <*impuesto*>; lift <*restricción*>; delete <*párrafo*>

supuesto *a* supposed; <*falso*> false. ● *m* assumption. ¡**por** ~! of course!

sur *m* south; (viento) south wind

surc|ar [7] *vt* plough; cut through <*agua*>. ~**o** *m* furrow; (de rueda) rut

surfear *vi* (Informática) surf

surgir [14] *vi* spring up; (elevarse) loom up; (aparecer) appear; <*dificultad, oportunidad*> arise

surrealis|mo *m* surrealism. ~**ta** *a* & *m* & *f* surrealist

surti|do *a* well-stocked; (variado) assorted. ● *m* assortment, selection. ~**dor** *m* (de gasolina) petrol pump (Brit), gas pump (Amer). ~**r** *vt* supply; have <*efecto*>. □ ~**rse** *vpr* provide o.s. (**de** with)

susceptib|ilidad *f* sensitivity. ~**le** *a* susceptible; (sensible) sensitive

suscitar *vt* provoke; arouse <*curiosidad, interés*>

suscr... ⇒SUBSCR...

susodicho *a* aforementioned

suspen|der *vt* suspend; stop <*tratamiento*>; call off <*viaje*>; (Escol) fail; (colgar) hang (**de** from). ~**se** *m* suspense. **novela de** ~**se** thriller. ~**sión** *f* suspension. ~**so** *m* fail; (LAm, en libro, película) suspense. **en** ~**so** suspended

suspir|ar *vi* sigh. ~**o** *m* sigh

sust... ⇒SUBST...

sustanci|a *f* substance. ~**al** *a* substantial. ~**oso** *a* substantial

sustantivo *m* noun

sustent|ación *f* support. ~**ar** *vt* support; (alimentar) sustain; (mantener) maintain. ~**o** *m* support; (alimento) sustenance

sustitu|ción *f* substitution; (permanente) replacement. ~**ir** [17] *vt* substitute, replace. ~**to** *m* substitute; (permanente) replacement

susto *m* fright

susurr|ar vi <persona> whisper; <agua> murmur; <hojas> rustle

sutil a fine; (fig) subtle. **~eza** f subtlety

suyo a & pron (de él) his; (de ella) hers; (de animal) its; (de Vd) yours; (de ellos, de ellas) theirs; (de Vds) yours. **un amigo ~** a friend of his, a friend of theirs, etc

tabac|alera f (state) tobacco monopoly. **~o** m tobacco; (cigarillos) cigarettes

tabern|a f bar. **~ero** m barman; (dueño) landlord

tabique m partition wall; (Mex, ladrillo) brick

tabl|a f plank; (del suelo) floorboard; (de vestido) pleat; (índice) index; (gráfico, en matemática etc) table. **hacer ~as** (en ajedrez) draw. **~a de surf** surfboard. **~ado** m platform; (en el teatro) stage. **~ao** m place where flamenco shows are held. **~ero** m board. **~ero de mandos** dashboard

tableta f tablet; (de chocolate) bar

tabl|illa f splint; (Mex, de chocolate) bar. **~ón** m plank. **~ón de anuncios** notice board (esp Brit), bulletin board (Amer)

tabú m (pl **~es**, **~s**) taboo

tabular vt tabulate

taburete m stool

tacaño a mean

tacha f stain, blemish. **sin ~** unblemished; <conducta>

irreproachable. **~r** vt (con raya) cross out; (Jurid) impeach. **~ de** accuse of

tácito a tacit

taciturno a taciturn; (triste) glum

taco m plug; (LAm, tacón) heel; (de billar) cue; (de billetes) book; (fig, 🔼, lío) mess; (palabrota) swearword; (Mex, Culin) taco, filled tortilla

tacón m heel

táctic|a f tactics. **~o** a tactical

táctil a tactile

tacto m touch; (fig) tact

tahúr m card-sharp

Tailandia f Thailand

tailandés a & m Thai

taimado a sly

taj|ada f slice. **sacar ~ada** profit. **~ante** a categorical; <tono> sharp. **~ear** vt (LAm) slash. **~o** m cut; (en mina) face

tal a such. **de ~ manera** in such a way. **un ~** someone called. ● pron. **como ~** as such. **y ~** and things like that. ● adv. **con ~ de que** as long as. **~ como** the way. **~ para cual** 🔼 two of a kind. **~ vez** maybe. **¿qué ~?** how are you? **¿qué ~ es ella?** what's she like?

taladr|ar vt drill. **~o** m drill

talante m mood. **de buen ~** <estar> in a good mood; <ayudar> willingly

talar vt fell

talco m talcum powder

talega f, **talego** m sack

talento m talent; (fig) talented person

talismán m talisman

talla f carving; (de diamante etc) cutting; (estatura) height; (tamaño) size. **~do** m carving; (de diamante etc) cutting. **~dor** m carver; (cortador) cutter; (LAm, de naipes) dealer. **~r** vt carve; sculpt

T

<esculptura>; cut <diamante>; (Mex, restregar) scrub. □ ~**rse** *vpr* (Mex) rub o.s.

tallarín *m* noodle

talle *m* waist; (figura) figure

taller *m* workshop; (de pintor etc) studio; (Auto) garage

tallo *m* stem, stalk

tal|ón *m* heel; (recibo) counterfoil; (cheque) cheque. ~**onario** *m* receipt book; (de cheques) cheque book

tamal *m* (LAm) tamale

tamaño *a* such a. ● *m* size. **de ~** **natural** life-size

tambalearse *vpr* (persona) stagger; <cosa> wobble

también *adv* also, too

tambor *m* drum. ~ **del freno** brake drum. ~**ilear** *vi* drum

tamiz *m* sieve. ~**ar** [10] *vt* sieve

tampoco *adv* neither, nor, not either. **yo ~ fui** I didn't go either

tampón *m* tampon; (para entintar) ink-pad

tan *adv* so. ~**... como** as... as. **¿qué ~...?** (LAm) how...?

tanda *f* group; (de obreros) shift

tang|ente *a & f* tangent. ~**ible** *a* tangible

tango *m* tango

tanque *m* tank

tante|ar *vt* estimate; sound up <persona>; (ensayar) test; (fig) weigh up; (LAm, palpar) feel. ● *vi* (LAm) feel one's way. ~**o** *m* estimate; (prueba) test; (en deportes) score

tanto *a* (en singular) so much; (en plural) so many; (comparación en singular) as much; (comparación en plural) as many. ● *pron* so much; (en plural) so many. ● *adv* so; (con verbo) so much. **hace ~ tiempo** it's been so long. ~**... como** both...and. **¿qué ~...?** (LAm) how

much...? ~ **como** as well as; (cantidad) as much as. ~ **más...** **cuanto que** all the more ... because. ~ **si... como si** whether ... or. **a ~s de** sometime in. **en ~** meanwhile. **en ~ que** while. **entre ~** meanwhile. **hasta ~ que** until. **no es para ~** it's not as bad as all that. **otro ~** the same; (el doble) as much again. **por (lo) ~** therefore. ● *m* certain amount; (punto) point; (gol) goal. **estar al ~ de** be up to date with

tañer [22] *vi* peal

tapa *f* lid; (de botella) top; (de libro) cover. ~**s** *fpl* savoury snacks. ~**dera** *f* cover, lid; (fig) cover. ~**r** *vt* cover; (abrigar) wrap up; (obturar) plug. ~**rrabos** *m invar* loincloth

tapete *m* (de mesa) table cover; (Mex, alfombra) rug

tapia *f* wall. ~**r** *vt* enclose

tapi|cería *f* tapestry; (de muebles) upholstery. ~**z** *m* tapestry. ~**ar** [10] *vt* upholster <muebles>

tapón *m* stopper; (Tec) plug

taqu|igrafía *f* shorthand. ~**ígrafo** *m* shorthand writer

taquill|a *f* ticket office; (fig, dinero) takings. ~**ero** *a* box-office

tara *f* (peso) tare; (defecto) defect

tarántula *f* tarantula

tararear *vt/i* hum

tarda|nza *f* delay. ~**r** *vt* take. ● *vi* (retrasarse) be late; (emplear mucho tiempo) take a long time. **a más ~r** at the latest. **sin ~r** without delay

tard|e *adv* late. ● *f* (antes del atardecer) afternoon; (después del atardecer) evening. ~**e o temprano** sooner or later. **de ~e en ~e** from time to time. **en la ~e** (LAm), **por la ~e** in the afternoon. ~**ío** *a* late

tarea *f* task, job

tarifa *f* rate; (en transporte) fare; (lista de precios) tariff

tarima f dais

tarjeta f card. ~ **de crédito** credit card. ~ **de fidelidad** loyalty card. ~ **postal** postcard. ~ **telefónica** phone card

tarro m jar; (Mex, taza) mug

tarta f cake; (con base de masa) tart. ~ **helada** ice-cream gateau

tartamud|ear vi stammer. ~**o** a. **es** ~**o** he stammers

tasa f valuation; (impuesto) tax; (índice) rate. ~**r** vt value; (limitar) ration

tasca f bar

tatarabuel|a f great-great-grandmother. ~**o** m great-great-grandfather

tatua|je m (acción) tattooing; (dibujo) tattoo. ~**r** [21] vt tattoo

taurino a bullfighting

Tauro m Taurus

tauromaquia f bullfighting

taxi m taxi. ~**ista** m & f taxi-driver

taz|a f cup. ~**ón** m bowl

te pron (acusativo) you; (dativo) (to) you; (reflexivo) (to) yourself

té m tea; (LAm, reunión) tea party

tea f torch

teatr|al a theatre; (exagerado) theatrical. ~**o** m theatre; (literatura) drama

tebeo m comic

tech|ado m roof. ~**ar** vt roof. ~**o** m (interior) ceiling; (LAm, tejado) roof. ~**umbre** f roof

tecl|a f key. ~**ado** m keyboard. ~**ear** vt key in

técnica f technique

tecnicismo m technical nature; (palabra) technical term

técnico a technical. ● m technician; (en deportes) trainer

tecnol|ogía f technology. ~**ógico** a technological

tecolote m (Mex) owl

teja f tile. ~**s de pizarra** slates. ~**do** m roof. **a toca** ~ cash

teje|dor m weaver. ~**r** vt weave; (hacer punto) knit

tejemaneje m 🄸 intrigue

tejido m material; (Anat, fig) tissue. ~**s** mpl textiles

tejón m badger

tela f material, fabric; (de araña) web; (en líquido) skin

telar m loom. ~**es** mpl textile mill

telaraña f spider's web, cobweb

tele f 🄸 TV, telly

tele|banca f telephone banking. ~**comunicación** f telecommunication. ~**diario** m television news. ~**dirigido** a remote-controlled; <misil> guided. ~**férico** m cable-car

tel|efonear vt/i telephone. ~**efónico** a telephone. ~**efonista** m & f telephonist. ~**éfono** m telephone

tel|egrafía f telegraphy. ~**égrafo** m telegraph. ~**egrama** m telegram

telenovela f television soap opera

teleobjetivo m telephoto lens

telep|atía f telepathy. ~**ático** a telepathic

telesc|ópico a telescopic. ~**opio** m telescope

telesilla m & f chair-lift

telespectador m viewer

telesquí m ski-lift

televi|dente m & f viewer. ~**sar** vt televise. ~**sión** f television. ~**sor** m television (set)

télex m invar telex

telón m curtain

tema m subject; (Mus) theme

tembl|ar [1] vi shake; (de miedo) tremble; (de frío) shiver. ~**or** m shaking; (de miedo) trembling; (de frío) shivering; **~or de tierra** earth tremor. **~oroso** a trembling

tem|er vt be afraid (of). ● vi be afraid. □ **~erse** vpr be afraid. **~erario** a reckless. **~eroso** a frightened. **~ible** a fearsome. **~or** m fear

témpano m floe

temperamento m temperament

temperatura f temperature

tempest|ad f storm. **~uoso** a stormy

templ|ado a (tibio) warm; <clima, tiempo> mild; (valiente) courageous. **~anza** f mildness. **~ar** vt temper; (calentar) warm up. **~e** m tempering; <coraje> courage; (humor) mood

templo m temple

tempora|da f season. **~l** a temporary. ● m storm

tempran|ero a <frutos> early. **ser ~ero** be an early riser. **~o** a & adv early

tenacidad f tenacity

tenacillas fpl tongs

tenaz a tenacious

tenaza f, **tenazas** fpl pliers; (de chimenea, Culin) tongs; (de cangrejo) pincer

tende|ncia f tendency. **~nte** a. **~nte a** aimed at. **~r** [1] vt spread (out); hang out <ropa a secar>; (colocar) lay. ● vi tend (**a** to). □ **~rse** vpr lie down

tender|ete m stall. **~o** m shopkeeper

tendido a spread out; <ropa> hung out; <persona> lying down. ● m (en plaza de toros) front rows

tendón m tendon

tenebroso a gloomy; <asunto> sinister

tenedor m fork; (poseedor) holder

---

tener [40]

●*verbo transitivo*

> [!] El presente del verbo **tener** admite dos traducciones: *to have* y *to have got*, este último de uso más extendido en el inglés británico

····▸ to have. **¿tienen hijos?** do you have any children?, have you got any children? **no tenemos coche** we don't have a car, we haven't got a car. **tiene gripe** he has (the) flu, he's got (the) flu

····▸ to be <dimensiones, edad>. **tiene 1 metro de largo** it's 1 metre long. **tengo 20 años** I'm 20 (years old)

····▸ (sentir) **tener** + nombre to be + adjective. **~ celos** to be jealous. **~ frío** to be cold

····▸ (sujetar, sostener) to hold. **tenme la escalera** hold the ladder for me

····▸ (indicando estado) **tiene las manos sucias** his hands are dirty. **me tiene preocupada** I'm worried about him. **me tuvo esperando** he kept me waiting

····▸ (llevar puesto) to be wearing, to have on. **¡qué zapatos más elegantes tienes!** those are very smart shoes you're wearing! **tienes el suéter al revés** you have your sweater on inside out

····▸ (considerar) **~ a uno por algo** to think s.o. is sth. **lo tenía por tímido** I thought he was shy

●*verbo auxiliar*

····▸ **~ quehacer algo** to have to do sth. **tengo que irme** I have to go

····▸ **tener** + participio pasado. **tengo pensado comprarlo** I'm thinking of buying it. **tenía entendido otra cosa** I understood something else

····➤ (LAm, con expresiones temporales) **tienen 2 años de estar aquí** they've been here for 2 months. **tiene mucho tiempo sin verlo** she hasn't seen him for a long time

····➤ (en locuciones) **aquí tiene** here you are. **¿qué tienes?** what's the matter with you? **¿ y eso qué tiene?** (LAm) and what's wrong with that?

□ **tenerse** *verbo pronominal*

····➤ (sostenerse) **no podía ∼se en pie** (de cansancio) he was dead on his feet; (de borracho) he could hardly stand

····➤ (considerarse) to consider o.s. **se tiene por afortunado** he considers himself lucky

tengo *vb* ⇒TENER

teniente *m* lieutenant

tenis *m* tennis. **∼ de mesa** table tennis. **∼ta** *m & f* tennis player

tenor *m* sense; (Mus) tenor. **a ∼ de** according to

tens|ión *f* tension; (arterial) blood pressure; (Elec) voltage; (estrés) strain. **∼o** *a* tense

tentación *f* temptation

tentáculo *m* tentacle

tenta|dor *a* tempting. **∼r** [1] *vt* tempt; (palpar) feel

tentativa *f* attempt

tenue *a* thin; <luz, voz> faint; <color> subdued

teñi|r [5 & 22] *vt* dye; (fig) tinge (de with). □ **∼rse** *vpr* dye one's hair

teología *f* theology

te|oría *f* theory. **∼órico** *a* theoretical

tequila *f* tequila

terap|euta *m & f* therapist. **∼éutico** *a* therapeutic. **∼ia** *f* therapy

terc|er *a* véase TERCERO. **∼era** *f* (Auto) third (gear). **∼ero** *a* (delante de nombre masculino en singular **tercer**) third. ● *m* third party. **∼io** *m* third

terciopelo *m* velvet

terco *a* obstinate

tergiversar *vt* distort

termal *a* thermal

térmico *a* thermal

termina|ción *f* ending; (conclusión) conclusion. **∼l** *a & m* terminal. **∼nte** *a* categorical. **∼r** *vt* finish, end. **∼r por** end up. □ **∼rse** *vpr* come to an end

término *m* end; (palabra) term; (plazo) period. **∼ medio** average. **dar ∼ a** finish off. **en primer ∼** first of all. **en último ∼** as a last resort. **estar en buenos ∼s con** be on good terms with. **llevar a ∼** carry out

terminología *f* terminology

termita *f* termite

termo *m* Thermos (P) flask, flask

termómetro *m* thermometer

termo|nuclear *a* thermonuclear. **∼stato** *m* thermostat

terner|a *f* (carne) veal. **∼o** *m* calf

ternura *f* tenderness

terquedad *f* stubbornness

terrado *m* flat roof

terraplén *m* embankment

terrateniente *m & f* landowner

terraza *f* terrace; (balcón) balcony; (terrado) flat roof

terremoto *m* earthquake

terre|no *a* earthly. ● *m* land; (solar) plot (fig) field. **∼stre** *a* land; (Mil) ground

terrible *a* terrible. **∼mente** *adv* awfully

T

territori|al *a* territorial. **~o** *m* territory

terrón *m* (de tierra) clod; (Culin) lump

terror *m* terror. **~ífico** *a* terrifying. **~ismo** *m* terrorism. **~ista** *m & f* terrorist

terso *a* smooth

tertulia *f* gathering

tesina *f* dissertation

tesón *m* tenacity

tesor|ería *f* treasury. **~ero** *m* treasurer. **~o** *m* treasure; (tesorería) treasury; (libro) thesaurus

testaferro *m* figurehead

testa|mento *m* will. **T~mento** (Relig) Testament. **~r** *vi* make a will

testarudo *a* stubborn

testículo *m* testicle

testi|ficar [7] *vt/i* testify. **~go** *m* witness. **~go ocular**, **~go presencial** eyewitness. **ser ~go de** witness. **~monio** *m* testimony

teta *f* tit (🅸 o vulg); (de biberón) teat

tétanos *m* tetanus

tetera *f* (para el té) teapot

tetilla *f* nipple; (de biberón) teat

tétrico *a* gloomy

textil *a & m* textile

text|o *m* text. **~ual** *a* textual; <traducción> literal; <palabras> exact

textura *f* texture

tez *f* complexion

ti *pron* you

tía *f* aunt; 🅸 woman

tiara *f* tiara

tibio *a* lukewarm

tiburón *m* shark

tiempo *m* time; (atmosférico) weather; (Mus) tempo; (Gram) tense; (en partido) half. **a su ~** in due course. **a ~** in time. **¿cuánto ~?** how long? **hace buen ~** the weather is fine. **hace ~** some

time ago. **mucho ~** a long time. **perder el ~** waste time

tienda *f* shop (esp Brit), store (esp Amer); (de campaña) tent. **~ de comestibles**, **~ de ultramarinos** grocer's (shop) (Brit), grocery store (Amer)

tiene *vb* ⇒TENER

tienta. **andar a ~s** feel one's way

tierno *a* tender; (joven) young

tierra *f* land; (planeta, Elec) earth; (suelo) ground; (Geol) soil, earth; (LAm, polvo) dust. **por ~** overland, by land

tieso *a* stiff; (engreído) conceited

tiesto *m* flowerpot

tifón *m* typhoon

tifus *m* typhus; (fiebre tifoidea) typhoid (fever)

tigre *m* tiger. **~sa** *f* tigress

tijera *f*, **tijeras** *fpl* scissors; (de jardín) shears

tijeretear *vt* snip

tila *f* (infusión) lime tea

tild|ar *vt*. **~ar de** (fig) brand as. **~e** *f* tilde

tilo *m* lime(-tree)

timar *vt* swindle

timbal *m* kettledrum; (Culin) timbale, meat pie. **~es** *mpl* (Mus) timpani

timbr|ar *vt* stamp. **~e** *m* (sello) fiscal stamp; (Mex) postage stamp; (Elec) bell; (sonido) timbre

timidez *f* shyness

tímido *a* shy

timo *m* swindle

timón *m* rudder; (rueda) wheel; (fig) helm

tímpano *m* eardrum

tina *f* tub. **~co** *m* (Mex) water tank. **~ja** *f* large earthenware jar

tinglado *m* mess; (asunto) racket

tinieblas *fpl* darkness; (fig) confusion

tino *f* good sense; (tacto) tact

tint|a *f* ink. **de buena ~a** on good authority. **~e** *m* dyeing; (color) dye; (fig) tinge. **~ero** *m* ink-well

tintinear *vi* tinkle; <*vasos*> chink, clink

tinto *a* <*vino*> red

tintorería *f* dry cleaner's

tintura *f* dyeing; (color) dye

tío *m* uncle; 🄸 man. **~s** *mpl* uncle and aunt

tiovivo *m* merry-go-round

típico *a* typical

tipo *m* type; (🄸, persona) person; (figura de mujer) figure; (figura de hombre) build; (Com) rate

tip|ografía *f* typography. **~ográfico** *a* typographic(al)

tira *f* strip. **la ~ de** lots of

tirabuzón *m* corkscrew; (de pelo) ringlet

tirad|a *f* distance; (serie) series; (de periódico etc) print-run. **de una ~a** in one go. **~o** *a* (barato) very cheap; (🄸, fácil) very easy. **~or** *m* (asa) handle

tiran|ía *f* tyranny. **~izar** [10] *vt* tyrannize. **~o** *a* tyrannical. ● *m* tyrant

tirante *a* tight; (fig) tense; <*relaciones*> strained. ● *m* strap. **~s** *mpl* braces (esp Brit), suspenders (Amer)

tirar *vt* throw; (desechar) throw away; (derribar) knock over; drop <*bomba*>; fire <*cohete*>; (imprimir) print. ● *vi* (disparar) shoot. **~ a** tend to (be); (parecerse a) resemble. **~ abajo** knock down. **~ de** pull. **a todo ~** at the most. **ir tirando** get by. □ **~se** *vpr* throw o.s.; (tumbarse) lie down

tirita *f* (sticking) plaster

tiritar *vi* shiver (**de** with)

tiro *m* throw; (disparo) shot. **~ libre** free kick. **a ~** within range. **errar el ~** miss. **pegarse un ~** shoot o.s.

tiroides *m* thyroid (gland)

tirón *m* tug. **de un ~** in one go

tirote|ar *vt* shoot at. **~o** *m* shooting

tisana *f* herb tea

tisú *m* (*pl* **~s**, **~es**) tissue

títere *m* puppet. **~s** *mpl* puppet show

titilar *vi* <*estrella*> twinkle

titiritero *m* puppeteer; (acróbata) acrobat

titube|ante *a* faltering; (fig) hesitant. **~ar** *vi* falter. **~o** *m* hesitation

titula|do *a* <*libro*> entitled; <*persona*> qualified. **~r** *m* headline; (persona) holder. ● *vt* call. □ **~rse** *vpr* be called; <*persona*> graduate

título *m* title; (académico) qualification; (Univ) degree. **a ~ de** as, by way of

tiza *f* chalk

tiz|nar *vt* dirty. **~ne** *m* soot

toall|a *f* towel. **~ero** *m* towel-rail

tobillo *m* ankle

tobogán *m* slide; (para la nieve) toboggan

tocadiscos *m invar* record-player

toca|do *a* touched 🄸. ● *m* headdress. **~dor** *m* dressing-table. **~nte** *a*. **en lo ~nte a** with regard to. **~r** [7] *vt* touch; (palpar) feel; (Mus) play; ring <*timbre*>; (mencionar) touch on; <*barco*> stop at. ● *vi* ring; (corresponder a uno) **te ~ a ti** it's your turn. **en lo que ~ a** as for. □ **~rse** *vpr* touch; <*personas*>; touch each other

tocayo *m* namesake

tocino *m* bacon

tocólogo *m* obstetrician

todavía *adv* still; (con negativos) yet. **~ no** not yet

T

todo, toda

● *adjetivo*

····▸ (la totalidad) all. ~ **el vino** all
the wine. ~**s los edificios** all the
buildings. ~ **ese dinero** all that
money. ~ **el mundo** everyone.
(como adv) **está toda sucia** it's all
dirty

····▸ (entero) whole. ~ **el día** the
whole day, all day. **toda su
familia** his whole family. ~ **el
tiempo** the whole time, all the
time

····▸ (cada, cualquiera) every. ~ **tipo
de coche** every type of car. ~**s
los días** every day

····▸ (enfático) **a toda velocidad** at top
speed. **es ~ un caballero** he's a
real gentleman

····▸ (en locuciones) **ante ~** above all.
a ~ esto meanwhile. **con ~** even
so. **del ~** totally. ~ **lo contrario**
quite the opposite

⇒ Para expresiones como **todo
recto, todo seguido** etc., ver
bajo el respectivo adjetivo

● *pronombre*

····▸ all; (todas las cosas) everything.
eso es ~ that's all. **lo perdieron ~**
they lost everything. **quiere
comprar ~** he wants to buy
everything

····▸ **todos, todas** all; (todo el mundo)
everyone. **los compró ~s** he
bought them all, he bought all
of them. ~**s queríamos ir** we all
wanted to go. **vinieron ~s**
everyone came

● *nombre masculino*

:···▸ **el/un ~** the/a whole

toldo *m* awning

tolera|ncia *f* tolerance. ~**nte** *a*
tolerant. ~**r** *vt* tolerate

toma *f* taking; (de universidad etc)
occupation; (Med) dose; (de agua)
intake; (Elec) socket; (LAm, acequia)
irrigation channel. ● *int* well!,
fancy that! ~ **de corriente** power
point. ~**dura** *f*. ~**dura de pelo**
hoax. ~**r** *vt* take; catch <*autobús,
tren*>; occupy <*universidad etc*>;
(beber) drink, have; (comer) eat,
have. ● *vi* take; (esp LAm, beber)
drink; (LAm, dirigirse) go. ~**r a bien**
take well. ~**r a mal** take badly. ~**r
en serio** take seriously. ~**rla con
uno** pick on s.o. ~**r por** take for.
~ **y daca** give and take. **¿qué va a
~r?** what would you like? □ ~**rse** *vpr* take; (beber) drink,
have; (comer) eat, have

tomate *m* tomato

tomillo *m* thyme

tomo *m* volume

ton: **sin ~ ni son** without rhyme
or reason

tonad|a *f* tune; (canción) popular
song; (LAm, acento) accent. ~**illa** *f*
tune

tonel *m* barrel. ~**ada** *f* ton. ~**aje**
m tonnage

tónic|a *f* trend; (bebida) tonic
water. ~**o** *a* tonic; <*sílaba*>
stressed. ● *m* tonic

tonificar [7] *vt* invigorate

tono *m* tone; (Mus, modo) key;
(color) shade

tont|ería *f* silliness; (cosa) silly
thing; (dicho) silly remark. **dejarse
de ~erías** stop fooling around.
~**o** *a* silly. ● *m* fool, idiot;
(payaso) clown. **hacer el ~o** act the
fool. **hacerse el ~o** act dumb

topacio *m* topaz

topar *vi*. ~ **con** run into

tope *a* maximum. ● *m* end; (de
tren) buffer; (Mex, Auto) speed
bump. **hasta los ~s** crammed full.
ir a ~ go flat out

tópico *a* trite. **de uso ~** (Med) for external use only. ● *m* cliché

topo *m* mole

topogr|afía *f* topography. **~áfico** *a* topographical

toque *m* touch; (sonido) sound; (de campana) peal; (de reloj) stroke. **~ de queda** curfew. **dar los últimos ~s a** put the finishing touches to. **~tear** *vt* fiddle with

toquilla *f* shawl

tórax *m invar* thorax

torcer [2 & 9] *vt* twist; (doblar) bend; wring out <*ropa*>. ● *vi* turn. □ **~se** *vpr* twist

tordo *a* dapple grey. ● *m* thrush

tore|ar *vt* fight; (evitar) dodge. ● *vi* fight (bulls). **~o** *m* bullfighting. **~ro** *m* bullfighter

torment|a *f* storm. **~o** *m* torture. **~oso** *a* stormy

tornado *m* tornado

tornasolado *a* irridescent

torneo *m* tournament

tornillo *m* screw

torniquete *m* (Med) tourniquet; (entrada) turnstile

torno *m* lathe; (de alfarero) wheel. **en ~ a** around

toro *m* bull. **los ~s** *mpl* bullfighting. **ir a los ~s** go to a bullfight

toronja *f* (LAm) grapefruit

torpe *a* clumsy; (estúpido) stupid

torpedo *m* torpedo

torpeza *f* clumsiness; (de inteligencia) slowness. **una ~** a blunder

torre *f* tower; (en ajedrez) castle, rook; (Elec) pylon; (edificio) tower block (Brit); apartment block (Amer)

torren|cial *a* torrential. **~te** *m* torrent; (circulatorio) bloodstream; (fig) flood

tórrido *a* torrid

torsión *f* twisting

torso *m* torso

torta *f* tart; (LAm, de verduras) pie; (golpe) slap, punch; (Mex, bocadillo) filled roll. **no entender ni ~** not understand a thing. **~zo** *m* slap, punch. **pegarse un ~zo** have a bad accident

tortícolis *f* stiff neck

tortilla *f* omelette; (Mex, de maíz) tortilla. **~ española** potato omelette. **~ francesa** plain omelette

tórtola *f* turtle-dove

tortuga *f* tortoise; (de mar) turtle

tortura *f* torture. **~r** *vt* torture

tos *f* cough. **~ ferina** whooping cough

tosco *a* crude; <*persona*> coarse

toser *vi* cough

tost|ada *f* piece of toast. **~adas** *fpl* toast; (Mex, de tortilla) fried tortillas. **~ado** *a* <*pan*> toasted; <*café*> roasted; <*persona, color*> tanned. **~ar** *vt* toast <*pan*>; roast <*café*>; tan <*piel*>

total *a* total. ● *adv* after all. **~ que** so, to cut a long story short. ● *m* total; (totalidad) whole. **~idad** *f* whole. **~itario** *a* totalitarian. **~izar** [10] *vt* total

tóxico *a* toxic

toxi|cómano *m* drug addict. **~na** *f* toxin

tozudo *a* stubborn

traba *f* catch; (fig, obstáculo) obstacle. **poner ~s a** hinder

trabaj|ador *a* hard-working. ● *m* worker. **~ar** *vt* work; knead <*masa*>. ● *vi* work (**de** as); <*actor*> act. **¿en qué ~as?** what do you do? **~o** *m* work. **costar ~o** be difficult. **~oso** *a* hard

trabalenguas *m invar* tonguetwister

traba|r *vt* (sujetar) fasten; (unir) join; (entablar) strike up. □ **~rse**

T

vpr get stuck. **trabársele la lengua** get tongue-tied

trácala *m* (Mex) cheat. ● *f* (Mex) trick

tracción *f* traction

tractor *m* tractor

tradic|ión *f* tradition. ~**onal** *a* traditional

traduc|ción *f* translation. ~**ir** [47] *vt* translate (**a** into). ~**tor** *m* translator

traer [41] *vt* bring; (llevar) carry; (causar) cause. **traérselas** be difficult

trafica|nte *m & f* dealer. ~**r** [7] *vi* deal

tráfico *m* traffic; (Com) trade

traga|luz *m* skylight. ~**perras** *f invar* slot-machine. ~**r** [12] *vt* swallow; (comer mucho) devour; (soportar) put up with. **no lo trago** I can't stand him. □ ~**rse** *vpr* swallow; (fig) swallow up

tragedia *f* tragedy

trágico *a* tragic. ● *m* tragedian

trag|o *m* swallow, gulp; (pequeña porción) sip; (fig, disgusto) blow; (LAm, bebida alcohólica) drink. **echar(se) un** ~**o** have a drink. ~**ón** *a* greedy. ● *m* glutton.

trai|ción *f* treachery; (Pol) treason. ~**cionar** *vt* betray. ~**cionero** *a* treacherous. ~**dor** *a* treacherous. ● *m* traitor

traigo *vb* ⇒TRAER

traje *m* dress; (de hombre) suit. ~ **de baño** swimming-costume. ~ **de etiqueta**, ~ **de noche** evening dress. ● *vb* ⇒TRAER

traj|ín *m* coming and going; (ajetreo) hustle and bustle. ~**inar** *vi* bustle about

trama *f* weft; (fig, argumento) plot. ~**r** *vt* weave; (fig) plot

tramitar *vt* negotiate

trámite *m* step. ~**s** *mpl* procedure

tramo *m* (parte) section; (de escalera) flight

tramp|a *f* trap; (fig) trick. **hacer** ~**a** cheat. ~**illa** *f* trapdoor

trampolín *m* trampoline; (de piscina) springboard; (rígido) diving board

tramposo *a* cheating. ● *m* cheat

tranca *f* bar. ~**r** *vt* bar

trance *m* moment; (hipnótico etc) trance

tranco *m* stride

tranquil|idad *f* peace; (de espíritu) peace of mind. **con** ~ calmly. ~**izar** [10] *vt* calm down; (reconfortar) reassure. ~**o** *a* calm; <lugar> quiet; <conciencia> clear. **estáte** ~**o** don't worry

transa|cción *f* transaction; (acuerdo) settlement. ~**r** *vi* (LAm) compromise

transatlántico *a* transatlantic. ● *m* (ocean) liner

transbord|ador *m* ferry. ~**ar** *vt* transfer. ~**o** *m* transfer. **hacer** ~**o** change (**en** at)

transcri|bir (*pp* **transcrito**) *vt* transcribe. ~**pción** *f* transcription

transcur|rir *vi* pass. ~**so** *m* course

transeúnte *m & f* passer-by

transfer|encia *f* transfer. ~**ir** [4] *vt* transfer

transforma|ción *f* transformation. ~**dor** *m* transformer. ~**r** *vt* transform

transfusión *f* transfusion

transgre|dir *vt* transgress. ~**sión** *f* transgression

transición *f* transition

transigir [14] *vi* give in, compromise

transistor *m* transistor

transita|ble *a* passable. ~**r** *vi* go

transitivo *a* transitive

tránsito *m* transit; (tráfico) traffic

transitorio *a* transitory

transmi|sión *f* transmission; (radio, TV) broadcast ~**sor** *m* transmitter. ~**sora** *f* broadcasting station. ~**tir** *vt* transmit; (radio, TV) broadcast; (fig) pass on

transparen|cia *f* transparency. ~**tar** *vt* show. ~**te** *a* transparent

transpira|ción *f* perspiration. ~**r** *vi* transpire; (sudar) sweat

transport|ar *vt* transport. ~**e** *m* transport. **empresa** *f* **de** ~**es** removals company

transversal *a* transverse. **una calle** ~ **a la Gran Vía** a street which crosses the Gran Vía

tranvía *m* tram

trapear *vt* (LAm) mop

trapecio *m* trapeze; (Math) trapezium

trapo *m* cloth. ~**s** *mpl* rags; (🄙, ropa) clothes. **a todo** ~ out of control

tráquea *f* windpipe, trachea

traquete|ar *vt* bang, rattle; <*persona*> rush around. ~**o** *m* banging, rattle

tras *prep* after; (detrás) behind

trascende|ncia *f* significance; (alcance) implication. ~**ntal** *a* transcendental; (importante) important. ~**r** [1] *vi* (saberse) become known; (extenderse) spread

trasero *a* back, rear. ● *m* (Anat) bottom

trasfondo *m* background

traslad|ar *vt* move; transfer <*empleado etc*>; (aplazar) postpone. ~**o** *m* transfer; (copia) copy. (mudanza) removal. **dar** ~**o** notify

trasl|úcido *a* translucent. ☐ ~**ucirse** [11] *vpr* be

translucent; (dejarse ver) show through; (fig, revelarse) be revealed. ~**uz** *m*. **al** ~**uz** against the light

trasmano. a ~ out of the way

trasnochar *vt* (acostarse tarde) go to bed late; (no acostarse) stay up all night; (no dormir) be unable to sleep

traspas|ar *vt* go through; (transferir) transfer; go beyond <*límite*>. **se** ~**a** for sale. ~**o** *m* transfer

traspié *m* trip; (fig) slip. **dar un** ~ stumble; (fig) slip up

trasplant|ar *vt* transplant. ~**e** *m* transplant

trastada *f* prank; (jugada) dirty trick

traste *m* fret. **dar al** ~ **con** ruin. **ir al** ~ fall through. ~**s** *mpl* (Mex) junk

trastero *m* storeroom

trasto *m* piece of junk. ● ~**s** *mpl* junk

trastorn|ado *a* mad. ~**ar** *vt* upset; (volver loco) drive mad; (fig, 🄙, gustar mucho) delight. ☐ ~**arse** *vpr* get upset; (volverse loco) go mad. ~**o** *m* (incl Med) upset; (Pol) disturbance; (fig) confusion

trat|able *a* friendly; (Med) treatable. ~**ado** *m* treatise; (acuerdo) treaty. ~**amiento** *m* treatment; (título) title. ~**ante** *m* & *f* dealer. ~**ar** *vt* (incl Med) treat; deal with <*asunto etc*>; (manejar) handle; (de tú, de Vd) address (**de** as). ● *vi* deal (with). ~**ar con** have to do with; (Com) deal in. ~**ar de** be about; (intentar) try. **¿de qué se** ~**a?** what's it about? ~**o** *m* treatment; (acuerdo) agreement; (título) title; (relación) relationship. **¡**~**o hecho!** agreed! ~**os** *mpl* dealings

traum|a *m* trauma. ~**ático** *a* traumatic

través: a ~ de through; (de lado a lado) crossways

travesaño *m* crossbeam; (de portería) crossbar

travesía *f* crossing; (calle) side street

trav|esura *f* prank. **~ieso** *a* <niño> mischievous, naughty

trayecto *m* (tramo) stretch; (ruta) route; (viaje) journey. **~ria** *f* trajectory; (fig) course

traz|a *f* (aspecto) appearance. **~as** *fpl* signs. **~ado** *m* plan. **~ar** [10] *vt* draw; (bosquejar) sketch. **~o** *m* stroke; (línea) line

trébol *m* clover. **~es** *mpl* (en naipes) clubs

trece *a & m* thirteen

trecho *m* stretch; (distancia) distance; (tiempo) while. **a ~s** here and there. **de ~ en ~** at intervals

tregua *f* truce; (fig) respite

treinta *a & m* thirty

tremendo *a* terrible; (extraordinario) terrific

tren *m* train. **~ de aterrizaje** landing gear. **~ de vida** lifestyle

tren|cilla *f* braid. **~za** *f* braid; (de pelo) plait. **~zar** [10] *vt* plait

trepa|dor *a* climbing. **~dora** *f* climber. **~r** *vt/i* climb. □ **~rse** *vpr* **~rse a** climb <árbol>; climb onto <silla etc>

tres *a & m* three. **~cientos** *a & m* three hundred. **~illo** *m* three-piece suite; (Mus) triplet

treta *f* trick

tri|angular *a* triangular. **~ángulo** *m* triangle

trib|al *a* tribal. **~u** *f* tribe

tribuna *f* platform; (de espectadores) stand. **~l** *m* court; (de examen etc) board; (fig) tribunal

tribut|ar *vt* pay. **~o** *m* tribute; (impuesto) tax

triciclo *m* tricycle

tricolor *a* three-coloured

tricotar *vt/i* knit

tridimensional *a* three-dimensional

trig|al *m* wheat field. **~o** *m* wheat

trigésimo *a* thirtieth

trigueño *a* olive-skinned; <pelo> dark blonde

trilla|do *a* (fig, manoseado) trite; (fig, conocido) well-known. **~r** *vt* thresh

trilogía *f* trilogy

trimestr|al *a* quarterly. **~e** *m* quarter; (Escol, Univ) term

trinar *vi* warble. **estar que trina** be furious

trinchar *vt* carve

trinchera *f* ditch; (Mil) trench; (abrigo) trench coat

trineo *m* sledge

trinidad *f* trinity

trino *m* warble

trío *m* trio

tripa *f* intestine; (fig, vientre) tummy, belly. **~s** *fpl* (de máquina etc) parts, workings. **revolver las ~s** turn one's stomach

tripl|e *a* triple. ● *m*. **el ~e (de)** three times as much (as). **~icado** *a*. **por ~icado** in triplicate. **~icar** [7] *vt* treble

tripula|ción *f* crew. **~nte** *m & f* member of the crew. **~r** *vt* man

tris *m*. **estar en un ~** be on the point of

triste *a* sad; <paisaje, tiempo etc> gloomy; (fig, insignificante) miserable. **~za** *f* sadness

triturar *vt* crush

triunf|al *a* triumphal. **~ante** *a* triumphant. **~ar** *vi* triumph (**de**, **sobre** over). **~o** *m* triumph

trivial *a* trivial. **~idad** *f* triviality

trizas: hacer algo ~ smash sth to pieces. **hacerse ~** smash

trocear *vt* cut up, chop

trocha f narrow path; (LAm, rail) gauge

trofeo m trophy

tromba f whirlwind; (marina) waterspout. ~ **de agua** heavy downpour

trombón m trombone

trombosis f invar thrombosis

trompa f horn; (de orquesta) French horn; (de elefante) trunk; (hocico) snout; (Anat) tube. **coger una ~** 🔢 get drunk. **~zo** m bump

trompet|a f trumpet; (músico) trumpet player; (Mil) trumpeter. **~illa** f ear-trumpet

trompo m (juguete) (spinning) top

tronar vt (Mex) shoot. ● vi thunder

tronchar vt bring down; (fig) cut short. **~se de risa** laugh a lot

tronco m trunk. **dormir como un ~** sleep like a log

trono m throne

trop|a f troops. **~el** m mob

tropez|ar [1 & 10] vi trip; (fig) slip up. **~ar con** run into. **~ón** m stumble; (fig) slip

tropical a tropical

trópico a tropical. ● m tropic

tropiezo m slip; (desgracia) hitch

trot|ar vi trot; (fig) toing and froing. **al ~e** at a trot; (de prisa) in a rush. **de mucho ~e** hard-wearing

trozo m piece, bit. **a ~s** in bits

trucha f trout

truco m trick. **coger el ~** get the knack

trueno m thunder; (estampido) bang

trueque m exchange; (Com) barter

trufa f truffle

truhán m rogue

truncar [7] vt truncate; (fig) cut short

tu a your

tú pron you

tuba f tuba

tubérculo m tuber

tuberculosis f tuberculosis

tub|ería f pipes; (oleoducto etc) pipeline. **~o** m tube. **~o de ensayo** test tube. **~o de escape** (Auto) exhaust (pipe). **~ular** a tubular

tuerca f nut

tuerto a one-eyed, blind in one eye. ● m one-eyed person

tuétano m marrow; (fig) heart. **hasta los ~s** completely

tufo m stench

tugurio m hovel

tul m tulle

tulipán m tulip

tulli|do a paralysed. **~r** [22] vt cripple

tumba f grave, tomb

tumb|ar vt knock over, knock down <estructura>; (fig, 🔢, en examen) fail. □ **~arse** vpr lie down. **~o** m jolt. **dar un ~o** tumble. **~ona** f sun lounger

tumor m tumour

tumulto m turmoil; (Pol) riot

tuna f prickly pear; (de estudiantes) student band

tunante m & f rogue

túnel m tunnel

túnica f tunic

tupé m toupee; (fig) nerve

tupido a thick

turba f peat; (muchedumbre) mob

turbado a upset

turbante m turban

turbar vt upset; (molestar) disturb. □ **~se** vpr be upset

turbina f turbine

turbi|o a cloudy; <vista> blurred; <asunto etc> shady. **~ón** m squall

T

turbulen|cia *f* turbulence; (disturbio) disturbance. **~te** *a* turbulent

turco *a* Turkish. ● *m* Turk; (lengua) Turkish

tur|ismo *m* tourism; (coche) car. **hacer ~** travel around. **~ista** *m* & *f* tourist. **~ístico** *a* tourist

turn|arse *vpr* take turns (**para** to). **~o** *m* turn; (de trabajo) shift. **de ~** on duty

turquesa *f* turquoise

Turquía *f* Turkey

turrón *m* nougat

tutear *vt* address as *tú*. □ **~se** *vpr* be on familiar terms

tutela *f* (Jurid) guardianship; (fig) protection

tutor *m* guardian; (Escol) form master

tuve *vb* ⇒TENER

tuyo *a* & *pron* yours. **un amigo ~** a friend of yours

u *conj* or

ubic|ar *vt* (LAm) place; (localizar) find. □ **~arse** *vpr* (LAm) be situated; (orientarse) find one's way around

ubre *f* udder

Ud. *abrev* (**Usted**) you

UE *abrev* (= **Unión Europea**) EU

uf *int* phew!; (de repugnancia) ugh!

ufan|arse *vpr* be proud (**con, de** of); (jactarse) boast (**con, de** about). **~o** *a* proud

úlcera *f* ulcer

últimamente *adv* (recientemente) recently; (finalmente) finally

ultim|ar *vt* complete; (LAm, matar) kill. **~átum** *m* ultimatum

último *a* last; (más reciente) latest; (más lejano) furthest; (más alto) top; (más bajo) bottom; (definitivo) final. ● *m* last one. **estar en las últimas** be on one's last legs; (sin dinero) be down to one's last penny. **por ~** finally. **vestido a la última** dressed in the latest fashion

ultra *a* ultra, extreme

ultraj|ante *a* offensive. **~e** *m* insult, outrage

ultramar *m*. **de ~** overseas; <productos> foreign. **tienda de ~inos** grocer's (shop) (Brit), grocery store (Amer)

ultranza. **a ~** (con decisión) decisively; (extremo) out-and-out

ultravioleta *a invar* ultraviolet

umbilical *a* umbilical

umbral *m* threshold

....

un, una

● *artículo indefinido*

! The masculine article **un** is also used before feminine nouns which begin with stressed **a** or **ha**, e.g. **un alma piadosa, un hada madrina**

····▸ (en sing) a; (antes de sonido vocálico) an. **un perro** a dog. **una hora** an hour

····▸ **unos, unas** (cantidad incierta) some. **compré ~os libros** I bought some books. (cantidad cierta) **tiene ~os ojos preciosos** she has beautiful eyes. **tiene ~os hijos muy buenos** her children are very good. (en aproximaciones)

about. **en ~as 3 horas** in about 3
hours

➡️ For further information see
uno

un|ánime *a* unanimous.
~animidad *f* unanimity
undécimo *a* eleventh
ungüento *m* ointment
únic|amente *adv* only. **~o** *a*
only; (fig, incomparable) unique
unicornio *m* unicorn
unid|ad *f* unit; (cualidad) unity.
~ad de disco disk drive. **~o** *a*
united
unifica|ción *f* unification. **~r** [7]
vt unite, unify
uniform|ar *vt* standardize. **~e** *a*
& m uniform. **~idad** *f* uniformity
unilateral *a* unilateral
uni|ón *f* union; (cualidad) unity;
(Tec) joint. **~r** *vt* join; mix
<líquidos>. ☐ **~rse** *vpr* join
together; *<caminos>* converge;
<compañías> merge
unísono *m* unison. **al ~** in unison
univers|al *a* universal. **~idad** *f*
university. **~itario** *a* university.
~o *m* universe

uno, una

● *adjetivo*

Note that **uno** becomes **un**
before masculine nouns

····▸ one. **una peseta** one peseta. **un
dólar** one dollar. **ni una persona**
not one person, not a single
person. **treinta y un años** thirty-
one years

● *pronombre*

····▸ one. **~ es mío** one (of them)
is mine. **es la una** it's one
o'clock. **se ayudan el ~ al otro**
they help one another, they

help each other. **lo que sienten el
~ por el otro** what they feel for
each other

····▸ (①, alguien) someone. **le
pregunté a ~** I asked someone

····▸ **unos, unas** some. **no tenía
vasos así es que le presté ~s** she
didn't have any glasses so I lent
her some. **a ~s les gusta, a otros
no** some like it, others don't. **los
~s a los otros** one another, each
other.

····▸ (impersonal) you. **~ no sabe qué
decir** you don't know what to say

untar *vt* grease; (cubrir) spread; (fig,
①, sobornar) bribe
uña *f* nail; (de animal) claw; (casco)
hoof
uranio *m* uranium
Urano *m* Uranus
urban|idad *f* politeness. **~ismo**
m town planning. **~ización** *f*
development. **~izar** [10] *vt*
develop. **~o** *a* urban
urbe *f* big city
urdir *vt* (fig) plot
urg|encia *f* urgency; (emergencia)
emergency. **~s** accident &
emergency, (Amer) emergency
room **~ente** *a* urgent; *<carta>*
express. **~ir** [14] *vi* be urgent.
urinario *m* urinal
urna *f* urn; (Pol) ballot box
urraca *f* magpie
URSS *abrev* (Historia) USSR
Uruguay *m*. **el ~** Uruguay
uruguayo *a & m* Uruguayan
us|ado *a* (con estar) used; *<ropa
etc>* worn; (con ser) secondhand.
~ar *vt* use; (llevar) wear. ☐ **~arse**
vpr (LAm) be in fashion. **~o** *m*
use; (costumbre) custom. **al ~o de**
in the style of
usted *pron* you. **~es** you

U

usual *a* usual

usuario *a* user

usur|a *f* usury. **~ero** *m* usurer

usurpar *vt* usurp

utensilio *m* utensil; (herramienta) tool

útero *m* womb, uterus

útil *a* useful. **~es** *mpl* implements; (equipo) equipment

utili|dad *f* usefulness. **~dades** *fpl* (LAm) profits. **~zación** *f* use, utilization. **~zar** [10] *vt* use, utilize

utopía *f* Utopia

uva *f* grape. **~ pasa** raisin. **mala ~** bad mood

vaca *f* cow. **carne de ~** beef

vacaciones *fpl* holiday(s), vacation(s) (Amer). **de ~** on holiday, on vacation (Amer)

vacante *a* vacant. ● *f* vacancy

vaciar [20] *vt* empty; (ahuecar) hollow out; (en molde) cast

vacila|ción *f* hesitation. **~nte** *a* unsteady; (fig) hesitant. **~r** *vi* hesitate (🄸, bromear) tease; (LAm, divertirse) have fun

vacío *a* empty; (frívolo) frivolous. ● *m* empty space; (estado) emptiness; (en física) vacuum; (fig) void

vacuna *f* vaccine. **~ción** *f* vaccination. **~r** *vt* vaccinate

vacuno *a* bovine

vad|ear *vt* ford. **~o** *m* ford

vaga|bundear *vi* wander. **~bundo** *a* vagrant; <perro> stray.

niño **~bundo** street urchin. ● *m* tramp, vagrant. **~ncia** *f* vagrancy; (fig) laziness. **~r** [12] *vi* wander (about)

vagina *f* vagina

vago *a* vague; (holgazán) lazy. ● *m* layabout

vag|ón *m* coach, carriage; (de mercancías) wagon. **~ón restaurante** dining-car. **~oneta** *f* small freight wagon; (Mex, para pasajeros) van

vaho *m* breath; (vapor) steam. **~s** *mpl* inhalation

vain|a *f* sheath; (Bot) pod. **~illa** *f* vanilla

vaiv|én *m* swinging; (de tren etc) rocking. **~enes** *mpl* (fig, de suerte) swings

vajilla *f* dishes, crockery

vale *m* voucher; (pagaré) IOU. **~dero** *a* valid

valenciano *a* from Valencia

valentía *f* bravery, courage

valer [42] *vt* be worth; (costar) cost; (fig, significar) mean. ● *vi* be worth; (costar) cost; (servir) be of use; (ser valedero) be valid; (estar permitido) be allowed. **~ la pena** be worthwhile, be worth it. **¿cuánto vale?** how much is it? **no ~ para nada** be useless. **eso no me vale** (Mex, 🄸) I don't give a damn about that. **¡vale!** all right!, OK! 🄸

valeroso *a* courageous

valgo *vb* ⇒ VALER

valía *f* worth

validez *f* validity. **dar ~ a** validate

válido *a* valid

valiente *a* brave; (en sentido irónico) fine. ● *m* brave person

valija *f* suitcase. **~ diplomática** diplomatic bag

valioso *a* valuable

valla *f* fence; (en atletismo) hurdle

valle *m* valley

valor *m* value, worth; (coraje) courage. **objetos** *mpl* **de** ~ valuables. **sin** ~ worthless. ~**es** *mpl* securities. ~**ación** *f* valuation. ~**ar** *vt* value

vals *m invar* waltz

válvula *f* valve

vampiro *m* vampire

vanagloriarse *vpr* boast

vandalismo *m* vandalism

vándalo *m & f* vandal

vanguardia *f* vanguard. **de** ~ (en arte, música etc) avant-garde

vani|**dad** *f* vanity. ~**doso** *a* vain. ~**o** *a* vain; (inútil) futile; <palabras> empty. **en** ~ in vain

vapor *m* steam, vapour; (Naut) steamer. **al** ~ (Culin) steamed. ~**izador** *m* vaporizer. ~**izar** [10] vaporize

vaquer|**o** *m* cowherd, cowboy. ~**os** *mpl* jeans

vara *f* stick; (de autoridad) staff (medida) yard

varar *vi* run aground

varia|**ble** *a & f* variable. ~**ción** *f* variation. ~**do** *a* varied. ~**nte** *f* variant; (Auto) by-pass. ~**ntes** *fpl* hors d'oeuvres. ~**r** [20] *vt* change; (dar variedad a) vary. ● *vi* vary; (cambiar) change

varicela *f* chickenpox

variedad *f* variety

varilla *f* stick; (de metal) rod

varios *a* several

varita *f* wand

variz *f* (*pl* **varices**, (LAm) **várices**) varicose vein

var|**ón** *a* male. ● *m* man; (niño) boy. ~**onil** *a* manly

vasco *a & m* Basque

vaselina *f* Vaseline (P), petroleum jelly

vasija *f* vessel, pot

vaso *m* glass; (Anat) vessel

vástago *m* shoot; (descendiente) descendant

vasto *a* vast

vaticin|**ar** *vt* forecast. ~**io** *m* prediction, forecast

vatio *m* watt

vaya *vb* ⇒IR

Vd. *abrev* (**Usted**) you

vecin|**al** *a* local. ~**dad** *f* neighbourhood; (vecinos) residents; (Mex, edificio) tenement house. ~**dario** *m* neighbourhood; (vecinos) residents. ~**o** *a* neighbouring. ● *m* neighbour; (de barrio, edificio) resident

veda *f* close season. ~**do** *m* reserve. ~**do de caza** game reserve. ~**r** *vt* prohibit

vega *f* fertile plain

vegeta|**ción** *f* vegetation. ~**l** *a & m* plant, vegetable. ~**r** *vi* grow; <persona> vegetate. ~**riano** *a & m* vegetarian

vehemente *a* vehement

vehículo *m* vehicle

veinte *a & m* twenty

veinti|**cinco** *a & m* twenty-five. ~**cuatro** *a & m* twenty-four. ~**dós** *a & m* twenty-two. ~**nueve** *a & m* twenty-nine. ~**ocho** *a & m* twenty-eight. ~**séis** *a & m* twenty-six. ~**siete** *a & m* twenty-seven. ~**trés** *a & m* twenty-three. ~**uno** *a & m* (delante de nombre masculino **veintiún**) twenty-one

vejar *vt* ill-treat

veje|**storio** *m* old crock; (LAm, cosa) old relic. ~**z** *f* old age

vejiga *f* bladder

vela *f* (Naut) sail; (de cera) candle; (vigilia) vigil. **pasar la noche en** ~ have a sleepless night

velada *f* evening

vela|**do** *a* veiled; (Foto) exposed. ~**r** *vt* watch over; hold a wake

V

velarse over <*difunto*>; (encubrir) veil; (Foto) expose. ● *vi* stay awake. ~**r por** look after. □ ~**rse** *vpr* (Foto) get exposed

velero *m* sailing-ship

veleta *f* weather vane

vell|o *m* hair; (pelusa) down. ~**ón** *m* fleece

velo *m* veil

veloc|idad *f* speed; (Auto, Mec) gear. **a toda ~idad** at full speed. ~**ímetro** *m* speedometer. ~**ista** *m & f* sprinter

velódromo *m* cycle-track

veloz *a* fast, quick

vena *f* vein; (en madera) grain. **estar de/en ~** be in the mood

venado *m* deer; (Culin) venison

vencedor *a* winning. ● *m* winner

venc|er [9] *vt* defeat; (superar) overcome. ● *vi* win; <*pasaporte*> expire. □ ~**erse** *vpr* collapse; (LAm, pasaporte) expire. ~**ido** *a* beaten; <*pasaporte*> expired; (Com, atrasado) in arrears. **darse por ~ido** give up. ~**imiento** *m* due date; (de pasaporte) expiry date

venda *f* bandage. ~**je** *m* dressing. ~**r** *vt* bandage

vendaval *m* gale

vende|dor *a* selling. ● *m* seller; (en tienda) salesperson. ~**dor ambulante** pedlar. ~**r** *vt* sell. **se ~** for sale. □ ~**rse** *vpr* <*persona*> sell out

vendimia *f* grape harvest

veneciano *a* Venetian

veneno *m* poison; (malevolencia) venom. ~**so** *a* poisonous

venera|ble *a* venerable. ~**ción** *f* reverence. ~**r** *vt* revere

venéreo *a* venereal

venezolano *a & m* Venezuelan

Venezuela *f* Venezuela

venga|nza *f* revenge. ~**r** [12] *vt* avenge. □ ~**rse** *vpr* take revenge (**de, por** for) (**en** on). ~**tivo** *a* vindictive

vengo *vb* ⇒VENIR

venia *f* (permiso) permission. ~**l** *a* venial

veni|da *f* arrival; (vuelta) return. ~**dero** *a* coming. ~**r** [53] *vi* come. ~**r bien** suit. **la semana que viene** next week. **¡venga!** come on!

venta *f* sale; (posada) inn. **en ~** for sale

ventaj|a *f* advantage. ~**oso** *a* advantageous

ventan|a *f* (inc informática) window; (de la nariz) nostril. ~**illa** *f* window

ventarrón *m* 🔟 strong wind

ventila|ción *f* ventilation. ~**dor** *m* fan. ~**r** *vt* air

vent|isca *f* blizzard. ~**olera** *f* gust of wind. ~**osa** *f* sucker. ~**osidad** *f* wind, flatulence. ~**oso** *a* windy

ventrílocuo *m* ventriloquist

ventur|a *f* happiness; (suerte) luck. **a la ~a** with no fixed plan. **echar la buena ~a a uno** tell s.o.'s fortune. **por ~a** fortunately; (acaso) perhaps. ~**oso** *a* happy, lucky

Venus *m* Venus

ver [43] *vt* see; watch <*televisión*>. ● *vi* see. **a mi modo de ~** in my view. **a ~** let's see. **dejarse ~** show. **no lo puedo ~** I can't stand him. **no tener nada que ~ con** have nothing to do with. **vamos a ~** let's see. **ya lo veo** that's obvious. **ya ~emos** we'll see. □ ~**se** *vpr* see o.s.; (encontrarse) find o.s.; <*dos personas*> meet; (LAm, parecer) look

veran|eante *m & f* holidaymaker, vacationer (Amer). ~**ear** *vi* spend one's summer holiday. ~**eo** *m*. **ir de ~eo** spend

one's summer holiday. **lugar** *m* de
~**eo** summer resort. ~**iego** *a*
summer. ~**o** *m* summer

vera|s. de ~s really; (verdadero)
real. ~**z** *a* truthful

verbal *a* verbal

verbena *f* (fiesta) fair; (baile) dance

verbo *m* verb. ~**so** *a* verbose

verdad *f* truth. **¿~?** isn't it?,
aren't they?, won't it? etc. **a decir**
~ to tell the truth. **de ~** really.
~**eramente** *adv* really. ~**ero** *a*
true; (fig) real

verd|e *a* green; *<fruta>* unripe;
<chiste> dirty. ● *m* green; (hierba)
grass. ~**or** *m* greenness

verdugo *m* executioner; (fig)
tyrant

verdu|lería *f* greengrocer's
(shop). ~**lero** *m* greengrocer

vereda *f* path; (LAm, acera)
pavement (Brit), sidewalk (Amer)

veredicto *m* verdict

verg|onzoso *a* shameful; (tímido)
shy. ~**üenza** *f* shame; (bochorno)
embarrassment. **¡es una ~üenza!**
it's a disgrace! **me da ~üenza** I'm
ashamed/embarrassed. **tener
~üenza** be ashamed/embarrassed

verídico *a* true

verifica|ción *f* verification. ~**r**
[7] *vt* check. □ ~**rse** *vpr* take
place; (resultar verdad) come true

verja *f* (cerca) railings; (puerta) iron
gate

vermú *m*, **vermut** *m* vermouth

verosímil *a* likely; *<relato>*
credible

verruga *f* wart

versa|do *a* versed. ~**r** *vi*. ~ **sobre**
deal with

versátil *a* versatile; (fig) fickle

versión *f* version; (traducción)
translation

verso *m* verse; (poema) poem

vértebra *f* vertebra

verte|dero *m* dump; (desagüe)
drain ~**r** [1] *vt* pour; (derramar)
spill ● *vi* flow

vertical *a* & *f* vertical

vértice *f* vertex

vertiente *f* slope

vertiginoso *a* dizzy

vértigo *m* (Med) vertigo. **dar ~**
make dizzy

vesícula *f* vesicle. ~ **biliar** gall
bladder

vespertino *a* evening

vestíbulo *m* hall; (de hotel, teatro)
foyer

vestido *m* dress

vestigio *m* trace. ~**s** *mpl*
remains

vest|imenta *f* clothes. ~**ir** [5] *vt*
(llevar) wear; dress *<niño etc>*. ●
vi dress. ~**ir de** wear. □ ~**irse** *vpr*
get dressed. ~**irse de** wear;
(disfrazarse) dress up as. ~**uario** *m*
wardrobe; (en gimnasio etc)
changing room (Brit), locker room
(Amer)

vetar *vt* veto

veterano *a* veteran

veterinari|a *f* veterinary science.
~**o** *a* veterinary. ● *m* vet Ⓘ,
veterinary surgeon (Brit),
veterinarian (Amer)

veto *m* veto

vez *f* time; (turno) turn. **a la ~** at
the same time. **alguna ~**
sometimes; (en preguntas) ever.
algunas veces sometimes. **a su ~**
in turn. **a veces** sometimes. **cada
~** each time. **cada ~ más** more
and more. **de una ~** in one go. **de
una ~ para siempre** once and for
all. **de ~ en cuando** from time to
time. **dos veces** twice. **en ~ de**
instead of. **érase una ~, había una
~** once upon a time there was.
otra ~ again. **pocas veces, rara ~**
seldom. **una ~ (que)** once

V

vía f road; (Rail) line; (Anat) tract; (fig) way. **estar en ~s de** be in the process of. ● prep via. **~ aérea** by air. **~ de comunicación** means of communication. **~ férrea** railway (Brit), railroad (Amer). **~ rápida** fast lane

viab|ilidad f viability. **~le** a viable

viaducto m viaduct

viaj|ante m & f commercial traveller. **~ar** vi travel. **~e** m journey; (corto) trip. **~e de novios** honeymoon. ¡buen **~e!** have a good journey!. **estar de ~** be away. **salir de ~** go on a trip. **~ero** m traveller; (pasajero) passenger

víbora f viper

vibra|ción f vibration. **~nte** a vibrant. **~r** vt/i vibrate

vicario m vicar

viceversa adv vice versa

vici|ado a <texto> corrupt; <aire> stale. **~ar** vt corrupt; (estropear) spoil. **~o** m vice; (mala costumbre) bad habit. **~oso** a dissolute; <círculo> vicious

víctima f victim; (de un accidente) casualty

victori|a f victory. **~oso** a victorious

vid f vine

vida f life; (duración) lifetime. ¡**~ mía!** my darling! **de por ~** for life. **en mi ~** never (in my life). **estar con ~** be still alive

vídeo m, (LAm) **video** m video; (cinta) videotape; (aparato) video recorder

videojuego m video game

vidri|era f stained glass window; (puerta) glass door; (LAm, escaparate) shop window. **~ería** f glass works. **~ero** m glazier. **~o** m glass; (LAm, en ventana) window

pane. **limpiar los ~os** clean the windows. **~oso** a glassy

vieira f scallop

viejo a old. ● m old person

viene vb ⇒VENIR

viento m wind. **hacer ~** be windy

vientre m stomach; (cavidad) abdomen; (matriz) womb; (intestino) bowels; (de vasija etc) belly

viernes m invar Friday. **V~ Santo** Good Friday

viga f beam; (de metal) girder

vigen|cia f validity. **~te** a valid; <ley> in force. **entrar en ~cia** come into force

vigésimo a twentieth

vigía f watch-tower. ● m & f (persona) lookout

vigil|ancia f vigilance. **~ante** a vigilant. ● m & f security guard; (nocturno) watchman. **~ar** vt keep an eye on. ● vi be vigilant; <vigía> keep watch. **~ia** f vigil; (Relig) fasting

vigor m vigour; (vigencia) force. **entrar en ~** come into force. **~oso** a vigorous

vil a vile. **~eza** f vileness; (acción) vile deed

villa f (casa) villa; (Historia) town. **la V~** Madrid

villancico m (Christmas) carol

villano a villanous; (Historia) peasant

vilo. en ~ in the air

vinagre m vinegar. **~ra** f vinegar bottle. **~ras** fpl cruet. **~ta** f vinaigrette

vincular vt bind

vínculo m tie, bond

vindicar [7] vt (rehabilitar) vindicate

vine vb ⇒VENIR

vinicult|or m wine-grower. **~ura** f wine growing

vino *m* wine. **~ de la casa** house wine. **~ de mesa** table wine. **~ tinto** red wine

viñ|a *f* vineyard. **~atero** *m* (LAm) wine-grower. **~edo** *m* vineyard

viola *f* viola

viola|ción *f* violation; (de una mujer) rape. **~r** *vt* violate; break <*ley*>; rape <*mujer*>

violen|cia *f* violence; (fuerza) force. □ **~tarse** *vpr* get embarrassed. **~to** *a* violent; (fig) awkward

violeta *a invar & f* violet

viol|ín *m* violin. ● *m & f* (músico) violinist. **~inista** *m & f* violinist. **~ón** *m* double bass. **~onc(h) elista** *m & f* cellist. **~onc(h)elo** *m* cello

vira|je *m* turn. **~r** *vt* turn. ● *vi* turn; (fig) change direction. **~r bruscamente** swerve

virg|en *a*. **ser ~en** be a virgin. ● *f* virgin. **~inal** *a* virginal. **~inidad** *f* virginity

Virgo *m* Virgo

viril *a* virile. **~idad** *f* virility

virtu|al *a* virtual. **~d** *f* virtue; (capacidad) power. **en ~d de** by virtue of. **~oso** *a* virtuous. ● *m* virtuoso

viruela *f* smallpox

virulento *a* virulent

virus *m invar* virus

visa *f* (LAm) visa. **~ado** *m* visa. **~r** *vt* endorse

vísceras *fpl* entrails

viscoso *a* viscous

visera *f* visor; (de gorra) peak

visib|ilidad *f* visibility. **~le** *a* visible

visillo *m* (cortina) net curtain

visi|ón *f* vision; (vista) sight. **~onario** *a & m* visionary

visita *f* visit; (visitante) visitor; (invitado) guest; (Internet) hit. **~nte** *m & f* visitor. **~r** *vt* visit

vislumbrar *vt* glimpse

viso *m* sheen; (aspecto) appearance

visón *m* mink

visor *m* viewfinder

víspera *f* day before, eve

vista *f* sight, vision; (aspecto, mirada) look; (panorama) view. **apartar la ~** look away. **a primera ~, a simple ~** at first sight. **con ~s a** with a view to. **en ~ de** in view of. **estar a la ~** be obvious. **hacer la ~ gorda** turn a blind eye. **perder la ~** lose one's sight. **tener a la ~** have in front of one. **volver la ~ atrás** look back. **~zo** *m* glance. **dar/echar un ~zo a** glance at

visto *a* seen; (poco original) common (considerado) considered. **~ que** since. **bien ~** acceptable. **está ~ que** it's obvious that. **mal ~** unacceptable. **por lo ~** apparently. ● *vb* ⇒VESTIR. **~ bueno** *m* approval. **~so** *a* colourful, bright

visual *a* visual. **campo ~** field of vision

vital *a* vital. **~icio** *a* life; <*cargo*> held for life. **~idad** *f* vitality

vitamina *f* vitamin

viticult|or *m* wine-grower. **~ura** *f* wine growing

vitorear *vt* cheer

vítreo *a* vitreous

vitrina *f* showcase; (en casa) glass cabinet; (LAm, escaparate) shop window

viud|a *f* widow. **~ez** *f* widowhood. **~o** *a* widowed. ● *m* widower

viva *m* cheer. **~cidad** *f* liveliness. **~mente** *adv* vividly. **~z** *a* lively

V

víveres *mpl* supplies

vivero *m* nursery; (de peces) hatchery; (de moluscos) bed

viveza *f* vividness; (de inteligencia) sharpness; (de carácter) liveliness

vívido *a* vivid

vividor *m* pleasure seeker

vivienda *f* housing; (casa) house; (piso) flat (Brit), apartment (esp Amer). **sin ~** homeless

viviente *a* living

vivificar [7] *vt* (animar) enliven

vivir *vt* live through. ● *vi* live; (estar vivo) be alive. **~ de** live on. ¡**viva!** hurray! ¡**viva el rey!** long live the king! ● *m* life. **de mal ~** dissolute

vivisección *f* vivisection

vivo *a* alive; (viviente) living; *<color>* bright; (listo) clever; (fig) lively. ● *m* sharp operator

vocab|lo *m* word. **~ulario** *m* vocabulary

vocación *f* vocation

vocal *a* vocal. ● *f* vowel. ● *m & f* member. **~ista** *m & f* vocalist

voce|ar *vt* call *<mercancías>*; (fig) proclaim; (Mex) page *<persona>*. ● *vi* shout. **~río** *m* shouting. **~ro** *m* (LAm) spokesperson

vociferar *vi* shout

vola|dor *a* flying. ● *m* rocket. **~ndas. en ~ndas** in the air. **~nte** *a* flying. ● *m* (Auto) steering-wheel; (nota) note; (rehilete) shuttlecock. **~r** [2] *vt* blow up. ● *vi* fly; (Ⅱ, desaparecer) disappear

volátil *a* volatile

volcán *m* volcano. **~ico** *a* volcanic

volcar [2 & 7] *vt* knock over; (vaciar) empty out; turn over *<molde>*. ● *vi* overturn. □ **~se** *vpr* fall over; *<vehículo>* overturn;

(fig) do one's utmost. **~se en** throw o.s. into

vóleibol *m*, (Mex) **volibol** *m* volleyball

voltaje *m* voltage

volte|ar *vt* turn over; (en el aire) toss; ring *<campanas>*; (LAm) turn over *<colchón etc>*. □ **~arse** *vpr* (LAm) turn around; *<carro>* overturn. **~reta** *f* somersault

voltio *m* volt

voluble *a* (fig) fickle

volum|en *m* volume. **~inoso** *a* voluminous

voluntad *f* will; (fuerza de voluntad) willpower; (deseo) wish; (intención) intention. **buena ~** goodwill. **mala ~** ill will

voluntario *a* voluntary. ● *m* volunteer

voluptuoso *a* voluptuous

volver [2] (*pp* vuelto) *vt* turn; (de arriba a abajo) turn over; (devolver) restore. ● *vi* return; (fig) revert. **~ a hacer algo** do sth again. **~ en sí** come round. □ **~se** *vpr* turn round; (hacerse) become

vomit|ar *vt* bring up. ● *vi* be sick, vomit. **~ivo** *a* disgusting

vómito *m* vomit; (acción) vomiting

voraz *a* voracious

vos *pron* (LAm) you. **~otros** *pron* you; (reflexivo) yourselves

vot|ación *f* voting; (voto) vote. **~ante** *m & f* voter. **~ar** *vt* vote for. ● *vi* vote (**por** for). **~o** *m* vote; (Relig) vow

voy *vb* ⇒IR

voz *f* voice; (rumor) rumour; (palabra) word. **~ pública** public opinion. **a media ~** softly. **a una ~** unanimously. **dar voces** shout. **en ~ alta** loudly

vuelco *m* upset. **el corazón me dio un ~** my heart missed a beat

vuelo *m* flight; (acción) flying; (de ropa) flare. **al ~** in flight; (fig) in passing

vuelta *f* turn; (curva) bend; (paseo) walk; (revolución) revolution; (regreso) return; (dinero) change. **a la ~** on one's return. **a la ~ de la esquina** round the corner. **dar la ~ al mundo** go round the world. **dar una ~** go for a walk. **estar de ~** be back

vuelvo *vb* ⇒VOLVER

vuestro *a* your. ● *pron* yours. **un amigo ~** a friend of yours

vulg|ar *a* vulgar; <*persona*> common. **~aridad** *f* vulgarity. **~arizar** [10] *vt* popularize. **~o** *m* common people

vulnerable *a* vulnerable

y *conj* and

ya *adv* already; (ahora) now; (con negativos) any more; (para afirmar) yes, sure; (en seguida) immediately; (pronto) soon. **~ mismo** (LAm) right away. ● *int* of course! **~ no** no longer. **~ que** since. ¡**~**, **~**! oh sure!

yacaré *m* (LAm) alligator

yac|er [44] *vi* lie. **~imiento** *m* deposit; (de petróleo) oilfield

yanqui *m & f* American, Yank(ee)

yate *m* yacht

yegua *f* mare

yelmo *m* helmet

yema *f* (Bot) bud; (de huevo) yolk; (golosina) sweet. **~ del dedo** fingertip

yerba *f* (LAm) grass; (Med) herb

yergo *vb* ⇒ERGUIR

yermo *a* uninhabited; (no cultivable) barren. ● *m* wasteland

yerno *m* son-in-law

yerro *m* mistake. ● *vb* ⇒ERRAR

yeso *m* plaster; (mineral) gypsum

yo *pron* I. **~ mismo** myself. ¿**quién, ~?** who, me? **soy ~** it's me

yodo *m* iodine

yoga *m* yoga

yogur *m* yog(h)urt

yuca *f* yucca

yugo *m* yoke

Yugoslavia *f* Yugoslavia

yugoslavo *a & m* Yugoslav

yunque *m* anvil

yunta *f* yoke

wáter /'(g)water/ *m* toilet

Web *m* /'(g)web/. **el ~** the Web

whisky /'(g)wiski/ *m* whisky

xenofobia *f* xenophobia

xilófono *m* xylophone

zafarrancho m (confusión) mess; (riña) quarrel

zafarse vpr escape; get out of <obligación etc>; (Mex, dislocarse) dislocate

zafiro m sapphire

zaga f rear; (en deportes) defence. **a la ~** behind

zaguán m hall

zaherir [4] vt hurt

zahorí m dowser

zaino a <caballo> chestnut; <vaca> black

zalamer|ía f flattery. **~o** a flattering. ● m flatterer

zamarra f (piel) sheepskin; (prenda) sheepskin jacket

zamarrear vt shake

zamba f South American dance

zambulli|da f dive; (baño) dip. □ **~rse** vpr dive

zamparse vpr gobble up

zanahoria f carrot

zancad|a f stride. **~illa** f trip. **hacer una ~illa a uno** trip s.o. up

zanc|o m stilt. **~udo** a long-legged; <ave> wading. ● m (LAm) mosquito

zanganear vi idle

zángano m drone. ● m & f (persona) idler

zangolotear vt shake. ● vi rattle; <persona> fidget

zanja f ditch; (para tuberías etc) trench. **~r** vt (fig) settle

zapat|ear vi tap with one's feet. **~ería** f shoe shop; (arte) shoemaking. **~ero** m shoemaker; (el que remienda zapatos) cobbler. **~illa** f slipper; (de deportes) trainer. **~ de ballet** ballet shoe. **~o** m shoe

zarand|a f sieve. **~ear** vt (sacudir) shake

zarcillo m earring

zarpa f paw

zarpar vi set sail, weigh anchor

zarza f bramble. **~mora** f blackberry

zarzuela f Spanish operetta

zigzag m zigzag. **~uear** vi zigzag

zinc m zinc

zócalo m skirting-board; (pedestal) plinth; (Mex, plaza) main square

zodiaco m, **zodíaco** m zodiac

zona f zone; (área) area

zoo m zoo. **~logía** f zoology. **~lógico** a zoological

zoólogo m zoologist

zopenco a stupid. ● m idiot

zoquete m blockhead

zorr|a f vixen **~illo** m (LAm) skunk. **~o** m fox

zorzal m thrush

zozobra f (fig) anxiety. **~r** vi founder

zueco m clog

zumb|ar vt Ⅰ give <golpe etc>. ● vi buzz. **~ido** m buzzing

zumo m juice

zurci|do m darning. **~r** [9] vt darn

zurdo a left-handed; <mano> left

zurrar vt (fig, Ⅰ, dar golpes) beat (up)

zutano m so-and-so

Test yourself with word games

This section contains a number of word games which will help you to use your dictionary more effectively and to build up your knowledge of Spanish vocabulary and usage in a fun and entertaining way. You will find answers to all puzzles and games at the end of the section.

1 X files

A freak power cut in the office has caused all the computers to go down. When they are re-booted, all the words on the screen have become mysteriously jumbled. Use the English to Spanish side of the dictionary to help you decipher these Spanish names of everyday office and computer equipment.

ZIPLÁ

ÓCNAJ

AERODONRD

PRACATE

ODCSI

MOAG

GLOBAFÍRO

TAPALLAN

2 Odd meaning Out

Watch out: one word can have different meanings. In the
following exercise, only two of the suggested translations are
correct. Use the dictionary to spot the odd one out, then find
the correct Spanish translation for it.

vela	**sail**
	veil
	candle
bote	**boot**
	jar
	boat
talón	**cheque**
	heel
	talon
suave	**smooth**
	suave
	soft
muelle	**wharf**
	mussel
	jetty
bufete	**buffet**
	writing desk
	lawyer's office

3 Mystery Word

The following crossword is composed entirely of musical
instruments. Put the Spanish translation of the pictures of
instruments in the right boxes to form the name of a Spanish
composer in the vertical column.

The composer is _ _ _ _ _ _   _ _ _ _ _ _ _ _ _ _ _ _ _ _ _ _ _ .

4 Doña Paquita's shooting stars

Doña Paquita is very good at predicting the future, but she is not very good at using the subjunctive. Help her to replace the verbs between brackets with the correct part of the present subjunctive.

ARIES: Estás en el apogeo de tu vida, tanto en tu carrera profesional como en el ámbito personal. Pero tienes que evitar que todo (echarse) a perder. Con la influencia maléfica de Saturnio situada actualmente en tu astro, siempre es posible que (suceder) algo negativo. Además, los aries son impacientes por naturaleza y quieren que las cosas (hacerse) lo antes posible. Por lo tanto te aconsejo que no (precipitarse) a la hora de tomar decisiones importantes. Aunque tu situación económica te (parecer) segura, no (contar) con el apoyo de los demás. Sin embargo, con el aspecto favorable de Venus es muy posible que dentro de poco (conocer) a tu pareja ideal. ¡No (dejar) de reconocerlo! ¡Suerte!

5 Write it right

A mother and daughter are getting a little bit annoyed with each other. In the fraught atmosphere, many of the Spanish accents and some punctuation marks have been left out of the dialogue. You have a box full of characters to be substituted or added in the right place in the text. They must all be used up.

— ¡Raquel! ¿Donde estás?

— Aquí, mama. ¿Que pasa? Por que me gritas así?

— Porque tu no me haces caso. Mira, ¿cuando vas a ordenar tu habitación?

— Cuando tenga tiempo. Quizá manana. No me des la lata ahora!

— Eso me dices todos los días, pero jamas lo haces. No me ayudas nada en la casa y encima me contestas mal. Eres una sinverguenza y pienso decirselo a tu padre cuando vuelva.

— Perdon, mama. Lo siento. Me pasé, lo se.

---

6 Crowded suitcase

You are at the airport on your way to visit your Welsh cousins in Patagonia when you are told that your suitcase is overweight. Luckily, you had packed a number of things you did not need because you had forgotten that it was wintertime in the southern hemisphere. Decide which 5 items to jettison from your luggage.

gafas de sol   calcetines de lana   alpargatas   camisón

esterilla   cepillo de dientes   camiseta

crema bronceadora   camisa de manga corta   cinturón

bañador   abrigo   unas revistas

pantalón corto   bufanda

7 Crossword

Across

1. we inhabit
7. dative of 'them'
9. scarcely
10. the letter 'n' as spoken (or written)
11. evade – present subjunctive
   (1st or 3rd person singular)
13. reindeer, in reverse
14. swim! – polite imperative (singular)
15. nor
16. clear
18. religious sister
20. go! – familiar imperative (plural)
21. I heard
22. woman's name
23. do! – familiar imperative (singular)
24. sarcasm

Down

2. mountaineers
3. to be unaware of
4. absence
5. wave (figurative sense)
6. paths
8. present subjunctive of 'ser'
   (1st or 3rd person singular)
12. you (singular) will be worth
13. half of the number eleven
17. they were hearing
19. ounce
21. plural of 'te'

8 Liar, liar

Miguel is telling his parents what he did on his day off while his younger brother Félix was meant to be at school, but he makes a blunder. Once the truth is out, as a punishment they both have to write out the story with the correct plural endings and pronouns. Use the verb tables at the back of the dictionary to help you make the necessary alterations to the text.

Iba andando a la playa cuando de repente me encontré con Paco. Me acompañó hasta la tienda de la esquina donde dijo:

—Mira, ¿quieres que te preste mi bicicleta para que llegues más rápido?

Estaba muy cansado y no quería seguir caminando así que acepté con mucho gusto y me fui contentísimo por el camino. Me costó un poco controlar la bici porque era tan grande y casi me caigo un par de veces. La gente me miraba como si estuviera loco y varias personas me gritaban "¡Bravo!"

Cuando estaba ya en la playa se me salieron los pies de los pedales y perdí el control. Bajaba a toda velocidad hacia el agua, de repente frené y - ¡plaf! - me caí al agua.

Más tarde, me dio vergüenza devolverle la bicicleta a Paco y naturalmente se echó a reír:

—Pero, ¿qué pasó? - me dijo - ¿te diste un buen baño? Le contesté:

—Fue culpa de él - y dije dándome la vuelta hacia atrás—¡Nunca más voy a montar en un tándem contigo, Félix!

9 Hidden words—false friends

Hidden in the grid are nine Spanish words. First look at the
list of false friends below - look up the translation of the
Spanish words listed, then using your own knowledge and the
dictionary, find the translations of the English to search for
in the grid.

O	S	É	T	R	O	C	S	E	D
H	I	G	A	E	C	Í	J	A	O
A	D	O	R	A	R	H	D	E	L
F	O	B	I	N	S	A	H	O	M
N	F	T	É	P	N	L	E	P	A
Ú	R	E	L	A	V	E	Ú	O	S
T	E	R	P	T	O	T	I	T	É
A	C	M	D	Z	A	A	S	I	T
M	E	A	C	R	X	P	O	N	U
S	R	O	J	O	N	Í	A	E	L

English	Spanish	
pie	pie	....
dote	dote	....
red	red	....
tuna	atún	....
lid	lid	....
fin	fin	....
rude	rudo	....
mole	mole	....
tea	tea	....

10 Word Families

It's good to build up word families to increase your vocabulary, but it's important to know the part of speech of each word and how it can fit into a sentence. Pick the right word from each family to go in the space. Everything you need to know for this exercise is in the dictionary.

le falta	preparado preparación preparó
tuverion que	esconder escondrijo esconderse
una mujer ... en años	entrada entró entrante
no se hace así en la ...	actualmente actualidad actualización
y por ... agregarla el agua	ultimar últimamente último
la industria ... de esa región	floreciente florista florida
su timidez me	desconcierto desconcertante deconcierta

11 My life's a mess

Pilar Jiménez has a busy schedule but she is a creature of habit and likes to stick to her daily routine. The order of her normal workday has been muddled up in the sentences below. Link up the matching halves of each sentence in the two columns and then try to put the complete sentences in sequence. Be careful, some can link up with more than one of the other column, so you'll have to do them all before you can be sure which go together best.

sólo lee el periódico	para comer
llega a casa	lee la correspondencia
nunca toma café durante	antes de las nueve y media
normalmente saca al perro	muy cansada
le gusta	durante el viaje de vuelta
primero	antes de acostarse
suele salir a mediodía	una reunión
prefiere ducharse antes	por la mañana
siempre entra al trabajo	dar una vuelta antes de volver a la oficina
insiste en tener las reuniones	de cenar

12 Recipe of the Week

The printers have left out some important words from this recipe. Can you supply the missing words from the jumble below?

COCINA: Receta de la semana

Limpiar y lavar los .... y cortarlos en rodajas finas. Calentar el ...... en una sartén de hierro y freír la ..... picada, los puerros y dos dientes de .... . Agregar el vaso de .... y dejar cocer a .... lento durante 10 minutos. Sazonar con ...., ... y ...... picado.

En otra sartén aparte, saltear los trocitos de ..... en el resto del aceite de oliva hasta que empiecen a dorarse. Regar con dos cucharadas de ..... y dejar cocer unos minutos más. Incorporar las .... y la ......

Distribuir los puerros uniformemente en platos calientes y colocar el pollo salteado encima. Salar al gusto. Servir acompañado de una guarnición de ...... al vapor.

puerros	aceite de oliva	**fuego**
cebolla	ajo	vino blanco	**sal**
pimienta	**pollo**	**perejil**	jerez
aceitunas	**nata**	patatas

13 Link-up

The Spanish nouns on the left-hand side are all made up of two separate words but they have been split apart. Try to link up the two halves of each compound, then do the same for the English compounds in the right-hand columns. Now you can match up the Spanish compounds with their English translations.

espanta	corchos	pencil	sport
sujeta	pipas	birth	cleaner
porta	césped	paper	screw
agua	aviones	flame	day
saca	años	spoil	crow
lanza	puntas	lawn	sharpener
limpia	fiestas	aircraft	thrower
corta	papeles	pipe	clip
cumple	llamas	scare	carrier
saca	pájaros	cork	mower

Answers

1

lápiz	disco
cajón	goma
ordenador	bolígrafo
carpeta	pantalla

2

veil – velo	suave – zalamero
boot – bota	mussel – mejillón
talon – garra	buffet – bufé

3

gaita	laúd
guitarra	pandereta
flauta	tambor
acordeón	castañuelas

The composer's name is Granados (1867-1916)

4

se eche	parezca
suceda	cuentes
se hagan	conozcas
te precipites	dejes

5

— ¡Raquel! ¿Dónde estás?
— Aquí, mamá. ¿Qué pasa? ¿Por qué me gritas así?
— Porque tú no me haces caso. Mira, ¿cuándo vas a ordenar tu
habitación?
— Cuando tenga tiempo. Quizá mañana. ¡No me des de la lata ahora!
— Eso me dices todos los días, pero jamás lo haces. No me ayudas nada
en la casa y encima me contestas mal. Eres una sinvergüenza y
pienso decírselo a tu padre cuando vuelva.
— Perdón, mamá. Lo siento. Me pasé, lo sé.

6

alpargatas
esterilla
crema bronceadora
camisa de manga corta
pantalón corto

7

Across	Down
1 habitamos	2 alpinistas
7 les	3 ignorar
9 apenas	4 ausencia
10 ene	5 oleada
11 evada	6 senderos
13 oner (=reno)	8 sea
14 nade	12 valdrás
15 ni	13 on (from
16 claro	('once')
18 sor	17 oían
20 id	19 onza
21 oí	21 os
22 Marisa	
23 haz	
24 sarcasmo	

8

There are two boys going to the beach, the narrator and Félix. The bike is a tandem.

Íbamos   nos encontramos   Nos acompañó   nos dijo

—Mirad, ¿queréis que os preste...?

Estábamos muy cansados y no queríamos   aceptamos

y nos fuimos contentísimos   Nos costó

casi nos caemos   nos miraba

como si estuviéramos locos   nos gritaban

estábamos   se nos salieron   perdimos el control

Bajábamos   frenamos   Nos dio vergüenza

¿os disteis un buen baño?

Note that the second person plural verb endings given here are all the `vosotros' form used in Spain. In Latin America this would be replaced by the `ustedes' form, as follows:

—Miren, ¿quieren que les preste ...?

¿se dieron un buen baño?

9

```
O  S  É  T  R  O  C  S  E  D
H  I  G  A  E  C  Í  J  A  O
A  D  O  R  A  R  H  D  E  L
F  O  B  I  N  S  A  H  O  M
N  F  T  Ë  P  N  L  E  P  A
Ú  R  E  L  A  V  E  Ú  O  S
T  E  R  P  T  O  T  I  T  É
A  C  M  D  Z  A  A  S  I  T
M  E  A  C  R  X  P  O  N  U
S  R  O  J  O  N  Í  A  E  L
```

foot	empanada
dowry	adorar
	(= dote on)
net	rojo
torch	té
fight	tapa
end	aleta
rough	descortés
prickly pear	atún
mass, bulk	topo

10

preparación
esconderse
entrada
actualidad
último
floreciente
desconcierta

11

siempre entra al trabajo antes de las nueve y media
primero lee la correspondencia
insiste en tener las reuniones por la mañana
nunca toma café durante una reunión
suele salir a mediodía para comer
le gusta dar una vuelta antes de volver a la oficina
sólo lee el periódico durante el viaje de vuelta
llega a casa muy cansada
prefiere ducharse antes de cenar
normalmente saca al perro antes de acostarse

12

Limpiar y lavar los PUERROS y cortarlos en rodajas finas.
Calentar el ACEITE DE OLIVA en una sartén de hierro y freír la
CEBOLLA picada, los puerros y dos dientes de AJO. Agregar el vaso de
VINO BLANCO y dejar cocer a FUEGO lento durante 10 minutos.
Sazonar con SAL, PIMIENTA y PEREJIL picado.

En otra sartén aparte, saltear los trocitos de POLLO en el resto del
aceite de oliva hasta que empiecen a dorarse. Regar con dos cucharadas
de JEREZ y dejar cocer unos minutos más. Incorporar las ACEITUNAS y
la NATA.

Distribuir los puerros uniformemente en platos calientes y colocar el
pollo salteado encima. Salar al gusto. Servir acompañado de una
guarnición de PATATAS al vapor.

13

espantapájaros	=	scarecrow
sujetapapeles	=	paper clip
portaaviones	=	aircraft carrier
aguafiestas	=	spoilsport
sacacorchos	=	corkscrew
lanzallamas	=	flame thrower
cumpleaños	=	birthday
limpiapipas	=	pipe cleaner
cortacésped	=	lawn-mower
sacapuntas	=	pencil sharpener

A–Z of the Spanish-speaking countries of the world

Argentina
Official Name: The Argentine Republic
Capital: Buenos Aires
Currency: peso
Area: 1,073,809 square miles (2,780,092 square kilometers)
Population: 35,672,000 (1997 estimate)

Bolivia
Official Name: Republic of Bolivia
Administrative capital: La Paz
Judicial and legal capital: Sucre
Currency: boliviano
Area: 424,162 square miles (1,098,580 square kilometers)
Population: 7,767,000 (1997 estimate)

Chile
Official Name: The Republic of Chile
Capital: Santiago
Currency: peso
Area: 292,132 square miles (756,622 square kilometers)
Population: 14,622,000 (1997 estimate)

Colombia
Official Name: The Republic of Colombia
Capital: Bogotá
Currency: peso
Area: 440,365 square miles (1,140,105 square kilometers)
Population: 40,214,723 (1997 estimate)

Costa Rica
Official Name: The Republic of Costa Rica
Capital: San José
Currency: colón
Area: 19,707 square miles (51,022 square kilometers)
Population: 3,464,000 (1997 estimate)

Cuba
Official Name: The Republic of Cuba
Capital: Havana/La Habana
Currency: peso
Area: 42,820 square miles (110,860 square kilometers)
Population: 11,059,000 (1997 estimate)

Dominican Republic/República Dominicana
Capital: Santo Domingo
Currency: peso
Area: 18,704 square miles (48,442 square kilometers)
Population: 8,190,000 (1997 estimate)

Ecuador
Official Name: The Republic of Ecuador
Capital: Quito
Currency: sucre
Area: 109,484 square miles (270,670 square kilometers)
Population: 12,174,628 (1998 estimate)

El Salvador

Official Name: The Republic of El Salvador
Capital: San Salvador
Currency: colón
Area: 8,260 square miles (21,393 square kilometers)
Population: 5,118,599 (1992)

Guatemala

Official Name: The Republic of Guatemala
Capital: Guatemala City/Ciudad de Guatemala
Currency: quetzal
Area: 42,056 square miles (108,889 square kilometers)
Population: 10,928,000 (1996 estimate)

Honduras

Official Name: The Republic of Honduras
Capital: Tegucigalpa
Currency: lempira
Area: 43,294 square miles (112,088 square kilometers)
Population: 5,294,000 (1994 estimate)

Mexico/México

Official Name: The United Mexican States
Capital: Mexico City/México
Currency: peso
Area: 756,200 square miles (1,958,200 square kilometers)
Population: 94,400,000 (1997 provisional estimate)

Nicaragua

Official Name: The Republic of Nicaragua
Capital: Managua
Currency: córdoba
Area: 46,448 square miles (120,254 square kilometers)
Population: 4,357,099 (1995)

Panama/Panamá

Official Name: The Republic of Panama
Capital: Panama City/Ciudad de Panamá
Currency: balboa
Area: 29,773 square miles (77,082 square kilometers)
Population: 2,719,000 (1997 estimate)

Paraguay

Official Name: The Republic of Paraguay
Capital: Asunción
Currency: guaraní
Area: 157,108 square miles (406,752 square kilometers)
Population: 5,085,000 (1997 estimate)

Peru/Perú

Official Name: The Republic of Peru
Capital: Lima
Currency: sol
Area: 496,414 square miles (1,285,216 square kilometers)
Population: 24,371,000 (1997 estimate)

Puerto Rico

Capital: San Juan
Currency: US dollar
Area: 3,460 square miles (8,959 square kilometers)
Population: 3,833,000 (1998 estimate)

Spain/España

Official Name: The Kingdom of Spain
Capital: Madrid
Currency: peseta
Area: 194,959 square miles

(505,750 square kilometers)
Population: 39,371,147 (1998
estimate)

Uruguay

Official Name: The Oriental
Republic of Uruguay
Capital: Montevideo
Currency: peso
Area: 68,063 square miles
(176,215 square kilometers)
Population: 3,221,000 (1997
estimate)

Venezuela

Official Name: The Republic of
Venezuela
Capital: Caracas
Currency: bolivar
Area: 352,279 square miles
(912,050 square kilometers)
Population: 22,777,000 (1997
estimate)

Calendar of traditions, festivals, and holidays in Spanish-speaking countries

January
1 8 15 22 29
2 9 16 23 30
3 10 17 24 31
4 11 18 25
5 12 19 26
6 13 **20** 27
7 14 21 28

February
1 8 15 22
2 9 16 23
3 10 17 24
4 11 18 25
5 12 19 **26**
6 13 20 27
7 14 **21** 28

March
1 8 15 22 29
2 9 16 23 30
3 10 17 24 31
4 11 18 25
5 12 19 26
6 13 20 27
7 14 21 28

April
1 8 15 22 29
2 9 16 **23** 30
3 10 17 24 31
4 11 18 25
5 12 19 26
7 **14** 21 28

May
1 8 15 22 29
2 9 16 23 30
3 10 17 24 31
4 11 18 **25**
5 12 19 26
6 13 20 27
7 14 21 28

June
1 8 15 22 29
2 9 16 23 30
3 10 17 **24**
4 11 18 25
5 12 19 26
6 13 **20** 27
7 14 21 28

July
1 8 15 22 29
2 **9** 16 23 30
3 10 17 24 31
4 11 18 **25**
5 12 19 26
6 13 20 27
7 14 21 **28**

August
1 8 15 22 29
2 9 16 23 30
3 **10 17** 24 31
4 11 18 **25**
5 12 19 26
6 13 20 27
7 14 21 28

September
1 8 **15** 22 29
2 9 16 23 30
3 10 17 24
4 **11 18** 25
5 12 19 26
6 **13** 20 27
7 14 21 28

October
1 8 15 22 29
2 9 16 23 30
3 10 17 24 **31**
4 11 18 25
5 **12** 19 26
6 13 20 27
7 14 21 28

November
1 8 15 22 29
2 9 16 23 30
3 **10** 17 24
4 11 18 25
5 12 19 26
6 13 **20** 27
7 14 21 28

December
1 8 15 22 29
2 9 16 23 30
3 10 17 24 **31**
4 11 18 **25**
5 12 19 26
6 13 20 27
7 14 21 **28**

1 January

Año Nuevo (New Year´s Day).
A public holiday in all Spanish-speaking countries.

5 January (Mexico)

Día de la Constitución
(Constitution Day). A public holiday.

6 January

Día de Reyes
(Epiphany/Twelfth Night).
In many Spanish-speaking countries, this is when presents are given, rather than on Christmas Day.

20 January

San Sebastián (Saint Sebastian's Day). Celebrated in Spain with parades, sporting events, and bullfights, it is also a day of celebration and dancing for the people of the Basque city that bears the name of the saint.

2 February

La Candelaria (Candlemas).
An occasion for celebrations and parades in many Spanish-speaking countries.

3 February

Fiesta de San Blas (patron saint of Paraguay). A public holiday.

21 February (Mexico)

Anniversary of the birth of Benito Juárez, a famous nineteenth-century statesman, who was twice president. A public holiday.

26 February

Aberri Eguna - Basque national day and a public holiday in the Basque country of Spain.

12–19 March

Las Fallas are one of the best known *fiestas* in Spain. They are held in Valencia in eastern Spain. The high point of the celebration is on the last night, when the *cabezudos* (carnival figures with large heads), which have been carefully prepared by the *falleros*, are paraded through the streets and then burned, all this to the accompaniment of an enormous fireworks display.

14 April (Paraguay)

Día de la Independencia.
A public holiday.

23 April

San Jordi The feast day of Catalonia's patron saint. According to custom, women give men books and men give women roses on this Catalan version of St Valentine´s Day.

1 May

Día del Trabajo (Labor Day).
A public holiday in all Spanish-speaking countries.

5 May (Mexico)

The anniversary of the victory of the state of Puebla against the French invasion of 1862. A public holiday.

25 May (Argentina)

The anniversary of the May revolution of 1810.

20 June (Argentina)

Día de la Bandera (Argentinian National Day). A public holiday.

(Colombia)

Día de la Independencia. A public holiday.

24 June

San Juan (Feast of St John). Traditionally fires are lit on the night of San Juan in order to keep away the cold of winter. In some places, people jump over the fires and in others the faithful will try to walk through them barefoot. The custom is slowly dying out, but continues in many parts of the Spanish-speaking world.

5 July (Venezuela)

Día de la Independencia. A public holiday.

6–14 July

Sanfermines. The festival of *el encierro* (the 'running of the bulls'), takes place in Pamplona in northern Spain. The animals are released into the barricaded streets and people run in front of them, in honor of the town´s patron saint, San Fermín, who was put to death by being dragged by bulls.

9 July (Argentina)

Día de la Independencia. A public holiday.

25 July

Fiesta de Santiago (Feast of St James). The famous *Camino de Santiago*, the pilgrimage of thousands of people from all over Spain and many other parts of Europe to the holy city of Santiago de Compostela, takes place in the week leading up to St James' Day, 25 July. The city also has its *fiestas* around this time. The streets are full of musicians and performers for two weeks of celebrations culminating in the *Festival del Apóstol*.

28 July (Peru)

Día de la Independencia. A public holiday.

6 August (Bolivia)

Día de la Independencia. A public holiday.

10 August (Ecuador)

Primer Grito de Independencia. A public holiday commemorating the first cry of independence in 1809.

17 August (Argentina)

A public holiday to celebrate the anniversary of the death of the San Martín who liberated Argentina from Spanish rule in 1816.

25 August (Uruguay)

Día de la Independencia. A public holiday.

11 September

Día Nacional de Cataluña.

Catalonian National Day and a public holiday in Catalonia.

13 September (Mexico)

Commemoration of the *Niños Héroes* (child heroes) who fell while defending the castle of Chapultepec against European invaders in 1847.

15 September (Mexico)

Conmemoración de la Proclamación de la Independencia. Throughout the country, at 11 o'clock at night, there is a communal shout, *El Grito*, in memory of Padre Hidalgo's cry of independence from the Spanish in the town of Dolores.

18 September (Chile)

Día de la Independencia. A public holiday.

12 October

Día de la Hispanidad. A public holiday, this is also **Columbus Day**, which is celebrated in all Spanish-speaking countries, as well as the US, in commemoration of the discovery of the Americas by Christopher Columbus in 1492. In Spanish-speaking countries of the Americas, it is also called the **Día de la Raza** (literally, Day of the Race) in celebration of the *mestizaje*, the mingling of races, which gave birth to the populations of today.

31 October

Todos los Santos (All Saints). People all over the Spanish-speaking world flock to the cemeteries on this and the following day *el día de los Difuntos/Muertos* to put flowers on the graves of relatives and friends and to remember the dead. In Mexico this is an important festival in which Catholic traditions are mixed with those of pre-Hispanic religions.

10 November (Argentina)

Fiesta de la Tradición. This festival takes place throughout the country but is especially important in the town of San Antonio de Areco, near Buenos Aires. The capital also holds a festival in November, the **Semana de Buenos Aires**, in honor of its patron saint San Martín de Tours.

20 November (Mexico)

Día de la Revolución de 1910. A public holiday to celebrate the revolution of 1910.

2 December (Mexico)

Virgen de Guadalupe. Celebrations are held in honor of the patron saint of the country, with music and dancers, in particular the *concheros*, who dance, wearing bells around their ankles, to the sound of stringed instruments and conches.

25 December

Navidad (Christmas Day). A time of great religious cele-bration in all Spanish-speaking countries. In many places, reenactments of the nativity are held, with a variety of traditions, parades, and costumes.

28 December

Día de los Inocentes. This is the equivalent to April Fool's Day. In most Spanish-speaking countries it is a day for playing tricks on people. And if you trick someone into lending you money for that day, you keep it and tell them *que te lo paguen los Santos Inocentes* (let the Holy Innocents pay you back).

31 December

La noche de Fin de Año.
This is often the occasion for parties, and at midnight the New Year is welcomed with much noise and merrymaking. In Spain and in many other Spanish-speaking countries, the families gather together twelve seconds before midnight *para tomar las uvas* (to see the New Year in by eating one grape on each chime of the clock) for good luck.

Movable feasts and holidays

Martes de Carnaval (Shrove Tuesday). The last Tuesday before the beginning of *Cuaresma* (Lent). *Carnaval* is celebrated in many Spanish-speaking countries just before this date. In many places, there are masked balls and parades. The biggest in Spain are those of Cádiz, on the south coast, and Madrid, where a strange ceremony called *el entierro de la sardina* (literally the burial of the sardine) takes place. In Mexico, the best-known are in Veracruz and Mazatlán.

Pascua (Easter) - **Semana Santa** (Holy Week). The week leading up to Easter Sunday is the most important time of religious celebration throughout the Spanish-speaking world. In many places, there are processions in which statues of Christ or the Virgin Mary, often

covered in jewels and flowers, are carried to the church.

Seville's famous **Feria de abril** (April festival) takes place in the week following Easter. The site of the *feria* is decked out with hundreds of *casetas* or small marquees, hired by companies or private individuals, in which people entertain, eat *tapas*, drink *manzanilla* (a pale dry sherry), play music, and dance *sevillanas*, the popular dances of Andalucía. Many people dress up in colourful traditional costumes, some of them on horseback or in horse-drawn carriages.

Corpus Christi - 9 weeks after Easter is celebrated in most Spanish-speaking countries with religious parades.

A–Z of Spanish life and culture

ABC
One of the Spanish national daily newspapers. *ABC* holds conservative political views and is a firm supporter of the monarchy. It is considered to be one of the high-quality newspapers in Spain.

aberzale or abertzale
This term is used to refer to the political and social ideology of Basque nationalism, and to its followers. It embraces different degrees of radicalism in the movement's objectives and in its support of violence as a means to achieve independence.

alcalde/alcaldesa
President of the AYUNTAMIENTO (local council), who is in charge of running the administration of the MUNICIPIO. The *alcalde* is elected by proportional representation from the candidates put forward by the political parties. The approximate equivalent position in Britain would be that of mayor.

ambulatorio (de la seguridad social)
Medical centre, part of the social security system, where people can go to see a MÉDICO DE CABECERA (general practitioner). It is a day centre and does not take in-patients. It has the same function as the CENTRO DE SALUD, but is generally bigger.

Antena 3
One of the main national Spanish commercial TV channels, broadcasting films and entertainment programmes.

As
Daily newspaper dealing exclusively with sports information and reports, mainly football. It is published in Madrid and distributed over the whole of Spain.

autonomía
One of the autonomous regions of which Spain is made up. There are 19 *autonomías* in Spain: Andalucía, Aragón, Baleares, Canarias, Cantabria, Castilla-La Mancha, Castilla y León, Cataluña, Ceuta, Comunidad Valenciana, Extremadura, Galicia, La Rioja, Madrid, Melilla, Navarra, PAÍS VASCO (or EUSKADI), Principado de Asturias, and Región de Murcia. Each *autonomía* has its own administrative, legislative, and judicial powers and its own assemblies or parliaments.

AVE
High-speed train that completes the Madrid-Seville route in two and a half hours. It was introduced to coincide with the international exhibition, Expo-92, that took place in Seville in 1992. It is the only high-speed train in use at the moment in

Spain, although there are plans to use them on other routes.

ayuntamiento

Governing body (similar to a council) that is in charge of the administration of a MUNICIPIO. It comprises the ALCALDE and the CONCEJALES, each of them with responsibility for a particular area of government. The building where the ALCALDE and CONCEJALES work is also called the *ayuntamiento*.

bable

Bable is spoken in Asturias. It is very similar to Castilian.

bacalao or bakalao

Name given in Spain to modern music that has a very strong repetitive rhythm, such as house music.

Bachillerato

Educational level that comes after the ESO and before the COU, for pupils between 16 and 18. It comprises two years of non-compulsory education. This level is normally taken by pupils who want to go on to university and it has an academic focus. Pupils can choose one from among several *modalidades* (groups of subjects) to study. These *modalidades* are made up of a small number of core subjects (such as Spanish language and the language of the AUTONOMÍA) common to all of them, plus a combination of subjects that are geared more to sciences or arts, etc., according to the pupils' interests and to what they want to study at university. In addition to these,

they can choose a number of optional subjects. The qualification that is awarded after completing these two years is called *Título de Bachiller*.

bar

In Spain a *bar* sells all types of drinks, hot and cold, alcoholic and non-alcoholic. *Bares* also sell snack food such as TAPAS or RACIONES, or *bocadillos* (sandwiches made with a baguette-type loaf), and pastries to have with coffee. They can also offer full meals at lunchtime. *Bares* open all day, from early in the morning, for people to have breakfast, till late in the evening (sometimes just before midnight). There is sometimes little distinction between a BAR and a CAFETERÍA.

barrio

Area of a city or town. Many of them have a very strong identity and they often have their own residents' association that organizes events.

BNG

Political party of Galicia with a nationalist ideology.

BOE – Boletín Oficial del Estado

Name of the official news bulletin published by the government. It publishes all general regulations and laws that have been passed by Parliament. A new law comes into effect 21 days after it has appeared in the BOE.

bonhotel or bonotel

Voucher with which the holder

can book nights in a hotel at a special rate. They are sold by travel agents and some department stores and banks.

bonobús
Special ticket that allows the purchaser to travel by bus a certain number of times (normally 10), at a cheaper rate than if individual tickets are purchased. On boarding the bus, the holder has to enter the ticket in a machine that punches out a small square in the ticket. *Bonobuses* can be bought in the ESTANCOS, at newspaper kiosks, and at special ticket stands.

bonoloto
National lottery that runs four times a week. The player has to bet on six numbers which he or she marks in a square consisting of forty-nine numbers. The winner is the person whose numbers coincide with the numbers that are drawn. The prizes are normally substantial.

bonometro
Special ticket that allows the purchaser to travel by bus or underground a certain number of times (normally 10), at a cheaper rate than if individual tickets are purchased. The ticket has to be put through a machine that registers the number of trips remaining and then prints the date and code of each journey. They can be bought in the ESTANCOS, at newspaper kiosks, and at special ticket stands.

BUP
The old educational level that used to exist in place of the current BACHILLERATO before the 1990 educational reform. The *BUP* used to last three years, whereas now the *Bachillerato* is only two, since the *reforma* (education reform) increased by one year the length of compulsory education. Like the current BACHILLERATO, it was taken by pupils who wanted to go on to university education.

cabalgata de Reyes
Parade that takes place in the streets of villages, towns, and cities on 5 January, the night before the DÍA DE REYES, the day on which Christmas presents are exchanged in Spain. The parade includes the *Reyes Magos* (the Three Wise Men) coming into the village, town, or city, with cartloads of presents to give to the people. It is an event aimed mainly at children, since they believe that it is the *Reyes Magos* who give out the presents.

Cadena SER
Commercial radio station offering a high level of information and political debate. Its political views are considered left of centre.

cafetería
Establishment with tables where you can sit down and have a coffee or other hot drink, and pastries or cakes. It also serves many other types of drink, such as soft drinks and beer. Often there is a

supplementary charge for sitting at a table. *Cafeterías* are often combined with BARES and there is often little distinction between them in terms of what you can have.

Cámara de los diputados

The lower of the two chambers that form the Spanish CORTES or Parliament. Its members, the *diputados*, are elected by proportional representation during the general elections and they meet to debate issues of current national and international politics and to vote on proposed legislation. The place where the *diputados* meet is also called *la Cámara de los diputados* or EL CONGRESO.

campamentos

Summer camps where groups of children go to spend their summer holidays. Every day there are different activities for the children, ranging from ceramics to survival games. Some *campamentos* are organized by large companies (such as CORREOS or banks), some by the councils.

Canal + (Canal plus)

Privately owned television channel specializing in showing films that have been recently released. It is paid for by subscription and the subscriber must have a decoder to be able to receive the channel. Films are shown on this channel before going to the national television channels.

Canal 9

Television channel of Cataluña, Valencia, and Baleares. It broadcasts in CATALÁN.

Canal Sur

Television channel of Andalucía.

CAP – Curso de adaptación pedagógica

Course taken by graduates who have a degree in a subject other than education, and who want to teach in COLEGIOS or INSTITUTOS.

carnaval

Popular festival that takes place before Lent. Schools give three or more days' holiday, depending on the AUTONOMÍA. During *carnaval* there are street parades and festivals in most towns and cities, at which people dress up in fancy dress. The *carnavales* in Cádiz and the Canary Islands are particularly spectacular.

carnet de conducir

The card given to people who have passed their driving test. It must always be carried with you when you are driving.

carnet de identidad

Identity card that is compulsory for all Spanish residents over 14 years of age. It is also called *DNI*, short for *Documento Nacional de Identidad* (National Identity Document). This card, which states the name of the person, their date of birth, their address, and the name of their parents, must be carried at all times. It also has a picture of the person and a code which refers to the person's fingerprints.

Each person is given an identity card number, consisting of a series of figures followed by a letter. The identity card number is the same as the NIF, and people are required to give it as proof of identity and as part of their personal details when filling in official forms, applying for a loan, etc.

castellano

The language that is spoken all over Spain and, with regional differences, in most of Latin America. It is also referred to as 'español'. A foreigner learning Spanish is learning *castellano*. *Castellano* is the official language of the whole of Spain and is a compulsory subject in schools in all AUTONOMÍAS. Like CATALÁN and GALLEGO, it is a member of the group of Romance languages that derived from Latin.

catalán

The main language spoken in Cataluña, and, with some regional differences, in Valencia and Baleares. In all these areas it is the official language, together with CASTELLANO (Castilian), and is an official requirement for many official and academic positions as well as a compulsory subject in school. *Catalán* is spoken by around 11 million people. A large number of books are published in *catalán*, either originally written in this language or translated into it. *Catalán*, like CASTELLANO and GALLEGO, is part of the group of Romance languages that are derived from Latin. The Catalan name for this language is *Catalá*.

cava

Spanish sparkling wine, made by the same method as Champagne. *Cava* is made in the area of Cataluña and produced to a very high standard. There are three types, depending on dryness: *Brut*, *Sec*, and *Semi-Sec*, *Brut* being the driest.

CC – Coalición Canaria

Political party of the Canary Islands with a nationalist ideology.

CCOO – Comisiones Obreros

One of the main trade unions in Spain. It is a unitary national organization, drawing its members from all occupations. It has historical links with the Spanish Communist Party. Nowadays, it is still considered to be associated with the current political parties of the left.

CEIP – Colegio de Educación Infantil y Primaria

Official name given to the COLEGIOS ESTATALES (state infant and primary schools).

centro de salud

Medical centre, part of the social security system, where people can go to see a MÉDICO DE CABECERA (general practitioner). It is a day centre and does not take in-patients. It has the same function as the AMBULATORIO, but is generally smaller.

charcutería

Name used to refer to a shop or supermarket counter selling pork products, such as *chorizo* (spicy cured sausage), cured and cooked ham, sausages, etc.

CiU

Political party in Cataluña. It has a nationalist ideology and is represented in the central parliament as well as in the GENERALITAT, the parliament of Cataluña. Its influence in central government has been considerable, as often the main political party in power (whether PSOE or PP) has been forced to form a pact with it in order to be able to outvote the opposition.

colegio concertado

School that is privately owned but receives a grant from central government. Parents have to pay a monthly fee for tuition, but not as much as in a COLEGIO PRIVADO. It normally covers all stages of education: EDUCACIÓN PRIMARIA, ESO, BACHILLER, and COU. Some might also offer classes for children aged 3-6, which is called EDUCACIÓN INFANTIL and is not compulsory. These schools have a reputation for a high standard of education, and often are, or were in the past, religious schools.

colegio estatal

Its official name is CEIP, Colegio de Educación Infantil y Primaria (School of Infant and Primary Education). It is part of the free state school system, meaning that parents do not have to pay for their children's education. It offers EDUCACIÓN PRIMARIA for children aged from 6 to 12. Some might also offer classes for children aged 3-6, which is called EDUCACIÓN INFANTIL and is not compulsory. After finishing the EDUCACIÓN PRIMARIA in a CEIP, children go to an INSTITUTO for their secondary education.

colegio privado

School that is privately owned and receives no money at all from central government. The costs of tuition are covered by the parents in the form of monthly fees, which are normally quite high. It usually covers all stages of education: EDUCACIÓN PRIMARIA, ESO, BACHILLER, and COU. Some might also offer classes for children aged 3-6, which is called EDUCACIÓN INFANTIL and is not compulsory.

comunidad de vecinos

Name given to the group of people who live in a block of flats. They have regular meetings to discuss and decide things concerning the maintenance of the building, lifts, central heating system, etc. Each of the tenants must also pay a sum of money every month into a fund that goes to pay for any repairs that are needed, as well as to cover the services of a PORTERO, if the building has one. This is called *pagar la comunidad* (to pay the community charge). Each *comunidad* must elect a president, who calls the meetings, and employs the services of an administrator, who is in charge of getting quotes, paying the salary of the PORTERO, etc.

concejal
Person in charge of an area of local government (such as town planning, traffic, or the environment) in a MUNICIPIO. They are appointed by the ALCALDE.

el Congreso
See CÁMARA DE LOS DIPUTADOS.

consejo escolar
Administrative body in a school comprising the school management team, representatives of teachers, parents, and students (although students cannot vote), and one representative of the council and one of the non-teaching staff. They meet to discuss and decide issues regarding the running of the school.

Correos
Name given to the state-run postal system in Spain. In Spain, stamps can be bought in ESTANCOS, although if you want to send a parcel or letter by registered or express post you need to go to an *estafeta de correos* (post office). Postboxes in Spain are yellow.

corrida
The Spanish word for a bullfight. *Toreo* (bullfighting) has ancient origins, with Phoenician and Roman roots, and is a very popular spectacle in Spain. *Corridas* are regularly broadcast on television when the season starts. During the *corrida* three *matadores* (bullfighters) fight a total of six bulls, two each.

las Cortes
The name by which the national parliament is known in Spain. The name derives from a body that existed in the old kingdoms of Castilla, Aragón, Valencia, Navarra, and Cataluña, formed by people who were authorized to take part in government business, either in a personal capacity or as representatives of a particular social or economic group. Today it is used to refer to the two bodies that form the Spanish parliament: the CÁMARA DE LOS DIPUTADOS and the SENADO.

COU – Curso de orientación universitaria
One-year course taken by students who wish to go to university. The course prepares students for the university entrance exam, SELECTIVIDAD. Students normally carry on studying the subjects they have chosen for the BACHILLERATO. However, the *COU* will be phased out as part of the changes introduced by the REFORMA.

créditos
Number of points or credits awarded for each subject studied at university. To get their degree, students must accumulate a certain number of these points.

Defensor del pueblo

Ombudsman who, in Spain, is nominated by the PARLAMENTO to preside over the institution in charge of defending the fundamental rights of Spanish citizens against the administration. Citizens can write to the *Defensor del pueblo* if they feel that their constitutional rights have not been respected. The *Defensor del pueblo* decides whether they are right or not, and, if they are, writes to the administration advising what steps should be taken to compensate them. He also reports to Parliament at least once a year or on request.

despacho de lotería y apuestas del estado

Often just called *despachos de lotería*, this is a shop licensed to sell tickets for a lottery, such as the BONOLOTO or the LOTERÍA DE NAVIDAD. Some people always like to buy their ticket from the same shop as they think this might bring them good luck. Also, the *despacho* that sells the GORDO DE NAVIDAD at Christmas time normally gets a lot of people buying from it the following year.

Día de Reyes

Name given in Spain to the Epiphany, 6 January. It is the day when Christmas presents are given and exchanged. Young children in Spain believe that the *Reyes Magos* (Three Wise Men) come to every house and leave presents for everybody. The night before, people leave a pair of shoes belonging to each member of the family close to a window or balcony door, which is how the *Reyes Magos* get into the house or flat. The *Reyes Magos* leave next to each pair of shoes the presents that correspond to that person. People also put out some Christmas sweets and spirits for the *Reyes Magos*, and some water for the camels. The tradition is based on the *Reyes Magos* (Three Wise Men) who came to offer presents to baby Jesus in Bethlehem.

Dicen

Daily newspaper dealing exclusively with sports information and reports, mainly football. It is published in Barcelona and distributed over the whole of Spain.

droguería

Shop selling household and cleaning products and utensils, as well as DIY products such as paint, plaster, etc.

duro

Informal name given to a five-peseta coin. 'Duro' is often used in conversation when talking about a relatively low amount of money. For instance, people very often say 'veinte duros' (= 'twenty duros') meaning 100 pesetas, or 'diez duros' (= 'ten duros') meaning 50 pesetas.

educación infantil

Period of pre-school education that is not part of the compulsory educational system but has a certain academic orientation and aims to prepare children for formal education. It provides care and education for

children from 0 to 6 years of age
(at 6 children will start formal
education). Parents wishing
their children to receive
educación infantil can take them
to those GUARDERÍAS that cater
for children up to 6 years of age
or to COLEGIOS (which only offer
educación infantil to children
from 3 to 6 years of age). Since
pre-school education is not
compulsory, parents must pay
for it. Depending on whether the
GUARDERÍAS are fully private or
run by the council, they can be
more or less expensive.

educación primaria, enseñanza primaria
See PRIMARIA

educación secundaria, enseñanza secundaria
See ESO

EGB – Enseñanza General Básica
The old level of compulsory
education that used to exist
before the REFORMA. It was for
pupils between 6 and 14 years of
age. Students who wished to
carry on studying could go on to
study FORMACIÓN PROFESIONAL,
which had a vocational focus, or
BUP, which had a more
academic approach.

EH – Euskal Herritarrok
EH is the political platform on
which the Basque political
party, HB, runs for elections. It
was formed by HB in 1998.

elecciones
There are three types of election
in Spain: *generales*,
autonómicas, and *municipales*.

The *elecciones generales* (general
elections) elect members to the
central PARLAMENTO of Spain.
The *elecciones autonómicas*
(elections in the autonomous
regions) elect members to the
parliaments of the AUTONOMÍAS,
Cataluña, Euskadi, Andalucía,
etc. The *elecciones municipales*
(local elections) elect the
ALCALDE and the party that will
be in charge of the local
government. The elections
normally take place at different
times, and they are held at least
every four years. All elections
follow a system of proportional
representation.

Ertzaintza
Regional police of the Basque
country. They come under the
authority of the parliament of
the PAÍS VASCO. Their members
are called *ertzainas*.

ESO – Enseñanza Secundaria Obligatoria
The name given to Spanish
secondary education, coming
after the ENSEÑANZA PRIMARIA,
for pupils from 12 to 16 years of
age. The *ESO* is compulsory, and
comprises two cycles of two
academic years each. At the end
of the *ESO* the student will get a
qualification called *Graduado
en Educación Secundaria*.
Students wishing to carry on
studying can then study either
FORMACIÓN PROFESIONAL, which
has a vocational focus, or
BACHILLERATO, which has a
more traditional academic
approach.

estanco

In Spain, many bars and restaurants sell cigarettes, either over the bar, or, more commonly nowadays, in cigarette machines. However, the main shop that sells cigarettes, cigars, pipe tobacco, etc. is an *estanco*. *Estancos* also sell stamps and some writing materials such as envelopes, pens, ink, etc. However, if you want to send a parcel or letter by registered or express post you need to go to an *estafeta de correos* (post office). In the *estancos* you can also buy the special 10-journey bus and metro tickets: BONOBÚS and BONOMETRO.

ETA – Euskadi Ta Askatasuna

Terrorist organization of a nationalist character, whose aim is to achieve political independence for the Basque Country (EUSKADI) from the Spanish central government.

ETB

Television channel of the Basque Country. It broadcasts only in the PAÍS VASCO and in the language of that region, EUSKERA.

Euskadi

Name in Basque (EUSKERA) for the Basque Country. See PAÍS VASCO.

euskera (Basque)

Language spoken in the Basque Country (EUSKADI) and parts of Navarra. Together with Castilian, it is the official language of this AUTONOMÍA and is a compulsory subject in schools. It is spoken by around 750,000 people and is an official requirement for many official and administrative positions in the Basque Country. A considerable number of books are published in *euskera*, either originally written in this language or translated into it. It is also spoken in the French Basque country, though there it is not an official language. *Euskera* is a language unrelated to the Romance languages derived from Latin which are spoken in Spain: GALLEGO, CASTELLANO, and CATALÁN. Its origins are, in fact, unknown. It has been linked to Caucasian, Asian, and North African languages, but there is no strong evidence relating it to any of them. Many think it is a language that preceded Indo-European languages. Current official *euskera* is a language that was 'created' by fusing the different dialects that already existed and it is called *euskera batua*.

facultad

Each of the branches of study that are offered in a university, such as medicine, architecture, social studies, etc. Each university offers a wide range of *facultades*. The buildings and departments where the study of a particular branch takes place are also called the *facultad* of that particular area of study. For instance, *Facultad de Medicina* (Faculty of Medicine) is where you go to study medicine.

fallas

Popular festival that takes place in Valencia on 19 March and the preceding days. Huge figures of papier maché are constructed during this time, often representing popular public figures, or making reference to social or political events. They are displayed and then burnt on the 19th in the streets. There are numerous street parties and other types of events during the period of the *fallas*.

farmacia

Shop licensed to sell drugs and medicines. The pharmacists must be graduates in pharmacy, as they are supposed to offer medical advice for simple ailments such as colds and headaches. Pharmacies can also sell cosmetics and hygiene products and are identified by a street sign with a green cross. Some are also *farmacias de guardia*, which means that they open outside the normal hours as part of a local rota, in order to sell medicines in cases of emergency. There is a notice outside each pharmacy indicating the *farmacia de guardia* for each day/week of the month and its address. The same information also appears in local newspapers.

fiesta

Every town and village in Spain has its *fiesta*. This is a period, lasting from a few days to a couple of weeks, that precedes the day of the saint of the locality, which can also be a holiday. During the *fiesta*, the town or village is decorated and various cultural and social events take place, such as communal dances, concerts, games, etc. Some of these events are very traditional, going back hundreds of years, and they can be something like a parade or the re-enacting of a historical event or battle. Some *fiestas* are very big and famous, even outside Spain, such as the FALLAS in Valencia or SAN FERMINES in Navarra.

flamenco

Style of songs and dance typical of the south of Spain, of GITANO origins. It is characterized by the passionate and powerful expression of feelings, often tragic.

Formación Profesional (FP)

After finishing the compulsory years of education (ESO), pupils can go on to the BACHILLERATO, which has a more traditional academic approach, or to the *Formación Profesional*, which has a vocational focus. *FP* comprises two cycles, one for students from 16 to 18 years of age and another which runs parallel to university education, for students of 18 years and upwards. For each of these stages pupils are given a qualification, either *técnico* or *asistente*, which qualifies them for a specific occupation or to continue to a more specialized course. It is possible to access the BACHILLERATO or university education from the *Formación Profesional*.

gallego (galego)

Language spoken in Galicia. It

is very similar to Portuguese, from which it derived in the 14th century. Together with Castilian, it is the official language of this AUTONOMÍA, where it is an official requirement for many official and academic positions, as well as a compulsory subject in school. It is spoken by around three million people in Galicia, but there is also a substantial number of speakers of *gallego* living outside Galicia, both in Spain and abroad, since in the past it was an area that produced a large number of emigrants. A considerable number of books are published in *gallego*, either originally written in this language or translated into it. *Gallego*, like CASTELLANO and CATALÁN, is part of the group of Romance languages that derived from Latin. The Galician name for the language is *galego*.

gazpacho
Traditional cold summer soup made with water, tomatoes, cucumber, green pepper, onion, garlic, and dry bread. It originated in the region of Andalucía but is very popular all over Spain.

Generalitat
Name given in Cataluña and Valencia to their parliaments.

gitano
Member of the Spanish gypsy community, which has its roots in a Hindu ethnic group that spread around the north of Africa and Europe. The gypsies

often live in camps and retain their nomadic habits, deriving a living from trading and selling things in markets. They also keep a lot of their customs and do not usually integrate into the mainstream of Spanish society. Flamenco dance and songs have gypsy origins and many of the best performers come from the *gitano* community.

El Gordo de Navidad
This name means 'the fat one of Christmas' and it is the name given to the biggest prize in the LOTERIA DE NAVIDAD (Christmas Lottery), which takes place shortly before 24 December.

Goyas
Prizes awarded by the AACC, *Academia de las Artes y las Ciencias Cinematográficas de España* (Academy of the Cinematographic Arts and Sciences of Spain) for achievement in the Spanish film industry. They are the Spanish equivalent of the Oscars and there are different categories such as best film, best main actor and actress, etc. The winners receive a replica bust of the painter *Goya*, hence the name of the prize.

guardería
Centre that looks after small children who are under the compulsory school age (6 years old). It is similar to a nursery in the UK. The *guarderías* normally look after children from a few months old up to 4 years, or sometimes up to 6. Some *guarderías* are private,

while some are run and subsidized by the council, or in some cases by the government, and are part of a COLEGIO, but parents must always pay a certain amount for their children to attend.

guardia civil

Military body in Spain which is in charge of security in rural areas and on the coast, and of the protection of the Spanish public bodies (*organismos públicos*). It has a military organization and a strong army ethos, even though it carries out police work. Its members are also called *guardia civiles* and they used to have a very characteristic three-pointed hat, called *tricornio*, as part of their uniform, but this is no longer used.

HB – Herri Batasuna

Coalition of nationalist political parties of Marxist-Leninist ideology formed in 1978. It is described as the 'political arm' of ETA and, like ETA, it aims to achieve political independence for the PAÍS VASCO (the Basque Country) from the Spanish central government. Its political platform is EH.

Iberia

Spanish national commercial airline company.

ikastola

School where the teaching is done in EUSKERA (Basque).

instituto

Centre of secondary education providing ESO (compulsory secondary education for children 12 to 16), the two years of BACHILLERATO (non-compulsory secondary education for children 16 to 18), and the one-year pre-university course, COU. These establishments are part of the state school system and therefore free of charge.

La 2

Spanish commercial television channel, broadcasting documentaries and educational and news programmes. It is considered to be the channel that maintains the highest quality in Spanish television.

lehendakari

President of the parliament of EUSKADI. Each party running for the ELECCIONES AUTONÓMICAS in the PAÍS VASCO nominates a person, who can also, but does not have to, be the leader of the party, to become the president in the event of the party winning the elections. Apart from presiding over Parliament and running the administration of the AUTONOMÍA of the PAÍS VASCO, the *lehendakari* has an important role in liaising with the president of the Spanish central government.

lotería de Navidad and lotería del Niño

Name given to the special national lottery draws that take place at Christmas time. There are two main draws: *Lotería de Navidad* (that takes place a couple of days before the 24th), and *Lotería del Niño* (that takes place on 5 January, before the DÍA DE REYES). The prizes may not be as big as the LOTERÍA PRIMITIVA or the BONOLOTO, but it is a big social event. It is traditional to buy tickets and give them as presents to friends and relatives, or for a group of friends or colleagues at work to buy a number together. This means that the prize is normally shared between people who are related or know each other. The draw, with children singing the numbers as they come out of the drum, is shown on television and later the winners are shown and interviewed on the national news.

lotería primitiva
This is the national lottery, which takes place three times a week. People playing have to bet on six numbers which they mark in a square consisting of 49 numbers. The winner is the person whose numbers coincide with the numbers that come out in the draw. The prizes are normally substantial.

Marca
Daily newspaper dealing exclusively with sports information and reports, mainly football. It is published in Madrid and distributed all over Spain. It is the highest-circulation newspaper in Spain, well ahead any of the daily non-sports newspapers, such as ABC or EL PAÍS.

médico de cabecera
Doctor who is a general practitioner. People go to see the médico de cabecera for common illnesses that are not of a serious nature, or to get referred to a specialist.

mercado
Even though every day there are more and more supermarkets in Spain, people still like, or even prefer, to buy in mercados (markets). The markets normally comprise a group of stalls set up in a covered square or in a building. They are open every day except Sunday.

Mossos d'Esquadra
The police force of Cataluña. It comes under the authority of the GENERALITAT, the parliament of Cataluña.

El Mundo
A Spanish daily national newspaper. It is considered to be close to the Conservative party, the PP.

municipio
Each of the administrative areas into which a PROVINCIA is divided. A municipio can be a town, a city, or a village. Each municipio has an ALCALDE and several CONCEJALES, who deal with the administration and government of the area. This governing body comprising the ALCALDE and the CONCEJALES is also called municipio.

NIF – Número de identificación fiscal
Tax identification code that all residents must have in Spain. People must give it as part of the personal details provided when applying for a loan, opening a

bank account, etc. It is the same number as a person's identity number (and passport number), with the addition of a letter. It is used to keep tax control over people's financial transactions.

ONG – Organización no Gubernamental

The *ONGs* (non-governmental organizations) are not set up by a government or any agreement between governments. They are non-profit-making and are partly financed by governments and administrative bodies, although mainly by the general public. They are normally concerned with social issues, such as homelessness or drug addiction. A lot of them work in Spain although many also work abroad in the developing world. There are currently around 70 *ONGs* in Spain.

oposición

This is a competitive exam for people wanting to get a job in the administration, or as a teacher in a secondary school (INSTITUTO), or to become a judge. The candidates are examined by a tribunal. When the candidate is applying for the position of a teacher in an INSTITUTO or to become a judge, passing the exam often means studying for several years and sitting more than once for the exam, as the exams are very hard and there are thousands of applicants for very few positions.

PA – Partido Andaluz

Nationalist political party of Andalucía. It is one of the main political parties of this autonomous region and has representatives both in the central parliament and in the parliament of Andalucía.

paga extra, paga extraordinaria

Name for a bonus payment that most people receive at work twice a year, at Christmas and in July before the summer holidays, on top of their monthly salary.

El País

A Spanish national newspaper which is published daily. Its political views are to the left of centre and it gives considerable coverage to social issues and the arts. It also publishes a number of supplements on different subjects such as the economy and culture. It was founded in 1976, just as Spain was starting the democratic process of transition following General Franco's dictatorship, and its importance and influence on Spanish society at that critical time was considerable. It is considered to represent a very high standard of journalism.

País Vasco

Name used in Spain to refer to the AUTONOMÍA formed by the provinces of Álava, Guipúzcoa, and Vizcaya, in the north of Spain. Some people consider that, for historical and cultural reasons, it extends on both sides of the Pyrenees where Basque or EUSKERA is spoken. Therefore, people also talk of the *País*

Vasco–Francés and *País
Vasco–Español*. The *País
Vasco–Francés* (French Basque
region) does not have
autonomous status, and Basque
is not recognized as an official
language there, whereas the
País Vasco–Español is an
autonomous region within the
Spanish State, with its own
parliament, and its own
administrative, legislative, and
judicial powers. The name given
to the *País Vasco* in EUSKERA
(the Basque language) is
EUSKADI.

parador
Hotel that is situated in a big
historic house, typical of the
region or area where it is
located, or sometimes in an old
palace, which has been
renovated, thus preserving the
character of the building.
Normally of very high quality,
they were created as a way of
giving buildings of historical or
architectural importance a new
lease of life. They used to be
controlled by the Ministry of
Tourism but are now
independent.

Parlamento
The Spanish parliament, also
known as *las Cortes*. It is formed
by two bodies: a Lower Chamber
or CÁMARA DE LOS DIPUTADOS
and an Upper Chamber or
SENADO.

paro
Name given in Spain to
unemployment and to the
unemployment benefit received
by people out of work. The
payment is not the same fixed
amount for everybody, but
varies according to the National
Insurance contributions that
have been made during the
period of employment. The
period during which
unemployment pay can be
claimed depends on the period
of time a person has been
working, and it can range from
three months to a maximum of
two years. Unemployment pay
also decreases over the period of
unemployment. For instance,
someone who has worked for six
months will receive three
months' unemployment pay, and
a maximum of 70% of their
salary, which might go down in
the following months. To receive
unemployment benefit is called
cobrar el paro.

payo
Name given by members of the
gypsy community to all non-
gypsies.

PNV – Partido Nacionalista Vasco
Main political party in the PAÍS
VASCO. It has a nationalist
ideology and is represented in
the central parliament as well as
in the parliament of the PAÍS
VASCO. Its influence in central
government has been
considerable, as often the main
political party in power
(whether PSOE or PP) has been
forced to enter into a pact with
it in order to be able to outvote
the opposition.

portero
The name given in Spain to the

caretaker of a block of flats who looks after the building, keeps it clean, and also keeps an eye on who comes and goes. *Porteros* are also in charge of collecting the rubbish and delivering the mail to each mailbox. Their salary comes from the money paid by the COMUNIDAD DE VECINOS and they are often given a flat in the building to live in, as part of their payment. However, a lot of buildings now do not have *porteros* and their inhabitants either share the cleaning by rota or employ someone to do it. Where there is no *portero*, access is regulated by an entryphone, which in Spain is called *portero automático* (automatic caretaker).

PP – Partido Popular
One of the two main political parties in Spain with representation in the central government and in the government of the AUTONOMÍAS. Its ideology is right of centre.

Premio Cervantes
Prize awarded in Spain for literary achievement. It is considered to be the most prestigious prize among Spanish intellectuals and writers. The prize is not awarded for a particular piece of writing, but for a writer's work as a whole.

Presidente del gobierno
President of the Spanish central parliament, the equivalent of the Prime Minister in the UK. Each party running for the ELECCIONES *generales* in Spain nominates a person, usually, but not necessarily, the leader of the party, to become the president in the event of that party winning the elections. Apart from presiding over the parliament and running the administration of the state, the *Presidente* has an important role in liaising and meeting with the prime ministers of other countries and with the presidents of the different AUTONOMÍAS of Spain.

Primaria
The name given in Spain to the first of the two compulsory levels of education. The *Primaria* is for pupils between 6 and 12 years of age and leads on to the ESO. It is compulsory and is taught in COLEGIOS.

provincia
Each of the different administrative areas into which Spain is divided. The current division was established in 1833. Each *provincia* includes a main city or town, sometimes more, depending on their social and economic power. Most AUTONOMÍAS comprise at least two or more *provincias*, except Madrid and Murcia, which consist of just one *provincia*. The city of Madrid is the capital of the province and of the AUTONOMÍA of Madrid, as well as being the capital of Spain.

PSOE – Partido Socialista Obrero Español
One of the two main political parties in Spain with representation in the central

government and in the governments of the AUTONOMÍAS. Its ideology is left of centre.

pub

Name used in Spain to refer to an establishment where drinks are served and sometimes also snacks. Although the name comes from English, Spanish *pubs* look very different from English pubs. They are usually decorated in a very stylish modern fashion, and are sometimes theme-based. Often concentrated in a particular area of a town or city, they are aimed at young people going out in the evening and are open till the early hours of the morning. They always have music, which can be very loud.

puente

Holidays in Spain are fixed on specific dates in the calendar. This means that each year the day of the week on which they fall will vary. If one year a holiday falls on a Tuesday or a Thursday, some companies and most schools will also give a holiday on the day between the holiday and the weekend (i.e. the Monday or the Friday). This is called a *puente* (bridge), while to give this holiday is called *dar puente* and to take this holiday is *hacer puente*.

quiniela

Name given to football and horse racing pools in Spain. The paper on which the bet is written is also called the *quiniela*. The punters must state

what they think will be the result of a match or a race. In the case of football pools, for each match, they must write 1, 2, or X: '1' if they think the home team is going to win, '2' if they think the away team is going to win, and 'X' if they think it is going to be a draw. The total number of matches is 14, and people who get either 13 or 14 correct results share the prize money.

ración

This is a small portion of food that you have in a bar with a drink. *Raciones* are bigger than TAPAS and normally shared between two or three people. It is common for a group of friends in Spain to meet and go out to a bar, or from one bar to another, having a drink and a selection of TAPAS and *raciones*, either as an aperitif before lunch or in the evening instead of having dinner.

RAE – Real Academia Española

Official body created in the 18th century with the aim of preserving the purity of the Spanish language. It is made up of *académicos*, who are normally well-known writers or academic experts on the Spanish language, both from Spain and abroad. The *RAE* has published different editions of a Dictionary of Spanish and a Spanish Grammar, incorporating changes that have taken place in the language. These books are regarded as an authority on what is acceptable and correct Spanish. However, the *RAE* is often criticized as being conservative and slow in accepting the changes that take place in the language. There are also *RAEs* in most Latin American countries.

rastro

Name given to an open-air flea market that normally takes place once a week and where all types of new and old items are sold, including a lot of handicrafts. The name *El rastro* is used to refer to a very big market of this type that takes place in an old and very traditional part of Madrid at the weekend, but smaller *rastros* take place all over Madrid and other towns and they are often called *rastrillos*.

la reforma (educativa)

Name used to refer to the change in the educational system that was introduced gradually from 1990 onwards. The main changes were the extension of compulsory education by one year (up to 16 years of age), with the introduction of the ESO that replaced EGB.

RENFE – Red Nacional de los Ferrocarriles Españoles

State-run railway system. Trains in Spain are often cheaper than in the UK, and it is a generally efficient system. The most common trains are *Intercity* and *TALGO*. Tickets can be booked over the phone, and then collected, or if you pay a supplement they are delivered to your address.

San Fermines

Popular festival that takes place in Pamplona on 7 July and the preceding days. During these days, a series of *encierros* take place, events in which people must run in front of a herd of bulls in narrow streets, leading them to the bullring where there is later a CORRIDA (bullfight). *San Fermines* is a very popular festival, well-known also abroad, and a lot of foreigners like to try their skill at running in front of the bulls.

santo

Day that has been assigned by the church to a particular saint. In Spain people celebrate their name days as well as birthdays, although this varies according to the region. Some saints' days are very important celebrations in certain areas, such as San Juan in Valencia (known locally as San Joan) and San Fermín in Pamplona (see SAN FERMINES).

Selectividad

Examination that takes place after COU, when students are normally 17 or 18. Students sit exams in the core subjects, such as history and Spanish language, which are common to all students, and in the subject they have chosen as their specialism (for example literature or chemistry). An average is taken of the results of the exams and this is worked out against the average of the year's results in BACHILLERATO. The final result is a figure out of

10, and this figure is taken as a qualification for entering university. So, for instance, different FACULTADES will only accept students who have obtained a grade in *Selectividad* above a certain figure.

Senado

The upper of the two chambers in LAS CORTES. Its members, the *senadores*, are elected during the general elections. The Senate's function is to discuss and either approve or suggest amendments to legislation passed by the CÁMARA DE LOS DIPUTADOS. The place where the *senadores* meet is also called the *Senado*.

senyera

Name given in Cataluña and Valencia to the flag of these autonomous regions.

siesta

Nap that some people in Spain take after lunch and especially at the weekends and in the heat of the summer. Nowadays it is not such a common practice, owing to the change in lifestyle and in working hours (in the past most jobs used to have a long break at lunch).

Sport

Daily newspaper dealing exclusively with sports information and reports, mainly football. It is published in Barcelona and distributed all over Spain.

tapas

Small snack eaten with a drink. *Tapas* is a popular form of food all over Spain. It is common for a group of friends in Spain to meet and go out to a bar, or from one bar to another, having a drink and a selection of *tapas*, either as an aperitif before lunch or in the evening instead of having dinner. This is called *ir de tapas*. You can also have RACIONES, which are bigger portions, on such outings.

Tele 5

One of the main national Spanish commercial TV channels, broadcasting films and entertainment programmes.

Telefónica (de Espana S.A.)

This is the largest telephone company in Spain. It used to be a state company but it was privatized in 1999. There are a number of other privately owned telephone companies now operating in Spain.

terraza

Area outside a bar, café, or restaurant where people can sit and have a drink or eat in the open air. Some *terrazas* are very trendy and popular among young people going out in the evening. These can be very large, open until late into the night, and they can even have music.

tiendas

Shops in Spain are open from nine or ten in the morning until one or two in the afternoon. They close for lunch and then are open again from five o'clock until eight or nine in the evening. Shops close on Sundays, except around

Christmas time. Big stores are only allowed to open a certain number of Sundays during the year, in order to protect small shops. There are a lot more small independent shops in Spain than in the UK.

turismo rural

Name used to refer to a form of tourism that rents out renovated houses in the country and in old Spanish villages to people on holiday. Houses are given a grant to be renovated on the condition that they are rented out for this purpose. The aim of the initiative was to promote tourism in rural areas, thereby providing an income to farmers and helping to preserve village architecture.

TV1

One of the main national Spanish commercial TV channels, broadcasting films and entertainment programmes.

TV-3

Television channel of Cataluña, Valencia, and Baleares. It broadcasts in CATALÁN.

TVAC

Television channel of the Canary Islands.

TVG

Television channel of Galicia. It broadcasts in GALLEGO.

UGT – Union General de Trabajadores

One of the main trade unions in Spain, traditionally linked to the Socialist party and movement. It is a unitary national organization, drawing its members from all occupations.

UNED – Universidad Nacional de Educación a Distancia

Spanish national university for distance learning. Students receive the booklist and the syllabus of the subject and submit their assignments by post. They also have regular meetings, individually or in small groups, with a tutor, and on occasions they also attend lectures.

universidad

Educational body in charge of higher education. It is made up of various FACULTADES and university schools, each offering a different branch of study. There are private universities and universities that form part of the state system of education. Students have to pay fees in both, but these are much higher in private universities. Since students are not given grants unless the income of their family falls below a certain level, they normally live at home with their parents while at university, usually attending the university that is nearest to their home. Language is also a deciding factor, since a student wishing to go to a university in Cataluña, for instance, would need to attend classes in CATALÁN. Students can choose different subjects within their degree, following a system of points called CRÉDITOS.

vacaciones de verano
In Spain a lot of companies allow their employees to take their summer holidays only during the months of July, August, and September. Some companies close during the month of August. This means that most people tend to have their summer holidays at the same time of the year. However, during the rest of the year people can have PUENTES, which are small holidays given around a bank holiday.

La Vanguardia
Daily newspaper published in Barcelona and distributed all over Spain. It is the newspaper with the largest number of subscribers and has a series of supplements on different subjects. It is a prestigious newspaper with a strong influence in Catalan society and is also published on the Internet.

Xunta
The parliament of Galicia.

Letter-writing

Holiday postcard

- Beginning (quite informal): this formula is used among young people, very close friends, and, generally speaking, when addressee and sender address each other using the familiar form tú. *Querido Juan* can also be used, or *Querida Ana* if the addressee is a woman. If addressed to two or more people, males and females or only males, the masculine plural *Queridos* is always used: *Queridos Juan y Ana, Queridos amigos, Queridos Juan y Pedro. Queridas* is used if the card or letter is addressed to more than one female: *Queridas chicas, Queridas Ana y Conchita*

- Address: Note that the title (*Sr., Sra., Srta.*) is always followed by a full stop and stands next to the name.

  The house number (sometimes also N° ...) comes after the street name. In addresses of apartments in Spain, this is often followed by a floor number and sometimes the apartment's position on the landing: *c/ Hermosilla 98, 6° Dcha.*

  The post code or zip code comes before the place

Hola Juan

¿Qué tal? Hemos llegado a esta maravilla de ciudad hace dos días y estamos disfrutando muchísimo de todo lo que vemos, ¡a pesar del tiempo! Ya sabes tú como es el clima por aquí.

Hemos visitado los baños romanos (por supuesto), la catedral y sus alrededores, Hicimos un paseo por el río en barca y hemos recorrido la ciudad a pie. Es la mejor forma de apreciar la increíble arquitectura de este lugar.

¡Ah! También tomamos un té inglés como es debido, con sándwichs de pepino incluidos, en la elegante "Pump Room". Mañana regresamos a Londres y luego de vuelta a la dura realidad.

Esperamos que todo te haya ido bien con el cambio de trabajo. Ya nos contarás.

Hasta pronto.

Ana y Eduardo

Bath, 8 de octubre 2001 **1**

Sr. Juan Elizalde

P° Pintor Rosales 101

28008 Madrid

Spain

- Endings (informal): *Un fuerte abrazo, Muchos saludos, Muchos besos y abrazos.* Also in Latin America: *Cariños* (NB not between men), *Hasta pronto* (See you soon).

1 Not only on postcards, but on most personal letters, Spanish speakers do not put the address at the top, but just the name of the place and the date. The sender's address is recorded on the back of the envelope.

Christmas and New Year wishes

On a card:

Feliz Navidad **1** y Próspero Año Nuevo **2**

Feliz Navidad **1** y los mejores deseos para el Año Nuevo **3**

1 Or: *Felices Pascuas, Felices Navidades.*

2 Or: *Próspero Año 2001.*

3 Or: *para el Año 2001.*

In a letter:

■ Beginning: the name on the first line is usually followed by a colon.

  4 This is a letter to friends who are addressed as *vosotros*, the plural of the familiar form *tú*. However, Latin American Spanish uses the formal plural *ustedes* instead of this form, so would replace the words marked * in the letter as follows: *vosotros* by *ustedes*, *vuestro* and *vuestra* by *su* or *de ustedes*, *os* by *les* or *los*. The verbs, marked **, should be replaced by the formal plural form, e.g. *estéis* by *estén*.

  5 Or (if the children are older): *para vosotros y los chicos* (or *y las chicas* if there are only females), *para vosotros y para toda la familia.*

  6 Or: *todos muy bien.*

Barcelona, 18 de diciembre de 2001

Queridos Juan y Elsa:

4 Antes que nada, os* deseamos a vosotros* y a los niños **5** unas muy felices Navidades y os* enviamos nuestros mejores deseos para el año 2000. Esperamos que estéis** todos estupendamente **6**. No sabéis** cómo nos alegramos con el anuncio de vuestro* viaje para enero. Ya tenemos pensado todo lo que podemos hacer durante vuestra* estancia aquí. Os* esperamos.

Conchita hizo los exámenes del último año de su carrera y sacó muy buenas notas. Ahora tiene que hacer su trabajo de práctica. Elena está bien y muy contenta en el colegio. Tiene muchísimos amigos y es muy buena chica. Luis y yo estamos bien también y sumamente felices con la reciente noticia del próximo ascenso de Luis.
En definitiva, 1999 ha sido un buen año y no nos podemos quejar. Confiamos en que el próximo será aún mejor.

Decidnos** con antelación la fecha de vuestro* viaje para que podamos ir a esperaros* al aeropuerto.

Recibid** todo nuestro cariño y un fuerte abrazo.

Luis y Ana.

Invitation (informal)

> Hamm, den 22.4.2000
>
> Madrid, 22 de abril del 2000
>
> Querido James:
>
> Te escribo para preguntarte si te apetecería **1** pasar las vacaciones de verano con nosostros. A Tito y a Pilar les haría mucha ilusión (y también a Juan y a mí, por supuesto). Pensamos ir al noreste del país a finales de julio o a principios de agosto. Es una región realmente hermosa y nos encantaría que tú también vinieras. Es muy probable que llevemos tiendas de campaña ¡espero que no te importe dormir en el suelo!
>
> Te agracedería que me avisaras lo más pronto posible si puedes venir.
>
> Un cariñoso saludo,
>
> Ana de Salas

1 Or (in Latin America and also in Spain): *si te gustaría*.

Invitation (formal)

Invitations to parties are usually by word of mouth, while for weddings announcements are usually sent out.

> Carmen S.de Pérez y Ramón Pérez Arrate, Lucía N.de Salas y Mario Salas Moro Participan a Ud. de la boda de sus hijos
>
> Consuelo y Hernán
>
> Y le invitan a la ceremonia religiosa que se efectuará en la Capilla del Sagrado Corazón, de Mirasierra, Madrid, el sábado 25 de julio del 2001 a las 7 p.m.
>
> Y luego a una recepción en la Sala de Banquetes del Restaurante Galán en C/Los Santos 10 de Majadahonda, Madrid.
>
> S.R.C.2

■ In Latin America invitations to the reception are sent to relatives and close friends in a separate smaller card enclosed with the announcement.

■ In Spanish-speaking countries, the answer is not usually given in writing.

2 In Latin America: R.S.V.P.

Accepting an invitation

Winchester, 2 de mayo del 2001

Estimada Sra. de Salas:

Muchísimas gracias por su amable carta y su invitación **1**.

No tengo nada planeado para las vacaciones de verano, así es que me encantaría acompañarles **2** *al norte. Desgraciadamente, no podré quedarme más de cinco o seis días debido a que mi madre no se encuentra muy bien y no me gustaría estar mucho tiempo fuera de casa.*

Por favor dígame lo que tengo que llevar. ¿Hace mucho calor en la región adonde vamos? ¿Hay mar o río donde se pueda nadar? En cuanto a hacer camping, no tengo ningún problema. Nosostros siempre llevamos nuestras tiendas de campaña a todas partes.

Esperando verles **3** *pronto otra vez,*

Un afectuoso saludo.

James

1 Since this is a letter from a younger person writing to the mother of a friend, he uses the formal *usted* form and the possessive *su*, and writes to her as *Sra. de Salas* and *Estimada*, which is normally used to begin a letter when the relationship is not too close. *Querida ...* could also be used (*Estimado Sr. ...* or *Querido Sr. ...* if the addressee is a man). On the other hand it was quite natural for *Sra. de Salas* to use the informal *tú* form to him.

2 In Latin America: *acompañarlos*.

3 In Latin America: *verlos*.

■ Ending: This is normally used when the relationship is not too close, generally when the person is known to you but the usted form would be used. *Un saludo muy afectuoso* is also possible.

Enquiry to a tourist office

■ This is a standard formula for starting a business letter addressed to a firm or organization, and not to a particular person. Alternatively, *Estimados señores* and, also in Latin America, *De nuestra mayor consideración*, could be used.

■ A simple business-style letter. The sender's address is on the top left-hand corner, the date is on the right, and the recipient's address is on the left, beneath the sender's address.

Sally McGregor
16 Victoria Road
Brixton
London SW2 5HU

4 de mayo del 2001

Oficina de Información y Turismo
Princesa 5
Oviedo

Muy señores míos:

Les agradecería me remitieran a la mayor brevedad una lista de hoteles y pensiones, de precio medio, en Oviedo y los pueblos de la provincia.

También me interesaría obtener información acerca de excursiones en autocar **1** a los lugares de interés de la zona durante la segunda mitad de agosto.

Agradeciendo de antemano su atención, les saluda atentamente,

Sally McGregor

■ *Les* (*Los* in Latin America) *saluda atentamente* is the standard ending for a formal or business letter. Other possibilities are: *Me despido de ustedes atentamente* or *Reciban un atento saludo de ...*

1 In Latin America: *autobús*.

Booking a hotel room

Luis Granados
C/Felipe V 32
Segovia

23 de abril del 2001

Sr. Director
Hotel Los Palomos
C/Piedrabuena 40
Cádiz

Apreciado señor: **1**

Su hotel aparece en un folleto turístico sobre la zona para el año 2001 y me ha causado muy buena impresión. Por ello le escribo para reservar una habitación doble con baño y una habitación individual **2** para nuestro hijo, desde el 2 hasta 11 de agosto (nueve noches). Preferiblemente ambas habitaciones con vista al mar.

Si tiene disponibilidad para esas fechas, le rogaría que me comunicara el precio y si se requiere depósito.

Sin otro particular le saluda **3** atentamente,

Luis Granados

---

1 Also: *Estimado Sr.*

2 Or: *una habitación doble y una individual para nuestro hijo, ambas con baño.*

3 In Latin America: *lo saluda ...*

Booking a campsite

Urbanización El Molino
Chalet 88
Villanueva de la Cañada
Madrid

25 de abril del 2001

Camping Loredo
Sr. Roberto Loredo
Nájera
La Rioja

Muy señor mío:

Un amigo que suele acampar en la zona me ha recomendado
su camping **1**, por lo que quisiera reservar una plaza para una tienda **2**, preferiblemente en un lugar abrigado **3**. Dos amigos y yo queremos pasar una semana allí, desde el 18 al 25 de julio inclusive.

Le agracedería que me confirmara la reserva lo antes posible y que me dijera si se requiere depósito. También le estaría muy agradecido si me enviara indicaciones para llegar al camping desde la carretera.

A la espera de su confirmación, le saluda **4** atentamente,

Pedro Salguedo

1 Or: *Su camping aparece anunciado en la revista Guía del Buen Campista.*

2 Other possibility: *para una caravana.*

3 Alternatively: *en un lugar sombreado/ cerca de la playa.*

4 In Latin America: *lo saluda ...*

Cancelling a reservation

Sra. Rosario de Barros
Av. Colonial
San Isidro
Lima

20 de julio de 2001

Estimada señora (de Barros):

Debido a circunstancias ajenas a nuestra voluntad **1**, nos hemos visto obligados a cambiar nuestros planes para las vacaciones, por lo que le rogaría cancelara la reserva **2** hecha a mi nombre para la semana del 7 al 14 de agosto.

Lamento muchísimo tener que hacer esta cancelación (tan a último momento) y espero que esto no le cause muchos inconvenientes.

La saluda atentamente,

Paul Roberts
2633 Higland Avenue
Urbandale, IA 51019
EEUU

■ In Latin America if the full address is given, it is usually written in the bottom left-hand corner, beneath the signature.

1 Or: *Debido al repentino fallecimiento de mi marido/a la hospitalización de mi hijo/a la enfermedad de mi marido* etc.

2 Also in Latin America: *reservación*.

Sending an e-mail

The illustration shows a typical interface for sending e-mail.

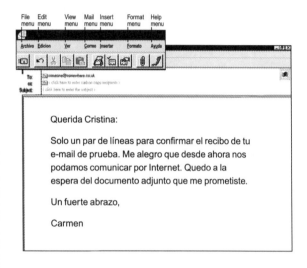

Querida Cristina:

Solo un par de líneas para confirmar el recibo de tu e-mail de prueba. Me alegro que desde ahora nos podamos comunicar por Internet. Quedo a la espera del documento adjunto que me prometiste.

Un fuerte abrazo,

Carmen

English–Spanish Dictionary

a

before vowel sound or silent 'h'
an

● *indefinite article*

⸱⸱⸱➤ un (*m*), una (*f*). **a problem** un problema. **an apple** una manzana. **have you got a pencil?** ¿tienes un lápiz?

❗ Feminine singular nouns beginning with stressed or accented *a* or *ha* take the article *un* instead of *una*, e.g. *un águila, un hada*

⸱⸱⸱➤ (when talking about prices and quantities) por. **30 miles an hour** 30 millas por hora. **twice a week** dos veces por semana, dos veces a la semana

❗ There are many cases in which **a** is not translated, such as when talking about people's professions, in exclamations, etc: **she's a lawyer** *es abogada*. **what a beautiful day!** *¡qué día más precioso!*. **have you got a car?** *¿tienes coche?* **half a cup** *media taza*

A & E *n.* urgencias *fpl*

aback *adv.* **be taken ~** quedar desconcertado

abandon *vt* abandonar. ● *n* abandono *m*, desenfado *m*. **~ed** *a* abandonado

abashed *a* confuso

abate *vi* disminuir; <*storm etc*> calmarse

abattoir *n* matadero *m*

abbess *n* abadesa *f*

abbey *n* abadía *f*

abbot *n* abad *m*

abbreviat|e *vt* abreviar. **~ion** *n* abreviatura *f*; (act) abreviación *f*

abdicat|e *vt/i* abdicar. **~ion** *n* abdicación *f*

abdom|en *n* abdomen *m*. **~inal** *a* abdominal

abduct *vt* secuestrar. **~ion** *n* secuestro *m*

abhor *vt* (*pt* **abhorred**) aborrecer. **~rence** *n* aborrecimiento *m*. **~rent** *a* aborrecible

abide *vt* (*pt* **abided**) soportar. ● *vi* (old use, *pt* **abode**) morar. ⬜ **~ by** *vt* atenerse a; cumplir <*promise*>

ability *n* capacidad *f*; (cleverness) habilidad *f*

abject *a* (wretched) miserable

ablaze *a* en llamas

able *a* (**-er, -est**) capaz. **be ~** poder; (know how to) saber. **~-bodied** *a* sano, no discapacitado

ably *adv* hábilmente

abnormal *a* anormal. **~ity** *n* anormalidad *f*

aboard *adv* a bordo. ● *prep* a bordo de

abode ⇒ABIDE. ● *n* (old use) domicilio *m*

aboli|sh *vt* abolir. **~tion** *n* abolición *f*

abominable *a* abominable

aborigin|al *a & n* aborigen (*m &
f*), indígena (*m & f*). ~**es** *npl*
aborígenes *mpl*

abort *vt* hacer abortar. ~**ion** *n*
aborto *m* provocado; (fig) aborto
m. **have an** ~**ion** hacerse un
aborto. ~**ive** *a* fracasado

abound *vi* abundar (**in** en)

about *adv* (approximately) alrededor
de; (here and there) por todas
partes; (in existence) por aquí. ~
here por aquí. **be** ~ **to** estar a
punto de. ● *prep* sobre; (around)
alrededor de; (somewhere in) en.
talk ~ hablar de. ~**-face**, ~**-turn**
n (fig) cambio *m* rotundo

above *adv* arriba. ● *prep* encima
de; (more than) más de. ~ **all** sobre
todo. ~ **board** *a* legítimo. ● *adv*
abiertamente. ~**-mentioned** *a*
susodicho

abrasi|on *n* abrasión *f*. ~**ve** *a*
abrasivo

abreast *adv*. **march four** ~
marchar en columna de cuatro
en fondo. **keep** ~ **of** mantenerse
al corriente de

abroad *adv* (be) en el extranjero;
(go) al extranjero; (far and wide) por
todas partes

abrupt *a* brusco. ~**ly** *adv*
(suddenly) repentinamente; (curtly)
bruscamente

abscess *n* absceso *m*

abscond *vi* fugarse

absen|ce *n* ausencia *f*; (lack) falta
f. ~**t** *a* ausente. ~**t-minded** *a*
distraído. ~**t-mindedness** *n*
distracción *f*, despiste *m*. ~**tee** *n*
ausente *m & f*. ~**teeism** *n*
absentismo *m*, ausentismo (LAm)

absolute *a* absoluto. ~**ly** *adv*
absolutamente

absolve *vt* (from sin) absolver; (from
obligation) liberar

absor|b *vt* absorber. ~**bent** *a*
absorbente. ~**bent cotton** *n*

(Amer) algodón *m* hidrófilo.
~**ption** *n* absorción *f*

abstain *vi* abstenerse (**from** de)

abstemious *a* abstemio

abstention *n* abstención *f*

abstract *a* abstracto. ● *n*
(summary) resumen *m*; (painting)
cuadro *m* abstracto. ● *vt* extraer;
(summarize) resumir. ~**ion** *n*
abstracción *f*

absurd *a* absurdo. ~**ity** *n*
absurdo *m*, disparate *m*

abundan|ce *n* abundancia *f*. ~**t**
a abundante

abus|e *vt* (misuse) abusar de; (ill-
treat) maltratar; (insult) insultar. ● *n*
abuso *m*; (insults) insultos *mpl*.
~**ive** *a* injurioso

abysmal *a* Ⓘ pésimo

abyss *n* abismo *m*

academic *a* académico; (pej)
teórico. ● *n* universitario *m*,
catedrático *m*

academy *n* academia *f*

accelerat|e *vt* acelerar. ● *vi*
acelerar; (Auto) apretar el
acelerador. ~**ion** *n* aceleración *f*.
~**or** *n* acelerador *m*

accent *n* acento *m*

accept *vt* aceptar. ~**able** *a*
aceptable. ~**ance** *n* aceptación *f*;
(approval) aprobación *f*

access *n* acceso *m*. ~**ible** *a*
accesible; <*person*> tratable

accession *n* (to power, throne etc)
ascenso *m*; (thing added)
adquisición *f*

accessory *a* accesorio. ● *n*
accesorio *m*, complemento *m*;
(Jurid) cómplice *m & f*

accident *n* accidente *m*; (chance)
casualidad *f*. **by** ~ sin querer; (by
chance) por casualidad. ~**al** *a*
accidental, fortuito. ~**ally** *adv* sin
querer; (by chance) por casualidad.

~-prone *a* propenso a los accidentes

acclaim *vt* aclamar. ● *n* aclamación *f*

accolade *n* (praise) encomio *m*

accommodat|e *vt* (give hospitality to) alojar; (adapt) acomodar; (oblige) complacer. **~ing** *a* complaciente. **~ion** *n*, **~ions** *npl* (Amer) alojamiento *m*

accompan|iment *n* acompañamiento *m*. **~ist** *n* acompañante *m & f*. **~y** *vt* acompañar

accomplice *n* cómplice *m & f*

accomplish *vt* (complete) acabar; (achieve) realizar; (carry out) llevar a cabo. **~ed** *a* consumado. **~ment** *n* realización *f*; (ability) talento *m*; (thing achieved) triunfo *m*, logro *m*

accord *vi* concordar. ● *vt* conceder. ● *n* acuerdo *m*; (harmony) armonía *f*. **of one's own ~** espontáneamente. **~ance** *n*. **in ~ance with** de acuerdo con. **~ing** *adv*. **~ing to** según. **~ingly** *adv* en conformidad; (therefore) por consiguiente

accordion *n* acordeón *m*

accost *vt* abordar

account *n* cuenta *f*; (description) relato *m*. **~s** *npl* (in business) contabilidad *f*. **on ~ of** a causa de. **on no ~** de ninguna manera. **on this ~** por eso. **take into ~** tener en cuenta. ● *vt* considerar. □ **~ for** *vt* dar cuenta de, explicar

accountan|cy *n* contabilidad *f*. **~t** *n* contable *m & f*, contador *m* (LAm)

accumulat|e *vt* acumular. ● *vi* acumularse. **~ion** *n* acumulación *f*

accura|cy *n* exactitud *f*, precisión *f*. **~te** *a* exacto, preciso

accus|ation *n* acusación *f*. **~e** *vt* acusar

accustom *vt* acostumbrar. **~ed** *a*. **be ~ed (to)** estar acostumbrado (a). **get ~ed (to)** acostumbrarse (a)

ace *n* as *m*

ache *n* dolor *m*. ● *vi* doler. **my leg ~s** me duele la pierna

achieve *vt* realizar; lograr *<success>*. **~ment** *n* realización *f*; (feat) proeza *f*; (thing achieved) logro *m*

acid *a & n* ácido (*m*). **~ic** *a* ácido. **~ rain** *n* lluvia *f* ácida

acknowledge *vt* reconocer. **~ receipt of** acusar recibo de. **~ment** *n* reconocimiento *m*; (Com) acuse *m* de recibo

acne *n* acné *m*

acorn *n* bellota *f*

acoustic *a* acústico. **~s** *npl* acústica *f*

acquaint *vt*. **~ s.o. with** poner a uno al corriente de. **be ~ed with** conocer *<person>*; saber *<fact>*. **~ance** *n* conocimiento *m*; (person) conocido *m*

acquiesce *vi* consentir (**in** en). **~nce** *n* aquiescencia *f*, consentimiento *m*

acqui|re *vt* adquirir; aprender *<language>*. **~re a taste for** tomar gusto a. **~sition** *n* adquisición *f*. **~sitive** *a* codicioso

acquit *vt* (*pt* **acquitted**) absolver. **~tal** *n* absolución *f*

acre *n* acre *m*

acrid *a* acre

acrimonious *a* cáustico, mordaz

acrobat *n* acróbata *m & f*. **~ic** *a* acrobático. **~ics** *npl* acrobacia *f*

acronym *n* acrónimo *m*, siglas *fpl*

across *adv & prep* (side to side) de un lado al otro; (on other side) al otro lado de; (crosswise) a través. **it is 20 metres ~** tiene 20 metros de ancho. **go** or **walk** ~ atravesar, cruzar

act n acto m; (action) acción f; (in variety show) número m; (decree) decreto m. ● vt hacer <part, role>. ● vi actuar; (pretend) fingir. ~ **as** actuar de; <object> servir de. ~ **for** representar. ~**ing** a interino. ● n (of play) representación f; (by actor) interpretación f; (profession) profesión f de actor

action n acción f; (Jurid) demanda f; (plot) argumento m. **out of** ~ (on sign) no funciona. **put out of** ~ inutilizar. **take** ~ tomar medidas. ~ **replay** n repetición f de la jugada

activate vt activar

activ|e a activo; (energetic) lleno de energía; <volcano> en actividad. ~**ist** n activista m & f. ~**ity** n actividad f

act|or n actor m. ~**ress** n actriz f

actual a verdadero. ~**ly** adv en realidad, efectivamente; (even) incluso

acute a agudo. ~**ly** adv agudamente

ad n 🔲 anuncio m, aviso m (LAm)

AD abbr (= **Anno Domini**) d. de J.C.

Adam's apple n nuez f (de Adán)

adapt vt adaptar. ● vi adaptarse. ~**ability** n adaptabilidad f. ~**able** a adaptable. ~**ation** n adaptación f; (of book etc) versión f. ~**or** n (Elec, with several sockets) enchufe m múltiple; (Elec, for different sockets) adaptador m

add vt añadir. ● vi sumar. □ ~ **up** vt sumar; (fig) tener sentido. ~ **up to** equivaler a

adder n víbora f

addict n adicto m; (fig) entusiasta m & f. ~**ed** a. ~**ed to** adicto a; (fig) fanático de. ~**ion** n (Med) dependencia f; (fig) afición f. ~**ive** a que crea adicción; (fig) que creahábito

addition n suma f. **in** ~ además. ~**al** a suplementario

address n dirección f; (on form) domicilio m; (speech) discurso m. ● vt poner la dirección en; (speak to) dirigirse a. ~ **book** n libreta f de direcciones. ~**ee** n destinatario m

adept a & n experto (m)

adequa|cy n suficiencia f. ~**te** a suficiente, adecuado. ~**tely** adv suficientemente, adecuadamente

adhere vi adherirse (**to** a); observar <rule>. ~**nce** n adhesión f; (to rules) observancia f

adhesi|on n adherencia f. ~**ve** a & n adhesivo (m)

adjacent a contiguo

adjective n adjetivo m

adjourn vt aplazar; suspender <meeting etc>. ● vi suspenderse

adjust vt ajustar <machine>; (arrange) arreglar. ● vi. ~ (**to**) adaptarse (a). ~**able** a ajustable. ~**ment** n adaptación f; (Tec) ajuste m

administer vt administrar

administrat|ion n administración f. ~**ive** a administrativo. ~**or** n administrador m

admirable a admirable

admiral n almirante m

admir|ation n admiración f. ~**e** vt admirar. ~**er** n admirador m

admission n admisión f; (entry) entrada f

admit vt (pt **admitted**) dejar entrar; (acknowledge) admitir, reconocer. ~ **to** confesar. **be** ~**ted** (to hospital etc) ingresar. ~**tance** n entrada *f*. ~**tedly** *adv* es verdad que

admonish *vt* reprender; (advise) aconsejar

ado *n* alboroto *m*; (trouble) dificultad *f*. **without more** or **further** ~ en seguida, sin más

adolescen|ce *n* adolescencia *f*. ~**t** *a* & *n* adolescente (*m* & *f*)

adopt *vt* adoptar. ~**ed** *a* <*child*> adoptivo. ~**ion** *n* adopción *f*

ador|able *a* adorable. ~**ation** *n* adoración *f*. ~**e** *vt* adorar

adorn *vt* adornar. ~**ment** *n* adorno *m*

adrift *a* & *adv* a la deriva

adult *a* & *n* adulto (*m*)

adulter|er *n* adúltero *m*. ~**ess** *n* adúltera *f*. ~**y** *n* adulterio *m*

advance *vt* adelantar. ● *vi* adelantarse. ● *n* adelanto *m*. **in** ~ con anticipación, por adelantado. ~**d** *a* avanzado; <*studies*> superior

advantage *n* ventaja *f*. **take** ~ **of** aprovecharse de; abusar de <*person*>. ~**ous** *a* ventajoso

advent *n* venida *f*. **A**~ *n* adviento *m*

adventur|e *n* aventura *f*. ~**er** *n* aventurero *m*. ~**ous** *a* <*person*> aventurero; <*thing*> arriesgado; (fig, bold) audaz

adverb *n* adverbio *m*

adversary *n* adversario *m*

advers|e *a* adverso, contrario, desfavorable. ~**ity** *n* infortunio *m*

advert *n* 🄸 anuncio *m*, aviso *m* (LAm). ~**ise** *vt* anunciar. ● *vi* hacer publicidad; (seek, sell) poner un anuncio. ~**isement** *n* anuncio *m*, aviso *m* (LAm). ~**iser** *n* anunciante *m* & *f*

advice *n* consejo *m*; (report) informe *m*

advis|able *a* aconsejable. ~**e** *vt* aconsejar; (inform) avisar. ~**e against** aconsejar en contra de. ~**er** *n* consejero *m*; (consultant) asesor *m*. ~**ory** *a* consultivo

advocate *n* defensor *m*; (Jurid) abogado *m*. ● *vt* recomendar

aerial *a* aéreo. ● *n* antena *f*

aerobics *npl* aeróbica *f*

aerodrome *n* aeródromo *m*

aerodynamic *a* aerodinámico

aeroplane *n* avión *m*

aerosol *n* aerosol *m*

aesthetic *a* estético

afar *adv* lejos

affable *a* afable

affair *n* asunto *m*. (love) ~ aventura *f*, amorío *m*. ~**s** *npl* (business) negocios *mpl*

affect *vt* afectar; (pretend) fingir. ~**ation** *n* afectación *f*. ~**ed** *a* afectado, amanerado

affection *n* cariño *m*. ~**ate** *a* cariñoso

affiliate *vt* afiliar

affirm *vt* afirmar. ~**ative** *a* afirmativo. ● *n* respuesta *f* afirmativa

afflict *vt* afligir. ~**ion** *n* aflicción *f*, pena *f*

affluen|ce *n* riqueza *f*. ~**t** *a* rico.

afford *vt* permitirse; (provide) dar. **he can't** ~ **a car** no le alcanza el dinero para comprar un coche

affront *n* afrenta *f*, ofensa *f*. ● *vt* afrentar, ofender

afield *adv*. **far** ~ muy lejos

afloat *adv* a flote

afraid *a*. **be** ~ tener miedo (**of** a); (be sorry) sentir, lamentar

afresh *adv* de nuevo

Africa *n* África *f*. ~**n** *a* & *n* africano (*m*). ~**n-American** *a* & *n* norteamericano (*m*) de origen africano

after *adv* después; (behind) detrás.
● *prep* después de; (behind) detrás
de. **it's twenty ~ four** (Amer) son
las cuatro y veinte. **be ~** (seek)
andar en busca de. ● *conj*
después de que. ● *a* posterior.
~-effect *n* consecuencia *f*, efecto
m secundario. **~math** *n* secuelas
fpl. **~noon** *n* tarde *f*. **~shave** *n*
loción *f* para después de
afeitarse. **~thought** *n* ocurrencia
f tardía. **~wards** *adv* después

again *adv* otra vez; (besides)
además. **do ~** volver a hacer,
hacer otra vez. **~ and ~** una y
otra vez

against *prep* contra; (in opposition
to) en contra de, contra

age *n* edad *f*. **at four years of ~** a
los cuatro años. **under ~** menor
de edad. **~s** *npl* 🄸 siglos *mpl*.
● *vt/i* (*pres p* **ageing**) envejecer.
~d *a* de … años. **~d 10** de 10
años. **~d** *a* (old) viejo, anciano

agency *n* agencia *f*; (department)
organismo *m*

agenda *n* orden *m* del día

agent *n* agente *m* & *f*;
(representative) representante *m* & *f*

aggravat|e *vt* agravar; (🄸, irritate)
irritar. **~ion** *n* agravación *f*; (🄸,
irritation) irritación *f*

aggress|ion *n* agresión *f*. **~ive** *a*
agresivo. **~iveness** *n* agresividad
f. **~or** *n* agresor *m*

aggrieved *a* apenado, ofendido

aghast *a* horrorizado

agil|e *a* ágil. **~ity** *n* agilidad *f*

aging *a* envejecido. ● *n*
envejecimiento *m*

agitat|e *vt* agitar. **~ed** *a*
nervioso. **~ion** *n* agitación *f*,
excitación *f*. **~or** *n* agitador *m*

ago *adv*. **a long time ~** hace
mucho tiempo. **3 days ~** hace 3
días

agon|ize *vi* atormentarse. **~izing**
a <pain> atroz; <experience>
angustioso. **~y** *n* dolor *m*
(agudo); (mental) angustia *f*

agree *vt* acordar. ● *vi* estar de
acuerdo; (of figures) concordar; (get
on) entenderse. □ **~ on** *vt* acordar
<date, details>. □ **~ with** *vt* (of
food etc) sentarle bien a. **~able** *a*
agradable. **be ~able** (willing) estar
de acuerdo. **~d** *a* <time, place>
convenido. **~ment** *n* acuerdo *m*.
in ~ment de acuerdo

agricultur|al *a* agrícola. **~e** *n*
agricultura *f*

aground *adv*. **run ~** (of ship) varar,
encallar

ahead *adv* delante; (in time) antes
de. **be ~** ir delante

aid *vt* ayudar. ● *n* ayuda *f*. **in ~ of**
a beneficio de

AIDS *n* sida *m*

ailment *n* enfermedad *f*

aim *vt* apuntar; (fig) dirigir. ● *vi*
apuntar; (fig) pretender. ● *n*
puntería *f*; (fig) objetivo *m*. **~less**
a, **~lessly** *adv* sin objeto, sin
rumbo

air *n* aire *m*. **be on the ~** (Radio, TV)
estar en el aire. **put on ~s** darse
aires. ● *vt* airear. **~ bag** *n* (Auto)
bolsa *f* de aire. **~ base** *n* base *f*
aérea. **~borne** *a* en el aire; (Mil)
aerotransportado.
~-conditioned *a* climatizado,
con aire acondicionado. **~
conditioning** *n* aire *m*
acondicionado. **~craft** *n* (*pl
invar*) avión *m*. **~craft carrier** *n*
portaaviones *m*. **~field** *n*
aeródromo *m*. **A~ Force** *n*
fuerzas *fpl* aéreas. **~ freshener**
n ambientador *m*. **~gun** *n*
escopeta *f* de aire comprimido. **~
hostess** *n* azafata *f*, aeromoza *f*
(LAm). **~line** *n* línea *f* aérea. **~
mail** *n* correo *m* aéreo. **~plane** *n*

(Amer) avión *m*. **~port** *n* aeropuerto *m*. **~sick** *a* mareado (*en un avión*). **~tight** *a* hermético. **~ traffic controller** *n* controlador *m* aéreo. **~y** *a* (**-ier**, **-iest**) aireado; <*manner*> desenfadado

aisle *n* nave *f* lateral; (gangway) pasillo *m*

ajar *a* entreabierto

alarm *n* alarma *f*. ● *vt* asustar. **~ clock** *n* despertador *m*. **~ist** *n* alarmista *m & f*

Albania *n* Albania *f*. **~n** *a & n* albanés (*m*)

albatross *n* albatros *m*

album *n* álbum *m*

alcohol *n* alcohol *m*. **~ic** *a & n* alcohólico (*m*)

alcove *n* nicho *m*

ale *n* cerveza *f*

alert *a* vivo; (watchful) vigilante. ● *n* alerta *f*. **on the ~** alerta. ● *vt* avisar

algebra *n* álgebra *f*

Algeria *n* Argelia *f*. **~n** *a & n* argelino (*m*)

alias *n* (*pl* **-ases**) alias *m*. ● *adv* alias

alibi *n* (*pl* **-is**) coartada *f*

alien *n* extranjero *m*. ● *a* ajeno. **~ate** *vt* enajenar. **~ation** *n* enajenación *f*

alienat|e *vt* enajenar. **~ion** *n* enajenación *f*

alight *a* ardiendo; <*light*> encendido

align *vt* alinear. **~ment** *n* alineación *f*

alike *a* parecido, semejante. **look or be ~** parecerse. ● *adv* de la misma manera

alive *a* vivo. **~ with** lleno de

alkali *n* (*pl* **-is**) álcali *m*. **~ne** *a* alcalino

all

● *adjective*

····▸ todo, -da; (pl) todos, -das. **~ day** todo el día. **~ the windows** todas las ventanas. **~ four of us went** fuimos los cuatro

● *pronoun*

····▸ (everything) todo. **that's ~** eso es todo. **I did ~ I could to persuade her** hice todo lo que pude para convencerla

····▸ (after pronoun) todo, -da; (pl) todos, -das. **he helped us ~** nos ayudó a todos

····▸ **all of** todo, -da, (pl) todos, -das. **~ of the paintings** todos los cuadros. **~ of the milk** toda la leche

····▸ (in phrases) **all in all** en general. **not at all** (in no way) de ninguna manera; (after thanks) de nada, no hay de qué. **it's not at ~ bad** no está nada mal. **I don't like it at ~** no me gusta nada

● *adverb*

····▸ (completely) completamente. **she was ~ alone** estaba completamente sola. **I got ~ dirty** me ensucié todo/toda. **I don't know him ~ that well** no lo conozco tan bien

····▸ (in scores) **the score was one ~** iban empatados uno a uno

····▸ (in phrases) **to be all for sth** estar completamente a favor de algo. **to be all in** 🔳 estar rendido

all-around *a* (Amer) completo

allay *vt* aliviar <*pain*>; aquietar <*fears etc*>

all-clear *n* fin *m* de (la) alarma; (permission) visto *m* bueno

alleg|ation n alegato m. ~**e** vt alegar. ~**edly** adv según se dice, supuestamente

allegiance n lealtad f

allegory n alegoría f

allerg|ic a alérgico (**to** a). ~**y** n alergia f

alleviate vt aliviar

alley (pl -**eys**), ~**way** ns callejuela f

alliance n alianza f

alligator n caimán m

allocat|e vt asignar; (share out) repartir. ~**ion** n asignación f; (distribution) reparto m

allot vt (pt **allotted**) asignar. ~**ment** n asignación f; (land) parcela f

allow vt permitir; (grant) conceder; (reckon on) prever; (agree) admitir. □ ~ **for** vt tener en cuenta. ~**ance** n concesión f; (pension) pensión f; (Com) rebaja f. **make** ~**ances for** ser indulgente con <person>; (take into account) tener en cuenta

alloy n aleación f

all: ~ **right** adj & adv bien. ● int ¡vale!, ¡okey! (esp LAm), ¡órale! (Mex). ~-**round** a completo

allusion n alusión f

ally n aliado m. ● vt. ~ **o.s.** aliarse (**with** con)

almighty a todopoderoso

almond n almendra f

almost adv casi

alms npl limosnas fpl

alone a solo. ● adv sólo, solamente

along prep por, a lo largo de. ● adv. ~ **with** junto con. **all** ~ todo el tiempo. **come** ~ venga. ~**side** adv (Naut) al costado. ● prep al lado de

aloof adv apartado. ● a reservado

aloud adv en voz alta

alphabet n alfabeto m. ~**ical** a alfabético

Alps npl. **the** ~ los Alpes

already adv ya

Alsatian n pastor m alemán

also adv también; (moreover) además

altar n altar m

alter vt cambiar. ● vi cambiarse. ~**ation** n modificación f; (to garment) arreglo m

alternate a alterno; (Amer) ⇒ALTERNATIVE. ● vt/i alternar. ~**ly** adv alternativamente

alternative a alternativo. ● n alternativa f. ~**ly** adv en cambio, por otra parte

although conj aunque

altitude n altitud f

altogether adv completamente; (on the whole) en total

aluminium, **aluminum** (Amer) n aluminio m

always adv siempre

am ⇒BE

a.m. abbr (= **ante meridiem**) de la mañana

amalgamate vt amalgamar. ● vi amalgamarse

amass vt acumular

amateur a & n amateur (m & f). ~**ish** a (pej) torpe, chapucero

amaz|e vt asombrar. ~**ed** a asombrado, estupefacto. **be** ~**ed at** quedarse asombrado de, asombrarse de. ~**ement** n asombro m. ~**ing** a increíble

ambassador n embajador m

ambigu|ity n ambigüedad f. ~**ous** a ambiguo

ambiti|on n ambición f. ~**ous** a ambicioso

ambivalent a ambivalente

amble vi andar despacio, andar sin prisa

ambulance n ambulancia f

ambush *n* emboscada *f*. ● *vt* tender una emboscada a

amen *int* amén

amend *vt* enmendar. ~**ment** *n* enmienda *f*. ~**s** *npl*. make ~**s** reparar

amenities *npl* servicios *mpl*; (of hotel, club) instalaciones *fpl*

America *n* (continent) América; (North America) Estados *mpl* Unidos, Norteamérica *f*. ~**n** *a & n* americano (*m*); (North American) estadounidense (*m & f*), norteamericano (*m*). ~**nism** *n* americanismo *m*

amiable *a* simpático

amicable *a* amistoso

amid(st) *prep* entre, en medio de

ammonia *n* amoníaco *m*, amoniaco *m*

ammunition *n* municiones *fpl*

amnesty *n* amnistía *f*

amok *adv*. run ~ volverse loco

among(st) *prep* entre

amount *n* cantidad *f*; (total) total *m*, suma *f*. □ ~ to *vt* sumar; (fig) equivaler a, significar

amp(ere) *n* amperio *m*

amphibi|an *n* anfibio *m*. ~**ous** *a* anfibio

amphitheatre *n* anfiteatro *m*

ampl|e (-er, -est) *a* amplio; (enough) suficiente; (plentiful) abundante. ~**y** *adv* ampliamente, bastante

amplif|ier *n* amplificador *m*. ~**y** *vt* amplificar

amputat|e *vt* amputar. ~**ion** *n* amputación *f*

amus|e *vt* divertir. ~**ed** *a* <*expression*> divertido. keep s.o. ~**ed** entretener a uno. ~**ement** *n* diversión *f*. ~**ing** *a* divertido

an ⇒A

anaemi|a *n* anemia *f*. ~**c** *a* anémico

anaesthe|tic *n* anestésico *m*. ~**tist** *n* anestesista *m & f*

anagram *n* anagrama *m*

analogy *n* analogía *f*

analy|se *vt* analizar. ~**sis** *n* (*pl* -ses) *n* análisis *m*. ~**st** *n* analista *m & f*. ~**tic(al)** *a* analítico

anarch|ist *n* anarquista *m & f*. ~**y** *n* anarquía *f*

anatom|ical *a* anatómico. ~**y** *n* anatomía *f*

ancest|or *n* antepasado *m*. ~**ral** *a* ancestral. ~**ry** *n* ascendencia *f*

anchor *n* ancla *f*. ● *vt* anclar; (fig) sujetar. ● *vi* anclar. ~**man** *n* (on TV) presentador *m*. ~**woman** *n* (on TV) presentadora *f*.

ancient *a* antiguo, viejo

ancillary *a* auxiliar

and *conj* y; (before **i-** and **hi-**) e. bread ~ butter pan *m* con mantequilla. go ~ see him ve a verlo. more ~ more cada vez más. try ~ come trata de venir

anecdot|al *a* anecdótico. ~**e** *n* anécdota *f*

anew *adv* de nuevo

angel *n* ángel *m*. ~**ic** *a* angélico

anger *n* ira *f*. ● *vt* enfadar, (esp LAm) enojar

angle *n* ángulo *m*; (fig) punto *m* de vista. ~**r** *n* pescador *m*

Anglican *a & n* anglicano (*m*)

angr|ily *adv* con enfado, (esp LAm) con enojo. ~**y** *a* (**-ier, -iest**) enfadado, (esp LAm) enojado. get ~**y** enfadarse, enojarse (esp LAm)

anguish *n* angustia *f*

animal *a & n* animal (*m*)

animat|e *vt* animar. ~**ion** *n* animación *f*

animosity *n* animosidad *f*

ankle *n* tobillo *m*. ~ boot botín *m*. ~ sock calcetín *m* corto

annexe *n* anexo *m*

annihilat|e *vt* aniquilar. **~ion** *n* aniquilación *f*

anniversary *n* aniversario *m*

announce *vt* anunciar, comunicar. **~ment** *n* anuncio *m*; (official) comunicado *m*. **~r** *n* (Radio, TV) locutor *m*

annoy *vt* molestar. **~ance** *n* molestia *m*. **~ed** *a* enfadado, enojado (LAm). **~ing** *a* molesto

annual *a* anual. ● *n* anuario *m*. **~ly** *adv* cada año

annul *vt* (*pt* **annulled**) anular

anonymous *a* anónimo

anorak *n* anorac *m*

another *a & pron* otro. **~ 10 minutes** 10 minutos más. **in ~ way** de otra manera. **one ~** el uno al otro; (*pl*) unos a otros

answer *n* respuesta *f*; (solution) solución *f*. ● *vt* contestar; escuchar, oír <*prayer*>. **~ the door** abrir la puerta. ● *vi* contestar. □ **~ back** *vi* contestar. □ **~ for** *vt* ser responsable de. **~able** *a* responsable. **~ing machine** *n* contestador *m* automático

ant *n* hormiga *f*

antagoni|sm *n* antagonismo *m*. **~stic** *a* antagónico, opuesto. **~ze** *vt* provocar la enemistad de

Antarctic *a* antártico. ● *n* **the ~** la región antártica

antelope *n* antílope *m*

antenatal *a* prenatal

antenna (*pl* **-nae**) (of insect etc) *n* antena *f*; (*pl* **-nas**) (of radio, TV) antena *f*

anthem *n* himno *m*

anthology *n* antología *f*

anthrax *n* ántrax *m*

anthropolog|ist *n* antropólogo *m*. **~y** *n* antropología *f*

anti-... *pref* anti... **~aircraft** *a* antiaéreo

antibiotic *a & n* antibiótico (*m*)

anticipat|e *vt* anticiparse a; (foresee) prever; (forestall) prevenir. **~ion** *n* (foresight) previsión *f*; (expectation) expectativa *f*

anti: ~climax *n* decepción *f*. **~clockwise** *adv & a* en sentido contrario al de las agujas del reloj

antidote *m* antídoto *m*

antifreeze *n* anticongelante *m*

antiperspirant *n* antitranspirante *m*

antiquated *a* anticuado

antique *a* antiguo. ● *n* antigüedad *f*. **~ dealer** anticuario *m*. **~ shop** tienda *f* de antigüedades

antiquity *n* antigüedad *f*

anti: ~septic *a & n* antiséptico (*m*). **~social** *a* antisocial

antlers *npl* cornamenta *f*

anus *n* ano *m*

anvil *n* yunque *m*

anxi|ety *n* ansiedad *f*; (worry) inquietud *f*; (eagerness) anhelo *m*. **~ous** *a* inquieto; (eager) deseoso. **~ously** *adv* con inquietud; (eagerly) con impaciencia

any *a* algún; (negative) ningún *m*; (whatever) cualquier; (every) todo. **at ~ moment** en cualquier momento. **have you ~ wine?** ¿tienes vino? ● *pron* alguno; (negative) ninguno. **have we ~?** ¿tenemos algunos? **not ~** ninguno. ● *adv* (a little) un poco, algo. **is it ~ better?** ¿está algo mejor?

anybody *pron* alguien; (*after negative*) nadie. **~ can do it** cualquiera puede hacerlo

anyhow *adv* de todas formas; (in spite of all) a pesar de todo; (badly) de cualquier manera

anyone *pron* ⇒ANYBODY

anything *pron* algo; (whatever) cualquier cosa; (after negative) nada. ~ **but** todo menos

anyway *adv* de todas formas

anywhere *adv* en cualquier parte; (after negative) en ningún sitio. ~ **else** en cualquier otro lugar. ~ **you go** dondequiera que vayas

apart *adv* aparte; (separated) separado. ~ **from** aparte de. **come** ~ romperse. **take** ~ desmontar

apartheid *n* apartheid *m*

apartment *n* (Amer) apartamento *m*, piso *m*. ~ **building** *n* (Amer) edificio *m* de apartamentos, casa *f* de pisos

apath|etic *a* apático. ~**y** *n* apatía *f*

ape *n* mono *m*. ● *vt* imitar

aperitif *n* aperitivo *m*

aperture *n* abertura *f*

apex *n* ápice *m*

aphrodisiac *a & n* afrodisíaco (*m*), afrodisiaco (*m*)

apolog|etic *a* lleno de disculpas. **be** ~**etic** disculparse. ~**ize** *vi* disculparse (for de). ~**y** *n* disculpa *f*

apostle *n* apóstol *m*

apostrophe *n* apóstrofo *m*

appal *vt* (pt **appalled**) horrorizar. ~**ling** *a* espantoso

apparatus *n* aparato *m*

apparel *n* (Amer) ropa *f*

apparent *a* aparente; (clear) evidente. ~**ly** *adv* por lo visto

apparition *n* aparición *f*

appeal *vi* apelar; (attract) atraer. ● *n* llamamiento *m*; (attraction) atractivo *m*; (Jurid) apelación *f*. ~**ing** *a* atrayente

appear *vi* aparecer; (seem) parecer; (in court) comparecer.

~**ance** *n* aparición *f*; (aspect) aspecto *m*; (in court) comparecencia *f*

appease *vt* aplacar; (pacify) apaciguar

append *vt* adjuntar

appendicitis *n* apendicitis *f*

appendix *n* (pl **-ices**) (of book) apéndice *m*. (pl **-ixes**) (Anat) apéndice *m*

appetite *n* apetito *m*

applau|d *vt/i* aplaudir. ~**se** *n* aplausos *mpl*. **round of** ~**se** aplauso *m*

apple *n* manzana *f*. ~ **tree** *n* manzano *m*

appliance *n* aparato *m*. **electrical** ~ electrodoméstico *m*

applic|able *a* aplicable; (relevant) pertinente. ~**ant** *n* candidato *m*, solicitante *m & f*. ~**ation** *n* aplicación *f*; (request) solicitud *f*. ~**ation form** formulario *m* (de solicitud)

appl|ied *a* aplicado. ~**y** *vt* aplicar. ● *vi* aplicarse; (ask) presentar una solicitud. ~**y for** solicitar <job etc>

appoint *vt* nombrar; (fix) señalar. ~**ment** *n* cita *f*

apprais|al *n* evaluación *f*. ~**e** *vt* evaluar

appreciable *a* (considerable) considerable

appreciat|e *vt* (value) apreciar; (understand) comprender; (be grateful for) agradecer. ~**ion** *n* aprecio *m*; (gratitude) agradecimiento *m*. ~**ive** *a* agradecido

apprehen|sion *n* (fear) recelo *f*. ~**sive** *a* aprensivo

apprentice *n* aprendiz *m*. ● *vt*. **be** ~**d to s.o.** estar de aprendiz con uno. ~**ship** *n* aprendizaje *m*

approach *vt* acercarse a. ● *vi* acercarse. ● *n* acercamiento *m*;

(to problem) enfoque *m*; (access) acceso *m*

appropriate *a* apropiado. ● *vt* apropiarse de. ~**ly** *adv* apropiadamente

approv|al *n* aprobación *f*. **on** ~**al** a prueba. ~**e** *vt/i* aprobar. ~**ingly** *adv* con aprobación

approximat|e *a* aproximado. ● *vt* aproximarse a. ~**ely** *adv* aproximadamente. ~**ion** *n* aproximación *f*

apricot *n* albaricoque *m*, chabacano *m* (Mex)

April *n* abril *m*. ~ **fool!** ¡inocentón!

apron *n* delantal *m*

apt *a* apropiado. **be** ~ **to** tener tendencia a. ~**itude** *n* aptitud *f*. ~**ly** *adv* acertadamente

aquarium *n* (*pl* -**ums**) acuario *m*

Aquarius *n* Acuario *m*

aquatic *a* acuático

aqueduct *n* acueducto *m*

Arab *a* & *n* árabe (*m* & *f*). ~**ian** *a* árabe. ~**ic** *a* & *n* árabe (*m*). ~**ic numerals** números *mpl* arábigos

arable *a* cultivable

arbitrary *a* arbitrario

arbitrat|e *vi* arbitrar. ~**ion** *n* arbitraje *m*. ~**or** *n* árbitro *m*

arc *n* arco *m*

arcade *n* arcada *f*; (around square) soportales *mpl*; (shops) galería *f*

arch *n* arco *m*. ● *vt* arquear. ● *vi* arquearse

archaeolog|ical *a* arqueológico. ~**ist** *n* arqueólogo *m*. ~**y** *n* arqueología *f*

archaic *a* arcaico

archbishop *n* arzobispo *m*

archer *n* arquero *m*. ~**y** *n* tiro *m* con arco

architect *n* arquitecto *m*. ~**ure** *n* arquitectura *f*. ~**ural** *a* arquitectónico

archives *npl* archivo *m*

archway *n* arco *m*

Arctic *a* ártico. ● *n*. **the** ~ el Ártico

ard|ent *a* fervoroso; <supporter, lover> apasionado. ~**our** *n* fervor *m*; (love) pasión *f*

arduous *a* arduo

are ⇒BE

area *n* (Math) superficie *f*; (of country) zona *f*; (of city) barrio *m*

arena *n* arena *f*; (scene of activity) ruedo *m*

aren't = **are not**

Argentin|a *n* Argentina *f*. ~**ian** *a* & *n* argentino (*m*)

argu|able *a* discutible. ~**e** *vi* discutir; (reason) razonar. ~**ment** *n* disputa *f*; (reasoning) argumento *m*. ~**mentative** *a* discutidor

arid *a* árido

Aries *n* Aries *m*

arise *vi* (*pt* **arose**, *pp* **arisen**) surgir (**from** de)

aristocra|cy *n* aristocracia *f*. ~**t** *n* aristócrata *m* & *f*. ~**tic** *a* aristocrático

arithmetic *n* aritmética *f*

ark *n* (Relig) arca *f*

arm *n* brazo *m*; (of garment) manga *f*. ~**s** *npl* armas *fpl*. ● *vt* armar

armament *n* armamento *m*

arm: ~**band** *n* brazalete *m*. ~**chair** *n* sillón *m*

armed *a* armado. ~ **robbery** *n* robo *m* a mano armada

armful *n* brazada *f*

armour *n* armadura *f*. ~**ed** *a* blindado. ~**y** *n* arsenal *m*

armpit *n* sobaco *m*, axila *f*

army *n* ejército *m*

aroma *n* aroma *m*

arose ⇒ARISE

around *adv* alrededor; (near) cerca. **all** ~ por todas partes.

● *prep* alrededor de; (with time) a eso de

arouse *vt* despertar

arrange *vt* arreglar; (fix) fijar. ~**ment** *n* arreglo *m*; (agreement) acuerdo *m*. ~**ments** *npl* (plans) preparativos *mpl*

arrears *npl* atrasos *mpl*. in ~ atrasado en el pago (with de)

arrest *vt* detener. ● *n* detención *f*. under ~ detenido

arriv|al *n* llegada *f*. new ~al recién llegado *m*. ~e *vi* llegar

arrogan|ce *n* arrogancia *f*. ~t *a* arrogante. ~tly *adv* con arrogancia

arrow *n* flecha *f*

arse *n* (vulg) culo *m*

arsenal *n* arsenal *m*

arsenic *n* arsénico *m*

arson *n* incendio *m* provocado. ~ist *n* incendiario *m*

art¹ *n* arte *m*. **A~s** *npl* (Univ) Filosofía y Letras *fpl*. fine ~s bellas artes *fpl*

art² (old use, with thou) ⇒ARE

artery *n* arteria *f*

art gallery *n* museo *m* de arte, pinacoteca *f*; <commercial> galería *f* de arte

arthritis *n* artritis *f*

article *n* artículo *m*. ~ of clothing prenda *f* de vestir

articulat|e *a* <utterance> articulado; <person> que sabe expresarse. ● *vt/i* articular. ~ed lorry *n* camión *m* articulado. ~ion *n* articulación *f*

artificial *a* artificial. ~ respiration respiración *f* artificial

artillery *n* artillería *f*

artist *n* artista *m* & *f*. ~tic *a* artístico. ~ry *n* arte *m*, habilidad *f*

as *adv* & *conj* como; (since) ya que; (while) mientras. ~ big ~ tan grande como. ~ far ~ (distance) hasta; (qualitative) en cuanto a. ~ far ~ I know que yo sepa. ~ if como si. ~ long ~ mientras. ~ much ~ tanto como. ~ soon ~ tan pronto como. ~ well también

asbestos *n* amianto *m*, asbesto *m*

ascen|d *vt/i* subir. **A~sion** *n*. the **A~sion** la Ascensión. ~t *n* subida *f*

ascertain *vt* averiguar

ash *n* ceniza *f*. ● *n*. ~ (tree) fresno *m*

ashamed *a* avergonzado (of de). be ~ of s.o. avergonzarse de uno

ashore *adv* a tierra. go ~ desembarcar

ash: ~tray *n* cenicero *m*. **A~ Wednesday** *n* Miércoles *m* de Ceniza

Asia *n* Asia *f*. ~n *a* & *n* asiático (*m*). ~tic *a* asiático

aside *adv* a un lado. ● *n* (in theatre) aparte *m*

ask *vt* pedir; hacer <question>; (invite) invitar. ~ about enterarse de. ~ s.o. to do something pedirle a uno quehaga algo. □ ~ after *vt* preguntar por. □ ~ for *vt*. ~ for help pedir ayuda. ~ for trouble buscarse problemas. □ ~ in *vt*. ~ s.o. in invitar a uno a pasar

askew *adv* & *a* torcido

asleep *adv* & *a* dormido. fall ~ dormirse

asparagus *n* espárrago *m*

aspect *n* aspecto *m*

asphalt *n* asfalto *m*. ● *vt* asfaltar

aspir|ation *n* aspiración *f*. ~e *vi* aspirar

aspirin *n* aspirina *f*

ass *n* asno *m*; (fig, 🛈) imbécil *m*; (Amer vulg) culo *m*

assassin *n* asesino *m*. ~ate *vt* asesinar. ~ation *n* asesinato *m*

assault n (Mil) ataque m; (Jurid) atentado m. ● vt asaltar

assembl|e vt reunir; (Mec) montar. ● vi reunirse. ~**y** n reunión f; (Pol etc) asamblea f. ~**y line** n línea f de montaje

assent n asentimiento m. ● vi asentir

assert vt afirmar; hacer valer <one's rights>. ~**ion** n afirmación f. ~**ive** a positivo, firme

assess vt evaluar; (determine) determinar; fijar <tax etc>. ~**ment** n evaluación f

asset n (advantage) ventaja f. ~**s** npl (Com) bienes mpl

assign vt asignar; (appoint) nombrar. ~**ment** n asignación f; (mission) misión f; (task) función f; (for school) trabajo m

assimilate vt asimilar. ● vi asimilarse

assist vt/i ayudar. ~**ance** n ayuda f. ~**ant** n ayudante m & f; (shop) dependienta f, dependiente m. ● a auxiliar, adjunto

associat|e vt asociar. ● vi asociarse. ● a asociado. ● n colega m & f; (Com) socio m. ~**ion** n asociación f.

assort|ed a surtido. ~**ment** n surtido m

assum|e vt suponer; tomar <power, attitude>; asumir <role, burden>. ~**ption** n suposición f

assur|ance n seguridad f; (insurance) seguro m. ~**e** vt asegurar. ~**ed** a seguro

asterisk n asterisco m

asthma n asma f. ~**tic** a & n asmático (m)

astonish vt asombrar. ~**ed** adj asombrado. ~**ing** a asombroso. ~**ment** n asombro m

astound vt asombrar. ~**ed** adj atónito. ~**ing** adj increíble

astray adv. go ~ extraviarse. lead ~ llevar por mal camino

astrology n astrología f

astronaut n astronauta m & f

astronom|er n astrónomo m. ~**ical** a astronómico. ~**y** n astronomía f

astute a astuto

asylum n asilo m. lunatic ~ manicomio m

....

at

● *preposition*

····▶ (location) en. **she's at the office** está en la oficina. **at home** en casa. **call me at the office** llámame a la oficina

➡ For translations of phrases such as **at the top, at the front of, at the back of** see entries **top, front** etc

····▶ (at the house of) en casa de. **I'll be at Rachel's** estaré en casa de Rachel

····▶ (in e-mails: @) arroba f

····▶ (talking about time) **at 7 o'clock** las siete. **at night** por la noche, de noche, en la noche (LAm). **at Christmas** en Navidad

····▶ (talking about age) a. **at six (years) of age)** a los seis años

····▶ (with measurements, numbers etc) a. **at 60 miles an hour** a 60 millas por hora. **at a depth of** a una profundidad de. **three at a time** de tres en tres

➡ For translations of phrasal verbs with **at**, such as **look at**, see entries for those verbs

....

ate ➡EAT

atheis|m n ateísmo m. ~**t** n ateo m

athlet|e n atleta m & f. ~**ic** a atlético. ~**ics** npl atletismo m; (Amer, Sport) deportes mpl

Atlantic a atlántico. ● n. the ~ (**Ocean**) el (Océano) Atlántico

atlas n atlas m

ATM abbr (= **automated teller machine**) cajero m automático

atmospher|e n atmósfera f; (fig) ambiente m. ~**ic** a atmosférico

atom n átomo m. ~**ic** a atómico

atroci|ous a atroz. ~**ty** n atrocidad f

attach vt sujetar; adjuntar <document etc>. **be ~ed to** (be fond of) tener cariño a. ~**ment** n (affection) cariño m; (tool) accesorio m

attack n ataque m. ● vt/i atacar. ~**er** n agresor m

attain vt conseguir. ~**able** a alcanzable

attempt vt intentar. ● n tentativa f; (attack) atentado m

attend vt asistir a; (escort) acompañar. ● vi prestar atención. □ ~ **to** vt (look after) ocuparse de. ~**ance** n asistencia f; (people present) concurrencia f

atten|tion n atención f. ~**tion!** (Mil) ¡firmes! **pay ~tion** prestar atención. ~**tive** a atento

attic n desván m

attire n atavío m. ● vt ataviar

attitude n postura f

attorney n (pl -**eys**) (Amer) abogado m

attract vt atraer. ~**ion** n atracción f; (charm) atractivo m. ~**ive** a atractivo; (interesting) atrayente

attribute vt atribuir. ● n atributo m

aubergine n berenjena f

auction n subasta f. ● vt subastar. ~**eer** n subastador m

audaci|ous a audaz. ~**ty** n audacia f

audible a audible

audience n (at play, film) público m; (TV) audiencia f; (interview) audiencia f

audiovisual a audiovisual

audit n revisión f de cuentas. ● vt revisar

audition n audición f. ● vt hacerle una audición a. ● vi dar una audición (**for** para)

auditor n interventor m de cuentas

auditorium (pl -**riums** or -**ria**) n sala f, auditorio m

augment vt aumentar

augur vt augurar. **it ~s well** es de buen agüero

August n agosto m

aunt n tía f

au pair n chica f au pair

aura n aura f, halo m

auster|e a austero. ~**ity** n austeridad f

Australia n Australia f. ~**n** a & n australiano (m)

Austria n Austria f. ~**n** a & n austríaco (m)

authentic a auténtico. ~**ate** vt autenticar. ~**ity** n autenticidad f

author n autor m. ~**ess** n autora f

authoritative a autorizado; <manner> autoritario

authority n autoridad f; (permission) autorización f

authoriz|ation n autorización f. ~**e** vt autorizar

autobiography n autobiografía f

autograph n autógrafo m. ● vt firmar, autografiar

automat|e vt automatizar. ~**ic** a automático. ~**ion** n automatización f. ~**on** n (pl -**tons** or -**ta**) autómata m

automobile n (Amer) coche m, carro m (LAm), automóvil m

autonom|ous a autónomo. **~y** n autonomía f

autopsy n autopsia f

autumn n otoño m. **~al** a otoñal

auxiliary a & n auxiliar (m & f)

avail n. to no ~ inútil

availab|ility n disponibilidad f. **~le** a disponible

avalanche n avalancha f

avaric|e n avaricia f. **~ious** a avaro

avenue n avenida f; (fig) vía f

average n promedio m. on ~ por término medio. ● a medio

avers|e a. be **~e** to ser reacio a. **~ion** n repugnancia f

avert vt (turn away) apartar; (ward off) desviar

aviation n aviación f

avid a ávido

avocado n (pl **-os**) aguacate m

avoid vt evitar. **~able** a evitable. **~ance** n el evitar

await vt esperar

awake vt/i (pt **awoke**, pp **awoken**) despertar. ● a despierto. **wide** ~ completamente despierto; (fig) despabilado. **~n** vt/i despertar. **~ning** n el despertar

award vt otorgar; (Jurid) adjudicar. ● n premio m; (Jurid) adjudicación f; (scholarship) beca f

aware a. be ~ of sth ser consciente de algo, darse cuenta de algo

awash a inundado

away adv (absent) fuera. **far** ~ muy lejos. ● a. ~ **match** partido m fuera de casa

awe n temor m. **~-inspiring** a impresionante. **~some** a imponente

awful a terrible, malísimo. **feel** ~ sentirse muy mal

awkward a difícil; (inconvenient) inoportuno; (clumsy) desmañado; (embarrassed) incómodo. **~ness** n dificultad f; (discomfort) molestia f; (clumsiness) torpeza f

awning n toldo m

awoke, awoken ⇒AWAKE

axe n hacha f. ● vt (pres p **axing**) cortar con hacha; (fig) recortar

axis n (pl **axes**) eje m

axle n eje m

BA abbr ⇒BACHELOR

babble vi balbucir; (chatter) parlotear; <stream> murmurar.

baboon n mandril m

baby n niño m, bebé m. ~ **buggy**, ~ **carriage** n (Amer) cochecito m. **~ish** a infantil. **~-sit** vi cuidar a los niños, hacer de canguro. **~-sitter** n baby sitter m & f, canguro m & f

bachelor n soltero m. **B~ of Arts (BA)** licenciado m en filosofía y letras. **B~ of Science (BSc)** licenciado m en ciencias

back n espalda f; (of car) parte f trasera; (of chair) respaldo m; (of cloth) revés m; (of house) parte f de atrás; (of animal, book) lomo m; (of hand, document) dorso m; (football) defensa m & f. **in the ~ of beyond** en el quinto infierno. ● a trasero. **the ~ door** la puerta trasera. ● adv atrás; (returned) de vuelta. ● vt apoyar; (betting) apostar a; da:

marcha atrás a <*car*>. ● *vi*
retroceder; <*car*> dar marcha
atrás. □ ~ **down** *vi* volverse
atrás. □ ~ **out** *vi* retirarse. □ ~
up *vt* apoyar; (Comp) hacer una
copia de seguridad de. ~**ache** *n*
dolor *m* de espalda. ~**bone** *n*
columna *f* vertebral; (fig) pilar *m*.
~**date** *vt* antedatar. ~**er** *n*
partidario *m*; (Com) financiador
m. ~**fire** *vi* (Auto) petardear; (fig)
fallar. **his plan ~fired on him** le
salió el tiro por la culata.
~**ground** *n* fondo *m*; (environment)
antecedentes *mpl*. ~**hand** *n*
(Sport) revés *m*. ~**ing** *n* apoyo *m*.
~**lash** *n* reacción *f*. ~**log** *n*
atrasos *mpl*. ~**side** *n* Ⅰ trasero
m. ~**stage** *a* de bastidores. ● *adv*
entre bastidores. ~**stroke** *n*
(tennis etc) revés *m*; (swimming)
estilo *m* espalda, estilo *m* dorso
(Mex). ~**up** *n* apoyo *m*; (Comp)
copia *f* de seguridad. ~**ward** *a*
<*step etc*> hacia atrás; (retarded)
retrasado;(undeveloped) atrasado.
● *adv* (Amer) ⇒BACKWARDS.
~**wards** *adv* hacia atrás; (fall) de
espaldas; (back to front) al revés. **go
~wards and forwards** ir de acá
para allá. ~**water** *n* agua *f*
estancada; (fig) lugar *m* apartado
bacon *n* tocino *m*
bacteria *npl* bacterias *fpl*
bad *a* (**worse, worst**) malo,
(before masculine singular noun) mal;
(serious) grave; (harmful) nocivo;
<*language*> indecente. **feel ~**
sentirse mal
bade ⇒BID
badge *n* distintivo *m*, chapa *f*
badger *n* tejón *m*. ● *vt* acosar
bad: ~ly *adv* mal. **want ~ly**
desear muchísimo. ~**ly injured**
gravemente herido. ~**ly off** mal
de dinero. ~**-mannered** *a* mal
educado

badminton *n* bádminton *m*
bad-tempered *a* (always) de mal
carácter; (temporarily) de mal
humor
baffle *vt* desconcertar. ~**d** *a*
perplejo
bag *n* bolsa *f*; (handbag) bolso *m*.
● *vt* (*pt* **bagged**) ensacar; (take)
coger (esp Spain), agarrar (LAm).
~**s** *npl* (luggage) equipaje *m*
baggage *n* equipaje *m*. ~ **room**
n (Amer) consigna *f*
baggy *a* <*clothes*> holgado
bagpipes *npl* gaita *f*
baguette *n* baguette *f*
bail¹ *n* fianza *f*. ● *vt* poner en
libertad bajo fianza. ~ **s.o. out**
pagar la fianza a uno
bail² *vt*. ~ **out** (Naut) achicar
bait *n* cebo *m*
bak|e *vt* cocer al horno. ● *vi*
cocerse. ~**er** *n* panadero *m*.
~**ery** *n* panadería *f*
balance *n* equilibrio *m*; (Com)
balance *m*; (sum) saldo *m*; (scales)
balanza *f*; (remainder) resto *m*. ● *vt*
equilibrar <*load*>; mantener en
equilibrio <*object*>; nivelar
<*budget*>. ● *vi* equilibrarse; (Com)
cuadrar. ~**d** *a* equilibrado
balcony *n* balcón *m*
bald *a* (**-er, -est**) calvo, pelón
(Mex)
bale *n* bala *f*, fardo *m*. ● *vi*. ~ **out**
lanzarse en paracaídas
Balearic *a*. **the ~ Islands** las Islas
fpl Baleares
ball *n* bola *f*; (tennis etc) pelota *f*;
(football etc) balón *m*, pelota *f* (esp
LAm); (of yarn) ovillo *m*; (*dance*)
baile *m*
ballad *n* balada *f*
ballast *n* lastre *m*
ball bearing *n* cojinete *m* de
bolas
ballerina *f* bailarina *f*

ballet n ballet m. ~ **dancer** n bailarín m de ballet, bailarina f de ballet

balloon n globo m

ballot n votación f. ~ **box** n urna f. ~ **paper** n papeleta f.

ball: ~**point** n. ~**point (pen)** bolígrafo m, pluma f atómica (Mex). ~**room** n salón m de baile

bamboo n bambú m

ban vt (pt banned) prohibir. ~ s.o. from sth prohibir algo a uno. ● n prohibición f

banal a banal. ~**ity** n banalidad f

banana n plátano m

band n (strip) banda f. ● n (Mus) orquesta f; (military, brass) banda f. □ ~ **together** vi juntarse

bandage n venda f. ● vt vendar

Band-Aid n (Amer, P) tirita f, curita f (LAm)

B & B abbr (= **bed and breakfast**) cama f y desayuno; (place) pensión f

bandit n bandido m

band: ~**stand** n quiosco m de música. ~**wagon** n. **jump on the** ~**wagon** (fig) subirse al carro

bandy a (-ier, -iest) patizambo

bang n (noise) ruido m; (blow) golpe m; (of gun) estampido m; (of door) golpe m. ● vt (strike) golpear. ~ **the door** dar un portazo. ● adv exactamente. ● int ¡pum! ~s npl (Amer) flequillo m, cerquillo m (LAm), fleco m (Mex)

banger n petardo m; (▣, Culin) salchicha f

bangle n brazalete m

banish vt desterrar

banisters npl pasamanos m

banjo n (pl -os) banjo m

bank n (Com) banco m; (of river) orilla f. ● vt depositar. ● vi (Aviat) ladearse. □ ~ **on** vt contar con. □ ~ **with** vi tener una cuenta

con. ~ **card** tarjeta f bancaria; (Amer) tarjeta f de crédito (expedida por un banco). ~**er** n banquero m. ~ **holiday** n día m festivo, día m feriado (LAm). ~**ing** n (Com) banca f. ~**note** n billete m de banco

bankrupt a & n quebrado (m). **go** ~ quebrar. ● vt hacer quebrar. ~**cy** n bancarrota f, quiebra f

bank statement n estado m de cuenta

banner n bandera f; (in demonstration) pancarta f

banquet n banquete m

banter n chanza f

bap n panecillo m blando

baptism n bautismo m; (act) bautizo m

Baptist n bautista m & f

baptize vt bautizar

bar n barra f; (on window) reja f; (of chocolate) tableta f; (of soap) pastilla f; (pub) bar m; (Mus) compás m; (Jurid) abogacía f; (fig) obstáculo m. ● vt (pt barred) arrancar <door>; (exclude) excluir; (prohibit) prohibir. ● prep excepto

barbar|ian a & n bárbaro (m). ~**ic** a bárbaro

barbecue n barbacoa f. ● vt asar a la parrilla

barbed wire n alambre m de púas

barber n peluquero m, barbero m

barbwire n (Amer) ⇒BARBED WIRE

bare a (-er, -est) desnudo; (room) con pocos muebles; (mere) simple; (empty) vacío. ● vt desnudar; (uncover) descubrir. ~ **one's teeth** mostrar los dientes. ~**back** adv a pelo. ~**faced** a descarado. ~**foot** a descalzo. ~**headed** a descubierto. ~**ly** adv apenas.

bargain n (agreement) pacto m; (good buy) ganga f. ● vi negociar;

B

(haggle) regatear. □ ~ **for** vt esperar, contar con

barge n barcaza f. ● vi. ~ **in** irrumpir

baritone n barítono m

bark n (of dog) ladrido m; (of tree) corteza f. ● vi ladrar

barley n cebada f

bar: ~**maid** n camarera f. ~**man** n camarero m, barman m

barmy a ⊠ chiflado

barn n granero m

barometer n barómetro m

baron n barón m. ~**ess** n baronesa f

barracks npl cuartel m

barrage n (Mil) barrera f; (dam) presa f. **a** ~ **of questions** un aluvión de preguntas

barrel n barril m; (of gun) cañón m

barren a estéril

barrette n (Amer) pasador m

barricade n barricada f. ● vt cerrar con barricadas

barrier n barrera f

barrister n abogado m

bartender n (Amer) (male) camarero m, barman m; (female) camarera f

barter n trueque m. ● vt trocar

base n base f. ● vt basar. ~**ball** n béisbol m, beisbol m (Mex)

basement n sótano m

bash vt golpear. ● n golpe m

bashful a tímido

basic a básico, fundamental. ~**ally** adv fundamentalmente

basin n (for washing) palangana f; (for food) cuenco m; (Geog) cuenca f

basis n (pl **bases**) base f

bask vi asolearse; (fig) gozar (**in** de)

basket n cesta f; (big) cesto m. ~**ball** n baloncesto m, básquetbol m (LAm)

bass[1] a bajo. ● n (Mus) bajo m

bass[2] n (fish) lubina f

barring prep salvo

bassoon n fagot m

bastard n bastardo m. **you** ~! (⊠ or vulg) ¡cabrón! (⊠ or vulg)

bat n (for baseball, cricket) bate m; (for table tennis) raqueta f; (mammal) murciélago m. **off one's own** ~ por sí solo. ● vt (pt **batted**) golpear. **without** ~**ting an eyelid** sin pestañear. ● vi batear

batch n (of people) grupo m; (of papers) pila f; (of goods) remesa f; (of bread) hornada f; (Comp) lote m

bated a. **with** ~ **breath** con aliento entrecortado

bath n (pl **-s**) baño m; (tub) bañera f, tina f (LAm). ~**s** npl (swimming pool) piscina f, alberca f (LAm). **have a** ~, **take a** ~ (Amer) bañarse. ● vt bañar. ● vi bañarse

bathe vt bañar. ● vi bañarse. ● n baño m. ~**r** n bañista m & f

bathing n baños mpl. ~ **costume**, ~ **suit** n traje m de baño

bathroom n cuarto m de baño; (Amer, toilet) servicio m, baño m (LAm)

batsman n (pl **-men**) bateador m

battalion n batallón m

batter vt (beat) apalear; (cover with batter) rebozar. ● n batido m para rebozar; (Amer, for cake) masa f. ~**ed** a <car etc> estropeado; <wife etc> maltratado

battery n (Mil, Auto) batería f; (of torch, radio) pila f

battle n batalla f; (fig) lucha f. ● vi luchar. ~**field** n campo m de batalla. ~**ship** n acorazado m

bawl vt/i gritar

bay n (Geog) bahía f; (for buses) dársena f. **keep at** ~ mantener a raya

bayonet n bayoneta f

bay window n ventana f salediza

bazaar n bazar m

BC abbr (= **before Christ**) a. de C., antes de Cristo

··

be

present **am, are, is**; past **was, were**; past participle **been**

● *intransitive verb*

❗ Spanish has two verbs meaning **be**, *ser* and *estar*. See those entries for further information about the differences between them.

····▶ (position, changed condition or state) estar. **where is the library?** ¿dónde está la biblioteca? **she's tired** está cansada. **how are you?** ¿cómo estás?

····▶ (identity, nature or permanent characteristics) ser. **she's tall** es alta. **he's Scottish** es escocés. **I'm a journalist** soy periodista. **he's very kind** es muy bondadoso

····▶ (feel) **to be** + *adjective* tener + *sustantivo*. **to be cold/hot** tener frío/calor. **he's hungry/thirsty** tiene hambre/sed

····▶ (age) **he's thirty** tiene treinta años

····▶ (weather) **it's cold/hot** hace frío/calor. **it was 40 degrees** hacía 40 grados

● *auxiliary verb*

····▶ (in tenses) estar. **I'm working** estoy trabajando. **they were singing** estaban cantando, cantaban

····▶ (in tag questions) **it's a beautiful house, isn't it?** es una casa preciosa, ¿verdad? or ¿no? or ¿no es cierto?

····▶ (in short answers) **are you disappointed? - yes, I am** ¿estás desilusionado? - sí (,lo estoy). **I'm surprised, aren't you?** estoy sorprendido, ¿tú no?

····▶ (in passive sentences) **it was built in 1834** fue construido en 1834, se construyó en 1834. **she was told that** ... le dijeron que..., se le dijo que ...

❗ Note that passive sentences in English are often translated using the pronoun se or using the third person plural.

··

beach n playa f

beacon n faro m

bead n cuenta f; (of glass) abalorio m

beak n pico m

beaker n taza f (alta y sin asa)

beam n (of wood) viga f; (of light) rayo m; (Naut) bao m. ● vt emitir. ● vi irradiar; (smile) sonreír

bean n alubia f, frijol m (LAm); (broad bean) haba f; (of coffee) grano m

bear vt (pt **bore**, pp **borne**) llevar; parir <niño>; (endure) soportar. ∼ **right** torcer a la derecha. ∼ **in mind** tener en cuenta. □ ∼ **with** vt tener paciencia con. ● n oso m. ∼**able** a soportable

beard n barba f. ∼**ed** a barbudo

bearer n portador m; (of passport) titular m & f

bearing n comportamiento m; (relevance) relación f; (Mec) cojinete m. **get one's** ∼**s** orientarse. **lose one's** ∼**s** desorientarse

beast n bestia f; (person) bruto m. ∼**ly** a (**-ier, -iest**) bestial; 🄸 horrible

beat vt (pt **beat**, pp **beaten**) (hit) pegar; (Culin) batir; (defeat) derrotar; (better) sobrepasar; batir <record>; (baffle) dejar perplejo. ~ **it** 🄵 largarse. ● vi <heart> latir. ● n latido m; (Mus) ritmo m; (of policeman) ronda f. □ ~ **up** vt darle una paliza a; (Culin) batir. ~ **up on** (Amer, 🄵) darle una paliza a. ~**er** n batidor m. ~**ing** n paliza f

beautician n esteticista m & f

beautiful a hermoso. ~**ly** adv maravillosamente

beauty n belleza f. ~ **salon**, ~ **shop** (Amer) n salón m de belleza. ~ **spot** n (on face) lunar m; (site) lugar m pintoresco

beaver n castor m

became ⇒BECOME

because conj porque. ● adv. ~ **of** por, a causa de

beckon vt/i. ~ **(to)** hacer señas (a)

become vi (pt **became**, pp **become**) hacerse, llegar a ser, volverse, convertirse en. **what has** ~ **of her?** ¿qué es de ella?

bed n cama f; (layer) estrato m; (of sea, river) fondo m; (of flowers) macizo m. **go to** ~ acostarse. ~ **and breakfast** (B & B) cama y desayuno; (place) pensión f. ~**bug** n chinche f. ~**clothes** npl, ~**ding** n ropa f de cama, cobijas fpl (LAm). ~**room** n dormitorio m, cuarto m, habitación f, recámara f (Mex). ~-**sitter** n habitación f con cama y uso de cocina y baño compartidos, estudio m. ~**spread** n colcha f. ~**time** n hora f de acostarse

bee n abeja f; (Amer, social gathering) círculo m

beech n haya f

beef n carne f de vaca, carne f de res (Mex). ● vi 🄵 quejarse.

~**burger** n hamburguesa f. ~**y** a (-**ier**, -**iest**) musculoso

bee: ~**hive** n colmena f. ~**line** n. **make a** ~**line for** ir en línea recta hacia

been ⇒BE

beer n cerveza f

beet n (Amer) remolacha f, betabel f (Mex)

beetle n escarabajo m

beetroot n invar remolacha f, betabel f (Mex)

befall vt (pt **befell**, pp **befallen**) ocurrirle a. ● vi ocurrir

before prep (time) antes de; (place) delante de. ~ **leaving** antes de marcharse. ● adv (place) delante; (time) antes. **a week** ~ una semana antes. **the week** ~ la semana anterior. ● conj (time) antes de que. ~ **he leaves** antes de que se vaya. ~**hand** adv de antemano

befriend vt hacerse amigo de

beg vt/i (pt **begged**) mendigar; (entreat) suplicar; (ask) pedir. ~ **s.o.'s pardon** pedir perdón a uno. I ~ **your pardon!** ¡perdone Vd! I ~ **your pardon?** ¿cómo?

began ⇒BEGIN

beggar n mendigo m

begin vt/i (pt **began**, pp **begun**, pres p **beginning**) comenzar, empezar. ~**ner** n principiante m & f. ~**ning** n principio m

begrudge vt envidiar; (give) dar de mala gana

begun ⇒BEGIN

behalf n. **on** ~ **of**, **in** ~ **of** (Amer) de parte de, en nombre de

behav|e vi comportarse, portarse. ~**e (o.s.)** portarse bien. ~**iour** n comportamiento m

behead vt decapitar

behind 338 **better**

behind *prep* detrás de, atrás de (LAm). ● *adv* detrás; (late) atrasado. ● *n* Ⅰ trasero *m*

beige *a & n* beige (*m*)

being *n* ser *m*. **come into ~** nacer

belated *a* tardío

belch *vi* eructar. □ **~ out** *vt* arrojar <*smoke*>

belfry *n* campanario *m*

Belgi|an *a & n* belga (*m & f*). **~um** *n* Bélgica *f*

belie|f *n* (trust) fe *f*; (opinion) creencia *f*. **~ve** *vt/i* creer. **~ve in** creer en. **make ~ve** fingir

belittle *vt* menospreciar <*achievements*>; denigrar <*person*>

bell *n* campana *f*; (on door, bicycle) timbre *m*

belligerent *a* beligerante

bellow *vt* gritar. ● *vi* bramar. **~s** *npl* fuelle *m*

bell pepper *n* (Amer) pimiento *m*

belly *n* barriga *f*

belong *vi* pertenecer (**to** a); (club) ser socio (**to** de); (have as usual place) ir. **~ings** *npl* pertenencias *fpl*. **personal ~ings** efectos *mpl* personales

beloved *a* querido

below *prep* debajo de, abajo de (LAm); (fig) inferior a. ● *adv* abajo

belt *n* cinturón *m*; (area) zona *f*. ● *vt* (fig) rodear; ✗ darle una paliza a. **~way** *n* (Amer) carretera *f* de circunvalación

bench *n* banco *m*

bend *n* curva *f*. ● *vt* (*pt & pp* **bent**) doblar; torcer <*arm, leg*>. ● *vi* doblarse; <*road*> torcerse. □ **~ down** *vi* inclinarse □ **~ over** *vi* agacharse

beneath *prep* debajo de; (fig) inferior a. ● *adv* abajo

beneficial *a* provechoso

beneficiary *n* beneficiario *m*

benefit *n* provecho *m*, ventaja *f*; (allowance) prestación *f*; (for unemployed) subsidio *m*; (perk) beneficio *m*. ● *vt* (*pt* **benefited**, *pres p* **benefiting**) beneficiar. ● *vi* beneficiarse

benevolent *a* benévolo

benign *a* benigno

bent ⇒BEND. ● *n* inclinación *f*. ● *a* torcido; (✗, corrupt) corrompido

bereave|d *n*. **the ~d** la familia del difunto. **~ment** *n* pérdida *f*; (mourning) luto *m*

beret *n* boina *f*

berry *n* baya *f*

berserk *a*. **go ~** volverse loco

berth *n* litera *f*; (anchorage) amarradero *m*. **give a wide ~ to** evitar. ● *vt/i* atracar

beside *prep* al lado de. **be ~ o.s.** estar fuera de sí

besides *prep* además de; (except) excepto. ● *adv* además

besiege *vt* sitiar, asediar; (fig) acosar

best *a* (el) mejor. **the ~ thing is to...** lo mejor es... ● *adv* mejor. **like ~** preferir. ● *n* lo mejor. **at ~** a lo más. **do one's ~** hacer todo lo posible. **make the ~ of** contentarse con. **~ man** *n* padrino *m* (de boda)

bestow *vt* conceder

bestseller *n* éxito *m* de librería, bestseller *m*

bet *n* apuesta *f*. ● *vt/i* (*pt* **bet** or **betted**) apostar

betray *vt* traicionar. **~al** *n* traición *f*

better *a & adv* mejor. **~ off** en mejores condiciones; (richer) más rico. **get ~** mejorar. **all the ~** tanto mejor. **I'd ~ be off** me tengo que ir. **the ~ part of** la mayor parte de. ● *vt* mejorar; (beat) sobrepasar. **~ o.s.** superarse. ● *n* superior *m*. **get the ~ of** vencer a. **my ~s** mis superiores *mpl*

between *prep* entre. ● *adv* en medio

beverage *n* bebida *f*

beware *vi* tener cuidado. ● *int* ¡cuidado!

bewilder *vt* desconcertar. **~ment** *n* aturdimiento *m*

bewitch *vt* hechizar; (delight) cautivar

beyond *prep* más allá de; (fig) fuera de. **~ doubt** sin lugar a duda. ● *adv* más allá

bias *n* tendencia *f*; (prejudice) prejuicio *m*. ● *vt* (*pt* **biased**) influir en. **~ed** *a* parcial

bib *n* babero *m*

Bible *n* Biblia *f*

biblical *a* bíblico

bibliography *n* bibliografía *f*

biceps *n invar* bíceps *m*

bicker *vi* altercar

bicycle *n* bicicleta *f*

bid *n* (offer) oferta *f*; (attempt) tentativa *f*. ● *vi* hacer una oferta. ● *vt* (*pt & pp* **bid**, *pres p* **bidding**) ofrecer; (*pt* **bid**, *pp* **bidden**, *pres p* **bidding**) mandar; dar <*welcome, good day etc*>. **~der** *n* postor *m*. **~ding** *n* (at auction) ofertas *fpl*; (order) mandato *m*

bide *vt*. **~ one's time** esperar el momento oportuno

bifocals *npl* gafas *fpl* bifocales, anteojos *mpl* bifocales (LAm)

big *a* (**bigger, biggest**) grande, (before singular noun) gran. ● *adv*. **talk ~** fanfarronear

bigam|ist *n* bígamo *m*. **~ous** *a* bígamo. **~y** *n* bigamia *f*

big-headed *a* engreído

bigot *n* fanático *m*. **~ed** *a* fanático

bike *n* 🄸 bici *f* 🄸

bikini *n* (*pl* **-is**) bikini *m*

bile *n* bilis *f*

bilingual *a* bilingüe

bill *n* cuenta *f*; (invoice) factura *f*; (notice) cartel *m*; (Amer, banknote) billete *m*; (Pol) proyecto *m* de ley; (of bird) pico *m*

billet *n* (Mil) alojamiento *m*. ● *vt* alojar

billfold *n* (Amer) cartera *f*, billetera *f*

billiards *n* billar *m*

billion *n* billón *m*; (Amer) mil millones *mpl*

bin *n* recipiente *m*; (for rubbish) cubo *m* de basura, bote *m* de basura (Mex); (for waste paper) papelera *f*

bind *vt* (*pt* **bound**) atar; encuadernar <*book*>; (Jurid) obligar. ● *n* 🄸 lata *f*. **~ing** *n* (of books) encuadernación *f*

binge *n* 🆇 (of food) comilona *f*; (of drink) borrachera *f*. **go on a ~** ir de juerga

bingo *n* bingo *m*

binoculars *npl* gemelos *mpl*

biograph|er *n* biógrafo *m*. **~y** *n* biografía *f*

biolog|ical *a* biológico. **~ist** *n* biólogo *m*. **~y** *n* biología *f*

birch *n* (tree) abedul *m*

bioterrorism *n* bioterrorismo *m*

bird *n* ave *f*; (small) pájaro *m*; (🆇, girl) chica *f*

Biro *n* (*pl* **-os**) (P) bolígrafo *m*

birth *n* nacimiento *m*. **give ~** dar a luz. **~ certificate** *n* partida *f* de nacimiento. **~ control** *n* control *m* de la natalidad. **~day** *n* cumpleaños *m*. **~mark** *n* marca *f* de nacimiento. **~place** *n* lugar *m* de nacimiento. **~ rate** *n* natalidad *f*

biscuit *n* galleta *f*

bisect *vt* bisecar

bishop n obispo m; (Chess) alfil m

bit ⇒BITE. ● n trozo m; (quantity) poco m; (of horse) bocado m; (Mec) broca f; (Comp) bit m

bitch n perra f; (🔒, woman) bruja f 🔒

bit|e vt/i (pt **bit**, pp **bitten**) morder; (insect) picar. ~**e one's nails** morderse las uñas. ● n mordisco m; (mouthful) bocado m; (of insect etc) picadura f. ~**ing** a mordaz

bitter a amargo; <weather> glacial. ● n cerveza f amarga. ~**ly** adv amargamente. **it's** ~**ly cold** hace un frío glacial. ~**ness** n amargor m; (resentment) amargura f

bizarre a extraño

black a (-**er**, -**est**) negro. ~ **and blue** amoratado. ● n negro m; (coffee) solo, negro (LAm). ● vt ennegrecer; limpiar <shoes>. ~ **out** vi desmayarse. ~ **and white** n blanco y negro m. ~-**and-white** adj en blanco y negro. ~**berry** n zarzamora f. ~**bird** n mirlo m. ~**board** n pizarra f. ~**currant** n grosella f negra. ~**en** vt ennegrecer. ~ **eye** n ojo m morado. ~**list** vt poner en la lista negra. ~**mail** n chantaje m. ● vt chantajear. ~**mailer** n chantajista m & f. ~**out** n apagón m; (Med) desmayo m; (of news) censura f. ~**smith** n herrero m

bladder n vejiga f

blade n (of knife, sword) hoja f. ~ **of grass** brizna f de hierba

blame vt echar la culpa a. **be to** ~ tener la culpa. ● n culpa f. ~**less** a inocente

bland a (-**er**, -**est**) suave

blank a <page, space> en blanco; <cassette> virgen; <cartridge> sin bala; (fig) vacío. ● n blanco m

blanket n manta f, cobija f (LAm), frazada (LAm); (fig) capa f. ● vt (pt **blanketed**) (fig) cubrir (**in, with** de)

blare vi sonar muy fuerte. ● n estrépito m

blasphem|e vt/i blasfemar. ~**ous** a blasfemo. ~**y** n blasfemia f

blast n explosión f; (gust) ráfaga f; (sound) toque m. ● vt volar. ~**ed** a maldito. ~-**off** n (of missile) despegue m

blatant a patente; (shameless) descarado

blaze n llamarada f; (of light) resplandor m; (fig) arranque m. ● vi arder en llamas; (fig) brillar

blazer n chaqueta f

bleach n lejía f, cloro m (LAm), blanqueador m (LAm). ● vt blanquear; decolorar <hair>.

bleak a (-**er**, -**est**) desolado; (fig) sombrío

bleat n balido m. ● vi balar

bleed vt/i (pt **bled**) sangrar

bleep n pitido m

blemish n mancha f

blend n mezcla f. ● vt mezclar. ● vi combinarse. ~**er** n licuadora f

bless vt bendecir. ~ **you!** (on sneezing) ¡Jesús!, ¡salud! (Mex). ~**ed** a bendito. ~**ing** n bendición f; (advantage) ventaja f

blew ⇒BLOW

blight n añublo m, tizón m; (fig) plaga f. ● vt añublar, atizonar; (fig) destrozar

blind a ciego. ~ **alley** callejón m sin salida. ● n persiana f; (fig) pretexto m. ● vt dejar ciego; (dazzle) deslumbrar. ~**fold** a & adv con los ojos vendados. ● n venda f. ● vt vendar los ojos a.

~ly *adv* a ciegas. **~ness** *n* ceguera *f*

blink *vi* parpadear; <*light*> centellear. **~ers** *npl* (on horse) anteojeras *fpl*

bliss *n* felicidad *f*. **~ful** *a* feliz

blister *n* ampolla *f*

blizzard *n* ventisca *f*

bloated *a* hinchado (**with** de)

blob *n* (drip) gota *f*; (stain) mancha *f*

bloc *n* (Pol) bloque *m*

block *n* bloque *m*; (of wood) zoquete *m*; (of buildings) manzana *f*, cuadra *f* (LAm). **in ~ letters** en letra de imprenta. **~ of flats** edificio *m* de apartamentos, casa *f* de pisos. ● *vt* bloquear. **~ade** *n* bloqueo *m*. ● *vt* bloquear. **~age** *n* obstrucción *f*. **~head** *n* 🗵 zopenco *m*

bloke *n* 🗵 tipo *m*, tío *m* 🗵

blond *a & n* rubio (*m*), güero (*m*) (Mex 🗵). **~e** *a & n* rubia (*f*), güera (*f*) (Mex 🗵)

blood *n* sangre *f*. **~bath** *n* masacre *m*. **~-curdling** *a* horripilante. **~hound** *n* sabueso *m*. **~ pressure** *n* tensión *f* arterial. **high ~ pressure** hipertensión *f*. **~shed** *n* derramamiento *m* de sangre. **~shot** *a* sanguinolento; <*eye*> inyectado de sangre. **~stream** *n* torrente *m* sanguíneo. **~thirsty** *a* sanguinario. **~y** *a* (**-ier, -iest**) sangriento; (stained) ensangrentado; 🗵 maldito

bloom *n* flor *f*. ● *vi* florecer

blossom *n* flor *f*. ● *vi* florecer. **~ (out) into** (fig) llegar a ser

blot *n* borrón *m*. ● *vt* (*pt* **blotted**) manchar; (dry) secar. ☐ **~ out** *vt* oscurecer

blotch *n* mancha *f*. **~y** *a* lleno de manchas

blotting-paper *n* papel *m* secante

blouse *n* blusa *f*

blow *vt* (*pt* **blew**, *pp* **blown**) soplar; fundir <*fuse*>; tocar <*trumpet*>. ● *vi* soplar; <*fuse*> fundirse; (sound) sonar. ● *n* golpe *m*. ☐ **~ down** *vt* derribar. ☐ **~ out** *vi* apagar <*candle*>. ☐ **~ over** *vi* pasar. ☐ **~ up** *vt* inflar; (explode) volar; (Photo) ampliar. *vi* (explode) estallar; (burst) reventar. **~-dry** *vt* secar con secador. **~lamp** *n* soplete *m*. **~out** *n* (of tyre) reventón *m*. **~ torch** *n* soplete *m*

blue *a* (**-er, -est**) azul; <*joke*> verde. ● *n* azul *m*. **out of the ~** totalmente inesperado. **~s** *npl*. **have the ~s** tener tristeza. **~bell** *n* campanilla *f*. **~bottle** *n* moscarda *f*. **~print** *n* plano *m*; (fig, plan) programa *m*

bluff *n* (poker) farol *m*, bluff *m* (LAm), blof *m* (Mex). ● *vt* engañar. ● *vi* tirarse un farol, hacer un bluf (LAm), blofear (Mex)

blunder *vi* cometer un error. ● *n* metedura *f* de pata

blunt *a* desafilado; <*person*> directo, abrupto. ● *vt* desafilar. **~ly** *adv* francamente

blur *n* impresión *f* indistinta. ● *vt* (*pt* **blurred**) hacer borroso

blurb *n* resumen *m* publicitario

blurt *vt*. **~ out** dejar escapar

blush *vi* ruborizarse. ● *n* rubor *m*

boar *n* verraco *m*. **wild ~** jabalí *m*

board *n* tabla *f*, tablero *m*; (for notices) tablón *m* de anuncios, tablero *m* de anuncios (LAm); (blackboard) pizarra *f*; (food) pensión *f*; (Admin) junta *f*. **~ and lodging** casa y comida. **full ~** pensión *f* completa. **go by the ~** ser abandonado. ● *vt* alojar; **~ a ship** embarcarse. ● *vi* alojarse (**with** en casa de); (at school) ser interno. **~er** *n* huésped *m & f*; (school) interno *m*. **~ing card** *n* tarjeta *f* de embarque. **~ing house** n casa f de huéspedes, pensión f. **~ing pass** n ⇨**~ing card**. **~ing school** n internado m

boast vt enorgullecerse de. ● vi jactarse. ● n jactancia f. **~ful** a jactancioso

boat n barco m; (small) bote m, barca f

bob vi (pt bobbed) menearse, subir y bajar. □ **~ up** vi presentarse súbitamente

bobbin n carrete m; (in sewing machine) canilla f, bobina f

bobby : **~ pin** n (Amer) horquilla f, pasador m (Mex). **~ sox** npl (Amer) calcetines mpl cortos

bobsleigh n bob(sleigh) m

bode vi. **~ well/ill** ser de buen/ mal agüero

bodice n corpiño m

bodily a físico, corporal. ● adv físicamente

body n cuerpo m; (dead) cadáver m. **~guard** n guardaespaldas m. **~work** n carrocería f

bog n ciénaga f. □ **~ down** vt (pt bogged). **get ~ged down** empantanarse

boggle vi sobresaltarse. **the mind ~s** uno se queda atónito

bogus a falso

boil vt/i hervir. **be ~ing hot** estar ardiendo; <weather> hacer mucho calor. ● n furúnculo m. □ **~ away** vi evaporarse. □ **~ down to** vt reducirse a. □ **~ over** vi rebosar. **~ed** a hervido; <egg> pasado por agua. **~er** n caldera f. **~er suit** n mono m, overol m (LAm)

boisterous a ruidoso, bullicioso

bold a (-er, -est) audaz. **~ly** adv con audacia, audazmente

Bolivia n Bolivia f. **~n** a & n boliviano (m)

bolster □ **~ up** vt sostener

bolt n (on door) cerrojo m; (for nut) perno m; (lightning) rayo m; (leap) fuga f. ● vt echar el cerrojo a <door>; engullir <food>. ● vi fugarse. ● adv. **~ upright** rígido

bomb n bomba f. ● vt bombardear. **~ard** vt bombardear **~er** n (plane) bombardero m; (terrorist) terrorista m & f. **~ing** n bombardeo m. **~shell** n bomba f

bond n (agreement) obligación f; (link) lazo m; (Com) bono m. ● vi (stick) adherirse. **~age** n esclavitud f

bone n hueso m; (of fish) espina f. ● vt deshuesar; quitar las espinas a <fish>. **~-dry** a completamente seco. **~ idle** a holgazán

bonfire n hoguera f, fogata f

bonnet n gorra f; (Auto) capó m, capote m (Mex)

bonus n (payment) bonificación f; (fig) ventaja f

bony a (-ier, -iest) huesudo; <fish> lleno de espinas

boo int ¡bu! ● vt/i abuchear

boob n (🅵, mistake) metedura f de pata. ● vi 🅵 meter la pata

booby : **~ prize** n premio m al peor. **~ trap** n trampa f; (bomb) bomba f trampa.

book n libro m; (of cheques etc) talonario m, chequera f; (notebook) libreta f; (exercise book) cuaderno m. **~s** (mpl) (Com) cuentas fpl. ● vt (enter) registrar; (reserve) reservar. ● vi reservar. **~case** n biblioteca f, librería f, librero m (Mex). **~ing** n reserva f, reservación f (LAm). **~ing office** n (in theatre) taquilla f, boletería f (LAm). **~keeping** n contabilidad f. **~let** n folleto m. **~maker** n corredor m de apuestas. **~mark** n señal f. **~seller** n librero m. **~shop**, (Amer) **~store** n librería

f. ~**worm** n (fig) ratón m de biblioteca

boom vi retumbar; (fig) prosperar. ● n estampido m; (Com) boom m

boost vt estimular; reforzar <*morale*>. ● n empuje m. ~**er** n (Med) revacunación f. ~**er cable** n (Amer) cable m de arranque

boot n bota f; (Auto) maletero m, cajuela f (Mex). □ ~ **up** vt (Comp) cargar

booth n cabina f; (at fair) puesto m

booze vi 🄸 beber mucho. ● n 🄸 alcohol m

border n borde m; (frontier) frontera f; (in garden) arriate m. □ ~ **on** vt lindar con. ~**line** n línea f divisoria. ~**line case** n caso m dudoso

bor|e ⇒BEAR. ● vt (annoy) aburrir; (Tec) taladrar. ● vi taladrar. ● n (person) pelmazo m; (thing) lata f. ~**ed** a aburrido. **be** ~**ed** estar aburrido. **get** ~**ed** aburrirse. ~**edom** n aburrimiento m. ~**ing** a aburrido, pesado

born a nato. **be** ~ nacer

borne ⇒BEAR

borough n municipio m

borrow vt pedir prestado

Bosnia : ~ Herzegovina n Bosnia Herzegovina f. ~**n** a & n bosnio (m)

boss n 🄸 jefe m. ● vt. ~ (**about**) 🄸 dar órdenes a. ~**y** a mandón

botan|ical a botánico. ~**ist** n botánico m. ~**y** n botánica f

both a & pron ambos (mpl), los dos (mpl). ● adv al mismo tiempo, a la vez. ~ **Ann and Brian came** tanto Ann como Bob vinieron

bother vt (inconvenience) molestar; (worry) preocupar. ~ **it!** ¡caramba! ● vi molestarse. ~ **about** preocuparse de. ~ **doing** tomarse

la molestia de hacer. ● n molestia f

bottle n botella, mamila f (Mex); (for baby) biberón m. ● vt embotellar. □ ~ **up** vt (fig) reprimir. ~**neck** n (traffic jam) embotellamiento m. ~ **opener** n abrebotellas m, destapador m (LAm)

bottom n fondo m; (of hill) pie m; (buttocks) trasero m. ● a de más abajo; <*price*> más bajo; <*lip, edge*> inferior. ~**less** a sin fondo

bough n rama f

bought ⇒BUY

boulder n canto m

bounce vt hacer rebotar. ● vi rebotar; <*person*> saltar; 🄸 <*cheque*> ser rechazado. ● n rebote m

bound ⇒BIND. ● vi saltar. ● n (jump) salto m. ~**s** npl (limits) límites mpl. **out of** ~**s** zona f prohibida. ● a. **be** ~ **for** dirigirse a. ~ **to** obligado a; (certain) seguro de

boundary n límite m

bouquet n ramo m; (of wine) buqué m, aroma m

bout n período m; (Med) ataque m; (Sport) encuentro m

bow[1] n (weapon, Mus) arco m; (knot) lazo m, moño m (LAm)

bow[2] n reverencia f; (Naut) proa f. ● vi inclinarse. ● vt inclinar

bowels npl intestinos mpl; (fig) entrañas fpl

bowl n (container) cuenco m; (for washing) palangana f; (ball) bola f. ● vt (cricket) arrojar. ● vi (cricket) arrojar la pelota. □ ~ **over** vt derribar

bowl: ~**er** n (cricket) lanzador m. ~**er** (**hat**) sombrero m de hongo, bombín m. ~**ing** n bolos mpl. ~**ing alley** n bolera f

bow tie n corbata f de lazo, pajarita f

box n caja f; (for jewels etc) estuche m; (in theatre) palco m. ● vt boxear contra. ~ **s.o.'s ears** dar una manotada a uno. ● vi boxear. ~**er** n boxeador m. ~**ing** n boxeo m. **B~ing Day** n el 26 de diciembre. ~ **office** n taquilla f, boletería f (LAm). ~ **room** n trastero m

boy n chico m, muchacho m; (young) niño m

boycott vt boicotear. ● n boicoteo m

boy: ~**friend** n novio m. ~**hood** n niñez f. ~**ish** a de muchacho; (childish) infantil

bra n sostén m, sujetador m, brasier m (Mex)

brace n abrazadera f. ● vt asegurar. ~ **o.s.** prepararse. ~**s** npl tirantes mpl; (Amer, dental) aparato(s) m(pl)

bracelet n pulsera f

bracken n helecho m

bracket n soporte m; (group) categoría f; (parenthesis) paréntesis m. **square** ~**s** corchetes mpl. ● vt poner entre paréntesis; (join together) agrupar

brag vi (pt **bragged**) jactarse (**about** de)

braid n galón m; (Amer, in hair) trenza f

brain n cerebro m. ● vt romper la cabeza a. ~**child** n invento m. ~ **drain** n 🄸 fuga f de cerebros. ~**storm** n ataque m de locura; (Amer, brainwave) idea f genial. ~**wash** vt lavar el cerebro. ~**wave** n idea f genial. ~**y** a (-ier, -iest) inteligente

brake n freno m. ● vt/i frenar. ~ **fluid** n líquido m de freno. ~ **lights** npl luces fpl de freno

bramble n zarza f

bran n salvado m

branch n rama f; (of road) bifurcación f; (Com) sucursal m; (fig) ramo m. □ ~ **off** vi bifurcarse. □ ~ **out** vi ramificarse

brand n marca f. ● vt marcar; (label) tildar de

brandish vt blandir

brand: ~ **name** n marca f. ~**-new** a flamante

brandy n coñac m

brash a descarado

brass n latón m. **get down to** ~ **tacks** (fig) ir al grano. ~ **band** n banda f de música

brassière n ⇒BRA

brat n (pej) mocoso m

bravado n bravata f

brave a (-er, -est) valiente. ● n (North American Indian) guerrero m indio. **the** ~ npl los valientes. ● vt afrontar. ~**ry** n valentía f, valor m

brawl n alboroto m. ● vi pelearse

brazen a descarado

Brazil n Brasil m. ~**ian** a & n brasileño (m)

breach n infracción f, violación f; (of contract) incumplimiento m; (gap) brecha f. ~ **of the peace** alteración f del orden público. ● vt abrir una brecha en

bread n pan m. **a loaf of** ~ un pan. ~**crumbs** npl migajas fpl; (Culin) pan m rallado, pan m molido (Mex)

breadth n anchura f

breadwinner n sostén m de la familia

break vt (pt **broke**, pp **broken**) romper; infringir, violar <law>; batir <record>; comunicar <news>; interrumpir <journey>. ● vi romperse; <news>

divulgarse. ● n ruptura f; (interval) intervalo m; (🔲, chance) oportunidad f; (in weather) cambio m. □ ~ **away** vi escapar. □ ~ **down** vt derribar; analizar *<figures>*. vi estropearse, descomponerse (LAm); (Auto) averiarse; (cry) deshacerse en lágrimas. □ ~ **in** vi *<intruder>* entrar (para robar). □ ~ **into** vt entrar en (para robar) *<house etc>*; (start doing) ponerse a. □ ~ **off** vi interrumpirse. □ ~ **out** vi *<war, disease>* estallar; (run away) escaparse. □ ~ **up** vi romperse; *<band, lovers>* separarse; *<schools>* terminar. ~**able** a frágil. ~**age** n rotura f. ~**down** n (Tec) falla f; (Med) colapso m, crisis f nerviosa; (of figures) análisis f. ~**er** n (wave) ola f grande

breakfast n desayuno m. **have ~** desayunar

break: ~**through** n adelanto m. ~**water** n rompeolas m

breast n pecho m; (of chicken etc) pechuga f. (estilo m) ~**stroke** n braza f, (estilo m) pecho m (LAm)

breath n aliento m, respiración f. **be out of ~** estar sin aliento. **hold one's ~** aguantar la respiración. **under one's ~** a media voz

breath|e vt/i respirar. ~**er** n descanso m, pausa f. ~**ing** n respiración f

breathtaking a impresionante

bred ⇒BREED

breed vt (pt bred) criar; (fig) engendrar. ● vi reproducirse. ● n raza f

breez|e n brisa f. ~**y** a de mucho viento

brew vt hacer *<beer>*; preparar *<tea>*. ● vi hacer cerveza; *<tea>* reposar; (fig) prepararse. ● n infusión f. ~**er** n cervecero m.

~**ery** n cervecería f, fábrica f de cerveza

bribe n soborno m. ● vt sobornar. ~**ry** n soborno m

brick n ladrillo m. ~**layer** n albañil m

bridal a nupcial

bride n novia f. ~**groom** n novio m. ~**smaid** n dama f de honor

bridge n puente m; (of nose) caballete m; (Cards) bridge m. ● vt tender un puente sobre. ~ **a gap** llenar un vacío

bridle n brida f. ~ **path** n camino m de herradura

brief a (-er, -est) breve. ● n (Jurid) escrito m. ● vt dar instrucciones a. ~**case** n maletín m, portafolio(s) m (LAm). ~**ly** adv brevemente. ~**s** npl (man's) calzoncillos mpl; (woman's) bragas fpl, calzones mpl (LAm), pantaletas fpl (Mex)

brigade n brigada f

bright a (-er, -est) brillante, claro; (clever) listo; (cheerful) alegre. ~**en** vt aclarar; hacer más alegre *<house etc>*. ● vi (weather) aclararse; *<face>* iluminarse

brillian|ce n brillantez f, brillo m. ~**t** a brillante

brim n borde m; (of hat) ala f. □ ~ **over** vi (pt **brimmed**) desbordarse

brine n salmuera f

bring vt (pt **brought**) traer; (lead) llevar. □ ~ **about** vt causar. □ ~ **back** vt devolver. □ ~ **down** vt derribar. □ ~ **off** vt lograr. □ ~ **on** vt causar. □ ~ **out** vt sacar; lanzar *<product>*; publicar *<book>*. □ ~ **round/to** vt hacer volver en sí. □ ~ **up** vt (Med) vomitar; educar *<children>*; plantear *<question>*

brink n borde m

brisk a (-er, -est) enérgico, vivo

bristle n cerda f. ● vi erizarse

Brit|ain n Gran Bretaña f. ~**ish** a británico. ● npl the ~**ish** los británicos. ~**on** n británico m
Brittany n Bretaña f
brittle a frágil, quebradizo
broach vt abordar
broad a (-er, -est) ancho. in ~ **daylight** a plena luz del día. ~ **bean** n haba f ~**cast** n emisión f. ● vt (pt broadcast) emitir. ● vi hablar por la radio. ~**caster** n locutor m. ~**casting** n radiodifusión f. ~**en** vt ensanchar. ● vi ensancharse. ~**ly** adv en general. ~**-minded** a de miras amplias, tolerante
broccoli n invar brécol m
brochure n folleto m
broil vt (Amer) asar a la parrilla. ~**er** n (Amer) parrilla f
broke ⇒BREAK. ● a 🄸 sin blanca, en la ruina
broken ⇒BREAK. ● a roto
broker n corredor m
brolly n 🄸 paraguas m
bronchitis n bronquitis f
bronze n bronce m. ● a de bronce
brooch n broche m
brood n cría f; (hum) prole m. ● vi empollar; (fig) meditar
brook n arroyo m. ● vt soportar
broom n escoba f. ~**stick** n palo m de escoba
broth n caldo m
brothel n burdel m
brother n hermano m. ~**hood** n fraternidad f. ~**in-law** (pl ~**s-in-law**) n cuñado m. ~**ly** a fraternal
brought ⇒BRING
brow n frente f; (of hill) cima f. ~**beat** vt (pt -beaten, pp -beat) intimidar
brown a (-er, -est) marrón, café (Mex); <hair> castaño; <skin> moreno; (tanned) bronceado. ● n marrón m, café m (Mex). ● vt poner moreno; (Culin) dorar. ~ **bread** n pan m integral. ~ **sugar** n azúcar m moreno
browse vi (in a shop) curiosear; <animal> pacer; (Comp) navegar. ~**r** (Comp) navegador m
bruise n magulladura f. ● vt magullar; machucar <fruit>
brunch n 🄸 desayuno m tardío
brunette n morena f
brunt n. bear o take the ~ of sth sufrir algo
brush n cepillo m; (large) escoba; (for decorating) brocha f; (artist's) pincel; (skirmish) escaramuza f. ● vt cepillar. □ ~ **against** vt rozar. □ ~ **aside** vt rechazar. □ ~ **off** vt (rebuff) desairar. □ ~ **up (on)** vt refrescar
brusque a brusco. ~**ly** adv bruscamente
Brussels n Bruselas f. ~ **sprout** n col f de Bruselas
brutal a brutal. ~**ity** n brutalidad f. ~**ly** adv brutalmente
brute n bestia f. ~ **force** fuerza f bruta
BSc abbr ⇒BACHELOR
BSE abbr (= bovine spongiform encephalopathy) encefalopatía f espongiforme bovina
bubbl|e n burbuja f. ● vi burbujear. □ ~ **over** vi desbordarse. ~**ly** a burbujeante
buck a macho. ● n (deer) ciervo m; (Amer 🄸) dólar m. **pass the** ~ pasar la pelota
bucket n balde m, cubo m
buckle n hebilla f. ● vt abrochar. ● vi torcerse
bud n brote m. ● vi (pt budded) brotar.
Buddhis|m n budismo m. ~**t** a & n budista (m & f)

budding *a* (fig) en ciernes

buddy *n* 🇺🇸 amigo *m*, cuate *m* (Mex)

budge *vt* mover. ● *vi* moverse

budgerigar *n* periquito *m*

budget *n* presupuesto *m*

buffalo *n* (*pl* **-oes** *or* **-o**) búfalo *m*

buffer *n* parachoques *m*

buffet¹ *n* (meal) buffet *m*; (in train) bar *m*

buffet² *n* golpe *m*; (slap) bofetada *f*. ● *vt* (*pt* **buffeted**) golpear

bug *n* bicho *m*; 🇺🇸, (germ) microbio *m*; (device) micrófono *m* oculto. ● *vt* (*pt* **bugged**) ocultar un micrófono en; (🇺🇸, bother) molestar

buggy *n*. **baby ~** sillita *f* de paseo (plegable); (Amer) cochecito *m*

bugle *n* corneta *f*

build *vt/i* (*pt* **built**) construir. ● *n* (of person) figura *f*, tipo *m*. □ **~ up** *vt/i* fortalecer; (increase) aumentar. **~er** *n* (contractor) contratista *m & f*; (labourer) albañil *m*. **~ing** *n* edificio *m*; (construction) construcción *f*. **~up** *n* aumento *m*; (of gas etc) acumulación *f*

built ⇒BUILD. **~-in** *a* empotrado. **~-up area** *n* zona *f* urbanizada

bulb *n* bulbo *m*; (Elec) bombilla *f*, foco *m* (Mex)

Bulgaria *n* Bulgaria *f*. **~n** *a & n* búlgaro (*m*)

bulge *n* protuberancia *f*. ● *vi* pandearse. **~ing** *a* abultado; <*eyes*> saltón

bulk *n* bulto *m*, volumen *m*. **in ~** a granel; (loose) suelto. **the ~ of** la mayor parte de. **~y** *a* voluminoso

bull *n* toro *m*. **~dog** *n* bulldog *m*. **~dozer** *n* bulldozer *m*

bullet *n* bala *f*

bulletin *n* anuncio *m*; (journal) boletín *m*. **~ board** *n* (Amer) tablón *m* de anuncios, tablero *m* de anuncios (LAm)

bulletproof *a* a prueba de balas

bullfight *n* corrida *f* (de toros). **~er** *n* torero *m*. **~ing** *n* (deporte *m* de) los toros

bull: **~ring** *n* plaza *f* de toros. **~'s-eye** *n* diana *f*. **~shit** *n* (vulg) sandeces *fpl* 🇺🇸, gillipolleces *fpl* ☒

bully *n* matón *m*. ● *vt* intimidar. **~ing** *n* intimidación *f*

bum *n* (🇺🇸, backside) trasero *m*; (Amer 🇺🇸) holgazán *m*

bumblebee *n* abejorro *m*

bump *vt* chocar contra. ● *vi* dar sacudidas. ● *n* (blow) golpe *m*; (jolt) sacudida *f*. □ **~ into** *vt* chocar contra; (meet) encontrar.

bumper *n* parachoques *m*. ● *a* récord. **~ edition** *n* edición *f* especial

bun *n* bollo *m*; (bread roll) panecillo *m*, bolillo *m* (Mex); (hair) moño *m*, chongo *m* (Mex)

bunch *n* (of people) grupo *m*; (of bananas, grapes) racimo *m*; (of flowers) ramo *m*

bundle *n* bulto *m*; (of papers) legajo *m*. □ **~ up** *vt* atar

bungalow *n* casa *f* de un solo piso

bungle *vt* echar a perder

bunk *n* litera *f*

bunker *n* carbonera *f*; (Golf, Mil) búnker *m*

bunny *n* conejito *m*

buoy *n* boya *f*. □ **~ up** *vt* hacer flotar; (fig) animar

buoyant *a* flotante; (fig) optimista

burden *n* carga *f*. ● *vt* cargar (with de)

bureau *n* (*pl* **-eaux**) agencia *f*; (desk) escritorio *m*; (Amer, chest of drawers) cómoda *f*

bureaucra|cy *n* burocracia *f*. **~t** *n* burócrata *m & f*. **~tic** *a* burocrático

burger n Ⓔ hamburguesa f

burgl|ar n ladrón m. ~**ar alarm** n alarma f antirrobo. ~**ary** n robo m (en casa o edificio). ~**e** vt entrar a robar en. **we were** ~**ed** nos entraron a robar

burial n entierro m

burly a (-ier, -iest) corpulento

burn vt (pt **burned** or **burnt**) quemar. ● vi quemarse. ● n quemadura f. ~ **down** vt incendiar. vi incendiarse

burnt ⇒BURN

burp n Ⓔ eructo m. ● vi Ⓔ eructar

burrow n madriguera f. ● vt excavar

burst vt (pt **burst**) reventar. ● vi reventarse. ~ **into tears** echarse a llorar. ~ **out laughing** echarse a reír. ● n (Mil) ráfaga f; (of activity) arrebato; (of applause) salva f

bury vt enterrar; (hide) ocultar

bus n (pl **buses**) autobús m, camión m (Mex)

bush n arbusto m; (land) monte m. ~**y** a espeso

business n negocio m; (Com) negocios mpl; (profession) ocupación f; (fig) asunto m. **mind one's own** ~ ocuparse de sus propios asuntos. ~**like** a práctico, serio. ~**man** n hombre m de negocios. ~**woman** n mujer f de negocios

busker n músico m ambulante

bus stop n parada f de autobús, paradero m de autobús (LAm)

bust n busto m; (chest) pecho m. ● vt (pt **busted** or **bust**) Ⓔ romper. ● vi romperse. ● a roto. **go** ~ Ⓔ quebrar

bust-up n Ⓔ riña f

busy a (-ier, -iest) ocupado; <street> concurrido. **be** ~ (Amer)

<phone> estar comunicando, estar ocupado (LAm). ● vt. ~ **o.s. with** ocuparse de. ~**body** n entrometido m

but conj pero; (after negative) sino. ● prep menos. ~ **for** si no fuera por. **last** ~ **one** penúltimo

butcher n carnicero m. ● vt matar; (fig) hacer una carnicería con

butler n mayordomo m

butt n (of gun) culata f; (of cigarette) colilla f; (target) blanco m; (Amer Ⓔ, backside) trasero m. ● vi topar. □ ~ **in** vi interrumpir

butter n mantequilla f. ● vt untar con mantequilla. ~**cup** n ranúnculo m. ~**fingers** n manazas m, torpe m. ~**fly** n mariposa f; (swimming) estilo m mariposa

buttock n nalga f

button n botón m. ● vt abotonar. ● vi abotonarse. ~**hole** n ojal m. ● vt (fig) detener

buy vt/i (pt **bought**) comprar. ● n compra f. ~**er** n comprador m

buzz n zumbido m. ● vi zumbar. □ ~ **off** vi ✖ largarse. ~**er** n timbre m

by prep por; (near) cerca de; (before) antes de; (according to) según. ~ **and large** en conjunto, en general. ~ **car** en coche. ~ **oneself** por sí solo

bye, bye-bye int Ⓔ ¡adiós!

by: ~**-election** n elección f parcial. ~**-law** n reglamento m (local). ~**pass** n carretera f de circunvalación. ● vt eludir; <road> circunvalar. ~**-product** n subproducto m. ~**stander** n espectador m

byte n (Comp) byte m, octeto m

cab *n* taxi *m*; (of lorry, train) cabina *f*

cabaret *n* cabaret *m*

cabbage *n* col *f*, repollo *m*

cabin *n* (house) cabaña *f*; (in ship) camarote *m*; (in plane) cabina *f*

cabinet *n* (cupboard) armario *m*; (for display) vitrina *f*. **C~** (Pol) gabinete *m*

cable *n* cable *m*. **~ car** *n* teleférico *m*. **~ TV** *n* televisión *f* por cable, cablevisión *f* (LAm)

cackle *n* (of hen) cacareo *m*; (laugh) risotada *f*. ● *vi* cacarear; (laugh) reírse a carcajadas

cactus *n* (*pl* **-ti** *or* **-tuses**) cacto *m*

caddie, caddy *n* (golf) portador *m* de palos

cadet *n* cadete *m*

cadge *vt/i* gorronear

café *n* cafetería *f*

cafeteria *n* restaurante *m* autoservicio

caffeine *n* cafeína *f*

cage *n* jaula *f*. ● *vt* enjaular

cake *n* pastel *m*, tarta *f*; (sponge) bizcocho *m*. **~ of soap** pastilla *f* de jabón

calamity *n* calamidad *f*

calcium *n* calcio *m*

calculat|e *vt/i* calcular. **~ion** *n* cálculo *m*. **~or** *n* calculadora *f*

calculus *n* (Math) cálculo *m*

calendar *n* calendario *m*

calf *n* (*pl* **calves**) (animal) ternero *m*; (of leg) pantorrilla *f*

calibre *n* calibre *m*

call *vt/i* llamar. ● *n* llamada *f*; (shout) grito *m*; (visit) visita *f*. **be on ~** estar de guardia. **long-distance ~** llamada *f* de larga distancia, conferencia *f*. □ **~ back** *vt* hacer volver; (on phone) volver a llamar. *vi* volver; (on phone) volver a llamar. □ **~ for** *vt* pedir; (fetch) ir a buscar. □ **~ off** *vt* suspender. □ **~ on** *vt* pasar a visitar. □ **~ out** *vi* dar voces. □ **~ together** *vt* convocar. □ **~ up** *vt* (Mil) llamar al servicio militar; (phone) llamar. **~ box** *n* cabina *f* telefónica. **~er** *n* visita *f*; (phone) el quellama *m*. **~ing** *n* vocación *f*

callous *a* insensible, cruel

calm *a* (**-er, -est**) tranquilo; <*sea*> en calma. ● *n* tranquilidad *f*, calma *f*. ● *vt* calmar. ● *vi* calmarse. **~ down** *vi* tranquilizarse. *vt* calmar. **~ly** *adv* con calma

calorie *n* caloría *f*

calves *npl* ⇒CALF

camcorder *n* videocámara *f*, camcórder *m*

came ⇒COME

camel *n* camello *m*

camera *n* cámara *f*, máquina *f* fotográfica. **~man** *n* camarógrafo *m*, cámara *m*

camouflage *n* camuflaje *m*. ● *vt* camuflar

camp *n* campamento *m*. ● *vi* acampar. **go ~ing** hacer camping

campaign *n* campaña *f*. ● *vi* hacer campaña

camp: ~bed *n* catre *m* de tijera. **~er** *n* campista *m* & *f*; (vehicle) cámper *m*. **~ground** *n* (Amer) ⇒~site. **~ing** *n* camping *m*. **~site** *n* camping *m*

campus *n* (*pl* **-puses**) campus *m*, ciudad *f* universitaria

can¹

negative **can't, cannot** (formal); past **could**

● *auxiliary verb*

····▸ (be able to) poder. **I ∼'t lift it** no lo puedo levantar. **she says she ∼ come** dice que puede venir

····▸ (be allowed to) poder. **∼ I smoke?** ¿puedo fumar?

····▸ (know how to) saber. **∼ you swim?** ¿sabes nadar?

····▸ (with verbs of perception) *not translated.* **I ∼'t see you** no te veo. **I ∼ hear you better now** ahora te oigo mejor

····▸ (in requests) **∼ I have a glass of water, please?** ¿me trae un vaso de agua, por favor?. **∼ I have a kilo of cheese, please?** ¿me da un kilo de queso, por favor?

····▸ (in offers) **∼ I help you?** ¿te ayudo?; (in shop) ¿lo/la atienden?

can² *n* lata *f*, bote *m*. ● *vt* (*pt* **canned**) enlatar. **∼ned music** música *f* grabada

Canad|a *n* (el) Canadá *m*. **∼ian** *a* & *n* canadiense (*m & f*)

canal *n* canal *m*

Canaries *npl* = CANARY ISLANDS

canary *n* canario *m*. **C∼ Islands** *npl*. **the C∼ Islands** las Islas Canarias

cancel *vt* (*pt* **cancelled**) cancelar; anular <*command, cheque*>; (delete) tachar. **∼lation** *n* cancelación *f*

cancer *n* cáncer *m*. **C∼** *n* (Astr) Cáncer *m*. **∼ous** *a* canceroso

candid *a* franco

candidate *n* candidato *m*

candle *n* vela *f*. **∼stick** *n* candelero *m*

candour *n* franqueza *f*

candy *n* (Amer) caramelo *m*, dulce *f* (LAm). **∼floss** *n* algodón *m* de azúcar

cane *n* caña *f*; (for baskets) mimbre *m*; (stick) bastón *m*; (for punishment) palmeta *f*. ● *vt* castigar con palmeta

canister *n* bote *m*

cannabis *n* cáñamo *m* índico, hachís *m*, cannabis *m*

cannibal *n* caníbal *m*. **∼ism** *n* canibalismo *m*

cannon *n invar* cañón *m*. **∼ ball** *n* bala *f* de cañón

cannot ⇒CAN¹

canoe *n* canoa *f*, piragua *f*. ● *vi* ir en canoa

canon *n* canon *m*; (person) canónigo *m*. **∼ize** *vt* canonizar

can opener *n* abrelatas *m*

canopy *n* dosel *m*

can't ⇒CAN¹

cantankerous *a* mal humorado

canteen *n* cantina *f*; (of cutlery) juego *m* de cubiertos

canter *n* medio galope *m*. ● *vi* ir a medio galope

canvas *n* lona *f*; (artist's) lienzo *m*

canvass *vi* hacer campaña, solicitar votos. **∼ing** *n* solicitación *f* (de votos)

canyon *n* cañón *m*

cap *n* gorra *f*; (lid) tapa *f*; (of cartridge) cápsula *f*; (of pen) capuchón *m*. ● *vt* (*pt* **capped**) tapar, poner cápsula a; (outdo) superar

capab|ility *n* capacidad *f*. **∼le** *a* capaz

capacity *n* capacidad *f*; (function) calidad *f*

cape *n* (cloak) capa *f*; (Geog) cabo *m*

capital *a* capital. **∼ letter** mayúscula *f*. ● *n* (town) capital *f*;

(money) capital *m.* ~**ism** *n* capitalismo *m.* ~**ist** *a & n* capitalista (*m & f.*) ~**ize** *vt* capitalizar; escribir con mayúsculas <*word*>. ● *vi.* ~**ize on** aprovechar

capitulat|e *vi* capitular. ~**ion** *n* capitulación *f*

Capricorn *n* Capricornio *m*

capsize *vt* hacer volcar. ● *vi* volcarse

capsule *n* cápsula *f*

captain *n* capitán *m*; (of plane) comandante *m & f.* ● *vt* capitanear

caption *n* (heading) título *m*; (of cartoon etc) leyenda *f*

captivate *vt* encantar

captiv|e *a & n* cautivo (*m*). ~**ity** *n* cautiverio *m*, cautividad *f*

capture *vt* capturar; atraer <*attention*>; (Mil) tomar. ● *n* apresamiento *m*; (Mil) toma *f*

car *n* coche *m*, carro *m* (LAm); (Amer, of train) vagón *m*

caramel *n* azúcar *m* quemado; (sweet) caramelo *m*, dulce *m* (LAm)

caravan *n* caravana *f*

carbohydrate *n* hidrato *m* de carbono

carbon *n* carbono *m*; (paper) carbón *m.* ~ **copy** *n* copia *f* al carbón. ~ **dioxide** *n* anhídrido *m* carbónico. ~ **monoxide** *n* monóxido de carbono

carburettor *n* carburador *m*

carcass *n* cuerpo *m* de animal muerto; (for meat) res *f* muerta

card *n* tarjeta *f*; (for games) carta *f*; (membership) carnet *m*; (records) ficha *f.* ~**board** *n* cartón *m*

cardigan *n* chaqueta *f* de punto, rebeca *f*

cardinal *a* cardinal. ● *n* cardenal *m*

care *n* cuidado *m*; (worry) preocupación *f*; (protection) cargo *m.* ~ **of** a cuidado de, en casa de. **take** ~ tener cuidado. **take** ~ **of** cuidar de <*person*>; ocuparse de <*matter*>. ● *vi* interesarse. **I don't** ~ me da igual. □ ~ **about** *vt* preocuparse por. □ ~ **for** *vt* cuidar de; (like) querer

career *n* carrera *f.* ● *vi* correr a toda velocidad

care: ~free *a* despreocupado. ~**ful** *a* cuidadoso; (cautious) prudente. **be ~ful** tener cuidado. ~**fully** *adv* con cuidado. ~**less** *a* negligente; (not worried) indiferente. ~**lessly** *adv* descuidadamente. ~**lessness** *n* descuido *m*

caress *n* caricia *f.* ● *vt* acariciar

caretaker *n* vigilante *m*; (of flats etc) portero *m*

car ferry *n* transbordador *m* de coches

cargo *n* (*pl* -oes) carga *f*

Caribbean *a* caribeño. **the** ~ (**Sea**) *n* el mar Caribe

caricature *n* caricatura *f.* ● *vt* caricaturizar

carnage *n* carnicería *f*, matanza *f*

carnation *n* clavel *m*

carnival *n* carnaval *m*

carol *n* villancico *m*

carousel *n* tiovivo *m*, carrusel *m* (LAm); (for baggage) cinta *f* transportadora

carp *n* *invar* carpa *f.* □ ~ **at** *vi* quejarse de

car park *n* aparcamiento *m*, estacionamiento *m*

carpent|er *n* carpintero *m.* ~**ry** *n* carpintería *f*

carpet *n* alfombra *f.* ~ **sweeper** *n* cepillo *m* mecánico

carriage *n* coche *m*; (Mec) carro *m*; (transport) transporte *m*; (cost,

bearing) porte m; (of train) vagón m.
∼**way** n calzada f, carretera f
carrier n transportista m & f;
(company) empresa f de
transportes; (Med) portador m. ∼
bag n bolsa f
carrot n zanahoria f
carry vt llevar; transportar
<*goods*>; (involve) llevar consigo,
implicar. ● vi <*sounds*> llegar,
oírse. □ ∼ **off** vt llevarse. □ ∼ **on**
vi seguir, continuar. □ ∼ **out** vt
realizar; cumplir <*promise,
threat*>. ∼ **cot** n cuna f portátil
carsick a mareado (*por viajar en
coche*)
cart n carro m; (Amer, in supermarket,
airport) carrito m. ● vt acarrear;
(⬛, carry) llevar
carton n caja f de cartón
cartoon n caricatura f, chiste m;
(strip) historieta f; (film) dibujos
mpl animados
cartridge n cartucho m
carve vt tallar; trinchar <*meat*>
cascade n cascada f. ● vi caer en
cascadas
case n caso m; (Jurid) proceso m;
(crate) cajón m; (box) caja f;
(suitcase) maleta f, petaca f (Mex).
in any ∼ en todo caso. **in** ∼ **he
comes** por si viene. **in** ∼ **of** en
caso de
cash n dinero m efectivo. **pay (in)**
∼ pagar al contado. ● vt cobrar.
∼ **in (on)** aprovecharse de. ∼
desk n caja f. ∼ **dispenser** n
cajero m automático
cashier n cajero m
cashpoint n cajero m automático
casino n (pl -os) casino m
cask n barril m
casket n cajita f; (Amer) ataúd m,
cajón m (LAm)
casserole n cacerola f; (stew)
guiso m, guisado m (Mex)

cassette n cassette m & f
cast vt (pt **cast**) arrojar; fundir
<*metal*>; emitir <*vote*>. ● n
lanzamiento m; (in play) reparto m;
(mould) molde m
castanets npl castañuelas fpl
castaway n náufrago m
caster n ruedecita f. ∼ **sugar** n
azúcar m extrafino
Castil|le n Castilla f. ∼**ian** a & n
castellano (m)
cast: ∼ **iron** n hierro m fundido.
∼**-iron** a (fig) sólido
castle n castillo m; (Chess) torre f
cast-offs npl desechos mpl
castrat|e vt castrar. ∼**ion** n
castración f
casual a casual; <*meeting*>
fortuito; <*work*> ocasional;
<*attitude*> despreocupado;
<*clothes*> informal, de sport. ∼**ly**
adv de paso
casualt|y n (injured) herido m;
(dead) víctima f; (in hospital)
urgencias fpl. ∼**ies** npl (Mil) bajas
fpl
cat n gato m
Catalan a & n catalán (m)
catalogue n catálogo m. ● vt
catalogar
Catalonia n Cataluña f
catalyst n catalizador m
catamaran n catamarán m
catapult n catapulta f; (child's)
tirachinas f, resortera f (Mex)
catarrh n catarro m
catastroph|e n catástrofe m. ∼**ic**
a catastrófico
catch vt (pt **caught**) coger (esp
Spain), agarrar; tomar <*train, bus*>;
(unawares) sorprender, pillar;
(understand) entender; contagiarse
de <*disease*>. ∼ **a cold** resfriarse.
∼ **sight of** avistar. ● vi (get stuck)
engancharse; <*fire*> prenderse.
● n (by goalkeeper) parada f; (of fish)

pesca *f*; (on door) pestillo *m*; (on window) cerradura *f*. □ ~ **on** *vi* ⚠ hacerse popular. □ ~ **up** *vi* poner al día. ~**ing** *a* contagioso. ~**phrase** *n* eslogan *m*. ~**y** *a* pegadizo

categor|ical *a* categórico. ~**y** *n* categoría *f*

cater *vi* encargarse del servicio de comida. ~ **for** proveer a <*needs*>. ~**er** *n* proveedor *m*

caterpillar *n* oruga *f*, azotador *m* (Mex)

cathedral *n* catedral *f*

catholic *a* universal. **C**~ *a & n* católico (*m*). **C**~**ism** *n* catolicismo *m*

cat: ~**nap** *n* sueñecito *m*. **C**~**seyes** *npl* (P) catafaros *mpl*

cattle *npl* ganado *m*

catwalk *n* pasarela *f*

Caucasian *n*. **a male** ~ (Amer) un hombre de raza blanca

caught ⇒CATCH

cauliflower *n* coliflor *f*

cause *n* causa *f*, motivo *m*. ● *vt* causar

cautio|n *n* cautela *f*; (warning) advertencia *f*. ● *vt* advertir; (Jurid) amonestar. ~**us** *a* cauteloso, prudente

cavalry *n* caballería *f*

cave *n* cueva *f*. □ ~ **in** *vi* hundirse. ~**man** *n* troglodita *m*

cavern *n* caverna *f*

caviare *n* caviar *m*

cavity *n* cavidad *f*; (dental) caries *f*

CCTV *abbr* (= **closed circuit television**) circuito *m* cerrado de televisión

CD *abbr* (= **compact disc**) CD *m*. ~ **player** (reproductor *m* de) compact-disc *m*. ~**-ROM** *n* CD-ROM

cease *vt/i* cesar. ~**fire** *n* alto *m* el fuego, cese *m* del fuego (LAm)

cedar *n* cedro *m*

ceiling *n* techo *m*

celebrat|e *vt* celebrar. ● *vi* divertirse. ~**ed** *a* célebre. ~**ion** *n* celebración *f*; (party) fiesta *f*

celebrity *n* celebridad *f*

celery *n* apio *m*

cell *n* celda *f*; (Biol, Elec) célula *f*

cellar *n* sótano *m*; (for wine) bodega *f*

cello *n* (*pl* **-os**) violonc(h)elo *m*, chelo *m*

Cellophane *n* (P) celofán *m* (P)

celluloid *n* celuloide *m*

Celsius *a*. **20 degrees** ~ 20 grados centígrados *or* Celsio(s)

cement *n* cemento *m*. ● *vt* cementar

cemetery *n* cementerio *m*

cens|or *n* censor *m*. ● *vt* censurar. ~**ship** *n* censura *f*. ~**ure** *vt* censurar

census *n* censo *m*

cent *n* ($) centavo *m*; (€) céntimo *m*

centenary *n* centenario *m*

centi|grade *a* centígrado. ~**litre** *n* centilitro *m*. ~**metre** *n* centímetro *m*. ~**pede** *n* ciempiés *m*

central *a* central; (of town) céntrico. ~ **heating** *n* calefacción *f* central. ~**ize** *vt* centralizar

centre *n* centro *m*. ● *vt* (*pt* **centred**) centrar. ● *vi* centrarse (**on** en)

century *n* siglo *m*

cereal *n* cereal *m*

ceremon|ial *a & n* ceremonial (*m*). ~**y** *n* ceremonia *f*

certain *a* cierto. **for** ~ seguro. **make** ~ **of** asegurarse de. ~**ly** *adv* desde luego. ~**ty** *n* certeza *f*

certificate *n* certificado *m*; (of birth, death etc) partida *f*

certify *vt* certificar

chafe *vt* rozar. ● *vi* rozarse

chaffinch n pinzón m

chagrin n disgusto m

chain n cadena f. ● vt encadenar. ~ **reaction** n reacción f en cadena. ~-**smoker** n fumador m que siempre tiene un cigarrillo encendido. ~ **store** n tienda f de una cadena

chair n silla f; (Univ) cátedra f. ● vt presidir. ~**lift** n telesquí m, telesilla m (LAm). ~**man** n presidente m

chalet n chalé m

chalk n (Geol) creta f; (stick) tiza f, gis m (Mex)

challeng|e n desafío m; (fig) reto m. ● vt desafiar; (question) poner en duda. ~**ing** a estimulante

chamber n (old use) cámara f. ~**maid** n camarera f. ~ **pot** n orinal m

champagne n champaña m, champán m

champion n campeón m. ● vt defender. ~**ship** n campeonato m

chance n casualidad f; (likelihood) posibilidad f; (opportunity) oportunidad f; (risk) riesgo m. **by** ~ por casualidad. ● a fortuito

chancellor n canciller m; (Univ) rector m. **C~ of the Exchequer** Ministro m de Hacienda

chandelier n araña f (de luces)

chang|e vt cambiar; (substitute) reemplazar. ~ **one's mind** cambiar de idea. ● vi cambiarse. ● n cambio m; (coins) cambio m, sencillo m (LAm), feria f (Mex); (money returned) cambio m, vuelta f, vuelto m (LAm). ~**eable** a cambiable; <weather> variable. ~**ing room** n (Sport) vestuario m, vestidor m (Mex); (in shop) probador m

channel n canal m; (fig) medio m. ● vt (pt **channelled**) acanalar; (fig) encauzar. **the (English) C~** el Canal de la Mancha. **C~ Islands** npl. **the C~ Islands** las islas Anglonormandas. **C~ Tunnel** n. **the C~ Tunnel** el Eurotúnel

chant n canto m. ● vt/i cantar

chao|s n caos m. ~**tic** a caótico

chap n ⓘ tipo m, tío m ⓘ. ● vt (pt **chapped**) agrietar. ● vi agrietarse

chapel n capilla f

chaperon n acompañante f

chapter n capítulo m

char vt (pt **charred**) carbonizar

character n carácter m; (in book, play) personaje m. **in** ~ característico. ~**istic** a típico. ● n característica f. ~**ize** vt caracterizar

charade n farsa f. ~**s** npl (game) charada f

charcoal n carbón m vegetal; (for drawing) carboncillo m

charge n precio m; (Elec, Mil) carga f; (Jurid) acusación f; (task, custody) encargo m; (responsibility) responsabilidad f. **in** ~ **of** responsable de, encargado de. **the person in** ~ la persona responsable. **take** ~ **of** encargarse de. ● vt pedir; (Elec, Mil) cargar; (Jurid) acusar. ● vi cargar; <animal> embestir (**at** contra)

charit|able a caritativo. ~**y** n caridad f; (society) institución f benéfica

charm n encanto m; (spell) hechizo m; (on bracelet) dije m, amuleto m. ● vt encantar. ~**ing** a encantador

chart n (Aviat, Naut) carta f de navegación; (table) tabla f

charter n carta f. ● vt alquilar <bus, train>; fletar <plane, ship>. ~ **flight** n vuelo m chárter

chase *vt* perseguir. ● *vi* correr
(**after** tras). ● *n* persecución *f*.
□ ~ **away**, ~ **off** *vt* ahuyentar

chassis *n* chasis *m*

chastise *vt* castigar

chastity *n* castidad *f*

chat *n* charla *f*, conversación *f*
(LAm), plática *f* (Mex). ● *vi* (*pt*
chatted) charlar, conversar
(LAm), platicar (Mex)

chatter *n* charla *f*. ● *vi* charlar.
his teeth are ~ing le castañetean
los dientes. ~**box** *n* parlanchín
m

chauffeur *n* chófer *m*

chauvinis|m *n* patriotería *f*;
(male) machismo *m*. ~**t** *n*
patriotero *m*; (male) machista *m*

cheap *a* (-**er**, -**est**) barato; (poor
quality) de baja calidad; <*rate*>
económico. ~(**ly**) *adv* barato, a
bajo precio

cheat *vt* defraudar; (deceive)
engañar. ● *vi* (at cards) hacer
trampas. ● *n* trampa *f*; (person)
tramposo *m*

check *vt* comprobar; (examine)
inspeccionar; (curb) frenar. ● *vi*
comprobar. ● *n* comprobación *f*;
(of tickets) control *m*; (curb) freno
m; (Chess) jaque *m*; (pattern) cuadro
m; (Amer, bill) cuenta *f*; (Amer,
cheque) cheque *m*. □ ~ **in** *vi*
registrarse; (at airport) facturar el
equipaje, chequear el equipaje
(LAm), registrar el equipaje (Mex).
□ ~ **out** *vi* pagar la cuenta y
marcharse. □ ~ **up** *vi* confirmar.
□ ~ **up on** *vt* investigar. ~**book**
n (Amer) ⇒CHEQUEBOOK. ~**ered** *a*
(Amer) ⇒CHEQUERED

checkers *n* (Amer) damas *fpl*

check: ~**mate** *n* jaque *m* mate.
● *vt* dar mate a. ~**out** *n* caja *f*.
~**point** control *m*. ~**up** *n*
chequeo *m*, revisión

cheek *n* mejilla *f*; (fig) descaro *m*.
~**bone** *n* pómulo *m*. ~**y** *a*
descarado

cheep *vi* piar

cheer *n* alegría *f*; (applause) viva
m. ~**s!** ¡salud!. ● *vt* alegrar;
(applaud) aplaudir. ● *vi* alegrarse;
(applaud) aplaudir. ~ **up!** ¡anímate!
~**ful** *a* alegre

cheerio *int* 🅸 ¡adiós!, ¡hasta
luego!

cheerless *a* triste

cheese *n* queso *m*

cheetah *n* guepardo *m*

chef *n* jefe *m* de cocina

chemical *a* químico. ● *n*
producto *m* químico

chemist *n* farmacéutico *m*;
(scientist) químico *m*. ~**ry** *n*
química *f*. ~**'s** (**shop**) *n* farmacia
f

cheque *n* cheque *m*, talón *m*.
~**book** *n* chequera *f*, talonario *m*

cherish *vt* cuidar; (love) querer;
abrigar <*hope*>

cherry *n* cereza *f*. ~ **tree** *n*
cerezo *m*

chess *n* ajedrez *m*. ~**board** *n*
tablero *m* de ajedrez

chest *n* pecho *m*; (box) cofre *m*,
cajón *m*

chestnut *n* castaña *f*. ● *a*
castaño. ~ **tree** *n* castaño *m*

chest of drawers *n* cómoda *f*

chew *vt* masticar. ~**ing gum** *n*
chicle *m*

chic *a* elegante

chick *n* polluelo *m*. ~**en** *n* pollo
m. ● *a* 🅸 cobarde. □ ~**en out** *vi*
🅸 acobardarse. ~**enpox** *n*
varicela *f*. ~**pea** *n* garbanzo *m*

chicory *n* (in coffee) achicoria *f*; (in
salad) escarola *f*

chief *n* jefe *m*. ● *a* principal. ~**ly**
adv principalmente

chilblain *n* sabañón *m*

child n (pl **children**) niño m; (offspring) hijo m. ~**birth** n parto m. ~**hood** n niñez f. ~**ish** a infantil. ~**less** a sin hijos. ~**like** a ingenuo, de niño

Chile n Chile m. ~**an** a & n chileno (m)

chill n frío m; (illness) resfriado m. ● a frío. ● vt enfriar; refrigerar <food>

chilli n (pl **-ies**) chile m

chilly a frío

chime n carillón m. ● vt tocar <bells>; dar <hours>. ● vi repicar

chimney n (pl **-eys**) chimenea f. ~ **sweep** n deshollinador m

chimpanzee n chimpancé m

chin n barbilla f

china n porcelana f

Chin|a n China f. ~**ese** a & n chino (m)

chink n (crack) grieta f; (sound) tintín m. ● vi tintinear

chip n pedacito m; (splinter) astilla f; (Culin) patata f frita, papa f frita (LAm); (in gambling) ficha f; (Comp) chip m. **have a** ~ **on one's shoulder** guardar rencor. ● vt (pt **chipped**) desportillar. □ ~ **in** vi 🄸 interrumpir; (with money) contribuir

chiropodist n callista m & f, pedicuro m

chirp n pío m. ● vi piar. ~**y** a alegre

chisel n formón m. ● vt (pt **chiselled**) cincelar

chivalr|ous a caballeroso. ~**y** n caballerosidad f

chlorine n cloro m

chock n cuña f. ~**-a-block** a, ~**-full** a atestado

chocolate n chocolate m; (individual sweet) bombón m, chocolate m (LAm)

choice n elección f; (preference) preferencia f. ● a escogido

choir n coro m

choke vt sofocar. ● vi sofocarse. ● n (Auto) choke m, estárter m, ahogador m (Mex)

cholera n cólera m

cholesterol n colesterol m

choose vt/i (pt **chose**, pp **chosen**) elegir, escoger. ~**y** a 🄸 exigente

chop vt (pt **chopped**) cortar. ● n (Culin) chuleta f. □ ~ **down** vt talar. □ ~ **off** vt cortar. ~**per** n hacha f; (butcher's) cuchilla f. ~**py** a picado

chord n (Mus) acorde m

chore n tarea f, faena f. **household** ~**s** npl quehaceres mpl domésticos

chorus n coro m; (of song) estribillo m

chose, chosen ⇒CHOOSE

Christ n Cristo m

christen vt bautizar. ~**ing** n bautizo m

Christian a & n cristiano (m). ~**ity** n cristianismo m. ~ **name** n nombre m de pila

Christmas n Navidad f. **Merry** ~! ¡Feliz Navidad!, ¡Felices Pascuas! **Father** ~ Papá m Noel. ● a de Navidad, navideño. ~ **card** n tarjeta f de Navidad f. ~ **day** n día m de Navidad. ~ **Eve** n Nochebuena f. ~ **tree** n árbol m de Navidad

chrom|e n cromo m. ~**ium** n cromo m

chromosome n cromosoma m

chronic a crónico; (🄸, bad) terrible

chronicle n crónica f. ● vt historiar

chronological a cronológico

chubby *a* (**-ier, -iest**) regordete; *<person>* gordinflón Ⓘ

chuck *vt* Ⓘ tirar. □ **∼ out** *vt* tirar

chuckle *n* risa *f* ahogada. ● *vi* reírse entre dientes

chug *vi* (*pt* **chugged**) (of motor) traquetear

chum *n* amigo *m*, compinche *m*, cuate *m* (Mex)

chunk *n* trozo *m* grueso. ∼**y** *a* macizo

church *n* iglesia *f*. ∼**yard** *n* cementerio *m*

churn *n* (for milk) lechera *f*, cántara *f*; (for making butter) mantequera *f*. ● *vt* agitar. □ **∼ out** *vt* producir en profusión

chute *n* tobogán *m*

cider *n* sidra *f*

cigar *n* puro *m*

cigarette *n* cigarrillo *m*. **∼ end** *n* colilla *f*. **∼ holder** *n* boquilla *f*. **∼ lighter** *n* mechero *m*, encendedor *m*

cinecamera *n* tomavistas *m*, filmadora *f* (LAm)

cinema *n* cine *m*

cipher *n* (Math, fig) cero *m*; (code) clave *f*

circle *n* círculo *m*; (in theatre) anfiteatro *m*. ● *vt* girar alrededor de. ● *vi* dar vueltas

circuit *n* circuito *m*

circular *a & n* circular (*f*)

circulat|e *vt* hacer circular. ● *vi* circular. ∼**ion** *n* circulación *f*; (number of copies) tirada *f*

circumcise *vt* circuncidar

circumference *n* circunferencia *f*

circumstance *n* circunstancia *f*. ∼**s** (means) *npl* situación *f* económica

circus *n* circo *m*

cistern *n* cisterna *f*

cite *vt* citar

citizen *n* ciudadano *m*; (inhabitant) habitante *m & f*

citrus *n*. **∼ fruits** cítricos *mpl*

city *n* ciudad *f*; **the C∼** el centro *m* financiero de Londres

civic *a* cívico

civil *a* civil; (polite) cortés

civilian *a & n* civil (*m & f*)

civiliz|ation *n* civilización *f*. ∼**ed** *a* civilizado.

civil: ∼ servant *n* funcionario *m* (del Estado), burócrata *m & f* (Mex). **∼ service** *n* administración *f* pública. **∼ war** *n* guerra *f* civil

clad ⇒CLOTHE

claim *vt* reclamar; (assert) pretender. ● *n* reclamación *f*; (right) derecho *m*; (Jurid) demanda *f*

clairvoyant *n* clarividente *m & f*

clam *n* almeja *f*. ● *vi* (*pt* **clammed**). **∼ up** Ⓘ ponerse muy poco comunicativo

clamber *vi* trepar a gatas

clammy *a* (**-ier, -iest**) húmedo

clamour *n* clamor *m*. ● *vi*. **∼ for** pedir a gritos

clamp *n* abrazadera *f*; (Auto) cepo *m*. ● *vt* sujetar con abrazadera; poner cepo a *<car>*. □ **∼ down on** *vt* reprimir

clan *n* clan *m*

clang *n* sonido *m* metálico

clap *vt* (*pt* **clapped**) aplaudir; batir *<hands>*. ● *vi* aplaudir. ● *n* palmada *f*; (of thunder) trueno *m*

clarif|ication *n* aclaración *f*. ∼**y** *vt* aclarar. ● *vi* aclararse

clarinet *n* clarinete *m*

clarity *n* claridad *f*

clash *n* choque *m*; (noise) estruendo *m*; (contrast) contraste *m*; (fig) conflicto *m*. ● *vt* golpear. ● *vi* encontrarse; *<colours>* desentonar

clasp n cierre m. ● vt agarrar; apretar <hand>

class n clase f. **evening ~** n clase nocturna. ● vt clasificar

classic a & n clásico (m). **~al** a clásico. **~s** npl estudios mpl clásicos

classif|ication n clasificación f. **~y** vt clasificar

class: **~room** n aula f, clase f. **~y** a 🆒 elegante

clatter n ruido m; (of train) traqueteo m. ● vi hacer ruido

clause n cláusula f; (Gram) oración f

claustrophobia n claustrofobia f

claw n garra f; (of cat) uña f; (of crab) pinza f. ● vt arañar

clay n arcilla f

clean a (-er, -est) limpio; <stroke> bien definido. ● adv completamente. ● vt limpiar. ● vi limpiar. □ **~ up** vt hacer la limpieza. **~er** n persona f quehace la limpieza. **~liness** n limpieza f

cleanse vt limpiar. **~er** n producto m de limpieza; (for skin) crema f de limpieza. **~ing cream** n crema f de limpieza

clear a (-er, -est) claro; (transparent) transparente; (without obstacles) libre; <profit> neto; <sky> despejado. **keep ~ of** evitar. ● adv claramente. ● vt despejar; liquidar <goods>; (Jurid) absolver; (jump over) saltar por encima de; quitar, levantar (LAm) <table>. □ **~ off** vi 🆒, **~ out** vi 🆒, (go away) largarse. □ **~ up** vt (tidy) ordenar; aclarar <mystery>. vi <weather> despejarse. **~ance** n (removal of obstructions) despeje m; (authorization) permiso m; (by security) acreditación f. **~ing** n claro m. **~ly** adv evidentemente. **~way** n carretera f en la que no se permite parar

cleavage n escote m

clef n (Mus) clave f

clench vt apretar

clergy n clero m. **~man** n clérigo m

cleric n clérigo m. **~al** a clerical; (of clerks) de oficina

clerk n empleado m; (Amer, salesclerk) vendedor m

clever a (-er, -est) inteligente; (skilful) hábil. **~ly** adv inteligentemente; (with skill) hábilmente. **~ness** n inteligencia f

cliché n lugar m común m, cliché m

click n golpecito m. ● vi chascar; 🆒 llevarse bien. ● vt chasquear. **~ on sth** hacer clic en algo

client n cliente m

cliff n acantilado m

climat|e n clima m. **~ic** a climático

climax n clímax m; (orgasm) orgasmo m

climb vt subir <stairs>; trepar <tree>; escalar <mountain>. ● vi subir. ● n subida f. □ **~ down** vi bajar; (fig) ceder. **~er** n (Sport) alpinista m & f, andinista m & f (LAm); (plant) trepadora f

clinch vt cerrar <deal>

cling vi (pt clung) agarrarse; (stick) pegarse

clinic n centro m médico; (private hospital) clínica f. **~al** a clínico

clink n tintineo m. ● vt hacer tintinear. ● vi tintinear

clip n <fastener> clip m; (for paper) sujetapapeles m; (for hair) horquilla f. ● vt (pt clipped) (cut) cortar; (join) sujetar. **~pers** npl (for hair) maquinilla f para cortar

el pelo; (for nails) cortaúñas *m*.
∼ping *n* recorte *m*

cloak *n* capa *f*. **∼room** *n*
guardarropa *m*; (toilet) lavabo *m*,
baño *m* (LAm)

clock *n* reloj *m*. **∼wise** *a/adv* en
el sentido de las agujas del reloj.
∼work *n* mecanismo *m* de
relojería. **like ∼work** con
precisión

clog *n* zueco *m*. ● *vt* (*pt* **clogged**)
atascar

clone *n* clon *m*

cloister *n* claustro *m*

close¹ *a* (**-er, -est**) cercano;
(together) apretado; <*friend*>
íntimo; <*weather*> bochornoso;
<*link etc*> estrecho; <*game, battle*>
reñido. **have a ∼ shave** (fig)
escaparse de milagro. ● *adv*
cerca. ● *n* recinto *m*

close² *vt* cerrar. ● *vi* cerrarse;
(end) terminar. **∼ down** *vt/i*
cerrar. ● *n* fin *m*. **∼d** *a* cerrado

closely *adv* estrechamente; (at a
short distance) de cerca; (with attention)
detenidamente

closet *n* (Amer) armario *m*; (for
clothes) armario *m*, closet *m* (LAm)

close-up *n* (Cinema etc) primer
plano *m*

closure *n* cierre *m*

clot *n* (Med) coágulo *m*; 🄸 tonto
m. ● *vi* (*pt* **clotted**) cuajarse;
<*blood*> coagularse

cloth *n* tela *f*; (duster) trapo *m*;
(tablecloth) mantel *m*

cloth|e *vt* (*pt* **clothed** or **clad**)
vestir. **∼es** *npl* ropa. **∼espeg**,
∼espin (Amer) *n* pinza *f* (para
tender la ropa). **∼ing** *n* ropa *f*

cloud *n* nube *f*. ● **∼ over** *vi*
nublarse. **∼y** *a* (**-ier, -iest**)
nublado; <*liquid*> turbio

clout *n* bofetada *f*. ● *vt* abofetear

clove *n* clavo *m*. **∼ of garlic** *n*
diente *m* de ajo

clover *n* trébol *m*

clown *n* payaso *m*. ● *vi* hacer el
payaso

club *n* club *m*; (weapon) porra *f*;
(golf club) palo *m* de golf; (at cards)
trébol *m*. ● *vt* (*pt* **clubbed**)
aporrear. □ **∼ together** *vi*
contribuir con dinero (**to** para)

cluck *vi* cloquear

clue *n* pista *f*; (in crosswords)
indicación *f*. **not to have a ∼** no
tener la menor idea

clump *n* grupo *m*. ● *vt* agrupar

clums|iness *n* torpeza *f*. **∼y** *a*
(**-ier, -iest**) torpe

clung ⇒CLING

cluster *n* grupo *m*. ● *vi*
agruparse

clutch *vt* agarrar. ● *n* (Auto)
embrague *m*

clutter *n* desorden *m*. ● *vt*. **∼**
(**up**) abarrotar. **∼ed** *a* abarratado
de cosas

coach *n* autocar *m*, autobús *m*; (of
train) vagón *m*; (horse-drawn) coche
m; (Sport) entrenador *m*. ● *vt*
(Sport) entrenar

coal *n* carbón *m*

coalition *n* coalición *f*

coarse *a* (**-er, -est**) grueso;
<*material*> basto; (person, language)
ordinario

coast *n* costa *f*. ● *vi* (with cycle)
deslizarse sin pedalear; (with car)
ir en punto muerto. **∼al** *a*
costero. **∼guard** *n* guardacostas
m. **∼line** *n* litoral *m*

coat *n* abrigo *m*; (jacket) chaqueta
f; (of animal) pelo *m*; (of paint) mano
f. ● *vt* cubrir, revestir. **∼hanger**
n percha *f*, gancho *m* (LAm). **∼ing**
n capa *f*. **∼ of arms** *n* escudo *m*
de armas

coax *vt* engatusar

cobbler *n* zapatero *m*
(remendón)

cobblestone n adoquín m
cobweb n telaraña f
cocaine n cocaína f
cock n (cockerel) gallo m; (male bird) macho m. ● vt amartillar <gun>; aguzar <ears>. ~**erel** n gallo m. ~**-eyed** a 🔁 torcido
cockney a & n (pl -**eys**) londinense (m & f) (del este de Londres)
cockpit n (in aircraft) cabina f del piloto
cockroach n cucaracha f
cocktail n cóctel m
cock-up n 🔀 lío m
cocky a (-**ier, -iest**) engreído
cocoa n cacao m; (drink) chocolate m, cocoa f (LAm)
coconut n coco m
cocoon n capullo m
cod n invar bacalao m
code n código m; (secret) clave f; **in** ~ en clave
coeducational a mixto
coerc|e vt coaccionar. ~**ion** n coacción f
coffee n café m. ~ **bean** n grano m de café. ~ **maker** n cafetera f. ~**pot** n cafetera f
coffin n ataúd m, cajón m (LAm)
cog n diente m; (fig) pieza f
coherent a coherente
coil vt enrollar. ● n rollo m; (one ring) vuelta f
coin n moneda f. ● vt acuñar
coincide vi coincidir. ~**nce** n casualidad f. ~**ntal** a casual
coke n (coal) coque m. **C**~ (P) Coca-Cola f (P)
colander n colador m
cold a (-**er, -est**) frío m. **be** ~ <person> tener frío. **it is** ~ (weather) hace frío. ● n frío m; (Med) resfriado m. **have a** ~ estar resfriado. ~**-blooded** a <animal> de sangre fría; <murder> a sangre

fría. ~**-shoulder** vt tratar con frialdad. ~ **sore** n herpes m labial. ~ **storage** n conservación f en frigorífico
coleslaw n ensalada f de col
collaborat|e vi colaborar. ~**ion** n colaboración f. ~**or** n colaborador m
collaps|e vi derrumbarse; (Med) sufrir un colapso. ● n derrumbamiento m; (Med) colapso m. ~**ible** a plegable
collar n cuello m; (for animals) collar m. ● vt 🔁 hurtar. ~**bone** n clavícula f
colleague n colega m & f
collect vt reunir; (hobby) coleccionar, juntar (LAm); (pick up) recoger; cobrar <rent>. ● vi <people> reunirse; <things> acumularse. ~**ion** n colección f; (in church) colecta f; (of post) recogida f. ~**or** n coleccionista m & f
college n colegio m; (of art, music etc) escuela f; (Amer) universidad f
colli|de vi chocar. ~**sion** n choque m
colloquial a coloquial
Colombia n Colombia f. ~**n** a & n colombiano (m)
colon n (Gram) dos puntos mpl; (Med) colon m
colonel n coronel m
colon|ial a colonial. ~**ize** vt colonizar. ~**y** n colonia f
colossal a colosal
colour n color m. **off** ~ (fig) indispuesto. ● a de color(es), en color(es) ● vt colorear; (dye) teñir. ~**-blind** a daltoniano. ~**ed** a de color. ~**ful** a lleno de color; (fig) pintoresco. ~**ing** n color; (food colouring) colorante m. ~**less** a incoloro
column n columna f. ~**ist** n columnista m & f

coma *n* coma *m*

comb *n* peine *m*. ● *vt* (search) registrar. ~ **one's hair** peinarse

combat *n* combate *m*. ● *vt* (*pt* **combated**) combatir

combination *n* combinación *f*

combine *vt* combinar. ● *vi* combinarse. ● *n* asociación *f*. ~ **harvester** *n* cosechadora *f*

combustion *n* combustión *f*

come *vi* (*pt* **came**, *pp* **come**) venir; (occur) pasar. □ ~ **across** *vt* encontrarse con <*person*>; encontrar <*object*>. □ ~ **apart** *vi* deshacerse. □ ~ **away** *vi* (leave) salir; (become detached) salirse. □ ~ **back** *vi* volver. □ ~ **by** *vt* obtener. □ ~ **down** *vi* bajar. □ ~ **in** *vi* entrar; (arrive) llegar. □ ~ **into** *vt* entrar en; heredar <*money*>. □ ~ **off** *vi* desprenderse; (succeed) tener éxito. *vt*. ~ **off it!** Ⓘ ¡no me vengas con eso! □ ~ **on** *vi* (start to work) encenderse. ~ **on, hurry up!** ¡vamos, date prisa! □ ~ **out** *vi* salir. □ ~ **round** *vi* (after fainting) volver en sí; (be converted) cambiar de idea; (visit) venir. □ ~ **to** *vt* llegar a <*decision etc*>. □ ~ **up** *vi* subir; (fig) surgir. □ ~ **up with** *vt* proponer <*idea*>. ~**back** *n* retorno *m*; (retort) réplica *f*

comedian *n* cómico *m*

comedy *n* comedia *f*

comet *n* cometa *m*

comfort *n* comodidad *f*; (consolation) consuelo *m*. ● *vt* consolar. ~**able** *a* cómodo. ~**er** *n* (for baby) chupete *m*, chupón *m* (LAm); (Amer, for bed) edredón *m*

comic *a* cómico. ● *n* cómico *m*; (periodical) revista *f* de historietas, tebeo *m*. ~**al** *a* cómico. ~ **strip** *n* tira *f* cómica

coming *n* llegada *f*. ~**s and goings** idas *fpl* y venidas. ● *a*

próximo; <*week, month etc*> que viene

comma *n* coma *f*

command *n* orden *f*; (mastery) dominio *m*. ● *vt* ordenar; imponer <*respect*>

commandeer *vt* requisar

command: ~**er** *n* comandante *m*. ~**ing** *a* imponente. ~**ment** *n* mandamiento *m*

commando *n* (*pl* -**os**) comando *m*

commemorat|**e** *vt* conmemorar. ~**ion** *n* conmemoración *f*. ~**ive** *a* conmemorativo

commence *vt* dar comienzo a. ● *vi* iniciarse

commend *vt* alabar. ~**able** *a* loable. ~**ation** *n* elogio *m*

comment *n* observación *f*. ● *vi* hacer observaciones (**on** sobre)

commentary *n* comentario *m*; (Radio, TV) reportaje *m*

commentat|**e** *vi* narrar. ~**or** *n* (Radio, TV) locutor *m*

commerc|**e** *n* comercio *m*. ~**ial** *a* comercial. ● *n* anuncio *m*; aviso *m* (LAm). ~**ialize** *vt* comercializar

commiserat|**e** *vi* compadecerse (**with** de). ~**ion** *n* conmiseración *f*

commission *n* comisión *f*. **out of** ~ fuera de servicio. ● *vt* encargar; (Mil) nombrar oficial

commissionaire *n* portero *m*

commit *vt* (*pt* **committed**) cometer; (entrust) confiar. ~ **o.s.** comprometerse. ~**ment** *n* compromiso *m*

committee *n* comité *m*

commodity *n* producto *m*, artículo *m*

common *a* (-**er**, -**est**) común; (usual) corriente; (vulgar) ordinario. ● *n*. **in** ~ en común. ~**er** *n* plebeyo *m*. ~ **law** *n* derecho *m* consuetudinario. ~**ly** *adv* comúnmente. **C~ Market** n Mercado m Común. **~place** a banal. ● n banalidad f. **~ room** n sala f común, salón m común. **C~s** n. **the (House of) C~s** la Cámara de los Comunes. **~ sense** n sentido m común. **C~wealth** n. **the C~wealth** la Mancomunidad f Británica

commotion n confusión f

commune n comuna f

communicat|e vt comunicar. ● vi comunicarse. **~ion** n comunicación f. **~ive** a comunicativo

communion n comunión f

communis|m n comunismo m. **~t** n comunista m & f

community n comunidad f. **~ centre** n centro m social

commute vi viajar diariamente (entre el lugar de residencia y el trabajo). ● vt (Jurid) conmutar. **~r** n viajero m diario

compact a compacto. ● n (for powder) polvera f. **~ disc**, **~ disk** n disco m compacto, compact-disc m. **~ disc player** n (reproductor m de) compact-disc

companion n compañero m. **~ship** n compañía f

company n compañía f; (guests) visita f; (Com) sociedad f

compar|able a comparable. **~ative** a comparativo; (fig) relativo. ● n (Gram) comparativo m. **~e** vt comparar. **~ison** n comparación f

compartment n compartim(i) ento m

compass n brújula f. **~es** npl compás m

compassion n compasión f. **~ate** a compasivo

compatible a compatible

compel vt (pt **compelled**) obligar. **~ling** a irresistible

compensat|e vt compensar; (for loss) indemnizar. ● vi. **~e for sth** compensar algo. **~ion** n compensación f; (financial) indemnización f

compère n presentador m. ● vt presentar

compete vi competir

competen|ce n competencia f. **~t** a competente

competit|ion n (contest) concurso m; (Sport) competición f, competencia f (LAm); (Com) competencia f. **~ive** a competidor; <price> competitivo. **~or** n competidor m; (in contest) concursante m & f

compile vt compilar

complacen|cy n autosuficiencia f. **~t** a satisfecho de sí mismo

complain vi. **~ (about)** quejarse (de). ● vt. **~ that** quejarse de que. **~t** n queja f; (Med) enfermedad f

complement n complemento m. ● vt complementar. **~ary** a complementario

complet|e a completo; (finished) acabado; (downright) total. ● vt acabar; llenar <a form>. **~ely** adv completamente. **~ion** n finalización f

complex a complejo. ● n complejo m

complexion n tez f; (fig) aspecto m

complexity n complejidad f

complicat|e vt complicar. **~ed** a complicado. **~ion** n complicación f

compliment n cumplido m; (amorous) piropo m. ● vt felicitar. **~ary** a halagador; (given free) de regalo. **~s** npl saludos mpl

comply vi. **~ with** conformarse con

component a & n componente (m)

compos|e vt componer. **be ~ed of** estar compuesto de. **~er** n compositor m. **~ition** n composición f

compost n abono m

composure n serenidad f

compound n compuesto m; (enclosure) recinto m. ● a compuesto; <fracture> complicado

comprehen|d vt comprender. **~sion** n comprensión f. **~sive** a extenso; <insurance> contra todo riesgo. **~sive (school)** n instituto m de enseñanza secundaria

compress n (Med) compresa f. ● vt comprimir. **~ion** n compresión f

comprise vt comprender

compromis|e n acuerdo m, compromiso m, arreglo m. ● vt comprometer. ● vi llegar a un acuerdo. **~ing** a <situation> comprometido

compuls|ion n (force) coacción f; (obsession) compulsión f. **~ive** a compulsivo. **~ory** a obligatorio

comput|er n ordenador m, computadora f (LAm). **~erize** vt computarizar, computerizar. **~er studies** n, **~ing** n informática f, computación f

comrade n camarada m & f

con vt (pt conned) ▯ estafar. ● n (fraud) estafa f; (objection) ⇒PRO

concave a cóncavo

conceal vt ocultar

concede vt conceder

conceit n vanidad f. **~ed** a engreído

conceiv|able a concebible. **~e** vt/i concebir

concentrat|e vt concentrar. ● vi concentrarse (**on** en). **~ion** n concentración f

concept n concepto m

conception n concepción f

concern n asunto m; (worry) preocupación f; (Com) empresa f. ● vt tener que ver con; (deal with) tratar de. **as far as I'm ~ed** en cuanto a mí. **be ~ed about** preocuparse por. **~ing** prep acerca de

concert n concierto m. **~ed** a concertado

concertina n concertina f

concerto n (pl **-os** or **-ti**) concierto m

concession n concesión f

concise a conciso

conclu|de vt/i concluir. **~ding** a final. **~sion** n conclusión f. **~sive** a decisivo. **~sively** adv concluyentemente

concoct vt confeccionar; (fig) inventar. **~ion** n mezcla f; (drink) brebaje m

concrete n hormigón m, concreto m (LAm). ● a concreto

concussion n conmoción f cerebral

condemn vt condenar. **~ation** n condena f

condens|ation n condensación f. **~e** vt condensar. ● vi condensarse

condescend vi dignarse (**to** a). **~ing** a superior

condition n condición f. **on ~ that** a condición de que. ● vt condicionar. **~al** a condicional. **~er** n (for hair) suavizante m, enjuague m (LAm)

condo n (pl **-os**) (Amer ▯) ⇒CONDOMINIUM

condolences npl pésame m

condom n condón m

condominium n (Amer) apartamento m, piso m (en régimen de propiedad horizontal)

condone vt condonar

conduct vt llevar a cabo <business, experiment>; conducir <electricity>; dirigir <orchestra>. ● n conducta f. ∼or n director m; (of bus) cobrador m. ∼ress n cobradora f

cone n cono m; (for ice cream) cucurucho m, barquillo m (Mex)

confectionery n productos mpl de confitería

confederation n confederación f

confess vt confesar. ● vi confesarse. ∼ion n confesión f

confetti n confeti m

confide vt/i confiar

confiden|ce n confianza f; (self-confidence) confianza f en sí mismo; (secret) confidencia f. ∼ce trick n estafa f, timo m. ∼t a seguro de sí mismo. be ∼t of confiar en

confidential a confidencial. ∼ity n confidencialidad f

confine vt confinar; (limit) limitar. ∼ment n (imprisonment) prisión f

confirm vt confirmar. ∼ation n confirmación f. ∼ed a inveterado

confiscat|e vt confiscar. ∼ion n confiscación f

conflict n conflicto m. ● vi chocar. ∼ing a contradictorio

conform vi conformarse. ∼ist n conformista m & f

confound vt confundir. ∼ed a 🅸 maldito

confront vt hacer frente a; (face) enfrentarse con. ∼ation n confrontación f

confus|e vt confundir. ∼ed a confundido. get ∼ed confundirse. ∼ing a confuso. ∼ion n confusión f

congeal vi coagularse

congest|ed a congestionado. ∼ion n congestión f

congratulat|e vt felicitar. ∼ions npl enhorabuena f, felicitaciones fpl (LAm)

congregat|e vi congregarse. ∼ion n asamblea f; (Relig) fieles mpl, feligreses mpl

congress n congreso m. C∼ (Amer) el Congreso. ∼man n (Amer) miembro m del Congreso. ∼woman n (Amer) miembro f del Congreso.

conifer n conífera f

conjugat|e vt conjugar. ∼ion n conjugación f

conjunction n conjunción f

conjur|e vi hacer juegos de manos. ● vt. □ ∼e up vt evocar. ∼er, ∼or n prestidigitador m

conk vi. ∼ out 🅸 fallar; <person> desmayarse

conker n 🅸 castaña f de Indias

conman n (pl -men) 🅸 estafador m, timador m

connect vt conectar; (associate) relacionar. ● vi (be fitted) estar conectado (to a). □ ∼ with vt <train> enlazar con. ∼ed a unido; (related) relacionado. be ∼ed with tener que ver con, estar emparentado con. ∼ion n conexión f; (Rail) enlace m; (fig) relación f. in ∼ion with a propósito de, con respecto a

connive vi. ∼e at ser cómplice en

connoisseur n experto m

connotation n connotación f

conquer vt conquistar; (fig) vencer. ∼or n conquistador m

conquest n conquista f

conscience n conciencia f

conscientious a concienzudo

conscious a consciente; (deliberate) intencional. ∼ly adv a sabiendas. ∼ness n consciencia f; (Med) conocimiento m

conscript n recluta m & f,
conscripto m (LAm). ● vt reclutar.
~**ion** n reclutamiento m,
conscripción f (LAm)

consecrate vt consagrar

consecutive a sucesivo

consensus n consenso m

consent vi consentir. ● n
consentimiento m

consequen|ce n consecuencia f.
~**t** a consiguiente. ~**tly** adv por
consiguiente

conservation n conservación f,
preservación f. ~**ist** n
conservacionista m & f

conservative a conservador;
(modest) prudente, moderado. **C~**
a & n conservador (m)

conservatory n invernadero m

conserve vt conservar

consider vt considerar; (take into
account) tomar en cuenta. ~**able** a
considerable. ~**ably** adv
considerablemente

considerat|e a considerado.
~**ion** n consideración f. **take sth
into** ~**ion** tomar algo en cuenta

considering prep teniendo en
cuenta. ● conj. ~ (**that**) teniendo
en cuenta que

consign vt consignar; (send)
enviar. ~**ment** n envío m

consist vi. ~ **of** consistir en.
~**ency** n consistencia f; (fig)
coherencia f. ~**ent** a coherente;
(unchanging) constante. ~**ent with**
compatible con. ~**ently** adv
constantemente

consolation n consuelo m

console vt consolar. ● n consola
f

consolidate vt consolidar

consonant n consonante f

conspicuous a (easily seen)
visible; (showy) llamativo;
(noteworthy) notable

conspir|acy n conspiración f.
~**ator** n conspirador m. ~**e** vi
conspirar

constable n agente m & f de
policía

constant a constante. ~**ly** adv
constantemente

constellation n constelación f

consternation n consternación f

constipat|ed a estreñido. ~**ion**
n estreñimiento m

constituen|cy n distrito m
electoral. ~**t** n (Pol) elector m. ● a
constituyente, constitutivo

constitut|e vt constituir. ~**ion** n
constitución f. ~**ional** a
constitucional. ● n paseo m

constrict vt apretar. ~**ion** n
constricción f

construct vt construir. ~**ion** n
construcción f. ~**ive** a
constructivo

consul n cónsul m & f. ~**ate** n
consulado m

consult vt/i consultar. ~**ancy** n
asesoría. ~**ant** n asesor m; (Med)
especialista m & f; (Tec) consejero
m técnico. ~**ation** n consulta f

consume vt consumir. ~**r** n
consumidor m. ● a de consumo

consummate a consumado. ● vt
consumar

consumption n consumo m

contact n contacto m. ● vt
ponerse en contacto con. ~ **lens**
n lentilla f, lente f de contacto
(LAm)

contagious a contagioso

contain vt contener. ~ **o.s.**
contenerse. ~**er** n recipiente m;
(Com) contenedor m

contaminat|e vt contaminar.
~**ion** n contaminación f

contemplate vt contemplar;
(consider) considerar

contemporary *a & n*
contemporáneo (*m*)

contempt *n* desprecio *m*. ~**ible**
a despreciable. ~**uous** *a*
desdeñoso

contend *vt* competir. ~**er** *n*
aspirante *m & f* (**for** a)

content *a* satisfecho. ● *n*
contenido *m*. ● *vt* contentar.
~**ed** *a* satisfecho. ~**ment** *n*
satisfacción *f*. ~**s** *n* contenido *m*;
(of book) índice *m* de materias

contest *n* (competition) concurso *m*;
(Sport) competición *f*, competencia
f (LAm). ● *vt* disputar. ~**ant** *n*
concursante *m & f*

context *n* contexto *m*

continent *n* continente *m*. **the**
C~ Europa *f*. ~**al** *a* continental.
~**al quilt** *n* edredón *m*

contingen|cy *n* contingencia *f*.
~**t** *a & n* contingente (*m*)

continu|al *a* continuo. ~**ally** *adv*
continuamente. ~**ation** *n*
continuación *f*. ~**e** *vt/i* continuar,
seguir. ~**ed** *a* continuo. ~**ity** *n*
continuidad *f*. ~**ous** *a* continuo.
~**ously** *adv* continuamente

contort *vt* retorcer. ~**ion** *n*
contorsión *f*. ~**ionist** *n*
contorsionista *m & f*

contour *n* contorno *m*

contraband *n* contrabando *m*

contracepti|on *n* anticoncepción
f. ~**ve** *a & n* anticonceptivo (*m*)

contract *n* contrato *m*. ● *vt*
contraer. ● *vi* contraerse. ~**ion** *n*
contracción *f*. ~**or** *n* contratista
m & f

contradict *vt* contradecir. ~**ion**
n contradicción *f*. ~**ory** *a*
contradictorio

contraption *n* 🄸 artilugio *m*

contrary *a* contrario. **the** ~ lo
contrario. **on the** ~ al contrario.
● *adv*. ~ **to** contrariamente a. ●
a (obstinate) terco

contrast *n* contraste *m*. ● *vt/i*
contrastar. ~**ing** *a* contrastante

contravene *vt* contravenir

contribut|e *vt* contribuir con.
● *vi* contribuir. ~**e to** escribir
para <*newspaper*>. ~**ion** *n*
contribución *f*. ~**or** *n*
contribuyente *m & f*; (to newspaper)
colaborador *m*

contrite *a* arrepentido, pesaroso

contriv|e *vt* idear. ~**e to**
conseguir. ~**ed** *a* artificioso

control *vt* (*pt* **controlled**)
controlar. ● *n* control *m*. ~**ler** *n*
director *m*. ~**s** *npl* (Mec) mandos
mpl

controvers|ial controvertido. ~**y**
n controversia *f*

conundrum *n* adivinanza *f*

convalesce *vi* convalecer. ~**nce**
n convalecencia *f*

convector *n* estufa *f* de
convección

convene *vt* convocar. ● *vi*
reunirse

convenien|ce *n* conveniencia *f*,
comodidad *f*. **all modern** ~**ces**
todas las comodidades. **at your**
~**ce** según le convenga. ~**ces**
npl servicios *mpl*, baños *mpl*
(LAm). ~**t** *a* conveniente; <*place*>
bien situado; <*time*> oportuno. **be**
~**t** convenir. ~**tly** *adv*
convenientemente

convent *n* convento *m*

convention *n* convención *f*. ~**al**
a convencional

converge *vi* converger

conversation *n* conversación *f*.
~**al** *a* familiar, coloquial.

converse *vi* conversar. ● *a*
inverso. ● *n* lo contrario. ~**ly** *adv*
a la inversa

conver|sion *n* conversión *f*. ~**t**
vt convertir. ● *n* converso *m*.

C

~**tible** a convertible. ●n (Auto) descapotable m, convertible m (LAm)

convex a convexo

convey vt transportar <goods, people>; comunicar <idea, feeling>. ~**or belt** n cinta f transportadora, banda f transportadora (LAm)

convict vt condenar. ● n presidiario m. ~**ion** n condena f; (belief) creencia f

convinc|e vt convencer. ~**ing** a convincente

convoluted a <argument> intrincado

convoy n convoy m

convuls|e vt convulsionar. **be ~ed with laughter** desternillarse de risa. ~**ion** n convulsión f

coo vi arrullar

cook vt hacer, preparar. ● vi cocinar; <food> hacerse. ● n cocinero m. □ ~ **up** vt 🄸 inventar. ~**book** n libro m de cocina. ~**er** n cocina f, estufa f (Mex). ~**ery** n cocina f

cookie n (Amer) galleta f

cool a (-er, -est) fresco; (calm) tranquilo; (unfriendly) frío. ● n fresco m; 🅇 calma f. ● vt enfriar. ● vi enfriarse. □ ~ **down** vi <person> calmarse. ~**ly** adv tranquilamente

coop n gallinero m. □ ~ **up** vt encerrar

co-op n cooperativa f

cooperat|e vi cooperar. ~**ion** n cooperación f. ~**ive** a cooperativo. ● n cooperativa f

co-opt vt cooptar

co-ordinat|e vt coordinar. ● n (Math) coordenada f. ~**es** npl prendas fpl para combinar. ~**ion** n coordinación f

cop n 🄸 poli m & f 🄸, tira m & f (Mex, 🄸)

cope vi arreglárselas. ~ **with** hacer frente a

copious a abundante

copper n cobre m; (coin) perra f; 🄸 poli m & f 🄸, tira m & f (Mex, 🄸). ● a de cobre

copy n copia f; (of book, newspaper) ejemplar m. ● vt copiar. ~**right** n derechos mpl de reproducción

coral n coral m

cord n cuerda f; (fabric) pana f; (Amer, Elec) cordón m, cable m

cordial a cordial. ● n refresco m (concentrado)

cordon n cordón m. □ ~ **off** vt acordonar

core n (of apple) corazón m; (of Earth) centro m; (of problem) meollo m

cork n corcho m. ~**screw** n sacacorchos m

corn n (wheat) trigo m; (Amer) maíz m; (hard skin) callo m

corned beef n carne f de vaca en lata

corner n ángulo m; (inside) rincón m; (outside) esquina f; (football) córner m. ● vt arrinconar; (Com) acaparar

cornet n (Mus) corneta f; (for ice cream) cucurucho m, barquillo m (Mex)

corn: ~flakes npl copos mpl de maíz. ~**flour** n maizena f (P)

Cornish a de Cornualles

cornstarch n (Amer) maizena f (P)

corny a (🄸, trite) gastado

coronation n coronación f

coroner n juez m de primera instancia

corporal n cabo m. ● a corporal

corporate a corporativo

corporation n corporación f;
(Amer) sociedad f anónima
corps n (pl **corps**) cuerpo m
corpse n cadáver m
corpulent a corpulento
corral n (Amer) corral m
correct a correcto; <time> exacto.
● vt corregir. ~**ion** n corrección f
correspond vi corresponder;
(write) escribirse. ~**ence** n
correspondencia f. ~**ent** n
corresponsal m & f
corridor n pasillo m
corro|de vt corroer. ● vi
corroerse. ~**sion** n corrosión f.
~**sive** a corrosivo
corrugated a ondulado. ~ **iron** n
chapa f de zinc
corrupt a corrompido. ● vt
corromper. ~**ion** n corrupción f
corset n corsé m
cosmetic a & n cosmético (m)
cosmic a cósmico
cosmopolitan a & n cosmopolita
(m & f)
cosmos n cosmos m
cosset vt (pt **cosseted**) mimar
cost vt (pt **cost**) costar; (pt
costed) calcular el coste de,
calcular el costo de (LAm). ● n
coste m, costo m (LAm). **at all** ~**s**
cueste lo que cueste. **to one's** ~ a
sus expensas. ~**s** npl (Jurid)
costas fpl
Costa Rica n Costa f Rica. ~**n** a
& n costarricense (m & f),
costarriqueño (m & f)
cost: ~**effective** a rentable.
~**ly** a (-ier, -iest) costoso
costume n traje m; (for party,
disguise) disfraz m
cosy a (-ier, -iest) acogedor. ● n
cubreteras m
cot n cuna f

cottage n casita f. ~ **cheese** n
requesón m. ~ **pie** n pastel m de
carne cubierta con puré
cotton n algodón m; (thread) hilo
m; (Amer) ⇒~ wool. □ ~ **on** vi
Ⅰ comprender. ~ **bud** n
bastoncillo m, cotonete m (Mex).
~ **candy** n (Amer) algodón m de
azúcar. ~ **swab** n (Amer) ⇒~
bud. ~ **wool** n algodón m
hidrófilo
couch n sofá m
cough vi toser. ● n tos f. □ ~ **up**
vt Ⅰ pagar. ~ **mixture** n jarabe
m para la tos
could pt of CAN¹
couldn't = **could not**
council n consejo m; (of town)
ayuntamiento m. ~ **house** n
vivienda f subvencionada. ~**lor** n
concejal m
counsel n consejo m; (pl invar)
(Jurid) abogado m. ● vt (pt
counselled) aconsejar. ~**ling** n
terapia f de apoyo. ~**lor** n
consejero m
count n recuento m; (nobleman)
conde m. ● vt/i contar. □ ~ **on** vt
contar. ~**down** n cuenta f atrás
counter n (in shop) mostrador m;
(in bank, post office) ventanilla f;
(token) ficha f. ● adv. ~ **to** en
contra de. ● a opuesto. ● vt
oponerse a; parar <blow>
counter... pref contra.... ~**act** vt
contrarrestar. ~**attack** n
contraataque m. ● vt/i
contraatacar. ~**balance** n
contrapeso m. ● vt/i contrapesar.
~**clockwise** a/adv (Amer) en
sentido contrario al de las agujas
del reloj
counterfeit a falsificado. ● n
falsificación f. ● vt falsificar
counterfoil n matriz f, talón m
(LAm)

counter-productive *a* contraproducente

countess *n* condesa *f*

countless *a* innumerable

country *n* (native land) país *m*; (countryside) campo *m*; (Mus) (música *f*) country *m*. **~-and-western** (música *f*) country *m*. **~man** *n* (of one's own country) compatriota *m*. **~side** *n* campo *m*; (landscape) paisaje *m*

county *n* condado *m*

coup *n* golpe *m*

couple *n* (of things) par *m*; (of people) pareja *f*; (married) matrimonio *m*. **a ~ of** un par de

coupon *n* cupón *m*

courage *n* valor *m*. **~ous** *a* valiente

courgette *n* calabacín *m*

courier *n* mensajero *m*; (for tourists) guía *m & f*

course *n* curso *m*; (behaviour) conducta *f*; (Aviat, Naut) rumbo *m*; (Culin) plato *m*; (for golf) campo *m*. **in due ~** a su debido tiempo. **in the ~ of** en el transcurso de, durante. **of ~** claro, por supuesto. **of ~ not** claro que no, por supuesto que no

court *n* corte *f*; (tennis) pista *f*; cancha *f* (LAm); (Jurid) tribunal *m*. ● *vt* cortejar; buscar *<danger>*

courteous *a* cortés

courtesy *n* cortesía *f*

courtier *n* (old use) cortesano *m*

court: **~ martial** *n* (*pl* **~s martial**) consejo *m* de guerra. **~-martial** *vt* (*pt* **~-martialled**) juzgar en consejo de guerra. **~ship** *n* cortejo *m*. **~yard** *n* patio *m*

cousin *n* primo *m*. **first ~** primo carnal. **second ~** primo segundo

cove *n* ensenada *f*, cala *f*

Coventry *n*. **send s.o. to ~** hacer el vacío a uno

cover *vt* cubrir. ● *n* cubierta *f*; (shelter) abrigo *m*; (lid) tapa *f*; (for furniture) funda *f*; (pretext) pretexto *m*; (of magazine) portada *f*. □ **~ up** *vt* cubrir; (fig) ocultar. **~ charge** *n* precio *m* del cubierto. **~ing** *n* cubierta *f*. **~ing letter** *n* carta *f* adjunta

covet *vt* codiciar

cow *n* vaca *f*

coward *n* cobarde *m*. **~ice** *n* cobardía *f*. **~ly** *a* cobarde.

cowboy *n* vaquero *m*

cower *vi* encogerse, acobardarse

coxswain *n* timonel *m*

coy *a* (**-er**, **-est**) (shy) tímido; (evasive) evasivo

crab *n* cangrejo *m*, jaiba *f* (LAm)

crack *n* grieta *f*; (noise) crujido *m*; (of whip) chasquido *m*; (drug) crack *m*. ● *a* 🄸 de primera. ● *vt* agrietar; chasquear *<whip, fingers>*; cascar *<nut>*; gastar *<joke>*; resolver *<problem>*. ● *vi* agrietarse. **get ~ing** 🄸 darse prisa. □ **~ down on** *vt* 🄸 tomar medidas enérgicas contra

cracker *n* (Culin) cracker *f*, galleta *f* (salada); (Christmas cracker) sorpresa *f* (que estalla al abrirla)

crackle *vi* crepitar. ● *n* crepitación *f*, crujido *m*

crackpot *n* 🄸 chiflado *m*

cradle *n* cuna *f*. ● *vt* acunar

craft *n* destreza *f*; (technique) arte *f*; (cunning) astucia *f*. ● *n invar* (boat) barco *m*

craftsman *n* (*pl* **-men**) artesano *m*. **~ship** *n* artesanía *f*

crafty *a* (**-ier**, **-iest**) astuto

cram *vt* (*pt* **crammed**) rellenar. **~ with** llenar de. ● *vi* (for exams) memorizar, empollar, zambutir (Mex)

cramp *n* calambre *m*

cramped *a* apretado

crane *n* grúa *f*. ● *vt* estirar *<neck>*

crank *n* manivela *f*; (person) excéntrico *m*. ~**y** *a* excéntrico

cranny *n* grieta *f*

crash *n* accidente *m*; (noise) estruendo *m*; (collision) choque *m*; (Com) quiebra *f*. ● *vt* estrellar. ● *vi* quebrar con estrépito; (have accident) tener un accidente; *<car etc>* estrellarse, chocar; (fail) fracasar. ~ **course** *n* curso intensivo. ~ **helmet** *n* casco *m* protector. ~**-land** *vi* hacer un aterrizaje forzoso

crass *a* craso, burdo

crate *n* cajón *m*. ● *vt* embalar

crater *n* cráter *m*

crav|e *vt* ansiar. ~**ing** *n* ansia *f*

crawl *vi* *<baby>* gatear; (move slowly) avanzar lentamente; (drag o.s.) arrastrarse. ~ **to** humillarse ante. ~ **with** hervir de. ● *n* (swimming) crol *m*. **at a** ~ a paso lento

crayon *n* lápiz *m* de color; (made of wax) lápiz *m* de cera, crayola *f* (P), crayón *m* (Mex)

craz|e *n* manía *f*. ~**y** *a* (**-ier**, **-iest**) loco. **be** ~**y about** estar loco por

creak *n* crujido *m*; (of hinge) chirrido *m*. ● *vi* crujir; *<hinge>* chirriar

cream *n* crema *f*; (fresh) nata *f*, crema *f* (LAm). ● *a* (colour) color crema. ● *vt* (beat) batir. ~ **cheese** *n* queso *m* para untar, queso *m* crema (LAm). ~**y** *a* cremoso

crease *n* raya *f*, pliegue *m* (Mex); (crumple) arruga *f*. ● *vt* plegar; (wrinkle) arrugar. ● *vi* arrugarse

creat|e *vt* crear. ~**ion** *n* creación *f*. ~**ive** *a* creativo. ~**or** *n* creador *m*

creature *n* criatura *f*

crèche *n* guardería *f* (infantil)

credib|ility *n* credibilidad *f*. ~**le** *a* creíble

credit *n* crédito *m*; (honour) mérito *m*. **take the** ~ **for** atribuirse el mérito de. ● *vt* (*pt* **credited**) acreditar; (believe) creer. ~ **s.o. with** atribuir a uno. ~ **card** *n* tarjeta *f* de crédito. ~**or** *n* acreedor *m*

creed *n* credo *m*

creek *n* ensenada *f*. **up the** ~ ⊠ en apuros

creep *vi* (*pt* **crept**) arrastrarse; (plant) trepar. ● *n* 🄸 adulador. ~**s** *npl*. **give s.o. the** ~**s** poner los pelos de punta a uno. ~**er** *n* enredadera *f*

cremat|e *vt* incinerar. ~**ion** *n* cremación *f*. ~**orium** *n* (*pl* **-ia**) crematorio *m*

crept ⇨CREEP

crescendo *n* (*pl* **-os**) crescendo *m*

crescent *n* media luna *f*; (street) calle *f* en forma de media luna

crest *n* cresta *f*; (on coat of arms) emblema *m*

crevice *n* grieta *f*

crew *n* tripulación *f*; (gang) pandilla *f*. ~ **cut** *n* corte *m* al rape

crib *n* (Amer) cuna *f*; (Relig) belén *m*. ● *vt/i* (*pt* **cribbed**) copiar

crick *n* calambre *m*; (in neck) tortícolis *f*

cricket *n* (Sport) críquet *m*; (insect) grillo *m*

crim|e *n* delito *m*; (murder) crimen *m*; (acts) delincuencia *f*. ~**inal** *a* & *n* criminal (*m* & *f*)

crimson *a* & *n* carmesí (*m*)

cringe *vi* encogerse; (fig) humillarse

crinkle vt arrugar. ● vi arrugarse. ● n arruga f

cripple n lisiado m. ● vt lisiar; (fig) paralizar

crisis n (pl **crises**) crisis f

crisp a (-er, -est) (Culin) crujiente; <air> vigorizador. ~s npl patatas fpl fritas, papas fpl fritas (LAm) (de bolsa)

crisscross a entrecruzado. ● vt entrecruzar. ● vi entrecruzarse

criterion n (pl -ia) criterio m

critic n crítico m. ~al a crítico. ~ally adv críticamente; (ill) gravemente

critici|sm n crítica f. ~ze vt/i criticar

croak n (of person) gruñido m; (of frog) canto m. ● vi gruñir; <frog> croar

Croat n croata m & f. ~ia n Croacia f. ~ian a croata

crochet n crochet m, ganchillo m. ● vt tejer a crochet or a ganchillo

crockery n loza f

crocodile n cocodrilo m. ~ tears npl lágrimas fpl de cocodrilo

crocus n (pl -es) azafrán m de primavera

crook n 🔢 sinvergüenza m & f. ~ed a torcido, chueco (LAm); (winding) tortuoso; (dishonest) deshonesto

crop n cosecha f; (haircut) corte m de pelo muy corto. ● vt (pt cropped) cortar. □ ~ **up** vi surgir

croquet n croquet m

cross n cruz f; (of animals) cruce m. ● vt cruzar; (oppose) contrariar. ~ **s.o.'s mind** ocurrírsele a uno. ~ vi cruzar. ~ **o.s.** santiguarse. ● a enfadado, enojado (esp LAm). □ ~ **out** vt tachar. ~**bar** n travesaño m. ~-**examine** vt interrogar. ~-**eyed** a bizco. ~**fire** n fuego m

cruzado. ~**ing** n (by boat) travesía f; (on road) cruce m peatonal. ~**ly** adv con enfado, con enojo (esp LAm). ~-**purposes** npl. **talk at** ~-**purposes** hablar sin entenderse. ~-**reference** n remisión f. ~**roads** n invar cruce m. ~-**section** n sección f transversal; (fig) muestra f representativa. ~**walk** n (Amer) paso de peatones. ~**word** n ~**word** (**puzzle**) crucigrama m

crotch n entrepiernas fpl

crouch vi agacharse

crow n cuervo m. **as the** ~ **flies** en línea recta. ● vi cacarear. ~**bar** n palanca f

crowd n muchedumbre f. ● vt amontonar; (fill) llenar. ● vi amontonarse; (gather) reunirse. ~**ed** a atestado

crown n corona f; (of hill) cumbre f; (of head) coronilla f. ● vt coronar

crucial a crucial

crucifix n crucifijo m. ~**ion** n crucifixión f

crucify vt crucificar

crude a (-er, -est) (raw) crudo; (rough) tosco; (vulgar) ordinario

cruel a (**crueller, cruellest**) cruel. ~**ty** n crueldad f

cruet n vinagrera f

cruise n crucero m. ● vi hacer un crucero; (of car) circular lentamente. ~**r** n crucero m

crumb n miga f

crumble vt desmenuzar. ● vi desmenuzarse; (collapse) derrumbarse

crummy a (-ier, -iest) ✖ miserable

crumpet n bollo m blando

crumple vt arrugar. ● vi arrugarse

crunch vt hacer crujir; (bite) masticar. ~**y** a crujiente

crusade n cruzada f. ~r n cruzado m

crush vt aplastar; arrugar <clothes>. ● n (crowd) aglomeración f. **have a ~ on** 🇬🇧 estar chiflado por

crust n corteza f. ~y a <bread> de corteza dura

crutch n muleta f; (Anat) entrepiernas fpl

crux n (pl **cruxes**). **the ~ (of the matter)** el quid (de la cuestión)

cry n grito m. **be a far ~ from** (fig) distar mucho de. ● vi llorar; (call out) gritar. □ **~ off** vi echarse atrás, rajarse. ~**baby** n llorón m

crypt n cripta f

cryptic a enigmático

crystal n cristal m. ~**lize** vi cristalizarse

cub n cachorro m. **C~ (Scout)** n lobato m

Cuba n Cuba f. ~**n** a & n cubano (m)

cubbyhole n cuchitril m

cub|e n cubo m. ~**ic** a cúbico

cubicle n cubículo m; (changing room) probador m

cuckoo n cuco m, cuclillo m

cucumber n pepino m

cuddl|e vt abrazar. ● vi abrazarse. ● n abrazo m. ~**y** a adorable

cue n (Mus) entrada f; (in theatre) pie m; (in snooker) taco m

cuff n puño m; (Amer, of trousers) vuelta f, dobladillo m; (blow) bofetada f. **speak off the ~** hablar de improviso. ● vt abofetear. ~**link** n gemelo m, mancuerna f (Mex)

cul-de-sac n callejón m sin salida

culinary a culinario

cull vt sacrificar en forma selectiva <animals>

culminat|e vi culminar. ~**ion** n culminación f

culprit n culpable m & f

cult n culto m

cultivat|e vt cultivar. ~**ion** n cultivo m

cultur|al a cultural. ~**e** n cultura f; (Bot etc) cultivo m. ~**ed** a cultivado; <person> culto

cumbersome a incómodo; (heavy) pesado

cunning a astuto. ● n astucia f

cup n taza f; (trophy) copa f

cupboard n armario m

curator n (of museum) conservador m

curb n freno m; (Amer) bordillo m (de la acera), borde m de la banqueta (Mex). ● vt refrenar

curdle vt cuajar. ● vi cuajarse; (go bad) cortarse

cure vt curar. ● n cura f

curfew n toque m de queda

curio|sity n curiosidad f. ~**us** a curioso

curl vt rizar, enchinar (Mex). ~ **o.s. up** acurrucarse. ● vi <hair> rizarse, enchinarse (Mex); <paper> ondularse. ● n rizo m, chino m (Mex). ~**er** n rulo m, chino m (Mex). ~**y** a (-**ier**, -**iest**) rizado, chino (Mex)

currant n pasa f de Corinto

currency n moneda f

current a & n corriente (f); (existing) actual. ~ **affairs** npl sucesos de actualidad. ~**ly** adv actualmente

curriculum n (pl -**la**) programa m de estudios. ~ **vitae** n currículum m vitae

curry n curry m. ● vt preparar al curry

curse n maldición f; (oath) palabrota f. ● vt maldecir. ● vi decir palabrotas

cursory *a* superficial

curt *a* brusco

curtain *n* cortina *f*; (in theatre) telón *m*

curtsey, **curtsy** *n* reverencia *f*. ● *vi* hacer una reverencia

curve *n* curva *f*. ● *vi* estar curvado; <*road*> torcerse

cushion *n* cojín *m*, almohadón *m*

cushy *a* (**-ier, -iest**) 🅸 fácil

custard *n* natillas *fpl*

custody *n* custodia *f*. **be in ∼** (Jurid) estar detenido

custom *n* costumbre *f*; (Com) clientela *f*. **∼ary** *a* acostumbrado. **∼er** *n* cliente *m*. **∼s** *npl* aduana *f*. **∼s officer** *n* aduanero *m*

cut *vt/i* (*pt* **cut**, *pres p* **cutting**) cortar; reducir <*prices*>. ● *n* corte *m*; (reduction) reducción *f*. □ **∼ across** *vt* cortar camino por. □ **∼ back, ∼ down** *vt* reducir. □ **∼ in** *vi* interrumpir. □ **∼ off** *vt* cortar; (phone) desconectar; (fig) aislar. □ **∼ out** *vt* recortar; (omit) suprimir. □ **∼ through** *vt* cortar camino por. □ **∼ up** *vt* cortar en pedazos

cute *a* (**-er, -est**) 🅸 mono, amoroso (LAm); (Amer, attractive) guapo, buen mozo (LAm)

cutlery *n* cubiertos *mpl*

cutlet *n* chuleta *f*

cut: ∼-price, (Amer) **∼-rate** *a* a precio reducido. **∼-throat** *a* despiadado. **∼ting** *a* cortante; <*remark*> mordaz. ● *n* (from newspaper) recorte *m*; (of plant) esqueje *m*

CV *n* (= curriculum vitae) currículum *m* (vitae)

cyberspace *n* ciberespacio *m*

cycl|e *n* ciclo *m*; (bicycle) bicicleta *f*. ● *vi* ir en bicicleta. **∼ing** *n* ciclismo *m*. **∼ist** *n* ciclista *m & f*

cylind|er *n* cilindro *m*. **∼er head** (Auto) *n* culata *f*. **∼rical** *a* cilíndrico

cymbal *n* címbalo *m*

cynic *n* cínico *m*. **∼al** *a* cínico. **∼ism** *n* cinismo *m*

Czech *a & n* checo (*m*). **∼oslovakia** *n* (History) Checoslovaquia *f*. **∼ Republic** *n*. **the ∼ Republic** *n* la República Checa

dab *vt* (*pt* **dabbed**) tocar ligeramente. ● *n* toque *m* suave. **a ∼ of** un poquito de

dad *n* 🅸 papá *m*. **∼dy** *n* papi *m*. **∼dy-long-legs** *n invar* (cranefly) típula *f*; (Amer, harvestman) segador *m*, falangio *m*

daffodil *n* narciso *m*

daft *a* (**-er, -est**) 🅸 tonto

dagger *n* daga *f*, puñal *m*

daily *a* diario. ● *adv* diariamente, cada día

dainty *a* (**-ier, -iest**) delicado

dairy *n* vaquería *f*; (shop) lechería *f*

daisy *n* margarita *f*

dam *n* presa *f*, represa *f* (LAm)

damag|e *n* daño *m*; **∼s** (*npl*, Jurid) daños *mpl* y perjuicios *mpl*. ● *vt* (fig) dañar, estropear. **∼ing** *a* perjudicial

dame *n* (old use) dama *f*; (Amer, ✖) chica *f*

damn *vt* condenar; (curse) maldecir. ● *int* 🅸 ¡caray! 🅸. ● *a* maldito. ● *n* I **don't give a ~** (no) me importa un comino

damp *n* humedad *f*. ● *a* (**-er, -est**) húmedo. ● *vt* mojar. **~ness** *n* humedad *f*

danc|e *vt/i* bailar. ● *n* baile *m*. **~e hall** *n* salón *m* de baile. **~er** *n* bailador *m*; (professional) bailarín *m*. **~ing** *n* baile *m*

dandelion *n* diente *m* de león

dandruff *n* caspa *f*

dandy *n* petimetre *m*

Dane *n* danés *m*

danger *n* peligro *m*; (risk) riesgo *m*. **~ous** *a* peligroso

dangle *vt* balancear. ● *vi* suspender, colgar

Danish *a* danés. ● *m* (Lang) danés *m*

dar|e *vt* desafiar. ● *vi* atreverse a. I **~ say** probablemente. ● *n* desafío *m*. **~edevil** *n* atrevido *m*. **~ing** *a* atrevido

dark *a* (**-er, -est**) oscuro; <*skin, hair*> moreno. ● *n* oscuridad *f*; (nightfall) atardecer. **in the ~** a oscuras. **~en** *vt* oscurecer. ● *vi* oscurecerse. **~ness** *n* oscuridad *f*. **~room** *n* cámara *f* oscura

darling *a* querido. ● *n* cariño *m*

darn *vt* zurcir

dart *n* dardo *m*. ● *vi* lanzarse; (run) precipitarse. **~board** *n* diana *f*. **~s** *npl* los dardos *mpl*

dash *vi* precipitarse. ● *vt* tirar; (break) romper; defraudar <*hopes*>. ● *n* (small amount) poquito *m*; (punctuation mark) guión *m*. □ **~ off** *vi* marcharse apresuradamente. **~ out** *vi* salir corriendo. **~board** *n* tablero *m* de mandos

data *npl* datos *mpl*. **~base** *n* base *f* de datos. **~ processing** *n* proceso *m* de datos

date *n* fecha *f*; (appointment) cita *f*; (fruit) dátil *m*. **to ~** hasta la fecha. ● *vt* fechar. ● *vi* datar; datar <*remains*>; (be old-fashioned) quedar anticuado. **~d** *a* pasado de moda

daub *vt* embadurnar

daughter *n* hija *f*. **~-in-law** *n* nuera *f*

dawdle *vi* andar despacio; (waste time) perder el tiempo

dawn *n* amanecer *m*. ● *vi* amanecer; (fig) nacer. **it ~ed on me that** caí en la cuenta de que

day *n* día *m*; (whole day) jornada *f*; (period) época *f*. **~break** *n* amanecer *m*. **~ care center** *n* (Amer) guardería *f* infantil. **~dream** *n* ensueño *m*. ● *vi* soñar despierto. **~light** *n* luz *f* del día. **~time** *n* día *m*

daze *vt* aturdir. ● *n* aturdimiento *m*. **in a ~** aturdido. **~d** *a* aturdido

dazzle *vt* deslumbrar

dead *a* muerto; (numb) dormido. ● *adv* justo; (🄸, completely) completamente. **~ beat** rendido. **~ slow** muy lento. **stop ~** parar en seco. **~en** *vt* amortiguar <*sound, blow*>; calmar <*pain*>. **~ end** *n* callejón *m* sin salida. **~line** *n* fecha *f* tope, plazo *m* de entrega. **~lock** *n* punto *m* muerto. **~ly** *a* (**-ier, -iest**) mortal

deaf *a* (**-er, -est**) sordo. **~en** *vt* ensordecer. **~ness** *n* sordera *f*

deal *n* (agreement) acuerdo *m*; (treatment) trato *m*. **a good ~** bastante. **a great ~ (of)** muchísimo. ● *vt* (*pt* **dealt**) dar <*blow, cards*>. ● *vi* (cards) dar, repartir. □ **~ in** *vt* comerciar en. □ **~ out** *vt* repartir, distribuir. □ **~ with** *vt* tratar con <*person*>; tratar de <*subject*>; ocuparse de <*problem*>. **~er** *n* comerciante *m*. **drug ~er** traficante *m & f* de drogas

D

dean n deán m; (Univ) decano m

dear a (-er, -est) querido; (expensive) caro. ● n querido m. ● adv caro. ● int. **oh** ∼! ¡ay por Dios! ∼ **me!** ¡Dios mío! ∼**ly** adv (pay) caro; (very much) muchísimo

death n muerte f. ∼ **sentence** n pena f de muerte. ∼ **trap** n lugar m peligroso

debat|able a discutible. ∼**e** n debate m. ● vt debatir, discutir

debauchery vt libertinaje m

debit n débito m. ● vt debitar, cargar. ∼ **card** n tarjeta f de cobro automático

debris n escombros mpl

debt n deuda f. **be in** ∼ tener deudas. ∼**or** n deudor m

decade n década f

decaden|ce n decadencia f. ∼**t** a decadente

decay vi descomponerse; <tooth> cariarse. ● n decomposición f; (of tooth) caries f

deceased a difunto

deceit n engaño m. ∼**ful** a falso. ∼**fully** adv falsamente

deceive vt engañar

December n diciembre m

decen|cy n decencia f. ∼**t** a decente; (🄸, good) bueno; (🄸, kind) amable. ∼**tly** adv decentemente

decepti|on n engaño m. ∼**ve** a engañoso

decibel n decibel(io) m

decide vt/i decidir. ∼**d** a resuelto; (unquestionable) indudable

decimal a & n decimal (m). ∼ **point** n coma f (decimal), punto m decimal

decipher vt descifrar

decis|ion n decisión f. ∼**ive** a decisivo; <manner> decidido

deck n (Naut) cubierta f; (Amer, of cards) baraja f; (of bus) piso m. ● vt adornar. ∼**chair** n tumbona f, silla f de playa

declar|ation n declaración f. ∼**e** vt declarar

decline vt rehusar; (Gram) declinar. ● vi disminuir; (deteriorate) deteriorarse. ● n decadencia f; (decrease) disminución f

decode vt descifrar

decompose vi descomponerse

décor n decoración f

decorat|e vt adornar, decorar (LAm); empapelar y pintar <room>. ∼**ion** n (act) decoración f; (ornament) adorno m. ∼**ive** a decorativo. ∼**or** n pintor m decorador

decoy n señuelo m. ● vt atraer con señuelo

decrease vt/i disminuir. ● n disminución f

decree n decreto m. ● vt decretar

decrepit a decrépito

decriminalize vt despenalizar

dedicat|e vt dedicar. ∼**ion** n dedicación f

deduce vt deducir

deduct vt deducir. ∼**ion** n deducción f

deed n hecho m; (Jurid) escritura f

deem vt juzgar, considerar

deep a (-er, -est) adv profundo. ● adv profundamente. **be** ∼ **in thought** estar absorto en sus pensamientos. ∼**en** vt hacer más profundo. ● vi hacerse más profundo. ∼**freeze** n congelador m, freezer m (LAm). ∼**ly** adv profundamente

deer n invar ciervo m

deface vt desfigurar

default vi faltar. ● n. opción f por defecto; **by** ∼ en rebeldía

defeat vt vencer; (frustrate) frustrar. ● n derrota f. ~ism n derrotismo m. ~ist n derrotista a & (m & f)

defect n defecto m. ● vi desertar. ~ to pasar a. ~ion n (Pol) defección f. ~ive a defectuoso

defence n defensa f. ~less a indefenso

defen|d vt defender. ~dant n (Jurid) acusado m. ~sive a defensivo. ● n defensiva f

defer vt (pt deferred) aplazar. ~ence n deferencia f. ~ential a deferente

defian|ce n desafío m. in ~ce of a despecho de. ~t a desafiante. ~tly adv con actitud desafiante

deficien|cy n falta f. ~t a deficiente. be ~t in carecer de

deficit n déficit m

define vt definir

definite a (final) definitivo; (certain) seguro; (clear) claro; (firm) firme. ~ly adv seguramente; (definitively) definitivamente

definition n definición f

definitive a definitivo

deflate vt desinflar. ● vi desinflarse

deflect vt desviar

deform vt deformar. ~ed a deforme. ~ity n deformidad f

defrost vt descongelar. ● vi descongelarse

deft a (-er, -est) hábil. ~ly adv hábilmente f

defuse vt desactivar <bomb>; (fig) calmar

defy vt desafiar

degenerate vi degenerar. ● a & n degenerado (m)

degrad|ation n degradación f. ~e vt degradar

degree n grado m; (Univ) licenciatura f; (rank) rango m. to a certain ~ hasta cierto punto

deign vi. ~ to dignarse

deity n deidad f

deject|ed a desanimado. ~ion n abatimiento m

delay vt retrasar, demorar (LAm). ● vi tardar, demorar (LAm). ● n retraso m, demora f (LAm)

delegat|e vt/i delegar. ● n delegado m. ~ion n delegación f

delet|e vt tachar. ~ion n supresión f

deliberat|e vt/i deliberar. ● a intencionado; <steps etc> pausado. ~ely adv a propósito. ~ion n deliberación f

delica|cy n delicadeza f; (food) manjar m. ~te a delicado

delicatessen n charcutería f, salchichonería f (Mex)

delicious a delicioso

delight n placer m. ● vt encantar. ● vi deleitarse. ~ed a encantado. ~ful a delicioso

deliri|ous a delirante. ~um n delirio m

deliver vt entregar; (distribute) repartir; (aim) lanzar; (Med) he ~ed the baby la asistió en el parto. ~ance n liberación f. ~y n entrega f; (of post) reparto m; (Med) parto m

delta n (Geog) delta m

delude vt engañar. ~ o.s. engañarse

deluge n diluvio m

delusion n ilusión f

deluxe a de lujo

delve vi hurgar. ~ into (investigate) ahondar en

demand vt exigir. ● n petición f, pedido m (LAm); (claim) exigencia f; (Com) demanda f. in ~ muy popular, muy solicitado. on ~ a solicitud. ~ing *a* exigente. ~s *npl* exigencias *fpl*

demented *a* demente

demo *n* (*pl* -os) 🄳 manifestación *f*

democra|cy *n* democracia *f*. ~t *n* demócrata *m & f*. D~t *a & n* (in US) demócrata (*m & f*). ~tic *a* democrático

demoli|sh *vt* derribar. ~tion *n* demolición *f*

demon *n* demonio *m*

demonstrat|e *vt* demostrar. ● *vi* manifestarse, hacer una manifestación. ~ion *n* demostración *f*; (Pol) manifestación *f*. ~or *n* (Pol) manifestante *m & f*; (marketing) demostrador *m*

demoralize *vt* desmoralizar

demote *vt* bajar de categoría

demure *a* recatado

den *n* (of animal) guarida *f*, madriguera *f*

denial *n* denegación *f*; (statement) desmentimiento *m*

denim *n* tela *f* vaquera *or* de jeans, mezclilla (Mex) *f*. ~s *npl* vaqueros *mpl*, jeans *mpl*, tejanos *mpl*, pantalones *mpl* de mezclilla (Mex)

Denmark *n* Dinamarca *f*

denote *vt* denotar

denounce *vt* denunciar

dens|e *a* (-er, -est) espeso; <*person*> torpe. ~ely *adv* densamente. ~ity *n* densidad *f*

dent *n* abolladura *f*. ● *vt* abollar

dental *a* dental. ~ **floss** *n* hilo *m* *or* seda *f* dental. ~ **surgeon** *n* dentista *m & f*

dentist *n* dentista *m & f*. ~ry *n* odontología *f*

dentures *npl* dentadura *f* postiza

deny *vt* negar; desmentir <*rumour*>; denegar <*request*>

deodorant *a & n* desodorante (*m*)

depart *vi* partir, salir. ~ from (deviate from) apartarse de

department *n* departamento *m*; (Pol) ministerio *m*, secretaría *f* (Mex). ~ **store** *n* grandes almacenes *mpl*, tienda *f* de departamentos (Mex)

departure *n* partida *f*; (of train etc) salida *f*

depend *vi* depender. ~ on depender de. ~able *a* digno de confianza. ~ant *n* familiar *m & f* dependiente. ~ence *n* dependencia *f*. ~ent *a* dependiente. be ~ent on depender de

depict *vt* representar; (in words) describir

deplete *vt* agotar

deplor|able *a* deplorable. ~e *vt* deplorar

deploy *vt* desplegar

deport *vt* deportar. ~ation *n* deportación *f*

depose *vt* deponer

deposit *vt* (*pt* **deposited**) depositar. ● *n* depósito *m*

depot *n* depósito *m*; (Amer) estación *f* de autobuses

deprav|ed *a* depravado. ~ity *n* depravación *f*

depress *vt* deprimir; (press down) apretar. ~ed *a* deprimido. ~ing *a* deprimente. ~ion *n* depresión *f*

depriv|ation *n* privación *f*. ~e *vt*. ~e of privar de. ~d *a* carenciado

depth *n* profundidad *f*. be out of one's ~ perder pie; (fig) meterse en honduras. in ~ a fondo

deput|ize *vi*. ~ize for sustituir a. ~y *n* sustituto *m*. ~y **chairman** *n* vicepresidente *m*

derail *vt* hacer descarrilar. ~ment *n* descarrilamiento *m*

derelict *a* abandonado y en ruinas

deri|de *vt* mofarse de. ~**sion** *n* mofa *f*. ~**sive** *a* burlón. ~**sory** *a* <*offer etc*> irrisorio

deriv|ation *n* derivación *f*. ~**ative** *n* derivado *m*. ~**e** *vt/i* derivar

derogatory *a* despectivo

descen|d *vt/i* descender, bajar. ~**dant** *n* descendiente *m & f*. ~**t** *n* descenso *m*, bajada *f*; (lineage) ascendencia *f*

descri|be *vt* describir. ~**ption** *n* descripción *f*. ~**ptive** *a* descriptivo

desecrate *vt* profanar

desert¹ *vt* abandonar. ● *vi* (Mil) desertar. ~**er** *n* desertor *m*

desert² *a & n* desierto (*m*)

deserts *npl* lo merecido. **get one's just** ~ llevarse su merecido

deserv|e *vt* merecer. ~**ing** *a* <*cause*> meritorio

design *n* diseño *m*; (plan) plan *m*. ~**s** (intentions) propósitos *mpl*. ● *vt* diseñar; (plan) planear

designate *vt* designar

designer *n* diseñador *m*; (fashion ~) diseñador *m* de modas. ● *a* <*clothes*> de diseño exclusivo

desirable *a* deseable

desire *n* deseo *m*. ● *vt* desear

desk *n* escritorio *m*; (at school) pupitre *m*; (in hotel) recepción *f*; (Com) caja *f*. ~**top publishing** *n* autoedición *f*, edición *f* electrónica

desolat|e *a* desolado; (uninhabited) deshabitado. ~**ion** *n* desolación *f*

despair *n* desesperación *f*. **be in** ~ estar desesperado. ● *vi.* ~ **of** desesperarse de

despatch *vt, n* ⇒DISPATCH

desperat|e *a* desesperado. ~**ely** *adv* desesperadamente. ~**ion** *n* desesperación *f*

despicable *a* despreciable

despise *vt* despreciar

despite *prep* a pesar de

despondent *a* abatido

despot *n* déspota *m*

dessert *n* postre *m*. ~**spoon** *n* cuchara *f* de postre

destination *n* destino *m*

destiny *n* destino *m*

destitute *a* indigente

destroy *vt* destruir. ~**er** *n* destructor *m*

destructi|on *n* destrucción *f*. ~**ve** *a* destructivo

desultory *a* desganado

detach *vt* separar. ~**able** *a* separable. ~**ed** *a* (aloof) distante; (house) no adosado. ~**ment** *n* desprendimiento *m*; (Mil) destacamento *m*; (aloofness) indiferencia *f*

detail *n* detalle *m*. **explain sth in** ~ explicar algo detalladamente. ● *vt* detallar; (Mil) destacar. ~**ed** *a* detallado

detain *vt* detener; (delay) retener. ~**ee** *n* detenido *m*

detect *vt* percibir; (discover) descubrir. ~**ive** *n* (private) detective *m*; (in police) agente *m & f*. ~**or** *n* detector *m*

detention *n* detención *f*

deter *vt* (*pt* **deterred**) disuadir; (prevent) impedir

detergent *a & n* detergente (*m*)

deteriorat|e *vi* deteriorarse. ~**ion** *n* deterioro *m*

determin|ation *n* determinación *f*. ~**e** *vt* determinar; (decide) decidir. ~**ed** *a* determinado; (resolute) decidido

deterrent *n* fuerza *f* de disuasión

detest vt aborrecer. ~**able** a odioso

detonat|e vt hacer detonar. ● vi detonar. ~**ion** n detonación f. ~**or** n detonador m

detour n rodeo m; (Amer, of transport) desvío m, desviación f. ● vt (Amer) desviar

detract vi. ~ **from** disminuir

detriment n. **to the** ~ **of** en perjuicio de. ~**al** a perjudicial

devalue vt desvalorizar

devastat|e vt devastar. ~**ing** a devastador; (fig) arrollador. ~**ion** n devastación f

develop vt desarrollar; contraer <*illness*>; urbanizar <*land*>. ● vi desarrollarse; (appear) surgir. ~**ing** a <*country*> en vías de desarrollo. ~**ment** n desarrollo m. (**new**) ~**ment** novedad f

deviant a desviado

deviat|e vi desviarse. ~**ion** n desviación f

device n dispositivo m; (scheme) estratagema f

devil n diablo m

devious a taimado

devise vt idear

devoid a. **be** ~ **of** carecer de

devolution n descentralización f; (of power) delegación f

devot|e vt dedicar. ~**ed** a <*couple*> unido; <*service*> leal. ~**ee** n partidario m. ~**ion** n devoción f

devour vt devorar

devout a devoto

dew n rocío m

dexterity n destreza f

diabet|es n diabetes f. ~**ic** a & n diabético (m)

diabolical a diabólico

diagnos|e vt diagnosticar. ~**is** n (pl -**oses**) diagnóstico m

diagonal a & n diagonal (f)

diagram n diagrama m

dial n cuadrante m; (on clock, watch) esfera f; (on phone) disco m. ● vt (pt **dialled**) marcar, discar (LAm)

dialect n dialecto m

dialling: ~ **code** n prefijo m, código m de la zona (LAm). ~ **tone** n tono m de marcar, tono m de discado (LAm)

dialogue n diálogo m

dial tone n (Amer) ⇒DIALLING TONE

diameter n diámetro m

diamond n diamante m; (shape) rombo m. ~**s** npl (Cards) diamantes mpl

diaper n (Amer) pañal m

diaphragm n diafragma m

diarrhoea n diarrea f

diary n diario m; (book) agenda f

dice n invar dado m. ● vt (Culin) cortar en cubitos

dictat|e vt/i dictar. ~**ion** n dictado m. ~**or** n dictador m. ~**orship** n dictadura f

dictionary n diccionario m

did ⇒DO

didn't = did not

die vi (pres p **dying**) morir. **be dying to** morirse por. □ ~ **down** vi irse apagando. □ ~ **out** vi extinguirse

diesel n (fuel) gasóleo m. ~ **engine** n motor m diesel

diet n alimentación f; (restricted) régimen m. **be on a** ~ estar a régimen. ● vi estar a régimen

differ vi ser distinto; (disagree) no estar de acuerdo. ~**ence** n diferencia f; (disagreement) desacuerdo m. ~**ent** a distinto, diferente. ~**ently** adv de otra manera

difficult a difícil. ~**y** n dificultad f

diffus|e a difuso. ● vt difundir. ● vi difundirse. ~**ion** n difusión f

dig n (poke) empujón m; (poke with elbow) codazo m; (remark) indirecta f. ~**s** npl 🎗 alojamiento m ● vt (pt **dug**, pres p **digging**) cavar; (thrust) empujar. ● vi cavar. □ ~ **out** vt extraer. □ ~ **up** vt desenterrar

digest n resumen m. ● vt digerir. ~**ion** n digestión f. ~**ive** a digestivo

digger n (Mec) excavadora f

digit n dígito m; (finger) dedo m. ~**al** a digital. ~ **camera** cámara f digital

dignified a solemne

dignitary n dignatario m

dignity n dignidad f

digress vi divagar. ~ **from** apartarse de. ~**ion** n digresión f

dike n dique m

dilapidated a ruinoso

dilate vt dilatar. ● vi dilatarse

dilemma n dilema m

diligent a diligente

dilute vt diluir

dim a (**dimmer, dimmest**) <light> débil; <room> oscuro; (🎗, stupid) torpe. ● vt (pt **dimmed**) atenuar. ~ **one's headlights** (Amer) poner las (luces) cortas or de cruce, poner las (luces) bajas (LAm). ● vi <light> irse atenuando

dime n (Amer) moneda de diez centavos

dimension n dimensión f

diminish vt/i disminuir

dimple n hoyuelo m

din n jaleo m

dine vi cenar. ~**r** n comensal m & f; (Amer, restaurant) cafetería f

dinghy n bote m; (inflatable) bote m neumático

dingy a (**-ier, -iest**) miserable, sucio

dining: ~ **car** n coche m restaurante. ~ **room** n comedor m

dinner n cena f, comida f (LAm). have ~ cenar, comer (LAm). ~ **party** n cena f, comida f (LAm)

dinosaur n dinosaurio m

dint n. by ~ of a fuerza de

dip vt (pt **dipped**) meter; (in liquid) mojar. ~ **one's headlights** poner las (luces) cortas or de cruce, poner las (luces) bajas (LAm). ● vi bajar. ● n (slope) inclinación f; (in sea) baño m. □ ~ **into** vt hojear <book>

diphthong n diptongo m

diploma n diploma m

diploma|cy n diplomacia f. ~**t** n diplomático m. ~**tic** a diplomático

dipstick n (Auto) varilla f del nivel de aceite

dire a (**-er, -est**) terrible; <need, poverty> extremo

direct a directo. ● adv directamente. ● vt dirigir; (show the way) indicar. ~**ion** n dirección f. ~**ions** npl instrucciones fpl. ~**ly** adv directamente; (at once) en seguida. ● conj 🎗 en cuanto. ~**or** n director m; (of company) directivo m

directory n guía f; (Comp) directorio m

dirt n suciedad f. ~**y** a (**-ier, -iest**) sucio. ● vt ensuciar

disab|ility n invalidez f. ~**le** vt incapacitar. ~**led** a minusválido

disadvantage n desventaja f. ~**d** a desfavorecido

disagree vi no estar de acuerdo (with con). ~ **with** <food, climate> sentarle mal a. ~**able** a desagradable. ~**ment** n desacuerdo m; (quarrel) riña f

disappear vi desaparecer. ~**ance** n desaparición f

disappoint vt decepcionar. ~ing a decepcionante. ~ment n decepción f

disapprov|al n desaprobación f. ~e vi. ~e of desaprobar. ~ing a de reproche

disarm vt desarmar. ● vi desarmarse. ~ament n desarme m

disarray n desorden m

disast|er n desastre m. ~rous a catastrófico

disband vt disolver. ● vi disolverse

disbelief n incredulidad f

disc n disco m

discard vt descartar; abandonar <beliefs etc>

discern vt percibir. ~ing a exigente; <ear, eye> educado

discharge vt descargar; cumplir <duty>; (Mil) licenciar. ● n descarga f; (Med) secreción f; (Mil) licenciamiento m

disciple n discípulo m

disciplin|ary a disciplinario. ~e n disciplina f. ● vt disciplinar; (punish) sancionar

disc jockey n pinchadiscos m & f

disclaim vt desconocer. ~er n (Jurid) descargo m de responsabilidad

disclos|e vt revelar. ~ure n revelación f

disco n (pl -os) 🔁 discoteca f

discolour vt decolorar. ● vi decolorarse

discomfort n malestar m; (lack of comfort) incomodidad f

disconcert vt desconcertar

disconnect vt separar; (Elec) desconectar

disconsolate a desconsolado

discontent n descontento m. ~ed a descontento

discontinue vt interrumpir

discord n discordia f; (Mus) disonancia f. ~ant a discorde; (Mus) disonante

discotheque n discoteca f

discount n descuento m. ● vt hacer caso omiso de; (Com) descontar

discourag|e vt desanimar; (dissuade) disuadir. ~ing a desalentador

discourteous a descortés

discover vt descubrir. ~y n descubrimiento m

discredit vt (pt discredited) desacreditar. ● n descrédito m

discreet a discreto. ~ly adv discretamente

discrepancy n discrepancia f

discretion n discreción f

discriminat|e vt discriminar. ~e between distinguir entre. ~ing a perspicaz. ~ion n discernimiento m; (bias) discriminación f

discus n disco m

discuss vt discutir. ~ion n discusión f

disdain n desdén m. ~ful a desdeñoso

disease n enfermedad f

disembark vi desembarcar

disenchant|ed a desilusionado. ~ment n desencanto m

disentangle vt desenredar

disfigure vt desfigurar

disgrace n vergüenza f. ● vt deshonrar. ~ful a vergonzoso

disgruntled a descontento

disguise vt disfrazar. ● n disfraz m. **in ~** disfrazado

disgust n repugnancia f, asco m. ● vt dar asco a. ~ed a indignado; (stronger) asqueado. ~ing a repugnante, asqueroso

dish n plato m. **wash** or **do the ~es** fregar los platos, lavar los trastes

(Mex). □ ~ **up** vt/i servir. ~**cloth** n bayeta f

disheartening a desalentador

dishonest a deshonesto. ~**y** n falta f de honradez

dishonour n deshonra f

dish: ~ **soap** n (Amer) lavavajillas m. ~ **towel** n paño m de cocina. ~**washer** n lavaplatos m, lavavajillas m. ~**washing liquid** n (Amer) ⇒~ **soap**

disillusion vt desilusionar. ~**ment** n desilusión f

disinfect vt desinfectar. ~**ant** n desinfectante m

disintegrate vt desintegrar. ●vi desintegrarse

disinterested a desinteresado

disjointed a inconexo

disk n disco m. ~ **drive** (Comp) unidad f de discos. ~**ette** n disquete m

dislike n aversión f. ●vt. I ~ **dogs** no me gustan los perros

dislocate vt dislocar(se) <limb>

dislodge vt sacar

disloyal a desleal. ~**ty** n deslealtad f

dismal a triste; (bad) fatal

dismantle vt desmontar

dismay n consternación f. ●vt consternar

dismiss vt despedir; (reject) rechazar. ~**al** n despido m; (of idea) rechazo m

dismount vi desmontar

disobe|dience n desobediencia f. ~**dient** a desobediente. ~**y** vt/i desobedecer

disorder n desorden m; (ailment) afección f. ~**ly** a desordenado

disorganized a desorganizado

disorientate vt desorientar

disown vt repudiar

disparaging a despreciativo

dispatch vt despachar. ●n despacho m. ~ **rider** n mensajero m

dispel vt (pt dispelled) disipar

dispens|able a prescindible. ~**e** vt distribuir; (Med) preparar. □ ~ **with** vt prescindir de

dispers|al n dispersión f. ~**e** vt dispersar. ●vi dispersarse

dispirited a desanimado

display vt exponer <goods>; demostrar <feelings>. ●n exposición f; (of feelings) demostración f

displeas|e vt desagradar. **be** ~**ed with** estar disgustado con. ~**ure** n desagrado m

dispos|able a desechable. ~**al** n (of waste) eliminación f. **at s.o.'s** ~**al** a la disposición de uno. ~**e of** vt deshacerse de

disproportionate a desproporcionado

disprove vt desmentir <claim>; refutar <theory>

dispute vt discutir. ●n disputa f. **in** ~ disputado

disqualif|ication n descalificación f. ~**y** vt incapacitar; (Sport) descalificar

disregard vt no hacer caso de. ●n indiferencia f (**for** a)

disreputable a de mala fama

disrespect n falta f de respeto

disrupt vt interrumpir; trastornar <plans>. ~**ion** n trastorno m. ~**ive** a <influence> perjudicial, negativo

dissatis|faction n descontento m. ~**fied** a descontento

dissect vt disecar

dissent vi disentir. ●n disentimiento m

dissertation n (Univ) tesis f

dissident a & n disidente (m & f)

dissimilar a distinto

dissolute a disoluto

dissolve vt disolver. ●vi disolverse

dissuade vt disuadir

distan|ce n distancia f. **from a ~ce** desde lejos. **in the ~ce** a lo lejos. **~t** a distante, lejano; (aloof) distante

distaste n desagrado m. **~ful** a desagradable

distil vt (pt **distilled**) destilar. **~lery** n destilería f

distinct a distinto; (clear) claro; (marked) marcado. **~ion** n distinción f; (in exam) sobresaliente m. **~ive** a distintivo

distinguish vt/i distinguir. **~ed** a distinguido

distort vt torcer. **~ion** n deformación f

distract vt distraer. **~ed** a distraído. **~ion** n distracción f; (confusion) aturdimiento m

distraught a consternado, angustiado

distress n angustia f. ●vt afligir. **~ed** a afligido. **~ing** a penoso

distribut|e vt repartir, distribuir. **~ion** n distribución f. **~or** n distribuidor m; (Auto) distribuidor m (del encendido)

district n zona f, región f; (of town) barrio m

distrust n desconfianza f. ●vt desconfiar de

disturb vt molestar; (perturb) inquietar; (move) desordenar; (interrupt) interrumpir. **~ance** n disturbio m; (tumult) alboroto m. **~ed** a trastornado. **~ing** a inquietante

disused a fuera de uso

ditch n zanja f; (for irrigation) acequia f. ●vt 🄘 abandonar

dither vi vacilar

ditto adv ídem

divan n diván m

dive vi tirarse (al agua), zambullirse; (rush) meterse (precipitadamente). ●n (into water) zambullida f; (Sport) salto m (de trampolín); (of plane) descenso m en picado, descenso m en picada (LAm); (🄘, place) antro m. **~r** n saltador m; (underwater) buzo m

diverge vi divergir. **~nt** a divergente

divers|e a diverso. **~ify** vt diversificar. **~ity** n diversidad f

diver|sion n desvío m; desviación f; (distraction) diversión f. **~t** vt desviar; (entertain) divertir

divide vt dividir. ●vi dividirse. **~d highway** n (Amer) autovía f, carretera f de doble pista

dividend n dividendo m

divine a divino

diving : **~ board** n trampolín m. **~ suit** n escafandra f

division n división f

divorce n divorcio m. ●vt divorciarse de. **get ~d** divorciarse. ●vi divorciarse. **~e** n divorciado m

divulge vt divulgar

DIY abbr ⇒DO-IT-YOURSELF

dizz|iness n vértigo m. **~y** a (-ier, -iest) mareado. **be** or **feel ~y** marearse

DJ abbr ⇒DISC JOCKEY

D

....

do

3rd pers sing present **does**; past **did**; past participle **done**

●transitive verb

····➤ hacer. **he does what he wants** hace lo que quiere. **to do one's homework** hacer los deberes. **to do the cooking** preparar la

comida, cocinar. **well done!** ¡muy
bien!

····➤ (clean) lavar <*dishes*>. limpiar
<*windows*>

····➤ (as job) **what does he do?** ¿en
qué trabaja?

····➤ (swindle) estafar. **I've been done!**
¡me han estafado!

····➤ (achieve) **she's done it!** ¡lo ha
logrado!

●*intransitive verb*

····➤ hacer. **do as you're told!** ¡haz
lo que se te dice!

····➤ (fare) **how are you doing?** (with a
task) ¿qué tal te va? **how do you
do?** (as greeting) mucho gusto,
encantado

····➤ (perform) **she did well/badly** le
fue bien/mal

····➤ (be suitable) **will this do?** ¿esto
sirve?

····➤ (be enough) ser suficiente,
bastar. **one box will do** con una
caja basta, con una caja es
suficiente

●*auxiliary verb*

····➤ (to form interrogative and negative)
do you speak Spanish? ¿hablas
español?. **I don't want to** no
quiero. **don't shut the door** no
cierres la puerta

····➤ (in tag questions) **you eat meat,
don't you?** ¿comes carne,
¿verdad? or ¿no? **he lives in
London, doesn't he?** vive en
Londres, ¿no? or ¿verdad? or
¿no es cierto?

····➤ (in short answers) **do you like it? -
yes, I do** ¿te gusta? - sí. **who
wrote it? - I did** ¿quién lo
escribió? - yo

····➤ (emphasizing) **do come in!** ¡pase
Ud!. **you do exaggerate!** ¡cómo
exageras!

□ **do away with** *vt* abolir. □ **do in**
vt (🗶, kill) eliminar. □ **do up** *vt*

abrochar <*coat etc*>; arreglar
<*house*>. □ **do with** *vt* (need) (with
can, could) necesitar; (expressing
connection) **it has nothing to do with
that** no tiene nada que ver con
eso. □ **do without** *vt* prescindir de

docile *a* dócil

dock *n* (Naut) dársena *f*; (wharf,
quay) muelle *m*; (Jurid) banquillo *m*
de los acusados. **~s** *npl* (port)
puerto *m*. ● *vt* cortar <*tail*>;
atracar <*ship*>. ● *vi* <*ship*>
atracar. **~er** *n* estibador *m*.
~yard *n* astillero *m*

doctor *n* médico *m*, doctor *m*

doctrine *n* doctrina *f*

document *n* documento *m*. **~ary**
a & n documental (*m*)

dodg|e *vt* esquivar. ● *vi*
esquivarse. ● *n* treta *f*. **~ems** *npl*
autos *mpl* de choque. **~y** *a* (**-ier,
-iest**) 🆃 (awkward) difícil

does ⇒DO

doesn't = **does not**

dog *n* perro *m*. ● *vt* (*pt* **dogged**)
perseguir

dogged *a* obstinado

doghouse *n* (Amer) casa *f* del
perro. **in the ~** 🆃 en desgracia

dogmatic *a* dogmático

do|ings *npl* actividades *fpl*. **~-it-
yourself** *n* bricolaje *m*

dole *n* 🆃 subsidio *m* de paro,
subsidio *m* de desempleo. □ **~
out** *vt* distribuir

doleful *a* triste

doll *n* muñeca *f*

dollar *n* dólar *m*

dollarization *n* dolarización *f*

dollop *n* 🆃 porción *f*

dolphin *n* delfín *m*

domain *n* dominio *m*; (fig) campo
m

dome *n* cúpula *f*

domestic *a* doméstico; *<trade, flights, etc>* nacional. ~**ated** *a* *<animal>* domesticado. ~**science** economía *f* doméstica

domin|ance *n* dominio *m*. ~**ant** *a* dominante. ~**ate** *vt/i* dominar. ~**ation** *n* dominación *f*. ~**eering** *a* dominante

Dominican Republic *n* República *f* Dominicana

dominion *n* dominio *m*

domino *n* (*pl* -**oes**) ficha *f* de dominó. ~**es** *npl* dominó *m*

donat|e *vt* donar. ~**ion** *n* donativo *m*, donación *f*

done ⇒DO

donkey *n* burro *m*, asno *m*. ~'s **years** Ⓘ siglos *mpl*

donor *n* donante *m & f*

don't = **do not**

doodle *vi/t* garrapatear

doom *n* destino *m*; (death) muerte *f*. ● *vt*. be ~ed to ser condenado a

door *n* puerta *f*. ~**bell** *n* timbre *m*. ~**knob** *n* pomo *m* (de la puerta). ~**mat** *n* felpudo *m*. ~**step** *n* peldaño *m*. ~**way** *n* entrada *f*

dope *n* Ⓘ droga *f*; (🗙, idiot) imbécil *m*. ● *vt* Ⓘ drogar

dormant *a* aletargado, *<volcano>* inactivo

dormice ⇒DORMOUSE

dormitory *n* dormitorio *m*

dormouse *n* (*pl* -**mice**) lirón *m*

DOS *abbr* (= **disc-operating system**) DOS *m*

dos|age *n* dosis *f*. ~**e** *n* dosis *f*

dot *n* punto *m*. on the ~ en punto. ~**-com company** empresa *f* punto com

dote *vi*. ~ on adorar

dotty *a* (-**ier**, -**iest**) Ⓘ chiflado

double *a* doble. ● *adv* el doble. ● *n* doble *m*; (person) doble *m & f*. at the ~ corriendo. ● *vt* doblar; redoblar *<efforts etc>*. ● *vi*

doblarse. ~ **bass** *n* contrabajo *m*. ~ **bed** *n* cama *f* de matrimonio, cama *f* de doa plazas (LAm). ~ **chin** *n* papada *f*. ~ **click** *vt* hacer doble clic en. ~**-cross** *vt* traicionar. ~**-decker** *n* autobús *m* de dos pisos. ~ **Dutch** *n* Ⓘ chino *m*. ~ **glazing** *n* doble ventana *f*. ~**s** *npl* (tennis) dobles *mpl*

doubly *adv* doblemente

doubt *n* duda *f*. ● *vt* dudar; (distrust) dudar de. ~**ful** *a* dudoso. ~**less** *adv* sin duda

dough *n* masa *f*; (🗙, money) pasta *f* Ⓘ, lana *f* (LAm Ⓘ). ~**nut** *n* donut *m*, dona *f* (Mex)

dove *n* paloma *f*

down *adv* abajo. ~ **with**. abajo. **come** ~ bajar. **go** ~ bajar; *<sun>* ponerse. ● *prep* abajo. ● *a* Ⓘ deprimido. ● *vt* derribar; (Ⓘ, drink) beber. ● *n* (feathers) plumón *m*. ~ **and out** *a* en la miseria. ~**cast** *a* abatido. ~**fall** *n* perdición *f*; (of king, dictator) caída *f*. ~**-hearted** *a* abatido. ~**hill** *adv* cuesta abajo. ~**load** *vt* (Comp) bajar. ~**market** *a* *<newspaper>* popular; *<store>* barato. ~ **payment** *n* depósito *m*. ~**pour** *n* aguacero *m*. ~**right** *a* completo. ● *adv* completamente. ~**s** *npl* colinas *fpl*. ~**stairs** *adv* abajo. ● *a* de abajo. ~**stream** *adv* río abajo. ~**-to-earth** *a* práctico. ~**town** *n* centro *m* (de la ciudad). ● *adv*. **go** ~**town** ir al centro. ~ **under** *adv* en las antípodas; (in Australia) en Australia. ~**ward** *a & adv*, ~**wards** *adv* hacia abajo

dowry *n* dote *f*

doze *vi* dormitar

dozen *n* docena *f*. **a** ~ **eggs** una docena de huevos. ~**s of** Ⓘ miles de, muchos

D

Dr *abbr* (= **Doctor**) Dr. ~ **Broadley** (el) Doctor Broadley

drab *a* monótono

draft *n* borrador *m*; (Com) letra *f* de cambio; (Amer, Mil) reclutamiento *m*; (Amer, of air) corriente *f* de aire. ● *vt* redactar el borrador de; (Amer, conscript) reclutar

drag *vt* (*pt* **dragged**) arrastrar. ● *n* 🄸 lata *f*

dragon *n* dragón *m*. ~**fly** *n* libélula *f*

drain *vt* vaciar <*tank, glass*>; drenar <*land*>; (fig) agotar. ● *vi* escurrirse. ● *n* (pipe) sumidero *m*, resumidero *m* (LAm); (plughole) desagüe *m*. ~**board** (Amer), ~**ing board** *n* escurridero *m*

drama *n* drama *m*; (art) arte *m* teatral. ~**tic** *a* dramático. ~**tist** *n* dramaturgo *m*. ~**tize** *vt* adaptar al teatro; (fig) dramatizar

drank ⇒DRINK

drape *vt* cubrir; (hang) colgar. ~**s** *npl* (Amer) cortinas *fpl*

drastic *a* drástico

draught *n* corriente *f* de aire. ~ **beer** *n* cerveza *f* de barril. ~**s** *npl* (game) juego *m* de damas *fpl*. ~**y** *a* lleno de corrientes de aire

draw *vt* (*pt* **drew**, *pp* **drawn**) tirar; (attract) atraer; dibujar <*picture*>; trazar <*line*>. ~ **the line** trazar el límite. ● *vi* (Art) dibujar; (Sport) empatar; ~ **near** acercarse. ● *n* (Sport) empate *m*; (in lottery) sorteo *m*. □ ~ **in** *vi* <*days*> acortarse. □ ~ **out** *vt* sacar <*money*>. □ ~ **up** *vi* pararse. *vt* redactar <*document*>; acercar <*chair*>. ~**back** *n* desventaja *f*. ~**bridge** *n* puente *m* levadizo

drawer *n* cajón *m*, gaveta *f* (Mex). ~**s** *npl* calzones *mpl*

drawing *n* dibujo *m*. ~ **pin** *n* tachuela *f*, chincheta *f*, chinche *f*. ~ **room** *n* salón *m*

drawl *n* habla *f* lenta

drawn ⇒DRAW

dread *n* terror *m*. ● *vt* temer. ~**ful** *a* terrible. ~**fully** *adv* terriblemente

dream *n* sueño *m*. ● *vt/i* (*pt* **dreamed** *or* **dreamt**) soñar. □ ~ **up** *vt* idear. *a* ideal. ~**er** *n* soñador *m*

dreary *a* (**-ier**, **-iest**) triste; (boring) monótono

dredge *n* draga *f*. ● *vt* dragar. ~**r** *n* draga *f*

dregs *npl* posos *mpl*, heces *fpl*; (fig) hez *f*

drench *vt* empapar

dress *n* vestido *m*; (clothing) ropa *f*. ● *vt* vestir; (decorate) adornar; (Med) vendar. ● *vi* vestirse. □ ~ **up** *vi* ponerse elegante. □ ~ **up as** disfrazarse de. ~ **circle** *n* primer palco *m*

dressing *n* (sauce) aliño *m*; (bandage) vendaje *m*. ~**-down** *n* rapapolvo *m*, reprensión *f*. ~ **gown** *n* bata *f*. ~ **room** *n* vestidor *m*; (in theatre) camarín *m*. ~ **table** *n* tocador *m*

dress: ~**maker** *n* modista *m* & *f*. ~**making** *n* costura *f*. ~ **rehearsal** *n* ensayo *m* general

drew ⇒DRAW

dribble *vi* <*baby*> babear; (in football) driblar, driblear

drie|d *a* <*food*> seco; <*milk*> en polvo. ~**r** *n* secador *m*

drift *vi* ir a la deriva; <*snow*> amontonarse. ● *n* (movement) dirección *f*; (of snow) montón *m*

drill *n* (tool) taladro *m*; (of dentist) torno *m*; (training) ejercicio *m*. ● *vt* taladrar, perforar; (train) entrenar. ● *vi* entrenarse

drink vt/i (pt **drank**, pp **drunk**) beber, tomar (LAm). ● n bebida f. ~**able** a bebible; <water> potable. ~**er** n bebedor m. ~**ing water** n agua f potable

drip vi (pt **dripped**) gotear. ● n gota f; (Med) goteo m intravenoso; (✕, person) soso m. ~**dry** a de lava y pon. ~**ping** a. be ~**ping wet** estar chorreando

drive vt (pt **drove**, pp **driven**) conducir, manejar (LAm) <car etc>. ~ **s.o. mad** volver loco a uno. ~ **s.o. to do sth** llevar a uno a hacer algo. ● vi conducir, manejar (LAm). ~ **at** querer decir. ~ **in** (in car) entrar en coche. ● n paseo m; (road) calle f; (private road) camino m de entrada; (fig) empuje m. ~**r** n conductor m, chofer m (LAm). ~**r's license** n (Amer) ⇒DRIVING LICENCE

drivel n tonterías fpl

driving n conducción f. ~ **licence** n permiso m de conducir, licencia f de conducción (LAm), licencia f (de manejar) (Mex). ~ **test** n examen m de conducir, examen m de manejar (LAm)

drizzle n llovizna f. ● vi lloviznar

drone n zumbido m. ● vi zumbar

drool vi babear

droop vi inclinarse; <flowers> marchitarse

drop n gota f; (fall) caída f; (decrease) descenso m. ● vt (pt **dropped**) dejar caer; (lower) bajar. ● vi caer. □ ~ **in on** vt pasar por casa de. □ ~ **off** vi (sleep) dormirse. □ ~ **out** vi retirarse; <student> abandonar los estudios. ~**out** n marginado m

drought n sequía f

drove ⇒DRIVE. ● n manada f

drown vt ahogar. ● vi ahogarse

drowsy a soñoliento

drudgery n trabajo m pesado

drug n droga f; (Med) medicamento m. ● vt (pt **drugged**) drogar. ~ **addict** n drogadicto m. ~**gist** n (Amer) farmacéutico m. ~**store** n (Amer) farmacia f (que vende otros artículos también)

drum n tambor m; (for oil) bidón m. ● vi (pt **drummed**) tocar el tambor. ● vt. ~ **sth into s.o.** hacerle aprender algo a uno a fuerza de repetírselo. ~**mer** n tambor m; (in group) batería f. ~**s** npl batería f. ~**stick** n baqueta f; (Culin) muslo m

drunk ⇒DRINK. ● a borracho. **get** ~ emborracharse. ● n borracho m. ~**ard** n borracho m. ~**en** a borracho

dry a (drier, driest) seco. ● vt secar. ● vi secarse. □ ~ **up** vi <stream> secarse; <funds> agotarse. ~**-clean** vt limpiar en seco. ~**-cleaner's** tintorería f. ~**er** n ⇒DRIER

dual a doble. ~ **carriageway** n autovía f, carretera f de doble pista

dub vt (pt **dubbed**) doblar <film>

dubious a dudoso; <person> sospechoso

duchess n duquesa f

duck n pato m. ● vt sumergir; bajar <head>. ● vi agacharse. ~**ling** n patito m

duct n conducto m

dud a inútil; <cheque> sin fondos

due a debido; (expected) esperado. ~ **to** debido a. ● adv. ~ **north** derecho hacia el norte. ~**s** npl derechos mpl

duel n duelo m

duet n dúo m

duffel, duffle : ~ **bag** n bolsa f de lona. ~ **coat** n trenca f

dug ⇒DIG

duke n duque m

dull a (-er, -est) <weather> gris; <colour> apagado; <person, play, etc> pesado; <sound> sordo

dumb a (-er, -est) mudo; ⓘ estúpido. ~ **down** vt reducir el valor intelectual de. ~**found** vt pasmar

dummy n muñeco m; (of tailor) maniquí m; (for baby) chupete m. ● a falso. ~ **run** prueba f

dump vt tirar, botar (LAm). ● n vertedero m, depósito m; ⓘ lugar m desagradable. **be down in the ~s** estar deprimido

Dumpster n (Amer, P) contenedor m (para escombros)

dumpy a (-ier, -iest) regordete

dunce n burro m

dung n (manure) estiércol m

dungarees npl mono m, peto m

dungeon n calabozo m

dunk vt remojar

dupe vt engañar. ● n inocentón m

duplicat|e a & n duplicado (m). ● vt duplicar; (on machine) reproducir. ~**ing machine**, ~**or** n multicopista f

durable a durable

duration n duración f

duress n. **under ~** bajo coacción

during prep durante

dusk n anochecer m

dust n polvo m. ● vt quitar el polvo a; (sprinkle) espolvorear (with con). ~**bin** n cubo m de la basura, bote m de la basura (Mex). ~ **cloth** (Amer), ~**er** n trapo m. ~**jacket** n sobrecubierta f. ~**man** n basurero m. ~**pan** n recogedor m. ~**y** a (-ier, -iest) polvoriento

Dutch a holandés. ● n (Lang) holandés m. **the ~** (people) los holandeses. ~**man** m holandés m. ~**woman** n holandesa f

duty n deber m; (tax) derechos mpl de aduana. **on ~** de servicio. ~**-free** a libre de impuestos

duvet n edredón m

dwarf n (pl -s or dwarves) enano m

dwell vi (pt dwelt or dwelled) morar. □ ~ **on** vt detenerse en. ~**ing** n morada f

dwindle vi disminuir

dye vt (pres p dyeing) teñir. ● n tinte m

dying ⇒DIE

dynamic a dinámico. ~**s** npl dinámica f

dynamite n dinamita f. ● vt dinamitar

dynamo n (pl -os) dinamo f, dínamo f, dinamo m (LAm), dínamo m (LAm)

dynasty n dinastía f

E abbr (= **East**) E

each a cada. ● pron cada uno. ~ **one** cada uno. ~ **other** uno a otro, el uno al otro. **they love ~ other** se aman

eager a impaciente; (enthusiastic) ávido. ~**ness** n impaciencia f; (enthusiasm) entusiasmo m

eagle n águila f

ear n oído m; (outer) oreja f; (of corn) espiga f. ~**ache** n dolor m de oído. ~**drum** n tímpano m

earl n conde m

early a (-ier, -iest) temprano; (before expected time) prematuro.

● *adv* temprano; (ahead of time) con anticipación

earn *vt* ganar; (deserve) merecer

earnest *a* serio. **in ~** en serio

earnings *npl* ingresos *mpl*; (Com) ganancias *fpl*

ear: ~phone *n* audífono *m*. **~ring** *n* pendiente *m*, arete *m* (LAm). **~shot** *n*. **within ~shot** al alcance del oído

earth *n* tierra *f*. **the E~** (planet) la Tierra. ● *vt* (Elec) conectar a tierra. **~quake** *n* terremoto *m*

earwig *n* tijereta *f*

ease *n* facilidad *f*; (comfort) tranquilidad *f*. **at ~** a gusto; (Mil) en posición de descanso. **ill at ~** molesto. **with ~** fácilmente. ● *vt* calmar; aliviar *<pain>*. ● *vi* calmarse; (lessen) disminuir

easel *n* caballete *m*

easily *adv* fácilmente

east *n* este *m*. ● *a* este, oriental; *<wind>* del este. ● *adv* hacia el este.

Easter *n* Semana *f* Santa; (Relig) Pascua *f* de Resurrección. **~ egg** *n* huevo *m* de Pascua

east: ~erly *a <wind>* del este. **~ern** *a* este, oriental. **~ward, ~wards** *adv* hacia el este

easy *a* (**-ier, -iest**) fácil. ● *adv*. **go ~ on sth** Ⅰ no pasarse con algo. **take it ~** tomarse las cosas con calma. ● *int* ¡despacio! **~ chair** *n* sillón *m*. **~going** *a* acomodadizo

eat *vt/i* (*pt* **ate**, *pp* **eaten**) comer. □ **~ into** *vt* corroer. **~er** *n* comedor *m*

eaves *npl* alero *m*. **~drop** *vi* (*pt* **-dropped**). **~drop (on)** escuchar a escondidas

ebb *n* reflujo *m*. ● *vi* bajar; (fig) decaer

ebola *n* Ébola *m*

ebony *n* ébano *m*

EC *abbr* (= **European Community**) CE *f* (Comunidad *f* Europea)

eccentric *a* & *n* excéntrico (*m*)

echo *n* (*pl* **-oes**) eco *m*. ● *vi* hacer eco

eclipse *n* eclipse *m*. ● *vt* eclipsar

ecolog|ical *a* ecológico. **~y** *n* ecología *f*

e-commerce *n* comercio *m* electrónico

econom|ic *a* económico. **~ical** *a* económico. **~ics** *n* economía *f*. **~ist** *n* economista *m* & *f*. **~ize** *vi* economizar. **~ize on sth** economizar algo. **~y** *n* economía *f*

ecsta|sy *n* éxtasis *f*

Ecuador *n* Ecuador *m*. **~ean** *a* & *n* ecuatoriano (*m*)

edg|e *n* borde *m*; (of knife) filo *m*; (of town) afueras *fpl*. **have the ~e on** Ⅰ llevar la ventaja a. **on ~e** nervioso. ● *vt* ribetear; (move) mover poco a poco. ● *vi* avanzar cautelosamente. **~y** *a* nervioso

edible *a* comestible

edit *vt* dirigir *<newspaper>*; preparar una edición de *<text>*; editar *<film>*. **~ion** *n* edición *f*. **~or** *n* (of newspaper) director *m*; (of text) redactor *m*. **~orial** *a* editorial. ● *n* artículo *m* de fondo

educat|e *vt* educar. **~ed** *a* culto. **~ion** *n* educación *f*; (knowledge, culture) cultura *f*. **~ional** *a* instructivo

EEC *abbr* (= **European Economic Community**) CEE *f* (Comunidad *f* Económica Europea)

eel *n* anguila *f*

eerie *a* (**-ier, -iest**) misterioso

effect *n* efecto *m*. **in ~** efectivamente. **take ~** entrar en

E

vigor. **~ive** a eficaz; (striking) impresionante; (real) efectivo. **~ively** adv eficazmente. **~iveness** n eficacia f

effeminate a afeminado

efficien|cy n eficiencia f; (Mec) rendimiento m. **~t** a eficiente. **~tly** adv eficientemente

effort n esfuerzo m. **~less** a fácil

e.g. abbr (= exempli gratia) p.ej., por ejemplo

egg n huevo m. □ ~ **on** vt 🔲 incitar. **~cup** n huevera f. **~plant** n (Amer) berenjena f. **~shell** n cáscara f de huevo

ego n (pl -os) yo m. **~ism** n egoísmo m. **~ist** n egoísta m & f. **~centric** a egocéntrico. **~tism** n egotismo m. **~tist** n egotista m & f

eh int 🔲 ¡eh!

eiderdown n edredón m

eight a & n ocho (m). **~een** a & n dieciocho (m). **~eenth** a decimoctavo. ● n dieciochavo m. **~h** a & n octavo (m) **~ieth** a octogésimo. ● n ochentavo m. **~y** a & n ochenta (m)

either a cualquiera de los dos; (negative) ninguno de los dos; (each) cada. ● pron uno u otro; (with negative) ni uno ni otro. ● adv (negative) tampoco. ● conj o. ~ **Tuesday or Wednesday** o el martes o el miércoles; (with negative) ni el martes ni el miércoles

eject vt expulsar

eke vt. ~ **out** hacer alcanzar <resources>. ~ **out a living** ganarse la vida a duras penas

elaborate a complicado. ● vt elaborar. ● vi explicarse

elapse vi transcurrir

elastic a & n elástico (m). ~ **band** n goma f (elástica), liga f (Mex)

elat|ed a regocijado. **~ion** n regocijo m

elbow n codo m. ● vt dar un codazo a

elder a mayor. ● n mayor m & f; (tree) saúco m. **~ly** a mayor, anciano

eldest a & n mayor (m & f)

elect vt elegir. ~ **to do** decidir hacer. ● a electo. **~ion** n elección f. **~or** n elector m. **~oral** a electoral. **~orate** n electorado m

electric a eléctrico. **~al** a eléctrico. ~ **blanket** n manta f eléctrica. **~ian** n electricista m & f. **~ity** n electricidad f

electrify vt electrificar; (fig) electrizar

electrocute vt electrocutar

electrode n electrodo m

electron n electrón m

electronic a electrónico. ~ **mail** n correo m electrónico. **~s** n electrónica f

elegan|ce n elegancia f. **~t** a elegante. **~tly** adv elegantemente

element n elemento m. **~ary** a elemental. **~ary school** n (Amer) escuela f primaria

elephant n elefante m

elevat|e vt elevar. **~ion** n elevación f. **~or** n (Amer) ascensor m

eleven a & n once (m). **~th** a undécimo. ● n onceavo m

elf n (pl elves) duende m

eligible a elegible. **be ~ for** tener derecho a

eliminat|e vt eliminar. **~ion** n eliminación f

élite n elite f, élite f

ellip|se n elipse f. **~tical** a elíptico

elm n olmo m

elope *vi* fugarse con el amante

eloquen|ce *n* elocuencia *f*. ∼t *a* elocuente

El Salvador *n* El Salvador

else *adv.* **somebody** ∼ otra persona. **everybody** ∼ todos los demás. **nobody** ∼ ningún otro, nadie más. **nothing** ∼ nada más. **or** ∼ o bien. **somewhere** ∼ en otra parte. ∼**where** *adv* en otra parte

elu|de *vt* eludir. ∼**sive** *a* esquivo

elves ⇒ELF

emaciated *a* consumido

email, e-mail *n* correo *m* electrónico, correo-e *m*. ● *vt* mandar por correo electrónico, emailear. ∼ **address** *n* casilla *f* electrónica, dirección *f* de correo electrónico

emancipat|e *vt* emancipar. ∼**ion** *n* emancipación *f*

embankment *n* terraplén *m*; (of river) dique *m*

embargo *n* (*pl* **-oes**) embargo *m*

embark *vi* embarcarse. ∼ **on** (fig) emprender. ∼**ation** *n* embarque *m*

embarrass *vt* avergonzar. ∼**ed** *a* avergonzado. ∼**ing** *a* embarazoso. ∼**ment** *n* vergüenza *f*

embassy *n* embajada *f*

embellish *vt* adornar. ∼**ment** *n* adorno *m*

embers *npl* ascuas *fpl*

embezzle *vt* desfalcar. ∼**ment** *n* desfalco *m*

emblem *n* emblema *m*

embrace *vt* abrazar; (fig) abarcar. ● *vi* abrazarse. ● *n* abrazo *m*

embroider *vt* bordar. ∼**y** *n* bordado *m*

embroil *vt* enredar

embryo *n* (*pl* **-os**) embrión *m*. ∼**nic** *a* embrionario

emend *vt* enmendar

emerald *n* esmeralda *f*

emerge *vi* salir. ∼**nce** *n* aparición *f*

emergency *n* emergencia *f*; (Med) urgencia *f*. **in an** ∼ en caso de emergencia. ∼ **exit** *n* salida *f* de emergencia. ∼ **room** *n* (Amer) urgencias *fpl*

emigra|nt *n* emigrante *m & f*. ∼**te** *vi* emigrar. ∼**tion** *n* emigración *f*

eminen|ce *n* eminencia *f*. ∼**t** *a* eminente

emi|ssion *n* emisión *f*. ∼**t** *vt* (*pt* **emitted**) emitir

emoti|on *n* emoción *f*. ∼**onal** *a* emocional; <*person*> emotivo; (moving) conmovedor. ∼**ve** *a* emotivo

empathy *n* empatía *f*

emperor *n* emperador *m*

empha|sis *n* (*pl* ∼**ses**) énfasis *m*. ∼**size** *vt* enfatizar. ∼**tic** *a* <*gesture*> enfático; <*assertion*> categórico

empire *n* imperio *m*

empirical *a* empírico

employ *vt* emplear. ∼**ee** *n* empleado *m*. ∼**er** *n* patrón *m*. ∼**ment** *n* empleo *m*. ∼**ment agency** *n* agencia *f* de trabajo

empower *vt* autorizar (**to do a** hacer)

empress *n* emperatriz *f*

empty *a* vacío; <*promise*> vano. **on an** ∼**y stomach** con el estómago vacío. ● *n* 🄴 envase *m* (vacío). ● *vt* vaciar. ● *vi* vaciarse

emulate *vt* emular

emulsion *n* emulsión *f*

enable *vt*. ∼ **s.o. to do sth** permitir a uno hacer algo

enact *vt* (Jurid) decretar; (in theatre) representar

enamel *n* esmalte *m*. ● *vt* (*pt* **enamelled**) esmaltar**

enchant *vt* encantar. ∼**ing** *a* encantador. ∼**ment** *n* encanto *m*

encircle *vt* rodear

enclave *n* enclave *m*

enclos|e *vt* cercar <*land*>; (Com) adjuntar. ∼**ed** *a* <*space*> cerrado; (Com) adjunto. ∼**ure** *n* cercamiento *m*

encode *vt* codificar, cifrar

encore *int* ¡otra! ● *n* bis *m*, repetición *f*

encounter *vt* encontrar. ● *n* encuentro *m*

encourag|e *vt* animar; (stimulate) fomentar. ∼**ement** *n* ánimo *m*. ∼**ing** *a* alentador

encroach *vi*. ∼ **on** invadir <*land*>; quitar <*time*>

encyclopaedi|a *n* enciclopedia *f*. ∼**c** *a* enciclopédico

end *n* fin *m*; (furthest point) extremo *m*. **in the** ∼ por fin. **make** ∼**s meet** poder llegar a fin de mes. **put an** ∼ **to** poner fin a. **no** ∼ **of** muchísimos. **on** ∼ de pie; (consecutive) seguido. ● *vt/i* terminar, acabar

endanger *vt* poner en peligro. ∼**ed** *a* <*species*> en peligro

endearing *a* simpático

endeavour *n* esfuerzo *m*, intento *m*. ● *vi*. ∼ **to** esforzarse por

ending *n* fin *m*

endless *a* interminable

endorse *vt* endosar; (fig) aprobar. ∼**ment** *n* endoso *m*; (fig) aprobación *f*; (Auto) nota *f* de inhabilitación

endur|ance *n* resistencia *f*. ∼**e** *vt* aguantar. ∼**ing** *a* perdurable

enemy *n* & *a* enemigo (*m*)

energ|etic *a* enérgico. ∼**y** *n* energía *f*

enforce *vt* hacer cumplir <*law*>; hacer valer <*claim*>. ∼**d** *a* forzado

engag|e *vt* emplear <*staff*>; captar <*attention*>; (Mec) hacer engranar. ● *vi* (Mec) engranar. ∼**e in** dedicarse a. ∼**ed** *a* prometido, comprometido (LAm); (busy) ocupado. **be** ∼**ed** (of phone) estar comunicando, estar ocupado (LAm). **get** ∼**ed** prometerse, comprometerse (LAm). ∼**ement** *n* compromiso *m*

engine *n* motor *m*; (of train) locomotora *f*. ∼ **driver** *n* maquinista *m*

engineer *n* ingeniero *m*; (mechanic) mecánico *m*; (Amer, Rail) maquinista *m*. ● *vt* (contrive) fraguar. ∼**ing** *n* ingeniería *f*

England *n* Inglaterra *f*

English *a* inglés. ● *n* (Lang) inglés *m*. ● *npl*. **the** ∼ los ingleses. ∼**man** *n* inglés *m*. ∼**woman** *n* inglesa *f*

engrav|e *vt* grabar. ∼**ing** *n* grabado *m*

engrossed *a* absorto

engulf *vt* envolver

enhance *vt* realzar; aumentar <*value*>

enigma *n* enigma *m*. ∼**tic** *a* enigmático

enjoy *vt*. **I** ∼ **reading** me gusta la lectura. ∼ **o.s.** divertirse. ∼**able** *a* agradable. ∼**ment** *n* placer *m*

enlarge *vt* agrandar; (Photo) ampliar. ● *vi* agrandarse. ∼ **upon** extenderse sobre. ∼**ment** *n* (Photo) ampliación *f*

enlighten *vt* ilustrar. ∼**ment** *n*. **the E**∼**ment** el siglo de la luces

enlist *vt* alistar; conseguir <*support*>. ● *vi* alistarse

enliven *vt* animar

enorm|ity *n* enormidad *f*. ∼**ous** *a* enorme. ∼**ously** *adv* enormemente

enough *a & adv* bastante. ● *n* bastante *m*, suficiente *m*. ● *int* ¡basta!

enquir|e *vt/i* preguntar. ~**e about** informarse de. ~**y** *n* pregunta *f*; (investigation) investigación *f*

enrage *vt* enfurecer

enrol *vt* (*pt* **enrolled**) inscribir, matricular *<student>*. ● *vi* inscribirse, matricularse

ensue *vi* seguir

ensure *vt* asegurar

entail *vt* suponer; acarrear *<expense>*

entangle *vt* enredar. ~**ment** *n* enredo *m*

enter *vt* entrar en, entrar a (esp LAm); presentarse a *<competition>*; inscribirse en *<race>*; (write) escribir. ● *vi* entrar

enterpris|e *n* empresa *f*; (fig) iniciativa *f*. ~**ing** *a* emprendedor

entertain *vt* entretener; recibir *<guests>*; abrigar *<ideas, hopes>*; (consider) considerar. ~**ing** *a* entretenido. ~**ment** *n* entretenimiento *m*; (show) espectáculo *m*

enthral *vt* (*pt* **enthralled**) cautivar

enthuse *vi* ~ **over** entusiasmarse por

enthusias|m *n* entusiasmo *m*. ~**t** *n* entusiasta *m & f*. ~**tic** *a* entusiasta. ~**tically** *adv* con entusiasmo

entice *vt* atraer

entire *a* entero. ~**ly** *adv* completamente. ~**ty** *n*. **in its** ~**ty** en su totalidad

entitle *vt* titular; (give a right) dar derecho a. **be** ~**d to** tener derecho a. ~**ment** *n* derecho *m*

entity *n* entidad *f*

entrails *npl* entrañas *fpl*

entrance *n* entrada *f*. ● *vt* encantar

entrant *n* participante *m & f*; (in exam) candidato *m*

entreat *vt* suplicar. ~**y** *n* súplica *f*

entrenched *a* *<position>* afianzado

entrust *vt* confiar

entry *n* entrada *f*

entwine *vt* entrelazar

enumerate *vt* enumerar

envelop *vt* envolver

envelope *n* sobre *m*

enviable *a* envidiable

envious *a* envidioso

environment *n* medio *m* ambiente. ~**al** *a* ambiental

envisage *vt* prever; (imagine) imaginar

envision *vt* (Amer) prever

envoy *n* enviado *m*

envy *n* envidia *f*. ● *vt* envidiar

enzyme *n* enzima *f*

ephemeral *a* efímero

epic *n* épica *f*. ● *a* épico

epidemic *n* epidemia *f*. ● *a* epidémico

epilep|sy *n* epilepsia *f*. ~**tic** *a & n* epiléptico (*m*)

epilogue *n* epílogo *m*

episode *n* episodio *m*

epitaph *n* epitafio *m*

epitom|e *n* personificación *f*, epítome *m*. ~**ize** *vt* ser la personificación de

epoch *n* época *f*

equal *a & n* igual (*m & f*). ~ **to** (a task) a la altura de. ● *vt* (*pt* **equalled**) ser igual a; (Math) ser. ~**ity** *n* igualdad *f*. ~**ize** *vt* igualar. ● *vi* (Sport) emapatar. ~**izer** *n* (Sport) gol *m* del empate. ~**ly** *adv* igualmente; *<share>* por igual

equation *n* ecuación *f*

equator n ecuador m. ∼ial a ecuatorial

equilibrium n equilibrio m

equinox n equinoccio m

equip vt (pt **equipped**) equipar. ∼ sth with proveer algo de. ∼ment n equipo m

equivalen|ce n equivalencia f. ∼t a & n equivalente (m). be ∼t to equivaler

equivocal a equívoco

era n era f

eradicate vt erradicar, extirpar

erase vt borrar. ∼r n goma f (de borrar)

erect a erguido. ● vt levantar. ∼ion n construcción f; (Anat) erección f

ero|de vt erosionar. ∼sion n erosión f

erotic a erótico

err vi errar; (sin) pecar

errand n recado m, mandado m (LAm)

erratic a desigual; <person> voluble

erroneous a erróneo

error n error m

erudit|e a erudito. ∼ion n erudición f

erupt vi entrar en erupción; (fig) estallar. ∼ion n erupción f

escalat|e vt intensificar. ● vi intensificarse. ∼ion n intensificación f. ∼or n escalera f mecánica

escapade n aventura f

escap|e vi escaparse. ● vt evitar. ● n fuga f; (of gas, water) escape m. have a narrow ∼e escapar por un pelo. ∼ism n escapismo m

escort n acompañante m; (Mil) escolta f. ● vt acompañar; (Mil) escoltar

Eskimo n (pl -os or invar) esquimal m & f

especial a especial. ∼ly adv especialmente

espionage n espionaje m

Esq. abbr (= **Esquire**) (in address) E. Ashton, ∼ Sr. Don E. Ashton

essay n ensayo m; (at school) composición f

essence n esencia f. in ∼ esencialmente

essential a esencial. ● n elemento m esencial. ∼ly adv esencialmente

establish vt establecer. ∼ment n establecimiento m. the E∼ment los que mandan, el sistema

estate n finca f; (housing estate) complejo m habitacional, urbanización f, fraccionamiento m (Mex); (possessions) bienes mpl. ∼ agent n agente m inmobiliario. ∼ car n ranchera f, (coche m) familiar m, camioneta f (LAm)

esteem n estimación f, estima f

estimat|e n cálculo m; (Com) presupuesto m. ● vt calcular. ∼ion n estima f, estimación f; (opinion) opinión f

estranged a alejado

estuary n estuario m

etc abbr (= **et cetera**) etc., etcétera

etching n aguafuerte m

etern|al a eterno. ∼ity n eternidad f

ether n éter m

ethic n ética f. ∼al a ético. ∼s npl ética f

ethnic a étnico

ethos n carácter m distintivo

etiquette n etiqueta f

etymology n etimología f

euphemism n eufemismo m

euphoria n euforia f

EU *abbr* (= European Union) UE (Unión Europea)

euro *n* euro *m*

Europe *n* Europa *f*. ∼**an** *a & n* europeo (*m*). ∼**an Union** *n* Unión *f* Europea

euthanasia *n* eutanasia *f*

evacuat|e *vt* evacuar; desocupar *<building>*. ∼**ion** *n* evacuación *f*

evade *vt* evadir

evaluate *vt* evaluar

evangelical *a* evangélico

evaporat|e *vi* evaporarse. ∼**ion** *n* evaporación *f*

evasi|on *n* evasión *f*. ∼**ve** *a* evasivo

eve *n* víspera *f*

even *a* (flat, smooth) plano; *<colour>* uniforme; *<distribution>* equitativo; *<number>* par. **get** ∼ **with** desquitarse con. ● *vt* nivelar. □ ∼ **up** *vt* equilibrar. ● *adv* aun, hasta, incluso. ∼ **if** aunque. ∼ **so** aun así. **not** ∼ ni siquiera

evening *n* tarde *f*; (after dark) noche *f*. ∼ **class** *n* clase *f* nocturna

event *n* acontecimiento *m*; (Sport) prueba *f*. **in the** ∼ **of** en caso de. ∼**ful** *a* lleno de acontecimientos

eventual *a* final, definitivo. ∼**ity** *n* eventualidad *f*. ∼**ly** *adv* finalmente

ever *adv* (negative) nunca, jamás; (at all times) siempre. **have you** ∼ **been to Greece?** ¿has estado (alguna vez) en Grecia? ∼ **after** desde entonces. ∼ **since** desde entonces. ∼ **so** Ⓘ muy. **for** ∼ para siempre. **hardly** ∼ casi nunca. ∼**green** *a* de hoja perenne. ● *n* árbol *m* de hoja perenne. ∼**lasting** *a* eterno.

every *a* cada, todo. ∼ **child** todos los niños. ∼ **one** cada uno. ∼ **other day** un día sí y otro no. ∼**body** *pron* todos, todo el

mundo. ∼**day** *a* de todos los días. ∼**one** *pron* todos, todo el mundo. ∼**thing** *pron* todo. ∼**where** *adv* (be) en todas partes; (go) a todos lados

evict *vt* desahuciar. ∼**ion** *n* desahucio *m*

eviden|ce *n* evidencia *f*; (proof) pruebas *fpl*; (Jurid) testimonio *m*; **give** ∼**ce** prestar declaración. ∼**ce of** señales de. **in** ∼**ce** visible. ∼**t** *a* evidente. ∼**tly** *adv* evidentemente

evil *a* malvado. ● *n* mal *m*

evoke *vt* evocar

evolution *n* evolución *f*

evolve *vi* evolucionar

ewe *n* oveja *f*

exact *a* exacto. ● *vt* exigir (**from** a). ∼**ing** *a* exigente. ∼**ly** *adv* exactamente

exaggerat|e *vt* exagerar. ∼**ion** *n* exageración *f*

exam *n* examen *m*. ∼**ination** *n* examen *m*. ∼**ine** *vt* examinar; interrogar *<witness>*. ∼**iner** *n* examinador *m*

example *n* ejemplo *m*. **for** ∼ por ejemplo. **make an** ∼ **of s.o.** darle un castigo ejemplar a uno

exasperat|e *vt* exasperar. ∼**ing** *a* exasperante. ∼**ion** *n* exasperación *f*

excavat|e *vt* excavar. ∼**ion** *n* excavación *f*

exceed *vt* exceder. ∼**ingly** *adv* sumamente

excel *vi* (*pt* **excelled**) sobresalir. ● *vt*. ∼ **o.s.** lucirse. ∼**lence** *n* excelencia *f*. ∼**lent** *a* excelente

except *prep* menos, excepto. ∼ **for** si no fuera por. ● *vt* exceptuar. ∼**ing** *prep* con excepción de

exception *n* excepción *f*. **take** ∼ **to** ofenderse por. ∼**al** *a*

E

excepcional. ~**ally** adv
excepcionalmente

excerpt n extracto m

excess n exceso m. ● a
excedente. ~ **fare** suplemento m.
~ **luggage** exceso m de
equipaje. ~**ive** a excesivo

exchange vt cambiar. ● n
intercambio m; (of money) cambio
m. (telephone) ~ central f
telefónica

excise n impuestos mpl interos.
● vt quitar

excit|able a excitable. ~**e** vt
emocionar; (stimulate) excitar. ~**ed**
a entusiasmado. **get** ~**ed**
entusiasmarse. ~**ement** n
emoción f; (enthusiasm) entusiasmo
m. ~**ing** a emocionante

excla|im vi/t exclamar. ~**mation**
n exclamación f. ~**mation mark**
n signo m de admiración f

exclu|de vt excluir. ~**sion** n
exclusión f. ~**sive** a exclusivo;
<club> selecto. ~**sive of**
excluyendo. ~**sively** adv
exclusivamente

excruciating a atroz,
insoportable

excursion n excursión f

excus|able a perdonable. ~**e** vt
perdonar.~**e from** dispensar de.
~**e me!** ¡perdón! ● n excusa f

ex-directory a que no figura en
la guía telefónica, privado (Mex)

execut|e vt ejecutar. ~**ion** n
ejecución f. ~**ioner** n verdugo m

executive a & n ejecutivo (m)

exempt a exento (from de). ● vt
dispensar. ~**ion** n exención f

exercise n ejercicio m. ● vt
ejercer. ● vi hacer ejercicio. ~
book n cuaderno m

exert vt ejercer. ~ **o.s.** hacer un
gran esfuerzo. ~**ion** n esfuerzo m

exhale vt/i exhalar

exhaust vt agotar. ● n (Auto) tubo
m de escape. ~**ed** a agotado.
~**ion** n agotamiento m. ~**ive** a
exhaustivo

exhibit vt exponer; (fig) mostrar.
● n objeto m expuesto; (Jurid)
documento m. ~**ion** n
exposición. ~**ionist** n
exhibicionista m & f. ~**or** n
expositor m

exhilarat|ing a excitante. ~**ion** n
regocijo m

exhort vt exhortar

exile n exilio m; (person) exiliado
m. ● vt desterrar

exist vi existir. ~**ence** n
existencia f. **in** ~**ence** existente

exit n salida f

exorbitant a exorbitante

exorcis|e vt exorcizar. ~**m** n
exorcismo m. ~**t** n exorcista m &
f

exotic a exótico

expand vt expandir; (develop)
desarrollar. ● vi expandirse

expanse n extensión f

expansion n expansión f

expatriate a & n expatriado (m)

expect vt esperar; (suppose)
suponer; (demand) contar con. **I** ~
so supongo que sí. ~**ancy** n
esperanza f. **life** ~**ancy** esperanza
f de vida. ~**ant** a expectante.
~**ant mother** n futura madre f

expectation n expectativa f

expedient a conveniente. ● n
expediente m

expedition n expedición f

expel vt (pt expelled) expulsar

expend vt gastar. ~**able** a
prescindible. ~**iture** n gastos mpl

expens|e n gasto m. **at s.o.'s** ~**e** a
costa de uno. ~**es** npl (Com)
gastos mpl. ~**ive** a caro

experience n experiencia. ● vt
experimentar. ~**d** a con

experiencia; <*driver*> experimentado

experiment n experimento m. ● vi experimentar. ~al a experimental

expert a & n experto (m). ~ise pericia f. ~ly adv hábilmente

expir|e vi <*passport, ticket*> caducar; <*contract*> vencer. ~y n vencimiento m, caducidad f

expla|in vt explicar. ~nation n explicación f. ~natory a explicativo

explicit a explícito

explode vt hacer explotar. ● vi estallar

exploit n hazaña f. ● vt explotar. ~ation n explotación f

explor|ation n exploración f. ~atory a exploratorio. ~e vt explorar. ~er n explorador m

explosi|on n explosión f. ~ve a & n explosivo (m)

export vt exportar. ● n exportación f; (item) artículo m de exportación. ~er exportador m

expos|e vt exponer; (reveal) descubrir. ~ure n exposición f. **die of** ~ure morir de frío

express vt expresar. ● a expreso; <*letter*> urgente. ● adv (by express post) por correo urgente. ● n (train) rápido m, expreso m. ~ion n expresión f. ~ive a expresivo. ~ly adv expresadamente. ~way n (Amer) autopista f

expulsion n expulsión f

exquisite a exquisito

exten|d vt extender; (prolong) prolongar; ampliar <*house*>. ● vi extenderse. ~sion n extensión f; (of road, time) prolongación f; (building) anejo m. ~sive a extenso. ~sively adv extensamente. ~t n extensión f; (fig) alcance m. **to a certain** ~t hasta cierto punto

exterior a & n exterior (m)

exterminat|e vt exterminar. ~ion n exterminio m

external a externo

extinct a extinto. ~ion n extinción f

extinguish vt extinguir. ~er n extintor m, extinguidor m (LAm)

extol vt (pt **extolled**) alabar

extort vt sacar por la fuerza. ~ion n exacción f. ~ionate a exorbitante

extra a de más. ● adv extraordinariamente. ● n suplemento m; (Cinema) extra m & f

extract n extracto m. ● vt extraer. ~ion n extracción f

extradit|e vt extraditar. ~ion n extradición f ~ordinary a extraordinario. ~-sensory a extrasensorial

extravagan|ce n prodigalidad f; (of gestures, dress) extravagancia f. ~t a pródigo; <*behaviour*> extravagante. ~za n gran espectáculo m

extrem|e a & n extremo (m). ~ely adv extremadamente. ~ist n extremista m & f

extricate vt desenredar, librar

extrovert n extrovertido m

exuberan|ce n exuberancia f. ~t a exuberante

exude vt rezumar

exult vi exultar. ~ation n exultación f

eye n ojo m. **keep an** ~ **on** no perder de vista. **see** ~ **to** ~ **with s.o.** estar de acuerdo con uno. ● vt (pt **eyed**, pres p **eyeing**) mirar. ~ball n globo m ocular. ~brow n ceja f. ~drops npl colirio m. ~lash n pestaña f. ~lid n párpado m. ~-opener n I revelación f. ~-shadow n sombra *f* de ojos. ~**sight** *n* vista *f*. ~**sore** *n* (fig, Ⅰ) monstruosidad *f*, adefesio *m*. ~**witness** *n* testigo *m* ocular

fable *n* fábula *f*

fabric *n* tejido *m*, tela *f*

fabricate *vt* inventar. ~**ation** *n* invención *f*

fabulous *a* fabuloso

facade *n* fachada *f*

face *n* cara *f*, rostro *m*; (of watch) esfera *f*, carátula *f* (Mex); (aspect) aspecto *m*. ~ **down(wards)** boca abajo. ~ **up(wards)** boca arriba. **in the ~ of** frente a. **lose ~** quedar mal. **pull ~s** hacer muecas. ●*vt* mirar hacia; <*house*> dar a; (confront) enfrentarse con. ●*vi* volverse. □ ~ **up to** *vt* enfrentarse con. ~ **flannel** *n* paño *m* (para lavarse la cara). ~**less** *a* anónimo. ~ **lift** *n* cirugía *f* estética en la cara

facetious *a* burlón

facial *a* facial

facile *a* superficial, simplista

facilitate *vt* facilitar

facility *n* facilidad *f*

fact *n* hecho *m*. **as a matter of ~**, **in ~** en realidad, de hecho

faction *n* facción *f*

factor *n* factor *m*

factory *n* fábrica *f*

factual *a* basado en hechos, factual

faculty *n* facultad *f*

fad *n* manía *f*, capricho *m*

fade *vi* <*colour*> desteñirse; <*flowers*> marchitarse; <*light*> apagarse; <*memory, sound*> desvanecerse

fag *n* (Ⅰ, chore) faena *f*; (Ⅹ, cigarette) cigarillo *m*, pitillo *m*

Fahrenheit *a* Fahrenheit

fail *vi* fracasar; <*brakes*> fallar; (in an exam) suspender, ser reprobado (LAm). **he ~ed to arrive** no llegó. ●*vt* suspender, ser reprobado en (LAm) <*exam*>; suspender, reprobar (LAm) <*candidate*>. ●*n*. **without ~** sin falta. ~**ing** *n* defecto *m*. ●*prep*. ~**ing that, ...** si eso no resulta.... ~**ure** *n* fracaso *m*

faint *a* (-er, -est) (weak) débil; (indistinct) indistinto. **feel ~** estar mareado. **the ~est idea** la más remota idea. ●*vi* desmayarse. ●*n* desmayo *m*. ~**hearted** *a* pusilánime, cobarde. ~**ly** *adv* (weakly) débilmente; (indistinctly) indistintamente; (slightly) ligeramente

fair *a* (-er, -est) (just) justo; <*weather*> bueno; <*amount*> razonable; <*hair*> rubio, güero (Mex Ⅰ); <*skin*> blanco. ●*adv* limpio. ●*n* feria *f*. ~**-haired** *a* rubio, güero (Mex Ⅰ). ~**ly** *adv* (justly) justamente; (rather) bastante. ~**ness** *n* justicia *f*. **in all ~ness** sinceramente. ~ **play** *n* juego *m* limpio

fairy *n* hada *f*. ~ **story,** ~ **tale** *n* cuento *m* de hadas

faith *n* (trust) confianza *f*; (Relig) fe *f*. ~**ful** *a* fiel. ~**fully** *adv* fielmente. **yours ~fully** (in letters) (le saluda) atentamente

fake *n* falsificación *f*; (person) farsante *m*. ●*a* falso. ●*vt* falsificar

falcon *n* halcón *m*

Falkland Islands *npl.* the **Falkland Islands**, **the Falklands** las (Islas) Malvinas

fall *vi* (*pt* **fell**, *pp* **fallen**) caer; (decrease) bajar. ●*n* caída *f*; (Amer, autumn) otoño *m*; (in price) bajada *f*. □ ~ **apart** *vi* deshacerse. □ ~ **back on** *vt* recurrir a. □ ~ **down** *vi* (fall) caerse. □ ~ **for** *vt* 🄸 enamorarse de <*person*>; dejarse engañar por <*trick*>. □ ~ **in** *vi* (Mil) formar filas. □ ~ **off** *vi* caerse; (diminish) disminuir. □ ~ **out** *vi* (quarrel) reñir (**with** con); (drop out) caerse; (Mil) romper filas. □ ~ **over** *vi* caerse. *vt* tropezar con. □ ~ **through** *vi* no salir adelante

fallacy *n* falacia *f*

fallible *a* falible

fallout *n* lluvia *f* radiactiva. ~ **shelter** *n* refugio *m* antinuclear

fallow *a* en barbecho

false *a* falso. ~ **alarm** *n* falsa alarma. ~**hood** *n* mentira *f*. ~**ly** *adv* falsamente. ~ **teeth** *npl* dentadura *f* postiza

falsify *vt* falsificar

falter *vi* vacilar

fame *n* fama *f*. ~**d** *a* famoso

familiar *a* familiar. **the name sounds** ~ el nombre me suena. **be** ~ **with** conocer. ~**ity** *n* familiaridad *f*. ~**ize** *vt* familiarizar

family *n* familia *f*. ●*a* de (la) familia, familiar. ~ **tree** *n* árbol *m* genealógico

famine *n* hambre *f*, hambruna *f*

famished *a* hambriento

famous *a* famoso

fan *n* abanico *m*; (Mec) ventilador *m*; (enthusiast) aficionado *m*; (of group, actor) fan *m* & *f*; (of sport, team) hincha *m* & *f*. ●*vt* (*pt* **fanned**) abanicar; avivar <*interest*>. □ ~ **out** *vi* desparramarse en forma de abanico

fanatic *n* fanático *m*. ~**al** *a* fanático. ~**ism** *n* fanatismo *m*

fan belt *n* correa *f* de ventilador, banda *f* del ventilador (Mex)

fanciful *a* (imaginative) imaginativo; (impractical) extravagante

fancy *n* imaginación *f*; (liking) gusto *m*. **take a** ~ **to** tomar cariño a <*person*>; aficionarse a <*thing*>. ●*a* de lujo. ●*vt* (imagine) imaginar; (believe) creer; (🄸, want) apetecer a. ~ **dress** *n* disfraz *m*

fanfare *n* fanfarria *f*

fang *n* (of animal) colmillo *m*; (of snake) diente *m*

fantasize *vi* fantasear

fantastic *a* fantástico

fantasy *n* fantasía *f*

far *adv* lejos; (much) mucho. **as** ~ **as** hasta. **as** ~ **as I know** que yo sepa. **by** ~ con mucho. ●*a* (**further**, **furthest** *or* **farther**, **farthest**) lejano. ~ **away** lejano

farc|e *n* farsa *f*. ~**ical** *a* ridículo

fare *n* (on bus) precio *m* del billete, precio *m* del boleto (LAm); (on train, plane) precio *m* del billete, precio *m* del pasaje (LAm); (food) comida *f*

Far East *n* Extremo *or* Lejano Oriente *m*

farewell *int* & *n* adiós (*m*)

far-fetched *a* improbable

farm *n* granja *f*. ●*vt* cultivar. □ ~ **out** *vt* encargar (*a terceros*). ●*vi* ser agricultor. ~**er** *n* agricultor *m*, granjero *m*. ~**house** *n* granja *f*. ~**ing** *n* agricultura *f*. ~**yard** *n* corral *m*

far: ~**-off** *a* lejano. ~**-reaching** *a* trascendental. ~**-sighted** *a* con visión del futuro; (Med, Amer) hipermétrope

farther, farthest ⇒FAR

F

fascinat|e *vt* fascinar. ~**ed** *a* fascinado. ~**ing** *a* fascinante. ~**ion** *n* fascinación *f*

fascis|m *n* fascismo *m*. ~**t** *a & n* fascista (*m & f*)

fashion *n* (manner) manera *f*; (vogue) moda *f*. **be in/out of** ~ estar de moda/estar pasado de moda. ~**able** *a* de moda

fast *a* (-**er**, -**est**) rápido; <*clock*> adelantado; (secure) fijo; <*colours*> sólido. ● *adv* rápidamente; (securely) firmemente. ~ **asleep** profundamente dormido. ● *vi* ayunar. ● *n* ayuno *m*

fasten *vt* sujetar; cerrar <*case*>; abrochar <*belt etc*>. ● *vi* <*case*> cerrar; <*belt etc*> cerrarse. ~**er**, ~**ing** *n* (on box, window) cierre *m*; (on door) cerrojo *m*

fat *n* grasa *f*. ● *a* (**fatter**, **fattest**) gordo; <*meat*> que tiene mucha grasa; (thick) grueso. **get** ~ engordar

fatal *a* mortal; (fateful) fatídico. ~**ity** *n* muerto *m*. ~**ly** *adv* mortalmente

fate *n* destino *m*; (one's lot) suerte *f*. ~**d** *a* predestinado. ~**ful** *a* fatídico

father *n* padre *m*. ~**hood** *m* paternidad *f*. ~**-in-law** *m* (*pl* ~**s-in-law**) *m* suegro *m*. ~**ly** *a* paternal

fathom *n* braza *f*. ● *vt.* ~ (**out**) comprender

fatigue *n* fatiga *f*. ● *vt* fatigar

fat|ten *vt.* ~**ten** (**up**) cebar <*animal*>. ~**tening** *a* que engorda. ~**ty** *a* graso, grasoso (LAm). ● *n* 🄸 gordinflón *m*

fatuous *a* fatuo

faucet *n* (Amer) grifo *m*, llave *f* (LAm)

fault *n* defecto *m*; (blame) culpa *f*; (tennis) falta *f*; (Geol) falla *f*. **at** ~

culpable. ● *vt* encontrarle defectos a. ~**less** *a* impecable. ~**y** *a* defectuoso

favour *n* favor *m*. ● *vt* favorecer; (support) estar a favor de; (prefer) preferir. ~**able** *a* favorable. ~**ably** *adv* favorablemente. ~**ite** *a & n* preferido (*m*). ~**itism** *n* favoritismo *m*

fawn *n* cervato *m*. ● *a* beige, beis. ● *vi.* ~ **on** adular

fax *n* fax *m*. ● *vt* faxear

fear *n* miedo *m*. ● *vt* temer. ~**ful** *a* (frightening) espantoso; (frightened) temeroso. ~**less** *a* intrépido. ~**some** *a* espantoso

feasib|ility *n* viabilidad *f*. ~**le** *a* factible; (likely) posible

feast *n* (Relig) fiesta *f*; (meal) banquete *m*

feat *n* hazaña *f*

feather *n* pluma *f*. ~**weight** *n* peso *m* pluma

feature *n* (on face) rasgo *m*; (characteristic) característica *f*; (in newspaper) artículo *m*; ~ (**film**) película *f* principal, largometraje *m*. ● *vt* presentar; (give prominence to) destacar

February *n* febrero *m*

fed ⇒FEED

feder|al *a* federal. ~**ation** *n* federación *f*

fed up *a* 🄸 harto (**with** de)

fee *n* (professional) honorarios *mpl*; (enrolment) derechos *mpl*; (club) cuota *f*

feeble *a* (-**er**, -**est**) débil

feed *vt* (*pt* **fed**) dar de comer a; (supply) alimentar. ● *vi* comer. ● *n* (for animals) pienso *m*; (for babies) comida *f*. ~**back** *n* reacción *f*

feel *vt* (*pt* **felt**) sentir; (touch) tocar; (think) considerar. **do you** ~ **it's a good idea?** ¿te parece buena idea? ~ **as if** tener la impresión de que. **~ hot/hungry** tener calor/hambre. **~ like** (I, want) tener ganas de. • n sensación f. **get the ~ of sth** acostumbrarse a algo. **~er** n (of insect) antena f. **~ing** n sentimiento m; (physical) sensación f

feet ⇒FOOT

feign vt fingir

feint n finta f

fell ⇒FALL. • vt derribar; talar <tree>

fellow n I tipo m; (comrade) compañero m; (of society) socio m. **~ countryman** n compatriota m. **~ passenger/traveller** n compañero m de viaje

felony n delito m grave

felt n ⇒FEEL. • n fieltro m

female a hembra; <voice, sex etc> femenino. • n mujer f; (animal) hembra f

femini|ne a & n femenino (m). **~nity** n feminidad f. **~st** a & n feminista m & f

fenc|e n cerca f, cerco m (LAm). • vt. **~e** (**in**) encerrar, cercar. • vi (Sport) practicar la esgrima. **~er** n esgrimidor m. **~ing** n (Sport) esgrima f

fend vi. **~ for o.s.** valerse por sí mismo. □ **~ off** vt defenderse de

fender n rejilla f; (Amer, Auto) guardabarros m, salpicadera f (Mex)

ferment vt/i fermentar. **~ation** n fermentación f

fern n helecho m

feroci|ous a feroz. **~ty** n ferocidad f

ferret n hurón m. • vi (pt ferreted) **~ about** husmear. • vt. **~ out** descubrir

ferry n ferry m. • vt transportar

fertil|e a fértil. **~ity** n fertilidad f. **~ize** vt fecundar, abonar <soil>. **~izer** n fertilizante m

ferv|ent a ferviente. **~our** n fervor m

fester vi enconarse

festival n fiesta f; (of arts) festival m

festiv|e a festivo. **the ~e season** n las Navidades. **~ity** n festividad f

fetch vt (go for) ir a buscar; (bring) traer; (be sold for) venderse en. **~ing** a atractivo

fête n fiesta f. • vt festejar

fetish n fetiche m

fetter vt encadenar

feud n contienda f

feudal a feudal. **~ism** n feudalismo m

fever n fiebre f. **~ish** a febril

few a pocos. **a ~ houses** algunas casas. • n pocos mpl. **a ~** unos (pocos). **a good ~, quite a ~** I muchos. **~er** a & n menos. **~est** a el menor número de

fiancé n novio m. **~e** n novia f

fiasco n (pl -os) fiasco m

fib n I mentirilla f. • vi I mentir, decir mentirillas

fibre n fibra f. **~glass** n fibra f de vidrio

fickle a inconstante

ficti|on n ficción f. (**works of**) **~on** novelas fpl. **~onal** a novelesco. **~tious** a ficticio

fiddle n I violín m; (I, swindle) trampa f. • vt I falsificar. **~ with** juguetear con

fidget vi (pt fidgeted) moverse, ponerse nervioso. **~ with** juguetear con. • n persona f inquieta. **~y** a inquieto

field n campo m. **~ day** n. **have a ~ day** hacer su agosto. **~**

glasses *npl* gemelos *mpl*. F~
Marshal *n* mariscal *m* de campo.
~ **trip** *n* viaje *m* de estudio.
~**work** *n* investigaciones *fpl* en
el terreno

fiend *n* demonio *m*. ~**ish** *a*
diabólico

fierce *a* (-er, -est) feroz; *<attack>*
violento. ~**ly** *adv* *<growl>* con
ferocidad; *<fight>* con fiereza

fiery *a* (-ier, -iest) ardiente;
<temper> exaltado

fifteen *a & n* quince (*m*). ~**th** *a*
decimoquinto. ● *n* quinceavo *m*

fifth *a & n* quinto (*m*)

fift|ieth *a* quincuagésimo. ● *n*
cincuentavo *m*. ~**y** *a & n*
cincuenta (*m*). ~**y**-~**y** *adv* mitad
y mitad, a medias. ● *a*. **a** ~**y**-~**y**
chance una posibilidad de cada
dos

fig *n* higo *m*

fight *vi* (*pt* fought) luchar;
(quarrel) disputar. ● *vt* luchar
contra. ● *n* pelea *m*; (struggle)
lucha *f*; (quarrel) disputa *f*; (Mil)
combate *m*. □ ~ **back** *vi*
defenderse. □ ~ **off** *vt* rechazar
<attack>; luchar contra *<illness>*.
~**er** *n* luchador *m*; (aircraft) avión
m de caza. ~**ing** *n* luchas *fpl*

figment *n*. ~ **of the imagination**
producto *m* de la imaginación

figurative *a* figurado

figure *n* (number) cifra *f*; (person)
figura *f*; (shape) forma *f*; (of woman)
tipo *m*. ● *vt* imaginar; (Amer 🔳,
reckon) calcular. ● *vi* figurar. **that**
~**s** 🔳 es lógico. □ ~ **out** *vt*
entender. ~**head** *n* testaferro *m*,
mascarón *m* de proa. ~ **of**
speech *n* figura *f* retórica

filch *vt* 🔳 hurtar

file *n* (tool, for nails) lima *f*; (folder)
carpeta *f*; (set of papers) expediente
m; (Comp) archivo *m*; (row) fila *f*. **in**
single ~ en fila india. ● *vt*

archivar *<papers>*; limar *<metal,
nails>*. ● ~ **in** *vi* entrar en fila. ~
past *vt* desfilar ante

filing cabinet *n* archivador *m*

fill *vt* llenar. ● *vi* llenarse. ● *n*. **eat**
one's ~ hartarse de comer. **have
had one's** ~ **of** estar harto de □ ~
in *vt* rellenar *<form, hole>*. □ ~
out *vt* rellenar *<form>*. *vi* (get
fatter) engordar. □ ~ **up** *vt* llenar.
vi llenarse

fillet *n* filete *m*. ● *vt* (*pt* filleted)
cortar en filetes *<meat>*; quitar la
espina a *<fish>*

filling *n* (in tooth) empaste *m*,
tapadura *f* (Mex). ~ **station** *n*
gasolinera *f*

film *n* película *f*. ● *vt* filmar. ~
star *n* estrella *f* de cine

filter *n* filtro *m*. ● *vt* filtrar. ● *vi*
filtrarse. ~**-tipped** *a* con filtro

filth *n* mugre *f*. ~**y** *a* mugriento

fin *n* aleta *f*

final *a* último; (conclusive) decisivo.
● *n* (Sport) final *f*. ~**s** *npl* (Schol)
exámenes *mpl* de fin de curso

finale *n* final *m*

final|ist *n* finalista *m & f*. ~**ize** *vt*
ultimar. ~**ly** *adv* (lastly)
finalmente, por fin

financ|e *n* finanzas *fpl*. ● *vt*
financiar. ~**ial** *a* financiero;
<difficulties> económico

find *vt* (*pt* found) encontrar. ~
out *vt* descubrir. ● *vi* (learn)
enterarse. ~**ings** *npl*
conclusiones *fpl*

fine *a* (-er, -est) (delicate) fino;
(excellent) excelente. ● *adv* muy
bien. ● *n* multa *f*. ● *vt* multar. ~
arts *npl* bellas artes *fpl*. ~**ly** *adv*
(cut) en trozos pequeños; *<adjust>*
con precisión

finger *n* dedo *m*. ● *vt* tocar. ~**nail**
n uña *f*. ~**print** *n* huella *f* digital.
~**tip** *n* punta *f* del dedo

finish *vt/i* terminar, acabar. ∼ **doing** terminar de hacer. ● *n* fin *m*; (of race) llegada *f*

finite *a* finito

Fin|land *n* Finlandia *f*. ∼**n** *n* finlandés *m*. ∼**nish** *a & n* finlandés (*m*)

fiord *n* fiordo *m*

fir *n* abeto *m*

fire *n* fuego *m*; (conflagration) incendio *m*. ● *vt* disparar <*gun*>; (dismiss) despedir; avivar <*imagination*>. ● *vi* disparar. ∼ **alarm** *n* alarma *f* contra incendios. ∼**arm** *n* arma *f* de fuego. ∼ **brigade**, **department** (Amer) *n* cuerpo *m* de bomberos. ∼ **engine** *n* coche *m* de bomberos, carro *m* de bomberos (Mex). ∼**-escape** *n* escalera *f* de incendios. ∼ **extinguisher** *n* extintor *m*, extinguidor *m* (LAm). ∼**fighter** *n* bombero *m*. ∼**man** *n* bombero *m*. ∼**place** *n* chimenea *f*. ∼**side** *n* hogar *m*. ∼ **truck** *n* (Amer) ⇒∼ engine. ∼**wood** *n* leña *f*. ∼**work** *n* fuego *m* artificial

firm *n* empresa *f*. ● *a* (**-er**, **-est**) firme. ∼**ly** *adv* firmemente

first *a* primero, (before masculine singular noun) primer. **at ∼ hand** directamente. ● *n* primero *m*. ● *adv* primero; (first time) por primera vez. ∼ **of all** primero. ∼ **aid** *n* primeros auxilios *mpl*. ∼ **aid kit** *n* botiquín *m*. ∼ **class** *adv* <*travel*> en primera clase. ∼**-class** *a* de primera clase. ∼ **floor** *n* primer piso *m*; (Amer) planta *f* baja. **F∼ Lady** *n* (Amer) Primera Dama *f*. ∼**ly** *adv* en primer lugar. ∼ **name** *n* nombre *m* de pila. ∼**-rate** *a* excelente

fish *n* (*pl invar or* **-es**) pez *m*; (as food) pescado *m*. ● *vi* pescar. **go**

∼**ing** ir de pesca. ▫ ∼ **out** *vt* sacar. ∼**erman** *n* pescador *m*. ∼**ing** *n* pesca *f*. ∼**ing pole** (Amer), ∼**ing rod** *n* caña *f* de pesca. ∼**monger** *n* pescadero *m*. ∼ **shop** *n* pescadería *f*. ∼**y** *a* <*smell*> a pescado; (🗉, questionable) sospechoso

fission *n* fisión *f*

fist *n* puño *m*

fit *a* (**fitter, fittest**) (healthy) en forma; (good enough) adecuado; (able) capaz. ● *n* (attack) ataque; (of clothes) corte *m*. ● *vt* (*pt* **fitted**) (adapt) adaptar; (be the right size for) quedarle bien a; (install) colocar. ● *vi* encajar; (in certain space) caber; <*clothes*> quedarle bien a uno. ▫ ∼ **in** *vi* caber. ∼**ful** *a* irregular. ∼**ness** *n* salud *f*; (Sport) (buena) forma *f* física. ∼**ting** *a* apropiado. ● *n* (of clothes) prueba *f*. ∼**ting room** *n* probador *m*

five *a & n* cinco (*m*)

fix *vt* fijar; (mend, deal with) arreglar. ● *n*. **in a ∼** en un aprieto. ∼**ed** *a* fijo. ∼**ture** *n* (Sport) partido *m*

fizz *vi* burbujear. ● *n* efervescencia *f*. ∼**le** *vi*. ∼**le out** fracasar. ∼**y** *a* efervescente; <*water*> con gas

fjord *n* fiordo *m*

flabbergasted *a* estupefacto

flabby *a* flojo

flag *n* bandera *f*. ● *vi* (*pt* **flagged**) (weaken) flaquear; <*conversation*> languidecer

flagon *n* botella *f* grande, jarro *m*

flagpole *n* asta *f* de bandera

flagrant *a* flagrante

flair *n* don *m* (**for** de)

flak|e *n* copo *m*; (of paint, metal) escama *f*. ● *vi* desconcharse. ∼**y** *a* escamoso

flamboyant *a* <*clothes*> vistoso; <*manner*> extravagante

flame *n* llama *f*. **go up in ∼s** incendiarse

flamingo *n* (*pl* -o(e)s) flamenco *m*

flammable *a* inflamable

flan *n* tartaleta *f*

flank *n* (of animal) ijada *f*; (of person) costado *m*; (Mil, Sport) flanco *m*

flannel *n* franela *f*; (for face) paño *m* (para lavarse la cara).

flap *vi* (*pt* **flapped**) ondear; <*wings*> aletear. ● *vt* batir <*wings*>; agitar <*arms*>. ● *n* (cover) tapa *f*; (of pocket) cartera *f*; (of table) ala *f*. **get into a ∼** 🄳 ponerse nervioso

flare ● *n* llamarada *f*; (Mil) bengala *f*; (in skirt) vuelo *m*. □ ∼ **up** *vi* llamear; <*fighting*> estallar; <*person*> encolerizarse

flash *vi* destellar. ● *vt* (aim torch) dirigir; (flaunt) hacer ostentación de. ∼ **past** pasar como un rayo. ● *n* destello *m*; (Photo) flash *m*. ∼**back** *n* escena *f* retrospectiva. ∼**light** *n* (Amer, torch) linterna *f*. ∼**y** *a* ostentoso

flask *n* frasco *m*; (vacuum flask) termo *m*

flat *a* (**flatter, flattest**) plano; <*tyre*> desinflado; <*refusal*> categórico; <*fare, rate*> fijo; (Mus) bemol. ● *adv* (Mus) demasiado bajo. ∼ **out** (at top speed) a toda velocidad. ● *n* (rooms) apartamento *m*, piso *m*; (Auto, esp Amer) 🄳 pinchazo *m*; (Mus) bemol *m*. ∼**ly** *adv* categóricamente. ∼**ten** *vt* allanar, aplanar

flatter *vt* adular. ∼**ing** *a* <*person*> lisonjero; <*clothes*> favorecedor. ∼**y** *n* adulación *f*

flaunt *vt* hacer ostentación de

flavour *n* sabor *m*. ● *vt* sazonar. ∼**ing** *n* condimento *m*

flaw *n* defecto *m*. ∼**less** *a* perfecto

flea *n* pulga *f*

fleck *n* mancha *f*, pinta *f*

fled ⇒FLEE

flee *vi* (*pt* **fled**) huir. ● *vt* huir de

fleece *n* vellón *m*. ● *vt* 🄳 desplumar

fleet *n* flota *f*; (of cars) parque *m* móvil

fleeting *a* fugaz

Flemish *a & n* flamenco (*m*)

flesh *n* carne *f*. **in the ∼** en persona

flew ⇒FLY

flex *vt* doblar; flexionar <*muscle*>. ● *n* (Elec) cable *m*

flexib|ility *n* flexibilidad *f*. ∼**le** *a* flexible

flexitime, (Amer) **flextime** *n* horario *m* flexible

flick *n* golpecito *m*. ● *vt* dar un golpecito a. □ ∼ **through** *vt* hojear

flicker *vi* parpadear. ● *n* parpadeo *m*; (of hope) resquicio *m*

flies *npl* (🄳, on trousers) bragueta *f*

flight *n* vuelo *m*; (fleeing) huida *f*, fuga *f*. ∼ **of stairs** tramo *m* de escalera *f*. **take (to) ∼** darse a la fuga. ∼ **attendant** *n* (male) sobrecargo *m*, aeromozo *m* (LAm); (female) azafata *f*, aeromoza *f* (LAm). ∼**-deck** *n* cubierta *f* de vuelo

flimsy *a* (**-ier, -iest**) flojo, débil, poco sólido

flinch *vi* retroceder (**from** ante)

fling *vt* (*pt* **flung**) arrojar. ● *n* (love affair) aventura *f*; (wild time) juerga *f*

flint *n* pedernal *m*; (for lighter) piedra *f*

flip *vt* (*pt* **flipped**) dar un golpecito a. ● *n* golpecito *m*. □ ∼ **through** *vt* hojear

flippant *a* poco serio

flipper *n* aleta *f*

flirt vi coquetear. ● n (woman) coqueta f; (man) coqueto m

flit vi (pt **flitted**) revolotear

float vi flotar. ● vt hacer flotar; introducir en Bolsa <company>. ● n flotador m; (cash) caja f chica

flock n (of birds) bandada f; (of sheep) rebaño m. ● vi congregarse

flog vt (pt **flogged**) (beat) azotar; (囗, sell) vender

flood n inundación f; (fig) avalancha f. ● vt inundar. ● vi <building etc> inundarse; <river> desbordar. ~**light** n foco m. ● vt (pt ~**lit**) iluminar (con focos)

floor n suelo m; (storey) piso m; (for dancing) pista f. ● vt derribar; (baffle) confundir

flop vi (pt **flopped**) dejarse caer pesadamente; (囗, fail) fracasar. ● n 囗 fracaso m. ~**py** a flojo. ● n ⇒~**py disk** n disquete m, floppy (disk) n

floral a floral

florid a florido

florist n florista m & f

flounder vi (in water) luchar para mantenerse a flote; <speaker> quedar sin saber qué decir

flour n harina f

flourish vi florecer; <business> prosperar. ● vt blandir. ● n ademán m elegante; (in handwriting) rasgo m. ~**ing** a próspero

flout vt burlarse de

flow vi fluir; <blood> correr; (hang loosely) caer. ● n flujo m; (stream) corriente f; (of traffic, information) circulación f. ~ **chart** n organigrama m

flower n flor f. ● vi florecer, florear (Mex). ~ **bed** n macizo m de flores. ~**y** a florido

flown ⇒FLY

flu n gripe f

fluctuat|e vi fluctuar. ~**ion** n fluctuación f

flue n tiro m

fluen|cy n fluidez f. ~**t** a <style> fluido; <speaker> elocuente. **be ~t in a language** hablar un idioma con fluidez. ~**tly** adv con fluidez

fluff n pelusa f. ~**y** a (-ier, -iest) velloso

fluid a & n fluido (m)

flung ⇒FLING

fluorescent a fluorescente

flush vi ruborizarse. ● vt. ~ **the toilet** tirar de la cadena, jalarle a la cadena (LAm). ● n (blush) rubor m

fluster vt poner nervioso

flute n flauta f

flutter vi ondear; <bird> revolotear. ● n (of wings) revoloteo m; (fig) agitación f

flux n flujo m. **be in a state of ~** estar siempre cambiando

fly vi (pt **flew**, pp **flown**) volar; <passenger> ir en avión; <flag> flotar; (rush) correr. ● vt pilotar, pilotear (LAm) <aircraft>; transportar en avión <passengers, goods>; izar <flag>. ● n mosca f; (of trousers) ⇒FLIES. ~**ing** a volante. ~**ing visit** visita f relámpago. ● n (activity) aviación f. ~**leaf** n guarda f. ~**over** n paso m elevado

foal n potro m

foam n espuma f. ● vi espumar. ~ **rubber** n goma f espuma, hule m espuma (Mex)

fob vt (pt **fobbed**). ~ **sth off onto s.o.** (palm off) encajarle algo a uno

focal a focal

focus n (pl **-cuses** or **-ci**) foco m; (fig) centro m. **in ~** enfocado. **out of ~** desenfocado. ● vt (pt **focused**) enfocar (fig) concentrar.

F

● *vi* enfocar; (fig) concentrarse (**on** en)

fodder *n* forraje *m*

foe *n* enemigo *m*

foetus *n* (*pl* **-tuses**) feto *m*

fog *n* niebla *f*

fog|gy *a* (**-ier**, **-iest**) nebuloso. **it is** ~**gy** hay niebla. ~**horn** *n* sirena *f* de niebla

foible *n* punto *m* débil

foil *vt* frustrar. ● *n* papel *m* de plata

foist *vt* encajar (**on** a)

fold *vt* doblar; cruzar <*arms*>. ● *vi* doblarse; (fail) fracasar. ● *n* pliegue *m*. (for sheep) redil *m*. ~**er** *n* carpeta *f*. ~**ing** *a* plegable

foliage *n* follaje *m*

folk *n* gente *f*. ● *a* popular. ~**lore** *n* folklore *m*. ~ **music** *n* música *f* folklórica; (modern) música *f* folk. ~**s** *npl* (one's relatives) familia *f*

follow *vt/i* seguir. □ ~ **up** *vt* seguir. ~**er** *n* seguidor *m*. ~**ing** *n* partidarios *mpl*. ● *a* siguiente. ● *prep* después de

folly *n* locura *f*

fond *a* (**-er**, **-est**) (loving) cariñoso; <*hope*> vivo. **be** ~ **of s.o.** tener(le) cariño a uno. **be** ~ **of sth** ser aficionado a algo

fondle *vt* acariciar

fondness *n* cariño *m*; (for things) afición *f*

font *n* pila *f* bautismal

food *n* comida *f*. ~ **poisoning** *n* intoxicación *f* alimenticia. ~ **processor** *n* robot *m* de cocina

fool *n* idiota *m & f* ● *vt* engañar. □ ~ **about** *vi* hacer payasadas. ~**hardy** *a* temerario. ~**ish** *a* tonto. ~**ishly** *adv* tontamente. ~**ishness** *n* tontería *f*. ~**proof** *a* infalible

foot *n* (*pl* **feet**) pie *m*; (measure) pie *m* (= 30,48cm); (of animal, furniture) pata *f*. **get under s.o.'s feet** estorbar a uno. **on** ~ a pie. **on/to one's feet** de pie. **put one's** ~ **in it** meter la pata. ● *vt* pagar <*bill*>. ~**age** *n* (of film) secuencia *f*. ~**-and-mouth disease** *n* fiebre *f* aftosa. ~**ball** *n* (ball) balón *m*; (game) fútbol *m*; (American ~ball) fútbol *m* americano. ~**baller** *n* futbolista *m & f*. ~**bridge** *n* puente *m* para peatones. ~**hills** *npl* estribaciones *fpl*. ~**hold** *n* punto *m* de apoyo. ~**ing** *n* pie *m*. **on an equal** ~**ing** en igualdad de condiciones. ~**lights** *npl* candilejas *fpl*. ~**man** *n* lacayo *m*. ~**note** *n* nota *f* (al pie de la página). ~**path** *n* (in country) senda *f*; (in town) acera *f*, banqueta *f* (Mex). ~**print** *n* huella *f*. ~**step** *n* paso *m*. ~**wear** *n* calzado *m*

for

● *preposition*

⋯▸ (intended for) para. **it's** ~ **my mother** es para mi madre. **she works** ~ **a multinacional** trabaja para una multinacional

⋯▸ (on behalf of) por. **I did it** ~ **you** lo hice por ti

⟹ See entries **para** and **por** for further information

⋯▸ (expressing purpose) para. **I use it** ~ **washing the car** lo uso para limpiar el coche. **what** ~? ¿para qué?. **to go out** ~ **a meal** salir a comer fuera

⋯▸ (in favour of) a favor de. **are you** ~ **or against the idea?** estás a favor o en contra de la idea?

⋯▸ (indicating cost, in exchage for) por. **I bought it** ~ **30 pounds** lo compré por 30 libras. **she left him** ~ **another man** lo dejó por otro. **thanks** ~ **everything** gracias por

todo. **what's the Spanish ~ 'toad'?**
¿cómo se dice 'toad' en español?

····▸ (expressing duration) **he read ~
two hours** leyó durante dos
horas. **how long are you going ~?**
¿por cuánto tiempo vas? **I've
been waiting ~ three hours** hace
tres horas que estoy esperando,
llevo tres horas esperando

····▸ (in the direction of) para. **the train
~ Santiago** el tren para Santiago

●*conjunction*

····▸ (because) porque, pues (literary
usage). **she left at once, ~ it was
getting late** se fue en seguida,
porque *or* pues se hacía tarde

forage *vi* forrajear. ● *n* forraje *m*
forbade ⇒FORBID
forbearance *n* paciencia *f*
forbid *vt* (*pt* **forbade**, *pp*
forbidden) prohibir (**s.o. to do a**
uno hacer). **~ s.o. sth** prohibir
algo a uno. **~ding** *a* imponente
force *n* fuerza *f*. **by ~** a la fuerza.
come into ~ entrar en vigor. **the
~s** las fuerzas *fpl* armadas. ● *vt*
forzar; (compel) obligar (**s.o. to do
sth** a uno a hacer algo). **~ on**
imponer a. **~ open** forzar. **~d** *a*
forzado. **~-feed** *vt* alimentar a la
fuerza. **~ful** *a* enérgico
forceps *n* fórceps *m*
forcibl|e *a* a la fuerza. **~y** *adv* a
la fuerza
ford *n* vado *m* ● *vt* vadear
fore *a* anterior. ● *n*. **come to the ~**
hacerse evidente
forearm *n* antebrazo *m*
foreboding *n* presentimiento *m*
forecast *vt* (*pt* **forecast**)
pronosticar *<weather>*; prever
<result>. ● *n* pronóstico *m*.
weather ~ pronóstico *m* del
tiempo
forecourt *n* patio *m* delantero

forefinger *n* (dedo *m*) índice *m*
forefront *n* vanguardia *f*. **in the ~**
a la vanguardia
forego *vt* (*pt* **forewent**, *pp*
foregone) ⇒FORGO
foregone *a*. **~ conclusion**
resultado *m* previsto
foreground *n*. **in the ~** en primer
plano
forehead *n* frente *f*
foreign *a* extranjero; *<trade>*
exterior; *<travel>* al extranjero,
en el extranjero. **~er** *n*
extranjero *m*
foreman (*pl* **-men**) *n* capataz *m*
foremost *a* primero. ● *adv*. **first
and ~** ante todo
forerunner *n* precursor *m*
foresee *vt* (*pt* **-saw**, *pp* **-seen**)
prever. **~able** *a* previsible
foresight *n* previsión *f*
forest *n* bosque *m*
forestall *vt* (prevent) prevenir;
(preempt) anticiparse
forestry *n* silvicultura *f*
foretaste *n* anticipo *m*
foretell *vt* (*pt* **foretold**) predecir
forever *adv* para siempre; (always)
siempre
forewarn *vt* advertir
forewent ⇒FOREGO
foreword *n* prefacio *m*
forfeit *n* (penalty) pena *f*; (in game)
prenda *f*. ● *vt* perder; perder el
derecho a *<property>*
forgave ⇒FORGIVE
forge *n* fragua *f*. ● *vt* fraguar;
(copy) falsificar. □ **~ ahead** *vi*
adelantarse rápidamente. **~r** *n*
falsificador *m*. **~ry** *n* falsificación
f
forget *vt* (*pt* **forgot**, *pp*
forgotten) olvidar, olvidarse de.
● *vi* olvidarse (**about** de). **I forgot**
se me olvidó. **~ful** *a* olvidadizo

F

forgive vt (pt **forgave**, pp **forgiven**) perdonar. ~ **s.o. for sth** perdonar algo a uno. ~**ness** n perdón m

forgo vt (pt **forwent**, pp **forgone**) renunciar a

fork n tenedor m; (for digging) horca f; (in road) bifurcación f. ● vi <road> bifurcarse. □ ~ **out** vt Ⓣ desembolsar, aflojar Ⓣ. ~**lift truck** n carretilla f elevadora

forlorn a <hope, attempt> desesperado; <smile> triste

form n forma f; (document) formulario m; (Schol) clase f. ● vt formar. ● vi formarse

formal a formal; <person> formalista; <dress> de etiqueta. ~**ity** n formalidad f. ~**ly** adv oficialmente

format n formato m. ● vt (pt **formatted**) (Comp) formatear

formation n formación f

former a anterior; (first of two) primero. ● n. **the ~** el primero m, la primera f, los primeros mpl, las primeras fpl. ~**ly** adv antes

formidable a formidable

formula n (pl **-ae** or **-as**) fórmula f. ~**te** vt formular

forsake vt (pt **forsook**, pp **forsaken**) abandonar

fort n fuerte m

forth adv. **and so ~** y así sucesivamente. ~**coming** a próximo, venidero; (sociable) comunicativo. ~**right** a directo. ~**with** adv inmediatamente

fortieth a cuadragésimo. ● n cuadragésima parte f

fortnight n quince días mpl, quincena f. ~**ly** a bimensual. ● adv cada quince días

fortress n fortaleza f

fortunate a afortunado. **be ~** tener suerte. ~**ly** adv afortunadamente

fortune n fortuna f. ~**-teller** n adivino m

forty a & n cuarenta (m). ~ **winks** un sueñecito

forum n foro m

forward a <movement> hacia adelante; (advanced) precoz; (pert) impertinente. ● n (Sport) delantero m. ● adv adelante. **go ~** avanzar. ● vt hacer seguir <letter>; enviar <goods>. ~**s** adv adelante

forwent ⇒FORGO

fossil a & n fósil (m)

foster vt (promote) fomentar; criar <child>. ~ **child** n hijo m adoptivo

fought ⇒FIGHT

foul a (-er, -est) <smell> nauseabundo; <weather> pésimo; <person> asqueroso; (dirty) sucio; <language> obsceno. ● n (Sport) falta f. ● vt contaminar; (entangle) enredar. ~ **play** n (Sport) jugada f sucia; (crime) delito m

found ⇒FIND. ● vt fundar.

foundation n fundación f; (basis) fundamento. (cosmetic) base f (de maquillaje). ~**s** npl (Archit) cimientos mpl

founder n fundador m. ● vi <ship> hundirse

fountain n fuente f. ~ **pen** n pluma f (estilográfica) f, estilográfica f

four a & n cuatro (m). ~**fold** a cuádruple. ● adv cuatro veces. ~**some** n grupo m de cuatro personas ~**teen** a & n catorce (m). ~**teenth** a & n decimocuarto m. ~**th** a & n cuarto (m). ~**-wheel drive** n tracción f integral

fowl n ave f

fox n zorro m, zorra f. ● vt
⚠ confundir

foyer n (of theatre) foyer m; (of hotel)
vestíbulo m

fraction n fracción f

fracture n fractura f. ● vt
fracturar. ● vi fracturarse

fragile a frágil

fragment n fragmento m. ~ary a
fragmentario

fragran|ce n fragancia f. ~t a
fragante

frail a (-er, -est) frágil

frame n (of picture, door, window)
marco m; (of spectacles) montura f;
(fig, structure) estructura f. ● vt
enmarcar <picture>; formular
<plan, question>; ⚠, (incriminate
unjustly) incriminar falsamente.
~work n estructura f; (context)
marco m

France n Francia f

frank a franco. ● vt franquear.
~ly adv francamente

frantic a frenético. ~ with loco de

fratern|al a fraternal. ~ity n
fraternidad f; (club) asociación f.
~ize vi fraternizar

fraud n fraude m; (person)
impostor m. ~ulent a
fraudulento

fraught a (tense) tenso. ~ with
cargado de

fray n riña f

freak n fenómeno m; (monster)
monstruo m. ● a anormal. ~ish a
anormal

freckle n peca f. ~d a pecoso

free a (freer, freest) libre; (gratis)
gratuito. ~ of charge gratis. ● vt
(pt freed) (set at liberty) poner en
libertad; (relieve from) liberar (from/
of de); (untangle) desenredar.
~dom n libertad f. ~hold n
propiedad f absoluta. ~ kick n
tiro m libre. ~lance a & adv por

cuenta propia. ~ly adv
libremente. ~mason n masón m.
~-range a <eggs> de granja. ~
speech n libertad f de expresión.
~style n estilo m libre. ~way n
(Amer) autopista f

freez|e vt (pt froze, pp frozen)
helar; congelar <food, wages>.
● vi helarse; (become motionless)
quedarse inmóvil. ● n (on wages,
prices) congelación f. ~er n
congelador m. ~ing a glacial.
● n. ~ing (point) punto m de
congelación f. **below** ~ing bajo
cero

freight n (goods) mercancías fpl.
~er n buque m de carga

French a francés. ● n (Lang)
francés m. ● npl. the ~ (people) los
franceses. ~ fries npl patatas fpl
fritas, papas fpl fritas (LAm).
~man n francés m. ~ window n
puerta f ventana. ~woman f
francesa f

frenz|ied a frenético. ~y n
frenesí m

frequency n frecuencia f

frequent vt frecuentar. ● a
frecuente. ~ly adv
frecuentemente

fresh a (-er, -est) fresco; (different,
additional) nuevo; <water> dulce.
~en vi refrescar. □ ~en up vi
<person> refrescarse. ~er n
⚠ ⇒~man. ~ly adv
recientemente. ~man n
estudiante m de primer año.
~ness n frescura f

fret vi (pt fretted) preocuparse.
~ful a (discontented) quejoso;
(irritable) irritable

friction n fricción f

Friday n viernes m

fridge n ⚠ frigorífico m, nevera f,
refrigerador m (LAm)

fried ⇒FRY. ● a frito

friend n amigo m. ~**liness** n simpatía f. ~**ly** a (**-ier, -iest**) simpático. ~**ship** n amistad f

fries npl ⇒FRENCH FRIES

frieze n friso m

frigate n fragata f

fright n miedo m; (shock) susto m. ~**en** vt asustar. □ ~ **off** vt ahuyentar. ~**ened** a asustado. be ~**ened** tener miedo (**of** de.) ~**ful** a espantoso, horrible. ~**fully** adv terriblemente

frigid a frígido

frill n volante m, olán m (Mex). ~**s** npl (fig) adornos mpl. **with no** ~**s** sencillo

fringe n (sewing) fleco m; (ornamental border) franja f; (of hair) flequillo m, cerquillo m (LAm), fleco m (Mex); (of area) periferia f; (of society) margen m

fritter n. □ ~ **away** vt desperdiciar <time>; malgastar <money>

frivol|ity n frivolidad f. ~**ous** a frívolo

fro ⇒TO AND FRO

frock n vestido m

frog n rana f. **have a** ~ **in one's throat** tener carraspera. ~**man** n hombre m rana. ~**spawn** n huevos mpl de rana

frolic vi (pt **frolicked**) retozar

from prep de; (indicating starting point) desde; (habit, conviction) por; ~ **then on** a partir de ahí

front n parte f delantera; (of building) fachada f; (of clothes) delantera f; (Mil, Pol) frente f; (of book) principio m; (fig, appearance) apariencia f; (seafront) paseo m marítimo, malecón m (LAm). **in** ~ **of** delante de. ● a delantero; (first) primero. ~**al** a frontal; <attack> de frente. ~ **door** n puerta f principal

frontier n frontera f

front page n (of newspaper) primera plana f

frost n (freezing) helada f; (frozen dew) escarcha f. ~**bite** n congelación f. ~**bitten** a congelado. ~**ed** a <glass> esmerilado. ~**ing** n (Amer) glaseado m. ~**y** a <weather> helado; <night> de helada; (fig) glacial

froth n espuma f. ● vi espumar. ~**y** a espumoso

frown vi fruncir el entrecejo ● n ceño m. □ ~ **on** vt desaprobar.

froze ⇒FREEZE. ~**n** ⇒FREEZE. ● a congelado; <region> helado

frugal a frugal

fruit n (Bot, on tree, fig) fruto m; (as food) fruta f. ~**ful** a fértil; (fig) fructífero. ~**ion** n. **come to** ~**ion** realizarse. ~**less** a infructuoso. ~ **salad** n macedonia f de frutas. ~**y** a que sabe a fruta

frustrat|e vt frustrar. ~**ion** n frustración f. ~**ed** a frustrado. ~**ing** a frustrante

fry vt (pt **fried**) freír. ● vi freírse. ~**ing pan** n sartén f, sartén m (LAm)

fudge n dulce m de azúcar

fuel n combustible m

fugitive a & n fugitivo (m)

fulfil vt (pt **fulfilled**) cumplir (con) <promise, obligation>; satisfacer <condition>; hacer realidad <ambition>. ~**ment** n (of promise, obligation) cumplimiento m; (of conditions) satisfacción f; (of hopes, plans) realización f

full a (**-er, -est**) lleno; <bus, hotel> completo; <account> detallado. **at** ~ **speed** a máxima velocidad. **be** ~ (**up**) (with food) no poder más. ● n. **in** ~ sin quitar nada. **to the** ~ completamente. **write in** ~ escribir con todas las letras.

~**back** n (Sport) defensa m & f.
~**-blown** a verdadero. ~**-fledged**
a (Amer) ⇒FULLY-FLEDGED. ~
moon n luna f llena. ~**-scale** a
<*drawing*> de tamaño natural;
(fig) amplio. ~ **stop** n punto m.
~**-time** a <*employment*> de
jornada completa. ● adv a tiempo
completo. ~**y** adv
completamente. ~**-fledged** a
<*chick*> capaz de volar; <*lawyer,
nurse*> hecho y derecho

fulsome a excesivo

fumble vi buscar (a tientas)

fume vi despedir gases; (fig, be
furious) estar furioso. ~**s** npl gases
mpl

fumigate vt fumigar

fun n (amusement) diversión f;
(merriment) alegría f. **for** ~ en
broma. **have** ~ divertirse. **make** ~
of burlarse de

function n (purpose, duty) función f;
(reception) recepción f. ● vi
funcionar. ~**al** a funcional

fund n fondo m. ● vt financiar

fundamental a fundamental.
~**ist** a & n fundamentalista (m &
f)

funeral n entierro m, funerales
mpl. ~ **director** n director m de
pompas fúnebres

funfair n feria f; (permanent)
parque m de atracciones, parque
m de diversiones (LAm)

fungus n (pl **-gi**) hongo m

funnel n (for pouring) embudo m; (of
ship) chimenea f

funn|ily adv (oddly) curiosamente.
~**y** a (**-ier, -iest**) divertido,
gracioso; (odd) curioso, raro

fur n pelo m; (pelt) piel f

furious a furioso. ~**ly** adv
furiosamente

furlough n (Amer) permiso m. **on**
~ de permiso

furnace n horno m

furnish vt amueblar, amoblar
(LAm); (supply) proveer. ~**ings** npl
muebles mpl, mobiliario m

furniture n muebles mpl,
mobiliario m. **a piece of** ~ un
mueble

furrow n surco m

furry a peludo

furthe|r a más lejano; (additional)
nuevo. ● adv más lejos; (more)
además. ● vt fomentar. ~**rmore**
adv además. ~**st** a más lejano.
● adv más lejos

furtive a furtivo

fury n furia f

fuse vt (melt) fundir; (fig, unite)
fusionar. ~ **the lights** fundir los
plomos. ● vi fundirse; (fig)
fusionarse. ● n fusible m, plomo
m; (of bomb) mecha f. ~**box** n caja
f de fusibles

fuselage n fuselaje m

fusion n fusión f

fuss n (commotion) jaleo m. **kick up**
a ~ armar un lío, armar una
bronca. **make a** ~ **of** tratar con
mucha atención. ● vi
preocuparse. ~**y** a (**-ier, -iest**)
(finicky) remilgado; (demanding)
exigente

futil|e a inútil, vano. ~**ity** n
inutilidad f

futur|e a futuro. ● n futuro m. **in**
~**e** de ahora en adelante. ~**istic**
a futurista

fuzz n pelusa f. ~**y** a <*hair*>
crespo; <*photograph*> borroso

F

gab n. have the gift of the ~ tener un pico de oro

gabardine n gabardina f

gabble vi hablar atropelladamente

gable n aguilón m

gad vi (pt **gadded**). ~ about callejear

gadget n chisme m

Gaelic a & n gaélico (m)

gaffe n plancha f, metedura f de pata, metida f de pata (LAm)

gag n mordaza f; (joke) chiste m. ● vt (pt **gagged**) amordazar. ● vi hacer arcadas

gaiety n alegría f

gaily adv alegremente

gain vt ganar; (acquire) adquirir; (obtain) conseguir. ● vi <clock> adelantar. ● n ganancia f; (increase) aumento m

gait n modo m de andar

gala n fiesta f. ~ **performance** (función f de) gala f

galaxy n galaxia f

gale n vendaval m

gall n bilis f; (fig) hiel f; (impudence) descaro m

gallant a (brave) valiente; (chivalrous) galante. ~**ry** n valor m

gall bladder n vesícula f biliar

gallery n galería f

galley n (ship) galera f; (ship's kitchen) cocina f. ~ **(proof)** n galerada f

gallivant vi 🔢 callejear

gallon n galón m (imperial = 4,546l; Amer = 3,785l)

gallop n galope m. ● vi (pt **galloped**) galopar

gallows n horca f

galore a en abundancia

galvanize vt galvanizar

gamb|le vi jugar. ~**e on** contar con. ● vt jugarse. ● n (venture) empresa f arriesgada; (bet) apuesta f; (risk) riesgo m. ~**er** n jugador m. ~**ing** n juego m

game n juego m; (match) partido m; (animals, birds) caza f. ● a valiente. ~ **for** listo para. ~**keeper** n guardabosque m. ~**s** n (in school) deportes mpl. ~**s console** n consola f de videojuegos

gammon n jamón m fresco

gander n ganso m

gang n pandilla f; (of workmen) equipo m. □ ~ **up** vi unirse (**on** contra)

gangling a larguirucho

gangrene n gangrena f

gangster n bandido m, gángster m & f

gangway n pasillo m; (of ship) pasarela f

gaol n cárcel f. ~**er** n carcelero m

gap n espacio m; (in fence, hedge) hueco m; (in time) intervalo m; (in knowledge) laguna f; (difference) diferencia f

gap|e vi quedarse boquiabierto; (be wide open) estar muy abierto. ~**ing** a abierto; (person) boquiabierto

garage n garaje m, garage m (LAm), cochera f (Mex); (petrol station) gasolinera f; (for repairs, sales) taller m, garage m (LAm)

garbage n basura f. ~ **can** n (Amer) cubo m de la basura, bote

m de la basura (Mex). ~
collector, ~ **man** *n* (Amer)
basurero *m*

garble *vt* tergiversar, embrollar

garden *n* (of flowers) jardín *m*; (of vegetables/fruit) huerto *m*. ● *vi* trabajar en el jardín. ~**er** *n* jardinero *m*. ~**ing** *n* jardinería *f*; (vegetable growing) horticultura *f*

gargle *vi* hacer gárgaras

gargoyle *n* gárgola *f*

garish *a* chillón

garland *n* guirnalda *f*

garlic *n* ajo *m*

garment *n* prenda *f* (de vestir)

garnish *vt* adornar, decorar. ● *n* adorno *m*

garret *n* buhardilla *f*

garrison *n* guarnición *f*

garrulous *a* hablador

garter *n* liga *f*

gas *n* (*pl* **gases**) gas *m*; (anaesthetic) anestésico *m*; (Amer, petrol) gasolina *f*. ● *vt* (*pt* **gassed**) asfixiar con gas

gash *n* tajo *m*. ● *vt* hacer un tajo de

gasket *n* junta *f*

gas: ~ **mask** *n* careta *f* antigás.
~ **meter** *n* contador *m* de gas

gasoline *n* (Amer) gasolina *f*

gasp *vi* jadear; (with surprise) dar un grito ahogado. ● *n* exclamación *f*, grito *m*

gas: ~ **ring** *n* hornillo *m* de gas.
~ **station** *n* (Amer) gasolinera *f*

gastric *a* gástrico

gate *n* puerta *f*; (of metal) verja *f*; (barrier) barrera *f*

gate: ~**crash** *vt* colarse en.
~**crasher** *n* intruso *m* (*que ha entrado sin ser invitado*). ~**way** *n* puerta *f*

gather *vt* reunir <*people, things*>; (accumulate) acumular; (pick up)

recoger; recoger <*flowers*>; (fig, infer) deducir; (sewing) fruncir. ~
speed acelerar. ● *vi* <*people*>
reunirse; <*things*> acumularse.
~**ing** *n* reunión *f*

gaudy *a* (**-ier, -iest**) chillón

gauge *n* (measurement) medida *f*; (Rail) entrevía *f*; (instrument) indicador *m*. ● *vt* medir; (fig) estimar

gaunt *a* descarnado; (from illness) demacrado

gauntlet *n*. **run the** ~ **of** aguantar el acoso de

gauze *n* gasa *f*

gave ⇒GIVE

gawky *a* (**-ier, -iest**) torpe

gawp *vi*. ~ **at** mirar como un tonto

gay *a* (**-er, -est**) (🄸, homosexual) homosexual, gay 🄸; (dated, joyful) alegre

gaze *vi*. ~ (**at**) mirar (fijamente).
● *n* mirada *f* (fija)

gazelle *n* (*pl invar* or **-s**) gacela *f*

GB *abbr* ⇒GREAT BRITAIN

gear *n* equipo *m*; (Tec) engranaje *m*; (Auto) marcha *f*, cambio *m*. **in** ~ engranado. **out of** ~ desengranado. **change** ~, **shift** ~ (Amer) cambiar de marcha. ● *vt* adaptar. ~**box** *n* (Auto) caja *f* de cambios

geese ⇒GOOSE

gel *n* gel *m*

gelatine *n* gelatina *f*

gelignite *n* gelignita *f*

gem *n* piedra *f* preciosa

Gemini *n* Géminis *mpl*

gender *n* género *m*

gene *n* gen *m*, gene *m*

genealogy *n* genealogía *f*

general *a* general. ● *n* general *m*.
in ~ en general. ~ **election** *n* elecciones *fpl* generales.
~**ization** *n* generalización *f*.

G

~ize vt/i generalizar. **~ knowledge** n cultura f general. **~ly** adv generalmente. **~ practitioner** n médico m de cabecera

generat|e vt generar. **~ion** n generación f. **~ion gap** n brecha f generacional. **~or** n generador m

genero|sity n generosidad f. **~us** a generoso; (plentiful) abundante

genetic a genético. **~s** n genética f

Geneva n Ginebra f

genial a simpático, afable

genital a genital. **~s** npl genitales mpl

genitive a & n genitivo (m)

genius n (pl **-uses**) genio m

genocide n genocidio m

genome n genoma m

genre n género m

gent n 🔲 señor m. **~s** n aseo m de caballeros

genteel a distinguido

gentl|e a (**-er, -est**) <person> dulce; <murmur, breeze> suave; <hint> discreto. **~eman** n señor m; (well-bred) caballero m. **~eness** n amabilidad f

genuine a verdadero; <person> sincero

geograph|er n geógrafo m. **~ical** a geográfico. **~y** n geografía f

geolog|ical a geológico. **~ist** n geólogo m. **~y** n geología f

geometr|ic(al) a geométrico. **~y** n geometría f

geranium n geranio m

geriatric a <patient> anciano; <ward> de geriatría. **~s** n geriatría f

germ n microbio m, germen m

German a & n alemán (m). **~ic** a germánico. **~ measles** n rubéola f. **~y** n Alemania f

germinate vi germinar

gesticulate vi hacer ademanes, gesticular

gesture n gesto m, ademán m; (fig) gesto m. ● vi hacer gestos

....

get

past **got**; past participle **got, gotten** (Amer); present participle **getting**

● transitive verb

····▸ (obtain) conseguir, obtener. **did you get the job?** ¿conseguiste el trabajo?

····▸ (buy) comprar. **I got it in the sales** lo compré en las rebajas

····▸ (achieve, win) sacar. **she got very good marks** sacó muy buenas notas

····▸ (receive) recibir. **I got a letter from Alex** recibí una carta de Alex

····▸ (fetch) ir a buscar. **~ your coat** vete a buscar tu abrigo

····▸ (experience) llevarse. **I got a terrible shock** me llevé un shock espantoso

····▸ (🔲, understand) entender. **I don't ~ what you mean** no entiendo lo que quieres decir

····▸ (ask or persuade) **to ~ s.o. to do sth** hacer que uno haga algo

Note that *hacer que* is followed by the subjunctive form of the verb

····▸ (cause to be done or happen) **I must ~ this watch fixed** tengo quellevar a arreglar este reloj. **they got the roof mended** hicieron arreglar el techo

● intransitive verb

····▶ (arrive, reach) llegar. **I got there late** llegué tarde. **how do you ~ to Paddington?** ¿cómo se llega a Paddington?

····▶ (become) **to ~ tired** cansarse. **she got very angry** se puso furiosa. **it's ~ting late** se está haciendo tarde

⟹ For translations of expressions such as **get better, get old** see entries **better, old** etc. See also **got**

····▶ **to get to do sth** (manage to) llegar a. **did you ~ to see him?** ¿llegaste a verlo?

□ **get along** vi (manage) arreglárselas; (progress) hacer progresos. □ **get along with** vt llevarse bien con. □ **get at** vt (reach) llegar a; (imply) querer decir. □ **get away** vi salir; (escape) escaparse. □ **get back** vi volver. vt (recover) recobrar. □ **get by** vi (manage) arreglárselas; (pass) pasar. □ **get down** vi bajar. vt (make depressed) deprimir. □ **get in** vi entrar. □ **get into** vt entrar en; subir a <car> □ **get off** vt bajar(se) de <train etc>. vi (from train etc) bajarse; (Jurid) salir absuelto. □ **get on** vi (progress) hacer progresos; (succeed) tener éxito. vt subirse a <train etc>. □ **get on with** vt (be on good terms with) llevarse bien con; (continue) seguir con. □ **get out** vi salir. vt (take out) sacar. □ **get out of** vt (fig) librarse de. □ **get over** vt reponerse de <illness>. □ **get round** vt soslayar <difficulty etc>; engatusar <person>. □ **get through** vi pasar; (on phone) comunicarse (**to** con). □ **get together** vi (meet up) reunirse. vt (assemble) reunir. □ **get up** vi levantarse; (climb) subir

geyser n géiser m

ghastly a (-ier, -iest) horrible

gherkin n pepinillo m

ghetto n (pl -os) gueto m

ghost n fantasma m. **~ly** a espectral

giant n gigante m. ● a gigantesco

gibberish n jerigonza f

gibe n pulla f

giblets npl menudillos mpl

gidd|iness n vértigo m. **~y** a (-ier, -iest) mareado. **be/feel ~y** estar/sentirse mareado

gift n regalo m; (ability) don m. **~ed** a dotado de talento. **~-wrap** vt envolver para regalo

gigantic a gigantesco

giggle vi reírse tontamente. ● n risita f

gild vt dorar

gills npl agallas fpl

gilt n dorado m. ● a dorado

gimmick n truco m

gin n ginebra f

ginger n jengibre m. ● a rojizo. **he has ~ hair** es pelirrojo. **~bread** n pan m de jengibre

gipsy n gitano m

giraffe n jirafa f

girder n viga f

girdle n (belt) cinturón m; (corset) corsé m

girl n chica f, muchacha f; (child) niña f. **~friend** n amiga f; (of boy) novia f. **~ish** a de niña; <boy> afeminado. **~ scout** n (Amer) exploradora f, guía f

giro n (pl -os) giro m (bancario)

girth n circunferencia f

gist n lo esencial

give vt (pt **gave**, pp **given**) dar; (deliver) entregar; regalar <present>; prestar <aid, attention>. **~ o.s. to** darse a. ● vi dar; (yield) ceder; (stretch) dar de sí. ● n elasticidad f. □ **~ away** vt regalar; revelar <*secret*>. □ ~ **back** vt devolver. □ ~ **in** vi ceder. □ ~ **off** vt emitir. □ ~ **out** vt distribuir. (become used up) agotarse. □ ~ **up** vt renunciar a; (yield) ceder. ~ **up doing sth** dejar de hacer algo. ~ **o.s. up** entregarse (**to** a). vi rendirse. ~n ⇨GIVE. ● a dado. ~n **name** n nombre m de pila

glacier n glaciar m

glad a contento. be ~ alegrarse (**about** de). ~**den** vt alegrar

gladly adv alegremente; (willingly) con mucho gusto

glamo|rous a glamoroso. ~**ur** n glamour m

glance n ojeada f. ● vi. ~ **at** dar un vistazo a

gland n glándula f

glar|e vi <*light*> deslumbrar; (stare angrily) mirar airadamente. ● n resplandor m; (stare) mirada f airada. ~**ing** a deslumbrante; (obvious) manifiesto

glass n (material) cristal m, vidrio m; (without stem or for wine) vaso m; (with stem) copa f; (for beer) caña f; (mirror) espejo m. ~**es** npl (spectacles) gafas fpl, lentes fpl (LAm), anteojos mpl (LAm). ~**y** a vítreo

glaze vt poner cristal(es) or vidrio(s) a <*windows, doors*>; vidriar <*pottery*>. ● vi. ~ (**over**) <*eyes*> vidriarse. ● n barniz m; (for pottery) esmalte m

gleam n destello m. ● vi destellar

glean vt espigar; recoger <*information*>

glee n regocijo m

glib a de mucha labia; <*reply*> fácil

glid|e vi deslizarse; (plane) planear. ~**er** n planeador m. ~**ing** n planeo m

glimmer n destello m. ● vi destellar

glimpse n. catch a ~ of vislumbrar, ver brevemente. ● vt vislumbrar

glint n destello m. ● vi destellar

glisten vi brillar

glitter vi brillar. ● n brillo m

gloat vi. ~ **on/over** regodearse sobre

glob|al a (worldwide) mundial; (all-embracing) global. ~**al warming** n calentamiento m global. ~**e** n globo m

gloom n oscuridad f; (sadness, fig) tristeza f. ~**y** a (**-ier**, **-iest**) triste; (pessimistic) pesimista

glor|ify vt glorificar. ~**ious** a espléndido; <*deed, hero etc*> glorioso. ~**y** n gloria f

gloss n lustre m. ~ (**paint**) (pintura f al or de) esmalte m. □ ~ **over** vt (make light of) minimizar; (cover up) encubrir

glossary n glosario m

glossy a brillante

glove n guante m. ~ **compartment** n (Auto) guantera f, gaveta f

glow vi brillar. ● n brillo m. ~**ing** a incandescente; <*account*> entusiasta; <*complexion*> rojo

glucose n glucosa f

glue n cola f, goma f de pegar. ● vt (pres p gluing) pegar

glum a (**glummer**, **glummest**) triste

glutton n glotón m

gnarled a nudoso

gnash vt. ~ **one's teeth** rechinar los dientes

gnat n jején m, mosquito m

gnaw vt roer. ● vi. ~ **at** roer

gnome n gnomo m

----

go

3rd pers sing present **goes**; past **went**; past participle **gone**

● *intransitive verb*

····▶ ir. **I'm going to France** voy a Francia. **to go shopping** ir de compras. **to go swimming** ir a nadar

····▶ (leave) irse. **we're going on Friday** nos vamos el viernes

····▶ (work, function) <*engine, clock*> funcionar

····▶ (become) **to go deaf** quedarse sordo. **to go mad** volverse loco. **his face went red** se puso colorado

····▶ (stop) <*headache, pain*> irse (+ me/te/le). **the pain's gone** se me ha ido el dolor

····▶ (turn out, progress) ir. **everything's going very well** todo va muy bien. **how did the exam go?** ¿qué tal te fue en el examen?

····▶ (match, suit) combinar. **the jacket and the trousers go well together** la chaqueta y los pantalones combinan bien.

····▶ (cease to function) <*bulb, fuse*> fundirse. **the brakes have gone** los frenos no funcionan

● *auxiliary verb*

to be going to + *infinitive* ir a + *infinitivo*. **it's going to rain** va a llover. **she's going to win!** ¡va a ganar!

● *noun* (*pl* **goes**)

····▶ (turn) turno m. **you have three goes** tienes tres turnos. **it's your go** te toca a ti

····▶ (attempt) **to have a go at doing sth** intentar hacer algo. **have another go** inténtalo de nuevo

····▶ (energy, drive) empuje m. **she has a lot of go** tiene mucho empuje

····▶ (in phrases) **I've been on the go all day** no he parado en todo el día. **to make a go of sth** sacar algo adelante

□ **go across** *vt/vi* cruzar. □ **go after** *vt* perseguir. □ **go away** *vi* irse. □ **go back** *vi* volver. □ **go back on** *vt* faltar a <*promise etc*>. □ **go by** *vi* pasar. □ **go down** *vt* bajar; <*sun*> ponerse. □ **go for** *vt* (🄵, attack) atacar. □ **go in** *vi* entrar. □ **go in for** *vt* presentarse para <*exam*>; participar en <*competition*>. □ **go off** *vi* (leave) irse; (go bad) pasarse; (explode) estallar; <*lights*> apagarse. □ **go on** *vi* seguir; (happen) pasar; (be switched on) encenderse, prenderse (LAm). □ **go out** *vi* salir; <*fire, light*> apagarse. □ **go over** *vt* (check) revisar; (revise) repasar. □ **go through** *vt* pasar por; (search) registrar; (check) examinar. □ **go up** *vi/vt* subir. □ **go without** *vt* pasar sin

----

goad *vt* aguijonear

go-ahead *n* luz *f* verde. ● *a* dinámico

goal *n* (Sport) gol *m*; (objective) meta *f*. ∼**ie** *n* 🄵, ∼**keeper** *n* portero *m*, arquero *m* (LAm). ∼**post** *n* poste *m* de la portería, poste *m* del arco (LAm)

goat *n* cabra *f*

gobble *vt* engullir

goblin *n* duende *m*

god *n* dios *m*. **G**∼ *n* Dios *m*. ∼**child** *n* ahijado *m*. ∼**-daughter** *n* ahijada *f*. ∼**dess** *n* diosa *f*. ∼**father** *n* padrino *m*. ∼**forsaken** *a* olvidado de Dios. ∼**mother** *n* madrina *f*. ∼**send** *n*

G

beneficio *m* inesperado. ~**son** *n* ahijado *m*

going *n* camino *m*; (racing) (estado *m* del) terreno *m*. **it is slow/hard** ~ es lento/difícil. ● *a* <*price*> actual; <*concern*> en funcionamiento

gold *n* oro *m*. ● *a* de oro. ~**en** *a* de oro; (in colour) dorado; <*opportunity*> único. ~**en wedding** *n* bodas *fpl* de oro. ~**fish** *n invar* pez *m* de colores. ~**mine** *n* mina *f* de oro; (fig) fuente *f* de gran riqueza. ~**plated** *a* chapado en oro. ~**smith** *n* orfebre *m*

golf *n* golf *m*. ~ **ball** *n* pelota *f* de golf. ~ **club** *n* palo *m* de golf; (place) club *m* de golf. ~**course** *n* campo *m* de golf. ~**er** *n* jugador *m* de golf

gondola *n* góndola *f*

gone ⇒GO. ● *a* pasado. ~ **six o'clock** después de las seis

gong *n* gong(o) *m*

good *a* (**better, best**) bueno, (*before masculine singular noun*) buen. ~ **afternoon** buenas tardes. ~ **evening** (before dark) buenas tardes; (after dark) buenas noches. ~ **morning** buenos días. ~ **night** buenas noches. **as** ~ **as** (almost) casi. **feel** ~ sentirse bien. **have a** ~ **time** divertirse. ● *n* bien *m*. **for** ~ para siempre. **it is no** ~ **shouting** es inútil gritar *etc.* ~**bye** *int* ¡adiós! ● *n* adiós *m*. **say** ~**bye to** despedirse de. ~**-for-nothing** *a* & *n* inútil (*m*). **G**~ **Friday** *n* Viernes *m* Santo. ~**looking** *a* guapo, buen mozo *m* (LAm), buena moza *f* (LAm). ~**ness** *n* bondad *f*. ~**ness!**, ~**ness gracious!**, ~**ness me!, my** ~**ness!** ¡Dios mío! ~**s** *npl* mercancías *fpl*. ~**will** *n* buena voluntad *f*. ~**y** *n*

(Culin, 🔢) golosina *f*; (in film) bueno *m*

gooey *a* (**gooier, gooiest**) 🔢 pegajoso; (fig) sentimental

goofy *a* (Amer) necio

goose *n* (*pl* **geese**) oca *f*, ganso *m*. ~**berry** *n* uva *f* espina, grosella *f* espinosa. ~**flesh** *n*, ~**pimples** *npl* carne *f* de gallina

gore *n* sangre *f*. ● *vt* cornear

gorge *n* (Geog) garganta *f*. ● *vt*. ~ **o.s.** hartarse (**on** de)

gorgeous *a* precioso; (splendid) magnífico

gorilla *n* gorila *m*

gorse *n* aulaga *f*

gory *a* (**-ier, -iest**) 🔢 sangriento

gosh *int* ¡caramba!

go-slow *n* huelga *f* de celo, huelga *f* pasiva

gospel *n* evangelio *m*

gossip *n* (chatter) chismorreo *m*; (person) chismoso *m*. ● *vi* (*pt* **gossiped**) (chatter) chismorrear; (repeat scandal) conta chismes

got ⇒GET. **have** ~ tener. **I've** ~ **to do it** tengo quehacerlo.

gotten ⇒GET

gouge *vt* abrir <*hole*>. ▫ ~ **out** *vt* sacar

gourmet *n* gastrónomo *m*

govern *vt/i* gobernar. ~**ess** *n* institutriz *f*. ~**ment** *n* gobierno *m*. ~**or** *n* gobernador *m*

gown *n* vestido *m*; (of judge, teacher) toga *f*

GP *abbr* ⇒GENERAL PRACTITIONER

grab *vt* (*pt* **grabbed**) agarrar

grace *n* gracia *f*. ~**ful** *a* elegante

gracious *a* (kind) amable; (elegant) elegante

grade *n* clase *f*, categoría *f*; (of goods) clase *f*, calidad *f*; (on scale) grado *m*; (school mark) nota *f*; (Amer, class) curso *m*, año *m*

gradient n pendiente f, gradiente f (LAm)

gradual a gradual. ~**ly** adv gradualmente, poco a poco

graduat|e n (Univ) licenciado. ● vi licenciarse. ~**ion** n graduación f

graffiti npl graffiti mpl, pintadas fpl

graft n (Med, Bot) injerto m; (Amer 🄸, bribery) chanchullos mpl. ● vt injertar

grain n grano m

gram n gramo m

gramma|r n gramática f. ~**tical** a gramatical

gramme n gramo m

grand a (-er, -est) magnífico; (🄸, excellent) estupendo. ~**child** n nieto m. ~**daughter** n nieta f. ~**eur** n grandiosidad f. ~**father** n abuelo m. ~**father clock** n reloj m de caja. ~**iose** a grandioso. ~**mother** n abuela f. ~**parents** npl abuelos mpl. ~**piano** n piano m de cola. ~**son** n nieto m. ~**stand** n tribuna f

granite n granito m

granny n 🄸 abuela f

grant vt conceder; (give) donar; (admit) admitir (**that** que). **take for ~ed** dar por sentado. ● n concesión f; (Univ) beca f

granule n gránulo m

grape n uva f. ~**fruit** n invar pomelo m, toronja f (LAm)

graph n gráfica f

graphic a gráfico. ~**s** npl diseño m gráfico; (Comp) gráficos mpl

grapple vi. ~ **with** forcejear con; (mentally) lidiar con

grasp vt agarrar. ● n (hold) agarro m; (fig) comprensión f. ~**ing** a avaro

grass n hierba f. ~**hopper** n saltamontes m. ~ **roots** npl base f popular. ● a de las bases. ~**y** a cubierto de hierba

grate n rejilla f; (fireplace) chimenea f. ● vt rallar. ● vi rechinar; (be irritating) ser crispante

grateful a agradecido. ~**ly** adv con gratitud

grater n rallador m

gratif|ied a contento. ~**y** vt satisfacer; (please) agradar a. ~**ying** a agradable

grating n reja f

gratitude n gratitud f

gratuitous a gratuito

gratuity n (tip) propina f

grave n sepultura f. ● a (-er, -est) (serious) grave

gravel n grava f

gravely adv (seriously) seriamente; (solemnly) con gravedad

grave: ~stone n lápida f. ~**yard** n cementerio m

gravitate vi gravitar

gravity n gravedad f

gravy n salsa f

gray a & n (Amer) ⇒GREY

graze vi (eat) pacer. ● vt (touch) rozar; (scrape) raspar. ● n rasguño m

greas|e n grasa f. ● vt engrasar. ~**eproof paper** n papel m encerado or de cera. ~**y** a <hands> grasiento; <food> graso; <hair, skin> graso, grasoso (LAm)

great a (-er, -est) grande, (before singular noun) gran; (🄸, very good) estupendo. **G~ Britain** n Gran Bretaña f. ~**grandfather** n bisabuelo m. ~**grandmother** n bisabuela f. ~**ly** adv (very) muy; (much) mucho

Greece n Grecia f

greed n avaricia f; (for food) glotonería f. ~**y** a avaro; (for food) glotón

Greek a & n griego (m)

green *a* (**-er, -est**) verde. ● *n* verde *m*; (grass) césped *m*. ~ **belt** *n* zona *f* verde. ~ **card** *n* (Amer) permiso *m* de residencia y trabajo. ~**ery** *n* verdor *m*. ~**gage** *n* claudia *f*. ~**grocer** *n* verdulero *m*. ~**house** *n* invernadero *m*. **the** ~**house effect** el efecto invernadero. ~ **light** *n* luz *f* verde. ~**s** *npl* verduras *fpl*

greet *vt* saludar; (receive) recibir. ~**ing** *n* saludo *m*

gregarious *a* gregario; <person> sociable

grenade *n* granada *f*

grew ⇒GROW

grey *a* (**-er, -est**) gris. **have** ~ **hair** ser canoso. ● *n* gris *m*. ~**hound** *n* galgo *m*

grid *n* reja *f*; (Elec, network) red *f*; (on map) cuadriculado *m*

grief *n* dolor *m*. **come to** ~ <person> acabar mal; (fail) fracasar

grievance *n* queja *f* formal

grieve *vt* apenar. ● *vi* afligirse. ~ **for** llorar

grievous *a* doloroso; (serious) grave. ~ **bodily harm** (Jurid) lesiones *fpl* (corporales) graves

grill *n* parrilla *f*. ● *vt* asar a la parrilla; (⏹, interrogate) interrogar

grille *n* rejilla *f*

grim *a* (**grimmer, grimmest**) severo

grimace *n* mueca *f*. ● *vi* hacer muecas

grim|e *n* mugre *f*. ~**y** *a* mugriento

grin *vt* (*pt* **grinned**) sonreír. ● *n* sonrisa *f* (abierta)

grind *vt* (*pt* **ground**) moler <coffee, corn etc>; (pulverize) pulverizar; (sharpen) afilar; (Amer) picar, moler <meat>

grip *vt* (*pt* **gripped**) agarrar; (interest) captar. ● *n* (hold) agarro *m*; (strength of hand) apretón *m*; (hairgrip) horquilla *f*, pasador *m* (Mex). **come to** ~**s with** entender <subject>

grisly *a* (**-ier, -iest**) horrible

gristle *n* cartílago *m*

grit *n* arenilla *f*; (fig) agallas *fpl*. ● *vt* (*pt* **gritted**) echar arena en <road>. ~ **one's teeth** (fig) acorazarse

groan *vi* gemir. ● *n* gemido *m*

grocer *n* tendero *m*, abarrotero *m* (Mex). ~**ies** *npl* comestibles *mpl*. ~**y** *n* tienda *f* de comestibles, tienda *f* de abarrotes (Mex)

groggy *a* (weak) débil; (unsteady) inseguro; (ill) malucho

groin *n* ingle *f*

groom *n* mozo *m* de caballos; (bridegroom) novio *m*. ● *vt* almohazar <horses>; (fig) preparar

groove *n* ranura *f*; (in record) surco *m*

grope *vi* (find one's way) moverse a tientas. ~ **for** buscar a tientas

gross *a* (**-er, -est**) (coarse) grosero; (Com) bruto; (fat) grueso; (flagrant) flagrante. ● *n invar* gruesa *f*. ~**ly** *adv* (very) enormemente

grotesque *a* grotesco

ground ⇒GRIND. ● *n* suelo *m*; (area) terreno *m*; (reason) razón *f*; (Amer, Elec) toma *f* de tierra. ● *vt* fundar <theory>; retirar del servicio <aircraft>. ~**s** *npl* jardines *mpl*; (sediment) poso *m*. ~ **beef** *n* (Amer) carne *f* picada, carne *f* molida. ~ **cloth** *n* (Amer) ⇒~sheet. ~ **floor** *n* planta *f* baja. ~**ing** *n* base *f*, conocimientos *mpl* (in de). ~**less** *a* infundado. ~**sheet** *n* suelo *m* impermeable (de una tienda de campaña). **∼work** n trabajo m preparatorio

group n grupo m. ● vt agrupar. ● vi agruparse

grouse n invar (bird) urogallo m. ● vi ⚡ rezongar

grovel vi (pt grovelled) postrarse; (fig) arrastrarse

grow vi (pt grew, pp grown) crecer; (become) volverse, ponerse. ● vt cultivar. **∼ a beard** dejarse (crecer) la barba. □ **∼ up** vi hacerse mayor. **∼ing** a <quantity> cada vez mayor; <influence> creciente

growl vi gruñir. ● n gruñido m

grown ⇒GROW. ● a adulto. **∼-up** a & n adulto (m)

growth n crecimiento m; (increase) aumento m; (development) desarrollo m; (Med) bulto m, tumor m

grub n (larva) larva f; (⚡, food) comida f

grubby a (-ier, -iest) mugriento

grudge vt ⇒BEGRUDGE. ● n rencilla f. **bear/have a ∼e against s.o.** guardarle rencor a uno. **∼ingly** adv de mala gana

gruelling a agotador

gruesome a horrible

gruff a (-er, -est) <manners> brusco; <voice> ronco

grumble vi rezongar

grumpy a (-ier, -iest) malhumorado

grunt vi gruñir. ● n gruñido m

guarant|ee n garantía f. ● vt garantizar. **∼or** n garante m & f

guard vt proteger; (watch) vigilar. ● n (vigilance, Mil group) guardia f; (person) guardia m; (on train) jefe m de tren. □ **∼ against** vt evitar; protegerse contra <risk>. **∼ed** a cauteloso. **∼ian** n guardián m; (of orphan) tutor m

Guatemala n Guatemala f. **∼n** a & n guatemalteco (m)

guer(r)illa n guerrillero m. **∼ warfare** n guerrilla f

guess vt adivinar; (Amer, suppose) suponer. ● n conjetura f. **∼work** n conjeturas fpl

guest n invitado m; (in hotel) huésped m. **∼ house** n casa f de huéspedes

guffaw n carcajada f. ● vi reírse a carcajadas

guidance n (advice) consejos mpl; (information) información f

guide n (person) guía m & f; (book) guía f. **Girl G∼** exploradora f, guía f. ● vt guiar. **∼book** n guía f. **∼ dog** n perro m guía, perro m lazarillo. **∼d missile** n proyectil m teledirigido. **∼lines** npl pauta f

guild n gremio m

guile n astucia f

guillotine n guillotina f

guilt n culpa f; (Jurid) culpabilidad f. **∼y** a culpable

guinea pig n (also fig) cobaya f

guitar n guitarra f. **∼ist** n guitarrista m & f

gulf n (part of sea) golfo m; (gap) abismo m

gull n gaviota f

gullet n garganta f, gaznate m ⚡

gullible a crédulo

gully n (ravine) barranco m

gulp vt. □ **∼ (down)** tragarse de prisa. ● vi tragar saliva. ● n trago m

gum n (Anat) encía f; (glue) goma f de pegar; (for chewing) chicle m. ● vt (pt gummed) engomar

gun n (pistol) pistola f; (rifle) fusil m, escopeta f; (artillery piece) cañón m. ● vt (pt gunned). □ **∼ down** vt abatir a tiros. **∼fire** n tiros mpl.

~**man** n pistolero m, gatillero m
(Mex). ~**powder** n pólvora f.
~**shot** n disparo m

gurgle vi <*liquid*> gorgotear;
<*baby*> gorjear

gush vi. ~ (**out**) salir a
borbotones. ● n (of liquid) chorro
m; (fig) torrente m

gusset n entretela f

gust n ráfaga f

gusto n entusiasmo m

gusty a borrascoso

gut n intestino m. ● vt (pt
gutted) destripar; <*fire*> destruir.
~**s** npl tripas fpl; (🅸, courage)
agallas fpl

gutter n (on roof) canalón m,
canaleta f; (in street) cuneta f; (fig,
🅇) arroyo m

guttural a gutural

guy n (🅸, man) tipo m 🅸, tío m 🅸

guzzle vt (drink) chupar 🅸; (eat)
tragarse

gym n 🅸 (gymnasium) gimnasio m;
(gymnastics) gimnasia f

gymnasium n gimnasio m

gymnast n gimnasta m & f. ~**ics**
npl gimnasia f

gymslip n túnica f (de gimnasia)

gynaecolog|ist n ginecólogo m.
~**y** n ginecología f

gypsy n gitano m

gyrate vi girar

haberdashery n mercería f;
(Amer, clothes) ropa f y accesorios
mpl para caballeros

habit n costumbre f; (Relig, costume)
hábito m. **be in the** ~ **of** (+
gerund) tener la costumbre de (+
infinitivo), soler (+ infinitivo). **get
into the** ~ **of** (+ gerund)
acostumbrarse a (+ infinitivo)

habitable a habitable

habitat n hábitat m

habitation n habitación f

habitual a habitual; <*liar*>
inveterado. ~**ly** adv de
costumbre

hack n (old horse) jamelgo m;
(writer) escritorzuelo m. ● vt
cortar. ~**er** n (Comp) pirata m
informático

hackneyed a manido

had ⇒HAVE

haddock n invar eglefino m

haemorrhage n hemorragia f

hag n bruja f

haggard a demacrado

hail n granizo m. ● vi granizar.
● vt (greet) saludar; llamar <*taxi*>.
□ ~ **from** vt venir de. ~**stone** n
grano m de granizo

hair n pelo m. ~**band** n cinta f,
banda f (Mex). ~**brush** n cepillo
m (para el pelo). ~**cut** n corte m
de pelo. **have a** ~**cut** cortarse el
pelo. ~**do** n 🅸 peinado m.
~**dresser** n peluquero m.
~**dresser's** (**shop**) n peluquería
f. ~**dryer** n secador m, secadora

f (Mex). **~grip** *n* horquilla *f*, pasador *m* (Mex). **~pin** *n* horquilla *f*. **~pin bend** *n* curva *f* cerrada. **~raising** *a* espeluznante. **~spray** *n* laca *f*, fijador *m* (para el pelo). **~style** *n* peinado *m*. **~y** *a* (**-ier**, **-iest**) peludo

half *n* (*pl* **halves**) mitad *f*. ● *a* medio. **~ a dozen** media docena *f*. **~ an hour** media hora *f*. ● *adv* medio, a medias. **~-hearted** *a* poco entusiasta. **~-mast** *n*. at **~-mast** a media asta. **~ term** *n* vacaciones *fpl* de medio trimestre. **~-time** *n* (Sport) descanso *m*, medio tiempo *m* (LAm). **~way** *a* medio. ● *adv* a medio camino

hall *n* (entrance) vestíbulo *m*; (for public events) sala *f*, salón *m*. **~ of residence** residencia *f* universitaria, colegio *m* mayor. **~mark** *n* (on gold, silver) contraste *m*; (fig) sello *m* (distintivo)

Hallowe'en *n* víspera *f* de Todos los Santos

hallucination *n* alucinación *f*

halo *n* (*pl* **-oes**) aureola *f*

halt *n*. **come to a ~** pararse. ● *vt* parar. ● *vi* pararse

halve *vt* reducir a la mitad; (divide into halves) partir por la mitad

halves ⇒HALF

ham *n* jamón *m*

hamburger *n* hamburguesa *f*

hammer *n* martillo *m*. ● *vt* martill(e)ar

hammock *n* hamaca *f*

hamper *n* cesta *f*. ● *vt* estorbar

hamster *n* hámster *m*

hand *n* mano *f*; (of clock, watch) manecilla *f*; (worker) obrero *m*. **by ~** a mano. **lend a ~** echar una mano. **on ~** a mano. **on the one ~... on the other ~** por un lado...

por otro. **out of ~** fuera de control. **to ~** a mano. ● *vt* pasar. □ **~ down** *vt* pasar. □ **~ in** *vt* entregar. □ **~ over** *vt* entregar. □ **~ out** *vt* distribuir. **~bag** *n* bolso *m*, cartera *f* (LAm), bolsa *f* (Mex). **~brake** *n* (in car) freno *m* de mano. **~cuffs** *npl* esposas *fpl*. **~ful** *n* puñado *m*; (🔢, person) persona *f* difícil

handicap *n* desventaja *f*; (Sport) hándicap *m*. **~ped** *a* minusválido

handicraft *n* artesanía *f*

handkerchief *n* (*pl* **-fs** or **-chieves**) pañuelo *m*

handle *n* (of door) picaporte *m*; (of drawer) tirador *m*; (of implement) mango *m*; (of cup, bag, jug) asa *f*. ● *vt* manejar; (touch) tocar. **~bars** *npl* manillar *m*, manubrio *m* (LAm).

handout *n* folleto *m*; (of money, food) dádiva *f*

hands-free *adj* manos libres *a invar*

handshake *n* apretón *m* de manos

handsome *a* (good-looking) guapo, buen mozo, buena moza (LAm); (generous) generoso

handwriting *n* letra *f*

handy *a* (**-ier**, **-iest**) (useful) práctico; <*person*> diestro; (near) a mano. **come in ~** venir muy bien. **~man** *n* hombre *m* habilidoso

hang *vt* (*pt* **hung**) colgar; (*pt* **hanged**) (capital punishment) ahorcar. ● *vi* colgar; <*clothing*> caer. ● *n*. **get the ~ of sth** coger el truco de algo. □ **~ about**, **~ around** *vi* holgazanear. □ **~ on** *vi* (wait) esperar. □ **~ out** *vt* tender <*washing*>. □ **~ up** *vi* (also telephone) colgar

hangar *n* hangar *m*

hang: **~er** *n* (for clothes) percha *f*. **~-glider** *n* alta *f* delta, deslizador m (Mex). ~**over** (after drinking) resaca f. ~-**up** n 🆒 complejo m

hankie, hanky n 🆒 pañuelo m

haphazard a fortuito. ~**ly** adv al azar

happen vi pasar, suceder, ocurrir. **if he ~s to come** si acaso viene. ~**ing** n acontecimiento m

happ|ily adv alegremente; (fortunately) afortunadamente. ~**iness** n felicidad f. ~**y** a (-ier, -iest) feliz; (satisfied) contento

harass vt acosar. ~**ment** n acoso m

harbour n puerto m

hard a (-er, -est) duro; (difficult) difícil. ● adv <work> mucho; (pull) con fuerza. ~ **done by** tratado injustamente. ~-**boiled egg** n huevo m duro. ~ **disk** n disco m duro. ~**en** vt endurecer. ● vi endurecerse. ~-**headed** a realista

hardly adv apenas. ~ **ever** casi nunca

hard: ~**ness** n dureza f. ~**ship** n apuro m. ~ **shoulder** n arcén m, acotamiento m (Mex). ~**ware** n ferretería f; (Comp) hardware m. ~**ware store** n (Amer) ferretería f. ~-**working** a trabajador

hardy a (-ier, -iest) fuerte; (Bot) resistente

hare n liebre f

hark vi escuchar. □ ~ **back to** vt volver a

harm n daño m. **there is no ~ in asking** con preguntar no se pierde nada. ● vt hacer daño a <person>; dañar <thing>; perjudicar <interests>. ~**ful** a perjudicial. ~**less** a inofensivo

harmonica n armónica f

harmon|ious a armonioso. ~**y** n armonía f

harness n arnés m. ● vt poner el arnés a <horse>; (fig) aprovechar

harp n arpa f. ● vi. ~ **on** (**about**) machacar (con)

harpoon n arpón m

harpsichord n clavicémbalo m, clave m

harrowing a desgarrador

harsh a (-er, -est) duro, severo; <light> fuerte; <climate> riguroso. ~**ly** adv severamente. ~**ness** n severidad f

harvest n cosecha f. ● vt cosechar

has ⇒HAVE

hassle n 🆒 lío m 🆒, rollo m 🆒. ● vt (harass) fastidiar

hast|e n prisa f, apuro m (LAm). **make ~e** darse prisa. ~**ily** adv de prisa. ~**y** a (-ier, -iest) rápido; (rash) precipitado

hat n sombrero m

hatch n (for food) ventanilla f; (Naut) escotilla f. ● vt empollar <eggs>; tramar <plot>. ● vi salir del cascarón. ~**back** n coche m con tres/cinco puertas; (door) puerta f trasera

hatchet n hacha f

hat|e n odio m. ● vt odiar. ~**eful** a odioso. ~**red** n odio m

haughty a (-ier, -iest) altivo

haul vt arrastrar; transportar <goods>. ● n (catch) redada f; (stolen goods) botín m; (journey) recorrido m. ~**age** n transporte m. ~**er** (Amer), ~**ier** n transportista m & f

haunt vt frecuentar; <ghost> rondar. ● n sitio m preferido. ~**ed** a <house> embrujado; <look> angustiado

have

3rd pers sing present **has**; past **had**

●*transitive verb*

····▸ tener. **I ~ three sisters** tengo tres hermanas. **do you ~ a credit card?** ¿tiene una tarjeta de crédito?

····▸ (in requests) **can I ~ a kilo of apples, please?** ¿me da un kilo de manzanas, por favor?

····▸ (eat) comer. **I had a pizza** comí una pizza

····▸ (drink) tomar. **come and ~ a drink** ven a tomar una copa

····▸ (smoke) fumar *<cigarette>*

····▸ (hold, organize) hacer *<party, meeting>*

····▸ (get, receive) **I had a letter from Tony yesterday** recibí una carta de Tony ayer. **we've had no news of her** no hemos tenido noticias suyas

····▸ (illness) tener *<flu, headache>*. **to ~ a cold** estar resfriado, tener catarro

····▸ **to have sth done: we had it painted** lo hicimos pintar. **I had my hair cut** me corté el pelo

····▸ **to have it in for s.o.** tenerle manía a uno

●*auxiliary verb*

····▸ haber. **I've seen her already** ya la he visto, ya la vi (LAm)

····▸ **to have just done sth** acabar de hacer algo. **I've just seen her** acabo de verla

····▸ **to have to do sth** tener quehacer algo. **I ~ to** or **I've got to go to the bank** tengo que ir al banco

····▸ (in tag questions) **you've met her, ~n't you?** ya la conoces, ¿no? or ¿verdad? or ¿no es cierto?

····▸ (in short answers) **you've forgotten something - have I?** has olvidado algo - ¿sí?

haven *n* puerto *m*; (refuge) refugio *m*

haversack *n* mochila *f*

havoc *n* estragos *mpl*

hawk *n* halcón *m*

hawthorn *n* espino *m*

hay *n* heno *m*. **~ fever** *n* fiebre *f* del heno. **~stack** *n* almiar *m*. **~wire** *a*. **go ~wire** (plans) desorganizarse; *<machine>* estropearse

hazard *n* riesgo *m*. **~ous** *a* arriesgado

haze *n* neblina *f*

hazel *n* avellano *m*. **~nut** *n* avellana *f*

hazy *a* (**-ier, -iest**) nebuloso

he *pron* él

head *n* cabeza *f*; (of family, government) jefe *m*; (of organization) director *m*; (of beer) espuma *f*. **~s or tails** cara o cruz. ● *a* principal. ● *vt* encabezar, cabecear *<ball>*. □ **~ for** *vt* dirigirse a. **~ache** *n* dolor *m* de cabeza. **~er** *n* (football) cabezazo *m*. **~first** *adv* de cabeza. **~ing** *n* título *m*, encabezamiento *m*. **~lamp** *n* faro *m*, foco *m* (LAm). **~land** *n* promontorio *m*. **~line** *n* titular *m*. **the news ~lines** el resumen informativo. **~long** *adv* de cabeza; (precipitately) precipitadamente. **~master** *n* director *m*. **~mistress** *n* directora *f*. **~-on** *a* & *adv* de frente. **~phones** *npl* auriculares *mpl*, cascos *mpl*. **~quarters** *n* (of business) oficina *f* central; (Mil) cuartel *m* general. **~strong** *a* testarudo. **~teacher** *n* director *m*. **~y** *a* (**-ier, -iest**) *<scent>* embriagador

heal vt curar. ● vi cicatrizarse

health n salud f. ~**y** a sano

heap n montón m. ● vt amontonar.

hear vt/i (pt heard) oír. ~, ~! ¡bravo! ~ **about** oír hablar de. ~ **from** recibir noticias de. ~**ing** n oído m; (Jurid) vista f. ~**ing-aid** n audífono m. ~**say** n rumores mpl

hearse n coche m fúnebre

heart n corazón m. **at** ~ en el fondo. **by** ~ de memoria. **lose** ~ descorazonarse. ~**ache** n congoja f. ~ **attack** n ataque m al corazón, infarto m. ~**break** n congoja f. ~**breaking** a desgarrador. ~**burn** n ardor m de estómago. ~**felt** a sincero

hearth n hogar m

heart: ~**ily** adv de buena gana. ~**less** a cruel. ~**y** a (welcome) caluroso; <meal> abundante

heat n calor m; (contest) (prueba f) eliminatoria f. ● vt calentar. ● vi calentarse. ~**ed** a (fig) acalorado. ~**er** n calentador m

heath n brezal m, monte m

heathen n & a pagano (m)

heather n brezo m

heat: ~**ing** n calefacción f. ~**stroke** n insolación f. ~**wave** n ola f de calor

heave vt (lift) levantar; exhalar <sigh>; (fam, throw) tirar. ● vi (pull) tirar, jalar (LAm); (fam, retch) dar arcadas

heaven n cielo m. ~**ly** a celestial; (astronomy) celeste; (fam, excellent) divino

heav|ily adv pesadamente; (smoke, drink) mucho. ~**y** a (-ier, -iest) pesado; <rain> fuerte; <traffic> denso. ~**yweight** n peso m pesado

heckle vt interrumpir

hectic a febril

he'd = he had, he would

hedge n seto m (vivo). ● vi escaparse por la tangente. ~**hog** n erizo m

heed vt hacer caso de. ● n. **take** ~ tener cuidado

heel n talón m; (of shoe) tacón m

hefty a (-ier, -iest) (sturdy) fuerte; (heavy) pesado

heifer n novilla f

height n altura f; (of person) estatura f; (of fame, glory) cumbre f. ~**en** vt elevar; (fig) aumentar

heir n heredero m. ~**ess** n heredera f. ~**loom** n reliquia f heredada

held ➡HOLD

helicopter n helicóptero m

hell n infierno m

he'll = he will

hello int ¡hola!; (Telephone, caller) ¡oiga!, ¡bueno! (Mex); (Telephone, person answering) ¡diga!, ¡bueno! (Mex). **say** ~ **to** saludar

helm n (Naut) timón m

helmet n casco m

help vt/i ayudar. **he cannot** ~ **laughing** no puede menos de reír. ~ **o.s. to** servirse. **it cannot be** ~**ed** no hay más remedio. ● n ayuda f. ● int ¡socorro! ~**er** n ayudante m. ~**ful** a útil; <person> amable. ~**ing** n porción f. ~**less** a (unable to manage) incapaz; (defenceless) indefenso

hem n dobladillo m

hemisphere n hemisferio m

hen n (chicken) gallina f; (female bird) hembra f

hence adv de aquí. ~**forth** adv de ahora en adelante

henpecked a dominado por su mujer

her pron (direct object) la; (indirect object) le; (after prep) ella. **I know** ~ la conozco. ● a su, sus pl

herb *n* hierba *f*. ~**al** *a* de hierbas

herd *n* (of cattle, pigs) manada *f*; (of goats) rebaño *m*. ● *vt* arrear. ~ **together** reunir

here *adv* aquí, acá (esp LAm). ~! (take this) ¡tenga! ~**abouts** *adv* por aquí. ~**after** *adv* en el futuro. ~**by** *adv* por este medio

heredit|ary *a* hereditario

here|sy *n* herejía *f*. ~**tic** *n* hereje *m & f*

herewith *adv* adjunto

heritage *n* herencia *f*; (fig) patrimonio *m*

hermetically *adv*. ~ **sealed** herméticamente cerrado

hermit *n* ermitaño *m*, eremita *m*

hernia *n* hernia *f*

hero *n* (*pl* -oes) héroe *m*. ~**ic** *a* heroico

heroin *n* heroína *f*

hero: ~ine *n* heroína *f*. ~**ism** *n* heroísmo *m*

heron *n* garza *f* (real)

herring *n* arenque *m*

hers *poss pron* (el) suyo *m*, (la) suya *f*, (los) suyos *mpl*, (las) suyas *fpl*

herself *pron* ella misma; (*reflexive*) se; (*after prep*) sí misma

he's = he is, he has

hesit|ant *a* vacilante. ~**ate** *vi* vacilar. ~**ation** *n* vacilación *f*

heterosexual *a & n* heterosexual (*m & f*)

het up *a* Ⅰ nervioso

hew *vt* (*pp* hewed *or* hewn) cortar; (cut into shape) tallar

hexagon *n* hexágono *m*. ~**al** *a* hexagonal

hey *int* ¡eh!; (expressing dismay, protest) ¡oye!

heyday *n* apogeo *m*

hi *int* Ⅰ ¡hola!

hibernat|e *vi* hibernar. ~**ion** *n* hibernación *f*

hiccough, hiccup *n* hipo *m*. **have (the) ~s** tener hipo. ● *vi* hipar

hide *vt* (*pt* hid, *pp* hidden) esconder. ● *vi* esconderse. ● *n* piel *f*; (tanned) cuero *m*. ~**-and-seek** *n*. **play ~-and-seek** jugar al escondite, jugar a las escondidas (LAm)

hideous *a* (dreadful) horrible; (ugly) feo

hideout *n* escondrijo *m*

hiding *n* (Ⅰ, thrashing) paliza *f*. **go into ~** esconderse. ~ **place** *n* escondite *m*, escondrijo *m*

hierarchy *n* jerarquía *f*

hieroglyphics *n* jeroglíficos *mpl*

hi-fi *a* de alta fidelidad. ● *n* equipo *m* de alta fidelidad, hi-fi *m*

high *a* (-er, -est) alto; <*ideals*> elevado; <*wind*> fuerte; (Ⅰ, drugged) drogado, colocado Ⅰ; <*voice*> agudo; <*meat*> pasado. ● *n* alto nivel *m*. **a (new) ~** un récord. ● *adv* alto. ~**er education** *n* enseñanza *f* superior. ~**-handed** *a* prepotente. ~ **heels** *npl* zapatos *mpl* de tacón alto. ~**lands** *npl* tierras *fpl* altas. ~**-level** *a* de alto nivel. ~**light** *n* punto *m* culminante. ● *vt* destacar; (Art) realzar. ~**ly** *adv* muy; <*paid*> muy bien. ~**ly strung** *a* nervioso. H~**ness** *n* (title) alteza *f*. ~**-rise** *a* <*building*> alto. ~ **school** *n* (Amer) instituto *m*, colegio *m* secundario. ~ **street** *n* calle *f* principal. ~**-strung** *a* (Amer) nervioso. ~**way** *n* carretera *f*

hijack *vt* secuestrar. ● *n* secuestro *m*. ~**er** *n* secuestrador

hike *n* caminata *f.* ● *vi* ir de caminata. ~**r** *n* excursionista *m* & *f*

hilarious *a* muy divertido

hill *n* colina *f*; (slope) cuesta *f.* ~**side** *n* ladera *f.* ~**y** *a* accidentado

hilt *n* (of sword) puño *m.* **to the** ~ (fig) totalmente

him *pron* (direct object) lo, le (only Spain); (indirect object) le; (after prep) él. **I know** ~ lo/le conozco. ~**self** *pron* él mismo; (reflexive) se; (after prep) sí mismo

hind|er *vt* estorbar. ~**rance** *n* obstáculo *m*

hindsight *n.* **with** ~ retrospectivamente

Hindu *n* & *a* hindú (*m* & *f*). ~**ism** *n* hinduismo *m*

hinge *n* bisagra *f*

hint *n* indirecta *f*; (advice) consejo *m.* ● *vi* soltar una indirecta. ~ **at** dar a entender

hip *n* cadera *f*

hippie *n* hippy *m* & *f*

hippopotamus *n* (*pl* **-muses** or **-mi**) hipopótamo *m*

hire *vt* alquilar <thing>; contratar <person>. ● *n* alquiler *m.* **car** ~ alquiler *m* de coches. ~ **purchase** *n* compra *f* a plazos

his *a* su, sus *pl.* ● *poss pron* (el) suyo *m*, (la) suya *f*, (los) suyos *mpl*, (las) suyas *fpl*

Hispan|ic *a* hispánico. ● *n* (Amer) hispano *m.* ~**ist** *n* hispanista *m* & *f*

hiss *n* silbido. ● *vt/i* silbar

histor|ian *n* historiador *m.* ~**ic(al)** *a* histórico. ~**y** *n* historia *f.*

hit *vt* (*pt* **hit**, *pres p* **hitting**) golpear <object>; pegarle a <person>; (collide with) chocar con; (affect) afectar. ~ **it off with** hacer buenas migas con. □ ~ **on** *vt* dar

con. ● *n* (blow) golpe *m*; (success) éxito *m*; (Internet) visita *f*

hitch *vt* (fasten) enganchar. ● *n* (snag) problema *m.* ~ **a lift,** ~ **a ride** (Amer) ⇒~**hike.** ~**hike** *vi* hacer autostop, hacer dedo, ir de aventón (Mex). ~**hiker** *n* autoestopista *m* & *f*

hither *adv* aquí, acá. ~ **and thither** acá y allá. ~**to** *adv* hasta ahora

hit-or-miss *a* <approach> poco científico

hive *n* colmena *f*

hoard *vt* acumular. ● *n* provisión *f*; (of money) tesoro *m*

hoarding *n* valla *f* publicitaria

hoarse *a* (-er, -est) ronco. ~**ly** *adv* con voz ronca

hoax *n* engaño *m.* ● *vt* engañar

hob *n* (of cooker) hornillos *mpl*, hornillas *fpl* (LAm)

hobble *vi* cojear, renguear (LAm)

hobby *n* pasatiempo *m.* ~**horse** *n* (toy) caballito *m* (de niño); (fixation) caballo *m* de batalla

hockey *n* hockey *m*; (Amer) hockey *m* sobre hielo

hoe *n* azada *f.* ● *vt* (*pres p* **hoeing**) azadonar

hog *n* (Amer) cerdo *m.* ● *vt* (*pt* **hogged**) 🅸 acaparar

hoist *vt* levantar; izar <flag>. ● *n* montacargas *m*

hold *vt* (*pt* **held**) tener; (grasp) coger (esp Spain), agarrar; (contain) contener; mantener <interest>; (believe) creer. ● *vi* mantenerse. ● *n* (influence) influencia *f*; (Naut, Aviat) bodega *f.* **get** ~ **of** agarrar; (fig, acquire) adquirir. □ ~ **back** *vt* (contain) contener. □ ~ **on** *vi* (stand firm) resistir; (wait) esperar. □ ~ **on to** *vt* (keep) guardar; (cling to) agarrarse a. □ ~ **out** *vt* (offer) ofrecer. *vi* (resist) resistir. □ ~ **up** *vt* (raise) levantar; (support) sostener; (delay) retrasar; (rob) atracar. **~all** n bolsa f (de viaje). **~er** n tenedor m; (of post) titular m; (wallet) funda f. **~up** atraco m

hole n agujero m; (in ground) hoyo m; (in road) bache m. ● vt agujerear

holiday n vacaciones fpl; (public) fiesta f. **go on ~** ir de vacaciones. **~maker** n veraneante m & f

holiness n santidad f

Holland n Holanda f

hollow a & n hueco (m)

holly n acebo m

holocaust n holocausto m

holster n pistolera f

holy a (-ier, -iest) santo, sagrado. **H~ Ghost** n, **H~ Spirit** n Espíritu m Santo. **~ water** n agua f bendita

homage n homenaje m. **pay ~ to** rendir homenaje a

home n casa f; (for old people) residencia f de ancianos; (native land) patria f. ● a <cooking> casero; (address) particular; <background> familiar; (Pol) interior; <match> de casa. ● adv. (at) **~** en casa. **~land** n patria f. **~less** a sin hogar. **~ly** a (-ier, -iest) casero; (Amer, ugly) feo. **~-made** a hecho en casa. **~ page** n (Comp) página f frontal. **~sick** a. **be ~sick** echar de menos a su familia/su país, extrañar a su familia/su país (LAm). **~ town** n ciudad f natal. **~work** n deberes mpl

homicide n homicidio m

homoeopathic a homeopático

homogeneous a homogéneo

homosexual a & n homosexual (m)

honest a honrado; (frank) sincero. **~ly** adv honradamente. **~y** n honradez f

honey n miel f. **~comb** n panal m. **~moon** n luna f de miel. **~suckle** n madreselva f

honorary a honorario

honour n honor m. ● vt honrar; cumplir (con) <promise>. **~able** a honorable

hood n capucha f; (car roof) capota f; (Amer, car bonnet) capó m, capote m (Mex)

hoodwink vt engañar

hoof n (pl **hoofs** or **hooves**) (of horse) casco m, pezuña f (Mex); (of cow) pezuña f

hook n gancho m; (on garment) corchete m; (for fishing) anzuelo m. **let s.o. off the ~** dejar salir a uno del atolladero. **off the ~** <telephone> descolgado. ● vt. **~ed on** 🅸 adicto a. ◻ **~ up** vt enganchar. **~ed** a <tool> en forma de gancho; <nose> aguileño

hookey n. **play ~** (Amer 🅸) faltar a clase, hacer novillos

hooligan n vándalo m, gamberro m

hoop n aro m

hooray int & n ¡viva! (m)

hoot n (of horn) bocinazo m; (of owl) ululato m. ● vi tocar la bocina; <owl> ulular

Hoover n (P) aspiradora f. ● vt pasar la aspiradora por, aspirar (LAm)

hooves ⇒HOOF

hop vi (pt **hopped**) saltar a la pata coja; <frog, rabbit> brincar, saltar; <bird> dar saltitos. ● n salto m; (flight) etapa f. **~(s)** (Bot) lúpulo m

hope n esperanza f. ● vt/i esperar. **~ for** esperar. **~ful** a (optimistic) esperanzado; (promising) esperanzador. **~fully** adv con optimismo; (it is hoped) se espera. **~less** a desesperado

horde n horda f

horizon n horizonte m

horizontal a horizontal. ∼ly adv horizontalmente

hormone n hormona f

horn n cuerno m, asta f, cacho m (LAm); (of car) bocina f; (Mus) trompa f. ∼ed a con cuernos

hornet n avispón m

horoscope n horóscopo m

horrible a horrible

horrid a horrible

horrific a horroroso

horrify vt horrorizar

horror n horror m

hors-d'oeuvre n (pl -s) entremés m, botana f (Mex)

horse n caballo m. ∼back n. on ∼back a caballo. ∼power n (unit) caballo m (de fuerza). ∼racing n carreras fpl de caballos. ∼shoe n herradura f

horticultur|al a hortícola. ∼e n horticultura f

hose n manguera f, manga f. ● vt. ∼ down lavar (con manguera). ∼pipe n manga f

hosiery n calcetería f

hospice n residencia f para enfermos desahuciados

hospitable a hospitalario

hospital n hospital m

hospitality n hospitalidad f

host n (master of house) anfitrión m; (Radio, TV) presentador m; (multitude) gran cantidad f; (Relig) hostia f

hostage n rehén m

hostel n (for students) residencia f; (for homeless people) hogar m

hostess n anfitriona f

hostil|e a hostil. ∼ity n hostilidad f

hot a (hotter, hottest) caliente; <weather, day> caluroso; <climate> cálido; (Culin) picante; <news> de última hora. be/feel ∼ tener calor. get ∼ calentarse. it is ∼ hace calor. ∼bed n (fig) semillero m

hotchpotch n mezcolanza f

hot dog n perrito m caliente

hotel n hotel m. ∼ier n hotelero m

hot: ∼house n invernadero m. ∼plate n placa f, hornilla f (LAm). ∼-water bottle n bolsa f de agua caliente

hound n perro m de caza. ● vt perseguir

hour n hora f. ∼ly a <rate> por hora. ● adv (every hour) cada hora; (by the hour) por hora

house n (pl -s) casa f; (Pol) cámara f. ● vt alojar; (keep) guardar. ∼hold n casa f. ∼holder n dueño m de una casa. ∼keeper n ama f de llaves. ∼maid n criada f, mucama f (LAm). ∼-proud a meticuloso. ∼warming (party) n fiesta de inauguración de una casa. ∼wife n ama f de casa. ∼work n tareas fpl domésticas

housing n alojamiento m. ∼ development (Amer), ∼ estate n complejo m habitacional, urbanización f

hovel n casucha f

hover vi <bird, threat etc> cernerse; (loiter) rondar. ∼craft n (pl invar or -crafts) aerodeslizador m

how adv cómo. ∼ about a walk? ¿qué te parece si damos un paseo? ∼ are you? ¿cómo está Vd? ∼ do you do? (in introduction) mucho gusto. ∼ long? (in time) ¿cuánto tiempo? ∼ long is the room? ¿cuánto mide de largo el cuarto? ∼ often? ¿cuántas veces?

however adv (nevertheless) no obstante, sin embargo; (with verb) de cualquier manera que (+ subjunctive); (with adjective or adverb) por... que (+ subjunctive). ~ **much it rains** por mucho quellueva

howl n aullido. ● vi aullar

hp abbr ⇒HORSEPOWER

HP abbr ⇒HIRE PURCHASE

hub n (of wheel) cubo m; (fig) centro m

hubcap n tapacubos m

huddle vi apiñarse

hue n (colour) color m

huff n. **be in a** ~ estar enfurruñado

hug vt (pt hugged) abrazar. ● n abrazo m

huge a enorme. ~**ly** adv enormemente

hulk n (of ship) barco m viejo

hull n (of ship) casco m

hullo int ⇒HELLO

hum vt/i (pt hummed) <person> canturrear; <insect, engine> zumbar. ● n zumbido m

human a & n humano (m). ~ **being** n ser m humano. ~**e** a humano. ~**itarian** a humanitario. ~**ity** n humanidad f

humbl|e a (-er, -est) humilde. ● vt humillar. ~**y** adv humildemente

humdrum a monótono

humid a húmedo. ~**ity** n humedad f

humiliat|e vt humillar. ~**ion** n humillación f

humility n humildad f

humongous adj 🔲 de primera

humo|rist n humorista m & f. ~**rous** a humorístico. ~**rously** adv con gracia. ~**ur** n humor m. **sense of** ~**ur** sentido m del humor

hump n (of person, camel) joroba f; (in ground) montículo m. ● vt encorvar. ~ (**about**) (🔲, carry) cargar

hunch vt encorvar. ● n presentimiento m; (lump) joroba f. ~**back** n jorobado m

hundred a ciento, (before noun) cien, **one** ~ **and ninety-eight** ciento noventa y ocho. **two** ~ doscientos. **three** ~ **pages** trescientas páginas. **four** ~ cuatrocientos. **five** ~ quinientos. ● n ciento m. ~**s of** centenares de. ~**th** a & n centésimo (m). ~**weight** n 50,8kg; (Amer) 45,36kg

hung ⇒HANG

Hungar|ian a & n húngaro (m). ~**y** n Hungría f

hung|er n hambre f. ● vi. ~**er for** tener hambre de. ~**rily** adv ávidamente. ~**ry** a (-ier, -iest) hambriento. **be** ~**ry** tener hambre

hunk n (buen) pedazo m

hunt vt cazar. ● vi cazar. ~ **for** buscar. ● n caza f. ~**er** n cazador m. ~**ing** n caza f. **go** ~**ing** ir de caza

hurl vt lanzar

hurrah, hurray int & n ¡viva! (m)

hurricane n huracán m

hurr|ied a apresurado. ~**iedly** adv apresuradamente. ~**y** vi darse prisa, apurarse (LAm). ● vt meter prisa a, apurar (LAm). ● n prisa f. **be in a** ~**y** tener prisa, estar apurado (LAm)

hurt vt (pt hurt) hacer daño a, lastimar (LAm). ~ **s.o.'s feelings** ofender a uno. ● vi doler. **my head** ~**s** me duele la cabeza. ~**ful** a hiriente

hurtle vt ir volando. ● vi. ~ **along** mover rápidamente

husband n marido m, esposo m

hush *vt* acallar. ● *n* silencio *m*.
□ ~ **up** *vt* acallar *<affair>*.
~-**hush** *a* 🄵 super secreto

husk *n* cáscara *f*

husky *a* (**-ier, -iest**) (hoarse) ronco

hustle *vt* (jostle) empujar. ● *vi*
(hurry) darse prisa, apurarse (LAm).
● *n* empuje *m*

hut *n* cabaña *f*

hutch *n* conejera *f*

hybrid *a* & *n* híbrido (*m*)

hydrangea *n* hortensia *f*

hydrant *n*. (fire) ~ *n* boca *f* de
riego, boca *f* de incendios (LAm)

hydraulic *a* hidráulico

hydroelectric *a* hidroeléctrico

hydrofoil *n* hidrodeslizador *m*

hydrogen *n* hidrógeno *m*

hyena *n* hiena *f*

hygien|e *n* higiene *f*. ~**ic** *a*
higiénico

hymn *n* himno *m*

hyper... *pref* hiper...

hyphen *n* guión *m*. ~**ate** *vt*
escribir con guión

hypno|sis *n* hipnosis *f*. ~**tic** *a*
hipnótico. ~**tism** *n* hipnotismo
m. ~**tist** *n* hipnotista *m* & *f*.
~**tize** *vt* hipnotizar

hypochondriac *n* hipocondríaco
m

hypocri|sy *n* hipocresía *f*. ~**te** *n*
hipócrita *m* & *f*. ~**tical** *a*
hipócrita

hypodermic *a* hipodérmico. ● *n*
hipodérmica *f*

hypothe|sis *n* (*pl* **-theses**)
hipótesis *f*. ~**tical** *a* hipotético

hysteri|a *n* histerismo *m*. ~**cal** *a*
histérico. ~**cs** *npl* histerismo *m*.
have ~**cs** ponerse histérico;
(laugh) morir de risa

I *pron* yo

ice *n* hielo *m*. ● *vt* helar; glasear
<cake>. ● *vi*. ~ (**up**) helarse,
congelarse. ~**berg** *n* iceberg *m*.
~ **box** *n* (compartment) congelador;
(Amer 🄵, refrigerator) frigorífico *m*,
refrigerador *m* (LAm). ~**cream** *n*
helado *m*. ~ **cube** *n* cubito *m* de
hielo

Iceland *n* Islandia *f*

ice: ~ **lolly** polo *m*, paleta *f*
helada (LAm). ~ **rink** *n* pista *f* de
hielo. ~ **skating** *n* patinaje *m*
sobre hielo

icicle *n* carámbano *m*

icing *n* glaseado *m*

icon *n* icono *m*

icy *a* (**-ier, -iest**) helado; (fig)
glacial

I'd = **I had, I would**

idea *n* idea *f*

ideal *a* & *n* ideal (*m*). ~**ism** *n*
idealismo *m*. ~**ist** *n* idealista *m* &
f. ~**istic** *a* idealista. ~**ize** *vt*
idealizar. ~**ly** *adv* idealmente

identical *a* idéntico. ~ **twins** *npl*
gemelos *mpl* idénticos, gemelos
mpl (LAm)

identif|ication *n* identificación *f*.
~**y** *vt* identificar. ● *vi*. ~**y with**
identificarse con

identity *n* identidad *f*. ~ **card** *n*
carné *m* de identidad

ideolog|ical *a* ideológico. ~**y** *n*
ideología *f*

idiocy *n* idiotez *f*

idiom *n* locución *f*. ~**atic** *a*
idiomático

idiot n idiota m & f. ~**ic** a idiota

idle a (**-er, -est**) ocioso; (lazy) holgazán; (out of work) desocupado; <machine> parado. ● vi <engine> andar al ralentí. ~**ness** n ociosidad f; (laziness) holgazanería f

idol n ídolo m. ~**ize** vt idolatrar

idyllic a idílico

i.e. abbr (= id est) es decir

if conj si

igloo n iglú m

ignit|e vt encender. ● vi encenderse. ~**ion** n ignición f; (Auto) encendido m. ~**ion key** n llave f de contacto

ignoramus n (pl **-muses**) ignorante

ignoran|ce n ignorancia f. ~**t** a ignorante

ignore vt no hacer caso de; hacer caso omiso de <warning>

ill a enfermo. ● adv mal. ● n mal m

I'll = **I will**

ill: ~-advised a imprudente. ~ **at ease** a incómodo. ~**-bred** a mal educado

illegal a ilegal

illegible a ilegible

illegitima|cy n ilegitimidad f. ~**te** a ilegítimo

illitera|cy n analfabetismo m. ~**te** a analfabeto

illness n enfermedad f

illogical a ilógico

illuminat|e vt iluminar. ~**ion** n iluminación f

illus|ion n ilusión f.

illustrat|e vt ilustrar. ~**ion** n ilustración f; (example) ejemplo m

illustrious a ilustre

ill will n mala voluntad f

I'm = **I am**

image n imagen f. ~**ry** n imágenes fpl

imagin|able a imaginable. ~**ary** a imaginario. ~**ation** n imaginación f. ~**ative** a imaginativo. ~**e** vt imaginar(se)

imbalance n desequilibrio m

imbecile n imbécil m & f

imitat|e vt imitar. ~**ion** n imitación f. ● a de imitación. ~**or** n imitador m

immaculate a inmaculado

immatur|e a inmaduro. ~**ity** n inmadurez f

immediate a inmediato. ~**ly** adv inmediatamente. ● conj en cuanto (+ subjunctive)

immens|e a inmenso. ~**ely** adv inmensamente; (▣, very much) muchísimo

immers|e vt sumergir. ~**ion** n inmersión f. ~**ion heater** n calentador m de inmersión

immigra|nt a & n inmigrante (m & f). ~**tion** n inmigración f

imminent a inminente

immobil|e a inmóvil. ~**ize** vt inmovilizar. ~**izer** n inmovilizador m

immoderate a inmoderado

immodest a inmodesto

immoral a inmoral. ~**ity** n inmoralidad f

immortal a inmortal. ~**ity** n inmortalidad f. ~**ize** vt inmortalizar

immun|e a inmune (**to** a). ~**ity** n inmunidad f. ~**ization** n inmunización f. ~**ize** vt inmunizar

imp n diablillo m

impact n impacto m

impair vt perjudicar

impale vt atravesar (**on** con)

impart vt comunicar <news>; impartir <knowledge>

impartial *a* imparcial. ~**ity** *n*
imparcialidad *f*

impassable *a* <*barrier etc*>
infranqueable; <*road*>
intransitable

impassive *a* impasible

impatien|ce *n* impaciencia *f*. ~**t**
a impaciente. **get** ~**t**
impacientarse. ~**tly** *adv* con
impaciencia

impeccable *a* impecable

impede *vt* estorbar

impediment *n* obstáculo *m*.
(speech) ~ defecto *m* del habla

impending *a* inminente

impenetrable *a* impenetrable

imperative *a* imprescindible. ● *n*
(Gram) imperativo *m*

imperceptible *a* imperceptible

imperfect *a* imperfecto. ~**ion** *n*
imperfección *f*

imperial *a* imperial. ~**ism** *n*
imperialismo *m*

impersonal *a* impersonal

impersonat|e *vt* hacerse pasar
por; (mimic) imitar. ~**ion** *n*
imitación *f*. ~**or** *n* imitador *m*

impertinen|ce *n* impertinencia *f*.
~**t** *a* impertinente

impervious *a*. ~ **to** impermeable
a

impetuous *a* impetuoso

impetus *n* ímpetu *m*

implacable *a* implacable

implant *vt* implantar

implement *n* instrumento *m*,
implemento *m* (LAm). ● *vt*
implementar

implicat|e *vt* implicar. ~**ion** *n*
implicación *f*

implicit *a* (implied) implícito;
(unquestioning) absoluto

implore *vt* implorar

imply *vt* (involve) implicar;
(insinuate) dar a entender, insinuar

impolite *a* mal educado

import *vt* importar. ● *n*
importación *f*; (item) artículo *m* de
importación; (meaning)
significación *f*

importan|ce *n* importancia *f*. ~**t**
a importante

importer *n* importador *m*

impos|e *vt* imponer. ● *vi*. ~**e on**
abusar de la amabilidad de. ~**ing**
a imponente. ~**ition** *n*
imposición *f*; (fig) abuso *m*

impossib|ility *n* imposibilidad *f*.
~**le** *a* imposible

impostor *n* impostor *m*

impoten|ce *n* impotencia *f*. ~**t** *a*
impotente

impound *vt* confiscar

impoverished *a* empobrecido

impractical *a* poco práctico

impregnable *a* inexpugnable

impregnate *vt* impregnar (with
con, de)

impress *vt* impresionar; (make
good impression) causar una buena
impresión a. ● *vi* impresionar

impression *n* impresión *f*. ~**able**
a impresionable. ~**ism** *n*
impresionismo *m*

impressive *a* impresionante

imprint *n* impresión *f*. ● *vt*
imprimir

imprison *vt* encarcelar. ~**ment** *n*
encarcelamiento *m*

improbab|ility *n* improbabilidad
f. ~**le** *a* improbable

impromptu *a* improvisado. ● *adv*
de improviso

improper *a* impropio; (incorrect)
incorrecto

improve *vt* mejorar. ● *vi* mejorar.
~**ment** *n* mejora *f*

improvis|ation *n* improvisación
f. ~**e** *vt/i* improvisar

impuden|ce *n* insolencia *f*. ~**t** *a*
insolente

impuls|e *n* impulso *m*. **on ~e** sin reflexionar. **~ive** *a* irreflexivo

impur|e *a* impuro. **~ity** *n* impureza *f*

in *prep* en; (within) dentro de. **~ a firm manner** de una manera terminante. **~ an hour('s time)** dentro de una hora. **~ doing** al hacer. **~ so far as** en la medida en que. **~ the evening** por la tarde. **~ the rain** bajo la lluvia. **~ the sun** en el sol. **one ~ ten** uno de cada diez. **the best ~ the world** el mejor del mundo. ● *adv* (inside) dentro; (at home) en casa. **come ~** entrar. ● *n*. **the ~s and outs of** los detalles de

inability *n* incapacidad *f*

inaccessible *a* inaccesible

inaccura|cy *n* inexactitud *f*. **~te** *a* inexacto

inactiv|e *a* inactivo. **~ity** *n* inactividad *f*

inadequa|cy *a* insuficiencia *f*. **~te** *a* insuficiente

inadvertently *adv* sin querer

inadvisable *a* desaconsejable

inane *a* estúpido

inanimate *a* inanimado

inappropriate *a* inoportuno

inarticulate *a* incapaz de expresarse claramente

inattentive *a* desatento

inaudible *a* inaudible

inaugurate *vt* inaugurar

inborn *a* innato

inbred *a* (inborn) innato; <social group> endogámico

Inc *abbr* (Amer) (= **Incorporated**) S.A., Sociedad Anónima

incalculable *a* incalculable

incapable *a* incapaz

incapacit|ate *vt* incapacitar. **~y** *n* incapacidad *f*

incarcerate *vt* encarcelar

incarnat|e *a* encarnado. **~ion** *n* encarnación *f*

incendiary *a* incendiario. **~ bomb** bomba *f* incendiaria

incense *n* incienso *m*. ● *vt* enfurecer

incentive *n* incentivo *m*

incessant *a* incesante. **~ly** *adv* sin cesar

incest *n* incesto *m*. **~uous** *a* incestuoso

inch *n* pulgada *f*; (= 2,54cm). ● *vi*. **~ forward** avanzar lentamente

incidence *n* frecuencia *f*

incident *n* incidente *m*

incidental *a* <effect> secundario; (minor) incidental. **~ly** *adv* a propósito

incinerat|e *vt* incinerar. **~or** *n* incinerador *m*

incision *n* incisión *f*

incite *vt* incitar. **~ment** *n* incitación *f*

inclination *n* inclinación *f*. **have no ~ to** no tener deseos de

incline *vt* inclinar. **be ~d to** tener tendencia a. ● *vi* inclinarse. ● *n* pendiente *f*

inclu|de *vt* incluir. **~ding** *prep* incluso. **~sion** *n* inclusión *f*. **~sive** *a* inclusivo

incognito *adv* de incógnito

incoherent *a* incoherente

incom|e *n* ingresos *mpl*. **~e tax** *n* impuesto *m* sobre la renta. **~ing** *a* <tide> ascendente

incomparable *a* incomparable

incompatible *a* incompatible

incompeten|ce *n* incompetencia *f*. **~t** *a* incompetente

incomplete *a* incompleto

incomprehensible *a* incomprensible

inconceivable *a* inconcebible

inconclusive *a* no concluyente

incongruous *a* incongruente

inconsiderate *a* desconsiderado

inconsisten|cy *n* inconsecuencia *f*. ~**t** *a* inconsecuente. be ~**t** with no concordar con

inconspicuous *a* que no llama la atención. ~**ly** *adv* sin llamar la atención

incontinent *a* incontinente

inconvenien|ce *a* inconveniencia *f*; (drawback) inconveniente *m*. ~**t** *a* inconveniente

incorporate *vt* incorporar; (include) incluir; (Com) constituir (en sociedad)

incorrect *a* incorrecto

increas|e *n* aumento *m* (in de). ● *vt/i* aumentar. ~**ing** *a* creciente. ~**ingly** *adv* cada vez más

incredible *a* increíble

incredulous *a* incrédulo

incriminat|e *vt* incriminar. ~**ing** *a* comprometedor

incubat|e *vt* incubar. ~**ion** *n* incubación *f*. ~**or** *n* incubadora *f*

incur *vt* (*pt* **incurred**) incurrir en; contraer <*debts*>

incurable *a* <*disease*> incurable; <*romantic*> empedernido

indebted *a*. be ~ to s.o. estar en deuda con uno

indecen|cy *n* indecencia *f*. ~**t** *a* indecente

indecisi|on *n* indecisión *f*. ~**ve** *a* indeciso

indeed *adv* en efecto; (really?) ¿de veras?

indefinable *a* indefinible

indefinite *a* indefinido. ~**ly** *adv* indefinidamente

indelible *a* indeleble

indemni|fy *vt* (insure) asegurar; (compensate) indemnizar. ~**ty** *n* (insurance) indemnidad *f*; (payment) indemnización *f*

indent *vt* sangrar <*text*>. ~**ation** *n* mella *f*

independen|ce *n* independencia *f*. ~**t** *a* independiente. ~**tly** *adv* independientemente

in-depth *a* a fondo

indescribable *a* indescriptible

indestructible *a* indestructible

indeterminate *a* indeterminado

index *n* (*pl* **indexes**) (in book) índice *m*; (*pl* **indexes** or **indices**) (Com, Math) índice *m*. ● *vt* poner índice a; (enter in index) poner en un índice. ~ **finger** *n* (dedo *m*) índice *m*. ~-**linked** *a* indexado

India *n* la India. ~**n** *a* & *n* indio (*m*)

indicat|e *vt* indicar. ~**ion** *n* indicación *f*. ~**ive** *a* & *n* indicativo (*m*). ~**or** *n* indicador *m*; (Auto) intermitente *m*

indices ⇒INDEX

indict *vt* acusar. ~**ment** *n* acusación *f*

indifferen|ce *n* indiferencia *f*. ~**t** *a* indiferente; (not good) mediocre

indigesti|ble *a* indigesto. ~**on** *n* indigestión *f*

indigna|nt *a* indignado. ~**tion** *n* indignación *f*

indirect *a* indirecto. ~**ly** *adv* indirectamente

indiscre|et *a* indiscreto. ~**tion** *n* indiscreción *f*

indiscriminate *a* indistinto. ~**ly** *adv* indistintamente

indispensable *a* indispensable, imprescindible

indisposed *a* indispuesto

indisputable *a* indiscutible

indistinguishable *a* indistinguible (from de)

individual *a* individual. ● *n* individuo *m*. ~**ly** *adv* individualmente

indoctrinat|e vt adoctrinar. ~**ion** n adoctrinamiento m

indolen|ce n indolencia f. ~**t** a indolente

indomitable a indómito

indoor a interior; <clothes etc> de casa; (covered) cubierto. ~**s** adv dentro, adentro (LAm)

induc|e vt inducir. ~**ement** n incentivo m

indulge vt satisfacer <desires>; complacer <person>. ● vi. ~ **in** permitirse. ~**nce** n (of desires) satisfacción f; (extravagance) lujo m. ~**nt** a indulgente

industrial a industrial; <unrest> laboral. ~**ist** n industrial m & f. ~**ized** a industrializado

industrious a trabajador

industry n industria f; (zeal) aplicación f

inebriated a beodo, ebrio

inedible a incomible

ineffective a ineficaz; <person> incompetente

ineffectual a ineficaz

inefficien|cy n ineficacia f; (of person) incompetencia f. ~**t** a ineficaz; <person> incompetente

ineligible a inelegible. **be ~ for** no tener derecho a

inept a inepto

inequality n desigualdad f

inert a inerte. ~**ia** n inercia f

inescapable a ineludible

inevitabl|e a inevitable. ● n. **the ~e** lo inevitable. ~**y** adv inevitablemente

inexact a inexacto

inexcusable a imperdonable

inexpensive a económico, barato

inexperience n falta f de experiencia. ~**d** a inexperto

inexplicable a inexplicable

infallib|ility n infalibilidad f. ~**le** a infalible

infam|ous a infame. ~**y** n infamia f

infan|cy n infancia f. ~**t** n niño m. ~**tile** a infantil

infantry n infantería f

infatuat|ed a. **be ~ed with** estar encaprichado con. ~**ion** n encaprichamiento m

infect vt infectar; (fig) contagiar. **~ s.o. with sth** contagiarle algo a uno. ~**ion** n infección f. ~**ious** a contagioso

infer vt (pt **inferred**) deducir

inferior a & n inferior (m & f). ~**ity** n inferioridad f

inferno n (pl **-os**) infierno m

infertil|e a estéril. ~**ity** n esterilidad f

infest vt infestar

infidelity n infidelidad f

infiltrat|e vt infiltrarse en. ● vi infiltrarse. ~**or** n infiltrado m

infinite a infinito. ~**ly** adv infinitamente

infinitesimal a infinitesimal

infinitive n infinitivo m

infinity n (infinite distance) infinito m; (infinite quantity) infinidad f

infirm a enfermizo. ~**ity** n enfermedad f

inflam|e vt inflamar. ~**mable** a inflamable. ~**mation** n inflamación f

inflat|e vt inflar. ~**ion** n inflación f. ~**ionary** a inflacionario

inflection n inflexión f

inflexible a inflexible

inflict vt infligir (on a)

influen|ce n influencia f. **under the ~ce** (Ⓕ, drunk) borracho. ● vt influir (en). ~**tial** a influyente

influenza n gripe f

influx n afluencia f

inform vt informar. keep ~ed tener al corriente. ● vi. ~ on s.o. delatar a uno

informal a informal; <language> familiar. ~ity n falta f de ceremonia. ~ly adv (casually) de manera informal; (unofficially) informalmente

inform|ation n información f. ~ation technology n informática f. ~ative a informativo. ~er n informante m

infrared a infrarrojo

infrequent a poco frecuente. ~ly adv raramente

infringe vt infringir. ~ on violar. ~ment n violación f

infuriat|e vt enfurecer. ~ing a exasperante

ingen|ious a ingenioso. ~uity n ingeniosidad f

ingot n lingote m

ingrained a (belief) arraigado

ingratiate vt. ~ o.s. with congraciarse con

ingratitude n ingratitud f

ingredient n ingrediente m

ingrowing, ingrown a. ~ nail n uñero m, uña f encarnada

inhabit vt habitar. ~able a habitable. ~ant n habitante m

inhale vt aspirar. ● vi (when smoking) aspirar el humo. ~r n inhalador m

inherent a inherente. ~ly adv intrínsecamente

inherit vt heredar. ~ance n herencia f

inhibit vt inhibir. ~ed a inhibido. ~ion n inhibición f

inhospitable a <place> inhóspito; <person> inhospitalario

inhuman a inhumano. ~e a inhumano. ~ity n inhumanidad f

initial n inicial f. ● vt (pt initialled) firmar con iniciales. ● a inicial. ~ly adv al principio

initiat|e vt iniciar; promover <scheme etc>. ~ion n iniciación f

initiative n iniciativa f. on one's own ~ por iniciativa propia. take the ~ tomar la iniciativa

inject vt inyectar. ~ion n inyección f

injur|e vt herir. ~y n herida f

injustice n injusticia f

ink n tinta f. ~well n tintero m. ~y a manchado de tinta

inland a interior. ● adv tierra adentro. I~ Revenue n (UK) Hacienda f

in-laws npl parientes mpl políticos

inlay vt (pt inlaid) taracear, incrustar. ● n taracea f, incrustación f

inlet n (in coastline) ensenada f; (of river, sea) brazo m

inmate n (of asylum) interno m; (of prison) preso m

inn n posada f

innate a innato

inner a interior; (fig) íntimo. ~most a más íntimo. ~ tube n cámara f

innocen|ce n inocencia f. ~t a & n inocente (m & f)

innocuous a inocuo

innovat|e vi innovar. ~ion n innovación f. ~ive a innovador. ~or n innovador m

innuendo n (pl -oes) insinuación f

innumerable a innumerable

inoculat|e vt inocular. ~ion n inoculación f

inoffensive a inofensivo

inopportune a inoportuno

input n aportación f, aporte m (LAm); (Comp) entrada f. ● vt (pt **input**, pres p **inputting**) entrar <data>

inquest n investigación f judicial

inquir|e vt/i preguntar. ~e about informarse de. ~y n pregunta f; (investigation) investigación f

inquisition n inquisición f

inquisitive a inquisitivo

insan|e a loco. ~ity n locura f

insatiable a insaciable

inscri|be vt inscribir <letters>; grabar <design>. ~ption n inscripción f

inscrutable a inescrutable

insect n insecto m. ~icide n insecticida f

insecur|e a inseguro. ~ity n inseguridad f

insensitive a insensible

inseparable a inseparable

insert n materia f insertada. ● vt insertar. ~ion n inserción f

inside n interior m. ~ out al revés; (thoroughly) a fondo. ● a interior. ● adv dentro, adentro (LAm). ● prep dentro de. ~s npl tripas fpl

insight n perspicacia f. gain an ~ into llegar a comprender bien

insignificant a insignificante

insincer|e a poco sincero. ~ity n falta f de sinceridad

insinuat|e vt insinuar. ~ion n insinuación f

insipid a insípido

insist vt insistir (that en que). ● vi insistir. ~ on insistir en. ~ence n insistencia f. ~ent a insistente. ~ently adv con insistencia

insolen|ce n insolencia f. ~t a insolente

insoluble a insoluble

insolvent a insolvente

insomnia n insomnio m. ~c n insomne m & f

inspect vt (officially) inspeccionar; (look at closely) revisar, examinar . ~ion n inspección f. ~or n inspector m; (on train, bus) revisor m, inspector m (LAm)

inspir|ation n inspiración f. ~e vt inspirar. ~ing a inspirador

instability n inestabilidad f

install vt instalar. ~ation n instalación f

instalment n (payment) plazo m; (of publication) entrega f; (of radio, TV serial) episodio m

instance n ejemplo m; (case) caso m. for ~ por ejemplo. in the first ~ en primer lugar

instant a instantáneo. ● n instante m. ~aneous a instantáneo

instead adv en cambio. ~ of en vez de, en lugar de

instigat|e vt instigar. ~ion n instigación f

instinct n instinto m. ~ive a instintivo

institut|e n instituto m. ● vt instituir; iniciar <enquiry etc>. ~ion n institución f. ~ional a institucional

instruct vt instruir; (order) mandar. ~ s.o. in sth enseñar algo a uno. ~ion n instrucción f. ~ions npl (for use) modo m de empleo. ~ive a instructivo. ~or n instructor m

instrument n instrumento m. ~al a instrumental. be ~al in jugar un papel decisivo en

insubordinat|e a insubordinado. ~ion n insubordinación f

insufferable a <person> insufrible; <heat> insoportable

insufficient a insuficiente

insular *a* insular; (narrow-minded) estrecho de miras

insulat|e *vt* aislar. ~**ion** *n* aislamiento *m*

insulin *n* insulina *f*

insult *vt* insultar. ● *n* insulto *m*. ~**ing** *a* insultante

insur|ance *n* seguro *m*. ~**e** *vt* (Com) asegurar; (Amer) ⇒ENSURE

insurmountable *a* insuperable

intact *a* intacto

integral *a* integral

integrat|e *vt* integrar. ● *vi* integrarse. ~**ion** *n* integración *f*

integrity *n* integridad *f*

intellect *n* intelecto *m*. ~**ual** *a* & *n* intelectual (*m*)

intelligen|ce *n* inteligencia *f*. ~**t** *a* inteligente. ~**tly** *adv* inteligentemente

intelligible *a* inteligible

intend *vt*. ~ **to do** pensar hacer

intens|e *a* intenso; <*person*> apasionado. ~**ely** *adv* intensamente; (very) sumamente. ~**ify** *vt* intensificar. ● *vi* intensificarse. ~**ity** *n* intensidad *f*

intensive *a* intensivo. ~ **care** *n* cuidados *mpl* intensivos

intent *n* propósito *m*. ● *a* atento. ~ **on** absorto en. ~ **on doing** resuelto a hacer

intention *n* intención *f*. ~**al** *a* intencional

intently *adv* atentamente

interact *vi* relacionarse. ~**ion** *n* interacción *f*

intercept *vt* interceptar. ~**ion** *n* interceptación *f*

interchange *vt* intercambiar. ● *n* intercambio *m*; (road junction) cruce *m*. ~**able** *a* intercambiable

intercity *a* rápido interurbano *m*

intercourse *n* trato *m*; (sexual) acto *m* sexual

interest *n* interés *m*. ● *vt* interesar. ~**ed** *a* interesado. be ~**ed** in interesarse por. ~**ing** *a* interesante

interfere *vi* entrometerse. ~ **in** entrometerse en. ~ **with** afectar (a); interferir <*radio*>. ~**nce** *n* intromisión *f*; (Radio) interferencia *f*

interior *a* & *n* interior (*m*)

interjection *n* interjección *f*

interlude *n* intervalo *m*; (theatre, music) interludio *m*

intermediary *a* & *n* intermediario (*m*)

interminable *a* interminable

intermittent *a* intermitente. ~**ly** *adv* con discontinuidad

intern *vt* internar. ● *n* (Amer, doctor) interno *m*

internal *a* interno. ~**ly** *adv* internamente. **I~ Revenue Service** *n* (Amer) Hacienda *f*

international *a* internacional

Internet *n*. the ~ el Internet

interpret *vt/i* interpretar. ~**ation** *n* interpretación *f*. ~**er** *n* intérprete *m* & *f*

interrogat|e *vt* interrogar. ~**ion** *n* interrogatorio *m*. ~**ive** *a* interrogativo

interrupt *vt/i* interrumpir. ~**ion** *n* interrupción *f*

intersect *vt* cruzar. ● *vi* <*roads*> cruzarse; (geometry) intersecarse. ~**ion** *n* (roads) cruce *m*; (geometry) intersección *f*

intersperse *vt* intercalar

interstate (highway) *n* (Amer) carretera *f* interestatal

intertwine *vt* entrelazar. ● *vi* entrelazarse

interval *n* intervalo *m*; (theatre) descanso *m*. at ~**s** a intervalos

interven|e *vi* intervenir. ~**tion** *n* intervención *f*

interview n entrevista f. ● vt entrevistar. ~ee n entrevistado m. ~er n entrevistador m

intestine n intestino m

intimacy n intimidad f

intimate a íntimo. ● vt (state) anunciar; (imply) dar a entender. ~ly adv íntimamente

intimidat|e vt intimidar. ~ion n intimidación f

into prep en; <translate> a

intolerable a intolerable

intoleran|ce n intolerancia f. ~t a intolerante

intoxicat|e vt embriagar; (Med) intoxicar. ~ed a ebrio. ~ing a <substance> estupefaciente. ~ion n embriaguez f; (Med) intoxicación f

intransitive a intransitivo

intravenous a intravenoso

intrepid a intrépido

intrica|cy n complejidad f. ~te a complejo

intrigu|e vt/i intrigar. ● n intriga f. ~ing a intrigante

intrinsic a intrínseco. ~ally adv intrínsecamente

introduc|e vt introducir; presentar <person>. ~tion n introducción f; (to person) presentación f. ~tory a preliminar; <course> de introducción

introvert n introvertido m

intru|de vi entrometerse; (disturb) importunar. ~der n intruso m. ~sion n intrusión f. ~sive a impertinente

intuiti|on n intuición f. ~ve a intuitivo

inundat|e vt inundar. ~ion n inundación f

invade vt invadir. ~r n invasor m

invalid n inválido m. ● a inválido. ~ate vt invalidar

invaluable a inestimable, invalorable (LAm)

invariabl|e a invariable. ~y adv invariablemente

invasion n invasión f

invent vt inventar. ~ion n invención f. ~ive a inventivo. ~or n inventor m

inventory n inventario m

invertebrate n invertebrado m

inverted commas npl comillas fpl

invest vt invertir. ● vi. ~ in hacer una inversión f

investigat|e vt investigar. ~ion n investigación f. **under ~ion** sometido a examen. ~or n investigador m

inveterate a inveterado

invidious a (hateful) odioso; (unfair) injusto

invigorating a vigorizante; (stimulating) estimulante

invincible a invencible

invisible a invisible

invit|ation n invitación f. ~e vt invitar; (ask for) pedir. ● n Ⓘ invitación f. ~ing a atrayente

invoice n factura f. ● vt. ~ s.o. (for sth) pasarle a uno factura (por algo)

involuntary a involuntario

involve vt (entail) suponer; (implicate) implicar. ~d in envuelto en. ~d a (complex) complicado. ~ment n participación f; (relationship) enredo m

inward a interior. ● adv hacia adentro. ~s adv hacia dentro

iodine n yodo m

ion n ion m

iota n (amount) pizca f

IOU abbr (= I owe you) pagaré m

IQ *abbr* (= **intelligence quotient**) CI *m*, cociente *m* intelectual

Iran *n* Irán *m*. ~**ian** *a* & *n* iraní (*m*)

Iraq *n* Irak *m*. ~**i** *a* & *n* iraquí (*m*)

irate *a* colérico

Ireland *n* Irlanda *f*

iris *n* (Anat) iris *m*; (Bot) lirio *m*

Irish *a* irlandés. ●*n* (Lang) irlandés *m*. *npl*. **the** ~ (people) los irlandeses. ~**man** *n* irlandés *m*. ~**woman** *n* irlandesa *f*

iron *n* hierro *m*; (appliance) plancha *f*. ●*a* de hierro. ●*vt* planchar. □ ~ **out** *vt* allanar

ironic *a* irónico. ~**ally** *adv* irónicamente

ironing board *n* tabla *f* de planchar, burro *m* de planchar (Mex)

iron: ~**monger** *n* ferretero *m*. ~**monger's** *n* ferretería *f*

irony *n* ironía *f*

irrational *a* irracional

irrefutable *a* irrefutable

irregular *a* irregular. ~**ity** *n* irregularidad *f*

irrelevan|ce *n* irrelevancia *f*. ~**t** *a* irrelevante

irreparable *a* irreparable

irreplaceable *a* irreemplazable

irresistible *a* irresistible

irrespective *a*. ~ **of** sin tomar en cuenta

irresponsible *a* irresponsable

irretrievable *a* irrecuperable

irreverent *a* irreverente

irrevocable *a* irrevocable

irrigat|e *vt* regar, irrigar. ~**ion** *n* riego *m*, irrigación *f*

irritable *a* irritable

irritat|e *vt* irritar. **be** ~**ed with** estar irritado con. ~**ing** *a* irritante. ~**ion** *n* irritación *f*

IRS *abbr* (Amer) ⇒INTERNAL REVENUE SERVICE

is ⇒BE

ISDN *abbr* (= **Integrated Services Digital Network**) RSDI

Islam *n* el Islam. ~**ic** *a* islámico

island *n* isla *f*. ~**er** *n* isleño *m*

isolat|e *vt* aislar. ~**ion** *n* aislamiento *m*

Israel *n* Israel *m*. ~**i** *a* & *n* israelí (*m*)

issue *n* tema *m*, asunto *m*; (of magazine etc) número *m*; (of stamps, bank notes) emisión *f*; (of documents) expedición *f*. **take** ~ **with** discrepar de. ●*vt* hacer público *<statement>*; expedir *<documents>*; emitir *<stamps etc>*; prestar *<library book>*

....

it

●*pronoun*

····➤ (as subject) *generally not translated*. **it's huge** es enorme. **where is it?** ¿dónde está? **it's all lies** son todas mentiras

····➤ (as direct object) lo (*m*), la (*f*). **he read it to me** me lo/la leyó. **give it to me** dámelo/dámela

····➤ (as indirect object) le. **I gave it another coat of paint** le di otra mano de pintura

····➤ (after a preposition) *generally not translated*. **there's nothing behind it** no hay nada detrás

! Note, however, that in some cases *él* or *ella* must be used e.g. **he picked up the spoon and hit me with it** agarró la cuchara y me golpeó con ella

····➤ (at door) **who is it?** ¿quién es?. **it's me** soy yo; (on telephone) **who is it, please?** ¿quién habla, por favor?; (before passing on to sb else) ¿de parte de quién, por favor?

it's **Carol** soy Carol (Spain), habla Carol
····▶ (in impersonal constructions) **it is well known that** ... bien se sabe que ... **it's five o'clock** son las cinco. **so it seems** así parece
····▶ **that's it** (that's right) eso es; (that's enough, that's finished) ya está

Italian *a & n* italiano (*m*)
italics *npl* (letra *f*) cursiva *f*
Italy *n* Italia *f*
itch *n* picazón *f*. ● *vi* picar. **I'm ~ing to** estoy que me muero por. **my arm ~es** me pica el brazo. **~y** *a* que pica. **I've got an ~y nose** me pica la nariz
it'd = **it had**, **it would**
item *n* artículo *m*; (on agenda) punto *m*. **news ~** *n* noticia *f*. **~ize** *vt* detallar
itinerary *n* itinerario *m*
it'll = **it will**
its *a* su, sus (*pl*). ● *pron* (el) suyo *m*, (la) suya *f*, (los) suyos *mpl*, (las) suyas *fpl*
it's = **it is**, **it has**
itself *pron* él mismo, ella misma, ello mismo; (reflexive) se; (after prep) sí mismo, sí misma
I've = **I have**
ivory *n* marfil *m*. ~ **tower** *n* torre *f* de marfil
ivy *n* hiedra *f*

jab *vt* (*pt* **jabbed**) pinchar; (thrust) hurgonear. ● *n* pinchazo *m*
jack *n* (Mec) gato *m*; (socket) enchufe *m* hembra; (Cards) sota *f*. □ ~ **up** *vt* alzar con gato
jackal *n* chacal *m*
jackdaw *n* grajilla *f*
jacket *n* chaqueta *f*; (casual) americana *f*, saco *m* (LAm); (Amer, of book) sobrecubierta *f*; (of record) funda *f*, carátula *f*
jack: ~ knife *vi* <lorry> plegarse. ~**pot** *n* premio *m* gordo. **hit the ~pot** sacar el premio gordo
jade *n* (stone) jade *m*
jagged *a* <edge, cut> irregular; <rock> recortado
jaguar *n* jaguar *m*
jail *n* cárcel *m*, prisión *f*. ● *vt* encarcelar. ~**er** *n* carcelero *m*. ~**house** *n* (Amer) cárcel *f*
jam *vt* (*pt* **jammed**) interferir con <radio>; atestar <road>. ~ **sth into** sth meter algo a la fuerza en algo. ● *vi* <brakes> bloquearse; <machine> trancarse. ● *n* mermelada *f*; (**I**, situation) apuro *m*
jangle *n* sonido *m* metálico (y áspero). ● *vi* hacer ruido (metálico)
janitor *n* portero *m*
January *n* enero *m*
Japan *n* (el) Japón *m*. ~**ese** *a & n invar* japonés (*m*)
jar *n* tarro *m*, bote *m*. ● *vi* (*pt* **jarred**) <clash> desentonar. ● *vt* sacudir

jargon n jerga f
jaundice n ictericia f
jaunt n excursión f
jaunty a (-ier, -iest) garboso
jaw n mandíbula f. ~s npl fauces fpl. ~**bone** n mandíbula f, maxilar m; (of animal) quijada f
jay n arrendajo m. ~**walk** vi cruzar la calle descuidadamente. ~**walker** n peatón m imprudente
jazz n jazz m. □ ~ **up** vt animar. ~**y** a chillón
jealous a celoso; (envious) envidioso. ~**y** n celos mpl
jeans npl vaqueros mpl, jeans mpl, tejanos mpl, pantalones mpl de mezclilla (Mex)
Jeep (P), **jeep** n Jeep m (P)
jeer vi. ~ **at** mofarse de; (boo) abuchear. ● n burla f; (boo) abucheo m
Jell-O n (P) (Amer) gelatina f (con sabor a frutas)
jelly n (clear jam) jalea f; (pudding) ⇒JELL-O; (substance) gelatina f. ~**fish** n (pl invar or -es) medusa f
jeopardize vt arriesgar
jerk n sacudida f; (⊠, fool) idiota m & f. ● vt sacudir
jersey n (pl -eys) jersey m, suéter m, pulóver m
jest n broma f. ● vi bromear
Jesus n Jesús m
jet n (stream) chorro m; (plane) avión m (con motor a reacción); (mineral) azabache m. ~-**black** a azabache negro a invar. ~ **lag** n jet lag m, desfase f horario. **have** ~ **lag** estar desfasado. ~-**propelled** a (de propulsión) a reacción
jettison vt echar al mar; (fig, discard) deshacerse de
jetty n muelle m
Jew n judío m

jewel n joya f. ~**ler** n joyero m. ~**lery** n joyas fpl
Jewish a judío
jiffy n momentito m. **do sth in a** ~ hacer algo en un santiamén
jig n (dance) giga f
jigsaw n. ~ (**puzzle**) rompecabezas m
jilt vt dejar plantado
jingle vt hacer sonar. ● vi tintinear. ● n tintineo m; (advert) jingle m (publicitario)
job n empleo m, trabajo m; (piece of work) trabajo m. **it is a good** ~ **that** menos mal que. ~**less** a desempleado
jockey n jockey m
jocular a jocoso
jog vt (pt **jogged**) empujar; refrescar <memory>. ● vi hacer footing, hacer jogging. ~**er** n persona f quehace footing. ~**ging** n footing m, jogging m. **go** ~**ging** salir a hacer footing or jogging
join vt (link) unir; hacerse socio de <club>; hacerse miembro de <political group>; alistarse en <army>; reunirse con <another person>. ● n juntura. ● vi. ~ **together** <parts> unirse; <roads etc> empalmar; <rivers> confluir. □ ~ **in** vi participar (en). □ ~ **up** vi (Mil) alistarse. ~**er** n carpintero m
joint a conjunto. ● n (join) unión f, junta f; (Anat) articulación f. (Culin) trozo m de carne (para asar). **out of** ~ descoyuntado. ~ **account** n cuenta f conjunta. ~**ly** adv conjuntamente. ~ **owner** n copropietario m.
joist n viga f
jok|e n (story) chiste m; (practical joke) broma f. ● vi bromear. ~**er** n bromista m & f; (Cards) comodín m. ~**y** a jocoso

jolly *a* (**-ier, -iest**) alegre. ● *adv* Ⓘ muy

jolt *vt* sacudir. ● *vi* <vehicle> dar una sacudida. ● *n* sacudida *f*

jostle *vt* empujar. ● *vi* empujarse

jot *n* pizca *f*. ● *vt* (*pt* **jotted**). □ ~ **down** *vt* apuntar (rápidamente). ~**ter** *n* bloc *m*

journal *n* (diary) diario *m*; (newspaper) periódico *m*; (magazine) revista *f*. ~**ism** *n* periodismo *m*. ~**ist** *n* periodista *m & f*

journey *n* viaje *m*. **go on a** ~ hacer un viaje. ● *vi* viajar

jovial *a* jovial

joy *n* alegría *f*. ~**ful** *a* feliz. ~**ous** *a* feliz. ~**rider** *n* joven *m* que roba un coche para dar una vuelta. ~**stick** *n* (Aviat) palanca *f* de mando; (Comp) mando *m*, joystick *m*

jubila|nt *a* jubiloso. ~**tion** *n* júbilo *m*

jubilee *n* aniversario *m* especial

Judaism *n* judaísmo *m*

judge *n* juez *m*. ● *vt* juzgar. ~**ment** *n* juicio *m*

judicia|l *a* judicial. ~**ry** *n* judicatura *f*

judo *n* judo *m*

jug *n* jarra *f*

juggernaut *n* camión *m* grande

juggle *vi* hacer malabarismos. ● *vt* hacer malabarismos con. ~**r** *n* malabarista *m & f*

juic|e *n* jugo *m*, zumo *m*. ~**y** *a* jugoso, zumoso; <story etc> Ⓘ picante

jukebox *n* máquina *f* de discos, rocola *f* (LAm)

July *n* julio *m*

jumble *vt*. ~ (**up**) mezclar. ● *n* (muddle) revoltijo *m*. ~ **sale** *n* venta *f* de objetos usados *m*

jumbo *a* gigante. ~ **jet** *n* jumbo *m*

jump *vt* saltar. ~ **rope** (Amer) saltar a la comba, saltar a la cuerda. ~ **the gun** obrar prematuramente. ~ **the queue** colarse. ● *vi* saltar; (start) sobresaltarse; <prices> alzarse. ~ **at an opportunity** apresurarse a aprovechar una oportunidad. ● *n* salto *m*; (start) susto *m*; (increase) aumento *m*. ~**er** *n* jersey *m*, suéter *m*, pulóver *m*; (Amer, dress) pichi *m*, jumper *m & f* (LAm). ~**er cables** (Amer), ~ **leads** *npl* cables *mpl* de arranque. ~ **rope** (Amer) comba *f*, cuerda *f*, reata *f* (Mex). ~**suit** *n* mono *m*. ~**y** *a* nervioso

junction *n* (of roads, rails) cruce *m*; (Elec) empalme *m*

June *n* junio *m*

jungle *n* selva *f*, jungla *f*

junior *a* (in age) más joven (**to** que); (in rank) subalterno. ● *n* menor *m*

junk *n* trastos *mpl* viejos; (worthless stuff) basura *f*. ● *vt* Ⓘ tirar. ~ **food** *n* comida *f* basura, alimento *m* chatarra (Mex). ~**ie** *n* Ⓘ drogadicto *m*, yonqui *m & f* Ⓘ. ~ **mail** *n* propaganda *f* que se recibe por correo. ~ **shop** *n* tienda *f* de trastos viejos

junta *n* junta *f* militar

Jupiter *n* Júpiter *m*

jurisdiction *n* jurisdicción *f*

jur|or *n* (miembro *m* de un) jurado *m*. ~**y** *n* jurado *m*

just *a* (fair) justo. ● *adv* exactamente, justo; (barely) justo; (only) sólo, solamente. ~ **as tall** tan alto (**as** como). ~ **listen!** ¡escucha! **he has** ~ **arrived** acaba de llegar, recién llegó (LAm)

justice *n* justicia *f*. **J**~ **of the Peace** juez *m* de paz

J

justif|iable *a* justificable. **~iably**
adv con razón. **~ication** *n*
justificación *f*. **~y** *vt* justificar
jut *vi* (*pt* **jutted**). **~** (**out**)
sobresalir

juvenile *a* juvenil; (childish)
infantil. ● *n* (Jurid) menor *m & f*

kaleidoscope *n* caleidoscopio *m*
kangaroo *n* canguro *m*
karate *n* kárate *m*, karate *m* (LAm)
keel *n* (of ship) quilla *f*. □ **~ over**
vi volcar(se)
keen *a* (**-er, -est**) <interest,
feeling> vivo; <wind, mind,
analysis> penetrante; <eyesight>
agudo; (eager) entusiasta. **I'm ~ on
golf** me encanta el golf. **he's ~ on
Shostakovich** le gusta
Shostakovich. **~ly** *adv*
vivamente; (enthusiastically) con
entusiasmo. **~ness** *n* intensidad
f; (enthusiasm) entusiasmo *m*.
keep *vt* (*pt* **kept**) guardar;
cumplir <promise>; tener <shop,
animals>; mantener <family>;
observar <rule>; (celebrate)
celebrar; (delay) detener; (prevent)
impedir. ● *vi* <food> conservarse;
(remain) quedarse; (continue) seguir.
~ doing seguir haciendo. ● *n*
subsistencia *f*; (of castle) torreón
m. **for ~s** 🄸 para siempre. □ **~
back** *vt* retener. ● *vi* no
acercarse. □ **~ in** *vt* no dejar
salir. □ **~ off** *vt* mantenerse
alejado de <land>. '**~ off the
grass**' 'prohibido pisar el césped'.
□ **~ on** *vi* seguir. **~ on doing sth**

seguir haciendo. □ **~ out** *vt* no
dejar entrar. □ **~ up** *vt*
mantener. □ **~ up with** *vt* estar
al día en

kennel *n* casa *f* del perro; (Amer,
for boarding) residencia *f* canina.
~s *n invar* residencia *f* canina
kept ⇒KEEP
kerb *n* bordillo *m* (de la acera),
borde *m* de la banqueta (Mex)
kerosene *n* queroseno *m*
ketchup *n* salsa *f* de tomate
kettle *n* pava *f*, tetera *f* (para
calentar agua)
key *n* llave *f*; (of computer, piano)
tecla *f*; (Mus) tono *m*. **be off ~** no
estar en el tono. ● *a* clave. □ **~
in** *vt* teclear. **~board** *n* teclado
m. **~hole** *n* ojo *m* de la
cerradura. **~ring** *n* llavero *m*
khaki *a* caqui
kick *vt* dar una patada a
<person>; patear <ball>. ● *vi* dar
patadas; <horse> cocear. ● *n*
patada *f*; (of horse) coz *f*; (🄸, thrill)
placer *m*. □ **~ out** *vt* 🄸 echar.
□ **~ up** *vt* armar <fuss etc>. **~off**
n (Sport) saque *m* inicial. **~ start**
vt arrancar (con el pedal de
arranque) <engine>
kid *n* (young goat) cabrito *m*; (🄸,
child) niño *m*, chaval *m*, escuincle
m (Mex). ● *vt* (*pt* **kidded**) tomar
el pelo a. ● *vi* bromear
kidnap *vt* (*pt* **kidnapped**)
secuestrar. **~per** *n* secuestrador
m. **~ping** *n* secuestro *m*
kidney *n* riñón *m*
kill *vt* matar; (fig) acabar con. ● *n*
matanza *f*. □ **~ off** *vt* matar. **~er**
n asesino *m*. **~ing** *n* matanza *f*;
(murder) asesinato *m*. **make a ~ing**
(fig) hacer un gran negocio
kiln *n* horno *m*
kilo *n* (*pl* **-os**) kilo *m*. **~gram(me)**
n kilogramo *m*. **~metre** *n*

kilómetro *m*. **~watt** *n* kilovatio *m*

kilt *n* falda *f* escocesa

kin *n* familiares *mpl*

kind *n* tipo *m*, clase *f*. **~ of** (🎓, somewhat) un poco. **in ~** en especie. **be two of a ~** ser tal para cual. ● *a* amable

kindergarten *n* jardín *m* de infancia

kind-hearted *a* bondadoso

kindle *vt* encender

kind|ly *a* (**-ier**, **-iest**) bondadoso. ● *adv* amablemente; (please) haga el favor de. **~ness** *n* bondad *f*; (act) favor *m*

king *n* rey *m*. **~dom** *n* reino *m*. **~fisher** *n* martín *m* pescador. **~-size(d)** *a* extragrande

kink *n* (in rope) vuelta *f*, curva *f*; (in hair) onda *f*. **~y** *a* 🎓 pervertido

kiosk *n* quiosco *m*

kipper *n* arenque *m* ahumado

kiss *n* beso *m*. ● *vt* besar. ● *vi* besarse

kit *n* avíos *mpl*. **tool ~** caja *f* de herramientas. ☐ **~ out** *vt* (*pt* **kitted**) equipar

kitchen *n* cocina *f*

kite *n* cometa *f*, papalote *m* (Mex)

kitten *n* gatito *m*

knack *n* truco *m*

knapsack *n* mochila *f*

knead *vt* amasar

knee *n* rodilla *f*. **~cap** *n* rótula *f*

kneel *vi* (*pt* **kneeled** *or* **knelt**). **~ (down)** arrodillarse; (be on one's knees) estar arrodillado

knelt ⇒KNEEL

knew ⇒KNOW

knickers *npl* bragas *fpl*, calzones *mpl* (LAm), pantaletas *fpl* (Mex)

knife *n* (*pl* **knives**) cuchillo *m*. ● *vt* acuchillar

knight *n* caballero *m*; (Chess) caballo *m*. ● *vt* conceder el título de Sir a. **~hood** *n* título *m* de Sir

knit *vt* (*pt* **knitted** *or* **knit**) hacer, tejer (LAm). ● *vi* tejer, hacer punto. **~ one's brow** fruncir el ceño. **~ting** *n* tejido *m*, punto *m*. **~ting needle** *n* aguja *f* de hacer punto, aguja *f* de tejer

knives ⇒KNIFE

knob *n* botón *m*; (of door, drawer etc) tirador *m*. **~bly** *a* nudoso

knock *vt* golpear; (criticize) criticar. ● *vi* golpear; (at door) llamar, golpear (LAm). ● *n* golpe *m*. ☐ **~ about** *vt* maltratar. ☐ **~ down** *vt* derribar; atropellar <*person*>. ☐ **~ off** *vt* hacer caer. *vi* (🎓, finish work) terminar, salir del trabajo. ☐ **~ out** *vt* (by blow) dejar sin sentido; (eliminate) eliminar. ☐ **~ over** *vt* tirar; atropellar <*person*>. **~er** *n* aldaba *f*. **~-kneed** *a* patizambo. **~out** *n* (Boxing) nocaut *m*

knot *n* nudo *m*. ● *vt* (*pt* **knotted**) anudar

know *vt* (*pt* **knew**) saber; (be acquainted with) conocer. **let s.o. ~ sth** decirle algo a uno; (warn) avisarle algo a uno. ● *vi* saber. **~ how to do sth** saber hacer algo. **~ about** entender de <*cars etc*>. **~ of** saber de. ● *n*. **be in the ~** estar enterado. **~-all** *n* *n* sabelotodo *m & f*. **~-how** *n* know-how *m*, conocimientos *mpl* y experiencia. **~ingly** *adv* a sabiendas. **~-it-all** *n* (Amer) ⇒**~-all**

knowledge *n* saber *m*; (awareness) conocimiento *m*; (learning) conocimientos *mpl*. **~able** *a* informado

known ⇒KNOW. ● *a* conocido

knuckle *n* nudillo *m*. ☐ **~ under** *vi* someterse

Korea n Corea f. ~**n** a & n coreano (m)

kudos n prestigio m

lab n 🔲 laboratorio m
label n etiqueta f. ● vt (pt labelled) poner etiqueta a; (fig, describe as) tachar de
laboratory n laboratorio m
laborious a penoso
labour n trabajo m; (workers) mano f de obra; (Med) parto m. **in** ~ de parto. ● vi trabajar. ● vt insistir en. **L**~ n el partido m laborista. ● a laborista. ~**er** n peón m
lace n encaje m; (of shoe) cordón m, agujeta f (Mex). ● vt (fasten) atar
lacerate vt lacerar
lack n falta f. **for** ~ **of** por falta de. ● vt faltarle a uno. **he** ~**s confidence** le falta confianza en sí mismo. ~**ing** a. **be** ~**ing** faltar. **be** ~**ing in** no tener
lad n muchacho m
ladder n escalera f (de mano); (in stocking) carrera f. ● vt hacerse una carrera en. ● vi hacérsele una carrera a
laden a cargado (**with** de)
ladle n cucharón m
lady n señora f. **young** ~ señorita f. ~**bird** n, ~**bug** n (Amer) mariquita f, catarina f (Mex). ~**-in-waiting** n dama f de honor. ~**like** a fino
lag vi (pt lagged). ~ (**behind**) retrasarse. ● vt revestir <pipes>. ● n (interval) intervalo m

lager n cerveza f (rubia)
lagging n revestimiento m
lagoon n laguna f
laid ⇒LAY
lain ⇒LIE¹
lair n guarida f
lake n lago m
lamb n cordero m
lame a (-er, -est) cojo, rengo (LAm); <excuse> pobre, malo
lament n lamento m. ● vt lamentar. ~**able** a lamentable
lamp n lámpara f
lamp: ~**post** n farol m. ~**shade** n pantalla f
lance n lanza f
land n tierra f; (country) país m; (plot) terreno m. ● vt desembarcar; (obtain) conseguir; dar <blow>. ● vi (from ship) desembarcar; <aircraft> aterrizar. □ ~ **up** vi ir a parar. ~**ing** n desembarque m; (Aviat) aterrizaje m; (top of stairs) descanso m. ~**lady** n casera f; (of inn) dueña f. ~**lord** n casero m, dueño m; (of inn) dueño m. ~**mark** n punto m destacado. ~**scape** n paisaje m. ~**slide** n desprendimiento m de tierras; (Pol) victoria f arrolladora
lane n (path, road) camino m, sendero m; (strip of road) carril m
language n idioma m; (speech, style) lenguaje m
lank a <hair> lacio. ~**y** a (-ier, -iest) larguirucho
lantern n linterna f
lap n (of body) rodillas fpl; (Sport) vuelta f. ● vi (pt lapped) <waves> chapotear. □ ~**up** beber a lengüetazos; (fig) aceptar con entusiasmo
lapel n solapa f
lapse vi (decline) degradarse; (expire) caducar; <time>

transcurrir. **~ into silence**
callarse. ● *n* error *m*; (of time)
intervalo *m*

laptop *n.* **~ (computer)** laptop *m*,
laptop *f* (LAm)

lard *n* manteca *f* de cerdo

larder *n* despensa *f*

large *a* (**-er, -est**) grande, (before
singular noun) gran. ● *n.* **at ~** en
libertad. **~ly** *adv* en gran parte

lark *n* (bird) alondra *f*; (joke) broma
f; (bit of fun) travesura *f*. □ **~
about** *vt* hacer el tonto 🆃

larva *n* (*pl* **-vae**) larva *f*

laser *n* láser *m*. **~ beam** *n* rayo
m láser. **~ printer** *n* impresora *f*
láser

lash *vt* azotar. □ **~ out** *vi* atacar.
~ out against *vt* atacar. ● *n*
latigazo *m*; (eyelash) pestaña *f*;
(whip) látigo *m*

lashings *npl.* **~ of** (🆇, cream etc)
montones de

lass *n* muchacha *f*

lasso *n* (*pl* **-os**) lazo *m*

last *a* último; *<week etc>* pasado.
~ Monday el lunes pasado. **~
night** anoche. ● *adv* por último;
(most recently) la última vez. **he
came ~** llegó el último. ● *n*
último *m*; (remainder) lo que queda.
~ but one penúltimo. **at (long) ~**
por fin. ● *vi/t* durar. □ **~ out** *vi*
sobrevivir. **~ing** *a* duradero. **~ly**
adv por último

latch *n* pestillo *m*

late *a* (**-er, -est**) (not on time) tarde;
(recent) reciente; (former) antiguo,
ex. **be ~** llegar tarde. **in ~ July** a
fines de julio. **the ~ Dr Phillips** el
difunto Dr. Phillips. ● *adv* tarde.
~ly *adv* últimamente

latent *a* latente

later *adv* más tarde

lateral *a* lateral

latest *a* último. ● *n.* **at the ~** a
más tardar

lathe *n* torno *m*

lather *n* espuma *f*

Latin *n* (Lang) latín *m*. ● *a* latino.
~ America *n* América *f* Latina,
Latinoamérica *f*. **~ American** *a*
& *n* latinoamericano *f*

latitude *n* latitud *m*

latter *a* último; (of two) segundo.
● *n.* **the ~** éste *m*, ésta *f*, éstos
mpl, éstas *fpl*

laugh *vi* reír(se). **~ at** reírse de.
● *n* risa *f*. **~able** *a* ridículo. **~ing
stock** *n* hazmerreír *m*. **~ter** *n*
risas *fpl*

launch *vt* lanzar; botar *<new
vessel>*. ● *n* lanzamiento *m*; (of
new vessel) botadura; (boat) lancha *f*
(a motor). **~ing pad**, **~ pad** *n*
plataforma *f* de lanzamiento

laund|er *vt* lavar (y planchar).
~erette, **L~romat** (Amer) (P) *n*
lavandería *f* automática. **~ry** *n*
(place) lavandería *f*; (dirty clothes)
ropa *f* sucia; (clean clothes) ropa *f*
limpia

lava *n* lava *f*

lavatory *n* (cuarto *m* de) baño *m*.
public ~ servicios *mpl*, baños *mpl*
(LAm)

lavish *a* *<lifestyle>* de derroche;
(meal) espléndido; (production)
fastuoso. ● *vt* prodigar (on a)

law *n* ley *f*; (profession, subject of
study) derecho *m*. **~ and order** *n*
orden *m* público. **~ court** *n*
tribunal *m*

lawn *n* césped *m*, pasto *m* (LAm).
~mower *n* cortacésped *f*,
cortadora *f* de pasto (LAm)

lawsuit *n* juicio *m*

lawyer *n* abogado *m*

lax *a* descuidado; *<morals etc>*
laxo

laxative *n* laxante *m*

lay ⇒LIE. ● vt (pt **laid**) poner <also table, eggs>; tender <trap>; formar <plan>. ~ **hands on** echar mano a. ~ **hold of** agarrar. ● a (non-clerical) laico; <opinion etc> profano. □ ~ **down** vt dejar a un lado; imponer <condition>. □ ~ **into** vt ⊠ dar una paliza a. □ ~ **off** vt despedir <worker>. ● Ⅱ terminar. □ ~ **on** vt (provide) proveer. □ ~ **out** vt (design) disponer; (display) exponer; gastar <money>. ~**about** n holgazán. ~**-by** n área f de reposo

layer n capa f

layette n canastilla f

layman n (pl **-men**) lego m

layout n disposición f

laz|e vi holgazanear; (relax) descansar. ~**iness** n pereza f. ~**y** a perezoso. ~**ybones** n holgazán m

lead¹ vt (pt **led**) conducir; dirigir <team>; llevar <life>; encabezar <parade, attack>. **I was led to believe that …** me dieron a entender que …. ● vi (go first) ir delante; (in race) aventajar. ● n mando m; (clue) pista f; (leash) correa f; (wire) cable m. **be in the** ~ llevar la delantera

lead² n plomo m; (of pencil) mina f. ~**ed** a <fuel> con plomo

lead|er n jefe m; (Pol) líder m & f; (of gang) cabecilla m. ~**ership** n dirección f. ~**ing** a principal; (in front) delantero

leaf n (pl **leaves**) hoja f. □ ~ **through** vt hojear ~**let** n folleto m. ~**y** a frondoso

league n liga f. **be in** ~ **with** estar aliado con

leak n (hole) agujero m; (of gas, liquid) escape m; (of information) filtración f; (in roof) gotera f; (in boat) vía f de agua. ● vi gotear; <liquid> salirse; <boat> hacer agua. ● vt perder; filtrar <information>. ~**y** a <receptacle> agujereado; <roof> que tiene goteras

lean (pt **leaned** or **leant**) vt apoyar. ● vi inclinarse. □ ~ **against** vt apoyarse en. □ ~ **on** vt apoyarse en. □ ~ **out** vt asomarse (of a). □ ~ **over** vi inclinarse ● a (-er, -est) <person> delgado; <animal> flaco; <meat> magro. ~**ing** a inclinado. ~**-to** n colgadizo m

leap vi (pt **leaped** or **leapt**) saltar. ● n salto m. ~**frog** n. **play** ~**frog** saltar al potro, jugar a la pídola, brincar al burro (Mex). ● vi (pt **-frogged**) saltar. ~ **year** n año m bisiesto

learn vt/i (pt **learned** or **learnt**) aprender (**to do** a hacer). ~**ed** a culto. ~**er** n principiante m & f; (apprentice) aprendiz m. ~**ing** n saber m

lease n arriendo m. ● vt arrendar

leash n correa f

least a (smallest amount of) mínimo; (slightest) menor; (smallest) más pequeño. ● n. **the** ~ lo menos. **at** ~ por lo menos. **not in the** ~ en absoluto. ● adv menos

leather n piel f, cuero m

leave vt (pt **left**) dejar; (depart from) salir de. ~ **alone** dejar de tocar <thing>; dejar en paz <person>. ● vi marcharse; <train> salir. ● n permiso m. □ ~ **behind** vt dejar. □ ~ **out** vt omitir. □ ~ **over** vt. **be left over** quedar. **on** ~ (Mil) de permiso

leaves ⇒LEAF

lecture n conferencia f; (Univ) clase f; (rebuke) sermón m. ● vi dar clase. ● vt (scold) sermonear. ~**r** n conferenciante m & f, conferencista m & f (LAm); (Univ) profesor m universitario

led ⇒LEAD¹

ledge *n* cornisa *f*; (of window) alféizar *m*

leek *n* puerro *m*

leer *vi*. ∼ **at** mirar impúdicamente. ● *n* mirada impúdica *f*

left ⇒LEAVE. *a* izquierdo. ● *adv* a la izquierda. ● *n* izquierda *f*. ∼**-handed** *a* zurdo. ∼ **luggage** *n* consigna *f*. ∼**overs** *npl* restos *mpl*. ∼**-wing** *a* izquierdista

leg *n* pierna *f*; (of animal, furniture) pata *f*; (of pork) pernil *m*; (of lamb) pierna *f*; (of journey) etapa *f*. **on its last** ∼**s** en las últimas. **pull s.o.'s** ∼ 🄸 tomarle el pelo a uno

legacy *n* herencia *f*

legal *a* (permitted by law) lícito; (recognized by law) legítimo; <system etc> jurídico. ∼**ity** *n* legalidad *f*. ∼**ize** *vt* legalizar. ∼**ly** *adv* legalmente

legend *n* leyenda *f*. ∼**ary** *a* legendario

legible *a* legible

legislat|e *vi* legislar. ∼**ion** *n* legislación *f*

legitimate *a* legítimo

leisure *n* ocio *m*. **at your** ∼ cuando le venga bien. ∼**ly** *a* lento, pausado

lemon *n* limón *m*. ∼**ade** *n* (fizzy) gaseosa *f* (de limón); (still) limonada *f*

lend *vt* (*pt* lent) prestar. ∼**ing** *n* préstamo *m*

length *n* largo *m*; (of time) duración *f*; (of cloth) largo *m*. **at** ∼ (at last) por fin. **at (great)** ∼ detalladamente. ∼**en** *vt* alargar. ● *vi* alargarse. ∼**ways** *adv* a lo largo. ∼**y** *a* largo

lenient *a* indulgente

lens *n* lente *f*; (of camera) objetivo *m*. (**contact**) ∼**es** *npl* lentillas *fpl*, lentes *mpl* de contacto (LAm)

lent ⇒LEND

Lent *n* cuaresma *f*

Leo *n* Leo *m*

leopard *n* leopardo *m*

leotard *n* malla *f*

lesbian *n* lesbiana *f*. ● *a* lesbiano

less *a & n & adv & prep* menos. ∼ **than** menos que; (with numbers) menos de. ∼ **and** ∼ cada vez menos. **none the** ∼ sin embargo. ∼**en** *vt/i* disminuir

lesson *n* clase *f*

lest *conj* no sea que (+ subjunctive)

let *vt* (*pt* let, *pres p* letting) dejar; (lease) alquilar. ∼ **me do it** déjame hacerlo. ● *v aux*. ∼'**s go!** ¡vamos!, ¡vámonos! ∼'**s see** (vamos) a ver. ∼'**s talk/drink** hablemos/bebamos. □ ∼ **down** *vt* bajar; (deflate) desinflar; (fig) defraudar. □ ∼ **go** *vt* soltar. □ ∼ **in** *vt* dejar entrar. □ ∼ **off** *vt* disparar <gun>; (cause to explode) hacer explotar; hacer estallar <firework>; (excuse) perdonar. □ ∼ **out** *vt* dejar salir. □ ∼ **through** *vt* dejar pasar. □ ∼ **up** *vi* disminuir. ∼**down** *n* desilusión *f*

lethal *a* <dose, wound> mortal; <weapon> mortífero

letharg|ic *a* letárgico. ∼**y** *n* letargo *m*

letter *n* (of alphabet) letra *f*; (written message) carta *f*. ∼ **bomb** *n* carta *f* bomba. ∼**box** *n* buzón *m*. ∼**ing** *n* letras *fpl*

lettuce *n* lechuga *f*

let-up *n* interrupción *f*

leukaemia *n* leucemia *f*

level *a* (flat, even) plano, parejo (LAm); <spoonful> raso. ∼ **with** (at

L

same height) al nivel de. ● *n* nivel *m*. ● *vt* (*pt* **levelled**) nivelar; (aim) apuntar. ~ **crossing** *n* paso *m* a nivel, crucero *m* (Mex)

lever *n* palanca *f*. ● *vt* apalancar. ~ **open** abrir haciendo palanca. ~**age** *n* apalancamiento *m*

levy *vt* imponer <*tax*>. ● *n* impuesto *m*

lewd *a* (**-er, -est**) lascivo

liab|lity *n* responsabilidad *f*; (🄸, disadvantage) lastre *m*. ~**ilities** *npl* (debts) deudas *fpl*. ~**le** *a*. be ~**le to do** tener tendencia a hacer. ~**le for** responsable de. ~**le to** susceptible de; expuesto a <*fine*>

liais|e *vi* actuar de enlace (**with** con). ~**on** *n* enlace *m*

liar *n* mentiroso *m*

libel *n* difamación *f*. ● *vt* (*pt* **libelled**) difamar (por escrito)

liberal *a* liberal; (generous) generoso. **L~** (Pol) del Partido Liberal. ● *n* liberal *m & f*. ~**ly** *adv* liberalmente; (generously) generosamente

liberat|e *vt* liberar. ~**ion** *n* liberación *f*

liberty *n* libertad *f*. **take liberties** tomarse libertades. **take the ~ of** tomarse la libertad de

Libra *n* Libra *f*

librar|ian *n* bibliotecario *m*. ~**y** *n* biblioteca *f*

lice ⇒LOUSE

licence *n* licencia *f*, permiso *m*

license *vt* autorizar. ● *n* (Amer) ⇒LICENCE. ~ **number** *n* (Amer) (número *m* de) matrícula *f*. ~ **plate** *n* (Amer) matrícula *f*, placa *f* (LAm)

lick *vt* lamer; (🄸, defeat) dar una paliza a. ● *n* lametón *m*

licorice *n* (Amer) regaliz *m*

lid *n* tapa *f*; (eyelid) párpado *m*

lie¹ *vi* (*pt* **lay**, *pp* **lain**, *pres p* **lying**) echarse, tenderse; (be in lying position) estar tendido; (be) estar, encontrarse. ~ **low** quedarse escondido. □ ~ **down** *vi* echarse, tenderse

lie² *n* mentira *f*. ● *vi* (*pt* **lied**, *pres p* **lying**) mentir

lie-in *n*. **have a ~** quedarse en la cama

lieutenant *n* (Mil) teniente *m*

life *n* (*pl* **lives**) vida *f*. ~ **belt** *n* salvavidas *m*. ~**boat** *n* lancha *f* de salvamento; (on ship) bote *m* salvavidas. ~**buoy** *n* boya *f* salvavidas. ~**guard** *n* salvavidas *m & f*. ~ **jacket** *n* chaleco *m* salvavidas. ~**less** *a* sin vida. ~**like** *a* verosímil. ~**line** *n* cuerda *f* de salvamento; (fig) tabla *f* de salvación. ~**long** *a* de toda la vida. ~ **preserver** *n* (Amer, buoy) ⇒~buoy; (jacket) ⇒~ jacket. ~ **ring** *n* (Amer) ⇒~ BELT. ~**saver** *n* (person) salvavidas *m & f*; (fig) salvación *f*. ~**-size(d)** *a* (de) tamaño natural. ~**time** *n* vida *f*. ~ **vest** *n* (Amer) ⇒~ JACKET

lift *vt* levantar. ● *vi* <*fog*> disiparse. ● *n* ascensor *m*. **give a ~ to s.o.** llevar a uno en su coche, dar aventón a uno (Mex). □ ~ **up** *vt* levantar. ~**-off** *n* despegue *m*

light *n* luz *f*; (lamp) lámpara *f*, luz *f*; (flame) fuego *m*. **come to ~** salir a la luz. **have you got a ~?** ¿tienes fuego? **the ~s** *npl* (traffic signals) el semáforo; (on vehicle) las luces. ● *a* (**-er, -est**) (in colour) claro; (not heavy) ligero. ● *vt* (*pt* **lit** or **lighted**) encender, prender (LAm); (illuminate) iluminar. ● *vi* encenderse, prenderse (LAm). ~ **up** *vt* iluminar. ● *vi* iluminarse. ~ **bulb** *n* bombilla *f*, foco *m* (Mex).

~en vt (make less heavy) aligerar, alivianar (LAm); (give light to) iluminar; (make brighter) aclarar. **~er** n (for cigarettes) mechero m, encendedor m. **~hearted** a alegre. **~house** n faro m. **~ly** adv ligeramente

lightning n. flash of **~** relámpago m. ● a relámpago

lightweight a ligero, liviano (LAm)

like a parecido. ● prep como. ● conj 🆃 como. ● vt. I **~** chocolate me gusta el chocolate. they **~** swimming (a ellos) les gusta nadar. would you **~** a coffee? ¿quieres un café? **~able** a simpático.

like|lihood n probabilidad f. **~ly** a (-ier, -iest) probable. he is **~ly** to come es probable que venga. ● adv probablemente. not **~ly!** ¡ni hablar! **~n** vt comparar (to con, a). **~ness** n parecido m. be a good **~ness** parecerse mucho. **~wise** adv (also) también; (the same way) lo mismo

liking n (for thing) afición f; (for person) simpatía f

lilac a lila. ● n lila f; (color) lila m

lily n lirio m; (white) azucena f

limb n miembro m. out on a **~** aislado

lime n (white substance) cal f; (fruit) lima f. **~light** n. be in the **~light** ser el centro de atención

limerick n quintilla f humorística

limit n límite m. ● vt limitar. **~ation** n limitación f. **~ed** a limitado. **~ed company** n sociedad f anónima

limousine n limusina f

limp vi cojear, renguear (LAm). ● n cojera f, renguera f (LAm). have a **~** cojear. ● a (-er, -est) flojo

linden n (Amer) tilo m

line n línea f; (track) vía f; (wrinkle) arruga f; (row) fila f; (of poem) verso m; (rope) cuerda f; (of goods) surtido m; (Amer, queue) cola f. stand in **~** (Amer) hacer cola. get in **~** (Amer) ponerse en la cola. cut in **~** (Amer) colarse. in **~** with de acuerdo con. ● vt forrar <skirt, box>; bordear <streets etc>. **□ ~ up** vi alinearse; (in queue) hacer cola. vt (form into line) poner en fila; (align) alinear. **~ a** <paper> con renglones; (with fabric) forrado

linen n (sheets etc) ropa f blanca; (material) lino m

liner n (ship) transatlántico m

linger vi tardar en marcharse. **~ (on)** <smells etc> persistir. **□ ~ over** vt dilatarse en

lingerie n lencería f

linguist n políglota m & f; lingüista m & f. **~ic** a lingüístico. **~ics** n lingüística f

lining n forro m

link n (of chain) eslabón m; (connection) conexión f; (bond) vínculo m; (transport, telecommunications) conexión f, enlace m. ● vt conectar; relacionar <facts, events>. **□ ~ up** vt/i conectar

lino n (pl **-os**) linóleo m

lint n (Med) hilas fpl

lion n león m. **~ess** n leona f

lip n labio m; (edge) borde m. **~read** vi leer los labios. **~salve** n crema f para los labios. **~ service** n. pay **~ service to** aprobar de boquilla, aprobar de los dientes para afuera (Mex). **~stick** n lápiz m de labios

liqueur n licor m

liquid a & n líquido (m)

liquidate vt liquidar

liquidize vt licuar. **~r** n licuadora f

liquor n bebidas fpl alcohólicas

L

liquorice *n* regaliz *m*

liquor store *n* (Amer) tienda *f* de bebidas alcohólicas

lisp *n* ceceo *m*. **speak with a ~** cecear. ● *vi* cecear

list *n* lista *f*. ● *vt* hacer una lista de; (enter in a list) inscribir. ● *vi* (ship) escorar

listen *vi* escuchar. **~ in (to)** escuchar. **~ to** escuchar. **~er** *n* oyente *m & f*

listless *a* apático

lit ⇒LIGHT

literacy *n* alfabetismo *m*

literal *a* literal. **~ly** *adv* literalmente

literary *a* literario

literate *a* alfabetizado

literature *n* literatura *f*; (fig) folletos *mpl*

lithe *a* ágil

litre *n* litro *m*

litter *n* basura *f*; (of animals) camada *f*. ● *vt* ensuciar; (scatter) esparcir. **~ed with** lleno de. **~ bin** *n* papelera *f*. **~bug, ~ lout** *n* persona *f* que tira basura en lugares públicos

little *a* pequeño; (not much) poco. **~ water** un poco de agua. ● *pron* poco, poca. **a ~** un poco. ● *adv* poco. **~ by ~** poco a poco. **~ finger** *n* (dedo *m*) meñique *m*

live *vt/i* vivir. □ **~ down** *vt* lograr borrar. □ **~ off** *vt* vivir a costa de <*family, friends*>; (feed on) alimentarse de. □ **~ on** *vt* (feed o.s. on) vivir de. *vi* <*memory*> seguir presente; <*tradition*> seguir existiendo. □ **~ up** *vt*. **~ it up** □ darse la gran vida. □ **~ up to** *vt* vivir de acuerdo con; cumplir <*promise*>. ● *a* vivo; <*wire*> con corriente; <*broadcast*> en directo

livelihood *n* sustento *m*

lively *a* (-ier, -iest) vivo

liven up *vt* animar. ● *vi* animar(se)

liver *n* hígado *m*

lives ⇒LIFE

livestock *n* animales *mpl* (de cría); (cattle) ganado *m*

livid *a* lívido; (⒤, angry) furioso

living *a* vivo. ● *n* vida *f*. **make a ~** ganarse la vida. **~ room** *n* salón *m*, sala *f* (de estar), living *m* (LAm)

lizard *n* lagartija *f*; (big) lagarto *m*

load *n* (also Elec) carga *f*; (quantity) cantidad *f*; (weight, strain) peso *m*. **~s of** ⒤ montones de. ● *vt* cargar. **~ed** *a* cargado

loaf *n* (*pl* **loaves**) pan *m*; (stick of bread) barra *f* de pan. ● *vi*. **~ (about)** holgazanear

loan *n* préstamo *m*. **on ~** prestado. ● *vt* prestar

loath|e *vt* odiar. **~ing** *n* odio *m* (of a). **~esome** *a* repugnante

lobby *n* vestíbulo *m*; (Pol) grupo *m* de presión. ● *vt* ejercer presión sobre. ● *vi*. **~ for sth** ejercer presión para obtener algo

lobe *n* lóbulo *m*

lobster *n* langosta *f*, bogavante *m*

local *a* local. **~ (phone) call** llamada *f* urbana. ● *n* (⒤, pub) bar *m*. **the ~s** los vecinos *mpl*. **~ government** *n* administración *f* municipal. **~ity** *n* localidad *f*. **~ly** *adv* <*live, work*> en la zona

locat|e *vt* (situate) situar, ubicar (LAm); (find) localizar, ubicar (LAm). **~ion** *n* situación *f*, ubicación *f* (LAm). **on ~ion** fuera del estudio. **to film on ~ion in Andalusia** rodar en Andalucía

lock *n* (of door etc) cerradura *f*; (on canal) esclusa *f*; (of hair) mechón *m*. ● *vt* cerrar con llave. ● *vi* cerrarse con llave. □ **~ in** *vt* encerrar. □ ~ **out** *vt* cerrar la puerta a. □ ~ **up** *vt* encerrar <*person*>; cerrar con llave <*building*>

locker *n* armario *m*, locker *m* (LAm). ~ **room** *n* (Amer) vestuario *m*, vestidor *m* (Mex)

locket *n* medallón *m*

lock: ~**out** *n* cierre *m* patronal, paro *m* patronal (LAm). ~**smith** *n* cerrajero *m*

locomotive *n* locomotora *f*

lodg|e *n* (of porter) portería *f*. ● *vt* alojar; presentar <*complaint*>. ~**er** *n* huésped *m*. ~**ings** *n* alojamiento *m*; (room) habitación *f* alquilada

loft *n* desván *m*, altillo *m* (LAm)

lofty *a* (**-ier**, **-iest**) elevado; (haughty) altanero

log *n* (of wood) tronco *m*; (as fuel) leño *m*; (record) diario *m*. **sleep like a ~** dormir como un tronco. ● *vt* (*pt* **logged**) registrar. □ ~ **in**, ~ **on** *vi* (Comp) entrar (al sistema). □ ~ **off**, ~ **out** *vi* (Comp) salir (del sistema)

logarithm *n* logaritmo *m*

loggerheads *npl*. **be at ~ with** estar a matar con

logic *a* lógica *f*. ~**al** *a* lógico. ~**ally** *adv* lógicamente

logistics *n* logística *f*. ● *npl* (practicalities) problemas *mpl* logísticos

logo *n* (*pl* **-os**) logo *m*

loin *n* (Culin) lomo *m*. ~**s** *npl* entrañas *fpl*

loiter *vi* perder el tiempo

loll *vi* repantigarse

loll|ipop *n* pirulí *m*. ~**y** *n* polo *m*, paleta *f* (helada) (LAm)

London *n* Londres *m*. ● *a* londinense. ~**er** *n* londinense *m* & *f*

lone *a* solitario. ~**ly** *a* (**-ier**, **-iest**) solitario. **feel ~ly** sentirse muy solo. ~**r** *n* solitario *m*. ~**some** *a* solitario

long *a* (**-er**, **-est**) largo. **a ~ time** mucho tiempo. **how ~ is it?** ¿cuánto tiene de largo? ● *adv* largo/mucho tiempo. **as ~ as** (while) mientras; (provided that) con tal que (+ *subjunctive*). **before ~** dentro de poco. **so ~!** ¡hasta luego! **so ~ as** (provided that) con tal que (+ *subjunctive*). □ ~ **for** *vi* anhelar. ~ **to do** estar deseando hacer. ~-**distance** *a* de larga distancia. ~-**distance phone call** llamada *f* de larga distancia, conferencia *f*. ~**er** *adv*. **no ~er** ya no. ~-**haul** *a* de larga distancia. ~**ing** *n* anhelo *m*, ansia *f*

longitude *n* longitud *f*

long: ~ **jump** *n* salto *m* de longitud. ~-**playing record** *n* elepé *m*. ~-**range** *a* de largo alcance. ~-**sighted** *a* hipermétrope. ~-**term** *a* a largo plazo. ~-**winded** *a* prolijo

loo *n* 🄸 váter *m*, baño *m* (LAm)

look *vt* mirar; representar <*age*>. ● *vi* mirar; (seem) parecer; (search) buscar. ● *n* mirada *f*; (appearance) aspecto *m*. **good ~s** belleza *f*. □ ~ **after** *vt* cuidar <*person*>; (be responsible for) encargarse de. □ ~ **at** *vt* mirar; (consider) considerar. □ ~ **down on** *vt* despreciar. □ ~ **for** *vt* buscar. □ ~ **forward to** *vt* esperar con ansia. □ ~ **into** *vt* investigar. □ ~ **like** *vt* parecerse a. □ ~ **on** *vi* mirar. □ ~ **out** *vi* tener cuidado. □ ~ **out for** *vt* buscar; (watch) tener cuidado con. □ ~ **round** *vi* volver la cabeza. □ ~ **through** *vt* hojear. □ ~ **up** *vt* buscar <*word*>; (visit) ir a ver. □ ~

up to vt admirar. ~**-alike** n 🔢 doble m & f. ~**out** n (Mil, person) vigía m. **be on the** ~**out for** andar a la caza de. ~**s** npl belleza f

loom n telar m. ● vi aparecerse

looney, loony a & n 🔳 chiflado (m) 🔢, loco (m)

loop n (shape) curva f ; (in string) lazada f. ● vt hacer una lazada con. ~**hole** n (in rule) escapatoria f

loose a (-er, -est) suelto; <garment, thread, hair> flojo; (inexact) vago; (not packed) suelto. **be at a** ~ **end** no tener qué quehacer. ~**ly** adv sueltamente; ~**n** vt aflojar

loot n botín m. ● vt/i saquear. ~**er** n saqueador m

lop vt (pt **lopped**). ~ **off** cortar

lop-sided a ladeado

lord n señor m; (British title) lord m. (**good**) **L**~! ¡Dios mío! **the L**~ el Señor. **the (House of) L**~**s** la Cámara de los Lores

lorry n camión m. ~ **driver** n camionero m

lose vt/i (pt **lost**) perder. ~**r** n perdedor m

loss n pérdida f. **be at a** ~ estar perplejo. **be at a** ~ **for words** no encontrar palabras

lost ⇒LOSE. ● a perdido. **get** ~ perderse. ~ **property** n, ~ **and found** (Amer) oficina f de objetos perdidos

lot n (fate) suerte f; (at auction) lote m; (land) solar m. **a** ~ (**of**) muchos. **quite a** ~ **of** 🔢 bastante. ~**s** (**of**) 🔢 muchos. **they ate the** ~ se lo comieron todo

lotion n loción f

lottery n lotería f

loud a (-er, -est) fuerte; (noisy) ruidoso; (gaudy) chillón. **out** ~ en voz alta. ~**hailer** n megáfono m.

~**ly** adv <speak> en voz alta; <shout> fuerte; <complain> a voz en grito. ~**speaker** n altavoz m, altoparlante m (LAm)

lounge vi repantigarse. ● n salón m, sala f (de estar), living m (LAm)

lous|e n (pl **lice**) piojo m. ~**y** a (-ier, -iest) (🔳, bad) malísimo

lout n patán m

lov|able a adorable. ~**e** n amor m; (tennis) cero m. **be in** ~**e** (**with**) estar enamorado (de). **fall in** ~**e** (**with**) enamorarse (de). ● vt querer, amar <person>. **I** ~**e milk** me encanta la leche. ~**e affair** n aventura f, amorío m

lovely a (-ier, -iest) <appearance> precioso, lindo (LAm); <person> encantador, amoroso (LAm)

lover n amante m & f

loving a cariñoso

low a & adv (-er, -est) bajo. ● vi <cattle> mugir. ~**er** vt bajar. ~**er o.s.** envilecerse. ~**-level** a a bajo nivel. ~**ly** a (-ier, -iest) humilde

loyal a leal, fiel. ~**ty** n lealtad f. ~**ty card** tarjeta f de fidelidad

lozenge n (shape) rombo m; (tablet) pastilla f

LP abbr (= **long-playing record**) elepé m

Ltd abbr (= **Limited**) S.A., Sociedad Anónima

lubricate vt lubricar

lucid a lúcido

luck n suerte f. **good** ~! ¡(buena) suerte! ~**ily** adv por suerte. ~**y** a (-ier, -iest) <person> con suerte. **be** ~**y** tener suerte. ~**y number** número m de la suerte

lucrative a lucrativo

ludicrous a ridículo

lug vt (pt **lugged**) 🔢 arrastrar

luggage n equipaje m. ~ **rack** n rejilla f

lukewarm *a* tibio; (fig) poco entusiasta

lull *vt* (soothe, send to sleep) adormecer; (calm) calmar. ● *n* periodo *m* de calma

lullaby *n* canción *f* de cuna

lumber *n* trastos *mpl* viejos; (wood) maderos *mpl*. ● *vt*. ~ **s.o. with sth** 🇬🇧 endilgar algo a uno. ~**jack** *n* leñador *m*

luminous *a* luminoso

lump *n* (swelling) bulto *m*; (as result of knock) chichón *m*; (in liquid) grumo *m*; (of sugar) terrón *m*. ● *vt*. ~ **together** agrupar. ~ **it** 🇬🇧 aguantarse. ~ **sum** *n* suma *f* global. ~**y** *a* <*sauce*> grumoso; <*mattress, cushions*> lleno de protuberancias

lunacy *n* locura *f*

lunar *a* lunar

lunatic *n* loco *m*

lunch *n* comida *f*, almuerzo *m*. **have** ~ comer, almorzar

luncheon *n* comida *f*, almuerzo *m*. ~ **voucher** *n* vale *m* de comida

lung *n* pulmón *m*

lunge *n* arremetida *f*. ● *vi*. ~ **at** arremeter contra

lurch *vi* tambalearse. ● *n*. **leave in the** ~ dejar plantado

lure *vt* atraer

lurid *a* <*colour*> chillón; (shocking) morboso

lurk *vi* merodear; (in ambush) estar al acecho

luscious *a* delicioso

lush *a* exuberante

lust *n* lujuria *f*; (craving) deseo *m*. ● *vi*. ~ **after** codiciar

lute *n* laúd *m*

Luxembourg, Luxemburg *n* Luxemburgo *m*

luxuriant *a* exuberante

luxur|ious *a* lujoso. ~**y** *n* lujo *m*. ● *a* de lujo

lying ⇒LIE[1], LIE[2]. ● *n* mentiras *fpl*. ● *a* mentiroso

lynch *vt* linchar

lyric *a* lírico. ~**al** *a* lírico. ~**s** *npl* letra *f*

MA *abbr* ⇒MASTER

mac *n* 🇬🇧 impermeable *m*

macabre *a* macabro

macaroni *n* macarrones *mpl*

mace *n* (staff) maza *f*; (spice) macis *f*. **M~** (P) (Amer) gas *m* para defensa personal

machine *n* máquina *f*. ~ **gun** *n* ametralladora *f*. ~**ry** *n* maquinaria *f*

mackintosh *n* impermeable *m*

macro *n* (*pl* -**os**) (Comp) macro *m*

macrobiotic *a* macrobiótico

mad *a* (**madder, maddest**) loco; (🇬🇧, angry) furioso. **be** ~ **about** estar loco por

madam *n* señora *f*

mad: ~**cap** *a* atolondrado. ~ **cow disease** *n* enfermedad *f* de las vacas locas. ~**den** *vt* (make mad) enloquecer; (make angry) enfurecer

made ⇒MAKE. ~**-to-measure** hecho a (la) medida

mad: ~**house** *n* manicomio *m*. ~**ly** *adv* (interested, in love etc) locamente; (frantically) como un loco. ~**man** *n* loco *m*. ~**ness** *n* locura *f*

Madonna *n*. **the** ~ (Relig) la Virgen

maestro n (pl **maestri** or **-os**) maestro m

Mafia n mafia f

magazine n revista f; (of gun) recámara f

magenta a magenta, morado

maggot n gusano m

magic n magia f. ● a mágico. ~**al** a mágico. ~**ian** n mago m

magistrate n juez m que conoce de faltas y asuntos civiles de menor importancia

magnet n imán m. ~**ic** a magnético; (fig) lleno de magnetismo. ~**ism** n magnetismo m. ~**ize** vt imantar, magnetizar

magnif|ication n aumento m. ~**y** vt aumentar. ~**ying glass** n lupa f

magnificen|ce a magnificencia f. ~**t** a magnífico

magnitude n magnitud f

magpie n urraca f

mahogany n caoba f

maid n (servant) criada f, sirvienta f; (girl, old use) doncella f. **old ~** solterona f

maiden n doncella f. ● a <voyage> inaugural. ~ **name** n apellido m de soltera

mail n correo m; (armour) (cota f de) malla f. ● a correo. ● vt echar al correo <letter>; (send) enviar por correo. ~**box** n (Amer) buzón m. ~**ing list** n lista f de direcciones. ~**man** n (Amer) cartero m. ~ **order** n venta f por correo

maim vt mutilar

main n. (water/gas) ~ cañería f principal. **in the ~** en su mayor parte. **the ~s** npl (Elec) la red f de suministro. ● a principal. ~ **course** n plato m principal, plato m fuerte. ~ **frame** n (Comp)

unidad f central. ~**land** n. the ~**land** la masa territorial de un país excluyendo sus islas. ● a. ~**land China** (la) China continental. ~**ly** adv principalmente. ~ **road** n carretera f principal. ~**stream** a <culture> establecido. ~ **street** n calle f principal

maint|ain vt mantener. ~**enance** n mantenimiento m

maisonette n (small house) casita f; (part of house) dúplex m

maize n maíz m

majestic a majestuoso

majesty n majestad f

major a (important) muy importante; (Mus) mayor. **a ~ road** una calle prioritaria. ● n comandante m & f, mayor m & f (LAm). ● vi. ~ **in** (Amer, Univ) especializarse en

Majorca n Mallorca f

majority n mayoría f. ● a mayoritario

make vt (pt made) hacer; (manufacture) fabricar; ganar <money>; tomar <decision>; llegar a <destination>. ~ **s.o. do sth** obligar a uno a hacer algo. **be made of** estar hecho de. **I ~ it two o'clock** yo tengo las dos. ~ **believe** fingir. ~ **do** (manage) arreglarse. ~ **do with** (content o.s.) contentarse con. ~ **it** llegar; (succeed) tener éxito. ● n marca f. ~ **for** vt dirigirse a. □ ~ **good** vt compensar; (repair) reparar. □ ~ **off** vi escaparse (**with** con). □ ~ **out** vt distinguir; (understand) entender; (write out) hacer; (assert) dar a entender. ~ **up** vt (constitute) formar; (prepare) preparar; inventar <story>; ~ **it up** (become reconciled) hacer las paces. ~ **up** (one's face) maquillarse. □ ~ **up**

for vt compensar. ~**-believe** a
fingido, simulado. n ficción f.
~**over** n (Amer) maquillaje m. ~**r**
n fabricante m & f. ~**shift** a
(temporary) provisional, provisorio
(LAm); (improvised) improvisado.
~**up** n maquillaje m. **put on** ~**up**
maquillarse.

making n. **he has the** ~**s of** tiene
madera de. **in the** ~ en vías de
formación

maladjusted a inadaptado

malaria n malaria f, paludismo m

Malaysia n Malasia f. ~**n** a & n
malaisio (m)

male a macho; <voice, attitude>
masculino. ● n macho m; (man)
varón m

malevolent a malévolo

malfunction vi fallar, funcionar
mal

malic|e n mala intención f,
maldad f. **bear s.o.** ~**e** guardar
rencor a uno. ~**ious** a
malintencionado. ~**iously** adv
con malevolencia

malignant a maligno

mallet n mazo m

malnutrition n desnutrición f

malpractice n mala práctica f
(en el ejercicio de una profesión)

malt n malta f

Malt|a n Malta f. ~**ese** a & n
maltés (m)

mammal n mamífero m

mammoth n mamut m. ● a
gigantesco

man n (pl **men**) hombre m;
(Chess) pieza f. ~ **in the street**
hombre m de la calle. ● vt (pt
manned) encargarse de
<switchboard>; tripular <ship>;
servir <guns>

manacles n (for wrists) esposas fpl;
(for legs) grillos mpl

manag|e vt dirigir; administrar
<land, finances>; (handle) manejar.
● vi (Com) dirigir; (cope)
arreglárselas. ~**e to do** lograr
hacer. ~**eable** a <task> posible
de alcanzar; <size> razonable.
~**ement** n dirección f. ~**er** n
director m; (of shop) encargado m;
(of soccer team) entrenador m,
director m técnico (LAm). ~**eress**
n encargada f. ~**erial** a directivo,
gerencial (LAm).~**ing director** n
director m ejecutivo

mandate n mandato m

mandatory a obligatorio

mane n (of horse) crin(es) f(pl); (of
lion) melena f

mangle n rodillo m (escurridor).
● vt destrozar

man: ~**handle** vt mover a pulso;
(treat roughly) maltratar. ~**hole** n
registro m. ~**hood** n madurez f;
(quality) virilidad f. ~**-hour** n hora
f hombre. ~**-hunt** n persecución
f

mania n manía f. ~**c** n maníaco
m

manicure n manicura f,
manicure f (LAm)

manifest a manifiesto. ● vt
manifestar. ~**ation** n
manifestación f

manifesto n (pl **-os**) manifiesto
m

manipulat|e vt manipular. ~**ion**
n manipulación f. ~**ive** a
manipulador

man: ~**kind** n humanidad f. ~**ly**
a viril. ~**-made** a artificial

manner n manera f; (demeanour)
actitud f; (kind) clase f. ~**ed** a
amanerado. ~**s** npl modales mpl,
educación f. **bad** ~**s** mala
educación

manoeuvre n maniobra f. ● vt/i
maniobrar

M

manor *n.* ~ **house** casa *f* solariega

manpower *n* mano *f* de obra

mansion *n* mansión *f*

man: ~**-size**(d) *a* grande. ~**slaughter** *n* homicidio *m* sin premeditación

mantelpiece *n* repisa *f* de la chimenea

manual *a* manual. ● *n* (handbook) manual *m*

manufacture *vt* fabricar. ● *n* fabricación *f*. ~**r** *n* fabricante *m* & *f*

manure *n* estiércol *m*

manuscript *n* manuscrito *m*

many *a* & *pron* muchos, muchas. ~ **people** mucha gente. **a great/good** ~ muchísimos. **how** ~? ¿cuántos? **so** ~ tantos. **too** ~ demasiados

map *n* mapa *m*; (of streets etc) plano *m*

mar *vt* (*pt* **marred**) estropear

marathon *n* maratón *m* & *f*

marble *n* mármol *m*; (for game) canica *f*

march *vi* (Mil) marchar. ~ **off** *vi* irse. ● *n* marcha *f*

March *n* marzo *m*

march-past *n* desfile *m*

mare *n* yegua *f*

margarine *n* margarina *f*

margin *n* margen *f*. ~**al** *a* marginal

marijuana *n* marihuana *f*

marina *n* puerto *m* deportivo

marine *a* marino. ● *n* (sailor) infante *m* de marina

marionette *n* marioneta *f*

marital status *n* estado *m* civil

mark *n* marca *f*; (stain) mancha *f*; (Schol) nota *f*; (target) blanco *m*. ● *vt* (indicate) señalar, marcar; (stain) manchar; corregir <*exam*>. ~ **time** marcar el paso. □ ~ **out**

vt (select) señalar; (distinguish) distinguir. ~**ed** *a* marcado. ~**edly** *adv* marcadamente. ~**er** *n* marcador *m*. ~**er** (**pen**) *n* rotulador *m*, marcador *m* (LAm)

market *n* mercado *m*. **on the** ~ en venta. ● *vt* comercializar. ~ **garden** *n* huerta *f*. ~**ing** *n* marketing *m*

marking *n* marcas *fpl*; (on animal, plant) mancha *f*

marksman *n* (*pl* **-men**) tirador *m*. ~**ship** *n* puntería *f*

marmalade *n* mermelada *f* (de cítricos)

maroon *a* & *n* granate (*m*). ● *vt* abandonar (en una isla desierta)

marquee *n* toldo *m*, entoldado *m*; (Amer, awning) marquesina *f*

marriage *n* matrimonio *m*; (ceremony) casamiento *m*

married *a* casado; <*life*> conyugal

marrow *n* (of bone) tuétano *m*; (vegetable) calabaza *f* verde alargada. ~ **squash** *n* (Amer) calabaza *f* verde alargada

marry *vt* casarse con; (give or unite in marriage) casar. ● *vi* casarse. **get married** casarse (**to** con)

Mars *n* Marte *m*

marsh *n* pantano *m*

marshal *n* (Mil) mariscal *m*; (Amer, police chief) jefe *m* de policía. ● *vt* (*pt* **marshalled**) reunir; poner en orden <*thoughts*>

marsh: ~ **mallow** *n* malvavisco *m*, bombón *m* (LAm). ~**y** *a* pantanoso

martial *a* marcial. ~ **arts** *npl* artes *fpl* marciales. ~ **law** *n* ley *f* marcial

martyr *n* mártir *m* & *f*

marvel *n* maravilla *f*. ● *vi* (*pt* **marvelled**) maravillarse (**at** de). ~**lous** *a* maravilloso

Marxis|m *n* marxismo *m*. **~t** *a* & *n* marxista (*m* & *f*)

marzipan *n* mazapán *m*

mascara *n* rímel *m* (P)

mascot *n* mascota *f*

masculin|e *a* & *n* masculino (*m*). **~ity** *n* masculinidad *f*

mash *n* (Br 🔲, potatoes) puré *m* de patatas, puré *m* de papas (LAm). ● *vt* hacer puré de, moler (Mex). **~ed potatoes** *npl* puré *m* de patatas, puré *m* de papas (LAm)

mask *n* máscara *f*; (Sport) careta *f*. ● *vt* ocultar

masochis|m *n* masoquismo *m*. **~t** *n* masoquista *m* & *f*. **~tic** *a* masoquista

mason *n* (stone ~) mampostero *m*. **M~** (freemason) masón *m*. **~ry** *n* albañilería *f*

masquerade *n* mascarada *f*. ● *vi*. **~ as** hacerse pasar por

mass *n* masa *f*; (Relig) misa *f*; (large quantity) montón *m*. **the ~es** las masas. ● *vi* concentrarse

massacre *n* masacre *f*, matanza *f*. ● *vt* masacrar

mass|age *n* masaje *m*. ● *vt* masajear. **~eur** *n* masajista *m*. **~euse** *n* masajista *f*

massive *a* masivo; (heavy) macizo; (huge) enorme

mass: **~ media** *n* medios *mpl* de comunicación. **~-produce** *vt* fabricar en serie

mast *n* mástil *m*; (for radio, TV) antena *f* repetidora

master *n* amo *m*; (expert) maestro *m*; (in secondary school) profesor *m*; (of ship) capitán *m*; (master copy) original *m*. **~'s degree** master *m*, maestría *f*. **M~ of Arts** (MA) poseedor *m* de una maestría en folosofía y letras. **M~ of Science** (MSc) poseedor *m* de una maestría en ciencias. ● *vt* llegar a dominar. **~ key** *n* llave *f*

maestra. **~mind** *n* cerebro *m*. ● *vt* dirigir. **~piece** *n* obra *f* maestra. **~stroke** *n* golpe *m* de maestro. **~y** *n* dominio *m*; (skill) maestría *f*

masturbat|e *vi* masturbarse. **~ion** *n* masturbación *f*

mat *n* estera *f*; (at door) felpudo *m*. ● *a* (Amer) ⇒MATT

match *n* (Sport) partido *m*; (for fire) cerilla *f*, fósforo *m* (LAm), cerillo *m* (Mex); (equal) igual *m*. ● *vt* emparejar; (equal) igualar; *<clothes, colours>* hacer juego con. ● *vi* hacer juego. **~box** *n* caja *f* de cerillas, caja *f* de fósforos (LAm), caja *f* de cerillos (Mex). **~ing** *a* quehace juego. **~stick** *n* cerilla *f*, fósforo *m* (LAm), cerillo *m* (Mex)

mate *n* (of person) pareja *f*; (of animals, male) macho *m*; (of animals, female) hembra *f*; (assistant) ayudante *m*; (🔲, friend) amigo *m*, cuate *m* (Mex); (Chess) (jaque *m*) mate *m*. ● *vi* aparearse

material *n* material *m*; (cloth) tela *f*. ● *a* material. **~istic** *a* materialista. **~ize** *vi* materializarse. **~s** *npl* materiales *mpl*

matern|al *a* maternal. **~ity** *n* maternidad *f*. ● *a* *<ward>* de obstetricia; *<clothes>* premamá, de embarazada

math *n* (Amer) ⇒MATHS

mathematic|ian *n* matemático *m*. **~al** *a* matemático. **~s** *n* matemática(s) *f(pl)*

maths *n* matemática(s) *f(pl)*

matinée, matinee *n* (Theatre) función *f* de tarde; (Cinema) primera sesión *f* (de la tarde)

matrices ⇒MATRIX

matriculat|e *vi* matricularse. **~ion** *n* matrícula *f*

M

matrimon|ial *a* matrimonial. ~y *n* matrimonio *m*

matrix *n* (*pl* **matrices**) matriz *f*

matron *n* (married, elderly) matrona *f*; (in school) ama *f* de llaves; (former use, in hospital) enfermera *f* jefe

matt, matte (Amer) *a* mate

matted *a* enmarañado y apelmazado

matter *n* (substance) materia *f*; (affair) asunto *m*; (pus) pus *m*. **as a ~ of fact** en realidad. **no ~** no importa. **what is the ~?** ¿qué pasa? **to make ~s worse** para colmo (de males). ● *vi* importar. **it doesn't ~** no importa. **~-of-fact** *a* <person> práctico

mattress *n* colchón *m*

matur|e *a* maduro. ● *vi* madurar. **~ity** *n* madurez *f*

maudlin *a* llorón

maul *vt* atacar (y herir)

mauve *a & n* malva (*m*)

maverick *n* inconformista *m & f*

maxim *n* máxima *f*

maxim|ize *vt* maximizar. **~um** *a & n* máximo (*m*)

- - -

may, past **might**

●*auxiliary verb*

····▸ (expressing possibility) **he ~ come** puede que venga, es posible que venga. **it ~ be true** puede ser verdad. **she ~ not have seen him** es posible que *or* puede que no lo haya visto

····▸ (asking for or giving permission) **~ I smoke?** ¿puedo fumar?, ¿se puede fumar? **~ I have your name and address, please?** ¿quiere darme su nombre y dirección, por favor?

····▸ (expressing a wish) **~ he be happy** que sea feliz

····▸ (conceding) **he ~ not have much experience, but he's very hardworking** no tendrá mucha experiencia, pero es muy trabajador. **that's as ~ be** puede ser

····▸ **I ~ as well stay** más vale quedarme

- - -

May *n* mayo *m*

maybe *adv* quizá(s), tal vez, a lo mejor

May Day *n* el primero de mayo

mayhem *n* caos *m*

mayonnaise *n* mayonesa *f*, mahonesa *f*

mayor *n* alcalde *m*, alcaldesa *f*. **~ess** *n* alcaldesa *f*

maze *n* laberinto *m*

me *pron* me; (after prep) mí. **he knows ~** me conoce. **it's ~** soy yo

meadow *n* prado *m*, pradera *f*

meagre *a* escaso

meal *n* comida *f*. **~time** *n* hora *f* de comer

mean *vt* (*pt* **meant**) (intend) tener la intención de, querer; (signify) querer decir, significar. **~ to do** tener la intención de hacer. **~ well** tener buenas intenciones. **be meant for** estar destinado a. ● *a* (-er, -est) (miserly) tacaño; (unkind) malo; (Math) medio. ● *n* media *f*; (average) promedio *m*

meander *vi* <river> serpentear

meaning *n* sentido *m*. **~ful** *a* significativo. **~less** *a* sin sentido

meanness *n* (miserliness) tacañería *f*; (unkindness) maldad *f*

means *n* medio *m*. **by ~ of** por medio de, mediante. **by all ~** por supuesto. **by no ~** de ninguna manera. ● *npl* (wealth) medios *mpl*, recursos *mpl*. **~ test** *n* investigación *f* de ingresos

meant ⇒MEAN

meantime *adv* mientras tanto, entretanto. ● *n.* in the ~ mientras tanto, entretanto

meanwhile *adv* mientras tanto, entretanto

measl|es *n* sarampión *m*. ~y *a* 🆔 miserable

measure *n* medida *f*; (ruler) regla *f*. ● *vt/i* medir. □ ~ **up to** *vt* estar a la altura de. ~**ment** *n* medida *f*

meat *n* carne *f*. ~**ball** *n* albóndiga *f*. ~y *a* <taste, smell> a carne; <soup, stew> con mucha carne

mechan|ic *n* mecánico *m*. ~**ical** *a* mecánico. ~**ics** *n* mecánica *f*. ~**ism** *n* mecanismo *m*. ~**ize** *vt* mecanizar

medal *n* medalla *f*. ~**list** *n* medallista *m & f*. **be a gold** ~**list** ganar una medalla de oro

meddle *vi* meterse, entrometerse (**in** en). ~ **with** (tinker) toquetear

media ⇒MEDIUM. ● *npl.* the ~ los medios de comunicación

mediat|e *vi* mediar. ~**ion** *n* mediación *f*. ~**or** *n* mediador *m*

medical *a* médico; <student> de medicina. ● *n* revisión *m* médica

medicat|ed *a* medicinal. ~**ion** *n* medicación *f*

medicin|al *a* medicinal. ~**e** *n* medicina *f*

medieval *a* medieval

mediocre *a* mediocre

meditat|e *vi* meditar. ~**ion** *n* meditación *f*

Mediterranean *a* mediterráneo. ● *n.* the ~ el Mediterráneo

medium *n* (*pl* media) medio *m*. **happy** ~ término *m* medio. ● *a* mediano. ~**-size(d)** *a* de tamaño mediano

medley *n* (Mus) popurrí *m*; (mixture) mezcla *f*

meek *a* (-er, -est) dócil

meet *vt* (*pt* met) encontrar; (bump into s.o.) encontrarse con; (fetch) ir a buscar; (get to know, be introduced to) conocer. ● *vi* encontrarse; (get to know) conocerse; (have meeting) reunirse. ~ **up** *vi* encontrarse (**with** con). □ ~ **with** *vt* ser recibido con; (Amer, meet) encontrarse con. ~**ing** *n* reunión *f*; (accidental between two people) encuentro *m*

megabyte *n* (Comp) megabyte *m*, megaocteto *m*

megaphone *n* megáfono *m*

melanchol|ic *a* melancólico. ~**y** *n* melancolía *f*. ● *a* melancólico

mellow *a* (-er, -est) <fruit> maduro; <sound> dulce; <colour> tenue; <person> apacible

melodrama *n* melodrama *m*. ~**tic** *a* melodramático

melody *n* melodía *f*

melon *n* melón *m*

melt *vt* (make liquid) derretir; fundir <metals>. ● *vi* (become liquid) derretirse; <metals> fundirse. □ ~ **down** *vt* fundir

member *n* miembro *m & f*; (of club) socio *m*. ~ **of staff** empleado *m*. **M~ of Congress** (Amer) miembro *m & f* del Congreso. **M~ of Parliament** *n* diputado *m*. ~**ship** *n* calidad *f* de socio; (members) socios *mpl*, membresía *f* (LAm)

membrane *n* membrana *f*

memento *n* (*pl* -os or -oes) recuerdo *m*

memo *n* (*pl* -os) memorándum *m*, memo *m*

memoir *n* memoria *f*

memorable *a* memorable

memorandum *n* (*pl* -ums or -da) memorándum *m*

memorial *n* monumento *m*. ● *a* conmemorativo

M

memor|ize vt aprender de memoria. **~y** n (faculty) memoria f; (thing remembered) recuerdo m. **from ~y** de memoria. **in ~y of** a la memoria de

men ⇒MAN

menac|e n amenaza f; (🄸, nuisance) peligro m público. ● vt amenazar. **~ing** a amenazador

mend vt reparar; arreglar <garment>. **~ one's ways** enmendarse. ● n remiendo m. **be on the ~** ir mejorando

menfolk n hombres mpl

menial a servil

meningitis n meningitis f

menopause n menopausia f

menstruat|e vi menstruar. **~ion** n menstruación f

mental a mental; <hospital> psiquiátrico. **~ity** n mentalidad f. **~ly** adv mentalmente. **be ~ly ill** ser un enfermo mental

mention vt mencionar. **don't ~ it!** ¡no hay de qué! ● n mención f

mentor n mentor m

menu n (set) menú m; (à la carte) carta f

meow n & vi ⇒MEW

mercenary a & n mercenario (m)

merchandise n mercancias fpl, mercadería f (LAm)

merchant n comerciante m. ● a <ship, navy> mercante. **~ bank** n banco m mercantil

merci|ful a misericordioso. **~less** a despiadado

mercury n mercurio m. **M~** (planet) Mercurio m

mercy n compasión f. **at the ~ of** a merced de

mere a simple. **~ly** adv simplemente

merge vt unir; fusionar <companies>. ● vi unirse; <companies> fusionarse. **~r** n fusión f

meridian n meridiano m

meringue n merengue m

merit n mérito m. ● vt (pt merited) merecer

mermaid n sirena f

merr|ily adv alegremente. **~iment** n alegría f. **~y** a (-ier, -iest) alegre. **make ~** divertirse. **~y-go-round** n tiovivo m, carrusel m (LAm). **~y-making** n jolgorio m

mesh n malla f

mesmerize vt cautivar

mess n desorden m; (dirt) suciedad f; (Mil) rancho m. **make a ~ of** estropear. □ **~ up** vt desordenar; (dirty) ensuciar; estropear <plans>. □ **~ about** vi tontear. □ **~ with** vt (tinker with) manosear

mess|age n mensaje m; (when phoning) recado m. **~enger** n mensajero m

Messiah n Mesías m

Messrs npl. **~ Smith** los señores Smith, los Sres. Smith

messy a (-ier, -iest) en desorden; (dirty) sucio

met ⇒MEET

metabolism n metabolismo m

metal n metal. ● a de metal. **~lic** a metálico

metaphor n metáfora f. **~ical** a metafórico

mete vt. **~ out** repartir; dar <punishment>

meteor n meteoro m. **~ic** a meteórico. **~ite** n meteorito m

meteorolog|ical a meteorológico. **~ist** n meteorólogo m. **~y** n meteorología f

meter n contador m, medidor m (LAm); (Amer) ⇒METRE

method n método m. **~ical** a
metódico. **M~ist** a & n metodista
(m & f)

methylated a. **~ spirit(s)** n
alcohol m desnaturalizado

meticulous a meticuloso

metre n metro m

metric a métrico

metropoli|s n metrópoli(s) f

mettle n. **be on one's ~** (fig) estar
dispuesto a dar lo mejor de sí

mew n maullido m. ● vi maullar

Mexic|an a & n mejicano (m),
mexicano (m). **~o** n Méjico m,
México m

miaow n & vi ⇒MEW

mice ⇒MOUSE

mickey n. **take the ~ out of**
🄸 tomar el pelo a

micro... pref micro...

microbe n microbio m

micro: ~chip n pastilla f. **~film**
n microfilme m. **~light** n
aeroligero m. **~phone** n
micrófono m. **~processor** n
microprocesador m. **~scope** n
microscopio m. **~scopic** a
microscópico. **~wave** n
microonda f. **~wave oven** n
horno m de microondas

mid- pref. **in ~ air** en pleno aire.
in ~ March a mediados de marzo

midday n mediodía m

middl|e a de en medio. ● n medio
m. **in the ~e of** en medio de.
~e-aged a de mediana edad.
M~e Ages npl Edad f Media. **~e
class** n clase f media. **~e-class**
a de la clase media. **M~e East** n
Oriente m Medio. **~eman** n
intermediario m. **~e name** n
segundo nombre m. **~ing** a
regular

midge n mosquito m

midget n enano m. ● a
minúsculo

Midlands npl región f central de
Inglaterra

midnight n medianoche f

midriff n diafragma m

midst n. **in our ~** entre nosotros.
in the ~ of en medio de

midsummer n pleno verano m;
(solstice) solsticio m de verano

midway adv a mitad de camino

Midwest región f central de los
EE.UU.

midwife n comadrona f, partera f

midwinter n pleno invierno m

might ⇒MAY. ● n (strength) fuerza
f; (power) poder m. **~y** a (strong)
fuerte; (powerful) poderoso. ● adv
🄸 muy

migraine n jaqueca f

migra|nt a migratorio. ● n (person)
emigrante m & f. **~te** vi emigrar.
~tion n migración f

mild a (-er, -est) <person> afable;
<climate> templado; (slight) ligero;
<taste, manner> suave

mildew n moho m; (on plants)
mildeu m, mildiu m

mildly adv (gently) suavemente;
(slightly) ligeramente

mile n milla f. **~s better** 🄸 mucho
mejor. **~s too big** 🄸 demasiado
grande. **~age** n (loosely)
kilometraje m. **~ometer** n
(loosely) cuentakilómetros m.
~stone n mojón m; (event, stage,
fig) hito m

militant a & n militante (m & f)

military a militar

militia n milicia f

milk n leche f. ● a <product>
lácteo; <chocolate> con leche. ● vt
ordeñar <cow>. **~man** n lechero
m. **~ shake** n batido m, (leche f)
malteada f (LAm), licuado m con
leche (LAm). **~y** a lechoso. **M~y
Way** n Vía f Láctea

M

mill *n* molino *m*; (for coffee, pepper) molinillo *m*; (factory) fábrica *f* de tejidos de algodón. ● *vt* moler. □ ~ **about, mill around** *vi* dar vueltas

millennium *n* (*pl* **-ia** *or* **-iums**) milenio *m*

miller *n* molinero *m*

milli... *pref* mili... ~**gram(me)** *n* miligramo *m*. ~**metre** *n* milímetro *m*

milliner *n* sombrerero *m*

million *n* millón *m*. **a** ~ **pounds** un millón de libras. ~**aire** *n* millonario *m*

millstone *n* muela *f* (de molino); (fig, burden) carga *f*

mime *n* mímica *f*. ● *vt* imitar, hacer la mímica de. ● *vi* hacer la mímica

mimic *vt* (*pt* **mimicked**) imitar. ● *n* imitador *m*. ~**ry** *n* imitación *f*

mince *vt* picar, moler (LAm) *<meat>*. **not to** ~ **matters/words** no andar(se) con rodeos. ● *n* carne *f* picada, carne *f* molida (LAm). ~ **pie** *n* pastelito *m* de Navidad (*pastelito relleno de picadillo de frutos secos*). ~**r** *n* máquina *f* de picar carne, máquina *f* de moler carne (LAm)

mind *n* mente *f*; (sanity) juicio *m*. **to my** ~ a mi parecer. **be on one's mind** preocuparle a uno. **make up one's** ~ decidirse. ● *vt* (look after) cuidar (de); atender *<shop>*. ~ **the steps!** ¡cuidado con las escaleras! **never** ~ **him** no le hagas caso. **I don't** ~ **the noise** no me molesta el ruido. **would you** ~ **closing the door?** ¿le importaría cerrar la puerta? ● *vi*. **never** ~ no importa, no te preocupes. **I don't** ~ (don't object) me da igual. **do you** ~ **if I smoke?** ¿le importa si fumo? ~**ful** *a* atento (**of** a). ~**less** *a*

<activity> mecánico; *<violence>* ciego

mine¹ *poss pron* (*sing*) mío, mía; (*pl*) míos, mías. **it is** ~ es mío. ~ **are blue** los míos/las mías son azules. **a friend of** ~ un amigo mío/una amiga mía

mine² *n* mina *f*; (Mil) mina *f*. ● *vt* extraer. ~**field** *n* campo *m* de minas. ~**r** *n* minero *m*

mineral *a & n* mineral (*m*). ~ **water** *n* agua *f* mineral

mingle *vi* mezclarse

mini... *pref* mini...

miniature *n* miniatura *f*. ● *a* en miniatura

mini: ~**bus** *n* microbús *m*. ~**cab** *n* taxi *m* (*que se pide por teléfono*)

minim|al *a* mínimo. ~**ize** *vt* reducir al mínimo. ~**um** *a & n* (*pl* **-ima**) mínimo (*m*)

mining *n* minería *f*. ● *a* minero

miniskirt *n* minifalda *f*

minist|er *n* ministro *m*, secretario *m* (Mex); (Relig) pastor *m*. ~**erial** *a* ministerial. ~**ry** *n* ministerio *m*, secretaría *f* (Mex)

mink *n* visón *m*

minor *a* (also Mus) menor; *<injury>* leve; *<change>* pequeño; *<operation>* de poca importancia. ● *n* menor *m & f* de edad. ~**ity** *n* minoría *f*. ● *a* minoritario

minstrel *n* juglar *m*

mint *n* (plant) menta *f*; (sweet) pastilla *f* de menta; (Finance) casa *f* de la moneda. **in** ~ **condition** como nuevo. ● *vt* acuñar

minus *prep* menos; (Ⅱ, without) sin. ● *n* (sign) menos *m*. **five** ~ **three is two** cinco menos tres es igual a dos. ~ **sign** *n* (signo *m* de) menos *m*

minute¹ *n* minuto *m*. **the** ~**s** *npl* (of meeting) el acta *f*

minute^2 *a* diminuto; (detailed) minucioso

mirac|le *n* milagro *m*. ~**ulous** *a* milagroso

mirage *n* espejismo *m*

mirror *n* espejo *m*; (driving ~) (espejo *m*) retrovisor *m*. ● *vt* reflejar

mirth *n* regocijo *m*; (laughter) risas *fpl*

misapprehension *n* malentendido *m*

misbehav|e *vi* portarse mal. ~**iour** *n* mala conducta

miscalculat|e *vt/i* calcular mal. ~**ion** *n* error *m* de cálculo

miscarr|iage *n* aborto *m* espontáneo. ~**iage of justice** *n* injusticia *f*. ~**y** *vi* abortar

miscellaneous *a* heterogéneo

mischie|f *n* (foolish conduct) travesura *f*; (harm) daño *m*. **get into** ~**f** hacer travesuras. **make** ~**f** causar daños. ~**vous** *a* travieso; <*grin*> pícaro

misconception *n* equivocación *f*

misconduct *n* mala conducta *f*

misdeed *n* fechoría *f*

misdemeanour *n* delito *m* menor, falta *f*

miser *n* avaro *m*

miserable *a* (sad) triste; (in low spirits) abatido; (wretched, poor) mísero; <*weather*> pésimo

miserly *a* avariento

misery *n* (unhappiness) tristeza *f*; (pain) sufrimiento *m*

misfire *vi* fallar

misfit *n* inadaptado *m*

misfortune *n* desgracia *f*

misgiving *n* recelo *m*

misguided *a* equivocado

mishap *n* percance *m*

misinform *vt* informar mal

misinterpret *vt* interpretar mal

misjudge *vt* juzgar mal; (miscalculate) calcular mal

mislay *vt* (*pt* **mislaid**) extraviar, perder

mislead *vt* (*pt* **misled**) engañar. ~**ing** *a* engañoso

mismanage *vt* administrar mal. ~**ment** *n* mala administración *f*

misplace *vt* (lose) extraviar, perder

misprint *n* errata *f*

miss *vt* (fail to hit) no dar en; (regret absence of) echar de menos, extrañar (LAm); perder <*train, party*>; perder <*chance*>. ~ **the point** no comprender. ● *vi* errar el tiro, fallar; <*bullet*> no dar en el blanco. ● *n* fallo *m*, falla *f* (LAm); (title) señorita *f*. □ ~ **out** *vt* saltarse <*line*>. ~**out on sth** perderse algo

misshapen *a* deforme

missile *n* (Mil) misil *m*

missing *a* (lost) perdido. **be** ~ faltar. **go** ~ desaparecer. ~ **person** desaparecido *m*

mission *n* misión *f*. ~**ary** *n* misionero *m*

mist *n* neblina *f*; (at sea) bruma *f*. □ ~ **up** *vi* empañarse

mistake *n* error *m*. **make a** ~ cometer un error. **by** ~ por error. ● *vt* (*pt* **mistook**, *pp* **mistaken**) confundir. ~ **for** confundir con. ~**n** *a* equivocado. **be** ~**n** equivocarse

mistletoe *n* muérdago *m*

mistreat *vt* maltratar

mistress *n* (of house) señora *f*; (lover) amante *f*

mistrust *vt* desconfiar de. ● *n* desconfianza *f*. ~**ful** *a* desconfiado

misty *a* (-**ier**, -**iest**) neblinoso; <*day*> de neblina. **it's** ~ hay neblina

M

misunderstand vt (pt **-stood**) entender mal. ~**ing** n malentendido m

misuse vt emplear mal; malversar <funds>. ● n mal uso m; (unfair use) abuso m; (of funds) malversación f

mite n (insect) ácaro m

mitten n mitón m

mix vt mezclar. ● vi mezclarse; (go together) combinar. ~ **with** tratarse con <people>. ● n mezcla f. □ ~ **up** vt mezclar; (confuse) confundir. ~**ed** a <school etc> mixto; (assorted) mezclado. be ~**ed up** estar confuso. ~**er** n (Culin) batidora f; (TV, machine) mezcladora f. ~**ture** n mezcla f. ~**-up** n lío m

moan n gemido m. ● vi gemir; (complain) quejarse (**about** de)

moat n foso m

mob n turba f. ● vt (pt **mobbed**) acosar

mobil|e a móvil. ~**e home** n caravana f fija, trailer m (LAm). ~**e** (**phone**) n (teléfono m) móvil m, (teléfono m) celular m (LAm). ● n móvil m. ~**ize** vt movilizar. ● vi movilizarse

mock vt burlarse de. ● a <anger> fingido; <exam> de práctica. ~**ery** n burla f. make a ~**ery of sth** ridiculizar algo

model n (example) modelo m; (mock-up) maqueta f; (person) modelo m. ● a (exemplary) modelo; <car etc> en miniatura. ● vt (pt **modelled**) modelar. ~ **o.s. on s.o.** tomar a uno como modelo

modem n (Comp) módem m

moderat|e a & n moderado (m). ● vt moderar. ~**ely** adv (fairly) medianamente. ~**ion** n moderación f. **in** ~**ion** con moderación

modern a moderno. ~**ize** vt modernizar

modest a modesto. ~**y** n modestia f

modif|ication n modificación f. ~**y** vt modificar

module n módulo m

moist a (-er, -est) húmedo. ~**en** vt humedecer

moistur|e n humedad f. ~**ize** vt hidratar. ~**izer**, ~**izing cream** n crema f hidratante

mole n (animal) topo m; (on skin) lunar m

molecule n molécula f

molest vt abusar (sexualmente) de

mollify vt aplacar

mollusc n molusco m

mollycoddle vt mimar

molten a fundido; <lava> líquido

mom n (Amer, 🔲) mamá f 🔲

moment n momento m. **at the** ~ en este momento. **for the** ~ de momento. ~**ary** a momentáneo

momentous a trascendental

momentum n momento m; (speed) velocidad f

mommy n (Amer, 🔲) mamá m 🔲

monarch n monarca m. ~**y** n monarquía f

monastery n monasterio m

Monday n lunes m

money n dinero m, plata f (LAm). ~**box** n hucha f, alcancía f (LAm). ~ **order** n giro m postal

mongrel n perro m mestizo, chucho m 🔲

monitor n (Tec) monitor m. ● vt observar <elections>; seguir <progress>; (electronically) monitorizar

monk n monje m. ~**fish** n rape m

monkey n mono m. ~**-nut** n cacahuete m, cacahuate m (Mex),

maní *m* (LAm). **~wrench** *n* llave *f* inglesa

mono *n* monofonía *f*

monologue *n* monólogo *m*

monopol|ize *vt* monopolizar; acaparar <*conversation*>. **~y** *n* monopolio *m*

monoton|e *n* tono *m* monocorde. **~ous** *a* monótono. **~y** *n* monotonía *f*

monsoon *n* monzón *m*

monst|er *n* monstruo *m*. **~rous** *a* monstruoso

month *n* mes *m*. **£200 a ~** 200 libras mensuales *or* al mes. **~ly** *a* mensual. **~ly payment** mensualidad *f*, cuota *f* mensual (LAm). ● *adv* mensualmente

monument *n* monumento *m*. **~al** *a* monumental

moo *n* mugido *m*. ● *vi* mugir

mood *n* humor *m*. **be in a good/bad ~** estar de buen/mal humor. **~y** *a* (**-ier, -iest**) temperamental; (bad-tempered) malhumorado

moon *n* luna *f*. **~light** *n* luz *f* de la luna. **~lighting** *n* pluriempleo *m*. **~lit** *a* iluminado por la luna; <*night*> de luna

moor *n* páramo *m*; (of heather) brezal *m*. ● *vt* amarrar. **~ing** *n* (place) amarradero *m*. **~ings** *npl* (ropes) amarras *fpl*

moose *n invar* alce *m* americano

mop *n* fregona *f*, trapeador *m* (LAm). **~ of hair** pelambrera *f*. ● *vt* (*pt* **mopped**). **~ (up)** limpiar

mope *vi* estar abatido

moped *n* ciclomotor *m*

moral *a* moral. ● *n* (of tale) moraleja *f*

morale *n* moral *f*

moral|ity *n* moralidad *f*. **~ly** *adv* moralmente. **~s** *npl* moralidad *f*

morbid *a* morboso

more *a* más. **two ~ bottles** dos botellas más ● *pron* más. **you ate ~ than me** comiste más que yo. **some ~** más. **~ than six** más de seis. **the ~ he has, the ~ he wants** cuánto más tiene, más quiere. ● *adv* más. **~ and ~** cada vez más. **~ or less** más o menos. **once ~** una vez más. **she doesn't live here any ~** ya no vive aquí. **~over** *adv* además

morgue *n* depósito *m* de cadáveres, morgue *f* (LAm)

morning *n* mañana *f*; (early hours) madrugada *f*. **at 11 o'clock in the ~** a las once de la mañana. **in the ~** por la mañana, en la mañana (LAm). **tomorrow/yesterday ~** mañana/ayer por la mañana *or* (LAm) en la mañana. **(good) ~!** ¡buenos días!

Morocc|an *a & n* marroquí (*m & f*). **~o** *n* Marruecos *m*

moron *n* imbécil *m & f*

morose *a* taciturno

Morse *n* Morse *m*. **in ~ (code)** *n* en (código) morse

morsel *n* bocado *m*

mortal *a & n* mortal (*m*). **~ity** *n* mortalidad *f*

mortar *n* (all senses) mortero *m*

mortgage *n* hipoteca *f*. ● *vt* hipotecar

mortify *vt* darle mucha vergüenza a

mortuary *n* depósito *m* de cadáveres, morgue *f* (LAm)

mosaic *n* mosaico *m*

mosque *n* mezquita *f*

mosquito *n* (*pl* **-oes**) mosquito *m*, zancudo *m* (LAm)

moss *n* musgo *m*

most *a* la mayoría de, la mayor parte de. **~ days** casi todos los días. ● *pron* la mayoría, la mayor parte. **at ~** como máximo. **make**

M

the ~ of aprovechar al máximo.
● *adv* más; (very) muy; (Amer, almost,) casi. ~**ly** *adv* principalmente

MOT *n*. ~ (test) ITV *f*, inspección *f* técnica de vehículos

motel *n* motel *m*

moth *n* mariposa *f* de la luz, palomilla *f*; (in clothes) polilla *f*

mother *n* madre *f*. ● *vt* mimar. ~**-in-law** *n* (*pl* ~**s-in-law**) suegra *f*. ~**land** *n* patria *f*. ~**ly** *a* maternal. ~**-of-pearl** *n* nácar *m*, madreperla *f*. **M**~**'s Day** *n* el día *m* de la Madre. ~**-to-be** *n* futura madre *f*. ~ **tongue** *n* lengua *f* materna

motif *n* motivo *m*

motion *n* movimiento *m*; (proposal) moción *f*. **put** *or* **set in** ~ poner algo en marcha. ● *vt/i*. ~ (**to**) **s.o. to** hacerle señas a uno para que. ~**less** *a* inmóvil

motiv|ate *vt* motivar. ~**ation** *n* motivación *f*. ~**e** *n* motivo *m*

motley *a* variopinto

motor *n* motor *m*. ● *a* motor; (fem) motora, motriz. ~ **bike** *n* Ⓔ motocicleta *f*, moto *f* Ⓔ. ~ **boat** *n* lancha *f* a motor. ~ **car** *n* automóvil *m*. ~ **cycle** *n* motocicleta *f*. ~**cyclist** *n* motociclista *m & f*. ~**ing** *n* automovilismo *m*. ~**ist** *n* automovilista *m & f*. ~**way** *n* autopista *f*

motto *n* (*pl* -**oes**) lema *m*

mould *n* molde *m*; (fungus) moho *m*. ● *vt* moldear; formar <*character*>. ~**ing** *n* (on wall etc) moldura *f*. ~**y** *a* mohoso

moult *vi* mudar de pelo/piel/plumas

mound *n* montículo *m*; (pile, fig) montón *m*

mount *vt* montar <*horse*>; engarzar <*gem*>; preparar

<*attack*>. ● *vi* subir, crecer. ● *n*. montura *f*; (mountain) monte *m*. □ ~ **up** *vi* irse acumulando

mountain *n* montaña *f*. ~**eer** *n* alpinista *m & f*. ~**eering** *n* alpinismo *m*. ~**ous** *a* montañoso

mourn *vt* llorar. ● *vi* lamentarse. ~ **for s.o.** llorar a uno. ~**er** *n* doliente *m & f*. ~**ful** *a* triste. ~**ing** *n* duelo *m*, luto *m*. **be in** ~**ing** estar de duelo

mouse *n* (*pl* **mice**) ratón *m*. ~**trap** *n* ratonera *f*

mousse *n* (Culin) mousse *or m*; (for hair) mousse *f*

moustache *n* bigote *m*

mouth *n* boca *f*; (of cave) entrada *f*; (of river) desembocadura *f*. ~**ful** *n* bocado *m*. ~**-organ** *n* armónica *f*. ~**wash** *n* enjuague *m* bucal

move *vt* mover; (relocate) trasladar; (with emotion) conmover; (propose) proponer. ~ **the television** cambiar de lugar la televisión. ~ **house** mudarse de casa. ● *vi* moverse; (be in motion) estar en movimiento; (take action) tomar medidas. ● *n* movimiento *m*; (in game) jugada *f*; (player's turn) turno *m*; (removal) mudanza *f*. □ ~ **away** *vi* alejarse. □ ~ **in** *vi* instalarse. ~ **in with s.o.** irse a vivir con uno. □ ~ **over** *vi* correrse. ~**ment** *n* movimiento *m*

movie *n* (Amer) película *f*. **the** ~**s** *npl* el cine. ~ **camera** *n* (Amer) tomavistas *m*, filmadora *f* (LAm)

moving *a* en movimiento; (touching) conmovedor

mow *vt* (*pt* **mowed** *or* **mown**) cortar <*lawn*>; segar <*hay*>. □ ~ **down** *vt* acribillar. ~**er** *n* (for lawn) cortacésped *m*

MP *abbr* ⇒MEMBER OF PARLIAMENT

Mr *abbr* (*pl* **Messrs**) (= **Mister**) Sr. ~ **Coldbeck** Sr. Coldbeck

Mrs *abbr* (*pl* **Mrs**) (= **Missis**) Sra. ~ **Andrews** Sra. Andrews

Ms *abbr* (*title of married or unmarried woman*)

MSc *abbr* ⇒MASTER

much *a & pron* mucho, mucha. ● *adv* mucho; (before pp) muy. ~ **as** por mucho que. ~ **the same** más o menos lo mismo. **how ~?** ¿cuánto?. **so ~** tanto. **too ~** demasiado

muck *n* estiércol *m*; (🆸, dirt) mugre *f*. □ ~ **about** *vi* 🆸 tontear

mud *n* barro *m*, lodo *m*

muddle *vt* embrollar. ● *n* desorden *m*; (mix-up) lío *m*. □ ~ **through** *vi* salir del paso

muddy *a* lodoso; *<hands etc>* cubierto de lodo. ~**guard** *n* guardabarros *m*, salpicadera *f* (Mex)

muffle *vt* amortiguar *<sound>*. ~**r** *n* (scarf) bufanda *f*; (Amer, Auto) silenciador *m*

mug *n* taza *f* (alta y sin platillo), tarro *m* (Mex); (for beer) jarra *f*; (🆸, face) cara *f*, jeta *f* 🆇; (🆸, fool) idiota *m & f*. ● *vt* (*pt* **mugged**) asaltar. ~**ger** *n* asaltante *m & f*. ~**ging** *n* asalto *m*

muggy *a* bochornoso

mule *n* mula *f*

mull (Amer), ~ **over** *vt* reflexionar sobre

multi|coloured *a* multicolor. ~**national** *a & n* multinacional (*f*)

multipl|e *a* múltiple. ● *n* múltiplo *m*. ~**ication** *n* multiplicación *f*. ~**y** *vt* multiplicar. ● *vi* (Math) multiplicar; (increase) multiplicarse

multitude *n*. **a ~ of problems** múltiples problemas

mum *n* 🆸 mamá *f* 🆸

mumble *vt* mascullar. ● *vi* hablar entre dientes

mummy *n* (🆸, mother) mamá *f* 🆸; (archaeology) momia *f*

mumps *n* paperas *fpl*

munch *vt/i* mascar

mundane *a* mundano

municipal *a* municipal

mural *a & n* mural (*f*)

murder *n* asesinato *m*. ● *vt* asesinar. ~**er** *n* asesino *m*

murky *a* (**-ier, -iest**) turbio

murmur *n* murmullo *m*. ● *vt/i* murmurar

musc|le *n* músculo *m*. ~**ular** *a* muscular; *<arm, body>* musculoso

muse *vi* meditar (**on** sobre)

museum *n* museo *m*

mush *n* papilla *f*

mushroom *n* champiñón *m*; (Bot) seta *f*. ● *vi* aparecer como hongos

mushy *a* blando

music *n* música *f*. ~**al** *a* musical. **be ~** tener sentido musical. ● *n* musical *m*. ~**ian** *n* músico *m*

Muslim *a & n* musulmán (*m*)

mussel *n* mejillón *m*

must *v aux* deber, tener que; (expressing supposition) deber (de). **he ~ be old** debe (de) ser viejo. **I ~ have done it** debo (de) haberlo hecho. ● *n*. **be a ~** ser imprescindible

mustache *n* (Amer) bigote *m*

mustard *n* mostaza *f*

muster *vt* reunir

musty *a* (**-ier, -iest**) que huele a humedad

mutation *n* mutación *f*

mute *a* mudo

mutilate *vt* mutilar

mutiny *n* motín *m*. ● *vi* amotinarse

mutter *vt/i* murmurar

mutton *n* carne *f* de ovino

M

mutual *a* mutuo; (🔲, common) común

muzzle *n* (snout) hocico *m*; (device) bozal *m*

my *a* (*sing*) mi; (*pl*) mis

myself *pron* (*reflexive*) me; (used for emphasis) yo mismo *m*, yo misma *f*. **I cut** ∼ me corté. **I made it** ∼ lo hice yo mismo/misma. **I was by** ∼ estaba solo/sola

myster|ious *a* misterioso. ∼**y** *n* misterio *m*

mystical *a* místico

mystify *vt* dejar perplejo

mystique *n* mística *f*

myth *n* mito *m*. ∼**ical** *a* mítico. ∼**ology** *n* mitología *f*

N *abbr* (= **north**) N

nab *vt* (*pt* **nabbed**) (🔲, arrest) pescar; (snatch) agarrar

nag *vt* (*pt* **nagged**) fastidiar; (scold) estarle encima a. ● *vi* criticar

nail *n* clavo *m*; (of finger, toe) uña *f*. ∼ **polish** esmalte *m* para las uñas. ● *vt.* ∼ (**down**) clavar

naive *a* ingenuo

naked *a* desnudo. **to the** ∼ **eye** a simple vista

name *n* nombre *m*; (of book, film) título *m*; (fig) fama *f*. **my** ∼ **is Chris** me llamo Chris. **good** ∼ buena reputación. ● *vt* ponerle nombre a; (appoint) nombrar. **a man** ∼**d Jones** un hombre llamado Jones. **she was** ∼**d after** *or* (Amer) **for her grandmother** le pusieron el nombre de su abuela. ∼**less** *a* anónimo. ∼**ly** *adv* a saber. ∼**sake** *n* (person) tocayo *m*

nanny *n* niñera *f*

nap *n* (sleep) sueñecito *m*; (after lunch) siesta *f*. **have a** ∼ echarse un sueño

napkin *n* servilleta *f*

nappy *n* pañal *m*

narcotic *a & n* narcótico (*m*)

narrat|e *vt* narrar. ∼**ive** *n* narración *f*. ∼**or** *n* narrador *m*

narrow *a* (**-er, -est**) estrecho, angosto (LAm). **have a** ∼ **escape** salvarse de milagro. ● *vt* estrechar; (limit) limitar. ● *vi* estrecharse. ∼**ly** *adv* (just) por poco. ∼**-minded** *a* de miras estrechas

nasal *a* nasal; <*voice*> gangoso

nasty *a* (**-ier, -iest**) desagradable; (spiteful) malo (**to** con); <*taste, smell*> asqueroso; <*cut*> feo

nation *n* nación *f*

national *a* nacional. ● *n* ciudadano *m*. ∼ **anthem** *n* himno *m* nacional. ∼**ism** *n* nacionalismo *m*. ∼**ity** *n* nacionalidad *f*. ∼**ize** *vt* nacionalizar. ∼**ly** *adv* a escala nacional

nationwide *a & adv* a escala nacional

native *n* natural *m & f*. **be a** ∼ **of** ser natural de. ● *a* nativo; <*country, town*> natal; <*language*> materno; <*plant, animal*> autóctono. **N**∼ **American** indio *m* americano

nativity *n*. **the N**∼ la Natividad *f*

NATO *abbr* (= **North Atlantic Treaty Organization**) OTAN *f*

natter 🔲 *vi* charlar. ● *n* charla *f*

natural *a* natural. ∼ **history** *n* historia *f* natural. ∼**ist** *n* naturalista *m & f*. ∼**ized** *a* <*citizen*> naturalizado. ∼**ly** *adv* (of course) naturalmente; (by nature) por naturaleza

nature *n* naturaleza *f*; (of person) carácter *m*; (of things) naturaleza *f*

naught *n* cero *m*

naughty *a* (**-ier, -iest**) malo, travieso

nause|a *n* náuseas *fpl*. **~ous** *a* nauseabundo

nautical *a* náutico. **~ mile** *n* milla *f* marina

naval *a* naval; <*officer*> de marina

nave *n* nave *f*

navel *n* ombligo *m*

naviga|ble *a* navegable. **~te** *vt* navegar por <*sea etc*>; gobernar <*ship*>. ● *vi* navegar. **~tion** *n* navegación *f*. **~tor** *n* oficial *m & f* de derrota

navy *n* marina *f* de guerra. **~ (blue)** *a & n* azul (*m*) marino

NE *abbr* (= **north-east**) NE

near *adv* cerca. **draw ~** acercarse. ● *prep.* **~ (to)** cerca de. **go ~ (to)** **sth** acercarse a algo. ● *a* cercano. ● *vt* acercarse a. **~by** *a* cercano. **~ly** *adv* casi. **he ~ly died** por poco se muere, casi se muere. **not ~ly** ni con mucho. **~sighted** *a* miope, corto de vista

neat *a* (**-er, -est**) <*person*> pulcro; <*room etc*> bien arreglado; (ingenious) hábil; <*whisky, gin*> solo; (Amer 🆃, great) fantástico 🆃. **~ly** *adv* pulcramente; <*organized*> cuidadosamente

necessar|ily *adv* necesariamente. **~y** *a* necesario

necessit|ate *vt* exigir. **~y** *n* necesidad *f*. **the bare ~ies** lo indispensable

neck *n* (of person, bottle, dress) cuello *m*; (of animal) pescuezo *m*. **~ and ~** a la par, parejos (LAm). **~lace** *n* collar *m*. **~line** *n* escote *m*

nectar *n* néctar *m*

nectarine *n* nectarina *f*

née *a* de soltera

need *n* necesidad *f* (**for** de). ● *vt* necesitar; (demand) exigir. **you ~ not speak** no tienes quehablar

needle *n* aguja *f*. ● *vt* (🆃, annoy) pinchar

needless *a* innecesario

needlework *n* labores *fpl* de aguja; (embroidery) bordado *m*

needy *a* (**-ier, -iest**) necesitado

negative *a* negativo. ● *n* (of photograph) negativo *m*; (no) negativa *f*

neglect *vt* descuidar <*house*>; desatender <*children*>; no cumplir con <*duty*>. ● *n* negligencia *f*. **(state of) ~** abandono *m*. **~ful** *a* negligente

neglig|ence *n* negligencia *f*, descuido *m*. **~ent** *a* negligente. **~ible** *a* insignificante

negotia|ble *a* negociable. **~te** *vt/i* negociar. **~tion** *n* negociación *f*. **~tor** *n* negociador *m*

neigh *vi* relinchar

neighbour *n* vecino *m*. **~hood** *n* vecindad *f*, barrio *m*. **in the ~hood of** alrededor de. **~ing** *a* vecino

neither *a*. **~ book** ninguno de los libros. ● *pron* ninguno, -na. ● *conj.* **neither...nor** ni...ni. **~ do I** yo tampoco

neon *n* neón *m*. ● *a* <*lamp etc*> de neón

nephew *n* sobrino *m*

Neptune *n* Neptuno *m*

nerv|e *n* nervio *m*; (courage) valor *m*; (calm) sangre *f* fría; (🆃, impudence) descaro *m*. **~es** *npl* (before exams etc) nervios *mpl*. **get on s.o.'s ~es** ponerle los nervios de punta a uno. **~e-racking** *a*

N

exasperante. ∼**ous** *a* nervioso.
be/feel ∼**ous** estar nervioso.
∼**ousness** *n* nerviosismo *m*. ∼**y**
a nervioso; (Amer 🄸) descarado

nest *n* nido *m*. ● *vi* anidar

nestle *vi* acurrucarse

net *n* red *f*. **the N**∼ (Comp) la Red.
● *vt* (*pt* **netted**) pescar (con red)
<*fish*>. ● *a* neto. ∼**ball** *n*
baloncesto *m*

Netherlands *npl.* **the** ∼ los
Países Bajos

netting *n* redes *fpl.* **wire** ∼ tela *f*
metálica

nettle *n* ortiga *f*

network *n* red *f*; (TV) cadena *f*

neuro|sis *n* (*pl* **-oses**) neurosis *f*.
∼**tic** *a & n* neurótico (*m*)

neuter *a & n* neutro (*m*). ● *vt*
castrar <*animals*>

neutral *a* neutral; <*colour*>
neutro; (Elec) neutro. ∼ (**gear**)
(Auto) punto *m* muerto. ∼**ize** *vt*
neutralizar

neutron *n* neutrón *m*

never *adv* nunca; (more emphatic)
jamás; (🄸, not) no. ∼ **again** nunca
más. **he** ∼ **smiles** no sonríe
nunca, nunca sonríe. **I** ∼ **saw him**
🄸 no lo vi. ∼**-ending** *a*
interminable. ∼**theless** *adv* sin
embargo, no obstante

new *a* (**-er, -est**) nuevo. ∼**born** *a*
recién nacido. ∼**comer** *n* recién
llegado *m*. ∼**fangled** *a* (pej)
moderno. ∼**ly** *adv* recién. ∼**ly-
weds** *npl* recién casados *mpl*

news *n*. **a piece of** ∼ una noticia.
good/bad ∼ buenas/malas
noticias. **the** ∼ (TV, Radio) las
noticias. ∼**agent** *n* vendedor *m*
de periódicos. ∼**caster** *n* locutor
m. ∼**dealer** *n* (Amer) ⇒∼agent.
∼**flash** *n* información *f* de última
hora. ∼**letter** *n* boletín *m*,
informativo *m*. ∼**paper** *n*

periódico *m*, diario *m*. ∼**reader** *n*
locutor *m*

newt *n* tritón *m*

New Year *n* Año *m* Nuevo. ∼**'s
Day** *n* día *m* de Año Nuevo. ∼**'s
Eve** *n* noche *f* vieja, noche *f* de
fin de Año

New Zealand *n* Nueva Zeland
(i)a *f*

next *a* próximo; <*week, month
etc*> que viene, próximo; (adjoining)
vecino; (following) siguiente. ● *adv*
luego, después. ∼ **to** al lado de.
when you see me ∼ la próxima
vez que me veas. ∼ **to nothing**
casi nada. ∼ **door** al lado (to de).
∼**-door** *a* de al lado. ∼ **of kin** *n*
familiar(es) *m(pl)* más cercano(s)

nib *n* plumilla *f*

nibble *vt/i* mordisquear. ● *n*
mordisco *m*

Nicaragua *n* Nicaragua *f*. ∼**n** *a
& n* nicaragüense (*m & f*)

nice *a* (**-er, -est**) agradable;
(likeable) simpático; (kind) amable;
<*weather, food*> bueno. **we had a**
∼ **time** lo pasamos bien. ∼**ly** *adv*
(kindly) amablemente; (politely) con
buenos modales

niche *n* nicho *m*

nick *n* corte *m* pequeño. **in the** ∼
of time justo a tiempo. ● *vt*
(🄳 steal) afanar 🄳

nickel *n* (metal) níquel *m*; (Amer)
moneda *f* de cinco centavos

nickname *n* apodo *m*. ● *vt*
apodar

nicotine *n* nicotina *f*

niece *n* sobrina *f*

niggling *a* <*doubt*> constante

night *n* noche *f*; (evening) tarde *f*.
at ∼ por la noche, de noche.
good ∼ ¡buenas noches! ● *a*
nocturno, de noche. ∼**cap** *n*
(drink) bebida *f* (tomada antes de
acostarse). ∼**club** *n* club *m*
nocturno. ∼**dress** *n* camisón *m*.

~**fall** n anochecer m. ~**gown**, ~**ie** 🔲 n camisón m. ~**life** n vida f nocturna. ~**ly** a de todas las noches. ~**mare** n pesadilla f. ~ **school** n escuela f nocturna. ~**-time** n noche f. ~**watchman** n sereno m

nil n nada f; (Sport) cero m

nimble a (-er, -est) ágil

nine a & n nueve (m). ~**teen** a & n diecinueve (m). ~**teenth** a decimonoveno. ● n diecinueveavo m. ~**tieth** a nonagésimo. ● n noventavo m. ~**ty** a & n noventa (m)

ninth a & n noveno (m)

nip vt (pt nipped) (pinch) pellizcar; (bite) mordisquear. ● vi (🔲, rush) correr

nipple n (of woman) pezón m; (of man) tetilla f; (of baby's bottle) tetina f, chupón m (Mex)

nippy a (-ier, -iest) (🔲, chilly) fresquito

nitrogen n nitrógeno m

no a ninguno, (before masculine singular noun) ningún. **I have ~ money** no tengo dinero. **there's ~ food left** no queda nada de comida. **it has ~ windows** no tiene ventanas. **I'm ~ expert** no soy ningún experto. ~ **smoking** prohibido fumar. ~ **way!** 🔲 ¡ni hablar! ● adv & int no. ● n (pl **noes**) no m

noble a (-er, -est) noble. ~**man** n noble m

nobody pron nadie. **there's ~ there** no hay nadie

nocturnal a nocturno

nod vt (pt nodded). ~ **one's head** asentir con la cabeza. ● vi (in agreement) asentir con la cabeza; (in greeting) saludar con la cabeza. □ ~ **off** vi dormirse

nois|e n ruido m. ~**ily** adv ruidosamente. ~**y** a (-ier, -iest) ruidoso. **it's too ~y here** hay demasiado ruido aquí

nomad n nómada m & f. ~**ic** a nómada

no man's land n tierra f de nadie

nominat|e vt (put forward) proponer; postular (LAm); (appoint) nombrar. ~**ion** n nombramiento m; (Amer, Pol) proclamación f

non-... pref no ...

nonchalant a despreocupado

non-committal a evasivo

nondescript a anodino

none pron ninguno, ninguna. **there were ~ left** no quedaba ninguno/ninguna. ~ **of us** ninguno de nosotros. ● adv no, de ninguna manera. **he is ~ the happier** no está más contento

nonentity n persona f insignificante

non-existent a inexistente

nonplussed a perplejo

nonsens|e n tonterías fpl, disparates mpl. ~**ical** a disparatado

non-smoker n no fumador m. **I'm a ~** no fumo

non-stop a <train> directo; <flight> sin escalas. ● adv sin parar; (by train) directamente; (by air) sin escalas

noodles npl fideos mpl

nook n rincón m

noon n mediodía m

no-one pron nadie

noose n soga f

nor conj ni, tampoco. **neither blue ~ red** ni azul ni rojo. **he doesn't play the piano, ~ do I** no sabe tocar el piano, ni yo tampoco

norm n norma f

normal a normal. ~**cy** n (Amer) normalidad f. ~**ity** n normalidad f. ~**ly** adv normalmente

N

north *n* norte *m*. ● *a* norte. ● *adv* hacia el norte. **N~ America** *n* América *f* del Norte, Norteamérica *f*. **N~ American** *a* & *n* norteamericano (*m*). **~east** *n* nor(d)este *m*. ● *a* nor(d)este. ● *adv* <*go*> hacia el nor(d)este. **it's ~east of Leeds** está al nor(d) este de Leeds. **~erly** *a* <*wind*> del norte. **~ern** *a* del norte. **~erner** *n* norteño *m*. **N~ern Ireland** *n* Irlanda *f* del Norte. **N~ Sea** *n* mar *m* del Norte. **~ward**, **~wards** *adv* hacia el norte. **~west** *n* noroeste *m*. ● *a* noroeste. ● *adv* hacia el noroeste

Norw|ay *n* Noruega *f*. **~egian** *a* & *n* noruego (*m*)

nose *n* nariz *f*. **~bleed** *n* hemorragia *f* nasal. **~dive** *vi* descender en picado, descender en picada (LAm)

nostalgi|a *n* nostalgia *f*. **~c** *a* nostálgico

nostril *n* ventana *f* de la nariz *f*

nosy *a* (**-ier**, **-iest**) Ⓘ entrometido, metiche (LAm)

··

not

> Cuando **not** va precedido del verbo auxiliar **do** or **have** o de un verbo modal como **should** etc se suele emplear la forma contraída **don't**, **haven't**, **shouldn't** etc

● *adverb*
····➤ no. **I don't know** no sé. **~ yet** todavía no. **~ me** yo no
····➤ (replacing a clause) **I suppose ~** supongo que no. **of course ~** por supuesto que no. **are you going to help me or ~?** ¿me vas a ayudar o no?
····➤ (emphatic) ni. **~ a penny more!** ¡ni un penique más!

····➤ (in phrases) **certainly ~** de ninguna manera . **~ you again!** ¡tú otra vez!
··

notabl|e *a* notable; <*author*> distinguido. **~y** *adv* notablemente; (in particular) particularmente

notch *n* muesca *f*. ⯐ **~ up** *vt* apuntarse

note *n* (incl Mus) nota *f*; (banknote) billete *m*. **take ~s** tomar apuntes. ● *vt* (notice) observar; (record) anotar. ⯐ **~ down** *vt* apuntar. **~book** *n* cuaderno *m*. **~d** *a* célebre. **~paper** *n* papel *m* de carta(s)

nothing *pron* nada. **he eats ~** no come nada. **for ~** (free) gratis; (in vain) en vano. **~ else** nada más. **~ much happened** no pasó gran cosa. **he does ~ but complain** no hace más que quejarse

notice *n* (sign) letrero *m*; (item of information) anuncio *m*; (notification) aviso *m*; (of termination of employment) preaviso *m*; **~** (of dismissal) despido *m*. **take ~ of** hacer caso a <*person*>. ● *vt* notar. ● *vi* darse cuenta. **~able** *a* perceptible. **~ably** *adv* perceptiblemente. **~board** *n* tablón *m* de anuncios, tablero *m* de anuncios (LAm)

notif|ication *n* notificación *f*. **~y** *vt* informar; (in writing) notificar. **~y s.o. of sth** comunicarle algo a uno

notion *n* (concept) concepto *m*; (idea) idea *f*

notorious *a* notorio

notwithstanding *prep* a pesar de. ● *adv* no obstante

nougat *n* turrón *m*

nought *n* cero *m*

noun *n* sustantivo *m*, nombre *m*

nourish *vt* alimentar. **~ment** *n* alimento *m*

novel *n* novela *f*. ● *a* original, novedoso. ~**ist** *n* novelista *m & f*. ~**ty** *n* novedad *f*

November *n* noviembre *m*

novice *n* principiante *m & f*

now *adv* ahora. ~ **and again**, ~ **and then** de vez en cuando. **right** ~ ahora mismo. **from** ~ **on** a partir de ahora. ● *conj.* ~ **(that)** ahora que. ~**adays** *adv* hoy (en) día

nowhere *adv* por ninguna parte, por ningún lado; (after motion towards) a ninguna parte, a ningún lado

nozzle *n* (on hose) boca *f*; (on fire extinguisher) boquilla *f*

nuance *n* matiz *m*

nuclear *a* nuclear

nucleus *n* (*pl* **-lei**) núcleo *m*

nude *a & n* desnudo (*m*). **in the** ~ desnudo

nudge *vt* codear (ligeramente). ● *n* golpe *m* (suave) con el codo

nudi|st *n* nudista *m & f*. ~**ty** *n* desnudez *f*

nuisance *n* (thing, event) molestia *f*, fastidio *m*; (person) pesado *m*

null *a* nulo

numb *a* entumecido. **go** ~ entumecerse ● *vt* entumecer

number *n* número *m*; (telephone number) número *m* de teléfono. **a** ~ **of people** varias personas. ● *vt* numerar; (count, include) contar. ~**plate** *n* matrícula *f*, placa *f* (LAm)

numer|al *n* número *m*. ~**ical** *a* numérico. ~**ous** *a* numeroso

nun *n* monja *f*

nurse *n* enfermero *m*, enfermera *f*; (nanny) niñera *f*. ● *vt* cuidar; abrigar <hope etc>

nursery *n* (for plants) vivero *m*; (day ~) guardería *f*. ~ **rhyme** *n*

canción *f* infantil. ~ **school** *n* jardín *m* de infancia, jardín *m* infantil (LAm)

nursing home *n* (for older people) residencia *f* de ancianos (*con mayor nivel de asistencia médica*)

nut *n* fruto *m* seco (nuez, almendra, avellana etc); (Tec) tuerca *f*. ~**case** *n* 🆃 chiflado *m*. ~**crackers** *npl* cascanueces *m*. ~**meg** *n* nuez *f* moscada

nutri|ent *n* nutriente *m*. ~**tion** *n* nutrición *f*. ~**tious** *a* nutritivo

nuts *a* (🆃, crazy) chiflado

nutshell *n* cáscara *f* de nuez. **in a** ~ en pocas palabras

NW *abbr* (= **north-west**) NO

nylon *n* nylon *m*

oaf *n* zoquete *m*

oak *n* roble *m*

OAP *abbr* (= **old-age pensioner**) *n* pensionista *m & f*, pensionado *m*

oar *n* remo *m*

oasis *n* (*pl* **oases**) oasis *m*

oath *n* juramento *m*

oat|meal *n* harina *f* de avena; (Amer, flakes) avena *f* (en copos). ~**s** *npl* avena *f*

obedien|ce *n* obediencia *f*. ~**t** *a* obediente. ~**tly** *adv* obedientemente

obes|e *a* obeso. ~**ity** *n* obesidad *f*

obey *vt/i* obedecer

obituary *n* nota *f* necrológica, obituario *m*

object n objeto m; (aim) objetivo m. ● vi oponerse (**to** a). ~**ion** n objeción f. ~**ionable** a censurable; (unpleasant) desagradable. ~**ive** a & n objetivo (m)

oblig|ation n obligación f. **be under an** ~**ation to** estar obligado a. ~**atory** a obligatorio. ~**e** vt obligar. **I'd be much** ~**ed if you could help me** le quedaría muy agradecido si pudiera ayudarme. ● vi hacer un favor. ~**ing** a atento

oblique a oblicuo

obliterate vt arrasar; (erase) borrar

oblivio|n n olvido m. ~**us** a (unaware) inconsciente (**to, of** de)

oblong a oblongo. ● n rectángulo m

obnoxious a odioso

oboe n oboe m

obscen|e a obsceno. ~**ity** n obscenidad f

obscur|e a oscuro. ● vt ocultar; impedir ver claramente <issue>. ~**ity** n oscuridad f

obsequious a servil

observ|ant a observador. ~**ation** n observación f. ~**atory** n observatorio m. ~**e** vt observar. ~**er** n observador m

obsess vt obsesionar. ~**ed** a obsesionado. ~**ion** n obsesión f. ~**ive** a obsesivo

obsolete a obsoleto

obstacle n obstáculo m

obstina|cy n obstinación f. ~**te** a obstinado. ~**tely** adv obstinadamente

obstruct vt obstruir; bloquear <traffic>. ~**ion** n obstrucción f

obtain vt conseguir, obtener. ~**able** a asequible

obtrusive a <presence> demasiado prominente; <noise> molesto

obtuse a obtuso

obvious a obvio. ~**ly** adv obviamente

occasion n ocasión f. ~**al** a esporádico. ~**ally** adv de vez en cuando

occult a oculto

occup|ant n ocupante m & f. ~**ation** n ocupación f. ~**ier** n ocupante m & f. ~**y** vt ocupar. **keep o.s.** ~**ied** entretenerse

occur vi (pt **occurred**) tener lugar, ocurrir; <change> producirse; (exist) encontrarse. **it** ~**red to me that** se me ocurrió que. ~**rence** n (incidence) incidencia f. **it is a rare** ~**rence** no es algo frecuente

ocean n océano m

o'clock adv. **it is 7** ~ son las siete. **it's one** ~ es la una

octagon n octágono m

octave n octava f

October n octubre m

octopus n (pl -**puses**) pulpo m

odd a (-**er, -est**) extraño, raro; <number> impar; (one of pair) desparejado. **smoke the** ~ **cigarette** fumarse algún que otro cigarrillo. **fifty-**~ unos cincuenta, cincuenta y pico. **the** ~ **one out** la excepción. ~**ity** n (thing) rareza f; (person) bicho m raro. ~**ly** adv de una manera extraña. ~**ly enough** por extraño que parezca. ~**ment** n retazo m. ~**s** npl probabilidades fpl; (in betting) apuesta f. **be at** ~**s** estar en desacuerdo. ~**s and ends** mpl ⚅ cosas fpl sueltas

odious a odioso

odometer n (Amer) cuentakilómetros m

odour *n* olor *m*

of

● *preposition*

····▸ de. **a pound of cheese** una libra de queso. **it's made of wood** es de madera. **a girl of ten** una niña de diez años

····▸ (in dates) de. **the fifth of November** el cinco de noviembre

····▸ (Amer, when telling the time) **it's ten (minutes) of five** son las cinco menos diez, son diez para las cinco (LAm)

! **of** is not translated in cases such as the following: **a colleague of mine** *un colega mío*; **there were six of us** *éramos seis*; **that's very kind of you** *es Ud muy amable*

off *prep* (from) de. **he picked it up ~ the floor** lo recogió del suelo; (distant from) **just ~ the coast of Texas** a poca distancia de la costa de Tejas. **2 ft ~ the ground** a dos pies del suelo; (absent from) **I've been ~ work for a week** hace una semana que no voy a trabajar. ● *adv* (removed) **the lid was ~** la tapa no estaba puesta; (distant) **some way ~** a cierta distancia; (leaving) **I'm ~** me voy; (switched off) <*light, TV*> apagado; <*water*> cortado; (cancelled) <*match*> cancelado; (not on duty) <*day*> libre. ● *adj*. **be ~** <*meat*> estar malo, estar pasado; <*milk*> estar cortado. **~-beat** *a* poco convencional. **~ chance** *n*. **on the ~ chance** por si acaso

offen|ce *n* (breach of law) infracción *f*; (criminal) delito *m*; (cause of outrage) atentado *m*; (Amer, attack) ataque *m*. **take ~ce** ofenderse.

~d *vt* ofender. **~der** delincuente *m & f*. **~sive** *a* ofensivo; (disgusting) desagradable

offer *vt* ofrecer. **~ to do sth** ofrecerse a hacer algo. ● *n* oferta *f*. **on ~** de oferta

offhand *a* (brusque) brusco

office *n* oficina *f*; (post) cargo *m*. **doctor's ~** (Amer) consultorio *m*, consulta *m*. **~ block** *n* edificio *m* de oficinas **~r** *n* oficial *m & f*; (police ~r) policía *m & f*; (as form of address) agente

offici|al *a* oficial. ● *n* funcionario *m* del Estado; (of party, union) dirigente *m & f*. **~ally** *adv* oficialmente. **~ous** *a* oficioso

offing *n*. **in the ~** en perspectiva

off: **~-licence** *n* tienda *f* de vinos y licores. **~-putting** *a* (disconcerting) desconcertante; (disagreeable) desagradable. **~set** *vt* (*pt* **-set**, *pres p* **-setting**) compensar. **~side** *a* (Sport) fuera de juego. **~spring** *n invar* prole *f*. **~stage** *adv* fuera del escenario. **~white** *a* color hueso

often *adv* a menudo, con frecuencia. **how ~?** ¿con qué frecuencia? **more ~** con más frecuencia

ogle *vt* comerse con los ojos

ogre *n* ogro *m*

oh *int* ¡ah!; (expressing dismay) ¡ay!

oil *n* aceite *m*; (petroleum) petróleo *m*; (on beach) chapapote *m*. ● *vt* lubricar. **~field** *n* yacimiento *m* petrolífero. **~ painting** *n* pintura *f* al óleo; (picture) óleo *m*. **~ rig** *n* plataforma *f* petrolífera. **~ slick** *m* marea *f* negra. **~y** *a* <*substance*> oleaginoso; <*food*> aceitoso

ointment *n* ungüento *m*

O

OK *int* ¡vale!, ¡de acuerdo!, ¡bueno! (LAm). ● **a** ~, **thanks** bien, gracias. **the job's** ~ el trabajo no está mal

old *a* (**-er, -est**) viejo; (not modern) antiguo; (former) antiguo; **an** ~ **friend** un viejo amigo. **how** ~ **is she?** ¿cuántos años tiene? **she is ten years** ~ tiene diez años. **his** ~**er sister** su hermana mayor. ~ **age** *n* vejez *f*. ~**-fashioned** *a* anticuado

olive *n* aceituna *f*.

Olympic *a* olímpico. **the** ~**s** *npl*, **the** ~ **Games** *npl* los Juegos Olímpicos

omelette *n* tortilla *f* francesa, omelette *m* (LAm)

omen *n* agüero *m*

omi|ssion *n* omisión *f*. ~**t** *vt* (*pt* **omitted**) omitir

on *prep* en, sobre; (about) sobre. ~ **foot** a pie. ~ **Monday** el lunes. ~ **seeing** al ver. **I heard it** ~ **the radio** lo oí por la radio. ● *adv* (light etc) encendido, prendido (LAm); (machine) en marcha; (tap) abierto. ~ **and** ~ sin cesar. **and so** ~ y así sucesivamente. **have a hat** ~ llevar (puesto) un sombrero. **further** ~ un poco más allá. **what's** ~ **at the Odeon?** ¿qué dan en el Odeon? **go** ~ continuar. **later** ~ más tarde

once *adv* una vez; (formerly) antes. **at** ~ inmediatamente. ~ **upon a time there was...** érase una vez.... ~ **and for all** de una vez por todas. ● *conj* una vez que

one *a* uno, (before masculine singular noun) un. **the** ~ **person I trusted** la única persona en la que confiaba.● *n* uno *m*. ~ **by** ~ uno a uno.. ● *pron* uno (*m*), una (*f*). **the blue** ~ el/la azul. **this** ~ éste/ ésta. ~ **another** el uno al otro.

onerous *a* <*task*> pesado

one: ~**self** *pron* (reflexive) se; (after prep) sí (mismo); (emphatic use) uno mismo, una misma. **by** ~**self** solo. ~**-way** *a* <*street*> de sentido único; <*ticket*> de ida, sencillo

onion *n* cebolla *f*

onlooker *n* espectador *m*

only *a* único. **she's an** ~ **child** es hija única. ● *adv* sólo, solamente. ~ **just** (barely) apenas. **I've** ~ **just arrived** acabo de llegar. ● *conj* pero, sólo que

onset *n* comienzo *m*; (of disease) aparición *f*

onslaught *n* ataque *m*

onus *n* responsabilidad *f*

onward(s) *a & adv* hacia adelante

ooze *vt/i* rezumar

opaque *a* opaco

open *a* abierto; <*question*> discutible. ● *n*. **in the** ~ al aire libre. ● *vt/i* abrir. ~**ing** *n* abertura *f*; (beginning) principio *m*. ~**ly** *adv* abiertamente. ~**-minded** *a* de actitud abierta

opera *n* ópera *f*

operate *vt* manejar, operar (Mex) <*machine*>. ● *vi* funcionar; <*company*> operar. ~ **(on)** (Med) operar (a)

operatic *a* operístico

operation *n* operación *f*; (Mec) funcionamiento *m*; (using of machine) manejo *m*. **he had an** ~ lo operaron. **in** ~ en vigor. ~**al** *a* operacional

operative *a*. **be** ~ estar en vigor

operator *n* operador *m*

opinion *n* opinión *f*. **in my** ~ en mi opinión, a mi parecer

opponent *n* adversario *m*; (in sport) contrincante *m & f*

opportun|e a oportuno. ~**ist** n oportunista m & f. ~**ity** n oportunidad f

oppos|e vt oponerse a. be ~ed to oponerse a, estar en contra de. ~**ing** a opuesto. ~**ite** a (contrary) opuesto; (facing) de enfrente. ● n. the ~ite lo contrario. quite the ~ite al contrario. ● adv enfrente. ● prep enfrente de. ~**ite number** n homólogo m. ~**ition** n oposición f; (resistance) resistencia f

oppress vt oprimir. ~**ion** n opresión f. ~**ive** a (cruel) opresivo; <heat> sofocante

opt vi. ~ to optar por. □ ~ **out** vi decidir no tomar parte

optic|al a óptico. ~**ian** n óptico m

optimis|m n optimismo m. ~**t** n optimista m & f. ~**tic** a optimista

option n opción f. ~**al** a facultativo

or conj o; (before o- and ho-) u; (after negative) ni. ~ **else** si no, o bien

oral a oral. ● n 🔁 examen m oral

orange n naranja f; (colour) naranja m. ● a naranja. ~**ade** n naranjada f

orbit n órbita f. ● vt orbitar

orchard n huerto m

orchestra n orquesta f; (Amer, in theatre) platea f. ~**l** a orquestal. ~**te** vt orquestar

orchid n orquídea f

ordain vt (Relig) ordenar; (decree) decretar

ordeal n dura prueba f

order n orden m; (Com) pedido m; (command) orden f. in ~ that para que. in ~ to para. ● vt (command) ordenar, mandar; (Com) pedir; (in restaurant) pedir, ordenar (LAm); encargar <book>; llamar, ordenar

(LAm) <taxi>. ~**ly** a ordenado. ● n camillero m

ordinary a corriente; (average) medio; (mediocre) ordinario

ore n mena f

organ n órgano m

organ|ic a orgánico. ~**ism** n organismo m. ~**ist** n organista m & f. ~**ization** n organización f. ~**ize** vt organizar. ~**izer** n organizador m

orgasm n orgasmo m

orgy n orgía f

Orient n Oriente m. ~**al** a oriental

orientat|e vt orientar. ~**ion** n orientación f

origin n origen m. ~**al** a original. ~**ally** adv originariamente. ~**ate** vi. ~**ate from** provenir de

ornament n adorno m. ~**al** a de adorno

ornate a ornamentado; <style> recargado

ornithology n ornitología f

orphan n huérfano m. ● vt. be ~ed quedar huérfano. ~**age** n orfanato m

orthodox a ortodoxo

oscillate vi oscilar

ostentatious a ostentoso

osteopath n osteópata m & f

ostracize vt hacerle vacío a

ostrich n avestruz m

other a & pron otro. ~ **than** aparte de. the ~ **one** el otro. ~**wise** adv de lo contrario, si no

otter n nutria f

ouch int ¡ay!

ought v aux. I ~ **to see it** debería verlo. he ~ **to have done it** debería haberlo hecho

ounce n onza f (= 28.35 gr.)

our a (sing) nuestro, nuestra, (pl) nuestros, nuestras. ~**s** poss pron

O

(*sing*) nuestro, nuestra; (*pl*) nuestros, nuestras. ~s is red el nuestro es rojo. a friend of ~s un amigo nuestro. ~**selves** *pron* (reflexive) nos; (used for emphasis and after prepositions) nosotros mismos, nosotras mismas. we behaved ~**selves** nos portamos bien. we did it ~**selves** lo hicimos nosotros mismos/nosotras mismas

oust *vt* desbancar; derrocar <*government*>

out *adv* (outside) fuera, afuera (LAm). (not lighted, not on) apagado; (in blossom) en flor; (in error) equivocado. he's ~ (not at home) no está; be ~ to estar resuelto a. ~ **of** *prep* (from inside) de; (outside) fuera, afuera (LAm). five ~ of six cinco de cada seis. made ~ of hecho de. we're ~ of bread nos hemos quedado sin pan. ~**break** *n* (of war) estallido *m*; (of disease) brote *m*. ~**burst** *n* arrebato *m*. ~**cast** *a* paria *m & f.* ~**come** *n* resultado *m*. ~**cry** *n* protesta *f*. ~**dated** *a* anticuado. ~**do** *vt* (*pt* **-did**, *pp* **-done**) superar. ~**door** *a* <*clothes*> de calle; <*pool*> descubierto. ~**doors** *adv* al aire libre

outer *a* exterior

out: ~**fit** *n* equipo *m*; (clothes) conjunto *m*. ~**going** *a* <*minister etc*> saliente; (sociable) abierto. ~**goings** *npl* gastos *mpl*. ~**grow** *vt* (*pt* **-grew**, *pp* **-grown**) crecer más que <*person*>. he's ~**grown** his new shoes le han quedado pequeños los zapatos nuevos. ~**ing** *n* excursión *f*

outlandish *a* extravagante

out: ~**law** *n* forajido *m*. ● *vt* proscribir. ~**lay** *n* gastos *mpl*. ~**let** *n* salida *f*; (Com) punto *m* de venta; (Amer, Elec) toma *f* de corriente. ~**line** *n* contorno *m*;

(summary) resumen *m*; (plan of project) esquema *m*. ● *vt* trazar; (summarize) esbozar. ~**live** *vt* sobrevivir a. ~**look** *n* perspectivas *fpl*; (attitude) punto *m* de vista. ~**lying** *a* alejado. ~**number** *vt* superar en número. ~-**of-date** *a* <*ideas*> desfasado; <*clothes*> pasado de moda. ~**patient** *n* paciente *m* externo. ~**post** *n* avanzada *f*. ~**put** *n* producción *f*; (of machine, worker) rendimiento *m*. ~**right** *adv* completamente; (frankly) abiertamente; <*kill*> en el acto. ● *a* completo; <*refusal*> rotundo. ~**set** *n* principio *m*. ~**side** *a & n* exterior (*m*). at the ~**side** como máximo. ● *adv* fuera, afuera (LAm). ● *prep* fuera de. ~**size** *a* de talla gigante. ~**skirts** *npl* afueras *fpl*. ~**spoken** *a* directo, franco. ~**standing** *a* excepcional; <*debt*> pendiente. ~**stretched** *a* extendido. ~**strip** *vt* (*pt* **-stripped**) (run faster than) tomarle la delantera a; (exceed)sobrepasar. ~**ward** *a* <*appearance*> exterior; <*sign*> externo; <*journey*> de ida. ~**wardly** *adv* por fuera, exteriormente. ~(s) *adv* hacia afuera. ~**weigh** *vt* ser mayor que. ~**wit** *vt* (*pt* **-witted**) burlar

oval *a* ovalado, oval. ● *n* óvalo *m*

ovary *n* ovario *m*

ovation *n* ovación *f*

oven *n* horno *m*

over *prep* por encima de; (across) al otro lado de; (during) durante; (more than) más de. ~ and above por encima de. ● *adv* por encima; (ended) terminado; (more) más; (in excess) de sobra. ~ again otra vez. ~ and ~ una y otra vez. ~ here por aquí. ~ there por allí. all ~

(finished) acabado; (everywhere) por todas partes

over... *pref* excesivamente, demasiado

over: ~**all** *a* global; <length, cost> total. ● *adv* en conjunto. ● *n*, ~**alls** *npl* mono *m*, overol *m* (LAm); (Amer, dungarees) peto *m*, overol *m*. ~**awe** *vt* intimidar. ~**balance** *vi* perder el equilibrio. ~**bearing** *a* dominante. ~**board** *adv* <throw> por la borda. ~**cast** *a* <day> nublado; <sky> cubierto. ~**charge** *vt* cobrarle de más. ~**coat** *n* abrigo *m*. ~**come** *vt* (*pt* -**came**, *pp* -**come**) superar, vencer. ~**crowded** *a* abarrotado (de gente). ~**do** *vt* (*pt* -**did**, *pp* -**done**) exagerar; (Culin) recocer. ~**dose** *n* sobredosis *f*. ~**draft** *n* descubierto *m*. ~**draw** *vt* (*pt* -**drew**, *pp* -**drawn**) girar en descubierto. be ~**drawn** tener un descubierto. ~**due** *a*. the book is a month ~**due** el plazo de devolución del libro venció hace un mes. ~**estimate** *vt* sobreestimar. ~**flow** *vi* desbordarse. ● *n* (excess) exceso *m*; (outlet) rebosadero *m*. ~**grown** *a* demasiado grande; <garden> lleno de maleza. ~**haul** *vt* revisar. ● *n* revisión *f*. ~**head** *adv* por encima. ● *a* de arriba. ~**heads** *npl*. ~**head** *n* (Amer) gastos *mpl* indirectos. ~**hear** *vt* (*pt* -**heard**) oír por casualidad. ~**joyed** *a* encantado. ~**land** *a*/ *adv* por tierra. ~**lap** *vi* (*pt* -**lapped**) traslaparse. ~**leaf** *adv* al dorso. ~**load** *vt* sobrecargar. ~**look** *vt* <room> dar a; (not notice) pasar por alto; (disregard) disculpar. ~**night** *adv* durante la noche. stay ~**night** quedarse a pasar la noche. ● *a* <journey> de

noche; <stay> de una noche. ~**pass** *n* paso *m* elevado, paso *m* a desnivel (Mex). ~**pay** *vt* (*pt* -**paid**) pagar demasiado. ~**power** *vt* dominar <opponent>; <emotion> abrumar. ~**powering** *a* <smell> muy fuerte; <desire> irresistible. ~**priced** *a* demasiado caro. ~**rated** *a* sobrevalorado. ~**react** *vi* reaccionar en forma exagerada. ~**ride** *vt* (*pt* -**rode**, *pp* -**ridden**) invalidar. ~**riding** *a* dominante. ~**rule** *vt* anular; rechazar <objection>. ~**run** *vt* (*pt* -**ran**, *pp* -**run**, *pres p* -**running**) invadir; exceder <limit>. ~**seas** *a* <trade> exterior; <investments> en el exterior; <visitor> extranjero. ● *adv* al extranjero. ~**see** *vt* (*pt* -**saw**, *pp* -**seen**) supervisar. ~**seer** *n* capataz *m* & *f*, supervisor *m*. ~**shadow** *vt* eclipsar. ~**shoot** *vt* (*pt* -**shot**) excederse. ~**sight** *n* descuido *m*. ~**sleep** *vi* (*pt* -**slept**) quedarse dormido. ~**step** *vt* (*pt* -**stepped**) sobrepasar. ~**step the mark** pasarse de la raya

overt *a* manifiesto

over: ~**take** *vt/i* (*pt* -**took**, *pp* -**taken**) sobrepasar; (Auto) adelantar, rebasar (Mex). ~**throw** *vt* (*pt* -**threw**, *pp* -**thrown**) derrocar. ~**time** *n* horas *fpl* extra

overture *n* obertura *f*

over: ~**turn** *vt* darle la vuelta a. ● *vi* volcar. ~**weight** *a* demasiado gordo. be ~**weight** pesar demasiado. ~**whelm** *vt* aplastar; (with emotion) abrumar. ~**whelming** *a* aplastante; (fig) abrumador. ~**work** *vt* hacer trabajar demasiado. ● *vi* trabajar demasiado. ● *n* agotamiento *m*

ow|e *vt* deber. ~**ing to** debido a

owl *n* búho *m*

own a propio. my ~ **house** mi propia casa. ● *pron.* it's my ~ es mío (propio)/mía (propia). on one's ~ solo. get one's ~ **back** 🄸 desquitarse. ● *vt* tener. □ ~ **up** *vi.* 🄸 confesarse culpable. ~**er** n propietario m, dueño m. ~**ership** n propiedad f

oxygen n oxígeno m

oyster n ostra f

p *abbr* (= **pence, penny**) penique (s) m(pl)

p. (*pl* **pp.**) (= **page**) pág., p.

pace n paso m. keep ~ **with s.o.** seguirle el ritmo a uno. ● *vi.* ~ **up and down** andar de un lado para otro. ~**maker** n (runner) liebre f; (Med) marcapasos m

Pacific n. the ~ (**Ocean**) el (Océano) Pacífico m

pacif|ist n pacifista m & f. ~**y** *vt* apaciguar

pack n fardo m; (of cigarettes) paquete m, cajetilla f; (of cards) baraja f; (of hounds) jauría f; (of wolves) manada f. a ~ **of lies** una sarta de mentiras. ● *vt* empaquetar; hacer <*suitcase*>; (press down) apisonar. ● *vi* hacer la maleta, empacar (LAm). ~**age** n paquete m. ~**age holiday** n vacaciones fpl organizadas. ~**ed** a lleno (de gente). ~**et** n paquete m

pact n pacto m, acuerdo m

pad n (for writing) bloc m. **shoulder** ~**s** hombreras fpl. ● *vt* (*pt* padded) rellenar

paddle n pala f. ● *vi* mojarse los pies; (in canoe) remar (*con pala*)

paddock n prado m

padlock n candado m. ● *vt* cerrar con candado

paed|iatrician n pediatra m & f. ~**ophile** n pedófilo m

pagan a & n pagano (m)

page n página f; (attendant) paje m; (in hotel) botones m. ● *vt* llamar por megafonía/por buscapersonas

paid ⇒PAY. ● a. put ~ **to** 🄸 acabar con

pail n balde m, cubo m

pain n dolor m. I have a ~ **in my back** me duele la espalda. m. be in ~ tener dolores. be a ~ **in the neck** 🄸 ser un pesado; (thing) ser una lata. ● *vt* doler. ~**ful** a doloroso. it's very ~**ful** duele mucho. ~-**killer** n analgésico m. ~**less** a indoloro. ~**staking** a concienzudo

paint n pintura f. ● *vt/i* pintar. ~**er** n pintor m. ~**ing** n (medium) pintura f; (picture) cuadro m

pair n par m; (of people) pareja f. a ~ **of trousers** unos pantalones. □ ~**off**, ~ **up** *vi* formar parejas

pajamas npl (Amer) pijama m

Pakistan n Pakistán m. ~**i** a & n paquistaní (m & f)

pal n 🄸 amigo m

palace n palacio m

palat|able a agradable. ~**e** n paladar m

pale a (-**er**, -**est**) pálido. go ~, turn ~ palidecer. ~**ness** n palidez f

Palestin|e n Palestina f. ~**ian** a & n palestino (m)

palette n paleta f

palm n palma f. □ ~ **off** vt encajar (**on** a). **P~ Sunday** n Domingo m de Ramos

palpable a palpable

palpitat|e vi palpitar. ~**ion** n palpitación f

pamper vt mimar

pamphlet n folleto m

pan n cacerola f; (for frying) sartén f

panacea n panacea f

Panama n Panamá m. ~**nian** a & n panameño (m)

pancake n crep(e) m, panqueque m (LAm)

panda n panda m

pandemonium n pandemonio m

pander vi. ~ **to s.o.** consentirle los caprichos a uno

pane n vidrio m, cristal m

panel n panel m; (group of people) jurado m. ~**ling** n paneles mpl

pang n punzada f

panic n pánico m. ● vi (pt **panicked**) dejarse llevar por el pánico. ~**-stricken** a aterrorizado

panoram|a n panorama m. ~**ic** a panorámico

pansy n (Bot) pensamiento m

pant vi jadear

panther n pantera f

panties npl bragas fpl, calzones mpl (LAm), pantaletas fpl (Mex)

pantihose npl ⇒PANTYHOSE

pantomime n pantomima f

pantry n despensa f

pants npl (man's) calzoncillos mpl; (woman's) bragas fpl, calzones mpl (LAm), pantaletas fpl (Mex); (Amer, trousers) pantalones mpl

pantyhose npl (Amer) panty m, medias fpl, pantimedias fpl (Mex)

paper n papel m; (newspaper) diario m, periódico m; (exam) examen m; (document) documento m. ● vt empapelar, tapizar (Mex).

~**back** n libro m en rústica. ~**clip** n sujetapapeles m, clip m. ~**weight** n pisapapeles m. ~**work** n papeleo m, trabajo m administrativo

parable n parábola f

parachut|e n paracaídas m. ● vi saltar en paracaídas. ~**ist** n paracaidista m & f

parade n desfile m; (Mil) formación f. ● vi desfilar. ● vt hacer alarde de

paradise n paraíso m

paraffin n queroseno m

paragraph n párrafo m

Paraguay n Paraguay m. ~**an** a & n paraguayo (m)

parallel a paralelo. ● n paralelo m; (line) paralela f

paraly|se vt paralizar. ~**sis** n (pl -ses) parálisis f

paranoia n paranoia f

parapet n parapeto m

paraphernalia n trastos mpl

parasite n parásito m

paratrooper n paracaidista m (del ejército)

parcel n paquete m

parch vt resecar. **be ~ed** 🛈 estar muerto de sed

parchment n pergamino m

pardon n perdón m; (Jurid) indulto m. **I beg your ~** perdón. (**I beg your**) ~? ¿cómo?, ¿mande? (Mex). ● vt perdonar; (Jurid) indultar. ~ **me?** (Amer) ¿cómo?

parent n (father) padre m; (mother) madre f. **my ~s** mis padres. ~**al** a de los padres

parenthesis n (pl -**theses**) paréntesis m

parenthood n el ser padre/madre

Paris n París m

parish n parroquia f; (municipal) distrito m. ~**ioner** n feligrés m

P

park n parque m. ● vt/i aparcar, estacionar (LAm)

parking : ~ **lot** n (Amer) aparcamiento m, estacionamiento m (LAm). ~ **meter** n parquímetro m

parkway n (Amer) carretera f ajardinada

parliament n parlamento m. ~**ary** a parlamentario

parlour n salón m

parochial a (fig) provinciano

parody n parodia f. ● vt parodiar

parole n libertad f condicional

parrot n loro m, papagayo m

parsley n perejil m

parsnip n pastinaca f

part n parte f; (of machine) pieza f; (of serial) episodio m; (in play) papel m; (Amer, in hair) raya f. **take** ~ **in** tomar parte en, participar en. **for the most** ~ en su mayor parte. ● adv en parte. ● vt separar. ● vi separarse. □ ~ **with** vt desprenderse de

partial a parcial. **be** ~ **to** tener debilidad por. ~**ly** adv parcialmente

participa|nt n participante m & f. ~**te** vi participar. ~**tion** n participación f

particle n partícula f

particular a particular; (precise) meticuloso; (fastidious) quisquilloso. **in** ~ en particular. ● n detalle m. ~**ly** adv particularmente; (specifically) específicamente

parting n despedida f; (in hair) raya f. ● a de despedida

partition n partición f; (wall) tabique m. ● vt dividir

partly adv en parte

partner n socio m; (Sport) pareja f. ~**ship** n asociación f; (Com) sociedad f

partridge n perdiz f

part-time a & adv a tiempo parcial, de medio tiempo (LAm)

party n reunión f, fiesta f; (group) grupo m; (Pol) partido m; (Jurid) parte f

pass vt (hand, convey) pasar; (go past) pasar por delante de; (overtake) adelantar, rebasar (Mex); (approve) aprobar <exam, bill, law>; pronunciar <judgement>. ● vi pasar; <pain> pasarse; (Sport) pasar la pelota. □ ~ **away** vi fallecer. □ ~ **down** vt transmitir. □ ~ **out** vi desmayarse. □ ~ **round** vt distribuir. □ ~ **up** vt Ⓘ dejar pasar. ● n (permit) pase m; (ticket) abono m; (in mountains) puerto m, desfiladero m; (Sport) pase m; (in exam) aprobado m. **make a** ~ **at** Ⓘ intentar besar. ~**able** a pasable; <road> transitable

passage n (voyage) travesía f; (corridor) pasillo m; (alleyway) pasaje m; (in book) pasaje m

passenger n pasajero m

passer-by n (pl **passers-by**) transeúnte m & f

passion n pasión f. ~**ate** a apasionado. ~**ately** adv apasionadamente

passive a pasivo

Passover n Pascua f de los hebreos

pass: ~**port** n pasaporte m. ~**word** n contraseña f

past a anterior; <life> pasado; <week, year> último. **in times** ~ en tiempos pasados. ● n pasado m. **in the** ~ (formerly) antes, antiguamente. ● prep por delante de; (beyond) más allá de. **it's twenty** ~ **four** son las cuatro y veinte. ● adv. **drive** ~ pasar en coche. **go** ~ pasar

paste n pasta f; (glue) engrudo m; (wallpaper ~) pegamento m; (jewellery) estrás m

pastel a & n pastel (m)

pasteurize vt pasteurizar

pastime n pasatiempo m

pastry n masa f; (cake) pastelito m

pasture n pasto(s) m(pl)

pasty n empanadilla f, empanada f (LAm)

pat vt (pt patted) darle palmaditas. ● n palmadita f; (of butter) porción f

patch n (on clothes) remiendo m, parche m; (over eye) parche m. **a bad ~** una mala racha. ● vt remendar. □ ~ **up** vt hacerle un arreglo a

patent a patente. ● n patente f. ● vt patentar. ~ **leather** n charol m. ~**ly** adv. **it's ~ly obvious that...** está clarísimo que...

patern|al a paterno. ~**ity** n paternidad f

path n (pl -s) sendero m; (Sport) pista f; (of rocket) trayectoria f; (fig) camino m

pathetic a (pitiful) patético; <excuse> pobre. **don't be so ~** no seas tan pusilánime

patien|ce n paciencia f. ~**t** a & n paciente (m & f). **be ~t with s.o.** tener paciencia con uno. ~**tly** adv pacientemente

patio n (pl -os) patio m

patriot n patriota m & f. ~**ic** a patriótico. ~**ism** n patriotismo m

patrol n patrulla f. ● vt/i patrullar

patron n (of the arts) mecenas m & f; (of charity) patrocinador m; (customer) cliente m & f. ~**age** (sponsorship) patrocinio m; (of the arts) mecenazgo m. ~**ize** vt ser cliente de; (fig) tratar con condescendencia. ~**izing** a condescendiente

pattern n diseño m; (sample) muestra f; (in dressmaking) patrón m

paunch n panza f

pause n pausa f. ● vi hacer una pausa

pave vt pavimentar; (with flagstones) enlosar. ~**ment** n pavimento m; (at side of road) acera f, banqueta f (Mex)

paving stone n losa f

paw n pata f

pawn n (Chess) peón m; (fig) títere m. ● vt empeñar. ~**broker** n prestamista m & f

pay vt (pt paid) pagar; prestar <attention>; hacer <compliment, visit>. ~ **cash** pagar al contado. ● vi pagar; (be profitable) rendir. ● n paga f. **in the ~ of** al servicio de. □ ~ **back** vt devolver; pagar <loan>. □ ~ **in** vt ingresar, depositar (LAm). □ ~ **off** vt cancelar, saldar <debt>. vi valer la pena. □ ~ **up** vi pagar. ~**able** a pagadero. ~**ment** n pago m. ~**roll** n nómina f

pea n guisante m, arveja f (LAm), chícharo m (Mex)

peace n paz f. ~ **of mind** tranquilidad f. ~**ful** a tranquilo. ~**maker** n conciliador m

peach n melocotón m, durazno m (LAm)

peacock n pavo m real

peak n cumbre f; (of career) apogeo m; (maximum) máximo m. ~ **hours** npl horas fpl de mayor demanda (o consumo etc)

peal n repique m. ~**s of laughter** risotadas fpl

peanut n cacahuete m, maní m (LAm), cacahuate m (Mex)

pear n pera f. ~ **(tree)** peral m

pearl n perla f

peasant n campesino m

peat n turba f

P

pebble n guijarro m

peck vt picotear. ● n picotazo m; (kiss) besito m

peculiar a raro; (special) especial. ~ity n rareza f; (feature) particularidad f

pedal n pedal m. ● vi pedalear

pedantic a pedante

peddle vt vender por las calles

pedestal n pedestal m

pedestrian n peatón m. ~ **crossing** paso m de peatones. ● a pedestre; (dull) prosaico

pedigree linaje m; (of animal) pedigrí m. ● a <animal> de raza

peek vi mirar a hurtadillas

peel n piel f, cáscara f. ● vt pelar <fruit, vegetables>. ● vi pelarse

peep vi. ~ **at** echarle un vistazo a. ● n (look) vistazo m; (bird sound) pío m

peer vi mirar. ~ **at** escudriñar. ● n (equal) par m & f; (contemporary) coetáneo m; (lord) par m. ~age n nobleza f

peg n (in ground) estaca f; (on violin) clavija f; (for washing) pinza f; (hook) gancho m; (for tent) estaquilla f. **off the** ~ de confección. ● vt (pt **pegged**) sujetar (con estacas, etc); fijar <precios>

pejorative a peyorativo, despectivo

pelican n pelícano m

pellet n bolita f; (for gun) perdigón m

pelt n pellejo m. ● vt. ~ **s.o. with sth** lanzarle algo a uno. ● vi. ~ **with rain**, ~ **down** llover a cántaros

pelvis n pelvis f

pen (for writing) pluma f; (ballpoint) bolígrafo m; (sheep ~) redil m; (cattle ~) corral m

penal a penal. ~ize vt sancionar. ~ty n pena f; (fine) multa f; (in soccer) penalty m; (in US football) castigo m. ~ty **kick** n (in soccer) penalty m

penance n penitencia f

pence ⇒PENNY

pencil n lápiz m. ● vt (pt **pencilled**) escribir con lápiz. ~-**sharpener** n sacapuntas m

pendulum n péndulo m

penetrat|e vt/i penetrar. ~ing a penetrante. ~ion n penetración f

penguin n pingüino m

penicillin n penicilina f

peninsula n península f

penis n pene m

pen: ~**knife** n (pl pen-knives) navaja f. ~-**name** n seudónimo m

penn|iless a sin un céntimo. ~y n (pl **pennies** or **pence**) penique m

pension n pensión f; (for retirement) pensión f de jubilación. ~er n jubilado m

pensive a pensativo

Pentecost n Pentecostés m

penthouse n penthouse m

pent-up a reprimido; (confined) encerrado

penultimate a penúltimo

people npl gente f; (citizens) pueblo m. ~ **say** (that) se dice que, dicen que. **English** ~ los ingleses. **young** ~ los jóvenes. **the** ~ (nation) el pueblo. ● vt poblar

pepper n pimienta f; (vegetable) pimiento m. ● vt (intersperse) salpicar (with de). ~**box** n (Amer) pimentero m. ~**corn** n grano m de pimienta. ~**mint** n menta f; (sweet) caramelo m de menta. ~**pot** n pimentero m

per prep por. ~ **annum** al año. ~ **cent** ⇒PERCENT. ~ **head** por cabeza, por persona. **ten miles** ~ **hour** diez millas por hora

perceive vt percibir; (notice) darse cuenta de

percent, per cent n (no pl) porcentaje m. ● adv por ciento. ~**age** n porcentaje m

percepti|ble a perceptible. ~**on** n percepción f. ~**ve** a perspicaz

perch n (of bird) percha f; (fish) perca f. ● vi <bird> posarse. ~ **on** <person> sentarse en el borde de

percolat|e vi filtrarse. ~**or** n cafetera f eléctrica

percussion n percusión f

perfect a perfecto; <place, day> ideal. ● vt perfeccionar. ~**ion** n perfección f. **to** ~**ion** a la perfección. ~**ly** adv perfectamente

perform vt desempeñar <function, role>; ejecutar <task>; realizar <experiment>; representar <play>; (Mus) interpretar. ~ **an operation** (Med) operar. ● vi <actor> actuar; <musician> tocar; (produce results) <vehicle> responder; <company> rendir. ~**ance** n ejecución f; (of play) representación f; (of actor, musician) interpretación f; (of team) actuación f; (of car) rendimiento m. ~**er** n (actor) actor m; (entertainer) artista m & f

perfume n perfume m

perhaps adv quizá(s), tal vez, a lo mejor

peril n peligro m. ~**ous** a arriesgado, peligroso

perimeter n perímetro m

period n período m; (in history) época f; (lesson) clase f; (Amer, Gram) punto m; (menstruation) período m, regla f. ● a de (la) época. ~**ic** a periódico. ~**ical** n revista f. ~**ically** adv periódico

peripher|al a secundario; (Comp) periférico. ~**y** n periferia f

perish vi perecer; (rot) deteriorarse. ~**able** a perecedero. ~**ing** a 🄸 glacial

perjur|e vr. ~**e o.s.** perjurarse. ~**y** n perjurio m

perk n gaje m. □ ~ **up** vt reanimar. vi reanimarse

perm n permanente f. ● vt. **have one's hair** ~**ed** hacerse la permanente

permanen|ce n permanencia f. ~**t** a permanente. ~**tly** adv permanentemente

permissible a permisible

permission n permiso m

permit vt (pt permitted) permitir. ● n permiso m

peroxide n peróxido m

perpendicular a & n perpendicular (f)

perpetrat|e vt cometer. ~**or** n autor m

perpetua|l a perpetuo. ~**te** vt perpetuar

perplex vt dejar perplejo. ~**ed** a perplejo

persecut|e vt perseguir. ~**ion** n persecución f

persever|ance n perseverancia f. ~**e** vi perseverar, persistir

Persian a persa. **the** ~ **Gulf** n el golfo Pérsico

persist vi persistir. ~**ence** n persistencia f. ~**ent** a persistente; (continual) continuo

person n persona f. **in** ~ en persona. ~**al** a personal; <call> particular; <property> privado. ~**al assistant** n secretario m personal. ~**ality** n personalidad f. ~**ally** adv personalmente. ~**nel** n personal m. **P~** (department) sección f de personal

perspective n perspectiva f

perspir|ation n transpiración f. ~**e** vi transpirar

P

persua|de vt convencer, persuadir. ~**de s.o. to do sth** convencer a uno para que haga algo. ~**sion** n persuasión f. ~**sive** a persuasivo

pertinent a pertinente. ~**ly** adv pertinentemente

perturb vt perturbar

Peru n el Perú m

peruse vt leer cuidadosamente

Peruvian a & n peruano (m)

perver|se a retorcido; (stubborn) obstinado. ~**sion** n perversión f. ~**t** vt pervertir. ● n pervertido m

pessimis|m n pesimismo m. ~**t** n pesimista m & f. ~**tic** a pesimista

pest n plaga f; (⬛, person, thing) peste f

pester vt importunar

pesticide n pesticida f

pet n animal m doméstico; (favourite) favorito m. ● a preferido. **my** ~ **hate** lo que más odio. ● vt (pt **petted**) acariciar

petal n pétalo m

petition n petición f

pet name n apodo m

petrified a (terrified) muerto de miedo; (Geol) petrificado

petrol n gasolina f. ~**eum** n petróleo m. ~ **pump** n surtidor m. ~ **station** n gasolinera f. ~ **tank** n depósito m de gasolina

petticoat n enagua f; (slip) combinación f

petty a (-ier, -iest) insignificante; (mean) mezquino. ~**y cash** n dinero m para gastos menores

petulant a irritable

pew n banco m (de iglesia)

phantom n fantasma m

pharma|ceutical a farmacéutico. ~**cist** n farmacéutico m. ~**cy** n farmacia f

phase n etapa f. □ ~ **out** vt retirar progresivamente

PhD abbr (= **Doctor of Philosophy**) n doctorado m; (person) Dr., Dra.

pheasant n faisán m

phenomen|al a fenomenal. ~**on** n (pl -**ena**) fenómeno m

philistine a & n filisteo (m)

philosoph|er n filósofo m. ~**ical** a filosófico. ~**y** n filosofía f

phlegm n flema f. ~**atic** a flemático

phobia n fobia f

phone n ⬛ teléfono m. ● vt/i llamar (por teléfono). ~ **back** (call again) volver a llamar; (return call) llamar (más tarde). ~ **book** n guía f telefónica, directorio m (LAm). ~ **booth**, ~ **box** n cabina f telefónica. ~ **call** n llamada f (telefónica). ~ **card** n tarjeta f telefónica. ~ **number** n número m de teléfono

phonetic a fonético. ~**s** n fonética f

phoney a (-ier, -iest) ⬛ falso

phosph|ate n fosfato m. ~**orus** n fósforo m

photo n (pl -**os**) ⬛ foto f. **take a** ~ sacar una foto. ~**copier** n fotocopiadora f. ~**copy** n fotocopia f. ● vt fotocopiar. ~**genic** a fotogénico. ~**graph** n fotografía f. ● vt fotografiar, sacarle una fotografía a. ~**grapher** n fotógrafo m. ~**graphic** a fotográfico. ~**graphy** n fotografía f

phrase n frase f. ● vt expresar. ~ **book** n manual m de conversación

physi|cal a físico. ~**cian** n médico m. ~**cist** n físico m. ~**cs** n física f. ~**ology** n fisiología f. ~**otherapist** n fisioterapeuta m

& *f.* ~**otherapy** *n* fisioterapia *f.*
~**que** *n* físico *m*

pian|ist *n* pianista *m & f.* ~**o** *n*
(*pl* -os) piano *m*

pick (*tool*) pico *m.* ● *vt* escoger;
cortar <*flowers*>; recoger <*fruit,
cotton*>; abrir con una ganzúa
<*lock*>. ~ **a quarrel** buscar
camorra. ~ **holes in** criticar. □ ~
on *vt* meterse con. □ ~ **out** *vt*
escoger; (identify) reconocer. □ ~
up *vt* recoger; (lift) levantar; (learn)
aprender; adquirir <*habit, etc*>;
contagiarse de <*illness*>. ● *vi*
mejorar; <*sales*> subir. ~**axe** *n*
pico *m*

picket *n* (group) piquete *m.* ~ **line**
n piquete *m.* ● *vt* formar un
piquete frente a

pickle *n* (in vinegar) encurtido *m*;
(Amer, gherkin) pepinillo *m*; (relish)
salsa *f* (a base de encurtidos). ● *vt*
encurtir

pick: ~**pocket** *n* carterista *m &
f.* ~**-up** *n* (truck) camioneta *f*

picnic *n* picnic *m*

picture *n* (painting) cuadro *m*;
(photo) foto *f*; (drawing) dibujo *m*;
(illustration) ilustración *f*; (film)
película *f*; (fig) descripción *f.* ● *vt*
imaginarse. ~**sque** *a* pintoresco

pie *n* empanada *f*; (sweet) pastel
m, tarta *f*

piece *n* pedazo *m*, trozo *m*; (part of
machine) pieza *f*; (coin) moneda *f*;
(in chess) figura *f*. **a** ~ **of advice** un
consejo. **a** ~ **of furniture** un
mueble. **a** ~ **of news** una noticia.
take to ~**s** desmontar. □ ~
together *vt* juntar. ~**meal** *a*
gradual; (unsystematic) poco
sistemático. ● *adv* poco a poco

pier *n* muelle *m*; (with amusements)
*paseo con atracciones sobre un
muelle*

pierc|e *vt* perforar. ~**ing** *a*
penetrante

piety *n* piedad *f*

pig *n* cerdo *m*, chancho *m* (LAm)

pigeon *n* paloma *f*; (Culin) pichón
m. ~**-hole** *n* casillero *m*; (fig)
casilla *f*

piggy *n* cerdito *m.* ~**back** *n.* **give
s.o. a** ~**back** llevar a uno a
cuestas. ~ **bank** *n* hucha *f*

pig-headed *a* terco

pigment *n* pigmento *m*

pig|sty *n* pocilga *f.* ~**tail** *n* (plait)
trenza *f*; (bunch) coleta *f*

pike *n invar* (fish) lucio *m*

pilchard *n* sardina *f*

pile *n* (heap) montón *m*; (of fabric)
pelo *m.* ● *vt* amontonar. ~ **it on**
exagerar. ● *vi* amontonarse. □ ~
up *vt* amontonar. ● *vi*
amontonarse. ~**s** *npl* (Med)
almorranas *fpl.* ~**-up** *n* choque *m*
múltiple

pilgrim *n* peregrino *m.* ~**age** *n*
peregrinación *f*

pill *n* pastilla *f*

pillar *n* columna *f.* ~ **box** *n*
buzón *m*

pillow *n* almohada *f.* ~**case** *n*
funda *f* de almohada

pilot *n* piloto *m.* ● *vt* pilotar. ~
light *n* fuego *m* piloto

pimple *n* grano *m*, espinilla *f*
(LAm)

pin *n* alfiler *m*; (Mec) perno *m.* ~**s
and needles** hormigueo *m.* ● *vt*
(*pt* **pinned**) prender con
alfileres; (fix) sujetar

PIN *n* (= personal identification
number) PIN *m*

pinafore *n* delantal *m.* ~ **dress** *n*
pichi *m*, jumper *m & f* (LAm)

pincers *npl* tenazas *fpl*

pinch *vt* pellizcar; (🄸, steal)
hurtar. ● *vi* <*shoe*> apretar. ● *n*
pellizco *m*; (small amount) pizca *f*. **at
a** ~ si fuera necesario

pine n pino m. ● vi. ~ **for sth** suspirar por algo. □ ~ **away** vi languidecer de añoranza. ~**apple** n piña f

ping-pong n ping-pong m

pink a & n rosa (m), rosado (m)

pinnacle n pináculo m

pin: ~**point** vt determinar con precisión f. ~**stripe** n raya f fina

pint n pinta f (= 0.57 litros)

pioneer n pionero m

pious a piadoso

pip n (seed) pepita f; (time signal) señal f

pipe n tubo m; (Mus) caramillo m; (for smoking) pipa f. ● vt llevar por tuberías. ~-**dream** n ilusión f. ~**line** n conducto m; (for oil) oleoducto m. **in the** ~**line** en preparación f

piping n tubería f. ● adv. ~ **hot** muy caliente, hirviendo

pira|cy n piratería f. ~**te** n pirata m

Pisces n Piscis m

piss vi ⊠ mear. □ ~ **off** vi ⊠. ~ **off!** ¡vete a la mierda! ~**ed** a (⊠, drunk) como una cuba; (Amer, fed up) cabreado

pistol n pistola f

piston n pistón m

pit n hoyo m; (mine) mina f; (Amer, in fruit) hueso m

pitch n (substance) brea f; (degree) grado m; (Mus) tono m; (Sport) campo m. ● vt (throw) lanzar; armar <tent>. ● vi <ship> cabecear. ~**black** a oscuro como boca de lobo. ~**er** n jarra f

pitfall n trampa f

pith n (of orange, lemon) médula f; (fig) meollo m

pitiful a lastimoso

pittance n miseria f

pity n lástima f, pena f; (compassion) piedad f. **it's a** ~ **you**

can't come es una lástima que no puedas venir. ● vt tenerle lástima a

pivot n pivote m. ● vi pivotar; (fig) depender (**on** de)

placard n pancarta f; (sign) letrero m

placate vt apaciguar

place n lugar m; (seat) asiento m; (in firm, team) puesto m; (🏠, house) casa f. **feel out of** ~ sentirse fuera de lugar. **take** ~ tener lugar. ● vt poner, colocar; (identify) identificar. **be** ~**d** (in race) colocarse. ~ **mat** n mantel m individual

placid a plácido

plague n peste f; (fig) plaga f. ● vt atormentar

plaice n invar platija f

plain a (-er, -est) (clear) claro; (simple) sencillo; (candid) franco; (ugly) feo. **in** ~ **clothes** de civil. ● adv totalmente. ● n llanura f. ~**ly** adv claramente; (frankly) francamente; (simply) con sencillez

plait vt trenzar. ● n trenza f

plan n plan m; (map) plano m; (of book, essay) esquema f. ● vt (pt **planned**) planear; planificar <strategies>. **I'm** ~**ning to go to Greece** pienso ir a Grecia

plane n (tree) plátano m; (level) nivel m; (Aviat) avión m; (tool) cepillo m. ● vt cepillar

planet n planeta m. ~**ary** a planetario

plank n tabla f

planning n planificación f. **family** ~ planificación familiar. **town** ~ urbanismo m

plant n planta f; (Mec) maquinaria f; (factory) fábrica f. ● vt plantar; (place in position) colocar. ~**ation** n plantación f

plaque n placa f

plasma n plasma m

plaster n yeso m; (on walls) revoque m; (sticking plaster) tirita f (P), curita f (P) (LAm); (for setting bones) yeso m, escayola f. ● vt revocar; rellenar con yeso <cracks>

plastic a & n plástico (m)

Plasticine n (P) plastilina f (P)

plastic surgery n cirugía f estética

plate n plato m; (of metal) chapa f; (silverware) vajilla f de plata; (in book) lámina f. ● vt recubrir (**with** de)

platform n plataforma f; (Rail) andén m

platinum n platino m

platitude n lugar m común

platonic a platónico

plausible a verosímil; <person> convincente

play vt jugar a <game, cards>; jugar a, jugar (LAm) <football, chess>; tocar <instrument>; (act role) representar el papel de. ● vi jugar. ● n juego m; (drama) obra f de teatro. □ ~ **down** vt minimizar. □ ~ **up** vi 🄸 <child> dar guerra; <car, TV> no funcionar bien. ~**er** n jugador m; (Mus) músico m. ~**ful** a juguetón. ~**ground** n parque m de juegos infantiles; (in school) patio m de recreo. ~**group** n jardín m de la infancia. ~**ing card** n naipe m. ~**ing field** n campo m de deportes. ~**pen** n corralito m. ~**wright** n dramaturgo m

plc abbr (= public limited company) S.A.

plea n súplica f; (excuse) excusa f; (Jurid) defensa f

plead vt (Jurid) alegar; (as excuse) pretextar. ● vi suplicar. ~ **with** suplicarle a. ~ **guilty** declararse culpable

pleasant a agradable

pleas|e int por favor. ● vt complacer; (satisfy) contentar. ● vi agradar; (wish) querer. ~**ed** a (satisfied) satisfecho; (happy) contento. ~**ed with** satisfecho de. ~**ing** a agradable; (news) grato. ~**ure** n placer m

pleat n pliegue m

pledge n cantidad f prometida

plenti|ful a abundante. ~**y** n abundancia f. ● pron. ~**y of** muchos, -chas; (of sth uncountable) mucho, -cha

pliable a flexible

pliers npl alicates mpl

plight n situación f difícil

plimsolls npl zapatillas fpl de lona

plod vi (pt **plodded**) caminar con paso pesado

plot n complot m; (of novel etc) argumento m; (piece of land) parcela f. ● vt (pt **plotted**) tramar; (mark out) trazar. ● vi conspirar

plough n arado m. ● vt/i arar. □ ~ **into** vt estrellarse contra. □ ~ **through** vt avanzar laboriosamente por

ploy n treta f

pluck vt arrancar; depilarse <eyebrows>; desplumar <bird>. ~ **up courage to** armarse de valor para. ● n valor m. ~**y** a (-**ier**, -**iest**) valiente

plug n (in bath) tapón m; (Elec) enchufe m; (spark ~) bujía f. ● vt (pt **plugged**) tapar; (🄸, advertise) hacerle propaganda a. □ ~ **in** vt (Elec) enchufar. ~**hole** n desagüe m

plum n ciruela f

plumage n plumaje m

plumb|er n fontanero m, plomero m (LAm). ~**ing** n instalación f sanitaria, instalación *f* de cañerías

plume *n* pluma *f*

plump *a* (-er, -est) rechoncho

plunge *vt* hundir <*knife*>; (in water) sumergir; (into state, condition) sumir. ● *vi* zambullirse; (fall) caer. ● *n* zambullida *f*

plural *n* plural *m*. ● *a* en plural

plus *prep* más. ● *a* positivo. ● *n* signo *m* de más; (fig) ventaja *f*

plush *a* lujoso

Pluto *n* Plutón *m*

plutonium *n* plutonio *m*

ply *vt* manejar <*tool*>; ejercer <*trade*>. ~ **s.o. with drink** dar continuamente de beber a uno. ~**wood** *n* contrachapado *m*

p.m. *abbr* (= *post meridiem*) de la tarde

pneumatic drill *a* martillo *m* neumático

pneumonia *n* pulmonía *f*

poach *vt* escalfar <*egg*>; cocer <*fish etc*>; (steal) cazar furtivamente. ~**er** *n* cazador *m* furtivo

PO box *n* Apdo. postal

pocket *n* bolsillo *m*; (of air, resistance) bolsa *f*. ● *vt* poner en el bolsillo. ~**book** *n* (notebook) libro *m* de bolsillo; (Amer, wallet) cartera *f*; (Amer, handbag) bolso *m*, cartera *f* (LAm), bolsa *f* (Mex). ~ **money** *n* dinero *m* de bolsillo, mesada *f* (LAm)

pod *n* vaina *f*

poem *n* poema *m*

poet *n* poeta *m*. ~**ic** *a* poético. ~**ry** *n* poesía *f*

poignant *a* conmovedor

point *n* (dot, on scale) punto *m*; (sharp end) punta *f*; (in time) momento *m*; (statement) observación; (on agenda, in discussion) punto *m*; (Elec) toma *f*

de corriente. **to the** ~ pertinente. **up to a** ~ hasta cierto punto. **be on the** ~ **of** estar a punto de. **get to the** ~ ir al grano. **there's no** ~ **(in) arguing** no sirve de nada discutir. ● *vt* (aim) apuntar; (show) indicar. ● *vi* señalar. ~ **at/to sth** señalar algo. □ ~ **out** *vt* señalar. ~-**blank** *a* & *adv* a quemarropa. ~**ed** *a* (chin, nose) puntiagudo; (fig) mordaz. ~**less** *a* inútil

poise *n* porte *m*; (composure) desenvoltura *f*

poison *n* veneno *m*. ● *vt* envenenar. ~**ous** *a* venenoso; <*chemical etc*> tóxico

poke *vt* empujar; atizar <*fire*>. ● *vi* hurgar; (pry) meterse. ● *n* golpe *m*. □ ~ **about** *vi* fisgonear. ~**r** *n* atizador *m*; (Cards) póquer *m*

poky *a* (-ier, -iest) diminuto

Poland *n* Polonia *f*

polar *a* polar. ~ **bear** *n* oso *m* blanco

pole *n* palo *m*; (fixed) poste *m*; (for flag) mástil *m*; (Geog) polo *m*

police *n* policía *f*. ~**man** *n* policía *m*, agente *m*. ~ **station** *n* comisaría *f*. ~**woman** *n* policía *f*, agente *f*

policy *n* política *f*; (insurance) póliza *f* (de seguros)

polish *n* (for shoes) betún *m*; (furniture ~) cera *f* para muebles; (floor ~) abrillantador *m* de suelos; (shine) brillo *m*; (fig) finura *f*. ● *vt* darle brillo a; limpiar <*shoes*>; (refine) pulir. □ ~ **off** *vt* despachar. ~**ed** *a* pulido

Polish *a* & *n* polaco (*m*)

polite *a* cortés. ~**ly** *adv* cortésmente. ~**ness** *n* cortesía *f*

politic|al *a* político. ~**ian** *n* político *m*. ~**s** *n* política *f*

poll *n* elección *f*; (survey) encuesta *f*. ● *vt* obtener <*votes*>

pollack n abadejo m

pollen n polen m

polling booth n cabina f de votar

pollut|e vt contaminar. ~**ion** n contaminación f

polo n polo m. ~ **neck** n cuello m vuelto

poly|styrene n poliestireno m. ~**thene** n plástico, polietileno m

pompous a pomposo

pond n (natural) laguna f; (artificial) estanque m

ponder vt considerar. ~**ous** a pesado

pony n poni m. ~**-tail** n cola f de caballo

poodle n caniche m

pool n charca f; (artificial) estanque m; (puddle) charco m. (common fund) fondos mpl comunes; (snooker) billar m americano. (**swimming**) ~ n piscina f, alberca f (Mex). ~**s** npl quinielas fpl. ● vt aunar

poor a (-er, -est) pobre; <quality, diet> malo. **be in ~ health** estar mal de salud. ~**ly** a 🄘 malito. ● adv mal

pop n (Mus) música f pop; (Amer 🄘, father) papá m. ● vt (pt popped) hacer reventar; (put) poner. □ ~ **in** vi (visit) pasar por. □ ~ **out** vi saltar; <person> salir un rato. □ ~ **up** vi surgir, aparecer

popcorn n palomitas fpl

pope n papa m

poplar n álamo m (blanco)

poppy n amapola f

popular a popular. ~**ity** n popularidad f. ~**ize** vt popularizar

populat|e vt poblar. ~**ion** n población f

porcelain n porcelana f

porch n porche m

porcupine n puerco m espín

pore n poro m

pork n carne f de cerdo m, carne f de puerco m (Mex)

porn n 🄘 pornografía f. ~**ographic** a pornográfico. ~**ography** n pornografía f

porpoise n marsopa f

porridge n avena f (cocida)

port n puerto m; (Naut) babor m; (Comp) puerto m; (Culin) oporto m

portable a portátil

porter n (for luggage) maletero m; (concierge) portero m

porthole n portilla f

portion n porción f; (part) parte f

portrait n retrato m

portray vt representar. ~**al** n representación f

Portug|al n Portugal m. ~**uese** a & n portugués (m)

pose n pose f, postura f. ● vt representar <threat>; plantear <problem, question>. ● vi posar. ~ **as** hacerse pasar por

posh a 🄘 elegante

position n posición f; (job) puesto m; (situation) situación f. ● vt colocar

positive a positivo; (real) auténtico; (certain) seguro. ● n (Photo) positiva f. ~**ly** adv positivamente

possess vt poseer. ~**ion** n posesión f; (Jurid) bien m. ~**ive** a posesivo

possib|ility n posibilidad f. ~**le** a posible. ~**ly** adv posiblemente

post n (pole) poste m; (job) puesto m; (mail) correo m. ● vt echar al correo <letter>; (send) enviar por correo. **keep s.o. ~ed** mantener a uno al corriente

post... pref post, pos

post: ~**age** n franqueo m. ~**al** a postal. ~**al order** n giro m

P

postal. ∼ **box** n buzón m.
∼**card** n (tarjeta f) postal f.
∼**code** n código m postal

poster n cartel m, póster m

posterity n posteridad f

posthumous a póstumo

post: ∼**man** n cartero m.
∼**mark** n matasellos m

post mortem n autopsia f

post office n oficina f de correos,
correos mpl, correo m (LAm)

postpone vt aplazar, posponer.
∼**ment** n aplazamiento m

postscript n posdata f

posture n postura f

posy n ramillete m

pot n (for cooking) olla f; (for jam,
honey) tarro m; (for flowers) tiesto m;
(in pottery) vasija f. ∼**s and pans**
cacharros mpl

potato n (pl -oes) patata f, papa
f (LAm)

potent a potente; <drink> fuerte

potential a & n potencial (m).
∼**ly** adv potencialmente

pot: ∼**hole** n cueva f
subterránea; (in road) bache m.
∼**holing** n espeleología f

potion n poción f

pot-shot n tiro m al azar

potter n alfarero m. ● vi hacer
pequeños trabajos agradables.
∼**y** n (pots) cerámica f; (workshop,
craft) alfarería f

potty a (-ier, -iest) 🄸 chiflado.
● n orinal m

pouch n bolsa f pequeña; (for
correspondence) valija f

poultry n aves fpl de corral

pounce vi saltar. ∼ **on**
abalanzarse sobre

pound n (weight) libra f (= 454g);
(money) libra f (esterlina); (for cars)
depósito m. ● vt (crush) machacar.
● vi aporrear; <heart> palpitar;
<sound> retumbar

pour vt verter; echar <salt>. ●
(out) servir <drink>. ● vi <blood>
manar; <water> salir; (rain) llover
a cántaros. □ ∼ **out** vi <people>
salir en tropel. ∼**ing** a. ∼**ing rain**
lluvia f torrencial

pout vi hacer pucheros

poverty n pobreza f

powder n polvo m; (cosmetic)
polvos mpl. ● vt empolvar. ∼
one's face ponerse polvos en la
cara. ∼**y** a como polvo

power n poder m; (energy) energía
f; (electricity) electricidad f; (nation)
potencia f. ● vt. ∼**ed by**
impulsado por ∼ **cut** n apagón
m. ∼**ed** a con motor. ∼**ful** a
poderoso. ∼**less** a impotente. ∼
plant, ∼**-station** n central f
eléctrica

PR = public relations

practicable a practicable

practical a práctico. ∼ **joke** n
broma f. ∼**ly** adv prácticamente

practi|ce n práctica f; (custom)
costumbre f; (exercise) ejercicio m;
(Sport) entrenamiento m; (clients)
clientela f. he's out of ∼ce le falta
práctica. in ∼ce (in fact) en la
práctica. ∼**se** vt practicar;
ensayar <act>; ejercer
<profession>. ● vi practicar;
<professional> ejercer. ∼**tioner** n
médico m

prairie n pradera f

praise vt (Relig) alabar; (compliment)
elogiar. ● n (credit) elogios mpl.
∼**worthy** a loable

pram n cochecito m

prank n travesura f

prawn n gamba f, camarón m
(LAm)

pray vi rezar (for por). ∼**er** n
oración f

pre.. pref pre...

preach *vt/i* predicar. **~er** *n* predicador *m*; (Amer, minister) pastor *m*

pre-arrange *vt* concertar de antemano

precarious *a* precario. **~ly** *adv* precariamente

precaution *n* precaución *f*

precede *vt* preceder. **~nce** *n* precedencia *f*. **~nt** *n* precedente *m*

preceding *a* anterior

precept *n* precepto *m*

precinct *n* recinto *m*; (Amer, police district) distrito *m* policial; (Amer, voting district) circunscripción *f*. **pedestrian ~** zona *f* peatonal. **~s** (of city) límites *mpl*

precious *a* precioso. ● *adv* 🔢 muy

precipice *n* precipicio *m*

precipitate *vt* precipitar. ● *n* precipitado *m*. ● *a* precipitado

precis|e *a* (accurate) exacto; (specific) preciso; (meticulous) minucioso. **~ely** *adv* con precisión. **~!** ¡exacto! **~ion** *n* precisión *f*

preclude *vt* excluir

precocious *a* precoz. **~ly** *adv* precozmente

preconce|ived *a* preconcebido. **~ption** *n* preconcepción *f*

precursor *n* precursor *m*

predator *n* depredador *m*. **~y** *a* predador

predecessor *n* predecesor *m*, antecesor *m*

predicament *n* aprieto *m*

predict *vt* predecir. **~ion** *n* predicción *f*

preen *vt* arreglar. **~ o.s.** atildarse

prefab *n* 🔢 casa *f* prefabricada. **~ricated** *a* prefabricado

preface *n* prefacio *m*; (to event) prólogo *m*

prefect *n* (Schol) monitor *m*; (official) prefecto *m*

prefer *vt* (*pt* **preferred**) preferir. **~ sth to sth** preferir algo a algo. **~able** *a* preferible. **~ence** *n* preferencia *f*. **~ential** *a* preferente

pregnan|cy *n* embarazo *m*. **~t** *a* embarazada

prehistoric *a* prehistórico

prejudge *vt* prejuzgar

prejudice *n* prejuicio *m*. ● *vt* predisponer; (harm) perjudicar. **~d** *a* lleno de prejuicios

preliminary *a* preliminar

prelude *n* preludio *m*

premature *a* prematuro

premeditated *a* premeditado

premier *n* (Pol) primer ministro *m*

première *n* estreno *m*

premise *n* premisa *f*. **~s** *npl* local *m*. **on the ~s** en el local

premium *n* (insurance ~) prima *f* de seguro. **be at a ~** escasear

premonition *n* premonición *f*, presentimiento *m*

preoccup|ation *n* (obsession) obsesión *f*; (concern) preocupación *f*. **~ied** *a* absorto; (worried) preocupado

preparat|ion *n* preparación *f*. **~ions** *npl* preparativos *mpl*. **~ory** *a* preparatorio

prepare *vt* preparar. ● *vi* prepararse. ● *a* preparado (willing). **be ~d to** estar dispuesto a

preposition *n* preposición *f*

preposterous *a* absurdo

prerequisite *n* requisito *m* esencial

prerogative *n* prerrogativa *f*

Presbyterian *a* & *n* presbiteriano (*m*)

prescri|be *vt* prescribir; (Med) recetar. **~ption** *n* (Med) receta *f*

P

presence n presencia f. ~ of mind presencia f de ánimo

present n (gift) regalo m; (current time) presente m. at ~ actualmente. for the ~ por ahora. ●a presente. ● vt presentar; (give) obsequiar. ~ s.o. with obsequiar a uno con. ~able a presentable. ~ation n presentación f; (ceremony) ceremonia f de entrega. ~er n presentador m. ~ly adv dentro de poco

preserv|ation n conservación f. ~ative n conservante m. ~e vt conservar; (maintain) mantener; (Culin) hacer conserva de. ●n coto m; (jam) confitura f. **wildlife** ~e (Amer) reserva f de animales

preside vi presidir. ~ over presidir

presiden|cy n presidencia f. ~t n presidente m. ~tial a presidencial

press vt apretar; prensar <grapes>; (put pressure on) presionar; (iron) planchar. be ~ed for time andar escaso de tiempo. ●vi apretar; <time> apremiar; (fig) urgir. ●n (Mec, newspapers) prensa f; (printing) imprenta f. □ ~ on vi seguir adelante (with con). ~ conference n rueda f de prensa. ~ cutting n recorte m de periódico. ~ing a urgente. ~-up n flexión f, fondo m

pressur|e n presión f. ●vt presionar. ~e-cooker n olla f a presión. ~ize vt presionar

prestig|e n prestigio m. ~ious a prestigioso

presum|ably adv. ~... supongo que..., me imagino que... ~e vt suponer. ~ptuous a impertinente

presuppose vt presuponer

preten|ce n fingimiento m; (claim) pretensión f; (pretext) pretexto m. ~d vt/i fingir. ~sion n pretensión f. ~tious a pretencioso

pretext n pretexto m

pretty a (-ier, -iest) adv bonito, lindo (esp LAm)

prevail vi predominar; (win) prevalecer. □ ~ on vt persuadir

prevalen|ce n (occurrence) preponderancia f; (predominance) predominio m. ~t a extendido

prevent vt (hinder) impedir; (forestall) prevenir, evitar. ~ion n prevención f. ~ive a preventivo

preview n preestreno m; (trailer) avance m

previous a anterior. ~ to antes de. ~ly adv antes

prey n presa f. **bird of** ~ ave f de rapiña

price n precio m. ●vt fijar el precio de. ~less a inestimable; (🄸, amusing) muy divertido. ~y a 🄸 carito

prick vt/i pinchar. ●n pinchazo m

prickl|e n (Bot) espina f; (of animal) púa f; (sensation) picor m. ~y a espinoso; <animal> con púas; (touchy) quisquilloso

pride n orgullo m. ●vr. ~ o.s. on enorgullecerse de

priest n sacerdote m. ~hood n sacerdocio m

prim a (primmer, primmest) mojigato; (affected) remilgado

primar|ily adv en primer lugar. ~y a (principal) primordial; (first, basic) primario. ~ school n escuela f primaria

prime vt cebar <gun>; (prepare) preparar; aprestar <surface>. ●a principal; (first rate) excelente. ~ minister n primer ministro m. ●n. be in one's ~ estar en la flor de la vida. **~r** n (paint) imprimación f.

primeval a primigenio

primitive a primitivo

primrose n primavera f

prince n príncipe m. **~ss** n princesa f

principal a principal. ● n (of school) director m; (of university) rector m. **~ly** adv principalmente

principle n principio m. **in ~** en principio. **on ~** por principio

print vt imprimir; (write in capitals) escribir con letras de molde. **~ed matter** impresos mpl. ● n (characters) letra f; (picture) grabado m; (Photo) copia f; (fabric) estampado m. **in ~** (published) publicado; (available) a la venta. **out of ~** agotado. **~er** n impresor m; (machine) impresora f. **~ing** n impresión f; (trade) imprenta f. **~out** n listado m

prion n prión m

prior n prior m. ● a previo. **~ to** antes de. **~ity** n prioridad f. **~y** n priorato m

prise vt. **~ open** abrir haciendo palanca

prison n cárcel m. **~er** n prisionero m; (in prison) preso m; (under arrest) detenido m. **~ officer** n funcionario m de prisiones

priva|cy n privacidad f. **~te** a privado; (confidential) personal; <lessons, house> particular. **in ~te** en privado; (secretly) en secreto. ● n soldado m raso. **~te detective** n detective m & f privado. **~tely** adv en privado. **~tion** n privación f

privilege n privilegio m. **~d** a privilegiado. **be ~d to** tener el privilegio de

prize n premio m. ● a <idiot etc> de remate. ● vt estimar

pro n. **~s and cons** los pros m y los contras

probab|ility n probabilidad f. **~le** a probable. **~ly** adv probablemente

probation n período m de prueba; (Jurid) libertad f condicional

probe n sonda f; (fig) investigación f. ● vt sondar. ● vi. **~ into** investigar

problem n problema m. ● a difícil. **~atic** a problemático

procedure n procedimiento m

proceed vi proceder; (move forward) avanzar. **~ings** npl (report) actas fpl; (Jurid) proceso m. **~s** npl. the **~s** lo recaudado

process n proceso m. **in the ~ of** en vías de. ● vt tratar; revelar <photo>; tramitar <order>. **~ion** n desfile m; (Relig) procesión f

procla|im vt proclamar. **~mation** n proclamación f

procure vt obtener

prod vt (pt prodded) (with sth sharp) pinchar; (with elbow) darle un codazo a. ● n (with sth sharp) pinchazo m; (with elbow) codazo m

produc|e vt producir <effect>; sacar <gun>; producir <film>; poner en escena <play>. ● n productos mpl. **~er** n (TV, Cinema) productor m; (in theatre) director m; (manufacturer) fabricante m & f. **~t** n producto m. **~tion** n (manufacture) fabricación f; (output) producción f; (of play) producción f. **~tive** a productivo. **~tivity** n productividad f

profess vt profesar; (pretend) pretender. **~ion** n profesión f. **~ional** a & n profesional (m & f). **~or** n catedrático m; (Amer) profesor m

proficient a competente

profile n perfil m

P

profit n (Com) ganancia f; (fig) provecho m. ● vi. ~ **from** sacar provecho de. ~**able** a provechoso

profound a profundo. ~**ly** adv profundamente

profus|e a profuso. ~**ely** adv profusamente

prognosis n (pl -oses) pronóstico m

program n (Comp) programa m; (Amer, course) curso m. ~**me** n programa m. ● vt (pt -med) programar. ~**mer** n programador m

progress n progreso m; (development) desarrollo m. **make** ~ hacer progresos. **in** ~ en curso. ● vi hacer progresos; (develop) desarrollarse. ~**ion** n progresión f; (advance) evolución f. ~**ive** a progresivo; (reforming) progresista. ~**ively** adv progresivamente

prohibit vt prohibir; (prevent) impedir. ~**ive** a prohibitivo

project vt proyectar. ● vi (stick out) sobresalir. ● n proyecto m; (Schol) trabajo m; (Amer, housing ~) complejo m de viviendas subvencionadas. ~**or** n proyector m

prolific a prolífico

prologue n prólogo m

prolong vt prolongar

prom n (Amer) baile m del colegio. ~**enade** n paseo m marítimo. ● vi pasearse.

prominen|ce n prominencia f; (fig) importancia f. ~**t** a prominente; (important) importante; (conspicuous) destacado

promiscu|ity n promiscuidad f. ~**ous** a promiscuo

promis|e n promesa f. ● vt/i prometer. ~**ing** a prometedor; <future> halagüeño

promot|e vt promover; promocionar <product>; (in rank) ascender. ~**ion** n promoción f; (in rank) ascenso m

prompt a rápido; (punctual) puntual. ● adv en punto. ● n (Comp) presto m. ● vt incitar; apuntar <actor>. ~**ly** adv puntualmente

prone a (tendido) boca abajo. **be** ~ **to** ser propenso a

pronoun n pronombre m

pronounc|e vt pronunciar; (declare) declarar. ~**ement** n declaración f. ~**ed** a pronunciado; (noticeable) marcado

pronunciation n pronunciación f

proof n prueba f, pruebas fpl; (of alcohol) graduación f normal. ● a. ~ **against** a prueba de. ~-**reading** n corrección f de pruebas

propaganda n propaganda f

propagate vt propagar. ● vi propagarse

propel vt (pt propelled) propulsar. ~**ler** n hélice f

proper a correcto; (suitable) apropiado; (Gram) propio; ([T], real) verdadero. ~**ly** adv correctamente; <eat, work> bien

property n propiedad f; (things owned) bienes mpl. ● a inmobiliario

prophe|cy n profecía f. ~**sy** vt/i profetizar. ~**t** n profeta m. ~**tic** a profético

proportion n proporción f. ~**al** a, ~**ate** a proporcional

propos|al n propuesta f; (of marriage) proposición f matrimonial. ~**e** vt proponer. ● vi. ~**e to s.o.** hacerle una oferta de matrimonio a una. ~**ition** n propuesta f; (offer) oferta f

proprietor n propietario m

pro rata adv a prorrata

prose n prosa f

prosecut|e vt procesar (for por); (carry on) proseguir. ~**ion** n proceso m. **the** ~ (side) la acusación. ~**or** n fiscal m & f; (in private prosecutions) abogado m de la acusación

prospect n (possibility) posibilidad f (of de); (situation envisaged) perspectiva f. ~**s** (chances) perspectivas fpl. ~**ive** a posible; (future) futuro. ~**or** n prospector m. ~**us** n folleto m informativo

prosper vi prosperar. ~**ity** n prosperidad f. ~**ous** a próspero

prostitut|e n prostituta f. ~**ion** n prostitución f

prostrate a postrado

protagonist n protagonista m & f

protect vt proteger. ~**ion** n protección f. ~**ive** a protector. ~**or** n protector m

protein n proteína f

protest n protesta f. **in** ~ (**against**) en señal de protesta (contra). **under** ~ bajo protesta. ● vt/i protestar

Protestant a & n protestante (m & f)

protester n manifestante m & f

protocol n protocolo m

protrud|e vi sobresalir. ~**ing** a <chin> prominente. ~**ing eyes** ojos saltones

proud a orgulloso. ~**ly** adv con orgullo; (arrogantly) orgullosamente

prove vt probar; demostrar <loyalty>. ● vi resultar. ~**n** a probado

proverb n refrán m, proverbio m

provide vt proporcionar; dar <accommodation>. ~ **s.o. with sth** proveer a uno de algo. ● vi. ~ **for** (allow for) prever; mantener <person>. ~**d** conj. ~**d** (**that**) con tal de que, siempre que

providen|ce n providencia f. ~**tial** a providencial

providing conj. ~ **that** con tal de que, siempre que

provinc|e n provincia f; (fig) competencia f. ~**ial** a provincial

provision n provisión f; (supply) suministro m; (stipulation) disposición f. ~**s** npl provisiones fpl, víveres mpl. ~**al** a provisional

provo|cation n provocación f. ~**cative** a provocador. ~**ke** vt provocar

prow n proa f

prowess n destreza f; (valour) valor m

prowl vi merodear. ~**er** n merodeador m

proximity n proximidad f

prude n mojigato m

pruden|ce n prudencia f. ~**t** a prudente. ~**tly** adv prudentemente

prudish a mojigato

prune n ciruela f pasa. ● vt podar

pry vi curiosear. ~ **into** algo entrometerse en algo. vt (Amer) ⇒PRISE

PS n (postscript) P.D.

psalm n salmo m

psychiatr|ic a psiquiátrico. ~**ist** n psiquiatra m & f. ~**y** n psiquiatría f

psychic a para(p)sicológico

psycho|analysis n (p)sicoanálisis m. ~**logical** a (p)sicológico. ~**logist** n (p)sicólogo m. ~**logy** n (p)sicología f. ~**therapy** n (p)sicoterapia f

pub n bar m

puberty n pubertad f

pubic a pubiano, púbico

public a público. ~**an** n tabernero m. ~**ation** n

P

publicación f. ~ **holiday** n día m festivo, día m feriado (LAm). ~ **house** n bar m. ~**ity** n publicidad f. ~**ize** vt hacer público. ~**ly** adv públicamente. ~ **school** n colegio m privado; (Amer) instituto m, escuela f pública

publish vt publicar. ~**er** n editor m. ~**ing** n publicación f. ~**ing house** editorial f

pudding n postre m; (steamed) budín m

puddle n charco m

Puerto Ric|an a & n portorriqueño (m), puertorriqueño (m). ~**o** n Puerto Rico m

puff n (of wind) ráfaga f; (of smoke) nube f; (action) soplo m; (on cigarette) chupada f, calada f. ● vt/i soplar. ~ **at** dar chupadas a <pipe>. ~ **out** (swell up) inflar, hinchar. ~**ed** a (out of breath) sin aliento. ~ **paste** (Amer), ~ **pastry** n hojaldre m. ~**y** a hinchado

pull vt tirar de, jalar (LAm); desgarrarse <muscle>. ~ **a face** hacer una mueca. ~ **a fast one** hacer una mala jugada. ● vi tirar, jalar (LAm). ~ **at** tirar de, jalar (LAm). ● n tirón m, jalón m (LAm); (pulling force) fuerza f; (influence) influencia f. □ ~ **away** vi (Auto) alejarse. □ ~ **back** vi retirarse. □ ~ **down** vt echar abajo <building>; (lower) bajar. □ ~ **in** vi (Auto) parar. □ ~ **off** vt (remove) quitar; (achieve) conseguir. □ ~ **out** vt sacar; retirar <team>. vi (Auto) salirse. □ ~ **through** vi recobrar la salud. □ ~ **up** vi (Auto) parar. vt (uproot) arrancar; (reprimand) regañar

pullover n suéter m, pulóver m, jersey m

pulp n pulpa f; (for paper) pasta f

pulpit n púlpito m

pulse n (Med) pulso m; (Culin) legumbre f

pummel vt (pt pummelled) aporrear

pump n bomba f; (for petrol) surtidor m. ● vt sacar con una bomba. □ ~ **up** vt inflar

pumpkin n calabaza f

pun n juego m de palabras

punch vt darle un puñetazo a; (perforate) perforar; hacer <hole>. ● n puñetazo m; (vigour) fuerza f; (device) perforadora f; (drink) ponche m. ~ **in** vi (Amer) fichar (al entrar al trabajo). ~ **out** vi (Amer) fichar (al salir del trabajo)

punctual a puntual. ~**ity** n puntualidad f. ~**ly** adv puntualmente

punctuat|e vt puntuar. ~**ion** n puntuación f

puncture n (in tyre) pinchazo m. **have a** ~ pinchar. ● vt pinchar. ● vi pincharse

punish vt castigar. ~**ment** n castigo m

punk n punk m & f, punki m & f; (Music) punk m; (Amer, hoodlum) vándalo m

punt n (boat) batea f. ~**er** n apostante m & f

puny a (-ier, -iest) enclenque

pup n cachorro m

pupil n alumno m; (of eye) pupila f

puppet n marioneta f, títere m; (glove ~) títere m

puppy n cachorro m

purchase vt adquirir. ● n adquisición f. ~**r** n comprador m

pur|e a (-er, -est) puro. ~**ity** n pureza f

purgatory n purgatorio m

purge vt purgar. ● n purga f

purif|ication n purificación f. ~**y** vt purificar

purist *n* purista *m & f*
puritan *n* puritano *m*. **~ical** *a*
puritano
purple *a* morado. ● *n* morado *m*,
púrpura *f*
purport *vt*. **~ to be** pretender ser
purpose *n* propósito *m*;
(determination) resolución *f*. **on ~** a
propósito. **serve a ~** servir de
algo. **~ful** *a* (resolute) resuelto.
~ly *adv* a propósito
purr *vi* ronronear
purse *n* monedero *m*; (Amer) bolso
m, cartera *f* (LAm), bolsa *f* (Mex)
pursu|e *vt* perseguir, continuar
con <*course of action*>. **~it** *n*
persecución *f*; (pastime) actividad *f*
pus *n* pus *m*
push *vt* empujar; apretar (button).
● *vi* empujar. ● *n* empujón *m*;
(effort) esfuerzo *m*. □ **~ back** *vt*
hacer retroceder. □ **~ off** *vi*
🅇 largarse. **~chair** *n* sillita *f* de
paseo, carreola *f* (Mex). **~y** *a* (pej)
ambicioso
pussy (*pl* **-sies**), **pussycat** *n*
🄸 minino *m*
put *vt* (*pt* put, *pres p* putting)
poner; (with care, precision) colocar;
(inside sth) meter; (express) decir.
□ **~ across** *vt* comunicar. □ **~
away** *vt* guardar. □ **~ back** *vt*
volver a poner; retrasar <*clock*>.
□ **~ by** *vt* guardar; ahorrar
<*money*>. □ **~ down** *vt* (on a
surface) dejar; colgar <*phone*>;
(suppress) sofocar; (write) apuntar;
(kill) sacrificar. □ **~ forward** *vt*
presentar <*plan*>; proponer
<*candidate*>; adelantar
<*clocks*>;adelantar <*meeting*>.
□ **~ in** *vt* (instal) poner; presentar
<*claim*>. □ **~ in for** *vt* solicitar.
□ **~ off** *vt* aplazar, posponer;
(disconcert) desconcertar. □ **~ on** *vt*
(wear) ponerse; poner <*CD,
music*>; encender <*light*>. □ **~

out** *vt* (extinguish) apagar;
(inconvenience) incomodar; extender
<*hand*>; (disconcert) desconcertar.
□ **~ through** *vt* (phone) poner,
pasar (**to** con). □ **~ up** *vt*
levantar; aumentar <*rent*>; subir
<*price*>; poner <*sign*>; alojar
<*guest*>. □ **~ up with** *vt*
aguantar, soportar
putrid *a* putrefacto
putt *n* (golf) golpe *m* suave
puzzl|e *n* misterio *m*; (game)
rompecabezas *m*. ● *vt* dejar
perplejo. **~ed** *a* <*expression*> de
desconcierto. **I'm ~ed about it** me
tiene perplejo. **~ing** *a*
incomprensible; (odd) curioso
pygmy *n* pigmeo *m*
pyjamas *npl* pijama *m*, piyama *m
or f* (LAm)
pylon *n* pilón *m*
pyramid *n* pirámide *f*
python *n* pitón *m*

quack *n* (of duck) graznido *m*;
(person) charlatán *m*. **~ doctor** *n*
curandero *m*
quadrangle *n* cuadrilátero *m*
quadruped *n* cuadrúpedo *m*
quadruple *a & n* cuádruplo (*m*).
● *vt* cuadruplicar
quagmire *n* lodazal *m*
quaint *a* (-er, -est) pintoresco;
(odd) curioso
quake *vi* temblar. ● *n*
🄸 terremoto *m*
qualif|ication *n* título *m*;
(requirement) requisito *m*; (ability)

capacidad *f*; (Sport) clasificación *f*;
(fig) reserva *f*. **~ied** *a* cualificado;
(with degree, diploma) titulado;
(competent) capacitado. **~y** *vt*
calificar; (limit) limitar. • *vi*
titularse; (Sport) clasificarse. **~y
for sth** (be entitled to) tener derecho
a algo
qualit|ative *a* cualitativo. **~y** *n*
calidad *f*; (attribute) cualidad *f*
qualm *n* reparo *m*
quandary *n* dilema *m*
quanti|fy *vt* cuantificar. **~ty** *n*
cantidad *f*
quarantine *n* cuarentena *f*. • *vt*
poner en cuarentena
quarrel *n* pelea *f*. • *vi* (*pt*
quarrelled) pelearse, discutir.
~some *a* pendenciero
quarry *n* (excavation) cantera *f*;
(prey) presa *f*
quart *n* cuarto *m* de galón
quarter *n* cuarto *m*; (of year)
trimestre *m*; (district) barrio *m*. **a ~
of an hour** un cuarto de hora. • *vt*
dividir en cuartos; (Mil)
acuartelar. **~-final** *n* cuarto *m* de
final. **~ly** *a* trimestral. • *adv*
trimestralmente
quartz *n* cuarzo *m*
quay *n* muelle *m*
queasy *a* mareado
queen *n* reina *f*. **~ mother** *n*
reina *f* madre
queer *a* (**-er, -est**) extraño
quench *vt* quitar <*thirst*>; sofocar
<*desire*>
query *n* pregunta *f*. • *vt*
preguntar; (doubt) poner en duda
quest *n* busca *f*
question *n* pregunta *f*; (for
discussion) cuestión *f*. **in ~** en
cuestión. **out of the ~** imposible.
without ~ sin duda. • *vt* hacer
preguntas a; <*police etc*>
interrogar; (doubt) poner en duda.

~able *a* discutible. **~ mark** *n*
signo *m* de interrogación. **~naire**
n cuestionario *m*
queue *n* cola *f*. • *vi* (*pres p*
queuing) hacer cola
quibble *vi* discutir; (split hairs)
sutilizar
quick *a* (**-er, -est**) rápido. **be ~**!
¡date prisa! • *adv* rápido. **~en** *vt*
acelerar. • *vi* acelerarse. **~ly**
adv rápido. **~sand** *n* arena *f*
movediza. **~-tempered** *a*
irascible
quid *n invar* ⊞ libra *f* (esterlina)
quiet *a* (**-er, -est**) tranquilo;
(silent) callado; (discreet) discreto.
• *n* tranquilidad *f*. • *vt/i* (Amer)
⇒QUIETEN. **~en** *vt* calmar. • *n*
calmarse. **~ly** *adv*
tranquilamente; (silently)
silenciosamente; (discreetly)
discretamente. **~ness** *n*
tranquilidad *f*
quilt *n* edredón *m*. **~ed** *a*
acolchado
quintet *n* quinteto *m*
quirk *n* peculiaridad *f*
quit *vt* (*pt* **quitted**) dejar. **~ doing**
(Amer, cease) dejar de hacer. • *vi*
(give in) abandonar; (stop) parar;
(resign) dimitir
quite *adv* bastante; (completely)
totalmente; (really)
verdaderamente. **~ (so!)** ¡claro!
~ a few bastante
quits *a*. **be ~** estar en paz. **call it
~** darlo por terminado
quiver *vi* temblar
quiz *n* (*pl* **quizzes**) serie *f* de
preguntas; (game) concurso *m*.
• *vt* (*pt* **quizzed**) interrogar.
~zical *a* burlón
quota *n* cuota *f*
quot|ation *n* cita *f*; (price)
presupuesto *m*. **~ation marks**
npl comillas *fpl*. **~e** *vt* citar; (Com)
cotizar. • *n* ⊞ cita *f*; (price)

presupuesto *m*. **in ~es** *npl* entre comillas

rabbi *n* rabino *m*

rabbit *n* conejo *m*

rabi|d *a* feroz; *<dog>* rabioso. **~es** *n* rabia *f*

race *n* (in sport) carrera *f*; (ethnic group) raza *f*. ●*vt* hacer correr *<horse>*. ●*vi* (run) correr, ir corriendo; (rush) ir de prisa. **~course** *n* hipódromo *m*. **~horse** *n* caballo *m* de carreras. **~ relations** *npl* relaciones *fpl* raciales. **~track** *n* hipódromo *m*

racial *a* racial

racing *n* carreras *fpl*. **~ car** *n* coche *m* de carreras

racis|m *n* racismo *m*. **~t** *a & n* racista (*m & f*)

rack¹ *n* (shelf) estante *m*; (for luggage) rejilla *f*; (for plates) escurreplatos *m*. ●*vt*. **~ one's brains** devanarse los sesos

rack² *n*. **go to ~ and ruin** quedarse en la ruina

racket *n* (for sports) raqueta; (din) alboroto *m*; (swindle) estafa *f*. **~eer** *n* estafador *m*

racy *a* (**-ier, -iest**) vivo

radar *n* radar *m*

radian|ce *n* resplandor *m*. **~t** *a* radiante

radiat|e *vt* irradiar. ●*vi* divergir. **~ion** *n* radiación *f*. **~or** *n* radiador *m*

radical *a & n* radical (*m*)

radio *n* (*pl* **-os**) radio *f or m*. ●*vt* transmitir por radio. **~active** *a* radiactivo. **~activity** *n* radiactividad *f*

radish *n* rábano *m*

radius *n* (*pl* **-dii**) radio *m*

raffle *n* rifa *f*

raft *n* balsa *f*

rafter *n* cabrio *m*

rag *n* andrajo *m*; (for wiping) trapo *m*. **in ~s** *<person>* andrajoso

rage *n* rabia *f*; (fashion) moda *f*. ●*vi* estar furioso; *<storm>* bramar

ragged *a* *<person>* andrajoso; *<clothes>* hecho jirones

raid *n* (Mil) incursión *f*; (by police etc) redada *f*; (by thieves) asalto *m*. ●*vt* (Mil) atacar; *<police>* hacer una redada en; *<thieves>* asaltar. **~er** *n* invasor *m*; (thief) ladrón *m*

rail *n* barandilla *f*; (for train) riel *m*; (rod) barra *f*. **by ~** por ferrocarril. **~ing** *n* barandilla *f*; (fence) verja *f*. **~road** *n* (Amer), **~way** *n* ferrocarril *m*. **~way station** *n* estación *f* de ferrocarril

rain *n* lluvia *f*. ●*vi* llover. **~bow** *n* arco *m* iris. **~coat** *n* impermeable *m*. **~fall** *n* precipitación *f*. **~y** *a* (**-ier, -iest**) lluvioso

raise *vt* levantar; (breed) criar; obtener *<money etc>*; formular *<question>*; plantear *<problem>*; subir *<price>*. ●*n* (Amer) aumento *m*

raisin *n* (uva *f*) pasa *f*

rake *n* rastrillo *m*. ●*vt* rastrillar; (search) buscar en. □ **~ up** *vt* remover

rally *vt* reunir; (revive) reanimar. ●*n* reunión *f*; (Auto) rally *m*

ram *n* carnero *m*. ●*vt* (*pt* **rammed**) (thrust) meter por la fuerza; (crash into) chocar con

RAM n (Comp) RAM f

ramble n excursión f a pie. ● vi ir de paseo; (in speech) divagar. □ ~e on vi divagar. ~er n excursionista m & f. ~ing a <speech> divagador

ramp n rampa f

rampage vi alborotarse. ● n. go on the ~ alborotarse

ramshackle a desvencijado

ran ⇒RUN

ranch n hacienda f

random a hecho al azar; (chance) fortuito. ● n. at ~ al azar

rang ⇒RING²

range n alcance m; (distance) distancia f; (series) serie f; (of mountains) cordillera f; (extent) extensión f; (Com) surtido m; (stove) cocina f económica. ● vi extenderse; (vary) variar. ~r n guardabosque m

rank n posición f, categoría f; (row) fila f; (for taxis) parada f. the ~ and file la masa f. ~s npl soldados mpl rasos. ● a (-er, -est) (smell) fétido; (fig) completo. ● vt clasificar. ● vi clasificarse

ransack vt registrar; (pillage) saquear

ransom n rescate m. hold s.o. to ~ exigir rescate por uno. ● vt rescatar; (redeem) redimir

rant vi despotricar

rap n golpe m seco. ● vt/i (pt rapped) golpear

rape vt violar. ● n violación f

rapid a rápido. ~s npl rápidos mpl

rapist n violador m

rapture n éxtasis m. ~ous a extático

rare a (-er, -est) raro; (Culin) poco hecho. ~fied a enrarecido. ~ly adv raramente

raring a ▣. ~ to impaciente por

rarity n rareza f

rascal n granuja m & f

rash a (-er, -est) precipitado, imprudente. ● n erupción f

rasher n loncha f

rashly adv precipitadamente, imprudentemente

rasp n (file) escofina f

raspberry n frambuesa f

rat n rata f

rate n (ratio) proporción f; (speed) velocidad f; (price) precio m; (of interest) tipo m. at any ~ de todas formas. at this ~ así. ~s npl (taxes) impuestos mpl municipales. ● vt valorar; (consider) considerar; (Amer, deserve) merecer. ● vi ser considerado

rather adv mejor dicho; (fairly) bastante; (a little) un poco. ● int claro. I would ~ not prefiero no

rating n clasificación f; (sailor) marinero m; (number, TV) índice m

ratio n (pl -os) proporción f

ration n ración f. ~s npl (provisions) víveres mpl. ● vt racionar

rational a racional. ~ize vt racionalizar

rattle vi traquetear. ● vt (shake) agitar; ▣ desconcertar. ● n traqueteo m; (toy) sonajero m. □ ~ off vt (fig) decir de corrida

raucous a estridente

ravage vt estragar

rave vi delirar; (in anger) despotricar. ~ about sth poner a algo por las nubes

raven n cuervo m

ravenous a voraz; <person> hambriento. be ~ morirse de hambre

ravine n barranco m

raving a. ~ mad loco de atar

ravishing a (enchanting) encantador

raw *a* (**-er -est**) crudo; <*sugar*> sin refinar; (inexperienced) inexperto. ~ **deal** *n* tratamiento *m* injusto, injusticia *f*. ~ **materials** *npl* materias *fpl* primas

ray *n* rayo *m*

raze *vt* arrasar

razor *n* navaja *f* de afeitar; (electric) maquinilla *f* de afeitar

Rd *abbr* (= **Road**) C/, Calle *f*

re *prep* con referencia a. ●*pref* re.

reach *vt* alcanzar; (extend) extender; (arrive at) llegar a; (achieve) lograr; (hand over) pasar, dar. ●*vi* extenderse. ●*n* alcance *m*. **within** ~ **of** al alcance de; (close to) a corta distancia de. □ ~ **out** *vi* alargar la mano

react *vi* reaccionar. ~**ion** *n* reacción *f*. ~**ionary** *a & n* reaccionario (*m*). ~**or** *n* reactor *m*

read *vt* (*pt* **read**) leer; (study) estudiar; (interpret) interpretar. ●*vi* leer; <*instrument*> indicar. □ ~ **out** *vt* leer en voz alta. ~**able** *a* (clear) legible. ~**er** *n* lector *m*

readily *adv* (willingly) de buena gana; (easily) fácilmente

reading *n* lectura *f*

readjust *vt* reajustar. ●*vi* readaptarse (**to** a)

ready *a* (**-ier -iest**) listo, preparado. **get** ~ prepararse. ~**-made** *a* confeccionado

real *a* verdadero. ●*adv* (Amer 🅸) verdaderamente. ~ **estate** *n* bienes *mpl* raíces, propiedad *f* inmobiliaria. ~ **estate agent** ⇒REALTOR. ~**ism** *n* realismo *m*. ~**ist** *n* realista *m & f*. ~**istic** *a* realista. ~**ity** *n* realidad *f*. ~**ization** *n* comprensión *f*. ~**ize** *vt* darse cuenta de; (fulfil, Com) realizar. ~**ly** *adv* verdaderamente

realm *n* reino *m*

realtor *n* (Amer) agente *m* inmobiliario

reap *vt* segar; (fig) cosechar

reappear *vi* reaparecer

rear *n* parte *f* de atrás. ●*a* posterior, trasero. ●*vt* (bring up, breed) criar. ● *vi* ~ (**up**) <*horse*> encabritarse

rearguard *n* retaguardia *f*

rearrange *vt* arreglar de otra manera

reason *n* razón *f*, motivo *m*. **within** ~ dentro de lo razonable. ●*vi* razonar. ~**able** *a* razonable. ~**ing** *n* razonamiento *m*

reassur|ance *n* promesa *f* tranquilizadora; (guarantee) garantía *f*. ~**e** *vt* tranquilizar

rebate *n* (discount) rebaja *f*

rebel *n* rebelde *m & f*. ● *vi* (*pt* **rebelled**) rebelarse. ~**lion** *n* rebelión *f*. ~**lious** *a* rebelde

rebound *vi* rebotar; (fig) recaer. ● *n* rebote *m*

rebuff *vt* rechazar. ●*n* desaire *m*

rebuild *vt* (*pt* **rebuilt**) reconstruir

rebuke *vt* reprender. ●*n* reprimenda *f*

recall *vt* (call s.o. back) llamar; (remember) recordar. ●*n* (of goods, ambassador) retirada *f*; (memory) memoria *f*

recap *vt/i* (*pt* **recapped**) 🅸 resumir

recapitulate *vt/i* resumir

recapture *vt* recobrar; (recall) hacer revivir

recede *vi* retroceder

receipt *n* recibo *m*. ~**s** *npl* (Com) ingresos *mpl*

receive *vt* recibir. ~**r** *n* (of stolen goods) perista *m & f*; (part of phone) auricular *m*

recent *a* reciente. ~**ly** *adv* recientemente

R

recept|ion n recepción f; (welcome) acogida f. **~ionist** n recepcionista m & f. **~ive** a receptivo

recess n hueco m; (holiday) vacaciones fpl. **~ion** n recesión f

recharge vt cargar de nuevo, recargar

recipe n receta f. **~ book** n libro m de cocina

recipient n recipiente m & f; (of letter) destinatario m

recit|al n (Mus) recital m. **~e** vt recitar; (list) enumerar

reckless a imprudente. **~ly** adv imprudentemente

reckon vt/i calcular; (consider) considerar; (think) pensar. □ **~ on** vt (rely) contar con

reclaim vt reclamar; recuperar <land>

reclin|e vi recostarse. **~ing** a acostado; <seat> reclinable

recluse n ermitaño m

recogni|tion n reconocimiento m. **beyond ~tion** irreconocible. **~ze** vt reconocer

recoil vi retroceder. ● n (of gun) culatazo m

recollect vt recordar. **~ion** n recuerdo m

recommend vt recomendar. **~ation** n recomendación f

reconcil|e vt reconciliar <people>; conciliar <facts>. **~e o.s.** resignarse (**to** a). **~iation** n reconciliación f

reconnaissance n reconocimiento m

reconnoitre vt (pres p -**tring**) (Mil) reconocer

re: ~consider vt volver a considerar. **~construct** vt reconstruir

record vt (in register) registrar; (in diary) apuntar; (Mus) grabar. ● n (document) documento m; (of events) registro m; (Mus) disco m; (Sport) récord m. **off the ~** en confianza. **~er** n registrador m; (Mus) flauta f dulce. **~ing** n grabación f. **~player** n tocadiscos m invar

recount vt contar, relatar

re-count vt volver a contar; recontar <votes>. ● n (Pol) recuento m

recover vt recuperar. ● vi reponerse. **~y** n recuperación f

recreation n recreo m. **~al** a de recreo

recruit n recluta m. ● vt reclutar; contratar <staff>. **~ment** n reclutamiento m

rectangle n rectángulo m. **~ular** a rectangular

rectify vt rectificar

rector n párroco m; (of college) rector m. **~y** n rectoría f

recuperat|e vt recuperar. ● vi reponerse. **~ion** n recuperación f

recur vi (pt **recurred**) repetirse. **~rence** n repetición f. **~rent** a repetido

recycle vt reciclar

red a (**redder**, **reddest**) rojo. ● n rojo. **be in the ~** estar en números rojos. **~den** vi enrojecerse. **~dish** a rojizo

redecorate vt pintar de nuevo

rede|em vt redimir. **~mption** n redención f

red: ~-handed a. **catch s.o. ~handed** agarrar a uno con las manos en la masa. **~ herring** n (fig) pista f falsa. **~-hot** a al rojo vivo; **~ light** n luz f roja

redo vt (pt **redid**, pp **redone**) rehacer

redouble vt redoblar

red tape n (fig) papeleo m

reduc|e *vt* reducir; aliviar *<pain>*. ●*vi* (Amer, slim) adelgazar. **~tion** *n* reducción *f*

redundan|cy *n* superfluidad *f*; (unemployment) despido *m*. **~t** superfluo. **she was made ~t** la despidieron por reducción de plantilla

reed *n* caña *f*; (Mus) lengüeta *f*

reef *n* arrecife *m*

reek *n* mal olor *m*. ●*vi*. **~ (of)** apestar (a)

reel *n* carrete *m*. ●*vi* dar vueltas; (stagger) tambalearse. □ **~ off** *vt* (fig) enumerar

refectory *n* refectorio *m*

refer *vt* (*pt* **referred**) remitir. ●*vi* referirse. **~ to** referirse a; (consult) consultar. **~ee** *n* árbitro *m*; (for job) referencia *f*. ●*vi* (*pt* **refereed**) arbitrar. **~ence** *n* referencia *f*. **~ence book** *n* libro *m* de consulta. **in ~ence to, with ~ence to** con referencia a; (Com) respecto a. **~endum** *n* (*pl* **-ums** *or* **-da**) referéndum *m*

refill *vt* volver a llenar. ● *n* recambio *m*

refine *vt* refinar. **~d** *a* refinado. **~ry** *n* refinería *f*

reflect *vt* reflejar. ●*vi* reflejarse; (think) reflexionar. □ **~ badly upon** perjudicar. **~ion** *n* reflexión *f*; (image) reflejo *m*. **~or** *n* reflector *m*

reflex *a* & *n* reflejo (*m*). **~ive** *a* (Gram) reflexivo

reform *vt* reformar. ●*vi* reformarse. ● *n* reforma *f*

refrain *n* estribillo *m*. ●*vi* abstenerse (from de)

refresh *vt* refrescar. **~ing** *a* refrescante. **~ments** *npl* (food and drink) refrigerio *m*

refrigerat|e *vt* refrigerar. **~or** *n* frigorífico *m*, refrigerador *m* (LAm)

refuel *vt/i* (*pt* **refuelled**) repostar

refuge *n* refugio *m*. **take ~** refugiarse. **~e** *n* refugiado *m*

refund *vt* reembolsar. ● *n* reembolso *m*

refusal *n* negativa *f*

refuse *vt* rehusar. ●*vi* negarse. ● *n* residuos *mpl*

refute *vt* refutar

regain *vt* recobrar

regal *a* real

regard *vt* considerar; (look at) contemplar. **as ~s** en lo que se refiere a. ●*n* (consideration) consideración *f*; (esteem) estima *f*. **~s** *npl* saludos *mpl*. **kind ~s** recuerdos. **~ing** *prep* en lo que se refiere a. **~less** *adv* a pesar de todo. **~less of** sin tener en cuenta

regatta *n* regata *f*

regime *n* régimen *m*

regiment *n* regimiento *m*. **~al** *a* del regimiento

region *n* región *f*. **in the ~ of** alrededor de. **~al** *a* regional

register *n* registro *m*. ●*vt* registrar; matricular *<vehicle>*; declarar *<birth>*; certificar *<letter>*; facturar *<luggage>*. ●*vi* (enrol) inscribirse; (fig) producir impresión

registrar *n* secretario *m* del registro civil; (Univ) secretario *m* general

registration *n* registración *f*; (in register) inscripción *f*. **~ number** *n* (Auto) (número de) matrícula *f*

registry *n*. **~ office** *n* registro *m* civil

regret *n* pesar *m*; (remorse) arrepentimiento *m*. ●*vt* (*pt* **regretted**) lamentar. **I ~ that** siento (que). **~table** *a* lamentable

regula|r *a* regular; (usual) habitual. ●*n* Ⓘ cliente *m*

R

habital. ~**rity** n regularidad f.
~**rly** adv con regularidad. ~**te** vt
regular. ~**tion** n regulación f;
(rule) regla f

rehears|al n ensayo m. ~**e** vt
ensayar

reign n reinado m. ● vi reinar

reindeer n invar reno m

reinforce vt reforzar. ~**ment** n
refuerzo m

reins npl riendas fpl

reiterate vt reiterar

reject vt rechazar. ● n producto
m defectuoso. ~**ion** n rechazo m;
(after job application) respuesta f
negativa

rejoice vi regocijarse

rejoin vt reunirse con

rejuvenate vt rejuvenecer

relapse n recaída f. ● vi recaer;
(into crime) reincidir

relat|e vt contar; (connect)
relacionar. ● vi relacionarse (**to**
con). ~**ed** a emparentado; <ideas
etc> relacionado. ~**ion** n relación
f; (person) pariente m & f.
~**ionship** n relación f; (blood tie)
parentesco m; (affair) relaciones
fpl. ~**ive** n pariente m & f. ● a
relativo. ~**ively** adv
relativamente

relax vt relajar. ● vi relajarse.
~**ation** n relajación f; (rest)
descanso m; (recreation) recreo m.
~**ing** a relajante

relay n relevo m. ~ (**race**) n
carrera f de relevos. ● vt
transmitir

release vt soltar; poner en
libertad <prisoner>; estrenar
<film>; (Mec) soltar; publicar
<news>. ● n liberación f; (of film)
estreno m; (record) disco m nuevo

relent vi ceder. ~**less** a
implacable; (continuous) incesante

relevan|ce n pertinencia f. ~**t** a
pertinente

relia|bility n fiabilidad f. ~**ble** a
<person> de confianza; <car>
fiable. ~**nce** n dependencia f;
(trust) confianza f. ~**nt** a confiado

relic n reliquia f

relie|f n alivio m; (assistance)
socorro m. **be on** ~**f** (Amer) recibir
prestaciones de la seguridad
social. ~**ve** vt aliviar; (take over
from) relevar. ~**ved** a aliviado.
feel ~**ved** sentir un gran alivio

religio|n n religión f. ~**us** a
religioso

relinquish vt abandonar,
renunciar

relish n gusto m; (Culin) salsa f.
● vt saborear

reluctan|ce n desgana f. ~**t** a
mal dispuesto. **be** ~**t to** no tener
ganas de. ~**tly** adv de mala gana

rely vi. ~ **on** contar con; (trust)
fiarse de; (depend) depender

remain vi (be left) quedar; (stay)
quedarse; (continue to be) seguir.
~**der** n resto m. ~**s** npl restos
mpl; (left-overs) sobras fpl

remand vt. ~ **in custody**
mantener bajo custodia. ● n. **on**
~ en prisión preventiva

remark n observación f. ● vt
observar. ~**able** a notable

remarry vi volver a casarse

remedy n remedio m. ● vt
remediar

remember vt acordarse de,
recordar. ● vi acordarse

remind vt recordar. ~**er** n
recordatorio m

reminisce vi rememorar los
viejos tiempos. ~**nces** npl
recuerdos mpl. ~**nt** a. **be** ~**nt of**
recordar

remnant n resto m; (of cloth)
retazo m; (trace) vestigio m

remorse n remordimiento m. ~ful a arrepentido. ~less a implacable

remote a remoto. ~ **control** n mando m a distancia. ~ly adv remotamente

remov|able a (detachable) de quita y pon; <handle> desmontable. ~al n eliminación f; (from house) mudanza f. ~e vt quitar; (dismiss) destituir; (get rid of) eliminar

render vt rendir <homage>; prestar <help etc>. ~ sth useless hacer que algo resulte inútil

rendezvous n (pl -vous) cita f

renegade n renegado

renew vt renovar; (resume) reanudar. ~al n renovación f

renounce vt renunciar a

renovat|e vt renovar. ~ion n renovación f

renown n renombre m. ~ed a de renombre

rent n alquiler m. ● vt alquilar. ~al n alquiler m. **car** ~ (Amer) alquiler m de coche

renunciation n renuncia f

reopen vt volver a abrir. ● vi reabrirse

reorganize vt reorganizar

rep n (Com) representante m & f

repair vt arreglar, reparar; arreglar <clothes, shoes>. ● n reparación f; (patch) remiendo m. **in good** ~ en buen estado. **it's beyond** ~ ya no tiene arreglo

repatriate vt repatriar

repay vt (pt **repaid**) reembolsar; pagar <debt>; corresponder a <kindness>. ~ment n pago m

repeal vt revocar. ● n revocación f

repeat vt repetir. ● vi repetir(se). ● n repetición f. ~edly adv repetidas veces

repel vt (pt **repelled**) repeler. ~lent a repelente

repent vi arrepentirse. ~ant a arrepentido

repercussion n repercusión f

repertoire n repertorio m

repetit|ion n repetición f. ~ious a, ~ive a repetitivo

replace vt reponer; cambiar <battery>; (take the place of) sustituir. ~ment n sustitución f; (person) sustituto m

replay n (Sport) repetición f del partido; (recording) repetición f inmediata

replenish vt reponer

replica n réplica f

reply vt/i responder, contestar. ~ **to sth** responder a algo, contestar algo. ● n respuesta f

report vt <reporter> informar sobre; informar de <accident>; (denounce) denunciar. ● vi informar; (present o.s.) presentarse. ● n informe m; (Schol) boletín m de notas; (rumour) rumor m; (in newspaper) reportaje m. ~ **card** (Amer) n boletín m de calificaciones. ~edly adv según se dice. ~er n periodista m & f, reportero m

reprehensible a reprensible

represent vt representar. ~ation n representación f. ~ative a representativo. ● n representante m & f; (Amer, in government) diputado m

repress vt reprimir. ~ion n represión f. ~ive a represivo

reprieve n indulto m; (fig) respiro m. ● vt indultar

reprimand vt reprender. ● n reprensión f

reprisal n represalia f

reproach vt reprochar. ● n reproche m. ~ful a de reproche

R

reproduc|e vt reproducir. ●vi reproducirse. ~**tion** n reproducción f. ~**tive** a reproductor

reprove vt reprender

reptile n reptil m

republic n república f. ~**an** a & n republicano (m). **R~** a & n (in US) republicano (m)

repugnan|ce n repugnancia f. ~**t** a repugnante

repuls|e vt rechazar, repulsar. ~**ion** n repulsión f. ~**ive** a repulsivo

reput|able a acreditado, reputado. ~**ation** n reputación f

request n petición f. ●vt pedir

require vt requerir; (need) necesitar; (demand) exigir. ~**d** a necesario. ~**ment** n requisito m

rescue vt rescatar, salvar. ●n rescate m. ~**r** n salvador m

research n investigación f. ●vt investigar. ~**er** n investigador m

resembl|ance n parecido m. ~**e** vt parecerse a

resent vt guardarle rencor a <*person*>. she ~ed his success le molestaba que él tuviera éxito. ~**ful** a resentido. ~**ment** n resentimiento m

reserv|ation n reserva f; (booking) reserva f. ~**e** vt reservar. ●n reserva f; (in sports) suplente m & f. ~**ed** a reservado. ~**oir** n embalse m

reshuffle n (Pol) reorganización f

residen|ce n residencia f. ~**t** a & n residente (m & f). ~**tial** a residencial

residue n residuo m

resign vt/i dimitir. ~ **o.s. to** resignarse a. ~**ation** n resignación f; (from job) dimisión f. ~**ed** a resignado

resilien|ce n elasticidad f; (of person) resistencia f. ~**t** a elástico; <*person*> resistente

resin n resina f

resist vt resistir. ●vi resistirse. ~**ance** n resistencia f. ~**ant** a resistente

resolut|e a resuelto. ~**ion** n resolución f

resolve vt resolver. ~ **to do** resolver a hacer. ●n resolución f

resort n recurso m; (place) lugar m turístico. **in the last ~** como último recurso. □ ~ **to** vt recurrir a.

resource n recurso m. ~**ful** a ingenioso

respect n (esteem) respeto m; (aspect) respecto m. **with ~ to** con respecto a. ●vt respetar. ~**able** a respetable. ~**ful** a respetuoso. ~**ive** a respectivo. ~**ively** adv respectivamente

respiration n respiración f

respite n respiro m

respon|d vi responder. ~**se** n respuesta f; (reaction) reacción f

responsib|ility n responsabilidad f. ~**le** a responsable; <*job*> de responsabilidad. ~**ly** adv con formalidad

responsive a que reacciona bien. ~ **to** sensible a

rest vt descansar; (lean) apoyar. ●vi descansar; (lean) apoyarse. ●n descanso m; (Mus) pausa f; (remainder) resto m, lo demás; (people) los demás, los otros mpl. **to have a ~** tomarse un descanso. □ ~ **up** vi (Amer) descansar

restaurant n restaurante m

rest: ~ful a sosegado. ~**ive** a impaciente. ~**less** a inquieto

restor|ation n restablecimiento m; (of building, monarch) restauración f.~e vt restablecer; restaurar <building>; devolver <confidence, health>

restrain vt contener. ~ **o.s.** contenerse.~ed a (moderate) moderado; (in control of self) comedido.~t n restricción f; (moderation) compostura f

restrict vt restringir.~ion n restricción f.~ive a restrictivo

rest room n (Amer) baño m, servicio m

result n resultado m. **as a ~ of** como consecuencia de. ● vi. ~ **from** resultar de. ~ **in** dar como resultado

resume vt reanudar. ● vi reanudarse

résumé n resumen m; (Amer, CV) currículum m, historial m personal

resurrect vt resucitar.~ion n resurrección f

resuscitat|e vt resucitar.~ion n resucitación f

retail n venta f al por menor. ● a & adv al por menor. ● vt vender al por menor. ● vi venderse al por menor.~er n minorista m & f

retain vt retener; conservar <heat>

retaliat|e vi desquitarse; (Mil) tomar represalias.~ion n represalias fpl

retarded a retrasado

rethink vt (pt **rethought**) reconsiderar

reticen|ce n reticencia f.~t a reticente

retina n retina f

retinue n séquito m

retir|e vi (from work) jubilarse; (withdraw) retirarse; (go to bed)

acostarse.~ed a jubilado. ~ement n jubilación f. ~ing a retraído

retort vt/i replicar. ● n réplica f

retrace vt. ~ **one's steps** volver sobre sus pasos

retract vt retirar <statement>. ● vi retractarse

retrain vi hacer un curso de reciclaje

retreat vi retirarse. ● n retirada f; (place) refugio m

retrial n nuevo juicio m

retriev|al n recuperación f.~e vt recuperar.~er n (dog) perro m cobrador

retro|grade a retrógrado. ~spect n. **in ~** en retrospectiva. ~spective a retrospectivo

return vi volver, regresar; <symptom> reaparecer. ● vt devolver; corresponder a <affection>. ● n regreso m, vuelta f; (Com) rendimiento m; (to owner) devolución f. **in ~ for** a cambio de. **many happy ~s!** ¡feliz cumpleaños! ~ **ticket** n billete m or (LAm) boleto m de ida y vuelta, boleto m redondo (Mex). ~s npl (Com) ingresos mpl

reun|ion n reunión f. ~ite vt reunir

rev n (Auto, 🔧) revolución f. ● vt/i. ~ (up) (pt **revved**) (Auto, 🔧) acelerar(se)

reveal vt revelar. ~ing a revelador

revel vi (pt **revelled**) tener un jolgorio. ~ **in** deleitarse en. ~ry n jolgorio m

revelation n revelación f

revenge n venganza f. **take ~** vengarse. ● vt vengar

revenue n ingresos mpl

revere vt venerar. ~nce n reverencia f.

R

Reverend a reverendo

reverent a reverente

reverie n ensueño m

revers|al n inversión f. ~e a inverso. ●n contrario m; (back) revés m; (Auto) marcha f atrás. ●vt invertir; anular <decision>; (Auto) dar marcha atrás a. ●vi (Auto) dar marcha atrás

revert vi. ~ to volver a; (Jurid) revertir a

review n revisión f; (Mil) revista f; (of book, play, etc) crítica f. ●vt examinar <situation>; reseñar <book, play, etc>; (Amer, for exam) repasar

revis|e vt revisar; (Schol) repasar. ~ion n revisión f; (Schol) repaso m

revive vt resucitar <person>

revolt vi sublevarse. ●n revuelta f. ~ing a asqueroso

revolution n revolución f. ~ary a & n revolucionario (m). ~ize vt revolucionar

revolv|e vi girar. ~er n revólver m. ~ing a giratorio

revue n revista f

revulsion n asco m

reward n recompensa f. ●vt recompensar. ~ing a gratificante

rewrite vt (pt **rewrote** pp **rewritten**) volver a escribir or redactar; (copy out) escribir otra vez

rhetoric n retórica f. ~al a retórico

rheumatism n reumatismo m

rhinoceros n (pl -oses or invar) rinoceronte m

rhubarb n ruibarbo m

rhyme n rima f; (poem) poesía f. ●vt/i rimar

rhythm n ritmo m. ~ic(al) a rítmico

rib n costilla f

ribbon n cinta f

rice n arroz m. ~ pudding n arroz con leche

rich a (-er -est) rico. ●n ricos mpl. ~es npl riquezas fpl

ricochet vi rebotar

rid vt (pt **rid** pres p **ridding**) librar (of de). get ~ of deshacerse de. ~dance n. good ~dance! ¡adiós y buen viaje!

ridden ⇒RIDE

riddle n acertijo m. ●vt acribillar. be ~d with estar lleno de

ride vi (pt **rode** pp **ridden**) (on horseback) montar a caballo; (go) ir (en bicicleta, a caballo etc). ●vt montar a <horse>; ir en <bicycle>; (Amer) ir en <bus, train>; recorrer <distance>. ●n (on horse) cabalgata f; (in car) paseo m en coche. take s.o. for a ~ 🄘 engañarle a uno. ~r n (on horse) jinete m; (cyclist) ciclista m & f

ridge n (of hills) cadena f; (hilltop) cresta f

ridicul|e n burlas fpl. ●vt ridiculizar. ~ous a ridículo

rife a difundido

rifle n fusil m

rift n grieta f; (fig) ruptura f

rig vt (pt **rigged**) (pej) amañar. ●n (at sea) plataforma f de perforación. □ ~ up vt improvisar

right a <answer> correcto; (morally) bueno; (not left) derecho; (suitable) adecuado. be ~ <person> tener razón; <clock> estar bien. it is ~ (just, moral) es justo. put ~ rectificar. the ~ person for the job la persona indicada para el puesto. ●n (entitlement) derecho m; (not left) derecha f; (not evil) bien m. ~ of way (Auto) prioridad f. be in the ~ tener razón. on the ~ a la derecha. ●vt enderezar; (fig) reparar. ● *adv* a la derecha; (directly) derecho; (completely) completamente. ~ **angle** *n* ángulo recto. ~ **away** *adv* inmediatamente. ~**eous** *a* recto; <*cause*> justo. ~**ful** *a* legítimo. ~**-handed** *a* diestro. ~**-hand man** *n* brazo *m* derecho. ~**ly** *adv* justamente. ~ **wing** *a* (Pol) derechista

rigid *a* rígido

rig|orous *a* riguroso. ~**our** *n* rigor *m*

rim *n* borde *m*; (of wheel) llanta *f*; (of glasses) montura *f*

rind *n* corteza *f*; (of fruit) cáscara *f*

ring¹ *n* (circle) círculo *m*; (circle of metal etc) aro *m*; (on finger) anillo *m*; (on finger with stone) sortija *f*; (Boxing) cuadrilátero *m*; (bullring) ruedo *m*; (for circus) pista *f*; ● *vt* cercar

ring² *n* (of bell) toque *m*; (tinkle) tintineo *m*; (telephone call) llamada *f*. ● *vt* (*pt* **rang**, *pp* **rung**) hacer sonar; (telephone) llamar por teléfono. ~ **the bell** tocar el timbre. ● *vi* sonar. ~ **back** *vt/i* volver a llamar. □ ~ **up** *vt* llamar por teléfono

ring: ~**leader** *n* cabecilla *m* & *f*. ~ **road** *n* carretera *f* de circunvalación

rink *n* pista *f*

rinse *vt* enjuagar. ● *n* aclarado *m*; (of dishes) enjuague *m*; (for hair) tintura *f* (no permanente)

riot *n* disturbio *m*; (of colours) profusión *f*. **run** ~ desenfrenarse. ● *vi* causar disturbios

rip *vt* (*pt* **ripped**) rasgar. ● *vi* rasgarse. ● *n* rasgón *m*. □ ~ **off** *vt* (pull off) arrancar; (🅇, cheat) robar

ripe *a* (**-er**, **-est**) maduro. ~**n** *vt/i* madurar

rip-off *n* 🅇 timo *m*

ripple *n* (on water) onda *f*

ris|e *vi* (*pt* **rose**, *pp* **risen**) subir; <*sun*> salir; <*river*> crecer; <*prices*> subir; <*land*> elevarse; (get up) levantarse. ● *n* subida *f*; (land) altura *f*; (increase) aumento *m*; (to power) ascenso *m*. **give** ~**e to** ocasionar. ~**er** *n*. **early** ~**er** *n* madrugador *m*. ~**ing** ● *a* <*sun*> naciente; <*number*> creciente; <*prices*> en alza

risk *n* riesgo *m*. ● *vt* arriesgar. ~**y** *a* (**-ier**, **-iest**) arriesgado

rite *n* rito *m*

ritual *a* & *n* ritual (*m*)

rival *a* & *n* rival (*m*). ~**ry** *n* rivalidad *f*

river *n* río *m*

rivet *n* remache *m*. ~**ing** *a* fascinante

road *n* (in town) calle *f*; (between towns) carretera *f*; (route, way) camino *m*. ~ **map** *n* mapa *m* de carreteras. ~**side** *n* borde *m* de la carretera. ~**works** *npl* obras *fpl*. ~**worthy** *a* <*vehicle*> apto para circular

roam *vi* vagar

roar *n* rugido *m*; (laughter) carcajada *f*. ● *vt/i* rugir. ~ **past** <*vehicles*> pasar con estruendo. ~ **with laughter** reírse a carcajadas. ~**ing** *a* <*trade etc*> activo

roast *vt* asar; tostar <*coffee*>. ● *a* & *n* asado (*m*). ~ **beef** *n* rosbif *m*

rob *vt* (*pt* **robbed**) atracar, asaltar <*bank*>; robarle a <*person*>. ~ **of** (deprive of) privar de. ~**ber** *n* ladrón *m*; (of bank) atracador *m*. ~**bery** *n* robo *m*; (of bank) atraco *m*

robe *n* bata *f*; (Univ etc) toga *f*

robin *n* petirrojo *m*

robot *n* robot *m*, autómata *m*

robust *a* robusto

rock *n* roca *f*; (crag, cliff) peñasco *m*. ● *vt* mecer; (shake) sacudir.

R

●*vi* mecerse; (shake) sacudirse.
●*n* (Mus) música *f* rock.
~-bottom *a* 🄸 bajísimo

rocket *n* cohete *m*

rock: **~ing-chair** *n* mecedora *f*.
~y (**-ier, -iest**) rocoso; (fig,
shaky) bamboleante

rod *n* vara *f*; (for fishing) caña *f*;
(metal) barra *f*

rode ⇒RIDE

rodent *n* roedor *m*

rogue *n* pícaro *m*

role *n* papel *m*

roll *vt* hacer rodar; (roll up)
enrollar; allanar <*lawn*>; aplanar
<*pastry*>. ●*vi* rodar; <*ship*>
balancearse; (on floor) revolcarse.
be ~ing in money 🄸 nadar en
dinero ●*n* rollo *m*; (of ship)
balanceo *m*; (of drum) redoble *m*;
(of thunder) retumbo *m*; (bread)
panecillo *m*, bolillo *m* (Mex). □ ~
over *vi* (turn over) dar una vuelta.
□ ~ **up** *vt* enrollar; arremangar
<*sleeve*>. **~-call** *n* lista *f*

roller *n* rodillo *m*; (wheel) rueda *f*;
(for hair) rulo *m*. **R~blades** (P) *npl*
patines *mpl* en línea. **~-coaster**
n montaña *f* rusa. **~-skate** *n*
patín *m* de ruedas. **~-skating**
patinaje *m* (*sobre ruedas*)

rolling *a* ondulado. **~-pin** *n*
rodillo *m*

ROM *n* (= **read-only memory**)
ROM *f*

Roman *a* & *n* romano (*m*). **~
Catholic** *a* & *n* católico (*m*)
(romano)

romance *n* novela *f* romántica;
(love) amor *m*; (affair) aventura *f*

Romania *n* Rumania *f*, Rumanía
f. **~n** *a* & *n* rumano (*m*)

romantic *a* romántico

Rome *n* Roma *f*

romp *vi* retozar

roof *n* techo *m*, tejado *m*; (of mouth)
paladar *m*. ●*vt* techar. ~ **rack** *n*
baca *f*. **~top** *n* tejado *m*

rook *n* grajo *m*; (in chess) torre *f*

room *n* cuarto *m*, habitación *f*;
(bedroom) dormitorio *m*; (space)
espacio *m*; (large hall) sala *f*. **~y** *a*
espacioso

roost *vi* posarse. **~er** *n* gallo *m*

root *n* raíz *f*. **take ~** echar raíces;
<*idea*> arraigarse. ●*vi* echar
raíces. ~ **about** *vi* hurgar. □ ~ **for**
vt 🄸 alentar. □ ~ **out** *vt* extirpar

rope *n* cuerda *f*. **know the ~s**
estar al corriente. ●*vt* atar; (Amer,
lasso) enlazar. □ ~ **in** *vt* agarrar

rose¹ *n* rosa *f*; (nozzle) roseta *f*

rose² ⇒RISE

rosé *n* (vino *m*) rosado *m*

rot *vt* (*pt* **rotted**) pudrir. ●*vi*
pudrirse. ●*n* putrefacción *f*

rota *n* lista *f* (de turnos)

rotary *a* rotatorio

rotat|e *vt* girar; (change round)
alternar. ●*vi* girar; (change round)
alternarse. **~ion** *n* rotación *f*

rote *n*. **by ~** de memoria

rotten *a* podrido; 🄸 pésimo 🄸;
<*weather*> horrible

rough *a* (**-er, -est**) áspero;
<*person*> tosco; (bad) malo;
<*ground*> accidentado; (violent)
brutal; (approximate) aproximado;
<*diamond*> bruto. ●*adv* duro. ~
copy, ~ draft borrador *m*. ●*vt*. ~
it vivir sin comodidades. **~age** *n*
fibra *f*. **~-and-ready** *a*
improvisado. **~ly** *adv*
bruscamente; (more or less)
aproximadamente

roulette *n* ruleta *f*

round *a* (**-er, -est**) redondo. ●*n*
círculo *m*; (of visits, drinks) ronda *f*;
(of competition) vuelta *f*; (Boxing)
asalto *m*. ●*prep* alrededor de.

● *adv* alrededor. **∼ about** (approximately) aproximadamente. **come ∼ to**, **go ∼ to** (a friend etc) pasar por casa de. ● *vt* doblar *<corner>*. □ **∼ off** *vt* terminar; redondear *<number>*. □ **∼ up** *vt* rodear *<cattle>*; hacer una redada de *<suspects>*. **∼about** *n* tiovivo *m*, carrusel *m* (LAm); (for traffic) glorieta *f*, rotonda *f*. ● *a* indirecto. **∼ trip** *n* viaje *m* de ida y vuelta. **∼-up** *n* resumen *m*; (of suspects) redada *f*

rous|e *vt* despertar. **∼ing** *a* enardecedor

route *n* ruta *f*; (Naut, Aviat) rumbo *m*; (of bus) línea *f*

routine *n* rutina *f*. ● *a* rutinario

row¹ *n* fila *f*. ● *vi* remar

row² *n* (🔲, noise) bulla *f* 🔲; (quarrel) pelea *f*. ● *vi* 🔲 pelearse

rowboat (Amer) *n* bote *m* de remos

rowdy *a* (-ier, -iest) *n* escandaloso, alborotador

rowing *n* remo *m*. **∼ boat** *n* bote *m* de remos

royal *a* real. **∼ist** *a & n* monárquico (*m*). **∼ly** *adv* magníficamente. **∼ty** *n* realeza *f*

rub *vt* (*pt* **rubbed**) frotar. □ **∼ out** *vt* borrar

rubber *n* goma *f*, caucho *m*, hule *m* (Mex); (eraser) goma *f* (de borrar). **∼ band** *n* goma *f* (elástica). **∼-stamp** *vt* (fig) autorizar. **∼y** *a* parecido al caucho

rubbish *n* basura *f*; (junk) trastos *mpl*; (fig) tonterías *fpl*. **∼ bin** *n* cubo *m* de la basura, bote *m* de la basura (Mex). **∼y** *a* sin valor

rubble *n* escombros *mpl*

ruby *n* rubí *m*

rucksack *n* mochila *f*

rudder *n* timón *m*

rude *a* (-er, -est) grosero, mal educado; (improper) indecente; (brusque) brusco. **∼ly** *adv* groseramente. **∼ness** *n* mala educación *f*

rudimentary *a* rudimentario

ruffian *n* rufián *m*

ruffle *vt* despeinar *<hair>*; arrugar *<clothes>*

rug *n* alfombra *f*, tapete *m* (Mex); (blanket) manta *f* de viaje

rugged *a* *<coast>* escarpado; *<landscape>* escabroso

ruin *n* ruina *f*. ● *vt* arruinar; (spoil) estropear

rul|e *n* regla *f*; (Pol) dominio *m*. **as a ∼** por regla general. ● *vt* gobernar; (master) dominar; (Jurid) dictaminar. **∼e out** *vt* descartar. **∼ed paper** *n* papel *m* rayado. **∼er** *n* (sovereign) soberano *m*; (leader) gobernante *m & f*; (measure) regla *f*. **∼ing** *a* *<class>* dirigente. ● *n* decisión *f*

rum *n* ron *m*

rumble *vi* retumbar; *<stomach>* hacer ruidos

rummage *vi* hurgar

rumour *n* rumor *m*. ● *vt*. **it is ∼ed that** se rumorea que

rump steak *n* filete *m* de cadera

run *vi* (*pt* **ran**, *pp* **run**, *pres p* **running**) correr; *<water>* correr; (function) funcionar; (melt) derretirse; *<makeup>* correrse; *<colour>* desteñir; *<bus etc>* circular; (in election) presentarse. ● *vt* correr *<race>*; dirigir *<business>*; correr *<risk>*; (move, pass) pasar; tender *<wire>*; preparar *<bath>*. **∼ a temperature** tener fiebre. ● *n* corrida *f*, carrera *f*; (outing) paseo *m* (en coche); (ski) pista *f*. **in the long ∼** a la larga. **be on the ∼** estar prófugo. □ **∼ away** *vi* huir, escaparse. □ **∼ down** *vi* bajar

R

corriendo; <*battery*> descargarse.
vt (Auto) atropellar; (belittle)
denigrar. □ ~ **in** *vi* entrar
corriendo. □ ~ **into** *vt* toparse
con <*friend*>; (hit) chocar con. □ ~
off *vt* sacar <*copies*>. □ ~ **out** *vi*
salir corriendo; <*liquid*> salirse;
(fig) agotarse. □ ~ **out of** *vt*
quedarse sin. □ ~ **over** *vt* (Auto)
atropellar. □ ~ **through** *vt* (review)
ensayar; (rehearse) repasar. □ ~
up *vt* ir acumulando <*bill*>. *vi*
subir corriendo. ~**away** *n*
fugitivo *m*. ~ **down** *a* <*person*>
agotado

rung¹ *n* (of ladder) peldaño *m*
rung² ⇒RING²

run: ~**ner** *n* corredor *m*; (on
sledge) patín *m*. ~**ner bean** *n*
judía *f* escarlata. ~**ner-up** *n*. **be**
~**er-up** quedar en segundo lugar.
~**ning** *n*. **be in the** ~**ning** tener
posibilidades de ganar. ● *a*
<*water*> corriente; <*commentary*>
en directo. **four times** ~**ning**
cuatro veces seguidas. ~**ny** *a*
líquido; <*nose*> que moquea.
~**way** *n* pista *f* de aterrizaje
rupture *n* ruptura *f*. ● *vt* romper
rural *a* rural
ruse *n* ardid *m*
rush *n* (haste) prisa *f*; (crush)
bullicio *m*; (plant) junco *m*. ● *vi*
precipitarse. ● *vt* apresurar; (Mil)
asaltar. ~**-hour** *n* hora *f* punta,
hora *f* pico (LAm)
Russia *n* Rusia *f*. ~**n** *a* & *n* ruso
(*m*)
rust *n* orín *m*. ● *vt* oxidar. ● *vi*
oxidarse
rustle *vt* hacer susurrar; (Amer)
robar. ● *vi* susurrar □ ~ **up** *vt*
🔲 preparar.
rust: ~**proof** *a* inoxidable. ~**y**
(**-ier, -iest**) oxidado
rut *n* surco *m*. **be in a** ~ estar
anquilosado

ruthless *a* despiadado
rye *n* centeno *m*

S *abbr* (= **south**) S
sabot|age *n* sabotaje *m*. ● *vt*
sabotear. ~**eur** *n* saboteador *m*
saccharin *n* sacarina *f*
sachet *n* bolsita *f*
sack *n* saco *m*. **get the** ~ 🔲 ser
despedido. ● *vt* 🔲 despedir.
sacrament *n* sacramento *m*
sacred *a* sagrado
sacrifice *n* sacrificio *m*. ● *vt*
sacrificar
sacrileg|e *n* sacrilegio *m*. ~**ious**
a sacrílego
sad *a* (**sadder, saddest**) triste.
~**den** *vt* entristecer
saddle *n* silla *f* de montar. ● *vt*
ensillar <*horse*>. ~ **s.o. with sth**
(fig) endilgarle algo a uno
sadist *n* sádico *m*. ~**tic** *a* sádico
sadly *adv* tristemente; (fig)
desgraciadamente. ~**ness** *n*
tristeza *f*
safe *a* (**-er, -est**) seguro; (out of
danger) salvo; (cautious) prudente.
~ **and sound** sano y salvo. ● *n*
caja *f* fuerte. ~ **deposit** *n* caja *f*
de seguridad. ~**guard** *n*
salvaguardia *f*. ● *vt* salvaguardar.
~**ly** *adv* sin peligro; (in safe place)
en lugar seguro. ~**ty** *n* seguridad
f. ~**ty belt** *n* cinturón *m* de
seguridad. ~**ty pin** *n* imperdible
m
sag *vi* (*pt* **sagged**) <*ceiling*>
combarse; <*bed*> hundirse

saga n saga f

Sagittarius n Sagitario m

said ⇒SAY

sail n vela f; (trip) paseo m (en barco). **set** ● zarpar. ● vi navegar; (leave) partir; (Sport) practicar la vela; (fig) deslizarse. **go ∼ing** salir a navegar. vt gobernar <boat>. **∼boat** n (Amer) barco m de vela. **∼ing** n (Sport) vela f. **∼ing boat** n, **∼ing ship** n barco m de vela. **∼or** n marinero m

saint n santo m. **∼ly** a santo

sake n. **for the ∼ of** por. **for God's ∼** por el amor de Dios

salad n ensalada f. **∼ bowl** n ensaladera f. **∼ dressing** n aliño m

salary n sueldo m

sale n venta f; (at reduced prices) liquidación f. **for ∼** (sign) se vende. **be for ∼** estar a la venta. **be on ∼** (Amer, reduced) estar en liquidación. **∼able** a vendible. (for sale) estar a la venta. **∼s clerk** n (Amer) dependiente m, dependienta f. **∼sman** n vendedor m; (in shop) dependiente m. **∼swoman** n vendedora f; (in shop) dependienta f

saliva n saliva f

salmon n invar salmón m

saloon n (on ship) salón m; (Amer, bar) bar m; (Auto) turismo m

salt n sal f. ● vt salar. **∼ cellar** n salero m. **∼y** a salado

salute n saludo m. ● vt saludar. ● vi hacer un saludo

Salvadorean, Salvadorian a & n salvadoreño (m)

salvage vt salvar

salvation n salvación f

same a igual (**as** que); (before noun) mismo (**as** que). **at the ∼**

time al mismo tiempo. ● pron. **the ∼** lo mismo. **all the ∼** de todas formas. ● adv. **the ∼** igual

sample n muestra f. ● vt degustar <food>

sanct|ify vt santificar. **∼ion** n sanción f. ● vt sancionar. **∼uary** n (Relig) santuario m; (for wildlife) reserva f; (refuge) asilo m

sand n arena f. ● vt pulir <floor>. □ **∼ down** vt lijar <wood>

sandal n sandalia f

sand: ∼castle n castillo m de arena. **∼paper** n papel m de lija. ● vt lijar. **∼storm** n tormenta f de arena

sandwich n bocadillo m, sandwich m. ● vt. **be ∼ed between** <person> estar apretujado entre

sandy a arenoso

sane a (-er, -est) <person> cuerdo; (sensible) sensato

sang ⇒SING

sanitary a higiénico; <system etc> sanitario. **∼ towel, ∼ napkin** n (Amer) compresa f (higiénica)

sanitation n higiene f; (drainage) sistema m sanitario

sanity n cordura f

sank ⇒SINK

Santa (Claus) n Papá m Noel

sap n (in plants) savia f

sapling n árbol m joven

sapphire n zafiro m

sarcas|m n sarcasmo m. **∼tic** a sarcástico

sardine n sardina f

sash n (over shoulder) banda f; (round waist) fajín m.

sat ⇒SIT

SAT abbr (Amer) = **Scholastic Aptitude Test**; (Brit) = **Standard Assessment Test**

satchel n cartera f

satellite n & a satélite (m). **∼ TV** n televisión f por satélite

satin n raso m. ● a de raso

S

satir|e n sátira f. ~**ical** a satírico.
~**ize** vt satirizar
satis|faction n satisfacción f.
~**factorily** adv
satisfactoriamente. ~**factory** a
satisfactorio. ~**fy** vt satisfacer;
(convince) convencer. ~**fying** a
satisfactorio
saturat|e vt saturar. ~**ed** a
saturado; (drenched) empapado
Saturday n sábado m
Saturn n Saturno m
sauce n salsa f; (cheek) descaro m.
~**pan** n cazo m, cacerola f. ~**r** n
platillo m
saucy a (**-ier, -iest**) descarado
Saudi a & n saudita (m & f). ~
Arabia n Arabia f Saudí
sauna n sauna f
saunter vi pasearse
sausage n salchicha f
savage a salvaje; (fierce) feroz.
● n salvaje m & f. ● vt atacar.
~**ry** n ferocidad f
sav|e vt (rescue) salvar; ahorrar
<money, time>; (prevent) evitar;
(Comp) guardar. ● n (football)
parada f. ● prep salvo, excepto.
□ ~**e up** vi/t ahorrar. ~**er** n
ahorrador m. ~**ing** n ahorro m.
~**ings** npl ahorros mpl
saviour n salvador m
savour vt saborear. ~**y** a
(appetizing) sabroso; (not sweet) no
dulce
saw¹ ⇒SEE¹
saw² n sierra f. ● vt (pt **sawed**,
pp **sawn**) serrar. ~**dust** n serrín
m. ~**n** ⇒SAW²
saxophone n saxofón m,
saxófono m
say vt/i (pt **said**) decir; rezar
<prayer>. ● n. have a ~ expresar
una opinión; (in decision) tener voz
en capítulo. have no ~ no tener
ni voz ni voto. ~**ing** n refrán m

scab n costra f; (🄸, blackleg)
esquirol m
scaffolding n andamios mpl
scald vt escaldar
scale n (also Mus) escala f; (of fish)
escama f. ● vt (climb) escalar. ~
down vt reducir (a escala)
<drawing>; recortar <operation>.
~**s** npl (for weighing) balanza f,
peso m
scallion n (Amer) cebolleta f
scalp vt quitar el cuero cabelludo
a
scamper vi. ~ **away** irse
correteando
scan vt (pt **scanned**) escudriñar;
(quickly) echar un vistazo a;
<radar> explorar
scandal n escándalo m; (gossip)
chismorreo m. ~**ize** vt
escandalizar. ~**ous** a
escandaloso
Scandinavia n Escandinavia f.
~**n** a & n escandinavo (m)
scant a escaso. ~**y** a (**-ier, -iest**)
escaso
scapegoat n cabeza f de turco
scar n cicatriz f
scarc|e a (**-er, -est**) escaso. be
~**e** escasear. make o.s. ~**e**
🄸 mantenerse lejos. ~**ely** adv
apenas. ~**ity** n escasez f
scare vt asustar. be ~**d** tener
miedo. be ~**d of sth** tenerle
miedo a algo. ● n susto m.
~**crow** n espantapájaros m
scarf n (pl **scarves**) bufanda f;
(over head) pañuelo m
scarlet a escarlata f. ~ **fever** n
escarlatina f
scarves ⇒SCARF
scary a (**-ier, -iest**) que da miedo
scathing a mordaz
scatter vt (throw) esparcir;
(disperse) dispersar. ● vi

dispersarse. ~ed *a* disperso; (occasional) esporádico

scavenge *vi* escarbar (en la basura)

scenario *n* (*pl* -os) perspectiva *f*; (of film) guión *m*

scen|e *n* escena *f*; (sight) vista *f*; (fuss) lío *m*. **behind the ~es** entre bastidores. ~ery *n* paisaje *m*; (in theatre) decorado *m*. ~ic *a* pintoresco

scent *n* olor *m*; (perfume) perfume *m*; (trail) pista *f*. ●*vt* intuir; (make fragrant) perfumar

sceptic *n* escéptico *m*. ~al *a* escéptico. ~ism *n* escepticismo *m*

sceptre *n* cetro *m*

schedule *n* programa *f*; (timetable) horario *m*. **behind ~** atrasado. **it's on ~** va de acuerdo a lo previsto. ●*vt* proyectar. ~d flight *n* vuelo *m* regular

scheme *n* proyecto *m*; (plot) intriga *f*. ●*vi* (pej) intrigar

schizophrenic *a & n* esquizofrénico (*m*)

scholar *n* erudito *m*. ~ly *a* erudito. ~ship *n* erudición *f*; (grant) beca *f*

school *n* escuela *f*; (Univ) facultad *f*. ●*a* <*age, holidays, year*> escolar. ●*vt* instruir; (train) capacitar. ~boy *n* colegial *m*. ~girl *n* colegiala *f*. ~ing *n* instrucción *f*. ~master *n* (primary) maestro *m*; (secondary) profesor *m*. ~mistress *n* (primary) maestra *f*; (secondary) profesora *f*. ~teacher *n* (primary) maestro *n* (secondary) profesor *m*

scien|ce *n* ciencia *f*. **study ~ce** estudiar ciencias. ~ce fiction *n* ciencia *f* ficción. ~tific *a* científico. ~tist *n* científico *m*

scissors *npl* tijeras *fpl*

scoff *vt* 🄸 zamparse. ●*vi*. ~ **at** mofarse de

scold *vt* regañar

scoop *n* pala *f*; (news) primicia *f*. ☐ ~ **out** *vt* sacar; excavar <*hole*>

scooter *n* escúter *m*; (for child) patinete *m*

scope *n* alcance *m*; (opportunity) oportunidad *f*

scorch *vt* chamuscar. ~ing *a* 🄸 de mucho calor

score *n* tanteo *m*; (Mus) partitura *f*; (twenty) veintena *f*. **on that ~** en cuanto a eso. **know the ~** 🄸 saber cómo son las cosas. ●*vt* marcar <*goal*>; anotarse <*points*>; (cut, mark) rayar; conseguir <*success*>. ●*vi* marcar

scorn *n* desdén *m*. ●*vt* desdeñar. ~ful *a* desdeñoso

Scorpio *n* Escorpio *m*, Escorpión *m*

scorpion *n* escorpión *m*

Scot *n* escocés *m*. ~ch *n* whisky *m*, güisqui *m*

scotch *vt* frustrar; acallar <*rumours*>

Scotch tape *n* (Amer) celo *m*, cinta *f* Scotch

Scot: ~land *n* Escocia *f*. ~s *a* escocés. ~tish *a* escocés

scoundrel *n* canalla *f*

scour *vt* fregar; (search) registrar. ~er *n* estropajo *m*

scourge *n* azote *m*

scout *n* explorador *m*. **Boy S~** explorador *m*

scowl *n* ceño *m* fruncido. ●*vi* fruncir el ceño

scram *vi* 🄸 largarse

scramble *vi* (clamber) gatear. ●*n* (difficult climb) subida *f* difícil; (struggle) rebatiña *f*. ~d egg *n* huevos *mpl* revueltos

scrap *n* pedacito *m*; (🄸, fight) pelea *f*. ●*vt* (*pt* **scrapped**)

S

desechar. **~book** n álbum m de recortes. **~s** npl sobras fpl

scrape n (fig) apuro m. ● vt raspar; (graze) rasparse; (rub) rascar. □ **~ through** vi/t aprobar por los pelos <exam>. □ **~ together** vt reunir. **~r** n rasqueta f

scrap: **~heap** n montón m de deshechos. **~ yard** n chatarrería f

scratch vt rayar <furniture, record>; (with nail etc) rascarse <itch>. ● vi arañar. ● n rayón m; (from nail etc) arañazo m. **start from ~** empezar desde cero. **be up to ~** dar la talla

scrawl n garabato m. ● vt/i garabatear

scream vt/i gritar. ● n grito m

screech vi chillar; <brakes etc> chirriar. ● n chillido m; (of brakes etc) chirrido m

screen n pantalla f; (folding) biombo m. ● vt (hide) ocultar; (protect) proteger; proyectar <film>

screw n tornillo m. ● vt atornillar. □ **~ up** vt atornillar; entornar <eyes>; torcer <face>; (🅇, ruin) fastidiar. **~driver** n destornillador m

scribble vt/i garabatear. ● n garrabato m

script n escritura f; (of film etc) guión m

scroll n rollo m (de pergamino). **~ down** vi retroceder la pantalla. **~ up** vi avanzar la pantalla

scrounge vt/i gorronear. **~r** n gorrón m

scrub n (land) maleza f. ● vt/i (pt scrubbed) fregar

scruff n. **by the ~ of the neck** por el pescuezo. **~y** a (-ier, -iest) desaliñado

scrup|le n escrúpulo m. **~ulous** a escrupuloso

scrutin|ize vt escudriñar; inspeccionar <document>. **~y** n examen m minucioso

scuffle n refriega f

sculpt vt/i esculpir. **~or** n escultor m. **~ure** n escultura f. ● vt/i esculpir

scum n espuma f; (people, pej) escoria f

scuttle n cubo m del carbón. ● vt barrenar <ship>. ● vi. **~ away** escabullirse rápidamente

scythe n guadaña f

SE abbr (= south-east) SE

sea n mar m. **at ~** en el mar; (fig) confuso. **by ~** por mar. **~food** n mariscos mpl. **~ front** n paseo m marítimo, malecón m (LAm). **~gull** n gaviota f. **~horse** n caballito m de mar

seal n sello m; (animal) foca f. ● vt sellar. □ **~ off** vt acordonar

sea level n nivel m del mar

sea lion n león m marino

seam n costura f; (of coal) veta f

seaman n (pl -men) marinero m

seamy a sórdido

seance n sesión f de espiritismo

search vt registrar; buscar en <records>. ● vi buscar. ● n (for sth) búsqueda f; (of sth) registro m; (Comp) búsqueda f. **in ~ of** en busca de. □ **~ for** vt buscar. **~ engine** n buscador m. **~ing** a penetrante. **~light** n reflector m. **~ party** n partida f de rescate

sea: **~shore** n orilla f del mar. **~sick** a mareado. **be ~sick** marearse. **~side** n playa f. **~ trout** n reo m

season n estación f; (period) temporada f. **high/low ~**

temporada *f* alta/baja. ●*vt* (Culin) sazonar. **~al** *a* estacional; <*demand*> de estación. **~ed** *a* (fig) avezado. **~ing** *n* condimento *m*. **~ ticket** *n* abono *m* (de temporada)

seat *n* asiento *m*; (place) lugar *m*; (in cinema, theatre) localidad *f*; (of trousers) fondillos *mpl*. **take a ~** sentarse. ●*vt* sentar; (have seats for) <*auditorium*> tener capacidad para; <*bus*> tener asientos para. **~belt** *n* cinturón *m* de seguridad

sea: ~-urchin *n* erizo *m* de mar. **~weed** *n* alga *f* marina. **~worthy** *a* en condiciones de navegar

seclu|ded *a* aislado. **~sion** *n* aislamiento *m*

second *a* & *n* segundo (*m*). **on ~ thoughts** pensándolo bien. ●*adv* (in race etc) en segundo lugar. ●*vt* secundar. **~s** *npl* (goods) artículos *mpl* de segunda calidad; (▯, more food) **have ~s** repetir. ● *vt* (transfer) trasladar temporalmente. **~ary** *a* secundario. **~ary school** *n* instituto *m* (de enseñanza secundaria)

second: ~-class *a* de segunda (clase). **~-hand** *a* de segunda mano. **~ly** *adv* en segundo lugar. **~-rate** *a* mediocre

secre|cy *n* secreto *m*. **~t** *a* & *n* secreto (*m*). **in ~t** en secreto

secretar|ial *a* de secretario; <*course*> de secretariado. **~y** *n* secretario *m*. **S~y of State** (in UK) ministro *m*: (in US) secretario *m* de Estado

secretive *a* reservado

sect *n* secta *f*. **~arian** *a* sectario

section *n* sección *f*; (part) parte *f*

sector *n* sector *m*

secular *a* secular

secur|e *a* seguro; <*shelf*> firme. ●*vt* asegurar; (obtain) obtener.

~ely *adv* seguramente. **~ity** *n* seguridad *f*; (for loan) garantía *f*

sedat|e *a* reposado. ●*vt* sedar. **~ion** *n* sedación *f*. **~ive** *a* & *n* sedante (*m*)

sediment *n* sedimento *m*

seduc|e *vt* seducir. **~er** *n* seductor *m*. **~tion** *n* seducción *f*. **~tive** *a* seductor

see ●*vt* (*pt* **saw**, *pp* **seen**) ver; (understand) comprender; (escort) acompañar. **~ing that** visto que. **~ you later!** ¡hasta luego! ●*vi* ver. □ **~ off** *vt* (say goodbye to) despedirse de. □ **~ through** *vt* llevar a cabo; calar <*person*>. □ **~ to** *vt* ocuparse de

seed *n* semilla *f*; (fig) germen *m*; (Amer, pip) pepita *f*. **go to ~** granar; (fig) echarse a perder. **~ling** *n* planta *f* de semillero. **~y** *a* (**-ier, -iest**) sórdido

seek *vt* (*pt* **sought**) buscar; pedir <*approval*>. □ **~ out** *vt* buscar

seem *vi* parecer

seen ⇒SEE

seep *vi* filtrarse

see-saw *n* balancín *m*

seethe *vi* (fig) estar furioso. **I was seething with anger** me hervía la sangre

see-through *a* transparente

segment *n* segmento *m*; (of orange) gajo *m*

segregat|e *vt* segregar. **~ion** *n* segregación *f*

seiz|e *vt* agarrar; (Jurid) incautar. **~e on** *vt* aprovechar <*chance*>. □ **~e up** *vi* (Tec) agarrotarse. **~ure** *n* incautación *f*; (Med) ataque *m*

seldom *adv* rara vez

select *vt* escoger; (Sport) seleccionar. ●*a* selecto; (exclusive)

S

exclusivo. ~**ion** n selección f.
~**ive** a selectivo

self n (pl **selves**). he's his old ~
again vuelve a ser el de antes.
~**-addressed** a con el nombre y
la dirección del remitente.
~**-catering** a con facilidades
para cocinar. ~**-centred** a
egocéntrico. ~**-confidence** n
confianza f en sí mismo.
~**-confident** a seguro de sí
mismo. ~**-conscious** a cohibido.
~**-contained** a independiente.
~**-control** n dominio m de sí
mismo. ~**-defence** n defensa f
propia. ~**-employed** a que
trabaja por cuenta propia.
~**-evident** a evidente.
~**-important** a presumido.
~**-indulgent** a inmoderado.
~**-interest** n interés m
(personal). ~**ish** a egoísta.
~**ishness** n egoísmo m. ~**-pity** n
autocompasión. ~**-portrait** n
autorretrato m. ~**-respect** n
amor m propio. ~**-righteous** a
santurrón. ~**-sacrifice** n
abnegación f. ~**-satisfied** a
satisfecho de sí mismo. ~**-serve**
(Amer), ~**-service** a & n
autoservicio (m). ~**-sufficient** a
independiente

sell vt (pt **sold**) vender. ● vi
venderse. □ ~ **off** vt liquidar. ~
out vi. we've sold out of gloves los
guantes están agotados. ~**-by**
date n fecha f límite de venta.
~**er** n vendedor m

Sellotape n (P) celo m, cinta f
Scotch

sell-out n (performance) éxito m de
taquilla; ([I], betrayal) capitulación f

semblance n apariencia f

semester n (Amer) semestre m

semi... pref semi...

semi|breve n redonda f. ~**circle**
n semicírculo m. ~**colon** n punto

m y coma. ~**-detached** a
<house> adosado. ~**final** n
semifinal f

seminar n seminario m

senat|e n senado m. the S~e
(Amer) el Senado. ~**or** n senador
m

send vt/i (pt **sent**) mandar,
enviar. □ ~ **away** vt despedir.
□ ~ **away for** vt pedir (por
correo). □ ~ **for** vt enviar a
buscar. □ ~ **off for** vt pedir (por
correo). □ ~ **up** vt [I] parodiar.
~**er** n remitente m. ~**-off** n
despedida f

senile a senil

senior a mayor; (in rank) superior;
<partner etc> principal. ● n
mayor m & f. ~ **citizen** n
jubilado m. ~ **high school** n
(Amer) colegio m secundario. ~**ity**
n antigüedad f

sensation n sensación f. ~**al** a
sensacional

sens|e n sentido m; (common sense)
juicio m; (feeling) sensación f.
make ~**e** vt tener sentido. **make**
~**e of sth** entender algo. ~**eless**
a sin sentido. ~**ible** a sensato;
<clothing> práctico. ~**itive** a
sensible; (touchy) susceptible.
~**itivity** n sensibilidad f. ~**ual** a
sensual. ~**uous** a sensual

sent ⇒SEND

sentence n frase f; (judgment)
sentencia f; (punishment) condena f.
● vt. ~ **to** condenar a

sentiment n sentimiento m;
(opinion) opinión f. ~**al** a
sentimental. ~**ality** n
sentimentalismo f

sentry n centinela f

separa|ble a separable. ~**te** a
separado; (independent)
independiente. ● vt separar. ● vi
separarse. ~**tely** adv por

separado. **~tion** n separación f.
~tist n separatista m & f
September n se(p)tiembre m
septic a séptico
sequel n continuación f; (later events) secuela f
sequence n sucesión f; (of film) secuencia f
Serb a & n ⇒SERBIAN. **~ian** n Serbia f **~ian** a & n serbio (m)
serenade n serenata f. ● vt dar serenata a
serene a sereno
sergeant n sargento m
serial n serie f. **~ize** vt serializar
series n serie f
serious a serio. **~ly** adv seriamente; (ill) gravemente. **take ~ly** tomar en serio
sermon n sermón m
serum n (pl -a) suero m
servant n criado m
serve vt servir; servir a <country>; cumplir <sentence>. **~ as** servir de. **it ~s you right** ¡bien te lo mereces! ● vi servir; (in tennis) sacar. ● n (in tennis) saque m. **~r** n (Comp) servidor m
service n servicio m; (of car etc) revisión f. ● vt revisar <car etc>. **~ charge** n (in restaurant) servicio m. **~s** npl (Mil) fuerzas fpl armadas. **~ station** n estación f de servicio
serviette n servilleta f
servile a servil
session n sesión f
set vt (pt set pres p setting) poner; poner en hora <clock etc>; fijar <limit etc>; (typeset) componer. **~ fire to** prender fuego a. **~ free** vt poner en libertad. ● vi <sun> ponerse; <jelly> cuajarse. ● n serie f; (of cutlery etc) juego m; (tennis) set m; (TV, Radio) aparato m; (in theatre)

decorado m; (of people) círculo m. ● a fijo. **be ~ on** estar resuelto a. □ **~ back** vt (delay) retardar; (**Ⅰ**, cost) costar. □ **~ off** vi salir. vt hacer sonar <alarm>; hacer explotar <bomb>. □ **~ out** vt exponer <argument>. vi (leave) salir. □ **~ up** vt establecer. **~back** n revés m
settee n sofá m
setting n (of dial, switch) posición f
settle vt (arrange) acordar; arreglar <matter>; resolver <dispute>; pagar <bill>; saldar <debt>. ● vi (live) establecerse. □ **~ down** vi calmarse; (become more responsible) sentar (la) cabeza. □ **~ for** vt aceptar. □ **~ up** vi arreglar cuentas. **~ment** n establecimiento m; (agreement) acuerdo m; (of debt) liquidación f; (colony) colonia f. **~r** n colono m
set: **~-to** n pelea f. **~-up** n **Ⅰ** sistema m; (con) tinglado m
seven a & n siete (m). **~teen** a & n diecisiete (m). **~teenth** a decimoséptimo. ● n diecisieteavo m. **~th** a & n séptimo (m). **~tieth** a septuagésimo. ● n setentavo m. **~ty** a & n setenta (m)
sever vt cortar; (fig) romper
several a & pron varios
sever|e a (-er, -est) severo; (serious) grave; <weather> riguroso. **~ely** adv severamente. **~ity** n severidad f; (seriousness) gravedad f
sew vt/i (pt sewed pp sewn or sewed) coser. □ **~ up** vt coser
sew|age n aguas fpl residuales. **~er** n cloaca f
sewing n costura f. **~-machine** n máquina f de coser
sewn ⇒SEW
sex n sexo m. **have ~** tener relaciones sexuales. ● a sexual.

~ist *a & n* sexista (*m & f*). **~ual** *a* sexual. **~ual intercourse** *n* relaciones *fpl* sexuales. **~uality** *n* sexualidad *f*. **~y** *a* (**-ier, -iest**) excitante, sexy, provocativo

shabby *a* (**-ier, -iest**) <*clothes*> gastado; <*person*> pobremente vestido

shack *n* choza *f*

shade *n* sombra *f*; (of colour) tono *m*; (for lamp) pantalla *f*; (nuance) matiz *m*; (Amer, over window) persiana *f*

shadow *n* sombra *f*. ● *vt* (follow) seguir de cerca a. **~y** *a* (fig) vago

shady *a* (**-ier, -iest**) sombreado; (fig) turbio; <*character*> sospechoso

shaft *n* (of arrow) astil *m*; (Mec) eje *m*; (of light) rayo *m*; (of lift, mine) pozo *m*

shaggy *a* (**-ier, -iest**) peludo

shake *vt* (*pt* **shook**, *pp* **shaken**) sacudir; agitar <*bottle*>; (shock) desconcertar. **~ hands with** estrechar la mano a. **~ one's head** negar con la cabeza; (Amer, meaning yes) asentir con la cabeza. ● *vi* temblar. □ **~ off** *vi* deshacerse de. ● *n* sacudida *f*.

shaky *a* (**-ier, -iest**) tembloroso; <*table etc*> inestable

shall *v aux*. we **~** see veremos. **~ we go to the cinema?** ¿vamos al cine?

shallow *a* (**-er, -est**) poco profundo; (fig) superficial

sham *n* farsa *f*. ● *a* fingido

shambles *npl* (🄵, mess) caos *m*

shame *n* (feeling) vergüenza *f*. **what a ~!** ¡qué lástima! ● *vt* avergonzar. **~ful** *a* vergonzoso. **~less** *a* desvergonzado

shampoo *n* champú *m*. ● *vt* lavar

shan't = shall not

shape *n* forma *f*. ● *vt* formar; determinar <*future*>. ● *vi* tomar forma. **~less** *a* informe

share *n* porción *f*; (Com) acción *f*. ● *vt* compartir; (divide) dividir. ● *vi* compartir. **~ in sth** participar en algo. □ **~ out** *vt* repartir. **~holder** *n* accionista *m & f*. **~-out** *n* reparto *m*

shark *n* tiburón *m*

sharp *a* (**-er, -est**) <*knife etc*> afilado; <*pin etc*> puntiagudo; <*pain, sound*> agudo; <*taste*> ácido; <*bend*> cerrado; <*contrast*> marcado; (clever) listo; (Mus) sostenido. ● *adv* en punto. **at seven o'clock ~** a las siete en punto. ● *n* (Mus) sostenido *m*. **~en** *vt* afilar; sacar punta a <*pencil*>. **~ener** *n* (Mec) afilador *m*; (for pencils) sacapuntas *m*. **~ly** *adv* bruscamente

shatter *vt* hacer añicos. **he was ~ed by the news** la noticia lo dejó destrozado. ● *vi* hacerse añicos. **~ed** *a* (exhausted) agotado

shav|e *vt* afeitar, rasurar (Mex). ● *vi* afeitarse, rasurarse (Mex). ● *n* afeitada *f*, rasurada *f* (Mex). **have a ~e** afeitarse. **~er** *n* maquinilla *f* (de afeitar). **~ing brush** *n* brocha *f* de afeitar. **~ing cream** *n* crema *f* de afeitar

shawl *n* chal *m*

she *pron* ella

sheaf *n* (*pl* **sheaves**) gavilla *f*

shear *vt* (*pp* **shorn** or **sheared**) esquilar. **~s** *npl* tijeras *fpl* grandes

shed *n* cobertizo *m*. ● *vt* (*pt* **shed**, *pres p* **shedding**) perder; derramar <*tears*>; despojarse de <*clothes*>. **~ light on** arrojar luz sobre

she'd = she had, she would

sheep *n invar* oveja *f*. **~dog** *n* perro *m* pastor. **~ish** *a* avergonzado

sheer *a* (as intensifier) puro; (steep) perpendicular

sheet *n* sábana *f*; (of paper) hoja *f*; (of glass) lámina *f*; (of ice) capa *f*

shelf *n* (*pl* **shelves**) estante *m*. **a set of shelves** unos estantes

shell *n* concha *f*; (of egg) cáscara *f*; (of crab, snail, tortoise) caparazón *m or f*; (explosive) proyectil *m*, obús *m*. ● *vt* pelar <*peas etc*>; (Mil) bombardear

she'll = **she had, she would**

shellfish *n invar* marisco *m*; (collectively) mariscos *mpl*

shelter *n* refugio *m*. **take ~** refugiarse. ● *vt* darle cobijo a <*fugitive*>; (protect from weather) resguardar. ● *vi* refugiarse. **~ed** *a* <*spot*> abrigado; <*life*> protegido

shelv|e *vt* (fig) dar carpetazo a. **~ing** *n* estantería *f*

shepherd *n* pastor *m*. **~ess** *n* pastora *f*

sherbet *n* (Amer, water ice) sorbete *m*

sheriff *n* (in US) sheriff *m*

sherry *n* (vino *m* de) jerez *m*

she's = **she is, she has**

shield *n* escudo *m*. ● *vt* proteger

shift *vt* cambiar; correr <*furniture etc*>. ● *vi* <*wind*> cambiar; <*attention, opinion*> pasar a; (Amer, change gear) cambiar de velocidad. ● *n* cambio *m*; (work) turno *m*; (workers) tanda *f*. **~y** *a* (**-ier, -iest**) furtivo

shilling *n* chelín *m*

shimmer *vi* rielar, relucir

shin *n* espinilla *f*

shine *vi* (*pt* **shone**) brillar. ● *vt* sacar brillo a. **~ a light on sth** alumbrar algo con una luz. ● *n* brillo *m*

shingle *n* (pebbles) guijarros *mpl*

shin|ing *a* brillante. **~y** *a* (**-ier, -iest**) brillante

ship *n* barco *m*, buque *m*. ● *vt* (*pt* **shipped**) transportar; (send) enviar; (load) embarcar. **~building** *n* construcción *f* naval. **~ment** *n* envío *m*. **~ping** *n* transporte *m*; (ships) barcos *mpl*. **~shape** *a* limpio y ordenado. **~wreck** *n* naufragio *m*. **~wrecked** *a* naufragado. **be ~wrecked** naufragar. **~yard** *n* astillero *m*

shirk *vt* esquivar

shirt *n* camisa *f*. **in ~-sleeves** en mangas de camisa

shit *n & int* (vulg) mierda (*f*). ● *vi* (vulg) (*pt* **shat**, *pres p* **shitting**) cagar

shiver *vi* temblar. ● *n* escalofrío *m*

shoal *n* banco *m*

shock *n* (of impact) choque *m*; (of earthquake) sacudida *f*; (surprise) shock *m*; (scare) susto *m*; (Elec) descarga *f*; (Med) shock *m*. **get a ~** llevarse un shock. ● *vt* escandalizar; (apall) horrorizar. **~ing** *a* escandaloso; 🇪🇸 espantoso

shod ⇒SHOE

shoddy *a* (**-ier, -iest**) mal hecho, de pacotilla

shoe *n* zapato *m*; (of horse) herradura *f*. ● *vt* (*pt* **shod**, *pres p* **shoeing**) herrar <*horse*>. **~horn** *n* calzador *m*. **~lace** *n* cordón *m* (de zapato). **~ polish** *n* betún *m*

shone ⇒SHINE

shoo *vt* ahuyentar

shook ⇒SHAKE

shoot *vt* (*pt* **shot**) disparar; rodar <*film*>. ● *vi* (hunt) cazar. ● *n* (Bot)

S

retoño m. □ **~ down** vt derribar. □ **~ out** vi (rush) salir disparado. □ **~ up** vi <prices> dispararse; (grow) crecer mucho

shop n tienda f. **go to the ~s** ir de compras. **talk ~** hablar del trabajo. ● vi (pt **shopping**) hacer compras. **go ~ping** ir de compras. □ **~ around** vi buscar el mejor precio. **~ assistant** n dependiente m, dependienta f, empleado m, empleada f (LAm). **~keeper** n comerciante m, tendero m. **~lifter** n ladrón m (que roba en las tiendas). **~lifting** n hurto m (en las tiendas). **~per** n comprador m. **~ping** (purchases) compras fpl. **do the ~ping** hacer la compra, hacer el mandado (Mex). **~ping bag** n bolsa f de la compra. **~ping cart** n (Amer) carrito m (de la compra). **~ping centre**, **~ping mall** (Amer) n centro m comercial. **~ping trolley** n carrito m de la compra. **~ steward** n enlace m sindical. **~ window** n escaparate m, vidriera f (LAm), aparador m (Mex)

shore n orilla f

shorn ⇒SHEAR

short a (-er, -est) corto; (not lasting) breve; <person> bajo; (curt) brusco. **a ~ time ago** hace poco. **be ~ of time/money** andar corto de tiempo/dinero. **Mick is ~ for Michael** Mick es el diminutivo de Michael. ● adv <stop> en seco. **we never went ~ of food** nunca nos faltó comida. ● n. **in ~** en resumen. **~age** n escasez f, falta f. **~bread** n galleta f (de mantequilla). **~ circuit** n cortocircuito m. **~coming** n defecto m. **~ cut** n atajo m. **~en** vt acortar. **~hand** n taquigrafía f. **~ly** adv (soon) dentro de poco. **~ly before midnight** poco antes de

la medianoche. **~s** npl pantalones m cortos, shorts mpl; (Amer, underwear) calzoncillos mpl. **~-sighted** a miope

shot ⇒SHOOT. ● n (from gun) disparo m; tiro m; (in soccer) tiro m, disparo m; (in other sports) tiro m; (Photo) foto f. **be a good/poor ~** ser un buen/mal tirador. **be off like a ~** salir disparado. **~gun** n escopeta f

should v aux. **I ~ go** debería ir. **you ~n't have said that** no deberías haber dicho eso. **I ~ like to see her** me gustaría verla. **if he ~ come** si viniese

shoulder n hombro m. ● vt cargar con <responsibility>; ponerse al hombro <burden>. **~ blade** n omóplato m

shout n grito m. ● vt/i gritar. **~ at s.o.** gritarle a uno

shove n empujón m. ● vt empujar; (I, put) poner. ● vi empujar. □ **~ off** vi 🔢 largarse

shovel n pala f. ● vt (pt shovelled) palear <coal>; espalar <snow>

show vt (pt **showed**, pp **shown**) mostrar; (put on display) exponer; poner <film>. **I'll ~ you to your room** lo acompaño a su cuarto. ● vi (be visible) verse. ● n muestra f; (exhibition) exposición f; (in theatre) espectáculo m; (on TV, radio) programa m; (ostentation) pompa f. **be on ~** estar expuesto. □ **~ off** vt (pej) lucir, presumir de. vi presumir, lucirse. □ **~ up** vi (be visible) notarse; (arrive) aparecer. vt (reveal) poner de manifiesto; (embarrass) hacer quedar mal. **~case** n vitrina f. **~down** n confrontación f

shower n (of rain) chaparrón m; (for washing) ducha f. **have a ~**, **take a ~** ducharse. ● vi ducharse

showjumping *n* concursos *mpl* hípicos.

shown ⇒SHOW

show: ~**-off** *n* fanfarrón *m*. ~**room** *n* sala *f* de exposición *f*. ~**y** *a* (**-ier, -iest**) llamativo; (attractive) ostentoso

shrank ⇒SHRINK

shred *n* pedazo *m*; (fig) pizca *f*. ● *vt* (*pt* **shredded**) hacer tiras; destruir, triturar <*documents*>. ~**der** *n* (for paper) trituradora *f*; (for vegetables) cortadora *f*

shrewd *a* (**-er, -est**) astuto

shriek *n* chillido *m*; (of pain) alarido *m*. ● *vt/i* chillar

shrift *n*. **give s.o. short** ~ despachar a uno con brusquedad. **give sth short** ~ desestimar algo de plano

shrill *a* agudo

shrimp *n* gamba *f*, camarón *m* (LAm); (Amer, large) langostino *m*

shrine *n* (place) santuario *m*; (tomb) sepulcro *m*

shrink *vt* (*pt* **shrank**, *pp* **shrunk**) encoger. ● *vi* encogerse; <*amount*> reducirse; retroceder (recoil)

shrivel *vi* (*pt* **shrivelled**). ~ (**up**) <*plant*> marchitarse; <*fruit*> resecarse y arrugarse

shroud *n* mortaja *f*; (fig) velo *m*. ● *vt* envolver

Shrove *n*. ~ **Tuesday** *n* martes *m* de carnaval

shrub *n* arbusto *m*

shrug *vt* (*pt* **shrugged**) encogerse de hombros

shrunk ⇒SHRINK. ~**en** *a* encogido

shudder *vi* estremecerse. ● *n* estremecimiento *m*

shuffle *vi* andar arrastrando los pies. ● *vt* barajar <*cards*>. ~ **one's feet** arrastrar los pies

shun *vt* (*pt* **shunned**) evitar

shunt *vt* cambiar de vía

shush *int* ¡chitón!

shut *vt* (*pt* **shut**, *pres p* **shutting**) cerrar. ● *vi* cerrarse. ● *a*. **be** ~ estar cerrado. □ ~ **down** *vt/i* cerrar. □ ~ **up** *vt* cerrar; ⊡ hacer callar. *vi* callarse. ~**ter** *n* contraventana *f*; (Photo) obturador *m*

shuttle *n* lanzadera *f*; (Aviat) puente *m* aéreo; (space ~) transbordador *m* espacial. ● *vi*. ~ (**back and forth**) ir y venir. ~**cock** *n* volante *m*. ~ **service** *n* servicio *m* de enlace

shy *a* (**-er, -est**) tímido. ● *vi* (*pt* **shied**) asustarse. ~**ness** *n* timidez *f*

sick *a* enfermo; <*humour*> negro; (⊡, fed up) harto. **be** ~ estar enfermo; (vomit) vomitar. **be** ~ **of** (fig) estar harto de. **feel** ~ sentir náuseas. **get** ~ (Amer) caer enfermo, enfermarse (LAm). ~ **leave** *n* permiso *m* por enfermedad, baja *f* por enfermedad. ~**ly** *a* (**-lier, -liest**) enfermizo; <*taste, smell etc*> nauseabundo. ~**ness** *n* enfermedad *f*

side *n* lado *m*; (of hill) ladera *f*; (of person) costado *m*; (team) equipo *m*; (fig) parte *f*. ~ **by** ~ uno al lado del otro. **take** ~s tomar partido. ● *a* lateral. □ ~ **with** *vt* ponerse de parte de. ~**board** *n* aparador *m*. ~ **dish** *n* acompañamiento *m*. ~**-effect** *n* efecto *m* secundario; (fig) consecuencia *f* indirecta. ~**line** *n* actividad *f* suplementaria. ~ **road** *n* calle *f* secundaria. ~**-step** *vt* eludir. ~**-track** *vt* desviar del tema. ~**walk** *n* (Amer) acera *f*, vereda *f* (LAm), banqueta *f* (Mex). ~**ways** *a* & *adv* de lado

S

siding *n* apartadero *m*

sidle *vi.* ~ **up to s.o.** acercarse furtivamente a uno

siege *n* sitio *m*

sieve *n* tamiz *m.* ● *vt* tamizar, cernir

sift *vt* tamizar, cernir. ● *vi.* ~ **through sth** pasar algo por el tamiz

sigh *n* suspiro. ● *vi* suspirar

sight *n* vista *f*; (spectacle) espectáculo *m*; (on gun) mira *f.* **at first** ~ a primera vista. **catch** ~ **of** ver; (in distance) avistar. **lose** ~ **of** perder de vista. **see the** ~**s** visitar los lugares de interés. **within** ~ **of** (near) cerca de. ● *vt* ver; divisar <*land*>. ~**seeing** *n.* **go** ~ ir a visitar los lugares de interés. ~**seer** *n* turista *m & f*

sign *n* (indication) señal *f*, indicio *m*; (gesture) señal *f*, seña *f*; (notice) letrero *m*; (Astr) signo *m.* ● *vt* firmar. □ ~ **on** *vi* (for unemployment benefit) anotarse para recibir el seguro de desempleo

signal *n* señal *f.* ● *vt* (*pt* **signalled**) señalar. ● *vi.* ~ **(to s.o.)** hacer señas (a uno); (Auto) poner el intermitente, señalizar

signature *n* firma *f.* ~ **tune** *n* sintonía *f*

significan|ce *n* importancia *f.* ~**t** *a* (important) importante; <*fact, remark*> significativo

signify *vt* significar

signpost *n* señal *f*, poste *m* indicador

silen|ce *n* silencio *m.* ● *vt* hacer callar. ~**cer** *n* (on gun and on car) silenciador *m.* ~**t** *a* silencioso; <*film*> mudo. **remain** ~**t** quedarse callado. ~**tly** *adv* silenciosamente

silhouette *n* silueta *f.* ● *vt.* **be** ~**d** perfilarse (**against** contra)

silicon *n* silicio *m.* ~ **chip** *n* pastilla *f* de silicio

silk *n* seda *f.* ~**y** *a* (of silk) de seda; (like silk) sedoso

silly *a* (**-ier, -iest**) tonto

silt *n* cieno *m*

silver *n* plata *f.* ● *a* de plata. ~**-plated** *a* bañado en plata, plateado. ~**ware** *n* platería *f*

simil|ar *a* parecido, similar. ~**arity** *n* parecido *m.* ~**arly** *adv* de igual manera. ~**e** *n* símil *m*

simmer *vt/i* hervir a fuego lento. □ ~ **down** *vi* calmarse

simpl|e *a* (**-er, -est**) sencillo, simple; <*person*> (humble) simple; (backward) simple. ~**e-minded** *a* ingenuo. ~**icity** *n* simplicidad *f*, sencillez *f.* ~**ify** *vt* simplificar. ~**y** *adv* sencillamente, simplemente; (absolutely) realmente

simulate *vt* simular

simultaneous *a* simultáneo. ~**ly** *adv* simultáneamente

sin *n* pecado *m.* ● *vi* (*pt* **sinned**) pecar

....

since

● *preposition*

····▸ desde. **he's been living here** ~ **1991** vive aquí desde 1991. ~ **Christmas** desde Navidad. ~ **then** desde entonces. **I haven't been feeling well** ~ **Sunday** desde el domingo que no me siento bien. **how long is it** ~ **your interview?** ¿cuánto (tiempo) hace de la entrevista?

● *adverb*

····▸ desde entonces. **I haven't spoken to her** ~ no he hablado con ella desde entonces

● *conjunction*

····▶ desde que. **I haven't seen her
~ she left** no la he visto desde
que se fue. **~ coming to
Manchester** desde que vine (*or*
vino *etc*) a Manchester. **it's ten
years ~ he died** hace diez años
que se murió

····▶ (because) como, ya que. **~ it
was quite late, I decided to stay**
como *or* ya que era bastante
tarde, decidí quedarme

sincer|e *a* sincero. **~ely** *adv*
sinceramente. **yours ~ely, ~ely
(yours)** (in letters) (saluda a usted
atentamente. **~ity** *n* sinceridad *f*

sinful *a* <*person*> pecador; <*act*>
pecaminoso

sing *vt/i* (*pt* **sang**, *pp* **sung**)
cantar

singe *vt* (*pres p* **singeing**)
chamuscar

singer *n* cantante *m & f*

single *a* solo; (not double) sencillo;
(unmarried) soltero; <*bed, room*>
individual, de una plaza (LAm);
<*ticket*> de ida, sencillo. **not a ~
house** ni una sola casa. **every ~
day** todos los días sin excepción.
● *n* (ticket) billete *m* sencillo,
boleto *m* de ida (LAm). □ ~ **out** *vt*
escoger; (distinguish) distinguir.
~-handed *a & adv* sin ayuda. **~s**
npl (Sport) individuales *mpl*

singular *n* singular *f*. ● *a*
singular; (unusual) raro; <*noun*> en
singular

sinister *a* siniestro

sink *vt* (*pt* **sank**, *pp* **sunk**)
hundir. ● *vi* hundirse. ● *n*
fregadero *m* (Amer, in bathroom)
lavabo *m*, lavamanos *m*. □ ~ **in** *vi*
penetrar

sinner *n* pecador *m*

sip *n* sorbo *m*. ● *vt* (*pt* **sipped**)
sorber

siphon *n* sifón *m*. **~ (out)** sacar
con sifón. □ ~ **off** *vt* desviar
<*money*>.

sir *n* señor *m*. **S~** *n* (title) sir *m*.
Dear S~, (in letters) De mi mayor
consideración:

siren *n* sirena *f*

sister *n* hermana *f*; (nurse)
enfermera *f* jefe. **~-in-law** *n* (*pl*
~s-in-law) cuñada *f*

sit *vi* (*pt* **sat**, *pres p* **sitting**)
sentarse; <*committee etc*>
reunirse en sesión. **be ~ting** estar
sentado. ● *vt* sentar; hacer
<*exam*>. □ ~ **back** *vi* (fig)
relajarse. □ ~ **down** *vi* sentarse.
be ~ting down estar sentado. □ ~
up *vi* (from lying) incorporarse;
(straighten back) ponerse derecho.
~-in *n* (strike) encierro *m*,
ocupación *f*

site *n* emplazamiento *m*; (piece of
land) terreno *m*; (archaeological)
yacimiento *m*. **building ~** *n* solar
m. ● *vt* situar

sit: ~ting *n* sesión *f*; (in restaurant)
turno *m*. **~ting room** *n* sala *f* de
estar, living *m*

situat|e *vt* situar. **~ion** *n*
situación *f*

six *a & n* seis (*m*). **~teen** *a & n*
dieciséis (*m*). **~teenth** *a*
decimosexto. ● *n* dieciseisavo *m*.
~th *a & n* sexto (*m*). **~tieth** *a*
sexagésimo. ● *n* sesentavo *m*.
~ty *a & n* sesenta (*m*)

size *n* tamaño *m*; (of clothes) talla *f*;
(of shoes) número *m*; (of problem,
operation) magnitud *f*. **what ~ do
you take?** (clothes) ¿qué talla
tiene?; (shoes) ¿qué número
calza?. □ ~ **up** *vt* 🛈 evaluar
<*problem*>; calar <*person*>

sizzle *vi* crepitar

skat|e *n* patín *m*.● *vi* patinar.
~eboard *n* monopatín *m*,

S

patineta *f* (Mex). **~er** *n* patinador *m*. **~ing** *n* patinaje *m*. **~ing-rink** *n* pista *f* de patinaje

skeleton *n* esqueleto *m*. **~ key** *n* llave *f* maestra

sketch *n* (drawing) dibujo *m*; (rougher) esbozo *m*; (TV, Theatre) sketch *m*. ● *vt* esbozar. ● *vi* dibujar. **~y** *a* (**-ier, -iest**) incompleto

ski *n* (*pl* **skis**) esquí *m*. ● *vi* (*pt* **skied**, *pres p* **skiing**) esquiar. **go ~ing** ir a esquiar

skid *vi* (*pt* **skidded**) patinar. ● *n* patinazo *m*

ski: ~er *n* esquiador *m*. **~ing** *n* esquí *m*

skilful *a* diestro

ski-lift *n* telesquí *m*

skill *n* habilidad *f*; (technical) destreza *f*. **~ed** *a* hábil; *<worker>* cualificado

skim *vt* (*pt* **skimmed**) espumar *<soup>*; desnatar, descremar *<milk>*; (glide over) pasar casi rozando. **~ milk** (Amer), **~med milk** *n* leche *f* desnatada, leche *f* descremada. **~ through** *vt* leer por encima

skimp *vi*. **~ on sth** escatimar algo. **~y** *a* (**-ier, -iest**) escaso; *<skirt, dress>* brevísimo

skin *n* piel *f*. ● *vt* (*pt* **skinned**) despellejar. **~-deep** *a* superficial. **~-diving** *n* submarinismo *m*. **~ny** *a* (**-ier, -iest**) flaco

skip *vi* (*pt* **skipped**) *vi* saltar; (with rope) saltar a la comba, saltar a la cuerda. ● *vt* saltarse *<chapter>*; faltar a *<class>*. ● *n* brinco *m*; (container) contenedor *m* (*para escombros*). **~per** *n* capitán *m*. **~ping-rope, ~rope** (Amer) *n* comba *f*, cuerda *f* de saltar, reata *f* (Mex)

skirmish *n* escaramuza *f*

skirt *n* falda *f*. ● *vt* bordear; (go round) ladear. **~ing-board** *n* rodapié *m*, zócalo *m*

skittle *n* bolo *m*

skive off (*vi* 🄻, disappear) escurrir el bulto; (stay away from work) no ir a trabajar

skulk *vi* (hide) esconderse. **~ around** *vi* merodear

skull *n* cráneo *m*; (remains) calavera *f*

sky *n* cielo *m*. **~lark** *n* alondra *f*. **~light** *n* tragaluz *m*. **~scraper** *n* rascacielos *m*

slab *n* (of concrete) bloque *m*; (of stone) losa *f*

slack *a* (**-er, -est**) flojo; *<person>* poco aplicado; *<period>* de poca actividad. ● *vi* flojear. **~en** *vt* aflojar. ● *vi* *<person>* descansar. ☐ **~en off** *vt/i* aflojar

slain ⇒SLAY

slake *vt* apagar

slam *vt* (*pt* **slammed**). **~ the door** dar un portazo. **~ the door shut** cerrar de un portazo. **~ on the brakes** pegar un frenazo; (🄴, criticize) atacar violentamente. ● *vi* cerrarse de un portazo

slander *n* calumnia *f*. ● *vt* difamar

slang *n* argot *m*

slant *vt* inclinar. ● *n* inclinación *f*

slap *vt* (*pt* **slapped**) (on face) pegarle una bofetada a; (put) tirar. **~ s.o. on the back** darle una palmada a uno en la espalda ● *n* bofetada *f*; (on back) palmada *f*. ● *adv* de lleno. **~dash** *a* descuidado; *<work>* chapucero

slash *vt* acuchillar; (fig) rebajar drásticamente. ● *n* cuchillada *f*

slat *n* tablilla *f*

slate *n* pizarra *f*. ● *vt* 🄴 poner por los suelos

slaughter vt matar salvajemente; matar <animal>. ● n carnicería f; (of animals) matanza f

slave n esclavo m. ● vi ~ (away) trabajar como un negro. ~-driver n 🔟 negrero m. ~ry n esclavitud f

slay vt (pt slew, pp slain) dar muerte a

sleazy a (-ier, -iest) 🔟 sórdido

sled (Amer), **sledge** n trineo m

sledge-hammer n mazo m, almádena f

sleek a (-er, -est) liso, brillante

sleep n sueño m. go to ~ dormirse. ● vi (pt slept) dormir. ● vt poder alojar. ~er n (on track) traviesa f, durmiente m. be a light/heavy ~er tener el sueño ligero/pesado. ~ing bag n saco m de dormir. ~ing pill n somnífero m. ~less a. have a ~less night pasar la noche en blanco. ~walk vi caminar dormido. ~y a (-ier, -iest) soñoliento. be/feel ~y tener sueño

sleet n aguanieve f

sleeve n manga f; (for record) funda f, carátula f. up one's ~ en reserva. ~less a sin mangas

sleigh n trineo m

slender a delgado; (fig) escaso

slept ⇒SLEEP

slew ⇒SLAY

slice n (of ham) lonja f; (of bread) rebanada f; (of meat) tajada f; (of cheese) trozo m; (of sth round) rodaja f. ● vt cortar (en rebanadas, tajadas etc)

slick a <performance> muy pulido. ● n. (oil) ~ marea f negra

slid|e vt (pt slid) deslizar. ● vi (intentionally) deslizarse; (unintentionally) resbalarse. ● n resbalón m; (in playground) tobogán m, resbaladilla f (Mex); (for hair)

pasador m, broche m (Mex); (Photo) diapositiva f. ~ing scale n escala f móvil

slight a (-er, -est) ligero; (slender) delgado. ● vt desairar. ● n desaire m. ~est a mínimo. not in the ~est en absoluto. ~ly adv un poco, ligeramente

slim a (slimmer, slimmest) delgado. ● vi (pt slimmed) (become slimmer) adelgazar; (diet) hacer régimen

slim|e n limo m; (of snail, slug) baba f. ~y a viscoso; (fig) excesivamente obsequioso

sling n (Med) cabestrillo m. ● vt (pt slung) lanzar

slip vt (pt slipped) deslizar. ~ s.o.'s mind olvidársele a uno. ● vi resbalarse. it ~ped out of my hands se me resbaló de las manos. he ~ped out the back door se deslizó por la puerta trasera ● n resbalón m; (mistake) error m; (petticoat) combinación f; (paper) trozo m. give s.o. the ~ lograr zafarse de uno. ~ of the tongue n lapsus m linguae. □ ~ away vi escabullirse. □ ~ up vi 🔟 equivocarse

slipper n zapatilla f

slippery a resbaladizo

slip: ~ road n rampa f de acceso. ~shod a descuidado. ~-up n 🔟 error m

slit n raja f; (cut) corte m. ● vt (pt slit, pres p slitting) rajar; (cut) cortar

slither vi deslizarse

slobber vi babear

slog vt (pt slogged) golpear. ● vi caminar trabajosamente. ● n golpetazo m; (hard work) trabajo m penoso. □ ~ away vi sudar tinta 🔟

slogan n eslogan m

S

slop vt (pt **slopped**) derramar.
● vi derramarse

slop|e vi inclinarse. ● vt inclinar.
● n declive m, pendiente f. ~**ing**
a inclinado

sloppy a (-**ier**, -**iest**) <work>
descuidado; <person> desaliñado

slosh vi 🛈 chapotear

slot n ranura f. ● vt (pt **slotted**)
encajar

slot-machine n distribuidor m
automático; (for gambling) máquina
f tragamonedas

slouch vi andar cargado de
espaldas; (in chair) repanchigarse

Slovak a & n eslovaco (m). ~**ia** n
Eslovaquia f

slovenly a <work> descuidado;
<person> desaliñado

slow a (-**er**, -**est**) lento. **be** ~
<clock> estar atrasado. **in** ~
motion a cámara lenta. ● adv
despacio. ● vt retardar. ● vi ir
más despacio. □ ~ **down**, ~ **up**
vt retardar. vi ir más despacio.
~**ly** adv despacio, lentamente

sludge n fango m

slug n babosa f. ~**gish** a lento

slum n barrio m bajo

slumber vi dormir

slump n baja f repentina; (in
business) depresión f. ● vi
desplomarse

slung ⇒SLING

slur vt (pt **slurred**). ~ **one's words**
arrastrar las palabras. ● n. **a**
racist ~ un comentario racista

slush n nieve f medio derretida.
~ **fund** n fondo m de reptiles

sly a (**slyer**, **slyest**) (crafty) astuto.
● n. **on the** ~ a hurtadillas. ~**ly**
adv astutamente

smack n manotazo m. ● adv 🛈 ~
in the middle justo en el medio. **he**

went ~ **into a tree** se dio contra un
árbol. ● vt pegarle a (con la
mano)

small a (-**er**, -**est**) pequeño, chico
(LAm). ● n. **the** ~ **of the back** la
región lumbar. ~ **ads** npl
anuncios mpl (clasificados),
avisos mpl (clasificados) (LAm). ~
change n suelto m. ~**pox** n
viruela f. ~ **talk** n charla f sobre
temas triviales

smart a (-**er**, -**est**) elegante;
(clever) listo; (brisk) rápido. ● vi
escocer. □ ~**en up** vt arreglar. vi
<person> mejorar su aspecto,
arreglarse. ~**ly** adv
elegantemente; (quickly)
rápidamente

smash vt romper; (into little pieces)
hacer pedazos; batir <record>.
● vi romperse; (collide) chocar
(into con). ● n (noise) estrépito m;
(collision) choque m; (in sport) smash
m. □ ~ **up** vt destrozar. ~**ing** a
🛈 estupendo

smattering n nociones fpl

smear vt untar (with de); (stain)
manchar (with de); (fig)
difamar. ● n mancha f

smell n olor m; (sense) olfato m.
● vt (pt **smelt**) oler; <animal>
olfatear. ● vi oler. ~ **of sth** oler a
algo. ~**y** a maloliente. **be** ~**y** oler
mal

smelt ⇒SMELL. ● vt fundir

smile n sonrisa f. ● vi sonreír. ~
at s.o. sonreírle a uno

smirk n sonrisita f (de suficiencia
etc)

smith n herrero m

smithereens npl. **smash sth to** ~
hacer algo añicos

smock n blusa f, bata f

smog n smog m

smok|e n humo m. ● vt fumar
<tobacco>; ahumar <food>. ● vi

fumar. ~**eless** *a* que arde sin humo. ~**er** *n* fumador *m*. ~**y** *a* <*room*> lleno de humo

smooth *a* (**-er**, **-est**) <*texture/ stone*> liso; <*skin*> suave; <*movement*> suave; <*sea*> tranquilo. ● *vt* alisar. □ ~ **out** *vt* allanar <*problems*>. ~**ly** *adv* suavemente; (without problems) sin problemas

smother *vt* asfixiar <*person*>. ~ **s.o. with kisses** cubrir a uno de besos

smoulder *vi* arder sin llama

smudge *n* borrón *m*. ● *vi* tiznarse

smug *a* (**smugger**, **smuggest**) pagado de sí mismo; <*expression*> de suficiencia

smuggl|e *vt* pasar de contrabando. ~**er** *n* contrabandista *m* & *f*. ~**ing** *n* contrabando *m*

snack *n* tentempié *m*. ~ **bar** *n* cafetería *f*

snag *n* problema *m*

snail *n* caracol *m*. **at a** ~**'s pace** a paso de tortuga

snake *n* culebra *f*, serpiente *f*

snap *vt* (*pt* **snapped**) (break) romper. ~ **one's fingers** chasquear los dedos. ● *vi* romperse; <*dog*> intentar morder; (say) contestar bruscamente. ~ **at** <*dog*> intentar morder; (say) contestar bruscamente. ● *n* chasquido *m*; (Photo) foto *f*. ● *a* instantáneo. □ ~ **up** *vt* no dejar escapar <*offer*>. ~**py** *a* (**-ier**, **-iest**) 🔲 rápido. **make it** ~**py!** ¡date prisa! ~**shot** *n* foto *f*

snare *n* trampa *f*

snarl *vi* gruñir

snatch *vt*. ~ **sth from s.o.** arrebatarle algo a uno; (steal) robar. ● *n* (short part) fragmento *m*

sneak *n* soplón *m*. ● *vi* (*past* & *pp* **sneaked** *or* 🔲 **snuck**) ~ **in**

entrar a hurtadillas. ~ **off** escabullirse. ~**ers** *npl* zapatillas *fpl* de deporte. ~**y** *a* artero

sneer *n* expresión *f* desdeñosa. ● *vi* hacer una mueca de desprecio. ~ **at** hablar con desprecio a

sneeze *n* estornudo *m*. ● *vi* estornudar

snide *a* insidioso

sniff *vt* oler. ● *vi* sorberse la nariz

snigger *n* risilla *f*. ● *vi* reírse (*por lo bajo*)

snip *vt* (*pt* **snipped**) dar un tijeretazo a. ● *n* tijeretazo *m*

sniper *n* francotirador *m*

snippet *n* (of conversation) trozo *m*. ~**s of information** datos *mpl* aislados

snivel *vi* (*pt* **snivelled**) lloriquear

snob *n* esnob *m* & *f*. ~**bery** *n* esnobismo *m*. ~**bish** *a* esnob

snooker *n* snooker *m*

snoop *vi* 🔲 husmear

snooze *n* sueñecito *m*. ● *vi* dormitar

snore *n* ronquido *m*. ● *vi* roncar

snorkel *n* esnórkel *m*

snort *n* bufido *m*. ● *vi* bufar

snout *n* hocico *m*

snow *n* nieve *f*. ● *vi* nevar. **be** ~**ed in** estar aislado por la nieve. **be** ~**ed under with work** estar agobiado de trabajo. ~**ball** *n* bola *f* de nieve. ~**drift** *n* nieve *f* amontonada. ~**fall** *n* nevada *f*. ~**flake** *n* copo *m* de nieve. ~**man** *n* muñeco *m* de nieve. ~**plough** *n* quitanieves *m*. ~**storm** *n* tormenta *f* de nieve. ~**y** *a* <*day, weather*> nevoso; <*landscape*> nevado

snub *vt* (*pt* **snubbed**) desairar. ● *n* desaire *m*. ~**-nosed** *a* chato

snuck ⇒SNEAK

snuff out *vt* apagar <*candle*>

S

snug *a* (**snugger**, **snuggest**) cómodo; (tight) ajustado

snuggle (**up**) *vi* acurrucarse

so *adv* (before a or adv) tan; (thus) así. ● *conj* (therefore) así que. ~ **am I** yo también. ~ **as to** para. ~ **far** *adv* (time) hasta ahora. ~ **far as I know** que yo sepa. ~ **long!** ¡hasta luego! **and** ~ **on**, **and** ~ **forth** etcétera (etcétera). **I think** ~ creo que sí. **or** ~ más o menos ~ **that** *conj* para que.

soak *vt* remojar. ● *vi* remojarse. □ ~ **in** *vi* penetrar. □ ~ **up** *vt* absorber. ~**ing** *a* empapado.

so-and-so *n* fulano *m*

soap *n* jabón *m*. ● *vt* enjabonar. ~ **opera** *n* telenovela *f*, culebrón *m*. ~ **powder** *n* jabón *m* en polvo. ~**y** *a* jabonoso

soar *vi* <bird/plane> planear; (rise) elevarse; <price> dispararse. ~**ing** *a* <inflation> galopante

sob *n* sollozo *m*. ● *vi* (*pt* **sobbed**) sollozar

sober *a* (not drunk) sobrio

so-called *a* llamado; (pej) supuesto

soccer *n* fútbol *m*, futbol *m* (Mex)

sociable *a* sociable

social *a* social; (sociable) sociable. ~**ism** *n* socialismo *m*. ~**ist** *a* & *n* socialista (*m* & *f*). ~**ize** *vt* socializar. ~ **security** *n* seguridad *f* social. ~ **worker** *n* asistente *m* social

society *n* sociedad *f*

sociolog|ical *a* sociológico. ~**ist** *n* sociólogo *m*. ~**y** *n* sociología *f*

sock *n* calcetín *m*

socket *n* (of joint) hueco *m*; (of eye) cuenca *f*; (wall plug) enchufe *m*; (for bulb) portalámparas *m*

soda *n* soda *f*. ~**-water** *n* soda *f*

sodium *n* sodio *m*

sofa *n* sofá *m*

soft *a* (**-er**, **-est**) blando; <light, colour> suave; (gentle) dulce, tierno; (not strict) blando. ~ **drink** *n* refresco *m*. ~**en** *vt* ablandar; suavizar <skin>. ● *vi* ablandarse. ~**ly** *adv* dulcemente; <speak> bajito. ~**ware** *n* software *m*

soggy *a* (**-ier**, **-iest**) empapado

soil *n* tierra *f*; (Amer, dirt) suciedad *f*. ● *vt* ensuciar

solar *a* solar

sold ⇒SELL

solder *vt* soldar

soldier *n* soldado *m*. □ ~ **on** *vi* 🔢 seguir al pie del cañón

sole *n* (of foot) planta *f*; (of shoe) suela *f*. ● *a* único, solo. ~**ly** *adv* únicamente

solemn *a* solemne

solicitor *n* abogado *m*; (notary) notario *m*

solid *a* sólido; <gold etc> macizo; (unanimous) unánime; <meal> sustancioso. ● *n* sólido *m*. ~**s** *npl* alimentos *mpl* sólidos. ~**arity** *n* solidaridad *f*. ~**ify** *vi* solidificarse

solitary *a* solitario

solitude *n* soledad *f*

solo *n* (*pl* **-os**) (Mus) solo *m*. ~**ist** *n* solista *m* & *f*

solstice *n* solsticio *m*

solu|ble *a* soluble. ~**tion** *n* solución *f*

solve *vt* solucionar <problem>; resolver <mystery>. ~**nt** *a* & *n* solvente (*m*)

sombre *a* sombrío

some

● *adjective*

····▶ (unspecified number) unos, unas. **he ate** ~ **olives** comió unas aceitunas

····▸ (unspecified amount) *not translated.* **I have to buy ~ bread** tengo que comprar pan. **would you like ~ coffee?** ¿quieres café?

····▸ (certain, not all) algunos, -nas. **I like ~ modern writers** algunos escritores modernos me gustan

····▸ (a little) algo de. **I eat ~ meat, but not much** como algo de carne, pero no mucho

····▸ (considerable amount of) **we've known each other for ~ time** ya hace tiempo que nos conocemos

····▸ (expressing admiration) **that's ~ car you've got!** ¡vaya coche que tienes!

● *pronoun*

····▸ (a number of things or people) algunos, -nas, unos, unas. **~ are mine and ~ aren't** algunos *or* unos son míos y otros no. **aren't there any apples? we bought ~ yesterday** ¿no hay manzanas? compramos algunas ayer

····▸ (part of an amount) **he wants ~** quiere un poco. **~ of what he said** parte *or* algo de lo que dijo

····▸ (certain people) algunos, -nas. **~ say that…** algunos dicen que…

● *adverb*

····▸ (approximately) unos, unas, alrededor de. **there were ~ fifty people there** había unas cincuenta personas, había alrededor de cincuenta personas

some: ~body *pron* alguien. **~how** *adv* de algún modo. **~how or other** de una manera u otra. **~one** *pron* alguien

somersault *n* salto *m* mortal.
● *vi* dar un salto mortal

some: ~thing *pron* algo *m*. **~thing like** (approximately) alrededor de. **~time** *a* ex. ● *adv* algún día. **~time next week** un día de la

semana que viene. **~times** *adv* a veces. **~where** *adv* en alguna parte, en algún lado

son *n* hijo *m*

sonata *n* sonata *f*

song *n* canción *f*

sonic *a* sónico

son-in-law *n* (*pl* **sons-in-law**) yerno *m*

sonnet *n* soneto *m*

son of a bitch *n* (*pl* **sons of bitches**) (esp Amer 🆇) hijo *m* de puta

soon *adv* (**-er, -est**) pronto; (in a short time) dentro de poco. **~ after** poco después. **~er or later** tarde o temprano. **as ~ as** en cuanto; **as ~ as possible** lo antes posible. **the ~er the better** cuanto antes mejor

soot *n* hollín *m*

sooth|e *vt* calmar; aliviar *<pain>*. **~ing** *a <medicine>* calmante; *<words>* tranquilizador

sooty *a* cubierto de hollín

sophisticated *a* sofisticado; (complex) complejo

sophomore *n* (Amer) estudiante *m & f* de segundo curso (*en la universidad*)

sopping *a*. **~ (wet)** empapado

soppy *a* (**-ier, -iest**) 🇮 sentimental

soprano *n* (*pl* **-os**) soprano *f*

sordid *a* sórdido

sore *a* (**-er, -est**) dolorido; (Amer 🇮, angry) **be ~ at s.o.** estar picado con uno. **~ throat** *n* dolor *m* de garganta. **I've got a ~ throat** me duele la garganta. ● *n* llaga *f*.

sorrow *n* pena *f*, pesar *m*

sorry *a* (**-ier, -ier**) arrepentido; (wretched) lamentable. **I'm ~** lo siento. **be ~ for s.o.** (pity) compadecer a uno. **I'm ~ you can't come** siento que no puedas venir. **say ~** pedir perdón. **~!**

S

(apologizing) ¡lo siento!, ¡perdón!
~? (asking s.o. to repeat) ¿cómo?
sort n tipo m, clase f; (I, person)
tipo m. **a ~ of** una especie de.
● vt clasificar. □ ~ **out** vt
(organize) ordenar; organizar
<finances>; (separate out) separar;
solucionar <problem>
so-so a regular
soufflé n suflé m
sought ⇒SEEK
soul n alma f
sound n sonido m; (noise) ruido m.
● vt tocar. ● vi sonar; (seem)
parecer (as if que). it ~s
interesting suena interesante.. ● a
(-er, -est) sano; <argument>
lógico; (secure) seguro. ● adv. ~
asleep profundamente dormido.
~ barrier n barrera f del sonido.
~ly adv sólidamente; (asleep)
profundamente. ~proof a
insonorizado. ~track n banda f
sonora
soup n sopa f
sour a (-er, -est) agrio; <milk>
cortado
source n fuente f
south n sur m. ● a sur a invar;
<wind> del sur. ● adv <go> hacia
el sur. it's ~ of está al sur de. S~
Africa n Sudáfrica f. S~
America n América f (del Sur),
Sudamérica f. S~ **American** a &
n sudamericano (m). ~-**east** n
sudeste m, sureste m. ~**erly**
<wind> del sur. ~**ern** a del sur,
meridional. ~**erner** n sureño m.
~**ward** , ~**wards** adv hacia el
sur. ~-**west** n sudoeste m,
suroeste m
souvenir n recuerdo m
sovereign n & a soberano (m)
Soviet a (History) soviético. **the ~**
Union n la Unión f Soviética
sow¹ vt (pt sowed, pp sowed or
sown) sembrar

sow² n cerda f
soy, soya n. ~ **bean** n soja f
spa n balneario m
space n espacio m; (room) espacio
m, lugar m. ● a <research etc>
espacial. ● vt espaciar. □ ~ **out**
vt espaciar. ~**craft**, ~**ship** n
nave f espacial
spacious a espacioso
spade n pala f. ~**s** npl (Cards)
picas fpl
spaghetti n espaguetis mpl
Spain n España f
spam n (Comp) correo m basura
span n (of arch) luz f; (of time)
espacio m; (of wings) envergadura
f. ● vt (pt **spanned**) extenderse
sobre. ● a ⇒SPICK
Spaniard n español m
spaniel n spaniel m
Spanish a español; (Lang)
castellano, español. ● n (Lang)
castellano m, español m. npl. the
~ (people) los españoles
spank vt pegarle a (en las nalgas)
spanner n llave f
spare vt. if you can ~ the time si
tienes tiempo. can you ~ me a
pound? ¿tienes una libra que me
des? ~ no effort no escatimar
esfuerzos. have money to ~ tener
dinero de sobra. ● a (not in use) de
más; (replacement) de repuesto;
(free) libre. ~ (**part**) n repuesto m.
~ **room** n cuarto m de
huéspedes. ~ **time** n tiempo m
libre. ~ **tyre** n neumático m de
repuesto
sparingly adv <use> con
moderación
spark n chispa f. ● vt provocar
<criticism>; suscitar <interest>.
~**ing plug** n (Auto) bujía f
spark|le vi centellear. ● n
destello m. ~**ing** a centelleante;
<wine> espumoso

spark plug n (Auto) bujía f

sparrow n gorrión m

sparse a escaso. ~**ly** adv escasamente

spasm n espasmo m; (of cough) acceso m. ~**odic** a espasmódico; (Med) irregular

spat ⇒SPIT

spate n racha f

spatial a espacial

spatter vt salpicar (with de)

spawn n huevas fpl. ● vt generar. ● vi desovar

speak vt/i (pt **spoke**, pp **spoken**) hablar. ~ **for s.o.** hablar en nombre de uno. □ ~ **up** vi hablar más fuerte. ~**er** n (in public) orador m; (loudspeaker) altavoz m; (of language) hablante m & f

spear n lanza f. ~**head** vt (lead) encabezar

special a especial. ~**ist** n especialista m & f. ~**ity** n especialidad f. ~**ization** n especialización f. ~**ize** vi especializarse. ~**ized** a especializado. ~**ly** adv especialmente. ~**ty** n especialidad f

species n especie f

specif|**ic** a específico. ~**ically** adv específicamente; <state> explícitamente. ~**ication** n especificación f. ~**y** vt especificar

specimen n muestra f

speck n (of dust) mota f; (in distance) punto m

specs npl 𝕀 ⇒SPECTACLES

spectac|**le** n espectáculo m. ~**les** npl gafas fpl, lentes fpl (LAm), anteojos mpl (LAm). ~**ular** a espectacular

spectator n espectador m

spectr|**e** n espectro m. ~**um** n (pl -**tra**) espectro m; (of views) gama f

speculat|**e** vi especular. ~**ion** n especulación f. ~**or** n especulador m

sped ⇒SPEED

speech n (faculty) habla f; (address) discurso m. ~**less** a mudo

speed n velocidad f; (rapidity) rapidez f. ● vi (pt **speeded**) (drive too fast) ir a exceso de velocidad. □ ~ **off**, ~ **away** (pt **sped**) vi alejarse a toda velocidad. □ ~ **by** (pt **sped**) vi <time> pasar volando. □ ~ **up** (pt **speeded**) vt acelerar. vi acelerarse. ~**boat** n lancha f motora. ~ **bump** n badén m, tope m (Mex). ~ **limit** n velocidad f máxima. ~**ometer** n velocímetro m. ~**way** n (Amer) autopista f. ~**y** a rápido

spell n (magic) hechizo m; (of weather, activity) período m. **go through a bad** ~ pasar por una mala racha. ● vt/i (pt **spelled** or **spelt**) escribir. □ ~ **out** vt deletrear; (fig) explicar. ~ **checker** n corrector m ortográfico. ~**ing** n ortografía f

spellbound a embelesado

spelt ⇒SPELL

spend vt (pt **spent**) gastar <money>; pasar <time>; dedicar <care>. ● vi gastar dinero

sperm n (pl **sperms** or **sperm**) esperma f; (individual) espermatozoide m

spew vt/i vomitar

spher|**e** n esfera f. ~**ical** a esférico

spice n especia f

spicy a picante

spider n araña f

spik|**e** n (of metal etc) punta f. ~**y** a puntiagudo

S

spill vt (pt **spilled** or **spilt**) derramar. ● vi derramarse. ~ **over** vi <container> desbordarse; <liquid> rebosar

spin vt (pt **spun**, pres p **spinning**) hacer girar; hilar <wool>; centrifugar <washing>. ● vi girar. ● n. give sth a ~ hacer girar algo. go for a ~ (Auto) ir a dar un paseo en coche

spinach n espinacas fpl

spindly a larguirucho

spin-drier n centrifugadora f (de ropa)

spine n columna f vertebral; (of book) lomo m; (on animal) púa f. ~**less** a (fig) sin carácter

spinning wheel n rueca f

spin-off n resultado m indirecto; (by-product) producto m derivado

spinster n soltera f

spiral a espiral; <shape> de espiral. ● n espiral f. ● vi (pt **spiralled**) <unemployment> escalar; <prices> dispararse. ~ **staircase** n escalera f de caracol

spire n aguja f

spirit n espíritu m. be in good ~s estar animado. in low ~s abatido. ~**ed** a animado, fogoso. ~**s** npl (drinks) bebidas fpl alcohólicas (de alta graduación). ~**ual** a espiritual

spit vt (pt **spat** or (Amer) **spit**, pres p **spitting**) escupir. ● vi escupir. it's ~**ting** caen algunas gotas. ● n saliva f; (for roasting) asador m

spite n rencor m. in ~ of a pesar de. ● vt fastidiar. ~**ful** a rencoroso

spittle n baba f

splash vt salpicar. ● vi <person> chapotear. ● n salpicadura f. a ~ of paint un poco de pintura. □ ~ **about** vi chapotear. □ ~ **down** vi

<spacecraft> amerizar. □ ~ **out** vi gastarse un dineral (on en)

splend|id a espléndido. ~**our** n esplendor m

splint n tablilla f

splinter n astilla f. ● vi astillarse

split vt (pt **split**, pres p **splitting**) partir; fisionar <atom>; reventar <trousers>; (divide) dividir. ● vi partirse; (divide) dividirse. a ~**ting headache** un dolor de cabeza espantoso. ● n (in garment) descosido m; (in wood, glass) rajadura f. □ ~ **up** vi separarse. ~ **second** n fracción f de segundo

splutter vi chisporrotear; <person> farfullar

spoil vt (pt **spoilt** or **spoiled**) estropear, echar a perder; (indulge) consentir, malcriar. ~**s** npl botín m. ~**-sport** n aguafiestas m & f

spoke¹ ⇒SPEAK

spoke² (of wheel) rayo m

spoken ⇒SPEAK

spokesman n (pl -men) portavoz m

sponge n esponja f. ● vt limpiar con una esponja. ~ **off**, ~ **on** vt vivir a costillas de. ~ **cake** n bizcocho m

sponsor n patrocinador m; (of the arts) mecenas m & f; (surety) garante m. ● vt patrocinar. ~**ship** n patrocinio m; (of the arts) mecenazgo m

spontaneous a espontáneo. ~**ously** adv espontáneamente

spoof n 🄸 parodia f

spooky a (-ier, -iest) 🄸 espeluznante

spool n carrete m

spoon n cuchara f. ~**ful** n cucharada f

sporadic a esporádico

sport n deporte m. ~**s car** n coche m deportivo. ~**s centre** n centro m deportivo. ~**sman** n, (pl **-men**), ~**swoman** n deportista m & f

spot n mancha f; (pimple) grano m; (place) lugar m; (in pattern) lunar m. **be in a** ~ Ⓘ estar en apuros. **on the** ~ allí mismo; <decide> en ese mismo momento. ● vt (pt **spotted**) manchar; (Ⓘ, notice) ver, divisar; descubrir <mistake>. ~ **check** n control m hecho al azar. ~**less** a <clothes> impecable; <house> limpísimo. ~**light** n reflector m; (in theatre) foco m. ~**ted** a moteado; <material> de lunares. ~**ty** a (**-ier, -iest**) <skin> lleno de granos; <youth> con la cara llena de granos

spouse n cónyuge m & f

spout n pico m; (jet) chorro m

sprain vt hacerse un esguince en. ● n esguince m

sprang ⇨SPRING

spray n (of flowers) ramillete m; (from sea) espuma f; (liquid in spray form) espray m; (device) rociador m. ● vt rociar

spread vt (pt **spread**) (stretch, extend) extender; desplegar <wings>; difundir <idea, news>. ~ **butter on a piece of toast** untar una tostada con mantequilla. ● vi extenderse; <disease> propagarse; <idea, news> difundirse. ● n (of ideas) difusión f; (of disease, fire) propagación f; (Ⓘ, feast) festín m. ▢ ~ **out** vi (move apart) desplegarse

spree n. **go on a shopping** ~ ir de expedición a las tiendas

sprightly a (**-ier, -iest**) vivo

spring n (season) primavera f; (device) resorte m; (in mattress) muelle m, resorte m (LAm); (elasticity) elasticidad f; (water)

manantial m. ● a primaveral. ● vi (pt **sprang**, pp **sprung**) saltar; (issue) brotar. ~ **from sth** <problem> provenir de algo. ▢ ~ **up** vi surgir. ~**board** n trampolín m. ~**-clean** vi hacer una limpieza general. ~ **onion** n cebolleta f. ~**time** n primavera f. ~**y** a (**-ier, -iest**) <mattress, grass> mullido

sprinkle vt salpicar; (with liquid) rociar. ● n salpicadura f; (of liquid) rociada f. ~**r** n regadera f

sprint n carrera f corta. ● vi (Sport) esprintar; (run fast) correr. ~**er** n corredor m

sprout vi brotar. ● n brote m. (**Brussels**) ~**s** npl coles fpl de Bruselas

sprung ⇨SPRING

spud n Ⓘ patata f, papa f (LAm)

spun ⇨SPIN

spur n espuela f; (stimulus) acicate m. **on the** ~ **of the moment** sin pensarlo. ● vt (pt **spurred**). ~ (**on**) espolear; (fig) estimular

spurn vt desdeñar; (reject) rechazar

spurt vi <liquid> salir a chorros. ● n chorro m; (of activity) racha f

spy n espía m & f. ● vt descubrir, ver. ● vi espiar. ~ **on s.o.** espiar a uno

squabble vi reñir

squad n (Mil) pelotón m; (of police) brigada f; (Sport) equipo m. ~ **car** m coche m patrulla. ~**ron** n (Mil, Aviat) escuadrón m; (Naut) escuadra f

squalid a miserable

squall n turbión m

squalor n miseria f

squander vt derrochar; desaprovechar <opportunity>

square n cuadrado m; (in town) plaza f. ● a cuadrado; <meal>

S

decente; (🗓, old-fashioned) chapado a la antigua. ● vt (settle) arreglar; (Math) elevar al cuadrado. ● vi (agree) cuadrar. ◻ ~ **up** vi arreglar cuentas (with con). ~**ly** adv directamente

squash vt aplastar; (suppress) acallar. ● n. it was a terrible ~ íbamos (or iban) terriblemente apretujados; (drink) **orange** ~ naranjada f; (Sport) squash m; (vegetable) calabaza f. ~**y** a blando

squat vi (pt **squatted**) ponerse en cuclillas; (occupy illegally) ocupar sin autorización. ● a rechoncho y bajo. ~**ter** n ocupante m & f ilegal, okupa m & f

squawk n graznido m. ● vi graznar

squeak n chillido m; (of door) chirrido m. ● vi chillar; <door> chirriar; <shoes> crujir. ~**y** a chirriante

squeal n chillido m ● vi chillar

squeamish a impresionable, delicado

squeeze vt apretar; exprimir <lemon etc>. ● vi. ~ **in** meterse. ● n estrujón m; (of hand) apretón m

squid n calamar m

squiggle n garabato m

squint vi bizquear; (trying to see) entrecerrar los ojos. ● n estrabismo m

squirm vi retorcerse

squirrel n ardilla f

squirt vt <liquid> echar un chorro de. ● vi salir a chorros. ● n chorrito m

St abbr (= **saint**) S, San(to); (= **street**) C/, Calle f

stab vt (pt **stabbed**) apuñalar. ● n puñalada f; (pain) punzada f. **have a** ~ **at sth** intentar algo

stabili|ty n estabilidad f. ~**ze** vt/i estabilizar

stable a (-**er**, -**est**) estable. ● n caballeriza f, cuadra f

stack n montón m. ● vt. ~ (**up**) amontonar

stadium n (pl -**diums** or -**dia**) estadio m

staff n (stick) palo m; (employees) personal m. **teaching** ~ personal m docente. **a member of** ~ un empleado

stag n ciervo m. ~-**night**, ~-**party** n (before wedding) fiesta f de despedida de soltero; (men-only party) fiesta f para hombres

stage n (in theatre) escenario f; (platform) plataforma f; (phase) etapa f. **the** ~ (profession, medium) el teatro. ● vt poner en escena <play>; (arrange) organizar; (pej) orquestar. ~**coach** n diligencia f

stagger vi tambalearse. ● vt dejar estupefacto; escalonar <holidays etc>. ~**ing** a asombroso

stagna|nt a estancado. ~**te** vi estancarse

staid a serio, formal

stain vt manchar; (colour) teñir. ● n mancha f; (dye) tintura f. ~**ed glass window** n vidriera f de colores. ~**less steel** n acero m inoxidable. ~ **remover** n quitamanchas m

stair n escalón m. ~**s** npl escalera f. ~**case**, ~**way** n escalera f

stake n estaca f; (wager) apuesta f; (Com) intereses mpl. **be at** ~ estar en juego. ● vt estacar; jugarse <reputation>. ~ **a claim** reclamar

stala|ctite n estalactita f. ~**gmite** n estalagmita f

stale a (-**er**, -**est**) no fresco; <bread> duro; <smell> viciado. ~**mate** n (Chess) ahogado m; (deadlock) punto m muerto

stalk n tallo m. ● vt acechar. ● vi irse indignado

stall *n* (in stable) compartimiento *m*; (in market) puesto *m*. **~s** *npl* (in theatre) platea *f*, patio *m* de butacas. ● *vt* parar <*engine*>. ● *vi* <*engine*> pararse; (fig) andar con rodeos

stallion *n* semental *m*

stalwart *a* <*supporter*> leal, incondicional

stamina *n* resistencia *f*

stammer *vi* tartamudear. ● *n* tartamudeo *m*

stamp *vt* (with feet) patear; (press) estampar; (with rubber stamp) sellar; (fig) señalar. ● *vi* dar patadas en el suelo. ● *n* sello *m*, estampilla *f* (LAm), timbre *m* (Mex); (on passport) sello *m*; (with foot) patada *f*; (mark) marca *f*, señal *f*. □ **~ out** *vt* (fig) erradicar. **~ed addressed envelope** *n* sobre *m* franqueado con su dirección

stampede *n* estampida *f*. ● *vi* salir en estampida

stance *n* postura *f*

stand *vi* (*pt* **stood**) estar de pie, estar parado (LAm); (rise) ponerse de pie, pararse; (be) encontrarse; (Pol) presentarse como candidato (**for** en). **the offer ~s** la oferta sigue en pie. **~ to reason** ser lógico. ● *vt* (endure) soportar; (place) colocar. **~ a chance** tener una posibilidad. ● *n* posición *f*, postura *f*; (for lamp etc) pie *m*, sostén *m*; (at market) puesto *m*; (booth) quiosco *m*; (Sport) tribuna *f*. **make a ~ against sth** oponer resistencia a algo. □ **~ back** *vi* apartarse. □ **~ by** *vi* estar preparado. *vt* (support) apoyar. □ **~ down** *vi* retirarse. □ **~ for** *vt* significar. □ **~ in for** *vt* suplir a. □ **~ out** *vi* destacarse. □ **~ up** *vi* ponerse de pie, pararse (LAm). □ **~ up for** *vt* defender. **~ up for**

oneself defenderse. □ **~ up to** *vt* resistir a

standard *n* norma *f*; (level) nivel *m*; (flag) estandarte *m*. ● *a* estándar *a invar*, normal. **~ize** *vt* estandarizar. **~ lamp** *n* lámpara *f* de pie. **~s** *npl* principios *mpl*

stand: **~-by** *n* (at airport) stand-by *m*. **be on ~-by** <*police*> estar en estado de alerta. **~-in** *n* suplente *m & f*. **~ing** *a* de pie, parado (LAm); (permanent) permanente *f*. ● *n* posición *f*; (prestige) prestigio *m*. **~off** *n* (Amer, draw) empate *m*; (deadlock) callejón *m* sin salida. **~point** *n* punto *m* de vista. **~still** *n*. **be at a ~still** estar paralizado. **come to a ~still** <*vehicle*> parar; <*city*> quedar paralizado

stank ⇒STINK

staple *a* principal. ● *n* grapa *f*. ● *vt* sujetar con una grapa. **~r** *n* grapadora *f*

star *n* (incl Cinema, Theatre) estrella *f*; (asterisk) asterisco *m*. ● *vi* (*pt* **starred**). **~ in a film** protagonizar una película. **~board** *n* estribor *m*.

starch *n* almidón *m*; (in food) fécula *f*. ● *vt* almidonar. **~y** *a* <*food*> a base de féculas

stardom *n* estrellato *m*

stare *n* mirada *f* fija. ● *vi*. **~ (at)** mirar fijamente

starfish *n* estrella *f* de mar

stark *a* (**-er**, **-est**) escueto. ● *adv* completamente

starling *n* estornino *m*

starry *a* estrellado

start *vt* empezar, comenzar; encender <*engine*>; arrancar <*car*>; (cause) provocar; abrir <*business*>. ● *vi* empezar; <*car etc*> arrancar; (jump) dar un respingo. **to ~ with** (as linker) para empezar. **~ off by doing sth**

S

empezar por hacer algo. ● *n* principio *m*; (Sport) ventaja *f*; (jump) susto *m*. **make an early ~** (on journey) salir temprano. **~er** *n* (Auto) motor *m* de arranque; (Culin) primer plato *m*. **~ing-point** *n* punto *m* de partida

startle *vt* asustar

starv|ation *n* hambre *f*, inanición *f*. **~e** *vt* hacer morir de hambre. ● *vi* morirse de hambre. **I'm ~ing** me muero de hambre

state *n* estado *m*. **be in a ~** estar agitado. **the S~** los Estados *mpl* Unidos. ● *vt* declarar; expresar <*views*>; (fix) fijar. ● *a* del Estado; (Schol) público; (with ceremony) de gala. **~ly** *a* (**-ier, -iest**) majestuoso. **~ly home** *n* casa *f* solariega. **~ment** *n* declaración *f*; (account) informe *m*. **~sman** *n* estadista *m*

static *a* estacionario. ● *n* (interference) estática *f*

station *n* estación *f*; (on radio) emisora *f*; (TV) canal *m*. ● *vt* colocar; (Mil) estacionar. **~ary** *a* estacionario. **~er's** (**shop**) *n* papelería *f*. **~ery** *n* artículos *mpl* de papelería. **~ wagon** *n* (Amer) ranchera *f*, (coche *m*) familiar *m*, camioneta *f* (LAm)

statistic *n* estadística *f*. **~al** *a* estadístico. **~s** *n* (science) estadística *f*

statue *n* estatua *f*

stature *n* talla *f*, estatura *f*

status *n* posición *f* social; (prestige) categoría *f*; (Jurid) estado *m*

statut|e *n* estatuto *m*. **~ory** *a* estatutario

staunch *a* (**-er, -est**) leal

stave *n* (Mus) pentagrama *m*. □ **~ off** *vt* evitar

stay *n* (of time) estancia *f*, estadía *f* (LAm); (Jurid) suspensión *f*. ● *vi*

quedarse; (reside) alojarse. **I'm ~ing in a hotel** estoy en un hotel. □ **~ in** *vi* quedarse en casa. □ **~ up** *vi* quedarse levantado

stead *n*. **in s.o.'s ~** en lugar de uno. **stand s.o. in good ~** resultarle muy útil a uno. **~ily** *adv* firmemente; (regularly) regularmente. **~y** *a* (**-ier, -iest**) firme; (regular) regular; <*flow*> continuo; <*worker*> serio

steak *n*. **a ~** un filete. **some ~** carne para guisar

steal *vt* (*pt* **stole**, *pp* **stolen**) robar. **~ in** *vi* entrar a hurtadillas

stealth *n*. **by ~** sigilosamente. **~y** *a* sigiloso

steam *n* vapor *m*. **let off ~** (fig) desahogarse. ● *vt* (cook) cocer al vapor. ● *vi* echar vapor. □ **~ up** *vi* empañarse. **~ engine** *n* máquina *f* de vapor. **~er** *n* (ship) barco *m* de vapor. **~roller** *n* apisonadora *f*. **~y** *a* lleno de vapor

steel *n* acero *m*. ● *vt*. **~ o.s.** armarse de valor. **~ industry** *n* industria *f* siderúrgica

steep ● *a* (**-er, -est**) empinado; <*increase*> considerable; <*price*> 🄸 excesivo

steeple *n* aguja *f*, campanario *m*

steeply *adv* abruptamente; <*increase*> considerablemente

steer *vt* dirigir; gobernar <*ship*>. ● *vi* (in ship) estar al timón. **~ clear of** evitar. **~ing** *n* (Auto) dirección *f*. **~ing wheel** *n* volante *m*

stem *n* (of plant) tallo *m*; (of glass) pie *m*; (of word) raíz *f*. ● *vt* (*pt* **stemmed**) contener <*bleeding*>. ● *vi*. **~ from** provenir de

stench *n* hedor *m*

stencil *n* plantilla *f*

stenographer *n* estenógrafo *m*

step vi (pt **stepped**). ~ **in** sth pisar algo. □ ~ **aside** vi hacerse a un lado. □ ~ **down** vi retirarse. □ ~ **in** vi (fig) intervenir. □ ~ **up** vt intensificar; redoblar <security>. ● n paso m; (stair) escalón m; (fig) medida f. take ~s tomar medidas. be in ~ llevar el paso. be out of ~ no llevar el paso. ~**brother** n hermanastro m. ~**daughter** n hijastra f. ~**father** n padrastro m. ~**ladder** n escalera f de tijera. ~**mother** n madrastra f. ~**ping-stone** n peldaño m. ~**sister** n hermanastra f. ~**son** n hijastro m

stereo n (pl **-os** estéreo m. ● a estéreo a invar. ~**type** n estereotipo m

steril|e a estéril. ~**ize** vt esterilizar

sterling n libras fpl esterlinas. ● a <pound> esterlina

stern n (of boat) popa f. ● a (**-er, -est**) severo

stethoscope n estetoscopio m

stew vt/i guisar. ● n estofado m, guiso m

steward n administrador m; (on ship) camarero m; (air steward) sobrecargo m, aeromozo m (LAm). ~**ess** n camarera f; (on aircraft) auxiliar f de vuelo, azafata f

stick n palo m; (for walking) bastón m; (of celery etc) tallo m. ● vt (pt **stuck**) (glue) pegar; (🄸, put) poner; (thrust) clavar; (🄸, endure) soportar. ● vi pegarse; (jam) atascarse. □ ~ **out** vi sobresalir. □ ~ **to** vt ceñirse a. □ ~ **up for** vt 🄸 defender. ~**er** n pegatina f. ~**ing plaster** n esparadrapo m; (individual) tirita f, curita f (LAm). ~**ler** n. be a ~**ler for** insistir en. ~**y** a (**-ier, -iest**) <surface> pegajoso; <label> engomado

stiff a (**-er, -est**) rígido; <joint, fabric> tieso; <muscle> entumecido; (difficult) difícil; <manner> estirado; <drink> fuerte. have a ~ neck tener tortícolis. ~**en** vi (become rigid) agarrotarse; (become firm) endurecerse. ~**ly** adv rígidamente

stifl|e vt sofocar. ~**ing** a sofocante

stiletto (**heel**) n (pl **-os**) tacón m de aguja

still a inmóvil; (peaceful) tranquilo; <drink> sin gas. sit ~, stand ~ quedarse tranquilo. ● adv todavía, aún; (nevertheless) sin embargo. ~**born** a nacido muerto. ~ **life** n (pl **-s**) bodegón m. ~**ness** n tranquilidad f

stilted a rebuscado; <conversation> forzado

stilts npl zancos mpl

stimul|ant n estimulante m. ~**ate** vt estimular. ~**ation** n estímulo m. ~**us** n (pl **-li**) estímulo m

sting n picadura f; (organ) aguijón m. ● vt/i (pt **stung**) picar

stingy a (**-ier, -iest**) tacaño

stink n hedor m. ● vi (pt **stank** or **stunk**, pp **stunk**) apestar, oler mal

stipulat|e vt/i estipular. ~**ion** n estipulación f

stir vt (pt **stirred**) remover, revolver; (move) agitar; estimular <imagination>. ● vi moverse. ~ **up trouble** armar lío 🄸. ● n revuelo m, conmoción f

stirrup n estribo m

stitch n (in sewing) puntada f; (in knitting) punto m; (pain) dolor m costado. be in ~**es** 🄸 desternillarse de risa. ● vt coser

S

stock n (Com, supplies) existencias fpl; (Com, variety) surtido m; (livestock) ganado m; (Culin) caldo m. ~s and shares, ~s and bonds (Amer) acciones fpl. out of ~ agotado. take ~ of sth (fig) hacer un balance de algo. ● a estándar a invar; (fig) trillado. ● vt surtir, abastecer (with de). □ ~ up vi abastecerse (with de). ~broker n corredor m de bolsa. S~ Exchange n ~ing n media f. ~pile n reservas fpl. ● vt almacenar. ~-still a inmóvil. ~-taking n (Com) inventario m. ~y a <-ier, -iest> bajo y fornido

stodgy (-dgier, -dgiest) a pesado

stoke vt echarle carbón (or leña) a

stole ⇒STEAL

stolen ⇒STEAL

stomach n estómago m. ● vt soportar. ~-ache n dolor m de estómago

ston|e n piedra f; (in fruit) hueso m; (weight, pl stone) unidad de peso equivalente a 14 libras o 6,35 kg. ● a de piedra. ● vt apedrear. ~e-deaf a sordo como una tapia. ~y a <silence> sepulcral

stood ⇒STAND

stool n taburete m

stoop vi agacharse; (fig) rebajarse. ● n. have a ~ ser cargado de espaldas

stop vt (pt stopped) (halt, switch off) parar; (cease) terminar; (prevent) impedir; (interrupt) interrumpir. ~ doing sth dejar de hacer algo. ~ it! ¡basta ya! ● vi <bus> parar, detenerse; <clock> pararse. it's ~ped raining ha dejado de llover. ● n (bus etc) parada f; (break on journey) parada f. put a ~ to sth poner fin a algo. come to a ~ detenerse. ~gap n remedio m provisional. ~over n

escala f. ~page n suspensión f; paradero m (LAm); (of work) huelga f, paro m (LAm); (interruption) interrupción f. ~per n tapón m. ~watch n cronómetro m

storage n almacenamiento m

store n provisión f; (depot) almacén m; (Amer, shop) tienda f; (fig) reserva f. in ~ en reserva. ● vt (for future) poner en reserva; (in warehouse) almacenar. □ ~ up vt (fig) ir acumulando. ~keeper n (Amer) tendero m, comerciante m & f. ~room n almacén m; (for food) despensa f

storey n (pl -eys) piso m, planta f

stork n cigüeña f

storm n tempestad f. ● vi rabiar. ● vt (Mil) asaltar. ~y a tormentoso; <sea, relationship> tempestuoso

story n historia f; (in newspaper) artículo m; (rumour) rumor m; (fam, lie) mentira f, cuento m. ~-teller n cuentista m & f

stout a (-er, -est) robusto, corpulento. ● n cerveza f negra

stove n estufa f

stow vt guardar; (hide) esconder. □ ~ away vi viajar de polizón. ~away n polizón m & f

straggl|e vi rezagarse. ~y a desordenado

straight a (-er, -est) recto; (tidy) en orden; (frank) franco; <hair> lacio; (fam, conventional) convencional. be ~ estar derecho. ● adv <sit up> derecho; (direct) directamente; (without delay) inmediatamente. ~ away en seguida, inmediatamente. ~ on todo recto. ~ out sin rodeos. ● n recta f. ~en vt enderezar. □ ~en up vt ordenar. ~forward a franco; (easy) sencillo

strain n (tension) tensión f; (injury) torcedura f. ● vt forzar <voice, eyesight>; someter a demasiada tensión <relations>; (sieve) colar. ~ one's back hacerse daño en la espalda. ~ a muscle hacerse un esguince. ~ed a forzado; <relations> tirante. ~er n colador m. ~s npl (Mus) acordes mpl

strait n estrecho m. be in dire ~s estar en grandes apuros. ~jacket n camisa f de fuerza

strand n (thread) hebra f. a ~ of hair un pelo. ● vt. be ~ed <ship> quedar encallado. I was left ~ed me abandonaron a mi suerte

strange a (-er, -est) raro, extraño; (not known) desconocido. ~ly adv de una manera rara. ~ly enough aunque parezca mentira. ~r n desconocido m; (from another place) forastero m

strangle vt estrangular

strap n correa f; (of garment) tirante m. ● vt (pt strapped) atar con una correa

strat|egic a estratégico. ~egy n estrategia f

straw n paja f; (drinking ~) pajita f, paja f, popote m (Mex). the last ~ el colmo. ~berry n fresa f; (large) fresón m

stray vi (wander away) apartarse; (get lost) extraviarse; (deviate) desviarse (from de). ● a <animal> (without owner) callejero; (lost) perdido. ● n (without owner) perro m/gato m callejero; (lost) perro m/ gato m perdido

streak n lista f, raya f; (in hair) reflejo m; (in personality) veta f

stream n arroyo m; (current) corriente f. a ~ of abuse una sarta de insultos. ● vi correr. □ ~ out vi <people> salir en tropel. ~er n (paper) serpentina f; (banner) banderín m. ~line vt dar

líneaaerodinámica a; (simplify) racionalizar. ~lined a aerodinámico

street n calle f. ~car n (Amer) tranvía m. ~ lamp n farol m. ~ map, ~ plan n plano m

strength n fuerza f; (of wall etc) solidez f. ~en vt reforzar <wall>; fortalecer <muscle>

strenuous a enérgico; (arduous) arduo; (tiring) fatigoso

stress n énfasis f; (Gram) acento m; (Mec, Med, tension) tensión f. ● vt insistir en

stretch vt estirar; (extend) extender; forzar <truth>; estirar <resources>. ● vi estirarse; (when sleepy) desperezarse; (extend) extenderse; (be elastic) estirarse. ● n (period) período m; (of road) tramo m. at a ~ sin parar. □ ~ out vi <person> tenderse. ~er n camilla f

strict a (-er, -est) estricto; <secrecy> absoluto. ~ly adv con se veridad; <rigorously> terminantemente. ~ly speaking en rigor

stridden ⇒STRIDE

stride vi (pt strode, pp stridden) andar a zancadas. ● n zancada f. take sth in one's ~ tomarse algo con calma. ~nt a estridente

strife n conflicto m

strike vt (pt struck) golpear; encender <match>; encontrar <gold, oil>; <clock> dar. it ~s me as odd me parece raro. ● vi golpear; (go on strike) declararse en huelga; (be on strike) estar en huelga; (attack) atacar; <clock> dar la hora. ● n (of workers) huelga f, paro m; (attack) ataque m. come out on ~ ir a la huelga. □ ~ off, ~ out vt tachar. ~ up a friendship trabar amistad. ~r n huelguista m & f; (Sport) artillero m

S

striking a <resemblance> sorprendente; <colour> llamativo

string n cordel m, mecate m (Mex); (Mus) cuerda f; (of lies, pearls) sarta f; (of people) sucesión f. □ ~ **along** vt 🔢 engañar

stringent a riguroso

strip vt (pt **stripped**) desnudar <person>; deshacer <bed>. ● vi desnudarse. ● n tira f; (of land) franja f. ~ **cartoon** n historieta f

stripe n raya f. ~**d** a a rayas, rayado

strip lighting n luz f fluorescente

strive vi (pt **strove**, pp **striven**). ~ **to** esforzarse por

strode ⇒STRIDE

stroke n golpe m; (in swimming) brazada f; (Med) ataque m de apoplejía; (of pen etc) trazo m; (of clock) campanada f; (caress) caricia f. a ~ **of luck** un golpe de suerte. ● vt acariciar

stroll vi pasearse. ● n paseo m. ~**er** n (Amer) sillita f de paseo, cochecito m

strong a (-**er**, -**est**) fuerte. ~**hold** n fortaleza f; (fig) baluarte m. ~**ly** adv (greatly) fuertemente; <protest> enérgicamente; (deeply) profundamente. ~**room** n cámara f acorazada

strove ⇒STRIVE

struck ⇒STRIKE

structur|al a estructural. ~**e** n estructura f

struggle vi luchar; (thrash around) forcejear. ● n lucha f

strum vt (pt **strummed**) rasguear

strung ⇒STRING

strut n (in building) puntal m. ● vi (pt **strutted**) pavonearse

stub n (of pencil, candle) cabo m; (counterfoil) talón m; (of cigarette) colilla f. □ ~ **out** (pt **stubbed**) vt apagar

stubble n rastrojo m; (beard) barba f de varios días

stubborn a terco

stuck ⇒STICK. ● a. **the drawer is** ~ el cajón se ha atascado. **the door is** ~ la puerta se ha atrancado. ~**-up** a 🔢 estirado

stud n tachuela f; (for collar) gemelo m.

student n estudiante m & f; (at school) alumno m. ~ **driver** n (Amer) persona que está aprendiendo a conducir

studio n (pl -**os**) estudio m. ~ **apartment**, ~ **flat** n estudio m

studious a estudioso

study n estudio m. ● vt/i estudiar

stuff n 🔢 cosas fpl. **what's this** ~ **called?** ¿cómo se llama esta cosa? ● vt rellenar; disecar <animal>; (cram) atiborrar; (put) meter de prisa. ~ **o.s.** 🔢 darse un atracón. ~**ing** n relleno m. ~**y** a (-**ier**, -**iest**) mal ventilado; (old-fashioned) acartonado. **it's** ~ **y in here** está muy cargado el ambiente

stumbl|e vi tropezar. ~**e across**, ~**e on** vt dar con. ~**ing-block** n tropiezo m, impedimento m

stump n (of limb) muñón m; (of tree) tocón m

stun vt (pt **stunned**) (daze) aturdir; (bewilder) dejar atónito. ~**ning** a sensacional

stung ⇒STING

stunk ⇒STINK

stunt n 🔢 ardid m publicitario. ● vt detener, atrofiar. ~**ed** a (growth) atrofiado; (body) raquítico. ~**man** n especialista m. ~**woman** n especialista f

stupendous a estupendo

stupid a (foolish) tonto; (unintelligent) estúpido. ~**ity** n estupidez f. ~**ly** adv estúpidamente

stupor n estupor m

sturdy *a* (**-ier, -iest**) robusto

stutter *vi* tartamudear. ● *n* tartamudeo *m*

sty *n* (*pl* **sties**) pocilga *f*; (Med) orzuelo *m*

styl|e *n* estilo *m*; (fashion) moda *f*; (design, type) diseño *m*. **in ∼** a lo grande. ● *vt* diseñar. **∼ish** *a* elegante. **∼ist** *n* estilista *m & f*. **hair ∼ist** estilista *m & f*

stylus *n* (*pl* **-uses**) aguja *f* (*de tocadiscos*)

suave *a* elegante y desenvuelto

subconscious *a & n* subconsciente (*m*)

subdivide *vt* subdividir

subdued *a* apagado

subject *a* sometido. **∼ to** sujeto a. ● *n* (theme) tema *m*; (Schol) asignatura *f*, materia *f* (LAm); (Gram) sujeto *m*; (Pol) súbdito *m*. ● *vt* someter. **∼ive** *a* subjetivo

subjunctive *a & n* subjuntivo (*m*)

sublime *a* sublime

submarine *n* submarino *m*

submerge *vt* sumergir. ● *vi* sumergirse

submi|ssion *n* sumisión *f*. **∼t** *vt* (*pt* **submitted**) (subject) someter; presentar <*application*>. ● *vi* rendirse

subordinate *a & n* subordinado (*m*). ● *vt* subordinar

subscri|be *vi* suscribir. **∼be to** suscribirse a <*magazine*>. **∼ber** *n* suscriptor *m*. **∼ption** *n* (to magazine) suscripción *f*

subsequent *a* posterior, subsiguiente. **∼ly** *adv* posteriormente

subside *vi* <*land*> hundirse; <*flood*> bajar; <*storm, wind*> amainar. **∼nce** *n* hundimiento *m*

subsidiary *a* secundario; <*subject*> complementario. ● *n* (Com) filial

subsid|ize *vt* subvencionar, subsidiar (LAm). **∼y** *n* subvención *f*, subsidio *m*

substance *n* sustancia *f*

substandard *a* de calidad inferior

substantial *a* (sturdy) sólido; <*meal*> sustancioso; (considerable) considerable

substitut|e *n* (person) substituto *m*; (thing) sucedáneo *m*. ● *vt/i* sustituir. **∼ion** *n* sustitución *f*

subterranean *a* subterráneo

subtitle *n* subtítulo *m*

subtle *a* (**-er, -est**) sutil; (tactful) discreto. **∼ty** *n* sutileza *f*

subtract *vt* restar. **∼ion** *n* resta *f*

suburb *n* barrio *m* residencial de las afueras, colonia *f*. **the ∼s** las afueras *fpl*. **∼an** *a* suburbano. **∼ia** *n* zonas residenciales de las afueras de una ciudad

subversive *a* subversivo

subway *n* paso *m* subterráneo; (Amer) metro *m*

succeed *vi* <*plan*> dar resultado; <*person*> tener éxito. **∼ in doing** lograr hacer. ● *vt* suceder

success *n* éxito *m*. **∼ful** *a* <*person*> de éxito, exitoso (LAm). **the ∼ful applicant** el candidato que obtenga el puesto. **∼fully** *a* satisfactoriamente. **∼ion** *n* sucesión *f*. **for 3 years in ∼ion** durante tres años consecutivos. **in rapid ∼ion** uno tras otro. **∼ive** *a* sucesivo. **∼or** *n* sucesor *m*

succulent *a* suculento

succumb *vi* sucumbir

such *a* tal (+ *noun*), tan (+ *adj*). **∼ a big house** una casa tan grande. ● *pron* tal. **∼ and ∼** tal o cual. **∼ as** como. **∼ as it is** tal como es

S

suck *vt* chupar *<sweet, thumb>*; sorber *<liquid>*. □ **~ up** *vt* *<vacuum cleaner>* aspirar; *<pump>* succionar. □ **~ up to** *vt* 🗵 dar coba a. **~er** *n* (plant) chupón *m*; (🗵, person) imbécil *m*

suckle *vt* amamantar

suction *n* succión *f*

sudden *a* repentino. **all of a ~** de repente. **~ly** *adv* de repente

suds *npl* espuma *f* de jabón

sue *vt* (*pres p* **suing**) demandar (**for** por)

suede *n* ante *m*

suet *n* sebo *m*

suffer *vt* sufrir; (tolerate) aguantar. ● *vi* sufrir; (be affected) resentirse

suffic|e *vi* bastar. **~ient** *a* suficiente, bastante. **~iently** *adv* (lo) suficientemente

suffix *n* (*pl* **-ixes**) sufijo *m*

suffocat|e *vt* asfixiar. ● *vi* asfixiarse. **~ion** *n* asfixia *f*

sugar *n* azúcar *m & f*. **~ bowl** *n* azucarero *m*. **~y** *a* azucarado.

suggest *vt* sugerir. **~ion** *n* sugerencia *f*

suicid|al *a* suicida. **~e** *n* suicidio *m*. **commit ~e** suicidarse

suit *n* traje *m*; (woman's) traje *m* de chaqueta; (Cards) palo *m*; (Jurid) pleito *m*. ● *vt* venirle bien a, convenirle a; *<clothes>* quedarle bien a; (adapt) adaptar. **be ~ed to** *<thing>* ser apropiado para. **I'm not ~ed to this kind of work** no sirvo para este tipo de trabajo. **~able** *a* apropiado, adecuado. **~ably** *adv* *<dressed>* apropiadamente; *<qualified>* adecuadamente. **~case** *n* maleta *f*, valija *f* (LAm)

suite *n* (of furniture) juego *m*; (of rooms) suite *f*

sulk *vi* enfurruñarse

sullen *a* hosco

sulphur *n* azufre *m*. **~ic acid** *n* ácido *m* sulfúrico

sultan *n* sultán *m*

sultana *n* pasa *f* de Esmirna

sultry *a* (**-ier, -iest**) *<weather>* bochornoso; (fig) sensual

sum *n* (of money) suma *f*, cantidad *f*; (Math) suma *f*. ● □ **~ up** (*pt* **summed**) *vt* resumir. ● *vi* recapitular

summar|ily *adv* sumariamente. **~ize** *vt* resumir. **~y** *n* resumen *m*

summer *n* verano *m*. **~ camp** *n* (in US) colonia *f* de vacaciones. **~time** *n* verano *m*. **~y** *a* veraniego

summit *n* (of mountain) cumbre *f*. **~ conference** *n* conferencia *f* cumbre

summon *vt* llamar; convocar *<meeting, s.o. to meeting>*; (Jurid) citar. □ **~ up** *vt* armarse de. **~s** *n* (Jurid) citación *f*. ● *vt* citar

sumptuous *a* suntuoso

sun *n* sol *m*. **~bathe** *vi* tomar el sol, asolearse (LAm). **~beam** *n* rayo *m* de sol. **~burn** *n* quemadura *f* de sol. **~burnt** *a* quemado por el sol

Sunday *n* domingo *m*

sunflower *n* girasol *m*

sung ⇒SING

sunglasses *npl* gafas *fpl* de sol, lentes *mpl* de sol (LAm)

sunk ⇒SINK. **~en** ● *a* hundido

sun: ~light *n* luz *f* del sol. **~ny** *a* (**-ier, -iest**) *<day>* de sol; (place) soleado. **it is ~ny** hace sol. **~rise** *n* salida *f* del sol. **at ~rise** al amanecer. **~roof** *n* techo *m* corredizo. **~set** *n* puesta *f* del sol. **~shine** *n* sol *m*. **~stroke** *n* insolación *f*. **~tan** *n* bronceado *m*. **get a ~tan** broncearse. **~tan lotion** *n* bronceador *m*

super *a* 🔲 genial, super *a invar*

superb *a* espléndido

supercilious *a* desdeñoso

superficial *a* superficial

superfluous *a* superfluo

superhighway *n* (Amer, Auto) autopista *f*; (Comp) **information ~** autopista *f* de la comunicación

superhuman *a* sobrehumano

superintendent *n* director *m*; (Amer, of building) portero *m*; (of police) comisario *m*; (in US) superintendente *m & f*

superior *a & n* superior (*m*). **~ity** *n* superioridad *f*

superlative *a* inigualable. ● *n* superlativo *m*

supermarket *n* supermercado *m*

supernatural *a* sobrenatural

superpower *n* superpotencia *f*

supersede *vt* reemplazar, sustituir

supersonic *a* supersónico

superstitio|n *n* superstición *f*. **~us** *a* supersticioso

supervis|e *vt* supervisar. **~ion** *n* supervisión *f*. **~or** *n* supervisor *m*

supper *n* cena *f* (ligera), comida *f* (ligera) (LAm)

supple *a* flexible

supplement *n* suplemento *m*; (to diet, income) complemento *m*. ● *vt* complementar <*diet, income*>. **~ary** *a* suplementario

suppl|ier *n* (Com) proveedor *m*. **~y** *vt* suministrar; proporcionar <*information*>. **~y s.o. with sth** <*equipment*> proveer a uno de algo; (in business) abastecer a uno de algo. ● *n* suministro *m*. **~y and demand** oferta *f* y demanda. **~ies** *npl* provisiones *mpl*, víveres *mpl*; (Mil) pertrechos *mpl*. **office ~ies** artículos *mpl* de oficina

support *vt* (hold up) sostener; (back) apoyar; mantener <*family*>. ● *n* apoyo *m*; (Tec) soporte *m*. **~er** *n* partidario *m*; (Sport) hincha *m & f*

suppos|e *vt* suponer, imaginarse; (think) creer. **I'm ~ed to start work at nine** se supone que tengo que empezar a trabajar a las nueve. **~edly** *adv* supuestamente. **~ition** *n* suposición *f*

suppress *vt* reprimir <*feelings*>; sofocar <*rebellion*>. **~ion** *n* represión *f*

suprem|acy *n* supremacía *f*. **~e** *a* supremo

sure *a* (-er, -est) seguro. **make ~ that** asegurarse de que. ● *adv* ¡claro! **~ly** *adv* (undoubtedly) seguramente; (gladly) desde luego. **~ly you don't believe that!** ¡no te creerás eso! **~ty** *n* garantía *f*

surf *n* oleaje *m*; (foam) espuma *f*. ● *vi* hacer surf. ● *vt* (Comp) surfear, navegar

surface *n* superficie *f*. ● *a* superficial. ● *vt* recubrir (with de). ● *vi* salir a la superficie

surfboard *n* tabla *f* de surf

surfeit *n* exceso *m*

surf: ~er *n* surfista *m & f*; (Internet) internauta *m & f*. **~ing** *n* surf *m*

surge *vi* <*crowd*> moverse en tropel; <*sea*> hincharse. ● *n* oleada *f*; (in demand, sales) aumento *m*

surg|eon *n* cirujano *m*. **~ery** *n* cirugía *f*; (consulting room) consultorio *m*; (consulting hours) consulta *f*. **~ical** *a* quirúrgico

surly *a* (-ier, -iest) hosco

surmise *vt* conjeturar

surmount *vt* superar

surname *n* apellido *m*

surpass *vt* superar

surplus *a & n* excedente (*m*)

surpris|e *n* sorpresa *f.* ● *vt* sorprender. ~**ed** *a* sorprendido. ~**ing** *a* sorprendente. ~**ingly** *adv* sorprendentemente

surrender *vt* entregar. ● *vi* rendirse. ● *n* rendición *f*

surreptitious *a* furtivo

surround *vt* rodear; (Mil) rodear, cercar. ~**ing** *a* circundante. ~**ings** *npl* alrededores *mpl*; (environment) ambiente *m*

surveillance *n* vigilancia *f*

survey *n* inspección *f*; (report) informe *m*; (general view) vista *f* general. ● *vt* inspeccionar; (measure) medir; (look at) contemplar. ~**or** *n* topógrafo *m*, agrimensor *m*; (of building) perito *m*

surviv|al *n* supervivencia *f.* ~**e** *vt/i* sobrevivir. ~**or** *n* superviviente *m & f*

susceptible *a.* ~ **to** propenso a

suspect *vt* sospechar; sospechar de <*person*>. ● *a & n* sospechoso (*m*)

suspen|d *vt* suspender. ~**ders** *npl* (Amer, braces) tirantes *mpl.* ~**se** *n* (in film etc) suspense *m*, suspenso *m* (LAm). **keep s.o. in** ~**se** mantener a uno sobre ascuas. ~**sion** *n* suspensión *f.* ~**sion bridge** *n* puente *m* colgante

suspici|on *n* (belief) sospecha *f*; (mistrust) desconfianza *f.* ~**ous** *a* desconfiado; (causing suspicion) sospechoso

sustain *vt* sostener; mantener <*conversation, interest*>; (suffer) sufrir

SW *abbr* (= **south-west**) SO

swab *n* (specimen) muestra *f*, frotis *m*

swagger *vi* pavonearse

swallow *vt/i* tragar. ● *n* trago *m*; (bird) golondrina *f*

swam ⇒SWIM

swamp *n* pantano *m*, ciénaga *f.* ● *vt* inundar. ~**y** *a* pantanoso

swan *n* cisne *m*

swap *vt/i* (*pt* **swapped**) intercambiar. ~ **sth for sth** cambiar algo por algo. ● *n* cambio *m*

swarm *n* enjambre *m.* ● *vi* <*bees*> enjambrar; (fig) hormiguear

swarthy *a* (**-ier**, **-iest**) moreno

swat *vt* (*pt* **swatted**) matar (*con matamoscas etc*)

sway *vi* balancearse; (gently) mecerse. ● *vt* (influence) influir en

swear *vt/i* (*pt* **swore**, *pp* **sworn**) jurar. ~**word** *n* palabrota *f*

sweat *n* sudor *m*, transpiración *f.* ● *vi* sudar

sweat|er *n* jersey *m*, suéter *m.* ~**shirt** *n* sudadera *f.* ~**suit** *n* (Amer) chándal *m*, equipo *m* de deportes

swede *n* nabo *m* sueco

Swede *n* sueco *m.* ~**n** *n* Suecia *f.* ~**ish** *a* sueco. ● *n* (Lang) sueco *m.* ● *npl.* **the** ~ (people) los suecos

sweep *vt* (*pt* **swept**) barrer; deshollinar <*chimney*>. ● *vi* barrer. ● *n* barrido *m.* ~ **away** *vt* (carry away) arrastrar; (abolish) erradicar. ~**er** *n* barrendero *m.* ~**ing** *a* <*gesture*> amplio; <*changes*> radical; <*statement*> demasiado general

sweet *a* (**-er**, **-est**) dulce; (fragrant) fragante; (pleasant) agradable; (kind, gentle) dulce; (cute) rico. **have a** ~ **tooth** ser dulcero. ● *n* caramelo *m*, dulce *m* (Mex); (dish) postre *m.* ~**en** *vt* endulzar. ~**heart** *n* enamorado *m*; (as form of address) amor *m.* ~**ly** *adv* dulcemente. ~ **potato** *n* boniato *m*, batata *f*

swell *vt* (*pt* **swelled**, *pp* **swollen** *or* **swelled**) hinchar; (increase)

aumentar. ● *vi* hincharse;
(increase) aumentar. ● *a* (Amer 🔅)
fenomenal. ● *n* (of sea) oleaje *m*.
~**ing** *n* hinchazón *m*
sweltering *adj* sofocante
swept ⇒SWEEP
swerve *vi* virar bruscamente
swift *a* (**-er, -est**) veloz, rápido;
<*reply*> rápido. ● *n* (bird) vencejo
m. ~**ly** *adv* rápidamente
swig *vt* (*pt* **swigged**) 🔅 beber a
grandes tragos. ● *n* 🔅 trago *m*
swim *vi* (*pt* **swam**, *pp* **swum**)
nadar. ● *n* baño *m*. ~**mer** *n*
nadador *m*. ~**ming** *n* natación *f*.
~**ming bath(s)** *n(pl)* piscina *f*
cubierta, alberca *f* techada (Mex).
~**ming pool** *n* piscina *f*, alberca *f*
(Mex). ~**ming trunks** *npl* bañador
m, traje *m* de baño ~**suit** *n* traje
m de baño, bañador *m*
swindle *vt* estafar. ● *n* estafa *f*.
~**r** *n* estafador *m*
swine *npl* cerdos *mpl*. ● *n* (*pl*
swine) (🔅, person) canalla *m* & *f*.
~ **fever** *n* fiebre *f* porcina
swing *vt* (*pt* **swung**) balancear;
(object on rope) hacer oscilar. ● *vi*
(dangle) balancearse; (swing on a
swing) columpiarse; <*pendulum*>
oscilar. ~ **open/shut** abrirse/
cerrarse. ● *n* oscilación *f*, vaivén
m; (seat) columpio *m*; (in opinion)
cambio *m*. **in full** ~ en plena
actividad
swipe *vt* darle un golpe a; (🔅,
snatch) birlar. ● *n* golpe *m*
Swiss *a* suizo (*m*). ● *npl*. **the** ~
los suizos
switch *n* (Elec) interruptor *m*;
(exchange) intercambio *m*; (Amer,
Rail) agujas *fpl*. ● *vt* cambiar;
(deviate) desviar. ◻ ~ **off** *vt* (Elec)
apagar <*light, TV, heating*>;
desconectar <*electricity*>. ◻ ~ **on**
vt encender, prender (LAm);
arrancar <*engine*>. ~**board** *n*
centralita *f*

Switzerland *n* Suiza *f*
swivel *vi* (*pt* **swivelled**) girar.
● *vt* hacer girar
swollen ⇒SWELL. ● *a* hinchado
swoop *vi* <*bird*> abatirse; <*police*>
llevar a cabo una redada. ● *n* (of
bird) descenso *m* en picado *or*
(LAm) picada; (by police) redada *f*
sword *n* espada *f*
swore ⇒SWEAR
sworn ⇒SWEAR. ● *a* <*enemy*>
declarado; <*statement*> jurado
swot *vt/i* (*pt* **swotted**) (Schol, 🔅)
empollar, estudiar como loco. ● *n*
(Schol, 🔅) empollón *m*, matado *m*
(Mex)
swum ⇒SWIM
swung ⇒SWING
syllable *n* sílaba *f*
syllabus *n* (*pl* **-buses**) plan *m* de
estudios; (of a particular subject)
programa *m*
symbol *n* símbolo *m*. ~**ic(al)** *a*
simbólico. ~**ism** *n* simbolismo *m*.
~**ize** *vt* simbolizar
symmetr|ical *a* simétrico. ~**y** *n*
simetría *f*
sympath|etic *a* comprensivo;
(showing pity) compasivo. ~**ize** *vi*
comprender; (commiserate) ~**ize**
with s.o. compadecer a uno. ~**y** *n*
comprensión *f*; (pity) compasión *f*;
(condolences) pésame *m*
symphony *n* sinfonía *f*
symptom *n* síntoma *m*. ~**atic** *a*
sintomático
synagogue *n* sinagoga *f*
synchronize *vt* sincronizar
syndicate *n* agrupación *f*; (Amer,
TV) agencia *f* de distribución
periodística
synonym *n* sinónimo *m*. ~**ous** *a*
sinónimo
syntax *n* sintaxis *f*

S

synthesi|s *n* (*pl* **-theses**) síntesis *f*. **~ze** *vt* sintetizar

synthetic *a* sintético

syringe *n* jeringa *f*, jeringuilla *f*

syrup *n* (sugar solution) almíbar *m*; (with other ingredients) jarabe *m*; (medicine) jarabe *m*

system *n* sistema *m*, método *m*; (Tec, Mec, Comp) sistema *m*. **the digestive ~** el aparato digestivo. **~atic** *a* sistemático. **~atically** *adv* sistemáticamente. **~s analyst** *n* analista *m & f* de sistemas

tab *n* (flap) lengüeta *f*; (label) etiqueta *f*

table *n* mesa *f*; (list) tabla *f*. **~cloth** *n* mantel *m*. **~ mat** *n* salvamanteles *m*. **~spoon** *n* cuchara *f* grande; (measure) cucharada *f* (grande)

tablet *n* pastilla *f*; (pill) comprimido *m*

table tennis *n* tenis *m* de mesa, ping-pong *m*

tabloid *n* tabloide *m*

taboo *a & n* tabú (*m*)

tacit *a* tácito

taciturn *a* taciturno

tack *n* tachuela *f*; (stitch) hilván *m*. ● *vt* clavar con tachuelas; (sew) hilvanar. ● *vi* (Naut) virar □ **~ on** *vt* añadir.

tackle *n* (equipment) equipo *m*; (soccer) entrada *f* fuerte; (US football, Rugby) placaje *m*. **fishing ~** aparejo *m* de pesca. ● *vt* abordar

<problem>; (in soccer) entrarle a; (in US football, Rugby) placar

tacky *a* pegajoso

tact *n* tacto *m*. **~ful** *a* diplomático

tactic|al *a* táctico. **~s** *npl* táctica *f*

tactless *a* indiscreto

tadpole *n* renacuajo *m*

tag *n* (label) etiqueta *f*. □ **~ along** (*pt* **tagged**) *vt* 🛈 seguir

tail *n* (of horse, fish, bird) cola *f*; (of dog, pig) rabo *m*. **~s** *npl* (tailcoat) frac *m*; (of coin) cruz *f*. ● *vt* seguir. □ **~ off** *vi* disminuir.

tailor *n* sastre *m*. **~ed** *a* entallado. **~-made** *n* hecho a (la) medida

taint *vt* contaminar

take *vt* (*pt* **took**, *pp* **taken**) tomar, coger (esp Spain), agarrar (esp LAm); (capture) capturar; (endure) aguantar; (require) requerir; llevar *<time>*; tomar *<bath>*; tomar *<medicine>*; (carry) llevar; aceptar *<cheque>*. **I ~ a size 10** uso la talla 14. ● *n* (Cinema) toma *f*. □ **~ after** *vt* parecerse a. □ **~ away** *vt* llevarse; (confiscate) quitar. □ **~ back** *vt* retirar *<statement etc>*. □ **~ in** *vt* achicar *<garment>*; (understand) asimilar; (deceive) engañar. □ **~ off** *vt* (remove) quitar, sacar; quitarse *<shoes, jacket>*; (mimic) imitar. *vi* (Aviat) despegar. □ **~ on** *vt* contratar *<employee>*. □ **~ out** *vt* sacar. □ **~ over** *vt* tomar posesión de; hacerse cargo de *<job>*. *vi* (assume control) asumir el poder. □ **~ up** *vt* empezar a hacer *<hobby>*; aceptar *<challenge>*; subir *<hem>*; llevar *<time>*; ocupar *<space>*. **~-off** *n* despegue *m*. **~-over** *n* (Com) absorción *f*

takings *npl* recaudación *f*; (at box office) taquilla *f*

talcum powder *n* polvos *mpl* de talco, talco *m* (LAm)

tale *n* cuento *m*

talent *n* talento *m*. ~**ed** *a* talentoso

talk *vt/i* hablar. ~ **to s.o.** hablar con uno. ~ **about** hablar de. ● *n* conversación *f*; (lecture) charla *f*. □ ~ **over** *vt* discutir. ~**ative** *a* hablador

tall *a* (-er, -est) alto. ~ **story** *n* 🔢 cuento *m*

tally *vi* coincidir (**with** con)

talon *n* garra *f*

tambourine *n* pandereta *f*

tame *a* (-er, -est) <*animal*> (by nature) manso; (tamed) domado. ● *vt* domar <*wild animal*>

tamper *vi*. ~ **with** tocar; (alter) alterar, falsificar

tampon *n* tampón *m*

tan *vi* (*pt* **tanned**) broncearse. ● *n* bronceado *m*. **get a** ~ broncearse. ● *a* habano

tang *n* sabor *m* fuerte

tangent *n* tangente *f*

tangerine *n* mandarina *f*

tangible *a* tangible

tangle *vt* enredar. **get** ~**d** (**up**) enredarse. ● *n* enredo *m*, maraña *f*

tango *n* (*pl* -os) tango *m*

tank *n* depósito *m*; (Auto) tanque *m*; (Mil) tanque *m*

tanker *n* (ship) buque *m* cisterna; (truck) camión *m* cisterna

tantrum *n* berrinche *m*, rabieta *f*

tap *n* grifo *m*, llave *f* (LAm); (knock) golpecito *m*. ● *vt* (*pt* **tapped**) (knock) dar un golpecito en; interceptar <*phone*>. ● *vi* dar golpecitos (**on** en). ~ **dancing** *n* claqué *m*

tape *n* cinta *f*; (Med) esparadrapo *m*. ● *vt* (record) grabar. ~**-measure** *n* cinta *f* métrica

taper *vt* afilar. ● *vi* afilarse. □ ~ **off** *vi* disminuir

tape recorder *n* magnetofón *m*, magnetófono *m*

tapestry *n* tapiz *m*

tar *n* alquitrán *m*. ● *vt* (*pt* **tarred**) alquitranar

target *n* blanco *m*; (fig) objetivo *m*

tarmac *n* pista *f*. **T**~ *n* (Amer, P) asfalto *m*

tarnish *vt* deslustrar; empañar <*reputation*>

tart *n* pastel *m*; (individual) pastelillo *m*; (🔣, woman) prostituta *f*, fulana *f* 🔢. ● *vt*. ~ **o.s. up** 🔢 engalanarse. ● *a* (-er, -est) ácido

tartan *n* tartán *m*, tela *f* escocesa

task *n* tarea *f*. **take to** ~ reprender

tassel *n* borla *f*

tast|e *n* sabor *m*, gusto *m*; (liking) gusto *m*. ● *vt* probar. ~ **of** saber a. ~**eful** *a* de buen gusto. ~**eless** *a* soso; (fig) de mal gusto. ~**y** *a* (-ier, -iest) sabroso

tat ⇒TIT FOR TAT

tatter|ed *a* hecho jirones. ~**s** *npl* andrajos *mpl*

tattoo *n* (on body) tatuaje *m*. ● *vt* tatuar

tatty *a* (-ier, -iest) gastado, estropeado

taught ⇒TEACH

taunt *vt* provocar mediante burlas. ● *n* pulla *f*

Taurus *n* Tauro *m*

taut *a* tenso

tavern *n* taberna *f*

tax *n* impuesto *m*. ● *vt* imponer contribuciones a <*person*>; gravar <*thing*>; (strain) poner a prueba. ~**able** *a* imponible. ~**ation** *n*

T

impuestos *mpl*; (system) sistema *m* tributario. ~ **collector** *n* recaudador *m* de impuestos. ~**-free** *a* libre de impuestos

taxi *n* (*pl* **-is**) taxi *m*. ● *vi* (*pt* **taxied**, *pres p* **taxiing**) <*aircraft*> rodar por la pista

taxpayer *n* contribuyente *m* & *f*

tea *n* té *m*; (afternoon tea) merienda *f*, té *m*. ~ **bag** *n* bolsita *f* de té

teach *vt* (*pt* **taught**) dar clases de, enseñar <*subject*>; dar clase a <*person*>. ~ **school** (Amer) dar clase(s) en un colegio. ● *vi* dar clase(s). ~**er** *n* profesor *m*; (primary) maestro *m*. ~**ing** *n* enseñanza *f*. ● *a* docente

tea: ~**cup** *n* taza *f* de té

team *n* equipo *m*. □ ~ **up** *vi* asociarse (with con). ~ **work** *n* trabajo *m* en equipo

teapot *n* tetera *f*

tear[1] *vt* (*pt* **tore**, *pp* **torn**) romper, rasgar. ● *vi* romperse, rasgarse. ● *n* rotura *f*; (rip) desgarrón *m*. □ ~ **along** *vi* ir a toda velocidad. □ ~ **apart** *vt* desgarrar. □ ~ **off**, ~ **out** *vt* arrancar. □ ~ **up** *vt* romper

tear[2] *n* lágrima *f*. **be in** ~**s** estar llorando. ~**ful** *a* lloroso <*farewell*> triste. ~ **gas** *n* gas *m* lacrimógeno

tease *vt* tomarle el pelo a

tea: ~ **set** *n* juego *m* de té. ~**spoon** *n* cucharita *f*, cucharilla *f*; (amount) cucharadita *f*

teat *n* (of animal) tetilla *f*; (for bottle) tetina *f*

tea towel *n* paño *m* de cocina

techni|cal *a* técnico. ~**cality** *n n* detalle *m* técnico. ~**cally** *adv* técnicamente. ~**cian** *n* técnico *m*.

technique *n* técnica *f*

technolog|ical *a* tecnológico. ~**y** *n* tecnología *f*

teddy bear *n* osito *m* de peluche

tedi|ous *a* tedioso

teem *vi* abundar (**with** en), estar repleto (**with** de)

teen|age *a* adolescente; (for teenagers) para jóvenes. ~**ager** *n* adolescente *m* & *f*. ~**s** *npl* adolescencia *f*

teeny *a* (**-ier**, **-iest**) ⊡ chiquito

teeter *vi* balancearse

teeth ⇒TOOTH. ~**e** *vi*. he's ~ing le están saliendo los dientes. ~**ing troubles** *npl* (fig) problemas *mpl* iniciales

tele|communications *npl* telecomunicaciones *fpl*. ~**gram** *n* telegrama *m*. ~**pathic** *a* telepático. ~**pathy** *n* telepatía *f*

telephon|e *n* teléfono *m*. ● *vt* llamar por teléfono. ~**e booth**, ~**e box** *n* cabina *f* telefónica. ~**e call** *n* llamada *f* telefónica. ~ **card** *n* tarjeta *f* telefónica. ~**e directory** *n* guía *f* telefónica. ~**e exchange** *n* central *f* telefónica. ~**ist** *n* telefonista *m* & *f*

tele|sales *npl* televentas *fpl*. ~**scope** *n* telescopio *m*. ~**scopic** *a* telescópico. ~**text** *n* teletex(to) *m*

televis|e *vt* televisar. ~**ion** *n* (medium) televisión *f*. ~**ion** (set) *n* televisor *m*

teleworking *n* teletrabajo *m*

telex *n* télex *m*

tell *vt* (*pt* **told**) decir; contar <*story, joke*>; (distinguish) distinguir. ~ **the difference** notar la diferencia. ~ **the time** decir la hora. ● *vi* (produce an effect) tener efecto; (know) saber. □ ~ **off** *vt* regañar. ~**ing** *a* revelador. ~**-tale** *n* soplón *m*. ● *a* revelador

telly *n* ⊡ tele *f*

temp *n* empleado *m* eventual *or* temporal

temper n (mood) humor m; (disposition) carácter m; (fit of anger) cólera f. **be in a ~** estar furioso. **lose one's ~** perder los estribos. **~ament** n temperamento m. **~amental** a temperamental. **~ate** a templado. **~ature** n temperatura f. **have a ~ature** tener fiebre

tempestuous a tempestuoso

temple n templo m; (Anat) sien f

tempo n (pl **-os** or **tempi**) ritmo m

temporar|ily adv temporalmente, temporariamente (LAm). **~y** a temporal, provisional; <job> eventual, temporal

tempt vt tentar. **~ation** n tentación f. **~ing** a tentador

ten a & n diez (m)

tenaci|ous a tenaz. **~ty** n tenacidad f

tenan|cy n inquilinato m. **~t** n inquilino m, arrendatorio m

tend vi. **~ to** tender a. ● vt cuidar (de). **~ency** n tendencia f

tender a (soft); (painful) sensible. ● n (Com) oferta f. **legal ~** n moneda f de curso legal. ● vt ofrecer, presentar. **~ly** adv tiernamente

tendon n tendón m

tennis n tenis m

tenor n tenor m

tens|e a (**-er**, **-est**) (taut) tenso, tirante; <person> tenso. ● n (Gram) tiempo m. **~ion** n tensión f; (between two parties) conflicto m

tent n tienda f (de campaña), carpa f (LAm)

tentacle n tentáculo m

tentative a <plan> provisional; <offer> tentativo; <person> indeciso

tenterhooks npl. **be on ~** estar en ascuas

tenth a & n décimo (m)

tenuous a <claim> poco fundado; <link> indirecto

tenure n tenencia f; (period of office) ejercicio m

tepid a tibio

term n (of time) período m; (Schol) trimestre m; (word etc) término m. **~s** npl condiciones fpl; (Com) precio m. **on good/bad ~s** en buenas/malas relaciones. ● vt calificar de

termin|al a terminal. ● n (transport) terminal f; (Comp, Elec) terminal m. **~ate** vt poner fin a; poner término a <contract>; (Amer, fire) despedir. ● vi terminarse. **~ology** n terminología f

terrace n terraza f; (houses) hilera f de casas

terrain n terreno m

terrestrial a terrestre

terribl|e a espantoso. **~y** adv terriblemente

terrif|ic a (🆃, excellent) estupendo; (🆃, huge) enorme. **~ied** a aterrorizado. **~y** vt aterrorizar. **~ying** a aterrador

territor|ial a territorial. **~y** n territorio m

terror n terror m. **~ism** n terrorismo m. **~ist** n terrorista m & f. **~ize** vt aterrorizar

terse a seco, lacónico

test n (of machine, drug) prueba f; (exam) prueba f, test m; (of blood) análisis m; (for eyes, hearing) examen m. ● vt probar, poner a prueba <product>; hacerle una prueba a <student>; evaluar <knowledge>; examinar <sight>

testament n (will) testamento m. **Old/New T~** Antiguo/Nuevo Testamento

testicle n testículo m

testify vt atestiguar. ● vi declarar

T

testimon|ial n recomendación f. **~y** n testimonio m

test: **~ match** n partido m internacional. **~ tube** n tubo m de ensayo, probeta f

tether vt atar. ●n. **be at the end of one's ~** no poder más

text n texto m. ●vt mandar un mensaje a. **~book** n libro m de texto

textile a & n textil (m)

texture n textura f

Thames n Támesis m

than conj que; (with quantity) de

thank vt darle las gracias a, agradecer. **~ you** gracias. **~ful** a agradecido. **~fully** adv (happily) gracias a Dios. **~less** a ingrato. **~s** npl agradecimiento m. **~s!** 🔲 ¡gracias!. **~s to** gracias a

Thanksgiving (Day) n (in US) el día de Acción de Gracias

that a (pl those) ese, aquel, esa, aquella. ●pron (pl those) ése, aquél, ésa, aquélla. **~ is** es decir. **~'s not true** eso no es cierto. **~'s why** por eso. **is ~ you?** ¿eres tú? **like ~** así. ●adv tan. ●rel pron que; (with prep) el que, la que, el cual, la cual. ●conj que

thatched a <roof> de paja; <cottage> con techo de paja

thaw vt descongelar. ●vi descongelarse; <snow> derretirse. ●n deshielo m

the

●definite article
····▶el (m), la (f), los (mpl), las (fpl). **~ building** el edificio. **~ windows** las ventanas

❗ Feminine singular nouns beginning with a stressed or accented a or ha take the article el instead of la, e.g.

~ soul el alma; **~ axe** el hacha. **~ eagle** el águila.

Note that when el follows the prepositions de and a, it combines to form del and al, e.g. **of ~ group** del grupo. **I went to ~ bank** fui al banco

····▶(before an ordinal number in names, titles) not translated. **Henry ~ Eighth** Enrique Octavo. **Elizabeth ~ Second** Isabel Segunda

····▶(in abstractions) lo. **~ impossible** lo imposible

theatr|e n teatro m; (Amer, movie theatre) cine m. **~ical** a teatral

theft n hurto m

their a su, sus pl. **~s** poss pron (el) suyo m, (la) suya f, (los) suyos mpl, (las) suyas fpl

them pron (accusative) los m, las f; (dative) les; (after prep) ellos m, ellas f

theme n tema m. **~ park** n parque m temático. **~ song** n motivo m principal

themselves pron ellos mismos m, ellas mismas f; (reflexive) se; (after prep) sí mismos m, sí mismas f

then adv entonces; (next) luego, después. **by ~** para entonces. **now and ~** de vez en cuando. **since ~** desde entonces. ●a entonces

theology n teología f

theor|etical a teórico. **~y** n teoría f

therap|eutic a terapéutico. **~ist** n terapeuta m & f. **~y** n terapia f

there adv ahí; (further away) allí, ahí; (less precise, further) allá. **~ is, ~ are** hay. **~ it is** ahí está. **down ~** ahí abajo. **up ~** ahí arriba. ●int. **~!** **that's the last box** ¡listo! ésa es la última caja. **~, ~, don't**

cry! vamos, no llores. **~abouts** *adv* por ahí. **~fore** *adv* por lo tanto.

thermometer *n* termómetro *m*

Thermos *n* (P) termo *m*

thermostat *n* termostato *m*

thesaurus *n* (*pl* **-ri**) diccionario *m* de sinónimos

these *a* estos, estas. ● *pron* éstos, éstas

thesis *n* (*pl* **theses**) tesis *f*

they *pron* ellos *m*, ellas *f*. **~ say that** dicen *or* se dice que

they'd = they had, they would

they'll = they will

they're = they are

they've = they have

thick *a* (**-er**, **-est**) <*layer, sweater*> grueso, gordo; <*sauce*> espeso; <*fog, smoke*> espeso, denso; <*fur*> tupido; ((I), stupid) burro. ● *adv* espesamente, densamente. ● *n*. **in the ~ of** en medio de. **~en** *vt* espesar. ● *vi* espesarse. **~et** *n* matorral *m*. **~ness** *n* (of fabric) grosor *m*; (of paper, wood, wall) espesor *m*

thief *n* (*pl* **thieves**) ladrón *m*

thigh *n* muslo *m*

thimble *n* dedal *m*

thin *a* (**thinner**, **thinnest**) <*person*> delgado, flaco; <*layer, slice*> fino; <*hair*> ralo

thing *n* cosa *f*. **it's a good ~ (that)...** menos mal que.... **just the ~** exactamente lo que se necesita. **poor ~!** ¡pobrecito!

think *vt* (*pt* **thought**) pensar, creer. ● *vi* pensar (**about** en); (carefully) reflexionar; (imagine) imaginarse. **I ~ so** creo que sí. **~ of s.o.** pensar en uno. **I hadn't thought of that** eso no se me ha ocurrido. **~ over** *vt* pensar bien. **~ up** *vt* idear, inventar. **~er** *n*

pensador *m*. **~-tank** *n* gabinete *m* estratégico

third *a* tercero, (before masculine singular noun) tercer. ● *n* tercio *m*, tercera parte *f*. **~ (gear)** *n* (Auto) tercera *f*. **~-rate** *a* muy inferior. **T~ World** *n* Tercer Mundo *m*

thirst *n* sed *f*. **~y** *a* sediento. **be ~y** tener sed

thirt|een *a* & *n* trece (*m*). **~teenth** *a* decimotercero. ● *n* treceavo *m* **~ieth** *a* trigésimo. ● *n* treintavo *m*. **~y** *a* & *n* treinta (*m*)

this *a* (*pl* **these**) este, esta. **~ one** éste, ésta. ● *pron* (*pl* **these**) éste, ésta, esto. **like ~** así

thistle *n* cardo *m*

thong *n* correa *f*; (Amer, sandal) chancla *f*

thorn *n* espina *f*. **~y** *a* espinoso

thorough *a* <*investigation*> riguroso; <*cleaning etc*> a fondo; <*person*> concienzudo. **~bred** *a* de pura sangre. **~fare** *n* vía *f* pública; (street) calle *f*. **no ~fare** prohibido el paso. **~ly** *adv* <*clean*> a fondo; <*examine*> minuciosamente; (completely) perfectamente

those *a* esos, esas, aquellos, aquellas. ● *pron* ésos, ésas, aquéllos, aquéllas

though *conj* aunque. ● *adv* sin embargo. **as ~** como si

thought ⇒THINK. ● *n* pensamiento *m*; (idea) idea *f*. **~ful** *a* pensativo; (considerate) atento. **~fully** *adv* pensativamente; (considerately) atentamente. **~less** *a* desconsiderado

thousand *a* & *n* mil (*m*). **~th** *a* & *n* milésimo (*m*)

thrash *vt* azotar; (defeat) derrotar

thread *n* hilo *m*; (of screw) rosca *f*. ● *vt* enhebrar <*needle*>; ensartar <*beads*>. **~bare** *a* gastado, raído

T

threat n amenaza f. ~**en** vt/i amenazar. ~**ening** a amenazador
three a & n tres (m). ~**fold** a triple. ● adv tres veces
threshold n umbral m
threw ⇒THROW
thrift n economía f, ahorro m. ~**y** a frugal
thrill n emoción f. ● vt emocionar. ~**ed** a contentísimo (**with** con). ~**er** n (book) libro m de suspense or (LAm) suspenso; (film) película f de suspense or (LAm) suspenso. ~**ing** a emocionante
thriv|e vi prosperar. ~**ing** a próspero
throat n garganta f
throb vi (pt **throbbed**) palpitar; (with pain) dar punzadas; <engine> vibrar. ~**bing** a <pain> punzante
throes npl. be in one's death ~ estar agonizando
throne n trono m
throng n multitud f
throttle n (Auto) acelerador m (que se acciona con la mano). ● vt estrangular
through prep por, a través de; (during) durante; (by means of) a través de; (Amer, until and including) **Monday** ~ **Friday** de lunes a viernes. ● adv de parte a parte, de un lado a otro; (entirely) completamente; (to the end) hasta el final. be ~ (finished) haber terminado. ● a <train etc> directo. no ~ road calle sin salida. ~**out** prep por todo; (time) durante todo. ~**out his career** a lo largo de su carrera
throve ⇒THRIVE
throw vt (pt **threw**, pp **thrown**) tirar, aventar (Mex); lanzar <grenade, javelin>; (disconcert) desconcertar; 🄵 hacer, dar <party>. ● n (of ball) tiro m; (of dice)

tirada f. □ ~ **away** vt tirar. □ ~ **up** vi (vomit) vomitar.
thrush n tordo m
thrust vt (pt **thrust**) empujar; (push in) clavar. ● n empujón m; (of sword) estocada f
thud n ruido m sordo
thug n matón m
thumb n pulgar m. ● vt. ~ **a lift** ir a dedo. ~**tack** n (Amer) chincheta f, tachuela f, chinche f (Mex)
thump vt golpear. ● vi <heart> latir fuertemente. ● n golpazo m
thunder n truenos mpl, (of traffic) estruendo m. ● vi tronar. ~**bolt** n rayo m. ~**storm** n tormenta f eléctrica. ~**y** a con truenos
Thursday n jueves m
thus adv así
thwart vt frustrar
tic n tic m
tick n (sound) tic m; (insect) garrapata f, (mark) marca f, visto m, palomita f (Mex); (instant) momentito m. ● vi hacer tictac. ● vt. ~ (**off**) marcar
ticket n (for bus, train) billete m, boleto m (LAm); (for plane) pasaje m, billete m; (for theatre, museum) entrada f; (for baggage, coat) ticket m; (fine) multa f. ~ **collector** n revisor m. ~ **office** n (transport) mostrador m de venta de billetes or (LAm) boletos; (in theatre) taquilla f, boletería f (LAm)
tickl|e vt hacerle cosquillas a. ● n cosquilleo m. ~**ish** a. be ~**ish** tener cosquillas
tidal wave n maremoto m
tide n marea f. **high/low** ~ marea alta/baja. □ ~ **over** vt ayudar a salir de un apuro
tid|ily adv ordenadamente. ~**iness** n orden m. ~**y** a (-**ier**, -**iest**) ordenado. ● vt/i ~**y** (**up**) ordenar, arreglar

tie vt (pres p **tying**) atar, amarrar (LAm); hacer <knot>. ● vi (Sport) empatar. ● n (constraint) atadura f; (bond) lazo m; (necktie) corbata f; (Sport) empate m. ~ **in with** vt concordar con. □ ~ **up** vt atar. **be** ~**d up** (busy) estar ocupado

tier n hilera f superpuesta; (in stadium etc) grada f; (of cake) piso m

tiger n tigre m

tight a (-er, -est) <clothes> ajustado, ceñido; (taut) tieso; <control> estricto; <knot, nut> apretado; (🇮, drunk) borracho. ~**en** vt apretar. □ ~**en up** vt hacer más estricto. ~**-fisted** a tacaño. ~**ly** adv bien, fuerte; <fastened> fuertemente. ~**rope** n cuerda f floja. ~**s** npl (for ballet etc) leotardo(s) m(pl); (pantyhose) medias fpl

tile n (decorative) azulejo m; (on roof) teja f; (on floor) baldosa f. ● vt azulejar; tejar <roof>; embaldosar <floor>

till prep hasta. ● conj hasta que. ● n caja f. ● vt cultivar

tilt vt inclinar. ● vi inclinarse. ● n inclinación f

timber n madera f (para construcción)

time n tiempo m; (moment) momento m; (occasion) ocasión f; (by clock) hora f; (epoch) época f; (rhythm) compás m. **at** ~**s** a veces. **for the** ~ **being** por el momento. **from** ~ **to** ~ de vez en cuando. **have a good** ~ divertirse, pasarlo bien. **in a year's** ~ dentro de un año. **in no** ~ en un abrir y cerrar de ojos. **in** ~ a tiempo; (eventually) con el tiempo. **arrive on** ~ llegar a tiempo. **it's** ~ **we left** es hora de irnos. ● vt tomar el tiempo a <runner>; cronometrar <race>. ~**bomb** n bomba f de tiempo. ~**ly** a oportuno. ~**r** n cronómetro m;

(Culin) avisador m; (with sand) reloj m de arena; (Elec) interruptor m de reloj. ~**s** prep. **2** ~**s 4 is 8** 2 (multiplicado) por 4 son 8. ~**table** n horario m

timid a tímido; (fearful) miedoso

tin n estaño m; (container) lata f. ~ **foil** n papel m de estaño

tinge vt. **be** ~**d with sth** estar matizado de algo. ● n matiz m

tingle vi sentir un hormigueo

tinker vi. ~ **with** juguetear con

tinkle vi tintinear

tinned a en lata, enlatado

tin opener n abrelatas m

tint n matiz m

tiny a (-ier, -iest) minúsculo, diminuto

tip n punta f. ● vt (pt **tipped**) (tilt) inclinar; (overturn) volcar; (pour) verter; (give gratuity to) darle (una) propina a. □ ~ **off** vt avisar. □ ~ **out** vt verter. □ ~ **over** vi caerse. n propina f; (advice) consejo m (práctico); (for rubbish) vertedero m. ~**ped** a <cigarette> con filtro

tipsy a achispado

tiptoe n. **on** ~ de puntillas

tiptop a 🇮 de primera. **in** ~ **condition** en excelente estado

tire n (Amer) ⇒TYRE. ● vt cansar. ● vi cansarse. ~**d** a cansado. **get** ~**d** cansarse. ~**d of** harto de. ~**d out** agotado. ~**less** a incansable; <efforts> inagotable. ~**some** a <person> pesado; <task> tedioso

tiring a cansado, cansador (LAm)

tissue n (Anat, Bot) tejido m; (paper handkerchief) pañuelo m de papel. ~ **paper** n papel m de seda

tit n (bird) paro m; (🅧, breast) teta f

titbit n exquisitez f

tit for tat n: **it was** ~ fue ojo por ojo, diente por diente

title n título m

to *prep* a; (towards) hacia; (in order to) para; (as far as) hasta; (of) de. **give it ~ me** dámelo. **what did you say ~ him?** ¿qué le dijiste?; **I don't want ~** no quiero. **it's twenty ~ seven** (by clock) son las siete menos veinte, son veinte para las siete (LAm). ●*adv.* **pull ~** cerrar. **~ and fro** *adv* de un lado a otro

toad *n* sapo *m*. **~stool** *n* hongo *m* (*no comestible*)

toast *n* pan *m* tostado, tostadas *fpl*; (drink) brindis *m*. **a piece of ~** una tostada, un pan tostado (Mex). **drink a ~ to** brindar por. ●*vt* (Culin) tostar; (drink to) brindar por. **~er** *n* tostadora *f* (eléctrica), tostador *m*

tobacco *n* tabaco *m*. **~nist** *n* estanquero *m*

toboggan *n* tobogán *m*

today *n & adv* hoy (*m*)

toddler *n* niño *m* pequeño (*entre un año y dos años y medio de edad*)

toe *n* dedo *m* (del pie); (of shoe) punta *f*. **big ~** dedo *m* gordo (del pie). **on one's ~s** (fig) alerta. ●*vt.* **~ the line** acatar la disciplina

toffee *n* toffee *m* (*golosina hecha con azúcar y mantequilla*)

together *adv* juntos; (at same time) a la vez. **~ with** junto con

toil *vi* afanarse. ●*n* trabajo *m* duro

toilet *n* servicio *m*, baño *m* (LAm). **~ paper** *n* papel *m* higiénico. **~ries** *npl* artículos *mpl* de tocador. **~ roll** *n* rollo *m* de papel higiénico

token *n* muestra *f*; (voucher) vale *m*; (coin) ficha *f*. ●*a* simbólico

told ⇒TELL

tolera|ble *a* tolerable; (not bad) pasable. **~nce** *n* tolerancia *f*. **~nt** *a* tolerante. **~te** *vt* tolerar. **~tion** *n* tolerancia *f*

toll *n* (on road) peaje *m*, cuota *f* (Mex). **death ~** número *m* de muertos. **~ call** *n* (Amer) llamada *f* interurbana, conferencia *f*. ●*vi* doblar, tocar a muerto

tomato *n* (*pl* **-oes**) tomate *m*, jitomate *m* (Mex)

tomb *n* tumba *f*, sepulcro *m*. **~stone** *n* lápida *f*

tomorrow *n & adv* mañana (*f*). **see you ~!** ¡hasta mañana!

ton *n* tonelada *f* (= 1,016kg). **~s of** 🄸 montones de. **metric ~** tonelada *f* (métrica) (= 1,000kg)

tone *n* tono *m*. □ **~ down** *vt* atenuar; moderar <*language*>. **~-deaf** *a* que no tiene oído (musical)

tongs *npl* tenacillas *fpl*

tongue *n* lengua *f*. **say sth ~ in cheek** decir algo medio burlándose. **~-tied** *a* cohibido. **~-twister** *n* trabalenguas *m*

tonic *a* tónico. ●*n* (Med, fig) tónico *m*. **~ (water)** *n* tónica *f*

tonight *adv & n* esta noche (*f*); (evening) esta tarde (*f*)

tonne *n* tonelada *f* (métrica)

tonsil *n* amígdala *f*. **~litis** *n* amigdalitis *f*

too *adv* (excessively) demasiado; (also) también. **I'm not ~ sure** no estoy muy seguro. **~ many** demasiados. **~ much** demasiado

took ⇒TAKE

tool *n* herramienta *f*

tooth *n* (*pl* **teeth**) diente *m*; (molar) muela *f*. **~ache** *n* dolor *m* de muelas. **~brush** *n* cepillo *m* de dientes. **~paste** *n* pasta *f* dentífrica, pasta *f* de dientes. **~pick** *n* palillo *m* (de dientes)

top *n* parte *f* superior, parte *f* de arriba; (of mountain) cima *f*; (of tree) copa *f*; (of page) parte *f* superior; (lid, of bottle) tapa *f*; (of pen) capuchón *m*; (spinning **~**) trompo *m*, peonza *f*. **be ∼ of the class** ser el primero de la clase. **from ∼ to bottom** de arriba abajo. **on ∼ of** encima de; (besides) además de. ● *a* más alto; <*shelf*> superior; <*speed*> máximo; (in rank) superior; (leading) más destacado. ● *vt* (*pt* **topped**) cubrir; (exceed) exceder. □ ∼ **up** *vt* llenar. ∼ **floor** *n* último piso *m*. ∼ **hat** *n* chistera *f*. ∼**heavy** *a* inestable (*por ser más pesado en su parte superior*)

topic *n* tema *m*. ∼**al** *a* de actualidad

topless *n* topless

topple *vi* (Pol) derribar; (overturn) volcar. ● *vi* caerse

top secret *a* secreto, reservado

torch *n* linterna *f*; (flaming) antorcha *f*

tore ⇒TEAR¹

torment *n* tormento *m*. ● *vt* atormentar

torn ⇒TEAR¹

tornado *n* (*pl* **-oes**) tornado *m*

torpedo *n* (*pl* **-oes**) torpedo *m*. ● *vt* torpedear

torrent *n* torrente *m*. ∼**ial** *a* torrencial

torrid *a* tórrido; <*affair*> apasionado

tortoise *n* tortuga *f*. ∼**shell** *n* carey *m*

tortuous *a* tortuoso

torture *n* tortura *f*. ● *vt* torturar

Tory *a & n* tory *m & f*

toss *vt* tirar, lanzar <*ball*>; (shake) sacudir. ● *vi*. ∼ **and turn** (in bed) dar vueltas

tot *n* pequeño *m*; (🄸, of liquor) trago *m*. ● *vt* (*pt* **totted**). ∼ **up** 🄸 sumar

total *a & n* total (*m*). ● *vt* (*pt* **totalled**) ascender a un total de;

(add up) totalizar. ∼**itarian** *a* totalitario. ∼**ly** *adv* totalmente

totter *vi* tambalearse

touch *vt* tocar; (move) conmover; (concern) afectar. ● *vi* tocar; <*wires*> tocarse. ● *n* toque *m*; (sense) tacto *m*; (contact) contacto *m*. **be/get/stay in ∼ with** estar/ponerse/mantenerse en contacto con. □ ∼ **down** *vi* <*aircraft*> aterrizar. □ ∼ **up** *vt* retocar. ∼**ing** *a* enternecedor. ∼**y** *a* quisquilloso

tough *a* (**-er, -est**) duro; (strong) fuerte, resistente; (difficult) difícil; (severe) severo. ∼**en**. ∼ **(up)** *vt* endurecer; hacer más fuerte <*person*>

tour *n* viaje *m*; (visit) visita *f*; (excursion) excursión *f*; (by team etc) gira *f*. **be on ∼** estar de gira. ● *vt* recorrer; (visit) visitar. ∼ **guide** *n* guía de turismo

touris|m *n* turismo *m*. ∼**t** *n* turista *m & f*. ● *a* turístico. ∼**t office** *n* oficina *f* de turismo

tournament *n* torneo *m*

tousle *vt* despeinar

tout *vi*. ∼ **(for)** solicitar

tow *vt* remolcar. ● *n* remolque *m*

toward(s) *prep* hacia. **his attitude ∼ her** su actitud para con ella

towel *n* toalla *f*

tower *n* torre *f*. ● *vi*. ∼ **above** <*building*> descollar sobre; <*person*> destacar sobre. ∼ **block** *n* edificio *m* or bloque *m* de apartamentos. ∼**ing** *a* altísimo; <*rage*> violento

town *n* ciudad *f*; (smaller) pueblo *m*. **go to ∼** 🄸 no escatimar dinero. ∼ **hall** *n* ayuntamiento *m*

toxic *a* tóxico

toy *n* juguete *m*. □ ∼ **with** *vt* juguetear con <*object*>; darle vueltas a <*idea*>. ∼**shop** *n* juguetería *f*

T

trac|e *n* señal *f*, rastro *m*. ●*vt* trazar; (draw) dibujar; (with tracing paper) calcar; (track down) localizar. **~ing paper** *n* papel *m* de calcar

track *n* pista *f*, huellas *fpl*; (path) sendero *m*; (Sport) pista *f*. **the ~(s)** la vía férrea; (Rail) vía *f*. **keep ~ of** seguirle la pista a <*person*>. ●*vt* seguirle la pista a. □ **~ down** *vt* localizar. **~ suit** *n* equipo *m* (de deportes), chándal *m*

tract *n* (land) extensión *f*; (pamphlet) tratado *m* breve

traction *n* tracción *f*

tractor *n* tractor *m*

trade *n* comercio *m*; (occupation) oficio *m*; (exchange) cambio *m*; (industry) industria *f*. ●*vt*. **~ sth for sth** cambiar algo por algo. ●*vi* comerciar. □ **~ in** *vt* (give in part-exchange) entregar como parte del pago. **~ mark** *n* marca *f* (de fábrica). **~r** *n* comerciante *m & f*. **~ union** *n* sindicato *m*

tradition *n* tradición *f*. **~al** *a* tradicional

traffic *n* tráfico *m*. ●*vi* (*pt* **trafficked**) comerciar (in en). **~ circle** *n* (Amer) glorieta *f*, rotonda *f*. **~ island** *n* isla *f* peatonal. **~ jam** *n* embotellamiento *m*, atasco *m*. **~ lights** *npl* semáforo *m*. **~ warden** *n* guardia *m*, controlador *m* de tráfico

trag|edy *n* tragedia *f*. **~ic** *a* trágico

trail *vi* arrastrarse; (lag) rezagarse. ●*vt* (track) seguir la pista de. ●*n* (left by animal, person) huellas *fpl*; (path) sendero *m*. **be on the ~ of s.o./sth** seguir la pista de uno/algo **~er** *n* remolque *m*; (Amer, caravan) caravana *f*, rulot *m*; (film) avance *m*

train *n* (Rail) tren *m*; (of events) serie *f*; (of dress) cola *f*. ●*vt* capacitar <*employee*>; adiestrar <*soldier*>; (Sport) entrenar; educar <*voice*>; guiar <*plant*>; amaestrar <*animal*>. ●*vi* estudiar; (Sport) entrenarse. **~ed** *a* (skilled) cualificado, calificado; <*doctor*> diplomado. **~ee** *n* aprendiz *m*; (Amer, Mil) recluta *m & f*. **~er** *n* (Sport) entrenador *m*; (of animals) amaestrador *m*. **~ers** *mpl* zapatillas *fpl* de deporte. **~ing** *n* capacitación *f*; (Sport) entrenamiento *m*

trait *n* rasgo *m*

traitor *n* traidor *m*

tram *n* tranvía *m*

tramp *vi*. **~ (along)** caminar pesadamente. ●*n* vagabundo *m*

trample *vt* pisotear. ●*vi*. **~ on** pisotear

trampoline *n* trampolín *m*

trance *n* trance *m*

tranquil *a* tranquilo. **~lity** *n* tranquilidad *f*; (of person) serenidad *f*. **~lize** *vt* sedar, dar un sedante a. **~lizer** *n* sedante *m*, tranquilizante *m*

transaction *n* transacción *f*, operación *f*

transatlantic *a* transatlántico

transcend *vt* (go beyond) exceder

transcript *n* transcripción *f*

transfer *vt* (*pt* **transferred**) trasladar; traspasar <*player*>; transferir <*funds, property*>; pasar <*call*>. ●*vi* trasladarse. ●*n* traslado *m*; (of player) traspaso *m*; (of funds, property) transferencia *f*; (paper) calcomanía *f*

transform *vt* transformar. **~ation** *n* transformación *f*. **~er** *n* transformador *m*

transfusion *n* transfusión *f*

transient *a* pasajero

transistor *n* transistor *m*

transit n tránsito m. ~**ion** n transición f. ~**ive** a transitivo

translat|e vt traducir. ~**ion** n traducción f. ~**or** n traductor m

transmission n transmisión f

transmit vt (pt **transmitted**) transmitir. ~**ter** n transmisor m

transparen|cy n transparencia f; (Photo) diapositiva f. ~**t** a transparente

transplant vt trasplantar. ● n trasplante m

transport vt transportar. ● n transporte m. ~**ation** n transporte m

trap n trampa f. ● vt (pt **trapped**) atrapar; (jam) atascar; (cut off) bloquear. ~**door** n trampilla f

trapeze n trapecio m

trash n basura f; (Amer, worthless people) escoria f. ~ **can** n (Amer) cubo m de la basura, bote m de la basura (Mex). ~**y** a <souvenir> de porquería; <magazine> malo

travel vi (pt **travelled**) viajar; <vehicle> desplazarse. ● vt recorrer. ● n viajes mpl. ~ **agency** n agencia f de viajes. ~**ler** n viajero m. ~**ler's cheque** n cheque m de viaje or viajero. ~**ling expenses** npl gastos mpl de viaje

trawler n barca f pesquera

tray n bandeja f

treacher|ous a traidor; (deceptive) engañoso. ~**y** n traición f

treacle n melaza f

tread vi (pt **trod**, pp **trodden**) pisar. ~ **on sth** pisar algo. ~ **carefully** andarse con cuidado. ● n (step) paso m; (of tyre) banda f de rodamiento

treason n traición f

treasur|e n tesoro m. ~**ed** a <possession> preciado. ~**er** n

tesorero m. ~**y** n erario m, tesoro m. **the T~y** el fisco, la hacienda pública. **Department of the T~y** (in US) Departamento m del Tesoro

treat vt tratar; (Med) tratar. ~ **s.o.** (to meal etc) invitar a uno. ● n placer m; (present) regalo m

treatise n tratado m

treatment n tratamiento m

treaty n tratado m

treble a triple; <clef> de sol; <voice> de tiple. ● vt triplicar. ● vi triplicarse. ● n tiple m & f

tree n árbol m

trek n caminata f. ● vi (pt **trekked**) caminar

trellis n enrejado m

tremble vi temblar

tremendous a formidable; (🄸, huge) tremendo. ~**ly** adv tremendamente

tremor n temblor m

trench n zanja f; (Mil) trinchera f

trend n tendencia f; (fashion) moda f. ~**y** a (-ier, -iest) 🄸 moderno

trepidation n inquietud f

trespass vi. ~ **on** entrar sin autorización (en propiedad ajena). ~**er** n intruso m

trial n prueba f; (Jurid) proceso m, juicio m; (ordeal) prueba f dura. **by ~ and error** por ensayo y error. **be on ~** estar a prueba; (Jurid) estar siendo procesado

triang|le n triángulo m. ~**ular** a triangular

trib|al a tribal. ~**e** n tribu f

tribulation n tribulación f

tribunal n tribunal m

tributary n (Geog) afluente m

tribute n tributo m; (acknowledgement) homenaje m. **pay ~ to** rendir homenaje a

trick n trampa f, ardid m; (joke) broma f; (feat) truco m; (in card

T

trickery *n* (games) baza *f*. **play a ~ on** gastar una broma a. ● *vt* engañar. **~ery** *n* engaño *m*

trickle *vi* gotear. **~ in** (fig) entrar poco a poco

trickster *n* estafador *m*

tricky *a* delicado, difícil

tricycle *n* triciclo *m*

tried ⇒TRY

trifl|e *n* nimiedad *f*; (Culin) *postre de bizcocho, jerez, frutas y nata.* ● *vi.* □ **~e with** *vt* jugar con. **~ing** *a* insignificante

trigger *n* (of gun) gatillo *m*. ● *vt.* **~ (off)** desencadenar

trim *a* (**trimmer, trimmest**) (slim) esbelto; (neat) elegante. ● *vt* (*pt* **trimmed**) (cut) recortar; (adorn) adornar. ● *n* (cut) recorte *m*. **in ~** en buen estado. **~mings** *npl* recortes *mpl*

trinity *n.* **the (Holy) T~** la (Santísima) Trinidad

trinket *n* chuchería *f*

trio *n* (*pl* **-os**) trío *m*

trip (*pt* **tripped**) *vt* **~ (up)** hacerle una zancadilla a, hacer tropezar ● *vi* tropezar. ● *n* (journey) viaje *m*; (outing) excursión *f*; (stumble) traspié *m*

tripe *n* callos *mpl*, mondongo *m* (LAm), pancita *f* (Mex); (🄵, nonsense) paparruchas *fpl*

triple *a* triple. ● *vt* triplicar. ● *vi* triplicarse. **~t** *n* trillizo *m*

triplicate *a* triplicado. **in ~** por triplicado

tripod *n* trípode *m*

trite *a* trillado

triumph *n* triunfo *m*. ● *vi* triunfar (**over** sobre). **~al** *a* triunfal. **~ant** *a* <*troops*> triunfador; <*moment*> triunfal; <*smile*> de triunfo

trivial *a* insignificante; <*concerns*> trivial. **~ity** *n* trivialidad *f*

trod, trodden ⇒TREAD

trolley *n* (*pl* **-eys**) carretón *m*; (in supermarket, airport) carrito *m*; (for food, drink) carrito *m*, mesa *f* rodante. **~ car** *n* (Amer) tranvía *f*

trombone *n* trombón *m*

troop *n* compañía *f*; (of cavalry) escuadrón *m*. ● *vi.* **~ in** entrar en tropel. **~ out** salir en tropel. **~er** *n* soldado *m* de caballería; (Amer, state police officer) agente *m & f*. **~s** *npl* (Mil) tropas *fpl*

trophy *n* trofeo *m*

tropic *n* trópico *m*. **~al** *a* tropical. **~s** *npl* trópicos *mpl*

trot *n* trote *m*. ● *vi* (*pt* **trotted**) trotar

trouble *n* problemas *mpl*; (awkward situation) apuro *m*; (inconvenience) molestia *f*. **be in ~** estar en apuros. **get into ~** meterse en problemas. **look for ~** buscar camorra. **take the ~ to do sth** molestarse en hacer algo. ● *vt* (bother) molestar; (worry) preocupar. **~maker** *n* alborotador *m*. **~some** *a* problemático. **~ spot** *n* punto *m* conflictivo

trough *n* (for drinking) abrevadero *m*; (for feeding) comedero *m*

troupe *n* compañía *f* teatral

trousers *npl* pantalón *m*, pantalones *mpl*

trout *n* (*pl* **trout**) trucha *f*

trowel *n* (garden) desplantador *m*; (for mortar) paleta *f*

truant *n.* **play ~** hacer novillos

truce *n* tregua *f*

truck *n* camión *m*; (Rail) vagón *m*, furgón *m*; (Amer, vegetables, fruit) productos *mpl* de la huerta. **~ driver, ~er** (Amer) *n* camionero

m. ~**ing** n transporte m por carretera

trudge vi andar penosamente

true a (-er, -est) verdadero; <story, account> verídico; <friend> auténtico, de verdad. ~ **to sth/s.o.** fiel a algo/uno. **be** ~ ser cierto. **come** ~ hacerse realidad

truffle n trufa f; (chocolate) trufa f de chocolate

truly adv verdaderamente; (sincerely) sinceramente. **yours** ~ (in letters) cordiales saludos

trump n (Cards) triunfo m; (fig) baza f

trumpet n trompeta f. ~**er** n trompetista m & f, trompeta m & f

truncheon n porra f

trunk n (of tree) tronco m; (box) baúl m; (of elephant) trompa f; (Amer, Auto) maletero m, cajuela f (Mex). ~**s** npl bañador m, traje m de baño

truss vt. **truss (up)** vt atar

trust n confianza f; (money, property) fondo m de inversiones; (institution) fundación f. **on** ~ a ojos cerrados; (Com) al fiado. ●vi. ~ **in s.o./sth** confiar en uno/algo. ●vt confiar en; (in negative sentences) fiarse; (hope) esperar. ~**ed** a leal. ~**ee** n fideicomisario m. ~**ful** a confiado. ~**ing** a confiado. ~**worthy**, ~**y** a digno de confianza

truth n (pl -s) verdad f; (of account, story) veracidad f. ~**ful** a veraz.

try vt (pt **tried**) intentar; probar <food, product>; (be a strain on) poner a prueba; (Jurid) procesar. ~ **to do sth** tratar de hacer algo, intentar hacer algo. ~ **not to forget** procura no olvidarte. ●n tentativa f, prueba f; (Rugby) ensayo m. □ ~ **on** vt probarse

<garment>. □ ~ **out** vt probar. ~**ing** a duro; (annoying) molesto

tsar n zar m

T-shirt n camiseta f

tub n cuba f; (for washing clothes) tina f; (bathtub) bañera f; (for ice cream) envase m, tarrina f

tuba n tuba f

tubby a (-ier, -iest) rechoncho

tube n tubo m; (𝕀, Rail) metro m; (Amer 𝕀, television) tele f. **inner** ~ n cámara f de aire

tuberculosis n tuberculosis f

tub|ing n tubería f. ~**ular** a tubular

tuck n (fold) jareta f. ●vt plegar; (put) meter. □ ~ **in(to)** vi (𝕀, eat) ponerse a comer. □ ~ **up** vt arropar <child>

Tuesday n martes m

tuft n (of hair) mechón m; (of feathers) penacho m; (of grass) mata f

tug vt (pt **tugged**) tirar de. ●vi. ~ **at sth** tirar de algo. ●n tirón m; (Naut) remolcador m. ~**-of-war** n juego de tira y afloja

tuition n clases fpl

tulip n tulipán m

tumble vi caerse. ●n caída f. ~**down** a en ruinas. ~**-drier** n secadora f. ~**r** n (glass) vaso m (de lados rectos)

tummy n 𝕀 barriga f

tumour n tumor m

tumult n tumulto m. ~**uous** a <applause> apoteósico

tuna n (pl **tuna**) atún m

tune n melodía f; (piece) tonada f. **be in** ~ estar afinado. **be out of** ~ estar desafinado. ●vt afinar, sintonizar <radio, TV>; (Mec) poner a punto. ●vi. ~ **in (to)** sintonizar (con). □ ~ **up** vt/i afinar. ~**ful** a melodioso. ~**r** n afinador m; (Radio) sintonizador m

T

tunic *n* túnica *f*

tunnel *n* túnel *m*. ● *vi* (*pt* **tunnelled**) abrir un túnel

turban *n* turbante *m*

turbine *n* turbina *f*

turbo *n* (*pl -os*) turbo(compresor) *m*

turbulen|ce *n* turbulencia *f*. **~t** *a* turbulento

turf *n* (*pl* **turfs** *or* **turves**) césped *m*; (segment of grass) tepe *m*. □ **~ out** *vt* 🗉 echar

turgid *a* <language> ampuloso

turkey *n* (*pl -eys*) pavo *m*

Turk|ey *f* Turquía *f*. **~ish** *a & n* turco (*m*)

turmoil *n* confusión *f*

turn *vt* hacer girar; volver <head, page>; doblar <corner>; (change) cambiar; (deflect) desviar. **~ sth into sth** convertir *or* transformar algo en algo. ● *vi* <handle> girar, dar vueltas; <person> volverse, darse la vuelta. **~ right** girar *or* doblar *or* torcer a la derecha. **~ red** ponerse rojo. **~ into sth** convertirse en algo. ● *n* vuelta *f*; (in road) curva *f*; (change) giro *m*; (sequence) turno *m*; (🗉, of illness) ataque *m*. **good ~** favor *m*. **in ~** a su vez. □ **~ down** *vt* (fold) doblar; (reduce) bajar; (reject) rechazar. □ **~ off** *vt* cerrar <tap>; apagar <light, TV, etc>. *vi* (from road) doblar. □ **~ on** *vt* abrir <tap>; encender, prender (LAm) <light etc>. □ **~ out** *vt* apagar <light etc>. *vi* (result) resultar. □ **~ round** *vi* darse la vuelta. □ **~ up** *vi* aparecer. *vt* (find) encontrar; levantar <collar>; subir <hem>; acortar <trousers>; poner más fuerte <gas>. **~ed-up** *a* <nose> respingón. **~ing** *n* (in town) bocacalle *f*. **we've missed the ~ing** nos hemos pasado la calle (*or*

carretera). **~ing-point** *n* momento *m* decisivo.

turnip *n* nabo *m*

turn: ~over *n* (Com) facturación *f*; (of staff) movimiento *m*. **~pike** *n* (Amer) autopista *f* de peaje. **~stile** *n* torniquete *m*. **~table** *n* platina *f*. **~up** *n* (of trousers) vuelta *f*, valenciana *f* (Mex)

turquoise *a & n* turquesa (*f*)

turret *n* torrecilla *f*

turtle *n* tortuga *f* de mar; (Amer, tortoise) tortuga *f*

turves ⇒TURF

tusk *n* colmillo *m*

tussle *n* lucha *f*

tutor *n* profesor *m* particular

tuxedo *n* (*pl -os*) (Amer) esmoquin *m*, smoking *m*

TV *n* televisión *f*, tele *f* 🗉

twang *n* tañido *m*; (in voice) gangueo *m*

tweet *n* piada *f*. ● *vi* piar

tweezers *npl* pinzas *fpl*

twel|fth *a* duodécimo. ● *n* doceavo *m*. **~ve** *a & n* doce (*m*)

twent|ieth *a* vigésimo. ● *n* veinteavo *m*. **~y** *a & n* veinte (*m*)

twice *adv* dos veces. **~ as many people** el doble de gente

twiddle *vt* (hacer) girar

twig *n* ramita *f*. ● *vi* (*pt* **twigged**) 🗉 caer, darse cuenta

twilight *n* crepúsculo *m*

twin *a & n* gemelo (*m*), mellizo (*m*) (LAm)

twine *n* cordel *m*, bramante *m*

twinge *n* punzada *f*; (of remorse) punzada *f*

twinkle *vi* centellear. ● *n* centelleo *m*; (in eye) brillo *m*

twirl *vt* (hacer) girar. ● *vi* girar. ● *n* vuelta *f*

twist *vt* retorcer; (roll) enrollar; girar <knob>; tergiversar

<words>; (distort) retorcer. ~ **one's
ankle** torcerse el tobillo. ●*vi*
<rope, wire> enrollarse; *<road,
river>* serpentear. ●*n* torsión *f*;
(curve) vuelta *f*

twit *n* 🛈 imbécil *m*

twitch *vi* moverse. ●*n* tic *m*

twitter *vi* gorjear

two *a & n* dos (*m*). ~**-bit** *a* (Amer)
de tres al cuarto. ~**-faced** *a*
falso, insincero. ~**fold** *a* doble.
●*adv* dos veces. ~**pence** *n* dos
peniques *mpl.* ~**-piece** (**suit**) *n*
traje *m* de dos piezas. ~**-way** *a*
<traffic> de doble sentido

tycoon *n* magnate *m*

tying ⇒TIE

type *n* tipo *m*. ●*vt/i* escribir a
máquina. ~**-cast** *a* *<actor>*
encasillado. ~**script** *n* texto *m*
mecanografiado, manuscrito *m*
(*de una obra, novela etc*).
~**writer** *n* máquina *f* de escribir.
~**written** *a* escrito a máquina,
mecanografiado

typhoon *n* tifón *m*

typical *a* típico. ~**ly** *adv*
típicamente

typify *vt* tipificar

typi|ng *n* mecanografía *f*. ~**st** *n*
mecanógrafo *m*

tyran|nical *a* tiránico. ~**ny** *n*
tiranía *f*. ~**t** *n* tirano *m*

tyre *n* neumático *m*, llanta *f* (LAm)

udder *n* ubre *f*

UFO *abbr* (= **unidentified flying
object**) OVNI *m* (*objeto volante
no identificado*)

ugly *a* (**-ier, -iest**) feo

UK *abbr* (= **United Kingdom**)
Reino *m* Unido

Ukraine *n* Ucrania *f*

ulcer *n* úlcera *f*; (external) llaga *f*

ultimate *a* (eventual) final; (utmost)
máximo. ~**ly** *adv* en última
instancia; (in the long run) a la larga

ultimatum *n* (*pl* **-ums**)
ultimátum *m*

ultra... *pref* ultra... ~**violet** *a*
ultravioleta

umbilical cord *n* cordón *m*
umbilical

umbrella *n* paraguas *m*

umpire *n* árbitro *m*. ●*vt* arbitrar

umpteen *a* 🛈 tropecientos 🛈.
~**th** *a* 🛈 enésimo

un... *pref* in..., des..., no, poco,
sin

UN *abbr* (= **United Nations**)
ONU *f* (*Organización de las
Naciones Unidas*)

unable *a*. be ~ to no poder; (be
incapable of) ser incapaz de

unacceptable *a* *<behaviour>*
inaceptable; *<terms>* inadmisible

unaccompanied *a* *<luggage>* no
acompañado; *<person,
instrument>* solo; *<singing>* sin
acompañamiento

unaccustomed *a*
desacostumbrado. **be ~ to** *a* no
estar acostumbrado a

unaffected *a* natural
unaided *a* sin ayuda
unanimous *a* unánime. ~**ly** *adv* unánimemente; <*elect*> por unanimidad
unarmed *a* desarmado
unattended *a* sin vigilar
unattractive *a* poco atractivo
unavoidabl|e *a* inevitable. ~**y** *adv*. **I was** ~**y delayed** no pude evitar llegar tarde
unaware *a*. **be** ~ **of** ignorar, no ser consciente de. ~**s** *adv* desprevenido
unbearabl|e *a* insoportable, inaguantable. ~**y** *adv* inaguantablemente
unbeat|able *a* <*quality*> insuperable; <*team*> invencible. ~**en** *a* no vencido; <*record*> insuperado
unbelievabl|e *a* increíble. ~**y** *adv* increíblemente
unbiased *a* imparcial
unblock *vt* desatascar
unbolt *vt* descorrer el pestillo de
unborn *a* que todavía no ha nacido
unbreakable *a* irrompible
unbroken *a* (intact) intacto; (continuous) ininterrumpido
unbutton *vt* desabotonar, desabrochar
uncalled-for *a* fuera de lugar
uncanny *a* (**ier**, **-iest**) raro, extraño
uncertain *a* incierto; (hesitant) vacilante. **be** ~ **of/about sth** no estar seguro de algo. ~**ty** *n* incertidumbre *f*
uncharitable *a* severo
uncivilized *a* incivilizado
uncle *n* tío *m*
unclean *a* impuro
unclear *a* poco claro
uncomfortable *a* incómodo

uncommon *a* poco común
uncompromising *a* intransigente
unconcerned *a* indiferente
unconditional *a* incondicional
unconnected *a* (unrelated) sin conexión. **the events are** ~ estos acontecimientos no guardan ninguna relación (entre sí)
unconscious *a* (Med) inconsciente. ~**ly** *adv* inconscientemente
unconventional *a* poco convencional
uncork *vt* descorchar
uncouth *a* zafio
uncover *vt* destapar; revelar <*plot, scandal*>
undaunted *a* impertérrito
undecided *a* indeciso
undeniabl|e *a* innegable. ~**y** *adv* sin lugar a dudas
under *prep* debajo de; (less than) menos de; <*heading*> bajo; (according to) según; (expressing movement) por debajo de. ● *adv* debajo, abajo
under... *pref* sub...
under: ~**carriage** *n* (Aviat) tren *m* de aterrizaje. ~**charge** *vt* cobrarle menos a. ~**clothes** *npl* ropa *f* interior. ~**coat**, ~**coating** (Amer) *n* (paint) pintura *f* base; (first coat) primera mano *f* de pintura. ~**cover** *a* secreto. ~**current** *n* corriente *f* submarina. ~**dog** *n*. **the** ~**dog** el que tiene menos posibilidades. **the** ~**dogs** *npl* los de abajo. ~**done** *a* <*meat*> poco hecho. ~**estimate** *vt* (underrate) subestimar. ~**fed** *a* subalimentado. ~**foot** *adv* debajo de los pies. ~**go** *vt* (*pt* -**went** *pp*-**gone**) sufrir. ~**graduate** *n* estudiante *m & f* universitario (no licenciado).

~ground *adv* bajo tierra; (in secret) clandestinamente. ● *a* subterráneo; (secret) clandestino. ● *n* metro *m*. **~growth** *n* maleza *f*. **~hand** *a* (secret) clandestino; (deceptive) fraudulento. **~lie** *vt* (*pt* **-lay** *pp* **-lain** *pres p* **-lying**) subyacer a. **~line** *vt* subrayar. **~lying** *a* subyacente. **~mine** *vt* socavar. **~neath** *prep* debajo de, abajo de (LAm). ● *adv* por debajo. **~paid** *a* mal pagado. **~pants** *npl* calzoncillos *mpl*. **~pass** *n* paso *m* subterráneo; (for traffic) paso *m* inferior. **~privileged** *a* desfavorecido. **~rate** *vt* subestimar. **~rated** *a* no debidamente apreciado. **~shirt** *n* (Amer) camiseta *f* (interior).

understand *vt* (*pt* **-stood**) entender; (empathize with) comprender, entender. ● *vi* entender, comprender. **~able** *a* comprensible. **~ing** *a* comprensivo. ● *n* (grasp) entendimiento *m*; (sympathy) comprensión *f*; (agreement) acuerdo *m*

under: **~statement** *n* subestimación *f*. **~take** (*pt* **-took** *pp* **-taken**) emprender *<task>*; asumir *<responsibility>*. **~take to do sth** comprometerse a hacer algo. **~taker** *n* director *m* de pompas fúnebres. **~taking** *n* empresa *f*; (promise) promesa *f*. **~tone** *n*. **in an ~tone** en voz baja. **~value** *vt* subvalorar. **~water** *a* submarino. ● *adv* debajo del agua. **~wear** *n* ropa *f* interior. **~weight** *a* de peso más bajo que el normal. **~went** ⇒UNDERGO. **~world** *n* (criminals) hampa *f*. **~write** *vt* (*pt* **-wrote** *pp* **-written**) (Com) asegurar; (guarantee financially) financiar

undeserved *a* inmerecido

undesirable *a* indeseable

undignified *a* indecoroso

undisputed *a* *<champion>* indiscutido; *<facts>* innegable

undo *vt* (*pt* **-did** *pp* **-done**) desabrochar *<button, jacket>*; abrir *<zip>*; desatar *<knot, laces>*

undoubted *a* indudable. **~ly** *adv* indudablemente, sin duda

undress *vt* desvestir, desnudar. ● *vi* desvestirse, desnudarse

undue *a* excesivo

undulate *vi* ondular

unduly *adv* excesivamente

unearth *vt* desenterrar; descubrir *<document>*

unearthly *a* sobrenatural. **at an ~ hour** a estas horas intempestivas

uneasy *a* incómodo

uneconomic *a* poco económico

uneducated *a* sin educación

unemploy|ed *a* desempleado, parado. **~ment** *n* desempleo *m*, paro *m*

unending *a* interminable, sin fin

unequal *a* desigual

unequivocal *a* inequívoco

unethical *a* poco ético, inmoral

uneven *a* desigual

unexpected *a* inesperado; *<result>* imprevisto. **~ly** *adv* *<arrive>* de improviso; *<happen>* de forma imprevista

unfair *a* injusto; improcedente *<dismissal>*. **~ly** *adv* injustamente

unfaithful *a* infiel

unfamiliar *a* desconocido. **be ~ with** desconocer

unfasten *vt* desabrochar *<clothes>*; (untie) desatar

unfavourable *a* desfavorable

unfeeling *a* insensible

unfit *a*. **I'm ~** no estoy en forma. **~ for human consumption** no apto para el consumo

U

unfold vt desdoblar; desplegar <wings>; (fig) revelar.● vi <leaf> abrirse; <events> desarrollarse

unforeseen a imprevisto

unforgettable a inolvidable

unforgivable a imperdonable

unfortunate a desafortunado; (regrettable) lamentable.~ly adv desafortunadamente; (stronger) por desgracia, desgraciadamente

unfounded a infundado

unfriendly a poco amistoso; (stronger) antipático

unfurl vt desplegar

ungainly a desgarbado

ungrateful a desagradecido, ingrato

unhapp|iness n infelicidad f, tristeza f.~y a (-ier, -iest) infeliz, triste; (unsuitable) inoportuno. be ~y about sth no estar contento con algo

unharmed a <person> ileso

unhealthy a (-ier, -iest) <person> de mala salud; <complexion> enfermizo; <conditions> poco saludable

unhurt a ileso

unification n unificación f

uniform a & n uniforme (m). ~ity n uniformidad f

unify vt unir

unilateral a unilateral

unimaginable a inimaginable

unimaginative a <person> poco imaginativo

unimportant a sin importancia

uninhabited a deshabitado; <island> despoblado

unintelligible a ininteligible

unintentional a involuntario

union n unión f; (trade union) sindicato m; (student ~) asociación f de estudiantes. U~ Jack n bandera f del Reino Unido

unique a único

unison n. in ~ al unísono

unit n unidad f; (of furniture etc) módulo m; (in course) módulo m

unite vt unir.● vi unirse. U~d Kingdom n Reino m Unido. U~d Nations n Organización f de las Naciones Unidas (ONU). U~d States (of America) n Estados mpl Unidos (de América)

unity n unidad f

univers|al a universal.~e n universo m

university n universidad f.● a universitario

unjust a injusto.~ified a injustificado

unkind a poco amable; (cruel) cruel; <remark> hiriente

unknown a desconocido

unlawful a ilegal

unleaded a <fuel> sin plomo

unleash vt soltar

unless conj a menos que, a no ser que

unlike prep diferente de. (in contrast to) a diferencia de.~ly a improbable

unlimited a ilimitado

unlisted a (Amer) que no figura en la guía telefónica, privado (Mex)

unload vt descargar

unlock vt abrir (con llave)

unluck|ily adv desgraciadamente. ~y a (-ier, -iest) <person> sin suerte, desafortunado. be ~y tener mala suerte; (bring bad luck) traer mala suerte

unmarried a soltero

unmask vt desenmascarar

unmentionable a inmencionable

unmistakable a inconfundible

unnatural a poco natural; (not normal) anormal

unnecessar|ily *adv* innecesariamente. **~y** *a* innecesario

unnerve *vt* desconcertar

unnoticed *a* inadvertido

unobtainable *a* imposible de conseguir

unobtrusive *a* discreto

unofficial *a* no oficial. **~ly** *adv* extraoficialmente

unpack *vt* sacar las cosas de *<bags>*; deshacer, desempacar (LAm) *<suitcase>*. ● *vi* deshacer las maletas

unpaid *a* *<work>* no retribuido, no remunerado; *<leave>* sin sueldo

unperturbed *a* impasible. **he carried on ~** siguió sin inmutarse

unpleasant *a* desagradable

unplug *vt* desenchufar

unpopular *a* impopular

unprecedented *a* sin precedentes

unpredictable *a* imprevisible

unprepared *a* no preparado; (unready) desprevenido

unprofessional *a* poco profesional

unprofitable *a* no rentable

unprotected *a* sin protección; *<sex>* sin el uso de preservativos

unqualified *a* sin título; (fig) absoluto

unquestion|able *a* incuestionable, innegable. **~ing** *a* *<obedience>* ciego; *<loyalty>* incondicional

unreal *a* irreal. **~istic** *a* poco realista

unreasonable *a* irrazonable

unrecognizable *a* irreconocible

unrelated *a* *<facts>* no relacionados (entre sí); *<people>* no emparentado

unreliable *a* *<person>* informal; *<machine>* poco fiable; *<information>* poco fidedigno

unrepentant *a* impenitente

unrest *n* (discontent) descontento *m*; (disturbances) disturbios *mpl*

unrivalled *a* incomparable

unroll *vt* desenrollar. ● *vi* desenrollarse

unruffled *<person>* sereno

unruly *a* *<class>* indisciplinado; *<child>* revoltoso

unsafe *a* inseguro

unsatisfactory *a* insatisfactorio

unsavoury *a* desagradable

unscathed *a* ileso

unscheduled *a* no programado, no previsto

unscrew *vt* destornillar; desenroscar *<lid>*

unscrupulous *a* inescrupuloso

unseemly *a* indecoroso

unseen *a* *<danger>* oculto; (unnoticed) sin ser visto

unselfish *a* *<act>* desinteresado; *<person>* nada egoísta

unsettle *vt* desestabilizar *<situation>*; alterar *<plans>*. **~d** *a* agitado; *<weather>* inestable; (undecided) pendiente (de resolución)

unshakeable *a* inquebrantable

unshaven *a* sin afeitar, sin rasurar (Mex)

unsightly *a* feo

unskilled *a* *<work>* no especializado; *<worker>* no cualificado, no calificado

unsociable *a* insociable

unsolved *a* no resuelto; *<murder>* sin esclarecerse

unsophisticated *a* sencillo

unsound *a* poco sólido

U

unspecified *a* no especificado

unstable *a* inestable

unsteady *a* inestable, poco firme

unstuck *a* despegado. **come ~** despegarse; (fail) fracasar

unsuccessful *a* <*attempt*> infructuoso. **be ~** no tener éxito, fracasar

unsuitable *a* <*clothing*> poco apropiado, poco adecuado; <*time*> inconveniente. **she is ~ for the job** no es la persona indicada para el trabajo

unsure *a* inseguro

unthinkable *a* inconcebible

untid|iness *n* desorden *m*. **~y** *a* (**-ier**, **-iest**) desordenado; <*appearance, writing*> descuidado

untie *vt* desatar, desamarrar (LAm)

until *prep* hasta. ● *conj* hasta que

untold *a* incalculable

untouched *a* intacto

untried *a* no probado

untrue *a* falso

unused *a* nuevo. ● *a*. **~ to** no acostumbrado a

unusual *a* poco común, poco corriente. **it's ~ to see so many people** es raro ver a tanta gente. **~ly** *adv* excepcionalmente, inusitadamente

unveil *vt* descubrir

unwanted *a* superfluo; <*child*> no deseado

unwelcome *a* <*news*> poco grato; <*guest*> inoportuno

unwell *a* indispuesto

unwieldy *a* pesado y difícil de manejar

unwilling *a* mal dispuesto. **be ~** no querer

unwind *vt* (*pt* **unwound**) desenrollar. ● *vi* (⧉, relax) relajarse

unwise *a* poco sensato

unworthy *a* indigno

unwrap *vt* (*pt* **unwrapped**) desenvolver

unwritten *a* no escrito; <*agreement*> verbal

up *adv* arriba; (upwards) hacia arriba; (higher) más arriba. **~ here** aquí arriba. **~ there** allí arriba. **~ to** hasta. **he's not ~ yet** todavía no se ha levantado. **be ~ against** enfrentarse con. **come ~** subir. **go ~** subir. **he's not ~ to the job** no tiene las condiciones necesarias para el trabajo. **it's ~ to you** depende de ti. **what's ~?** ¿qué pasa? ● *prep*. **go ~ the stairs** subir la escalera. **it's just ~ the road** está un poco más allá. ● *vt* (*pt* **upped**) aumentar. ● *n*. **~s and downs** *npl* altibajos *mpl*; (of life) vicisitudes *fpl*. **~bringing** *n* educación *f*. **~date** *vt* poner al día. **~grade** *vt* elevar de categoría <*person*>; mejorar <*equipment*>. **~heaval** *n* trastorno *m*. **~hill** *adv* cuesta arriba. **~hold** *vt* (*pt* **upheld**) mantener <*principle*>; confirmar <*decision*>. **~holster** *vt* tapizar. **~holstery** *n* tapicería *f*. **~keep** *n* mantenimiento *m*. **~-market** *a* de categoría

upon *prep* sobre. **once ~ a time** érase una vez

upper *a* superior. **~ class** *n* clase *f* alta

up: ~right *a* vertical; <*citizen*> recto. **place sth ~right** poner algo de pie. **~rising** *n* levantamiento *m*. **~roar** *n* tumulto *m*

upset *vt* (*pt* **upset**, *pres p* **upsetting**) (hurt) disgustar; (offend) ofender; (distress) alterar; desbaratar <*plans*>. ● *a* (hurt) disgustado; (distressed) alterado; (offended) ofendido; (disappointed) desilusionado. ● *n* trastorno *m*.

have a stomach ~ estar mal del estómago

up: ~**shot** n resultado m. ~**side down** adv al revés (con la parte de arriba abajo); (in disorder) patas arriba. **turn sth** ~**side down** poner algo boca abajo. ~**stairs** adv arriba. **go** ~**stairs** subir. ● a de arriba. ~**start** n advenedizo m. ~**state** adv (Amer). **I live** ~**state** vivo en el norte del estado. ~**stream** adv río arriba. ~**take** n. **be quick on the** ~**take** agarrar las cosas al vuelo. ~**-to-date** a al día; <news> de última hora. ~**turn** n repunte m, mejora f. ~**ward** <movement> ascendente; <direction> hacia arriba. ● adv hacia arriba. ~**wards** adv hacia arriba

uranium n uranio m

Uranus n Urano m

urban a urbano

urchin n pilluelo m

urge vt instar. ~ **s.o. to do sth** instar a uno a quehaga algo. ● n impulso m; (wish, whim) ganas fpl. □ ~ **on** vt animar

urgen|cy n urgencia f. ~**t** a urgente. ~**tly** adv urgentemente, con urgencia

urin|ate vi orinar. ~**e** n orina f

Uruguay n Uruguay m. ~**an** a & n uruguayo (m)

us pron nos; (after prep) nosotros m, nosotras f

US(A) abbr (= **United States (of America)**) EE.UU. (only written), Estados mpl Unidos

usage n uso m

use vt usar; utilizar <service, facilities>; consumir <fuel>. ● n uso m, empleo m. **be of** ~ servir. **it is no** ~ es inútil. □ ~ **up** vt agotar, consumir. ~**d** a usado. ● v mod ~ **to.** he ~**d to say** decía, solía decir. **there** ~**d to be** (antes)

había. ● a. **be** ~**d to** estar acostumbrado a. ~**ful** a útil. ~**fully** adv útilmente. ~**less** a inútil; <person> incompetente. ~**r** n usuario m. **drug** ~ n consumidor m de drogas

usher n (in theatre etc) acomodador m. □ ~ **in** vt hacer pasar; marcar el comienzo de <new era>. ~**ette** n acomodadora f

USSR abbr (History) (= **Union of Soviet Socialist Republics**) URSS

usual a usual; (habitual) acostumbrado, habitual; <place, route> de siempre. **as** ~ como de costumbre, como siempre. ~**ly** adv normalmente. **he** ~**ly wakes up early** suele despertarse temprano

utensil n utensilio m

utilize vt utilizar

utmost a sumo. ● n. **do one's** ~ hacer todo lo posible (**to** para)

utter a completo. ● vt pronunciar <word>; dar <cry>. ~**ly** adv totalmente

U-turn n cambio m de sentido

vacan|cy n (job) vacante f; (room) habitación f libre. ~**t** a <building> desocupado; <seat> libre; <post> vacante; <look> ausente

vacate vt dejar

vacation n (Amer) vacaciones fpl. **go on** ~ ir de vacaciones. ~**er** n (Amer) veraneante m & f

vaccin|ate vt vacunar. ~**ation** n vacunación f. ~**e** n vacuna f

vacuum n vacío m. ~ **cleaner** n aspiradora f

vagina n vagina f

vague a (**-er, -est**) vago; <outline> borroso; <person, expression> despistado. ~**ly** adv vagamente

vain a (**-er, -est**) vanidoso; (useless) vano. **in** ~ en vano

Valentine's Day n el día de San Valentín

valiant a valeroso

valid a válido. ~**ate** vt dar validez a; validar <contract>. ~**ity** n validez f

valley n (pl **-eys**) valle m

valour n valor m

valu|able a valioso. ~**ables** npl objetos mpl de valor. ~**ation** n valoración f. ~**e** n valor m. ●vt valorar; tasar, valorar, avaluar (LAm) <property>. ~**e added tax** n impuesto m sobre el valor añadido

valve n válvula f

vampire n vampiro m

van n furgoneta f, camioneta f; (Rail) furgón m

vandal n vándalo m. ~**ism** n vandalismo m. ~**ize** vt destruir

vanilla n vainilla f

vanish vi desaparecer

vanity n vanidad f. ~ **case** n neceser m

vapour n vapor m

varia|ble a variable. ~**nce** n. **at** ~**ce** en desacuerdo. ~**nt** n variante f. ~**tion** n variación f

vari|ed a variado. ~**ety** n variedad f. ~**ety show** n espectáculo m de variedades. ~**ous** a (several) varios; (different) diversos

varnish n barniz m; (for nails) esmalte m. ●vt barnizar; pintar <nails>

vary vt/i variar

vase n, (Amer) n (for flowers) florero m; (ornamental) jarrón m

vast a vasto, extenso; <size> inmenso. ~**ly** adv infinitamente

vat n cuba f

VAT abbr (= **value added tax**) IVA m

vault n (roof) bóveda f; (in bank) cámara f acorazada; (tomb) cripta f. ●vt/i saltar

VCR n = **videocassette recorder**

VDU n = **visual display unit**

veal n ternera f

veer vi dar un viraje, virar

vegeta|ble a vegetal. ●n verdura f. ~**rian** a & n vegetariano (m). ~**tion** n vegetación f

vehement a vehemente. ~**tly** adv con vehemencia

vehicle n vehículo m

veil n velo m

vein n vena f; (in marble) veta f

velocity n velocidad f

velvet n terciopelo m

vendetta n vendetta f

vend|ing machine n distribuidor m automático. ~**or** n vendedor m

veneer n chapa f, enchapado m; (fig) barniz m, apariencia f

venerate vt venerar

venereal a venéreo

Venetian blind n persiana f veneciana

Venezuela n Venezuela f. ~**n** a & n venezolano (m)

vengeance n venganza f. **with a** ~ (fig) con ganas

venom n veneno m. ~**ous** a venenoso

vent n (conducto m de) ventilación; (air ~) respiradero m.

give $\sim$ to dar rienda suelta a.● vt descargar

ventilat|e vt ventilar.$\sim$**ion** n ventilación f

ventriloquist n ventrílocuo m

venture n empresa f.● vt aventurar.● vi atreverse

venue n (for concert) lugar m de actuación

Venus n Venus m

veranda n galería f

verb n verbo m.$\sim$**al** a verbal.

verdict n veredicto m; (opinion) opinión f

verge n borde m.□ $\sim$ **on** vt rayar en

verify vt (confirm) confirmar; (check) verificar

vermin n alimañas fpl

versatil|e a versátil.$\sim$**ity** n versatilidad f

verse n estrofa f; (poetry) poesías fpl.$\sim$**d** a. be well-$\sim$ed in ser muy versado en.$\sim$**ion** n versión f

versus prep contra

vertebra n (pl-brae) vértebra f. $\sim$**te** n vertebrado m

vertical a & n vertical (f).$\sim$**ly** adv verticalmente

vertigo n vértigo m

verve n brío m

very adv muy. $\sim$ **much** muchísimo. $\sim$ **well** muy bien. the $\sim$ **first** el primero de todos.● a mismo. the $\sim$ **thing** exactamente lo quehace falta

vessel n (receptacle) recipiente m; (ship) navío m, nave f

vest n camiseta f; (Amer) chaleco m.

vestige n vestigio m

vet n veterinario m; (Amer 🅣, veteran) veterano m.● vt (pt vetted) someter a investigación <applicant>

veteran n veterano m

veterinary a veterinario.$\sim$ **surgeon** n veterinario m

veto n (pl-oes) veto m.● vt vetar

vex vt fastidiar

via prep por, por vía de

viable a viable

viaduct n viaducto m

vibrat|e vt/i vibrar.$\sim$**ion** n vibración f

vicar n párroco m.$\sim$**age** n casa f del párroco

vice n vicio m; (Tec) torno m de banco

vice versa adv viceversa

vicinity n vecindad f. in the $\sim$ of cerca de

vicious a <attack> feroz; <dog> fiero; <rumour> malicioso.$\sim$ **circle** n círculo m vicioso

victim n víctima f.$\sim$**ize** vt victimizar

victor n vencedor m

Victorian a victoriano

victor|ious a <army> victorioso; <team> vencedor.$\sim$**y** n victoria f

video n (pl-os) vídeo m, video m (LAm).$\sim$ **camera** n videocámara f.$\sim$**(cassette) recorder** n magnetoscopio m.$\sim$**tape** n videocassette f

vie vi (pres p vying) rivalizar

Vietnam n Vietnam m.$\sim$**ese** a & n vietnamita (m & f)

view n vista f; (mental survey) visión f de conjunto; (opinion) opinión f. in my $\sim$ a mi juicio. in $\sim$ of en vista de. on $\sim$ expuesto.● vt ver <scene, property>; (consider) considerar.$\sim$**er** n (TV) televidente m & f.$\sim$**finder** n visor m.$\sim$**point** n punto m de vista

vigil|ance n vigilancia f.$\sim$**ant** a vigilante

V

vigorousa enérgico; <growth> vigoroso. ~urn vigor m

vilea (base) vil; <food> asqueroso; <weather, temper> horrible

villagen pueblo m; (small) aldea f. ~rn vecino m del pueblo; (of small village) aldeano m

villainn maleante m & f; (in story etc) villano m

vindicatevt justificar

vindictivea vengativo

vinen (on ground) vid f; (climbing) parra f

vinegarn vinagre m

vineyardn viña f

vintagen (year) cosecha f. ●a <wine> añejo; <car> de época

vinyln vinilo m

violan viola f

violat|evt violar. ~ionn violación f

violen|cen violencia f. ~ta violento. ~tlyadv violentamente

violeta & n violeta (f); (colour) violeta (m)

violinn violín m. ~istn violinista m & f

VIPabbr (= **very important person**) VIP m

vipern víbora f

virgina & n virgen (f)

Virgon Virgo f

virilea viril

virtuala. **traffic is at a ~ standstill** el tráfico está prácticamente paralizado. ~ **reality**n realidad f virtual. ~lyadv prácticamente

virtuen virtud f. **by ~ of** en virtud de

virtuousa virtuoso

virulenta virulento

virusn (pl **-uses**) virus m

visan visado m, visa f (LAm)

visen (Amer) torno m de banco

visib|ilityn visibilidad f. ~lea visible; <sign, improvement> evidente

visionn visión f; (sight) vista f

visitvt visitar; hacer una visita a <person>. ●vi hacer visitas. ~ **with s.o.** (Amer) ir a ver a uno. ●n visita f. **pay s.o. a ~** hacerle una visita a uno. ~orn visitante m & f; (guest) visita f

visorn visera f

visuala visual. ~izevt imaginar (se); (foresee) prever

vitala (essential) esencial; <factor> de vital importancia; <organ> vital. ~ityn vitalidad f

vitaminn vitamina f.

vivaciousa vivaz

vivida vivo. ~lyadv intensamente; (describe) gráficamente

vivisectionn vivisección f

vocabularyn vocabulario m

vocala vocal. ~istn cantante m & f

vocationn vocación f. ~ala profesional

vociferousa vociferador

voguen moda f, boga f

voicen voz f. ●vt expresar

voida (not valid) nulo. ●n vacío m

volatilea volátil; <person> imprevisible

volcan|ica volcánico. ~on (pl **-oes**) volcán m

volleyn (pl **-eys**) (of gunfire) descarga f cerrada; (sport) volea f. ~balln vóleibol m

voltn voltio m. ~agen voltaje m

volumen volumen m; (book) tomo m

voluntar|ilyadv voluntariamente. ~ya voluntario; <organization> de beneficencia

volunteern voluntario m. ●vt ofrecer. ●vi. ~ **(to)** ofrecerse (a)

vomit *vt/i* vomitar. ● *n* vómito *m*

voracious *a* voraz

vot|e *n* voto *m*; (right) derecho *m* al voto; (act) votación *f*. ● *vi* votar. **~er** *n* votante *m & f*. **~ing** *n* votación *f*

vouch *vi*. **~ for s.o.** responder por uno. **~er** *n* vale *m*

vow *n* voto *m*. ● *vi* jurar

vowel *n* vocal *f*

voyage *n* viaje *m*; (by sea) travesía *f*

vulgar *a* (coarse) grosero, vulgar; (tasteless) de mal gusto. **~ity** *n* vulgaridad *f*

vulnerable *a* vulnerable

vulture *n* buitre *m*

vying ⇒VIE

W *abbr* (=**West**) O

wad *n* (of notes) fajo *m*; (tied together) lío *m*; (papers) montón *m*

waddle *vi* contonearse

wade *vi* caminar (*por el agua etc*)

wafer *n* galleta *f* de barquillo

waffle *n* ⓘ palabrería *f*. ● *vi* ⓘ divagar; (in essay, exam) meter paja ⓘ. ● *n* (Culin) gofre *m*, wafle *m* (LAm)

waft *vi* flotar

wag *vt* (*pt* **wagged**) menear. ● *vi* menearse

wage *n* sueldo *m*. **~s** *npl* salario *m*, sueldo *m*. **~r** *n* apuesta *f*

waggle *vt* menear. ● *vi* menearse

wagon *n* carro *m*; (Rail) vagón *m*; (Amer, delivery truck) furgoneta *f* de reparto

wail *vi* llorar

waist *n* cintura *f*. **~coat** *n* chaleco *m*. **~line** *n* cintura *f*

wait *vi* esperar; (at table) servir. **~ for** esperar. **~ on s.o.** atender a uno. ● *vt* (await) esperar <*chance, turn*>. **~ table** (Amer) servir a la mesa. **I can't ~ to see him** me muero de ganas de verlo. ● *n* espera *f*. **lie in ~** acechar

waiter *n* camarero *m*, mesero *m* (LAm)

wait: **~ing-list** *n* lista *f* de espera. **~ing-room** *n* sala *f* de espera

waitress *n* camarera *f*, mesera *f* (LAm)

waive *vt* renunciar a

wake *vt* (*pt* **woke**, *pp* **woken**) despertar. ● *vi* despertarse. ● *n* (Naut) estela *f*. **in the ~ of** como resultado de. ▢ **~ up** *vt* despertar. *vi* despertarse

Wales *n* (el país de) Gales

walk *vi* andar, caminar; (not ride) ir a pie; (stroll) pasear. ● *vt* andar por <*streets*>; llevar de paseo <*dog*>. ● *n* paseo *m*; (long) caminata *f*; (gait) manera *f* de andar. ▢ **~ out** *vi* salir; <*workers*> declararse en huelga. ▢ **~ out on** *vt* abandonar. **~er** *n* excursionista *m & f*

walkie-talkie *n* walkie-talkie *m*

walk: **~ing-stick** *n* bastón *m*. **W~man** *n* Walkman *m* (P). **~out** *n* retirada *f* en señal de protesta; (strike) abandono *m* del trabajo

wall *n* (interior) pared *f*; (exterior) muro *m*

wallet *n* cartera *f*, billetera *f*

wallop *vt* (*pt* **walloped**) ⓘ darle un golpazo a.

wallow *vi* revolcarse

wallpaper *n* papel *m* pintado

walnut *n* nuez *f*; (tree) nogal *m*

walrus *n* morsa *f*

waltz *n* vals *m*. ●*vi* valsar

wand *n* varita *f* (mágica)

wander *vi* vagar; (stroll) pasear; (digress) divagar. ●*n* vuelta *f*, paseo *m*. ~**er** *n* trotamundos *m*

wane *vi* <moon> menguar; <interest> decaer. ●*n*. be on the ~ <popularity> estar decayendo

wangle *vt* ⒤ agenciarse

want *vt* querer; (need) necesitar. ●*vi*. ~ **for** carecer de. ●*n* necesidad *f*; (lack) falta *f*. ~**ed** *a* <criminal> buscado

war *n* guerra *f*. **at** ~ en guerra

warble *vi* trinar, gorjear

ward *n* (in hospital) sala *f*; (child) pupilo *m*. □~ **off** *vt* conjurar <danger>; rechazar <attack>

warden *n* guarda *m*

warder *n* celador *m* (de una cárcel)

wardrobe *n* armario *m*; (clothes) guardarropa *f*, vestuario *m*

warehouse *n* depósito *m*, almacén *m*

wares *npl* mercancía(s) *f(pl)*

war: ~**fare** *n* guerra *f*. ~**head** *n* cabeza *f*, ojiva *f*

warm *a* (-er -est) <water, day> tibio, templado; <room> caliente; <climate, wind> cálido; <clothes> de abrigo; <welcome> caluroso. **be** ~ <person> tener calor. **it's** ~ **today** hoy hace calor. ●*vt*. ~ (**up**) calentar <room>; recalentar <food>; (fig) animar. ●*vi*. ~ (**up**) calentarse; (fig) animarse. ~-**blooded** *a* de sangre caliente. ~**ly** *adv* (heartily) calurosamente. ~**th** *n* calor *m*; (of colour, atmosphere) calidez *f*

warn *vt* advertir. ~**ing** *n* advertencia *f*; (notice) aviso *m*

warp *vt* alabear. ~**ed** *a* <wood> alabeado; <mind> retorcido

warrant *n* orden *f* judicial; (search ~) orden *f* de registro; (for arrest) orden *f* de arresto. ●*vt* justificar. ~**y** *n* garantía *f*

warrior *n* guerrero *m*

warship *n* buque *m* de guerra

wart *n* verruga *f*

wartime *n* tiempo *m* de guerra

wary *a* (-ier -iest) cauteloso. **be** ~ **of** recelar de

was ⇒BE

wash *vt* lavar; fregar, lavar (LAm) <floor>. ~ **one's face** lavarse la cara. ●*vi* lavarse. ●*n* (in washing machine) lavado *m*. **have a** ~ lavarse. **I gave the car a** ~ lavé el coche. □~ **out** *vt* (clean) lavar; (rinse) enjuagar. □~ **up** *vi* fregar los platos, lavar los trastes (Mex); (Amer, wash face and hands) lavarse. ~**able** *a* lavable. ~**basin** ~**bowl** (Amer) *n* lavabo *m*. ~**er** *n* arandela *f*. ~**ing** *n* lavado *m*; (dirty clothes) ropa *f* para lavar; (wet clothes) ropa *f* lavada. **do the** ~**ing** lavar la ropa, hacer la colada. ~**ing-machine** *n* máquina *f* de lavar, lavadora *f*. ~**ing-powder** *n* jabón *m* en polvo. ~**ing-up** *n*. **do the** ~**ing-up** lavar los platos, fregar (los platos). ~**ing-up liquid** *n* lavavajillas *m*. ~**out** *n* ⒤ desastre *m*. ~**room** *n* (Amer) baños *mpl*, servicios *mpl*

wasp *n* avispa *f*

waste ●*a* <matter> de desecho; <land> (barren) yermo; (uncultivated) baldío. ●*n* (of materials) desperdicio *m*; (of time) pérdida *f*; (refuse) residuos *mpl*. ●*vt* despilfarrar <electricity, money>; desperdiciar <talent, effort>; perder <time>. ●*vi*. ~-**disposal unit** *n* trituradora *f* de desperdicios. ~**ful** *a* poco

económico; *person*
despilfarrador. **~-paper basket**
n papelera *f*

watch *vt* mirar; observar
person, expression; ver *TV*;
(keep an eye on) vigilar; (take heed)
tener cuidado con. ● *vi* mirar. ● *n*
(observation) vigilancia *f*; (period of
duty) guardia *f*; (timepiece) reloj *m*.
~ **out** *vi* (be careful) tener cuidado;
(look carefully) estarse atento. **~dog**
n perro *m* guardián. **~man** *n* (*pl*
-men) vigilante *m*.

water *n* agua *f*. ● *vt* regar *plants
etc*. ● *vi* *eyes* llorar. **make s.o.'s
mouth ~** hacérsele la boca agua,
hacérsele agua la boca (LAm). **~
down** *vt* diluir; aguar *wine*.
~-colour *n* acuarela *f*. **~cress** *n*
berro *m*. **~fall** *n* cascada *f*; (large)
catarata *f*. **~ing-can** *n* regadera
f. **~ lily** *n* nenúfar *m*. **~logged** *a*
anegado; *shoes* empapado.
~proof *a* impermeable; *watch*
sumergible. **~-skiing** *n* esquí *m*
acuático. **~tight** *a* hermético;
boat estanco; *argument*
irrebatible. **~way** *n* canal *m*
navegable. **~y** *a* acuoso; *eyes*
lloroso

watt *n* vatio *m*

wave *n* onda *f*; (of hand) señal *f*;
(fig) oleada *f*. ● *vt* agitar; (curl)
ondular *hair*. ● *vi* (signal) hacer
señales con la mano; ondear
flag. **~band** *n* banda *f* de
frecuencia. **~length** *n* longitud *f*
de onda

waver *vi* (be indecisive) vacilar;
(falter) flaquear

wavy *a* (**-ier**, **-iest**) ondulado

wax *n* cera *f*. ● *vi* *moon* crecer.
~work *n* figura *f* de cera.
~works *npl* museo *m* de cera

way *n* (route) camino *m*; (manner)
manera *f*, forma *f*, modo *m*;

(direction) dirección *f*; (habit)
costumbre *f*. **it's a long ~ from
here** queda muy lejos de aquí. **be
in the ~** estorbar. **by the ~** a
propósito. **either ~** de cualquier
manera. **give ~** (collapse) ceder,
romperse; (Auto) ceder el paso. **in
a ~** en cierta manera. **in some ~s**
en ciertos modos. **make ~** dejar
paso a. **no ~!** ¡ni hablar! **on my ~
to** de camino a. **out of the ~**
remoto; (extraordinary) fuera de lo
común. **that ~** por allí. **this ~** por
aquí. **~ in** *n* entrada *f*. **~-lay** *vt*
(*pt* **-laid**) abordar. **~ out** *n* salida
f. **~-out** *a* ultramoderno, original.
~s *npl* costumbres *fpl*

we *pron* nosotros *m*, nosotras *f*

weak *a* (**-er**, **-est**) débil;
structure poco sólido;
performance, student flojo;
coffee poco cargado; *solution*
diluido; *beer* suave; (pej)
aguado. **~en** *vt* debilitar. ● *vi*
resolve flaquear. **~ling** *n*
alfeñique *m*. **~ness** *n* debilidad *f*

wealth *n* riqueza *f*. **~y** *a* (**-ier**,
-iest) rico

weapon *n* arma *f*

wear *vt* (*pt* **wore**, *pp* **worn**)
llevar; vestirse *black, red,
etc*; (usually) usar. **I've got nothing
to ~** no tengo nada que
ponerme. ● *vi* (through use)
gastarse; (last) durar. ● *n* uso *m*;
(damage) desgaste *m*; **~ and tear**
desgaste *m* natural. □ **~ out** *vt*
gastar; (tire) agotar. *vi* gastarse

weary *a* (**-ier**, **-iest**) cansado. ● *vt*
cansar. ● *vi* cansarse. **~ of**
cansarse de

weather *n* tiempo *m*. **what's the
~ like?** ¿qué tiempo hace?. **the ~
was bad** hizo mal tiempo. **be
under the ~** 🔢 no andar muy
bien 🔢. ● *vt* (survive) sobrellevar.
~-beaten *a* curtido. **~ forecast**

W

n pronóstico *m* del tiempo.
~**-vane** *n* veleta *f*

weave *vt* (*pt* **wove**, *pp* **woven**)
tejer; entretejer <*threads*>. ~
one's way abrirse paso. ●*vi*
<*person*> zigzaguear; <*road*>
serpentear. ~**r** *n* tejedor *m*

web *n* (of spider) telaraña *f*; (of
intrigue) red *f*. ~**cam** *n* cámara *f*
web. ~**master** *n* administrador
m de web. ~ **page** *n* página *f*
web. ~ **site** *n* sitio web *m*

wed *vt* (*pt* **wedded**) casarse con.
●*vi* casarse.

we'd = **we had**, **we would**

wedding *n* boda *f*, casamiento *m*.
~**-cake** *n* pastel *m* de boda.
~**-ring** *n* anillo *m* de boda

wedge *n* cuña *f*

Wednesday *n* miércoles *m*

wee *a* 🄸 pequeñito. ●*n*. **have a ~**
🄸 hacer pis 🄸

weed *n* mala hierba *f*. ●*vt*
desherbar. □ ~ **out** *vt* eliminar.
~**killer** *n* herbicida *m*. ~**y** *a*
<*person*> enclenque; (Amer, lanky)
larguirucho 🄸

week *n* semana *f*. ~**day** *n* día *m*
de semana. ~**end** *n* fin *m* de
semana. ~**ly** *a* semanal. ●*n*
semanario *m*. ●*adv*
semanalmente

weep *vi* (*pt* **wept**) llorar

weigh *vt/i* pesar. ~ **anchor** levar
anclas. □ ~ **down** *vt* (fig) oprimir.
□ ~ **up** *vt* pesar; (fig) considerar

weight *n* peso *m*; (sport) pesa *f*.
put on ~ engordar. **lose ~**
adelgazar. ~**-lifting** *n* halterofilia
f, levantamiento *m* de pesos

weir *n* presa *f*

weird *a* (**-er**, **-est**) raro, extraño;
(unearthly) misterioso

welcom|e *a* bienvenido. **you're**
~**!** (after thank you) ¡de nada! ●*n*
bienvenida *f*; (reception) acogida *f*.

●*vt* dar la bienvenida a;
(appreciate) alegrarse de

weld *vt* soldar. ●*n* soldadura *f*.
~**er** *n* soldador *m*

welfare *n* bienestar *m*; (aid)
asistencia *f* social. **W~ State** *n*
estado *m* benefactor

well *adv* (**better**, **best**) bien. ~
done! ¡muy bien!, ¡bravo! **as ~**
también. **as ~ as** además de. **we
may as ~ go tomorrow** más vale
que vayamos mañana. **do ~**
(succeed) tener éxito. **very ~** muy
bien. ● *a* bien. **I'm very ~** estoy
muy bien. ● *int* (introducing,
continuing sentence) bueno; (surprise)
¡vaya!; (indignation, resignation)
bueno. ~ **I never!** ¡no me digas!
●*n* pozo *m*

we'll = **we will**

well: ~**-behaved** *a* que se porta
bien, bueno. ~**-educated** *a*
culto.

wellington (**boot**) *n* bota *f* de
goma *or* de agua

well: ~**-known** *a* conocido. ~
off *a* adinerado. ~**-stocked** *a*
bien provisto. ~**-to-do** *a*
adinerado

Welsh *a* & *n* galés (*m*). **the ~** *n*
los galeses

went ⇒GO

wept ⇒WEEP

were ⇒BE

we're = **we are**

west *n* oeste *m*. **the W~** el
Occidente *m*. ●*a* oeste; <*wind*>
del oeste, al oeste. ●*adv* <*go*> hacia el
oeste, al oeste. **it's ~ of York** está
al oeste de York. ~**erly** *a* <*wind*>
del oeste. ~**ern** *a* occidental. ●*n*
(film) película *f* del Oeste. ~**erner**
n occidental *m* & *f*. **W~ Indian** *a*
& *n* antillano (*m*). **W~ Indies** *npl*
Antillas *fpl*. ~**ward(s)** *adv* hacia
el oeste

wet *a* (**wetter**, **wettest**) mojado;
(rainy) lluvioso; (🄸, person) soso. '~

paint' 'pintura fresca'. **get ~** mojarse. **he got his feet ~** se mojó los pies. ●*vt* (*pt* **wetted**) mojar; (dampen) humedecer. **~ o.s.** orinarse. **~back** *n* espalda *f* mojada. **~ blanket** *n* aguafiestas *m* & *f*. **~ suit** *n* traje *m* de neopreno

we've = we have

whack *vt* 🇬🇧 golpear. ●*n* 🇬🇧 golpe *m*.

whale *n* ballena *f*. **we had a ~ of a time** 🇬🇧 lo pasamos bomba 🇬🇧

wham *int* ¡zas!

wharf *n* (*pl* **wharves** or **wharfs**) muelle *m*

---

what

●*adjective*

····▸ (in questions) qué. **~ perfume are you wearing?** ¿qué perfume llevas?. **~ colour are the walls?** ¿de qué color son las paredes?

····▸ (in exclamations) qué. **~ a beautiful house!** ¡qué casa más linda!. **~ a lot of people!** ¡cuánta gente!

····▸ (in indirect speech) qué. **I'll ask him ~ bus to take** le preguntaré qué autobús hay que tomar. **do you know ~ time it leaves?** ¿sabes a qué hora sale?

●*pronoun*

····▸ (in questions) qué. **~ is it?** ¿qué es? **~ for?** ¿para qué?. **~'s the problem?** ¿cuál es el problema? **~'s he like?** ¿cómo es? **what?** (say that again) ¿cómo?, ¿qué?

····▸ (in indirect questions) qué. **I didn't know ~ to do** no sabía qué hacer

····▸ (relative) lo que. **I did ~ I could** hice lo que pude. **~ I need is a new car** lo que necesito es un coche nuevo

····▸ (in phrases) **~ about me?** ¿y yo qué? **~ if she doesn't come?** ¿y si no viene?

---

whatever *a* cualquiera. ●*pron* (todo) lo que, cualquier cosa que

whatsoever *a* & *pron* = **whatever**

wheat *n* trigo *m*

wheel *n* rueda *f*. **at the ~** al volante. ●*vt* empujar <*bicycle etc*>; llevar (*en silla de ruedas etc*) <*person*>. **~barrow** *n* carretilla *f*. **~chair** *n* silla *f* de ruedas

wheeze *vi* respirar con dificultad

when *adv* cuándo. ●*conj* cuando. **~ever** *adv* (every time that) cada vez que, siempre que; (at whatever time) **we'll go ~ever you're ready** saldremos cuando estés listo

where *adv* & *conj* donde; (interrogative) dónde. **~ are you going?** ¿adónde vas? **~ are you from?** ¿de dónde eres?. **~abouts** *adv* en qué parte. ●*n* paradero *m*. **~as** *conj* por cuanto; (in contrast) mientras (que). **~ver** *adv* (in questions) dónde; (no matter where) en cualquier parte. ●*conj* donde (+ *subjunctive*), dondequiera (+ *subjunctive*)

whet *vt* (*pt* **whetted**) abrir <*appetite*>

whether *conj* si. **I don't know ~ she will like it** no sé si le gustará. **~ you like it or not** te guste o no te guste

which *a* (in questions) (*sing*) qué, cuál; (*pl*) qué, cuáles. **~ one** cuál. **~ one of you** cuál de ustedes. ●*pron* (in questions) (*sing*) cuál; (*pl*) cuáles; (relative) que; (object) el cual, la cual, lo cual, los cuales, las cuales. **~ever** *a* cualquier. ●*pron* cualquiera que, el que, la que; (in questions) cuál; (*pl*) cuáles

W

while n rato m. **a ~ ago** hace un rato. ● conj mientras; (although) aunque. □ **~ away** vt pasar <time>

whilst conj ⇒WHILE

whim n capricho m

whimper vi gimotear. ● n quejido m

whine vi <person> gemir; <child> lloriquear; <dog> aullar

whip n látigo m; (for punishment) azote m. ● vt (pt **whipped**) fustigar, pegarle a (con la fusta) <horse>; azotar <person>; (Culin) batir

whirl vi girar rápidamente. **~pool** n remolino m. **~wind** n torbellino m

whirr n zumbido m. ● vi zumbar

whisk vt (Culin) batir. ● n (Culin) batidor m. **~ away** llevarse

whisker n pelo m. **~s** npl (of cat etc) bigotes mpl

whisky n whisky m, güisqui m

whisper vi susurrar. ● vi cuchichear. ● n susurro m

whistle n silbido m; (loud) chiflado m; (instrument) silbato m, pito m. ● vi silbar; (loudly) chiflar

white a (-er, -est) blanco. **go ~** ponerse pálido. ● n blanco; (of egg) clara f. **~ coffee** n café m con leche. **~-collar worker** n empleado m de oficina. **~ elephant** n objeto m inútil y costoso. **~-hot** a <metal> al rojo blanco. **~ lie** n mentirijilla f. **~n** vt/i blanquear. **~wash** n cal f; (cover-up) tapadera f 🆃. ● vt blanquear, encalar

Whitsun n Pentecostés m

whiz vi (pt **whizzed**). **~ by**, **~ past** pasar zumbando. **~-kid** n 🆃 lince m 🆃

who pron (in questions) quién; (pl) quiénes; (as relative) que; **the girl ~** lives there la chica que vive allí. **those ~** can't come tomorrow los que no puedan venir mañana. **~ever** pron quienquiera que; (interrogative) quién

whole a. **the ~ country** todo el país. **there's a ~ bottle left** queda una botella entera. ● n todo m, conjunto m; (total) total m. **on the ~** en general. **~-hearted** a <support> incondicional; <approval> sin reservar. **~meal** a integral. **~sale** n venta f al por mayor. ● a & adv al por mayor. **~some** a sano

wholly adv completamente

whom pron que, a quien; (in questions) a quién

whooping cough n tos f convulsa

whore n puta f

whose pron de quién; (pl) de quiénes. ● a (in questions) de quién; (pl) de quiénes; (relative) cuyo; (pl) cuyos

why adv por qué. **~ not?** ¿por qué no? **that's ~ I couldn't go** por eso no pude ir. ● int ¡vaya!

wick n mecha f

wicked a malo; (mischievous) travieso; (🆃, very bad) malísimo

wicker n mimbre m & f. ● a de mimbre. **~work** n artículos mpl de mimbre

wicket n (cricket) rastrillo m

wide a (-er, -est) ancho; <range, experience> amplio; (off target) desviado. **it's four metres ~** tiene cuatro metros de ancho. ● adv. **open ~!** abra bien la boca. **~ awake** a completamente despierto; (fig) despabilado. **I left the door ~ open** dejé la puerta abierta de par en par. **~ly** adv extensamente; (believed) generalmente; (different) muy. **~n** vt ensanchar. ● vi ensancharse

∼spread a extendido; (fig) difundido

widow n viuda f. **∼er** n viudo m.

width n anchura f. **in ∼** de ancho

wield vt manejar; ejercer <power>

wife n (pl **wives**) mujer f, esposa f

wig n peluca f

wiggle vt menear. ●vi menearse

wild a (**-er -est**) <animal> salvaje; <flower> silvestre; <country> agreste; (enraged) furioso; <idea> extravagante; (with joy) loco. **a ∼ guess** una conjetura hecha totalmente al azar. **I'm not ∼ about the idea** la idea no me enloquece. ●adv en estado salvaje. **run ∼** <children> criarse como salvajes. **∼s** npl regiones fpl salvajes. **∼erness** n páramo m. **∼fire** n. **spread like ∼fire** correr como un reguero de pólvora. **∼-goose chase** n empresa f inútil. **∼life** n fauna f. **∼ly** adv violentamente; (fig) locamente

....

will

●*auxiliary verb*

past **would**; contracted forms **I'll, you'll, etc = I will, you will,** etc.; **won't = will not**

····▸(talking about the future)

❗ The Spanish future tense is not always the first option for translating the English future tense. The present tense of *ir a + a + verb* is commonly used instead, particularly in Latin American countries. **he'll be here on Tuesday** *estará el martes, va a estar el*

martes; **she won't agree** *no va a aceptar, no aceptará*

····▸(in invitations and requests) **∼ you have some wine?** ¿quieres (un poco de) vino? **you'll stay for dinner, won't you?** te quedas a cenar, ¿no?

····▸(in tag questions) **you ∼ be back soon, won't you?** vas a volver pronto, ¿no?

····▸(in short answers) **will it be ready by Monday? - yes, it ∼** ¿estará listo para el lunes? - sí

●*noun*

····▸(mental power) voluntad f

····▸(document) testamento m

....

willing a complaciente. **∼ to** dispuesto a. **∼ly** adv de buena gana

willow n sauce m

will-power n fuerza f de voluntad

wilt vi marchitarse

win vt (pt **won** pres p **winning**) ganar; (achieve, obtain) conseguir. ●vi ganar. ●n victoria f. □ **∼ over** vt ganarse a

wince vi hacer una mueca de dolor

winch n cabrestante m

wind[1] n viento m; (in stomach) gases mpl. **∼ instrument** instrumento m de viento. ●vt dejar sin aliento; <blow> cortarle la respiración a

wind[2] vt (pt **wound**) (wrap around) enrollar; dar cuerda a <clock etc>. ●vi <road etc> serpentear. □ **∼ up** vt dar cuerda a <watch, clock>; (fig) terminar, concluir

wind : ∼cheater n cazadora f. **∼fall** n (fig) suerte f inesperada. **∼ farm** n parque m eólico

winding a tortuoso

windmill n molino m (de viento)

window n ventana f; (in shop) escaparate m, vitrina f (LAm), vidriera f (LAm), aparador m (Mex); (of vehicle, booking-office) ventanilla f; (Comp) ventana f, window m. ~ **box** n jardinera f. ~**shop** vi mirar los escaparates. ~**sill** n alféizar m or repisa f de la ventana

wind : ~**pipe** n tráquea f. ~**screen** n, ~**shield** n (Amer) parabrisas m. ~**screen wiper** n limpiaparabrisas m. ~**swept** a azotado por el viento. ~**y** a (**-ier**, **-iest**) <day> ventoso, de viento. **it's** ~**y** hace viento

wine n vino m. ~**cellar** n bodega f. ~**glass** n copa f de vino. ~**growing** n vinicultura f. ● a vinícola. ~ **list** n lista f de vinos. ~**tasting** n cata f de vinos

wing n ala f; (Auto) aleta f. **under one's** ~ bajo la protección de uno. ~**er** n (Sport) ala m & f. ~**s** npl (in theatre) bastidores mpl

wink vi guiñar el ojo; <light etc> centellear. ● n guiño m. **not to sleep a** ~ no pegar ojo

win : ~**ner** n ganador m. ~**ning-post** n poste m de llegada. ~**nings** npl ganancias fpl

wint|er n invierno m. ● vi invernar. ~**ry** a invernal

wipe vt limpiar, pasarle un trapo a; (dry) secar. ~ **one's nose** limpiarse la nariz. ● n. **give sth a** ~ limpiar algo, pasarle un trapo a algo. □ ~ **out** vt (cancel) cancelar; (destroy) destruir; (obliterate) borrar. □ ~ **up** vt limpiar

wir|e n alambre m; (Elec) cable m. ~**ing** n instalación f eléctrica

wisdom n sabiduría f. ~ **tooth** n muela f del juicio

wise a (**-er**, **-est**) sabio; (sensible) prudente; <decision, choice>

acertado. ~**ly** adv sabiamente; (sensibly) prudentemente

wish n deseo m; (greeting) saludo m. **make a** ~ pedir un deseo. **best** ~**es, John** (in letters) saludos de John, un abrazo de John. ● vt desear. ~ **s.o. well** desear buena suerte a uno. **I** ~ **I were rich** ¡ojalá fuera rico! **he** ~**ed he hadn't told her** lamentó habérselo dicho. ~**ful thinking** n ilusiones fpl

wistful a melancólico

wit n gracia f; (intelligence) ingenio m. **be at one's** ~**s' end** no saber más qué hacer

witch n bruja f. ~**craft** n brujería f.

with prep con; (cause, having) de. **come** ~ **me** ven conmigo. **take it** ~ **you** llévalo contigo; (formal) llévelo consigo. **the man** ~ **the beard** el hombre de la barba. **trembling** ~ **fear** temblando de miedo

withdraw vt (pt **withdrew**, pp **withdrawn**) retirar. ● vi apartarse. ~**al** n retirada f. ~**n** a <person> retraído

wither vi marchitarse

withhold vt (pt **withheld**) retener; (conceal) ocultar (**from** a)

within prep dentro de. ● adv dentro. ~ **sight** a la vista

without prep sin. ~ **paying** sin pagar

withstand vt (pt **-stood**) resistir

witness n testigo m; (proof) testimonio m. ● vt presenciar; atestiguar <signature>. ~**-box** n tribuna f de los testigos

witt|icism n ocurrencia f. ~**y** a (**-ier**, **-iest**) gracioso

wives ⇒WIFE

wizard n hechicero m

wizened a arrugado

wobble vi <*chair*> tambalearse; <*bicycle*> bambolearse; <*voice, jelly, hand*> temblar. ~y a <*chair etc*> cojo

woe n aflicción f

woke woken ⇒WAKE

wolf n (pl **wolves**) lobo m

woman n (pl **women**) mujer f

womb n matriz f

women npl ⇒WOMAN

won ⇒WIN

wonder n maravilla f; (bewilderment) asombro m. **no ~** no es de extrañarse (**that** que). ●vt (ask oneself) preguntarse. **I ~ whose book this is** me pregunto de quién será este libro; (in polite requests) **I ~ if you could help me?** ¿me podría ayudar? ~**ful** a maravilloso. ~**fully** adv maravillosamente

won't = will not

wood n madera f; (for burning) leña f; (area) bosque m. ~**ed** a poblado de árboles, boscoso. ~**en** a de madera. ~**land** n bosque m. ~**wind** n instrumentos mpl de viento de madera. ~**work** n carpintería f; (in room etc) maderaje m. ~**worm** n carcoma f. ~**y** a leñoso

wool n lana f. **pull the ~ over s.o.'s eyes** engañar a uno. ~**len** a de lana. ~**ly** a (-**ier** -**iest**) de lana; (unclear) vago. ●n jersey m

word n palabra f; (news) noticia f. **by ~ of mouth** de palabra. **I didn't say a ~** yo no dije nada. **in other ~s** es decir. ●vt expresar. ~**ing** n redacción f; (of question) formulación f. **~ processor** n procesador m de textos. ~**y** a prolijo

wore ⇒WEAR

work n trabajo m; (arts) obra f. **be out of ~** estar sin trabajo, estar

desocupado. ●vt hacer trabajar; manejar <*machine*>. ●vi trabajar; <*machine*> funcionar; <*student*> estudiar; <*drug etc*> surtir efecto. □ **~ off** vt desahogar. □ **~ out** vt resolver <*problem*>; (calculate) calcular; (understand) entender. vi (succeed) salir bien; (Sport) entrenarse. □ **~ up** vt. **get ~ed up** exaltarse. ~**able** a <*project, solution*> factible. ~**er** n trabajador m; (manual) obrero m; (in office, bank) empleado m. ~**ing** a <*day*> laborable; <*clothes etc*> de trabajo. **in ~ing order** en estado de funcionamiento. ~**ing class** n clase f obrera. ~**ing-class** a de la clase obrera. ~**man** n (pl -**men**) obrero m. ~**manship** n destreza f. ~**s** npl (building) fábrica f; (Mec) mecanismo m. ~**shop** n taller m

world n mundo m. **out of this ~** maravilloso. ●a mundial. **W~ Cup** n. **the W~ Cup** la Copa del Mundo. ~**ly** a mundano. ~**wide** a universal. **W~ Wide Web** n World Wide Web m

worm n gusano m, lombriz f

worn ⇒WEAR. ●a gastado. ~-**out** a gastado; <*person*> rendido

worr|ied a preocupado. ~**y** vt preocupar; (annoy) molestar. ●vi preocuparse. ●n preocupación f. ~**ying** a inquietante

worse a peor. **get ~** empeorar. ●adv peor; (more) más. ~**n** vt/i empeorar

worship n culto m; (title) Su Señoría. ●vt (pt **worshipped**) adorar

worst a peor. **he's the ~ in the class** es el peor de la clase. ●adv peor. ●n. **the ~** lo peor

worth n valor m. ●a. **be ~** valer. **it's ~ trying** vale la pena

W

probarlo. **it was ~ my while** (me) valió la pena.**~less** *a* sin valor. **~while** *a* que vale la pena.**~y** *a* meritorio; (respectable) respetable; (laudable) loable

would *v aux*. (in conditional sentences) **~ you go?** ¿irías tú? **he ~ come if he could** vendría si pudiera; (in reported speech) **I thought you'd forget** pensé que te olvidarías; (in requests, invitations) **~ you come here, please?** ¿quieres venir aquí? **~ you switch the television off?** ¿podrías apagar la televisión?; (be prepared to) **he ~n't listen to me** no me quería escuchar

wound[1] *n* herida *f*. ● *vt* herir

wound[2] ⇒WIND[2]

wove, woven ⇒WEAVE

wow *int* ¡ah!

wrangle *vi* reñir. ● *n* riña *f*

wrap *vt* (*pt* **wrapped**) envolver. ● *n* bata *f*; (shawl) chal *m*.**~per** *n*, **~ping** *n* envoltura *f*

wrath *n* ira *f*

wreak *vt* sembrar. **~ havoc** causar estragos

wreath *n* (*pl* -**ths**) corona *f*

wreck *n* (ship) restos *mpl* de un naufragio; (vehicle) restos *mpl* de un avión siniestrado. **be a nervous ~** tener los nervios destrozados. ● *vt* provocar el naufragio de <*ship*>; destrozar <*car*>; (Amer, demolish) demoler; (fig) destrozar. **~age** *n* restos *mpl*; (of building) ruinas *fpl*

wrench *vt* arrancar; (sprain) desgarrarse; dislocarse <*joint*>. ● *n* tirón *m*; (emotional) dolor *m* (*causado por una separación*); (tool) llave *f* inglesa

wrestl|e *vi* luchar.**~er** *n* luchador *m*.**~ing** *n* lucha *f*

wretch *n* (despicable person) desgraciado *m*; (unfortunate person)

desdichado *m* & *f*.**~ed** *a* desdichado; <*weather*> horrible

wriggle *vi* retorcerse. **~ out of** escaparse de

wring *vt* (*pt* **wrung**) retorcer <*neck*>. **~ out of** (obtain from) arrancar. □ **~ out** *vt* retorcer

wrinkl|e *n* arruga *f*. ● *vt* arrugar. ● *vi* arrugarse.**~y** *a* arrugado

wrist *n* muñeca *f*.**~watch** *n* reloj *m* de pulsera

writ *n* orden *m* judicial

write *vt/i* (*pt* **wrote**, *pp* **written**, *pres p* **writing**) escribir. □ **~ down** *vt* anotar. □ **~ off** *vt* cancelar <*debt*>.**~-off** *n*. **the car was a ~-off** el coche fue declarado un siniestro total.**~r** *n* escritor *m*

writhe *vi* retorcerse

writing *n* (script) escritura *f*; (handwriting) letra *f*. **in ~** por escrito.**~s** *npl* obra *f*, escritos *mpl*.**~ desk** *n* escritorio *m*.**~ pad** *n* bloc *m*.**~ paper** *n* papel *m* de escribir

written ⇒WRITE

wrong *a* equivocado, incorrecto; (not just) injusto; (mistaken) equivocado. **be ~** no tener razón; (be mistaken) equivocarse. **what's ~?** ¿qué pasa? **it's ~ to steal** robar está mal. **what's ~ with that?** ¿qué hay de malo en eso?. ● *adv* mal. **go ~** equivocarse; <*plan*> salir mal. ● *n* injusticia *f*; (evil) mal *m*. **in the ~** equivocado. ● *vt* ser injusto con.**~ful** *a* injusto.**~ly** *adv* mal; (unfairly) injustamente

wrote ⇒WRITE

wrought iron *n* hierro *m* forjado

wrung ⇒WRING

wry *a* (**wryer**, **wryest**) irónico. **make a ~ face** torcer el gesto

xerox vt fotocopiar, xerografiar
Xmas n abbr (**Christmas**) Navidad f
X-ray n (ray) rayo m X; (photograph) radiografía f. ~**s** npl rayos mpl. ●vt hacer una radiografía de
xylophone n xilofón m, xilófono m

yacht n yate m. ~**ing** n navegación f a vela
yank vt 🄸 tirar de (*violentamente*)
Yankee n 🄸 yanqui m & f
yap vi (pt **yapped**) <*dog*> ladrar (*con ladridos agudos*)
yard n patio m; (Amer, garden) jardín m; (measurement) yarda f (= 0.9144 metre)
yarn n hilo m; (🄸, tale) cuento m
yawn vi bostezar. ●n bostezo m
year n año m. **be three ~s old** tener tres años. ~**ly** a anual. ●adv cada año
yearn vi. ~ **to do sth** anhelar hacer algo. ~ **for sth** añorar algo. ~**ing** n anhelo m, ansia f
yeast n levadura f
yell vi gritar. ●n grito m
yellow a & n amarillo (m)

yelp n gañido m. ●vi gañir
yes int & n sí (m)
yesterday adv & n ayer (m). **the day before ~** anteayer m. ~ **morning** ayer por la mañana, ayer en la mañana (LAm)
yet adv todavía, aún; (already) ya. **as ~** hasta ahora; (as a linker) sin embargo. ●conj pero
Yiddish n yídish m
yield vt (surrender) ceder; producir <*crop/mineral*>; dar <*results*>. ●vi ceder. **'yield'** (Amer, traffic sign) ceda el paso. ●n rendimiento m
yoga n yoga m
yoghurt n yogur m
yoke n (fig also) yugo m
yokel n palurdo m
yolk n yema f (de huevo)

. . . .
you
. . . . :

●*pronoun*
····▶ (as the subject) (familiar form) (*sing*) tú, vos (River Plate and parts of Central America); (*pl*) vosotros, -tras (Spain), ustedes (LAm); (formal) (*sing*) usted; (*pl*) ustedes

❗ In Spanish the subject pronoun is usually only used to give emphasis or mark contrast.

····▶ (as the direct object) (familiar form) (*sing*) te; (*pl*) os (Spain), los, las (LAm); (formal) (*sing*) lo or (Spain) le, la; (*pl*) los or (Spain) les, las. **I love ~** te quiero
····▶ (as the indirect object) (familiar form) (*sing*) te; (*pl*) os (Spain), les (LAm); (formal) (*sing*) le; (*pl*) les. **I sent ~ the book yesterday** te mandé el libro ayer

❗ The pronoun se replaces the indirect object pronoun le or les when the latter is used with the direct object pronoun (*lo*, *la* etc), e.g. **I gave it to** ∼ *se lo di*

····▸ (when used after a preposition) (*familiar form*) (*sing*) ti, vos (River Plate and parts of Central America); (*pl*) vosotros, -tras (Spain), ustedes (LAm); (*formal*) (*sing*) usted; (*pl*) ustedes

····▸ (generalizing) uno, tú (*esp* Spain). ∼ **feel very proud** uno se siente muy orgulloso, te sientes muy orgulloso (*esp* Spain). ∼ **have to be patient** hay que tener paciencia

you'd = you had, you would

you'll = you will

young *a* (**-er**, **-est**) joven. **my** ∼**er sister** mi hermana menor. **he's a year** ∼**er than me** tiene un año menos que yo. ∼ **lady** *n* señorita *f*. ∼ **man** *n* joven *m*. ∼**ster** *n* joven *m*

your *a* (belonging to one person) (*sing, familiar*) tu; (*pl, familiar*) tus; (*sing, formal*) su; (*pl, formal*) sus; (belonging to more than one person) (*sing, familiar*) vuestro, -tra, su (LAm); (*pl, familiar*) vuestros, -tras, sus (LAm); (*sing, formal*) su; (*pl, formal*) sus

you're = you are

yours *poss pron* (belonging to one person) (*sing, familiar*) tuyo, -ya; (*pl, familiar*) tuyos, -yas; (*sing, formal*) suyo, -ya; (*pl, formal*) suyos, -yas. (belonging to more than one person) (*sing, familiar*) vuestro, -tra; (*pl, familiar*) vuestros, -tras, suyos, -yas (LAm); (*sing, formal*) suyo, -ya; (*pl, formal*) suyos, -yas. **an aunt of** ∼ una tía tuya; ∼ **is here** el tuyo está aquí

yourself *pron* (*reflexive*). (emphatic use) 🅸 tú mismo, tú misma; (formal) usted mismo, usted misma. **describe** ∼**f** descríbete;

(Ud form) descríbase. **stop thinking about** ∼**f** deja de pensar en tí mismo; (formal) deje de pensar en sí mismo; **by** ∼**f** solo, sola. ∼**ves** *pron* vosotros mismos, vosotras mismas (familiar), ustedes mismos, ustedes mismas (LAm familiar), ustedes mismos, ustedes mismas (formal); (*reflexive*). **behave** ∼**ves** ¡portaos bien (familiar), ¡pórtense bien! (formal, LAm familiar). **by** ∼**ves** solos, solas

youth *n* (*pl* **youths**) (early life) juventud *f*; (boy) joven *m*; (young people) juventud *f*. ∼**ful** *a* joven, juvenil. ∼ **hostel** *n* albergue *m* juvenil

you've = you have

Yugoslav *a & n* yugoslavo (*m*). ∼**ia** *n* Yugoslavia *f*

zeal *n* fervor *m*, celo *m*

zeal|ot *n* fanático *m*. ∼**ous** *a* ferviente; (worker) que pone gran celo en su trabajo

zebra *n* cebra *f*. ∼ **crossing** *n* paso *m* de cebra

zenith *n* cenit *m*

zero *n* (*pl* **-os**) cero *m*

zest *n* entusiasmo *m*; (peel) cáscara *f*

zigzag *n* zigzag *m*. ● *vi* (*pt* **zigzagged**) zigzaguear

zilch *n* 🆇 nada de nada

zinc *n* cinc *m*

zip *n* cremallera *f*, cierre *m* (LAm), zíper *m* (Mex). ● *vt*. ~ **(up)** cerrar (la cremallera). ~ **code** *n* (Amer) código *m* postal. ~ **fastener** *n* cremallera *f*. ~**per** *n/vt* ⇒ZIP

zodiac *n* zodíaco *m*, zodiaco *m*

zombie *n* zombi *m* & *f*

zone *n* zona *f*. **time** ~ *n* huso *m* horario

zoo *n* zoo *m*, zoológico *m*. ~**logical** *a* zoológico. ~**logist** *n* zoólogo *m*. ~**logy** *n* zoología *f*

zoom . □ ~ **in** *vi* (Photo) hacer un zoom in (**on** sobre). □ ~ **past** *vi/t* pasar zumbando. ~ **lens** *n* teleobjetivo *m*, zoom *m*

zucchini *n* (*invar or* ~**s**) (Amer) calabacín *m*

Z

Summary of Spanish grammar

The following section lists the most basic rules of Spanish grammar. It does not include all the exceptions that you will come across later in your studies. There are one or two differences between European and Latin-American Spanish which are mentioned below.

Spelling: basic rules

- The sound of *c* as in English *cat* is spelt **c** before **a**, **o**, or **u**, but **qu** before **e** or **i** (the **u** is not pronounced): **cama** *bed*, **cómo** *how*, but **pequeño** *small*, **aquí** *here*.

- The sound *th* as in English *think* is spelt **z** before **a**, **o**, and **u**, but **c** before **e** or **i**: **caza** *hunting*, **brazo** *arm*, but **cero** *zero*, **hace** *he/she does*.

- The sound 'kh' (like Scottish ch in *loch*) is spelt **j** before **a**, **o**, and **u**, but usually **g** before **e** and **i**: **jardín** *garden*, **hija** *daughter*, but **general** *general*, **gimnasio** *gym*. There are some exceptions like **Jesús** *Jesús*, **dije** *I said*.

Accents

The acute accent (the sign over **á**, **ó**, **é**, etc.) shows where the stress falls, i.e. which part of a Spanish word is spoken loudest. In both English and Spanish shifting the stress can change the meaning, as can be seen in the English *the invalid had an invalid ticket*. We must write an accent on the stressed vowel in a Spanish word when:

- It ends in a vowel (**a**, **e**, **i**, **o**, or **u**), or **n** or **s**, and it is not stressed on the last vowel but one: **habló** *he/she spoke*, **Canadá** *Canada*, **inglés** *English*, **acción** *action*, **dámelo** *give it to me*.

- It does not end in a vowel or **n** or **s**, and it is not stressed on the last vowel: **revólver** *revolver*, **récord** *sports record*, **álbum** *album*, **córner** *corner* (in soccer).

- A few words have an accent to distinguish them from other similar words: **de** = *of* and **dé** = *give!*, **si** = *if* and **sí** = *yes*, **sólo** = *only* and **solo** = *alone*.

! Note: The letters **i** and **u** do not count as vowels when they are pronounced *y* or *w*, so the following do not require accents (the stressed vowel is underlined): **Francia** *France*, **importancia** *importance*, **continuo** *continuous*.

Question marks and exclamation marks

We write upside-down question marks or exclamation marks at the beginning of Spanish questions and exclamations (words spoken in surprise, fear, or anger): **¿quién es?** *who is it?*, **¿dónde está?** *where is it?*, **¡socorro!** *help!*, **¡déjame en paz!** *leave me alone!*

Nouns

Nouns are the names of things, people, places, or abstract ideas like 'liberty', 'justice', 'happiness'. All Spanish nouns are either masculine or feminine in gender, including nouns referring to objects or ideas. For this reason learn every Spanish noun with the word for 'the' in front of it: **la piedra** (fem.)= *the stone*, **el coche** (masc.)= *the car*, **la mesa** (fem.)= *the table*, **el escritorio** (masc.)= *the desk*. The gender of nouns is shown in dictionaries, but the following general rules will help you to guess the gender of many nouns:

The following nouns are masculine:

- Male humans and male animals: **el hombre** *man*, **el muchacho** *boy*, **el toro** *bull*, **el león** *lion*, **el gallo** *cockerel*

- Nouns ending in –o; **el libro** *book*, **el vídeo** *video*, **el bolígrafo** *ball-point pen*. Exceptions: **la mano** *hand*, **la radio** *radio*, **la foto** *photo*, **la moto** *motor-bike*

- Nouns ending in –aje: **el viaje** *journey*, **el equipaje** *luggage*

- Nouns ending in a stressed vowel (i.e. a vowel with an accent on it): **el tisú** *tissue*, **el menú** *menu*, **el sofá** *sofa*

- Days of the week and months: **el lunes** *Monday*, **los domingos** *Sundays*, **un diciembre frío** *a cold December*

The following nouns are feminine:

- Female humans and female animals: **la mujer** *woman*, **la actriz** *actress*, **la vaca** *cow*, **la gallina** *chicken*

- Nouns ending in –a (but see 'Gender problems' below for words ending in -ma): **la casa** *house*, **la comida** *meal*, **la camiseta** *tee-shirt*. Exceptions: **el día** *day*, **el mapa** *map*, **el planeta** *planet*, **el tranvía** *tramway*

- Nouns ending in –ción: **la nación** *nation*, **la calefacción** *heating*, **la elección** *election*

- Nouns ending in –dad, -tad, -tud, or -is; **la ciudad** *city*, **la libertad** *liberty*, **la actitud** *attitude*, **la crisis** *crisis*, **la apendicitis** *appendicitis*. Exceptions: **el análisis** *analysis*, **el tenis** *tennis*

Gender problems

- About half of the nouns ending in –ma are masculine, e.g. **el programa** *programme*, **el diagrama** *diagram*, **el clima** *climate*,

el problema *problem*. Common feminine nouns ending in –**ma** are: **la cama** *bed*, **la llama** *flame*, **la rama** *branch*, **la forma** *shape*, **la lágrima** *tear* (the sort one cries).

■ Some nouns change their meaning according to their gender: **el corte** = *cut*, but **la corte** = *court* (i.e. the royal court), **el margen** = *margin*, but **la margen** = *river-bank*.

Plural of nouns

The plural indicates more than one of a thing, and, as in English, it usually ends in –**s** in Spanish. The two most important ways of making Spanish plurals are:

■ If a noun ends in a vowel (**a**, **e**, **i**, **o**, or **u**), simply add –**s**: **la casa-las casas** *house-houses*, **el hombre-los hombres** *man-men*, **el taxi-los taxis** *taxi-taxis*, **el tisú-los tisús** *tissue-tissues*.

■ If a noun ends in a consonant (any letter except a vowel), add –**es**: **el ordenador-los ordenadores** *computer-computers*, **el español-los españoles** *Spaniard-Spaniards*, **el inglés-los ingleses** *English person-English people*. Note! If the last consonant of the singular is **z**, the plural ends in –**ces**; **la voz-las voces** *voice-voices*.

Exception: If the singular already ends in –**s** and the last vowel in the word does not have an accent, the plural is the same as the singular: **el martes-los martes** *Tuesday-Tuesdays*, **la crisis-las crisis** *crisis-crises*.

Adjectives

Adjectives describe the qualities of nouns or pronouns, as in *a **tall** tree*, ***beautiful** girls*, *she is **blond***. Spanish adjectives are different from English ones in two ways:

■ They usually come after the noun: **un libro interesante** *an interesting book*, **el pan blanco** *white bread*, **los pantalones azules** *blue trousers*. But some, like **grande** *big* or **pequeño** *small*, often come before the noun: **un gran escritor** *a great writer*, **un pequeño problema** *a small problem*.

■ They 'agree' with the noun or pronoun they describe. This means that if the noun is plural the adjective in Spanish must also be plural, and if the noun is feminine the adjective must also be feminine—if it has a special feminine form

un hombre delgado *a thin man*	**una mujer delgada** *a thin woman*
hombres delgados *thin men*	**mujeres delgadas** *thin women*

un coche nuevo	**tres coches nuevos**
a new car	*three new cars*
una camisa nueva	**camisas nuevas**
a new shirt	*new shirts*

The following adjectives agree in both number **and** gender:

- Adjectives that end in –**o**. Add –**s** for the plural, change the –**o** to –**a** for the feminine: **el pañuelo blanco-los pañuelos blancos** *white handkerchief-white handkerchiefs*, **la bandera blanca-las banderas blancas** *white flag-white flags*.

- Adjectives that end in –**és**. Add –**a** for the feminine, and –**es** for the masculine plural. Note the disappearing accent! **el vino francés-los vinos franceses** *French wine-French wines*, **la bandera inglesa-las banderas inglesas** *the English flag-the English flags*. Exception: **cortés** *polite* and **descortés** *impolite*. These have no separate feminine form, and the plural is **corteses/descorteses**.

- Most adjectives ending in –**n**: **alemán-alemana-alemanes-alemanas** *German*. Exception: **marrón** (masc. and fem.) *brown*, plural **marrones** (masc. and fem.)

- **Español-española-españoles-españolas** *Spanish*, **andaluz-andaluza-andaluces-andaluzas** *Andalusian* (i.e. belonging to Southern Spain).

The rest do not have a separate feminine form. Those ending in a vowel (usually –**e**) simply add –**s** for the plural; those ending in anything else add –**es**. If the singular ends in –**z**, the plural ends in –**ces**:

Singular masc. & fem.	Plural masc. & fem.	Meaning
grande	**grandes**	*big*
difícil	**difíciles**	*difficult*
superior	**superiores**	*superior/higher*
feroz	**feroces**	*ferocious*

Exception: adjectives ending in –**dor** add –**a** to show the feminine: **tranquilizador-tranquilizadora-tranquilizadores-tranquilizadoras** *comforting/soothing*.

Shortened adjectives

A few adjectives have a short form used immediately before a noun. The most important are:

	Short form	When used
grande *big*	**gran**	before all singular nouns

cualquiera *any*	**cualquier**	before all singular nouns	
bueno *good*	**buen**	before singular masculine nouns	
malo *bad*	**mal**	"	"
primero *first*	**primer**	"	"
tercero *third*	**tercer**	"	"

Compare **un buen libro** *a good book* and **una buena respuesta** *a good answer*.

Comparison of adjectives

To compare two things, simply put **más** *more*, or **menos** *less* in front of the adjective: **Luis es más/menos alto que ella** *Luis is taller/less tall than her*. To indicate the *most*...or *least*... of three or more things, put **el más/el menos** (or **la más, los más, las más**, according to gender) before the adjective: **pero ella es** *la más alta* **de todos** *but she is the tallest of all*.

! Note: the following two special forms must be learned:

		singular	plural	
bueno/buen	*good*	**mejor**	**mejores**	*better/best*
malo/mal	*bad/badly*	**peor**	**peores**	*worse/worst*

Example: **San Miguel es una de** *las mejores* **cervezas españolas** *San Miguel is one of the best Spanish beers*.

'as...as' and 'the more... the more...'

*She is **as** tall **as** John* is translated **ella es** *tan* **alta** *como* **Juan**. *The more you work the more you earn* is *cuanto más* **trabajas** *más* **ganas**. *The less you work the less you earn* is *cuanto menos* **trabajas** *menos* **ganas**.

'the' and 'a'

These words, called 'articles' in linguistics, vary in Spanish according to whether the following noun is masculine or feminine or singular or plural:

	Singular	Plural	English equivalent
Masculine	**el**	**los**	*the*
Feminine	**la**	**las**	

	Singular	Plural	
Masculine	**un**	**unos**	*a* or *an*
Feminine	**una**	**unas**	

They are used in more or less the same way as their English equivalents: *el* hombre compró *una* camisa y *la* mujer compró *unos* zapatos y *un* sombrero *the man bought a shirt, and the woman bought a pair of shoes and a hat.* **Unos/unas** means *a pair of* before things that come in pairs like shoes or trousers (**unos pantalones** = *a pair of trousers*). It means *some* before other plural nouns: **unos peniques** *a few pennies,* **unas muchachas** *a few girls.*

But note the following points!

■ We always use **el** and **un** before nouns that begin with **a-** or **ha-** when the **a** is stressed, even though these words may be feminine: *el* **agua** *water,* *el/un* **arma** *weapon,* *el* **hambre** *hunger.* These are all feminine nouns, and their plural would be **las aguas, las armas, las hambres.** Compare the following feminine nouns, where the accent does not fall on the first **a**: **la actitud** *attitude,* **la habitación** *room.*

■ **De** *of* + **el** is shortened to **del**: **el coche del profesor** *the teacher's car.* **A** *to* + **el** is shortened to **al**: **doy el libro al profesor** *I give the book to the teacher.*

■ We use the Spanish for *the* before nouns that refer to things in general: *doctors say apples are good for children* means doctors, apples, and children in general, so we must say **los médicos dicen que las manzanas son buenas para los niños.** In the same way **el amor** = *love,* **la libertad** = *freedom,* **la justicia** = *justice.*

■ We do not use the word for *a* in Spanish before professions: **es profesora** = *she is a teacher,* **soy estudiante** = *I am a student.*

Saying 'this book', 'that girl'

The words for *this* and *that* must agree in number and gender with the following noun. Note that in Spanish there are two words for *that,* the second of which refers to something far away from the speaker:

	Singular	Plural	
Masculine	**este**	**estos**	*this/these*
Feminine	**esta**	**estas**	
Masculine	**ese**	**esos**	*that/those*
Feminine	**esa**	**esas**	
Masculine	**aquel**	**aquellos**	*that/those* **over there**
Feminine	**aquella**	**aquellas**	

Beginners can manage without using **aquel** because **ese** is often used even for distant things: ¿ves **esa** (or **aquella**) **estrella**? *can you see that star?*

- When these words are used to mean *this one* or *that one*, most people write them with an accent. **¿ves estos dos coches? Éste es amarillo y ése es rojo** *do you see these two cars? This one is yellow and that one is red.* However, the Spanish Academy nowadays says that these accents are not necessary, so follow your teacher's advice on this point.

- When these words do not refer to any noun in particular, a special genderless form must be used, **esto**, **eso**, or **aquello**: **esto es terrible** *this is terrible*, **no quiero hablar de eso** *I don't want to talk about that*. (**Éste es terrible** means *this one is terrible* and would refer to something masculine. **No quiero hablar de ésa** means *I don't want to talk about that girl* or some other feminine noun.)

'My', 'your', 'his', 'her', 'our', 'their'

In Spanish these words (called 'possessive adjectives' in linguistics) agree in number with the thing that you possess, not with the person that possesses them, so we say **mi mano** *my hand* and **mis manos** *my hands*, **tu libro** *your book* but **tus libros** *your books*. Only **nuestro** and **vuestro** have special feminine forms: **nuestra casa** *our house*, **vuestras amigas** *your female friends*. Note: Spanish has no separate words for *his*, *her*, or *their*: **su/sus** cover all these meanings:

Singular	Plural	
mi	**mis**	*my*
tu	**tus**	*your* (when speaking to a friend or relative)
su	**sus**	*his/her/their/your* (use it for *your* when speaking to older strangers)
nuestro	**nuestros**	*our* (before masc. nouns)
nuestra	**nuestras**	*our* (before fem. nouns)
vuestro	**vuestros**	*your* (before masc. nouns)
vuestra	**vuestras**	*your* (before fem. nouns)

- **Vuestro** is used in Spain when speaking to more than one friend or relative. Latin Americans never use **vuestro** and always use **su** for *your* when speaking to more than one person.

- We do not use these words with parts of the body or intimate possessions. Spanish says 'put up the hand' for *put up your hand* **levanta la mano**, 'put on the shirt' for *put on your shirt* **ponte la camisa**.

'Mine', 'your', 'his', 'hers', 'ours', 'theirs'

To translate sentences like *this coat is **mine**, those pencils are **yours***,

we use special Spanish words. These all agree in gender and number
with the noun that they refer to:

| masc. | **mío** | **míos** | *mine* |
| fem. | **mía** | **mías** | |

| masc. | **tuyo** | **tuyos** | *yours* (only to a friend or relative) |
| fem. | **tuya** | **tuyas** | |

| masc. | **suyo** | **suyos** | *his/hers/theirs/yours* (use it for |
| fem. | **suya** | **suyas** | *yours* when speaking to older strangers) |

| masc. | **nuestro** | **nuestros** | *ours* |
| fem. | **nuestra** | **nuestras** | |

| masc. | **vuestro** | **vuestros** | *yours* |
| fem. | **vuestra** | **vuestras** | |

- See the note above for when to use **vuestro**.

- Examples: **este abrigo es mío/tuyo** *this coat is mine/yours*, **estas
llaves son suyas** *these keys are his/hers/yours/theirs*, **esta
dirección es nuestra** *this address is ours*. After a preposition
(see page 604) we must add the word for *the*: **no vamos en tu
coche, vamos en el mío** *we're not going in your car, we're going
in mine*.

Personal pronouns

Personal pronouns are used to replace nouns: if they did not exist we
would constantly have to repeat nouns, as in '*John saw Jill and John
kissed Jill*'. Obviously we would replace the second mention of John
and Jill with pronouns: *John saw Jill and he kissed her*.

The most important Spanish personal pronouns are the ones used
to translate *me, him, her, us, them* in sentences like *John saw me,
Anne knows us, Jenny met them*. These are called 'direct object
pronouns' and they stand for the person or thing to whom the action
is done:

me *me*	**nos** *us*
te *you* (a friend or relative only)	**os** *you* (friends or relatives only)
lo *him, you* (a male stranger), or *it*	**los** *them* (masc.) or *you* (male strangers)
la *her, you* (a female stranger), or *it*	**las** *them* (fem.) or *you* (female strangers)

- ! Note: in Spain, **le** is constantly used for *him/you* (male) instead
of **lo**, but **lo** must be used for *it* when it refers to a masculine

thing like a book (**el libro**). Latin Americans use only **lo**. Both forms are considered correct, so imitate your teacher on this point.

- **Os** is not used in Latin America. Latin Americans say **los** for males, **las** for females.

- These words come directly before verbs: **me ve** *he/she sees me*, **los veo** *I see them*. However, they are joined to the end of infinitives, gerunds, and imperatives (see below): **quiero verla** *I want to see her*, **estoy haciéndolo** *I'm doing it*, **cómpralo** *buy it*.

- Note how Spanish says *it's me*, *it's you*: **soy yo** (= 'I am I'), **eres tú** ('you are you').

Saying 'to me', 'to you', 'to him', etc.
We use the same forms as above: **me da cien libras** *he gives £100 to me*, **te manda una carta** *he sends a letter to you*, **nos dicen todo** *they tell everything to us*. These forms are called 'indirect object pronouns' in linguistics.

! Note: There are two special indirect object forms, **le** and **les**. **Le** means *to him*, *to her*, or *to you* (speaking to one stranger). **Les** means *to them* and also *to you* when talking to strangers: **le dije** *I said to him* or *to her* or *to you* (one person), **les dije** *I said to them* or *to you* (two or more people).

Saying 'it to me', 'them to you', etc.
We can combine these pronouns, but the order is indirect object first, then direct object, i.e.

    me or **te** or **nos** or **os** first   then **lo**, **la**, **los**, or **las**

Examples: **me lo dan** *they give it to me*, **te lo dicen** *they say it to you*, **nos los mandan** *they send them to us*.

- !! The rule of two L's. It is an important rule of Spanish that when **le** or **les** is followed by **lo**, **la**, **los**, or **las**, the **le** or **les** changes into **se**. In other words, two pronouns beginning with L can never stand side-by-side: **se lo doy** *I give it to him/to her/to you/to them*, not 'le lo doy'. Note that the word **se** has four possible meanings here.

How to say 'I', 'you', 'he', 'she', 'we', 'they'
We do not need these words very often in Spanish, because the ending of the verb does their work: **hablo** already means *I speak*, **vas** already means *you go*, **compramos** means *we buy*. You must learn not to say **yo hablo**, **tú vas**, **nosotros compramos**: it is usually unnecessary and it confuses Spanish-speakers. But we do sometimes need these words, and their forms are as follows:

yo *I*	**nosotros** (males) *we*, **nosotras** (women) *we*
tú *you* (friends and relatives only)	**vosotros** (to two or more males) *you*, **vosotras** (two or more females) *you*
usted *you* (to an older stranger)	**ustedes** *you* (to older strangers)
él *he* **ella** *she*	**ellos** *they* (males) **ellas** *they* (females)

- **Vosotros** or **vosotras** are not used in Latin America, where they always say **ustedes** to two or more persons.

- **Tú** (note the accent!) and **vosotros** or **vosotras** are used only for friends (and anyone of your own age group if you are young), relatives, animals, and children. Nowadays Spaniards use them more and more even to complete strangers as a way of being friendly, but you must use **usted**, **ustedes** to older strangers, officials, policemen, etc.

- We only use these words (a) when there is no following verb: —¿**quién lo hizo?** —**Yo** *'Who did it?' 'I did.'* (b) to contrast one person with another: **yo trabajo en casa y *ella* va a la oficina** *I work at home and she goes to the office.*

- **Usted** and **ustedes** are followed by third-person verb forms (i.e. the forms used for *he* and *them*): **usted habla** = *you speak*, **ustedes hablan** *you* (more than one) *speak.*

- We do not usually use any word for *it* or *they* when these words stand for things and not for people: **llueve** *it's raining*, **contienen dinero** *they contain money.*

The Spanish words *mí* and *ti*

These are special forms meaning *me* and *you* (to a friend or relative) that we use after certain prepositions, e.g. after **de** *of/about*, **contra** *against*, **para** *for*, **por** *because of/on behalf of*, **sin** *without*: **hablamos de ti** (no accent!) *we're talking about you*, **esto es para mí** (accent!) *this is for me.* For other persons use the forms **él**, **ella**, **nosotros/nosotras**, **vosotros/vosotras**, **usted/ustedes**, **ellos**, **ellas** described in the previous section.

! Note: there are two special words: **conmigo** *with me*, and **contigo** *with you* (a friend or relative): **Miguel va conmigo de vacaciones** *Miguel is going with me on holiday.*

'There is' and 'there are'

There is and *there are* are **hay** in Spanish: **hay lobos en España** *there are wolves in Spain*, **no hay pan** *there is no bread. There was* and *there were* are **había** (not **habían!**): **había osos en Inglaterra** *there were* (or *there used to be*) *bears in England.* For sudden, short events in the past we say **hubo**: **hubo una explosión/un accidente** *there was an explosion/accident.* There will be is **habrá**.

'To be'

Spanish has two words meaning *to be*: **ser** and **estar** (their forms are shown on pages 619 and 617), and you must learn to use them correctly.

Ser is basically used to show what sort of thing something is: **esto es mermelada** *this is jam*, **Manuel es piloto** *Manuel is a pilot*, **soy inglesa** *I'm English* (girl speaking).

Estar is used to show how or where something is: **estoy cansado** *I'm tired*, **la radio está rota** *the radio is broken*, **Madrid está en España.** **Estar** therefore refers to temporary or passing states like tiredness, illness, anger, but there are exceptions, e.g. **Napoleón está muerto** *Napoleon is dead*, **soy feliz** *I'm happy*.

- ! Note: when we want to say where an event is taking place we use **ser**: —¿**dónde *es* la fiesta esta noche?** —*Es* **en casa de Antonio** 'where's the party tonight?' 'It's in Antonio's house'. A party is an event, not an object. Compare ¿**dónde *está* tu coche?** *where is your car?*

- We use the verb **hacer** to talk about the weather: **hace frío** *it's cold*, **hacía demasiado calor** *it was too hot.*

Question words

These are written with an accent:

¿cómo? *how?*	¿cuánto? *how much?,*	¿por qué? *why?*
¿cuál? *which?*	*how many?*	¿qué? *what?*
¿cuándo? *when?*	¿de quién? *whose?*	¿quién? *who?*

¿**Cuál?** and ¿**quién?** become ¿**cuáles?** and ¿**quiénes?** when they refer to more than one thing or person: ¿**quiénes son?** *who are they?*, **no sé cuáles quiero** *I don't know which ones I want.* ¿**Cuánto?** agrees in number and gender with what it refers to: ¿**cuánto dinero?** *how much money?*, ¿**cuántos sellos?** *how many stamps?*, ¿**cuántas chicas?** *how many girls?*

- Note: the meaning of these words changes when no accent is used: **como** = *as* or *like* (**habla como un niño** = *he talks like a little boy*), **porque** (one word!) = *because*, **que** = *that* as in **dice que está enfermo** *he says that he is ill.*

Personal *a*

Note carefully the difference between these two sentences: **vi tu**

casa *I saw your house*, and **vi *a* tu madre** *I saw your mother*. The **a** is necessary in the second example because the thing seen was a human being. So: **no conozco *a* María** *I don't know María*, **admiro *al* profesor** *I admire the teacher*, but **no conozco la ciudad** *I don't know the city*. Pets are also treated like humans: **paseo *al* perro** *I take the dog for a walk*.

Prepositions

These are short words placed before nouns and pronouns to link them to the meaning of the rest of the sentence. The main Spanish prepositions are:

a *to, at*	**desde** *from*	*as*
con *with*	**detrás de** *behind*	**para** *for*
contra *against*	**durante** *during*	**por** *on behalf of,*
de *of*	**en** *in, on, at*	*through, by*
debajo de *underneath*	**entre** *between, among*	**según** *according to*
delante de *in front of*	**hacia** *towards*	**sin** *without*
	hasta *until, as far*	**sobre** *over, on, about*

These are all used in more or less the same way as their English equivalents except that:

- **a** basically means *to*, not *at*, which is usually **en** in Spanish: **en la estación** = *in the station* or *at the station*. *At the bus-stop* is **en la parada de autobús**, *at the traffic-lights* is **en el semáforo**. **A** means *at* only when movement is involved, as in **tiró una flecha *al* blanco** *he fired an arrow at the target*.

- **en** therefore has three meanings: *in, on,* and *at*. Spanish-speakers have trouble distinguishing between our words *on* and *in* as in *on a record* (**en un disco**), *in a film* (**en una película**).

- **para** means *for*, as in **este dinero es para ti** *this money is for you*. **Por** means, among other things, *because of*: **lo hago por amor, no por dinero** *I do it for love not for money* (it really means *because of love, because of money*), **lo hice para ti** = *I made it for you*, **lo hice por ti** = *I did it because of you*, or *...for your sake*. **Para** and **por** have other meanings, which you will learn as you progress in Spanish.

Numbers

The numbers from one to twenty are: **uno, dos, tres, cuatro, cinco, seis, siete, ocho, nueve, diez, once, doce, trece, catorce, quince, dieciséis, diecisiete, dieciocho, diecinueve, veinte**. **Un** is used before a masculine noun and **una** is used before a feminine noun: **un**

zapato *one shoe*, **una falda** *one skirt*. When no noun follows, **uno** (masculine) or **una** (feminine) is used, depending on the gender of the noun referred to: **yo quiero comprar uno de esos melones** *I want to buy one of those melons*, **en este pueblo no hay iglesia, pero en San Pedro hay una** *there is no church in this village, but there is one in San Pedro*.

21 to 29 are: **veintiuno/veintiuna, veintidós, veintitrés, veinticuatro, veinticinco, veintiséis, veintisiete, veintiocho, veintinueve** (all written as one word).

The other tens are: 30 **treinta**, 40 **cuarenta**, 50 **cincuenta**, 60 **sesenta**, 70 **setenta**, 80 **ochenta**, 90 **noventa**. 31 is **treinta y uno/una**, 32 **treinta y dos**, 33 **treinta y tres**, 45 is **cuarenta y cinco** and so on.

100 is **cien**—**cien hombres** = *100 men*. But it becomes **ciento** before another number: **ciento dos** = 102, **ciento setenta y ocho** = 178.

There are special words for 200 to 900, but only three of them are unexpected: 200 **doscientos**, 300 **trescientos**, 400 **cuatrocientos**, 500 **quinientos**, 600 **seiscientos**, 700 *setecientos*, 800 **ochocientos**, 900 *novecientos*. Note! The last **o** of these words changes to **a** before feminine nouns: **setecientos hombres** *700 men*, but **setecientas mujeres** *700 women*.

1000 is **mil**. 2003 = **dos mil tres**, 4056 = **cuatro mil cincuenta y seis**, 6225 = **seis mil doscientos veinticinco** (seis mil doscientas veinticinco before a feminine noun). **Un millón de libras** = £1,000,000. Note! Most students forget that **un billón** is a million million in Spanish. In English it is a thousand million.

Verbs

Verbs are words that describe actions or events: *he drinks, you walk, I'm writing, it rained*. Words meaning *to be* are also considered to be verbs: the Spanish equivalents of the English *to be* are described on page 603.

Actions and events can take place in the present, in the past, or in the future. In English and Spanish verbs appear in different forms (known as 'tenses') to show us the time of the action: *he speaks, he spoke, he will speak*, **habla, habló, hablará**. These different forms are rather more complicated in Spanish than in English.

English and Spanish verbs also change their shape to show us who or what is performing the action: compare *I speak* and *he speaks*. This happens far more often in Spanish: **hablo** = *I speak*, **hablas** = *you speak*, **habló** = *he/she/it spoke*, **hablábamos** = *we spoke*, **hablarán** = *they will speak*, etc. Because of these different endings, Spanish usually does not need extra words like 'I', 'you', 'he' to show who is performing the action, as explained on page 601.

Unfortunately these Spanish endings are not always very precise.

A word like **va** means *he goes*, or *she goes*, or *it goes*, or even *you go* (i.e. **usted va**). English-speaking students often feel that something is missing here to make the meaning clear, but the context of the conversation nearly always makes it obvious who we are talking about, as in the following example: —**¿Dónde está tu mujer?** —**Está enferma** *'where's your wife?'* *'She's ill/off sick'* (it obviously can't mean 'he's sick'!)

'Reflexive' verbs

These are verbs which have a personal pronoun that refers to the person or thing that also performs the action, as in English *I shave* **myself**, *they admire* **themselves**. This kind of verb is much more common in Spanish than in English. Here is the present tense of **lavarse** *to wash oneself*:

me lavo	**nos lavamos**
I wash myself	*we wash ourselves*
te lavas	**os laváis** (Spain only)
you wash yourself	*you wash yourselves*
se lava	**se lavan**
he washes himself or *she washes herself* or *you* (**usted**) *wash yourself*	*they wash themselves* or *you* (**ustedes**) *wash yourselves*

This kind of verb has various uses in Spanish. The following are the most important for beginners:

- If a human or an animal performs the action, it usually shows that the action is done to myself, yourself, himself, itself, etc. as in the **lavarse** example just shown.

- If more than one human or animal is performing the action, it often shows that they are doing the action to one another: **se escriben mucho** *they write to one another a lot*.

- Sometimes the reflexive form shows that you are not doing the action to someone or something else: **me caso** *I'm getting married*.

- Sometimes the 'reflexive' form is the only one used, as in **me atrevo** 'I dare', or **te arrepientes** 'you regret' (having done something).

- If no human or animal is involved, then the verb often has to be understood as a 'passive', as the translation shows: **este libro se publicó en Argentina** *this book was published in Argentina*, **se dijeron muchas cosas en la reunión** *many things were said in the meeting*.

- With many verbs, the 'reflexive' form simply alters the meaning: **ir** = *to go*, **irse** = *to go away*; **caer** = *to fall*, **caerse** = *to fall over*.

Apart from **irse**, these verbs are rather advanced for a beginners' course.

Tenses of verbs

Talking about actions that take place in the present (the 'present tense')

We tend to talk most about things that are happening *now*, so the forms of the verb used to describe present actions are the most common ones. They are shown on page 614.

English has two forms for describing present actions: compare *I smoke*, which describes a habit, and *I'm smoking*, which shows that you are smoking right now. Spanish has the same system: **fumo** = *I smoke*, **estoy fumando** = *I am smoking* (right now). However, the second of these forms is used less than in English and beginners can use the simple form, **fumo**, for both meanings, as is clear in these examples:

—¿Qué haces? —Fumo	*'What are you doing?' 'I'm smoking'*
Hablan mucho	*They talk a lot* (or *they are talking a lot*)
Vamos al cine	*We go to the cinema* (or *we're going to the cinema*)

As was said earlier, the present tense usually describes actions that are happening in the present or which happen always or usually (habits): **Marcos abre la puerta** *Marcos opens* (or *is opening the door*), **trabajas demasiado** *you work too much*, **los tigres comen carne** *tigers eat meat*.

However, despite its name, the Spanish present tense can be used to talk about events in the future: **mañana vamos a Devon** *tomorrow we're going to Devon*, **te llamo esta noche** *I'll phone you tonight*. See below, page 610, for details.

Talking about past events (the past tenses)

We often need to describe things that happened in the past, and in English there are several different verb forms that we use to show different ways of looking at past events. Compare *I did it, I have done it, I was doing it,* and *I had done it*. Spanish also has several ways of describing past events:

(a) The 'preterite' tense: **hablé** *I spoke*, **llegaron** *they arrived*, **compraste** *you bought*.

(b) The 'imperfect' tense: **hablaba** *I was speaking* or *I used to speak*, **llegaban** *they were arriving* or *they used to arrive*, **comprabas** *you were buying* or *you used to buy*.

(c) The 'perfect' tense: **he hablado** *I have spoken*, **han llegado** *they have arrived*, **has comprado** *you have bought*.

(d) The 'pluperfect' tense: **había hablado** *I had spoken*, **habían llegado** *they had arrived*, **habías comprado** *you had bought*.

The two most used past tenses in Spanish are the preterite and the imperfect.

The preterite and the imperfect tenses compared

We use the preterite forms to describe actions that took place **once** or a **specific number** of times in the past:

Ayer compré un nuevo ordenador	*I bought a new computer yesterday*
Ganó la lotería	*He/She won the lottery*
Fue presidente durante tres años	*(S)he was President for three years*
Estuve enfermo hace tres meses	*I was ill three months ago*
Dije "hola" tres veces	*I said 'hi' three times*

We use the imperfect forms to describe actions or events that were not yet finished at the time we are talking about:

Miguel fumaba demasiado	*Miguel was smoking too much/Miguel used to smoke too much* (and he probably went on smoking after)
Mi hermana iba mucho a la disco	*My sister used to go/was going a lot to the Disco* (and probably went on going)
Roberto era alto y moreno	*Roberto was tall and dark-skinned* (and went on being tall and dark)

In these three examples we either don't know how many times the event happened, or, in the case of Roberto, he obviously wasn't tall and dark once or three times, so in all cases the imperfect must be used.

If an event happened once or a specific number of times we always use the preterite tense, regardless of how long it went on for: **los dinosaurios reinaron sobre la tierra durante millones de años** *the dinosaurs reigned on earth for millions of years* (it only happened once), **ocurrió más de mil veces** *it happened more than a thousand times* (but it happened a specific number of times).

We must use the imperfect to show that an event was interrupted by another event. This is because interrupted events were not fully completed in the past: **yo dormía cuando empezó la tormenta** *I was sleeping when the storm started*. Here we use the imperfect of

dormir because when the storm started I was still sleeping. Even if I woke up I must still use the imperfect, because at the time I hadn't finished sleeping.

The perfect tense

In English this is formed by using the present tense of *have*, and in Spanish by using the present tense of **haber**, with the 'past participle' of the verb, which, in Spanish, usually ends with –**ado**, -**ido**, or –**isto**, as shown on pages 614–621. As a rule, whenever you would say 'I **have** been', 'she **has** done', 'we **have** seen', etc. in English, you use the same tense in Spanish: **he sido**, **ha hecho**, **hemos visto**.

Nunca he bebido vodka	*I have never drunk vodka*
He estado tres veces en Chicago	*I've been in Chicago three times*
¿Has visto La guerra de las galaxias?	*Have you seen Star Wars?*
Hemos ido tres veces esta semana	*We've been three times this week*

Many Latin Americans replace this tense by the preterite tense described earlier: **nunca bebí vodka, estuve tres veces en Chicago, ¿viste La guerra de las galaxias?, fuimos tres veces esta semana**. If your teacher is Latin American, imitate him or her on this point.

! Note: If you are studying the Spanish of Spain you will notice one crucial difference between English and Spanish: the latter often uses the perfect tense for any event that has happened since midnight: **esta mañana me he duchado, he desayunado, he cogido el metro y he llegado aquí a las nueve** *this morning I had a shower, I had breakfast, I caught the underground, and I got here at nine o'clock.*

Important. If you are also studying French, do not make the mistake of using the perfect when you should use the preterite. French says '*I have seen him* (**je l'ai vu**) *last year*'. Both English and Spanish must say *I saw him last year*, **lo** (or **le**) **vi el año pasado**.

The pluperfect tense

This is almost exactly equivalent to the English tense made with *had*: *I had seen, they had eaten*, **había visto, habían comido**. It is used in both languages to show that an event **had** finished before another past event happened: **mamá ya se había ido cuando llegué a casa** *mother **had** already **gone** when I got home*, **yo iba a mandarles una tarjeta, pero mi hermano ya lo había hecho** *I was going to send them a card, but my brother had already done it.*

Talking about events in the future (the future tenses)

There are several ways in English and Spanish of showing that an event is still in the future:

(a) **We're going to arrive** tomorrow mañana	**Vamos a llegar** (ir + infinitive)
(b) **We are arriving** tomorrow	**Llegamos mañana** (present tense)
(c) **We will arrive** tomorrow	**Llegaremos mañana** (future tense)

The first two are more or less the same in both languages. (b) is used when an event is more or less pre-arranged or programmed, as in *we're going to the theatre tonight* **vamos al teatro esta noche** (you've probably booked tickets or made some other arrangement).

Form (c) involves learning the forms of the future tense (shown on page 614), and is normally used where English uses *will*, and it is especially used in promises and forecasts as in **te pagaré el dinero mañana** *I will pay you the money tomorrow*, and **el viernes hará buen tiempo** *the weather will be fine on Friday*.

The conditional tense

This tense, whose forms are shown on page 614, indicates an event that *would* happen, **estarías más guapa con el pelo recogido** *you would be* more attractive with your hair up, **en ese caso te costaría menos** *in that case it would cost you less*.

Giving orders and making requests

We use a special form of the verb (called 'the imperative' in linguistics) to give orders or to ask someone to do something. The forms of the verb used vary:

■ If we are speaking to one friend or relative, the form is made by dropping the –s from the **tú** form of the present tense: **das** = *you give*, so *give* is **da**; similarly **hablas** > **habla** *speak*, **comes** > **come** *eat*. There are eight exceptions that you must learn:

decir *to say* **di**	**poner** *to put* **pon**	**tener** *to have* **ten**
hacer *to make* **haz**	**salir** *to go out* **sal**	**venir** *to come* **ven**
ir *to go* **ve**	**ser** *to be* **sé**	

■ If we are speaking to one stranger we must use the **usted** form, which is the same as the present subjunctive form for *he* when talking to one person. To more than one stranger we must use the **ustedes** form, which is the *they* form of the present subjunctive. These forms are shown on page 614. Examples: **¡venga! come!**,

¡conteste! *answer!*, ¡vengan! (to more than one person) *give!*,
¡contesten! *answer!*

- In Spain, if we are talking to more than one person who is a
  friend or relative, we must use the **vosotros** form of the
  imperative, which is easily formed by replacing the –**r** of the
  infinitive form (the form shown in dictionaries) by –**d**. There are
  no important exceptions: ¡venid! *come!*, ¡contestad! *answer!*,
  ¡dad! *give!* This form is never used in Latin America, where they
  replace it with the **ustedes** form.

- To tell someone not to do something, we must always use the
  present subjunctive form of the verb: ¡no vengas! (tú), ¡no
  venga! (usted), ¡no vengan! (ustedes), ¡no vengáis! (vosotros).
  These all mean *don't come!*, but the form varies in Spanish
  according to whom you are talking.

- If we need to add pronouns, for example to translate *give her it*,
  sell me them, these are tacked on to the end of the imperative. In
  these examples the **lo** and the **los** refer to some masculine noun
  like **libros** *books*. Note the accents:

to 1 friend	to 1 stranger	to 2+ strangers	to 2+ friends (Spain only)
dámelo	**démelo**	**dénmelo**	**dádmelo** = *give it to me*
mándanoslos	**mándenoslos**	**mándennoslos**	**mandádnoslos** = *send them to us*

But if we make the order negative (i.e. put **no** in front of it), the
pronouns then come in front of the present subjunctive of the verb:

no me lo des	**no me lo dé**	**no me lo den**	**no me lo deis** = *don't give it to me*

The infinitive

The infinitive is the dictionary form of a verb, and it always ends in
–**r** in Spanish: **hablar** *to speak*, **comer** *to eat*, **tener** *to say*, **ser** *to be*.
Its form never changes. It has the following uses:

- It stands for the name of an action (i.e. it is a masculine noun):
  fumar es **malo** *smoking is bad*, mi pasatiempo es *escuchar*
  música *my hobby is listening to music*.

- It is used after prepositions (see page 604): estoy cansado de
  andar *I'm tired of walking*, voy a *hacerlo* *I'm going to do it* (note
  that the pronoun **lo** is added to the end of an infinitive).

- It is used after many verbs, of which the following are common:
  puedo *I can*, **quiero** *I want to*, **debo** *I must*, **hay que** *it is
  necessary to*, **acabo de** *I have just…*, e.g. **quiero ir al cine** *I want*

to go to the cinema, **debes hacerlo así** *you have to do it like this*, **acabo de verla** *I've just seen her*.

The gerund (or –ndo form of verbs)

This form of Spanish verbs always ends in **–ando** or **–iendo** and it never changes. It is used:

- With the verb **estar** to stress the fact that an action is actually going on right now, or was in the middle of happening: **estoy comiendo** *I'm eating* (right now), **estabas durmiendo** *you were* (*in the middle of*) *sleeping*. It must not be used for actions in the future: **voy a Madrid mañana** (not "estoy yendo") *I'm going to Madrid tomorrow*.

- To show that another action happens at the same time as the main action: **entré silbando** *I went in whistling*, **María salió llorando del cine** *María came out of the cinema crying*.

The subjunctive

You will probably not cover the subjunctive in GCSE or other beginners' courses, but you will eventually have to learn to use it since it is important in Spanish. The forms of the present subjunctive are shown on page 614. The present subjunctive is used:

- To make all negative orders, i.e. to tell someone not to do something: see the previous section on the imperative. This use is important, even at beginners' level, so it is necessary to learn the forms of the present subjunctive as soon as possible.

- In a sentence consisting of a present-tense negative verb + **que** + another verb, the second verb is in the subjunctive: compare **creo que está enferma** *I think that she is ill* and **no creo que esté enferma** *I don't think that she is ill*.

- After the present tense of verbs meaning *want* or *hope* + **que**: **quiero que *vengas* a mi casa** *I want you to come to my house*, **espero que *ganes*** *I hope you win*. But if the person doing the wanting is the same person that is going to perform the action of the second verb, we must use the infinitive (-**r** form) for the second verb: **quiero *ir* a mi casa** *I want to go to my house*, **espero ganar** *I hope I'll win/I hope to win*.

- After emotional reactions followed by **que**: **es una pena que no *trabajes* más** *it's a shame that you don't work more*, **estoy muy contento de que no *haya* llovido** *I'm very pleased that it hasn't rained* (**haya** is the subjunctive of **haber**).

- After certain words, when the action following them still hasn't happened. The most important of these are **cuando** *when*, **en cuanto** or **apenas** *as soon as*: **te daré el dinero cuando *llegues***

I'll give you the money when you arrive, **te llamaré apenas *encuentre* mi móvil** *I'll ring you as soon as I find my mobile phone*.

- Always after these words: **antes de que** *before*, **para que** *in order to*, **sin que** *without*, **con tal de que** *provided that*: **llegaremos antes de que *salga* el tren** *we'll arrive before the train leaves*, **te doy el dinero con tal de que me lo *devuelvas*** *I'll give you the money provided that you give it back to me*.

Spanish verbs

Regular verbs:

in -ar (e.g. comprar)
Present: compr|o, ~as, ~a, ~amos, ~áis, ~an
Future: comprar|é, ~ás, ~á, ~emos, ~éis, ~án
Imperfect: compr|aba, ~abas, ~aba, ~ábamos, ~abais, ~aban
Preterite: compr|é, ~aste, ~ó, ~amos, ~asteis, ~aron
Present subjunctive: compr|e, ~es, ~e, ~emos, ~éis, ~en
Imperfect subjunctive: compr|ara, ~aras ~ara, ~áramos, ~arais, ~aran
compr|ase, ~ases, ~ase, ~ásemos, ~aseis, ~asen
Conditional: comprar|ía, ~ías, ~ía, ~íamos, ~íais, ~ían
Present participle: comprando
Past participle: comprado
Imperative: compra, comprad

in -er (e.g. beber)
Present: beb|o, ~es, ~e, ~emos, ~éis, ~en
Future: beber|é, ~ás, ~á, ~emos, ~éis, ~án
Imperfect: beb|ía, ~ías, ~ía, ~íamos, ~íais, ~ían
Preterite: beb|í, ~iste, ~ió, ~imos, ~isteis, ~ieron
Present subjunctive: beb|a, ~as, ~a, ~amos, ~áis, ~an
Imperfect subjunctive: beb|iera, ~ieras, ~iera, ~iéramos, ~ierais, ~ieran beb|iese, ~ieses, ~iese, ~iésemos, ~ieseis, ~iesen
Conditional: beber|ía, ~ías, ~ía, ~íamos, ~íais, ~ían
Present participle: bebiendo
Past participle: bebido
Imperative: bebe, bebed

in -ir (e.g. vivir)
Present: viv|o, ~es, ~e, ~imos, ~ís, ~en
Future: vivir|é, ~ás, ~á, ~emos, ~éis, ~án
Imperfect: viv|ía, ~ías, ~ía, ~íamos, ~íais, ~ían
Preterite: viv|í, ~iste, ~ió, ~imos, ~isteis, ~ieron
Present subjunctive: viv|a, ~as, ~a, ~amos, ~áis, ~an
Imperfect subjunctive: viv|iera, ~ieras, ~iera, ~iéramos, ~ierais, ~ieran
viv|iese, ~ieses, ~iese, ~iésemos, ~ieseis, ~iesen
Conditional: vivir|ía, ~ías, ~ía, ~íamos, ~íais, ~ían
Present participle: viviendo
Past participle: vivido
Imperative: vive, vivid

Irregular verbs:

[1] cerrar
Present: cierro, cierras, cierra, cerramos, cerráis, cierran
Present subjunctive: cierre, cierres, cierre, cerremos, cerréis, cierren
Imperative: cierra, cerrad

[2] contar, mover
Present: cuento, cuentas, cuenta, contamos, contáis, cuentan

muevo, mueves, mueve,
movemos, movéis, mueven
Present subjunctive: cuente,
cuentes, cuente, contemos,
contéis, cuenten
mueva, muevas, mueva,
movamos, mováis, muevan
Imperative: cuenta, contad
mueve, moved

[3] jugar

Present: juego, juegas, juega,
jugamos, jugáis, juegan
Preterite: jugué, jugaste, jugó,
jugamos, jugasteis, jugaron
Present subjunctive: juegue,
juegues, juegue, juguemos,
juguéis, jueguen

[4] sentir

Present: siento, sientes, siente,
sentimos, sentís, sienten
Preterite: sentí, sentiste, sintió,
sentimos, sentisteis, sintieron
Present subjunctive: sienta,
sientas, sienta, sintamos,
sintáis, sientan
Imperfect subjunctive: sint I iera,
~ieras, ~iera, ~iéramos,
~ierais, ~ieran
sint I iese, ~ieses, ~iese,
~iésemos, ~ieseis, ~iesen
Present participle: sintiendo
Imperative: siente, sentid

[5] pedir

Present: pido, pides, pide,
pedimos, pedís, piden
Preterite: pedí, pediste, pidió,
pedimos, pedisteis, pidieron
Present subjunctive: pid I a, ~as,
~a, ~amos, ~áis, ~an
Imperfect subjunctive: pid I iera,
~ieras, ~iera, ~iéramos,
~ierais, ~ieran
pid I iese, ~ieses, ~iese,
~iésemos, ~ieseis, ~iesen
Present participle: pidiendo

Imperative: pide, pedid

[6] dormir

Present: duermo, duermes,
duerme, dormimos, dormís,
duermen
Preterite: dormí, dormiste,
durmió, dormimos,
dormisteis, durmieron
Present subjunctive: duerma,
duermas, duerma, durmamos,
durmáis, duerman
Imperfect subjunctive:
durm I iera, ~ieras, ~iera,
~iéramos, ~ierais, ~ieran
durm I iese, ~ieses, ~iese,
~iésemos, ~ieseis, ~iesen
Present participle: durmiendo
Imperative: duerme, dormid

[7] dedicar

Preterite: dediqué, dedicaste,
dedicó, dedicamos, dedicasteis,
dedicaron
Present subjunctive: dediqu I e,
~es, ~e, ~emos, ~éis, ~en

[8] delinquir

Present: delinco, delinques,
delinque, delinquimos,
delinquís, delinquen
Present subjunctive: delinc I a,
~as, ~a, ~amos, ~áis, ~an

[9] vencer, esparcir

Present: venzo, vences, vence,
vencemos, vencéis, vencen
esparzo, esparces, esparce,
esparcimos, esparcís, esparcen
Present subjunctive:
venz I a, ~as, ~a, ~amos, ~áis,
~an
esparz I a, ~as, ~a, ~amos, ~áis,
~an

[10] rechazar

Preterite: rechacé, rechazaste,
rechazó, rechazamos,
rechazasteis, rechazaron

Present subjunctive: rechac|e, ~es, ~e, ~emos, ~éis, ~en

[11] conocer, lucir
Present: conozco, conoces, conoce, conocemos, conocéis, conocen
luzco, luces, luce, lucimos, lucís, lucen
Present subjunctive:
conozc|a, ~as, ~a, ~amos, ~áis, ~an
luzc|a, ~as, ~a, ~amos, ~áis, ~an

[12] pagar
Preterite: pagué, pagaste, pagó, pagamos, pagasteis, pagaron
Present subjunctive: pagu|e, ~es, ~e, ~emos, ~éis, ~en

[13] distinguir
Present: distingo, distingues, distingue, distinguimos, distinguís, distinguen
Present subjunctive: disting|a, ~as, ~a, ~amos, ~áis, ~an

[14] acoger, afligir
Present: acojo, acoges, acoge, acogemos, acogéis, acogen
aflijo, afliges, aflige, afligimos, afligís, afligen
Present subjunctive:
acoj|a, ~as, ~a, ~amos, ~áis, ~an
aflij|a, ~as, ~a, ~amos, ~áis, ~an

[15] averiguar
Preterite: averigüé, averiguaste, averiguó, averiguamos, averiguasteis, averiguaron
Present subjunctive: averigü|e, ~es, ~e, ~emos, ~éis, ~en

[16] agorar
Present: agüero, agüeras, agüera, agoramos, agoráis, agüeran
Present subjunctive: agüere, agüeres, agüere, agoremos, agoréis, agüeren
Imperative: agüera, agorad

[17] huir
Present: huyo, huyes, huye, huimos, huís, huyen
Preterite: huí, huiste, huyó, huimos, huisteis, huyeron
Present subjunctive:
huy|a, ~as, ~a, ~amos, ~áis, ~an
Imperfect subjunctive:
huy|era, ~eras, ~era, ~éramos, ~erais, ~eran
huy|ese, ~eses, ~ese, ~ésemos, ~eseis, ~esen
Present participle: huyendo
Imperative: huye, huid

[18] creer
Preterite: creí, creíste, creyó, creímos, creísteis, creyeron
Imperfect subjunctive: crey|era, ~eras, ~era, ~éramos, ~erais, ~eran crey|ese, ~eses, ~ese, ~ésemos, ~eseis, ~esen
Present participle: creyendo
Past participle: creído

[19] argüir
Present: arguyo, arguyes, arguye, argüimos, argüís, arguyen
Preterite: argüí, argüiste, arguyó, argüimos, argüisteis, arguyeron
Present subjunctive: arguy|a, ~as, ~a, ~amos, ~áis, ~an
Imperfect subjunctive: arguy|era, ~eras, ~era, ~éramos, ~erais, ~eran arguy|ese, ~eses, ~ese, ~ésemos, ~eseis, ~esen
Present participle: arguyendo
Imperative: arguye, argüid

[20] vaciar
Present: vacío, vacías, vacía, vaciamos, vaciáis, vacían
Present subjunctive: vacíe,

vacíes, vacíe, vaciemos,
vaciéis, vacíen
Imperative: vacía, vaciad

[21] acentuar

Present: acentúo, acentúas,
acentúa, acentuamos,
acentuáis, acentúan
Present subjunctive:
acentúe, acentúes, acentúe,
acentuemos, acentuéis,
acentúen
Imperative: acentúa, acentuad

[22] atañer, engullir

Preterite:
atañ|i, ~iste, ~ó, ~imos,
~isteis, ~eron
engull|í ~iste, ~ó, ~imos,
~isteis, ~eron
Imperfect subjunctive:
atañ|era, ~eras, ~era,
~éramos, ~erais, ~eran
atañ|ese, ~eses, ~ese, ~ésemos,
~eseis, ~esen
engull|era, ~eras, ~era,
~éramos, ~erais, ~eran
engull|ese, ~eses, ~ese,
~ésemos, ~eseis, ~esen
Present participle: atañendo
engullendo

[23] aislar, aullar

Present: aíslo, aíslas, aísla,
aislamos, aisláis, aíslan
aúllo, aúllas, aúlla, aullamos
aulláis, aúllan
Present subjunctive: aísle, aísles,
aísle, aislemos, aisléis, aíslen
aúlle, aúlles, aúlle, aullemos,
aulléis, aúllen
Imperative: aísla, aislad
aúlla, aullad

[24] abolir

Present: abolimos, abolís
Present subjunctive: not used
Imperative: abolid

[25] andar

Preterite: anduv|e, ~iste, ~o,
~imos, ~isteis, ~ieron
Imperfect subjunctive:
anduv|iera, ~ieras, ~iera,
~iéramos, ~ierais, ~ieran
anduv|iese, ~ieses, ~iese,
~iésemos, ~ieseis, ~iesen

[26] dar

Present: doy, das, da, damos,
dais, dan
Preterite: di, diste, dio, dimos,
disteis, dieron
Present subjunctive: dé, des, dé,
demos, deis, den
Imperfect subjunctive: diera,
dieras, diera, diéramos,
dierais, dieran
diese, dieses, diese, diésemos,
dieseis, diesen

[27] estar

Present: estoy, estás, está,
estamos, estáis, están
Preterite: estuv|e, ~iste, ~o,
~imos, ~isteis, ~ieron
Present subjunctive: esté, estés,
esté, estemos, estéis, estén
Imperfect subjunctive:
estuv|iera, ~ieras, ~iera,
~iéramos, ~ierais, ~ieran
estuv|iese, ~ieses, ~iese,
~iésemos, ~ieseis, ~iesen
Imperative: está, estad

[28] caber

Present: quepo, cabes, cabe,
cabemos, cabéis, caben
Future: cabr|é, ~ás, ~á, ~emos,
~éis, ~án
Preterite: cup|e, ~iste, ~o, ~imos,
~isteis, ~ieron
Present subjunctive: quep|a, ~as,
~a, ~amos, ~áis, ~an
Imperfect subjunctive: cup|iera,
~ieras, ~iera, ~iéramos,
~ierais, ~ieran
cup|iese, ~ieses, ~iese,

~iésemos, ~ieseis, ~iesen
Conditional: cabr|ía, ~ías, ~ía,
~íamos, ~íais, ~ían

[29] caer

Present: caigo, caes, cae, caemos,
caéis, caen
Preterite: caí, caiste, cayó,
caímos, caísteis, cayeron
Present subjunctive: caig|a, ~as,
~a, ~amos, ~áis, ~an
Imperfect subjunctive:
cay|era, ~eras, ~era, ~éramos,
~erais, ~eran
cay|ese, ~eses, ~ese, ~ésemos,
~eseis, ~esen
Present participle: cayendo
Past participle: caído

[30] haber

Present: he, has, ha, hemos,
habéis, han
Future: habr|é ~ás, ~á, ~emos,
~éis, ~án
Preterite: hub|e, ~iste, ~o,
~imos, ~isteis, ~ieron
Present subjunctive: hay|a, ~as,
~a, ~amos, ~áis, ~an
Imperfect subjunctive: hub|iera,
~ieras, ~iera, ~iéramos,
~ierais, ~ieran
hub|iese, ~ieses, ~iese,
~iésemos, ~ieseis, ~iesen
Conditional: habr|ía, ~ías, ~ía,
~íamos, ~íais, ~ían
Imperative: he, habed

[31] hacer

Present: hago, haces, hace,
hacemos, hacéis, hacen
Future: har|é, ~ás, ~á, ~emos,
~éis, ~án
Preterite: hice, hiciste, hizo,
hicimos, hicisteis, hicieron
Present subjunctive:
hag|a, ~as, ~a, ~amos, ~áis,
~an
Imperfect subjunctive:

hic|iera, ~ieras, ~iera,
~iéramos, ~ierais, ~ieran
hic|iese, ~ieses, ~iese,
~iésemos, ~ieseis, ~iesen
Conditional: har|ía,
~ías, ~ía, ~íamos, ~íais, ~ían
Past participle: hecho
Imperative: haz, haced

[32] placer

Present subjunctive: plazca
Imperfect subjunctive: placiera,
placiese

[33] poder

Present: puedo, puedes,
puede, podemos, podéis,
pueden
Future: podr|é, ~ás, ~á, ~emos,
~éis, ~án
Preterite: pud|e, ~iste, ~o, ~imos,
~isteis, ~ieron
Present subjunctive:
pueda, puedas, pueda,
podamos, podáis, puedan
Imperfect subjunctive: pud|iera,
~ieras, ~iera, ~iéramos,
~ierais, ~ieran
pud|iese, ~ieses, ~iese,
~iésemos, ~ieseis, ~iesen
Conditional: podr|ía, ~ías, ~ía,
~íamos, ~íais, ~ían
Past participle: pudiendo

[34] poner

Present: pongo, pones, pone,
ponemos, ponéis, ponen
Future: pondr|é, ~ás, ~á, ~emos,
~éis, ~án
Preterite: pus|e, ~iste,
~o, ~imos, ~isteis, ~ieron
Present subjunctive: pong|a, ~as,
~a, ~amos, ~áis, ~an
Imperfect subjunctive: pus|iera,
~ieras, ~iera, ~iéramos,
~ierais, ~ieran
pus|iese, ~ieses, ~iese,
~iésemos, ~ieseis, ~iesen

Conditional: pondr|ía, ~ías, ~ía,
~íamos, ~íais, ~ían
Past participle: puesto
Imperative: pon, poned

[35] querer
Present: quiero, quieres,
quiere, queremos, queréis,
quieren
Future: querr|é, ~ás, ~á, ~emos,
~éis, ~án
Preterite: quis|e, ~iste, ~o,
~imos, ~isteis, ~ieron
Present subjunctive:
quiera, quieras, quiera,
queramos, queráis,
quieran
Imperfect subjunctive: quis|iera,
~ieras, ~iera, ~iéramos,
~ierais, ~ieran
quis|iese, ~ieses, ~iese,
~iésemos, ~ieseis, ~iesen
Conditional: querr|ía, ~ías, ~ía,
~íamos, ~íais, ~ían
Imperative: quiere, quered

[36] raer
Present: raigo/rayo, raes, rae,
raemos, raéis, raen
Preterite: raí, raíste, rayó,
raímos, raísteis, rayeron
Present subjunctive:
raig|a, ~as, ~a, ~amos, ~áis,
~an
ray|a, ~as, ~a, ~amos, ~áis,
~an
Imperfect subjunctive:
ray|era, ~eras, ~era, ~éramos,
~erais, ~eran ray|ese, ~eses,
~ese, ~ésemos, ~eseis, ~esen
Present participle: rayendo
Past participle: raído

[37] roer
Present: roo, roes, roe, roemos,
roéis, roen
Preterite: roí, roíste, royó,
roímos, roísteis, royeron

Present subjunctive: ro|a, ~as,
~a, ~amos, ~áis, ~an
Imperfect subjunctive:
roy|era, ~eras, ~era, ~éramos,
~erais, ~eran
roy|ese, ~eses, ~ese, ~ésemos,
~eseis, ~esen
Present participle: royendo
Past participle: roído

[38] saber
Present: sé, sabes, sabe, sabemos,
sabéis, saben
Future: sabr|é, ~ás, ~á, ~emos,
~éis, ~án
Preterite: sup|e, ~iste,
~o, ~imos, ~isteis, ~ieron
Present subjunctive: sep|a, ~as,
~a, ~amos, ~áis, ~an
Imperfect subjunctive: sup|iera,
~ieras, ~iera, ~iéramos,
~ierais, ~ieran
sup|iese, ~ieses, ~iese,
~iésemos, ~ieseis, ~iesen
Conditional: sabr|ía, ~ías, ~ía,
~íamos, ~íais, ~ían

[39] ser
Present: soy, eres, es, somos, sois,
son
Imperfect: era, eras, era, éramos,
erais, eran
Preterite: fui, fuiste, fue, fuimos,
fuisteis, fueron
Present subjunctive: se|a, ~as,
~a, ~amos, ~áis, ~an
Imperfect subjunctive: fu|era,
~eras, ~era, ~éramos, ~erais,
~eran
fu|ese, ~eses, ~ese, ~ésemos,
~eseis, ~esen
Imperative: sé, sed

[40] tener
Present: tengo, tienes,
tiene, tenemos, tenéis,
tienen
Future: tendr|é, ~ás, ~á, ~emos,

Preterite: tuv|e, ~iste, ~o, ~imos,
~isteis, ~ieron
Present subjunctive: teng|a, ~as,
~a, ~amos, ~áis, ~an
Imperfect subjunctive: tuv|iera,
~ieras, ~iera, ~iéramos,
~ierais, ~ieran
tuv|iese, ~ieses, ~iese,
~iésemos, ~ieseis, ~iesen
Conditional: tendr|ía, ~ías, ~ía,
~íamos, ~íais, ~ían
Imperative: ten, tened

[41] traer

Present: traigo, traes, trae,
traemos, traéis, traen
Preterite: traj|e, ~iste, ~o, ~imos,
~isteis, ~eron
Present subjunctive: traig|a, ~as,
~a, ~amos, ~áis, ~an
Imperfect subjunctive:
traj|era, ~eras, ~era, ~éramos,
~erais, ~eran traj|ese, ~eses,
~ese, ~ésemos, ~eseis, ~esen
Present participle: trayendo
Past participle: traído

[42] valer

Present: valgo, vales, vale,
valemos, valéis, valen
Future: vald|ré, ~ás, ~á, ~emos,
~éis, ~án
Present subjunctive: valg|a, ~as,
~a, ~amos ~áis, ~an
Conditional: vald|ría, ~ías, ~ía,
~íamos, ~íais, ~ían
Imperative: vale, valed

[43] ver

Present: veo, ves, ve,vemos,
veis, ven
Imperfect: ve|ía, ~ías, ~ía,
~íamos, ~íais, ~ían
Preterite: vi, viste, vio, vimos,
visteis, vieron
Present subjunctive: ve|a, ~as,
~a, ~amos, ~áis, ~an

Past participle: visto

[44] yacer

Present: yazco, yaces, yace,
yacemos, yacéis, yacen
Present subjunctive: yazc|a, ~as,
~a, ~amos, ~áis, ~an
Imperative: yace, yaced

[45] asir

Present: asgo, ases, ase, asimos,
asís, asen
Present subjunctive: asg|a, ~as,
~a, ~amos, ~áis, ~an

[46] decir

Present: digo, dices, dice,
decimos, decís, dicen
Future: dir|é, ~ás, ~á, ~emos,
~éis, ~án
Preterite: dij|e, ~iste, ~o, ~imos,
~isteis, ~eron
Present subjunctive: dig|a, ~as,
~a, ~amos, ~áis, ~an
Imperfect subjunctive:
dij|era, ~eras, ~era, ~éramos,
~erais,~eran
dij|ese, ~eses, ~ese, ~ésemos,
~eseis, ~esen
Conditional: dir|ía, ~ías, ~ía,
~íamos, ~íais, ~ían
Present participle: dicho
Imperative: di, decid

[47] reducir

Present: reduzco, reduces,
reduce, reducimos, reducís,
reducen
Preterite: reduj|e, ~iste, ~o,
~imos, ~isteis, ~eron
Present subjunctive: reduzc|a,
~as, ~a, ~amos, ~áis, ~an
Imperfect subjunctive: reduj|era,
~eras, ~era, ~éramos, ~erais,
~eran
reduj|ese, ~eses, ~ese,
~ésemos, ~eseis, ~esen

[48] erguir

Present: yergo, yergues, yergue, erguimos, erguís, yerguen
Preterite: erguí, erguiste, irguió, erguimos, erguisteis, irguieron
Present subjunctive: yerg|a, ~as, ~a, ~amos, ~áis, ~an
Imperfect subjunctive: irgu|iera, ~ieras, ~iera, ~iéramos, ~ierais, ~ieran
irgu|iese, ~ieses, ~iese, ~iésemos, ~ieseis, ~iesen
Present participle: irguiendo
Imperative: yergue, erguid

[49] ir

Present: voy, vas, va, vamos, vais, van
Imperfect: iba, ibas, iba, íbamos, ibais, iban
Preterite: fui, fuiste, fue, fuimos, fuisteis, fueron
Present subjunctive: vay|a, ~as, ~a, ~amos, ~áis, ~an
Imperfect subjunctive: fu|era, ~eras, ~era, ~éramos, ~erais, ~eran fu|ese, ~eses, ~ese, ~ésemos, ~eseis, ~esen
Present participle: yendo
Imperative: ve, id

[50] oír

Present: oigo, oyes, oye, oímos, oís, oyen
Preterite: oí, oíste, oyó, oímos, oísteis, oyeron
Present subjunctive: oig|a, ~as, ~a, ~amos, ~áis, ~an
Imperfect subjunctive: oy|era, ~eras, ~era, ~éramos, ~erais, ~eran
oy|ese, ~eses, ~ese, ~ésemos, ~eseis, ~esen
Present participle: oyendo
Past participle: oído
Imperative: oye, oíd

[51] reír

Present: río, ríes, ríe, reímos, reís, ríen
Preterite: reí, reíste, rió, reímos, reísteis, rieron
Present subjunctive: ría, rías, ría, riamos, riáis, rían
Present participle: riendo
Past participle: reído
Imperative: ríe, reíd

[52] salir

Present: salgo, sales, sale, salimos, salís, salen
Future: saldr|é, ~ás, ~á, ~emos, ~éis, ~án
Present subjunctive: salg|a, ~as, ~a, ~amos, ~áis, ~an
Conditional: saldr|ía, ~ías, ~ía, ~íamos, ~íais, ~ían
Imperative: sal, salid

[53] venir

Present: vengo, vienes, viene, venimos, venís, vienen
Future: vendr|é, ~ás, ~á, ~emos, ~éis, ~án
Preterite: vin|e, ~iste, ~o, ~imos, ~isteis, ~ieron
Present subjunctive: veng|a, ~as, ~a, ~amos, ~áis, ~an
Imperfect subjunctive: vin|iera, ~ieras, ~iera, ~iéramos, ~ierais, ~ieran
vin|iese, ~ieses, ~iese, ~iésemos, ~ieseis, ~iesen
Conditional: vendr|ía, ~ías, ~ía, ~íamos, ~íais, ~ían
Present participle: viniendo
Imperative: ven, venid

aloja|miento *m* accommodation.
∼**r** *vt* put up. □ ∼**rse** *vpr* stay
alondra *f* lark
alpaca *f* alpaca
alpargata *f* canvas shoe,
espadrille
alpin|ismo *m* mountaineering,
climbing. ∼**ista** *m & f*
mountaineer, climber. ∼**o** *a*
Alpine
alpiste *m* birdseed
alquil|ar *vt* (tomar en alquiler) hire
<*vehículo*>, rent <*piso, casa*>; (dar
en alquiler) hire (out) <*vehículo*>,
rent (out) <*piso, casa*>. **se alquila**
to let (Brit), for rent (Amer). ∼**er** *m*
(acción — de alquilar un piso etc)
renting; (— de alquilar un vehículo)
hiring; (precio — por el que se alquila
un piso etc) rent; (— por el que se
alquila un vehículo) hire charge. **de**
∼**er** for hire
alquimi|a *f* alchemy. ∼**sta** *m*
alchemist
alquitrán *m* tar
alrededor *adv* around. ∼ **de**
around; (con números) about. ∼**es**
mpl surroundings; (de una ciudad)
outskirts
alta *f* discharge
altaner|ía *f* (arrogancia) arrogance.
∼**o** *a* arrogant, haughty
altar *m* altar
altavoz *m* loudspeaker
altera|ble *a* changeable. ∼**ción** *f*
change, alteration. ∼**r** *vt* change,
alter; (perturbar) disturb; (enfadar)
anger, irritate. □ ∼**rse** *vpr*
change, alter; (agitarse) get upset;
(enfadarse) get angry; <*comida*> go
off
altercado *m* argument
altern|ar *vt/i* alternate. □ ∼**arse**
vpr take turns. ∼**ativa** *f*
alternative. ∼**ativo** *a* alternating.
∼**o** *a* alternate; (Elec) alternating

Alteza *f* (título) Highness
altibajos *mpl* (de terreno)
unevenness; (fig) ups and downs
altiplanicie *f*, **altiplano** *m* high
plateau
altisonante *a* pompous
altitud *f* altitude
altiv|ez *f* arrogance. ∼**o** *a*
arrogant
alto *a* high; <*persona, edificio*>
tall; <*voz*> loud; (fig, elevado) lofty;
(Mus) <*nota*> high(-pitched); (Mus)
<*voz, instrumento*> alto; <*horas*>
early. ● *adv* high; (de sonidos)
loud(ly). ● *m* height; (de un edificio)
top floor; (viola) viola; (voz) alto;
(parada) stop. ● *int* halt!, stop! **en
lo** ∼ **de** on the top of. **tiene 3
metros de** ∼ it is 3 metres high
altoparlante *m* (esp LAm)
loudspeaker
altruis|mo *m* altruism. ∼**ta** *a*
altruistic. ●*m & f* altruist
altura *f* height; (Aviac, Geog)
altitude; (de agua) depth; (fig, cielo)
sky. **a estas** ∼**s** at this stage. **tiene
3 metros de** ∼ it is 3 metres high
alubia *f* (haricot) bean
alucinación *f* hallucination
alud *m* avalanche
aludi|do *a* in question. **darse por**
∼**do** take it personally. **no darse
por** ∼**do** turn a deaf ear. ∼**r** *vi*
mention
alumbra|do *a* lit. ● *m* lighting.
∼**miento** *m* lighting; (parto)
childbirth. ∼**r** *vt* light
aluminio *m* aluminium (Brit),
aluminum (Amer)
alumno *m* pupil; (Univ) student
aluniza|je *m* landing on the
moon. ∼**r** [10] *vi* land on the
moon
alusi|ón *f* allusion. ∼**vo** *a*
allusive

alza *f* rise. **~da** *f* (de caballo) height; (Jurid) appeal. **~do** *a* raised; (Mex, soberbio) vain; <*precio*> fixed. **~miento** *m* (Pol) uprising. **~r** [10] *vt* raise, lift (up); raise <*precios*>. □ **~rse** *vpr* (Pol) rise up

ama *f* lady of the house. **~ de casa** housewife. **~ de cría** wet-nurse. **~ de llaves** housekeeper

amab|ilidad *f* kindness. **~le** *a* kind; (simpático) nice

amaestra|do *a* trained. **~r** *vt* train

amag|ar [12] *vt* (mostrar intención de) make as if to; (Mex, amenazar) threaten. ● *vi* threaten; <*algo bueno*> be in the offing. ● **~o** *m* threat; (señal) sign; (Med) symptom

amainar *vi* let up

amalgama *f* amalgam. **~r** *vt* amalgamate

amamantar *vt/i* breast-feed; <*animal*> to suckle

amanecer *m* dawn. ● *vi* dawn; <*persona*> wake up. **al ~** at dawn, at daybreak. □ **~se** *vpr* (Mex) stay up all night

amanera|do *a* affected. □ **~rse** *vpr* become affected

amansar *vt* tame; break in <*un caballo*>; soothe <*dolor etc*>. □ **~se** *vpr* calm down

amante *a* fond. ● *m & f* lover

amapola *f* poppy

amar *vt* love

amara|je *m* landing on water; (de astronave) splash-down. **~r** *vi* land on water; <*astronave*> splash down

amarg|ado *a* embittered. **~ar** [12] *vt* make bitter; embitter <*persona*>. □ **~arse** *vpr* become bitter. **~o** *a* bitter. **~ura** *f* bitterness

amariconado *a* 🔟 effeminate

amarill|ento *a* yellowish; <*tez*> sallow. **~o** *a* & *m* yellow

amarra|s *fpl.* **soltar las ~s** cast off. **~do** *a* (LAm) mean. **~r** *vt* moor; (esp LAm, atar) tie. □ **~rse** *vpr* LAm tie up

amas|ar *vt* knead; (acumular) to amass. **~ijo** *m* dough; (acción) kneading; (fig, 🔟, mezcla) hotchpotch

amate *m* (Mex) fig tree

amateur *a* & *m & f* amateur

amazona *f* Amazon; (jinete) horsewoman

ámbar *m* amber

ambici|ón *f* ambition. **~onar** *vt* aspire to. **~onar ser** have an ambition to be. **~oso** *a* ambitious. ● *m* ambitious person

ambidextro *a* ambidextrous. ● *m* ambidextrous person

ambient|ar *vt* give an atmosphere to. □ **~arse** *vpr* adapt o.s. **~e** *m* atmosphere; (entorno) environment

ambig|üedad *f* ambiguity. **~uo** *a* ambiguous

ámbito *m* sphere; (alcance) scope

ambos *a* & *pron* both

ambulancia *f* ambulance

ambulante *a* travelling

ambulatorio *m* out-patients' department

amedrentar *vt* frighten, scare. □ **~se** *vpr* be frightened

amén *m* amen. ● *int* amen! **en un decir ~** in an instant

amenaza *f* threat. **~r** [10] *vt* threaten

amen|idad *f* pleasantness. **~izar** [10] *vt* brighten up. **~o** *a* pleasant

América *f* America. **~ Central** Central America. **~ del Norte** North America. **~ del Sur** South America. **~ Latina** Latin America

american|a*f* jacket. **∼ismo** *m* Americanism. **∼o** *a* American

amerita|**do** *a* (LAm) meritorious. **∼r** *vt* (LAm) deserve

amerizaje *m* ⇒AMARAJE

ametralla|**dora** *f* machine-gun. **∼r** *vt* machine-gun

amianto *m* asbestos

amig|**a** *f* friend; (novia) girl-friend; (amante) lover. **∼able** *a* friendly. **∼ablemente** *adv* amicably

am|**ígdala** *f* tonsil. **∼igdalitis** *f* tonsillitis

amigo *a* friendly. ● *m* friend; (novio) boyfriend; (amante) lover. **ser ∼ de** be fond of. **ser muy ∼s** be close friends

amilanar *vt* daunt. □ **∼se** *vpr* be daunted

aminorar *vt* lessen; reduce <*velocidad*>

amist|**ad** *f* friendship. **∼ades** *fpl* friends. **∼osa** *a* friendly

amn|**esia** *f* amnesia. **∼ésico** *a* amnesiac

amnist|**ía** *f* amnesty. **∼iar** [20] *vt* grant an amnesty to

amo *m* master; (dueño) owner

amodorrarse *vpr* feel sleepy

amoldar *vt* mould; (adaptar) adapt; (acomodar) fit. □ **∼se** *vpr* adapt

amonestar *vt* rebuke, reprimand; (anunciar la boda) publish the banns of

amoniaco amoníaco *m* ammonia

amontonar *vt* pile up; (fig, acumular) accumulate. □ **∼se** *vpr* pile up; <*gente*> crowd together

amor *m* love. **∼es** *mpl* (relaciones amorosas) love affairs. **∼ propio** pride. **con mil ∼es, de mil ∼es** with (the greatest of) pleasure. **hacer el ∼** make love. **por (el) ∼ de Dios** for God's sake

amoratado *a* purple; (de frío) blue

amordazar [10] *vt* gag; (fig) silence

amorfo *a* amorphous, shapeless

amor|**ío** *m* affair. **∼oso** *a* loving; <*cartas*> love; (LAm, encantador) cute

amortajar *vt* shroud

amortigua|**dora** deadening. ● *m* (Auto) shock absorber. **∼r** [15] *vt* deaden <*ruido*>; dim <*luz*>; cushion <*golpe*>; tone down <*color*>

amortiza|**ble** *a* redeemable. **∼ción** *f* (de una deuda) repayment; (de bono etc) redemption. **∼r** [10] *vt* repay <*una deuda*>

amotinar *vt* incite to riot. □ **∼se** *vpr* rebel; (Mil) mutiny

ampar|**ar** *vt* help; (proteger) protect. □ **∼arse** *vpr* seek protection; (de la lluvia) shelter. **∼o** *m* protection; (de la lluvia) shelter. **al ∼o de** under the protection of

amperio *m* ampere, amp

amplia|**ción** *f* extension; (photo) enlargement. **∼r** [20] *vt* enlarge, extend; (photo) enlarge

amplifica|**ción** *f* amplification. **∼dor** *m* amplifier. **∼r** [7] amplify

ampli|**o** *a* wide; (espacioso) spacious; <*ropa*> loose-fitting. **∼tud** *f* extent; (espaciosidad) spaciousness; (espacio) space

ampolla *f* (Med) blister; (de medicamento) ampoule, phial

ampuloso *a* pompous

amputar *vt* amputate; (fig) delete

amueblar *vt* furnish

amuleto *m* charm, amulet

amuralla|**do** *a* walled. **∼r** *vt* build a wall around

anacr|**ónico** *a* anachronistic. **∼onismo** *m* anachronism

anales *mpl* annals

analfabet|**ismo** *m* illiteracy. **∼o** *a & m* illiterate

analgésico *a* analgesic. ● *m* painkiller

an|álisis *m invar* analysis. **~álisis de sangre** blood test. **~alista** *m & f* analyst. **~alítico** *a* analytical. **~alizar** [10] *vt* analyze

an|alogía *f* analogy. **~álogo** *a* analogous

anaranjado *a* orangey

an|arquía *f* anarchy. **~árquico** *a* anarchic. **~arquismo** *m* anarchism. **~arquista** *a* anarchistic. ● *m & f* anarchist

anat|omía *f* anatomy. **~ómico** *a* anatomical

anca *f* haunch; (parte superior) rump; (**🄸**, nalgas) bottom. **en ~s** (LAm) on the crupper

ancestro *m* ancestor

ancho *a* wide; <ropa> loose-fitting; (fig) relieved; (demasiado grande) too big; (ufano) smug. ● *m* width; (Rail) gauge. **tiene 3 metros de ~** it is 3 metres wide. **~ de banda** bandwidth.

anchoa *f* anchovy

anchura *f* width; (medida) measurement

ancian|o *a* elderly, old. ● *m* elderly man, old man. **~a** *f* elderly woman, old woman. **los ~os** old people

ancla *f* anchor. **echar ~s** drop anchor. **levar ~s** weigh anchor. **~r** *vi* anchor

andad|eras *fpl* (Mex) baby-walker. **~or** *m* baby-walker

Andalucía *f* Andalusia

andaluz *a & m* Andalusian

andamio *m* platform. **~s** *mpl* scaffolding

and|anzas *fpl* adventures. **~ar** [25] *vt* (recorrer) cover, go. ● *vi* walk; <máquina> go, work; (estar) be; (moverse) move. **~ar a caballo** (LAm) ride a horse. **~ar en bicicleta** (LAm) ride a bicycle. **¡anda!** go on!, come on! **~ar por** be about. □ **~arse** *vpr* (LAm, en imperativo) **¡ándate!** go away!. ● *m* walk. **~ariego** *a* fond of walking

andén *m* platform

Andes *mpl*. **los ~** the Andes

andin|o *a* Andean. **~ismo** *m* (LAm) mountaineering, climbing. **~ista** *m & f* (LAm) mountaineer, climber

andrajo *m* rag. **~so** *a* ragged

anduve *vb* ⇒ANDAR

anécdota *f* anecdote

anecdótico *a* anecdotal

anegar [12] *vt* flood. □ **~rse** *vpr* be flooded, flood

anejo *a* ⇒ANEXO

an|emia *f* anaemia. **~émico** *a* anaemic

anest|esia *f* anaesthesia; (droga) anaesthetic. **~esiar** *vt* anaesthetize. **~ésico** *a & m* anaesthetic. **~esista** *m & f* anaesthetist

anex|ar *vt* annex. **~o** *a* attached. ● *m* annexe

anfibio *a* amphibious. ● *m* amphibian

anfiteatro *m* amphitheatre; (en un teatro) upper circle

anfitri|ón *m* host. **~ona** *f* hostess

ángel *m* angel; (encanto) charm

angelical *a*, **angélico** *a* angelic

angina *f*. **~ de pecho** angina (pectoris). **tener ~s** have tonsillitis

anglicano *a & m* Anglican

angl|icismo *m* Anglicism. **~ófilo** *a & m* Anglophile. **~ohispánico** *a* Anglo-Spanish. **~osajón** *a & m* Anglo-Saxon

angosto *a* narrow

angu|ila *f* eel. **~la** *f* elver, baby eel

ángulo *m* angle; (rincón, esquina) corner; (curva) bend

angusti|a *f* anguish. **~ar** *vt* distress; (inquietar) worry. □ **~arse** *vpr* get distressed; (inquietarse) get worried. **~oso** *a* anguished; (que causa angustia) distressing

anhel|ar *vt* (+ *nombre*) long for; (+ *verbo*) long to. **~o** *m* (fig) yearning

anidar *vi* nest

anill|a *f* ring. **~o** *m* ring. **~o de boda** wedding ring

ánima *f* soul

anima|ción *f* (de personas) life; (de cosas) liveliness; (bullicio) bustle; (en el cine) animation. **~do** *a* lively; <*sitio etc*> busy. **~dor** *m* host. **~dora** *f* hostess; (de un equipo) cheerleader

animadversión *f* ill will

animal *a* animal; (fig, 🄵, torpe) stupid. ● *m* animal; (fig, 🄵, idiota) idiot; (fig, 🄵, bruto) brute

animar *vt* give life to; (dar ánimo) encourage; (dar vivacidad) liven up. □ **~se** *vpr* (decidirse) decide; (ponerse alegre) cheer up. **¿te animas a ir al cine?** do you feel like going to the cinema?

ánimo *m* soul; (mente) mind; (valor) courage; (intención) intention. **¡~!** come on!, cheer up! **dar ~s** encourage

animos|idad *f* animosity. **~o** *a* brave; (resuelto) determined

aniquilar *vt* annihilate; (acabar con) ruin

anís *m* aniseed; (licor) anisette

aniversario *m* anniversary

anoche *adv* last night, yesterday evening

anochecer [11] *vi* get dark. **anochecí en Madrid** I was in Madrid at dusk. ● *m* nightfall, dusk. **al ~** at nightfall

anodino *a* bland

an|omalía *f* anomaly. **~ómalo** *a* anomalous

an|onimato *m* anonymity. **~ónimo** *a* anonymous; <*sociedad*> limited. ● *m* (carta) anonymous letter

anormal *a* abnormal. ● *m & f* 🄵 idiot. **~idad** *f* abnormality

anota|ción *f* (nota) note; (acción de poner notas) annotation. **~r** *vt* (poner nota) annotate; (apuntar) make a note of; (LAm) score <*un gol*>

anquilosa|miento *m* (fig) paralysis. □ **~rse** *vpr* become paralyzed

ansi|a *f* anxiety, worry; (anhelo) yearning. **~ar** [20] *vt* long for. **~edad** *f* anxiety. **~oso** *a* anxious; (deseoso) eager

antag|ónico *a* antagonistic. **~onismo** *m* antagonism. **~onista** *m & f* antagonist

antaño *adv* in days gone by

antártico *a & m* Antarctic

ante *prep* in front of, before; (frente a) in the face of; (en vista de) in view of. ● *m* elk; (piel) suede. **~anoche** *adv* the night before last. **~ayer** *adv* the day before yesterday. **~brazo** *m* forearm

antece|dente *a* previous. ● *m* antecedent. **~dentes** *mpl* history, background. **~dentes penales** criminal record. **~der** *vt* precede. **~sor** *m* predecessor; (antepasado) ancestor

antelación *f* (advance) notice. **con ~** in advance

antemano *adv* **de ~** beforehand

antena *f* antenna; (radio, TV) aerial

antenoche *adv* (LAm) the night before last

anteoj|eras *fpl* blinkers. **~o** *m* telescope. **~os** *mpl* binoculars; (LAm, gafas) glasses, spectacles. **~os de sol** sunglasses

ante|pasados *mpl* forebears, ancestors. ~**poner** [34] *vt* put in front (**a** of); (fig) put before, prefer. ~**proyecto** *m* preliminary sketch; (fig) blueprint

anterior *a* previous; (delantero) front. ~**idad** *f*. **con** ~**idad** previously. **con** ~**idad a** prior to

antes *adv* before; (antiguamente) in the past; (mejor) rather; (primero) first. ~ **de** before. ~ **de ayer** the day before yesterday. ~ **de que** + *subj* before. ~ **de quellegue** before he arrives. **cuanto** ~, **lo** ~ **posible** as soon as possible

anti|aéreo *a* anti-aircraft. ~**biótico** *a* & *m* antibiotic. ~**ciclón** *m* anticyclone

anticip|ación *f*. **con** ~**ación** in advance. **con mediahora de** ~**ación** half an hour early. ~**ado** *a* advance. **por** ~**ado** in advance. ~**ar** *vt* bring forward; advance <*dinero*>. □ ~**arse** *vpr* be early. ~**o** *m* (dinero) advance; (fig) foretaste

anti|conceptivo *a* & *m* contraceptive. ~**congelante** *m* antifreeze

anticua|do *a* old-fashioned. ~**rio** *m* antique dealer

anticuerpo *m* antibody

antídoto *m* antidote

anti|estético *a* ugly. ~**faz** *m* mask

antig|ualla *f* old relic. ~**uamente** *adv* formerly; (hace mucho tiempo) long ago. ~**üedad** *f* antiquity; (objeto) antique; (en un empleo) length of service. ~**uo** *a* old; <*ruinas*> ancient; <*mueble*> antique

Antillas *fpl*. **las** ~ the West Indies

antílope *m* antelope

antinatural *a* unnatural

anti|patía *f* dislike; (cualidad de antipático) unpleasantness. ~**ático** *a* unpleasant, unfriendly

anti|semita *m* & *f* anti-Semite. ~**séptico** *a* & *m* antiseptic. ~**social** *a* antisocial

antítesis *f invar* antithesis

antoj|adizo *a* capricious. □ ~**arse** *vpr* fancy. **se le** ~**a un caramelo** he fancies a sweet. ~**itos** *mpl* (Mex) snacks bought at street stands. ~**o** *m* whim; (de embarazada) craving

antología *f* anthology

antorcha *f* torch

ántrax *m* anthrax

antro *m* (fig) dump, hole. ~ **de perversión** den of iniquity

antrop|ología *f* anthropology. ~**ólogo** *m* anthropologist

anua|l *a* annual. ~**lidad** *f* annuity. ~**lmente** *adv* yearly. ~**rio** *m* yearbook

anudar *vt* tie, knot. □ ~**se** *vpr* tie

anula|ción *f* annulment, cancellation. ~**r** *vt* annul, cancel. ● *a* <*dedo*> ring. ● *m* ring finger

anunci|ante *m* & *f* advertiser. ~**ar** *vt* announce; advertise <*producto comercial*>; (presagiar) be a sign of. ~**o** *m* announcement; (para vender algo) advertisement, advert Ⓘ; (cartel) poster

anzuelo *m* (fish)hook; (fig) bait. **tragar el** ~ swallow the bait

añadi|dura *f* addition. **por** ~**dura** in addition. ~**r** *vt* add

añejo *a* <*vino*> mature

añicos *mpl*. **hacer(se)** ~ smash to pieces

año *m* year. ~ **bisiesto** leap year. ~ **nuevo** new year. **al** ~ per year, a year. **¿cuántos** ~**s tiene?** how old is he? **tiene 5** ~**s** he's 5 (years old). **el** ~ **pasado** last year. **el** ~ **que viene** next year. **entrado en** ~**s** elderly. **los** ~**s 60** the sixties

añora|nza f nostalgia. ~**r** vt miss

apabulla|nte a overwhelming. ~**r** vt overwhelm

apacible a gentle; <clima> mild

apaciguar [15] vt pacify; (calmar) calm; relieve <dolor etc>. □~**se** vpr calm down

apadrinar vt sponsor; be godfather to <a un niño>

apag|ado a extinguished; <color> dull; <aparato eléctrico, luz> off; <persona> lifeless; <sonido> muffled. ~**ar** [12] vt put out <fuego, incendio>; turn off, switch off <aparato eléctrico, luz>; quench <sed>; muffle <sonido>. □~**arse** vpr <fuego, luz> go out; <sonido> die away. ~**ón** m blackout

apalabrar vt make a verbal agreement; (contratar) engage

apalear vt winnow <grano>; beat <alfombra, frutos, persona>

apantallar vt (Mex) impress

apañ|ar vt (arreglar) fix; (remendar) mend; (agarrar) grasp, take hold of. □~**se** vpr get along, manage

apapachar vt (Mex) cuddle

aparador m sideboard; (Mex, de tienda) shop window

aparato m apparatus; (máquina) machine; (doméstico) appliance; (teléfono) telephone; (radio, TV) set; (ostentación) show, pomp. ~**so** a showy, ostentatious; <caída> spectacular

aparca|miento m car park (Brit), parking lot (Amer). ~**r** [7] vt/i park

aparear vt mate <animales>.□~**se** vpr mate

aparecer [11] vi appear. □~**se** vpr appear

aparej|ado a. llevar ~**ado**, traer ~**ado** mean, entail. ~**o** m (avíos) equipment; (de caballo) tack; (de pesca) tackle

aparent|ar vt (afectar) feign; (parecer) look. ● vi show off. ~**a 20 años** she looks like she's 20. ~**e** a apparent

apari|ción f appearance; (visión) apparition. ~**encia** f appearance; (fig) show. **guardar las** ~**encias** keep up appearances

apartado a separated; (aislado) isolated. ● m (de un texto) section. ~ **(de correos)** post-office box, PO box

apartamento m apartment, flat (Brit)

apart|ar vt separate; (alejar) move away; (quitar) remove; (guardar) set aside. □~**arse** vpr leave; (quitarse de en medio) get out of the way; (aislarse) cut o.s. off. ~**e** adv apart, (por separado) separately; (además) besides. ● m aside; (párrafo) new paragraph. ~**e de** apart from. **dejar** ~**e** leave aside. **eso** ~**e** apart from that

apasiona|do a passionate; (entusiasta) enthusiastic; (falto de objetividad) biased. ● m. ~**do de** lover. ~**miento** m passion. ~**r** vt excite. □~**rse** vpr be mad (**por** about); (ser parcial) become biased

ap|atía f apathy. ~**ático** a apathetic

apea|dero m (Rail) halt. □~**rse** vpr get off

apechugar [12] vi 🆒 ~ **con** put up with

apedrear vt stone

apeg|ado a attached (**a** to). ~**o** m 🆒 attachment. **tener** ~**o a** be a fond of

apela|ción f appeal. ~**r** vi appeal; (recurrir) resort (**a** to). ● vt (apodar) call. ~**tivo** m (nick)name

apellid|ar vt call. □~**arse** vpr be called. **¿cómo te apellidas?** what's your surname? ~**o** m surname

apelmazarse *vpr* <*lana*> get matted

apenar *vt* sadden; (LAm, avergonzar) embarrass. □ ~**se** *vpr* be sad; (LAm, avergonzarse) be embarrassed

apenas *adv* hardly, scarcely; (Mex, sólo) only. ● *conj* (esp LAm, en cuanto) as soon as. ~ **si** Ⅱ hardly

ap|éndice *m* appendix. ~**endicitis** *f* appendicitis

apergaminado *a* <*piel*> wrinkled

aperitivo *m* (bebida) aperitif; (comida) appetizer

aperos *mpl* implements; (de labranza) agricultural equipment; (LAm, de un caballo) tack

apertura *f* opening

apesadumbrar *vt* upset. □ ~**se** *vpr* sadden

apestar *vt* infect. ● *vi* stink (**a** of)

apet|ecer [11] *vi.* ¿**te** ~**ece una copa?** do you fancy a drink? do you feel like a drink?. **no me** ~**ece** I don't feel like it. ~**ecible** *a* attractive. ~**ito** *m* appetite; (fig) desire. ~**itoso** *a* appetizing

apiadarse *vpr* feel sorry (**de** for)

ápice *m* (nada, en frases negativas) anything. **no ceder un** ~ not give an inch

apilar *vt* pile up

apiñar *vt* pack in. □ ~**se** *vpr* <*personas*> crowd together; <*cosas*> be packed tight

apio *m* celery

aplacar [7] *vt* placate; soothe <*dolor*>

aplanar *vt* level. ~ **calles** (LAm Ⅰ) loaf around

aplasta|nte *a* overwhelming. ~**r** *vt* crush. □ ~**rse** *vpr* flatten o.s.

aplau|dir *vt* clap, applaud; (fig) applaud. ~**so** *m* applause; (fig) praise

aplaza|miento *m* postponement. ~**r** [10] *vt* postpone; defer <*pago*>

aplica|ble *a* applicable. ~**ción** *f* application. ~**do** *a* <*persona*> diligent. ~**r** [7] *vt* apply. ● *vi* (LAm, a un puesto) apply (for). □ ~**rse** *vpr* apply o.s.

aplom|ado *a* composed. ~**o** *m* composure

apocado *a* timid

apocar [7] *vt* belittle <*persona*>. □ ~**se** *vpr* feel small

apodar *vt* nickname

apodera|do *m* representative. □ ~**rse** *vpr* seize

apodo *m* nickname

apogeo *m* (fig) height

apolilla|do *a* moth-eaten. □ ~**rse** *vpr* get moth-eaten

apolítico *a* non-political

apología *f* defence

apoltronarse *vpr* settle o.s. down

apoplejía *f* stroke

aporrear *vt* hit, thump; beat up <*persona*>

aport|ación *f* contribution. ~**ar** *vt* contribute. ~**e** *m* (LAm) contribution

aposta *adv* on purpose

apostar¹ [2] *vt/i* bet

apostar² *vt* station. □ ~**se** *vpr* station o.s.

apóstol *m* apostle

apóstrofo *m* apostrophe

apoy|ar *vt* lean (**en** against); (descansar) rest; (asentar) base; (reforzar) support. □ ~**arse** *vpr* lean, rest. ~**o** *m* support

apreci|able *a* appreciable; (digno de estima) worthy. ~**ación** *f* appreciation; (valoración) appraisal. ~**ar** *vt* value; (estimar) appreciate. ~**o** *m* appraisal; (fig) esteem

apremi|ante *a* urgent, pressing.
~ar *vt* urge; (obligar) compel; (dar
prisa a) hurry up. ● *vi* be urgent.
~o *m* urgency; (obligación)
obligation

aprender *vt/i* learn. □ **~se** *vpr*
learn

aprendiz *m* apprentice. **~aje** *m*
learning; (período) apprenticeship

aprensi|ón *f* apprehension;
(miedo) fear. **~vo** *a* apprehensive,
fearful

apresar *vt* seize; (capturar) capture

aprestar *vt* prepare. □ **~se** *vpr*
prepare

apresura|do *a* in a hurry; (hecho
con prisa) hurried. **~r** *vt* hurry.
□ **~rse** *vpr* hurry up

apret|ado *a* tight; (difícil) difficult;
(tacaño) stingy, mean. **~ar** [1] *vt*
tighten; press *<botón>*; squeeze
<persona>; (comprimir) press down.
● *vi* be too tight. □ **~arse** *vpr*
crowd together. **~ón** *m* squeeze.
~ón de manos handshake

aprieto *m* difficulty. **verse en un
~** be in a tight spot

aprisa *adv* quickly

aprisionar *vt* trap

aproba|ción *f* approval. **~r** [2] *vt*
approve (of); pass *<examen>*. ●
vi pass

apropia|ción *f* appropriation.
~do *a* appropriate. **~rse** *vpr*.
~rse de appropriate, take

aprovecha|ble *a* usable. **~do** *a*
(aplicado) diligent; (ingenioso)
resourceful; (oportunista)
opportunist. **bien ~do** well spent.
~miento *m* advantage; (uso) use.
~r *vt* take advantage of; (utilizar)
make use of. ● *vi* make the most
of it. **¡que aproveche!** enjoy your
meal! □ **~rse** *vpr*. **~rse de** take
advantage of

aprovisionar *vt* provision (**con**,
de with). □ **~se** *vpr* stock up

aproxima|ción *f* approximation;
(proximidad) closeness; (en la lotería)
consolation prize. **~damente**
adv roughly, approximately. **~do**
a approximate, rough. **~r** *vt*
bring near; (fig) bring together
<personas>. □ **~rse** *vpr* come
closer, approach

apt|itud *f* suitability; (capacidad)
ability. **~o** *a* (capaz) capable;
(adecuado) suitable

apuesta *f* bet

apuesto *m* handsome. ● *vb*
⇒APOSTAR [1]

apuntalar *vt* shore up

apunt|ar *vt* aim *<arma>*; (señalar)
point at; (anotar) make a note of,
note down; (inscribir) enrol; (en el
teatro) prompt. ● *vi* (con un arma) to
aim (**a** at). □ **~arse** *vpr* put one's
name down; score *<triunfo, tanto
etc>*. **~e** *m* note; (bosquejo) sketch.
tomar ~s take notes

apuñalar *vt* stab

apur|ado *a* difficult; (sin dinero)
hard up; (LAm, con prisa) in a
hurry. **~ar** *vt* (acabar) finish;
drain *<vaso etc>*; (causar vergüenza)
embarrass; (LAm, apresurar) hurry.
□ **~arse** *vpr* worry; (LAm,
apresurarse) hurry up. **~o** *m* tight
spot, difficult situation; (vergüenza)
embarrassment; (estrechez)
hardship, want; (LAm, prisa) hurry

aquejar *vt* afflict

aquel *a* (*f* **aquella**, *mpl*
aquellos, *fpl* **aquellas**) that; (en
plural) those

aquél *pron* (*f* **aquélla**, *mpl*
aquéllos, *fpl* **aquéllas**) that one;
(en plural) those

aquello *pron* that; (asunto) that
business

aquí *adv* here. **de ~** from here. **de
~ a 15 días** in a fortnight's time.
~ mismo right here. **de ~ para
allá** to and fro. **de ~ que** that is

why. **hasta** ~ until now. **por** ~
around here

aquietar vt calm (down)

árabe a & m & f Arab; (lengua)
Arabic

Arabia f Arabia. ~ **Saudita**, ~
Saudí Saudi Arabia

arado m plough. ~**r** m
ploughman

arancel m tariff; (impuesto) duty.
~**ario** a tariff

arandela f washer

araña f spider; (lámpara)
chandelier. ~**r** vt scratch

arar vt plough

arbitra|je m arbitration; (en
deportes) refereeing. ~**r** vt/i
arbitrate; (en fútbol etc) referee; (en
tenis etc) umpire

arbitr|ariedad f arbitrariness.
~**ario** a arbitrary. ~**io** m (free)
will

árbitro m arbitrator; (en fútbol etc)
referee; (en tenis etc) umpire

árbol m tree; (eje) axle; (palo)
mast. ~ **genealógico** family tree.
~ **de Navidad** Christmas tree

arbol|ado m trees. ~**eda** f wood

arbusto m bush

arca f (caja) chest. ~ **de Noé**
Noah's ark

arcada f arcade; (de un puente)
arch; (náuseas) retching

arcaico a archaic

arce m maple (tree)

arcén m (de autopista) hard
shoulder; (de carretera) verge

archipiélago m archipelago

archiv|ador m filing cabinet. ~**ar**
vt file (away). ~**o** m file; (de
documentos históricos) archives

arcilla f clay

arco m arch; (Elec, Mat) arc; (Mus,
arma) bow; (LAm, en fútbol) goal. ~
iris rainbow

arder vi burn; (LAm, escocer) sting;
(fig, de ira) seethe. **estar que arde** be
very tense

ardid m trick, scheme

ardiente a burning

ardilla f squirrel

ardor m heat; (fig) ardour; (LAm,
escozor) smarting. ~ **de
estómago** heartburn

arduo a arduous

área f area

arena f sand; (en deportes) arena;
(en los toros) (bull)ring. ~ **movediza**
quicksand

arenoso a sandy

arenque m herring. ~ **ahumado**
kipper

arete m (Mex) earring

Argel m Algiers. ~**ia** f Algeria

Argentina f Argentina

argentino a Argentinian,
Argentine. ● m Argentinian

argolla f ring. ~ **de matrimonio**
(LAm) wedding ring

arg|ot m slang. ~**ótico** a slang

argucia f cunning argument

argüir [19] vt (probar) prove, show;
(argumentar) argue. ● vi argue

argument|ación f argument.
~**ar** vt/i argue. ~**o** m argument;
(de libro, película etc) story, plot

aria f aria

aridez f aridity, dryness

árido a arid, dry. ~**s** mpl dry
goods

Aries m Aries

arisco a unfriendly

arist|ocracia f aristocracy.
~**ócrata** m & f aristocrat.
~**ocrático** a aristocratic

aritmética f arithmetic

arma f arm, weapon; (sección)
section. ~ **de fuego** firearm. ~**da**
f navy; (flota) fleet. ~**do** a armed
(**de** with). ~**dura** f armour; (de
gafas etc) frame; (Tec) framework.

~mentismo *m* build-up of arms.

~mento *m* arms, armaments; (acción de armar) armament. **~r** *vt* arm (**de** with); (montar) put together. **~r un lío** kick up a fuss

armario *m* cupboard; (para ropa) wardrobe (Brit), closet (Amer)

armatoste *m* huge great thing

armazón *m & f* frame(work)

armiño *m* ermine

armisticio *m* armistice

armonía *f* harmony

armónica *f* harmonica, mouth organ

armoni|oso *a* harmonious. **~zar** [10] *vt* harmonize. ● *vi* harmonize; <personas> get on well (**con** with); <colores> go well (**con** with)

arn|és *m* armour. **~eses** *mpl* harness

aro *m* ring, hoop

arom|a *m* aroma; (de flores) scent; (de vino) bouquet. **~ático** *a* aromatic

arpa *f* harp

arpía *f* harpy; (fig) hag

arpillera *f* sackcloth, sacking

arpón *m* harpoon

arquear *vt* arch, bend. □ **~se** *vpr* arch, bend

arque|ología *f* archaeology. **~ológico** *a* archaeological. **~ólogo** *m* archaeologist

arquero *m* archer; (LAm, en fútbol) goalkeeper

arquitect|o *m* architect. **~ónico** *a* architectural. **~ura** *f* architecture

arrabal *m* suburb; (barrio pobre) poor area. **~es** *mpl* outskirts. **~ero** *a* suburban; (de modales groseros) common

arraiga|do *a* deeply rooted. **~r** [12] *vi* take root. □ **~rse** *vpr* take root; (fig) settle

arran|car [7] *vt* pull up <planta>; pull out <diente>; (arrebatar) snatch; (Auto) start. ● *vi* start. □ **~carse** *vpr* pull out. **~que** *m* sudden start; (Auto) start; (fig) outburst

arras *fpl* deposit, security

arrasar *vt* level, smooth; raze to the ground <edificio etc>; (llenar) fill to the brim. ● *vi* (en deportes) sweep to victory; (en política) win a landslide victory

arrastr|ar *vt* pull; (por el suelo) drag (along); give rise to <consecuencias>. ● *vi* trail on the ground. □ **~arse** *vpr* crawl; (humillarse) grovel. **~e** *m* dragging; (transporte) haulage. **estar para el ~e** 🔢 be done in

arre *int* gee up! **~ar** *vt* urge on

arrebat|ado *a* (irreflexivo) impetuous. **~ar** *vt* snatch (away); (fig) win (over); (cautivar) captivate <corazón etc>. □ **~arse** *vpr* get carried away. **~o** *m* (de cólera etc) fit; (éxtasis) extasy

arrech|ar *vt* (LAm 🔢, enfurecer) to infuriate. □ **~se** *vpr* get furious. **~o** *a* furious

arrecife *m* reef

arregl|ado *a* neat; (bien vestido) well-dressed; (LAm, amañado) fixed. **~ar** *vt* arrange; (poner en orden) tidy up; sort out <asunto, problema etc>; (reparar) mend. □ **~arse** *vpr* (solucionarse) get sorted out; (prepararse) get ready; (apañarse) manage, make do; (ponerse de acuerdo) come to an agreement. **~árselas** manage, get by. **~o** *m* (incl Mus) arrangement; (acción de reparar) repair; (acuerdo) agreement; (solución) solution. **con ~o a** according to

arrellanarse *vpr* settle o.s. (**en** into)

arremangar [12] vt roll up
<*mangas*>; tuck up <*falda*>.
□ ~**se** vpr roll up one's sleeves

arremeter vi charge (**contra** at);
(atacar) attack

arremolinarse vpr mill about;
<*el agua*> to swirl

arrenda|dor m landlord. ~**dora** f
landlady. ~**miento** m renting;
(contrato) lease; (precio) rent. ~**r** [1]
vt (dar casa en alquiler) let; (dar cosa
en alquiler) hire out; (tomar en alquiler)
rent. ~**tario** m tenant

arreos mpl tack

arrepenti|miento m repentance,
regret. ~**rse** [4] vpr (retractarse) to
change one's mind; (lamentarse) be
sorry. ~**rse de** regret; repent of
<*pecados*>

arrest|ar vt arrest, detain;
(encarcelar) imprison. ~**o** m arrest;
(encarcelamiento) imprisonment

arriar [20] vt lower <*bandera,
vela*>

arriba adv up; (dirección)
up(wards); (en casa) upstairs. ●
int up with; (¡levántate!) up you
get!; (¡ánimo!) come on! ¡~ **España**!
long live Spain! ~ **de** (LAm) on
top of. ~ **mencionado**
aforementioned. **calle** ~ up the
street. **de** ~ **abajo** from top to
bottom. **de 100 pesetas para** ~
over 100 pesetas. **escaleras** ~
upstairs. **la parte de** ~ the top
part. **los de** ~ those at the top.
más ~ higher up

arrib|ar vi <*barco*> reach port;
(esp LAm, llegar) arrive. ~**ista** m & f
social climber. ~**o** m (esp LAm)
arrival

arriesga|do a risky; <*person*>
daring. ~**r** [12] vt risk; (aventurar)
venture. □ ~**rse** vpr take a risk

arrim|ar vt bring close(r).
□ ~**arse** vpr come closer,
approach; (apoyarse) lean (**a** on).

~**o** m protection. **al** ~**o de** with
the help of

arrincona|do a forgotten;
(acorralado) cornered. ~**r** vt put in
a corner; (perseguir) corner
(arrumbar) put aside. □ ~**rse** vpr
become a recluse

arroba f (Internet) at (@); *measure of
weight*

arrodillarse vpr kneel (down)

arrogan|cia f arrogance; (orgullo)
pride. ~**te** a arrogant; (orgulloso)
proud

arroj|ar vt throw; (emitir) give off,
throw out; (producir) produce. ●vi
(esp LAm, vomitar) throw up.
□ ~**arse** vpr throw o.s. ~**o** m
courage

arrollar vt roll (up); (atropellar) run
over; (vencer) crush

arropar vt wrap up; (en la cama)
tuck up. □ ~**se** vpr wrap (o.s.) up

arroy|o m stream; (de una calle)
gutter. ~**uelo** m small stream

arroz m rice. ~ **con leche** rice
pudding. ~**al** m rice field

arruga f (en la piel) wrinkle, line;
(en tela) crease. ~**r** [12] vt
wrinkle; crumple <*papel*>; crease
<*tela*>. □ ~**rse** vpr <*la piel*>
become wrinkled; <*tela*> crease,
get creased

arruinar vt ruin; (destruir) destroy.
□ ~**se** vpr <*persona*> be ruined

arrullar vt lull to sleep. ● vi
<*palomas*> coo

arrumbar vt put aside

arsenal m (astillero) shipyard; (de
armas) arsenal; (fig) mine

arsénico m arsenic

arte m (f en plural) art; (habilidad)
skill; (astucia) cunning. **bellas** ~**s**
fine arts. **con** ~ skilfully. **malas**
~**s** trickery. **por amor al** ~ for the
fun of it

artefacto m device

arteria *f* artery; (fig, calle) main road

artesan|al *a* craft.**~ía** *f* handicrafts. **objeto** *m* **de ~ía** traditional craft object.**~o** *m* artisan, craftsman

ártico *a* Arctic.**Á~** *m*. **el Á~** the Arctic

articula|ción *f* joint; (pronunciación) articulation.**~do** *a* articulated; *<lenguaje>* articulate.**~r** *vt* articulate

artículo *m* article.**~s** *mpl* (géneros) goods. **~ de exportación** export product. **~ de fondo** editorial, leader

artífice *m & f* artist; (creador) architect

artificial *a* artificial.**~o** *m* (habilidad) skill; (dispositivo) device; (engaño) trick

artiller|ía *f* artillery.**~o** *m* artilleryman, gunner

artilugio *m* gadget

artimaña *f* trick

art|ista *m & f* artist.**~ístico** *a* artistic

artritis *f* arthritis

arveja *f* (LAm) pea

arzobispo *m* archbishop

as *m* ace

asa *f* handle

asado *a* roast(ed).● *m* roast (meat), joint; (LAm, reunión) barbecue. **~o a la parrilla** grilled meat; (LAm) barbecued meat

asalariado *a* salaried.● *m* employee

asalt|ante *m* attacker; (de un banco) robber.**~ar** *vt* storm *<fortaleza>*; attack *<persona>*; raid *<banco etc>*; (fig) *<duda>* assail; (fig) *<idea etc>* cross one's mind.**~o** *m* attack; (robo) robbery; (en boxeo) round

asamblea *f* assembly; (reunión) meeting

asar *vt* roast.□**~se** *vpr* be very hot. **~ a la parrilla** grill; (LAm) barbecue. **~ al horno** (sin grasa) bake; (con grasa) roast

asbesto *m* asbestos

ascend|encia *f* descent; (LAm, influencia) influencia.**~ente** *a* ascending.**~er** [1] *vt* promote.● *vi* go up, ascend; *<cuenta etc>* come to, amount to; (ser ascendido) be promoted.**~iente** *m & f* ancestor; (influencia) influence

ascens|ión *f* ascent; (de grado) promotion. **día** *m* **de la A~ión** Ascension Day.**~o** *m* ascent; (de grado) promotion

ascensor *m* lift (Brit), elevator (Amer).**~ista** *m & f* lift attendant (Brit), elevator operator (Amer)

asco *m* disgust. **dar ~** be disgusting; (fig, causar enfado) be infuriating. **estar hecho un ~** be disgusting. **me da ~** it makes me feel sick. **¡qué ~!** how disgusting! **ser un ~** be disgusting

ascua *f* ember. **estar en ~s** be on tenterhooks

asea|do *a* clean; (arreglado) neat. **~r** *vt* (lavar) wash; (limpiar) clean; (arreglar) tidy up

asedi|ar *vt* besiege; (fig) pester. **~o** *m* siege

asegura|do *a & m* insured.**~dor** *m* insurer.**~r** *vt* secure, make safe; (decir) assure; (concertar un seguro) insure; (preservar) safeguard.□**~rse** *vpr* make sure

asemejarse *vpr* be alike

asenta|do *a* situated; (arraigado) established.**~r** [1] *vt* place; (asegurar) settle; (anotar) note down; (Mex, afirmar) state.□**~rse** *vpr* settle; (estar situado) be situated; (esp LAm, sentar cabeza) settle down

asentir[4] *vi* agree (a to). ~ con la cabeza nod

aseo *m* cleanliness. ~s *mpl* toilets

asequible *a* obtainable; <*precio*> reasonable; <*persona*> approachable

asesin|ar *vt* murder; (Pol) assassinate. ~ato *m* murder; (Pol) assassination. ~o *m* murderer; (Pol) assassin

asesor *m* adviser, consultant. ~ar *vt* advise. □ ~arse *vpr*. ~arse con consult. ~ía *f* consultancy; (oficina) consultant's office

asfalt|ado *a* asphalt. ~ar *vt* asphalt. ~o *m* asphalt

asfixia *f* suffocation. ~nte *a* suffocating. ~r *vt* suffocate. □ ~rse *vpr* suffocate

así *adv* (de esta manera) like this, like that. ●*a* such. ~ ~ so-so. ~ como just as. ~ como ~, (LAm) nomás just like that. ~ ... como both ... and. ~ que so. ~ que so; (en cuanto) as soon as. ~ sea so be it. ~ y todo even so. aun ~ even so. ¿no es ~? isn't that right? si es ~ if that is the case. y ~ (sucesivamente) and so on

Asia *f* Asia

asiático *a & m* Asian

asidero *m* handle; (fig, pretexto) excuse

asidu|amente *adv* regularly. ~o *a & m* regular

asiento *m* seat; (en contabilidad) entry. ~ delantero front seat. ~ trasero back seat

asignar *vt* assign; allot <*porción, tiempo etc*>

asignatura *f* subject. ~ pendiente (Escol) failed subject; (fig) matter still to be resolved

asil|ado *m* inmate; (Pol) refugee. ~o *m* asylum; (fig) shelter; (de ancianos etc) home. pedir ~o político ask for political asylum

asimétrico *a* asymmetrical

asimila|ción *f* assimilation. ~r *vt* assimilate

asimismo *adv* also; (igualmente) in the same way, likewise

asir[45] *vt* grasp

asist|encia *f* attendance; (gente) people (present); (en un teatro etc) audience; (ayuda) assistance. ~encia médica medical care. ~enta *f* (mujer de la limpieza) cleaning lady. ~ente *m & f* assistant. ~ente social social worker. ~ido *a* assisted. ~ir *vt* assist, help. ●*vi.* ~ir a attend, be present at

asm|a *f* asthma. ~ático *a & m* asthmatic

asno *m* donkey; (fig) ass

asocia|ción *f* association; (Com) partnership. ~do *a* associated; <*socio*> associate. ●*m* associate. ~r *vt* associate; (Com) take into partnership. □ ~rse *vpr* associate; (Com) become a partner

asolar[1] *vt* devastate

asomar *vt* show. ●*vi* appear, show. □ ~se *vpr* <*persona*> lean out (a, por of); <*cosa*> appear

asombr|ar *vt* (pasmar) amaze; (sorprender) surprise. □ ~arse *vpr* be amazed; (sorprenderse) be surprised. ~o *m* amazement, surprise. ~oso *a* amazing, astonishing

asomo *m* sign. ni por ~ by no means

aspa *f* cross, X-shape; (de molino) (windmill) sail. en ~ X-shaped

aspaviento *m* show, fuss. ~s *mpl* gestures. hacer ~s make a big fuss

aspecto *m* look, appearance; (fig) aspect

aspereza f roughness; (de sabor etc) sourness

áspero a rough; <sabor etc> bitter

aspersión f sprinkling

aspiración f breath; (deseo) ambition

aspirador m, **aspiradora** f vacuum cleaner

aspira|nte m & f candidate. ~r vt breathe in; <máquina> suck up. ● vi breathe in; <máquina> suck. ~r a aspire to

aspirina f aspirin

asquear vt sicken. ● vi be sickening. □~se vpr be disgusted

asqueroso a disgusting

asta f spear; (de la bandera) flagpole; (cuerno) horn. **a media ~** at half-mast. ~**bandera** f (Mex) flagpole

asterisco m asterisk

astilla f splinter. ~s fpl firewood

astillero m shipyard

astringente a & m astringent

astr|o m star. ~**ología** f astrology. ~**ólogo** m astrologer. ~**onauta** m & f astronaut. ~**onave** f spaceship. ~**onomía** f astronomy. ~**ónomo** m astronomer

astu|cia f cleverness; (ardid) cunning trick. ~**to** a astute; (taimado) cunning

asumir vt assume

asunción f assumption. **la A~** the Assumption

asunto m (cuestión) matter; (de una novela) plot; (negocio) business. ~**s** mpl **exteriores** foreign affairs. **el ~ es que** the fact is that

asusta|dizo a easily frightened. ~**r** vt frighten. □~**rse** vpr be frightened

ataca|nte m & f attacker. ~**r** [7] vt attack

atad|o a tied. ● m bundle. ~**ura** f tie

ataj|ar vi take a short cut; (Mex, en tenis) pick up the balls. ● vt (LAm, agarrar) catch. ~**o** m short cut

atañer [22] vt concern

ataque m attack; (Med) fit, attack. ~ **al corazón** heart attack. ~ **de nervios** fit of hysterics

atar vt tie. □~**se** vpr tie up

atarantar vt (LAm) fluster. □~**se** vpr (LAm) get flustered

atardecer [11] vi get dark. ● m dusk. **al ~** at dusk

atareado a busy

atasc|ar [7] vt block; (fig) hinder. □~**arse** vpr get stuck; <tubo etc> block. ~**o** m blockage; (Auto) traffic jam

ataúd m coffin

atav|iar [20] vt dress up. □~**iarse** vpr dress up, get dressed up. ~**ío** m dress, attire

atemorizar [10] vt frighten. □~**se** vpr be frightened

atención f attention; (cortesía) courtesy, kindness; (interés) interest. **¡~!** look out! **llamar la ~** attract attention, catch the eye; **prestar ~** pay attention

atender [1] vt attend to; (cuidar) look after. ● vi pay attention

atenerse [40] vpr abide (**a** by)

atentado m (ataque) attack; (afrenta) affront (**contra** to). ~ **contra la vida de uno** attempt on s.o.'s life

atentamente adv attentively; (con cortesía) politely; (con amabilidad) kindly. **lo saluda ~** (en cartas) yours faithfully

atentar vi. ~ **contra** threaten. ~ **contra la vida de uno** make an attempt on s.o.'s life

atento *a* attentive; (cortés) polite; (amable) kind

atenua|nte *a* extenuating. ● *f* extenuating circumstance. **~r** [21] *vt* attenuate; (hacer menor) diminish, lessen

ateo *a* atheistic. ● *m* atheist

aterciopelado *a* velvety

aterra|dor *a* terrifying. **~r** *vt* terrify

aterriza|je *m* landing. **~je forzoso** emergency landing. **~r** [10] *vt* land

aterrorizar [10] *vt* terrify

atesorar *vt* hoard; amass *<fortuna>*

atesta|do *a* packed, full up. ● *m* sworn statement. **~r** *vt* fill up, pack; (Jurid) testify

atestiguar [15] *vt* testify to; (fig) prove

atiborrar *vt* fill, stuff. □ **~se** *vpr* stuff o.s.

ático *m* attic

atina|do *a* right; (juicioso) wise, sensible. **~r** *vt/i* hit upon; (acertar) guess right

atizar [10] *vt* poke; (fig) stir up

atlántico *a* Atlantic. **el (océano) A~** the Atlantic (Ocean)

atlas *m* atlas

atl|eta *m & f* athlete. **~ético** *a* athletic. **~etismo** *m* athletics

atmósfera *f* atmosphere

atole *m* (LAm) boiled maize drink

atolladero *m* bog; (fig) tight corner

atolondra|do *a* scatter-brained; (aturdido) stunned. **~r** *vt* fluster; (pasmar) stun. □ **~se** *vpr* get flustered

at|ómico *a* atomic. **~omizador** *m* spray, atomizer

átomo *m* atom

atónito *m* amazed

atonta|do *a* stunned; (tonto) stupid. **~r** *vt* stun. □ **~se** *vpr* get confused

atorar *vt* (esp LAm) to block; (Mex, sujetar) secure. □ **~se** *vpr* (esp LAm, atragantarse) choke; (atascarse) get blocked; *<puerta>* get jammed

atormentar *vt* torture. □ **~se** *vpr* worry, torment o.s.

atornillar *vt* screw on

atosigar [12] *vt* pester

atraca|dor *m* mugger; (de banco) bank robber. **~r** [7] *vt* dock; (arrimar) bring alongside; hold up *<banco>*; mug *<persona>*. ● *vi* *<barco>* dock

atracci|ón *f* attraction. **~ones** *fpl* entertainment, amusements

atrac|o *m* hold-up, robbery. **~ón** *m*. **darse un ~ón** stuff o.s. (de with)

atractivo *a* attractive. ● *m* attraction; (encanto) charm

atraer [41] *vt* attract

atragantarse *vpr* choke (con on). **la historia se me atraganta** I can't stand history

atrancar [7] *vt* bolt *<puerta>*. □ **~se** *vpr* get stuck

atrapar *vt* catch; (encerrar) trap

atrás *adv* back; (tiempo) previously, before. **años ~** years ago. **~ de** (LAm) behind. **dar un paso ~** step backwards. **hacia ~, para ~** backwards

atras|ado *a* behind; *<reloj>* slow; (con deudas) in arrears; *<país>* backward. **llegar ~ado** (esp LAm) arrive late. **~ar** *vt* put back *<reloj>*; (demorar) delay, postpone. ● *vi* *<reloj>* be slow. □ **~arse** *vpr* be late; *<reloj>* be slow; (quedarse atrás) fall behind. **~o** *m* delay; (de un reloj) slowness; (de un país) backwardness. **~os** *mpl* (Com) arrears

atravesa|do *a* lying across. **~r** [1] *vt* cross; (traspasar) go through (poner transversalmente) lay across. □ **~rse** *vpr* get stuck, stick (en la garganta) get stuck, stick

atrayente *a* attractive

atrev|erse *vpr* dare. **~erse con** tackle. **~ido** *a* daring; (insolente) insolent. **~imiento** *m* daring; (descaro) insolence

atribu|ción *f* attribution. **~ciones** *fpl* authority. **~ir** [17] *vt* attribute; confer <función>. □ **~irse** *vpr* claim

atribulado *a* afflicted

atributo *m* attribute

atril *m* lectern; (Mus) music stand

atrocidad *f* atrocity. ¡qué **~**! how awful!

atrofiarse *vpr* atrophy

atropell|ado *a* hasty. **~ar** *vt* knock down; (por encima) run over; (empujar) push aside; (fig) outrage, insult. □ **~arse** *vpr* rush. **~o** *m* (Auto) accident; (fig) outrage

atroz *a* appalling; (fig) atrocious

atuendo *m* dress, attire

atún *m* tuna (fish)

aturdi|do *a* bewildered; (por golpe) stunned. **~r** *vt* bewilder; <golpe> stun; <ruido> deafen

auda|cia *f* boldness, audacity. **~z** *a* bold

audi|ble *a* audible. **~ción** *f* hearing; (prueba) audition. **~encia** *f* audience; (tribunal) court; (sesión) hearing

auditor *m* auditor. **~io** *m* audience; (sala) auditorium

auge *m* peak; (Com) boom

augur|ar *vt* predict; <cosas> augur. **~io** *m* prediction. **con nuestros mejores ~ios para** with our best wishes for. **mal ~** bad omen

aula *f* class-room; (Univ) lecture room

aull|ar [23] *vi* howl. **~ido** *m* howl

aument|ar *vt* increase; magnify <imagen>. ● *vi* increase. **~o** *m* increase; (de sueldo) rise

aun *adv* even. **~ así** even so. **~ cuando** although. **más ~** even more. **ni ~** not even

aún *adv* still, yet. **no ha llegado ~** it still hasn't arrived, it hasn't arrived yet

aunar [23] *vt* join. □ **~se** *vpr* join together

aunque *conj* although, (even) though

aúpa *int* up! **de ~** wonderful

aureola *f* halo

auricular *m* (de teléfono) receiver. **~es** *mpl* headphones

aurora *f* dawn

ausen|cia *f* absence. **en ~cia de** in the absence of. □ **~tarse** *vpr* leave. **~te** *a* absent. ● *m & f* absentee; (Jurid) missing person. **~tismo** *m* (LAm) absenteeism

auspici|ador *m* sponsor. **~ar** *vt* sponsor. **~o** *m* sponsorship; (signo) omen. **bajo los ~s de** sponsored by

auster|idad *f* austerity. **~o** *a* austere

austral *a* southern

Australia *m* Australia

australiano *a & m* Australian

Austria *f* Austria

austriaco, austríaco *a & m* Austrian

aut|enticar [7] authenticate. **~enticidad** *f* authenticity. **~éntico** *a* authentic

auto *m* (Jurid) decision; (orden) order; (Auto, ⬛) car. **~s** *mpl* proceedings

auto|abastecimiento m self-sufficiency. **~biografía** f autobiography

autobús m bus. **en ~** by bus

autocar m (long-distance) bus, coach (Brit)

autocontrol m self-control

autóctono a indigenous

auto|determinación f self-determination. **~didacta** a self-taught. ● m & f self-taught person. **~escuela** f driving school. **~financiamiento** m self-financing

autógrafo m autograph

autómata m robot

autom|ático a automatic. ● m press-stud. **~atización** f automation

automotor m diesel train

autom|óvil a motor. ● m car. **~ovilismo** m motoring. **~ovilista** m & f driver, motorist

aut|onomía f autonomy. **~onómico** a, **~ónomo** a autonomous

autopista f motorway (Brit), freeway (Amer)

autopsia f autopsy

autor m author. **~a** f author(ess)

autori|dad f authority. **~tario** a authoritarian

autoriza|ción f authorization. **~do** a authorized, official; <opinión etc> authoritative. **~r** [10] vt authorize

auto|rretrato m self-portrait. **~servicio** m self-service restaurant. **~stop** m hitch-hiking. **hacer ~stop** hitch-hike

autosuficiente a self-sufficient

autovía f dual carriageway

auxili|ar a auxiliary; <profesor> assistant. ● m & f assistant. ● vt

help. **~o** m help. **¡~o!** help! **en ~o de** in aid of. **pedir ~o** shout for help. **primeros ~os** first aid

Av. abrev (**Avenida**) Ave

aval m guarantee

avalancha f avalanche

avalar vt guarantee

aval|uar vt [21] (LAm) value. **~úo** m valuation

avance m advance; (en el cine) trailer. **~s** mpl (Mex) trailer

avanzar [10] vt move forward; **~ la pantalla** scroll up. ● vi advance

avar|icia f avarice. **~icioso** a, **~iento** a greedy; (tacaño) miserly. **~o** a miserly. ● m miser

avasallar vt dominate

Avda. abrev (**Avenida**) Ave

ave f bird. **~ de paso** (incl fig) bird of passage. **~ de rapiña** bird of prey

avecinarse vpr approach

avejentar vt age

avellan|a f hazel-nut. **~o** m hazel (tree)

avemaría f Hail Mary

avena f oats

avenida f (calle) avenue

avenir [53] vt reconcile. □ **~se** vpr come to an agreement; (entenderse) get on well (**con** with)

aventaja|do a outstanding. **~r** vt be ahead of; (superar) surpass

avent|ar [1] vt fan; winnow <grano etc>; (Mex, lanzar) throw; (Mex, empujar) push. □ **~arse** vpr (Mex) throw o.s.; (atreverse) dare. **~ón** m (Mex) ride, lift (Brit)

aventur|a f adventure. **~a amorosa** love affair. **~ado** a risky. **~ero** a adventurous. ● m adventurer

avergonzar [10 & 16] vt shame; (abochornar) embarrass. □ **~se** vpr be ashamed; (abochornarse) be embarrassed

aver|íaf (Auto) breakdown; (en máquina) failure. **~iado**a broken down. □ **~iarse**[20] vpr break down

averigua|ciónf inquiry; (Mex, disputa) argument. **~r**[15] vt find out. ● vi (Mex) argue

aversiónf aversion (**a, hacia, por** to)

avestruzm ostrich

avia|ciónf aviation; (Mil) air force. **~dor**m (piloto) pilot

av|ícolaa poultry. **~icultura**f poultry farming

avidezf eagerness, greed

ávidoa eager, greedy

avinagra|doa sour. □ **~rse**vpr go sour; (fig) become embittered

avi|ónm aeroplane (Brit), airplane (Amer); (Mex, juego) hopscotch. **~onazo**m (Mex) plane crash

avis|arvt warn; (informar) notify, inform; call <médico etc>. **~o**m warning; (comunicación) notice; (LAm, anuncio, cartel) advertisement; (en televisión) commercial. **estar sobre ~o** be on the alert. **sin previo ~** without prior warning

avisp|af wasp. **~ado**a sharp. **~ero**m wasps' nest; (fig) mess. **~ón**m hornet

avistarvt catch sight of

avivarvt stoke up <fuego>; brighten up <color>; arouse <interés, pasión>; intensify <dolor>. □ **~se**vpr revive; (animarse) cheer up; (LAm, despabilarse) wise up

axilaf armpit, axilla

axiomam axiom

ayint (de dolor) ouch!; (de susto) oh!; (de pena) oh dear! ¡**~ de ti!** poor you!

ayaf governess

ayeradv yesterday. ● m past. **antes de ~** the day before

yesterday. **~ por la mañana**, (LAm) **~ en la mañana** yesterday morning

ayudaf help, aid. **~ de cámara** valet. **~nta**f, **~nte**m assistant; (Mil) adjutant. **~r**vt help

ayun|arvi fast. **~as**fpl. estar en **~as** have had nothing to eat or drink; (fig, ⓘ) be in the dark. **~o**m fasting

ayuntamientom town council, city council; (edificio) town hall

azabachem jet

azad|af hoe. **~ón**m (large) hoe

azafataf air hostess

azafatem (LAm) tray

azafránm saffron

azaharm orange blossom; (del limonero) lemon blossom

azarm chance; (desgracia) misfortune. **al ~** at random. **por ~** by chance. **~es**mpl ups and downs

azaros|amenteadv hazardously. **~o**a hazardous, risky; <vida> eventful

azorarvt embarrass. □ **~rse**vpr be embarrassed

Azoresfpl. **las ~** the Azores

azotadorm (Mex) caterpillar

azot|arvt whip, beat; (Mex, puerta) slam. **~e**m whip; (golpe) smack; (fig, calamidad) calamity

azoteaf flat roof

aztecaa & m & f Aztec

az|úcarm & f sugar. **~ucarado**a sweet, sugary. **~ucarar**vt sweeten. **~ucarero**m sugar bowl

azucenaf (white) lily

azufrem sulphur

azula & m blue. **~ado**a bluish. **~ marino** navy blue

azulejom tile

azuzar[10] vt urge on, incite

bab|a f spittle.~**ear** vi drool, slobber; <niño> dribble. **caérsele la ~a a uno** be delighted.~**eo** m drooling; (de un niño) dribbling. ~**ero** m bib

babor m port. **a ~** to port, on the port side

babosa f slug

babosada f (Mex) drivel

babos|ear vt slobber over; <niño> dribble over.● vi (Mex) day dream.~**o** a slimy; (LAm, tonto) silly

babucha f slipper

baca f luggage rack

bacalao m cod

bache m pothole; (fig) bad patch

bachillerato m school-leaving examination

bacteria f bacterium

bagaje m. **~ cultural** cultural knowledge; (de un pueblo) cultural heritage

bahía f bay

bail|able a dance.~**aor** m Flamenco dancer.~**ar** vt/i dance. **ir a ~ar** go dancing.~**arín** m dancer.~**arina** f dancer; (de ballet) ballerina.~**e** m dance; (actividad) dancing. ~**e de etiqueta** ball

baja f drop, fall; (Mil) casualty. **~ por maternidad** maternity leave. **darse de ~** take sick leave.~**da** f slope; (acto de bajar) descent; (camino) way down.~**r** vt lower; (llevar abajo) get down; go down <escalera>; bow <la cabeza>.● vi go down; <temperatura, precio> fall.□ ~**rse** vpr pull down <pantalones>. ~**r(se) de** get out of <coche>; get off <autobús, caballo, tren, bicicleta>

bajeza f vile deed

bajío m shallows; (de arena) sandbank; (LAm, terreno bajo) low-lying area

bajo a low; (de estatura) short, small; <cabeza, ojos> lowered; (humilde) humble, low; (vil) vile, low; <voz> low; (Mus) deep.● m lowland; (Mus) bass.● adv quietly; <volar> low.● prep under. **~ cero** below zero. **~ la lluvia** in the rain. **los ~s** (LAm) ground floor (Brit), first floor (Amer); **los ~s fondos** the underworld

bajón m sharp drop; (de salud) sudden decline

bala f bullet; (de algodón etc) bale. (LAm, en atletismo) shot. **como una ~** like a shot. **lanzamiento de ~** (LAm) shot put

balada f ballad

balan|ce m balance; (documento) balance sheet; (resultado) outcome. ~**cear** vt balance.□ ~**cearse** vpr swing.~**ceo** m swinging. ~**cín** m rocking chair; (de niños) seesaw.~**za** f scales; (Com) balance

balar vi bleat

balazo m (disparo) shot; (herida) bullet wound

balboa f (unidad monetaria panameña) balboa

balbuc|ear vt/i stammer; <niño> babble.~**eo** m stammering; (de niño) babbling.~**ir** [24] vt/i stammer; <niño> babble

balcón m balcony

balda f shelf

balde m bucket. **de ~** free (of charge). **en ~** in vain

baldío *a* <*terreno*> waste

baldosa *f* (floor) tile; (losa) flagstone

bale|ar *a* Balearic. **las (Islas) B~ares** the Balearics, the Balearic Islands. ● *vt* (LAm) to shoot. **~o** *m* (LAm, tiroteo) shooting

balero *m* (Mex) cup and ball toy; (rodamiento) bearing

balido *m* bleat; (varios sonidos) bleating

balística *f* ballistics

baliza *f* (Naut) buoy; (Aviac) beacon

ballena *f* whale

ballet /ba'le/ (*pl* ~s) *m* ballet

balneario *m* spa; (con playa) seaside resort

balompié *m* soccer, football (Brit)

bal|ón *m* ball. **~oncesto** *m* basketball. **~onmano** *m* handball. **~onvolea** *m* volleyball

balotaje *m* (LAm) voting

balsa *f* (de agua) pool; (plataforma flotante) raft

bálsamo *m* balsam; (fig) balm

baluarte *m* (incl fig) bastion

bambalina *f* drop curtain. **entre ~s** behind the scenes

bambole|ar *vi* sway. □ **~arse** *vpr* sway; <*mesa etc*> wobble; <*barco*> rock. **~o** *m* swaying; (de mesa etc) wobbling; (de barco) rocking

bambú *m* (*pl* ~es) bamboo

banal *a* banal. **~idad** *f* banality

banan|a *f* (esp LAm) banana. **~ero** *a* banana. **~o** *m* (LAm) banana tree

banc|a *f* banking; (conjunto de bancos) banks; (en juegos) bank; (LAm, asiento) bench. **~ario** *a* bank, banking. **~arrota** *f* bankruptcy. **hacer ~arrota, ir a la ~arrota** go bankrupt. **~o** *m* (asiento) bench; (Com) bank; (bajío) sandbank; (de peces) shoal

banda *f* (incl Mus, Radio) band; (Mex, para el pelo) hair band; (raya ancha) stripe; (cinta ancha) sash; (grupo) gang, group. **~ sonora** soundtrack. **~da** *f* (de pájaros) flock; (de peces) shoal

bandeja *f* tray

bandejón *m* (Mex) central reservation (Brit), median strip (Amer)

bander|a *f* flag. **~illa** *f* banderilla. **~ear** *vt* stick the banderillas in. **~ero** *m* banderillero. **~ín** *m* pennant, small flag

bandido *m* bandit

bando *m* edict, proclamation; (facción) camp, side. **~s** *mpl* banns. **pasarse al otro ~** go over to the other side

bandolero *m* bandit

bandoneón *m* large accordion

banjo *m* banjo

banquero *m* banker

banquete *m* banquet; (de boda) wedding reception

banquillo *m* bench; (Jurid) dock; (taburete) footstool

bañ|ador *m* (de mujer) swimming costume; (de hombre) swimming trunks. **~ar** *vt* bath <*niño*>; (Culin, recubrir) coat. □ **~arse** *vpr* go swimming, have a swim; (en casa) have a bath. **~era** *f* bath(tub). **~ista** *m & f* bather. **~o** *m* bath; (en piscina, mar etc) swim; (cuarto) bathroom; (LAm, wáter) toilet; (bañera) bath(tub); (capa) coat(ing)

baqueano (LAm) **baquiano** *m* guide

bar *m* bar

baraja *f* pack of cards. **~r** *vt* shuffle; juggle <*cifras etc*>; consider <*posibilidades*>; (Mex, explicar) explain

baranda, barandilla *f* rail; (de escalera) banisters

barat|a *f* (Mex) sale. **~ija** *f* trinket. **~illo** *m* junk shop; (géneros) cheap goods. **~o** *a* cheap. ● *adv* cheap(ly)

barba *f* chin; (pelo) beard

barbacoa *f* barbecue; (carne) barbecued meat

barbari|dad *f* atrocity; (fam, mucho) awful lot fam. **¡qué ~dad!** how awful! **~e** *f* barbarity; (fig) ignorance. **~smo** *m* barbarism

bárbaro *a* barbaric, cruel; (bruto) uncouth; (fam, estupendo) terrific fam ● *m* barbarian. **¡qué ~!** how marvellous!

barbear *vt* (Mex, lisonjear) suck up to

barbecho *m*. **en ~** fallow

barber|ía *f* barber's (shop). **~o** *m* barber; (Mex, adulador) creep

barbilla *f* chin

barbitúrico *m* barbiturate

barbudo *a* bearded

barca *f* (small) boat. **~ de pasaje** ferry. **~za** *f* barge

barcelonés *a* of Barcelona, from Barcelona. ● *m* native of Barcelona

barco *m* boat; (navío) ship. **~ cisterna** tanker. **~ de vapor** steamer. **~ de vela** sailing boat. **ir en ~** go by boat

barda *f* (Mex) wall; (de madera) fence

barítono *a & m* baritone

barman *m* (*pl* ~s) barman

barniz *m* varnish; (para loza etc) glaze; (fig) veneer. **~ar** [10] *vt* varnish; glaze <loza etc>

barómetro *m* barometer

bar|ón *m* baron. **~onesa** *f* baroness

barquero *m* boatman

barquillo *m* wafer; (Mex, de helado) ice-cream cone

barra *f* bar; (pan) loaf of French bread; (palanca) lever; (de arena) sandbank; (LAm, de hinchas) supporters. **~ de labios** lipstick

barrabasada *f* mischief, prank

barraca *f* hut; (vivienda pobre) shack, shanty

barranco *m* ravine, gully; (despeñadero) cliff, precipice

barrer *vt* sweep; thrash <rival>

barrera *f* barrier. **~ del sonido** sound barrier

barriada *f* district; (LAm, barrio marginal) slum

barrial *m* (LAm) quagmire

barrida *f* sweep; (LAm, redada) police raid

barrig|a *f* belly. **~ón** *a*, **~udo** *a* pot-bellied

barril *m* barrel

barrio *m* district, area. **~s bajos** poor quarter, poor area. **el otro ~** (fig, fam) the other world. **~bajero** *a* vulgar, common

barro *m* mud; (arcilla) clay; (arcilla cocida) earthenware

barroco *a* Baroque. ● *m* Baroque style

barrote *m* bar

bartola *f*. **tirarse a la ~** take it easy

bártulos *mpl* things. **liar los ~** pack one's bags

barullo *m* racket; (confusión) confusion. **a ~** galore

basar *vt* base. □ **~se** *vpr*. **~se en** be based on

báscula *f* scales

base *f* base; (fig) basis, foundation. **a ~ de** thanks to; (mediante) by means of; (en una receta) mainly consisting of. **~ de datos** database. **partiendo de la ~ de, tomando como ~** on the basis of

básico *a* basic

basílica f basilica

básquetbol, basquetbol m (LAm) basketball

---

bastante

● *adjetivo/pronombre*

····▸ (suficiente) enough. **¿hay ~s sillas?** are there enough chairs? **ya tengo ~** I have enough already

····▸ (mucho) quite a lot. **vino ~ gente** quite a lot of people came. **tiene ~s amigos** he has quite a lot of friends **¿te gusta?- sí, ~** do you like it? - yes, quite a lot

● *adverbio*

····▸ (suficientemente) enough. **no has estudiado ~** you haven't studied enough. **no es lo ~ inteligente** he's not clever enough (**como para** to)

····▸ **bastante +** *adjetivo/adverbio* (modificando la intensidad) quite, fairly. **parece ~ simpático** he looks quite friendly. **es ~ fácil de hacer** it's quite easy to do. **canta ~ bien** he sings quite well

····▸ **bastante** *con verbo* (considerablemente) quite a lot. **el lugar ha cambiado ~** the place has changed quite a lot

bastar vi be enough. **¡basta!** that's enough! **basta con decir que** suffice it to say that. **basta y sobra** that's more than enough

bastardilla f italics

bastardo a & m bastard

bastidor m frame; (Auto) chassis. **~es** mpl (en el teatro) wings. **entre ~es** behind the scenes

basto a coarse. **~s** mpl (naipes) clubs

bast|ón m walking stick; (de esquí) ski pole. **~onazo** m blow with a stick; (de mando) staff of office

basur|a f rubbish, garbage (Amer); (en la calle) litter. **~al** m (LAm, lugar) rubbish dump. **~ero** m dustman (Brit), garbage collector (Amer); (sitio) rubbish dump; (Mex, recipiente) dustbin (Brit), garbage can (Amer)

bata f dressing-gown; (de médico etc) white coat; (esp LAm, de baño) bathrobe

batahola f (LAm) pandemonium

batall|a f battle. **~a campal** pitched battle. **de ~a** everyday. **~ador** a fighting. ● m fighter. **~ar** vi battle, fight. **~ón** m battalion

batata f sweet potato

bate m bat. **~ador** m batter; (cricket) batsman. **~ar** vi bat

batería f battery; (Mus) drums. ● m & f drummer. **~ de cocina** kitchen utensils, pots and pans

baterista m & f drummer

batid|o a beaten; <nata> whipped. ● m batter; (bebida) milk shake. **~ra** f (food) mixer

batir vt beat; break <récord>; whip <nata>. **~ palmas** clap. □ **~se** vpr fight

batuta f baton. **llevar la ~** be in command, be the boss

baúl m trunk

bauti|smal a baptismal. **~smo** m baptism, christening. **~zar** [10] vt baptize, christen. **~zo** m christening

baya f berry

bayeta f cloth

bayoneta f bayonet

baza f (naipes) trick; (fig) advantage. **meter ~** interfere

bazar m bazaar

bazofia *f* revolting food; (fig) rubbish

beato *a* blessed; (piadoso) devout; (pey) overpious

bebé *m* baby

beb|edero *m* drinking trough; (sitio) watering place. **~edizo** *m* potion; (veneno) poison. **~edor** *m* heavy drinker. **~er** *vt/i* drink. **~ida** *f* drink. **~ido** *a* drunk

beca *f* grant, scholarship. **~do** *m* (LAm) scholarship holder, scholar. **~r** [7] *vt* give a scholarship to. **~rio** *m* scholarship holder, scholar

beige /beis, beʒ/ *a & m* beige

béisbol, (Mex) **beisbol** *m* baseball

belén *m* crib, nativity scene

belga *a & m & f* Belgian

Bélgica *f* Belgium

bélico *a*, **belicoso** *a* warlike

bell|eza *f* beauty. **~o** *a* beautiful. **~as artes** *fpl* fine arts

bellota *f* acorn

bemol *m* flat. **tener (muchos) ~es** be difficult

bend|ecir [46] (*pero imperativo* **bendice**, *futuro, condicional y pp regulares*) *vt* bless. **~ición** *f* blessing. **~ito** *a* blessed; (que tiene suerte) lucky; (feliz) happy

benefactor *m* benefactor

benefic|encia *f* charity. **de ~encia** charitable. **~iar** *vt* benefit. □ **~iarse** *vpr* benefit. **~iario** *m* beneficiary; (de un cheque etc) payee. **~io** *m* benefit; (ventaja) advantage; (ganancia) profit, gain. **~ioso** *a* beneficial

benéfico *a* beneficial; (de beneficencia) charitable

ben|evolencia *f* benevolence. **~évolo** *a* benevolent

bengala *f* flare. **luz** *f* **de ~** flare

benigno *a* kind; (moderado) gentle, mild; <*tumor*> benign

berberecho *m* cockle

berenjena *f* aubergine (Brit), eggplant (Amer)

berr|ear *vi* <*animales*> bellow; <*niño*> bawl. **~ido** *m* bellow; (de niño) bawling

berrinche *m* temper; (de un niño) tantrum

berro *m* watercress

besamel(a) *f* white sauce

bes|ar *vt* kiss. □ **~arse** *vpr* kiss (each other). **~o** *m* kiss

bestia *f* beast; (bruto) brute; (idiota) idiot. **~ de carga** beast of burden. **~l** *a* bestial, animal; (fig, 🄸) terrific. **~lidad** *f* (acción brutal) horrid thing; (insensatez) stupidity

besugo *m* red bream

besuquear *vt* cover with kisses

betabel *f* (Mex) beetroot

betún *m* (para el calzado) shoe polish

biberón *m* feeding-bottle

Biblia *f* Bible

bibliografía *f* bibliography

biblioteca *f* library; (mueble) bookcase. **~ de consulta** reference library. **~rio** *m* librarian

bicarbonato *m* bicarbonate

bicho *m* insect, bug; (animal) small animal, creature. **~ raro** odd sort

bici *f* 🄸 bike. **~cleta** *f* bicycle. **ir en ~cleta** cycle. **~moto** (LAm) moped

bidé, **bidet** *m* /bi'ðe/ bidet

bidón *m* drum, can

bien *adv* well; (muy) very, quite; (correctamente) right; (de buena gana) willingly. ● *m* good; (efectos) property. **¡~!** fine!, OK!, good! **~... (o) ~** either... or. **¡está ~!** fine!, alright!; (basta) that is enough!. **más ~** rather. **¡muy ~!**

good! **no ~** as soon as. **¡qué ~!** marvellous! **ᵢ. si ~** although
bienal *a* biennial
bien|aventurado *a* fortunate. **~estar** *m* well-being. **~hablado** *a* well-spoken. **~hechor** *m* benefactor. **~intencionado** *a* well-meaning
bienio *m* two-year period
bienvenid|a *f* welcome. **dar la ~a a uno** welcome s.o. **~o** *a* welcome. **¡~o!** welcome!
bifurca|ción *f* junction. □ **~rse** [7] *vpr* fork; (rail) branch off
b|igamia *f* bigamy. **~ígamo** *a* bigamous. ● *m* bigamist
bigot|e *m* moustache. **~ón** *a* (Mex), **~udo** *a* with a big moustache
bikini *m* bikini
bilingüe *a* bilingual
billar *m* billiards
billete *m* ticket; (de banco) (bank) note (Brit), bill (Amer). **~ de ida y vuelta** return ticket (Brit), round-trip ticket (Amer). **~ sencillo** single ticket (Brit), one-way ticket (Amer). **~ra** *f*, **~ro** *m* wallet, billfold (Amer)
billón *m* billion (Brit), trillion (Amer)
bi|mensual *a* fortnightly, twice-monthly. **~mestral** *a* two-monthly. **~mestre** *m* two-month period. **~motor** *a* twin-engined. ● *m* twin-engined plane
binoculares *mpl* binoculars
bi|ografía *f* biography. **~ográfico** *a* biographical
bi|ología *f* biology. **~ológico** *a* biological. **~ólogo** *m* biologist
biombo *m* folding screen
biopsia *f* biopsy
bioterrorismo *m* bioterrorism
biplaza *m* two-seater
biquini *m* bikini

birlar *vt* ᵢ steal, pinch ᵢ
bis *m* encore. **¡~!** encore! **vivo en el 3 ~** I live at 3A
bisabuel|a *f* great-grandmother. **~o** *m* great-grandfather. **~os** *mpl* great-grandparents
bisagra *f* hinge
bisiesto *a*. **año** *m* **~** leap year
bisniet|a *f* great-granddaughter. **~o** *m* great-grandson. **~os** *mpl* great-grandchildren
bisonte *m* bison
bisoño *a* inexperienced
bisté, bistec *m* steak
bisturí *m* scalpel
bisutería *f* imitation jewellery, costume jewellery
bitácora *f* binnacle
bizco *a* cross-eyed
bizcocho *m* sponge (cake)
bizquear *vi* squint
blanc|a *f* white woman; (Mus) minim. **~o** *a* white; <*tez*> fair. ● *m* white; (persona) white man; (espacio) blank; (objetivo) target. **dar en el ~o** hit the mark. **dejar en ~o** leave blank. **pasar la noche en ~o** have a sleepless night. **~ura** *f* whiteness
blandir [24] *vt* brandish
bland|o *a* soft; <*carácter*> weak; (cobarde) cowardly; <*carne*> tender. **~ura** *f* softness; (de carne) tenderness
blanque|ar *vt* whiten; whitewash <*paredes*>; bleach <*tela*>; launder <*dinero*>. ● *vi* turn white. **~o** *m* whitening; (de dinero) laundering
blasón *m* coat of arms
bledo *m*. **me importa un ~** I couldn't care less
blinda|je *m* armour (plating). **~r** *vt* armour(-plate)
bloc *m* (*pl* **~s**) pad
bloque *m* block; (Pol) bloc. **en ~** en bloc. **~ar** *vt* block; (Mil)

blockade; (Com) freeze. **~o** m blockade; (Com) freezing

blusa f blouse

bob|ada f silly thing. **decir ~adas** talk nonsense. **~ería** f silly thing

bobina f reel; (Elec) coil

bobo a silly, stupid. ● m idiot, fool

boca f mouth; (fig, entrada) entrance; (de buzón) slot; (de cañón) muzzle. **~ abajo** face down. **~ arriba** face up

bocacalle f junction. **la primera ~ a la derecha** the first turning on the right

bocad|illo m (filled) roll; (⊞, comida ligera) snack. **~o** m mouthful; (mordisco) bite; (de caballo) bit

boca|jarro. a ~jarro point-blank. **~manga** f cuff

bocanada f puff; (de vino etc) mouthful; (ráfaga) gust

bocata f sandwich

bocatería f sandwich bar

bocazas m & f invar big mouth

boceto m sketch; (de proyecto) outline

bochinche m row; (alboroto) racket. **~ro** a (LAm) rowdy

bochorno m sultry weather; (fig, vergüenza) embarrassment. **¡qué ~!** how embarrassing!. **~so** a oppressive; (fig) embarrassing

bocina f horn; (LAm, auricular) receiver. **tocar la ~** sound one's horn. **~zo** m toot

boda f wedding

bodeg|a f cellar; (de vino) wine cellar; (LAm, almacén) warehouse; (de un barco) hold. **~ón** m cheap restaurant; (pintura) still life

bodoque m & f (⊞, tonto) thickhead; (Mex, niño) kid

bofes mpl lights. **echar los ~** slog away

bofet|ada f slap; (fig) blow. **~ón** m punch

boga f (moda) fashion. **estar en ~** be in fashion, be in vogue. **~r** [12] vt row. **~vante** m (crustáceo) lobster

Bogotá f Bogotá

bogotano a from Bogotá. ● m native of Bogotá

bohemio a & m Bohemian

bohío m (LAm) hut

boicot m (pl ~s) boycott. **~ear** vt boycott. **~eo** m boycott. **hacer un ~** boycott

boina f beret

bola f ball; (canica) marble; (mentira) fib; (Mex, reunión desordenada) rowdy party; (Mex, montón) heap. **una ~ de** a bunch of; (Mex, revolución) revolution; (Mex, brillo) shine

boleadoras (LAm) fpl bolas

bolear vt (Mex) polish, shine

bolera f bowling alley

bolero m (baile, chaquetilla) bolero; (fig, ⊞, mentiroso) liar; (Mex, limpiabotas) bootblack

bole|ta f (LAm, de rifa) ticket; (Mex, de notas) (school) report; (Mex, electoral) ballot paper. **~taje** m (Mex) tickets. **~tería** f (LAm) ticket office; (de teatro, cine) box office. **~tero** m (LAm) ticket-seller

boletín m bulletin; (publicación periódica) journal; (de notas) report

boleto m (esp LAm) ticket; (Mex, de avión) (air) ticket. **~ de ida y vuelta**, (Mex) **~ redondo** return ticket (Brit), round-trip ticket (Amer). **~ sencillo** single ticket (Brit), one-way ticket (Amer)

boli m ⊞ Biro (P), ball-point pen

boliche m (juego) bowls; (bolera) bowling alley

bolígrafo *m* Biro (P), ball-point pen

bolillo *m* bobbin; (Mex, pan) (bread) roll

bolívar *m* (unidad monetaria venezolana) bolívar

Bolivia *f* Bolivia

boliviano *a* Bolivian. ● *m* Bolivian; (unidad monetaria de Bolivia) boliviano

boll|ería *f* baker's shop. ~o *m* roll; (con azúcar) bun

bolo *m* skittle; (Mex, en bautizo) coins. ~s *mpl* (juego) bowling

bols|a *f* bag; (Mex, bolsillo) pocket; (Mex, de mujer) handbag; (Com) stock exchange; (cavidad) cavity. ~a de agua caliente hot-water bottle. ~illo *m* pocket. de ~illo pocket. ~o *m* (de mujer) handbag. ~o de mano, ~o de viaje (overnight) bag

bomba *f* bomb; (máquina) pump; (noticia) bombshell. ~ de aceite (Auto) oil pump. ~ de agua (Auto) water pump. pasarlo ~ have a marvellous time

bombachos *mpl* baggy trousers, baggy pants (Amer)

bombarde|ar *vt* bombard; (desde avión) bomb. ~o *m* bombardment; (desde avión) bombing. ~ro *m* (avión) bomber

bombazo *m* explosion

bombear *vt* pump

bombero *m* fireman. cuerpo *m* de ~s fire brigade (Brit), fire department (Amer)

bombilla *f* (light) bulb; (LAm, para mate) pipe for drinking maté

bombín *m* pump; (🅸, sombrero) bowler (hat) (Brit), derby (Amer)

bombo *m* (tambor) bass drum. a ~ y platillos with a lot of fuss

bomb|ón *m* chocolate; (Mex, malvavisco) marshmallow. ~ona *f* gas cylinder

bonachón *a* easygoing; (bueno) good-natured

bonaerense *a* from Buenos Aires. ● *m* native of Buenos Aires

bondad *f* goodness; (amabilidad) kindness; (del clima) mildness. tenga la ~ de would you be kind enough to. ~oso *a* kind

boniato *m* sweet potato

bonito *a* nice; (mono) pretty. ¡muy ~!, ¡qué ~! that's nice!, very nice! ● *m* bonito

bono *m* voucher; (título) bond. ~ del Tesoro government bond

boñiga *f* dung

boqueada *f* gasp. dar la última ~ be dying

boquerón *m* anchovy

boquete *m* hole; (brecha) breach

boquiabierto *a* open-mouthed; (fig) amazed, dumbfounded. quedarse ~ be amazed

boquilla *f* mouthpiece; (para cigarrillos) cigarette-holder; (filtro de cigarrillo) tip

borbotón *m*. hablar a borbotones gabble. salir a borbotones gush out

borda|do *a* embroidered. ● *m* embroidery. ~r *vt* embroider

bord|e *m* edge; (de carretera) side; (de plato etc) rim; (de un vestido) hem. al ~e de on the edge of; (fig) on the brink of. ~ear *vt* go round; (fig) border on. ~illo *m* kerb (Brit), curb (esp Amer)

bordo *m*. a ~ on board

borla *f* tassel

borrach|era *f* drunkenness. pegarse una ~era get drunk. ~ín *m* drunk; (habitual) drunkard. ∼**o** *a* drunk. ● *m* drunkard. **estar** ∼**o** be drunk. **ser** ∼**o** be a drunkard

borrador *m* rough draft; (de contrato) draft; (para la pizarra) (black)board rubber; (goma) eraser

borrar *vt* rub out; (tachar) cross out; delete <*información*>

borrasc|a *f* depression; (tormenta) storm. ∼**oso** *a* stormy

borrego *m* year-old lamb; (Mex, noticia falsa) canard

borrico *m* donkey; (fig, 🚹) ass

borrón *m* smudge; (de tinta) inkblot. ∼ **y cuenta nueva** let's forget about it!

borroso *a* blurred; (fig) vague

bos|coso *a* wooded. ∼**que** *m* wood, forest

bosquej|ar *vt* sketch; outline <*plan*>. ∼**o** *m* sketch; (de plan) outline

bosta *f* dung

bostez|ar [10] *vi* yawn. ∼**o** *m* yawn

bota *f* boot; (recipiente) wineskin

botana *f* (Mex) snack, appetizer

botánic|a *f* botany. ∼**o** *a* botanical. ● *m* botanist

botar *vt* launch; bounce <*pelota*>; (esp LAm, tirar) throw away. ● *vi* bounce

botarate *m* irresponsible person; (esp LAm, derrochador) spendthrift

bote *m* boat; (de una pelota) bounce; (lata) tin, can; (vasija) jar. ∼ **de la basura** (Mex) rubbish bin (Brit), trash can (Amer). ∼ **salvavidas** lifeboat. **de** ∼ **en** ∼ packed

botella *f* bottle

botica *f* chemist's (shop) (Brit), drugstore (Amer). ∼**rio** *m* chemist (Brit), druggist (Amer)

botijo *m* earthenware jug

botín *m* half boot; (de guerra) booty; (de ladrones) haul

botiquín *m* medicine chest; (de primeros auxilios) first aid kit

bot|ón *m* button; (yema) bud; (LAm, insignia) badge. ∼**ones** *m invar* bellboy (Brit), bellhop (Amer)

bóveda *f* vault

boxe|ador *m* boxer. ∼**ar** *vi* box. ∼**o** *m* boxing

boya *f* buoy; (corcho) float. ∼**nte** *a* buoyant

bozal *m* (de perro etc) muzzle; (de caballo) halter

bracear *vi* wave one's arms; (nadar) swim, crawl

bracero *m* seasonal farm labourer

braga(s) *f(pl)* panties, knickers (Brit)

bragueta *f* flies

bram|ar *vi* bellow. ∼**ido** *m* bellowing

branquia *f* gill

bras|a *f* ember. **a la** ∼**a** grilled. ∼**ero** *m* brazier

brasier *m* (Mex) bra

Brasil *m*. (el) ∼ Brazil

brasile|ño *a & m* Brazilian. ∼**ro** *a & m* (LAm) Brazilian

bravío *a* wild

brav|o *a* fierce; (valeroso) brave; <*mar*> rough. ¡∼**o**! *int* well done!, bravo! ∼**ura** *f* ferocity; (valor) bravery

braz|a *f* fathom. **nadar a** ∼**a** swim breast-stroke. ∼**ada** *f* (en natación) stroke. ∼**alete** *m* bracelet; (brazal) arm-band. ∼**o** *m* arm; (de caballo) foreleg; (rama) branch. ∼**o derecho** right-hand man. **del** ∼**o** arm in arm

brea *f* tar, pitch

brebaje *m* potion; (pej) concoction

brecha *f* opening; (Mil) breach; (Med) gash. ~ **generacional** generation gap. **estar en la** ~ be in the thick of it

brega *f* struggle. **andar a la** ~ work hard

breva *f* early fig

breve *a* short. **en** ~ soon, shortly. **en** ~**s momentos** soon. ~**dad** *f* shortness

brib|ón *m* rogue, rascal. ~**onada** *f* dirty trick

brida *f* bridle

brigad|a *f* squad; (Mil) brigade. ~**ier** *m* brigadier (Brit), brigadier-general (Amer)

brill|ante *a* bright; (lustroso) shiny; <*persona*> brilliant. ● *m* diamond. ~**ar** *vi* shine; (centellear) sparkle. ~**o** *m* shine; (brillantez) brilliance; (centelleo) sparkle. **sacar** ~**o** polish. ~**oso** *a* (LAm) shiny

brinc|ar [7] *vi* jump up and down. ~**o** *m* jump. **dar un** ~**o, pegar un** ~**o** jump

brind|ar *vt* offer. ● *vi*. ~**ar por** toast, drink a toast to. ~**is** *m* toast

br|ío *m* energy; (decisión) determination. ~**ioso** *a* spirited; (garboso) elegant

brisa *f* breeze

británico *a* British. ● *m* Briton, British person

brocha *f* paintbrush; (para afeitarse) shaving-brush

broche *m* clasp, fastener; (joya) brooch; (Mex, para el pelo) hairslide (Brit), barrete (Amer)

brocheta *f* skewer; (plato) kebab

brócoli *m* broccoli

brom|a *f* joke. ~**a pesada** practical joke. **en** ~**a** in fun. **ni de** ~**a** no way. ~**ear** *vi* joke. ~**ista** *a* fond of joking. ● *m & f* joker

bronca *f* row; (reprensión) telling-off; (LAm, rabia) foul mood. **dar** ~ **a uno** bug s.o.

bronce *m* bronze; (LAm) brass. ~**ado** *a* bronze; (por el sol) tanned. ~**ar** *vt* tan <*piel*>. □ ~**arse** *vpr* get a suntan

bronquitis *f* bronchitis

brot|ar *vi* (plantas) sprout; (Med) break out; <*líquido*> gush forth; <*lágrimas*> well up. ~**e** *m* shoot; (Med) outbreak

bruces: **de** ~ face down(wards). **caer de** ~ fall flat on one's face

bruj|a *f* witch. ~**ería** *f* witchcraft. ~**o** *m* wizard, magician. ● *a* (Mex) broke

brújula *f* compass

brum|a *f* mist; (fig) confusion. ~**oso** *a* misty, foggy

brusco *a* (repentino) sudden; <*persona*> brusque

Bruselas *f* Brussels

brusquedad *f* roughness; (de movimiento) abruptness

brut|al *a* brutal. ~**alidad** *f* brutality; (estupidez) stupidity. ~**o** *a* ignorant; (tosco) rough; <*peso, sueldo*> gross

bucal *a* oral; <*lesión*> mouth

buce|ar *vi* dive; (nadar) swim under water. ~**o** *m* diving; (natación) underwater swimming

bucle *m* ringlet

budín *m* pudding

budis|mo *m* Buddhism. ~**ta** *m & f* Buddhist

buen ⇒BUENO

buenaventura *f* good luck; (adivinación) fortune

bueno *a* (delante de nombre masculino en singular **buen**) good; (agradable) nice; <*tiempo*> fine. ● *int* well!; (de acuerdo) OK!, very well! **¡buena la has hecho!** you've gone and done it now! **¡buenas noches!**

good night! ¡buenas tardes! (antes del atardecer) good afternoon!; (después del atardecer) good evening! ¡~s días! good morning! estar de buenas be in a good mood. por las buenas willingly. ¡qué bueno! (LAm) great!

Buenos Aires *m* Buenos Aires

buey *m* ox

búfalo *m* buffalo

bufanda *f* scarf

bufar *vi* snort

bufete *m* (mesa) writing-desk; (despacho) lawyer's office

buf|o *a* comic. ~**ón** *a* comical. ● *m* buffoon; (Historia) jester

buhardilla *f* attic; (ventana) dormer window

búho *m* owl

buhonero *m* pedlar

buitre *m* vulture

bujía *f* (Auto) spark plug

bulbo *m* bulb

bulevar *m* avenue, boulevard

Bulgaria *f* Bulgaria

búlgaro *a & m* Bulgarian

bull|a *f* noise. ~**icio** *m* hubbub; (movimiento) bustle. ~**icioso** *a* bustling; (ruidoso) noisy

bullir [22] *vi* boil; (burbujear) bubble; (fig) bustle

bulto *m* (volumen) bulk; (forma) shape; (paquete) package; (maleta etc) piece of luggage; (protuberancia) lump

buñuelo *m* fritter

BUP *abrev* (**Bachillerato Unificado Polivalente**) secondary school education

buque *m* ship, boat

burbuj|a *f* bubble. ~**ear** *vi* bubble; <vino> sparkle

burdel *m* brothel

burdo *a* rough, coarse; <excusa> clumsy

burgu|és *a* middle-class, bourgeois. ● *m* middle-class person. ~**esía** *f* middle class, bourgeoisie

burla *f* taunt; (broma) joke; (engaño) trick. ~**r** *vt* evade. □ ~**rse** *vpr*. ~**rse de** mock, make fun of

burlesco *a* (en literatura) burlesque

burlón *a* mocking

bur|ocracia *f* bureaucracy; (Mex, funcionariado) civil service. ~**ócrata** *m & f* bureaucrat; (Mex, funcionario) civil servant. ~**ocrático** *a* bureaucratic; (Mex) <empleado> government

burro *a* stupid; (obstinado) pigheaded. ●*m* donkey; (fig) ass

bursátil *a* stock-exchange

bus *m* bus

busca *f* search. a la ~ de in search of. en ~ de in search of. ●*m* beeper

buscador *m* search engine

buscapleitos *m & f invar* (LAm) trouble-maker

buscar [7] *vt* look for. ●*vi* look. buscársela ask for it; ir a ~ a uno fetch s.o.

búsqueda *f* search

busto *m* bust

butaca *f* armchair; (en el teatro etc) seat

buzo *m* diver

buzón *m* postbox (Brit), mailbox (Amer)

C/ *abrev* (**Calle**) St, Rd

cabal *a* exact; (completo) complete. **no estar en sus ~es** not be in one's right mind

cabalga|dura *f* mount, horse. **~r** [12] *vt* ride. ● *vi* ride, go riding. **~ta** *f* ride; (desfile) procession

caballa *f* mackerel

caballerango *m* (Mex) groom

caballeresco *a* gentlemanly. **literatura** *f* **caballeresca** books of chivalry

caballer|ía *f* mount, horse. **~iza** *f* stable. **~izo** *m* groom

caballero *m* gentleman; (de orden de caballería) knight; (tratamiento) sir. **~so** *a* gentlemanly

caballete *m* (del tejado) ridge; (para mesa) trestle; (de pintor) easel

caballito *m* pony. **~ del diablo** dragonfly. **~ de mar** sea-horse. **~s** *mpl* (carrusel) merry-go-round

caballo *m* horse; (del ajedrez) knight; (de la baraja española) queen. **~ de fuerza** horsepower. **a ~** on horseback

cabaña *f* hut

cabaret /kaba're/ *m* (*pl* **~s**) night-club

cabecear *vi* nod off; (en fútbol) head the ball; <*caballo*> toss its head

cabecera *f* (de la cama) headboard; (de la mesa) head; (en un impreso) heading

cabecilla *m* ringleader

cabello *m* hair. **~s** *mpl* hair

caber [28] *vi* fit (en into). **no cabe duda** there's no doubt

cabestr|illo *m* sling. **~o** *m* halter

cabeza *f* head; (fig, inteligencia) intelligence. **andar de ~** have a lot to do. **~da** *f* nod. **dar una ~da** nod off. **~zo** *m* butt; (en fútbol) header

cabida *f* capacity; (extensión) area; (espacio) room. **dar ~ a** have room for, accommodate

cabina *f* (de pasajeros) cabin; (de pilotos) cockpit; (electoral) booth; (de camión) cab. **~ telefónica** telephone box (Brit), telephone booth (Amer)

cabizbajo *a* crestfallen

cable *m* cable

cabo *m* end; (trozo) bit; (Mil) corporal; (mango) handle; (Geog) cape; (Naut) rope. **al ~ de** after. **de ~ a rabo** from beginning to end. **llevar a ~** carry out

cabr|a *f* goat. **~iola** *f* jump, skip. **~itilla** *f* kid. **~ito** *m* kid

cábula *m* (Mex) crook

cacahuate, (Mex) **cacahuete** *m* peanut

cacalote *m* (Mex) crow

cacao *m* (planta y semillas) cacao; (polvo) cocoa; (fig) confusion

cacarear *vt* boast about. ● *vi* <*gallo*> crow; <*gallina*> cluck

cacería *f* hunt. **ir de ~** go hunting

cacerola *f* saucepan, casserole

cacharro *m* (earthenware) pot; (coche estropeado) wreck; (cosa inútil) piece of junk; (chisme) thing. **~s** *mpl* pots and pans

cachear *vt* frisk

cachemir *m*, **cachemira** *f* cashmere

cacheo *m* frisking

cachetada *f* (LAm) slap

cache|te *m* slap; (esp LAm, mejilla) cheek. **~tear** *vt* (LAm) slap. **~tón** *a* (LAm) chubby-cheeked

cachimba *f* pipe

cachiporra *f* club, truncheon

cachivache *m* piece of junk. **~s** *mpl* junk

cacho *m* bit, piece; (LAm, cuerno) horn

cachondeo *m* 🔲 joking, joke

cachorro *m* (perrito) puppy; (de león, tigre) cub

cachucha *f* (Mex) cup

caciqu|e *m* cacique, chief; (Pol) local political boss; (hombre poderoso) tyrant. **~il** *a* despotic. **~ismo** *m* despotism

caco *m* thief

cacofonía *f* cacophony

cacto *m*, **cactus** *m invar* cactus

cada *a invar* each, every. **~ uno** each one, everyone. **uno de ~ cinco** one in five. **~ vez más** more and more

cadáver *m* corpse

cadena *f* chain; (TV) channel. **~ de fabricación** production line. **~ de montañas** mountain range. **~ perpetua** life imprisonment

cadera *f* hip

cadete *m* cadet

caduc|ar [7] *vi* expire. **~idad** *f*. **fecha** *f* **de ~idad** sell-by date. **~o** *a* outdated

cae|r [29] *vi* fall. **dejar ~r** drop. **este vestido no me ~ bien** this dress doesn't suit me. **hacer ~r** knock over. **Juan me ~ bien** I like Juan. **su cumpleaños cayó en martes** his birthday fell on a Tuesday. **se le cayó** he dropped it

café *m* coffee; (cafetería) café; (Mex, marrón) brown. ● *a*. **color ~** coffee-coloured. **~ con leche** white coffee. **~ cortado** coffee

with a little milk. **~ negro** (LAm) expresso. **~ solo** black coffee

cafe|ína *f* caffeine. **~tal** *m* coffee plantation. **~tera** *f* coffee-pot. **~tería** *f* café. **~tero** *a* coffee

caíd|a *f* fall; (disminución) drop; (pendiente) slope. **~o** *a* fallen

caigo *vb* ⇒CAER

caimán *m* cayman, alligator

caj|a *f* box; (de botellas) case; (ataúd) coffin; (en tienda) cash desk; (en supermercado) check-out; (en banco) cashier's desk. **~a de ahorros** savings bank. **~a de cambios** gearbox. **~a de caudales**, **~a fuerte** safe. **~a registradora** till. **~ero** *m* cashier. **~ero automático** cash dispenser. **~etilla** *f* packet. **~ita** *f* small box. **~ón** *m* (de mueble) drawer; (caja grande) crate; (LAm, ataúd) coffin; (Mex, en estacionamiento) parking space. **ser de ~ón** be obvious. **~uela** *f* (Mex) boot (Brit), trunk (Amer)

cal *m* lime

cala *f* cove

calaba|cín *m*, **~cita** *f* (Mex) courgette (Brit), zucchini (Amer). **~za** *f* pumpkin; (fig, 🔲, idiota) idiot. **dar ~zas a uno** give s.o. the brush-off

calabozo *m* prison; (celda) cell

calado *a* soaked. **estar ~ hasta los huesos** be soaked to the skin. ● *m* (Naut) draught

calamar *m* squid

calambre *m* cramp

calami|dad *f* calamity, disaster. **~toso** *a* calamitous

calaña *f* sort

calar *vt* soak; (penetrar) pierce; (fig, penetrar) see through; rumble <persona>; sample <fruta>. ▢ **~se** *vpr* get soaked; <zapatos> leak; (Auto) stall

calavera *f* skull; (Mex, Auto) taillight

calcar [7] *vt* trace; (fig) copy

calcet|a *f*. hacer ∼ knit. ∼**ín** *m* sock

calcetín *m* sock

calcinar *vt* burn

calcio *m* calcium

calcomanía *f* transfer

calcula|dor *a* calculating. ∼**dora** *f* calculator. ∼**r** *vt* calculate; (suponer) reckon, think; (imaginar) imagine

cálculo *m* calculation; (Med) stone

caldear *vt* heat, warm. □ ∼**se** *vpr* get hot

caldera *f* boiler

calderilla *f* small change

caldo *m* stock; (sopa) clear soup, broth

calefacción *f* heating. ∼ **central** central heating

caleidoscopio *m* kaleidoscope

calendario *m* calendar; (programa) schedule

calent|ador *m* heater. ∼**amiento** *m* warming; (en deportes) warm-up. ∼**ar** [1] *vt* heat; (templar) warm. □ ∼**arse** *vpr* get hot; (templarse) warm up; (LAm, enojarse) get mad. ∼**ura** *f* fever, (high) temperature. ∼**uriento** *a* feverish

calibr|ar *vt* calibrate; (fig) weigh up. ∼**e** *m* calibre; (diámetro) diameter; (fig) importance

calidad *f* quality; (condición) capacity. **en** ∼ **de** as

calidez *f* (LAm) warmth

cálido *a* warm

caliente *a* hot; <habitación, ropa> warm; (LAm, enojado) angry

califica|ción *f* qualification; (evaluación) assessment; (nota) mark. ∼**do** *a* (esp LAm) qualified; (mano de obra) skilled. ∼**r** [7] *vt* qualify; (evaluar) assess; mark <examen etc>. ∼**r de** describe as, label

cáliz *m* chalice; (Bot) calyx

caliz|a *f* limestone. ∼**o** *a* lime

calla|do *a* quiet. ∼**r** *vt* silence; keep <secreto>; hush up <asunto>. ● *vi* be quiet, keep quiet, shut up 🅸. □ ∼**rse** *vpr* be quiet, keep quiet, shut up 🅸 ¡cállate! be quiet!, shut up! 🅸

calle *f* street, road; (en deportes, autopista) lane. ∼ **de dirección única** one-way street. ∼ **mayor** high street, main street. **de** ∼ everyday. ∼**ja** *f* narrow street. ∼**jear** *vi* hang out on the streets. ∼**jero** *a* street. ● *m* street plan. ∼**jón** *m* alley. ∼**jón sin salida** dead end. ∼**juela** *f* back street, side street

call|ista *m & f* chiropodist. ∼**o** *m* corn, callus. ∼**os** *mpl* tripe. ∼**osidad** *f* callus

calm|a *f* calm. ¡∼**a**! calm down!. **en** ∼**a** calm. **perder la** ∼**a** lose one's composure. ∼**ante** *m* tranquillizer; (para el dolor) painkiller. ∼**ar** *vt* calm; (aliviar) soothe. ● *vi* <viento> abate. □ ∼**arse** *vpr* calm down; <viento> abate. ∼**o** *a* calm. ∼**oso** *a* calm; (🅸, flemático) slow

calor *m* heat; (afecto) warmth. **hace** ∼ it's hot. **tener** ∼ be hot. ∼**ía** *f* calorie. ∼**ífero** *a* heat-producing. ∼**ico** *a* calorific

calumni|a *f* calumny; (oral) slander; (escrita) libel. ∼**ar** *vt* slander; (por escrito) libel. ∼**oso** *a* slanderous; <cosa escrita> libellous

caluroso *a* warm; <clima> hot

calv|a *f* bald head; (parte sin pelo) bald patch. ∼**icie** *f* baldness. ∼**o** *a* bald

calza *f* wedge

calzada *f* road; (en autopista) carriageway

calza|do *a* wearing shoes. ● *m* footwear, shoe. **~dor** *m* shoehorn. **~r** [10] *vt* put shoes on; (llevar) wear. **¿qué número calza Vd?** what size shoe do you take? ● *vi* wear shoes. □ **~rse** *vpr* put on

calz|ón *m* shorts. **~ones** *mpl* shorts; (LAm, ropa interior) panties. **~oncillos** *mpl* underpants

cama *f* bed. **~ de matrimonio** double bed. **~ individual** single bed. **guardar ~** stay in bed

camada *f* litter

camafeo *m* cameo

camaleón *m* chameleon

cámara *f* (aposento) chamber; (fotográfica) camera **~ digital** digital camera. **~ fotográfica** camera. **a ~ lenta** in slow motion **~ web** webcam

camarad|a *m & f* colleague; (de colegio) schoolfriend; (Pol) comrade. **~ería** *f* camaraderie

camarer|a *f* chambermaid; (de restaurante etc) waitress. **~o** *m* waiter

camarógrafo *m* cameraman

camarón *m* shrimp

camarote *m* cabin

cambi|able *a* changeable; (Com etc) exchangeable. **~ante** *a* variable; <persona> moody. **~ar** *vt* change; (trocar) exchange. ● *vi* change. **~ar de idea** change one's mind. □ **~arse** *vpr* change. **~o** *m* change; (Com) exchange rate; (moneda menuda) (small) change; (Auto) gear. **en ~o** on the other hand

camello *m* camel

camellón *m* (Mex) traffic island

camerino *m* dressing room

camilla *f* stretcher

camin|ante *m* traveller. **~ar** *vt/i* walk. **~ata** *f* long walk. **~o** *m* road; (sendero) path, track;

(dirección, ruta) way. **~o de** towards, on the way to. **abrir ~o** make way. **a medio ~o, a la mitad del ~o** half-way. **de ~o** on the way

cami|ón *m* lorry; (Mex, autobús) bus. **~onero** *m* lorry-driver; (Mex, de autobús) bus driver. **~oneta** *f* van; (LAm, coche familiar) estate car

camis|a *f* shirt. **~a de fuerza** strait-jacket. **~ería** *f* shirtmaker's. **~eta** *f* T-shirt; (ropa interior) vest. **~ón** *m* nightdress

camorra *f* 🔲 row. **buscar ~** look for a fight

camote *m* (LAm) sweet potato

campamento *m* camp. **de ~** *a* camping

campan|a *f* bell. **~ada** *f* stroke. **~ario** *m* bell tower, belfry. **~illa** *f* bell

campaña *f* campaign

campe|ón *a & m* champion. **~onato** *m* championship

campes|ino *a* country. ● *m* peasant. **~tre** *a* country

camping /'kampin/ *m* (pl **~s**) camping; (lugar) campsite. **hacer ~** go camping

camp|iña *f* countryside. **~o** *m* country; (agricultura, fig) field; (de fútbol) pitch; (de golf) course. **~osanto** *m* cemetery

camufla|je *m* camouflage. **~r** *vt* camouflage

cana *f* grey hair, white hair. **peinar ~s** be getting old

Canadá *m.* **el ~** Canada

canadiense *a & m & f* Canadian

canal *m* (incl TV) channel; (artificial) canal; (del tejado) gutter. **~ de la Mancha** English Channel. **~ de Panamá** Panama Canal. **~ón** *m* gutter; (vertical) drain-pipe

canalla *f* rabble. ● *m* (fig, 🔲) swine. **~da** *f* dirty trick

canapé *m* sofa, couch; (Culin) canapé

Canarias *fpl.* **las (islas)** ~ the Canary Islands, the Canaries

canario *a* of the Canary Islands. ● *m* native of the Canary Islands; (pájaro) canary

canast|a *f* (large) basket ~**illa** *f* small basket; (para un bebé) layette. ~**illo** *m* small basket. ~**o** *m* (large) basket

cancela|ción *f* cancellation. ~**r** *vt* cancel; write off *<deuda>*

cáncer *m* cancer. **C**~ Cancer

cancha *f* court; (LAm, de fútbol, rugby) pitch, ground

canciller *m* chancellor; (LAm, ministro) Minister of Foreign Affairs

canci|ón *f* song. ~**ón de cuna** lullaby. ~**onero** *m* song-book

candado *m* padlock

candel|a *f* candle. ~**abro** *m* candelabra. ~**ero** *m* candlestick

candente *a* (rojo) red-hot; (fig) burning

candidato *m* candidate

candidez *f* innocence; (ingenuidad) naivety

cándido *a* naive

candil *m* oil lamp. ~**ejas** *fpl* footlights

candor *m* innocence; (ingenuidad) naivety

canela *f* cinnamon

cangrejo *m* crab. ~ **de río** crayfish

canguro *m* kangaroo. ● *m & f* (persona) baby-sitter

caníbal *a & m & f* cannibal

canica *f* marble

canijo *a* weak; (Mex, terco) stubborn; (Mex, intenso) incredible

canilla *f* (LAm) shinbone

canino *a* canine. ● *m* canine (tooth)

canje *m* exchange. ~**ar** *vt* exchange

cano *a* grey. **de pelo** ~ grey-haired

canoa *f* canoe

can|ónigo *m* canon. ~**onizar** [10] *vt* canonize

canoso *a* grey-haired

cansa|do *a* tired; (que cansa) tiring. ~**dor** (LAm) tiring. ~**ncio** *m* tiredness. ~**r** *vt* tire; (aburrir) bore. ● *vi* be tiring; (aburrir) get boring. □ ~**rse** *vpr* get tired

canta|nte *a* singing. ● *m & f* singer. ~**or** *m* Flamenco singer. ~**r** *vt/i* sing. ~**rlas claras** speak frankly. ● *m* singing; (poema) poem

cántaro *m* pitcher. **llover a** ~**s** pour down

cante *m* folk song. ~ **flamenco**, ~ **jondo** Flamenco singing

cantera *f* quarry

cantidad *f* quantity; (número) number; (de dinero) sum. **una** ~ **de** lots of

cantimplora *f* water-bottle

cantina *f* canteen; (Rail) buffet; (LAm, bar) bar

cant|inela *f* song. ~**o** *m* singing; (canción) chant; (borde) edge; (de un cuchillo) blunt edge. ~**o rodado** boulder; (guijarro) pebble. **de** ~**o** on edge

canturre|ar *vt/i* hum. ~**o** *m* humming

canuto *m* tube

caña *f* (planta) reed; (del trigo) stalk; (del bambú) cane; (de pescar) rod; (de la bota) leg; (vaso) glass. ~ **de azúcar** sugar-cane. ~**da** *f* ravine; (camino) track; (LAm, arroyo) stream

cáñamo *m* hemp. ~ **indio** cannabis

cañ|ería *f* pipe; (tubería) piping. ~**o** *m* pipe, tube; (de fuente) jet.

∼**ón** m (de pluma) quill; (de artillería) cannon; (de arma de fuego) barrel; (desfiladero) canyon. ∼**onera** f gunboat

caoba f mahogany

ca|os m chaos. ∼**ótico** a chaotic

capa f layer; (de pintura) coat; (Culin) coating; (prenda) cloak; (más corta) cape; (Geol) stratum

capaci|dad f capacity; (fig) ability. ∼**tar** vt qualify, enable; (instruir) train

caparazón m shell

capataz m foreman

capaz a capable, able

capcioso a sly, insidious

capellán m chaplain

caperuza f hood; (de bolígrafo) cap

capilla f chapel

capital a capital, very important. ● m (dinero) capital. ● f (ciudad) capital. ∼ **de provincia** county town. ∼**ino** a (LAm) of/from the capital. ∼**ismo** m capitalism. ∼**ista** a & m & f capitalist. ∼**izar** [10] vt capitalize

capit|án m captain; (de pesquero) skipper. ∼**anear** vt lead, command; skipper <pesquero>; captain <un equipo>

capitel m (Arquit) capital

capitulaci|ón f surrender. ∼**ones** fpl marriage contract

capítulo m chapter; (de serie) episode

capó m bonnet (Brit), hood (Amer)

capón m (pollo) capon

caporal m (Mex) foreman

capot|a f (de mujer) bonnet; (Auto) folding top; (de cochecito) hood. ∼**e** m cape; (Mex, de coche) bonnet (Brit), hood (Amer)

capricho m whim. ∼**so** a capricious, whimsical

Capricornio m Capricorn

cápsula f capsule

captar vt harness <agua>; grasp <sentido>; capture <atención>; win <confianza>; (radio) pick up

captura f capture. ∼**r** vt capture

capucha f hood

capullo m bud; (de insecto) cocoon

caqui m khaki

cara f face; (de una moneda) heads; (de un objeto) side; (aspecto) look, appearance; (descaro) cheek. ∼ **a** facing. ∼ **a** face to face. ∼ **dura** ⇒ CARADURA. ∼ **o cruz** heads or tails. **dar la** ∼ face up to. **hacer** ∼ **a** face. **tener mala** ∼ look ill. **volver la** ∼ look the other way

carabela f caravel

carabina f carbine; (fig, 🄵, señora) chaperone

caracol m snail; (de mar) winkle; (LAm, concha) conch; (de pelo) curl. ¡∼**es!** Good Heavens!. ∼**a** f conch

carácter m (pl **caracteres**) character; (índole) nature. **con** ∼ **de** as

característic|a f characteristic. ∼**o** a characteristic, typical

caracteriza|do a characterized; (prestigioso) distinguished. ∼**r** [10] vt characterize

caradura f cheek, nerve. ● m & f cheeky person

caramba int good heavens!

carambola f (en billar) cannon; (Mex, choque múltiple) pile-up. **de** ∼ by pure chance

caramelo m sweet (Brit), candy (Amer); (azúcar fundido) caramel

caraqueño a from Caracas

carátula f (de disco) sleeve (Brit), jacket (Amer); (de video) case; (de libro) cover; (Mex, del reloj) face

caravana f caravan; (de vehículos) convoy; (Auto) long line, traffic jam; (remolque) caravan (Brit), trailer (Amer); (Mex, reverencia) bow

caray *int* ☒ good heavens!

carb|ón *m* coal; (para dibujar) charcoal. **~ de leña** charcoal. **~oncillo** *m* charcoal. **~onero** *a* coal. ● *m* coal-merchant. **~onizar** [10] *vt* (fig) burn (to a cinder). **~ono** *m* carbon

carbura|dor *m* carburettor. **~nte** *m* fuel

carcajada *f* guffaw. **reírse a ~s** roar with laughter. **soltar una ~** burst out laughing

cárcel *f* prison, jail

carcelero *m* jailer

carcom|er *vt* eat away; (fig) undermine. □ **~erse** *vpr* be eaten away; (fig) waste away

cardenal *m* cardinal; (contusión) bruise

cardiaco, cardíaco *a* cardiac, heart

cardinal *a* cardinal

cardo *m* thistle

carear *vt* bring face to face *<personas>*; compare *<cosas>*

care|cer [11] *vi*. **~cer de** lack. **~cer de sentido** not to make sense. **~ncia** *f* lack. **~nte** *a* lacking

care|ro *a* pricey. **~stía** *f* (elevado) high cost

careta *f* mask

carey *m* tortoiseshell

carga *f* load; (fig) burden; (acción) loading; (de barco, avión) cargo; (de tren) freight; (de arma) charge; (Elec, ataque) charge; (obligación) obligation. **llevar la ~ de algo** be responsible for sth. **~da** *f* (Mex, Pol) supporters. **~do** *a* loaded; (fig) burdened; *<atmósfera>* heavy; *<café>* strong; *<pila>* charged. **~mento** *m* load; (acción) loading; (de un barco) cargo. **~r** [12] *vt* load; (fig) burden; (Elec, atacar) charge; fill *<pluma etc>*. ● *vi* load. **~r con** carry. □ **~rse** *vpr*

<pila> charge. **~rse de** to load s.o. down with

cargo *m* (puesto) post; (acusación) charge. **a ~ de** in the charge of. **hacerse ~ de** take responsibility for. **tener a su ~** be in charge of

carguero *m* (Naut) cargo ship

caria|do *a* decayed. □ **~rse** *vpr* decay

caribeño *a* Caribbean

caricatura *f* caricature

caricia *f* caress; (a animal) stroke

caridad *f* charity. **¡por ~!** for goodness sake!

caries *f invar* tooth decay; (lesión) cavity

cariño *m* affection; (caricia) caress. **~ mío** my darling. **con mucho ~** (en carta) with love from. **tener ~ a** be fond of. **tomar ~ a** become fond of. **~so** *a* affectionate

carisma *m* charisma

caritativo *a* charitable

cariz *m* look

carmesí *a & m* crimson

carmín *m* (de labios) lipstick; (color) red

carnal *a* carnal. **primo ~** first cousin

carnaval *m* carnival. **~esco** *a* carnival

carne *f* meat; (Anat, de frutos, pescado) flesh. **~ de cerdo** pork. **~ de cordero** lamb. **~ de gallina** goose pimples. **~ molida** (LAm), **~ picada** mince (Brit), ground beef (Amer). **~ de ternera** veal. **~ de vaca** beef. **me pone la ~ de gallina** it gives me the creeps. **ser de ~ y hueso** be only human

carné, carnet *m* card. **~ de conducir** driving licence (Brit), driver's license (Amer) **~ de identidad** identity card. **~ de manejar** (LAm) driving license

(Brit), driver's license (Amer). ~ de
socio membership card

carnero *m* ram

carnicer|ía *f* butcher's (shop);
(fig) massacre. ~o *a* carnivorous.
● *m* butcher

carnívoro *a* carnivorous. ● *m*
carnivore

carnoso *a* fleshy; <*pollo*> meaty

caro *a* expensive. ● *adv* dear,
dearly. **costar ~ a uno** cost s.o.
dear.

carpa *f* carp; (LAm, tienda) tent

carpeta *f* folder, file. ~zo *m*. dar
~zo a shelve

carpinter|ía *f* carpentry. ~o *m*
carpenter, joiner

carraspe|ar *vi* clear one's throat.
~ra *f*. tener ~ra have a frog in
one's throat

carrera *f* run; (prisa) rush;
(concurso) race; (estudios) degree
course; (profesión) career; (de taxi)
journey

carreta *f* cart. ~da *f* cartload

carrete *m* reel; (película) film

carretear *vi* (LAm) taxi

carretera *f* road. ~ de
circunvalación bypass, ring road.
~ nacional A road (Brit), highway
(Amer)

carretilla *f* wheelbarrow

carril *m* lane; (Rail) rail

carrito *m* (en supermercado, para
equipaje) trolley (Brit), cart (Amer)

carro *m* cart; (LAm, coche) car; (Mex,
vagón) coach. ~ de combate tank.
~cería *f* (Auto) bodywork

carroña *f* carrion

carroza *f* coach, carriage; (en
desfile de fiesta) float

carruaje *m* carriage

carrusel *m* merry-go-round

cart|a *f* letter; (lista de platos) menu;
(lista de vinos) list; (Geog) map;

(naipe) card. ~a blanca free hand.
~a de crédito letter of credit.
~earse *vpr* correspond

cartel *m* poster; (letrero) sign.
~era *f* hoarding; (en periódico)
listings; (LAm en escuela, oficina)
notice board (Brit), bulletin board
(Amer). de ~ celebrated

carter|a *f* wallet; (de colegial)
satchel; (para documentos) briefcase;
(LAm, de mujer) handbag (Brit),
purse (Amer). ~ista *m & f*
pickpocket

cartero *m* postman, mailman
(Amer)

cartílago *m* cartilage

cartilla *f* first reading book. ~ de
ahorros savings book. leerle la ~ a
uno tell s.o. off

cartón *m* cardboard

cartucho *m* cartridge

cartulina *f* card

casa *f* house; (hogar) home;
(empresa) firm. ~ de huéspedes
boarding-house. ~ de socorro
first aid post. ir a ~ go home.
salir de ~ go out

casaca *f* jacket

casado *a* married. los recién ~os
the newly-weds

casa|mentero *m* matchmaker.
~miento *m* marriage; (ceremonia)
wedding. ~r *vt* marry. □ ~rse
vpr get married

cascabel *m* small bell; (de
serpiente) rattle

cascada *f* waterfall

casca|nueces *m invar*
nutcrackers. ~r [7] *vt* crack
<*nuez, huevo*>; (pegar) beat.
□ ~rse *vpr* crack

cáscara *f* (de huevo, nuez) shell; (de
naranja) peel; (de plátano) skin

cascarrabias *a invar* grumpy

casco *m* helmet; (de cerámica etc)
piece, fragment; (cabeza) scalp; (de

barco) hull; (envase) empty bottle; (de caballo) hoof; (de una ciudad) part, area

cascote *m* piece of rubble. **~s** *mpl* rubble

caserío *m* country house; (poblado) hamlet

casero *a* home-made; (doméstico) domestic; (amante del hogar) home-loving; *<reunión>* family. ● *m* owner; (vigilante) caretaker

caseta *f* hut; (puesto) stand. **~ de baño** bathing hut

casete *m & f* cassette

casi *adv* almost, nearly; (en frases negativas) hardly. **~ ~** very nearly. **~ nada** hardly any. **¡~ nada!** is that all? **~ nunca** hardly ever

casill|a *f* hut; (en ajedrez etc) square; (en formulario) box; (compartmento) pigeonhole. **~ electrónica** e-mail address. **~ero** *m* pigeonholes; (compartimento) pigeonhole

casino *m* casino; (club social) club

caso *m* case. **el ~ es que** the fact is that. **en ~ de** in the event of. **en cualquier ~** in any case, whatever happens. **en ese ~** in that case. **en todo ~** in any case. **en último ~** as a last resort. **hacer ~ de** take notice of. **poner por ~** suppose

caspa *f* dandruff

casquivana *f* flirt

cassette *m & f* cassette

casta *f* (de animal) breed; (de persona) descent; (grupo social) caste

castaña *f* chestnut

castañetear *vi* *<dientes>* chatter

castaño *a* chestnut; *<ojos>* brown. ● *m* chestnut (tree)

castañuela *f* castanet

castellano *a* Castilian. ● *m* (persona) Castilian; (lengua) Castilian, Spanish. **~parlante** *a* Castilian-speaking, Spanish-speaking. **¿habla Vd ~?** do you speak Spanish?

castidad *f* chastity

castig|ar [12] *vt* punish; (en deportes) penalize. **~o** *m* punishment; (en deportes) penalty

castillo *m* castle

cast|izo *a* traditional; (puro) pure. **~o** *a* chaste

castor *m* beaver

castrar *vt* castrate

castrense *m* military

casual *a* chance, accidental. **~idad** *f* chance, coincidence. **dar la ~idad** happen. **de ~idad, por ~idad** by chance. **¡qué ~idad!** what a coincidence!. **~mente** *adv* by chance; (precisamente) actually

cataclismo *m* cataclysm

catador *m* taster

catalán *a & m* Catalan

catalizador *m* catalyst

cat|alogar [12] *vt* catalogue; (fig) classify. **~álogo** *m* catalogue

Cataluña *f* Catalonia

catamarán *m* catamaran

catapulta *f* catapult

catar *vt* taste, try

catarata *f* waterfall, falls; (Med) cataract

catarro *m* cold

cat|ástrofe *m* catastrophe. **~astrófico** *a* catastrophic

catecismo *m* catechism

cátedra *f* (en universidad) professorship, chair; (en colegio) post of head of department

catedral *f* cathedral

catedrático *m* professor; (de colegio) teacher, head of department

categ|oría *f* category; (clase) class. **de ~oría** important. **de**

primera ~**oría** first-class. ~**órico** a categorical

cat|olicismo m catholicism. ~**ólico** a (Roman) Catholic ● m (Roman) Catholic

catorce a & m fourteen

cauce m river bed; (fig, artificial) channel

caucho m rubber

caudal m (de río) volume of flow; (riqueza) wealth. ~**oso** a <río> large

caudillo m leader

causa f cause; (motivo) reason; (Jurid) trial. **a ~ de, por ~ de** because of. ~**r** vt cause

cautel|la f caution. ~**oso** a cautious, wary

cauterizar [10] vt cauterize

cautiv|ar vt capture; (fig, fascinar) captivate. ~**erio** m, ~**idad** f captivity. ~**o** a & m captive

cauto a cautious

cavar vt/i dig

caverna f cave, cavern

caviar m caviare

cavidad f cavity

caza f hunting; (con fusil) shooting; (animales) game. ● m fighter. **andar a (la) ~ de** be in search of. **~ mayor** game hunting. **dar ~** chase, go after. **ir de ~** go hunting/shooting. ~**dor** m hunter. ~**dora** f jacket. ~**r** [10] vt hunt; (con fusil) shoot; (fig) track down; (obtener) catch, get

caz|o m saucepan; (cucharón) ladle. ~**oleta** f (small) saucepan. ~**uela** f casserole

cebada f barley

ceb|ar vt fatten (up); bait <anzuelo>; prime <arma de fuego>. ~**o** m bait; (de arma de fuego) charge

ceboll|a f onion. ~**eta** f spring onion (Brit), scallion (Amer). ~**ino** m chive

cebra f zebra

cece|ar vi lisp. ~**o** m lisp

cedazo m sieve

ceder vt give up; (transferir) transfer. ● vi give in; (disminuir) ease off; (romperse) give way, collapse. **ceda el paso** give way (Brit), yield (Amer)

cedro m cedar

cédula f bond. **~ de identidad** identity card

CE(E) abrev (**Comunidad (Económica) Europea**) E(E)C

ceg|ador a blinding. ~**ar** [1 & 12] vt blind; (tapar) block up. □ ~**arse** vpr be blinded (**de** by). ~**uera** f blindness

ceja f eyebrow

cejar vi give way

celada f ambush; (fig) trap

cela|dor m (de cárcel) prison warder; (de museo etc) security guard. ~**r** vt watch

celda f cell

celebra|ción f celebration. ~**r** vt celebrate; (alabar) praise. □ ~**rse** vpr take place

célebre a famous

celebridad f fame; (persona) celebrity

celest|e a heavenly; <vestido> pale blue. **azul ~e** sky-blue. ~**ial** a heavenly

celibato m celibacy

célibe a celibate

celo m zeal; (de las hembras) heat; (de los machos) rut; (cinta adhesiva) Sellotape (P) (Brit), Scotch (P) tape (Amer). ~**s** mpl jealousy. **dar ~s** make jealous. **tener ~s** be jealous

celofán m cellophane

celoso *a* conscientious; (que tiene celos) jealous

celta *a & m* (lengua) Celtic. ● *m & f* Celt

célula *f* cell

celular *a* cellular. ● *m* (LAm) mobile phone

celulosa *f* cellulose

cementerio *m* cemetery

cemento *m* cement; (hormigón) concrete; (LAm, cola) glue

cena *f* dinner; (comida ligera) supper

cenag|al *m* marsh, bog; (fig) tight spot. **~oso** *a* boggy

cenar *vt* have for dinner; (en cena ligera) have for supper. ● *vi* have dinner; (tomar cena ligera) have supper

cenicero *m* ashtray

ceniza *f* ash

censo *m* census. **~ electoral** electoral roll

censura *f* censure; (de prensa etc) censorship. **~r** *vt* censure; censor *<prensa etc>*

centavo *a & m* hundredth; (moneda) centavo

centell|a *f* flash; (chispa) spark. **~ar**, **~ear** *vi* sparkle

centena *f* hundred. **~r** *m* hundred. **a ~res** by the hundred. **~rio** *a* centenarian. ● *m* centenary; (persona) centenarian

centeno *m* rye

centésim|a *f* hundredth. **~o** *a* hundredth

cent|ígrado *a* centigrade, Celsius. ● *m* centigrade. **~igramo** *m* centigram. **~ilitro** *m* centilitre. **~ímetro** *m* centimetre

céntimo *a* hundredth. ● *m* cent

centinela *f* sentry

centolla *f*, **centollo** *m* spider crab

central *a* central. ● *f* head office. **~ de correos** general post office. **~ eléctrica** power station. **~ nuclear** nuclear power station. **~ telefónica** telephone exchange. **~ita** *f* switchboard

centraliza|ción *f* centralization. **~r** [10] *vt* centralize

centrar *vt* centre

céntrico *a* central

centrífugo *a* centrifugal

centro *m* centre. **~ comercial** shopping centre (Brit), shopping mall (Amer)

Centroamérica *f* Central America

centroamericano *a & m* Central American

ceñi|do *a* tight. **~r** [5 & 22] *vt* take *<corona>*; *<vestido>* cling to. □ **~rse** *vpr* limit o.s. (**a** to)

ceñ|o *m* frown. **fruncir el ~o** frown. **~udo** *a* frowning

cepill|ar *vt* brush; (en carpintería) plane. **~o** *m* brush; (en carpintería) plane. **~o de dientes** toothbrush

cera *f* wax

cerámic|a *f* ceramics; (materia) pottery; (objeto) piece of pottery. **~o** *a* ceramic

cerca *f* fence; (de piedra) wall. ● *adv* near, close. **~ de** close to, close up, closely

cercan|ía *f* nearness, proximity. **~ías** *fpl* vicinity. **tren** *m* **de ~ías** local train. **~o** *a* near, close.

cercar [7] *vt* fence in, enclose; *<gente>* surround; (asediar) besiege

cerciorar *vt* convince. □ **~se** *vpr* make sure

cerco *m* (asedio) siege; (círculo) ring; (LAm, valla) fence; (LAm, seto) hedge

cerdo *m* pig; (carne) pork

cereal *m* cereal

cerebr|al *a* cerebral. **~o** *m* brain; (persona) brains

ceremoni|a *f* ceremony. **~al** *a* ceremonial. **~oso** *a* ceremonious

cerez|a *f* cherry. **~o** *m* cherry tree

cerill|a *f* match. **~o** *m* (Mex) match

cern|er [1] *vt* sieve. □ **~erse** *vpr* hover. **~idor** *m* sieve

cero *m* nought, zero; (fútbol) nil (Brit), zero (Amer); (tenis) love; (persona) nonentity

cerquillo *m* (LAm, flequillo) fringe (Brit), bangs (Amer)

cerra|do *a* shut, closed; (espacio) shut in, enclosed; *<cielo>* overcast; *<curva>* sharp. **~dura** *f* lock; (acción de cerrar) shutting, closing. **~jero** *m* locksmith. **~r** [1] *vt* shut, close; (con llave) lock; (cercar) enclose; turn off *<grifo>*; block up *<agujero etc>*. ● *vi* shut, close. □ **~rse** *vpr* shut, close; *<herida>* heal. **~r con llave** lock

cerro *m* hill

cerrojo *m* bolt. echar el **~** bolt

certamen *m* competition, contest

certero *a* accurate

certeza, certidumbre *f* certainty

certifica|do *a* *<carta etc>* registered. ● *m* certificate. **~r** [7] *vt* certify

certitud *f* certainty

cervatillo, cervato *m* fawn

cerve|cería *f* beerhouse, bar; (fábrica) brewery. **~za** *f* beer. **~za de barril** draught beer. **~za rubia** lager

cesa|ción *f* cessation, suspension. **~nte** *a* redundant. **~r** *vt* stop. ● *vi* stop, cease; (dejar un empleo) resign. sin **~r** incessantly

cesárea *f* caesarian (section)

cese *m* cessation; (de un empleo) dismissal. **~ del fuego** (LAm) ceasefire

césped *m* grass, lawn

cest|a *f* basket. **~o** *m* basket. **~o de los papeles** waste-paper basket

chabacano *a* common; *<chiste etc>* vulgar. ● *m* (Mex, albaricoque) apricot

chabola *f* shack. **~s** *fpl* shanty town

cháchara *f* 🗊 chatter; (Mex, objetos sin valor) junk

chacharear *vt* (Mex) sell. ● *vi* 🗊 chatter

chacra *f* (LAm) farm

chal *m* shawl

chalado *a* 🗊 crazy

chalé *m* house (with a garden), villa

chaleco *m* waistcoat, vest (Amer). **~ salvavidas** life-jacket

chalet *m* (*pl* **~s**) house (with a garden), villa

chalote *m* shallot

chamac|a *f* (esp Mex) girl. **~o** *m* (esp Mex) boy

chamarra *f* sheepskin jacket; (Mex, chaqueta corta) jacket

chamb|a *f* (Mex, trabajo) work. por **~a** by fluke. **~ear** *vi* (Mex, 🗊) work

champán *m*, **champaña** *m & f* champagne

champiñón *m* mushroom

champú *m* (*pl* **~es** *o* **~s**) shampoo

chamuscar [7] *vt* scorch

chance *m* (esp LAm) chance

chancho *m* (LAm) pig

chanchullo *m* 🗊 swindle, fiddle 🗊

chanclo *m* clog; (de caucho) rubber overshoe

chándal *m* (*pl* **~s**) tracksuit

chantaje *m* blackmail. **~ar** *vt* blackmail

chanza *f* joke

chapa *f* plate, sheet; (de madera) plywood; (de botella) metal top; (carrocería) bodywork; (LAm cerradura) lock. **~do** *a* plated. **~do a la antigua** old-fashioned. **~do en oro** gold-plated

chaparro *a* (LAm) short, squat

chaparrón *m* downpour

chapapote *m* oil (*on beach*)

chapopote *m* (Mex) tar

chapotear *vi* splash

chapucero *a* <*persona*> slapdash; <*trabajo*> shoddy

chapulín *m* (Mex) locust; (saltamontes) grasshopper

chapurrar, chapurrear *vt* have a smattering of, speak a little

chapuza *f* botched job; (trabajo ocasional) odd job

chaqueta *f* jacket. **cambiar de ~a** change sides. **~ón** *m* three-quarter length coat

charca *f* pond, pool. **~o** *m* puddle, pool

charcutería *f* delicatessen

charla *f* chat; (conferencia) talk. **~dor** *a* talkative. **~r** *vi* 🛈 chat. **~tán** *a* talkative. ● *m* chatterbox; (vendedor) cunning hawker; (curandero) charlatan

charol *m* varnish; (cuero) patent leather. **~a** *f* (Mex) tray

charra *f* (Mex) horsewoman, cowgirl. **~o** *m* (Mex) horseman, cowboy

chascar [7] *vt* crack <*látigo*>; click <*lengua*>; snap <*dedos*>. ● *vi* <*madera*> creak. **~ con la lengua** click one's tongue

chasco *m* disappointment

chasis *m* (Auto) chassis

chasquear *vt* crack <*látigo*>; click <*lengua*>; snap <*dedos*>. ● *vi* <*madera*> creak. **~ con la lengua** click one's tongue. **~ido** *m* crack; (de la lengua) click; (de los dedos) snap

chatarra *f* scrap iron; (fig) scrap

chato *a* <*nariz*> snub; <*objetos*> flat. ● *m* wine glass

chav|a *f* (Mex) girl, lass. **~al** *m* 🛈 boy, lad. **~o** *m* (Mex) boy, lad.

checa|da *f* (Mex) check; (Mex, Med) checkup. **~r** [7] *vt* (Mex) check; (vigilar) check up on. **~r tarjeta** clock in

checo *a* & *m* Czech. **~slovaco** *a* & *m* (History) Czechoslovak

chelín *m* shilling

chelo *m* cello

cheque *m* cheque. **~ de viaje** traveller's cheque. **~ar** *vt* check; (LAm) check in <*equipaje*>. **~o** *m* check; (Med) checkup. **~ra** *f* cheque-book

chévere *a* (LAm) great

chica *f* girl; (criada) maid, servant

chicano *a* & *m* Chicano, Mexican-American

chícharo *m* (Mex) pea

chicharra *f* cicada; (timbre) buzzer

chichón *m* bump

chicle *m* chewing-gum

chico *a* 🛈 small; (esp LAm, de edad) young. ● *m* boy. **~s** *mpl* children

chicoria *f* chicory

chifla|do *a* 🛈 crazy, daft. **~r** *vt* whistle at, boo. ● *vi* (LAm) whistle; (🛈, gustar mucho) **me chifla el chocolate** I'm mad about chocolate. □ **~rse** *vpr* be mad (por about)

chilango *a* (Mex) from Mexico City

chile *m* chilli

Chile *m* Chile

chileno *a* & *m* Chilean

chill|ar vi scream, shriek; <*ratón*> squeak; <*cerdo*> squeal. **~ido** m scream, screech. **~ón** a noisy; <*colores*> loud; <*sonido*> shrill

chimenea f chimney; (hogar) fireplace

chimpancé m chimpanzee

china f Chinese (woman)

China f China

chinche m drawing-pin (Brit), thumbtack (Amer); (insecto) bedbug; (fig) nuisance. **~eta** f drawing-pin (Brit), thumbtack (Amer)

chinela f slipper

chino a Chinese; (Mex rizado) curly. ● m Chinese (man); (Mex, de pelo rizado) curly-haired person

chipriota a & m & f Cypriot

chiquero m pen; (LAm, pocilga) pigsty (Brit), pigpen (Amer)

chirimoya f custard apple

chiripa f fluke

chirri|ar [20] vi creak; <*frenos*> screech; <*pájaro*> chirp. **~do** m creaking; (de frenos) screech; (de pájaros) chirping

chis int sh!, hush!; (□, para llamar a uno) hey!, psst!

chism|e m gadget, thingumajig □; (chismorreo) piece of gossip. **~es** mpl things, bits and pieces. **~orreo** m gossip. **~oso** a gossipy.● m gossip

chisp|a f spark; (pizca) drop; (gracia) wit; (fig) sparkle. **estar que echa ~a(s)** be furious. **~eante** a sparkling. **~ear** vi spark; (lloviznar) drizzle; (fig) sparkle. **~orrotear** vt throw out sparks; <*fuego*> crackle; <*aceite*> spit

chistar vi. **ni chistó** he didn't say a word. **sin ~** without saying a word

chiste m joke, funny story. **tener ~** be funny

chistera f top hat

chistoso a funny

chiva|rse vpr tip-off; <*niño*> tell. **~tazo** m tip-off. **~to** m informer; (niño) telltale

chivo m kid; (LAm, macho cabrío) billy goat

choca|nte a shocking; (Mex, desagradable) unpleasant. **~r** [7] vt clink <*vasos*>; (LAm) crash <*vehículo*>. **¡chócala!** give me five! ● vi collide, hit. **~r con**, **~r contra** crash into

choch|ear vi be gaga. **~o** a gaga; (fig) soft

choclo m (LAm) corn on the cob

chocolate m chocolate. **tableta** f **de ~** bar of chocolate

chófer, (LAm) **chofer** m chauffeur; (conductor) driver

cholo a & m (LAm) half-breed

chopo m poplar

choque m collision; (fig) clash; (eléctrico) shock; (Auto, Rail etc) crash, accident; (sacudida) jolt

chorizo m chorizo

chorro m jet, stream; (caudal pequeño) trickle; (fig) stream. **a ~** <*avión*> jet. **a ~os** (fig) in abundance

chovinista a chauvinistic. ● m & f chauvinist

choza f hut

chubas|co m squall, heavy shower. **~quero** m raincoat, anorak

chuchería f trinket

chueco a (LAm) crooked

chufa f tiger nut

chuleta f chop

chulo a cocky; (bonito) lovely (Brit), neat (Amer); (Mex, atractivo) cute. ● m tough guy; (proxeneta) pimp

chup|ada f suck; (al helado) lick; (al cigarro) puff. **~ado** a skinny; (□, fácil) very easy. ~**ar** *vt* suck; puff at <*cigarro etc*>; (absorber) absorb. ~**ete** *m* dummy (Brit), pacifier (Amer). ~**ón** *m* sucker; (LAm) dummy (Brit), pacifier (Amer); (Mex, del biberón) teat

churrasco *m* barbecued steak; (LAm) steak

churro *m* fritter; 🅸 mess

chut|ar *vi* shoot. ~**e** *m* shot

cianuro *m* cyanide

cibernética *f* cybernetics

cicatriz *f* scar. ~**ar** [10] *vt/i* heal. □ ~**arse** *vpr* heal

cíclico *a* cyclic(al)

ciclis|mo *m* cycling. ~**ta** *a* cycle. ● *m & f* cyclist

ciclo *m* cycle; (de películas, conciertos) season; (de conferencias) series

ciclomotor *m* moped

ciclón *m* cyclone

ciego *a* blind. ● *m* blind man, blind person. **a ciegas** in the dark

cielo *m* sky; (Relig) heaven; (persona) darling. ¡~**s!** good heavens!, goodness me!

ciempiés *m invar* centipede

cien *a* a hundred. ~ **por** ~ one hundred per cent

ciénaga *f* bog, swamp

ciencia *f* science; (fig) knowledge. ~**s** *fpl* (Univ etc) science. ~**s empresariales** business studies. **a** ~ **cierta** for certain

cieno *m* mud

científico *a* scientific. ● *m* scientist

ciento *a & m* a hundred, one hundred. ~**s de** hundreds of. **por** ~ per cent

cierre *m* fastener; (acción de cerrar) shutting, closing; (LAm, cremallera) zip, zipper (Amer)

cierro *vb* ⇒CERRAR

cierto *a* certain; (verdad) true. **estar en lo** ~ be right. **lo** ~ **es que**

the fact is that. **no es** ~ that's not true. ¿**no es** ~? isn't that right? **por** ~ by the way. **si bien es** ~ **que** although

ciervo *m* deer

cifra *f* figure, number; (cantidad) sum. **en** ~ coded, in code. ~**do** *a* coded. ~**r** *vt* code

cigala *f* crayfish

cigarra *f* cicada

cigarr|illera *f* cigarette box; (de bolsillo) cigarette case. ~**illo** *m* cigarette. ~**o** *m* (cigarrillo) cigarette; (puro) cigar

cigüeña *f* stork

cilantro *m* coriander

cil|índrico *a* cylindrical. ~**indro** *m* cylinder

cima *f* top; (fig) summit

cimbr|ear *vt* shake. □ ~**earse** *vpr* sway. ~**onada** *f*, ~**onazo** *m* (LAm) jolt; (de explosión) blast

cimentar [1] *vt* lay the foundations of; (fig, reforzar) strengthen

cimientos *mpl* foundations

cinc *m* zinc

cincel *m* chisel. ~**ar** *vt* chisel

cinco *a & m* five; (en fechas) fifth

cincuent|a *a & m* fifty; (quincuagésimo) fiftieth. ~**ón** *a* in his fifties

cine *m* cinema; (local) cinema (Brit), movie theater (Amer). ~**asta** *m & f* film maker (Brit), movie maker (Amer). ~**matográfico** *a* film (Brit), movie (Amer)

cínico *a* cynical. ● *m* cynic

cinismo *m* cynicism

cinta *f* ribbon; (película) film (Brit), movie (Amer); (para grabar, en carreras) tape. ~ **aislante** insulating tape. ~ **métrica** tape measure. ~ **virgen** blank tape

C

cintur|a *f* waist. **~ón** *m* belt. **~ón de seguridad** safety belt. **~ón salvavidas** lifebelt

ciprés *m* cypress (tree)

circo *m* circus

circuito *m* circuit; (viaje) tour. **~ cerrado** closed circuit. **corto ~** short circuit

circula|ción *f* circulation; (vehículos) traffic. **~r** *a* circular. ● *vi* circulate; <líquidos> flow; (conducir) drive; (caminar) walk; <autobús> run

círculo *m* circle. **~ vicioso** vicious circle. **en ~** in a circle

circunci|dar *vt* circumcise. **~sión** *f* circumcision

circunferencia *f* circumference

circunflejo *m* circumflex

circunscri|bir (*pp* **circunscrito**) *vt* confine. □ **~birse** *vpr* confine o.s. (a to). **~pción** *f* (distrito) district. **~pción electoral** constituency

circunspecto *a* circumspect

circunstancia *f* circumstance

circunv|alar *vt* bypass. **~olar** *vt* [2] circle

cirio *m* candle

ciruela *f* plum. **~ pasa** prune

ciru|gía *f* surgery. **~jano** *m* surgeon

cisne *m* swan

cisterna *f* tank, cistern

cita *f* appointment; (entre chico y chica) date; (referencia) quotation. **~ción** *f* quotation; (Jurid) summons. **~do** *a* aforementioned. **~r** *vt* make an appointment with; (mencionar) quote; (Jurid) summons. □ **~rse** *vpr* arrange to meet

cítara *f* zither

ciudad *f* town; (grande) city. **~ balneario** (LAm) coastal resort. **~ perdida** (Mex) shanty town. **~ universitaria** university campus. **~anía** *f* citizenship; (habitantes) citizens. **~ano** *a* civic. ● *m* citizen, inhabitant

cívico *a* civic

civil *a* civil. ● *m & f* civil guard; (persona no militar) civilian

civiliza|ción *f* civilization. **~r** [10] *vt* civilize. □ **~rse** *vpr* become civilized

civismo *m* community spirit

clam|ar *vi* cry out, clamour. **~or** *m* clamour; (protesta) outcry. **~oroso** *a* noisy; (éxito) resounding

clandestino *a* clandestine, secret; <periódico> underground

clara *f* (de huevo) egg white

claraboya *f* skylight

clarear *vi* dawn; (aclarar) brighten up

clarete *m* rosé

claridad *f* clarity; (luz) light

clarifica|ción *f* clarification. **~r** [7] *vt* clarify

clar|ín *m* bugle. **~inete** *m* clarinet. **~inetista** *m & f* clarinettist

clarividen|cia *f* clairvoyance; (fig) far-sightedness. **~te** *a* clairvoyant; (fig) far-sighted

claro *a* clear; (luminoso) bright; <colores> light; <líquido> thin. ● *m* (en bosque etc) clearing; (espacio) gap. ● *adv* clearly. ● *int* of course! ¡**~ que sí**! yes, of course! ¡**~ que no**! of course not!

clase *f* class; (tipo) kind, sort; (aula) classroom. **~ media** middle class. **~ obrera** working class. **~ social** social class. **dar ~s** teach

clásico *a* classical; (típico) classic. ● *m* classic

C

clasifica|ción f classification; (deportes) league. ~**r** [7] vt classify; (seleccionar) sort

claustro m cloister; (Univ) staff

claustrof|obia f claustrophobia. ~**óbico** a claustrophobic

cláusula f clause

clausura f closure; (ceremonia) closing ceremony. ~**r** vt close

clava|do a fixed; (con clavo) nailed. **es** ~**do a su padre** he's the spitting image of his father. ● m (LAm) dive. ~**r** vt knock in <clavo>; stick in <cuchillo>; (fijar) fix; (juntar) nail together

clave f key; (Mus) clef; (instrumento) harpsichord. ~**cín** m harpsichord

clavel m carnation

clavícula f collarbone, clavicle

clav|ija f peg; (Elec) plug. ~**o** m nail; (Culin) clove

claxon m /'klakson/ (pl ~**s**) horn

clementina f clementine

cleptómano m kleptomaniac

clerical a clerical

clérigo m priest

clero m clergy

clic m: **hacer** ~ **en** click on

cliché m cliché; (Foto) negative

cliente m customer; (de médico) patient; (de abogado) client. ~**la** f clientele, customers; (de médico) patients

clim|a m climate; (ambiente) atmosphere. ~**ático** a climatic. ~**atizado** a air-conditioned

clínic|a f clinic. ~**o** a clinical

cloaca f drain, sewer

clon m clone

cloro m chlorine

club m (pl ~**s** o ~**es**) club

coacci|ón f coercion. ~**onar** vt coerce

coagular vt coagulate; clot <sangre>; curdle <leche>. □ ~**se**

vpr coagulate; <sangre> clot; <leche> curdle

coalición f coalition

coarta|da f alibi. ~**r** vt hinder; restrict <libertad etc>

cobard|e a cowardly. ● m coward. ~**ía** f cowardice

cobert|izo m shed. ~**ura** f covering

cobij|a f (Mex, manta) blanket. ~**as** fpl (LAm, ropa de cama) bedclothes. ~**ar** vt shelter. □ ~**arse** vpr (take) shelter. ~**o** m shelter

cobra f cobra

cobra|dor m collector; (de autobús) conductor. ~**r** vt collect; (ganar) earn; charge <precio>; cash <cheque>; (recuperar) recover. ● vi be paid

cobr|e m copper. ~**izo** a coppery

cobro m collection; (de cheque) cashing; (pago) payment. **presentar al** ~ cash

cocaína f cocaine

cocción f cooking; (Tec) firing

coc|er [2 & 9] vt/i cook; (hervir) boil; (Tec) fire. ~**ido** m stew

coche m car, automobile (Amer); (de tren) coach, carriage; (de bebé) pram (Brit), baby carriage (Amer). ~**-cama** sleeper. ~ **fúnebre** hearse. ~ **restaurante** dining-car. ~**s de choque** dodgems. ~**ra** f garage; (de autobuses) depot

cochin|ada f dirty thing. ~**o** a dirty, filthy. ● m pig

cociente m quotient. ~ **intelectual** intelligence quotient, IQ

cocin|a f kitchen; (arte) cookery, cuisine; (aparato) cooker. ~**a de gas** gas cooker. ~**a eléctrica** electric cooker. ~**ar** vt/i cook. ~**ero** m cook

coco m coconut; (árbol) coconut palm; (cabeza) head; (que mete

miedo) bogeyman. **comerse el ~**
think hard

cocoa f (LAm) cocoa

cocodrilo m crocodile

cocotero m coconut palm

cóctel m (pl ~**s** o ~**es**) cocktail

cod|azo m nudge (with one's
elbow). ~**ear** vt/i elbow, nudge.
□ ~**arse** vpr rub shoulders (**con**
with)

codici|a f greed. ~**ado** a coveted,
sought after. ~**ar** vt covet. ~**oso**
a greedy

código m code. ~ **de la circulación**
Highway Code

codo m elbow; (dobladura) bend. ~
a ~ side by side. **hablar (hasta)
por los ~s** talk too much

codorniz m quail

coeficiente m coefficient. ~
intelectual intelligence quotient,
IQ

coerción f constraint

coetáneo a & m contemporary

coexist|encia f coexistence. ~**ir**
vi coexist

cofradía f brotherhood

cofre m chest; (Mex, capó) bonnet
(Brit), hood (Amer)

coger [14] vt (esp Esp) take; catch
<tren, autobús, pelota, catarro>;
(agarrar) take hold of; (del suelo)
pick up; pick <frutos etc>. □ ~**se**
vpr trap, catch; (agarrarse) hold on

cogollo m (de lechuga etc) heart;
(brote) bud

cogote m nape; (LAm, cuello) neck

cohech|ar vt bribe. ~**o** m
bribery

cohe|rente a coherent. ~**sión** f
cohesion

cohete m rocket

cohibi|do a shy; (inhibido)
awkward; (incómodo) awkward. ~**r**
vt inhibit; (incomodar) make s.o.
feel embarrassed. □ ~**rse** vpr
feel inhibited

coima f (LAm) bribe

coincid|encia f coincidence. **dar
la ~encia** happen. ~**ir** vt coincide

coje|ar vt limp; <mueble> wobble.
~**ra** f lameness

coj|ín m cushion. ~**inete** m small
cushion

cojo a lame; <mueble> wobbly. ●
m lame person

col f cabbage. ~**es de Bruselas**
Brussel sprouts

cola f tail; (fila) queue; (para pegar)
glue. **a la ~** at the end. **hacer ~**
queue (up) (Brit), line up (Amer)

colabora|ción f collaboration.
~**dor** m collaborator. ~**r** vi
collaborate

colada f washing. **hacer la ~** do
the washing

colador m strainer

colapso m collapse; (fig)
standstill

colar [2] vt strain; pass <moneda
falsa etc>. ● vi <líquido> seep
through; (fig) be believed. □ ~**se**
vpr slip; (en una cola) jump the
queue; (en fiesta) gatecrash

colch|a f bedspread. ~**ón** m
mattress. ~**oneta** f air bed; (en
gimnasio) mat.

colear vi wag its tail; <asunto>
not be resolved. **vivito y coleando**
alive and kicking

colecci|ón f collection. ~**onar** vt
collect. ~**onista** m & f collector

colecta f collection

colectivo a collective

colega m & f colleague

colegi|al m schoolboy. ~**ala** f
schoolgirl. ~**o** m school; (de ciertas
profesiones) college. ~**o mayor** hall
of residence

cólera *m* cholera. ● *f* anger, fury. **montar en** ~ fly into a rage

colérico *a* furious, irate

colesterol *m* cholesterol

coleta *f* pigtail

colga|nte *a* hanging. ● *m* pendant. ~**r** [2 & 12] *vt* hang; hang up <*ropa lavada*>; hang up <*abrigo etc*>; put down <*teléfono*>. ● *vi* hang; (teléfono) hang up. □ ~**rse** *vpr* hang o.s. **dejar a uno** ~**do** let s.o. down

colibrí *m* hummingbird

cólico *m* colic

coliflor *f* cauliflower

colilla *f* cigarette end

colina *f* hill

colinda|nte *a* adjoining. ~**r** *vt* border (**con** on)

colisión *f* collision, crash; (fig) clash

collar *m* necklace; (de perro) collar

colmar *vt* fill to the brim; try <*paciencia*>; (fig) fulfill. ~ **a uno de atenciones** lavish attention on s.o.

colmena *f* beehive, hive

colmillo *m* eye tooth, canine (tooth); (de elefante) tusk; (de carnívoro) fang

colmo *m* height. **ser el** ~ be the limit, be the last straw

coloca|ción *f* positioning; (empleo) job, place; (buscar empleo) find ~**r** [7] *vt* put, place; (buscar empleo) find work for. □ ~**rse** *vpr* find a job

Colombia *f* Colombia

colombiano *a & m* Colombian

colon *m* colon

colón *m* (unidad monetaria de Costa Rica y El Salvador) colon

colon|ia *f* colony; (comunidad) community; (agua de colonia) cologne; (Mex, barrio) residential suburb. ~**a de verano** holiday camp. ~**iaje** *m* (LAm) colonial period. ~**ial** *a* colonial. ~**ialista** *m & f* colonialist. ~**ización** *f* colonization. ~**izar** [10] colonize. ~**o** *m* colonist, settler; (labrador) tenant farmer

coloqui|al *a* colloquial. ~**o** *m* conversation; (congreso) conference

color *m* colour. **de** ~ colour. **en** ~(**es**) <*fotos, película*> colour. ~**ado** *a* (rojo) red. ~**ante** *m* colouring. ~**ear** *vt/i* colour. ~**ete** *m* blusher. ~**ido** *m* colour

colosal *a* colossal; (fig, 🄵, magnífico) terrific

columna *f* column; (Anat) spine. ~ **vertebral** spinal column; (fig) backbone

columpi|ar *vt* swing. □ ~**arse** *vpr* swing. ~**o** *m* swing

coma *f* comma; (Mat) point. ● *m* (Med) coma

comadre *f* (madrina) godmother; (amiga) friend. ~**ar** *vi* gossip

comadreja *f* weasel

comadrona *f* midwife

comal *m* (Mex) griddle

comand|ancia *f* command. ~**ante** *m & f* commander. ~**o** *m* command; (Mil, soldado) commando; (de terroristas) cell

comarca *f* area, region

comba *f* bend; (juguete) skipping-rope; (de viga) sag. **saltar a la** ~ skip. □ ~**rse** *vpr* bend; <*viga*> sag

combat|e *m* combat; (pelea) fight. ~**iente** *m* fighter. ~**ir** *vt/i* fight

combina|ción *f* combination; (enlace) connection; (prenda) slip. ~**r** *vt* combine; put together <*colores*>

combustible *m* fuel

comedia *f* comedy; (cualquier obra de teatro) play; (LAm, telenovela) soap (opera)

comedi|do a restrained; (LAm, atento) obliging. □ **~rse** [5] vpr show restraint

comedor m dining-room; (restaurante) restaurant

comensal m companion at table, fellow diner

comentar vt comment on; discuss <tema>; (mencionar) mention. **~io** m commentary; (observación) comment. **~ios** mpl gossip. **~ista** m & f commentator

comenzar [1 & 10] vt/i begin

comer vt eat; (a mediodía) have for lunch; (esp LAm, cenar) have for dinner; (corroer) eat away; (en ajedrez) take. ● vi eat; (a mediodía) have lunch; (esp LAm, cenar) have dinner. **dar de ~ a** feed. □ **~se** vpr eat (up)

comerci|al a commercial; <ruta> trade; <nombre, trato> business. ● m (LAm) commercial, ad. **~ante** m trader; (de tienda) shopkeeper. **~ar** vi trade (**con** with, **en** in); (con otra persona) do business. **~o** m commerce; (actividad) trade; (tienda) shop; (negocios) business

comestible a edible. **~s** mpl food. **tienda de ~s** grocer's (shop) (Brit), grocery (Amer)

cometa m comet. ● f kite

comet|er vt commit; make <falta>. **~ido** m task

comezón m itch

comicios mpl elections

cómico a comic; (gracioso) funny. ● m comic actor; (humorista) comedian

comida f food; (a mediodía) lunch; (esp LAm, cena) dinner; (acto) meal. **~ corrida** (Mex) set menu

comidilla f. **ser la ~ del pueblo** be the talk of the town

comienzo m beginning, start

comillas fpl inverted commas

comil|ón a greedy. **~ona** f feast

comino m cumin. **(no) me importa un ~** I couldn't care less

comisar|ía f police station. **~io** m commissioner; (deportes) steward

comisión f assignment; (organismo) commission, committee; (Com) commission

comisura f corner. **~ de los labios** corner of the mouth

comité m committee

como prep as; (comparación) like. ● adv about. ● conj as. **~ quieras** as you like. **~ si** as if

. . . .

cómo

● adverbio

····▶ how. ¿**~ se llega?** how do you get there? ¿**~ es de alto?** how tall is it? **sé ~ pasó** I know how it happened

! Cuando **cómo** va seguido del verbo **llamar** se traduce por *what*, p. ej. ¿**~ te llamas?** *what's your name?*

····▶ **cómo + ser** (sugiriendo descripción) ¿**~ es su marido?** what's her husband like?; (físicamente) what does her husband look like? **no sé ~ es la comida** I don't know what the food's like

····▶ (por qué) why. ¿**~ no actuaron antes?** why didn't they act sooner?

····▶ (pidiendo que se repita) sorry?, pardon? ¿**~? no te escuché** sorry? I didn't hear you

····▶ (en exclamaciones) ¡**~ llueve!** it's really pouring! ¡**~!** ¿**que no lo sabes?** what! you mean you don't know? ¡**~ no!** of course!

. . . .

cómoda f chest of drawers

comodidad *f* comfort. **a su** ∼ at your convenience

cómodo *a* comfortable; (*conveniente*) convenient

comoquiera *conj.* ∼ **que sea** however it may be

compacto *a* compact; (*denso*) dense; *<líneas etc>* close

compadecer [11] *vt* feel sorry for. □ ∼**se** *vpr*. ∼**se de** feel sorry for

compadre *m* godfather; (*amigo*) friend

compañero *m* companion; (*de trabajo*) colleague; (*de clase*) classmate; (*pareja*) partner. ∼**ía** *f* company. **en** ∼**ía de** with

comparable *a* comparable. ∼**ción** *f* comparison. ∼**r** *vt* compare. ∼**tivo** *a* & *m* comparative

comparecer [11] *vi* appear

comparsa *f* group. ● *m* & *f* (en el teatro) extra

compartim(i)ento *m* compartment

compartir *vt* share

compás *m* (*instrumento*) (pair of) compasses; (*ritmo*) rhythm; (*división*) bar (Brit), measure (Amer); (Naut) compass. **a** ∼ in time

compasión *f* compassion, pity. **tener** ∼**ón de** feel sorry for. ∼**vo** *a* compassionate

compatibilidad *f* compatibility. ∼**le** *a* compatible

compatriota *m* & *f* compatriot

compendio *m* summary

compensación *f* compensation. ∼**ción por despido** redundancy payment. ∼**r** *vt* compensate

competencia *f* competition; (*capacidad*) competence; (*poder*) authority; (*incumbencia*) jurisdiction. ∼**te** *a* competent

competición *f* competition. ∼**dor** *m* competitor. ∼**r** [5] *vi* compete

compinche *m* accomplice; (fam, amigo) friend, mate 🔲

complacer [32] *vt* please. □ ∼**erse** *vpr* be pleased. ∼**iente** *a* obliging; *<marido>* complaisant

complejidad *f* complexity. ∼**o** *a* & *m* complex

complementario *a* complementary. ∼**o** *m* complement; (Gram) object, complement

completar *vt* complete. ∼**o** *a* complete; (*lleno*) full; (*exhaustivo*) comprehensive

complexión *f* build

complicación *f* complication; (esp AmL, *implicación*) involvement. ∼**r** [7] *vt* complicate; involve *<persona>*. □ ∼**rse** *vpr* become complicated; (*implicarse*) get involved

cómplice *m* & *f* accomplice

complot *m* (*pl* ∼**s**) plot

componente *a* component. ● *m* component; (*miembro*) member. ∼**er** [34] *vt* make up; (Mus, Literatura etc) write, compose; (esp LAm, *reparar*) mend; (LAm) set *<hueso>*; settle *<estómago>*. □ ∼**erse** *vpr* be made up; (*arreglarse*) get better. ∼**érselas** manage

comportamiento *m* behaviour. □ ∼**rse** *vpr* behave. ∼**rse mal** misbehave

composición *f* composition. ∼**tor** *m* composer

compostura *f* composure; (LAm, *arreglo*) repair

compota *f* stewed fruit

compra *f* purchase. ∼ **a plazos** hire purchase. **hacer la(s)** ∼**(s)** do the shopping. **ir de** ∼**s** go shopping. ∼**dor** *m* buyer. ∼**r** *vt* buy. **~venta** f buying and selling; (Jurid) sale and purchase contract. **negocio** m **de ~venta** second-hand shop

compren|der vt understand; (incluir) include. **~sión** f understanding. **~sivo** a understanding

compresa f compress; (de mujer) sanitary towel

compr|esión f compression. **~imido** a compressed. ● m pill, tablet. **~imir** vt compress

comproba|nte m proof; (recibo) receipt. **~r** vt check; (demostrar) prove

comprom|eter vt compromise; (arriesgar) jeopardize. □ **~eterse** vpr compromise o.s.; (obligarse) agree to; <novios> get engaged. **~etido** a <situación> awkward, delicate; <autor> politically committed. **~iso** m obligation; (apuro) predicament; (cita) appointment; (acuerdo) agreement. **sin ~iso** without obligation

compuesto a compound; <persona> smart. ● m compound

computa|ción f (esp LAm) computing. **curso** m **de ~ción** computer course. **~dor** m, **~dora** f computer. **~r** vt calculate. **~rizar, computerizar** [10] vt computerize

cómputo m calculation

comulgar [12] vi take Communion

común a common; (compartido) joint. **en ~** in common. **por lo ~** generally. ● m. **el ~ de** most

comunal a communal

comunica|ción f communication. **~do** m communiqué. **~do de prensa** press release. **~r** [7] vt communicate; (informar) inform; (LAm, por teléfono) put through. **está** **~ndo** <teléfono> it's engaged. □ **~rse** vpr communicate; (ponerse en contacto) get in touch. **~tivo** a communicative

comunidad f community. **~ de vecinos** residents' association. **C~ (Económica) Europea** European (Economic) Community. **en ~** together

comunión f communion; (Relig) (Holy) Communion

comunis|mo m communism. **~ta** a & m & f communist

con prep with; (+ infinitivo) by. **~ decir la verdad** by telling the truth. **~ que** so. **~ tal que** as long as

concebir [5] vt/i conceive

conceder vt concede, grant; award <premio>; (admitir) admit

concej|al m councillor. **~ero** m (LAm) councillor. **~o** m council

concentra|ción f concentration; (Pol) rally. **~r** vt concentrate; assemble <personas>. □ **~rse** vpr concentrate

concep|ción f conception. **~to** m concept; (opinión) opinion. **bajo ningún ~to** in no way

concerniente a. **en lo ~ a** with regard to

concertar [1] vt arrange; agree (upon) <plan>

concesión f concession

concha f shell; (carey) tortoiseshell

conciencia f conscience; (conocimiento) awareness. **~ limpia** clear conscience. **~ sucia** guilty conscience. **a ~ de que** fully aware that. **en ~** honestly. **tener ~ de** be aware of. **tomar ~ de** become aware of. **~r** vt make aware. **~rse** vpr become aware

concientizar [10] vt (esp LAm) make aware. □ **~se** vpr become aware

conciezudo *a* conscientious

concierto *m* concert; (acuerdo) agreement; (Mus, composición) concerto

concilia|ción *f* reconciliation. **~r** *vt* reconcile. **~r el sueño** get to sleep. □ **~rse** *vpr* gain

concilio *m* council

conciso *a* concise

conclu|ir [17] *vt* finish; (deducir) conclude. ● *vi* finish, end. **~sión** *f* conclusion. **~yente** *a* conclusive

concord|ancia *f* agreement. **~ar** [2] *vt* reconcile. ● *vi* agree. **~e** *a* in agreement. **~ia** *f* harmony

concret|amente *adv* specifically, to be exact. **~ar** *vt* make specific. **~arse** *vpr* become definite; (limitarse) confine o.s. **~o** *a* concrete; (determinado) specific, particular. **en ~o** definite; (concretamente) to be exact; (en resumen) in short. ● *m* (LAm, hormigón) concrete

concurr|encia *f* concurrence; (reunión) audience. **~ido** *a* crowded, busy. **~ir** *vi* meet; ; (coincidir) agree. **~ a** (asistir a) attend

concurs|ante *m & f* competitor, contestant. **~ar** *vi* compete, take part. **~o** *m* competition; (ayuda) help

cond|ado *m* county. **~e** *m* earl, count

condena *f* sentence. **~ción** *f* condemnation. **~do** *m* convicted person. **~r** *vt* condemn; (Jurid) convict

condensa|ción *f* condensation. **~r** *vt* condense

condesa *f* countess

condescende|ncia *f* condescension; (tolerancia) indulgence. **~r** [1] *vi* agree; (dignarse) condescend

condici|ón *f* condition. **a ~ón de (que)** on condition that. **~onal** *a* conditional. **~onar** *vt* condition

condiment|ar *vt* season. **~o** *m* seasoning

condolencia *f* condolence

condominio *m* joint ownership; (LAm, edificio) block of flats (Brit), condominium (esp Amer)

condón *m* condom

condonar *vt* (perdonar) reprieve; cancel <*deuda*>

conducir [47] *vt* drive <*vehículo*>; carry <*electricidad, gas, agua*>. ● *vi* drive; (fig, llevar) lead. **¿a qué conduce?** what's the point? □ **~se** *vpr* behave

conducta *f* behaviour

conducto *m* pipe, tube; (Anat) duct. **por ~ de** through. **~r** *m* driver; (jefe) leader; (Elec) conductor

conduzco *vb* ⇒CONDUCIR

conectar *vt/i* connect

conejo *m* rabbit

conexión *f* connection

confabularse *vpr* plot

confecci|ón *f* (de trajes) tailoring; (de vestidos) dressmaking. **~ones** *fpl* clothing, clothes. **de ~ón** ready-to-wear. **~onar** *vt* make

confederación *f* confederation

conferencia *f* conference; (al teléfono) long-distance call; (Univ) lecture. **~ en la cima**, **~ (en la) cumbre** summit conference. **~nte** *m & f* lecturer

conferir [4] *vt* confer; award <*premio*>

confes|ar [1] *vt/i* confess. □ **~arse** *vpr* confess. **~ión** *f* confession. **~ionario** *m* confessional. **~or** *m* confessor

confeti *m* confetti

confia|do *a* trusting; (seguro de sí mismo) self-confident. **~nza** *f* trust; (en sí mismo) confidence; (intimidad) familiarity. **~r** [20] *vt* entrust. ● *vi*. **~r en** trust

confiden|cia *f* confidence, secret. **~cial** *a* confidential. **~te** *m* confidant. ●*f* confidante

conf|ín *m* border. **~ines** *mpl* outermost parts. **~inar** *vt* confine; (desterrar) banish

confirma|ción *f* confirmation. **~r** *vt* confirm

confiscar [7] *vt* confiscate

confit|ería *f* sweet-shop (Brit), candy store (Amer). **~ura** *f* jam

conflict|ivo *a* difficult; <*época*> troubled; (polémico) controversial. **~o** *m* conflict

confluencia *f* confluence

conform|ación *f* conformation, shape. **~ar** *vt* (acomodar) adjust. ● *vi* agree. □ **~arse** *vpr* conform. **~e** *a* in agreement; (contento) happy, satisfied; (según) according (**con** to). **~e a** in accordance with, according to. ● *conj* as. ● *int* OK!. **~idad** *f* agreement; (tolerancia) resignation. **~ista** *m & f* conformist

conforta|ble *a* comfortable. **~nte** *a* comforting. **~r** *vt* comfort

confronta|ción *f* confrontation. **~r** *vt* confront

confu|ndir *vt* (equivocar) mistake, confuse; (mezclar) mix up, confuse; (turbar) embarrass. □ **~ndirse** *vpr* become confused; (equivocarse) make a mistake. **~sión** *f* confusion; (vergüenza) embarrassment. **~so** *a* confused; (borroso) blurred

congela|do *a* frozen. **~dor** *m* freezer. **~r** *vt* freeze

congeniar *vi* get on

congesti|ón *f* congestion. **~onado** *a* congested. □ **~onarse** *vpr* become congested

congoja *f* distress; (pena) grief

congraciarse *vpr* ingratiate o.s.

congratular *vt* congratulate

congrega|ción *f* gathering; (Relig) congregation. □ **~rse** [12] *vpr* gather, assemble

congres|ista *m & f* delegate, member of a congress. **~o** *m* congress, conference. C**~o** Parliament. C**~o de los Diputados** Chamber of Deputies

cónico *a* conical

conifer|a *f* conifer. **~o** *a* coniferous

conjetura *f* conjecture, guess. **~r** *vt* conjecture, guess

conjuga|ción *f* conjugation. **~r** [12] *vt* conjugate

conjunción *f* conjunction

conjunto *a* joint. ● *m* collection; (Mus) band; (ropa) suit, outfit. **en ~** altogether

conjurar *vt* exorcise; avert <*peligro*>. ● *vi* plot, conspire

conllevar *vt* to entail

conmemora|ción *f* commemoration. **~r** *vt* commemorate

conmigo *pron* with me

conmo|ción *f* shock; (tumulto) upheaval. **~ cerebral** concussion. **~cionar** *vt* shock. **~ver** [2] *vt* shake; (emocionar) move

conmuta|dor *m* switch; (LAm, de teléfonos) switchboard. **~r** *vt* exchange

connota|ción *f* connotation. **~do** *a* (LAm, destacado) distinguished. **~r** *vt* connote

cono *m* cone

conoc|edor *a & m* expert. **~er** [11] *vt* know; (por primera vez) meet; (reconocer) recognize, know. **se conoce que** apparently. **dar a ~er** make known. □ **~erse** *vpr* know o.s.; <*dos personas*> know each other; (notarse) be obvious. **~ido** *a*

well-known. ● *m* acquaintance.
~imiento *m* knowledge; (sentido)
consciousness. **sin ~imiento**
unconscious. **tener ~imiento de**
know about

conozco *vb* ⇒CONOCER

conque *conj* so

conquista *f* conquest. **~dor** *a*
conquering. ● *m* conqueror; (de
América) conquistador. **~r** *vt*
conquer, win

consabido *a* usual, habitual

consagra|ción *f* consecration.
~r *vt* consecrate; (fig) devote.
□ **~rse** *vpr* devote o.s.

consanguíneo *m* blood relation

consciente *a* conscious

consecuen|cia *f* consequence;
(coherencia) consistency. **a ~cia de**
as a result of. **~te** *a* consistent

consecutivo *a* consecutive

conseguir [5 & 13] *vt* get, obtain;
(lograr) manage; achieve <*objetivo*>

consej|ero *m* adviser; (miembro de
consejo) member. **~o** *m* piece of
advice; (Pol) council. **~o de
ministros** cabinet

consenso *m* assent, consent

consenti|do *a* <*niño*> spoilt.
~miento *m* consent. **~r** [4] *vt*
allow; spoil <*niño*>. ● *vi* consent

conserje *m* porter, caretaker.
~ría *f* porter's office

conserva *f* (mermelada) preserve;
(en lata) tinned food. **en ~** tinned
(Brit), canned. **~ción** *f*
conservation; (de alimentos)
preservation

conservador *a & m* (Pol)
conservative

conservar *vt* keep; preserve
<*alimentos*>. □ **~se** *vpr* keep;
<*costumbre*> survive

conservatorio *m* conservatory

considera|ble *a* considerable.
~ción *f* consideration; (respeto)

respect. **de ~ción** serious. **de mi
~ción** (LAm, en cartas) Dear Sir.
~do *a* considerate; (respetado)
respected. **~r** *vt* consider;
(respetar) respect

consigna *f* order; (para equipaje)
left luggage office (Brit), baggage
room (Amer); (eslogan) slogan

consigo *pron* (él) with him; (ella)
with her; (Ud, Uds) with you; (uno
mismo) with o.s.

consiguiente *a* consequent. **por
~** consequently

consist|encia *f* consistency.
~ente *a* consisting (en of); (firme)
solid; (LAm, congruente) consistent.
~ir *vi*. **~ en** consist of; (radicar en)
be due to

consola|ción *f* consolation. **~r**
[2] *vt* console, comfort. □ **~rse**
vpr console o.s.

consolidar *vt* consolidate. □ **~se**
vpr consolidate

consomé *m* clear soup,
consommé

consonante *a* consonant. ● *f*
consonant

consorcio *m* consortium

conspira|ción *f* conspiracy.
~dor *m* conspirator. **~r** *vi*
conspire

consta|ncia *f* constancy; (prueba)
proof; (LAm, documento) written
evidence. **~nte** *a* constant. **~r** *vi*
be clear; (figurar) appear, figure;
(componerse) consist. **hacer ~r**
state; (por escrito) put on record.
me ~ que I'm sure that. **que
conste que** believe me

constatar *vt* check; (confirmar)
confirm

constipa|do *m* cold. ● *a*. **estar
~do** have a cold; (LAm, estreñido)
be constipated. □ **~rse** *vpr* catch
a cold

constitu|ción *f* constitution;
(establecimiento) setting up.

∼cional a constitutional. **∼ir** [17] vt constitute; (formar) form; (crear) set up, establish. □ **∼irse** vpr set o.s. up (en as). **∼tivo** a, **∼yente** a constituent

constru|cción f construction. **∼ctor** m builder. **∼ir** [17] vt construct; build <edificio>

consuelo m consolation

consuetudinario a customary

cónsul m & f consul

consulado m consulate

consult|a f consultation. **horas** fpl **de ∼a** surgery hours. **obra** f **de ∼a** reference book. **∼ar** vt consult. **∼orio** m surgery

consumar vt complete; commit <crimen>; carry out <robo>; consummate <matrimonio>

consum|ición f consumption; (bebida) drink; (comida) food. **∼ición mínima** minimum charge. **∼ido** a <persona> skinny, wasted. **∼idor** m consumer. **∼ir** vt consume. □ **∼irse** vpr <persona> waste away; <vela, cigarillo> burn down; <líquido> dry up. **∼ismo** m consumerism. **∼o** m consumption; (LAm, en restaurante etc) (bebida) drink; (comida) food. **∼o mínimo** minimum charge

contab|ilidad f book-keeping; (profesión) accountancy. **∼le** m & f accountant

contacto m contact. **ponerse en ∼ con** get in touch with

conta|do a. **al ∼** cash. **∼s** a pl few. **tiene los días ∼s** his days are numbered. **∼dor** m meter; (LAm, persona) accountant

contagi|ar vt infect <persona>; pass on <enfermedad>; (fig) contaminate. **∼o** m infection; (directo) contagion. **∼oso** a infectious; (por contacto directo) contagious

contamina|ción f contamination, pollution. **∼r** vt contaminate, pollute

contante a. **dinero** m **∼** cash

contar [2] vt count; tell <relato>. **se cuenta que** it's said that. ● vi count. **∼ con** rely on, count on. □ **∼se** vpr be included (**entre** among)

contempla|ción f contemplation. **sin ∼ciones** unceremoniously. **∼r** vt look at; (fig) contemplate

contemporáneo a & m contemporary

conten|er [40] vt contain; hold <respiración>. □ **∼erse** vpr contain o.s. **∼ido** a contained. ● m contents

content|ar vt please. □ **∼arse** vpr. **∼arse con** be satisfied with, be pleased with. **∼o** a (alegre) happy; (satisfecho) pleased

contesta|ción f answer. **∼dor** m. **∼ automático** answering machine. **∼r** vt/i answer; (replicar) answer back

contexto m context

contienda f conflict; (lucha) contest

contigo pron with you

contiguo a adjacent

continen|tal a continental. **∼te** m continent

continu|ación f continuation. **a ∼ación** immediately after. **∼ar** [21] vt continue, resume. ● vi continue. **∼idad** f continuity. **∼o** a continuous; (frecuente) continual. **corriente** f **∼a** direct current

contorno m outline; (de árbol) girth; (de caderas) measurement. **∼s** mpl surrounding area

contorsión f contortion

contra prep against. **en ∼** against. ● m cons. ● f snag. **llevar la ∼** contradict

contraata|car [7] *vt/i* counter-attack. **~que** *m* counter-attack.

contrabaj|ista *m & f* double-bass player. **~o** *m* double-bass; (persona) double-bass player

contraband|ista *m & f* smuggler. **~o** *m* contraband

contracción *f* contraction

contrad|ecir [46] *vt* contradict. **~icción** *f* contradiction. **~ictorio** *a* contradictory

contraer [41] *vt* contract. **~matrimonio** marry. □ **~se** *vpr* contract

contralto *m* counter tenor. ● *f* contralto

contra|mano. a ~ in the wrong direction. **~partida** *f* compensation. **~pelo. a ~** the wrong way

contrapes|ar *vt* counterweight. **~o** *m* counterweight

contraproducente *a* counter-productive

contrari|a *f*. **llevar la ~a** contradict. **~ado** *a* upset; (enojado) annoyed. **~ar** [20] *vt* upset; (enojar) annoy. **~edad** *f* setback; (disgusto) annoyance. **~o** *a* contrary (**a** to); <*dirección*> opposite. **al ~o** on the contrary. **al ~o de** contrary to. **de lo ~o** otherwise. **por el ~o** on the contrary. **ser ~o a** be opposed to, be against

contrarrestar *vt* counteract

contrasentido *m* contradiction

contraseña *f* (palabra) password; (en cine) stub

contrast|ar *vt* check, verify. ● *vi* contrast. **~e** *m* contrast; (en oro, plata) hallmark

contratar *vt* contract <*servicio*>; hire, take on <*empleados*>; sign up <*jugador*>

contratiempo *m* setback; (accidente) mishap

contrat|ista *m & f* contractor. **~o** *m* contract

contraven|ción *f* contravention. **~ir** [53] *vt* contravene

contraventana *f* shutter

contribu|ción *f* contribution; (tributo) tax. **~ir** [17] *vt/i* contribute. **~yente** *m & f* contributor; (que paga impuestos) taxpayer

contrincante *m* rival, opponent

control *m* control; (vigilancia) check; (lugar) checkpoint. **~ar** *vt* control; (vigilar) check. □ **~se** *vpr* control s.o.

controversia *f* controversy

contundente *a* <*arma*> blunt; <*argumento*> convincing

contusión *f* bruise

convalec|encia *f* convalescence. **~er** [11] *vi* convalesce. **~iente** *a* & *m & f* convalescent

convalidar *vt* recognize <*título*>

convenc|er [9] *vt* convince. **~imiento** *m* conviction

convenci|ón *f* convention. **~onal** *a* conventional

conveni|encia *f* convenience; (aptitud) suitability. **~ente** *a* suitable; (aconsejable) advisable; (provechoso) useful. **~o** *m* agreement. **~r** [53] *vt* agree. ● *vi* agree (**en** on); (ser conveniente) be convenient for, suit; (ser aconsejable) be advisable

convento *m* (de monjes) monastery; (de monjas) convent

conversa|ción *f* conversation. **~ciones** *fpl* talks. **~r** *vi* converse, talk

conver|sión *f* conversion. **~so** *a* converted. ● *m* convert. **~tible** *a* convertible. ● *m* (LAm) convertible. **~tir** [4] *vt* convert. □ **~tirse** *vpr*. **~tirse en** turn into; (Relig) convert

convic|ción f conviction. **~to** a convicted

convida|do m guest. **~r** vt invite

convincente a convincing

conviv|encia f coexistence; (de parejas) life together. **~ir** vi live together; (coexistir) coexist

convocar [7] vt call <huelga, elecciones>; convene <reunión>; summon <personas>

convulsión f convulsion

conyugal a marital, conjugal; <vida> married

cónyuge m spouse. **~s** mpl married couple

coñac m (pl ~s) brandy

coopera|ción f cooperation. **~r** vi cooperate. **~tiva** f cooperative. **~tivo** a cooperative

coordinar vt coordinate

copa f glass; (deportes, fig) cup; (de árbol) top. **~s** fpl (naipes) hearts. **tomar una ~** have a drink

copia f copy. **~ en limpio** fair copy. **sacar una ~** make a copy. **~r** vt copy

copioso a copious; <lluvia, nevada etc> heavy

copla f verse; (canción) folksong

copo m flake. **~ de nieve** snowflake. **~s de maíz** cornflakes

coquet|a f flirt; (mueble) dressing-table. **~ear** vi flirt. **~o** a flirtatious

coraje m courage; (rabia) anger

coral a choral. ● m coral; (Mus) chorale

coraza f cuirass; (Naut) armour-plating; (de tortuga) shell

coraz|ón m heart; (persona) darling. **sin ~ón** heartless. **tener buen ~ón** be good-hearted. **~onada** f hunch; (impulso) impulse

corbata f tie, necktie (esp Amer). **~ de lazo** bow tie

corche|a f quaver. **~te** m fastener, hook and eye; (gancho) hook; (paréntesis) square bracket

corcho m cork. **~lata** f (Mex) (crown) cap

corcovado a hunchbacked

cordel m cord, string

cordero m lamb

cordial a cordial, friendly. ● m tonic. **~idad** f cordiality, warmth

cordillera f mountain range

córdoba m (unidad monetaria de Nicaragua) córdoba

cordón m string; (de zapatos) lace; (cable) cord; (fig) cordon. **~ umbilical** umbilical cord

coreografía f choreography

corista f (bailarina) chorus girl

cornet|a f bugle; (Mex, de coche) horn. **~ín** m cornet

coro m (Arquit, Mus) choir; (en teatro) chorus

corona f crown; (de flores) wreath, garland. **~ción** f coronation. **~r** vt crown

coronel m colonel

coronilla f crown. **estar hasta la ~** be fed up

corpora|ción f corporation. **~l** a <castigo> corporal; <trabajo> physical

corpulento a stout

corral m farmyard. **aves** fpl **de ~** poultry

correa f strap; (de perro) lead; (cinturón) belt

correc|ción f correction; (cortesía) good manners. **~to** a correct; (cortés) polite

corrector ortográfico m spell checker

corre|dizo a running. **nudo** m **~dizo** slip knot. **puerta** f **~diza** sliding door. **~dor** m runner; (pasillo) corridor; (agente) agent, broker. **~dor de coches** racing driver

corregir [5 & 14] vt correct

correlación f correlation

correo m post, mail; (persona) courier; (LAm, oficina) post office. **~s** mpl post office. **~ electrónico** e-mail. **echar al ~** post

correr vt run; (mover) move; draw <cortinas>. ● vi run; <agua, electricidad etc> flow; <tiempo> pass. □ **~se** vpr (apartarse) move along; <colores> run

correspond|encia f correspondence. **~er** vi correspond; (ser adecuado) be fitting; (contestar) reply; (pertenecer) belong; (incumbir) fall to. □ **~erse** vpr (amarse) love one another. **~iente** a corresponding

corresponsal m correspondent

corrid|a f run. **~a de toros** bullfight. **de ~a** from memory. **~o** a (continuo) continuous

corriente a <agua> running; <monedas, publicación, cuenta, año> current; (ordinario) ordinary. ● f current; (de aire) draught; (fig) tendency. ● m current month. **al ~** (al día) up-to-date; (enterado) aware

corr|illo m small group. **~o** m circle

corroborar vt corroborate

corroer [24 & 37] vt corrode; (Geol) erode; (fig) eat away

corromper vt corrupt, rot <materia>. □ **~se** vpr become corrupted; <materia> rot; <alimentos> go bad

corrosi|ón f corrosion. **~vo** a corrosive

corrupción f corruption; (de materia etc) rot

corsé m corset

cortacésped m inv lawn-mower

corta|do a cut; <carretera> closed; <leche> curdled; (avergonzado) embarrassed; (confuso) confused. ● m coffee with a little milk. **~dura** f cut. **~nte** a sharp; <viento> biting; <frío> bitter. **~r** vt cut; (recortar) cut out; (aislar, separar, interrumpir) cut off. ● vi cut; <novios> break up. □ **~rse** vpr cut o.s.; <leche etc> curdle; (fig) be embarrassed. **~rse el pelo** have one's hair cut. **~rse las uñas** cut one's nails. **~uñas** m invar nail-clippers

corte m cut; (de tela) length. **~ de luz** power cut. **~ y confección** dressmaking. ● f court; (LAm, tribunal) Court of Appeal. **hacer la ~** court. **las C~s** the Spanish parliament. **la C~ Suprema** the Supreme Court

cortej|ar vt court. **~o** m (de rey etc) entourage. **~o fúnebre** cortège, funeral procession

cortés a polite

cortesía f courtesy

corteza f bark; (de queso) rind; (de pan) crust

cortijo m farm; (casa) farmhouse

cortina f curtain

corto a short; (apocado) shy. **~ de** short of. **~ de alcances** dim, thick. **~ de vista** short-sighted. **a la corta o a la larga** sooner or later. **quedarse ~** fall short; (miscalcular) underestimate. **~circuito** m short circuit

Coruña f. **La ~** Corunna

cosa f thing; (asunto) business; (idea) idea. **como si tal ~** just like that; (como si no hubiera pasado nada) as if nothing had happened. **decirle a uno cuatro ~s** tell s.o. a thing or two

cosecha f harvest; (de vino) vintage. **~r** vt harvest

coser vt sew; sew on <botón>; stitch <herida>. ● vi sew. □ ~**se** vpr stick to s.o.

cosmético a & m cosmetic

cósmico a cosmic

cosmo|polita a & m & f cosmopolitan. ~**s** m cosmos

cosquillas fpl. **dar** ~ tickle. **hacer** ~ tickle. **tener** ~ be ticklish

costa f coast. **a** ~ **de** at the expense of. **a toda** ~ at any cost

costado m side

costal m sack

costar [2] vt cost. ● vi cost; (resultar difícil) to be hard. ~ **caro** be expensive. **cueste lo que cueste** at any cost

costarricense a & m, **costarriqueño** a & m Costa Rican

cost|as fpl (Jurid) costs. ~**e** m cost. ~**ear** vt pay for; (Naut) sail along the coast

costero a coastal

costilla f rib; (chuleta) chop

costo m cost. ~**so** a expensive

costumbre f custom; (de persona) habit. **de** ~ usual; (como adv) usually

costur|a f sewing; (línea) seam; (confección) dressmaking. ~**era** f dressmaker. ~**ero** m sewing box

cotejar vt compare

cotidiano a daily

cotille|ar vt gossip. ~**o** m gossip

cotiza|ción f quotation, price. ~**r** [10] vt (en la bolsa) quote. ● vi pay contributions. □ ~**rse** vpr fetch; (en la bolsa) stand at; (fig) be valued

coto m enclosure; (de caza) preserve. ~ **de caza** game preserve

cotorr|a f parrot; (fig) chatterbox. ~**ear** vi chatter

coyuntura f joint

coz f kick

cráneo m skull

cráter m crater

crea|ción f creation. ~**dor** a creative. ● m creator. ~**r** vt create

crec|er [11] vi grow; (aumentar) increase; <río> rise. ~**ida** f (de río) flood. ~**ido** a <persona> grown-up; <número> large, considerable; <plantas> fully-grown. ~**iente** a growing; <luna> crescent. ~**imiento** m growth

credencial f document. ● a. **cartas** fpl ~**es** credentials

credibilidad f credibility

crédito m credit; (préstamo) loan. **digno de** ~ reliable

credo m creed

crédulo a credulous

cre|encia f belief. ~**er** [18] vt/i believe; (pensar) think. ~**o que no** I don't think so, I think not. ~**o que sí** I think so. **no.** ~**o** I don't think so. **¡ya lo** ~**o!** I should think so!. □ ~**erse** vpr consider o.s. **no me lo** ~**o** I don't believe it. ~**íble** a credible

crema f cream; (Culin) custard; (LAm, de la leche) cream. ~ **batida** (LAm) whipped cream. ~ **bronceadora** sun-tan cream

cremallera f zip (Brit), zipper (Amer)

crematorio m crematorium

crepitar vi crackle

crepúsculo m twilight

crespo a frizzy; (LAm, rizado) curly. ● m (LAm) curl

cresta f crest; (de gallo) comb

creyente m believer

cría f breeding; (animal) baby animal. **las** ~**s** the young

cria|da f maid, servant. ~**dero** m (de pollos etc) farm; (de ostras) bed;

(Bot) nursery. ● *m* servant. **~dor**
m breeder. **~nza** *f* breeding. **~r**
[20] *vt* suckle; grow *<plantas>*;
breed *<animales>*; (educar) bring
up (Brit), raise (esp Amer). □ **~rse**
vpr grow up

criatura *f* creature; (niño) baby

crim|en *m* (serious) crime;
(asesinato) murder; (fig) crime.
~inal *a* & *m* & *f* criminal

crin *f* mane

crío *m* child

criollo *a* Creole; (LAm), *<música,
comida>* traditional. ● *m* Creole;
(LAm, nativo) Peruvian, Chilean etc

crisantemo *m* chrysanthemum

crisis *f invar* crisis

crispar *vt* twitch; (🔒, irritar) annoy.
~le los nervios a uno get on s.o.'s
nerves

cristal *m* crystal; (Esp, vidrio) glass;
(Esp, de una ventana) pane of glass.
limpiar los ~es (Esp) clean the
windows. **~ino** *a* crystalline; (fig)
crystal-clear. **~izar** [10]
crystallize

cristian|dad *f* Christendom.
~ismo *m* Christianity. **~o** *a*
Christian. ● *m* Christian

cristo *m* crucifix

Cristo *m* Christ

criterio *m* criterion; (discernimiento)
judgement; (opinión) opinion

cr|ítica *f* criticism; (reseña) review.
~iticar [7] *vt* criticize. **~ítico** *a*
critical. ● *m* critic

croar *vi* croak

crom|ado *a* chromium-plated.
~o *m* chromium, chrome

crónic|a *f* chronicle; (de radio, TV)
report; (de periódico) feature. **~a
deportiva** sport section. **~o** *a*
chronic

cronista *m* & *f* reporter

cronología *f* chronology

cron|ometrar *vt* time. **~ómetro**
m (en deportes) stop-watch

croqueta *f* croquette

cruce *m* crossing; (de calles,
carreteras) crossroads; (de peatones)
(pedestrian) crossing

crucero *m* cruise; (buque) cruiser;
(Mex) crossroads

crucial *a* crucial

crucifi|car [7] *vt* crucify. **~jo** *m*
crucifix

crucigrama *m* crossword
(puzzle)

crudo *a* raw; (fig) harsh. ● *m*
crude (oil)

cruel *a* cruel. **~dad** *f* cruelty

cruji|do *m* (de seda, de hojas secas)
rustle; (de muebles) creak. **~r** *vi*
<seda, hojas secas> rustle;
<muebles> creak

cruz *f* cross; (de moneda) tails. **~
gamada** swastika. **la C~ Roja** the
Red Cross

cruza|da *f* crusade. **~r** [10] *vt*
cross; exchange *<palabras>*.
□ **~rse** *vpr* cross; (pasar en la calle)
pass each other. **~rse con** pass

cuaderno *m* exercise book; (para
apuntes) notebook

cuadra *f* (caballeriza) stable; (LAm,
distancia) block

cuadrado *a* & *m* square

cuadragésimo *a* fortieth

cuadr|ar *vt* square. ● *vi* suit;
<cuentas> tally. □ **~arse** *vpr* (Mil)
stand to attention; (fig) dig one's
heels in. **~ilátero** *m*
quadrilateral; (Boxeo) ring

cuadrilla *f* group; (pandilla) gang

cuadro *m* square; (pintura)
painting; (Teatro) scene; (de
números) table; (de mando etc) panel;
(conjunto del personal) staff. **~ de
distribución** switchboard. **a ~s, de
~s** check. **¡qué ~!, ¡vaya un ~!**
what a sight!

cuadrúpedo *m* quadruped

cuádruple *a & m* quadruple

cuajar *vt* congeal <*sangre*>; curdle <*leche*>; (llenar) fill up. ● *vi* <*nieve*> settle; (fig, 🔲) work out. **cuajado de** full of. □ ~**se** *vpr* coagulate; <*sangre*> clot; <*leche*> curdle

cual *pron* el ~, la ~ etc (animales y cosas) that, which; (personas, sujeto) who, that; (personas, objeto) whom. ● *a* (LAm, qué) what. ~ **si** as if. **cada** ~ everyone. **lo** ~ which. **por lo** ~ because of which. **sea** ~ **sea** whatever

cuál *pron* which

cualidad *f* quality

cualquiera *a* (delante de nombres **cualquier,** *pl* **cualesquiera**) any. ● *pron* (*pl* **cualesquiera**) anyone, anybody; (cosas) whatever, whichever. **un** ~ a nobody. **una** ~ a slut

cuando *adv* when. ● *conj* when; (si) if. ~ **más** at the most. ~ **menos** at the least. **aun** ~ even if. **de** ~ **en** ~ from time to time

cuándo *adv & conj* when. ¿**de** ~ **acá?**, ¿**desde** ~? since when? ¡~ **no!** (LAm) as usual!, typical!

cuant|ía *f* quantity; (extensión) extent. ~**ioso** *a* abundant. ~**o** *a* as much … as, as many … as. ● *pron* as much as, as many as. ● *adv* as much as. ~**o antes** as soon as possible. ~**o más, mejor** the more the merrier. **en** ~**o** as soon as. **en** ~**o a** as for. **por** ~**o** since. **unos** ~**os** a few, some

cuánto *a* (interrogativo) how much?; (interrogativo en plural) how many?; (exclamativo) what a lot of! ● *pron* how much?; (en plural) how many? ● *adv* how much. ¿~ **mides?** how tall are you? ¿~ **tiempo?** how long? ¡~ **tiempo sin verte!** it's been a long time! ¿**a** ~**s estamos?**

what's the date today? **un Sr. no sé** ~**s** Mr So-and-So

cuáquero *m* Quaker

cuarent|a *a & m* forty; (cuadragésimo) fortieth. ~**ena** *f* (Med) quarantine. ~**ón** *a* about forty

cuaresma *f* Lent

cuarta *f* (palmo) span

cuartel *m* (Mil) barracks. ~ **general** headquarters

cuarteto *m* quartet

cuarto *a* fourth. ● *m* quarter; (habitación) room. ~ **de baño** bathroom. ~ **de estar** living room. ~ **de hora** quarter of an hour. **estar sin un** ~ be broke. **y** ~ (a) quarter past

cuarzo *m* quartz

cuate *m* (Mex) twin; (amigo) friend; (🔲, tipo) guy

cuatro *a & m* four. ~**cientos** *a & m* four hundred

Cuba *f* Cuba

cuba|libre *m* rum and Coke (P). ~**no** *a & m* Cuban

cúbico *a* cubic

cubículo *m* cubicle

cubiert|a *f* cover; (neumático) tyre; (Naut) deck. ~**o** *a* covered; <*cielo*> overcast. ● *m* place setting, piece of cutlery; (en restaurante) cover charge. **a** ~**o** under cover

cubilete *m* bowl; (molde) mould; (para los dados) cup

cubis|mo *m* cubism. ~**ta** *a & m & f* cubist

cubo *m* bucket; (Mat) cube

cubrecama *m* bedspread

cubrir (*pp* **cubierto**) *vt* cover; fill <*vacante*>. □ ~**se** *vpr* cover o.s.; (ponerse el sombrero) put on one's hat; <*el cielo*> cloud over, become overcast

cucaracha *f* cockroach

cuchar|a *f* spoon. **~ada** *f* spoonful. **~adita** *f* teaspoonful. **~illa**, **~ita** *f* teaspoon. **~ón** *m* ladle

cuchichear *vi* whisper

cuchill|a *f* large knife; (de carnicero) cleaver; (hoja de afeitar) razor blade. **~ada** *f* stab; (herida) knife wound. **~o** *m* knife

cuchitril *m* (fig) hovel

cuclillas: **en ~** *adv* squatting

cuco *a* shrewd; (mono) pretty, nice. ● *m* cuckoo

cucurucho *m* cornet

cuello *m* neck; (de camisa) collar. **cortar(le) el ~ a uno** cut s.o.'s throat

cuenc|a *f* (del ojo) (eye) socket; (Geog) basin. **~o** *m* hollow; (vasija) bowl

cuenta *f* count; (acción de contar) counting; (cálculo) calculation; (factura) bill; (en banco, relato) account; (de collar) bead. **~ corriente** current account, checking account (Amer). **dar ~ de** give an account of. **darse ~ de** realize. **en resumidas ~s** in short. **por mi propia ~** on my own account. **tener en ~** bear in mind

cuentakilómetros *m invar* milometer

cuent|ista *m & f* story-writer; (de mentiras) fibber. **~o** *m* story; (mentira) fib, tall story. **~ de hadas** fairy tale. ● *vb* ⇒CONTAR

cuerda *f* rope; (más fina) string; (Mus) string. **~ floja** tightrope. **dar ~ a** wind up *<un reloj>*

cuerdo *a* *<persona>* sane; *<acción>* sensible

cuerno *m* horn

cuero *m* leather; (piel) skin; (del grifo) washer. **~ cabelludo** scalp. **en ~s (vivos)** stark naked

cuerpo *m* body

cuervo *m* crow

cuesta *f* slope, hill. **~ abajo** downhill. **~ arriba** uphill. **a ~s** on one's back

cuestión *f* matter; (problema) problem; (cosa) thing

cueva *f* cave

cuida|do *m* care; (preocupación) worry. **~do!** watch out!. **tener ~do** be careful. **~doso** *a* careful. **~r** *vt* look after. ● *vi*. **~r de** look after. □ **~rse** *vpr* look after o.s. **~rse de** be careful to

culata *f* (de revólver, fusil) butt. **~zo** *m* recoil

culebr|a *f* snake. **~ón** *m* soap opera

culinario *a* culinary

culminar *vi* culminate

culo *m* 🔲 bottom; (LAm vulg) arse (Brit vulg), ass (Amer vulg)

culpa *f* fault. **echar la ~** blame. **por ~ de** because of. **tener la ~** be to blame (**de** for). **~bilidad** *f* guilt. **~ble** *a* guilty. ● *m & f* culprit. **~r** *vt* blame (**de** for)

cultiv|ar *vt* farm; grow *<plantas>*; (fig) cultivate. **~o** *m* farming; (de plantas) growing

cult|o *a* *<persona>* educated. ● *m* cult; (homenaje) worship. **~ura** *f* culture. **~ural** *a* cultural

culturismo *m* body-building

cumbre *f* summit

cumpleaños *m invar* birthday

cumplido *a* perfect; (cortés) polite. ● *m* compliment. **de ~** courtesy. **por ~** out of a sense of duty. **~r** *a* reliable

cumpli|miento *m* fulfilment; (de ley) observance; (de orden) carrying out. **~r** *vt* carry out; observe *<ley>*; serve *<condena>*; reach *<años>*; keep *<promesa>*. **hoy cumple 3 años** he's 3 (years old) today. ● *vi* do one's duty. **por ~r**

as a mere formality. □ **~rse** *vpr*
expire; (realizarse) be fulfilled
cuna *f* cradle; (fig, nacimiento)
birthplace
cundir *vi* spread; (rendir) go a long
way
cuneta *f* ditch
cuña *f* wedge
cuñad|a *f* sister-in-law. **~o** *m*
brother-in-law
cuño *m* stamp. **de nuevo ~** new
cuota *f* quota; (de sociedad etc)
membership, fee; (LAm, plazo)
instalment; (Mex, peaje) toll
cupe *vb* ⇒CABER
cupo *m* cuota; (LAm, capacidad)
room; (Mex, plaza) place
cupón *m* coupon
cúpula *f* dome
cura *f* cure; (tratamiento) treatment.
● *m* priest. **~ción** *f* healing.
~ndero *m* faith-healer. **~r** *vt* (incl
Culin) cure; dress <*herida*>; (tratar)
treat; (fig) remedy; tan <*pieles*>.
□ **~rse** *vpr* get better
curios|ear *vi* pry; (mirar) browse.
~idad *f* curiosity. **~o** *a* curious;
(raro) odd, unusual. ● *m* onlooker;
(fisgón) busybody
curita *f* (LAm) (sticking) plaster
curriculum (vitae) *m*
curriculum vitae, CV
cursar *vt* issue; (estudiar) study
cursi *a* pretentious, showy
cursillo *m* short course
cursiva *f* italics
curso *m* course; (Univ etc) year. **en
~** under way; <*año etc*> current
cursor *m* cursor
curtir *vt* tan; (fig) harden. □ **~se**
vpr become tanned; (fig) become
hardened
curv|a *f* curve; (de carretera) bend.
~ar *vt* bend; bow <*estante*>.
~arse *vpr* bend; <*estante*> bow;
<*madera*> warp. **~ilíneo** *a*

curvilinear; <*mujer*> curvaceous.
~o *a* curved
cúspide *f* top; (fig) pinnacle
custodi|a *f* safe-keeping; (Jurid)
custody. **~ar** *vt* guard; (guardar)
look after. **~o** *m* guardian
cutáneo *a* skin
cutis *m* skin, complexion
cuyo *pron* (de persona) whose, of
whom; (de cosa) whose, of which.
en ~ caso in which case

Dd

dactilógrafo *m* typist
dado *m* dice. ● *a* given. **~ que**
since, given that
daltónico *a* colour-blind
dama *f* lady. **~ de honor**
bridesmaid. **~s** *fpl* draughts (Brit),
checkers (Amer)
damasco *m* damask; (LAm, fruta)
apricot
danés *a* Danish. ● *m* Dane;
(idioma) Danish
danza *f* dance; (acción) dancing.
~r [10] *vt/i* dance
dañ|ar *vt* damage. □ **~se** *vpr* get
damaged. **~ino** *a* harmful. **~o** *m*
damage; (a una persona) harm.
~os y perjuicios damages. **hacer
~o a** harm, hurt. **hacerse ~o** hurt
o.s.
dar [26] *vt* give; bear <*frutos*>;
give out <*calor*>; strike <*la hora*>.
● *vi* give. **da igual** it doesn't
matter. **¡dale!** go on! **da lo mismo**
it doesn't matter. **~ a** <*ventana*>
look on to; <*edificio*> face. **~ a luz**
give birth. **~ con** meet <*persona*>;

find <*cosa*>. ¿**qué más da?** it
doesn't matter! □ ~**se** *vpr* have
<*baño*>. **dárselas de** make o.s. out
to be. ~**se por** consider o.s.

dardo *m* dart

datar *vi*. ~ **de** date from

dátil *m* date

dato *m* piece of information. ~**s**
mpl data, information. ~**s**
personales personal details

....

de

●*preposición*

Note that **de** before **el** becomes
del, e.g. **es del norte**

····▸ (contenido, material) of. **un vaso**
de agua a glass of water. **es de**
madera it's made of wood

····▸ (pertenencia) **el coche de Juan**
Juan's car. **es de ella** it's hers. **es**
de María it's María's. **las llaves del**
coche the car keys

····▸ (procedencia, origen, época) from.
soy de Madrid I'm from Madrid.
una llamada de Lima a call from
Lima. **es del siglo V** it's from the
5th century

····▸ (causa, modo) **se murió de cáncer**
he died of cancer. **temblar de**
miedo to tremble with fear. **de**
dos en dos two by two

····▸ (parte del día, hora) **de noche** at
night. **de madrugada** early in the
morning. **las diez de la mañana**
ten (o'clock) in the morning. **de**
9 a 12 from 9 to 12

····▸ (en oraciones pasivas) by. **rodeado**
de agua surrounded by water. **va**
seguido de coma it's followed by
a comma. **es de Mozart** it's by
Mozart

····▸ (al especificar) **el cajón de arriba**
the top drawer. **la clase de inglés**

the English lesson. **la chica de**
verde the girl in green. **el de**
debajo the one underneath

····▸ (en calidad de) as. **trabaja de**
oficinista he works as a clerk.
vino de chaperón he came as a
chaperon

····▸ (en comparaciones) than. **pesa**
más de un kilo it weighs more
than a kilo

····▸ (con superlativo) **el más alto del**
mundo the tallest in the world. **el**
mejor de todos the best of all

····▸ (sentido condicional) if. **de haberlo**
sabido if I had known. **de**
continuar así if this goes on

⇨Cuando la preposición **de** se
emplea como parte de
expresiones como **de prisa,**
de acuerdo etc., y de
nombres compuestos como
hombre de negocios, saco
de dormir etc., ver bajo el
respectivo nombre

....

deambular *vi* roam (**por** about)

debajo *adv* underneath. ~ **de**
under(neath). **el de** ~ the one
underneath. **por** ~ underneath.
por ~ **de** below

debat|e *m* debate. ~**ir** *vt* debate

deber *vt* owe. ●*v aux* have to,
must; (en condicional) should. **debo**
marcharme I must go, I have to
go. ● *m* duty. ~**es** *mpl*
homework. □ ~**se** *vpr*. ~**se a** be
due to

debido *a* due; (correcto) proper. ~
a due to. **como es** ~ as is proper

débil *a* weak; <*sonido*> faint;
<*luz*> dim

debili|dad *f* weakness. ~**tar** *vt*
weaken. □ ~**tarse** *vpr* weaken,
get weak

débito *m* debit. ~ **bancario** (LAm)
direct debit

debutar *vi* make one's debut

década *f* decade

deca|dencia *f* decline. **~dente** *a* decadent. **~er** [29] *vi* decline; (debilitarse) weaken. **~ído** *a* in low spirits. **~imiento** *m* decline, weakening

decano *m* dean; (miembro más antiguo) senior member

decapitar *vt* behead

decena *f* ten. **una ~ de** about ten

decencia *f* decency

decenio *m* decade

decente *a* decent; (decoroso) respectable; (limpio) clean, tidy

decepci|ón *f* disappointment. **~onar** *vt* disappoint

decidi|do *a* decided; <persona> determined, resolute. **~r** *vt* decide; settle <cuestión etc>. ● *vi* decide. **~rse** *vpr* make up one's mind

decimal *a & m* decimal

décimo *a & m* tenth. ● *m* (de lotería) tenth part of a lottery ticket

decir [46] *vt* say; (contar) tell. ● *m* saying. **~ que no** say no. **~ que sí** say yes. **dicho de otro modo** in other words. **dicho y hecho** no sooner said than done. **¿dígame?** can I help you? **¡dígame!** (al teléfono) hello! **digamos** let's say. **es ~** that is to say. **mejor dicho** rather. **¡no me digas!** you don't say!, really! **por así ~, por lo así ~** so to speak, as it were. **querer ~** mean. **se dice que** it is said that, they say that

decisi|ón *f* decision. **~vo** *a* decisive

declara|ción *f* declaration; (a autoridad, prensa) statement. **~ción de renta** income tax return. **~r** *vt/i* declare. □ **~rse** *vpr* declare o.s.; <epidemia etc> break out

declinar *vt* turn down; (Gram) decline

declive *m* slope; (fig) decline. **en ~** sloping

decola|je *m* (LAm) take-off. **~r** *vi* (LAm) take off

decolorarse *vpr* become discoloured, fade

decora|ción *f* decoration. **~do** *m* (en el teatro) set. **~r** *vt* decorate. **~tivo** *a* decorative

decoro *m* decorum. **~so** *a* decent, respectable

decrépito *a* decrepit

decret|ar *vt* decree. **~o** *m* decree

dedal *m* thimble

dedica|ción *f* dedication. **~r** [7] *vt* dedicate; devote <tiempo>. □ **~rse** *vpr*. **~rse a** devote o.s. to. **¿a qué se dedica?** what does he do? **~toria** *f* dedication

dedo *m* finger; (del pie) toe. **~ anular** ring finger. **~ corazón** middle finger. **~ gordo** thumb; (del pie) big toe. **~ índice** index finger. **~ meñique** little finger. **~ pulgar** thumb

deduc|ción *f* deduction. **~ir** [47] *vt* deduce; (descontar) deduct

defect|o *m* fault, defect. **~uoso** *a* defective

defen|der [1] *vt* defend. **~sa** *f* defence. □ **~derse** *vpr* defend o.s. **~sivo** *a* defensive. **~sor** *m* defender. **abogado** *m* **~sor** defence counsel

defeño *m* (Mex) person from the Federal District

deficien|cia *f* deficiency. **~cia mental** mental handicap. **~te** *a* poor, deficient. ● *m & f.* **~te mental** mentally handicapped person

déficit *m invar* deficit

defini|ción f definition. **~do** a defined. **~r** vt define. **~tivo** a definitive. **en ~tiva** all in all

deform|ación f deformation; (de imagen etc) distortion. **~ar** vt deform; distort <*imagen, metal*>. □ **~arse** vpr go out of shape. **~e** a deformed

defraudar vt defraud; (decepcionar) disappoint

defunción f death

degenera|ción f degeneration; (cualidad) degeneracy. **~do** a degenerate. **~r** vi degenerate

degollar [16] vt cut s.o.'s throat

degradar vt degrade; (Mil) demote. □ **~se** vpr demean o.s..

degusta|ción f tasting. **~r** vt taste

dehesa f pasture

deja|dez f slovenliness; (pereza) laziness. **~do** a slovenly; (descuidado) slack, negligent. **~r** vt leave; (abandonar) abandon; give up <*estudios*>; (prestar) lend; (permitir) let. **~r a un lado** leave aside. **~r de** stop

dejo m aftertaste; (tonillo) slight accent; (toque) touch

del = **de** + **el**

delantal m apron

delante adv in front. **~** **de** in front of. **de ~** front. **~ra** f front; (de teatro etc) front row; (ventaja) lead; (de equipo) forward line. **llevar la ~ra** be in the lead. **~ro** a front. ● m forward

delat|ar vt denounce. **~or** m informer

delega|ción f delegation; (oficina) regional office; (Mex, comisaría) police station. **~do** m delegate; (Com) agent, representative. **~r** [12] vt delegate

deleit|ar vt delight. **~e** m delight

deletrear vt spell (out)

delfín m dolphin

delgad|ez f thinness. **~o** a thin; (esbelto) slim. **~ucho** a skinny

delibera|ción f deliberation. **~do** a deliberate. **~r** vi deliberate (**sobre** on)

delicad|eza f gentleness; (fragilidad) frailty; (tacto) tact. **falta de ~eza** tactlessness. **tener la ~ de** have the courtesy to. **~o** a delicate; (refinado) refined; (sensible) sensitive

delici|a f delight. **~oso** a delightful; <*sabor etc*> delicious

delimitar vt delimit

delincuen|cia f delinquency. **~te** m & f criminal, delinquent

delinquir [8] vi commit a criminal offence

delir|ante a delirious. **~ar** vi be delirious; (fig) talk nonsense. **~io** m delirium; (fig) frenzy

delito m crime, offence

demacrado a haggard

demagogo m demagogue

demanda f demand; (Jurid) lawsuit. **~do** m defendant. **~nte** m & f (Jurid) plaintiff. **~r** vt (Jurid) sue; (LAm, requerir) require

demarcación f demarcation

demás a rest of the, other. ● pron rest, others. **lo ~** the rest. **por ~** extremely. **por lo ~** otherwise

demas|ía f. **en ~ía** in excess. **~iado** a too much; (en plural) too many. ● adv too much; (con adjetivo) too

demen|cia f madness. **~te** a demented, mad

dem|ocracia f democracy. **~ócrata** m & f democrat. **~ocrático** a democratic

demol|er [2] vt demolish. **~ición** f demolition

demonio *m* devil, demon. ¡**~s!** hell! ¿cómo **~s?** how the hell? ¡qué **~s!** what the hell!

demora *f* delay. **~r** *vt* delay. ● *vi* stay on. □ **~rse** *vpr* be too long; (LAm, cierto tiempo). **se ~ una hora en llegar** it takes him an hour to get there

demostra|ción *f* demonstration, show. **~r** [2] *vt* demonstrate; (mostrar) show; (probar) prove. **~tivo** *a* demonstrative

dengue *m* dengue fever

denigrar *vt* denigrate

dens|idad *f* density. **~o** *a* dense, thick

denta|dura *f* teeth. **~dura postiza** dentures, false teeth. **~l** *a* dental

dent|era *f.* **darle ~era a uno** set s.o.'s teeth on edge. **~ífrico** *m* toothpaste. **~ista** *m & f* dentist

dentro *adv* inside; (de un edificio) indoors. **~ de** in. **~ de poco** soon. **por ~** inside

denuncia *f* report; (acusación) accusation. **~r** *vt* report; <periódico etc> denounce

departamento *m* department; (LAm, apartamento) flat (Brit), apartment (Amer)

depend|encia *f* dependence; (sección) section; (oficina) office. **~encias** *fpl* buildings. **~er** *vi* depend (**de** on). **~ienta** *f* shop assistant. **~iente** *a* dependent (**de** on). ● *m* shop assistant

depila|r *vt* depilate. **~torio** *a* depilatory

deplora|ble *a* deplorable. **~r** *vt* deplore, regret

deponer [34] *vt* remove from office; depose <rey>; lay down <armas>. ● *vi* give evidence

deporta|ción *f* deportation. **~r** *vt* deport

deport|e *m* sport. **hacer ~e** take part in sports. **~ista** *m*

sportsman. ● *f* sportswoman. **~ivo** *a* sports. ● *m* sports car

dep|ositante *m & f* depositor. **~ositar** *vt* deposit; (poner) put, place. **~ósito** *m* deposit; (almacén) warehouse; (Mil) depot; (de líquidos) tank

depravado *a* depraved

deprecia|ción *f* depreciation. **~r** *vt* depreciate. □ **~rse** *vpr* depreciate

depr|esión *f* depression. **~imido** *a* depressed. **~imir** *vt* depress. □ **~imirse** *vpr* get depressed

depura|ción *f* purification. **~do** *a* refined. **~r** *vt* purify; (Pol) purge; refine <estilo>

derech|a *f* (mano) right hand; (lado) right. **a la ~a** on the right; (hacia el lado derecho) to the right. **~ista** *a* right-wing. ● *m & f* right-winger. **~o** *a* right; (vertical) upright; (recto) straight. ● *adv* straight. **todo ~o** straight on. ● *m* right; (Jurid) law; (lado) right side. **~os** *mpl* dues. **~os de autor** royalties

deriva *f* drift. **a la ~** drifting, adrift

deriva|do *a* derived. ● *m* derivative, by-product. **~r** *vt* divert. ● *vi.* **~r de** derive from, be derived from. □ **~rse** *vpr.* **~se de** be derived from

derram|amiento *m* spilling. **~amiento de sangre** bloodshed. **~ar** *vt* spill; shed <lágrimas>. □ **~arse** *vpr* spill. **~e** *m* spilling; (pérdida) leakage; (Med) discharge; (Med, de sangre) haemorrhage

derretir [5] *vt* melt

derribar *vt* knock down; bring down, overthrow <gobierno etc>

derrocar [7] *vt* bring down, overthrow <gobierno etc>

derroch|ar *vt* squander. **~e** *m* waste

derrot|a *f* defeat. **~ar** *vt* defeat. **~ado** *a* defeated. **~ero** *m* course

derrumba|r *vt* knock down. □ **~rse** *vpr* collapse; *<persona>* go to pieces

desabotonar *vt* unbutton, undo. □ **~se** *vpr* come undone; *<persona>* undo

desabrido *a* tasteless; *<persona>* surly; (LAm) dull

desabrochar *vt* undo. □ **~se** *vpr* come undone; *<persona>* undo

desacato *m* defiance; (Jurid) contempt of court

desac|ertado *a* ill-advised; (erróneo) wrong. **~ierto** *m* mistake

desacreditar *vt* discredit

desactivar *vt* defuse

desacuerdo *m* disagreement

desafiar [20] *vt* challenge; (afrontar) defy

desafina|do *a* out of tune. **~r** *vi* be out of tune. □ **~rse** *vpr* go out of tune

desafío *m* challenge; (a la muerte) defiance; (combate) duel

desafortunad|amente *adv* unfortunately. **~o** *a* unfortunate

desagrada|ble *a* unpleasant. **~r** *vt* displease. ● *vi* be unpleasant. **me ~ el sabor** I don't like the taste

desagradecido *a* ungrateful

desagrado *m* displeasure. **con ~** unwillingly

desagüe *m* drain; (acción) drainage. **tubo** *m* **de ~** drain-pipe

desahog|ado *a* roomy; (acomodado) comfortable. **~ar** [12] *vt* vent. □ **~arse** *vpr* let off steam. **~o** *m* comfort; (alivio) relief

desahuci|ar *vt* declare terminally ill *<enfermo>*; evict *<inquilino>*. **~o** *m* eviction

desair|ar *vt* snub. **~e** *m* snub

desajuste *m* maladjustment; (desequilibrio) imbalance

desal|entador *a* disheartening. **~entar** [1] *vt* discourage. **~iento** *m* discouragement

desaliñado *a* slovenly

desalmado *a* heartless

desalojar *vt* *<ocupantes>* evacuate; *<policía>* to clear; (LAm) evict *<inquilino>*

desampar|ado *a* helpless; *<lugar>* unprotected. **~ar** *vt* abandon. **~o** *m* helplessness; (abandono) lack of protection

desangrar *vt* bleed. □ **~se** *vpr* bleed

desanima|do *a* down-hearted. **~r** *vt* discourage. □ **~rse** *vpr* lose heart

desapar|ecer [11] *vi* disappear; *<efecto>* wear off. **~ecido** *a* missing. ● *m* missing person. **~ición** *f* disappearance

desapego *m* indifference

desapercibido *a*. **pasar ~** go unnoticed

desaprobar [2] *vt* disapprove of

desarm|able *a* collapsible; *<estante>* easy to dismantle. **~ar** *vt* disarm; (desmontar) dismantle; take apart; (LAm) take down *<carpa>*. **~e** *m* disarmament

desarraig|ado *a* rootless. **~ar** [12] *vt* uproot. **~o** *m* uprooting

desarregl|ar *vt* mess up; (alterar) disrupt. **~o** *m* disorder

desarroll|ar *vt* develop. □ **~arse** *vpr* (incl Foto) develop; *<suceso>* take place. **~o** *m* development

desaseado *a* dirty; (desordenado) untidy

desasosiego *m* anxiety; (intranquilidad) restlessness

desastr|ado *a* scruffy. **~e** *m* disaster. **~oso** *a* disastrous

desatar vt untie; (fig, soltar) unleash. □ ~se vpr come undone; to undo <zapatos>

desatascar [7] vt unblock

desaten|der [1] vt not pay attention to; neglect <deber etc>. ~to a inattentive; (descortés) discourteous

desatin|ado a silly. ~o m silliness; (error) mistake

desatornillar vt unscrew

desautorizar [10] vt declare unauthorized; discredit <persona>; (desmentir) deny

desavenencia f disagreement

desayun|ar vt have for breakfast. ● vi have breakfast. ~o m breakfast

desazón m (fig) unease

desbandarse vpr (Mil) disband; (dispersarse) disperse

desbarajust|ar vt mess up. ~e m mess

desbaratar vt spoil; (Mex) mess up <papeles>

desbloquear vt clear; release <mecanismo>; unfreeze <cuenta>

desbocado a <caballo> runaway; <escote> wide

desbordarse vpr overflow; <río> burst its banks

descabellado a crazy

descafeinado a decaffeinated. ● m decaffeinated coffee

descalabro m disaster

descalificar [7] vt disqualify; (desacreditar) discredit

descalz|ar [10] vt take off <zapatos>. ~o a barefoot

descampado m open ground. al ~ (LAm) in the open air

descans|ado a rested; <trabajo> easy. ~ar vt/i rest. ~illo m landing. ~o m rest; (del trabajo) break; (LAm, rellano) landing; (en deportes) half-time; (en el teatro etc) interval

descapotable a convertible

descarado a cheeky; (sin vergüenza) shameless

descarg|a f unloading; (Mil, Elec) discharge. ~ar [12] vt unload; (Mil, Elec) discharge; (Informática) download. ~o m (recibo) receipt; (Jurid) evidence

descaro m cheek, nerve

descarriarse [20] vpr go the wrong way; <res> stray; (fig) go astray

descarrila|miento m derailment. ~r vi be derailed. □ ~se vpr (LAm) be derailed

descartar vt rule out

descascararse vpr <pintura> peel; <taza> chip

descen|dencia f descent; (personas) descendants. ~der [1] vt go down <escalera etc>. ● vi go down; <temperatura> fall, drop; (provenir) be descended (de from). ~diente m & f descendant. ~so m descent; (de temperatura, fiebre etc) fall, drop

descifrar vt decipher; decode <clave>

descolgar [2 & 12] vt take down; pick up <el teléfono>. □ ~se vpr lower o.s.

descolor|ar vt discolour, fade. ~ido a discoloured, faded; <persona> pale

descomp|oner [34] vt break down; decompose <materia>; upset <estómago>; (esp LAm, estropear) break; (esp LAm, desarreglar) mess up. □ ~onerse vpr decompose; (esp LAm, estropearse) break down; <persona> feel sick. ~ostura f (esp LAm, de máquina) breakdown; (esp LAm, náuseas) sickness; (esp LAm, diarrea) diarrhoea; (LAm, falla) fault.

~uesto a decomposed; (encolerizado) angry; (esp LAm, estropeado) broken. **estar ~uesto** (del estómago) have diarrhoea

descomunal a enormous

desconc|ertante a disconcerting. **~ertar** [1] vt disconcert; (dejar perplejo) puzzle. □ **~ertarse** vpr be put out, be disconcerted

desconectar vt disconnect

desconfia|do a distrustful. **~nza** f distrust, suspicion. **~r** [20] vi. **~r de** mistrust; (no creer) doubt

descongelar vt defrost; (Com) unfreeze

desconoc|er [11] vt not know, not recognize. **~ido** a unknown; (cambiado) unrecognizable. ● m stranger. **~imiento** m ignorance

desconsidera|ción f lack of consideration. **~do** a inconsiderate

descons|olado a distressed. **~uelo** m distress; (tristeza) sadness

desconta|do a. **dar por ~do (que)** take for granted (that). **~r** [2] vt discount; deduct <impuestos etc>

descontento a unhappy (con with), dissatisfied (con with). ● m discontent

descorazonar vt discourage. □ **~se** vpr lose heart

descorchar vt uncork

descorrer vt draw <cortina>. **~ el cerrojo** unbolt the door

descort|és a rude, discourteous. **~esía** f rudeness

descos|er vt unpick. □ **~erse** vpr come undone. **~ido** a unstitched

descrédito m disrepute. **ir en ~ de** damage the reputation of

descremado a skimmed

descri|bir (pp **descrito**) vt describe. **~pción** f description

descuartizar [10] vt cut up

descubierto a discovered; (no cubierto) uncovered; <vehículo> open-top; <piscina> open-air; <cielo> clear; <cabeza> bare. ● m overdraft. **poner al ~** expose

descubri|miento m discovery. **~r** (pp **descubierto**) vt discover; (destapar) uncover; (revelar) reveal; unveil <estatua>. □ **~rse** vpr (quitarse el sombrero) take off one's hat

descuento m discount; (del sueldo) deduction

descuid|ado a careless; <aspecto etc> untidy; (desprevenido) unprepared. **~ar** vt neglect. ● vi not worry. **¡~a!** don't worry! □ **~arse** vpr be careless **~o** m carelessness; (negligencia) negligence

desde prep (lugar etc) from; (tiempo) since, from. **~ ahora** from now on. **~ hace un mes** for a month. **~ luego** of course. **~ Madrid hasta Barcelona** from Madrid to Barcelona. **~ niño** since childhood

desdecirse [46] vpr. **~ de** take back <palabras etc>; go back on <promesa>

desd|én m scorn. **~eñable** a insignificant. **nada ~eñable** significant. **~eñar** vt scorn

desdicha f misfortune. **por ~** unfortunately. **~do** a unfortunate

desdoblar vt (desplegar) unfold

desear vt want; wish <suerte etc>. **le deseo un buen viaje** I hope you have a good journey. **¿qué desea Vd?** can I help you?

desech|able a disposable. **~ar** vt throw out; (rechazar) reject. **~o** m waste

desembalar *vt* unpack

desembarcar [7] *vt* unload. ● *vi* disembark

desemboca|dura *f* (de río) mouth; (de calle) opening. **~r** [7] *vi*. **~r en** <*río*> flow into; <*calle*> lead to

desembolso *m* payment

desembragar [12] *vi* declutch

desempaquetar *vt* unwrap

desempat|ar *vi* break a tie. **~e** *m* tie-breaker

desempeñ|ar *vt* redeem; play <*papel*>; hold <*cargo*>; perform, carry out <*deber etc*>. □ **~arse** *vpr* (LAm) perform. **~arse bien** manage well. **~o** *m* redemption; (de un deber, una función) discharge; (LAm, actuación) performance

desemple|ado *a* unemployed. ● *m* unemployed person. **los ~ados** the unemployed. **~o** *m* unemployment

desencadenar *vt* unchain <*preso*>; unleash <*perro*>; (causar) trigger. □ **~se** *vpr* be triggered off; <*guerra etc*> break out

desencajar *vt* dislocate; (desconectar) disconnect. □ **~se** *vpr* become dislocated

desenchufar *vt* unplug

desenfad|ado *a* uninhibited; (desenvuelto) self-assured. **~o** *m* lack of inhibition; (desenvoltura) self-assurance

desenfocado *a* out of focus

desenfren|ado *a* unrestrained. **~o** *m* licentiousness

desenganchar *vt* unhook; uncouple <*vagón*>

desengañ|ar *vt* disillusion. □ **~arse** *vpr* become disillusioned; (darse cuenta) realize. **~o** *m* disillusionment, disappointment

desenlace *m* outcome

desenmascarar *vt* unmask

desenredar *vt* untangle. □ **~se** *vpr* untangle

desenro|llar *vt* unroll, unwind. **~scar** [7] *vt* unscrew

desentend|erse [1] *vpr* want nothing to do with. **~ido** *m*. **hacerse el ~ido** (fingir no oír) pretend not to hear; (fingir ignorancia) pretend not to know

desenterrar [1] *vt* exhume; (fig) unearth

desentonar *vi* be out of tune; <*colores*> clash

desenvoltura *f* ease; (falta de timidez) confidence

desenvolver [2] (*pp* **desenvuelto**) *vt* unwrap; expound <*idea etc*>. □ **~se** *vpr* perform; (manejarse) manage

deseo *m* wish, desire. **~so** *a* eager. **estar ~so de** be eager to

desequilibr|ado *a* unbalanced. **~io** *m* imbalance

des|ertar *vt* desert; (Pol) defect. **~értico** *a* desert-like. **~ertor** *m* deserter; (Pol) defector

desespera|ción *f* despair. **~do** *a* desperate. **~nte** *a* infuriating. **~r** *vt* drive to despair. □ **~rse** *vpr* despair

desestimar *vt* (rechazar) reject

desfachat|ado *a* brazen, shameless. **~ez** *f* nerve, cheek

desfallec|er [11] *vt* weaken. ● *vi* become weak; (desmayarse) faint. **~imiento** *m* weakness; (desmayo) faint

desfasado *a* out of phase; <*idea*> outdated; <*persona*> out of touch

desfavorable *a* unfavourable

desfil|adero *m* narrow mountain pass; (cañón) narrow gorge. **~ar** *vi* march (past). **~e** *m* procession, parade. **~e de modelos** fashion show

desgana f. (LAm) **desgano** m (falta de apetito) lack of appetite; (Med) weakness, faintness; (fig) unwillingness

desgarr|ador a heart-rending. **~ar** vt tear; (fig) break <corazón>. **~o** m tear, rip

desgast|ar vt wear away; wear out <ropa>. □ **~arse** vpr wear away; <ropa> be worn out; <persona> wear o.s. out. **~e** m wear

desgracia f misfortune; (accidente) accident; **por ~** unfortunately. **¡qué ~!** what a shame!. **~do** a unlucky; (pobre) poor. ● m unfortunate person, poor devil Ⅰ

desgranar vt shell <habas etc>

desgreñado a ruffled, dishevelled

deshabitado a uninhabited; <edificio> unoccupied

deshacer [31] vt undo; strip <cama>; unpack <maleta>; (desmontar) take to pieces; break <trato>; (derretir) melt; (disolver) dissolve. □ **~se** vpr come undone; (disolverse) dissolve; (derretirse) melt. **~se de algo** get rid of sth. **~se en lágrimas** dissolve into tears. **~se por hacer algo** go out of one's way to do sth

desheredar vt disinherit

deshidratarse vpr become dehydrated

deshielo m thaw

deshilachado a frayed

deshincha|do a <neumático> flat. **~r** vt deflate; (Med) reduce the swelling in. □ **~rse** vpr go down

deshollinador m chimney sweep

deshon|esto a dishonest; (obsceno) indecent. **~ra** f disgrace. **~rar** vt dishonour

deshora f. **a ~** out of hours. **comer a ~s** eat between meals

deshuesar vt bone <carne>; stone <fruta>

desidia f slackness; <pereza> laziness

desierto a deserted. ● m desert

designar vt designate; (fijar) fix

desigual a unequal; <terreno> uneven; (distinto) different. **~dad** f inequality

desilusi|ón f disappointment; (pérdida de ilusiones) disillusionment. **~onar** vt disappoint; (quitar las ilusiones) disillusion. □ **~onarse** vpr be disappointed; (perder las ilusiones) become disillusioned

desinfecta|nte m disinfectant. **~r** vt disinfect

desinflar vt deflate. □ **~se** vpr go down

desinhibido a uninhibited

desintegrar vt disintegrate. □ **~se** vpr disintegrate

desinter|és m lack of interest; (generosidad) unselfishness. **~esado** a uninterested; (liberal) unselfish

desistir vi. **~ de** give up

desleal a disloyal. **~tad** f disloyalty

desligar [12] vt untie; (separar) separate; (fig, librar) free. □ **~se** vpr break away; (de un compromiso) free o.s. (**de** from)

desliza|dor m (Mex) hang glider. **~r** [10] vt slide, slip. □ **~se** vpr slide, slip; <patinador> glide; <tiempo> slip by, pass; (fluir) flow

deslucido a tarnished; (gastado) worn out; (fig) undistinguished

deslumbrar vt dazzle

desmadr|arse vpr get out of control. **~e** m excess

desmán m outrage

desmanchar vt (LAm) remove the stains from

desmantelar vt dismantle; (despojar) strip

desmaquillador m make-up remover

desmay|ado a unconscious. □ ~arse vpr faint. ~o m faint

desmedido a excessive

desmemoriado a forgetful

desmenti|do m denial. ~r [4] vt deny; (contradecir) contradict

desmenuzar [10] vt crumble; shred <carne etc>

desmerecer [11] vi. no ~ de compare favourably with

desmesurado a excessive; (enorme) enormous

desmonta|ble a collapsible; <armario> easy to dismantle; (separable) removable. ~r vt (quitar) remove; (desarmar) dismantle, take apart. ● vi dismount

desmoralizar [10] vt demoralize

desmoronarse vpr crumble; <edificio> collapse

desnatado a skimmed

desnivel m unevenness; (fig) difference, inequality

desnud|ar vt strip; undress, strip <persona>. □ ~arse vpr undress. ~ez f nudity. ~o a naked; (fig) bare. ● m nude

desnutri|ción f malnutrition. ~do a undernourished

desobed|ecer [11] vt disobey. ~iencia f disobedience

desocupa|do a <asiento etc> vacant, free; (sin trabajo) unemployed; (ocioso) idle. ~r vt vacate; (desalojar) clear

desodorante m deodorant

desolado a desolate; <persona> sorry, sad

desorbitante a excessive

desorden m disorder, untidiness; (confusión) confusion. ~ado a

untidy. ~ar vt disarrange, make a mess of

desorganizar [10] vt disorganize; (trastornar) disturb

desorienta|do a confused. ~r vt disorientate. □ ~rse vpr lose one's bearings

despabila|do a wide awake; (listo) quick. ~r vt (despertar) wake up; (avivar) wise up. □ ~rse vpr wake up; (avivarse) wise up

despach|ar vt finish; (tratar con) deal with; (atender) serve; (vender) sell; (enviar) send; (despedir) fire. ~o m dispatch; (oficina) office; (venta) sale; (de localidades) box office

despacio adv slowly

despampanante a stunning

desparpajo m confidence; (descaro) impudence

desparramar vt scatter; spill <líquidos>

despavorido a terrified

despecho m spite. a ~ de in spite of. por ~ out of spite

despectivo a contemptuous; <sentido etc> pejorative

despedazar [10] vt tear to pieces

despedi|da f goodbye, farewell. ~da de soltero stag-party. ~r [5] vt say goodbye to, see off; dismiss <empleado>; evict <inquilino>; (arrojar) throw; give off <olor etc>. □ ~rse vpr say goodbye (de to)

despeg|ar [12] vt unstick. ● vi <avión> take off. ~ue m take-off

despeinar vt ruffle the hair of

despeja|do a clear; <persona> wide awake. ~r vt clear; (aclarar) clarify. ● vi clear. □ ~rse vpr (aclararse) become clear; <tiempo> clear up

despellejar vt skin

despenalizar vt decriminalize

despensa f pantry, larder

despeñadero *m* cliff

desperdici|ar *vt* waste. **~o** *m* waste. **~os** *mpl* rubbish

desperta|dor *m* alarm clock. **~r** [1] *vt* wake (up); (fig) awaken. □ **~rse** *vpr* wake up

despiadado *a* merciless

despido *m* dismissal

despierto *a* awake; (listo) bright

despilfarr|ar *vt* waste. **~o** *m* squandering; (gasto innecesario) extravagance

despintarse *vpr* (Mex) run

despista|do *a* (con estar) confused; (con ser) absent-minded. **~r** *vt* throw off the scent; (fig) mislead. □ **~rse** *vpr* go wrong; (fig) get confused

despiste *m* mistake; (confusión) muddle

desplaza|miento *m* displacement; (de opinión etc) swing, shift. **~r** [10] *vt* displace. □ **~rse** *vpr* travel

desplegar [1 & 12] *vt* open out; spread <*alas*>; (fig) show

desplomarse *vpr* collapse

despoblado *m* deserted area

despoj|ar *vt* deprive <*persona*>; strip <*cosa*>. **~os** *mpl* remains; (de res) offal; (de ave) giblets

despreci|able *a* despicable; <*cantidad*> negligible. **~ar** *vt* despise; (rechazar) scorn. **~o** *m* contempt; (desaire) snub

desprender *vt* remove; give off <*olor*>. □ **~se** *vpr* fall off; (fig) part with; (deducirse) follow

despreocupa|do *a* unconcerned; (descuidado) careless. □ **~rse** *vpr* not worry

desprestigiar *vt* discredit

desprevenido *a* unprepared. **pillar a uno ~** catch s.o. unawares

desproporcionado *a* disproportionate

desprovisto *a*. **~ de** lacking in, without

después *adv* after, afterwards; (más tarde) later; (a continuación) then. **~ de** after. **~ de comer** after eating. **~ de todo** after all. **~ (de) que** after. **poco ~** soon after

desquit|arse *vpr* get even (**de** with). **~e** *m* revenge

destaca|do *a* outstanding. **~r** [7] *vt* emphasize. ● *vi* stand out. □ **~rse** *vpr* stand out. **~se en** excel at

destajo *m*. **trabajar a ~** do piece-work

destap|ar *vt* uncover; open <*botella*>. □ **~arse** *vpr* reveal one's true self. **~e** *m* (fig) permissiveness

destartalado *a* <*coche*> clapped-out; <*casa*> ramshackle

destello *m* sparkle; (de estrella) twinkle; (fig) glimmer

destemplado *a* discordant; <*nervios*> frayed

desteñir [5 & 22] *vt* fade. ● *vi* fade; <*color*> run. □ **~se** *vpr* fade; <*color*> run

desterra|do *m* exile. **~r** [1] *vt* banish

destetar *vt* wean

destiempo *m*. **a ~** at the wrong moment; (Mus) out of time

destierro *m* exile

destil|ar *vt* distil. **~ería** *f* distillery

destin|ar *vt* destine; (nombrar) post. **~atario** *m* addressee. **~o** *m* (uso) use, function; (lugar) destination; (suerte) destiny. **con ~ a** (going) to

destituir [17] *vt* dismiss

destornilla|dor *m* screwdriver. **~r** *vt* unscrew

destreza *f* skill

destroz|ar [10] *vt* destroy; (fig) shatter. **~os** *mpl* destruction, damage

destru|cción *f* destruction. **~ir** [17] *vt* destroy

desus|ado *a* old-fashioned; (insólito) unusual. **~o** *m* disuse. **caer en ~o** fall into disuse

desvalido *a* needy, destitute

desvalijar *vt* rob; ransack *<casa>*

desvalorizar [10] *vt* devalue

desván *m* loft

desvanec|er [11] *vt* make disappear; (borrar) blur; (fig) dispel. □ **~erse** *vpr* disappear; (desmayarse) faint. **~imiento** *m* (Med) faint

desvariar [20] *vi* be delirious; (fig) talk nonsense

desvel|ar *vt* keep awake. □ **~arse** *vpr* stay awake, have a sleepless night. **~o** *m* sleeplessness

desvencijado *a* *<mueble>* rickety

desventaja *f* disadvantage

desventura *f* misfortune. **~do** *a* unfortunate

desverg|onzado *a* impudent, cheeky. **~üenza** *f* impudence, cheek

desvestirse [5] *vpr* undress

desv|iación *f* deviation; (Auto) diversion. **~iar** [20] *vt* divert; deflect *<pelota>*. □ **~iarse** *vpr* *<carretera>* branch off; (del camino) make a detour; (del tema) stray. **~ío** *m* diversion

desvivirse *vpr.* **~se por** be completely devoted to; (esforzarse) go out of one's way to

detall|ar *vt* relate in detail. **~e** *m* detail; (fig) gesture. **al ~e** retail. **entrar en ~es** go into detail. **¡qué ~e!** how thoughtful! **~ista** *m & f* retailer

detect|ar *vt* detect. **~ive** *m* detective

deten|ción *f* stopping; (Jurid) arrest; (en la cárcel) detention. **~er** [40] *vt* stop; (Jurid) arrest; (encarcelar) detain; (retrasar) delay. □ **~erse** *vpr* stop; (entretenerse) spend a lot of time. **~idamente** *adv* at length. **~ido** *a* (Jurid) under arrest. ● *m* prisoner

detergente *a & m* detergent

deterior|ar *vt* damage, spoil. □ **~arse** *vpr* deteriorate. **~o** *m* deterioration

determina|ción *f* determination; (decisión) decison. **~nte** *a* decisive. **~r** *vt* determine; (decidir) decide

detestar *vt* detest

detrás *adv* behind; (en la parte posterior) on the back. **~ de** behind. **por ~** at the back; (por la espalda) from behind

detrimento *m* detriment. **en ~ de** to the detriment of

deud|a *f* debt. **~or** *m* debtor

devalua|ción *f* devaluation. **~r** [21] *vt* devalue. □ **~se** *vpr* depreciate

devastador *a* devastating

devoción *f* devotion

devol|ución *f* return; (Com) repayment, refund. **~ver** [5] (*pp* **devuelto**) *vt* return; (Com) repay, refund. ● *vi* be sick

devorar *vt* devour

devoto *a* devout; *<amigo etc>* devoted. ● *m* admirer

di *vb* ⇒DAR, DECIR

día *m* day. **~ de fiesta** (public) holiday. **~ del santo** saint's day. **~ feriado** (LAm), **~ festivo** (public) holiday. **al ~** up to date. **al ~ siguiente** (on) the following day. **¡buenos ~s!** good morning! **de ~** by day. **el ~ de hoy** today. **el ~ de mañana** tomorrow. **un ~ sí y otro**

no every other day. **vivir al ~** live from hand to mouth

diab|etes *f* diabetes.**~ético** *a* diabetic

diab|lo *m* devil.**~lura** *f* mischief. **~ólico** *a* diabolical

diadema *f* diadem

diáfano *a* diaphanous; <cielo> clear

diafragma *m* diaphragm

diagn|osis *f* diagnosis.**~osticar** [7] *vt* diagnose.**~óstico** *m* diagnosis

diagonal *a & f* diagonal

diagrama *m* diagram

dialecto *m* dialect

di|alogar [12] *vi* talk.**~álogo** *m* dialogue; (Pol) talks

diamante *m* diamond

diámetro *m* diameter

diana *f* reveille; (blanco) bull's-eye

diapositiva *f* slide, transparency

diario *a* daily. ● *m* newspaper; (libro) diary. **a ~o** daily. **de ~o** everyday, ordinary

diarrea *f* diarrhoea

dibuj|ante *m* draughtsman. ● *f* draughtswoman. **~ar** *vt* draw. **~o** *m* drawing. **~os animados** cartoons

diccionario *m* dictionary

dich|a *f* happiness. **por ~a** fortunately.**~o** *a* said; (tal) such. ● *m* saying. **~o y hecho** no sooner said than done. **mejor ~o** rather. **propiamente ~o** strictly speaking.**~oso** *a* happy; (afortunado) fortunate

diciembre *m* December

dicta|do *m* dictation.**~dor** *m* dictator.**~dura** *f* dictatorship. **~men** *m* opinion; (informe) report. **~r** *vt* dictate; pronounce <sentencia etc>; (LAm) give <clase>

didáctico *a* didactic

dieci|nueve *a & m* nineteen. **~ocho** *a & m* eighteen.**~séis** *a & m* sixteen. **~siete** *a & m* seventeen

diente *m* tooth; (de tenedor) prong; (de ajo) clove. **~ de león** dandelion. **hablar entre ~s** mumble

diestro *a* right-handed; (hábil) skilful

dieta *f* diet

diez *a & m* ten

diezmar *vt* decimate

difamación *f* (con palabras) slander; (por escrito) libel

diferen|cia *f* difference; (desacuerdo) disagreement.**~ciar** *vt* differentiate between. □ **~ciarse** *vpr* differ.**~te** *a* different; (diversos) various

diferido *a* (TV etc). **en ~** recorded

dif|ícil *a* difficult; (poco probable) unlikely.**~icultad** *f* difficulty. **~icultar** *vt* make difficult

difteria *f* diphtheria

difundir *vt* spread; (TV etc) broadcast

difunto *a* late, deceased. ● *m* deceased

difusión *f* spreading

dige|rir [4] *vt* digest.**~stión** *f* digestion.**~stivo** *a* digestive

digital *a* digital; (de los dedos) finger

dign|arse *vpr* deign to.**~atario** *m* dignitary.**~idad** *f* dignity.**~o** *a* honourable; (decoroso) decent; (merecedor) worthy (**de** of). **~ de elogio** praiseworthy

digo *vb* ⇒DECIR

dije *vb* ⇒DECIR

dilatar *vt* expand; (Med) dilate; (prolongar) prolong. □ **~se** *vpr* expand; (Med) dilate; (extenderse) extend; (Mex, demorarse) be late

dilema *m* dilemma

diligen|cia f diligence; (gestión) job; (carruaje) stagecoach. **~te** a diligent

dilucidar vt clarify; solve <misterio>

diluir [17] vt dilute

diluvio m flood

dimensión f dimension; (tamaño) size

diminut|ivo a & m diminutive. **~o** a minute

dimitir vt/i resign

Dinamarca f Denmark

dinamarqués a Danish. ● m Dane

dinámic|a f dynamics. **~o** a dynamic

dinamita f dynamite

dínamo m dynamo

dinastía f dynasty

diner|al m fortune. **~o** m money. **~o efectivo** cash. **~o suelto** change

dinosaurio m dinosaur

dios m god. **~a** f goddess. **¡D~ mío!** good heavens! **¡gracias a D~!** thank God!

diplom|a m diploma. **~acia** f diplomacy. **~ado** a qualified. □ **~arse** vpr (LAm) graduate. **~ático** a diplomatic. ● m diplomat

diptongo m diphthong

diputa|ción f delegation. **~ción provincial** county council. **~do** m deputy; (Pol, en España) member of the Cortes; (Pol, en Inglaterra) Member of Parliament; (Pol, en Estados Unidos) congressman

dique m dike

direc|ción f direction; (señas) address; (los que dirigen) management; (Pol) leadership; (Auto) steering. **~ción prohibida** no entry. **~ción única** one-way. **~ta** f (Auto) top gear. **~tiva** f board;

(Pol) executive committee. **~tivas** fpl guidelines. **~to** a direct; <línea> straight; <tren> through. **en ~to** (TV etc) live. **~tor** m director; (Mus) conductor; (de escuela) headmaster; (de periódico) editor; (gerente) manager. **~tora** f (de escuela etc) headmistress. **~torio** m board of directors; (LAm, de teléfonos) telephone directory

dirig|ente a ruling. ● m & f leader; (de empresa) manager. **~ir** [14] vt direct; (Mus) conduct; run <empresa etc>; address <carta etc>. □ **~irse** vpr make one's way; (hablar) address

disciplina f discipline. **~r** vt discipline. **~rio** a disciplinary

discípulo m disciple; (alumno) pupil

disco m disc; (Mus) record; (deportes) discus; (de teléfono) dial; (de tráfico) sign; (Rail) signal. **~ duro** hard disk. **~ flexible** floppy disk

disconforme a not in agreement

discord|e a discordant. **~ia** f discord

discoteca f discothèque, disco Ⅰ; (colección de discos) record collection

discreción f discretion

discrepa|ncia f discrepancy; (desacuerdo) disagreement. **~r** vi differ

discreto a discreet; (moderado) moderate

discrimina|ción f discrimination. **~r** vt (distinguir) discriminate between; (tratar injustamente) discriminate against

disculpa f apology; (excusa) excuse. **pedir ~s** apologize. **~r** vt excuse, forgive. □ **~rse** vpr apologize

discurs|ar *vi* speak (**sobre** about). **~o** *m* speech

discusión *f* discussion; (riña) argument

discuti|ble *a* debatable. **~r** *vt* discuss; (contradecir) contradict. ● *vi* argue (**por** about)

disecar [7] *vt* stuff; (cortar) dissect

diseminar *vt* disseminate, spread

disentir [4] *vi* disagree (**de** with, **en** on)

diseñ|ador *m* designer. **~ar** *vt* design. **~o** *m* design; (fig) sketch

disertación *f* dissertation

disfraz *m* fancy dress; (para engañar) disguise. **~ar** [10] *vt* dress up; (para engañar) disguise. □ **~arse** *vpr*. **~arse de** dress up as; (para engañar) disguise o.s. as.

disfrutar *vt* enjoy. ● *vi* enjoy o.s. **~ de** enjoy

disgust|ar *vt* displease; (molestar) annoy. □ **~arse** *vpr* get annoyed, get upset; <dos personas> fall out. **~o** *m* annoyance; (problema) trouble; (riña) quarrel; (dolor) sorrow, grief

disidente *a & m & f* dissident

disimular *vt* conceal. ● *vi* pretend

disipar *vt* dissipate; (derrochar) squander

dislocarse [7] *vpr* dislocate

disminu|ción *f* decrease. **~ir** [17] *vi* diminish

disolver [2] (*pp* **disuelto**) *vt* dissolve. □ **~se** *vpr* dissolve

dispar *a* different

disparar *vt* fire; (Mex, pagar) buy. ● *vi* shoot (**contra** at)

disparate *m* silly thing; (error) mistake. **decir ~s** talk nonsense. **¡qué ~!** how ridiculous!

disparidad *f* disparity

disparo *m* (acción) firing; (tiro) shot

dispensar *vt* give; (eximir) exempt. ● *vi*. **¡Vd dispense!** forgive me

dispers|ar *vt* scatter, disperse. □ **~arse** *vpr* scatter, disperse. **~ión** *f* dispersion. **~o** *a* scattered

dispon|er [34] *vt* arrange; (Jurid) order. ● *vi*. **~er de** have; (vender etc) dispose of. □ **~erse** *vpr* prepare (**a** to). **~ibilidad** *f* availability. **~ible** *a* available

disposición *f* arrangement; (aptitud) talent; (disponibilidad) disposal; (Jurid) order, decree. **~ de ánimo** frame of mind. **a la ~ de** at the disposal of. **a su ~** at your service

dispositivo *m* device

dispuesto *a* ready; <persona> disposed (**a** to); (servicial) helpful

disputa *f* dispute; (pelea) argument

disquete *m* diskette, floppy disk

dista|ncia *f* distance. **a ~ncia** from a distance. **guardar las ~ncias** keep one's distance. **~nciar** *vt* space out; distance <amigos>. □ **~nciarse** *vpr* <dos personas> fall out. **~nte** *a* distant. **~r** *vi* be away; (fig) be far. **~ 5 kilómetros** it's 5 kilometres away

distin|ción *f* distinction; (honor) award. **~guido** *a* distinguished. **~guir** [13] *vt/i* distinguish. □ **~guirse** *vpr* distinguish o.s.; (diferenciarse) differ. **~tivo** *a* distinctive. ● *m* badge. **~to** *a* different, distinct

distra|cción *f* amusement; (descuido) absent-mindedness, inattention. **~er** [41] *vt* distract; (divertir) amuse. □ **~erse** *vpr* amuse o.s.; (descuidarse) not pay attention. **~ido** *a* (desatento) absent-minded

D

distribu|ción f distribution.
 ~idor m distributor. **~ir** [17] vt
 distribute
distrito m district
disturbio m disturbance
disuadir vt deter, dissuade
diurno a daytime
divagar [12] vi digress; (hablar sin
 sentido) ramble
diván m settee, sofa
diversi|dad f diversity. **~ficar**
 [7] vt diversify
diversión f amusement,
 entertainment; (pasatiempo)
 pastime
diverso a different
diverti|do a amusing; (que tiene
 gracia) funny. **~r** [4] vt amuse,
 entertain. □ **~rse** vpr enjoy o.s.
dividir vt divide; (repartir) share out
divino a divine
divisa f emblem. **~s** fpl currency
divisar vt make out
división f division
divorci|ado a divorced. ●m
 divorcee. **~ar** vt divorce.
 □ **~arse** vpr get divorced. **~o** m
 divorce
divulgar [12] vt spread; divulge
 <secreto>
dizque adv (LAm) apparently;
 (supuestamente) supposedly
do m C; (solfa) doh
dobl|adillo m hem; (de pantalón)
 turn-up (Brit), cuff (Amer). **~ar** vt
 double; (plegar) fold; (torcer) bend;
 turn <esquina>; dub <película>. ●
 vi turn; <campana> toll. □ **~arse**
 vpr double; (curvarse) bend. **~e** a
 double. ● m double. **el ~e** twice
 as much (**de**, **que** as). **~egar** [12]
 vt (fig) force to give in.
 □ **~egarse** vpr give in
doce a & m twelve. **~na** f dozen
docente a teaching. ● m & f
 teacher

dócil a obedient
doctor m doctor. **~ado** m
 doctorate
doctrina f doctrine
document|ación f
 documentation, papers. **~al** a &
 m documentary. **~o** m document.
 D~o Nacional de Identidad
 national identity card
dólar m dollar
dolarizar vt dollarize
dol|er [2] vi hurt, ache; (fig)
 grieve. **me duele la cabeza** I have a
 headache. **le duele el estómago** he
 has (a) stomach-ache. **~or** m
 pain; (sordo) ache; (fig) sorrow.
 ~or de cabeza headache. **~or de
 muelas** toothache. **~oroso** a
 painful
domar vt tame; break in
 <caballo>
dom|esticar [7] vt domesticate.
 ~éstico a domestic
domicili|ar vt. **~ar los pagos** pay
 by direct debit. **~o** m address.
 ~o particular home address.
 reparto a ~o home delivery
 service
domina|nte a dominant;
 <persona> domineering. **~r** vt
 dominate; (contener) control;
 (conocer) have a good command
 of. ●vi dominate. □ **~rse** vpr
 control o.s.
domingo m Sunday
dominio m authority; (territorio)
 domain; (fig) command
dominó m (pl **~s**) domino
don m talent, gift; (en un sobre) Mr.
 ~ Pedro Pedro
donación f donation
donaire m grace, charm
dona|nte m & f (de sangre) donor.
 ~r vt donate
doncella f maiden; (criada) maid
donde adv where

dónde *adv* where?; (LAm, cómo) how; ¿hasta ∼? how far? ¿por ∼? whereabouts?; (por qué camino?) which way? ¿a ∼ vas? where are you going? ¿de ∼ eres? where are you from?

dondequiera *adv*. ∼ que wherever. por ∼ everywhere

doña *f* (en un sobre) Mrs. ∼ María María

dora|do *a* golden; (cubierto de oro) gilt. ∼r *vt* gilt; (Culin) brown

dormi|do *a* asleep. quedarse ∼do fall asleep; (no despertar) oversleep. ∼r [6] *vt* send to sleep. ∼r la siesta have an afternoon nap, have a siesta. ● *vi* sleep. □ ∼rse *vpr* fall asleep. ∼tar *vi* doze. ∼torio *m* bedroom

dors|al *a* back. ● *m* (en deportes) number. ∼o *m* back. nadar de ∼ (Mex) do (the) backstroke

dos *a & m* two. de ∼ en ∼ in twos, in pairs. los ∼, las ∼ both (of them). ∼cientos *a & m* two hundred

dosi|ficar [7] *vt* dose; (fig) measure out. ∼s *f invar* dose

dot|ado *a* gifted. ∼ar *vt* give a dowry; (proveer) provide (de with). ∼e *m* dowry

doy *vb* ⇒DAR

dragar [12] *vt* dredge

drama *m* drama; (obra de teatro) play. ∼turgo *m* playwright

drástico *a* drastic

droga *f* drug. ∼dicto *m* drug addict. ∼do *m* drug addict. ∼r [12] *vt* drug. □ ∼rse *vpr* take drugs

droguería *f* hardware store

ducha *f* shower. □ ∼rse *vpr* have a shower

dud|a *f* doubt. poner en ∼a question. sin ∼a (alguna) without a doubt. ∼ar *vt/i* doubt. ∼oso *a* doubtful; (sospechoso) dubious

duelo *m* duel; (luto) mourning

duende *m* imp

dueñ|a *f* owner, proprietress; (de una pensión) landlady. ∼o *m* owner, proprietor; (de una pensión) landlord

duermo *vb* ⇒DORMIR

dul|ce *a* sweet; <*agua*> fresh; (suave) soft, gentle. ● *m* (LAm) sweet. ∼zura *f* sweetness; (fig) gentleness

duna *f* dune

dúo *m* duet, duo

duplica|do *a* duplicated. por ∼ in duplicate. ●*m* duplicate. ∼r [7] *vt* duplicate. □ ∼rse *vpr* double

duque *m* duke. ∼sa *f* duchess

dura|ción *f* duration, length. ∼dero *a* lasting. ∼nte *prep* during; (medida de tiempo) for. ∼ todo el año all year round. ∼r *vi* last

durazno *m* (LAm, fruta) peach

dureza *f* hardness; (Culin) toughness; (fig) harshness

duro *a* hard; (Culin) tough; (fig) harsh. ● *adv* (esp LAm) hard

e *conj* and

Ébola *m* ebola

ebrio *a* drunk

ebullición *f* boiling

eccema *m* eczema

echar *vt* throw; post <*carta*>; give off <*olor*>; pour <*líquido*>; (expulsar) expel; (de recinto) throw out; fire <*empleado*>; (poner) put on; get <*gasolina*>; put out

<raíces>; show *<película>*. ~ a start. ~ a perder spoil. ~ de menos miss. ~se atrás (fig) back down. echárselas de feign. □ ~se *vpr* throw o.s.; (tumbarse) lie down

eclesiástico *a* ecclesiastical

eclipse *m* eclipse

eco *m* echo. hacerse ~ de echo

ecolog|ía *f* ecology. ~ista *m & f* ecologist

economato *m* cooperative store

econ|omía *f* economy; (ciencia) economics. ~ómico *a* economic; (no caro) inexpensive. ~omista *m & f* economist. ~omizar [10] *vt/i* economize

ecuación *f* equation

ecuador *m* equator. el E~ the Equator. E~ (país) Ecuador

ecuánime *a* level-headed; (imparcial) impartial

ecuatoriano *a & m* Ecuadorian

ecuestre *a* equestrian

edad *f* age. ~ avanzada old age. E~ de Piedra Stone Age. E~ Media Middle Ages. ¿qué ~ tiene? how old is he?

edición *f* edition; (publicación) publication

edicto *m* edict

edific|ación *f* building. ~ante *a* edifying. ~ar [7] *vt* build; (fig) edify. ~io *m* building; (fig) structure

edit|ar *vt* edit; (publicar) publish. ~or *a* publishing. ● *m* editor; (que publica) publisher. ~orial *a* editorial. ● *m* leading article. ● *f* publishing house

edredón *m* duvet

educa|ción *f* upbringing; (modales) (good) manners; (enseñanza) education. falta de ~ción rudeness, bad manners. ~do *a* polite. bien ~do polite. mal ~do rude. ~r [7] *vt* bring up;

(enseñar) educate. ~tivo *a* educational

edulcorante *m* sweetener

EE.UU. *abrev* (Estados Unidos) USA

efect|ivamente *adv* really; (por supuesto) indeed. ~ivo *a* effective; (auténtico) real. ● *m* cash. ~o *m* effect; (impresión) impression. en ~o really; (como respuesta) indeed. ~os *mpl* belongings; (Com) goods. ~uar [21] *vt* carry out; make *<viaje, compras etc>*

efervescente *a* effervescent; *<bebidas>* fizzy

efica|cia *f* effectiveness; (de persona) efficiency. ~z *a* effective; *<persona>* efficient

eficien|cia *f* efficiency. ~te *a* efficient

efímero *a* ephemeral

efusi|vidad *f* effusiveness. ~vo *a* effusive; *<persona>* demonstrative

egipcio *a & m* Egyptian

Egipto *m* Egypt

ego|ísmo *m* selfishness, egotism. ~ísta *a* selfish

egresar *vi* (LAm) graduate; (de colegio) leave school, graduate Amer

eje *m* axis; (Tec) axle

ejecu|ción *f* execution; (Mus) performance. ~tar *vt* carry out; (Mus) perform; (matar) execute. ~tivo *m* executive

ejempl|ar *a* exemplary; (ideal) model. ● *m* specimen; (libro) copy; (revista) issue, number. ~ificar [7] *vt* exemplify. ~o *m* example. dar (el) ~o set an example. por ~o for example

ejerc|er [9] *vt* exercise; practise *<profesión>*; exert *<influencia>*. ● *vi* practise. ~icio *m* exercise; (de profesión) practice. hacer ~icios take exercise. ~itar *vt* exercise

ejército *m* army
ejido *m* (Mex) cooperative
ejote *m* (Mex) green bean

....

el

●*artículo definido masculino* (*pl* **los**)

The masculine article **el** is also used before feminine nouns which begin with stressed **a** or **ha**, e.g. **el ala derecha**, **el hada madrina**. Also, preceded by **de**, **el** becomes **del**, and preceded by **a**, **el** becomes **al**

····▶the. **el tren de las seis** the six o'clock train. **el vecino de al lado** the next-door neighbour. **cerca del hospital** near the hospital *No se traduce en los siguientes casos:*

····▶(con nombre abstracto, genérico) **el tiempo vuela** time flies. **odio el queso** I hate cheese. **el hilo es muy durable** linen is very durable

····▶(con colores, días de la semana) **el rojo está de moda** red is in fashion. **el lunes es fiesta** Monday is a holiday

····▶(con algunas instituciones) **termino el colegio mañana** I finish school tomorrow. **lo ingresaron en el hospital** he was admitted to hospital

····▶(con nombres propios) **el Sr. Díaz** Mr Díaz. **el doctor Lara** Doctor Lara

····▶(antes de infinitivo) **es muy cuidadosa en el vestir** she takes great care in the way she dresses. **me di cuenta al verlo** I realized when I saw him

····▶(con partes del cuerpo, artículos personales) *se traduce por un*

posesivo. **apretó el puño** he clenched his fist. **tienes el zapato desatado** your shoe is undone

····▶**el + de. es el de Pedro** it's Pedro's. **el del sombrero** the one with the hat

····▶**el + que** (persona) **el que me atendió** the one who served me. (cosa) **el que se rompió** the one that broke.

····▶**el + que** + *subjuntivo* (quienquiera) whoever. **el que gane la lotería** whoever wins the lottery. (cualquiera) whichever. **compra el que sea más barato** buy whichever is cheaper

....

él *pron* (persona) he; (persona con prep) him; (cosa) it. **es de ~** it's his
elabora|ción *f* elaboration; (fabricación) manufacture. **~r** *vt* elaborate; manufacture <*producto*>; (producir) produce
el|asticidad *f* elasticity. **~ástico** *a & m* elastic
elec|ción *f* choice; (de político etc) election. **~ciones** *fpl* (Pol) election. **~tor** *m* voter. **~torado** *m* electorate. **~toral** *a* electoral; <*campaña*> election
electrici|dad *f* electricity. **~sta** *m & f* electrician
eléctrico *a* electric; <*aparato*> electrical
electri|ficar[7] *vt* electrify. **~zar** [10] *vt* electrify
electrocutar *vt* electrocute. □ **~se** *vpr* be electrocuted
electrodoméstico *a* electrical appliance
electrónic|a *f* electronics. **~o** *a* electronic
elefante *m* elephant
elegan|cia *f* elegance. **~te** *a* elegant
elegía *f* elegy

elegi|ble *a* eligible.~**do** *a* chosen.~**r** [5 & 14] *vt* choose; (por votación) elect

element|al *a* elementary; (esencial) fundamental.~**o** *m* element; (persona) person, bloke (Brit, ▯).~**os** *mpl* (nociones) basic principles

elenco *m* (en el teatro) cast

eleva|ción *f* elevation; (de precios) rise, increase; (acción) raising. ~**dor** *m* (Mex) lift (Brit), elevator (Amer).~**r** *vt* raise; (promover) promote

elimina|ción *f* elimination.~**r** *vt* eliminate; (Informática) delete. ~**toria** *f* preliminary heat

élite /e'lit, e'lite/ *f* elite

ella *pron* (persona) she; (persona con prep) her; (cosa) it. **es de ~** it's hers.~**s** *pron pl* they; (con prep) them. **es de ~s** it's theirs

ello *pron* it

ellos *pron pl* they; (con prep) them. **es de ~** it's theirs

elocuen|cia *f* eloquence.~**te** *a* eloquent

elogi|ar *vt* praise.~**o** *m* praise

elote *m* (Mex) corncob; (Culin) corn on the cob

eludir *vt* avoid, elude

emanar *vi* emanate (**de** from); (originarse) originate (**de** from, in)

emancipa|ción *f* emancipation. ~**r** *vt* emancipate.◻~**rse** *vpr* become emancipated

embadurnar *vt* smear

embajad|a *f* embassy.~**or** *m* ambassador

embalar *vt* pack

embaldosar *vt* tile

embalsamar *vt* embalm

embalse *m* reservoir

embaraz|ada *a* pregnant.● *f* pregnant woman.~**ar** [10] *vt* get pregnant.~**o** *m* pregnancy; (apuro) embarrassment; (estorbo) hindrance.~**oso** *a* awkward, embarrassing

embar|cación *f* vessel.~**cadero** *m* jetty, pier.~**car** [7] *vt* load <*mercancías etc*>.◻~**carse** *vpr* board. ~**carse en** (fig) embark upon

embargo *m* embargo; (Jurid) seizure. **sin ~** however

embarque *m* loading; (de pasajeros) boarding

embaucar [7] *vt* trick

embelesar *vt* captivate

embellecer [11] *vt* make beautiful

embesti|da *f* charge.~**r** [5] *vt/i* charge

emblema *m* emblem

embolsarse *vpr* pocket

embonar *vt* (Mex) fit

emborrachar *vt* get drunk. ◻~**se** *vpr* get drunk

emboscada *f* ambush

embotar *vt* dull

embotella|miento *m* (de vehículos) traffic jam.~**r** *vt* bottle

embrague *m* clutch

embriag|arse [12] *vpr* get drunk. ~**uez** *f* drunkenness

embrión *m* embryo

embroll|ar *vt* mix up; involve <*persona*>.◻~**arse** *vpr* get into a muddle; (en un asunto) get involved.~**o** *m* tangle; (fig) muddle

embruj|ado *a* bewitched; <*casa*> haunted.~**ar** *vt* bewitch.~**o** *m* spell

embrutecer [11] *vt* brutalize

embudo *m* funnel

embuste *m* lie.~**ro** *a* deceitful. ● *m* liar

embuti|do *m* (Culin) sausage.~**r** *vt* stuff

emergencia f emergency

emerger [14] vi appear, emerge

emigra|ción f emigration. ~**nte** a & m & f emigrant. ~**r** vi emigrate

eminen|cia f eminence. ~**te** a eminent

emisario m emissary

emi|sión f emission; (de dinero) issue; (TV etc) broadcast. ~**sor** a issuing; (TV etc) broadcasting. ~**sora** f radio station. ~**tir** vt emit, give out; (TV etc) broadcast; cast <voto>; (poner en circulación) issue

emoci|ón f emotion; (excitación) excitement. ¡qué ~**ón!** how exciting! ~**onado** a moved. ~**onante** a exciting; (conmovedor) moving. ~**onar** vt move. □ ~**onarse** vpr get excited; (conmoverse) be moved

emotivo a emotional; (conmovedor) moving

empacar [7] vt (LAm) pack

empacho m indigestion

empadronar vt register. □ ~**se** vpr register

empalagoso a sickly; <persona> cloying

empalizada f fence

empalm|ar vt connect, join. ● vi meet. ~**e** m junction; (de trenes) connection

empan|ada f (savoury) pie; (LAm, individual) pasty. ~**adilla** f pasty

empantanarse vpr become swamped; <coche> get bogged down

empañar vt steam up; (fig) tarnish. □ ~**se** vpr steam up

empapar vt soak. ~**se** vpr get soaked

empapela|do m wallpaper. ~**r** vt wallpaper

empaquetar vt package

emparedado m sandwich

emparentado a related

empast|ar vt fill <muela>. ~**e** m filling

empat|ar vi draw. ~**e** m draw

empedernido a confirmed; <bebedor> inveterate

empedrar [1] vt pave

empeine m instep

empeñ|ado a in debt; (decidido) determined (en to). ~**ar** vt pawn; pledge <palabra>. □ ~**arse** vpr get into debt; (estar decidido a) be determined (en to). ~**o** m pledge; (resolución) determination. casa f de ~**s** pawnshop. ~**oso** a (LAm) hardworking

empeorar vt make worse. ● vi get worse. □ ~**se** vpr get worse

empequeñecer [11] vt become smaller; (fig) belittle

empera|dor m emperor. ~**triz** f empress

empezar [1 & 10] vt/i start, begin. **para** ~ to begin with

empina|do a <cuesta> steep. ~**r** vt raise. □ ~**rse** vpr <persona> stand on tiptoe

empírico a empirical

emplasto m plaster

emplaza|miento m (Jurid) summons; (lugar) site. ~**r** [10] vt summon; (situar) site

emple|ada f employee; (doméstica) maid. ~**ado** m employee. ~**ar** vt use; employ <persona>; spend <tiempo>. □ ~**arse** vpr get a job. ~**o** m use; (trabajo) employment; (puesto) job

empobrecer [11] vt impoverish. □ ~**se** vpr become poor

empoll|ar vt incubate <huevos>; (🖩, estudiar) cram 🄸. ● vi <ave> sit; <estudiante> 🄸 cram. ~**ón** m 🄸 swot (Brit 🄸), grind (Amer 🄸)

empolvarse vpr powder

E

empotra|do *a* built-in, fitted. ~**r** *vt* fit

emprende|dor *a* enterprising. ~**r** *vt* undertake; set out on <*viaje*>. ~**rla con uno** pick a fight with s.o.

empresa *f* undertaking; (Com) company, firm. ~ **puntocom** dotcom company. ~**rio** *m* businessman; (patrón) employer; (de teatro etc) impresario

empuj|ar *vt* push. ~**e** *m* (fig) drive. ~**ón** *m* push, shove

empuña|dura *f* handle

emular *vt* emulate

en *prep* in; (sobre) on; (dentro) inside, in; (medio de transporte) by. ~ **casa** at home. ~ **coche** by car. ~ **10 días** in 10 days. **de pueblo ~ pueblo** from town to town

enagua *f* petticoat

enajena|ción *f* alienation. ~**ción mental** insanity. ~**r** *vt* alienate; (volver loco) derange

enamora|do *a* in love. ● *m* lover. ~**r** *vt* win the love of. □ ~**rse** *vpr* fall in love (**de** with)

enano *a & m* dwarf

enardecer [11] *vt* inflame. □ ~**se** *vpr* get excited (**por** about)

encabeza|do *m* (Mex) headline. ~**miento** *m* heading; (de periódico) headline. ~**r** [10] *vt* head; lead <*revolución etc*>

encabritarse *vpr* rear up

encadenar *vt* chain; (fig) tie down

encaj|ar *vt* fit; fit together <*varias piezas*>. ● *vi* fit; (cuadrar) tally. □ ~**arse** *vpr* put on. ~**e** *m* lace; (Com) reserve

encaminar *vt* direct. □ ~**se** *vpr* make one's way

encandilar *vt* dazzle; (estimular) stimulate

encant|ado *a* enchanted; <*persona*> delighted. **¡~ado!** pleased to meet you! ~**ador** *a* charming. ~**amiento** *m* spell. ~**ar** *vt* bewitch; (fig) charm, delight. **me ~a la leche** I love milk. ~**o** *m* spell; (fig) delight

encapricharse *vpr*. ~ **con** take a fancy to

encarar *vt* face; (LAm) stand up to <*persona*>. □ ~**se** *vpr*. ~**se con** stand up to

encarcelar *vt* imprison

encarecer [11] *vt* put up the price of. □ ~**se** *vpr* become more expensive

encarg|ado *a* in charge. ● *m* manager, person in charge. ~**ar** [12] *vt* entrust; (pedir) order. □ ~**arse** *vpr* take charge (de of). ~**o** *m* job; (Com) order; (recado) errand. **hecho de ~o** made to measure

encariñarse *vpr*. ~ **con** take to, become fond of

encarna|ción *f* incarnation. ~**do** *a* incarnate; (rojo) red; <*uña*> ingrowing. ● *m* red

encarnizado *a* bitter

encarpetar *vt* file; (LAm, dar carpetazo) shelve

encarrilar *vt* put back on the rails; (fig) direct, put on the right track

encasillar *vt* classify; (fig) pigeonhole

encauzar [10] *vt* channel

enceguecer *vt* [11] (LAm) blind

encend|edor *m* lighter. ~**er** [1] *vt* light; switch on, turn on <*aparato eléctrico*>; start <*motor*>; (fig) arouse. □ ~**erse** *vpr* light; <*aparato eléctrico*> come on; (excitarse) get excited; (ruborizarse) blush. ~**ido** *a* lit; <*aparato eléctrico*> on; (rojo) bright red. ● *m* (Auto) ignition

encera|do *a* waxed. ● *m* (pizarra) blackboard. ~*r vt* wax

encerr|ar [1] *vt* shut in; (con llave) lock up; (fig, contener) contain. ~**ona** *f* trap

enchilar *vt* (Mex) add chili to

enchinar *vt* (Mex) perm

enchuf|ado *a* switched on. ~**ar** *vt* plug in; fit together <*tubos etc*>. ~**e** *m* socket; (clavija) plug; (de tubos etc) joint; (▯, influencia) contact. **tener** ~**e** have friends in the right places

encía *f* gum

enciclopedia *f* encyclopaedia

encierro *m* confinement; (cárcel) prison

encim|a *adv* on top; (arriba) above. ~ **de** on, on top of; (sobre) over; (además de) besides, as well as. **por** ~ on top; (a la ligera) superficially. **por** ~ **de todo** above all. ~**ar** *vt* (Mex) stack up. ~**era** *f* worktop

encina *f* holm oak

encinta *a* pregnant

enclenque *a* weak; (enfermizo) sickly

encoger [14] *vt* shrink; (contraer) contract. □ ~**se** *vpr* shrink. ~**erse de hombros** shrug one's shoulders

encolar *vt* glue; (pegar) stick

encolerizar [10] *vt* make angry. □ ~**se** *vpr* get furious

encomendar [1] *vt* entrust

encomi|ar *vt* praise. ~**o** *m* praise. ~**oso** *a* (LAm) complimentary

encono *m* bitterness, ill will

encontra|do *a* contrary, conflicting. ~**r** [2] *vt* find; (tropezar con) meet. □ ~**rse** *vpr* meet; (hallarse) be. **no** ~**rse** feel uncomfortable

encorvar *vt* hunch. □ ~**se** *vpr* stoop

encrespa|do *a* <*pelo*> curly; <*mar*> rough. ~**r** *vt* curl <*pelo*>; make rough <*mar*>

encrucijada *f* crossroads

encuaderna|ción *f* binding. ~**dor** *m* bookbinder. ~**r** *vt* bind

encub|ierto *a* hidden. ~**rir** (*pp* **encubierto**) *vt* hide, conceal; cover up <*delito*>; shelter <*delincuente*>

encuentro *m* meeting; (en deportes) match; (Mil) encounter

encuesta *f* survey; (investigación) inquiry

encumbrado *a* eminent; (alto) high

encurtidos *mpl* pickles

endeble *a* weak

endemoniado *a* possessed; (muy malo) wretched

enderezar [10] *vt* straighten out; (poner vertical) put upright; (fig, arreglar) put right, sort out; (dirigir) direct. □ ~**se** *vpr* straighten out

endeudarse *vpr* get into debt

endiablado *a* possessed; (malo) terrible; (difícil) difficult

endosar *vt* endorse <*cheque*>

endulzar [10] *vt* sweeten; (fig) soften

endurecer [11] *vt* harden. □ ~**se** *vpr* harden

enemi|go *a* enemy. ● *m* enemy. ~**stad** *f* enmity. ~**star** *vt* make an enemy of. □ ~**starse** *vpr* fall out (**con** with)

en|ergía *f* energy. ~**érgico** *a* <*persona*> lively; <*decisión*> forceful

energúmeno *m* madman

enero *m* January

enésimo *a* nth, umpteenth ▯

enfada|do *a* angry; (molesto) annoyed. ~**ar** *vt* make cross,

anger; (molestar) annoy. □ **~arse**
vpr get angry; (molestarse) get
annoyed. **~o** *m* anger; (molestia)
annoyance

énfasis *m invar* emphasis, stress.
poner ~ en stress, emphasize

enfático *a* emphatic

enferm|ar *vi* fall ill. □ **~arse** *vpr*
(LAm) fall ill. **~edad** *f* illness.
~era *f* nurse. **~ería** *f* sick bay;
(carrera) nursing. **~ero** *m* (male)
nurse **~izo** *a* sickly. **~o** *a* ill. ●
m patient

enflaquecer [11] *vt* make thin.
● *vi* lose weight

enfo|car [7] *vt* shine on; focus
<*lente*>; (fig) approach. **~que** *m*
focus; (fig) approach

enfrentar *vt* face, confront; (poner
frente a frente) bring face to face.
□ **~se** *vpr*. **~se con** confront; (en
deportes) meet

enfrente *adv* opposite. **~ de**
opposite. **de ~** opposite

enfria|miento *m* cooling; (catarro)
cold. **~r** [20] *vt* cool (down); (fig)
cool down. □ **~rse** *vpr* go cold;
(fig) cool off

enfurecer [11] *vt* infuriate.
□ **~se** *vpr* get furious

engalanar *vt* adorn. □ **~se** *vpr*
dress up

enganchar *vt* hook; hang up
<*ropa*>. □ **~se** *vpr* get caught;
(Mil) enlist

engañ|ar *vt* deceive, trick; (ser
infiel) be unfaithful. □ **~arse** *vpr*
be wrong, be mistaken; (no admitir
la verdad) deceive o.s. **~o** *m* deceit,
trickery; (error) mistake. **~oso** *a*
deceptive; <*persona*> deceitful

engarzar [10] *vt* string <*cuentas*>;
set <*joyas*>

engatusar *vt* 🄵 coax

engendr|ar *vt* father; (fig) breed.
~o *m* (monstruo) monster; (fig)
brainchild

englobar *vt* include

engomar *vt* glue

engordar *vt* fatten, gain <*kilo*>. ●
vi get fatter, put on weight

engorro *m* nuisance

engranaje *m* (Auto) gear

engrandecer [11] *vt* (enaltecer)
exalt, raise

engrasar *vt* grease; (con aceite) oil;
(ensuciar) get grease on

engreído *a* arrogant

engullir [22] *vt* gulp down

enhebrar *vt* thread

enhorabuena *f* congratulations.
dar la ~ congratulate

enigm|a *m* enigma. **~ático** *a*
enigmatic

enjabonar *vt* soap. □ **~se** *vpr* to
soap o.s.

enjambre *m* swarm

enjaular *vt* put in a cage

enjuag|ar [12] *vt* rinse. **~ue** *m*
rinsing; (para la boca) mouthwash

enjugar [12] *vt* wipe (away)

enjuiciar *vt* pass judgement on

enjuto *a* <*persona*> skinny

enlace *m* connection; (matrimonial)
wedding

enlatar *vt* tin, can

enlazar [10] *vt* link; tie together
<*cintas*>; (Mex, casar) marry

enlodar *vt*, **enlodazar** [10] *vt*
cover in mud

enloquecer [11] *vt* drive mad. ●
vi go mad. □ **~se** *vpr* go mad

enlosar *vt* (con losas) pave; (con
baldosas) tile

enmarañar *vt* tangle (up);
entangle; (confundir) confuse.
□ **~se** *vpr* get into a tangle;
(confundirse) get confused

enmarcar [7] *vt* frame

enm|endar *vt* correct.
□ **~endarse** *vpr* mend one's

ways. **~ienda** f correction; (de ley etc) amendment

enmohecerse [11] vpr (con óxido) go rusty; (con hongos) go mouldy

enmudecer [11] vi be dumbstruck; (callar) fall silent

ennegrecer [11] vt blacken

ennoblecer [11] vt ennoble; (fig) add style to

enoj|adizo a irritable. **~ado** a angry; (molesto) annoyed. **~ar** a anger; (molestar) annoy. □ **~arse** vpr get angry; (molestarse) get annoyed. **~o** m anger; (molestia) annoyance. **~oso** a annoying

enorgullecerse [11] vpr be proud

enorm|e a huge, enormous. **~emente** adv enormously. **~idad** f immensity; (de crimen) enormity

enraizado a deeply rooted

enrarecido a rarefied

enred|adera f creeper. **~ar** vt tangle (up), entangle; (confundir) confuse; (involucrar) involve. □ **~arse** vpr get tangled; (confundirse) get confused; <persona> get involved (**con** with). **~o** m tangle; (fig) muddle, mess

enrejado m bars

enriquecer [11] vt make rich; (fig) enrich. □ **~se** vpr get rich

enrojecerse [11] vpr <persona> go red, blush

enrolar vt enlist

enrollar vt roll (up), wind <hilo etc>

enroscar [7] vt coil; (atornillar) screw in

ensalad|a f salad. **armar una ~a** make a mess. **~era** f salad bowl. **~illa** f Russian salad

ensalzar [10] vt praise; (enaltecer) exalt

ensambla|dura f, **ensamblaje** m (acción) assembling; (efecto) joint. **~r** vt join

ensanch|ar vt widen; (agrandar) enlarge. □ **~arse** vpr get wider. **~e** m widening

ensangrentar [1] vt stain with blood

ensañarse vpr. **~ con** treat cruelly

ensartar vt string <cuentas etc>

ensay|ar vt test; rehearse <obra de teatro etc>. **~o** m test, trial; (composición literaria) essay

enseguida adv at once, immediately

ensenada f inlet, cove

enseña|nza f education; (acción de enseñar) teaching. **~nza media** secondary education. **~r** vt teach; (mostrar) show

enseres mpl equipment

ensillar vt saddle

ensimismarse vpr be lost in thought

ensombrecer [11] vt darken

ensordecer [11] vt deafen. ● vi go deaf

ensuciar vt dirty. □ **~se** vpr get dirty

ensueño m dream

entablar vt (empezar) start

entablillar vt put in a splint

entallar vt tailor <un vestido>. ● vi fit

entarimado m parquet; (plataforma) platform

ente m entity, being; (fam, persona rara) weirdo; (Com) firm, company

entend|er [1] vt understand; (opinar) believe, think. ● vi understand. **~er de** know about. **a mi ~er** in my opinion. **dar a ~er** hint. **darse a ~er** (LAm) make o.s. understood □ **~erse** vpr make o.s. understood; (comprenderse) be understood. **~erse con** get on with. **~ido** *a* understood; (enterado) well-informed. **no darse por ~ido** pretend not to understand. ● *interj* agreed!, OK! 🔲 **~imiento** *m* understanding

entera|do *a* well-informed; (que sabe) aware. **darse por ~do** take the hint. **~r** vt inform (**de** of). 🔲 **~rse** *vpr*. **~rse de** find out about, hear of. **¡entérate!** listen! **¿te ~s?** do you understand?

entereza *f* (carácter) strength of character

enternecer [11] *vt* (fig) move, touch. 🔲 **~se** *vpr* be moved, be touched

entero *a* entire, whole. **por ~** entirely, completely

enterra|dor *m* gravedigger. **~r** [1] *vt* bury

entibiar *vt* (enfriar) cool; (calentar) warm (up). 🔲 **~se** *vpr* (enfriarse) cool down; (fig) cool; (calentarse) get warm

entidad *f* entity; (organización) organization; (Com) company; (importancia) significance

entierro *m* burial; (ceremonia) funeral

entona|ción *f* intonation. **~r** vt intone; sing <*nota*>. ● *vi* (Mus) be in tune; <*colores*> match. 🔲 **~rse** *vpr* (emborracharse) get tipsy

entonces *adv* then. **en aquel ~** at that time, then

entorn|ado *a* <*puerta*> ajar; <*ventana*> slightly open. **~o** *m* environment; (en literatura) setting

entorpecer [11] *vt* dull; slow down <*tráfico*>; (dificultar) hinder

entra|da *f* entrance; (incorporación) admission, entry; (para cine etc) ticket; (de datos, Tec) input; (de una comida) starter. **de ~da** right away. **~do** *a*. **~do en años** elderly. **ya**

~da la noche late at night. **~nte** *a* next, coming

entraña *f* (fig) heart. **~s** *fpl* entrails; (fig) heart. **~ble** *a* <*cariño*> deep; <*amigo*> close. **~r** vt involve

entrar vt (traer) bring in; (llevar) take in. ● *vi* go in, enter; (venir) come in, enter; (empezar) start, begin; (incorporarse) join. **~ en**, (LAm) **~ a** go into

entre *prep* (dos personas o cosas) between; (más de dos) among(st)

entre|abierto *a* half-open. **~abrir** (*pp* entreabierto) *vt* half open. **~acto** *m* interval. **~cejo** *m* forehead. **fruncir el ~cejo** frown. **~cerrar** [1] *vt* (LAm) half close. **~cortado** *a* <*voz*> faltering; <*respiración*> laboured. **~cruzar** [10] *vt* intertwine

entrega *f* handing over; (de mercancías etc) delivery; (de novela etc) instalment; (dedicación) commitment. **~r** [12] *vt* deliver; (dar) give; hand in <*deberes*>; hand over <*poder*>. 🔲 **~rse** *vpr* surrender, give o.s. up; (dedicarse) devote o.s. (**a** to)

entre|lazar [10] *vt* intertwine. **~més** *m* hors-d'oeuvre; (en el teatro) short comedy. **~mezclar** vt intermingle

entrena|dor *m* trainer. **~miento** *m* training. **~r** vt train. 🔲 **~rse** *vpr* train

entre|pierna *f* crotch. **~piso** *m* (LAm) mezzanine. **~sacar** [7] *vt* pick out. **~suelo** *m* mezzanine. **~tanto** *adv* meanwhile. **~tejer** vt interweave

entreten|ción *f* (LAm) entertainment. **~er** [40] *vt* entertain, amuse; (detener) delay, keep. 🔲 **~erse** *vpr* amuse o.s.; (tardar) delay, linger. **~ido** *a* (con ser) entertaining; (con estar) busy. **~imiento** m entertainment

entrever [43] vt make out, glimpse

entrevista f interview; (reunión) meeting. □ **~rse** vpr have an interview

entristecer [11] vt sadden, make sad. □ **~se** vpr grow sad

entromet|erse vpr interfere. **~ido** a interfering

entronque m link; (AmL) junction

entumec|erse [11] vpr go numb. **~ido** a numb

enturbiar vt cloud

entusi|asmar vt fill with enthusiasm; (gustar mucho) delight. □ **~asmarse** vpr. **~asmarse con** get enthusiastic about. **~asmo** m enthusiasm. **~asta** a enthusiastic. ● m & f enthusiast

enumerar vt enumerate

envalentonar vt encourage. □ **~se** vpr become bolder

envas|ado m packaging; (en latas) canning; (en botellas) bottling. **~ar** vt package; (en latas) tin, can; (en botellas) bottle. **~e** m packing; (lata) tin, can; (botella) bottle

envejec|er [11] vt make (look) older. ● vi age, grow old. □ **~erse** vpr age, grow old

envenenar vt poison

envergadura f importance

envia|do m envoy; (de la prensa) correspondent. **~r** [20] vt send

enviciarse vpr become addicted (con to)

envidi|a f envy; (celos) jealousy. **~ar** vt envy, be envious of. **~oso** a envious; (celoso) jealous. **tener ~a a** a envy

envío m sending, dispatch; (de mercancías) consignment; (de dinero) remittance. **~ contra reembolso** cash on delivery. **gastos** mpl **de ~** postage and packing (costs)

enviudar vi be widowed

env|oltura f wrapping. **~olver** [2] (pp envuelto) vt wrap; (cubrir) cover; (rodear) surround; (fig, enredar) involve. **~uelto** a wrapped (up)

enyesar vt plaster; (Med) put in plaster

épica f epic

épico a epic

epid|emia f epidemic. **~émico** a epidemic

epil|epsia f epilepsy. **~éptico** a epileptic

epílogo m epilogue

episodio m episode

epístola f epistle

epitafio m epitaph

época f age; (período) period. **hacer ~** make history

equidad f equity

equilibr|ado a (well-)balanced. **~ar** vt balance. **~io** m balance; (de balanza) equilibrium. **~ista** m & f tightrope walker

equinoccio m equinox

equipaje m luggage (esp Brit), baggage (esp Amer)

equipar vt equip; (de ropa) fit out

equiparar vt make equal; (comparar) compare

equipo m equipment; (de personas) team

equitación f riding

equivale|nte a equivalent. **~r** [42] vi be equivalent; (significar) mean

equivoca|ción f mistake, error. **~do** a wrong. □ **~rse** vpr make a mistake; (estar en error) be wrong, be mistaken. **~rse de** be wrong about. **~rse de número** dial the wrong number. **si no me equivoco** if I'm not mistaken

E

equívoco *a* equivocal; (sospechoso) suspicious ● *m* misunderstanding; (error) mistake

era *f* era. ● *vb* ⇒SER

erario *m* treasury

erección *f* erection

eres *vb* ⇒SER

erguir [48] *vt* raise. □ ~**se** *vpr* raise

erigir [14] *vt* erect. □ ~**se** *vpr*. ~**se en** set o.s. up as; (llegar a ser) become

eriza|do *a* prickly. □ ~**rse** [10] *vpr* stand on end; (LAm) <persona> get goose pimples

erizo *m* hedgehog; (de mar) sea urchin. ~ **de mar** sea urchin

ermita *f* hermitage. ~**ño** *m* hermit

erosi|ón *f* erosion. ~**onar** *vt* erode

er|ótico *a* erotic. ~**otismo** *m* eroticism

err|ar [1] (la i inicial pasa a ser y) *vt* miss. ● *vi* wander; (equivocarse) make a mistake, be wrong. ~**ata** *f* misprint. ~**óneo** *a* erroneous, wrong. ~**or** *m* error, mistake. **estar en un** ~**or** be wrong, be mistaken

eruct|ar *vi* belch. ~**o** *m* belch

erudi|ción *f* learning, erudition. ~**to** *a* learned; <palabra> erudite

erupción *f* eruption; (Med) rash

es *vb* ⇒SER

esa *a* ⇒ESE

ésa *pron* ⇒ÉSE

esbelto *a* slender, slim

esboz|ar [10] *vt* sketch, outline. ~**o** *m* sketch, outline

escabeche *m* brine. **en** ~ pickled

escabroso *a* <terreno> rough; <asunto> difficult; (atrevido) crude

escabullirse [22] *vpr* slip away

escafandra *f* diving-suit

escala *f* scale; (escalera de mano) ladder; (Aviac) stopover. **hacer** ~ **en** stop at. **vuelo sin** ~**s** non-stop flight. ~**da** *f* climbing; (Pol) escalation. ~**r** *vt* climb; break into <una casa>. ● *vi* climb, go climbing

escaldar *vt* scald

escalera *f* staircase, stairs; (de mano) ladder. ~ **de caracol** spiral staircase. ~ **de incendios** fire escape. ~ **de tijera** step-ladder. ~ **mecánica** escalator

escalfa|do *a* poached. ~**r** *vt* poach

escalinata *f* flight of steps

escalofrío *m* shiver. **tener** ~**s** be shivering

escalón *m* step, stair; (de escala) rung

escalope *m* escalope

escam|a *f* scale; (de jabón, de la piel) flake. ~**oso** *a* scaly; <piel> flaky

escamotear *vt* make disappear; (robar) steal, pinch

escampar *vi* stop raining

esc|andalizar [10] *vt* scandalize, shock. □ ~**andalizarse** *vpr* be shocked. ~**ándalo** *m* scandal; (alboroto) commotion, racket. **armar un** ~ make a scene. ~**andaloso** *a* scandalous; (alborotador) noisy

escandinavo *a & m* Scandinavian

escaño *m* bench; (Pol) seat

escapa|da *f* escape; (visita) flying visit. ~**r** *vi* escape. **dejar** ~**r** let out. □ ~**rse** *vpr* escape; <líquido, gas> leak

escaparate *m* (shop) window

escap|atoria *f* (fig) way out. ~**e** *m* (de gas, de líquido) leak; (fuga) escape; (Auto) exhaust

escarabajo *m* beetle

escaramuza *f* skirmish

escarbar vt scratch; pick <dientes, herida>; (fig, escudriñar) pry (**en** into). □ ~**se** vpr pick

escarcha f frost. ~**do** a <fruta> crystallized

escarlat|a a invar scarlet. ~**ina** f scarlet fever

escarm|entar [1] vt teach a lesson to. ● vi learn one's lesson. ~**iento** m punishment; (lección) lesson

escarola f endive

escarpado a steep

escas|ear vi be scarce. ~**ez** f scarcity, shortage; (pobreza) poverty. ~**o** a scarce; (poco) little; (muy justo) barely. ~**o de** short of

escatimar vt be sparing with

escayola f plaster

esc|ena f scene; (escenario) stage. ~**enario** m stage; (fig) scene. ~**énico** a stage. ~**enografía** f set design

esc|epticismo m scepticism. ~**éptico** a sceptical. ● m sceptic

esclarecer [11] vt (fig) throw light on, clarify

esclav|itud f slavery. ~**izar** [10] vt enslave. ~**o** a scarce; slave

esclusa f lock; (de presa) floodgate

escoba f broom

escocer [2 & 9] vi sting

escocés a Scottish. ● m Scot

Escocia f Scotland

escog|er [14] vt choose. ~**ido** a chosen; <mercancía> choice; <clientela> select

escolar a school. ● m schoolboy. ● f schoolgirl

escolta f escort

escombros mpl rubble

escond|er vt hide. □ ~**erse** vpr hide. ~**idas** fpl (LAm, juego) hide-and-seek. **a** ~**idas** secretly. ~**ite** m hiding place; (juego) hide-and-seek. ~**rijo** m hiding place

escopeta f shotgun

escoria f slag; (fig) dregs

escorpión m scorpion

Escorpión m Scorpio

escot|ado a low-cut. ~**e** m low neckline. **pagar a** ~**e** share the expenses

escozor m stinging

escri|bano m clerk. ~**bir** (pp **escrito**) vt/i write. ~**bir a máquina** type. ¿**cómo se escribe...?** how do you spell...? □ ~**birse** vpr write to each other. ~**to** a written. **por** ~**to** in writing. ● m document. ~**tor** m writer. ~**torio** m desk; (oficina) office; (LAm, en una casa) study. ~**tura** f (hand) writing; (Jurid) deed

escr|úpulo m scruple. ~**upuloso** a scrupulous

escrut|ar vt scrutinize; count <votos>. ~**inio** m count

escuadr|a f (instrumento) square; (Mil) squad; (Naut) fleet. ~**ón** m squadron

escuálido a skinny

escuchar vt listen to; (esp LAm, oír) hear. ● vi listen

escudo m shield. ~ **de armas** coat of arms

escudriñar vt examine

escuela f school. ~ **normal** teachers' training college

escueto a simple

escuincle m (Mex **I**) kid **I**

escul|pir vt sculpture. ~**tor** m sculptor. ~**tora** f sculptress. ~**tura** f sculpture

escupir vt/i spit

escurr|eplatos m invar plate rack. ~**idizo** a slippery. ~**ir** vt drain; wring out <ropa>. ● vi drain; <ropa> drip. □ ~**irse** vpr slip

ese a (f **esa**) that; (mpl **esos**, fpl **esas**) those

ése *pron* (*f* **ésa**) that one: (*mpl* **ésos**, *fpl* **ésas**) those; (primero de dos) the former

esencia *f* essence. ~**l** *a* essential. **lo** ~**l** the main thing

esf|era *f* sphere; (de reloj) face. ~**érico** *a* spherical

esf|orzarse [2 & 10] *vpr* make an effort. ~**uerzo** *m* effort

esfumarse *vpr* fade away; <*persona*> vanish

esgrim|a *f* fencing. ~**ir** *vt* brandish; (fig) use

esguince *m* sprain

eslabón *m* link

eslavo *a* Slavic, Slavonic

eslogan *m* slogan

esmalt|ar *vt* enamel. ~**e** *m* enamel. ~**e de uñas** nail polish

esmerado *a* careful; <*persona*> painstaking

esmeralda *f* emerald

esmer|arse *vpr* take care (**en** over). ~**o** *m* care

esmero *m* care

esmoquin (*pl* **esmóquines**) *m* dinner jacket, tuxedo (Amer)

esnob *a invar* snobbish. ● *m & f* (*pl* ~**s**) snob. ~**ismo** *m* snobbery

esnórkel *m* snorkel

eso *pron* that. ¡~ **es!** that's it! ~ **mismo** exactly. **a** ~ **de** about. **en** ~ at that moment. ¿**no es** ~**?** isn't that right? **por** ~ that's why. **y** ~ **que** even though

esos *a pl* ⇒ESE

ésos *pron pl* ⇒ÉSE

espabila|do *a* bright; (despierto) awake. ~**r** *vt* (avivar) brighten up; (despertar) wake up. □ ~**rse** *vpr* wake up; (avivarse) wise up; (apresurarse) hurry up

espaci|al *a* space. ~**ar** *vt* space out. ~**o** *m* space. ~**oso** *a* spacious

espada *f* sword. ~**s** *fpl* (en naipes) spades

espaguetis *mpl* spaghetti

espald|a *f* back. **a** ~**as de uno** behind s.o.'s back. **volver la(s)** ~**a(s) a uno** give s.o. the cold shoulder. ~ **mojada** wetback. ~**illa** *f* shoulder-blade

espant|ajo *m*, ~**apájaros** *m invar* scarecrow. ~**ar** *vt* frighten; (ahuyentar) frighten away. □ ~**arse** *vpr* be frightened; (ahuyentarse) be frightened away. ~**o** *m* terror; (horror) horror. ¡**qué** ~**o!** how awful! ~**oso** *a* horrific; (terrible) terrible

España *f* Spain

español *a* Spanish. ● *m* (persona) Spaniard; (lengua) Spanish. **los** ~**es** the Spanish

esparadrapo *m* (sticking) plaster

esparcir [9] *vt* scatter; (difundir) spread. □ ~**rse** *vpr* be scattered; (difundirse) spread; (divertirse) enjoy o.s.

espárrago *m* asparagus

espasm|o *m* spasm. ~**ódico** *a* spasmodic

espátula *f* spatula; (en pintura) palette knife

especia *f* spice

especial *a* special. **en** ~ especially. ~**idad** *f* speciality (Brit), specialty (Amer). ~**ista** *a & m & f* specialist. ~**ización** *f* specialization. □ ~**izarse** [10] *vpr* specialize. ~**mente** *adv* especially

especie *f* kind, sort; (Biol) species. **en** ~ in kind

especifica|ción *f* specification. ~**r** [7] *vt* specify

específico *a* a specific

espect|áculo *m* sight; (de circo etc) show. ~**acular** *a* spectacular. ~**ador** *m & f* spectator

espectro m spectre; (en física) spectrum

especula|dor m speculator. **~r** vi speculate

espej|ismo m mirage. **~o** m mirror. **~o retrovisor** (Auto) rear-view mirror

espeluznante a horrifying

espera f wait. **a la ~** waiting (**de** for). **~nza** f hope. **~r** vt hope; (aguardar) wait for; expect <visita, carta, bebé>. **espero que no** I hope not. **espero que sí** I hope so. ● vi (aguardar) wait. □ **~rse** vpr hang on; (prever) expect

esperma f sperm

esperpento m fright

espes|ar vt/i thicken. □ **~arse** vpr thicken. **~o** a thick. **~or** m thickness

espetón m spit

esp|ía f spy. **~iar** [20] vt spy on. ● vi spy

espiga f (de trigo etc) ear

espina f thorn; (de pez) bone; (Anat) spine. **~ dorsal** spine

espinaca f spinach

espinazo m spine

espinilla f shin; (Med) blackhead; (LAm, grano) spot

espino m hawthorn. **~so** a thorny; (fig) difficult

espionaje m espionage

espiral a & f spiral

esp|iritista m & f spiritualist. **~íritu** m spirit; (mente) mind. **~iritual** a spiritual

espl|éndido a splendid; <persona> generous. **~endor** m splendour

espolear vt spur (on)

espolvorear vt sprinkle

esponj|a f sponge. **~oso** a spongy

espont|aneidad f spontaneity. **~áneo** a spontaneous

esporádico a sporadic

espos|a f wife. **~as** fpl handcuffs. **~ar** vt handcuff. **~o** m husband

espuela f spur; (fig) incentive

espum|a f foam; (en bebidas) froth; (de jabón) lather; (de las olas) surf. **echar ~a** foam, froth. **~oso** a <vino> sparkling

esqueleto m skeleton; (estructura) framework

esquema m outline

esqu|í m (pl ~is, ~íes) ski; (deporte) skiing. **~iar** [20] vi ski

esquilar vt shear

esquimal a & m Eskimo

esquina f corner

esquiv|ar vt avoid; dodge <golpe>. **~o** a elusive

esquizofrénico a & m schizophrenic

esta a ⇒ESTE

ésta pron ⇒ÉSTE

estab|ilidad f stability. **~le** a stable

establec|er [11] vt establish. □ **~erse** vpr settle; (Com) set up. **~imiento** m establishment

establo m cattleshed

estaca f stake

estación f station; (del año) season. **~ de invierno** winter (sports) resort. **~ de servicio** service station

estaciona|miento m parking; (LAm, lugar) car park (Brit), parking lot (Amer). **~r** vt station; (Auto) park. **~rio** a stationary

estadía f (LAm) stay

estadio m stadium; (fase) stage

estadista m statesman. ● f stateswoman

estadístic|a f statistics; (cifra) statistic. **~o** a statistical

estado m state; (Med) condition. **~ civil** marital status. **~ de ánimo**

E

frame of mind. **~ de cuenta** bank statement. **~ mayor** (Mil) staff. **en buen ~** in good condition

Estados Unidos *mpl* United States

estadounidense *a* American, United States. ● *m & f* American

estafa *f* swindle. **~r** *vt* swindle

estafeta *f* (oficina de correos) (sub-) post office

estala|ctita *f* stalactite. **~gmita** *f* stalagmite

estall|ar *vi* explode; *<olas>* break; *<guerra etc>* break out; (fig) burst. **~ar en llanto** burst into tears. **~ar de risa** burst out laughing. **~ido** *m* explosion; (de guerra etc) outbreak

estamp|a *f* print; (aspecto) appearance. **~ado** *a* printed. ● *m* printing; (motivo) pattern; (tela) cotton print. **~ar** *vt* stamp; (imprimir) print

estampido *m* bang

estampilla *f* (LAm, de correos) (postage) stamp

estanca|do *a* stagnant. **~r** [7] *vt* stem. □ **~rse** *vpr* stagnate

estancia *f* stay; (cuarto) large room

estanco *a* watertight. ● *m* tobacconist's (shop)

estandarte *m* standard, banner

estanque *m* pond; (depósito de agua) (water) tank

estanquero *m* tobacconist

estante *m* shelf. **~ría** *f* shelves; (para libros) bookcase

estaño *m* tin

∴∴∴∴∴∴∴∴∴∴∴∴∴∴∴∴∴∴

estar [27]

● *verbo intransitivo*

····▸ to be. **¿cómo estás?** how are you? **estoy enfermo** I'm ill. **está**

muy cerca it's very near. **¿está Pedro?** is Pedro in? **¿cómo está el tiempo?** what's the weather like? **ya estamos en invierno** it's winter already

····▸ (quedarse) to stay. **sólo ~é una semana** I'll only be staying for a week. **estoy en un hotel** I'm staying in a hotel

····▸ (con fecha) **¿a cuánto estamos?** what's the date today? **estamos a 8 de mayo** it's the 8th of May.

····▸ (en locuciones) **¿estamos?** all right? **¡ahí está!** that's it! **~ por** (apoyar a) to support; (LAm, encontrarse a punto de) to be about to; (quedar por) **eso está por verse** that remains to be seen. **son cuentas que están por pagar** they're bills still to be paid

● *verbo auxiliar*

····▸ (con gerundio) **estaba estudiando** I was studying

····▸ (con participio) **está condenado a muerte** he's been sentenced to death. **está mal traducido** it's wrongly translated.

□ **estarse** *verbo pronominal* to stay. **no se está quieto** he won't stay still

⟹ Cuando el verbo **estar** forma parte de expresiones como **estar de acuerdo, estar a la vista, estar constipado,** etc., ver bajo el respectivo nombre o adjetivo

∴∴∴∴∴∴∴∴∴∴∴∴∴∴∴∴∴∴

estatal *a* state

estático *a* static

estatua *f* statue

estatura *f* height

estatuto *m* statute; (norma) rule

este *a* <*región*> eastern; <*viento, lado*> east. ● *m* east. ● *a* (*f* **esta**) this; (*mpl* **estos,** *fpl* **estas**) these; (LAm, como muletilla) well, er

éste *pron* (*f* **ésta**) this one; (*mpl* **éstos**, *fpl* **éstas**) these; (segundo de dos) the latter

estela *f* wake; (de avión) trail; (Arquit) carved stone

estera *f* mat; (tejido) matting

est|éreo *a* stereo. **~ereofónico** *a* stereo, stereophonic

estereotipo *m* stereotype

estéril *a* sterile; <*terreno*> barren

esterilla *f* mat

esterlina *a*. **libra** *f* **~** pound sterling

estético *a* aesthetic

estiércol *m* dung; (abono) manure

estigma *m* stigma. **~s** *mpl* (Relig) stigmata

estil|arse *vpr* be used. **~o** *m* style; (en natación) stroke. **~ mariposa** butterfly. **~ pecho** (LAm) breaststroke. **por el ~o** of that sort

estilográfica *f* fountain pen

estima *f* esteem. **~do** *a* <*amigo, colega*> valued. **~do señor** (en cartas) Dear Sir. **~r** *vt* esteem; have great respect for <*persona*>; (valorar) value; (juzgar) consider

est|imulante *a* stimulating. ● *m* stimulant. **~imular** *vt* stimulate; (incitar) incite. **~ímulo** *m* stimulus

estir|ado *a* stretched; <*persona*> haughty. **~ar** *vt* stretch; (fig) stretch out. **~ón** *m* pull, tug; (crecimiento) sudden growth

estirpe *m* stock

esto *pron neutro* this; (este asunto) this business. **en ~** at this point. **en ~ de** in this business of. **por ~** therefore

estofa|do *a* stewed. ● *m* stew. **~r** *vt* stew

estómago *m* stomach. **dolor** *m* **de ~** stomach ache

estorb|ar *vt* obstruct; (molestar) bother. ● *vi* be in the way. **~o** *m* hindrance; (molestia) nuisance

estornud|ar *vi* sneeze. **~o** *m* sneeze

estos *a mpl* ⇒ESTE

éstos *pron mpl* ⇒ÉSTE

estoy *vb* ⇒ESTAR

estrabismo *m* squint

estrado *m* stage; (Mus) bandstand

estrafalario *a* eccentric; <*ropa*> outlandish

estrago *m* devastation. **hacer ~os** devastate

estragón *m* tarragon

estrambótico *a* eccentric; <*ropa*> outlandish

estrangula|dor *m* strangler; (Auto) choke. **~r** *vt* strangle

estratagema *f* stratagem

estrat|ega *m & f* strategist. **~egia** *f* strategy. **~égico** *a* strategic

estrato *m* stratum

estrech|ar *vt* make narrower; take in <*vestido*>; embrace <*persona*>. **~ar la mano a uno** shake hands with s.o. □ **~arse** *vpr* become narrower; (abrazarse) embrace. **~ez** *f* narrowness. **~eces** *fpl* financial difficulties. **~o** *a* narrow; <*vestido etc*> tight; (fig, íntimo) close. **~o de miras** narrow-minded. ● *m* strait(s)

estrella *f* star. **~ de mar** starfish. **~ado** *a* starry

estrellar *vt* smash; crash <*coche*>. □ **~se** *vpr* crash (**contra** into)

estremec|er [11] *vt* shake. □ **~erse** *vpr* shake; (de emoción etc) tremble (**de** with). **~imiento** *m* shaking

estren|ar *vt* wear for the first time <*vestido etc*>; show for the

first time <_película_>. □ **~arse** _vpr_
make one's début. **~o** _m_ (de
película) première; (de obra de teatro)
first night; (de persona) debut

estreñi|do _a_ constipated.
~miento _m_ constipation

estrés _m_ stress

estría _f_ groove; (de la piel) stretch
mark

estribillo _m_ (incl Mus) refrain

estribo _m_ stirrup; (de coche). step.
perder los ~s lose one's temper

estribor _m_ starboard

estricto _a_ strict

estridente _a_ strident, raucous

estrofa _f_ stanza, verse

estropajo _m_ scourer

estropear _vt_ damage; (plan) spoil;
ruin <_ropa_>. □ **~se** _vpr_ be
damaged; (averiarse) break down;
<_ropa_> get ruined; <_fruta etc_> go
bad; (fracasar) fail

estructura _f_ structure. **~l** _a_
structural

estruendo _m_ roar; (de mucha gente)
uproar

estrujar _vt_ squeeze; wring (out)
<_ropa_>; (fig) drain

estuario _m_ estuary

estuche _m_ case

estudi|ante _m & f_ student.
~antil _a_ student. **~ar** _vt_ study.
~o _m_ study; (de artista) studio.
~oso _a_ studious

estufa _f_ heater; (Mex, cocina)
cooker

estupefac|iente _m_ narcotic. **~to**
_a_ astonished

estupendo _a_ marvellous;
<_persona_> fantastic; **¡~!** that's
great!

est|upidez _f_ stupidity; (acto)
stupid thing. **~úpido** _a_ stupid

estupor _m_ amazement

etapa _f_ stage. **por ~s** in stages

etc _abrev_ (**etcétera**) etc

etéreo _a_ ethereal

etern|idad _f_ eternity. **~o** _a_
eternal

étic|a _f_ ethics. **~o** _a_ ethical

etimología _f_ etymology

etiqueta _f_ ticket, tag; (ceremonial)
etiquette. **de ~** formal

étnico _a_ ethnic

eucalipto _m_ eucalyptus

eufemismo _m_ euphemism

euforia _f_ euphoria

euro _m_ euro

Europa _f_ Europe

europeo _a & m_ European

eurozona _f_ eurozone

eutanasia _f_ euthanasia

evacua|ción _f_ evacuation. **~r**
[21] _vt_ evacuate

evadir _vt_ avoid; evade
<_impuestos_>. □ **~se** _vpr_ escape

evaluar [21] _vt_ assess; evaluate
<_datos_>

evangeli|o _m_ gospel. **~sta** _m & f_
evangelist; (Mex, escribiente) scribe

evapora|ción _f_ evaporation.
□ **~rse** _vpr_ evaporate; (fig)
disappear

evasi|ón _f_ evasion; (fuga) escape.
~vo _a_ evasive

evento _m_ event; (caso) case

eventual _a_ possible. **~idad** _f_
eventuality

eviden|cia _f_ evidence. **poner en
~cia a uno** show s.o. up. **~ciar** _vt_
show. □ **~ciarse** _vpr_ be obvious.
~te _a_ obvious. **~temente** _adv_
obviously

evitar _vt_ avoid; (ahorrar) spare;
(prevenir) prevent

evocar [7] _vt_ evoke

evoluci|ón _f_ evolution. **~onar** _vi_
evolve; (Mil) manoeuvre

ex _pref_ ex-, former

exacerbar _vt_ exacerbate

exact|amente _adv_ exactly.
~itud _f_ exactness. **~o** _a_ exact;

(preciso) accurate; (puntual) punctual. ¡~! exactly!

exagera|ción f exaggeration. ~**do** a exaggerated. ~**r** vt/i exaggerate

exalta|do a exalted; (excitado) (over-)excited; (fanático) hot-headed. ~**r** vt exalt. □ ~**rse** vpr get excited

exam|en m exam, examination. ~**inar** vt examine. □ ~**inarse** vpr take an exam

exasperar vt exasperate. □ ~**se** vpr get exasperated

excarcela|ción f release (from prison). ~**r** vt release

excava|ción f excavation. ~**dora** f digger. ~**r** vt excavate

excede|ncia f leave of absence. ~**nte** a & m surplus. ~**r** vi exceed. □ ~**rse** vpr go too far

excelen|cia f excellence; (tratamiento) Excellency. ~**te** a excellent

exc|entricidad f eccentricity. ~**éntrico** a & m eccentric

excepci|ón f exception. ~**onal** a exceptional. **a** ~**ón de, con** ~**ón de** except (for)

except|o prep except (for). ~**uar** [21] vt except

exces|ivo a excessive. ~**o** m excess. ~**o de equipaje** excess luggage (esp Brit), excess baggage (esp Amer)

excita|ción f excitement. ~**r** vt excite; (incitar) incite. □ ~**rse** vpr get excited

exclama|ción f exclamation. ~**r** vi exclaim

exclu|ir [17] vt exclude. ~**sión** f exclusion. ~**siva** f sole right; (reportaje) exclusive (story). ~**sivo** a exclusive

excomu|lgar [12] vt excommunicate. ~**nión** f excommunication

excremento m excrement

excursi|ón f excursion, outing. ~**onista** m & f day-tripper

excusa f excuse; (disculpa) apology. **presentar sus** ~**s** apologize. ~**r** vt excuse

exento a exempt; (libre) free

exhalar vt exhale, breath out; give off <olor etc>

exhaust|ivo a exhaustive. ~**o** a exhausted

exhibi|ción f exhibition; (demostración) display. ~**cionista** m & f exhibitionist. ~**r** vt exhibit. □ ~**rse** vpr show o.s.; (hacerse notar) draw attention to o.s.

exhumar vt exhume; (fig) dig up

exig|encia f demand. ~**ente** a demanding. ~**ir** [14] vt demand

exiguo a meagre

exil|(i)ado a exiled. ● m exile. □ ~**(i)arse** vpr go into exile. ~**io** m exile

exim|ente m reason for exemption; (Jurid) grounds for acquittal. ~**ir** vt exempt

existencia f existence. ~**s** fpl stock. ~**lismo** m existentialism

exist|ente a existing. ~**ir** vi exist

éxito m success. **no tener** ~ fail. **tener** ~ be successful

exitoso a successful

éxodo m exodus

exonerar vt exonerate

exorbitante a exorbitant

exorci|smo m exorcism. ~**zar** [10] vt exorcise

exótico a exotic

expan|dir vt expand; (fig) spread. □ ~**dirse** vpr expand. ~**sión** f expansion. ~**sivo** a expansive

expatria|do a & m expatriate. □ ~**rse** vpr emigrate; (exiliarse) go into exile

E

expectativa *f* prospect; (esperanza) expectation. **estar a la ∼** be waiting

expedi|ción *f* expedition; (de documento) issue; (de mercancías) dispatch. **∼r** [5] *vt* issue; (enviar) dispatch, send. **∼to** *a* clear; (LAm, fácil) easy

expeler *vt* expel

expend|edor *m* dealer. **∼dor automático** vending machine. **∼io** *m* (LAm) shop; (venta) sale

expensas *fpl* (Jurid) costs. **a ∼ de** at the expense of. **a mis ∼** at my expense

experiencia *f* experience

experiment|al *a* experimental. **∼ar** *vt* test, experiment with; (sentir) experience. **∼o** *m* experiment

experto *a & m* expert

expiar [20] *vt* atone for

expirar *vi* expire

explanada *f* levelled area; (paseo) esplanade

explayarse *vpr* speak at length; (desahogarse) unburden o.s. (**con** to)

explica|ción *f* explanation. **∼r** [7] *vt* explain. □ **∼rse** *vpr* understand; (hacerse comprender) explain o.s. **no me lo explico** I can't understand it

explícito *a* explicit

explora|ción *f* exploration. **∼dor** *m* explorer; (muchacho) boy scout. **∼r** *vt* explore

explosi|ón *f* explosion; (fig) outburst. **∼onar** *vt* blow up. **∼vo** *a & m* explosive

explota|ción *f* working; (abuso) exploitation. **∼r** *vt* work <*mina*>; farm <*tierra*>; (abusar) exploit. ● *vi* explode

expone|nte *m* exponent. **∼r** [34] *vt* expose; display <*mercancías*>; present <*tema*>; set out <*hechos*>; exhibit <*cuadros etc*>; (arriesgar) risk. ● *vi* exhibit. □ **∼rse** *vpr*. **∼se a que** run the risk of

exporta|ción *f* export. **∼dor** *m* exporter. **∼r** *vt* export

exposición *f* exposure; (de cuadros etc) exhibition; (de hechos) exposition

expres|ar *vt* express. □ **∼arse** *vpr* express o.s. **∼ión** *f* expression. **∼ivo** *a* expressive; (cariñoso) affectionate

expreso *a* express. ● *m* express; (café) expresso

exprimi|dor *m* squeezer. **∼r** *vt* squeeze

expropiar *vt* expropriate

expuesto *a* on display; <*lugar etc*> exposed; (peligroso) dangerous. **estar ∼ a** be exposed to

expuls|ar *vt* expel; throw out <*persona*>; send off <*jugador*>. **∼ión** *f* expulsion

exquisito *a* exquisite; (de sabor) delicious

éxtasis *m invar* ecstasy

extend|er [1] *vt* spread (out); (ampliar) extend; issue <*documento*>. □ **∼erse** *vpr* spread; <*paisaje etc*> extend, stretch. **∼ido** *a* spread out; (generalizado) widespread; <*brazos*> outstretched

extens|amente *adv* widely; (detalladamente) in full. **∼ión** *f* extension; (área) expanse; (largo) length. **∼o** *a* extensive

extenuar [21] *vt* exhaust

exterior *a* external, exterior; (del extranjero) foreign; <*aspecto etc*> outward. ● *m* outside, exterior; (países extranjeros) abroad

extermin|ación f extermination. ~ar vt exterminate. ~io m extermination

externo a external; <signo etc> outward. ● m day pupil

extin|ción f extinction. ~guidor m (LAm) fire extinguisher. ~guir [13] vt extinguish. □ ~guirse vpr die out; <fuego> go out. ~to a <raza etc> extinct. ~tor m fire extinguisher

extirpar vt eradicate; remove <tumor>

extorsión f extortion

extra a invar extra; (de buena calidad) good-quality; <huevos> large. **paga** f ~ bonus

extracto m extract

extradición f extradition

extraer [41] vt extract

extranjero a foreign. ● m foreigner; (países) foreign countries. **del** ~ from abroad. **en el** ~, **por el** ~ abroad

extrañ|ar vt surprise; (encontrar extraño) find strange; (LAm, echar de menos) miss. □ ~arse vpr be surprised (de at). ~eza f strangeness; (asombro) surprise. ~o a strange. ● m stranger

extraoficial a unofficial

extraordinario a extraordinary

extrarradio m outlying districts

extraterrestre a extraterrestrial. ● m alien

extravagan|cia f oddness, eccentricity. ~te a odd, eccentric

extrav|iado a lost. ~iar [20] vt lose. □ ~iarse vpr get lost; <objetos> go missing. ~io m loss

extremar vt take extra <precauciones>; tighten up <vigilancia>. □ ~se vpr make every effort

extremeño a from Extremadura

extrem|idad f end. ~idades fpl extremities. ~ista a & m & f extremist. ~o a extreme. ● m end; (colmo) extreme. **en** ~o extremely. **en último** ~o as a last resort

extrovertido a & m extrovert

exuberan|cia f exuberance. ~te a exuberant

eyacular vt/i ejaculate

fa m ; (solfa) fah

fabada f bean and pork stew

fábrica f factory. **marca** f **de** ~ trade mark

fabrica|ción f manufacture. ~ción en serie mass production. ~nte m & f manufacturer. ~r [7] vt manufacture

fábula f fable; (mentira) fabrication

fabuloso a fabulous

facci|ón f faction. ~ones fpl (de la cara) features

faceta f facet

facha f (fam, aspecto) look. ~da f façade

fácil a easy; (probable) likely

facili|dad f ease; (disposición) aptitude. ~dades fpl facilities. ~tar vt facilitate; (proporcionar) provide

factible a feasible

factor m factor

factura f bill, invoice. ~r vt (hacer la factura) invoice; (Aviat) check in

faculta|d f faculty; (capacidad) ability; (poder) power. ~tivo a optional

faena *f* job. **~s domésticas** housework

faisán *m* pheasant

faja *f* (de tierra) strip; (corsé) corset; (Mil etc) sash

fajo *m* bundle; (de billetes) wad

falda *f* skirt; (de montaña) side

falla *f* fault; (defecto) flaw. **~ humana** (LAm) human error. **~r** *vi* fail. **me falló** he let me down. **sin ~r** without fail. ● *vt* (errar) miss

fallec|er [11] *vi* die. **~ido** *m* deceased

fallido *a* vain; (fracasado) unsuccessful

fallo *m* (defecto) fault; (error) mistake. **~ humano** human error; (en certamen) decision; (Jurid) ruling

falluca *f* (Mex) smuggled goods

fals|ear *vt* falsify, distort. **~ificación** *f* forgery. **~ificador** *m* forger. **~ificar** [7] *vt* forge. **~o** *a* false; (falsificado) forged; *<joya>* fake

falt|a *f* lack; (ausencia) absence; (escasez) shortage; (defecto) fault, defect; (culpa) fault; (error) mistake; (en fútbol etc) foul; (en tenis) fault. **a ~a de** for lack of. **echar en ~a** miss. **hacer ~a** be necessary. **me hace ~a** I need. **sacar ~as** find fault. **~o** *a* lacking (**de** in)

....

faltar

● *verbo intransitivo*

!   Cuando el verbo **faltar** va precedido del complemento indirecto **le** (o **les, nos** etc) el sujeto en español pasa a ser el objeto en inglés p.ej: **les falta experiencia** *they lack experience*

····➤ (no estar) to be missing **¿quién falta?** who's missing? **falta una de** **las chicas** one of the girls is missing. **al abrigo le faltan 3 botones** the coat has three buttons missing. **~ a algo** (no asistir) to be absent from sth; (no acudir) to miss sth

····➤ (no haber suficiente) **va a ~ leche** there won't be enough milk. **nos faltó tiempo** we didn't have enough time

····➤ (no tener) **le falta cariño** he lacks affection

····➤ (hacer falta) **le falta sal** it needs more salt. **¡es lo que nos faltaba!** that's all we needed!

····➤ (quedar) **¿te falta mucho?** are you going to be much longer? **falta poco para Navidad** it's not long until Christmas. **aún falta mucho** (distancia) there's a long way to go yet **¡no faltaba más!** of course!

....

fama *f* fame; (reputación) reputation

famélico *a* starving

familia *f* family; (hijos) children. **~ numerosa** large family. **~r** *a* familiar; (de la familia) family; (sin ceremonia) informal; *<lenguaje>* colloquial. ● *m & f* relative. **~ridad** *f* familiarity. □ **~rizarse** [10] *vpr* become familiar (**con** with)

famoso *a* famous

fanático *a* fanatical. ● *m* fanatic

fanfarr|ón *a* boastful. ● *m* braggart. **~onear** *vi* show off

fango *m* mud. **~so** *a* muddy

fantasía *f* fantasy. **de ~** fancy; *<joya>* imitation

fantasma *m* ghost

fantástico *a* fantastic

fardo *m* bundle

faringe *f* pharynx

farmac|éutico *m* chemist (Brit), pharmacist, druggist (Amer). **~ia** *f* (ciencia) pharmacy; (tienda) chemist's (shop) (Brit), pharmacy

faro *m* lighthouse; (Aviac) beacon; (Auto) headlight

farol *m* lantern; (de la calle) street lamp. **~a** *f* street lamp

farr|a *f* partying. **~ear** *vi* (LAm) go out partying

farsa *f* farce. **~nte** *m & f* fraud

fascículo *m* instalment

fascinar *vt* fascinate

fascista *a & m & f* fascist

fase *f* phase

fastidi|ar *vt* annoy; (estropear) spoil. □ **~arse** *vpr* <*máquina*> break down; hurt <*pierna*>; (LAm, molestarse) get annoyed. **¡para que te ~es!** so there!. **~o** *m* nuisance; (aburrimiento) boredom. **~oso** *a* annoying

fatal *a* fateful; (mortal) fatal; (𝕀, pésimo) terrible. **~idad** *f* fate; (desgracia) misfortune

fatig|a *f* fatigue. **~ar** [12] *vt* tire. □ **~arse** *vpr* get tired. **~oso** *a* tiring

fauna *f* fauna

favor *m* favour. **a ~ de, en ~ de** in favour of. **haga el ~ de** would you be so kind as to, please. **por ~** please

favorec|er [11] *vt* favour; <*vestido, peinado etc*> suit

favorito *a & m* favourite

fax *m* fax

faxear *vt* fax

faz *f* face

fe *f* faith. **dar ~ de** certify. **de buena ~** in good faith

fealdad *f* ugliness

febrero *m* February

febril *a* feverish

fecha *f* date. **a estas ~s** now; (todavía) still. **hasta la ~** so far. **poner la ~** date. **~r** *vt* date

fecund|ación *f* fertilization. **~ación artificial** artificial insemination. **~ar** *vt* fertilize. **~o** *a* fertile; (fig) prolific

federa|ción *f* federation. **~l** *a* federal

felici|dad *f* happiness. **~dades** *fpl* best wishes; (congratulaciones) congratulations. **~tación** *f* letter of congratulation. **¡~taciones!** (LAm) congratulations! **~tar** *vt* congratulate

feligrés *m* parishioner

feliz *a* happy; (afortunado) lucky. **¡Felices Pascuas!** Happy Christmas! **¡F~ Año Nuevo!** Happy New Year!

felpudo *m* doormat

fem|enil *a* (Mex) women's. **~enino** *a* feminine; <*equipo*> women's; (Biol, Bot) female. ● *m* feminine. **~inista** *a & m & f* feminist.

fen|omenal *a* phenomenal. **~ómeno** *m* phenomenon; (monstruo) freak

feo *a* ugly; (desagradable) nasty. ● *adv* (LAm, mal) bad

feria *f* fair; (verbena) carnival; (Mex, cambio) small change. **~do** *m* (LAm) public holiday

ferment|ar *vt/i* ferment. **~o** *m* ferment

fero|cidad *f* ferocity. **~z** *a* fierce

férreo *a* iron; <*disciplina*> strict

ferreter|ía *f* hardware store, ironmonger's (Brit). **~o** *m* hardware dealer, ironmonger (Brit)

ferro|carril *m* railway (Brit), railroad (Amer). **~viario** *a* rail. ● *m* railwayman (Brit), railroader (Amer)

fértil *a* fertile

fertili|dad *f* fertility. **~zante** *m* fertilizer. **~zar** [10] *vt* fertilize

F

ferv|iente *a* fervent. ~**or** *m*
fervour

festej|ar *vt* celebrate; entertain
<*persona*>. ~**o** *m* celebration

festiv|al *m* festival. ~**idad** *f*
festivity. ~**o** *a* festive. ● *m* public
holiday

fétido *a* stinking

feto *m* foetus

fiable *a* reliable

fiado *m*. **al** ~ on credit. ~**r** *m*
(Jurid) guarantor

fiambre *m* cold meat. ~**ría** *f*
(LAm) delicatessen

fianza *f* (dinero) deposit; (objeto)
surety. **bajo** ~ on bail

fiar [20] *vt* (vender) sell on credit.
● *vi* give credit. **ser de** ~ be
trustworthy. □ ~**se** *vpr*. ~**se de**
trust

fibra *f* fibre. ~ **de vidrio** fibreglass

fic|ción *f* fiction

fich|a *f* token; (tarjeta) index card;
(en juegos) counter. ~**ar** *vt* open a
file on. **estar** ~**ado** have a (police)
record. ~**ero** *m* card index; (en
informática) file

fidedigno *a* reliable

fidelidad *f* faithfulness. **alta** ~
hi-fi 🄣, high fidelity

fideos *mpl* noodles

fiebre *f* fever. ~ **aftosa** foot-and-
mouth disease. ~ **del heno** hay
fever. ~ **porcina** swine fever.
tener ~ have a temperature

fiel *a* faithful; <*memoria, relato
etc*> reliable. ● *m* believer; (de
balanza) needle

fieltro *m* felt

fier|a *f* wild animal. ~**o** *a* fierce

fierro *m* (LAm) metal bar; (hierro)
iron

fiesta *f* party; (día festivo) holiday.
~**s** *fpl* celebrations

figura *f* figure; (forma) shape. ~**r**
vi appear; (destacar) show off.

□ ~**rse** *vpr* imagine

fij|ación *f* fixing; (obsesión)
fixation. ~**ar** *vt* fix; establish
<*residencia*>. □ ~**arse** *vpr* (poner
atención) pay attention; (percatarse)
notice. **¡fíjate!** just imagine! ~**o** *a*
fixed; (firme) stable; (permanente)
permanent. ● *adv*. **mirar** ~**o** stare

fila *f* line; (de soldados etc) file; (en el
teatro, cine etc) row; (cola) queue.
ponerse en ~ line up

filántropo *m* philanthropist

filat|elia *f* stamp collecting,
philately. ~**élico** *a* philatelic. ●
m stamp collector, philatelist

filete *m* fillet

filial *a* filial. ● *f* subsidiary

Filipinas *fpl*. **las (islas)** ~ the
Philippines

filipino *a* Philippine, Filipino

filmar *vt* film; shoot <*película*>

filo *m* edge; (de hoja) cutting edge.
al ~ **de las doce** at exactly twelve
o'clock. **sacar** ~ **a** sharpen

filología *f* philology

filón *m* vein; (fig) gold-mine

fil|osofía *f* philosophy. ~**ósofo** *m*
philosopher

filtr|ar *vt* filter. □ ~**arse** *vpr* filter;
<*dinero*> disappear; <*noticia*>
leak. ~**o** *m* filter; (bebida) philtre.
~ **solar** sunscreen

fin *m* end; (objetivo) aim. ~ **de
semana** weekend. **a** ~ **de** in order
to. **a** ~ **de cuentas** at the end of
the day. **a** ~ **de que** in order that.
a ~**es de** at the end of. **al** ~
finally. **al** ~ **y al cabo** after all. **dar**
~ **a** end. **en** ~ in short. **por** ~
finally. **sin** ~ endless

final *a* final. ● *m* end. ● *f* final.
~**idad** *f* aim. ~**ista** *m & f*
finalist. ~**izar** [10] *vt* finish. ● *vi*
end

financi|ación f financing; (fondos) funds; (facilidades) credit facilities. ~**ar** vt finance. ~**ero** a financial. ● m financier

finca f property; (tierras) estate; (rural) farm; (de recreo) country house

fingir [14] vt feign; (simular) simulate. ● vi pretend. □ ~**se** vpr pretend to be

finlandés a Finnish. ● m (persona) Finn; (lengua) Finnish

Finlandia f Finland

fino a fine; (delgado) thin; <oído> acute; (de modales) refined; (sútil) subtle

firma f signature; (acto) signing; (empresa) firm

firmar vt/i sign

firme a firm; (estable) stable, steady; <color> fast. ● m (pavimento) (road) surface. ● adv hard. ~**za** f firmness

fisc|al a fiscal, tax. ● m & f public prosecutor. ~**o** m treasury

fisg|ar [12] vi snoop (around). ~**ón** a nosy. ● m snooper

físic|a f physics. ~**o** a physical. ● m physique; (persona) physicist

fisonomista m & f. ser buen ~ be good at remembering faces

fistol m (Mex) tiepin

flaco a thin, skinny; (débil) weak

flagelo m scourge

flagrante a flagrant. en ~ redhanded

flama f (Mex) flame

flamante a splendid; (nuevo) brand-new

flamear vi flame; <bandera etc> flap

flamenco a flamenco; (de Flandes) Flemish. ● m (ave) flamingo; (música etc) flamenco; (idioma) Flemish

flan m crème caramel

flaqueza f thinness; (debilidad) weakness

flauta f flute

flecha f arrow. ~**zo** m love at first sight

fleco m fringe; (Mex, en el pelo) fringe (Brit), bangs (Amer)

flem|a f phlegm. ~**ático** a phlegmatic

flequillo m fringe (Brit), bangs (Amer)

fletar vt charter; (LAm, transportar) transport

flexible a flexible

flirte|ar vi flirt. ~**o** m flirting

floj|ear vi flag; (holgazanear) laze around. ~**o** a loose; (poco fuerte) weak; (perezoso) lazy

flor f flower. la ~ **y nata** the cream. ~**a** f flora. ~**ecer** [11] vi flower, bloom; (fig) flourish. ~**eciente** a (fig) flourishing. ~**ero** m flower vase. ~**ista** m & f florist

flot|a f fleet. ~**ador** m float; (de niño) rubber band. ~**ar** vi float. ~**e** m. **a** ~**e** afloat

fluctua|ción f fluctuation. ~**r** [21] vi fluctuate

flu|idez f fluidity; (fig) fluency. ~**ido** a fluid; (fig) fluent. ● m fluid. ~**ir** [17] vi flow

fluoruro m fluoride

fluvial a river

fobia f phobia

foca f seal

foco m focus; (lámpara) floodlight; (LAm, de coche) (head)light; (Mex, bombilla) light bulb

fogón m cooker; (LAm, fogata) bonfire

folio m sheet

folklórico a folk

follaje m foliage

follet|ín m newspaper serial. ~**o** m pamphlet

F

follón *m* 🆘 mess; (alboroto) row; (problema) trouble

fomentar *vt* promote; boost *<ahorro>*; stir up *<odio>*

fonda *f* (pensión) boarding-house; (LAm, restaurant) cheap restaurant

fondo *m* bottom; (de calle, pasillo) end; (de sala etc) back; (de escenario, pintura etc) background. ~ **de reptiles** slush fund. ~**s** *mpl* funds, money. **a** ~ thoroughly

fonétic|a *f* phonetics. ~**o** *a* phonetic

fontanero *m* plumber

footing /'futin/ *m* jogging

forastero *m* stranger

forcejear *vi* struggle

forense *a* forensic. ● *m & f* forensic scientist

forjar *vt* forge. □ ~**se** *vpr* forge; build up *<ilusiones>*

forma *f* form; (contorno) shape; (modo) way; (Mex, formulario) form. ~**s** *fpl* conventions. **de todas** ~**s** anyway. **estar en** ~ be in good form. ~**ción** *f* formation; (educación) training. ~**l** *a* formal; (de fiar) reliable; (serio) serious. ~**lidad** *f* formality; (fiabilidad) reliability; (seriedad) seriousness. ~**r** *vt* form; (componer) make up; (enseñar) train. □ ~**rse** *vpr* form; (desarrollarse) develop; (educarse) to be educated. ~**to** *m* format

formidable *a* formidable; (muy grande) enormous

fórmula *f* formula; (sistema) way. ~ **de cortesía** polite expression

formular *vt* formulate; make *<queja etc>*. ~**io** *m* form

fornido *a* well-built

forr|ar *vt* (en el interior) line; (en el exterior) cover. ~**o** *m* lining; (cubierta) cover

fortale|cer [11] *vt* strengthen. ~**za** *f* strength; (Mil) fortress; (fuerza moral) fortitude

fortuito *a* fortuitous; *<encuentro>* chance

fortuna *f* fortune; (suerte) luck

forz|ar [2 & 10] *vt* force; strain *<vista>*. ~**osamente** *adv* necessarily. ~**oso** *a* necessary

fosa *f* ditch; (tumba) grave. ~**s nasales** nostrils

fósforo *m* phosphorus; (cerilla) match

fósil *a & m* fossil

foso *m* ditch; (en castillo) moat; (de teatro) pit

foto *f* photo. **sacar** ~**s** take photos

fotocopia *f* photocopy. ~**dora** *f* photocopier. ~**r** *vt* photocopy

fotogénico *a* photogenic

fot|ografía *f* photography; (Foto) photograph. ~**ografiar** [20] *vt* photograph. ~**ógrafo** *m* photographer

foul /faʊl/ *m* (*pl* ~**s**) (LAm) foul

frac *m* (*pl* ~**s** *o* **fraques**) tails

fracas|ar *vi* fail. ~**o** *m* failure

fracción *f* fraction; (Pol) faction

fractura *f* fracture. ~**r** *vt* fracture. □ ~**rse** *vpr* fracture

fragan|cia *f* fragrance. ~**te** *a* fragrant

frágil *a* fragile

fragmento *m* fragment; (de canción etc) extract

fragua *f* forge. ~**r** [15] *vt* forge; (fig) concoct. ● *vi* set

fraile *m* friar; (monje) monk

frambuesa *f* raspberry

franc|és *a* French. ● *m* (persona) Frenchman; (lengua) French. ~**esa** *f* Frenchwoman

Francia *f* France

franco *a* frank; (evidente) marked; (Com) free. ● *m* (moneda) franc

francotirador *m* sniper

franela *f* flannel

franja *f* border; (banda) stripe; (de terreno) strip

franque|ar *vt* clear; (atravesar) cross; pay the postage on *<carta>*. **~o** *m* postage

franqueza *f* frankness

frasco *m* bottle; (de mermelada etc) jar

frase *f* phrase; (oración) sentence. **~ hecha** set phrase

fratern|al *a* fraternal. **~idad** *f* fraternity

fraud|e *m* fraud. **~ulento** *a* fraudulent

fray *m* brother, friar

frecuen|cia *f* frequency. **con ~cia** frequently. **~tar** *vt* frequent. **~te** *a* frequent

frega|dero *m* sink. **~r** [1 & 12] *vt* scrub; wash *<los platos>*; mop *<el suelo>*; (LAm, 🔲, molestar) annoy

freír [51] (*pp* **frito**) *vt* fry. □ **~se** *vpr* fry; *<persona>* roast

frenar *vt* brake; (fig) check

frenético *a* frenzied; (furioso) furious

freno *m* (de caballería) bit; (Auto) brake; (fig) check

frente *m* front. **~ a** opposite. **~ a ~** face to face. **al ~** at the head; (hacia delante) forward. **chocar de ~** crash head on. **de ~ a** (LAm) facing. **hacer ~ a** face *<cosa>*; stand up to *<persona>*. ● *f* forehead. **arrugar la ~** frown

fresa *f* strawberry

fresc|o *a* (frío) cool; (reciente) fresh; (descarado) cheeky. ● *m* fresh air; (frescor) coolness; (mural) fresco; (persona) impudent person. **al ~o** in the open air. **hacer ~o** be cool. **tomar el ~o** get some fresh air. **~or** *m* coolness. **~ura** *f* freshness; (frío) coolness; (descaro) cheek

frialdad *f* coldness; (fig) indifference

fricci|ón *f* rubbing; (fig, Tec) friction; (masaje) massage. **~onar** *vt* rub

frigidez *f* frigidity

frígido *a* frigid

frigorífico *m* fridge, refrigerator

frijol *m* (LAm) bean. **~es refritos** (Mex) fried purée of beans

frío *a* & *m* cold. **tomar ~** catch cold. **hacer ~** be cold. **tener ~** be cold

frito *a* fried; (🔲, harto) fed up. **me tiene ~** I'm sick of him

fr|ivolidad *f* frivolity. **~ívolo** *a* frivolous

fronter|a *f* border, frontier. **~izo** *a* border; *<país>* bordering

frontón *m* pelota court; (pared) fronton

frotar *vt* rub; strike *<cerilla>*

fructífero *a* fruitful

fruncir [9] *vt* gather *<tela>*. **~ el ceño** frown

frustra|ción *f* frustration. **~r** *vt* frustrate. □ **~rse** *vpr* (fracasar) fail. **quedar ~do** be disappointed

frut|a *f* fruit. **~al** *a* fruit. **~ería** *f* fruit shop. **~ero** *m* fruit seller; (recipiente) fruit bowl; **~icultura** *f* fruit-growing. **~o** *m* fruit

fucsia *f* fuchsia. ● *m* fuchsia

fuego *m* fire. **~s artificiales** fireworks. **a ~ lento** on a low heat. **tener ~** have a light

fuente *f* fountain; (manantial) spring; (plato) serving dish; (fig) source

fuera *adv* out; (al exterior) outside; (en otra parte) away; (en el extranjero) abroad. **~ de** outside; (excepto) except for, besides. **por ~** on the outside. ● *vb* ⇒IR y SER

fuerte *a* strong; *<color>* bright; *<sonido>* loud; *<dolor>* severe;

(duro) hard; (grande) large; <*lluvia, nevada*> heavy. ● *m* fort; (fig) strong point. ● *adv* hard; (con hablar etc) loudly; <*llover*> heavily; (mucho) a lot

fuerza *f* strength; (poder) power; (en física) force; (Mil) forces. ~ **de voluntad** will-power. **a ~ de** by (dint of). **a la ~** by necessity. **por ~** by force; (por necesidad) by necessity. **tener ~s para** have the strength to

fuese *vb* ⇒IR *y* SER

fug|a *f* flight, escape; (de gas etc) leak; (Mus) fugue. □ ~**arse** [12] *vpr* flee, escape. ~**az** *a* fleeting. ~**itivo** *a & m* fugitive

fui *vb* ⇒IR, SER

fulano *m* so-and-so. ~**, mengano y zutano** every Tom, Dick and Harry

fulminar *vt* (fig, con mirada) look daggers at

fuma|dor *a* smoking. ● *m* smoker. ~**r** *vt/i* smoke. ~**r en pipa** smoke a pipe. □ ~**rse** *vpr* smoke. ~**rada** *f* puff of smoke

funci|ón *f* function; (de un cargo etc) duty; (de teatro) show, performance. ~**onal** *a* functional. ~**onar** *vi* work, function. **no ~ona** out of order. ~**onario** *m* civil servant

funda *f* cover. ~ **de almohada** pillowcase

funda|ción *f* foundation. ~**mental** *a* fundamental. ~**mentar** *vt* base (**en** on). ~**mento** *m* foundation. ~**r** *vt* found; (fig) base. □ ~**rse** *vpr* be based

fundi|ción *f* melting; (de metales) smelting; (taller) foundry. ~**r** *vt* melt; smelt <*metales*>; cast <*objeto*>; blend <*colores*>; (fusionar) merge; (Elec) blow; (LAm) seize up

<*motor*>. □ ~**rse** *vpr* melt; (unirse) merge

fúnebre *a* funeral; (sombrío) gloomy

funeral *a* funeral. ● *m* funeral. ~**es** *mpl* funeral

funicular *a & m* funicular

furg|ón *m* van. ~**oneta** *f* van

fur|ia *f* fury; (violencia) violence. ~**ibundo** *a* furious. ~**ioso** *a* furious. ~**or** *m* fury

furtivo *a* furtive. **cazador ~** poacher

furúnculo *m* boil

fusible *m* fuse

fusil *m* rifle. ~**ar** *vt* shoot

fusión *f* melting; (unión) fusion; (Com) merger

fútbol *m*, (Mex) **futbol** *m* football

futbolista *m & f* footballer

futur|ista *a* futuristic. ● *m & f* futurist. ~**o** *a & m* future

Gg

gabardina *f* raincoat

gabinete *m* (Pol) cabinet; (en museo etc) room; (de dentista, médico etc) consulting room

gaceta *f* gazette

gafa *f* hook. ~**s** *fpl* glasses, spectacles. ~**s de sol** sunglasses

gaf|ar *vt* 🅸 bring bad luck to. ~**e** *m* jinx

gaita *f* bagpipes

gajo *m* segment

gala *f* gala. ~**s** *fpl* finery, best clothes. **estar de ~** be dressed up. **hacer ~ de** show off

galán *m* (en el teatro) (romantic) hero; (enamorado) lover

galante *a* gallant. ∼**ar** *vt* court. ∼**ría** *f* gallantry

galápago *m* turtle

galardón *m* award

galaxia *f* galaxy

galera *f* galley

galer|ía *f* gallery. ∼**ía comercial** (shopping) arcade. ∼**ón** *m* (Mex) hall

Gales *m* Wales. **país de** ∼ Wales

gal|és *a* Welsh. ● *m* Welshman; (lengua) Welsh. ∼**esa** *f* Welshwoman

galgo *m* greyhound

Galicia *f* Galicia

galimatías *m invar* gibberish

gallard|ía *f* elegance. ∼**o** *a* elegant

gallego *a & m* Galician

galleta *f* biscuit (Brit), cookie (Amer)

gall|ina *f* hen, chicken; (fig, 🄸) coward. ∼**o** *m* cock

galón *m* gallon; (cinta) braid; (Mil) stripe

galop|ar *vi* gallop. ∼**e** *m* gallop

gama *f* scale; (fig) range

gamba *f* prawn (Brit), shrimp (Amer)

gamberro *m* hooligan

gamuza *f* (piel) chamois leather; (de otro animal) suede

gana *f* wish, desire; (apetito) appetite. **de buena** ∼ willingly. **de mala** ∼ reluctantly. **no me da la** ∼ I don't feel like it. **tener** ∼**s de** (+ *infinitivo*) feel like (+ *gerundio*)

ganad|ería *f* cattle raising; (ganado) livestock. ∼**o** *m* livestock. ∼**o lanar** sheep. ∼**o porcino** pigs. ∼**o vacuno** cattle

gana|dor *a* winning. ● *m* winner. ∼**ncia** *f* gain; (Com) profit. ∼**r** *vt*

earn; (en concurso, juego etc) win; (alcanzar) reach. ● *vi* (vencer) win; (mejorar) improve. ∼**rle a uno** beat s.o. ∼**rse la vida** earn a living. **salir** ∼**ndo** come out better off

ganch|illo *m* crochet. **hacer** ∼**illo** crochet. ∼**o** *m* hook; (LAm, colgador) hanger. **tener** ∼**o** be very attractive

ganga *f* bargain

ganso *m* goose

garabat|ear *vt/i* scribble. ∼**o** *m* scribble

garaje *m* garage

garant|e *m & f* guarantor. ∼**ía** *f* guarantee. ∼**izar** [10] *vt* guarantee

garapiña *f* (Mex) pineapple squash. ∼**do** *a*. **almendras** *fpl* ∼**das** sugared almonds

garbanzo *m* chick-pea

garbo *m* poise; (de escrito) style. ∼**so** *a* elegant

garganta *f* throat; (Geog) gorge

gárgaras *fpl*. **hacer** ∼ gargle

garita *f* hut; (de centinela) sentry box

garra *f* (de animal) claw; (de ave) talon

garrafa *f* carafe

garrafal *a* huge

garrapata *f* tick

garrapat|ear *vi* scribble. ∼**o** *m* scribble

garrote *m* club, cudgel; (tormento) garrotte

gar|úa *f* (LAm) drizzle. ∼**uar** *vi* [21] (LAm) drizzle

garza *f* heron

gas *m* gas. **con** ∼ fizzy. **sin** ∼ still

gasa *f* gauze

gaseosa *f* fizzy drink

gas|óleo *m* diesel. ∼**olina** *f* petrol (Brit), gasoline (Amer), gas (Amer). ∼**olinera** *f* petrol station (Brit), gas station (Amer)

G

gast|ado a spent; *<vestido etc>* worn out. **~ador** m spendthrift. **~ar** vt spend; (consumir) use; (malgastar) waste; (desgastar) wear out; wear *<vestido etc>*; crack *<broma>*. □ **~arse** vpr wear out. **~o** m expense; (acción de gastar) spending

gastronomía f gastronomy.

gat|a f cat. **a ~as** on all fours. **~ear** vi crawl

gatillo m trigger

gat|ito m kitten. **~o** m cat. **dar ~o por liebre** take s.o. in

gaucho m Gaucho

gaveta f drawer

gaviota f seagull

gazpacho m gazpacho

gelatina f gelatine; (jalea) jelly

gema f gem

gemelo m twin. **~s** mpl (anteojos) binoculars; (de camisa) cuff-links

gemido m groan

Géminis m Gemini

gemir [5] vi moan; *<animal>* whine, howl

gen m, **gene** m gene

geneal|ogía f genealogy. **~ógico** a genealogical. **árbol** m **~ógico** family tree

generaci|ón f generation. **~onal** a generation

general a general. **en ~** in general. **por lo ~** generally. ● m general. **~izar** [10] vt/i generalize. **~mente** adv generally

generar vt generate

género m type, sort; (Biol) genus; (Gram) gender; (en literatura etc) genre; (producto) product; (tela) material. **~s de punto** knitwear. **~ humano** mankind

generos|idad f generosity. **~o** a generous

genétic|a f genetics. **~o** a genetic

geni|al a brilliant; (divertido) funny. **~o** m temper; (carácter) nature; (talento, persona) genius

genital a genital. **~es** mpl genitals

genoma m genome

gente f people; (nación) nation; (🄵, familia) family, folks; (Mex, persona) person. ● a (LAm) respectable; (amable) kind

gentil a charming. **~eza** f kindness. **tener la ~eza de** be kind enough to

genuflexión f genuflection

genuino a genuine

ge|ografía f geography. **~ográfico** a geographical.

ge|ología f geology. **~ólogo** m geologist

geom|etría f geometry. **~étrico** a geometrical

geranio m geranium

geren|cia f management. **~ciar** vt (LAm) manage. **~te** m & f manager

germen m germ

germinar vi germinate

gestación f gestation

gesticula|ción f gesticulation. **~r** vi gesticulate

gesti|ón f step; (administración) management. **~onar** vt take steps to arrange; (dirigir) manage

gesto m expression; (ademán) gesture; (mueca) grimace

gibraltareño a & m Gibraltarian

gigante a gigantic. ● m giant. **~sco** a gigantic

gimn|asia f gymnastics. **~asio** m gymnasium, gym 🄵. **~asta** m & f gymnast. **~ástic** a gymnastic

gimotear vi whine

ginebra f gin

ginecólogo m gynaecologist

gira f tour. ~**r** vt spin; draw <*cheque*>; transfer <*dinero*>. ● vi rotate, go round; <*en camino*> turn

girasol m sunflower

gir|atorio a revolving. ~**o** m turn; (Com) draft; (locución) expression. ~**o postal** money order

gitano a & m gypsy

glacia|l a icy. ~**r** m glacier

glándula f gland

glasear vt glaze; (Culin) ice

glob|al a global; (fig) overall. ~**o** m globe; (aerostato, juguete) balloon

glóbulo m globule

gloria f glory; (placer) delight. □ ~**rse** vpr boast (**de** about)

glorieta f square; (Auto) roundabout (Brit), (traffic) circle (Amer)

glorificar [7] vt glorify

glorioso a glorious

glotón a gluttonous. ● m glutton

gnomo /'nomo/ m gnome

gob|ernación f government. **Ministerio m de la G~ernación** Home Office (Brit), Department of the Interior (Amer). ~**ernador** a governing. ● m governor. ~**ernante** a governing. ● m & f leader. ~**ernar** [1] vt govern. ~**ierno** m government

goce m enjoyment

gol m goal

golf m golf

golfo m gulf; (niño) urchin; (holgazán) layabout

golondrina f swallow

golos|ina f titbit; (dulce) sweet. ~**o** a fond of sweets

golpe m blow; (puñetazo) punch; (choque) bump; (de emoción) shock; (✗, atraco) job ⧉; (en golf, en tenis, de remo) stroke. ~ **de estado** coup d'etat. ~ **de fortuna** stroke of luck.

~ **de vista** glance. ~ **militar** military coup. **de** ~ suddenly. **de un** ~ in one go. ~**ar** vt hit; (dar varios golpes) beat; (con mucho ruido) bang; (con el puño) punch. ● vi knock

goma f rubber; (para pegar) glue; (banda) rubber band; (de borrar) eraser. ~**a de mascar** chewing gum. ~**a espuma** foam rubber

gord|a f (Mex) small thick tortilla. ~**o** a <*persona*> (con ser) fat; (con estar) have put on weight; <*carne*> fatty; (grueso) thick; (grande) large, big. ● m first prize. ~**ura** f fatness; (grasa) fat

gorila f gorilla

gorje|ar vi chirp. ~**o** m chirping

gorra f cap. ~ **de baño** (LAm) bathing cap

gorrión m sparrow

gorro m cap; (de niño) bonnet. ~ **de baño** bathing cap

got|a f drop; (Med) gout. **ni** ~**a** nothing. ~**ear** vi drip. ~**era** f leak

gozar [10] vt enjoy. ● vi. ~ **de** enjoy

gozne m hinge

gozo m pleasure; (alegría) joy. ~**so** a delighted

graba|ción f recording. ~**do** m engraving, print; (en libro) illustration. ~**dora** f tape-recorder. ~**r** vt engrave; record <*discos etc*>

graci|a f grace; (favor) favour; (humor) wit. ~**as** fpl thanks. ¡~**as!** thank you!, thanks! **dar las** ~**as** thank. **hacer** ~**a** amuse; (gustar) please. ¡**muchas** ~**as!** thank you very much! **tener** ~**a** be funny. ~**oso** a funny. ● m fool, comic character

grad|a f step. ~**as** fpl stand(s). ~**ación** f gradation. ~**o** m degree; (Escol) year (Brit), grade (Amer). **de buen ~o** willingly

gradua|ción f graduation; (de alcohol) proof. **~do** m graduate. **~l** a gradual. **~r** [21] vt graduate; (regular) adjust. □ **~rse** vpr graduate

gráfic|a f graph. **~o** a graphic. ● m graph

gram|ática f grammar. **~atical** a grammatical

gramo m gram, gramme (Brit)

gran a véase GRANDE

grana f (color) deep red

granada f pomegranate; (Mil) grenade

granate m (color) maroon

Gran Bretaña f Great Britain

grande a (delante de nombre en singular **gran**) big, large; (alto) tall; (fig) great; (LAm, de edad) grown up. **~za** f greatness

grandioso a magnificent

granel m. **a ~** in bulk; (suelto) loose; (fig) in abundance

granero m barn

granito m granite; (grano) small grain

graniz|ado m iced drink. **~ar** [10] vi hail. **~o** m hail

granj|a f farm. **~ero** m farmer

grano m grain; (semilla) seed; (de café) bean; (Med) spot. **~s** mpl cereals

granuja m & f rogue

grapa f staple. **~r** vt staple

gras|a f grease; (Culin) fat. **~iento** a greasy

gratifica|ción f (de sueldo) bonus (recompensa) reward. **~r** [7] vt reward

grat|is adv free. **~itud** f gratitude. **~o** a pleasant **~uito** a free; (fig) uncalled for

grava|men m tax; (carga) burden; (sobre inmueble) encumbrance. **~r** vt tax; (cargar) burden

grave a serious; <voz> deep; <sonido> low; <acento> grave. **~dad** f gravity

gravilla f gravel

gravitar vi gravitate; (apoyarse) rest (**sobre** on); <peligro> hang (**sobre** over)

gravoso a costly

graznar vi <cuervo> caw; <pato> quack; honk <ganso>

Grecia f Greece

gremio m union

greña f mop of hair

gresca f rumpus; (riña) quarrel

griego a & m Greek

grieta f crack

grifo m tap, faucet (Amer)

grilletes mpl shackles

grillo m cricket. **~s** mpl shackles

gringo m (LAm) foreigner; (norteamericano) Yankee 🄸

gripe f flu

gris a grey. ● m grey; (🄸, policía) policeman

grit|ar vi shout. **~ería** f, **~erío** m uproar. **~o** m shout; (de dolor, sorpresa) cry; (chillido) scream. **dar ~s** shout

grosella f redcurrant. **~ negra** blackcurrant

groser|ía f rudeness; (ordinariez) coarseness; (comentario etc) coarse remark; (palabra) swearword. **~o** a coarse; (descortés) rude

grosor m thickness

grotesco a grotesque

grúa f crane

grueso a thick; <persona> fat, stout. ● m thickness; (fig) main body

grumo m lump

gruñi|do m grunt; (de perro) growl. **~r** [22] vi grunt; <perro> growl

grupa *f* hindquarters

grupo *m* group

gruta *f* grotto

guacamole *m* guacamole

guadaña *f* scythe

guaje *m* (Mex) gourd

guajolote *m* (Mex) turkey

guante *m* glove

guapo *a* good-looking; <*chica*> pretty; (elegante) smart

guarda *m & f* guard; (de parque etc) keeper. **∼barros** *m invar* mudguard. **∼bosque** *m* gamekeeper. **∼costas** *m invar* coastguard vessel. **∼espaldas** *m invar* bodyguard. **∼meta** *m* goalkeeper. **∼r** *vt* keep; (proteger) protect; (en un lugar) put away; (reservar) save, keep. □ **∼rse** *vpr*. **∼rse de** (+ *infinitivo*) avoid (+ *gerundio*). **∼rropa** *m* wardrobe; (en local público) cloakroom. **∼vallas** *m invar* (LAm) goalkeeper

guardería *f* nursery

guardia *f* guard; (policía) policewoman; (de médico) shift. **G∼ Civil** Civil Guard. **∼ municipal** police. **estar de ∼** be on duty. **estar en ∼** be on one's guard. **montar la ∼** mount guard. ● *m* policeman. **∼ jurado** *m & f* security guard. **∼ de tráfico** *m* traffic policeman. ● *f* traffic policewoman

guardián *m* guardian; (de parque etc) keeper; (de edificio) security guard

guar|ecer [11] *vt* (albergar) give shelter to. □ **∼ecerse** *vpr* take shelter. **∼ida** *f* den, lair; (de personas) hideout

guarn|ecer [11] *vt* (adornar) adorn; (Culin) garnish. **∼ición** *m* adornment; (de caballo) harness; (Culin) garnish; (Mil) garrison; (de piedra preciosa) setting

guas|a *f* joke. **∼ón** *a* humorous. ● *m* joker

Guatemala *f* Guatemala

guatemalteco *a & m* Guatemalan

guateque *m* party, bash

guayab|a *f* guava; (dulce) guava jelly. **∼era** *f* lightweight jacket

gubernatura *f* (Mex) government

güero *a* (Mex) fair

guerr|a *f* war; (método) warfare. **dar ∼a** annoy. **∼ero** *a* warlike; (belicoso) fighting. ● *m* warrior. **∼illa** *f* band of guerrillas. **∼illero** *m* guerrilla

guía *m & f* guide. ● *f* guidebook; (de teléfonos) directory

guiar [20] *vt* guide; (llevar) lead; (Auto) drive. □ **∼se** *vpr* be guided (por by)

guijarro *m* pebble

guillotina *f* guillotine

guind|a *f* morello cherry. **∼illa** *f* chilli

guiñapo *m* rag; (fig, persona) wreck

guiñ|ar *vt/i* wink. **∼o** *m* wink. **hacer ∼os** wink

gui|ón *m* hyphen, dash; (de película etc) script. **∼onista** *m & f* scriptwriter

guirnalda *f* garland

guisado *m* stew

guisante *m* pea. **∼ de olor** sweet pea

guis|ar *vt/i* cook. **∼o** *m* stew

guitarr|a *f* guitar. **∼ista** *m & f* guitarist

gula *f* gluttony

gusano *m* worm; (larva de mosca) maggot

G

----

gustar

● *verbo intransitivo*

! Cuando el verbo **gustar** va precedido del complemento indirecto **le** (o **les, nos** etc), el sujeto en español pasa a ser el objeto en inglés. **me gusta mucho la música** *I like music very much.* **le gustan los helados** *he likes ice cream.* **a Juan no le gusta** *Juan doesn't like it* (or *her* etc.)

····▸ **gustar** + *infinitivo.* **les gusta ver televisión** they like watching television

····▸ **gustar que** + *subjuntivo.* **me ~ía que vinieras** I'd like you to come. **no le gusta que lo corrijan** he doesn't like being corrected. **¿te ~ía que te lo comprara?** would you like me to buy it for you?

····▸ **gustar de algo** to like sth. **gustan de las fiestas** they like parties

····▸ (tener acogida) to go down well. **ese tipo de cosas siempre gusta** those sort of things always go down well. **el libro no gustó** the book didn't go down well

····▸ (en frases de cortesía) to wish. **como guste** as you wish. **cuando gustes** whenever you wish

●*verbo transitivo*

····▸ (LAm, querer) **¿gusta un café?** would you like a coffee? **¿gustan pasar?** would you like to come in?

□ **gustarse** *verbo pronominal* to like each other

gusto *m* taste; (placer) pleasure. **a ~** comfortable. **a mi ~** to my liking. **buen ~** good taste. **con mucho ~** with pleasure. **dar ~** please. **mucho ~** pleased to meet

you. **~so** *a* tasty; (de buen grado) willingly
gutural *a* guttural

ha *vb* ⇒HABER
haba *f* broad bean
Habana *f.* **La ~** Havana
habano *m* (puro) Havana
haber *v aux* [30] have. ●*v impersonal (presente s & pl* **hay**, *imperfecto s & pl* **había**, *pretérito s & pl* **hubo**). **hay una carta para ti** there's a letter for you. **hay 5 bancos en la plaza** there are 5 banks in the square. **hay quehacerlo** it must be done, you have to do it. **he aquí** here is, here are. **no hay de qué** don't mention it, not at all. **¿qué hay?** (¿qué pasa?) what's the matter?; (¿qué tal?) how are you?
habichuela *f* bean
hábil *a* skilful; (listo) clever; <*día*> working; (Jurid) competent
habili|dad *f* skill; (astucia) cleverness; (Jurid) competence. **~tar** *vt* qualify
habita|ción *f* room; (dormitorio) bedroom; (en biología) habitat. **~ción de matrimonio, ~ción doble** double room. **~ción individual, ~ción sencilla** single room. **~do** *a* inhabited. **~nte** *m* inhabitant. **~r** *vt* live in. ●*vi* live
hábito *m* habit
habitua|l *a* usual, habitual; <*cliente*> regular. **~r** [21] *vt* accustom. □ **~rse** *vpr*. **~rse a** get used to

habla f speech; (idioma) language; (dialecto) dialect. **al ~** (al teléfono) speaking. **ponerse al ~ con** get in touch with. **~dor** a talkative. ● m chatterbox. **~duría** f rumour. **~durías** fpl gossip. **~nte** a speaking. ● m & f speaker. **~r** vt speak. ● vi speak, talk (**con** to); (Mex, por teléfono) call. **¡ni ~r!** out of the question! **se ~ español** Spanish spoken

hacend|ado m landowner; (LAm) farmer. **~oso** a hard-working

hacer [31]

● verbo transitivo

····▸ to do. **¿qué haces?** what are you doing? **~ los deberes** to do one's homework. **no sé qué ~** I don't know what to do. **hazme un favor** can you do me a favour?

····▸ (fabricar, preparar, producir) to make. **me hizo un vestido** she made me a dress. **~ un café** to make a (cup of) coffee. **no hagas tanto ruido** don't make so much noise

····▸ (construir) to build <casa, puente>

····▸ **hacer que uno haga algo** to make s.o. do sth. **haz que se vaya** make him leave. **hizo que se equivocara** he made her go wrong

····▸ **hacer hacer algo** to have sth done. **hizo arreglar el techo** he had the roof repaired

➡️ Cuando el verbo **hacer** se emplea en expresiones como **hacer una pregunta**, **hacer trampa** etc., ver bajo el respectivo nombre

● verbo intransitivo

····▸ (actuar, obrar) to do. **hiciste bien en llamar** you did the right thing

to call. **¿cómo haces para parecer tan joven?** what do you do to look so young?

····▸ (fingir, simular) **hacer como que** to pretend. **hizo como que no me conocía** he pretended not to know me. **haz como que estás dormido** pretend you're asleep

····▸ **hacer de** (en teatro) to play the part of; (ejercer la función de) to act as

····▸ (LAm, sentar) **tanta sal hace mal** so much salt is not good for you. **dormir le hizo bien** the sleep did him good. **el pepino me hace mal** cucumber doesn't agree with me

● verbo impersonal

····▸ (hablando del tiempo atmosférico) to be. **hace sol** it's sunny. **hace 3 grados** it's 3 degrees

····▸ (con expresiones temporales) **hace una hora que espero** I've been waiting for an hour. **llegó hace 3 días** he arrived 3 days ago. **hace mucho tiempo** a long time ago. **hasta hace poco** until recently

□ **hacerse** verbo pronominal

····▸ (para sí) to make o.s. <falda, café>

····▸ (hacer que otro haga) **se hizo la permanente** she had her hair permed. **me hice una piscina** I had a swimming pool built

····▸ (convertirse en) to become. **se hicieron amigos** they became friends

····▸ (acostumbrarse) **~se a algo** to get used to sth

····▸ (fingirse) to pretend. **~se el enfermo** to pretend to be ill

····▸ (moverse) to move. **hazte para atrás** move back

····▸ **hacerse de** (LAm) to make <amigo, dinero>

hacha f axe; (antorcha) torch

hacia *prep* towards; (cerca de) near; (con tiempo) at about. ~ **abajo** downwards. ~ **arriba** upwards. ~ **atrás** backwards. ~ **las dos** (at) about two o'clock

hacienda *f* country estate; (en LAm) ranch; **la ~ pública** the Treasury. **Ministerio** *m* **de H~** Ministry of Finance; (en Gran Bretaña) Exchequer; (en Estados Unidos) Treasury

hada *f* fairy. **el ~ madrina** the fairy godmother

hago *vb* ⇒HACER

Haití *m* Haiti

halag|ar [12] *vt* flatter. ~**üeño** *a* flattering; (esperanzador) promising

halcón *m* falcon

halla|r *vt* find; (descubrir) discover. □ ~**rse** *vpr* be. ~**zgo** *m* discovery

hamaca *f* hammock; (asiento) deck-chair

hambr|e *f* hunger; (de muchos) famine. **tener ~e** be hungry. ~**iento** *a* starving

hamburguesa *f* hamburger

harag|án *a* lazy, idle. ● *m* layabout. ~**anear** *vi* laze around

harap|iento *a* in rags. ~**o** *m* rag

harina *f* flour

hart|ar *vt* (fastidiar) annoy. **me estás** ~**ando** you're annoying me. □ ~**arse** *vpr* (llenarse) gorge o.s. (**de** on); (cansarse) get fed up (**de** with). ~**o** *a* full; (cansado) tired; (fastidiado) fed up (**de** with). ● *adv* (LAm) (muy) very; (mucho) a lot

hasta *prep* as far as; (en el tiempo) until, till; (Mex) not until. ● *adv* even. **¡~ la vista!** goodbye!, see you! **⯐ ¡~ luego!** see you later! **¡~ mañana!** see you tomorrow! **¡~ pronto!** see you soon!

hast|iar [20] *vt* (cansar) weary, tire; (aburrir) bore. □ ~**iarse** *vpr*

get fed up (**de** with). ~**ío** *m* weariness; (aburrimiento) boredom

haya *f* beech (tree). ● *vb* ⇒HABER

hazaña *f* exploit

hazmerreír *m* laughing stock

he *vb* ⇒HABER

hebilla *f* buckle

hebra *f* thread; (fibra) fibre

hebreo *a* & *m* Hebrew

hechi|cera *f* witch. ~**cería** *f* witchcraft. ~**cero** *m* wizard. ~**zar** [10] *vt* cast a spell on; (fig) captivate. ~**zo** *m* spell; (fig) charm

hech|o *pp de* **hacer**. ● *a* (manufacturado) made; (terminado) done; <vestidos etc> ready-made; (Culin) done. ● *m* fact; (acto) deed; (cuestión) matter; (suceso) event. **de** ~**o** in fact. ~**ura** *f* making; (forma) form; (del cuerpo) build; (calidad de fabricación) workmanship

hed|er [1] *vi* stink. ~**iondez** *f* stench. ~**iondo** *a* stinking, smelly. ~**or** *m* stench

hela|da *f* frost. ~**dera** *f* (LAm) fridge, refrigerator. ~**dería** *f* ice-cream shop. ~**do** *a* freezing; (congelado) frozen; (LAm, bebida) chilled. ● *m* ice-cream. ~**r** [1] *vt/i* freeze. **anoche heló** there was a frost last night. □ ~**rse** *vpr* freeze

helecho *m* fern

hélice *f* propeller

helicóptero *m* helicopter

hembra *f* female; (mujer) woman

hemorr|agia *f* haemorrhage. ~**oides** *fpl* haemorrhoids

hendidura *f* crack, split; (Geol) fissure

heno *m* hay

heráldica *f* heraldry

hered|ar vt/i inherit. **~era** f heiress. **~ero** m heir. **~itario** a hereditary

herej|e m heretic. **~ía** f heresy

herencia f inheritance; (fig) heritage

heri|da f injury; (con arma) wound. **~do** a injured; (con arma) wounded; (fig) hurt. ● m injured person. **~r** [4] vt injure; (con arma) wound; (fig) hurt. □ **~rse** vpr hurt o.s.

herman|a f sister. **~a política** sister-in-law. **~astra** f stepsister. **~astro** m stepbrother. **~o** m brother. **~o político** brother-in-law. **~os** mpl brothers; (chicos y chicas) brothers and sisters. **~os gemelos** twins

hermético a hermetic; (fig) watertight

hermos|o a beautiful; (espléndido) splendid. **~ura** f beauty

héroe m hero

hero|ico a heroic. **~ína** f heroine; (droga) heroin. **~ísmo** m heroism

herr|adura f horseshoe. **~amienta** f tool. **~ero** m blacksmith

herv|idero m (fig) hotbed; (multitud) throng. **~ir** [4] vt/i boil. **~or** m (fig) ardour. **romper el ~** come to the boil

hiberna|ción f hibernation. **~r** vi hibernate

híbrido a & m hybrid

hice vb ⇒HACER

hidalgo m nobleman

hidrata|nte a moisturizing. **~r** vt hydrate; <crema etc> moisturize

hidráulico a hydraulic

hid|roavión m seaplane. **~oeléctrico** a hydroelectric. **~ofobia** f rabies. **~ófobo** a rabid. **~ógeno** m hydrogen

hiedra f ivy

hielo m ice

hiena f hyena

hierba f grass; (Culin, Med) herb. **mala ~** weed. **~buena** f mint

hierro m iron

hígado m liver

higi|ene f hygiene. **~énico** a hygienic

hig|o m fig. **~uera** f fig tree

hij|a f daughter. **~astra** f stepdaughter. **~astro** m stepson. **~o** m son. **~os** mpl sons; (chicos y chicas) children

hilar vt spin. **~ delgado** split hairs

hilera f row; (Mil) file

hilo m thread; (Elec) wire; (de líquido) trickle; (lino) linen

hilv|án m tacking. **~anar** vt tack; (fig) put together

himno m hymn. **~ nacional** anthem

hincapié m. **hacer ~ en** stress, insist on

hincar [7] vt drive <estaca> (en into). □ **~se** vpr. **~se de rodillas** kneel down

hincha f 🔢 grudge. ● m & f (🔢, aficionado) fan

hincha|do a inflated; (Med) swollen. **~r** vt inflate, blow up. □ **~rse** vpr swell up; (fig, 🔢, comer mucho) gorge o.s. **~zón** f swelling

hinojo m fennel

hiper|mercado m hypermarket. **~sensible** a hypersensitive. **~tensión** f high blood pressure

hípic|a f horse racing. **~o** a horse

hipn|osis f hypnosis. **~otismo** m hypnotism. **~otizar** [10] vt hypnotize

hipo m hiccup. **tener ~** have hiccups

hipo|alérgeno *a* hypoallergenic. **∼condríaco** *a & m* hypochondriac

hip|ocresía *f* hypocrisy. **∼ócrita** *a* hypocritical. ● *m & f* hypocrite

hipódromo *m* racecourse

hipopótamo *m* hippopotamus

hipoteca *f* mortgage. **∼r** [7] *vt* mortgage

hip|ótesis *f invar* hypothesis. **∼otético** *a* hypothetical

hiriente *a* offensive, wounding

hirsuto *a* <barba> bristly; <pelo> wiry

hispánico *a* Hispanic

Hispanoamérica *f* Spanish America

hispano|americano *a* Spanish American. **∼hablante** *a* Spanish-speaking

hist|eria *f* hysteria. **∼érico** *a* hysterical

hist|oria *f* history; (relato) story; (excusa) tale, excuse. **pasar a la ∼oria** go down in history. **∼oriador** *m* historian. **∼órico** *a* historical. **∼orieta** *f* tale; (con dibujos) strip cartoon

hito *m* milestone

hizo *vb* ⇒HACER

hocico *m* snout

hockey /'(x)oki/ *m* hockey. **∼ sobre hielo** ice hockey

hogar *m* home; (chimenea) hearth. **∼eño** *a* domestic; <persona> home-loving

hoguera *f* bonfire

hoja *f* leaf; (de papel, metal etc) sheet; (de cuchillo, espada etc) blade. **∼ de afeitar** razor blade. **∼lata** *f* tin

hojaldre *m* puff pastry

hojear *vt* leaf through

hola *int* hello!

Holanda *f* Holland

holand|és *a* Dutch. ● *m* Dutchman; (lengua) Dutch. **∼esa** *f* Dutchwoman. **los ∼eses** the Dutch

holg|ado *a* loose; (fig) comfortable. **∼ar** [2 & 12] *vi*. **huelga decir que** needless to say. **∼azán** *a* lazy. ● *m* idler. **∼ura** *f* looseness; (fig) comfort

hollín *m* soot

hombre *m* man; (especiehumana) man(kind). ● *int* Good Heavens!; (de duda) well. **∼ de negocios** businessman. **∼ rana** frogman

hombr|era *f* shoulder pad. **∼o** *m* shoulder

homenaje *m* homage, tribute. **rendir ∼ a** pay tribute to

home|ópata *m* homoeopath. **∼opatía** *f* homoeopathy. **∼opático** *a* homoeopathic

homicid|a *a* murderous. ● *m & f* murderer. **∼io** *m* murder

homosexual *a & m & f* homosexual. **∼idad** *f* homosexuality

hond|o *a* deep. **∼onada** *f* hollow

Honduras *f* Honduras

hondureño *a & m* Honduran

honest|idad *f* honesty. **∼o** *a* honest

hongo *m* fungus; (LAm, Culin) mushroom; (venenoso) toadstool

hon|or *m* honour. **∼orable** *a* honourable. **∼orario** *a* honorary. **∼orarios** *mpl* fees. **∼ra** *f* honour; (buena fama) good name. **∼radez** *f* honesty. **∼rado** *a* honest. **∼rar** *vt* honour

hora *f* hour; (momento puntual) time; (cita) appointment. **∼ pico, ∼ punta** rush hour. **∼s fpl de trabajo** working hours. **∼s fpl extraordinarias** overtime. **∼s fpl libres** free time. **a estas ∼s** now. **¿a qué ∼?** (at) what time? **a última ∼** at the last moment. **de**

última ~ last-minute. **en buena ~** at the right time. **media ~** half an hour. **pedir ~** to make an appointment. **¿qué ~ es?** what time is it?

horario *a* hourly. ● *m* timetable. **~ de trabajo** working hours

horca *f* gallows

horcajadas *fpl.* **a ~** astride

horchata *f* tiger-nut milk

horizont|al *a & f* horizontal. **~e** *m* horizon

horma *f* mould; (para fabricar calzado) last; (para conservar su forma) shoe-tree. **de ~ ancha** broad-fitting

hormiga *f* ant

hormigón *m* concrete

hormigue|ar *vi* tingle; (bullir) swarm. **me ~a la mano** I've got pins and needles in my hand. **~o** *m* tingling; (fig) anxiety

hormiguero *m* anthill; (de gente) swarm

hormona *f* hormone

horn|ada *f* batch. **~illa** *f* (LAm) burner. **~illo** *m* burner; (cocina portátil) portable electric cooker. **~o** *m* oven; (para cerámica etc) kiln; (Tec) furnace

horóscopo *m* horoscope

horquilla *f* pitchfork; (para el pelo) hairpin

horr|endo *a* awful. **~ible** *a* horrible. **~ipilante** *a* terrifying. **~or** *m* horror; (atrocidad) atrocity. **¡qué ~or!** how awful!. **~orizar** [10] *vt* horrify. □ **~orizarse** *vpr* be horrified. **~oroso** *a* horrifying

hort|aliza *f* vegetable. **~elano** *m* market gardener

hosco *a* surly

hospeda|je *m* accommodation. **~r** *vt* put up. □ **~rse** *vpr* stay

hospital *m* hospital. **~ario** *a* hospitable. **~idad** *f* hospitality

hostal *m* boarding-house

hostería *f* inn

hostia *f* (Relig) host

hostigar [12] *vt* whip; (fig, molestar) pester

hostil *a* hostile. **~idad** *f* hostility

hotel *m* hotel. **~ero** *a* hotel. ● *m* hotelier

hoy *adv* today. **~ (en) día** nowadays. **~ por ~** at the present time. **de ~ en adelante** from now on

hoy|o *m* hole. **~uelo** *m* dimple

hoz *f* sickle

hube *vb* ⇒HABER

hucha *f* money box

hueco *a* hollow; <palabras> empty; <voz> resonant; <persona> superficial. ● *m* hollow; (espacio) space; (vacío) gap

huelg|a *f* strike. **~a de brazos caídos** sit-down strike. **~a de hambre** hunger strike. **declararse en ~a** come out on strike. **~uista** *m & f* striker

huella *f* footprint; (de animal, vehículo etc) track. **~ digital** fingerprint

huelo *vb* ⇒OLER

huérfano *a* orphaned. ● *m* orphan. **~ de** without

huert|a *f* market garden (Brit), truck farm (Amer); (terreno de regadío) irrigated plain. **~o** *m* vegetable garden; (de árboles frutales) orchard

hueso *m* bone; (de fruta) stone

huésped *m* guest; (que paga) lodger

huesudo *a* bony

huev|a *f* roe. **~o** *m* egg. **~o duro** hard-boiled egg. **~o escalfado** poached egg. **~o estrellado, ~o frito** fried egg. **~o pasado por agua** boiled egg. **~os revueltos**

scrambled eggs. **~o tibio** (Mex) boiled egg

hui|da *f* flight, escape. **~dizo** *a* (tímido) shy; (esquivo) elusive

huipil *m* (Mex) traditional embroidered smock

huir *vi* [17] flee, run away; (evitar). **~ de** avoid. **me huye** he avoids me

huitlacoche *m* (Mex) edible black fungus

hule *m* oilcloth; (Mex, goma) rubber

human|idad *f* mankind; (fig) humanity. **~itario** *a* humanitarian. **~o** *a* human; (benévolo) humane

humareda *f* cloud of smoke

humed|ad *f* dampness; (en meteorología) humidity; (gotitas de agua) moisture. **~ecer** [11] *vt* moisten. □ **~ecerse** *vpr* become moist

húmedo *a* damp; *<clima>* humid; *<labios>* moist; (mojado) wet

humi|ldad *f* humility. **~lde** *a* humble. **~llación** *f* humiliation. **~llar** *vt* humiliate. □ **~llarse** *vpr* lower o.s.

humo *m* smoke; (vapor) steam; (gas nocivo) fumes. **~s** *mpl* airs

humor *m* mood, temper; (gracia) humour. **estar de mal ~** be in a bad mood. **~ista** *m & f* humorist. **~ístico** *a* humorous

hundi|miento *m* sinking. **~r** *vt* sink; destroy *<persona>*. □ **~rse** *vpr* sink; *<edificio>* collapse

húngaro *a & m* Hungarian

Hungría *f* Hungary

huracán *m* hurricane

huraño *a* unsociable

hurgar [12] *vi* rummage (en through). □ **~se** *vpr*. **~se la nariz** pick one's nose

hurra *int* hurray!

hurtadillas *fpl*. **a ~** stealthily

hurt|ar *vt* steal. **~o** *m* theft; (cosa robada) stolen object

husmear *vt* sniff out; (fig) pry into

huyo *vb* ⇒HUIR

iba *vb* ⇒IR

ibérico *a* Iberian

iberoamericano *a & m* Latin American

iceberg /iθ'ber/ *m* (*pl* **~s**) iceberg

ictericia *f* jaundice

ida *f* outward journey; (partida) departure. **de ~ y vuelta** *<billete>* return (Brit), round-trip (Amer); *<viaje>* round

idea *f* idea; (opinión) opinion. **cambiar de ~** change one's mind. **no tener la más remota ~, no tener la menor ~** not have the slightest idea, not have a clue Ⓘ

ideal *a & m* ideal. **~ista** *m & f* idealist. **~izar** [10] *vt* idealize

idear *vt* think up, conceive; (inventar) invent

ídem *pron & adv* the same

idéntico *a* identical

identi|dad *f* identity. **~ficación** *f* identification. **~ficar** [7] *vt* identify. □ **~ficarse** *vpr* identify o.s. **~ficarse con** identify with

ideolo|gía *f* ideology. **~ógico** *a* ideological

idílico *a* idyllic

idilio *m* idyll

idiom|a *m* language. **~ático** *a* idiomatic

idiosincrasia f idiosyncrasy
idiot|a a idiotic. ● m & f idiot.
~**ez** f stupidity
idolatrar vt worship; (fig) idolize
idolo m idol
idóneo a suitable (**para** for)
iglesia f church
iglú m igloo
ignora|ncia f ignorance. ~**nte** a
ignorant. ● m ignoramus. ~**r** vt
not know, be unaware of; (no hacer
caso de) ignore
igual a equal; (mismo) the same;
(similar) like; (llano) even; (liso)
smooth. ● adv the same. ● m
equal. ~ **que** (the same) as. **al** ~
que the same as. **da** ~, **es** ~ it
doesn't matter. **sin** ~ unequalled
igual|ar vt make equal; equal
<éxito, récord>; (allanar) level.
□ ~**arse** vpr be equal. ~**dad** f
equality. ~**mente** adv equally;
(también) also, likewise; (respuesta de
cortesía) the same to you
ilegal a illegal
ilegible a illegible
ilegítimo a illegitimate
ileso a unhurt
ilícito a illicit
ilimitado a unlimited
ilógico a illogical
ilumina|ción f illumination;
(alumbrado) lighting. ~**r** vt light
(up). □ ~**rse** vpr light up
ilusi|ón f illusion; (sueño) dream;
(alegría) joy. **hacerse** ~**ones** build
up one's hopes. **me hace** ~**ón** I'm
thrilled; I'm looking forward to
<algo en el futuro>. ~**onado** a
excited. ~**onar** vt give false
hope. □ ~**onarse** vpr have false
hopes
ilusionis|mo m conjuring. ~**ta** m
& f conjurer
iluso a naive. ● m dreamer. ~**rio** a
illusory

ilustra|ción f learning; (dibujo)
illustration. ~**do** a learned; (con
dibujos) illustrated. ~**r** vt explain;
(instruir) instruct; (añadir dibujos etc)
illustrate. □ ~**rse** vpr acquire
knowledge. ~**tivo** a illustrative
ilustre a illustrious
imagen f image; (TV etc) picture
imagina|ble a imaginable.
~**ción** f imagination. ~**r** vt
imagine. □ ~**rse** vpr imagine.
~**rio** m imaginary. ~**tivo** a
imaginative
imán m magnet
imbécil a stupid. ● m & f idiot
imborrable a indelible; <recuerdo
etc> unforgettable
imita|ción f imitation. ~**r** vt
imitate
impacien|cia f impatience.
□ ~**tarse** vpr lose one's patience.
~**te** a impatient
impacto m impact; (huella) mark.
~ **de bala** bullet hole
impar a odd
imparcial a impartial. ~**idad** f
impartiality
impartir vt impart, give
impasible a impassive
impávido a fearless; (impasible)
impassive
impecable a impeccable
impedi|do a disabled. ~**mento** m
impediment. ~**r** [5] vt prevent;
(obstruir) hinder
impenetrable a impenetrable
impensa|ble a unthinkable. ~**do**
a unexpected
impera|r vi prevail. ~**tivo** a
imperative; <necesidad> urgent
imperceptible a imperceptible
imperdible m safety pin
imperdonable a unforgivable
imperfec|ción f imperfection.
~**to** a imperfect

I

imperi|al *a* imperial. **~alismo** *m* imperialism. **~o** *m* empire; (poder) rule. **~oso** *a* imperious

impermeable *a* waterproof. ● *m* raincoat

impersonal *a* impersonal

impertinen|cia *f* impertinence. **~te** *a* impertinent

imperturbable *a* imperturbable

ímpetu *m* impetus; (impulso) impulse; (violencia) force

impetuos|idad *f* impetuosity. **~o** *a* impetuous

implacable *a* implacable

implantar *vt* introduce

implica|ción *f* implication. **~r** [7] *vt* implicate; (significar) imply

implícito *a* implicit

implorar *vt* implore

impon|ente *a* imposing; Ⓘ terrific. **~er** [34] *vt* impose; (requerir) demand; deposit <*dinero*>. □ **~erse** *vpr* (hacerse obedecer) assert o.s.; (hacerse respetar) command respect; (prevalecer) prevail. **~ible** *a* taxable

importa|ción *f* importation; (artículo) import. **~ciones** *fpl* imports. **~dor** *a* importing. ● *m* importer

importa|ncia *f* importance. **~nte** *a* important; (en cantidad) considerable. **~r** *vt* import; (ascender a) amount to. ● *vi* be important, matter. ¿le **~ría...?** would you mind...? **no ~** it doesn't matter

importe *m* price; (total) amount

importun|ar *vt* bother. **~o** *a* troublesome; (inoportuno) inopportune

imposib|ilidad *f* impossibility. **~le** *a* impossible. **hacer lo ~le para** do all one can to

imposición *f* imposition; (impuesto) tax

impostor *m* impostor

impoten|cia *f* impotence. **~te** *a* impotent

impracticable *a* impracticable; (intransitable) unpassable

imprecis|ión *f* vagueness; (error) inaccuracy. **~o** *a* imprecise

impregnar *vt* impregnate; (empapar) soak

imprenta *f* printing; (taller) printing house, printer's

imprescindible *a* indispensable, essential

impresi|ón *f* impression; (acción de imprimir) printing; (tirada) edition; (huella) imprint. **~onable** *a* impressionable. **~onante** *a* impressive; (espantoso) frightening. **~onar** *vt* impress; (negativamente) shock; (conmover) move; (Foto) expose. □ **~onarse** *vpr* be impressed; (negativamente) be shocked; (conmover) be moved

impresionis|mo *m* impressionism. **~ta** *a & m & f* impressionist

impreso *a* printed. ● *m* form. **~s** *mpl* printed matter. **~ra** *f* printer

imprevis|ible *a* unforeseeable. **~to** *a* unforeseen

imprimir (*pp* **impreso**) *vt* print <*libro etc*>

improbab|ilidad *f* improbability. **~le** *a* unlikely, improbable

improcedente *a* inadmissible; <*conducta*> improper; <*despido*> unfair

improductivo *a* unproductive

improperio *m* insult. **~s** *mpl* abuse

impropio *a* improper

improvis|ación *f* improvisation. **~ado** *a* improvised. **~ar** *vt* improvise. ~o a. de ~o unexpectedly

impruden|cia f imprudence. ~te a imprudent

imp|udicia f indecency; (desvergüenza) shamelessness. ~údico a indecent; (desvergonzado) shameless. ~udor m indecency; (desvergüenza) shamelessness

impuesto a imposed. ● m tax. ~ a la renta income tax. ~ sobre el valor agregado (LAm), ~ sobre el valor añadido VAT, value added tax

impuls|ar vt propel; drive <persona>; boost <producción etc>. ~ividad f impulsiveness. ~ivo a impulsive. ~o m impulse

impun|e a unpunished. ~idad f impunity

impur|eza f impurity. ~o a impure

imputa|ción f charge. ~r vt attribute; (acusar) charge

inaccesible a inaccessible

inaceptable a unacceptable

inactiv|idad f inactivity. ~o a inactive

inadaptado a maladjusted

inadecuado a inadequate; (inapropiado) unsuitable

inadmisible a inadmissible; (inaceptable) unacceptable

inadvertido a distracted. pasar ~ go unnoticed

inagotable a inexhaustible

inaguantable a unbearable

inalter|able a impassive; <color> fast; <convicción> unalterable. ~do a unchanged

inapreciable a invaluable; (imperceptible) imperceptible

inapropiado a inappropriate

inasequible a out of reach

inaudito a unprecedented

inaugura|ción f inauguration. ~l a inaugural. ~r vt inaugurate

inca a & m & f Inca. ~ico a Inca

incalculable a incalculable

incandescente a incandescent

incansable a tireless

incapa|cidad f incapacity; (física) disability. ~citado a disabled. ~citar vt incapacitate. ~z a incapable

incauto a unwary; (fácil de engañar) gullible

incendi|ar vt set fire to. □ ~arse vpr catch fire. ~ario a incendiary. ● m arsonist. ~o m fire

incentivo m incentive

incertidumbre f uncertainty

incesante a incessant

incest|o m incest. ~uoso a incestuous

inciden|cia f incidence; (efecto) impact; (incidente) incident. ~tal a incidental. ~te m incident

incidir vi fall (en into); (influir) influence

incienso m incense

incierto a uncertain

incinera|dor m incinerator. ~r vt incinerate; cremate <cadáver>

incipiente a incipient

incisi|ón f incision. ~vo a incisive. ● m incisor

incitar vt incite

inclemen|cia f harshness. ~te a harsh

inclina|ción f slope; (de la cabeza) nod; (fig) inclination. ~r vt tilt; (inducir) incline. ~rse vpr lean; (en saludo) bow; (tender) be inclined (a to)

inclu|ido a included; <precio> inclusive. ~ir [17] vt include; (en cartas) enclose. ~sión f inclusion. ~sive adv inclusive. hasta el lunes ~**sive** up to and including Monday. ~**so** adv even

incógnito a unknown. **de ~** incognito

incoheren|cia f incoherence. ~**te** a incoherent

incoloro a colourless

incomestible a, **incomible** a uneatable, inedible

incomodar vt inconvenience; (causar vergüenza) make feel uncomfortable. □ ~**se** vpr feel uncomfortable; (enojarse) get angry

incómodo a uncomfortable; (inconveniente) inconvenient

incomparable a incomparable

incompatib|ilidad f incompatibility. ~**le** a incompatible

incompleto a incomplete

incompren|dido a misunderstood. ~**sible** a incomprehensible. ~**sión** f incomprehension

incomunicado a cut off; <preso> in solitary confinement

inconcebible a inconceivable

inconcluso a unfinished

incondicional a unconditional

inconfundible a unmistakable

incongruente a incoherent; (contradictorio) inconsistent

inconmensurable a immeasurable

inconscien|cia f unconsciousness; (irreflexión) recklessness. ~**te** a unconscious; (irreflexivo) reckless

inconsecuente a inconsistent

inconsistente a flimsy

inconsolable a unconsolable

inconstan|cia f lack of perseverance. ~**te** a changeable; <persona> lacking in perseverance; (voluble) fickle

incontable a countless

incontenible a irrepressible

incontinen|cia f incontinence. ~**te** a incontinent

inconvenien|cia f inconvenience. ~**te** a inconvenient; (inapropiado) inappropriate; (incorrecto) improper. ● m problem; (desventaja) drawback

incorpora|ción f incorporation. ~**r** vt incorporate; (Culin) add. □ ~**rse** vpr sit up; join <sociedad, regimiento etc>

incorrecto a incorrect; (descortés) discourteous

incorregible a incorrigible

incorruptible a incorruptible

incrédulo a sceptical; <mirada, gesto> incredulous

increíble a incredible

increment|ar vt increase. ~**o** m increase

incriminar vt incriminate

incrustar vt encrust

incuba|ción f incubation. ~**dora** f incubator. ~**r** vt incubate; (fig) hatch

incuestionable a unquestionable

inculcar [7] vt inculcate

inculpar vt accuse

inculto a uneducated

incumplimiento m non-fulfilment; (de un contrato) breach

incurable a incurable

incurrir vi. ~ **en** incur <gasto>; fall into <error>; commit <crimen>

incursión f raid

indagar [12] vt investigate

indebido a unjust; <uso> improper

indecen|cia f indecency. ~**te** a indecent

indecible a indescribable

indecis|ión f indecision. ~**o** a (con ser) indecisive; (con estar) undecided

indefenso a defenceless

indefini|ble a indefinable. ~**do** a indefinite; (impreciso) undefined

indemnizar [10] vt compensate

independ|encia f independence. ~**iente** a independent. ~**izarse** [10] vpr become independent

indes|cifrable a indecipherable. ~**criptible** a indescribable

indeseable a undesirable

indestructible a indestructible

indetermina|ble a indeterminable. ~**do** a indeterminate; <tiempo> indefinite

India f. **la ~** India

indica|ción f indication; (señal) signal. ~**ciones** fpl directions. ~**dor** m indicator; (Tec) gauge. ~**r** [7] vt show, indicate; (apuntar) point at; (hacer saber) point out; (aconsejar) advise. ~**tivo** a indicative. ● m indicative; (al teléfono) dialling code

índice m index; (dedo) index finger; (catálogo) catalogue; (indicación) indication; (aguja) pointer

indicio m indication, sign; (vestigio) trace

indiferen|cia f indifference. ~**te** a indifferent. **me es ~te** it's all the same to me

indígena a indigenous. ● m & f native

indigen|cia f poverty. ~**te** a needy

indigest|ión f indigestion. ~**o** a indigestible

indign|ación f indignation. ~**ado** a indignant. ~**ar** vt make indignant. □ ~**arse** vpr become indignant. ~**o** a unworthy; (despreciable) contemptible

indio a & m Indian

indirect|a f hint. ~**o** a indirect

indisciplinado a undisciplined

indiscre|ción f indiscretion. ~**to** a indiscreet

indiscutible a unquestionable

indisoluble a indissoluble

indispensable a indispensable

indisp|oner [34] vt (enemistar) set against. □ ~**onerse** vpr (ponerse enfermo) fall ill. ~**osición** f indisposition. ~**uesto** a indisposed

individu|al a individual; <cama> single. ● m (en tenis etc) singles. ~**alidad** f individuality. ~**alista** m & f individualist. ~**alizar** [10] vt individualize. ~**o** m individual

índole f nature; (clase) type

indolen|cia f indolence. ~**te** a indolent

indoloro a painless

indomable a untameable

inducir [47] vt induce. ~ **a error** be misleading

indudable a undoubted

indulgen|cia f indulgence. ~**te** a indulgent

indult|ar vt pardon. ~**o** m pardon

industria f industry. ~**l** a industrial. ● m & f industrialist. ~**lización** f industrialization. ~**lizar** [10] vt industrialize

inédito a unpublished; (fig) unknown

inefable a indescribable

ineficaz a ineffective; <sistema etc> inefficient

ineficiente a inefficient

ineludible a inescapable, unavoidable

inept|itud *f* ineptitude. ~**o** *a* inept

inequívoco *a* unequivocal

inercia *f* inertia

inerte *a* inert; (sin vida) lifeless

inesperado *a* unexpected

inestable *a* unstable

inestimable *a* inestimable

inevitable *a* inevitable

inexistente *a* non-existent

inexorable *a* inexorable

inexper|iencia *f* inexperience. ~**to** *a* inexperienced

inexplicable *a* inexplicable

infalible *a* infallible

infam|ar *vt* defame. ~**atorio** *a* defamatory. ~**e** *a* infamous; (fig, 🇮, muy malo) awful. ~**ia** *f* infamy

infancia *f* infancy

infant|a *f* infanta, princess. ~**e** *m* infante, prince. ~**ería** *f* infantry. ~**il** *a* children's; <*población*> child; <*actitud etc*> childish, infantile

infarto *m* heart attack

infec|ción *f* infection. ~**cioso** *a* infectious. ~**tar** *vt* infect. □ ~**tarse** *vpr* become infected. ~**to** *a* infected; 🇮 disgusting

infeli|cidad *f* unhappiness. ~**z** *a* unhappy

inferior *a* inferior. ● *m & f* inferior. ~**idad** *f* inferiority

infernal *a* infernal, hellish

infestar *vt* infest; (fig) inundate

infi|delidad *f* unfaithfulness. ~**el** *a* unfaithful

infierno *m* hell

infiltra|ción *f* infiltration. □ ~**rse** *vpr* infiltrate

ínfimo *a* lowest; <*calidad*> very poor

infini|dad *f* infinity. ~**tivo** *m* infinitive. ~**to** *a* infinite. ● *m*. el ~**to** the infinite; (en matemáticas) infinity. ~**dad de** countless

inflación *f* inflation

inflama|ble *a* (in)flammable ~**ción** *f* inflammation. ~**r** *vt* set on fire; (fig, Med) inflame. □ ~**rse** *vpr* catch fire; (Med) become inflamed

inflar *vt* inflate; blow up <*globo*>; (fig, exagerar) exaggerate

inflexi|ble *a* inflexible. ~**ón** *f* inflexion

influ|encia *f* influence (en on). ~**ir** [17] *vt* influence. ● *vi*. ~ **en** influence. ~**jo** *m* influence. ~**yente** *a* influential

informa|ción *f* information; (noticias) news; (en aeropuerto etc) information desk; (de teléfonos) directory enquiries. ~**dor** *m* informant

informal *a* informal; <*persona*> unreliable

inform|ante *m & f* informant. ~**ar** *vt/i* inform. □ ~**arse** *vpr* find out. ~**ática** *f* information technology, computing. ~**ativo** *a* informative; <*programa*> news. ~**atizar** [10] *vt* computerize

informe *a* shapeless. ● *m* report. ~**s** *fpl* references, information

infracción *f* infringement. ~ **de tráfico** traffic offence

infraestructura *f* infrastructure

infranqueable *a* impassable; (fig) insuperable

infrarrojo *a* infrared

infringir [14] *vt* infringe

infructuoso *a* fruitless

ínfulas *fpl*. darse ~ give o.s. airs. tener ~ de fancy o.s. as

infundado *a* unfounded

infu|ndir *vt* instil. ~**sión** *f* infusion

ingeni|ar *vt* invent. ~**árselas para** find a way to

ingenier|ía *f* engineering. ~**o** *m* engineer

ingenio *m* ingenuity; (agudeza) wit; (LAm, de azúcar) refinery. **~so** *a* ingenious

ingenu|idad *f* naivety. **~o** *a* naive

Inglaterra *f* England

ingl|és *a* English. ● *m* Englishman; (lengua) English. **~esa** *f* Englishwoman. **los ~eses** the English

ingrat|itud *f* ingratitude. **~o** *a* ungrateful; (desagradable) thankless

ingrediente *m* ingredient

ingres|ar *vt* deposit. ● *vi.* **~ar en** come in, enter; join <*sociedad*>. **~o** *m* entrance; (de dinero) deposit; (en sociedad, hospital) admission. **~os** *mpl* income

inh|ábil *a* unskilful; (no apto) unfit. **~abilidad** *f* unskilfulness; (para cargo) ineligibility

inhabitable *a* uninhabitable

inhala|dor *m* inhaler. **~r** *vt* inhale

inherente *a* inherent

inhibi|ción *f* inhibition. **~r** *vt* inhibit

inhóspito *a* inhospitable

inhumano *a* inhuman

inici|ación *f* beginning. **~al** *a* & *f* initial. **~ar** *vt* initiate; (comenzar) begin, start. **~ativa** *f* initiative. **~o** *m* beginning

inigualado *a* unequalled

ininterrumpido *a* uninterrupted

injert|ar *vt* graft. **~to** *m* graft

injuri|a *f* insult. **~ar** *vt* insult. **~oso** *a* insulting

injust|icia *f* injustice. **~o** *a* unjust, unfair

inmaculado *a* immaculate

inmaduro *a* unripe; <*persona*> immature

inmediaciones *fpl.* **las ~** the vicinity, the surrounding area

inmediat|amente *adv* immediately. **~o** *a* immediate; (contiguo) next. **de ~o** immediately

inmejorable *a* excellent

inmemorable *a* immemorial

inmens|idad *f* immensity. **~o** *a* immense

inmersión *f* immersion

inmigra|ción *f* immigration. **~nte** *a* & *m* & *f* immigrant. **~r** *vt* immigrate

inminen|cia *f* imminence. **~te** *a* imminent

inmiscuirse [17] *vpr* interfere

inmobiliario *a* property

inmolar *vt* sacrifice

inmoral *a* immoral. **~idad** *f* immorality

inmortal *a* immortal. **~izar** [10] *vt* immortalize

inmóvil *a* immobile

inmovilizador *m* immobilizer

inmueble *a.* **bienes ~s** property

inmun|e *a* immune. **~idad** *f* immunity. **~ización** *f* immunization. **~izar** [10] *vt* immunize

inmuta|ble *a* unchangeable. □ **~rse** *vpr* be perturbed. **sin ~rse** unperturbed

innato *a* innate

innecesario *a* unnecessary

innegable *a* undeniable

innova|ción *f* innovation. **~r** *vi* innovate. ● *vt* make innovations in

innumerable *a* innumerable

inocen|cia *f* innocence. **~tada** *f* practical joke. **~te** *a* innocent. **~tón** *a* naïve

inocuo *a* innocuous

inodoro *a* odourless. ● *m* toilet

inofensivo *a* inoffensive

inolvidable *a* unforgettable

inoperable *a* inoperable

inoportuno *a* untimely; *<comentario>* ill-timed

inoxidable *a* stainless

inquiet|ar *vt* worry. □ **~arse** *vpr* get worried. **~o** *a* worried; (agitado) restless. **~ud** *f* anxiety

inquilino *m* tenant

inquirir [4] *vt* enquire into, investigate

insaciable *a* insatiable

insalubre *a* unhealthy

insatisfecho *a* unsatisfied; (descontento) dissatisfied

inscri|bir (*pp* inscrito) *vt* (en registro) register; (en curso) enrol; (grabar) inscribe. □ **~birse** *vpr* register. **~pción** *f* inscription; (registro) registration

insect|icida *m* insecticide. **~o** *m* insect

insegur|idad *f* insecurity. **~o** *a* insecure; *<ciudad>* unsafe, dangerous

insemina|ción *f* insemination. **~r** *vt* inseminate

insensato *a* foolish

insensible *a* insensitive

inseparable *a* inseparable

insertar *vt* insert

insidi|a *f* malice. **~oso** *a* insidious

insigne *a* famous

insignia *f* badge; (bandera) flag

insignificante *a* insignificant

insinu|ación *f* insinuation. **~ante** *a* insinuating. **~ar** [21] *vt* imply; insinuate *<algo ofensivo>*. □ **~arse** *vpr*. **~ársele a** make a pass at

insípido *a* insipid

insist|encia *f* insistence. **~ente** *a* insistent. **~ir** *vi* insist; (hacer hincapié) stress

insolación *f* sunstroke

insolen|cia *f* rudeness, insolence. **~te** *a* rude, insolent

insólito *a* unusual

insolven|cia *f* insolvency. **~te** *a* & *m* & *f* insolvent

insomn|e *a* sleepless. ● *m* & *f* insomniac. **~io** *m* insomnia

insondable *a* unfathomable

insoportable *a* unbearable

insospechado *a* unexpected

insostenible *a* untenable

inspec|ción *f* inspection. **~cionar** *vt* inspect. **~tor** *m* inspector

inspira|ción *f* inspiration. **~r** *vt* inspire. □ **~rse** *vpr* be inspired

instala|ción *f* installation. **~r** *vt* install. □ **~rse** *vpr* settle

instancia *f* request. **en última ~** as a last resort

instant|ánea *f* snapshot. **~áneo** *a* instantaneous; *<café etc>* instant. **~e** *m* instant. **a cada ~e** constantly. **al ~e** immediately

instaura|ción *f* establishment. **~r** *vt* establish

instiga|ción *f* instigation. **~dor** *m* instigator. **~r** [12] *vt* instigate; (incitar) incite

instint|ivo *a* instinctive. **~o** *m* instinct

institu|ción *f* institution. **~cional** *a* institutional. **~ir** [17] *vt* establish. **~to** *m* institute; (Escol) (secondary) school. **~triz** *f* governess

instru|cción *f* education; (Mil) training. **~cciones** *fpl* instruction. **~ctivo** *a* instructive; *<película etc>* educational. **~ctor** *m* instructor. **~ir** [17] *vt* instruct, teach; (Mil) train

instrument|ación *f* instrumentation. **~al** *a* instrumental. **~o** *m* instrument; (herramienta) tool

insubordina|ción *f*
insubordination. **~r** *vt* stir up.
□ **~rse** *vpr* rebel

insuficien|cia *f* insufficiency;
(inadecuación) inadequacy. **~te** *a*
insufficient

insufrible *a* insufferable

insular *a* insular

insulina *f* insulin

insulso *a* tasteless; (fig) insipid

insult|ar *vt* insult. **~o** *m* insult

insuperable *a* insuperable;
(inmejorable) unbeatable

insurgente *a* insurgent

insurrec|ción *f* insurrection.
~to *a* insurgent

intachable *a* irreproachable

intacto *a* intact

intangible *a* intangible

integra|ción *f* integration. **~l** *a*
integral; (completo) complete;
(incorporado) built-in; <*pan*>
wholemeal (Brit), wholewheat
(Amer). **~r** *vt* make up

integridad *f* integrity; (entereza)
wholeness

íntegro *a* complete; (fig) upright

intelect|o *m* intellect. **~ual** *a* &
m & *f* intellectual

inteligen|cia *f* intelligence. **~te**
a intelligent

inteligible *a* intelligible

intemperie *f*. **a la ~** in the open

intempestivo *a* untimely

intenci|ón *f* intention. **con doble
~ón** implying sth else. **~onado**
a deliberate. **bien ~onado** well-
meaning. **mal ~onado** malicious.
~onal *a* intentional

intens|idad *f* intensity. **~ificar**
[7] *vt* intensify. **~ivo** *a* intensive.
~o *a* intense

intent|ar *vt* try. **~o** *m* attempt;
(Mex, propósito) intention

inter|calar *vt* insert. **~cambio** *m*
exchange. **~ceder** *vt* intercede

interceptar *vt* intercept

interdicto *m* ban

inter|és *m* interest; (egoísmo) self-
interest. **~esado** *a* interested;
(parcial) biassed; (egoísta) selfish.
~esante *a* interesting. **~esar** *vt*
interest; (afectar) concern. ● *vi* be
of interest. □ **~esarse** *vpr* take
an interest (**por** in)

interfer|encia *f* interference. **~ir**
[4] *vi* interfere

interfono *m* intercom

interino *a* temporary; <*persona*>
acting. ● *m* stand-in; (médico)
locum

interior *a* interior; <*comercio etc*>
domestic. ● *m* inside. **Ministerio
del I~** Ministry of the Interior

interjección *f* interjection

inter|locutor *m* speaker.
~mediario *a* & *m* intermediary.
~medio *a* intermediate. ● *m*
interval

interminable *a* interminable

intermitente *a* intermittent. ●
m indicator

internacional *a* international

intern|ado *m* (Escol) boarding-
school. **~ar** *vt* (en manicomio)
commit; (en hospital) admit.
□ **~arse** *vpr* penetrate

internauta *m* & *f* Internet user

Internet *m* Internet

interno *a* internal; (Escol)
boarding. ● *m* (Escol) boarder

interponer [34] *vt* interpose.
□ **~se** *vpr* intervene

int|erpretación *f* interpretation.
~erpretar *vt* interpret; (Mús etc)
play. **~érprete** *m* interpreter;
(Mus) performer

interroga|ción *f* interrogation;
(signo) question mark. **~r** [12] *vt*
question. **~tivo** *a* interrogative

interru|mpir *vt* interrupt; cut off
<*suministro*>; cut short <*viaje*>

etc>; block *<tráfico>*. **~pción** *f*
interruption. **~ptor** *m* switch

inter|sección *f* intersection.
~urbano *a* inter-city; *<llamada>*
long-distance

intervalo *m* interval; (espacio)
space. **a ~s** at intervals

interven|ir [53] *vt* control; (Med)
operate on. ● *vi* intervene;
(participar) take part. **~tor** *m*
inspector; (Com) auditor

intestino *m* intestine

intim|ar *vi* become friendly.
~idad *f* intimacy

intimidar *vt* intimidate

íntimo *a* intimate; *<amigo>* close.
● *m* close friend

intolera|ble *a* intolerable. **~nte**
a intolerant

intoxicar [7] *vt* poison

intranquilo *a* worried

intransigente *a* intransigent

intransitable *a* impassable

intransitivo *a* intransitive

intratable *a* impossible

intrépido *a* intrepid

intriga *f* intrigue. **~nte** *a*
intriguing. **~r** [12] *vt* intrigue

intrincado *a* intricate

intrínseco *a* intrinsic

introduc|ción *f* introduction. **~ir**
[47] *vt* introduce; (meter) insert.
□ **~irse** *vpr* get into

intromisión *f* interference

introvertido *a* introverted. ● *m*
introvert

intruso *m* intruder

intui|ción *f* intuition. **~r** [17] *vt*
sense. **~tivo** *a* intuitive

inunda|ción *f* flooding. **~r** *vt*
flood

inusitado *a* unusual

in|útil *a* useless; (vano) futile.
~utilidad *f* uselessness

invadir *vt* invade

inv|alidez *f* invalidity; (Med)
disability. **~álido** *a & m* invalid

invariable *a* invariable

invas|ión *f* invasion. **~or** *a*
invading. ● *m* invader

invencible *a* invincible

inven|ción *f* invention. **~tar** *vt*
invent

inventario *m* inventory

invent|iva *f* inventiveness. **~ivo**
a inventive. **~or** *m* inventor

invernadero *m* greenhouse

invernal *a* winter

inverosímil *a* implausible

inversión *f* inversion; (Com)
investment

inverso *a* inverse; (contrario)
opposite. **a la inversa** the other
way round. **a la inversa de**
contrary to

invertir [4] *vt* reverse; (Com)
invest; put in *<tiempo>*

investidura *f* investiture

investiga|ción *f* investigation;
(Univ) research. **~dor** *m*
investigator; (Univ) researcher. **~r**
[12] *vt* investigate; (Univ) research

investir [5] *vt* invest

invicto *a* unbeaten

invierno *m* winter

inviolable *a* inviolate

invisible *a* invisible

invita|ción *f* invitation. **~do** *m*
guest. **~r** *vt* invite. **te invito a una
copa** I'll buy you a drink

invocar [7] *vt* invoke

involuntario *a* involuntary

invulnerable *a* invulnerable

inyec|ción *f* injection. **~tar** *vt*
inject

ir [49]

● *verbo intransitivo*

····▸ to go. **fui a verla** I went to see
her. **ir a pie** to go on foot. **ir en**

coche to go by car. **vamos a casa** let's go home. **fue (a) por el pan** he went to get some bread

! Cuando la acción del verbo **ir** significa trasladarse hacia o con el interlocutor la traducción es *to come*, p.ej: **¡ya voy!** *I'm coming!* **yo voy contigo** *I'll come with you*

••••➤ (estar) to be. **iba con su novio** she was with her boyfriend. **¿cómo te va?** how are you?

••••➤ (sentar) to suit. **ese color no le va** that colour doesn't suit her. **no me va ni me viene** I don't mind at all

••••➤ (Méx, apoyar) **irle a** to support. **le va al equipo local** he supports the local team

••••➤ (en exclamaciones) **¡vamos!** come on! **¡vaya!** what a surprise!; (contrariedad) oh, dear! **¡vaya noche!** what a night! **¡qué va!** nonsense!

➡Cuando el verbo intransitivo se emplea con expresiones como **ir de paseo, ir de compras, ir tirando** etc., ver bajo el respectivo nombre, verbo etc.

● *verbo auxiliar*

••••➤ **ir a** + *infinitivo* (para expresar futuro, propósito) to be going to + *infinitive;* (al prevenir) **no te vayas a caer** be careful you don't fall. **no vaya a ser que llueva** in case it rains. (en sugerencias) **vamos a dormir** let's go to sleep. **vamos a ver** let's see

••••➤ **ir** + *gerundio.* **ve arreglándote** start getting ready. **el tiempo va mejorando** the weather is gradually getting better. ◻ **irse** *verbo pronominal*

••••➤ to go. **vete a la cama** go to bed. **se ha ido a casa** he's gone home

••••➤ (marcharse) to leave. **se fue sin despedirse** he left without saying goodbye. **se fue de casa** she left home

ira *f* anger. **∼cundo** *a* irascible
Irak *m* Iraq
Irán *m* Iran
iraní *a & m & f* Iranian
iraquí *a & m & f* Iraqi
iris *m* (Anat) iris
Irlanda *f* Ireland
irland|és *a* Irish. ● *m* Irishman; (lengua) Irish. **∼esa** *f* Irishwoman. **los ∼eses** the Irish
ir|onía *f* irony. **∼ónico** *a* ironic
irracional *a* irrational
irradiar *vt* radiate
irreal *a* unreal. **∼idad** *f* unreality
irrealizable *a* unattainable
irreconciliable *a* irreconcilable
irreconocible *a* unrecognizable
irrecuperable *a* irretrievable
irreflexión *f* impetuosity
irregular *a* irregular. **∼idad** *f* irregularity
irreparable *a* irreparable
irreprimible *a* irrepressible
irreprochable *a* irreproachable
irresistible *a* irresistible
irrespetuoso *a* disrespectful
irresponsable *a* irresponsible
irriga|ción *f* irrigation. **∼r** [12] *vt* irrigate
irrisorio *a* derisory
irrita|ble *a* irritable. **∼ción** *f* irritation. **∼r** *vt* irritate. ◻ **∼rse** *vpr* get annoyed
irrumpir *vi* burst (en in)
isla *f* island. **las I∼s Británicas** the British Isles
islámico *a* Islamic
islandés *a* Icelandic. ● *m* Icelander; (lengua) Icelandic
Islandia *f* Iceland

isleño *a* island. ● *m* islander
Israel *m* Israel
israelí *a & m* Israeli
Italia *f* Italy
italiano *a & m* Italian
itinerario *a* itinerary
IVA *abrev* (**impuesto sobre el valor agregado** (LAm), **impuesto sobre el valor añadido**) VAT
izar [10] *vt* hoist
izquierd|a *f*. **la ~a** the left hand; (Pol) left. **a la ~a** on the left; (con movimiento) to the left. **de ~a** left-wing. **~ista** *m & f* leftist. **~o** *a* left

ja *int* ha!
jabalí *m* (*pl* ~es) wild boar
jabalina *f* javelin
jab|ón *m* soap. **~onar** *vt* soap. **~onoso** *a* soapy
jaca *f* pony
jacinto *m* hyacinth
jactarse *vpr* boast
jadea|nte *a* panting. **~r** *vi* pant
jaguar *m* jaguar
jaiba *f* (LAm) crab
jalar *vt* (LAm) pull
jalea *f* jelly
jaleo *m* row, uproar. **armar un ~** kick up a fuss
jalón *m* (LAm, tirón) pull; (Mex 🄸, trago) drink; (Mex, tramo) stretch
jamás *adv* never. **nunca ~** never ever
jamelgo *m* nag
jamón *m* ham. **~ de York** boiled ham. **~ serrano** cured ham

Japón *m*. **el ~** Japan
japonés *a & m* Japanese
jaque *m* check. **~ mate** checkmate
jaqueca *f* migraine
jarabe *m* syrup
jardín *m* garden. **~ de la infancia**, (Mex) **~ de niños** kindergarten, nursery school
jardiner|ía *f* gardening. **~o** *m* gardener
jarr|a *f* jug. **en ~as** with hands on hips. **~o** *m* jug. **caer como un ~o de agua fría** come as a shock. **~ón** *m* vase
jaula *f* cage
jauría *f* pack of hounds
jazmín *m* jasmine
jef|a *f* boss. **~atura** *f* leadership; (sede) headquarters. **~e** *m* boss; (Pol etc) leader. **~e de camareros** head waiter. **~e de estación** station-master. **~e de ventas** sales manager
jengibre *m* ginger
jer|arquía *f* hierarchy. **~árquico** *a* hierarchical
jerez *m* sherry. **al ~** with sherry
jerga *f* coarse cloth; (argot) jargon
jerigonza *f* jargon; (galimatías) gibberish
jeringa *f* syringe; (LAm 🄸, molestia) nuisance. **~r** [12] *vt* (fig, 🄸, molestar) annoy
jeroglífico *m* hieroglyph(ic)
jersey *m* (*pl* ~s) jersey
Jesucristo *m* Jesus Christ. **antes de ~** BC, before Christ
jesuita *a & m* Jesuit
Jesús *m* Jesus. ● *int* good heavens!; (al estornudar) bless you!
jícara *f* (Mex) gourd
jilguero *m* goldfinch
jinete *m & f* rider
jipijapa *m* panama hat